GMAT®

Prep Plus

2020

Editor, 2020 Edition
Paula L. Fleming, MA, MBA

Contributing Editor
Ethan A. Weber

Special thanks to our faculty authors and reviewers
Steve Bartley; Harry Broome; James Carney; Chris Cosci; Amy T. Craddock; Emily Graves; Jack Hayes, MBA; Jo L'Abbate; Gordon Spector; Chris Sun; Caroline Sykes; Mary Toro

Additional special thanks to
Naomi Beesen; Kim Bowers; Robin Garmise; Rita Garthaffner; Joanna Graham; M. L. (Lisa) Liu; Mandy Luk; Jennifer Moore; Monica Ostolaza; Anne Pennick; Carly Schnur; Sascha Strelka; Noah Teitelbaum, MSEd, MBA; Michael Wolff; Amy Zarkos; and the countless others who made this project possible.

TABLE OF CONTENTS

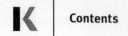

How to Use This Book

WELCOME TO KAPLAN'S GMAT PREP PLUS 2020

Congratulations on your decision to pursue an MBA or other graduate management degree and thank you for choosing Kaplan for your GMAT preparation.

You've made the right choice in acquiring this book—you're now armed with a comprehensive GMAT program that is the result of decades of researching the GMAT and teaching many thousands of students the skills they need to succeed. You have what you need to score higher; the next step is to make the commitment to your study plan, which, according to the GMAT test maker, averages about 100 hours of preparation for 600+ and 700+ scorers.

Let's start by walking you through everything you need to know to take advantage of this book and your online resources.

LEARNING OBJECTIVES

In this section, you will learn how to:

- Identify the types of study resources this book contains, including instruction covering everything tested on the GMAT, strategies for every question type, and practice questions of all types

- Explain how to register and access this book's online resources, which include full-length computer adaptive tests, analysis of your results, answers and explanations, video workshops, and more

- Create a study plan that lets you start your preparation for the GMAT with confidence

---

Your Book

There are two main components to your *GMAT Prep Plus* study package: your book and your online resources. This book contains:

- Detailed instruction covering the essential verbal, math, and writing concepts
- Time-tested and effective Kaplan Methods and strategies for every question type
- Over 350 practice questions, followed by detailed answer explanations

Your Online Resources

Your Kaplan online resources give you access to additional instruction and practice materials to reinforce key concepts and sharpen your GMAT skills. The following list summarizes the resources available to you:

- Six full-length computer-adaptive practice tests (CATs). Take one at the beginning of your studies to discover your strengths and weaknesses. Later in your prep, take practice tests every week or two to become thoroughly familiar with the test's format and timing and to measure your progress.
- Analysis of your performance on each practice test, including detailed answer explanations
- Practice sets for the Verbal, Quantitative, Analytical Writing, and Integrated Reasoning sections of the GMAT
- A 500-question Qbank for additional targeted practice
- Video workshops featuring veteran GMAT instructors
- The GMAT Strategy Sheet

GETTING STARTED

Studying for the GMAT can be daunting, and with so many resources available to you, it may not be clear where to begin. Don't worry; we'll break it down one step at a time, just as we'll do with the GMAT questions that you will soon be on your way to mastering.

> ### GETTING STARTED
>
> 1. Register your online resources.
> 2. Sign up for a free Live Online event.
> 3. Take a computer-adaptive GMAT practice test to identify your strengths and weaknesses.
> 4. Create a study plan.
> 5. Learn and practice using this book and your online resources.
> 6. Take more computer-adaptive practice tests to gauge your progress.

Step 1: Register Your Online Resources

Register your online resources using these simple steps:

1. Go to **kaptest.com/moreonline**.
2. Follow the on-screen instructions. Please have a copy of your book available.

Access to the online resources is limited to the original owner of this book and is nontransferable. Kaplan is not responsible for providing access to the online resources to customers who purchase or borrow used copies of this book. Access to the online resources expires one year after you register.

Step 2: Sign Up for a Free Live Online Event

Kaplan's GMAT Live Online events are interactive, instructor-led GMAT training sessions that you can join from anywhere you can access the internet.

Live Online events are held in a state-of-the-art virtual classroom in real time, just like a physical classroom experience. You'll interact with your teacher and other classmates using audio, instant chat, whiteboard, polling, and screen sharing. And just like in-person courses, a GMAT Live Online event is led by an experienced Kaplan instructor.

To register for a free GMAT Live Online event, go to **KaplanGMAT.com** and search for a free event. Look for events such as GMAT Bootcamps and GMAT Lessons. (The free GMAT practice tests draw from the same question pool as the tests in your online resources, so you should use the online tests that come with this book.) Live Online events are available for all locations.

Step 3: Take a GMAT Practice Test

It's essential to take a practice test early on. Doing so will give you the initial feedback and diagnostic information that you will need to achieve your maximum score. Taking a full-length test right at the start can be intimidating, but remember: your practice test scores don't count. During your first practice test—and any practice test you take—turn off your cell phone, give the test your full attention, and learn from your performance.

Your diagnostic test is Practice Test 1, and you'll find it in your online resources under **Get Started**. Practice Test 1, like all of Kaplan's online full-length tests, is a computer-adaptive test (CAT), which is the same format as the actual GMAT. The computer-adaptive format presents distinct challenges for time management, because you can only move forward through the test. Because you can't skip a question and come back to it later, you need to decide for each question how much time to spend trying to get it right and when you should just guess and move on. This ability to triage questions as you meet them is key to maximizing your GMAT score, and you can only practice it in an adaptive online test.

After taking Practice Test 1, review the detailed answer explanations to better understand your performance. Our explanations label each question according to its question type and topic; these labels align with the material covered throughout this book. Look for patterns in the questions you answered correctly and incorrectly. Were you stronger in some areas than others? This analysis will help you target your practice time to specific concepts.

Step 4: Create a Study Plan

Use what you've learned from your initial practice test to identify areas for closer study and practice. Take time to familiarize yourself with the key components of your book and online resources. Think about how many hours you can consistently devote to GMAT study. We have found that most students have success with about three months of committed preparation before Test Day.

Consider the following statistic as you build your study plan: according to the GMAT test makers, the average 600+ or 700+ scorer prepares for the GMAT for about 100 hours. We recommend you add 20 percent to this figure and plan to put in 120 total hours of practice before Test Day. Roughly estimated, if you spend an average of 2 hours per chapter in this book, that gets you to over 50 hours. The six computer-adaptive practice tests are each about 3.0 hours, if you do the writing section and Integrated Reasoning, followed by about 1.5 hours of review. All told, that gets you to about 80 hours of preparation. That 80 hours may be enough for some test takers, and it will be more than enough to give you an indication of where you stand relative to your GMAT goals. The most convenient way to bulk up your study plan is to enroll in one of Kaplan's GMAT self-guided options. For more information on GMAT self-guided practice tools and courses, as well as instructor-led courses, visit **KaplanGMAT.com**.

Schedule time for study, practice, and review. Many people find it works best to block out short, frequent periods of study time throughout the week. Also, keep a log of questions you find challenging or simply interesting. Come back to these questions every week or two until you feel you've learned all you can from them. Then check them off or cross them out and focus on the new questions you've added to your log. Check in with yourself often to make sure you're not falling behind your plan or forgetting about any of your resources.

Step 5: Learn and Practice

Your book and online resources come with many opportunities to develop and practice the skills you'll need on Test Day. Read each chapter of this book and complete the practice questions. Depending on how much time you have to study, you can do this work methodically, covering every chapter, or you can focus your study on those question types and content areas that are most challenging for you. You will inevitably need more work in some areas than in others, but know that the more thoroughly you prepare, the better your score will be.

Remember also to take and review the practice sets in your online resources, as well as using your Qbank to make custom quizzes. These additional test-like questions allow you to put into practice the skills you are learning. As always, review the explanations closely.

Initially, your practice should focus on mastering the needed skills and not on speed. Become more conscious of timing as you become more proficient.

Step 6: Take More Computer-Adaptive Practice Tests

Once you feel you have addressed the areas that gave you trouble on Practice Test 1, take another full-length practice test, also available in your online resources. You will learn more about CATs in Chapters 1 and 2 of this book. The Kaplan CATs are realistic practice tests, and taking the two full-length tests that come with this book is one of the best ways to prepare fully for what you will face on the real GMAT.

Always review your practice test results thoroughly to make sure you are addressing the areas that are most important to your score. Allot time to review the detailed explanations so that you can learn from your mistakes and not make these errors when it actually matters, on Test Day. After your second practice test, you'll probably find that some of your initial weaknesses aren't weaknesses anymore. Now, to continue to build your score, you'll probably want to adjust your study plan to focus on some different areas. Continue taking full-length practice tests every week or two leading up to Test Day.

If you would like access to more of Kaplan's CATs and quizzes, as well as in-depth instruction on the question types and strategies, look into the variety of practice resources and course options available at **KaplanGMAT.com**.

Thanks for choosing Kaplan. We wish you the best of luck on your journey to business school.

Changes and Corrections

The material in this book is accurate and up-to-date at the time of printing. However, the Graduate Management Admission Council may have instituted changes in the tests or test registration process after this book was published. Be sure to read carefully the materials you receive when you register for the test.

If there are any important late-breaking developments, we will post that information online at **KaplanGMAT.com**.

If there are changes or corrections to the materials in this book, these can be found at **kaptest.com/ publishing**.

PART ONE

The GMAT

CHAPTER 1

Introduction to the GMAT

LEARNING OBJECTIVES

After studying this chapter, you will be able to:

- List the four sections of the GMAT and explain the order in which they are presented
- Describe the 200–800 point scoring scale, including which sections contribute to it, and describe the scoring scales for the other sections
- Describe the materials you will use when taking the GMAT
- Explain when and how to register for the GMAT

Let's start with the basics. The GMAT is, among other things, an endurance test. It is a computerized test consisting of 127 minutes of multiple-choice math and verbal questions, a 30-minute reasoning section, and a 30-minute analytical essay. Add in the administrative details, plus two 8-minute breaks, and you can count on being in the testing center for about 3.5 hours.

It's a grueling experience, to say the least. And if you don't approach it with confidence and rigor, you'll quickly lose your composure. That's why it's so important that you take control of the test, just as you take control of the rest of your business school application process.

Here are the basics.

GMAT Format

The GMAT consists of four sections, and you can choose your section order on Test Day. Before you begin your test, you'll be presented with three orders and asked to select one:

- Analytical Writing Assessment (AWA), Integrated Reasoning (IR), Quantitative, Verbal
- Verbal, Quantitative, Integrated Reasoning, Analytical Writing Assessment
- Quantitative, Verbal, Integrated Reasoning, Analytical Writing Assessment

If you do not choose an order, then after 1 minute, the first order—beginning with Analytical Writing—will be chosen for you.

The order you take the sections in will not appear on your score report, and the test maker's research has not shown that section order gives one test taker a statistical advantage over another. If you are especially concerned about a section and want to take it when you are mentally freshest, then choose the order that puts that section first. If you want to build confidence by completing other sections first, then choose an order that puts that section later. And if you don't care what order you take the sections in, that's perfectly okay—just choose whichever order you have practiced most.

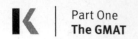

The Analytical Writing Assessment (AWA) requires you to complete an essay, typing it into the computer using a simple word processing program. You are given 30 minutes for this essay, during which you have to analyze the flawed reasoning behind a given argument and recommend how to improve the argument.

The Integrated Reasoning section is 30 minutes long. This section has 12 questions, each of which may require more than one response. The questions in this section ask you to draw conclusions based on information in tables, interpret graphs, understand information presented across different layouts, and find two answers that lead to a single solution.

The Quantitative section contains 31 questions in two formats, Problem Solving and Data Sufficiency, which are mixed together throughout the section. The Verbal section contains 36 questions in three formats, Reading Comprehension, Sentence Correction, and Critical Reasoning, which are also mixed throughout the section.

GMAT exam section	Questions	Time
Analytical Writing Assessment	1	30 minutes
Integrated Reasoning	12	30 minutes
Quantitative	31	62 minutes
Verbal	36	65 minutes
Total Testing Time		**3 hours, 7 minutes**

Length of Sections on the GMAT

You will also get two optional 8-minute breaks between sections. Kaplan recommends that you take these breaks. Also, note that a few experimental questions will be scattered throughout; they look just like the other questions but won't contribute to your score.

Order A	Order B	Order C
Analytical Writing Assessment	Verbal	Quantitative
Integrated Reasoning		
8-minute break (optional)		
Quantitative	Quantitative	Verbal
8-minute break (optional)		
Verbal	Integrated Reasoning	Integrated Reasoning
	Analytical Writing Assessment	Analytical Writing Assessment

Breaks on the GMAT by Section Order

We'll talk more about each of the question types in later chapters. For now, note the following: you'll be answering 79 multiple-choice questions in about 2.5 hours. Clearly, you'll have to move fast. But you can't let yourself get careless. Taking control of the GMAT means increasing the speed of your work without sacrificing accuracy.

GMAT Scoring

The most important score on the GMAT is the total score, which ranges from 200 to 800. Schools primarily look at this number. More than half of all GMAT test takers score within 120 points of 561, the approximate mean. Pulling yourself out of that cluster is an important part of distinguishing your application.

Percentile	Score
99%	760–800
90%	710
80%	670
66%	630
52%	590

Some GMAT Percentiles vs. Total Scores

The total score is calculated from "scaled scores" from the Quantitative section and Verbal section. These scores are meant to provide a timeless, absolute measure of skill. For example, a Quant score of 40 in 2009 represents the same level of ability as does a Quant score of 40 in 2019.

While the scaled scores haven't changed over time, the population of test takers has. Quant performance has gone up, and Verbal performance has gone down. While Verbal section scores still follow a fairly even distribution, Quantitative scaled scores now skew high. Thus, percentiles have shifted.

Schools view your percentile performance (which is the same thing as a "percent ranking") overall and on each section of the GMAT. The relationship between the section percentiles and the overall percentile is not simple. We're frequently asked, "One of my scaled scores is 82nd percentile and the other is 85th percentile. How can my overall score be 87th percentile?" An example shows how this works. Imagine that of 100 students taking the test, 50 people got a 51 Quant and an 11 Verbal, while the other 50 people got an 11 Quant and a 51 Verbal. You take the same test and get 40 Quant and 40 Verbal. You'd be 50th percentile on each section, because 50 percent of test takers in this sample group scored worse than you. However, your total score would put you higher than anyone else on the test—99th percentile.

Quantitative		Verbal	
Percentile	Score	Percentile	Score
96%	51	99%	45–51
85%	50	96%	42
74%	49	90%	40
67%	48	85%	38
61%	47	80%	36
58%	46	71%	34
55%	45	61%	31
50%	44	51%	28

Some Percentiles vs. Scaled Scores
for the Quantitative and Verbal Sections

Let's note two key takeaways about percentiles. The first is that your overall score is about balanced performance on the two sections. Generally, you will not win on the GMAT by nailing one section and hoping your performance will overcome a deficit on the other. The second key point is that admissions officers often look at Quant and Verbal percentiles separately and may reject a candidate who does not meet a certain threshold for either subscore. This is especially true for Quantitative percentiles, particularly at programs with a strong analytical focus.

The Analytical Writing Assessment (AWA) is scored separately from the rest of the GMAT. Unlike the total and scaled scores, AWA scores aren't available on Test Day. When you do get your score, it will take the form of a number from 1 to 6 in increments of 0.5 (you get a zero if you write off topic or in a foreign language). The magic number here is 4. Although you should strive for the best score possible, an essay graded 4 is considered "satisfactory" according to the grading rubric, and an essay graded 3 is not.

AWA	
Percentile	**Score**
88%	6
79%	5.5
53%	5
42%	4.5
17%	4
11%	3.5
4%	3

Some Percentiles vs. Scaled Scores for the AWA

Percentiles give a slightly different perspective on the AWA. An AWA score of 4 ranks at a shockingly low 17th percentile. To break the median, you have to score a 5 or higher. The good news is that few programs, in our experience, use the AWA score to differentiate candidates' competitiveness. It's more of a reality check against the writing skills that you demonstrate in your application essays. Here's a little-noticed fact: business schools receive the actual text of your AWA essay in the official score report.

Finally, you'll receive a score for the Integrated Reasoning section. As with the Quant and Verbal sections, Integrated Reasoning scores are available on Test Day. Like the AWA, the Integrated Reasoning section has its own scoring scale, independent of the 200 to 800 scale. You'll receive a score from 1 to 8, in whole-point increments. The magic number this time is 5, as this is the score at which you beat the median.

Integrated Reasoning	
Percentile	**Score**
92%	8
82%	7
70%	6
54%	5
38%	4
24%	3
11%	2
0%	1

*Percentiles vs. Scaled Scores for the
Integrated Reasoning Section*

You will want to show schools that you're in the better half of the Integrated Reasoning field, but at the same time, an exceptional 200–800 score will do more for your application than will an exceptional Integrated Reasoning score, and you should prioritize your study time accordingly.

The 1–8 score is derived from 12 questions, nearly all of which have multiple parts, and there is no partial credit. Integrated Reasoning questions come in four types, described in more detail in the Integrated Reasoning chapter of this book: Graphics Interpretation, Multi-Source Reasoning, Table Analysis, and Two-Part Analysis.

Unlike the Quantitative and Verbal sections of the GMAT, the Integrated Reasoning section isn't adaptive: you'll see a predetermined sequence of 12 questions no matter how many you get right and wrong as you go along. However, despite not being adaptive, the Integrated Reasoning section does not let test takers skip questions or return to previously answered questions. As a result, it's often advantageous to guess quickly on a tough question early in the section to make sure you get to easier questions toward the end of the section with enough time to do them.

Score Reports

Within 20 days after your test date, your official score report will be available online. You'll receive an email when yours is ready. Reports will only be mailed to candidates who request that service. The official score report includes your scores for the Analytical Writing Assessment, Integrated Reasoning, Verbal, and Quantitative sections, as well as your total score and percentile ranking.

Your report also includes the results of all the GMAT exams you've taken in the previous five years, not including cancellations. Any additional reports are US$35 each. All score report requests are final and cannot be canceled.

GMAT Strategies and Attitude

In the chapters that follow, we'll cover techniques for answering the GMAT questions. But you'll also need to go into the test with a certain attitude and approach. Here are some strategies.

Use the Erasable Notepads

Test takers are given notepads, which are spiral-bound booklets of laminated paper, and a black wet-erase pen. Here are the specs so you know what to expect on Test Day.

Notepad

- Five sheets, 10 numbered pages
- Spiral-bound at top
- Legal-sized (8.5" × 14") in United States, Canada, and Mexico; A4 elsewhere
- First page has test instructions and is not suitable for scratchwork
- Pages 2–10 consist of a gridded work surface
- Pale yellow in United States, Canada, and Mexico; may be a different color elsewhere

Pen

- Black fine-print Staedtler wet-erase pen

You will not be given an eraser, and you are not allowed to reuse the notepad. The administrator will replace your used notepad with a clean one upon request. You can also request a new pen, if necessary. The notepad cannot be removed from the test room during or after the exam, and you must return it to the administrator when your exam is complete.

We know how important it is for test takers to be as prepared as possible for the actual testing experience. That's why we have always recommended that students use separate scratch material with our GMAT preparation program, including with the practice questions and tests in this book. We suggest that you use an eraser board (or anything with a similar surface) and a nonpermanent marker while doing the practice tests. Even if you practice with the notepad and marker until you are comfortable, there are still some snags you may encounter on Test Day. Here are some tips on how to handle them:

1. **Erasable ink you're not supposed to erase:** Say you make a mistake during a calculation or you smudge your work with your hand. The notepad's surface won't lend itself to quick-and-easy erasing. You can't write on top of the smudge or error because you'll just be left with a blob of ink that you can't read. So what should you do? Just start over. Seriously. Think of it this way—you won't waste precious time in a futile attempt to save a sinking ship. Left-handed test takers (and some right-handed ones, too) might find that their writing styles make them particularly susceptible to smudging. If this sounds like you, practicing with an eraser board or something similar will help you work out any such problems before Test Day.

2. **A problematic pen:** Difficulties with pens are not common. Keep in mind that you should recap your pen when you are not using it so that it doesn't dry out. However, you could get a pen that's simply dry from the get-go or dries out quickly no matter how careful you are. Don't sweat it. The best thing to do is just to get a new pen. Should you be saddled with a pen that leaves wayward blobs of ink, don't waste time with this either. Ask the administrator for a new pen as soon as it starts to act up.

More Notepad Strategies

Using one booklet for an entire section and requesting a replacement during breaks is the most efficient method for using the notepads. Since you are given nine pages to write on, this technique can be used without difficulty, especially with planning and practice. However, should you need a new notepad (or pen) during a section, hold the used one in the air to let the proctor know what you need (rather than just raising your hand). Then the proctor can bring it to you immediately.

Be Systematic

Use your notepad to organize your thinking. To facilitate eliminating choices, especially on the Verbal section, draw an answer choice grid, cross off choices as you rule them out, and guess intelligently. Make sure to leave enough time to answer every question in the section. You'll be penalized for questions you don't get to.

Pace Yourself

Of course, the last thing you want to happen is to run out of time before you've done all the questions. Pace yourself so that this doesn't happen. We're not saying you have to spend exactly 120 seconds, for instance, on every Critical Reasoning question. But you should have a sense of how much time to spend on each question. (We'll talk about general timing guidelines later.)

Turn Off the Clock

The timer in the corner of the GMAT screen can work to your advantage, but if you find yourself looking at it so often that it becomes a distraction, turn it off for 10 or 15 minutes and try to refocus. Even if you lose track a bit without the clock, there is no replacement for focus and accuracy. Some people work best with the clock off from the beginning. If that's you, be sure to check in with the clock every five questions. You don't want to fall too far behind. No matter what your preference is for the clock, when there are 5 minutes left, the clock turns on permanently, counts down the seconds, turns red, and flashes.

Don't Waste Time on Questions You Can't Do

Skipping a tough question is easier said than done. It's natural to want to answer every question as it appears. But that doesn't pay off here. We'll discuss in Chapter 2 why it's sometimes best to move on and avoid running out of time on a section. Some strategic guesses are often necessary to get a top score on the GMAT.

Remain Calm

It's imperative that you remain calm and composed during the test. You can't let yourself get rattled by one hard question to the degree that it throws off your performance on the rest of the section.

When you face a tough question, remember that you're surely not the only one finding it difficult. The test is designed to challenge everyone who takes it. Having trouble with a difficult question isn't going to ruin your score, but getting upset and letting it throw you off track will. When you understand that part of the test maker's goal is to reward those who keep their composure, you'll recognize the importance of keeping your cool when you run into challenging material.

GMAT Checklist

The GMAT is offered by appointment, at your convenience, almost every day of the year. You will be required to register online before making an appointment.

Choose a Testing Center

Before you register, find a testing center that's convenient for you and determine whether that site has available seats. Each testing center operates on its own schedule and can accommodate varying numbers of test takers. To locate a testing center near you, go to **mba.com**.

Register and Schedule Your Appointment

Available time slots change continuously as people register for the test. You will find out what times are available at your chosen testing center when you register. You may be able to schedule an appointment within a few days of your desired test date, but popular dates and times (especially weekday evenings and weekends) fill up quickly.

Admissions deadlines for business schools vary. Check with the schools and make your test appointment early enough to allow your scores to be reported before the schools' application deadlines.

You may register and schedule your appointment online, by phone, by mail, or by fax:

- Online: Go to **mba.com** and create an account.
- Phone (you may be charged a US$10 fee):
  - The Americas: Call toll-free (within the United States and Canada only) 800-717-GMAT (4628), Monday to Friday, 7:00 a.m. to 7:00 p.m. CST.
  - Asia Pacific: 852-3077-4926, 9:00 a.m. to 6:00 p.m. AEST
  - China: 86-10-82345675, Monday to Friday, 8:30 a.m. to 5:00 p.m. China Standard Time
  - India: 91 120 439 7830, 9:00 a.m. to 6:00 p.m. Indian Standard Time
  - Europe/Middle East/Africa: 44 (0) 161 855 7219, 9:00 a.m. to 5:00 p.m. GMT

- Fax or postal mail (slowest options):
  - Look up your desired test center(s) in the Test Center List and get the GMAT Appointment Scheduling form, available from GMAC at **mba.com**.
  - Fill out the GMAT Appointment Scheduling form.
  - If you wish to fax your form, use the appropriate fax number:
    — The Americas: (952) 681-3680 or (952) 681-3681
    — Asia Pacific and India: 91 120 400 1660
    — China: 86-10-61957800
    — Europe/Middle East/Africa: 44 (0) 161 855 7301
  - If you wish to mail your form, send your completed form to the following address. Keep in mind that mail from some countries can take as long as eight weeks to arrive in the United States:

    Pearson VUE—GMAT Program
    5601 Green Valley Drive, Suite 300
    Bloomington, MN 55437
    USA

The fee to take the GMAT is US$250 worldwide (as this book goes to press). It is payable by credit card online or by mailing in a check. If you have questions about GMAT registration, visit **mba.com** or call 800-717-GMAT (4628).

Identify Yourself Correctly

When scheduling your test appointment, be sure that the spelling of your name and your stated date of birth match the ID you will present at the testing center. If those do not match, you will not be permitted to take the test, and your test fee will be forfeited.

Rescheduling or Canceling an Appointment

If you need to reschedule the date, time, or location of your appointment, there is a US$60 fee (as this book goes to press) as long as you reschedule at least seven days before your original appointment. If you need to reschedule fewer than seven days before your original date, you have to pay the full registration amount again. Rescheduling can be done online at **mba.com** or by calling one of the numbers listed previously. If you reschedule over the phone, you may be subject to an additional fee. You cannot reschedule an appointment by mail or fax.

If you need to cancel your appointment, you will receive a US$80 refund (as this book goes to press) as long as you cancel at least seven days before your original appointment. If you cancel fewer than seven days before your original date, you forfeit the entire registration fee. For registration fees paid by credit card, the refund amount will be credited to the card. If the fee was paid by check or money order, you will receive a check in the mail. Cancellations can be made online at **mba.com** or by calling one of the numbers listed previously, based on your location. If you cancel over the phone, you may be subject to an additional fee. You cannot cancel an appointment by mail or fax.

The Day of the Test

You should arrive at your testing center 30 minutes before the time of your scheduled appointment. You must complete a number of security measures before you will be allowed to take the exam. A late arrival (15 minutes or more) may result in your being turned away from the testing center and forfeiting your test fee.

Presentation of Proper Identification

You will be asked to present ID—no exceptions. The following are the only acceptable forms:

- Passport
- Government-issued driver's license or (US only) laminated learner's permit
- Government-issued national/state/province identity card (including European ID card)
- Military ID card
- Permanent resident/green card (US only)

If you aren't a citizen of the country in which you take your test, you'll need your passport. In some countries, even if you are a citizen, a passport is required. Visit **mba.com** for the current requirements.

The ID must be current (not expired) and legible, and it should contain all four of the elements listed below. If you do not have one ID with all four of these elements, you will need to bring a second ID (also from the list above) that shows the missing elements.

1. Your name in the Roman alphabet. It must be exactly the same as what you provided when you made your appointment, including the order and placement of the names.
2. Your date of birth. The date of birth must also exactly match the date provided when you made your appointment.
3. A recent, recognizable photograph
4. Your signature

If these elements do not match what the test administrator has on file for you, you will not be allowed to take the GMAT, and your test fee will be forfeited.

Before you schedule your test appointment, make sure you understand all the requirements that are particular to your situation and have acquired or renewed the ID you will use. Also, note that if your ID is found to be fraudulent or invalid after you take the exam, your scores will be canceled and your test fee forfeited.

Palm Scan, Signature, and Photograph

Once your government-issued ID is approved, the administrator will take your palm scan, signature, and photograph using digital equipment. The testing rooms are also equipped with audio and video recorders, which are active during the exam. If you do not complete the entire check-in process or refuse to be recorded, you will not be allowed to take the GMAT, and your test fee will be forfeited.

Agreements

When you arrive at the center, you will be asked to agree to the GMAT Test Taker Rules & Agreement. Once you are seated at a workstation, you will electronically confirm that you agree to the GMAT Non-Disclosure Agreement and General Terms of Use statement. If you do not agree, you will not be allowed to take the GMAT, and your test fee will be forfeited. If you are caught violating the agreement, the business schools that you're applying to will be informed of this fact.

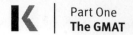
Prohibited Items

The following items cannot be brought into the testing room:

- Electronics of any kind, including cell phones, media players, cameras, radios, and photographic devices
- Any timepieces, including wristwatches, stopwatches, and watch alarms
- Notes, scratch paper, books, pamphlets, dictionaries, translators, and thesauruses
- Pens and pencils
- Measuring tools such as rulers
- Calculators and watch calculators

Essentially, you can't bring anything that may cause distractions, provide aid during testing, or be used to remove exam content from the testing room. (Note that you are not permitted to use a calculator for the Quantitative section, though there is an onscreen calculator available for the Integrated Reasoning section.) It is possible that your testing center has storage space available, such as lockers, where you can leave possessions that are prohibited from the testing room. However, this may not be the case at all centers. Call your testing center to inquire about storage and plan accordingly.

Disruptive Behavior

You will not be allowed to smoke, eat, drink, or use a cell phone in the testing room. In fact, you won't be allowed to use a phone or send a text message at all once the test has begun, even during breaks.

You also cannot leave the testing room without the administrator's permission. Some testing centers provide earplugs to keep noise to a minimum; if this interests you, call your testing center for details. Should you have any questions or problems during the exam, raise your hand and wait for the administrator to approach you.

Breaks

The length of your appointment is approximately 3.5 hours. Two breaks are scheduled into the exam. Each time you leave and return to the testing room, your palm will be scanned. If you exceed the allotted break time, the excess time will be deducted from the next section of your exam. For more information on administrative regulations and testing procedures, visit **mba.com**.

Know the Names of Up to Five Business Schools You Wish to Receive Your Scores

You may select up to five schools to receive your scores before you take the test. Your registration fee will cover that cost. Before Test Day, decide which schools you want to get your GMAT scores and bring that list with you. You will not be able to change the list once you have made your selection.

CHAPTER 2

Understanding the CAT

The GMAT is a computer-adaptive test, or CAT. The test is called "adaptive" because, in the course of a section, the test notices whether you answered the previous question correctly or incorrectly and "adapts" in its selection of the next question.

A few basic rules make the adaptive format possible:

- You're presented with one question at a time, and you must answer it to move on to the next question.
- You can't return to previously answered questions within a section.
- You can't skip questions—or rather, the only questions that can be skipped or omitted are any questions at the end of a section that you leave unanswered.
- Within a section (Quantitative or Verbal), the questions are not grouped by topic or type. You don't, for example, finish Reading Comprehension and then move on to Sentence Correction and then to Critical Reasoning; those three question types are interspersed with one another throughout the section.

The CAT Explained

Here's how the adapting works. You start the section (Quantitative or Verbal) with questions of about medium difficulty; about half of test takers get them right, and half get them wrong. Those who answer correctly begin to get harder questions, and those who answer incorrectly get easier items. This pattern continues: Throughout the section, if you got the previous question right, generally you'll get a harder question next. Conversely, if you got the previous question wrong, generally you'll get an easier one next. In this way, you'll follow a generally upward, downward, or flat trajectory through the questions. The test homes in on the difficulty level that is best matched to your performance; at that difficulty level, generally, you'll be getting about half the questions correct and half incorrect. Your score is determined by how high on the difficulty scale you end up, along with how many questions you answer. There is a significant penalty for leaving questions unanswered at the end of a section.

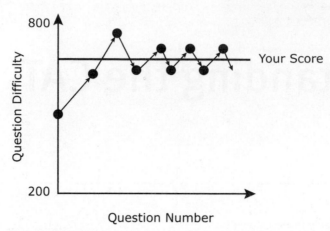

A Rough Schematic of How Adaptive Scoring Works on a CAT

The adaptive design of the test has two purposes:

1. **Accuracy:** A CAT is allegedly more accurate than a "linear" (i.e., nonadaptive) test because it zeros in on a test taker's ability level. Lucky guesses cause the GMAT to give lucky testers harder questions that they cannot answer correctly, thus eliminating any gains resulting from chance. Conversely, unlucky arithmetic errors on tough problems give unlucky testers easier problems, and these unlucky testers should be able to get the easier questions right, thus correcting the nonrepresentative drop in score.

2. **Time:** CATs can be made shorter than comparable linear tests, and the shorter duration is a benefit both to you and the test maker. The reason for this efficiency is that a CAT does not waste questions. If you get most of the questions right, you pretty much never see an easy one, and if you get most of the questions wrong, you pretty much never see a hard one. On a linear test, on the other hand, everyone gets the same mix of easy and hard questions. On such a test, students struggling on the easy questions will do little better than chance on the challenging problems, while high-scoring students will get close to 100 percent of the easy questions correct. Thus, giving low-scoring questions to high-scoring students (and vice versa) doesn't actually provide much useful statistical data. In this respect, many questions are "wasted," whereas the CAT can afford to be a much shorter test at equal accuracy.

Those points define the basic pattern of the CAT, but there are additional bells and whistles in the algorithm. One of the most important details to be aware of is that the test does not always adjust difficulty level question by question. Therefore, avoid the temptation to assess the difficulty level of a question you're on or to infer whether you got the previous question correct. Even if you could precisely assess a question's difficulty level (and you can't, in practice, for reasons we discuss partly later), you wouldn't be able to draw any conclusions, since the test doesn't always adapt immediately.

The experimental questions are another refinement to the CAT formula. Some of the questions in each section do not count toward your score. The test maker must try future questions out on people who do not know that they are experimental in order to determine the validity and difficulty of the questions. We'll talk more about this topic later, but we'll give away one headline early: do not try to guess which questions are experimental.

Are the First Questions More Important?

One of the most frequently asked questions about GMAT scoring is "Are the first 10 or so questions more important than the rest?"

As we've discussed, the GMAT adaptive algorithm starts with medium-difficulty questions. If you get questions right, your next questions are harder, and if you get questions wrong, your next questions are easier. The swings are relatively large at first but become smaller as the test zeros in on an estimate of your performance. For that reason, you may find it tempting to spend lots of extra time at the beginning of the test.

The short word on that idea: don't.

The test maker concedes that the computer-adaptive testing algorithm uses the first 10 questions to obtain an initial estimate of your ability. The key word, though, is *initial*. As you continue to answer questions, the algorithm self-corrects by computing an updated estimate on the basis of how many questions you have answered, and then it administers items that are closely matched to this new estimate of your ability. Your final score is based on your responses, the difficulty of all the questions you answered, and the number of questions left unanswered. Taking additional time on the first 10 questions will not "game the system" and can hurt your ability to finish the test.

The test maker insists that, despite persistent rumors to the contrary, you can't outsmart the GMAT by spending extra time at the beginning. The reason for this is timing: if you answer more questions correctly than you should in more time than you should, then you will face much harder questions, under more time pressure, in the rest of the section. Your short-term gains will be erased.

However, you still want to adjust your test prep strategy to account for those early swings. Specifically, remember that even when your test-taking skills have become so strong that most of your test will be made up of challenging, high-reward problems, you'll still have to go through some simpler problems to get there—don't rush or become overconfident just because those first few questions are easier.

A good comparison is to a sporting event. Are the first innings or is the first quarter of a game more important than the following ones? Perhaps, since the early part of the game sets the tone for the game and gives the leading team options. But doing well during the first part of a game does not guarantee a win; you need to start strong *and* finish strong.

The cost of not finishing strong on the GMAT is substantial. If you don't answer all the questions, a penalty is assessed that will precipitously lower your score. In fact, this effect is more exaggerated in the case of high scorers. As an example, provided by GMAC, if you are at the 91st percentile but then fail to answer five questions, your score could drop to the 77th percentile. A score difference of that magnitude is substantial.

The Importance of Pacing

The GMAT is a test of both accuracy and speed. There is a substantial penalty for not finishing a section, as we've seen. But there is no need to think of the GMAT as a race. In fact, according to the test maker, the GMAT is created to be optimally timed so that most test takers finish the first time they sit for the test. Those who don't finish the GMAT the first time often retake the test, and almost all finish the second time.

You want to be in the group that finishes the test on the first try. Also, while you don't want to rush or make sloppy guesses, you do need to finish the test on time in order to maximize your score.

The graph below is an illustration of the penalty incurred by test takers who leave a string of unanswered questions at the end of a CAT section. Even if you had previously been performing well on questions at a high level of difficulty, running out of time will lead to a severe drop in your score. Fortunately, pacing can be improved through practicing some key principles of time management.

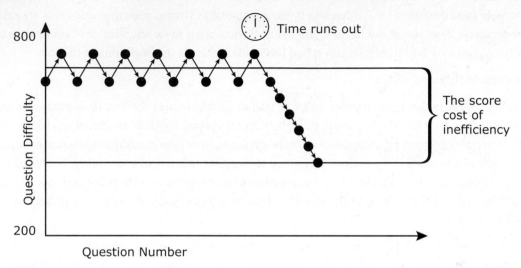

Spending Extra Time at the Beginning of a Section Can Lead to Failure at the End of the Section

You can pace yourself on both the Quantitative and Verbal sections, broadly speaking, by dividing each section into three parts:

1. The first 10 questions
2. The last 10 questions
3. Everything in between

Each part has its own strategy.

- **The first 10 questions:** Given what we've covered above, you now have an idea of how to pace yourself on the first 10 questions. To recap: the first questions are likely to produce some large swings in your score, but it's important to finish just as strong as you start. The theme of these 10 questions: proceed diligently, keep an eye out for pitfalls, and avoid preventable errors.

- **The middle segment:** Regardless of how the first 10 questions go, you're almost certain to find some challenges in this segment. Most test takers will "top out." Topping out means that you will be unable to solve any more difficult problems and you will begin to hover around your skill level, getting about half of the questions right and half of them wrong. The great danger at this point in the test is that you will feel you ought to be able to "get" every problem and you will spend too much time on some of them. Since time spent here takes away from the time you have for the later questions in the section, you may need to guess on a few questions to stay on pace. Fortunately, if you've budgeted your minutes well, you will have some time to give your guesses a little thought. The theme of the middle segment: stay on pace, keep your morale high, and make strategic guesses where necessary.

- **The final 10 questions** are the home stretch. You're trying to finish before the bell rings. Here you must pick your battles. Make an effort not to guess on more than one or two questions in a row. As the end draws nigh, alternate any guesses that you need to make, rather than saving them for a series at the end. Doing so will increase your options to solve without guessing, decrease the odds of accidentally running out of time, and most likely reduce the score drop from questions answered incorrectly. The theme of this segment: choose your questions and finish on time.

Now you're done. You've maximized your payoff. It can be exciting to set a pace and stick to it, and giving yourself permission to guess on the trickiest questions can reduce your anxiety and frustration.

Other CAT Strategies

In addition to the strategies mentioned earlier about pacing, keep in mind other CAT-specific strategies that will have a direct, positive impact on your score:

- Because the level of difficulty of questions on the CAT is not predictable, always be on the lookout for answer-choice traps.

- Because each right or wrong answer affects the next question you get, the CAT does not allow you to return to questions you've already answered. In other words, you cannot go back to double-check your work. So be as sure as you can be about your answer before moving on.

- If you're given a question you cannot answer, you'll have to guess. Guess intelligently and strategically by eliminating any answer choices that you know are wrong and guessing among those remaining. The faster you can determine that you can't answer a question, the more time you'll save by guessing; that's more time to spend on other questions that you *can* get right.

- Don't get rattled if you keep seeing really tough questions. It can mean you're doing very well. Keep it up—you're on your way to a great GMAT score!

Practice these strategies each time you take a CAT in your online resources, and you'll have the right mindset for success on Test Day.

 GO ONLINE

kaptest.com/login

PART TWO

Diagnostic Test

CHAPTER 3

GMAT Diagnostic Test

LEARNING OBJECTIVES

After studying this chapter, you will be able to:

- Complete a GMAT practice test in a test-like environment
- Self-assess your strengths and opportunities after gaining familiarity with GMAT test questions
- Create a goal-oriented study plan

How to Take This Test

To take Practice Test 1 (Diagnostic Test), log in to your online resources at **kaptest.com/login**. (If you have not yet registered your book, go to **kaptest.com/moreonline** to do so.)

GO ONLINE

kaptest.com/login

Before taking the diagnostic test, find a quiet place where you can work without interruptions for a little over 3 hours. If you cannot set aside this much time in a block, you can take the test in multiple sessions by using the Suspend button. However, this button will not be available during the actual test, so your experience will be more test-like—and you'll build more mental endurance—if you take the entire test in one sitting.

Make sure you have a comfortable desk, scratch paper or an erasable noteboard, and something to write with. To avoid a frustrating experience, use a strong internet connection; a weak connection can cause the test to think you've quit. Close all other apps on your device and all other tabs in your browser to avoid distracting content. If your device has a calculator app, do not use it during the Quantitative section, as you will not be permitted to use a calculator of any kind during this section on the actual GMAT.

The diagnostic test accurately reflects the question types and content of the GMAT Analytical Writing Assessment, Integrated Reasoning, Quantitative, and Verbal sections. The number of questions and timing of each section are also just like those of the real exam. And you'll be able to choose in which order you want to take the sections, just like on Test Day.

You'll gain several important benefits from taking this test. One is familiarity with the test format and content. This will give you context for the studying you're about to embark on, because you'll be able to relate what you learn to the hands-on experience of taking the test. Another benefit is an assessment of your strengths and areas of opportunity. This will provide important guidance as you plan your studying, allowing you to invest your time where it will yield the biggest score payoff.

If you have not already done so, read Chapters 1 and 2 about the GMAT and the nature of computer-adaptive tests. The information in these chapters will prepare you to get the most out of your diagnostic test experience.

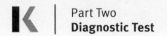
Review and Reflect

Taking a practice test is useful, but even more valuable is your review of the test—if you do it right.

How to Interpret Your Results

The most important thing to remember about your practice test results is that *they don't count*. They represent your skill at the test right now, but they don't reflect the scores you will earn on Test Day after you have put in many hours of practice.

More than your overall 200–800 score, pay attention to what types of questions you were most and least likely to get correct. First, did you perform better on the Verbal section or the Quantitative section, or did you do about the same on both? As shown in "GMAT Scoring" in Chapter 1, the same subscore means very different things on these two sections. For example, a subscore of 40 on the Verbal section represents quite strong performance, but a subscore of 40 on the Quant section is well below the 50th percentile. So when comparing your performance on these sections, use percentiles rather than subscores in order to compare "apples to apples." Both these sections are important for your overall score, and business schools look at the scores on both sections, so if you are much weaker on one than the other, you should plan to spend proportionally more time practicing for that section.

Then within each section, look for patterns in which questions you got right and wrong. Did you struggle with Critical Reasoning, for example, but do pretty well on Reading Comprehension and Sentence Correction? Or did you find Data Sufficiency questions challenging? Or are there certain areas of math that you don't remember well from whenever you last had a math class? Once you've identified the questions that give you the most trouble, plan to study the related book chapters early in your prep. That way, you'll be able to spiral back and review them several times before Test Day; this spiral approach is a proven technique for boosting your learning and your score.

How to Review the Test

The explanations themselves are valuable learning tools. Review all the explanations, both for the questions you answered incorrectly *and* those you got right. For the questions you missed, once you understand how to arrive at the correct answer, hide the explanation and redo the question. By actually doing the question correctly, you'll build "mental muscle memory" of doing it right. This is much more powerful than simply reading about how you could have done it right. Now, having successfully worked from the information given to the correct answer, you'll be more likely to be able to do it again on a similar question—on Test Day.

For the questions you got correct, first confirm that you answered correctly for the right reasons and not just based on a lucky hunch. Then consider whether the explanation offers a more efficient path to the right answer that you can add to your toolbox. If so, then practice redoing the question the same as if you'd missed it, in order to master the alternative approach. Or maybe you aced the question! Even in this case, reviewing the explanation will reinforce your successful approach, helping you be even more confident and efficient the next time you see a similar question.

As you review these explanations, you may not understand everything they say. Don't worry! The GMAT tests many concepts, and you haven't yet begun to learn all the valuable Kaplan Methods and strategies contained in this book. You may find it useful to return to these explanations later in your studies, once you've read and practiced with this book and your online resources. It's likely that by that point, things that were confusing at first will have become much clearer. It will also be a great confidence booster to see how far you've come in your mastery of the GMAT!

How to Plan Your Practice

No matter what your performance is on the diagnostic test, you can and will improve if you set aside time to study for the GMAT. Block out study time on your calendar, just as you would write down any other appointment. These blocks of time are appointments with yourself, so keep them!

Research shows that people learn better in shorter, more frequent study sessions. Therefore, plan to study at least three days a week for one to three hours, rather than one or two days a week for four or more hours. Sometimes students avoid studying because they feel too tired at the end of a long day at work, but that's often because they think "studying" means spending several hours focusing on tough academic material. Remember that putting in even 30 minutes—perhaps reading one section in your book, doing a handful of questions, or even reviewing questions you've done before—moves you forward toward your goal. Plus, it's much better to do a little and feel good about it than to feel overwhelmed from falling behind. Making time to study will help you feel motivated to study even more.

Every time you sit down to study, set a specific goal for each chunk of study time that addresses a skill you need to develop to score higher. Here are some examples of goals:

- Study the "Averages" section in the Math Formulas chapter, complete the accompanying practice set, and review the explanations, noting challenging questions in my question log.

- Review again the Reading Comprehension Strategy chapter to reinforce my understanding of strategic reading. Then practice using a passage set in the online Qbank, reviewing the explanations thoroughly.

- Complete five Problem Solving and five Data Sufficiency questions from the Quantitative Reasoning—Advanced Practice chapter. Review the explanations, noting challenging questions in my question log.

How you put together your study plan will depend on three factors:

1. How much improvement you want to achieve
2. When you want to take your test
3. How much time you have each week for GMAT practice

Clearly, these factors are interdependent. If you want to see a big score increase and you need to take your test in four weeks to meet an application deadline, then you'll probably need to put in at least 25 hours each week to meet your goal. In this case, if you weren't able to study that much in the next month, this would be a good time to reconsider how you will travel your path toward business school. By thinking through these three factors now, you will set yourself up for success and avoid frustration.

If you have ample time before Test Day, you will benefit from working through each chapter in this book, taking full advantage of the strategic explanations, and using your online resources at **kaptest.com/login** for further practice. If, however, you have more limited time to prepare, you may need to prioritize your studies to make sure you address the areas in which you are struggling the most—thereby making the most of your opportunities for score improvement.

And again, don't concern yourself with how many questions you got right or missed on this test. You've still got a lot to learn about the GMAT, but you have good tools to help you on your journey—and taking and reviewing your diagnostic test is a great first step. Just remember to be patient with yourself as you make mistakes. Everyone does—making mistakes is an essential part of learning. But consider this: every wrong answer you choose, *and then learn from*, reduces the chance that you'll get a similar question wrong on the one and only day when wrong answers matter. So make mistakes willingly and even happily now, while they don't count. Just resolve to learn from every one of them.

Happy studying!

PART THREE

Verbal Section and Strategies

CHAPTER 4

Verbal Section Overview

LEARNING OBJECTIVES

After studying this chapter, you will be able to:

- List important attributes of the Verbal section including question formats, timing demands, and the scoring method
- Articulate how key reasoning skills can help you manage the Verbal section

---

The Quantitative and Verbal sections contribute about equally to your overall 200–800 score. If your performance on the Verbal section is a strength, make sure to leverage that strength by including some Verbal practice in your study plan. If you're concerned about your Verbal score, know that the chapters in this part of the book will give you strategic approaches that work for every Verbal question type.

Composition of the Verbal Section

LEARNING OBJECTIVES

In this section, you will learn how to:

- Name the three different question formats found in the Verbal section
- Enumerate approximately how many questions of each format are found in the Verbal section
- Describe the nature and purpose of the experimental questions

---

A little more than half of the multiple-choice questions that count toward your overall score appear in the Verbal section. You have 65 minutes to answer 36 Verbal questions in three formats: Reading Comprehension, Sentence Correction, and Critical Reasoning. These three types of questions are mingled throughout the Verbal section, so you never know what's coming next. Here's what you can expect to see:

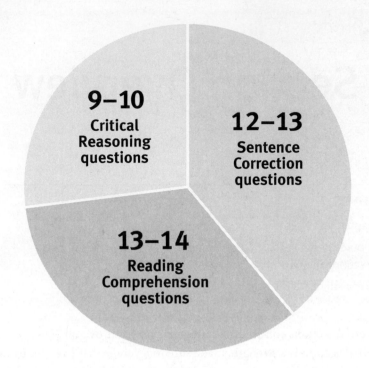

The Approximate Mix of Questions on the GMAT Verbal Section

You may see more of one question type and fewer of another. Don't worry: the GMAT is a standardized test, so the number of each kind of question won't vary too far from what you expect and have studied for.

In the next three chapters, you'll learn strategies for each of these question types. But first, let's look at some techniques for managing the Verbal section as a whole.

Experimental Questions

Some questions on the GMAT are experimental. These questions are not factored into your score. They are questions that the test maker is evaluating for possible use on future tests. To get good data, the test maker has to test each question against the whole range of test takers—that is, high and low scorers. Therefore, you could be on your way to an 800 and suddenly come across an easy question, leading you to question how you think you are doing.

Don't panic; just do your best on the question in front of you and keep going. The difficulty level of the experimental questions you see has little to do with how you're currently scoring. Remember, there is no way for you to know whether a question is experimental or not, so approach every question as if it were scored.

Furthermore, keep in mind that it's hard to judge the difficulty level of a question. A question that seems easy to you may simply be playing to your personal strengths and be very difficult for other test takers. So don't waste time speculating about the difficulty of the questions you're seeing and what that implies about your performance. Rather, focus your energy on answering the question on the screen as efficiently as possible.

Pacing on the Verbal Section

> **LEARNING OBJECTIVES**
>
> In this section, you will learn how to:
>
> - Predict how much time to spend on different kinds of questions on the Verbal section
> - Identify a strategy for pacing your work on the Verbal section
> - Articulate an appropriate guessing strategy for the Verbal section

The GMAT will give you about four Reading Comprehension passages. With less than 2 minutes per question on the Verbal section, where will you find the time to read those passages?

Part of the answer is that the Reading Comprehension chapter of this book will give you great tips about how to read the passages efficiently. Another big part, though, is how you will handle Sentence Correction. Follow the Kaplan Method for Sentence Correction, which you will see in the chapter devoted to that question type, and through practice you will bring your average time down to 60 seconds per Sentence Correction question. Moving through Sentence Correction questions efficiently will allow you the time you'll need to read long Reading Comprehension passages and take apart complex arguments in Critical Reasoning.

Here are Kaplan's timing recommendations for the Verbal section of the GMAT. While it's far more important at first that you practice to build mastery of the strategies, it's also a good idea to keep these timing recommendations in mind. Then, by incorporating more timed practice as you progress in your GMAT prep, you will grow comfortable reading and answering questions at the suggested pace, setting yourself up for success on Test Day.

Verbal Section Timing	
Question type	**Average time you should spend**
Sentence Correction	1 minute per question
Critical Reasoning	2 minutes per question
Reading Comprehension	4 minutes per passage and a little less than 1.5 minutes per question

Following these timing guidelines will also help you pace yourself so that you have time to work on the questions at the end of the section. One of the most persistent bits of bad advice out there is that you should take more time at the beginning of the test. Don't fall for this myth! Running short of time at the end of the test will cost you much more than you may gain from a few extra right answers up front. The test maker imposes heavy score penalties for not reaching all questions in a section, and long strings of wrong answers due to guessing or rushing will hurt your score as well.

What this all means is that you are under some conflicting pressures. It might seem like a good idea to take extra time at the beginning to ensure that you get all the early questions right, since then the test would give you those difficult, high-value questions. But if you use up a lot of time early on, you won't have time to finish, and your score will suffer a severe penalty. Just a handful of unanswered final questions can lower a score from the mid-90th percentile to the mid-70th percentile. Plus, if you spend all that time early on, you won't have time to solve the hard questions you may receive as a result of your careful work, so you won't be able to take advantage of their extra value.

So if taking more time at the beginning isn't a good idea, does that mean you should rush through the beginning? This is also not the case. Rushing almost guarantees that you will miss some crucial aspect of a question. If you get a lot of midlevel questions wrong, the test will never give you those difficult, high-value questions that you want to reach.

If you are stuck on a question, make a guess. Even the best test takers occasionally guess, and it's still possible to achieve an elite score if you are strategic about when and how you guess. If you start to fall behind pace, look for good guessing questions. That way, you'll reach the end of the section and have the time to earn the points for all the questions that you are capable of answering correctly and efficiently. What kinds of questions are good candidates for guessing? Ones that you know play to your weaknesses, ones that require lots of reading, or ones that look like they will involve separate evaluation of each answer choice.

Strategic Guessing

Whether because you're running short of time or you've encountered a question that totally flummoxes you, you will have to guess occasionally. But first, try to narrow down the answer choices. This will greatly improve your chances of guessing the right answer. When you guess, follow this plan:

1. **Eliminate answer choices you know are wrong.** Even if you don't know the right answer, you can often tell that some of the choices are wrong. For instance, on Sentence Correction questions, you can eliminate (A) as soon as you find an error in the original sentence, thus reducing the number of choices to consider.

2. **Avoid answer choices that make you suspicious.** These are the choices that just "look wrong" or conform to a common wrong-answer type. For example, if an answer choice in a Reading Comprehension question mentions a concept you don't remember from the passage, chances are it is wrong. (The next three chapters contain more information about common wrong-answer types on the Verbal section.)

3. **Choose one of the remaining answer choices.** The fewer options you have to choose from, the higher your chances of selecting the right answer.

How the Verbal Section Is Scored

LEARNING OBJECTIVE

In this section, you will learn how to:

- Describe the process by which the GMAT's computer-adaptive test (CAT) functions to score your performance

The Verbal section of the GMAT is quite different from the verbal sections of paper-and-pencil tests you may have taken. The major difference between the test formats is that the GMAT computer-adaptive test adapts to your performance. Each test taker is given a different mix of questions, depending on how well he or she is doing on the test. In other words, the questions get harder or easier depending on whether you answer them correctly or incorrectly. Your GMAT score is not determined by the number of questions you get right but rather by the difficulty level of the questions you get right.

When you begin a section, the computer:

- Assumes you have an average score (about 590).
- Gives you a medium-difficulty question. About half the people who take the test will get this question right, and half will get it wrong. What happens next depends on whether you answer the question correctly.

If you answer the question correctly:

- Your score goes up.
- You are given a slightly harder question.

If you answer the question incorrectly:

- Your score goes down.
- You are given a slightly easier question.

This pattern continues for the rest of the section. As you get questions right, the computer raises your score and gives you harder questions. As you get questions wrong, the computer lowers your score and gives you easier questions. In this way, the computer homes in on your score.

If you feel like you're struggling at the end of the section, don't worry! Because the CAT adapts to find the outer edge of your abilities, the test will feel hard; it's designed to be difficult for everyone, even the highest scorers.

Core Competencies on the Verbal Section

LEARNING OBJECTIVE

In this section, you will learn how to:

- Describe how Critical Thinking, Pattern Recognition, Paraphrasing, and Attention to the Right Detail are relevant to the Verbal section

Unlike most subject-specific tests you have taken throughout your academic career, the scope of knowledge that the GMAT requires of you is fairly limited. In fact, you don't need any background knowledge or expertise beyond fundamental math and verbal skills. While mastering those fundamentals is essential to your success on the GMAT—and this book is concerned in part with helping you develop or refresh those skills— the GMAT does *not* primarily seek to reward test takers for content-specific knowledge. Rather, the GMAT is a test of high-level thinking and reasoning abilities; it uses math and verbal subject matter as a platform to build questions that test your critical-thinking and problem-solving capabilities. As you prepare for the GMAT, you will notice that similar analytical skills come into play across the various question types and sections of the test.

Kaplan has adopted the term "Core Competencies" to refer to the four bedrock thinking skills rewarded by the GMAT: Critical Thinking, Pattern Recognition, Paraphrasing, and Attention to the Right Detail. The Kaplan Methods and strategies presented throughout this book will help you demonstrate these all-important skills. Let's dig into each of the Core Competencies in turn and discuss how each applies to the Verbal section.

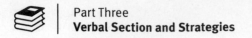

Critical Thinking

Most potential MBA students are adept at creative problem solving, and the GMAT offers many opportunities to demonstrate this skill. You probably already have experience assessing situations to see when data are inadequate; synthesizing information into valid deductions; finding creative solutions to complex problems; and avoiding unnecessary, redundant labor.

In GMAT terms, a critical thinker is a creative problem solver who engages in critical inquiry. One of the hallmarks of successful test takers is their skill at asking the right questions. GMAT critical thinkers first consider what they're being asked to do, then study the given information and ask the right questions, especially, "How can I get the answer in the most direct way?" and "How can I use the question format to my advantage?"

For instance, as you examine a Reading Comprehension passage, you'll interrogate the author: "Why are you writing about Walt Whitman?" or "Why have you included this detail in paragraph 2?" For Sentence Correction questions, you'll ask: "Why do three of the five answer choices share the same grammatical construction?" or "Is there a better way to express the idea?" For Critical Reasoning, you'll ask the author of the argument: "What's your main point?" or "What evidence have you presented to convince me to agree with you?"

Those test takers who learn to ask the right questions become creative problem solvers—and GMAT champs. Let's see how to apply the GMAT Core Competency of Critical Thinking to a sample Critical Reasoning question:

1. One problem with labor unions today is that their top staffs consist of college-trained lawyers, economists, and labor relations experts who cannot understand the concerns of real workers. One goal of union reform movements should be to build staffs out of workers who have come up from the ranks of the industry involved.

   The argument above depends primarily upon which one of the following assumptions?

   ○   Higher education lessens people's identification with their class background.

   ○   Union staffs should include more people with firsthand industrial supervisory experience.

   ○   Some people who have worked in a given industry can understand the concerns of workers in that industry.

   ○   Most labor unions today do not fairly represent workers' interests.

   ○   A goal of union reform movements should be to make unions more democratic.

This question asks you to identify what the author is assuming. You'll learn more about assumptions in the Critical Reasoning chapter of this book, but for now, know that an "assumption" is something the author *must* believe but doesn't state directly. A skilled critical thinker will approach this task by asking questions to uncover the author's unstated assumption.

First of all, what does the author want to see happen? The author argues that unions should get more "workers who have come up through the ranks" into leadership. What's her reason for this claim? She asserts that the lawyers and experts don't understand what real workers worry about.

So if her solution is to get more rank-and-file workers into top union staffs, then what must she think these rank-and-file are capable of? The author is assuming that, unlike the college-trained experts, "workers who have come up through the ranks" can understand the concerns of the "real workers" whom the unions are supposed to represent. Scanning the answer choices, the one that matches this prediction is choice (**C**).

Notice how efficiently you can move through a question like this one when you engage in critical inquiry—no rereading, no falling for answer choice traps, no time wasted. As you move through this book, you'll learn how to identify the most helpful questions to ask depending on how the test question is constructed.

Pattern Recognition

Most people fail to appreciate the level of constraint standardization places on test makers. Because the test makers must give reliable, valid, and comparable scores to many thousands of students each year, they're forced to reward the same skills on every test. They do so by repeating the same kinds of questions with the same traps and pitfalls, which are susceptible to the same strategic solutions.

Inexperienced test takers treat every problem as if it were a brand-new task, whereas the GMAT rewards those who spot the patterns and use them to their advantage. Of course, Pattern Recognition is a key business skill in its own right: executives who recognize familiar situations and apply proven solutions to them will outperform those who reinvent the wheel every time.

Even the smartest test taker will struggle if he approaches each GMAT question as a novel exercise. But the GMAT features nothing novel—just repeated patterns. Kaplan knows this test inside and out, and we'll show you which patterns you will encounter on Test Day. You will know the test better than your competition does. Let's see how to apply the GMAT Core Competency of Pattern Recognition to a sample Sentence Correction question:

2. A major pharmaceutical company, in cooperation with an international public health organization and the medical research departments of two large universities, <u>is expected to announce tomorrow that it will transfer the</u> rights to manufacture a number of tuberculosis drugs to several smaller companies.

   ○   is expected to announce tomorrow that it will transfer the

   ○   are expected to announce tomorrow that they will transfer their

   ○   are expected to announce tomorrow that they will transfer the

   ○   is expected to announce tomorrow that they will transfer the

   ○   is expected to announce tomorrow that there would be a transfer of the

Many people will look at this problem and start thinking about grammar classes they haven't had for years. Then they'll plug every answer choice back into the sentence to see which one works best. Did you find yourself doing that during your diagnostic test?

There are two important patterns at work in this question that you should recognize from now on. First, choice (**A**) on Sentence Correction questions will always repeat the underlined portion of the original sentence. You should only ever choose (**A**) if there's no error in the original sentence. If you've already read the original sentence, there's never any reason to spend time reading through choice (**A**).

Second, notice the pronoun *it* in the underlined portion. Pronouns are one of seven grammar and usage topics that together make up 93 percent of the Sentence Correction issues on the GMAT. Whenever a pronoun appears in the underlined portion of the sentence, you should check whether it's correct. Here, ask yourself what *it* refers to. In this case, *it* is the pharmaceutical company. Notice in scanning the answer choices that they, too, fall into patterns: some use *it*, and others use *they*. Recognizing this pattern lets you know what question to ask next: "To refer to a company, is the correct pronoun *it* or *they*?" For a singular noun, the correct pronoun is *it*. Eliminate (**B**), (**C**), and (**D**), which all use *they*.

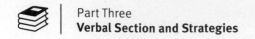
Having narrowed down the choices to just two, (**A**) and (**E**), you can eliminate (**E**) because it uses an awkward, lengthy phrase that makes it less clear *who* will "transfer the rights." The answer is (**A**); the sentence is correct as written.

Notice how efficiently you can find the correct answer when you recognize the patterns. Meanwhile, your competition, not recognizing how the GMAT works, would waste time floundering through each answer choice in turn.

Paraphrasing

Yet another Core Competency is Paraphrasing: the GMAT rewards those who can reduce difficult, abstract, or polysyllabic prose to simple terms. Paraphrasing is, of course, an essential business skill: executives must be able to define clear tasks based on complicated requirements and accurately summarize mountains of detail.

The test isn't going to make it easy for you to understand questions and passages. But you won't be overwhelmed by the complicated prose of Critical Reasoning or Reading Comprehension questions if you endeavor to make your own straightforward mental translations. Habitually putting complex ideas and convoluted wording into your own simple, accurate terms will ensure that you "get it"—that you understand the information well enough to drive to the correct answer.

Let's see how to apply the GMAT Core Competency of Paraphrasing to the first paragraph of a sample Reading Comprehension passage. You will return to this passage in full in the Reading Comprehension chapter of this book. For now, use the first paragraph to see how Paraphrasing helps you synthesize ideas by putting them in your own words:

> The informal sector of the economy involves activities that, in both developed and underdeveloped countries, are outside the arena of the normal, regulated economy and thus escape official record keeping. These activities, which include such practices as off-the-books hiring and cash payments, occur mainly in service industries such as construction, hotels, and restaurants. Many economists think that the informal sector is an insignificant supplement to the larger formal economy. They base this belief on three assumptions that have been derived from theories of industrial development. But empirical evidence suggests that these assumptions are not valid.

One of the most crucial ways to paraphrase on the GMAT is to summarize the main idea of a paragraph. When you learn about passage mapping in the Reading Comprehension chapter of this book, you will see how helpful it is to write a short summary of each paragraph. Clearly, however, you do not want to waste time copying down whole sentences or phrases from the passage verbatim. Paraphrasing helps you simultaneously identify quick, short ways to record main ideas and reinforce your understanding of those ideas.

You don't need to be an expert on economic policy to identify the main ideas in this paragraph and put them into your own words. The paragraph defines the informal sector, gives examples, then sets the stage for a debate between "many economists" and the author over how big or important the informal sector is.

On Test Day, you might write the following shorthand notes in your passage map for this paragraph:

¶1: Informal sector jobs; examps; econs think minor (based on 3 assumps); author disagrees

As you work through the Verbal chapters of this book, you will learn more about Paraphrasing for Reading Comprehension passages. You will also develop techniques for Paraphrasing the content of Critical Reasoning questions and interpreting the gist of what a Sentence Correction sentence is trying to say so that you can choose the answer choice that most accurately and concisely expresses that meaning.

Attention to the Right Detail

Details present a dilemma: missing them can cost you points. But if you try to absorb every fact in a Reading Comprehension passage or Critical Reasoning stimulus, you may find yourself swamped, delayed, and still unready for the questions that follow, because the relevant and irrelevant details are all mixed together in your mind. Throughout this book, you will learn how to discern the essential details from those that can slow you down or confuse you. The GMAT test maker rewards examinees for paying attention to the right details—the ones that make the difference between right and wrong answers.

Attention to the Right Detail distinguishes great administrators from poor ones in the business world as well. Just ask anyone who's had a boss who had the wrong priorities or who was so bogged down in minutiae that the department stopped functioning.

Not all details are created equal, and there are mountains of them on the test. Learn to target only what will turn into correct answers. Let's see how to apply the GMAT Core Competency of Attention to the Right Detail to a sample Critical Reasoning question:

3. Police officers in Smith County who receive Special Weapons and Tactics (SWAT) training spend considerable time in weapons instruction and practice. This time spent developing expertise in the use of guns affects the instincts of Smith County officers, making them too reliant on firearms. In the past year in Smith County, in 12 of the 14 cases in which police officers shot a suspect while attempting to make an arrest, the officer involved had received SWAT training, although only 5 percent of the police force as a whole in the county had received such training.

    Which of the following, if true, most strengthens the argument above?

    ○ In an adjacent county, all of the cases in which police shot suspects involved officers with SWAT training.

    ○ SWAT training stresses the need for surprise, speed, and aggression when approaching suspects.

    ○ Only 15 percent of Smith County's SWAT training course is devoted to firearms lessons.

    ○ Among officers involved in the arrest of suspects in Smith County in the past year, the proportion who had received SWAT training was similar to the proportion who had received SWAT training in the police force as a whole.

    ○ Some Smith County officers without SWAT training have not been on a firing range in years.

You will learn more about strengthening arguments in the Critical Reasoning chapter of this book; for now, focus on finding the detail that makes a difference.

SWAT training, the author concludes in the second sentence, is making Smith County officers too reliant on firearms. The evidence in the third sentence presents you with many different numbers and figures. However, the important thing to note here is the shift in scope between the conclusion, which is about Smith County police officers in general, and the evidence, which is about the 14 cases that involved shootings during an arrest.

That scope shift signals that you've found the right detail to focus on. If the author is using data from arrests to make a point about the effects of SWAT training on the police force as a whole, it will make a difference if, for example, a disproportionate number of officers involved in making arrests have received SWAT training. Since you're looking for the answer choice that strengthens the argument, you need one that equates officers making arrests to officers at large.

Choice **(D)** is the correct answer. If **(D)** is true, then the officers in the 14 cases are representative of officers as a whole, and the argument is strengthened.

Notice that paying Attention to the Right Detail—the one that the question hinges upon—enables you to form a prediction of what the correct answer will contain. Selecting an answer then becomes a straightforward matter of finding the choice that matches your prediction, rather than a time-consuming process of debating the pros and cons of each answer choice in turn. Throughout this book, you will learn to distinguish the important from the inconsequential on the GMAT.

Introduction to Strategic Reading

LEARNING OBJECTIVES

In this section, you will learn how to:

- Describe how attending to key words will help you read with a strategic purpose .
- Identify several categories of key words

Since you're reading this book and aspire to go to business school, it goes without saying that you can read. What needs saying is that the way of reading for which you've been rewarded throughout your academic and professional careers is likely not the best way to read on Test Day.

Normally, when you read for school, pleasure, or even work, the main things you try to get from the text are the facts—the story, who did what, what's true or false. That way of reading may have served you well throughout your life, but on the GMAT you must read strategically.

Because Kaplan knows the test so well, we've identified the key structures that will get you points on the test. More importantly, we've identified the key words that signal those structures and tell you what to do with them. Strategic Reading means using structural key words to zero in on what the test will ask you about. Usually, it's great to read in order to broaden your horizons. On Test Day, you haven't got time for anything that doesn't pay off in right answers.

KEY WORDS

- Key words determine the structure of a passage.
- Key words highlight lines in the text that are crucial to the author's message.

As you see from the bullet points, key words help you see the structure of the passage. That, in turn, tells you what part of the text is crucial to the author's point of view, which is what the test consistently rewards you for noticing.

On the GMAT, questions could give the same facts, but the correct answers could vary depending on the author's point of view. To see how this works, take a look at the following two facts about Bob:

Bob got a great GMAT score.

He is going to East Main State Business School.

The meaning depends on the key word that links these facts. Fill in the supported inference for each case:

Bob got a great GMAT score. Therefore, he is going to East Main State Business School.

Supported inference about East Main State: _____

Bob got a great GMAT score. Nevertheless, he is going to East Main State Business School.

Supported inference about East Main State: _____

For the first example, you can infer that East Main State must be a good school, or at least Bob must think it is; because he got a good score, that's where he's going. Based on the second example, however, you can infer that East Main State must not be the kind of school where people with good scores usually go; it must not be very competitive to get in there. Notice that the facts didn't change. The key words "therefore" and "nevertheless" made all the difference to the correct GMAT inference.

This distinction is important because almost all GMAT questions hinge on key words. Because it cannot reward test takers for outside knowledge, the GMAT cannot ask what you already know about East Main State—but it *will* ask questions to assess how well you understand what the author says about East Main State.

In Reading Comprehension and Critical Reasoning, key words highlight the author's opinion and logic, and they may indicate contrast, illustration, continuation, and sequence. As you continue your GMAT prep, pay close attention to key words you encounter and what they tell you about the relationship between the information that comes before and after the key words. Here are the most important categories of key words and some examples of words that fall into each category.

KEY WORD CATEGORIES

Contrast: Nevertheless, despite, although, but, yet, on the other hand

Continuation: Furthermore, moreover, additionally, also, and

Logic: Therefore, thus, consequently, it follows that, because, since

Illustration: For example, we can see this by, this shows, to illustrate

Sequence/Timing: First, second, finally, in the 1920s, several steps, later

Emphasis/Opinion: Unfortunately, happily, crucial, very important, a near disaster, unsuccessful, they even _____

To see how key words separate the useful from the useless on the GMAT, take a look at the following Critical Reasoning question—without the answer choices for the moment. You will learn more about analyzing arguments in the Critical Reasoning chapter of this book, but for now, the questions within this question will guide you through the process of breaking down an argument using key words:

What does this word tell us about the relationship between "artistic quality" and "marketing tool"? _____

What does this word tell us about the purpose of this sentence? _____

4. In recent years, many advertisements have won awards for their artistic quality. But since advertising must serve as a marketing tool, advertising executives must exercise their craft with an eye to the effectiveness of their advertisement. For this reason , advertising is not art.

What reason is this phrase referring to?

_____

_____

Paraphrase this argument: _____

_____

_____

_____

_____

The argument above depends on which of the following assumptions ?

What is the author assuming? _____

_____

Let's walk through the above questions in boxes, starting with the question that refers to the word "but." You may have noted that "but" is a contrast key word. This tells you that the author believes the terms "artistic quality" and "marketing tool" to be opposed or incompatible.

The next question refers to the word "since," which falls under the logic category of key words. Like the word "because," "since" signals a reason; in terms of an argument, "since" introduces the author's evidence.

The phrase "for this reason" refers to the evidence that came immediately beforehand—that ad executives must be concerned with effectiveness. "For this reason" also signals that the final sentence contains the argument's conclusion.

The next box asks you to paraphrase the argument. This means that you should put the evidence and conclusion into your own succinct words: *Ads aren't art [conclusion] because they must take effectiveness into account [evidence].*

Before looking at the answer choices, you need to predict exactly what you're looking for: "What is the author assuming?" Look for the gap in your paraphrase above. The author must believe that something judged on its effectiveness cannot be art.

Now take a look at the answer choices and identify which one matches your prediction.

4. In recent years, many advertisements have won awards for their artistic quality. But since advertising must serve as a marketing tool, advertising executives must exercise their craft with an eye to the effectiveness of their advertisement. For this reason, advertising is not art.

   The argument above depends on which of the following assumptions?

   ○ Some advertisements are made to be displayed solely as art.

   ○ Some advertising executives are more concerned than others with the effectiveness of their product.

   ○ Advertising executives ought to be more concerned than they currently are with the artistic dimension of advertising.

   ○ Something is not "art" if its creator must be concerned with its practical effect.

   ○ Artists are not concerned with the monetary value of their work.

Choice (**D**) matches the prediction and is the correct answer.

By attending to the key words, you zeroed in on just what's important to the test maker—with no wasted effort or rereading. Strategic Reading embodies all four GMAT Core Competencies: Critical Thinking, Pattern Recognition, Paraphrasing, and Attention to the Right Detail.

CHAPTER 5

Critical Reasoning Strategy

LEARNING OBJECTIVES

After studying this chapter, you will be able to:

- Describe the format of a Critical Reasoning question
- State the steps of the Kaplan Method for Critical Reasoning
- Define *argument* as it is used in Critical Reasoning questions on the Verbal section

Below is a typical Critical Reasoning question. In this chapter, we'll look at how to apply the Kaplan Method to this question, discuss the logical structures being tested, and go over the basic principles and strategies that you want to keep in mind on every Critical Reasoning question.

A study of 20 overweight males revealed that each man experienced significant weight loss after adding SlimDown, an artificial food supplement, to his daily diet. For three months, each man consumed one SlimDown portion every morning after exercising and then followed his normal diet for the rest of the day. Clearly, all adult males who consume one portion of SlimDown every day for at least three months will lose weight and will look and feel their best.

Which one of the following is an assumption on which the argument depends?

- ⭘ The men in the study will gain back the weight they lost if they discontinue the SlimDown program.
- ⭘ No other dietary supplement will have the same effect on overweight men.
- ⭘ The daily exercise regimen was not responsible for the effects noted in the study.
- ⭘ Women will not experience similar weight reductions if they adhere to the SlimDown program for three months.
- ⭘ Overweight men will achieve only partial weight loss if they do not remain on the SlimDown program for a full three months.

Before you move on, take a minute to think about what you see in this question and answer some questions about how you think it works:

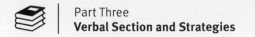

- The question refers to the paragraph as an "argument." What does this term mean?

- What does it mean for an argument to depend on an assumption?

- Notice that the question comes after the argument. Is it a better idea to read the argument first or the question first?

- What GMAT Core Competencies are most essential to success on this question?

Previewing Critical Reasoning

LEARNING OBJECTIVES

In this section, you will learn how to:

- Describe the concepts of evidence and conclusion in an argument

- Define an assumption and explain how it relates to an author's argument

- Identify where to start with a Critical Reasoning question

- Explain how Core Competencies will help you tackle Critical Reasoning questions

Here are the answers to the questions you considered above.

The Question Refers to the Paragraph as an "Argument." What Does This Term Mean?

Over 70 percent of Critical Reasoning questions are based on arguments, so understanding what they are and how they work will be of great help on Test Day.

When the GMAT refers to an *argument*, it doesn't mean a conversation in which two people shout at each other. An argument in Critical Reasoning means any piece of text in which an author puts forth a set of ideas or a point of view and attempts to support it. A statement such as "Small dogs make better pets than large dogs" is not an argument—it's just an opinion. An argument must make some attempt to persuade. For instance, if this opinion statement included a reason or two to support its point of view, then it would become a simple argument: "Small dogs make better pets than large dogs, because small dogs are easier to clean up after and generally have longer life spans than do large dogs." Later in this chapter, you will learn to refer to these main parts of the argument as the *conclusion* (the author's main point) and the *evidence* (the support for that point).

What Does It Mean for an Argument to Depend on an Assumption?

In everyday life, the verb *to assume* is used to mean "to take for granted" or "to presume" that something is the case. Likewise, *to depend on* something is to "need" or "rely on" that thing. Fortunately, the meaning of the word *assumption* in the context of a GMAT argument is much the same. Critical Reasoning questions that ask for an argument's assumption could be paraphrased as follows: "What important fact does the author of the argument take for granted but not directly state?" or "What else would need to be true in order for this argument to hold?" Throughout this chapter, you will see how identifying the central assumption is key to answering Critical Reasoning questions that involve arguments.

The Question Comes After the Text. Is It a Better Idea to Read the Text or the Question First?

It might be your natural instinct to start reading from the beginning of the paragraph, but the most efficient approach is to read the question (which we call the *question stem*) before the paragraph that precedes it (which we call the *stimulus*). By starting with the question stem and identifying the task it poses, you will be able to read the stimulus strategically—targeting the information you need to answer the question without wasting time rereading.

What GMAT Core Competencies Are Most Essential to Success on This Question?

As you may have surmised from the previous paragraphs, Critical Reasoning questions are full of rewards for test takers with a firm handle on all four Core Competencies—the bedrock analytical skills that the GMAT measures. Critical Thinking will enable you to analyze the structure of arguments, such as the one at the beginning of this chapter, and identify any gaps or errors in the author's logic. Your Pattern Recognition skills will help you take advantage of patterns of argumentation that come up again and again, as well as enable you to spot common wrong answer types quickly. Paraphrasing is essential to untangling tough text, such as the description of study results in this stimulus, by putting it in your own words. Finally, Attention to the Right Detail will let you zero in on the most important parts of Critical Reasoning stimuli, often signaled by key words, and determine which facts are crucial to the correct answer. In this and the following chapters, you will learn how to apply these skills to every type of Critical Reasoning question you may see on Test Day.

What Do Critical Reasoning Questions Test?

LEARNING OBJECTIVE

In this section, you will learn how to:

- Articulate the thinking skills that will help you tackle Critical Reasoning questions

About 10 Critical Reasoning questions appear on the Verbal section of the GMAT. Critical Reasoning (CR) tests reasoning skills involved in making arguments, evaluating arguments, and formulating or evaluating a plan of action. These questions are based on materials from a variety of sources, though you will not need to be familiar with any subject matter beforehand.

Specifically, you are measured on your ability to reason in the following areas:

- **Understanding the argument's construction:** Recognizing the basic structure of an argument, properly drawn conclusions, underlying assumptions, explanatory hypotheses, or parallels between structurally similar arguments

- **Evaluating the argument:** Analyzing an argument, recognizing elements that would strengthen or weaken it, identifying reasoning errors or aspects of the argument's development

- **Formulating and evaluating a plan of action:** Recognizing the relative appropriateness, effectiveness, and efficiency of different plans of action, as well as factors that would strengthen or weaken a proposed plan of action

The directions for Critical Reasoning questions are short and to the point. They look like this:

Directions: Select the best of the answer choices given.

On the GMAT, in business school, and in your career, you'll need the ability to recognize and understand complex reasoning. It's not enough to sense whether an argument is strong or weak; you'll need to analyze precisely why it is so. This presumes a fundamental skill that's called on by nearly every Critical Reasoning question—the ability to isolate and identify the various components of any given argument. And that brings us to the basic principles of Critical Reasoning.

The Basic Principles of Critical Reasoning

LEARNING OBJECTIVES

In this section, you will learn how to:

- Use the question stem to identify the specific task at hand
- Draw upon strategic reading skills in order to pay attention to the right details in the stimulus
- Distinguish an argument's evidence from its conclusion
- Predict potential problems with an argument

Here are the basic skills that you need to succeed on Critical Reasoning questions.

Understand the Structure of an Argument

As you learned earlier in this chapter, an argument is an author's attempt to convince you of a point. You must know how arguments are structured so that you can break them down into their core components. Every GMAT argument is made up of two basic parts:

1. The conclusion (the point that the author is trying to make)
2. The evidence (the support that the author offers for the conclusion)

Success on these questions hinges on your ability to identify the parts of the argument. There is no general rule about where the conclusion and evidence appear in the argument—the conclusion could be first, followed by the evidence, or it could be the other way around. Sometimes the conclusion will even be expressed in the question stem rather than in the stimulus. Consider the following CR stimulus:

The Brookdale Public Library will require extensive physical rehabilitation to meet the new building codes passed by the town council. For one thing, the electrical system is inadequate, causing the lights to flicker sporadically. Furthermore, there are too few emergency exits, and those few that exist are poorly marked and sometimes locked.

Suppose that the author of this argument was allowed only one sentence to convey her meaning. Do you think she would waste her time with the following statement? Would she walk away satisfied that her main point was communicated?

The electrical system [at the Brookdale Public Library] is inadequate, causing the lights to flicker sporadically.

No. Given a single opportunity, she would have to state the first sentence to convey her real purpose:

> The Brookdale Public Library will require extensive physical rehabilitation . . .

That is the conclusion. If you pressed the author to state her reasons for making that statement, she would then cite the electrical and structural problems with the building. That is the evidence for her conclusion.

But does that mean that a statement like "The electrical system is inadequate" can't be a conclusion? Not necessarily—it's just not the conclusion for this particular argument. Every idea, every new statement, must be evaluated in the context of the stimulus in which it appears.

For the statement above to serve as the conclusion, the stimulus could be the following:

> The electrical wiring at the Brookdale Public Library was installed more than 40 years ago and appears to be corroded in some places [evidence]. An electrician, upon inspection of the system, found a few frayed wires as well as some blown fuses [evidence]. Clearly, the electrical system at the Brookdale Public Library is inadequate [conclusion].

To succeed in Critical Reasoning, you'll have to be able to determine the precise function of every sentence. The easiest way to do this is to use structural signals, or *key words* as we call them at Kaplan, to identify conclusion and evidence. You read about key words in the Verbal Section Overview chapter of this book. Not every Critical Reasoning stimulus will have these key words, but most do. Look for them every time, because using them to identify the conclusion and evidence will greatly increase not only your ability to get the right answer but also your ability to do so quickly. Key words such as *because, for, since, as a result of,* and *due to* are clear indications of evidence; key words such as *therefore, hence, thus, so, clearly,* and *consequently* usually signal the conclusion. Notice how the "[c]learly" in the argument above provides a strong signal that the last sentence is the conclusion.

Finally, take a look at a way a question might be formatted to put the conclusion in the question stem:

> The electrical wiring at the Brookdale Public Library was installed more than 40 years ago and appears to be corroded in some places [evidence]. An electrician, upon inspection of the system, found a few frayed wires as well as some blown fuses [evidence].
>
> Which of the following, if true, provides the strongest support for a prediction that Brookdale Public Library will replace its electrical system [conclusion]?

The author could have ended the stimulus with the sentence *Therefore, the Brookdale Public Library is likely to replace its electrical system.* Instead, this conclusion, a prediction based on the evidence about the dilapidated state of the wiring and fuses, appears in the question stem. A conclusion you find in the question stem plays the same role in the argument as a conclusion you find in the stimulus.

Study the Question First

As you learned earlier in this chapter, you should always look over the question stem before you read the stimulus. Doing so will give you some idea of what you need to look for as you read. Suppose the question with the first library argument above asked:

> Which of the following, if true, most seriously weakens the argument that Brookdale Public Library must undergo rehabilitation?

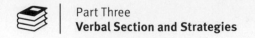

If you read the question before the stimulus, you'll know what to look for in advance—you know the conclusion (the library needs work), and you know the logic of the argument isn't entirely sound or you wouldn't be able to weaken it. As you read, you'll be able to zero in on the gap the authors left between evidence and conclusion. But suppose the question were this:

> Which of the following, if true, most helps to explain why the Brookdale Public Library still needs rehabilitation despite the passage of new building codes by the town council?

Now you already know most of the plot of this story—and you know there's a bit of a mystery that you'll need to solve. As you read, you can focus on thinking about why the library might be out of compliance with the building codes.

Reading the question first allows you to save valuable time because you will know how to attack the stimulus. As you'll see in the next chapter, this technique will be especially handy when you have a great working knowledge of the strategies for the different types of Critical Reasoning questions.

Read Strategically

As you learned in the Verbal Section Overview chapter of this book, Strategic Reading means reading for structure and for the author's point of view, since these are the things the GMAT most rewards test takers for noticing. On Critical Reasoning questions in particular, this means using key words to identify the most important parts of the stimulus (often an argument) and paraphrasing the main ideas. Let's examine how to read strategically on Critical Reasoning questions.

Paraphrase the Argument

In Critical Reasoning, you should paraphrase the author's main argument to yourself after reading the stimulus. As discussed in the Verbal Section Overview chapter, the Core Competency of Paraphrasing is a valuable tool. If you can't accurately paraphrase the stimulus, you probably don't understand it yet. Frequently, the authors in Critical Reasoning say pretty simple things in complex ways. So if you mentally translate the language into a simpler form, the whole thing will become more manageable.

In the first library argument, for instance, there's no advantage to grappling with the full complexity of the author's stated conclusion:

> The Brookdale Public Library will require extensive physical rehabilitation to meet the new building codes passed by the town council.

Instead, you want to paraphrase a much simpler point: *the library will need fixing up to meet new codes.*

Similarly, the evidence is pretty bulky:

> For one thing, the electrical system is inadequate, causing the lights to flicker sporadically. Furthermore, there are too few emergency exits, and those few that exist are poorly marked and sometimes locked.

You could paraphrase it like this: *the library's electrical system is bad, and the emergency exits are too few, hard to find, and locked.*

So the whole argument might be said simply as follows: the library's electrical system is bad, and the emergency exits are too few, hard to find, and locked. Therefore, the library will need fixing up to meet new codes.

Often, by the time you begin reading through the answer choices, you run the risk of losing sight of the gist of the stimulus. So restating the argument in your own words will not only help you get the author's point in the first place but also help you hold on to it until you've found the correct answer. Keep in mind that it's the *meaning* of the answer choices that matters. Since Critical Reasoning questions hinge on logic, you will be better able to choose the correct answer if you have paraphrased the ideas in the stimulus; doing so will keep you from becoming derailed if the correct choice doesn't use the exact wording you might expect.

Hunt for Potential Problems with the Argument

You must read actively, not passively, on the GMAT. Active readers are always attacking the passage, analyzing the text, and forming reactions as they go along. Instead of accepting an argument at face value, they look for potential problems. Active reading pays huge dividends on most Critical Reasoning questions.

Here are some common potential problems in Critical Reasoning passages:

- **Shifts of scope:** In its conclusion, the argument suddenly introduces a new term or idea that isn't mentioned in the evidence.

- **Mistaking correlation for causation:** Just because two things happen at the same time doesn't mean that one caused the other.

- **Plans and predictions:** Could there be something inherently self-defeating about a proposed course of action? Any unintended consequences? Any important factors unaccounted for? The GMAT asks many questions about plans and predictions because they are like miniature business plans.

Consider the argument about the library again. Seems pretty reasonable at first glance—good lighting and working emergency exits are pretty important for a public building. But the critical reader might think, "Wait a second—I've got a lot of information about the problems but no information about the codes. Do the codes apply to flickering lights, for example?"

Since part of what you're called on to do here is to evaluate arguments, don't let yourself fall into the bad habits of the passive reader—reading solely for the purpose of getting through the stimulus. Those who read this way invariably find themselves having to read stimuli two or even three times. Then they're caught short on time. Read the stimulus right the first time—with a critical eye and an active mind.

Answer the Question Being Asked

One of the most disheartening experiences in Critical Reasoning is to understand the author's argument fully but then supply an answer to a question that wasn't asked.

The classic example of this error occurs on Strengthen/Weaken questions, one of the common CR question types we will cover in the next chapter. When you're asked to strengthen or weaken an argument, you can be sure that there will be at least one answer choice that does the opposite of what's asked. Choosing such a wrong choice is less a matter of failing to understand the argument than of failing to remember the task at hand.

The question stem will always ask for something very specific. It's your job to follow the test makers' line of reasoning to the credited response.

Also, as you read the question stem, be on the lookout for words such as *not* and *except*. These little words are easy to miss, but they entirely change the kind of statement you're looking for among the choices.

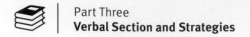

Try to Predict an Answer

This principle, which is really an extension of the last one, is crucial. You must approach the answer choices with at least a faint idea of what the answer should look like. That is, predict the answer in your own mind before looking at the choices. This isn't to say you should ponder the question for minutes—it's still a multiple-choice test, so the right answer is on the screen. Just get in the habit of framing an answer in your head.

Once you have made a prediction, scan the choices. Sure, the correct choice on the exam will be worded differently and may be more fleshed out than your prediction. But if it matches your thought, you'll know it in a second. And you'll find that there's no more satisfying feeling in Critical Reasoning than predicting correctly and then finding the correct answer quickly and confidently.

Continuing with the library situation, suppose you were asked this question:

> The author's argument depends on which of the following assumptions about the new building codes?

Having hunted for potential problems and realized that the argument gave no information about whether the codes applied to the problems in the library, you could quickly predict that the answer must say something like *The new building codes apply in this situation*. Then an answer like this one would jump off the screen as clearly correct:

○   The new codes apply to existing buildings, as well as to buildings under construction.

Alternatively, the correct answer could be worded like this:

○   The new codes require that all buildings have stable electrical systems as well as clearly marked, easily accessible emergency exits.

The most effective predictions are general enough to fit with unexpected ideas (such as "existing buildings" in the example above) but specific enough about the scope of the argument to allow you to eliminate most wrong answers.

Keep the Scope of the Stimulus in Mind

When you're at the point of selecting one of the answer choices, focus on the scope of the stimulus. Most of the wrong choices for CR questions are wrong because they are irrelevant to the argument's conclusion or, in the case of Inference questions, are unsupported by the stimulus. In other words, the wrong answer choices contain elements that don't match the author's ideas or that go beyond the context provided.

Some answer choices are too narrow or too broad, or they have nothing to do with the author's points. Others are too extreme to match the scope—they're usually signaled by such words as *all*, *always*, *never*, *none*, and so on. For arguments that are moderate in tone, correct answers are more qualified and contain such words as *usually*, *sometimes*, and *probably*.

To illustrate the concept of scope, let's look again at the question mentioned above:

> The author's argument depends on which of the following assumptions about the new building codes?

Let's say one of the answer choices reads as follows:

○   The new building codes are far too stringent.

Knowing the scope of the argument would help you to eliminate this choice very quickly. You know that this argument is just a claim about what the new codes will require: that the library be rehabilitated. It's not an argument about whether the requirements of the new codes are good, or justifiable, or ridiculously strict. That kind of value judgment is irrelevant to this argument.

Recognizing scope problems is a great way to eliminate wrong answers quickly. However, don't jump to eliminate an answer choice simply because it introduces a new term into discussion. A common error is to think that scope is purely about terminology. It's much more about the relationship of the ideas in the answer choice to the ideas in the stimulus. If your choice has the right relationship, the answer is relevant, regardless of its terminology. This fact reinforces the importance of using your Paraphrasing skills to clearly grasp how the ideas in a stimulus relate to one another.

The Kaplan Method for Critical Reasoning

LEARNING OBJECTIVES

In this section, you will learn how to:

- List the steps of the Kaplan Method for Critical Reasoning
- Explain the purpose of each step of the Kaplan Method for Critical Reasoning
- Perform the steps of the Kaplan Method for Critical Reasoning

Now it's time to learn how to orchestrate all of these basic principles into a consistent protocol for approaching Critical Reasoning questions. Kaplan has developed a Method for Critical Reasoning that you can use to attack each and every CR question.

> **THE KAPLAN METHOD FOR CRITICAL REASONING**
>
> 1. Identify the question type.
> 2. Untangle the stimulus.
> 3. Predict the answer.
> 4. Evaluate the choices.

STEP 1: IDENTIFY THE QUESTION TYPE

As you read in the introduction of basic Critical Reasoning principles, reading the question stem first is the best way to focus your reading of the stimulus. Determine the question type, and you'll know exactly what you're looking for. The next chapter is devoted to a thorough analysis of each type of CR question, including practice questions for each type. There may also be other important information in the question stem— possibly the conclusion of the argument or a particular aspect of the stimulus that you will need to focus on.

STEP 2: UNTANGLE THE STIMULUS

With the question stem in mind, read the stimulus. Read actively, paraphrasing to make sure you understand the construction of the stimulus and hunting for any potential problems. Most CR stimuli contain arguments, but many will not. Depending on the type of question that you identified in step 1 of the Method, you will look to gather different information from the stimulus.

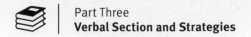
STEP 3: PREDICT THE ANSWER

Form an idea of what the right answer choice should say or do. How you form your prediction will vary depending on the specific question type. For some question types, it can be difficult to form a specific prediction of what the correct answer choice will say, but based on your analysis in steps 1 and 2, you will always know at least what function the correct answer will accomplish. Following this discussion of the steps of the Method is a chart that summarizes how to predict answers for different question types; you will learn about and practice all of these in depth in the next chapter.

STEP 4: EVALUATE THE CHOICES

Attack each answer choice critically. Keep your prediction in mind and see whether the answer choices match it. If you don't find a "clear winner," read through the answers that you haven't eliminated yet. You know what you *like* about each; now focus on what might be *wrong*.

STEPS 3 AND 4, BY QUESTION TYPE

You will look for different things in steps 3 and 4 of the Method, depending on the question type.

- **Assumption:** Identify the argument's central assumption and hunt for the answer choice that matches your prediction. If that fails, use the Denial Test on each answer choice.

- **Strengthen/Weaken:** Identify the argument's conclusion and predict an answer that gives a reason that the conclusion is more (for a Strengthen question) or less (for a Weaken question) likely to be true.

- **Evaluation:** Identify the argument's central assumption and hunt for the answer choice that identifies missing information that would help assess the validity of that assumption.

- **Flaw:** Identify the argument's central assumption and predict the error in the argument's reasoning.

- **Explain:** Predict the answer that explains how two seemingly discrepant facts can both be true. If it's difficult to form a specific prediction, work through the answers one by one, eliminating choices that are clearly wrong, until you find the one that reconciles both parts of the supposed paradox.

- **Inference:** It's often difficult to form a prediction beyond *the right answer* must be true *based on what the stimulus states*. Mentally catalog what you know to be true based on the stimulus. Then work through the answers one by one, eliminating choices that contradict or just don't align with what's known.

- **Bolded Statement:** Predict an answer based on the logic and structure of the stimulus.

Applying the Kaplan Method for Critical Reasoning

Now let's apply the Kaplan Method to the Critical Reasoning question you saw at the beginning of the chapter:

> A study of 20 overweight males revealed that each man experienced significant weight loss after adding SlimDown, an artificial food supplement, to his daily diet. For three months, each man consumed one SlimDown portion every morning after exercising and then followed his normal diet for the rest of the day. Clearly, all adult males who consume one portion of SlimDown every day for at least three months will lose weight and will look and feel their best.
>
> Which one of the following is an assumption on which the argument depends?
>
> O   The men in the study will gain back the weight they lost if they discontinue the SlimDown program.
>
> O   No other dietary supplement will have the same effect on overweight men.
>
> O   The daily exercise regimen was not responsible for the effects noted in the study.
>
> O   Women will not experience similar weight reductions if they adhere to the SlimDown program for three months.
>
> O   Overweight men will achieve only partial weight loss if they do not remain on the SlimDown program for a full three months.

STEP 1: IDENTIFY THE QUESTION TYPE

The question stem indicates directly that this is an Assumption question. Don't worry if you don't yet know much about Assumption questions; we will cover them in depth in the next chapter. For now, just focus on applying each step of the Method. You know from the mention of an "assumption" in this question stem that the argument in the stimulus will be missing a link in the chain of reasoning—some piece of support that the author takes for granted without which the conclusion wouldn't be valid. You will now turn to the stimulus, ready to find that link.

STEP 2: UNTANGLE THE STIMULUS

Sentence 1 introduces a study of 20 men who used a certain food supplement product. All 20 lost weight. Sentence 2 describes how they used it: once a day, for three months, after morning exercise. So far so good; it feels as if the argument is building up to something. The key word *clearly* usually indicates that some sort of conclusion follows, and that's the case here: in sentence 3, the author predicts that any adult who has one portion of the product daily for three months will lose weight, too.

You might paraphrase the argument like this:

> Each of 20 overweight men lost weight after taking SlimDown every morning after exercise (but otherwise eating normally). So any guy who consumes SlimDown will lose weight.

Reading strategically, do you see any scope shifts or other potential problems? Sure—what happened to the exercise? It's in the evidence as part of the study regimen but is totally dropped from the conclusion. That's a pretty significant change in scope, and you can use that scope shift as the basis for your prediction in step 3.

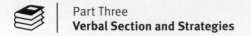

You could also look at the argument even more abstractly:

> A bunch of guys did *A* and *B* and had *X* result. So if another guy does *A*, he'll get *X* result, too.

This argument structure seems pretty weak: Who says *A* (SlimDown) caused *X* (weight loss)? Why couldn't *B* (exercise) have been the cause? The argument asserts that there could only be one cause for a certain effect even though other causes might, in reality, be possible. This kind of sloppy thinking about causality is a common GMAT pattern that you can use to help form your paraphrase.

You can use this insight to make a prediction in step 3, too. No matter how abstract or concrete your prediction is, you arrive at the same basic issue—that the author isn't accounting for the exercise. There's rarely one "perfect way" to figure out the right answer; as long as you read critically, you'll be moving in the right direction.

STEP 3: PREDICT THE ANSWER

You've realized that the argument forgot to consider the exercise. So you might predict something like *The author assumes exercise doesn't matter*. That's it. There's no need to paraphrase with something fancy or complicated. A simple paraphrase, as long as it reflects the scope of the stimulus, is enough to help you find the right answer.

STEP 4: EVALUATE THE CHOICES

Judge the answer choices based on how well they fulfill the requirements of your prediction. Sure enough, only **(C)** even mentions the exercise regimen. Reading it closely, you see it fits the prediction perfectly, clearing up the question of whether the exercise caused the weight loss.

Since the difficulty of Critical Reasoning is often in the wording of the answer choices (rather than the stimulus), you can't let them make you indecisive. Predicting the answer lets you know exactly what you're looking for, so you'll know it when you see it. You can choose **(C)** with confidence and move on.

Practice Set: The Kaplan Method for Critical Reasoning

1.   Residents of Cordoba County who receive unemployment benefits are allowed to attend courses on job search skills at the local community college at no charge. In addition, the unemployment benefits office offers free assistance with résumé writing. Many retail employees were recently laid off due to the closure of five Boxia Stores locations. Of the affected employees, those who live in Cordoba County will certainly not rely solely on their own resources as they look for new jobs.

   Which of the following is an assumption that is required for the conclusion of the argument?

   O   If an unemployed worker has access to job search resources, the worker will take advantage of those resources.

   O   Retail employees have more difficulty finding new jobs after being laid off than do workers in other occupations.

   O   In Cordoba County, the usual cost for job search skills courses and résumé writing assistance is too great for most people to afford.

   O   When it closed several locations, Boxia Stores laid off some employees who will have difficulty finding new employment if they do not receive assistance.

   O   The job search skills courses at the local community college and the résumé-writing assistance offered at the unemployment benefits office are usually helpful for individuals seeking employment.

2.   A business owner noticed that many of her employees exhibited signs of fatigue throughout the workday. To combat this, the business owner has partnered with a local gym to offer employees a discounted rate on annual memberships. The business owner is confident this program will help to lessen employee fatigue, as studies have shown that people who exercise regularly have higher energy levels than people who do not.

   Which of the following, if true, would most seriously call into question the claim that the business owner's plan will reduce fatigue?

   O   Making minor changes to one's diet can boost energy as effectively as can regular exercise.

   O   The discount offered is so small that most employees will not be encouraged to purchase an annual membership.

   O   Employees with higher energy levels are not necessarily more productive at work.

   O   The local gym would have to offer more classes to accommodate the increase in membership.

   O   There is no way to eliminate fatigue altogether.

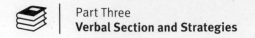

3. Last month, a group of salespeople from a software firm attended a seminar on persuasive speaking. In the weeks following the seminar, the salespeople who attended the seminar have made more sales, on average, than those who did not attend the seminar. To increase sales, the sales manager plans to send the remaining salespeople to the same seminar next month.

    Which of the following, if true, would most support the prediction that the sales manager's plan will achieve its goal?

    O   Last month's seminar focused solely on tactics relevant to the work at the particular company.

    O   Total company sales last month were higher than sales from the month prior to the seminar.

    O   To prepare for the seminar, the attending salespeople read a book on improving communication skills.

    O   Over the last month, the company's sales were greater than the sales of its largest competitor.

    O   Invitations to last month's seminar were not accepted solely by salespeople with above-average sales.

4. Some scientists are researching how to manipulate viruses so as to be useful in nanotechnology applications, particularly in the human body. Since viruses do not engage in metabolic activity to survive and reproduce, they may be durable building blocks for composite materials. Viruses can be altered to serve human purposes through two approaches, chemical modification and genetic engineering. To make a virus into an effective nanotechnological structure, it is necessary to determine how to attach biological interfaces to the surface of the virus's protein coat.

    The discussion above most strongly supports which of the following statements?

    O   Research into nanotechnology is likely to produce useful applications in the human body.

    O   Viruses are the best choice to make composite materials on a nanotechnological scale.

    O   The protein coats of viruses naturally lack biological interfaces.

    O   Composite materials are of interest primarily due to their potential uses in the human body.

    O   For their research to be successful, scientists must figure out how to make attachments to the protein coats of viruses.

Answers and explanations follow on the next page. ▶ ▶ ▶

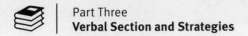

Answer Key

Practice Set: The Kaplan Method for Critical Reasoning

1. A
2. B
3. E
4. E

Answers and Explanations

Practice Set: The Kaplan Method for Critical Reasoning

1.   **(A)**

Residents of Cordoba County who receive unemployment benefits are allowed to attend courses on job search skills at the local community college at no charge. In addition, the unemployment benefits office offers free assistance with résumé writing. Many retail employees were recently laid off due to the closure of five Boxia Stores locations. Of the affected employees, those who live in Cordoba County will certainly not rely solely on their own resources as they look for new jobs.

Which of the following is an assumption that is required for the conclusion of the argument?

O   If an unemployed worker has access to job search resources, the worker will take advantage of those resources.

O   Retail employees have more difficulty finding new jobs after being laid off than do workers in other occupations.

O   In Cordoba County, the usual cost for job search skills courses and résumé writing assistance is too great for most people to afford.

O   When it closed several locations, Boxia Stores laid off some employees who will have difficulty finding new employment if they do not receive assistance.

O   The job search skills courses at the local community college and the résumé-writing assistance offered at the unemployment benefits office are usually helpful for individuals seeking employment.

STEP 1: IDENTIFY THE QUESTION TYPE

The question stem asks for an "assumption," so this is an Assumption question. The correct answer will be something the author does not say that must be true for the author's conclusion to follow from the evidence provided.

STEP 2: UNTANGLE THE STIMULUS

The author makes a strong prediction about the future with the language "will certainly": the author claims that certain recently unemployed people will get help finding jobs. The evidence is the two forms of no-cost job search assistance that are offered to these folks.

STEP 3: PREDICT THE ANSWER

The evidence is about assistance that is available, but the conclusion is an unqualified prediction that they will use that assistance. Thus, the author is assuming that if help is offered, it will be taken. To put this in perspective, consider that you have probably received many free offers that you've declined for one reason or another.

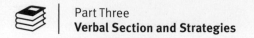

STEP 4: EVALUATE THE CHOICES

(A) matches the prediction and is correct. **(B)** is an irrelevant comparison between the laid-off workers in the stimulus and other workers who are not a subject of this argument. **(C)** discusses job search services that are not free, but the argument is based only on the use of free services. **(D)** speaks to how hard it may be for some workers to find new jobs, but the argument is about whether they'll use job search services, not about whether their job search will be fruitful. **(E)** is wrong for a similar reason as **(D)**: if the assistance offered is known to be helpful, this knowledge might influence unemployed people to use it—but it also might not. There may be other factors that people weigh when deciding whether to use the assistance. A choice that requires you to make a further assumption is not the correct answer to an Assumption question.

2.   **(B)**

A business owner noticed that many of her employees exhibited signs of fatigue throughout the workday. To combat this, the business owner has partnered with a local gym to offer employees a discounted rate on annual memberships. The business owner is confident this program will help to lessen employee fatigue, as studies have shown that people who exercise regularly have higher energy levels than people who do not.

Which of the following, if true, would most seriously call into question the claim that the business owner's plan will reduce fatigue?

- ○   Making minor changes to one's diet can boost energy as effectively as can regular exercise.
- ○   The discount offered is so small that most employees will not be encouraged to purchase an annual membership.
- ○   Employees with higher energy levels are not necessarily more productive at work.
- ○   The local gym would have to offer more classes to accommodate the increase in membership.
- ○   There is no way to eliminate fatigue altogether.

STEP 1: IDENTIFY THE QUESTION TYPE

This asks for something that would "call into question" the business owner's claim, so it's a Weaken question.

STEP 2: UNTANGLE THE STIMULUS

The business owner argues that partnering with a local gym to offer employees a discounted membership will help reduce fatigue. As evidence, the owner cites a correlation between exercise and high energy levels. The owner assumes that exercise is what causes people who exercise to have high energy levels.

There is another assumption as well. The owner makes a plan based on a prediction, which means the author assumes there are no factors that would affect the predicted outcome of the plan.

STEP 3: PREDICT THE ANSWER

To weaken the assumption of causation, it could be shown that the high energy levels in exercisers were caused by something else (e.g., caffeine, protein diets, medication). It could also be shown that the author has misunderstood the direction of causality: perhaps people exercise because they already have more energy, not the other way around. Or perhaps increased exercise and increased energy are both just effects of another variable (e.g., motivation).

To show that the author's predicted outcome might not occur, you could find a problem with the plan—something that shows it might not help reduce fatigue. Maybe employees will get the gym membership but not exercise more (how many people join a gym but don't actually go?), or maybe the membership will be unappealing even with the discount.

STEP 4: EVALUATE THE CHOICES

(B) matches the second prediction. It shows how the discount will not encourage people to go to the gym, making it less likely they will feel more energetic. **(A)** suggests there are other ways to achieve the same results, but that doesn't mean the owner's plan won't work. **(C)** is irrelevant. Higher productivity might be a nice side effect, but it's not the owner's stated goal. She is discounting gym memberships to reduce fatigue. **(D)** is irrelevant. Any extra burden on the gym has no effect on whether the plan will work. If anything, this supports the owner's thinking by implying that people will exercise more. **(E)** uses extreme language. The issue is whether fatigue can be reduced, not whether it can be eradicated completely.

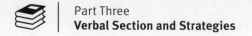
3. **(E)**

Last month, a group of salespeople from a software firm attended a seminar on persuasive speaking. In the weeks following the seminar, the salespeople who attended the seminar have made more sales, on average, than those who did not attend the seminar. To increase sales, the sales manager plans to send the remaining salespeople to the same seminar next month.

Which of the following, if true, would most support the prediction that the sales manager's plan will achieve its goal?

- ○ Last month's seminar focused solely on tactics relevant to the work at the particular company.
- ○ Total company sales last month were higher than sales from the month prior to the seminar.
- ○ To prepare for the seminar, the attending salespeople read a book on improving communication skills.
- ○ Over the last month, the company's sales were greater than the sales of its largest competitor.
- ○ Invitations to last month's seminar were not accepted solely by salespeople with above-average sales.

STEP 1: IDENTIFY THE QUESTION TYPE

This asks for something that supports a prediction, so it's a Strengthen question.

STEP 2: UNTANGLE THE STIMULUS

The sales manager's goal is to increase sales by having the salespeople who didn't attend the seminar on persuasive speaking attend the next seminar. The implied opinion is that the seminar will make employees better salespeople; in other words, it will cause sales to increase. The evidence provided for this argument is that the salespeople who did attend the seminar had better sales than did non-attendees. However, this is only a correlation. There could be some other reason for the good performance (e.g., other seminars, better leads, luck). It's also possible the author's logic is backward: perhaps the attendees were already above average. Maybe that's why they were chosen to attend the seminar in the first place, or perhaps more highly motivated people both choose to attend seminars and get more sales. The sales manager assumes these factors did not play an important role in the increased sales and that the seminar was responsible.

STEP 3: PREDICT THE ANSWER

Since the goal is to strengthen the sales manager's position, the correct answer will need to show that at least part of the manager's assumption was correct; it will eliminate one or more of the alternative causes from consideration.

STEP 4: EVALUATE THE CHOICES

(**E**) is correct; if the attendees weren't already top salespeople, it's at least somewhat more likely that the seminar helped improve their performance. (**A**) doesn't establish that these tactics actually helped sales—perhaps the salespeople already knew these tactics. Moreover, this choice describes the last seminar, but the argument is about the benefits of attending the next seminar. (**B**) does not help make the case for attending the seminar. The author's argument rests on the assumption that those who attended the seminar improved while those who didn't attend did not improve. (**B**) does not address the comparison. Indeed, if overall sales were up, then it's possible everyone did better and not just people who attended the seminar. (**C**) weakens the argument by bringing up a potential alternative explanation. Maybe the book was responsible and not the seminar itself. (**D**) is an irrelevant comparison. How the sales manager's company compares to other companies has nothing to do with whether the seminar was effective.

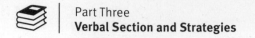

4.   **(E)**

Some scientists are researching how to manipulate viruses so as to be useful in nanotechnology applications, particularly in the human body. Since viruses do not engage in metabolic activity to survive and reproduce, they may be durable building blocks for composite materials. Viruses can be altered to serve human purposes through two approaches, chemical modification and genetic engineering. To make a virus into an effective nanotechnological structure, it is necessary to determine how to attach biological interfaces to the surface of the virus's protein coat.

The discussion above most strongly supports which of the following statements?

○   Research into nanotechnology is likely to produce useful applications in the human body.

○   Viruses are the best choice to make composite materials on a nanotechnological scale.

○   The protein coats of viruses naturally lack biological interfaces.

○   Composite materials are of interest primarily due to their potential uses in the human body.

○   For their research to be successful, scientists must figure out how to make attachments to the protein coats of viruses.

STEP 1: IDENTIFY THE QUESTION TYPE

The question stem indicates that you are to consider the stimulus as support, or evidence, for your answer choice. Therefore, this is an Inference question. The correct answer will be fully supported by the information provided.

STEP 2: UNTANGLE THE STIMULUS

The stimulus explains one reason scientists are interested in viruses. Don't get caught up in trying to understand all the details here; you're taking the GMAT, not a molecular biology exam. You might paraphrase the stimulus this way: viruses may be useful in nanotechnology because "composite materials" can be built from them. But viruses can only be useful in this way after people attach stuff to them, using one of two approaches.

STEP 3: PREDICT THE ANSWER

Because the question stem lacks specific clues, it will be difficult to make a specific prediction. But do have firmly in mind what the stimulus says—and what it doesn't say—as you evaluate the choices. Note, for example, the tentative language "[viruses] *may* be durable building blocks." So there's no guarantee that viruses will be used successfully in nanotechnology. But also note the definite "it is *necessary* [to attach stuff to the viruses]." If progress is going to be made in this area, scientists have to figure out how to do this.

STEP 4: EVALUATE THE CHOICES

(E) connects the idea in the first sentence of the stimulus—scientists are investigating how to make viruses useful in nanotechnology—with the idea in the last sentence, which is that the way to make viruses useful requires figuring out how to attach things to them. This statement is fully supported by the stimulus and is correct. **(A)** is a distortion; scientists are interested in pursuing this avenue of research, but nothing in the stimulus indicates that useful applications are "likely." It's possible that the scientists' research will yield no useful results. **(B)** is extreme; viruses may be a good choice for composite materials, according to the stimulus, but there is no evidence that they are the "best" choice. **(C)** is not supported. The stimulus says that biological interfaces need to be added to viruses for them to be useful in nanotechnology, but it does not say the viruses have no such interfaces now. Perhaps scientists need to attach particular interfaces to get the viruses to do a desired task. **(D)** is a distortion because of the word "primarily." While it is inferable that composite materials have potential uses in the human body, nothing in the stimulus indicates that this is the main reason they are useful.

Critical Reasoning Question Types

Now that you're familiar with the basic principles of Critical Reasoning and the Kaplan Method, let's look at the most common types of questions. Certain question types appear again and again on the GMAT, so it pays to understand them beforehand.

Here are the types of Critical Reasoning questions that the GMAT asks:

- Assumption
- Strengthen or Weaken
- Evaluate
- Flaw
- Explain
- Inference
- Bolded Statement

You saw many references to arguments in the previous chapter, and indeed analyzing arguments is the most important—though not the only—skill you need to possess for Critical Reasoning on the GMAT. Of the question types listed above, Assumption, Strengthen, Weaken, Evaluate, and Flaw questions are based on arguments. For these five question types, the way you will analyze the argument is quite similar. In all cases, the correct answer will depend on identifying and understanding the argument's conclusion, evidence, and assumption(s).

> ### GMAT ARGUMENTS
>
> - GMAT arguments (given in the stimuli) are usually two to four sentences long.
> - GMAT arguments vary in soundness: some are fairly sensible, while others make a big leap from evidence to conclusion.
> - To untangle the stimulus, find the conclusion, evidence, and the author's central assumption.

Let's examine in depth Kaplan's strategies for the different types of CR questions based on arguments, starting with Assumption questions.

Assumption Questions

> **LEARNING OBJECTIVES**
>
> In this section, you will learn how to:
> - Identify Assumption questions by the question stem
> - Distinguish evidence from conclusion in order to predict an argument's assumption
> - Apply the Kaplan Method for Critical Reasoning to Assumption questions

Assumption questions ask you for a piece of support that isn't explicitly stated but is necessary for the argument to remain valid. When a question asks you for what's missing from the argument or what the argument depends on, then it's asking you to find the author's necessary assumption.

Untangling the Stimulus for Assumption Questions

By first analyzing the question stem, you'll know what to look for in the stimulus. For Assumption questions—and all questions based on arguments—untangling the stimulus consists of identifying the three parts of a GMAT argument: conclusion, evidence, and assumption.

Conclusion

The conclusion is the main point of the author's argument. It's the thing that the author is seeking to convince you of. There are three ways to identify the conclusions of arguments:

1. **Conclusion key words or phrases:** As you learned in the Verbal Section Overview chapter of this book, key words are clues to the structure of a passage or argument. They tell you how the author's ideas relate to one another. Key words and phrases that signal an argument's conclusion include the following: *thus, therefore, so, hence, consequently, in conclusion, clearly, for this reason.*

2. **The one-sentence test:** You can also identify the author's conclusion by asking, "If the author had to boil this entire argument down to one sentence that expresses the main point, which sentence would it be?"

3. **Fact vs. opinion:** The conclusion of the argument is always a reflection of the author's opinion. This opinion can take several forms; it could be the author's plan, proposal, prediction, or value judgment or simply her interpretation or analysis of the evidence. As discussed next, evidence may also be an opinion, but it may also be, and usually is, factual. Therefore, if a statement presents a fact, it is not the conclusion.

Evidence

Evidence is provided to support the conclusion. GMAT arguments usually have little filler, so what isn't the conclusion is typically evidence. Evidence can take the form of data, such as statistics, surveys, polls, or historical facts. Sometimes, however, the evidence is merely a conjecture or an opinion. The best way to identify an argument's evidence is by examining its function within the argument: any material in the stimulus that provides support for the author's conclusion is evidence.

Assumption

All GMAT arguments contain one or more assumptions; identifying the assumptions is an essential step when answering any Critical Reasoning question based on an argument. An assumption is the unstated evidence necessary to make the argument work. It bridges the gap between two pieces of the argument, usually between conclusion and evidence but occasionally between two unconnected pieces of evidence. Without the assumption, the argument falls apart. You can think of it as something the author *must* believe but doesn't directly state.

You can visualize the relationship between the various parts of an argument as follows:

Evidence + Assumption(s) → Conclusion

Predicting the Answer for Assumption Questions

As you saw in the question about SlimDown diet supplement earlier in this chapter, you can usually predict an answer to an Assumption question. Your prediction is simply the argument's assumption, which you already identified when you untangled the stimulus during step 2 of the Kaplan Method.

Let's practice the whole process of untangling the stimulus and predicting the answer using this simple stimulus:

> Allyson plays volleyball for Central High School. Therefore, Allyson must be over 6 feet tall.

The conclusion is the second sentence (signaled by the key word "[t]herefore"), and the evidence is the first. Is there a gap, or assumption, in this argument? Well, who's to say that all high school volleyball players have to be over 6 feet tall? So you can confidently predict that the answer to an Assumption question would say something like this:

> All volleyball players at Central High School are over 6 feet tall.

But what if the assumption doesn't just jump out at you? How can you track it down? One of the most common ways the GMAT uses assumptions is to cover over mismatched concepts between evidence and conclusion. Notice that the argument above starts by talking about playing volleyball and then all of a sudden is talking about being over 6 feet tall. When tackling an Assumption question, look closely at the terms in each part of the argument. Is the scope of the evidence different, even if just slightly, from that of the conclusion?

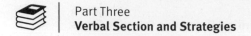

Consider this seemingly solid argument:

> Candidate A won the presidential election, carrying 40 out of 50 states. Clearly, Candidate A has a strong mandate to push for her legislative agenda.

At first glance, this sounds pretty good. But take a close look at the terms of the argument. The evidence is a win representing a sizable majority of states. The conclusion is about a strong mandate for an agenda. Even if you don't notice the subtle difference between these two things, you could still make a prediction like this: *Candidate A's big victory means she has a mandate for her agenda.* You'd be much more likely to recognize the right answer between these two possibilities:

- ○ No other candidate in the last 24 years has won as many states as did Candidate A.
- ○ Most of the people who voted for Candidate A support her legislative agenda.

The first answer choice doesn't deal with Candidate A's agenda at all. The second one shows a connection between her victory and her agenda, so it must be the right answer.

But what if you still aren't sure that your answer choice is correct? Or what if the assumption is so subtle that you can't predict the answer? In those cases, you can use the Denial Test.

The Denial Test

An assumption must be true in order for the conclusion to follow logically from the evidence. Therefore, in an Assumption question, you can test each answer choice by negating it—in other words, imagining that the information given in the answer choice is false. If this negation makes the author's argument fall apart, then the answer choice is a necessary assumption. If the argument is unaffected, then the choice is wrong. Let's look at what you predicted earlier as the assumption in the volleyball argument:

> All volleyball players at Central High School are over 6 feet tall.

Now let's negate it:

> Some volleyball players at Central High School are not over 6 feet tall.

Would Allyson still have to be over 6 feet tall? Not anymore. That's why that prediction would be a necessary assumption. Keep in mind not to be too extreme when negating answer choices. The denial of *hot* isn't *cold* but rather *not hot*. Similarly, the denial of *all are* isn't *none are* but rather *some aren't*.

Now let's take another look at the answer choices for the question about Candidate A:

- ○ No other candidate in the last 24 years has won as many states as did Candidate A.
- ○ Most of the people who voted for Candidate A support her legislative agenda.

And now we'll negate them:

- ○ Some candidates in the last 24 years have won as many states as did Candidate A.

Could Candidate A still enjoy a strong mandate? Definitely. Just because others in the past were as popular doesn't mean that she doesn't enjoy support for her agenda as well.

O   A majority of those who voted for Candidate A do not actually support her legislative agenda.

Now can Candidate A claim a mandate for her agenda? No, she can't. That's why the second choice is the correct answer for this Assumption question.

Give the Denial Test a try on your own using the following argument. Negate each answer choice and then ask, "Can the evidence still lead to the conclusion?"

I live in the city of Corpus Christi, so I also live in Texas.

The argument assumes which of the following?

O   Corpus Christi is the only city in Texas.

O   The only city named Corpus Christi is located in Texas.

O   If you have not been to Corpus Christi, you have not been to Texas.

The argument here is short and sweet, but it has all the essential elements of any GMAT argument. The conclusion is signaled by the key word *so*: the author lives in Texas. The author's evidence is the claim in the first part of the sentence: he lives in Corpus Christi.

Rather than predict the correct answer right away, let's test the answer choice statements using the Denial Test.

Negation of statement (A): Corpus Christi is not the only city in Texas

Does that threaten the argument? No. There could be other cities in Texas, and it could still be valid to say that living in Corpus Christi proves that the author lives in Texas. The evidence could still lead to the conclusion, so choice (**A**) is not the assumption.

Negation of statement (B): There is at least one other city named Corpus Christi that is not located in Texas.

If this is true, does the conclusion still follow logically from the evidence? No. In this case, if there is another town named Corpus Christi located in, say, California or Florida, it would no longer be logically valid to say that the author must live in Texas because he lives in Corpus Christi. Choice (**B**) is a necessary assumption for the argument.

Negation of statement (C): If you have not been to Corpus Christi, you still could have been to Texas.

Note that when you are denying an if/then statement, you should deny the "then," or result, portion of the statement. What impact does this negation have on the argument? None. Someone else could visit other cities in Texas, and still it may or may not be valid for the author to say, "I live in Texas because I live in Corpus Christi." Choice (**C**) is not the necessary assumption.

Argument Analysis Exercise

Answers are on the following page.

Now it's time to put all these skills together and practice breaking down some arguments. First find the conclusion, then identify the evidence that supports that conclusion, and finally determine the central assumption(s). Once you've identified the assumption, try the Denial Test to confirm that the assumption you've identified is necessary for the argument to hold:

1. A major car manufacturer produces two editions of its most popular model: the GK and the LK. Since both editions were made available, the manufacturer has sold nearly twice as many GK editions each year as it has LK editions. However, it is likely that the LK edition will outsell the GK edition next year. After all, the GK edition has always sold for significantly less than the LK edition, but the manufacturer is making modifications to the GK edition next year that will raise its selling price to a value exceeding that of the LK edition.

Conclusion:

Evidence:

Assumption(s):

2. Movie studio executive: Last summer, our studio released one of the most popular science fiction movies of the year. This summer, our studio released a critically praised war documentary. Unfortunately, ticket sales for this war documentary were 40 percent lower than that of last year's science fiction movie. Thus, it is clear that movie studios can be more profitable if they do not change the genre of movies they produce.

Conclusion:

Evidence:

Assumption(s):

Argument Analysis Exercise: Answers

1. **Conclusion:** The manufacturer will likely sell more LK editions than GK editions next year.
   Evidence: The GK edition will be more expensive next year.
   Assumption: Price is the most significant factor affecting a customer's car-buying decision.

2. **Conclusion:** Movie studios can be more profitable if they choose a movie genre and stick with it.
   Evidence: The war documentary released this year by the executive's studio made less money than the science fiction movie it released last year.
   Assumptions: In this case, the author is taking several things for granted. Lower ticket sales mean the studio made less profit (perhaps the documentary cost much less than the science fiction film to make and was thus more profitable). Another science fiction movie would have performed better than the war documentary this year (perhaps movie receipts were down in general this year, or perhaps another studio offered a great sci-fi film this year and audiences would have ignored a sci fi movie by this studio). What happened in this situation is representative of what would happen for film studios in general. The lower ticket sales were due to the genre of the film and no other factor (e.g., unpopular or challenging subject matter).

Sample Question Stems

There are many ways to write a Critical Reasoning question. Any wording that suggests that you need to find a missing but vital piece of information indicates an Assumption question. Assumption questions are worded in some of the following ways:

- Which one of the following is assumed by the author?
- Upon which one of the following assumptions does the author rely?
- The argument depends on the assumption that...
- Which one of the following, if added to the passage, would make the conclusion logical?
- The validity of the argument depends on which one of the following?
- The argument presupposes which one of the following?

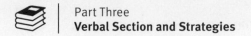

Applying the Kaplan Method: Assumption Questions

Now let's use the Kaplan Method for Critical Reasoning to solve an Assumption question:

> When unemployment rates are high, people with full-time jobs tend to take fewer and shorter vacations. When unemployment rates are low, people tend to vacation more often and go away for longer periods of time. Thus, it can be concluded that full-time workers' perceptions of their own job security influence the frequency and duration of their vacations.
>
> The argument above assumes that
>
> ○ the people who take the longest vacations when unemployment rates are low have no fear of losing their jobs
>
> ○ travel costs are lower during times of low unemployment
>
> ○ most people prefer to work full-time jobs
>
> ○ workers' perceptions of their own job security are in some way related to the unemployment rate
>
> ○ workers' fears of losing their jobs have increased recently

STEP 1: IDENTIFY THE QUESTION TYPE

The word "assumes" in the question stem is a clear indication of an Assumption question.

STEP 2: UNTANGLE THE STIMULUS

"Thus" signals the argument's conclusion. You could paraphrase it as follows: *how much vacation time full-time workers take depends on how secure they feel in their jobs.* The author's evidence for this conclusion is the relationship between vacations and unemployment. When unemployment is high, workers take fewer and shorter vacations; when unemployment is low, the opposite happens.

STEP 3: PREDICT THE ANSWER

To find the central assumption, use Critical Thinking to link the terms in the evidence with the terms in the conclusion. Since the evidence centers on employment levels and vacations, while the conclusion centers on job security and vacations, the central assumption must center on the connection between employment levels and job security.

STEP 4: EVALUATE THE CHOICES

Choice **(D)** matches this prediction, bridging the terms of the evidence with the terms of the conclusion. The Denial Test can help confirm **(D)** as the correct answer; if there were no relationship between workers' perceptions of job security and the unemployment rate, then it would no longer make sense for the author to use evidence about the unemployment rate to support a conclusion about workers' perceptions of job security. **(D)** is an assumption necessary for the argument to hold.

The other choices are all incorrect in some definable way. It's great practice to identify exactly why each wrong choice is wrong. Doing so will help you develop your Pattern Recognition skills so you can identify common wrong answer types on Test Day. (A) is too extreme ("*no* fear of losing their jobs") to be the necessary assumption. (B) introduces the idea of travel costs, which have no necessary connection to job security in the conclusion. (C) is incorrect because whether those people who work full-time jobs prefer to work them is irrelevant. (E) tells us that workers' perceptions of their job security have deteriorated lately, but that has no necessary connection to the unemployment rate. Remember that the assumption must successfully link the evidence to the conclusion.

TAKEAWAYS: ASSUMPTION QUESTIONS

- On Assumption questions, identify the argument's conclusion and evidence, determine the central assumption, and predict the answer. Evaluate the answer choices and select the one that matches your prediction.

- If you read the answer choices and can't find your prediction, try eliminating choices by asking whether they are necessary for the argument to hold.

- The Denial Test discriminates between right and wrong answers; when you deny the correct answer to an Assumption question, the argument falls apart.

Practice Set: Assumption Questions

1.   To protect the environment, paper towels in public restrooms should be banned and replaced with hot-air dryers. The use of such dryers would reduce the need to cut down trees to turn into paper towels. Furthermore, since fewer paper towels would be needed, the environmental impact of the emissions from the paper-manufacturing process would be lessened.

     Which of the following is an assumption upon which the above proposal depends?

     O   The operating expenses related to hot-air dryers are no greater than those related to paper towels.

     O   The manufacture and operation of hot-air dryers use fewer natural resources than do the manufacture and use of paper towels.

     O   Hot-air dryers are the only viable alternative to paper towels in public restrooms.

     O   Hot-air dryers are at least as effective at drying the hands as are paper towels.

     O   The operators of public restrooms are willing to replace paper towels with hot-air dryers.

2.   A company's health program offers medical coverage for all of its full-time employees. As part of the program, employees can choose from one of three plans, each of which offers a different mix of medical benefits depending on an individual's particular needs. Thus, all full-time employees who take advantage of the company's program are sure to be covered for most, if not all, of their medical needs.

     Which of the following is an assumption on which the argument relies?

     O   Part-time employees can also receive coverage from the company's health program.

     O   None of the three plans costs the company significantly more than the other plans.

     O   There are no full-time employees whose medical needs are mostly uncovered by each of the three available plans.

     O   There is no alternative plan that would cover more medical needs than the plans in the current program.

     O   At least one of the three plans offers dental coverage for full-time employees whose health is impacted by their dental needs.

3. A local hardware store is concerned that its sales will diminish when a competing hardware store opens in the same area next month. However, it is actually more likely that the existing store's sales will increase. Over the next few months, due to high demand for mixed-use residential and commercial buildings, over three times as many construction projects will be started in the area as were started over the past five years.

The argument above depends on which of the following assumptions?

○   The managers of the new construction projects will purchase an equal amount of material from both hardware stores.

○   The construction projects will require the purchase of materials that are sold at the existing hardware store.

○   The materials sold at the existing store are higher in quality than those to be sold at the new hardware store.

○   The area revitalization spurred by new mixed-use developments will encourage local residents to perform improvements on their own homes.

○   The existing hardware store will lower its prices below those of its competitors to attract new customers.

Strengthen and Weaken Questions

> **LEARNING OBJECTIVES**
>
> In this section, you will learn how to:
>
> - Identify Strengthen and Weaken questions by the question stem
> - Predict the kind of evidence that would make a conclusion more or less likely to be true
> - Apply the Kaplan Method for Critical Reasoning questions to Strengthen and Weaken questions

Determining an argument's necessary assumption, as you've just seen, is required to answer an Assumption question. But this skill can also be used to answer two other common types of question: Strengthen and Weaken.

Strengthen and Weaken questions are, as their names imply, all about the strength of the author's position. In the stimulus, the author makes a claim of some sort; for instance, it may be a plan of action, a recommendation, or an explanation for a particular phenomenon. In a Strengthen question, the correct answer is the one that makes the claim more likely to be true, while in a Weaken question, the correct answer makes the claim less likely to be true. It's important to note that the right answers to these questions will not necessarily prove or disprove the claim; they will likely just be evidence for or against the claim.

In many cases, the strength or weakness of the author's claim rests on the validity of her assumption. When the author gives evidence for her claim, use the skills you learned for tackling Assumption questions to find the gap between evidence and conclusion. The answer to many Weaken questions is the one that reveals an author's assumption to be unreasonable or untrue; conversely, the answer to many Strengthen questions provides additional support for the argument by affirming the truth of an assumption.

Sometimes, however, the correct answer might not focus on an assumption made by the author. In a Strengthen question, the right answer may be an independent piece of evidence, that, when added to the author's stated evidence, makes the conclusion more likely to be true. Similarly, the answer to a Weaken question may merely be a fact that casts doubt upon the conclusion.

There may be occasions in which the author presents no evidence at all to back up his claim; he may simply state that his proposed course of action will lead to a certain outcome. In that case, focus on the effect each choice would have on the proposal's likelihood of success. Also helpful in answering these types of questions are the strategies for plans, proposals, and predictions that are discussed in detail in Chapter 7. These strategies are all about how to untangle stimuli that deal with the predicted outcome of future events, so they'll provide some guidance on how to predict the kinds of evidence that will strengthen or weaken the proposal.

Let's return to a stimulus we've seen before and consider it in the context of Strengthen and Weaken questions:

> Allyson plays volleyball for Central High School. Therefore, Allyson must be over 6 feet tall.

Remember which assumption holds this argument together? It is that all volleyball players for Central High are over 6 feet tall. That assumption makes or breaks the argument. So if you're asked to weaken the argument, you'll want to attack that assumption:

> Which one of the following, if true, would most weaken the argument?

Prediction: Not all volleyball players at Central High School are over 6 feet tall.

Correct Answer:

    O   Some volleyball players at Central High School are under 6 feet tall.

Notice that we don't have to prove the conclusion wrong, just make it less likely. We've called into doubt the author's basic assumption, thus damaging the argument. Allyson still *could* be over 6 feet tall, but now she doesn't have to be.

What if the question asked you to strengthen the argument? Again, the key would be the necessary assumption:

    Which one of the following, if true, would most strengthen the argument?

Prediction: All volleyball players at Central High School are over 6 feet tall.

Correct Answer:

    O   No member of the Central High School volleyball team is under 6'2".

Here, by confirming the author's assumption, you've in effect bolstered the argument.

Strengthening and Weakening Arguments Exercise

Answers are on the page following this exercise.

Now it's time to put all these skills together and practice analyzing arguments and identifying possible strengtheners and weakeners. Find the conclusion, evidence (if any), and any assumption(s) that the author may be making for each of the following. Then predict what a correct answer choice might contain for a Strengthen question and for a Weaken question.

1. Mailing tubes are the safest and most convenient way for people to mail posters and art prints. Over the past six months, post offices and office supply stores throughout the nation have reported a significant increase in the sale of mailing tubes. It is obvious that people are mailing a greater number of posters and art prints.

Conclusion:

Evidence:

Assumption(s):

Predict strengtheners:

Predict weakeners:

2. Last month, a local newspaper published an editorial criticizing a prominent mayoral candidate for refusing to endorse a proposal to renovate the city's primary railroad station. This editorial was ultimately responsible for the candidate's losing the mayoral election. After all, before the editorial was published, the candidate was leading in opinion polls, while after the editorial was published, the candidate's approval ratings dropped sharply.

Conclusion:

Evidence:

Assumption(s):

Predict strengtheners:

Predict weakeners:

3. In the current economic recession in Kelrovia, many companies have chosen to reduce their expenditures in order to avoid bankruptcy. However, one company claims that increasing its research and development budget for its newest smartphone model will lead to increased profits.

    Conclusion:

    Evidence:

    Assumption(s):

    Predict strengtheners:

    Predict weakeners:

4. According to a recent study, the majority of people in a large city believe that most homeless people are drug addicts who could get jobs if they wanted to work. However, the public is misinformed. The city's Coalition for the Homeless estimates that over 85 percent of the homeless population is moderately to severely mentally ill.

    Conclusion:

    Evidence:

    Assumption(s):

    Predict strengtheners:

    Predict weakeners:

Strengthening and Weakening Arguments Exercise: Answers

1. **Conclusion:** People are mailing more posters and art prints.

   Evidence: The sale of mailing tubes has increased.

   Assumption: The people buying mailing tubes are using them to mail posters and art prints.

   Possible strengthener: When asked about the contents of their packages, almost all customers who use mailing tubes claim they are shipping posters or art prints (or any other evidence that suggests this is how the mailing tubes are being used).

   Possible weakener: Many people have recently started buying mailing tubes in bulk for craft projects at home (or for any reason other than mailing posters and art prints).

2. **Conclusion:** The editorial was responsible for the candidate's loss.

   Evidence: The candidate was leading in polls before the editorial was published, then dropped in popularity afterward.

   Assumption: The change in public opinion was caused by the editorial and not something else.

   Possible strengthener: Most of the city's residents claim that the railroad station renovation is very important to them (or any other reason the editorial would have influenced the election).

   Possible weakener: On the same day the editorial was published, reports were released implicating the candidate in a major tax evasion scandal (or any other reason besides the editorial that people did not vote for the candidate).

3. **Conclusion:** Even in a recession, spending more money on R & D will lead to increased profits for a particular company.

   Evidence: None; there's no support for why the company believes its profits will increase.

   Assumption: Since there's no evidence, there's also no assumption.

   Possible strengthener: The increased budget will allow the company to add features that make the smartphone especially useful to those searching for and applying to new jobs (or any other reason the smartphone will be profitable, especially given the recession).

   Possible weakener: In order to recoup the increased costs of producing the phone, the company will have to sell the smartphone at a price that is unaffordable to most Kelrovians (or any other reason the smartphone will not be profitable, especially given economic conditions).

4. **Conclusion:** The public is misinformed in its belief that the homeless are drug addicts who don't want to work; in other words, homeless people are not drug addicts and/or do want to work.

   Evidence: An estimate from Coalition for the Homeless that says the vast majority of homeless people are mentally ill.

   Assumption: If a homeless person is mentally ill, he or she is not a drug addict who is able to work.

   Possible strengthener: Moderate to severe mental illness makes it impossible to obtain or maintain employment (or any other evidence that connects mental illness to unemployment or that counters other reasons the homeless don't work).

   Possible weakener: The mentally ill are capable of maintaining employment if they want to, or many mentally ill people who could work are also drug addicts.

Sample Stems

The stems associated with these two question types may use the word *weaken* or *strengthen*, or they may use other phrasing. Here's a list of some you can expect to see on Test Day.

Weaken:

- Which one of the following, if true, would most weaken the argument?
- Which one of the following, if true, would most seriously damage the argument?
- Which one of the following, if true, casts the most doubt on the argument?
- Which of the following, if true, would most seriously call into question the plan outlined by the consultant?

Strengthen:

- Which one of the following, if true, would most strengthen the argument?
- Which one of the following, if true, would provide the most support for the conclusion in the argument?
- The argument would be more persuasive if which one of the following were found to be true?

There is some variance in the way these questions are asked. It's common for the question stem to refer explicitly to part of the argument. You might, for example, see something like this:

> Which of the following, if true, casts the most doubt on the author's conclusion that the Brookdale Public Library does not meet the requirements of the new building codes?

A Strengthen question may ask you to fill in the blank at the end of an argument, where the blank is preceded by a key word signaling evidence, such as *since*. As with other Strengthen questions, you must choose the answer that supplies evidence that supports the author's conclusion.

You may also see other slight variations on how Strengthen and Weaken questions are asked; for instance, you may be asked for a choice that would strengthen one conclusion and weaken another one. With such variations, simply pay attention to what effect the answer choice will have on the claims made in the stimulus and use the same strategies to evaluate the choices as you would for a more traditional question.

When you identify the question type during step 1 of the Method, make sure you understand what effect the correct answer will have on the argument. Wrong answers that have the opposite of the desired effect are called 180s, and they're extremely common on Strengthen and Weaken questions. If you're asked to weaken an argument, watch out for wrong answers that would strengthen it. Asked to strengthen? Be wary of weakeners. Pay close attention to what the question asks so you can avoid this trap.

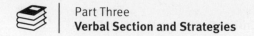

Applying the Kaplan Method: Strengthen and Weaken Questions

Now let's use the Kaplan Method for Critical Reasoning to solve a Strengthen or Weaken question:

> Due to recent success, Lawton, a contractor, can be more selective than in the past regarding the types of clients he chooses to service. If he restricts his business to commercial clients and only those residential clients requiring $10,000 of work or more, he would cease doing most of the kind of residential work he currently does, which would allow him to earn a higher average profit margin per job.
>
> Which of the following, if true, would most strengthen the conclusion that limiting his service in the manner cited would increase Lawton's average profit margin per job?
>
> ○ Lawton's recent success is due primarily to an upsurge in the number of residential clients he services.
>
> ○ Lawton's commercial clients would prefer that he focus more of his time and energy on their projects and less on the concerns of his residential clients.
>
> ○ Residential work for which Lawton cannot bill more than $10,000 comprises a significant proportion of his low-profit-margin work.
>
> ○ Due to the use of a more efficient cost-accounting system, Lawton's average profit margin per job has increased in each of the last three years.
>
> ○ Commercial jobs typically take longer to complete than residential jobs.

STEP 1: IDENTIFY THE QUESTION TYPE

In addition to containing the telltale word "strengthen," the question stem helps you by identifying the conclusion. When the GMAT gives you a gift like this, accept it!

STEP 2: UNTANGLE THE STIMULUS

The conclusion has been handed to you by the question stem: by restricting his work to commercial projects and expensive ($10,000+) residential projects, Lawton will increase his average profit margin. The only evidence is the first sentence, which informs you that due to recent success, Lawton can restrict his work to certain clients if he chooses.

STEP 3: PREDICT THE ANSWER

The evidence proves that Lawton can be selective. However, it does not establish that restricting his business will actually improve his profit margin. The author's claim depends on an assumption: inexpensive residential jobs have lower profit margins than do commercial jobs and pricey residential jobs.

STEP 4: EVALUATE THE CHOICES

Choice (**C**) supports the assumption, thereby strengthening the argument, and is the correct answer.

Wrong answer choices on Strengthen and Weaken questions commonly provide facts that are irrelevant to the argument; since such choices have no direct bearing on the argument, there's no way they could strengthen or weaken it. (**A**) is incorrect because the source of Lawton's recent success is irrelevant and has no connection to higher profit margins. (**B**) discusses the preferences of Lawton's commercial clients, which are also irrelevant. (**D**) credits a new accounting system with an increase in Lawton's profit margin per job. This statement doesn't tell us whether expensive jobs have a higher profit margin than do small residential jobs, so it doesn't help the argument. Furthermore, **(D)** focuses on past improvements, which have no bearing on whether his future plans will be successful. **(E)** tells us that commercial jobs will take longer to complete, but the profit margin of the jobs, not their duration, is what matters in this argument.

TAKEAWAYS: STRENGTHEN AND WEAKEN QUESTIONS

- On Strengthen and Weaken questions featuring an argument, determine the conclusion, evidence, and assumption. Predict that the strengthening or weakening answer may be based on the assumption, but be open to an independent fact that has the appropriate effect on the conclusion.

- Weakening an argument is not the same as disproving a conclusion—and strengthening is not the same as proving it. A weakener tips the scale toward doubting the conclusion, while a strengthener tips the scale toward believing in the validity of the conclusion.

- The words "if true" in the question stem remind you that the correct answers should be treated as facts that can make the argument more or less likely to be true.

- Some Strengthen or Weaken questions provide the conclusion in the stem; use such cases to your advantage.

- Common wrong answers in Strengthen and Weaken questions include irrelevant choices and 180s.

Practice Set: Strengthen and Weaken Questions

4. Earlier this year, our city's three main reservoirs had unusually low water levels. As a result, city officials initiated a program that encouraged residents to reduce their water usage by 20 percent. Since the program was announced, the water level at all three reservoirs has returned to normal. Our city officials should be applauded for their role in preventing a crisis.

    Which of the following, if true, casts the most doubt on the efficacy of the officials' program?

    ○   The current water level in the reservoirs is lower than it was at the same time last year.

    ○   Other nearby reservoirs recovered from lower water levels this year, even though those reservoirs provide water to cities that did not enact water restriction policies.

    ○   Residents reduced their water usage for lawn maintenance significantly more than they did for washing clothes.

    ○   Imposing stiff penalties on residents who did not conserve water would have resulted in even higher water levels in the reservoirs.

    ○   Water usage in the city dropped steadily during the first two weeks of the program before leveling off.

5. To attract new visitors, the local zoo is planning to offer new experiences. One proposal involves allowing visitors to assist in feeding the big cats, such as the lions and the tigers. However, unlike the zookeepers, visitors do not spend time interacting with the cats and becoming familiar to them. Enacting this plan would be like inviting people to enter the home of a well-armed stranger without knocking.

    Which of the following statements, if true, would most strengthen the argument?

    ○   Visitors have not spent as much time studying the behavior of big cats as the zookeepers have.

    ○   Those who would be most interested in opportunities to assist in feeding big cats are already regular visitors and would not bring along new visitors.

    ○   Burglars who are attacked by an occupant during a home invasion usually incur serious injuries requiring emergency treatment.

    ○   People who visit zoos have less experience interacting with wild animals than do people who do not visit zoos.

    ○   Feeding big cats requires entering their habitat, which can only be done safely after previous interaction with the animals.

6. The city of Northtown collects an average of $2.2 million in business taxes per year. Neighboring Southtown collects an average of $1.8 million in business taxes per year. Both cities assess business taxes on net profits. In an attempt to attract new businesses to Southtown, the spokesperson for the chamber of commerce of that city uses these statistics to claim that Southtown's lower business tax rate offers a more favorable environment for business than can be found in Northtown.

Which of the following, if true, would most seriously undermine the spokesperson's argument?

   ○   Most tax revenue collected in Northtown comes from business taxes.

   ○   Most tax revenue collected in Southtown comes from business taxes.

   ○   The net profits generated by Northtown businesses are currently twice those of Southtown businesses.

   ○   Northtown has twice the population of Southtown.

   ○   Southtown businesses generate twice as much sales revenue as do Northtown businesses.

7. Public interest law focuses on the legal issues that affect the entire community or involve broad areas of public concern, such as illegal discrimination, environmental protection, child welfare, and domestic violence. A particular nonprofit agency focusing on public interest law is woefully understaffed; many lawyers are urgently needed to continue its important work providing low-cost legal services to residents who are unable to afford a private attorney. In order to fill these vacancies as efficiently as possible, the agency should advertise the jobs to students in this year's graduating class at the local law school to encourage them to enter the field of public interest law.

Each of the following, if true, weakens the recommendation above EXCEPT:

   ○   Positions in corporate law that are advertised at the local law school have higher average salaries than do legal positions at nonprofit agencies.

   ○   The local law school maintains an active placement service for its graduates and publicizes job openings in the community to its graduating class.

   ○   The open positions at the nonprofit agency require several years of prior experience in the practice of law.

   ○   Several lawyers recently left the nonprofit agency because the agency's salaries did not enable the lawyers to make their student loan payments.

   ○   The local law school is ranked third highest in the country, and graduates of the school aspire to work for large, highly rated law firms located in major cities.

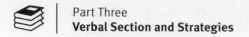

Evaluation Questions

> ### LEARNING OBJECTIVES
>
> In this section, you will learn how to:
>
> - Identify an Evaluation question by its question stem
> - Draw upon the author's conclusion and evidence in order to evaluate the validity of an argument
> - Apply the Kaplan Method for Critical Reasoning to Evaluation questions

An Evaluation question asks you to identify information that would help you assess an argument's strength. The correct answer won't strengthen or weaken the author's reasoning or supply a missing assumption. Instead, the right answer will specify the kind of evidence that would help you judge the validity of the author's argument.

Since the needed information will usually fill a gap in the argument, the correct answer to an Evaluation question typically relates in some way to the assumption. For example, let's say that a stimulus could be paraphrased in the following way: *Because country Y has many business-friendly policies, a recent increase in minimum wage will not affect the willingness of businesses to relocate their operations here.* This argument assumes that the advantages conferred by the country's other policies outweigh the increased labor costs. A Strengthen or Weaken answer choice would likely provide evidence to either support or refute this assumption. An Evaluation answer choice, however, would instead claim that it would be most useful to know *whether factors besides labor costs affect the decisions of certain businesses to relocate their operations to country Y.* If there are no other factors besides labor costs, the argument would be weakened, and if there are other factors, it would be strengthened. Incorrect Evaluation answer choices are generally irrelevant; the information they ask for would have little or no effect on the argument.

Sample Stems

Here are some example question stems that indicate an Evaluation question:

- Which of the following would it be most useful to know in order to evaluate the argument?
- The answer to which of the following questions would be most important in evaluating the proposal?
- To assess the likelihood that the plan will achieve its objective, it would be most useful to determine which of the following?
- To evaluate the author's reasoning, it would be most useful to compare...
- Which of the following must be studied in order to evaluate the argument presented above?

Applying the Kaplan Method: Evaluation Questions

Now let's use the Kaplan Method for Critical Reasoning to solve an Evaluation question:

> Committee member: Last week, committee members were encouraged to nominate candidates for the position of committee chairperson. So far, seven members have submitted nominations. That means we can expect contentious lead-up to the election. After all, such contention always occurs before an election whenever there are more than three candidates for any elected position.
>
> Which of the following would be most useful to know in order to evaluate the likelihood of the committee member's prediction?
>
> O   Whether any of the nominated members are known for arguing frequently with other members
>
> O   Whether a candidate can be nominated by more than one committee member
>
> O   Whether any more nominations for chairperson will be made
>
> O   Whether members were allowed to nominate themselves for chairperson
>
> O   Whether there has ever been contention before an election with only two candidates

STEP 1: IDENTIFY THE QUESTION TYPE

The question asks for something that would be useful "to evaluate" a position. That signals an Evaluation question.

STEP 2: UNTANGLE THE STIMULUS

The committee member predicts that there is likely to be a lot of contention before the upcoming election for committee chairperson. The evidence is that contention occurs any time there are more than three candidates, and seven nominations have already been made.

STEP 3: PREDICT THE ANSWER

There are two assumptions here, both based on the suggestion that contention arises when there are more than three candidates for a position. First, the evidence only says seven *nominations* were made. That doesn't mean those people are actually going to run in the election. Maybe some will decline the nomination, or maybe some will accept but then drop out. Second, there are seven nominations, but that doesn't mean they are for seven different people. Perhaps everyone nominated the same member and that person will run unopposed. So the author is assuming both that the nominated members will be candidates and that more than three people were nominated. The correct answer will question whether either one of these assumptions is valid.

STEP 4: EVALUATE THE CHOICES

(B) is correct, as it questions the assumption about duplicated nominations. If candidates can receive multiple nominations, then the seven nominations need not be for more than three candidates. That would make the argument less convincing. However, if there is no duplication, then there are seven different people nominated, and the argument is strengthened. **(A)** is irrelevant. Contention is said to be based on the number of candidates in the election, not how argumentative those candidates are. **(C)** is irrelevant. There are already seven nominations. If that includes more than three distinct candidates, then it doesn't matter how many more nominations, if any, are made. The prediction is valid either way. **(D)** is irrelevant. The contention is said to be based on the number of candidates, not on who nominated them. **(E)** is irrelevant. The argument is based on the assumption that there will be more than three candidates. It doesn't matter what happens when there are only two candidates.

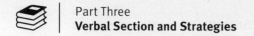
TAKEAWAYS: EVALUATION QUESTIONS

- Evaluation questions ask you to determine what information would most help to evaluate the argument.

- Untangle the stimulus the same way you do for other argument-based questions: identify the conclusion, evidence, and assumption(s).

- Choose the answer choice that would best fill in the gap in logic created by the central assumption.

Practice Set: Evaluation Questions

8. Soil quality is one of the most important factors affecting the growth of crops. Farmers often look for ways to improve soil conditions in order to increase crop production. One possibility involves the planting of dynamic accumulators—plants, such as comfrey, that may draw up significant quantities of beneficial nutrients from beneath the topsoil. Numerous reports have shown that plants grown in areas alongside dynamic accumulators are healthier and more abundant than those grown in areas without dynamic accumulators.

    Which of the following would be most useful in evaluating the claim that planting dynamic accumulators would help farmers increase crop production?

    ○   Would tending to dynamic accumulators increase the costs of crop production?

    ○   Are there solutions other than planting dynamic accumulators that would be more effective at increasing the farmers' crop production?

    ○   Are there plants other than comfrey that would draw up a greater number of nutrients?

    ○   Are any of the plants in the reports the types of crops grown by farmers?

    ○   Would planting dynamic accumulators provide any additional benefits to farmers other than increased soil quality?

9. A grain-processing company is considering purchasing a catfish farm in an attempt to reduce waste by using the by-products of its grain processing as fish food. Catfish whose diet includes grain by-products have been found to reach marketable size in five months, and restaurants have expressed interest in having a reliable source for catfish.

    ○   The answer to which of the following questions is LEAST directly relevant to the grain-processing company's consideration of whether fish farming is a preferable alternative to discarding grain by-products?

    ○   How does the cost of discarding grain by-products compare to the operating costs of a fish farm?

    ○   How many pounds of catfish are served by restaurants locally and nationally each year?

    ○   Are there government regulations that apply to the production and transportation of fish?

    ○   Do catfish require nutrients not supplied by grain by-products?

    ○   In how many months do wild catfish reach marketable size?

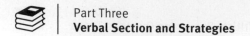

Flaw Questions

Flaw questions are similar to Weaken questions, but instead of asking you for some new fact that, if true, would make the argument questionable, Flaw questions ask what's already wrong with the argument. So your prediction should focus on reasoning errors the author makes.

The good news is that the GMAT uses a handful of common flaws over and over. Here are the two general categories of errors in reasoning:

1. Unsupportable shifts between the concepts in the evidence and conclusion
2. Overlooked alternatives

And here are some common patterns that show up:

- Confusing correlation and causation
- Confusing percent and actual value
- Inappropriate analogies (comparing things that aren't comparable)
- Inappropriate conflation/distinction of terms

All of these flaws and any others you find in GMAT Critical Reasoning questions center on the author's assumption, so you should handle them similarly to how you've handled all the other argument-based questions so far: by identifying the conclusion, evidence, and assumption.

Sample Stems

Here are some example question stems that indicate a Flaw question:

- Which of the following is a flaw in the reasoning above?
- The argument above is vulnerable to which of the following criticisms?

Applying the Kaplan Method: Flaw Questions

Now let's use the Kaplan Method for Critical Reasoning to solve a Flaw question:

> The public service advertising campaign promoting the use of helmets has improved bicycle safety dramatically. Over the past 12 months, the number of serious bicycling injuries has been reduced by nearly 70 percent. Unfortunately, helmet usage has not reduced the number of all types of bike injuries. While serious head trauma has decreased by nearly 85 percent, broken bones now represent 20 percent of all reported bicycling injuries. This is a significant increase from last year's 14 percent.

> The reasoning in the argument is flawed because the argument does which of the following?

- ○ It fails to include information about any types of bicycle injuries other than head trauma and broken bones.
- ○ It implies that the same conclusion can result from two different sets of causes.
- ○ It fails to take into account any possible increase in the number of people riding bicycles over the past 12 months.
- ○ It presumes that an increase in the percentage of injuries involving broken bones precludes a decrease in the actual number of such injuries.
- ○ It ignores the fact that a 70 percent overall decrease in injuries would not allow for an 85 percent decrease in one specific type of injury.

STEP 1: IDENTIFY THE QUESTION TYPE

The question stem alerts you to the idea that this argument is flawed, so Flaw is definitely the question type here.

STEP 2: UNTANGLE THE STIMULUS

The author concludes that the number of broken-bone bicycle injuries has gone up from last year to this year. The evidence for this is that broken bones made up 20 percent of this year's total bicycle-related injuries but were only 14 percent of last year's total.

STEP 3: PREDICT THE ANSWER

As soon as you see both percentages and numbers mentioned in the stimulus for a Flaw question, beware. In the Quantitative section, you will learn, if you have not already, that you must be careful when working with percentages. Twenty percent is guaranteed to equal a higher number than 14 percent only if those percentages are of the same total. And since the total number of injuries is much lower this year than last year, 20 percent of a much lower total could actually equal a lower number than 14 percent of last year's higher total.

If you're having trouble seeing this, you can use the Quant strategy of Picking Numbers. Suppose there were 100 bicycle injuries last year. That means that 14 percent, or 14 total, of those injuries involved broken bones. You know that this year, injuries have been reduced by 70 percent. In this example, that means there were a total of 30 bicycle injuries this year. Twenty percent of the new, lower total is 6 broken-bone injuries, a significantly lower number than last year's 14. The flaw here is the author's assumption that an increase in percentage cannot be consistent with a decrease in actual number.

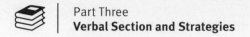

STEP 4: EVALUATE THE CHOICES

Only (**D**) accurately captures the logical flaw in this argument—confusing percent and actual value. (**D**) is the correct answer.

The fact that the author mentions only two types of injuries, as (**A**) says, is not a flaw in the argument, which concerns only whether or not the number of broken bones has been reduced. Other types of injuries are irrelevant. Since two sets of causes aren't discussed, you can rule out (**B**). Causation does figure in many GMAT flaws, but not this one. (**C**) might seem tempting, since it does relate to the "percentage versus actual number" issue, but if the total number of bicyclists increased over the past year, the reduction in the number of total injuries would actually be greater. And since a 70 percent overall decrease in injuries could, in fact, allow for an 85 percent decrease in one specific type of injury, (**E**) can be ruled out as well.

TAKEAWAYS: FLAW QUESTIONS

- Flaw questions ask you to describe how the author's reasoning has gone awry. Identifying the author's assumption will reveal the flawed thinking.

- Some classic flaws include mistaking correlation for causation and confusing actual value with percent.

- On Flaw questions, determine the conclusion, evidence, and central assumption(s). Then predict an answer describing the reasoning error in the author's assumption.

Practice Set: Flaw Questions

10. Our legislature is considering passing legislation to ban skateboarding on city streets, citing safety concerns. However, a review of public health records reveals that the legislature's concern is misplaced. Each year, many more people are injured while jogging than are injured while skateboarding. So in fact, skateboarding is safer than jogging.

    Which of the following indicates a flaw in the reasoning above?

    ○   It fails to distinguish professional skateboarders who attempt very dangerous maneuvers from amateurs who are comparatively cautious.

    ○   It assumes without warrant that no one who skateboards also jogs.

    ○   It fails to consider the number of people who skateboard as compared with the number of people who jog.

    ○   It ignores the possibility that other activities cause even more injuries than either skateboarding or jogging.

    ○   It fails to address the issue and instead attacks the character of the legislature.

11. Solo concert pianists, by convention, are not permitted to use musical scores during their performances. However, most members of chamber groups and orchestras are permitted to use sheet music during performances and perform well as a result. Therefore, all solo concert pianists should also be allowed to consult their musical scores during performances.

    The argument is most vulnerable to criticism on which of these grounds?

    ○   It overlooks the possibility that some solo concert pianists prefer performing without consulting musical scores.

    ○   It takes for granted that members of a chamber group or orchestra are less skilled than solo musicians and thus have more need for musical scores.

    ○   It overlooks the possibility that some solo concert pianists have broken with tradition and used musical scores during their performances.

    ○   It takes for granted that a solo concert pianist would use a musical score in the same way as does a member of a chamber group or orchestra.

    ○   It overlooks the possibility that performing in an orchestra is difficult despite the ability to use a musical score during the performance.

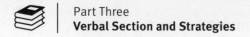

Explain Questions

> **LEARNING OBJECTIVES**
>
> In this section, you will learn how to:
>
> - Distinguish between argument-based and non-argument-based Critical Reasoning questions
> - Identify Explain questions by the question stem
> - Recognize apparent contradictions in the stimulus and predict possible resolutions
> - Apply the Kaplan Method for Critical Reasoning to Explain questions

Questions based on arguments (Assumption, Strengthen, Weaken, Evaluation, and Flaw) make up over 70 percent of all Critical Reasoning questions, but you will likely run into other question types on Test Day that are not based on arguments.

Explain question stimuli are not argumentative. Rather, they present a seeming discrepancy and ask you to find an explanation for the paradox. Your Paraphrasing skills and Attention to the Right Detail are the key to this question type—in your own simple but accurate words, restate not only the details in the stimulus but also the nature of the apparent contradiction. Once you've summed up the nature of the discrepancy, look for an answer choice that explains how the apparently contradictory facts in the stimulus could both be true.

It's sometimes difficult to predict exactly what the correct answer will contain, since an apparent contradiction can often be resolved in a number of different ways. On questions for which there could be multiple ways for the test maker to phrase the correct answer, predictions must be in the form of characterizing what the right answer will mean or do, not the words it will use. Again, Paraphrasing is crucial.

Sample Stems

Here are some example question stems that indicate an Explain question:

- Which of the following, if true, would best explain the discrepancy between customer satisfaction and sales?
- Which of the following, if true, would best resolve the paradox described above?

Applying the Kaplan Method: Explain Questions

Now let's use the Kaplan Method for Critical Reasoning to solve an Explain question:

Over an extended period of time, the average seawater temperature in a region of an ocean increased by over 1 degree Celsius. During that same time, the average size of the haddock population in the region decreased by more than 25 percent. This observation led scientists to hypothesize that warmer waters favored smaller fish because their bodies were less energy intensive and better able to adapt to the warmer water. However, long-term laboratory experiments showed no changes in the average size of haddock as water temperatures were increased.

Which of the following best explains the differences between the observations in nature and those in the laboratory experiments?

O   The measurements of fish size in the ocean were made by oceanographers, but the ones in the laboratory were made by biologists.

O   Measurements were made more frequently in the laboratory experiments than in the ocean.

O   A change in marine fishing regulations during the period allowed the use of nets with a more tightly spaced mesh than had previously been permitted.

O   The population in the ocean of predators that feed on smaller haddock increased during the period.

O   The water salinity measured in the laboratory exactly matched that of the ocean.

STEP 1: IDENTIFY THE QUESTION TYPE

The wording of this stem signals that there were differences between actual observations and the results of laboratory experiments. Your task is to seek a possible explanation for the different results. Any question that asks you to account for a set of potentially contradictory findings is an Explain question.

STEP 2: UNTANGLE THE STIMULUS

When untangling the stimulus, paraphrase the given information and make sure you understand the paradox. The findings described in this stimulus seem to be contradictory: average haddock size and water temperature were negatively related in the ocean, leading scientists to form a hypothesis as to why this occurred, but there was no correlation between size and temperature in the laboratory.

STEP 3: PREDICT THE ANSWER

There could be many reasons why this happened, so you cannot predict the exact answer here. But no matter how the right answer is phrased, you know that it will concern a difference between the real-world and laboratory environments that is relevant to fish size.

STEP 4: EVALUATE THE CHOICES

If the spacing of the mesh in fishing nets decreases, that means that relatively large fish that used to be able to escape the nets are now going to be caught and thus be taken out of the general population of haddock. This phenomenon would reduce the average size of the population. This spacing decrease is what (**C**) describes, so it's the correct answer.

Remember that for an answer choice to be correct, it must relate logically to the seeming contradiction in the stimulus. The incorrect choices here fail to resolve the paradox. The idea that if different kinds of scientists make the measurements, the results would be different requires an assumption that one or the other group is unlikely to report accurate results, so (**A**) does not explain the discrepancy. The frequency of the measurements, per (**B**), would not have any effect on the end results in either environment. Although (**D**) does not address predators in the laboratory environment, if there were more predators of smaller haddock in the ocean, one would expect the average size of fish there to *increase*. This is the opposite, or 180 degrees, from what was observed, so it certainly does not explain the discrepancy. (**E**) describes a variable that was the same in both the ocean and the laboratory, so it cannot explain the different outcomes.

TAKEAWAYS: EXPLAIN QUESTIONS

- Explain questions require test takers to choose an answer choice that best explains why all the information in the stimulus is true.

- In many instances, the Explain question stimulus contains a paradox or discrepancy. The correct answer reconciles the information in the stimulus without contradicting it.

- On Explain questions, identify the seeming paradox and predict an answer that addresses the paradox but does not contradict the evidence at hand.

Practice Set: Explain Questions

12. Sales of yoga mats from Daniel's yoga studio this year were double those of the prior year. However, average enrollment per class at Daniel's studio decreased from the prior year, despite Daniel's studio being the only yoga studio in town.

Which of the following, if true, most helps to explain the discrepancy in sales?

○   Daniel offered a greater variety of yoga mats for sale than he had offered the previous year.

○   The prices of yoga mats in Daniel's studio increased from the previous year.

○   Daniel began to teach additional styles of yoga this year, increasing the number of classes offered and attracting new students.

○   Daniel increased the cost of each of his yoga classes from the previous year.

○   Daniel's studio requires that an individual bring his or her own yoga mat to each of the classes.

13. A certain town's pizza shop initiated an advertising campaign to bring in new customers and increase sales in December. The advertising campaign consisted of sending emails that promoted a two-for-one deal on sheet pizzas. Even though the pizza shop sent out thousands of these email advertisements, sales remained about the same in December as they had been in previous months.

Which of the following, if true, most helps to explain the apparent discrepancy between the volume of advertisements and the volume of sales?

○   The emails did not list every type of pizza on the pizza shop's menu.

○   In December, a new coffee shop opened in the same neighborhood as the pizza shop.

○   Not every resident in the pizza shop's delivery area had an email address.

○   The pizza shop had email addresses only for customers who were members of its rewards club, which offers members weekly specials.

○   The other two pizza shops in town specialize in gourmet pizzas, which are more expensive on average than items on this pizza shop's menu.

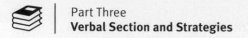

Inference Questions

A question type common to both Critical Reasoning and Reading Comprehension is the Inference question. The process of inferring is a matter of considering one or more statements as evidence and then drawing a conclusion from them. A valid inference is something that must be true if the statements in the stimulus are true—not *might* be true, not *probably* is true, but *must* be true.

Think of an inference as a conclusion that you draw based on the information, or evidence, given. It is your job on these questions to choose the inference that requires no assumption whatsoever; the correct answer will follow directly from the stimulus. But the answer to an Inference question is just as likely to be drawn from only one or two details as it is to take into account the stimulus as a whole. For this reason, it can be very difficult to predict an exact answer. Nevertheless, you can make a general prediction: the answer is the one that *must* be true based on the facts in the stimulus. You can use this prediction to help eliminate choices answer by answer, ruling out options that clearly don't match the facts as you paraphrased them. This is the beauty of a multiple-choice test—find four wrong answers, and you've also found the right one!

Let's examine a somewhat expanded version of the volleyball team argument:

> Allyson plays volleyball for Central High School, despite the team's rule against participation by nonstudents. Therefore, Allyson must be over 6 feet tall.

Wrong answer:

○   Allyson is the best player on the Central High School volleyball team.

Certainly Allyson *might* be the best player on the team. It's tempting to think that this would *probably* be true—otherwise the team would not risk whatever penalties violating the rule might entail. But *must* it be true? No. Allyson could be the second best. Or the third best. Or perhaps the coach owed Allyson's dad a favor. We have no support for the idea that she's the best on the team, so we can't infer this answer choice from the stimulus.

Valid inference:

○   Allyson is not a student at Central High School.

Clearly, if Allyson plays volleyball *despite* the team's rule against participation by nonstudents, she must not be a student. Otherwise, she wouldn't be playing despite the rule; she'd be playing in accordance with the rule. But note that this inference is not a necessary assumption of the argument because the conclusion about Allyson's height doesn't depend on it.

So be careful: unlike an assumption, an inference need not have anything to do with the author's conclusion. In fact, many Inference stimuli don't have conclusions at all—they consist not of arguments but of a series of facts. Make sure you are prepared for Inference questions, as they require a different approach than do other Critical Reasoning questions. Remember, everything that you need will be contained in the stimulus, so focus on the information as it's presented and avoid answers that twist the facts (or make up new ones).

Sample Stems

Inference questions probably have the most varied wording of all the Critical Reasoning question stems. Some question stems denote inference fairly obviously. Others are more subtle, and still others may look like other question types entirely. The bottom line is that if a question asks you to take the stimulus as fact and find something based on it, then you're looking at an Inference question. Here's a quick rundown of various Inference question stems that you may see on your test:

- Which one of the following can be inferred from the argument above?
- Which one of the following is implied by the argument above?
- If all the statements above are true, which one of the following must also be true?
- The statements above, if true, best support the argument that _____ .
- Which of the following is the conclusion toward which the author is probably moving?
- The statements above best support which of the following conclusions?

Applying the Kaplan Method: Inference Questions

Now let's use the Kaplan Method for Critical Reasoning to solve an Inference question:

A new electronic security system will only allow a single person at a time to pass through a secure door. A computer decides whether or not to unlock a secure door on the basis of visual clues, which it uses to identify people with proper clearance. The shape of the head, the shape and color of the eyes, the shape and color of the lips, and other characteristics of a person's head and face are analyzed to determine his or her identity. Only if the person trying to open a secure door has the required clearance will the door unlock. Because this new system never fails, an unauthorized person can never enter a secure door equipped with the system.

If the statements above are true, which of the following conclusions can be most properly drawn?

O   The new system is sure to be enormously successful and revolutionize the entire security industry.

O   The new system can differentiate between people who are seeking to open a secure door and people passing by a secure door.

O   No two people have any facial features that are identical, for example, identical lips.

O   High costs will not make the new security system economically unviable.

O   The new computer system is able to identify some slight facial differences between people who look very similar, such as identical twins.

STEP 1: IDENTIFY THE QUESTION TYPE

Since the stem asks you to accept the statements as true and draw a conclusion on the basis of them, this is an Inference question.

STEP 2: UNTANGLE THE STIMULUS

When untangling the stimulus of an Inference question, briefly paraphrase the important facts to ensure you understand them. The stimulus tells you that a new electronic security system is completely fail-safe and will never allow an unauthorized person through a door equipped with the system. The system allows an authorized person to enter solely on the basis of the person's appearance and facial features.

STEP 3: PREDICT THE ANSWER

Attempting to predict the correct inference is difficult here, but on the GMAT, remember that an inference is something that must be true, not just something that could or might be true. It's crucial to approach the answer choices with this definition in mind.

STEP 4: EVALUATE THE CHOICES

(A) is unsupported. There is no evidence of how the security industry is going to respond to the new system, so you can't say that this statement must be true based on what the stimulus states. **(B)** also doesn't need to be true. The new system doesn't need to differentiate between people passing by the door and people trying to enter, so long as it lets authorized people in and keeps unauthorized people out. **(C)** is too extreme. According to the stimulus, the security system examines multiple facial features to determine identity. You don't know that any *one* feature cannot be the same. All you know is that *all* of the features can't be the same. As for **(D)**, the stimulus only discusses the likelihood that unauthorized people will be able to get past the security system and through a secure door; there is no support for a statement about costs.

That means the correct inference must be **(E)**: if one twin is authorized and the other isn't, you know the system must be able to tell them apart, because the stimulus states that the security system never fails.

TAKEAWAYS: INFERENCE QUESTIONS
• Inference stimuli seldom contain complete arguments. Rather, they contain statements from which you must make a deduction.
• On an Inference question, you want the choice that *must* follow from the stimulus—not a choice that *might* or *could* follow.
• On Inference questions, determine which answer choice must be true, based on the stimulus.
• An inference need not be based on the entire stimulus. An inference may follow from a single sentence or fact.
• Some Inference question stems require you to complete a train of thought.

Practice Set: Inference Questions

14. Hyperkalemia occurs when the body contains an excessive amount of potassium. In severe circumstances, hyperkalemia can lead to abnormal heart rhythms. Lowering potassium levels is essential to treating those who suffer from hyperkalemia. However, patients with severe hyperkalemia are initially given an injection of calcium, even though calcium does not lower the body's potassium levels. Instead, the calcium protects the heart from the negative effects of excess potassium. Patients are then given doses of a medicine, such as insulin or albuterol, that help reduce potassium levels.

    The information given, if true, most strongly supports which of the following?

    O   If an injection of calcium is not given first, medicines such as insulin or albuterol could exacerbate the conditions of severe hyperkalemia.

    O   Patients with mild to moderate hyperkalemia are not given calcium to protect their heart.

    O   Patients given calcium injections cannot be given insulin until the calcium has provided its full effect.

    O   Not all treatments for hyperkalemia are intended to address the root cause of the condition.

    O   Patients cannot reduce their potassium levels without a sufficient intake of calcium.

15. A local department store hires college students for one month every spring to audit its unsold inventory. It costs the department store 20 percent less to pay wages to students than it would cost to hire outside auditors from a temporary service. Even after factoring in the costs of training and insuring the students against work-related injury, the department store spends less money by hiring its own auditors than it would by hiring auditors from the temporary service.

    The statements above, if true, best support which of the following assertions?

    O   The amount spent on insurance for college-student auditors is more than 20 percent of the cost of paying the college students' basic wages.

    O   It takes 20 percent less time for the college students to audit the unsold inventory than it does for the outside auditors.

    O   The department store pays its college-student auditors 20 percent less than the temporary service pays its auditors.

    O   By hiring college students, the department store will cause 20 percent of the auditors at the temporary service to lose their jobs.

    O   The cost of training its own college-student auditors is less than 20 percent of the cost of hiring auditors from the temporary service.

16. The Internal Revenue Service (IRS) has a mandate to operate more efficiently. However, if taxpayers did not have a respectful fear of the IRS, the timely collection of taxes could not be maintained. For the last 10 years, polls have shown that most American taxpayers fear the fines and late fees that can follow an IRS audit.

The statements above, if true, would best serve as an argument that

○ most American taxpayers are not concerned with receiving tax credits or refunds

○ those American taxpayers who comply voluntarily with the tax laws do not fear the potential consequences of an audit

○ projecting a friendlier public image would likely be counterproductive for the IRS

○ more American taxpayers fear the IRS today than feared it 10 years ago

○ collecting delinquent taxes costs the IRS more than does collecting taxes on time

Bolded Statement Questions

> **LEARNING OBJECTIVES**
>
> In this section, you will learn how to:
>
> - Identify a Bolded Statement question by its question stem
> - Classify in general terms the role a given statement serves in an argument
> - Apply the Kaplan Method for Critical Reasoning to Bolded Statement questions

Bolded Statement questions are usually based on stimuli that contain arguments, but the way you will analyze these arguments is different from what you have learned for other argument-based questions. Bolded Statement questions focus more on the structure than the substance of the stimulus.

A Bolded Statement question asks for the role that specific sentences play in an argument. The relevant sentences are, as the name implies, written in bold font. There are usually two bolded statements in the stimulus, but you may see questions with only one bolded statement. The answers to these questions will be abstract, using language such as "The first provides a counterexample to an opinion, while the second reaffirms that opinion by dismissing the counterexample." This technical language can make these questions seem intimidating.

Fortunately, these questions appear only occasionally. Moreover, if you do see any of these questions on Test Day, they shouldn't be nearly as difficult as they look. Remind yourself that Bolded Statement questions test the same core skill as much of the rest of the Critical Reasoning section: the ability to identify the evidence and the conclusion of an argument.

One caution: Unlike most GMAT stimuli, Bolded Statement questions often contain multiple arguments. Make sure that you note not only which parts of the argument are evidence and which are conclusions but also which evidence is connected to which conclusion. In addition, use key words in the stimulus to identify which conclusion (if any) the author agrees with. Once you've done so, you should be able to make a prediction about the role of the bolded statements. Then you can turn these difficult questions into points.

Sample Stem

Bolded Statement question stems can't really avoid referring directly to the part(s) of the argument in bold type, so these stems are among the easiest to identify. A Bolded Statement question stem will look something like this:

- The portions of the argument in boldface play which of the following roles?

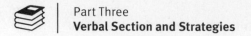
Applying the Kaplan Method: Bolded Statement Questions

Now let's use the Kaplan Method for Critical Reasoning to solve a Bolded Statement question:

> Auto manufacturer: For the past three years, the Micro has been our best-selling car. This year, however, sales of the Micro have been down for two consecutive quarters. Therefore, we are going to make certain features, like leather seats and CD players, standard on the Micro, rather than require buyers to pay extra for them. **This will make the Micro more attractive to buyers, thus stimulating sales.**
>
> Auto dealer: Most people who buy the Micro do so because of its low cost. **Adding new standard features will raise the base price of the Micro,** costing us sales.
>
> In the argument above, the two statements in **bold** play which of the following roles?

- ○ The first is a conclusion; the second suggests that this conclusion is based on evidence that is irrelevant to the issue at hand.
- ○ The first presents a hypothesis; the second casts doubt on the evidence on which that hypothesis is based.
- ○ The first provides a conclusion; the second weakens the assumption on which that conclusion relies.
- ○ The first offers evidence that is disproved by the second.
- ○ The first presents a conclusion; the second supports the conclusion but offers a different interpretation of how it will impact the speakers' business.

STEP 1: IDENTIFY THE QUESTION TYPE

This stem offers standard language for a Bolded Statement question—it asks you to determine the roles played in the arguments by each of the boldface statements.

STEP 2: UNTANGLE THE STIMULUS

The stimulus is organized as a dialogue. This is a rare stimulus format, but it does occasionally turn up on the GMAT. Here, the manufacturer has devised a solution to revive flagging sales of the Micro: to make certain features standard that used to cost buyers extra. The auto dealer, on the other hand, posits that adding new standard features will increase the price of the Micro, thereby hurting sales.

STEP 3: PREDICT THE ANSWER

Predict the answer by identifying the function of each of the bolded statements within the context of the argument-counterargument structure. The first bolded statement is a prediction that serves as the auto manufacturer's conclusion: adding more standard features to the Micro will stimulate sales. The manufacturer's conclusion relies on one of two assumptions: either that the added features will not result in an increase to the Micro's base price or that car buyers interested in the Micro are willing and able to pay more for a version of the car with added features. However, as the auto dealer states, people who buy the Micro do so primarily because of its low price. Because the addition of more standard features will result in an increase in price, the manufacturer's proposal will actually lower sales. The second bolded statement, therefore, weakens the manufacturer's prediction by challenging her assumption.

STEP 4: EVALUATE THE CHOICES

Only **(C)** matches this analysis of the arguments and is correct. **(A)** begins correctly, but the second bolded statement does not challenge any of the manufacturer's evidence (that the Micro was the best-selling model for three years, that sales of the Micro have been down for two quarters, and that the company is planning to add new standard features to the Micro). **(B)** can also be eliminated for this reason. **(D)** is incorrect because the first bolded statement is not the manufacturer's evidence but her conclusion. **(E)** might also have appealed to you, since the auto dealer does offer a different point of view on how these new standard features will affect sales of the Micro. However, the dealer's point of view is actually the opposite of the manufacturer's conclusion, so saying that the second statement "supports the conclusion" of the first is incorrect.

TAKEAWAYS: BOLDED STATEMENT QUESTIONS

- Bolded Statement questions commonly ask test takers to choose the answer that describes a connection between two parts of the stimulus that are in boldface.
- Predicting will help you deal with the wordy and difficult answer choices.
- On Bolded Statement questions, identify the purpose of every sentence in the stimulus and select the answer that matches your description of the bolded statements.
- The most challenging questions may present multiple points of view, often an argument and a counterargument.

Practice Set: Bolded Statement Questions

17. The use of fingerprint analysis to identify criminal suspects dates back to the late 1800s, although the theory behind the technique existed long before it was actually used in practice. **In fact, the hypothetical possibility was so intriguing to Mark Twain that he used fingerprint identification as a plot device in his quasi-memoir *Life on the Mississippi* nearly a decade before fingerprints were used to solve a crime in real life.** Since then, fingerprint analysis has become a standard law enforcement technique for real and fictional detectives alike. Yet, despite its widespread use, the practice has never been subjected to rigorous scientific study, and some of the assumptions that underpin its use—such as the notion that each person has a unique set of fingerprints—may not be accurate. **The time has come for the legal community to acknowledge that fingerprint analysis is an unsubstantiated forensic science and to advocate for more research in the field.**

    In the argument given, the two portions in boldface play which of the following roles?

    ○　The first is a detail that supports the author's main idea, and the second raises a contrary opinion.

    ○　The first is a detail that supports one opinion, and the second is a contrary opinion held by the author.

    ○　The first introduces an opinion, and the second contradicts that opinion.

    ○　The first is a detail that supports the author's main idea, and the second is additional evidence for the author's main idea.

    ○　The first is a detail that supports a claim made in the argument, and the second is the author's main point.

18. Historian: It is often claimed that in many ancient societies, spices were used to disguise the taste of spoiled meat. This claim should, however, be evaluated in its full economic context. **In the early days of the Roman Empire, a pound of ginger could cost as much as 5,000 times the average daily wage.** Surely, anyone who could afford such a luxury would simply buy fresh meat rather than attempting to hide unpleasant flavors in rotten meat.

    In the above argument, the statement in **boldface** plays which of the following roles?

    ○　It is data in support of a claim that the historian is attempting to refute.

    ○　It is evidence that supports the historian's conclusion.

    ○　It is the conclusion of the historian's argument.

    ○　It is a claim that the historian is attempting to refute.

    ○　It is data whose accuracy the historian questions.

Question Type Identification Exercise

LEARNING OBJECTIVE

In this section, you will learn how to:

- Identify which type of Critical Reasoning question has been asked based on the question stem

Answers are on the page following this exercise.

Identifying the question type during step 1 of the Kaplan Method for Critical Reasoning puts you in control of the entire process that follows: what to read for in the stimulus, how to frame your prediction, and how to evaluate answer choices. This exercise will help you practice identifying the key words that signal the question type. Note that often, the stem in actual questions will be more detailed than the examples below and will reference parts of the stimulus.

For the questions that follow, analyze key words in the question stem and determine what task the question is setting you. Based on this analysis, choose the correct question type from the list of choices.

1. Which of the following, if true, provides the best support for the author's position?

   O Assumption
   O Explain
   O Inference
   O Strengthen
   O Weaken

2. Which of the following is an assumption upon which the argument is based?

   O Assumption
   O Evaluate
   O Explain
   O Inference
   O Strengthen

3. Which of the following, if true, most seriously calls into question the author's conclusion?

   O Assumption
   O Explain
   O Flaw
   O Inference
   O Weaken

4. If the above statements are true, they provide the best support for which of the following?

   O Assumption
   O Explain
   O Inference
   O Strengthen
   O Weaken

5. Which of the following points out a serious shortcoming in the author's argument?

   O Evaluation
   O Explain
   O Flaw
   O Inference
   O Weaken

6. Which of the following would be most useful to investigate for the purpose of determining the validity of XXXXXXX?

   O Assumption
   O Evaluation
   O Explain
   O Strengthen
   O Weaken

7. Each of the following, if true, casts doubt upon the author's argument EXCEPT

    ○ Explain
    ○ Flaw
    ○ Inference
    ○ Strengthen
    ○ Weaken

8. Which of the following, if true, best explains the seeming contradiction described by the author?

    ○ Bolded Statement
    ○ Evaluation
    ○ Explain
    ○ Strengthen
    ○ Weaken

9. The portions of the argument in boldface play which of the following roles?

    ○ Bolded Statement
    ○ Evaluation
    ○ Explain
    ○ Inference
    ○ Strengthen

10. Which of the following, if true, provides the strongest grounds for the author's prediction that XXXXXXX will occur?

    ○ Assumption
    ○ Evaluate
    ○ Explain
    ○ Inference
    ○ Strengthen

11. The argument is most vulnerable to which of the following criticisms?

    ○ Evaluation
    ○ Explain
    ○ Flaw
    ○ Inference
    ○ Weaken

12. In order for the author's conclusion to be correct, which of the following statements must be true?

    ○ Assumption
    ○ Explain
    ○ Inference
    ○ Strengthen
    ○ Weaken

13. Which of the following, if true, increases the likelihood that the author's conclusion is correct?

    ○ Explain
    ○ Flaw
    ○ Inference
    ○ Strengthen
    ○ Weaken

14. If the above statements are true, then which of the following must also be true?

    ○ Assumption
    ○ Evaluate
    ○ Inference
    ○ Strengthen
    ○ Weaken

15. Which of the following, if true, contributes most strongly to the point of view of those critical of the author's position?

    ○ Evaluation
    ○ Explain
    ○ Flaw
    ○ Inference
    ○ Weaken

16. Which of the following, if true, most helps to justify the author's opinion?

    ○ Assumption
    ○ Evaluation
    ○ Explain
    ○ Inference
    ○ Strengthen

Question Type Identification Exercise: Answers

1. D

When the stem asks for what supports the conclusion, you are dealing with a Strengthen question.

2. A

Often, an Assumption question will actually use the word "assumption" in the stem.

3. E

Any outside information (as indicated by "if true") that "calls into question" the conclusion would certainly weaken that conclusion. This is a Weaken question.

4. C

Notice that "if...true" in this stem refers to the stimulus. Although "support" is frequently associated with a Strengthen question, in this case the question asks which of the choices is supported by the stimulus, meaning which can be inferred. So this is an Inference question.

5. C

The question points you toward identifying a "shortcoming" in the argument as it currently exists, rather than bringing in outside information to weaken it, so you are looking for an error in the reasoning that supports the conclusion. This is a Flaw question.

6. B

The phrase "most useful to investigate" means that you are looking for something that would be helpful in evaluating the argument. Thus, this is an Evaluation question.

7. E

The words "cast doubt" mean that this is a Weaken question. However, since the question uses EXCEPT, you are looking for the choice that either does not affect the conclusion or actually strengthens it.

8. C

As is often the case, the word "explains" in the stem tells you that this is an Explain question.

9. A

Boldface questions will be directly identified as such, since they refer to the parts of the stem that are in boldface.

10. E

Since the stem mentions the author's "prediction," the argument is in the category of Plans, Proposals, and Predictions, and the prediction is the author's conclusion. You're asked for the "strongest grounds" for that conclusion, so this is a Strengthen question.

11. C

If the argument is "vulnerable" to criticism, that means that there can be some truth to the criticism and the argument is thus flawed. This is a Flaw question.

12. A

For a conclusion to be correct, the underlying assumption must be valid. Therefore, this is an Assumption question.

13. D

If a statement "increases the likelihood" that the conclusion is correct, then it strengthens the argument. This is a Strengthen question.

14. C

This is an Inference question. The stem starts by telling you that the stimulus is true and requires you to use that as the basis to determine which of the choices must be true.

15. E

If a statement strengthens the argument of those who oppose the author, then it makes the author's opinion less strong. This is a Weaken question.

16. E

If a statement helps to "justify" the author's opinion, then it makes the argument stronger. This is a Strengthen question.

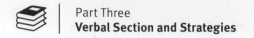
Congratulations on completing the Question Type Identification Exercise! As you've seen in this chapter, different types of Critical Reasoning questions ask you to approach the stimulus and answer choices differently. By executing step 1 of the Kaplan Method for Critical Reasoning—by understanding the specific task each question is asking you to perform—you will put yourself in a good position to be successful with these questions and earn a strong Verbal score.

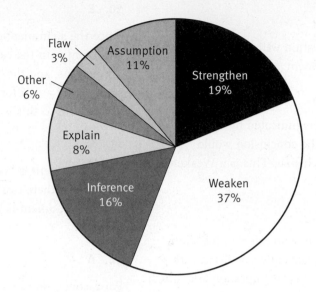

The Approximate Distribution of GMAT Critical Reasoning Questions

Following are the answers and explanations for the practice sets in this chapter.

Answer Key

Practice Set: Assumption Questions

1. B
2. C
3. B

Practice Set: Strengthen and Weaken Questions

4. B
5. E
6. C
7. A

Practice Set: Evaluation Questions

8. D
9. E

Practice Set: Flaw Questions

10. C
11. D

Practice Set: Explain Questions

12. C
13. D

Practice Set: Inference Questions

14. D
15. E
16. C

Practice Set: Bolded Statement Questions

17. E
18. B

Answers and Explanations

Practice Set: Assumption Questions

1. **(B)**

   To protect the environment, paper towels in public restrooms should be banned and replaced with hot-air dryers. The use of such dryers would reduce the need to cut down trees to turn into paper towels. Furthermore, since fewer paper towels would be needed, the environmental impact of the emissions from the paper-manufacturing process would be lessened.

   Which of the following is an assumption upon which the above proposal depends?

   ○ The operating expenses related to hot-air dryers are no greater than those related to paper towels.

   ○ The manufacture and operation of hot-air dryers use fewer natural resources than do the manufacture and use of paper towels.

   ○ Hot-air dryers are the only viable alternative to paper towels in public restrooms.

   ○ Hot-air dryers are at least as effective at drying the hands as are paper towels.

   ○ The operators of public restrooms are willing to replace paper towels with hot-air dryers.

STEP 1: IDENTIFY THE QUESTION TYPE

The question stem, in addition to asking for a necessary assumption, indicates that a proposal has been made.

STEP 2: UNTANGLE THE STIMULUS

The proposal is a ban on paper towels, which would be replaced by hot-air dryers; the purpose of this ban is to reduce environmental impact. The evidence used to support this proposal is that the manufacture of paper towels uses natural resources and causes emissions.

STEP 3: PREDICT THE ANSWER

To recommend the proposal, the author must assume that the environmental benefits of hot-air dryers outweigh any disadvantages. A good prediction would be that there's nothing about hot-air dryers that would make them worse for the environment than paper towels.

STEP 4: EVALUATE THE CHOICES

(B) matches this prediction and is thus correct; since one of the stated goals of the plan is to protect the environment and this will be achieved, in part, by cutting down fewer trees, the author must be assuming that hot-air dryers use fewer natural resources than do paper towels. If increased use of hot-air dryers would cause, for example, the mining of metals for their manufacture or of coal or uranium to produce electricity, then their environmental impact might not be less than that of paper towels, and the argument would fall apart. **(A)** is irrelevant; the fact that costs won't increase might be an additional benefit of the proposal, but since the argument is strictly about environmental impact, the author isn't assuming anything about the cost of the change. **(C)** is incorrect because it's not necessary for dryers to be the only alternative to towels for them to be the better alternative. **(D)** is wrong because effectiveness is irrelevant to an argument that is based on environmental concerns. **(E)** may be tempting because it might seem that the proposal won't be effective if people aren't willing to implement it. However, the proposal is that paper towels *should* be banned; even if the ban isn't enacted, the author could still think it's a good idea.

2.   **(C)**

A company's health program offers medical coverage for all of its full-time employees. As part of the program, employees can choose from one of three plans, each of which offers a different mix of medical benefits depending on an individual's particular needs. Thus, all full-time employees who take advantage of the company's program are sure to be covered for most, if not all, of their medical needs.

Which of the following is an assumption on which the argument relies?

- ○   Part-time employees can also receive coverage from the company's health program.
- ○   None of the three plans costs the company significantly more than the other plans.
- ○   There are no full-time employees whose medical needs are mostly uncovered by each of the three available plans.
- ○   There is no alternative plan that would cover more medical needs than the plans in the current program.
- ○   At least one of the three plans offers dental coverage for full-time employees whose health is impacted by their dental needs.

STEP 1: IDENTIFY THE QUESTION TYPE

The question directly asks for an "assumption," making this an Assumption question.

STEP 2: UNTANGLE THE STIMULUS

"Thus" indicates the author's conclusion: full-time employees who take advantage of the company's health program will have most or all of their medical needs covered. The evidence is that employees can choose from one of three plans, each of which offers a different mix of benefits.

STEP 3: PREDICT THE ANSWER

For the conclusion to be valid, each employee would have access to a plan that covers all or most of that employee's individual medical needs. However, despite the variety among the available plans, there are still only three to choose from. The author fails to consider that some people may have a set of medical needs that are not adequately covered by any of the three available options. For this argument to work, the author must assume that every employee will find what he or she needs in at least one of those three options.

STEP 4: EVALUATE THE CHOICES

(C) is correct. If nobody has all or most of their needs uncovered, that's just another way of saying that they all will have their needs covered. **(A)** is irrelevant. The argument is about full-time employees, so it doesn't matter what's available for part-time employees. **(B)** is irrelevant. The argument is only about whether employees will have coverage, not how much it will cost the company. **(D)** is not an assumption that is necessary for the argument. The author is not saying the health program is the best possible program. The author is only arguing that it will provide sufficient coverage, and that could be valid even if better options exist. **(E)** is not necessary. The argument does not claim that *everything* has to be covered. It only has to be true that *most* needs are covered. So there doesn't have to be dental coverage for this argument to work.

3. **(B)**

A local hardware store is concerned that its sales will diminish when a competing hardware store opens in the same area next month. However, it is actually more likely that the existing store's sales will increase. Over the next few months, due to high demand for mixed-use residential and commercial buildings, over three times as many construction projects will be started in the area as were started over the past five years.

The argument above depends on which of the following assumptions?

- O The managers of the new construction projects will purchase an equal amount of material from both hardware stores.
- O The construction projects will require the purchase of materials that are sold at the existing hardware store.
- O The materials sold at the existing store are higher in quality than those to be sold at the new hardware store.
- O The area revitalization spurred by new mixed-use developments will encourage local residents to perform improvements on their own homes.
- O The existing hardware store will lower its prices below those of its competitors to attract new customers.

STEP 1: IDENTIFY THE QUESTION TYPE

The question directly asks for an assumption, making this an Assumption question.

STEP 2: UNTANGLE THE STIMULUS

Despite the local hardware store's concerns about a competitor's impact on sales, the author concludes that the store's sales are actually likely to increase. To support this claim, the author points out a boom of construction projects in the area.

STEP 3: PREDICT THE ANSWER

A boom in construction projects might seem like a boon for a hardware store. However, what if those construction projects require special materials that the local store cannot provide? Or what if the construction crews already own the equipment they need and have no need to go shopping for new stuff? Or maybe the construction companies have preexisting contracts with national hardware chains and don't buy from local stores at all. In that case, the local store would gain no benefit from these new projects. For this argument to work, the author must assume that the construction projects will provide sales opportunities for the local store.

STEP 4: EVALUATE THE CHOICES

(B) is correct. If the construction projects don't need anything the local store is selling, then the local store will gain nothing. The author must assume the new projects will lead to sales. **(A)** is not necessary. The local store and the incoming competition don't have to have equal sales. If the construction projects lead to a large enough increase in overall sales, then the local store could increase sales even it takes in a smaller percentage of overall sales. **(C)** is irrelevant. There's no guarantee that higher quality would lead to higher sales. In addition, there are many scenarios under which the local store could increase sales even if its materials were of equal or lesser quality to those sold by the competitor. **(D)** is not necessary. While an increase in personal home improvement projects might well benefit the hardware store, they wouldn't be needed if the new mixed-use developments have the anticipated demand for the store's products. **(E)** is not necessary. While lower prices might be a great way to boost sales, there are many other reasons sales could increase—including those major construction projects that the author uses as evidence.

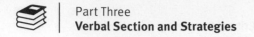

Practice Set: Strengthen and Weaken Questions

4. **(B)**

Earlier this year, our city's three main reservoirs had unusually low water levels. As a result, city officials initiated a program that encouraged residents to reduce their water usage by 20 percent. Since the program was announced, the water level at all three reservoirs has returned to normal. Our city officials should be applauded for their role in preventing a crisis.

Which of the following, if true, casts the most doubt on the efficacy of the officials' program?

- ○ The current water level in the reservoirs is lower than it was at the same time last year.
- ○ Other nearby reservoirs recovered from lower water levels this year, even though those reservoirs provide water to cities that did not enact water restriction policies.
- ○ Residents reduced their water usage for lawn maintenance significantly more than they did for washing clothes.
- ○ Imposing stiff penalties on residents who did not conserve water would have resulted in even higher water levels in the reservoirs.
- ○ Water usage in the city dropped steadily during the first two weeks of the program before leveling off.

STEP 1: IDENTIFY THE QUESTION TYPE

The question stem asks for something that reduces the likelihood that the officials' program was effective. Thus, this is a Weaken question.

STEP 2: UNTANGLE THE STIMULUS

The city officials instituted a program that called for reduced water usage, and the water levels did return to normal. The author concludes that the water reduction program was responsible for this result.

STEP 3: PREDICT THE ANSWER

This a classic example of an unsupported cause-and-effect argument. The author assumes that the program caused the levels to return to normal and that nothing else was responsible. Your prediction should be along the lines of "something other than the program led to the increased water level."

STEP 4: EVALUATE THE CHOICES

(B) matches this prediction. It doesn't outright state what the other factor was. However, if other reservoirs in the area recovered without a water usage program in place, then some other factor must have been involved. **(A)** makes an irrelevant comparison between this year and last year. Even if last year's levels were higher, it's still possible that the program helped the reservoirs return to normal this year. **(C)** is another irrelevant comparison: as long as people reduced water usage overall, the program still could have worked. **(D)** suggests that there could have been a more effective plan, but that doesn't mean that the city officials' plan was ineffective. And the timing of the drop in water usage, in **(E)**, does not affect the argument that the plan caused the reduction and that this reduction caused reservoir levels to rise.

5. **(E)**

To attract new visitors, the local zoo is planning to offer new experiences. One proposal involves allowing visitors to assist in feeding the big cats, such as the lions and the tigers. However, unlike the zookeepers, visitors do not spend time interacting with the cats and becoming familiar to them. Enacting this plan would be like inviting people to enter the home of a well-armed stranger without knocking.

Which of the following statements, if true, would most strengthen the argument?

- O   Visitors have not spent as much time studying the behavior of big cats as the zookeepers have.

- O   Those who would be most interested in opportunities to assist in feeding big cats are already regular visitors and would not bring along new visitors.

- O   Burglars who are attacked by an occupant during a home invasion usually incur serious injuries requiring emergency treatment.

- O   People who visit zoos have less experience interacting with wild animals than do people who do not visit zoos.

- O   Feeding big cats requires entering their habitat, which can only be done safely after previous interaction with the animals.

STEP 1: IDENTIFY THE QUESTION TYPE

This is a Strengthen question; you'll need to find something in the answer choices that supports the argument in the stimulus.

STEP 2: UNTANGLE THE STIMULUS

The author uses an analogy to argue that allowing visitors to help feed the big cats would be dangerous. The reason is that the cats don't get to know the visitors like they do the zookeepers.

STEP 3: PREDICT THE ANSWER

What if people could help feed the cats without actually interacting with the animals? That would take away the danger, making the author's argument fall apart. So to strengthen the argument, show that feeding the cats involves a risk of physical contact.

STEP 4: EVALUATE THE CHOICES

(E) does exactly that, making it correct. **(A)** states that visitors are not as knowledgeable as the zookeepers. However, the argument hinges on how well the cats know the people feeding them, not the other way around. Moreover, this statement still provides no evidence that visitors—well-informed or not—would be put in any danger, as the author concludes. **(B)** addresses the wrong idea. The zoo may be looking to attract new visitors, but the author is only concerned about safety, not whether the zoo is successful in increasing attendance. **(C)** confirms the potential danger of entering a stranger's home unannounced. However, the author brings up this situation as an analogy, and knowing more about the danger of committing a home invasion does not confirm that feeding big cats is equivalently dangerous. **(D)** mentions people's experience interacting with wild animals in general, while the argument is about whether the big cats in this zoo will have had prior exposure to the visitors. More importantly, this comparison of visitors to non-visitors is irrelevant as it still does not make a connection between greater interaction and safety.

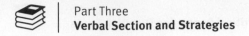
6. (C)

The city of Northtown collects an average of $2.2 million in business taxes per year. Neighboring Southtown collects an average of $1.8 million in business taxes per year. Both cities assess business taxes on net profits. In an attempt to attract new businesses to Southtown, the spokesperson for the chamber of commerce of that city uses these statistics to claim that Southtown's lower business tax rate offers a more favorable environment for business than can be found in Northtown.

Which of the following, if true, would most seriously undermine the spokesperson's argument?

- ○ Most tax revenue collected in Northtown comes from business taxes.
- ○ Most tax revenue collected in Southtown comes from business taxes.
- ○ The net profits generated by Northtown businesses are currently twice those of Southtown businesses.
- ○ Northtown has twice the population of Southtown.
- ○ Southtown businesses generate twice as much sales revenue as do Northtown businesses.

STEP 1: IDENTIFY THE QUESTION TYPE

The question stem asks you to identify the fact that will most undermine the spokesperson's argument, so this is a Weaken question.

STEP 2: UNTANGLE THE STIMULUS

The spokesperson claims that Southtown's lower business tax rate creates a better business environment. The evidence is the lower amount of business taxes collected in Southtown. Thus, the spokesperson is equating lower total business tax receipts with a lesser impact on an individual business that might start up in Southtown.

STEP 3: PREDICT THE ANSWER

While the amount of taxes collected is lower, that doesn't mean that Southtown has the lower tax rate. Perhaps Southtown has fewer businesses and collected the smaller amount by taking a larger percentage of taxes from those businesses. A good prediction would be "anything that says Southtown may have a smaller amount of business profits to tax or a higher rate of taxation."

STEP 4: EVALUATE THE CHOICES

(C) matches the prediction and is correct. If Northtown has twice the business profits and doesn't collect twice the tax revenue of Southtown, then Northtown has the lower tax rate. Thus, a business that started in Northtown would pay less taxes. The argument is only about the impact of business taxes, so whether a smaller or larger proportion of all taxes are business taxes has nothing to do with tax rates and is irrelevant to the conclusion; eliminate **(A)** and **(B)**. **(D)** is irrelevant because the size of the population does not necessarily correspond to the amount of business profits or business taxes collected. **(E)** is irrelevant because business taxes are not assessed on sales but on profits, and if they were assessed on sales, this choice would strengthen, not weaken, the argument.

7. **(A)**

Public interest law focuses on the legal issues that affect the entire community or involve broad areas of public concern, such as illegal discrimination, environmental protection, child welfare, and domestic violence. A particular nonprofit agency focusing on public interest law is woefully understaffed; many lawyers are urgently needed to continue its important work providing low-cost legal services to residents who are unable to afford a private attorney. In order to fill these vacancies as efficiently as possible, the agency should advertise the jobs to students in this year's graduating class at the local law school to encourage them to enter the field of public interest law.

Each of the following, if true, weakens the recommendation above EXCEPT:

- ○ Positions in corporate law that are advertised at the local law school have higher average salaries than do legal positions at nonprofit agencies.

- ○ The local law school maintains an active placement service for its graduates and publicizes job openings in the community to its graduating class.

- ○ The open positions at the nonprofit agency require several years of prior experience in the practice of law.

- ○ Several lawyers recently left the nonprofit agency because the agency's salaries did not enable the lawyers to make their student loan payments.

- ○ The local law school is ranked third highest in the country, and graduates of the school aspire to work for large, highly rated law firms located in major cities.

STEP 1: IDENTIFY THE QUESTION TYPE

This is a Weaken EXCEPT question. Look for an answer that strengthens the argument or that simply has no effect on the argument.

STEP 2: UNTANGLE THE STIMULUS

The recommendation is the final sentence, identified by the key word "should." The conclusion states that "the agency should advertise" the available jobs to "this year's graduating class at the local law school" and that this is the most efficient way to fill the vacancies. The evidence is that "many lawyers are urgently needed" to fill open positions at the agency.

STEP 3: PREDICT THE ANSWER

In this argument, the central assumption is that advertising to the local law school's current graduating class is the most efficient way to fill the agency's vacancies. The four incorrect answers will make the assumption less likely, thus weakening the recommendation. The one correct answer will either make it more likely that advertising in the recommended way will be the most efficient way to fill the vacancies or will be irrelevant to the conclusion.

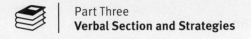
STEP 4: EVALUATE THE CHOICES

(A) has no effect on the conclusion and is correct. The agency doesn't need to attract every or even many graduates for advertising at the law school to be the most effective strategy to fill its positions, and while corporate salaries may be higher, public interest salaries may still be high enough to attract enough new lawyers. **(B)** points out that the local law school is already providing information about the positions to its graduating class, making it less likely that the advertising will have any effect. **(C)** suggests that the graduating students would not be qualified to fill the positions at the agency and thus weakens the argument. **(D)** states that several of the agency's vacancies are due to lawyers leaving the agency because of low pay, making it more likely that salaries, not advertising, are the issue. **(E)** makes it less likely that the agency's advertising will have a receptive audience.

Practice Set: Evaluation Questions

8.   (D)

Soil quality is one of the most important factors affecting the growth of crops. Farmers often look for ways to improve soil conditions in order to increase crop production. One possibility involves the planting of dynamic accumulators—plants, such as comfrey, that may draw up significant quantities of beneficial nutrients from beneath the topsoil. Numerous reports have shown that plants grown in areas alongside dynamic accumulators are healthier and more abundant than those grown in areas without dynamic accumulators.

Which of the following would be most useful in evaluating the claim that planting dynamic accumulators would help farmers increase crop production?

○   Would tending to dynamic accumulators increase the costs of crop production?

○   Are there solutions other than planting dynamic accumulators that would be more effective at increasing the farmers' crop production?

○   Are there plants other than comfrey that would draw up a greater number of nutrients?

○   Are any of the plants in the reports the types of crops grown by farmers?

○   Would planting dynamic accumulators provide any additional benefits to farmers other than increased soil quality?

STEP 1: IDENTIFY THE QUESTION TYPE

The question asks for something that would "most useful in evaluating" a claim, making this an Evaluation question. It's useful to notice that the claim being evaluated is in the question stem itself, not in the stimulus. The claim is that dynamic accumulators would help increase crop production.

STEP 2: UNTANGLE THE STIMULUS

According to the author, successful crop growth depends on having good soil, which is a consistent concern for farmers. The author offers a solution: dynamic accumulators (plants that gather nutrients). As evidence that this would help, the author cites reports of increased plant growth in places with dynamic accumulators.

STEP 3: PREDICT THE ANSWER

The reports seem to offer some support for using dynamic accumulators. Unfortunately, the reports merely mention "plants" without indicating what kinds of plants are being grown. The claim in question is concerned specifically with farmers' crops. If the reports are based solely on plants that farmers don't grow, then the reports may not be representative of what would happen with crops. The correct answer should question whether or not the reports adequately represent what would happen to farmers' crops.

STEP 4: EVALUATE THE CHOICES

(D) is correct. If none of the reports involve crops used by farmers, then the reports are irrelevant and provide no support for the claim in question. However, if such crops are examined in the reports, then that information does support the claim. **(A)** is irrelevant. While perhaps a source of concern for some farmers, costs do not impact whether the plants would help or not. **(B)** is irrelevant. Whether or not better solutions exist does not have a bearing on whether dynamic accumulators could help. **(C)** is irrelevant. Comfrey is just one example of a potential dynamic accumulator. The claim is not about comfrey, specifically. **(E)** is irrelevant. The only benefit that matters here is improving soil conditions. As long as that happens, then it doesn't matter whether or not there are any other benefits.

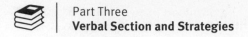

9.   **(E)**

A grain-processing company is considering purchasing a catfish farm in an attempt to reduce waste by using the by-products of its grain processing as fish food. Catfish whose diet includes grain by-products have been found to reach marketable size in five months, and restaurants have expressed interest in having a reliable source for catfish.

○   The answer to which of the following questions is LEAST directly relevant to the grain-processing company's consideration of whether fish farming is a preferable alternative to discarding grain by-products?

○   How does the cost of discarding grain by-products compare to the operating costs of a fish farm?

○   How many pounds of catfish are served by restaurants locally and nationally each year?

○   Are there government regulations that apply to the production and transportation of fish?

○   Do catfish require nutrients not supplied by grain by-products?

○   In how many months do wild catfish reach marketable size?

STEP 1: IDENTIFY THE QUESTION TYPE

This is an Evaluation question with a twist: you need to find the one question whose answer would *not* help you decide whether the grain-processing company should discard its grain by-products or recycle those products to feed catfish.

STEP 2: UNTANGLE THE STIMULUS

One piece of evidence for success of the plan is that fish with grain by-products in their diets reach marketable size; this establishes that catfish eat the by-products and grow large enough to be sold. Another piece of evidence is that restaurants want a steady supply of catfish.

STEP 3: PREDICT THE ANSWER

These facts are both promising, but do they make operating a fish farm a better choice than just throwing away the by-products? As with any question that asks you to evaluate a plan, consider other factors that might influence whether the plan is the better choice or feasible at all.

STEP 4: EVALUATE THE CHOICES

(E) is the correct answer because the time it takes for catfish to mature in the wild is irrelevant to whether the company should farm them. Even if catfish mature much more quickly in the wild, they may be difficult to harvest, expensive to transport, or not found in sufficient numbers. Even if they mature much more slowly, they may be less prone to disease and thus be a more reliable supply, or they may taste better. An answer to this question about wild catfish does not help evaluate the plan concerning farmed catfish. With **(A)**, if the costs of operating the fish farm were less than the costs of discarding the by-products, the plan would be more attractive. **(B)** is an important question that speaks to how much fish the company could sell to earn revenue and offset the costs of running the farm. An answer to **(C)** would provide information about regulations that could increase the costs and reduce the feasibility of fish farming. Although the author says that some fish fed with grain by-products grow up, it doesn't say their entire diet is grain by-products. Thus, an answer to **(D)** would provide information about whether the grain company would need to buy other foods or supplements, making the project more expensive.

Practice Set: Flaw Questions

10. (C)

Our legislature is considering passing legislation to ban skateboarding on city streets, citing safety concerns. However, a review of public health records reveals that the legislature's concern is misplaced. Each year, many more people are injured while jogging than are injured while skateboarding. So in fact, skateboarding is safer than jogging.

Which of the following indicates a flaw in the reasoning above?

- ○ It fails to distinguish professional skateboarders who attempt very dangerous maneuvers from amateurs who are comparatively cautious.
- ○ It assumes without warrant that no one who skateboards also jogs.
- ○ It fails to consider the number of people who skateboard as compared with the number of people who jog.
- ○ It ignores the possibility that other activities cause even more injuries than either skateboarding or jogging.
- ○ It fails to address the issue and instead attacks the character of the legislature.

STEP 1: IDENTIFY THE QUESTION TYPE

The word "flaw" in the question stem indicates that this is a Flaw question. You'll be looking for the argument's faulty assumption.

STEP 2: UNTANGLE THE STIMULUS

In Flaw questions, just as in Assumption questions, you need to identify the argument's conclusion and evidence. In this argument, the conclusion is the final sentence: skateboarding is safer than jogging. The evidence is that more people are injured while jogging than while skateboarding.

STEP 3: PREDICT THE ANSWER

In Flaw questions, expect that the conclusion will not follow logically from the evidence because the author makes an inappropriate assumption. Here, the author incorrectly assumes that a higher number of people injured means a higher percentage of people injured, which is not necessarily the case. Picking numbers clarifies the issue. Let's say that 100 people skateboard in a given city, while 10,000 people jog. In that case, if 200 people are injured by jogging while only 10 are injured by skateboarding, jogging would actually be the far safer sport because 2 percent of joggers but 10 percent of skateboarders have sustained injuries. The flaw in the argument, then, is that it fails to provide you with the relative numbers of joggers versus skateboarders.

STEP 4: EVALUATE THE CHOICES

(C) matches the prediction and is correct. **(A)** is an irrelevant comparison between professional and amateur skateboarders. **(B)** is incorrect because the evidence explicitly states that more people are hurt while jogging than while skateboarding. Even if some people do engage in both activities, the conclusion is based on evidence about which activity they were doing when they were injured, so it makes no difference whether there is any overlap between joggers and skateboarders. **(D)** is incorrect because activities other than jogging and skateboarding are irrelevant to the stimulus. **(E)** is incorrect because there is no attack on anybody's character in the argument.

11. (D)

Solo concert pianists, by convention, are not permitted to use musical scores during their performances. However, most members of chamber groups and orchestras are permitted to use sheet music during performances and perform well as a result. Therefore, all solo concert pianists should also be allowed to consult their musical scores during performances.

The argument is most vulnerable to criticism on which of these grounds?

○ It overlooks the possibility that some solo concert pianists prefer performing without consulting musical scores.

○ It takes for granted that members of a chamber group or orchestra are less skilled than solo musicians and thus have more need for musical scores.

○ It overlooks the possibility that some solo concert pianists have broken with tradition and used musical scores during their performances.

○ It takes for granted that a solo concert pianist would use a musical score in the same way as does a member of a chamber group or orchestra.

○ It overlooks the possibility that performing in an orchestra is difficult despite the ability to use a musical score during the performance.

STEP 1: IDENTIFY THE QUESTION TYPE

The question asks how the argument is "vulnerable to criticism," so this is a Flaw question.

STEP 2: UNTANGLE THE STIMULUS

The author concludes that solo concert pianists should be allowed to use musical scores during their performances. The author supports this conclusion by drawing an analogy: members of chamber groups and orchestras are allowed to consult musical scores during their performances and perform well as a result.

STEP 3: PREDICT THE ANSWER

Flaws in arguments arise from an author's faulty assumptions. In an argument that relies on an analogy, such as this one, the assumption is that the two things being compared are sufficiently alike. Predict that the correct answer will state that the author has overlooked a relevant difference between solo pianists and performers in ensembles.

STEP 4: EVALUATE THE CHOICES

(D) reflects the prediction and is correct. If a pianist would not use a score in the same way as, say, a violinist in an orchestra, then the analogy the argument relies on is not valid. As for **(A)**, it doesn't matter to the argument whether or not solo concert pianists prefer using musical scores; the author's argument states that they should be allowed to use them because they would perform better if they did. **(B)** is an irrelevant comparison; the argument does not rely on the relative skill levels of the two kinds of musicians. If anything, the author would take for granted that solo pianists are less skilled, since that might explain why they should be allowed to use sheet music. **(C)** mentions that some solo concert pianists may have used musical scores even though they're not supposed to; however, the author is arguing that these musicians *should* be allowed to perform with a score in front of them. **(E)** is incorrect because the author's assumption is that performing is less difficult with scores than without, not that it is easy.

Practice Set: Explain Questions

12. (C)

> Sales of yoga mats from Daniel's yoga studio this year were double those of the prior year. However, average enrollment per class at Daniel's studio decreased from the prior year, despite Daniel's studio being the only yoga studio in town.
>
> Which of the following, if true, most helps to explain the discrepancy in sales?

- O   Daniel offered a greater variety of yoga mats for sale than he had offered the previous year.
- O   The prices of yoga mats in Daniel's studio increased from the previous year.
- O   Daniel began to teach additional styles of yoga this year, increasing the number of classes offered and attracting new students.
- O   Daniel increased the cost of each of his yoga classes from the previous year.
- O   Daniel's studio requires that an individual bring his or her own yoga mat to each of the classes.

STEP 1: IDENTIFY THE QUESTION TYPE

This asks you to explain a discrepancy, so it's an Explain question.

STEP 2: UNTANGLE THE STIMULUS

The key word "[h]owever" identifies the discrepancy here: despite a decline in enrollments in each yoga class at a particular studio, sales of yoga mats increased.

STEP 3: PREDICT THE ANSWER

Consider possible explanations: it might be that more people are taking up yoga outside a studio or at a studio outside of town, people are using yoga mats for non-yoga-related activities, more classes are being offered such that per-class enrollment is down but overall enrollment is up, or people now want a different mat for each day of the week—or perhaps there are other explanations. There's no way to know exactly what will show up in the correct answer, so predict *anything that would increase demand for yoga mats without increasing class size*.

STEP 4: EVALUATE THE CHOICES

An increase in the number of classes as well as the addition of new students, **(C)**, explains the discrepancy. Even if per-class enrollment is down, more classes means overall enrollment could be up, and new students probably don't already have mats and need to buy them. **(A)** only explains the increase in sales if you further assume that people like to buy different types of mats when they are available, and there is no evidence for this. **(B)** deepens the mystery; if the price of mats has gone up, then all else being equal, you'd expect sales to go down. **(D)** may explain the decrease in yoga class enrollment, but it does not address the increase in yoga mat sales. **(E)** would only work if this requirement were new this year; however, the stimulus does not say this is the case.

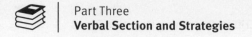

13. (D)

A certain town's pizza shop initiated an advertising campaign to bring in new customers and increase sales in December. The advertising campaign consisted of sending emails that promoted a two-for-one deal on sheet pizzas. Even though the pizza shop sent out thousands of these email advertisements, sales remained about the same in December as they had been in previous months.

Which of the following, if true, most helps to explain the apparent discrepancy between the volume of advertisements and the volume of sales?

- ○ The emails did not list every type of pizza on the pizza shop's menu.
- ○ In December, a new coffee shop opened in the same neighborhood as the pizza shop.
- ○ Not every resident in the pizza shop's delivery area had an email address.
- ○ The pizza shop had email addresses only for customers who were members of its rewards club, which offers members weekly specials.
- ○ The other two pizza shops in town specialize in gourmet pizzas, which are more expensive on average than items on this pizza shop's menu.

Step 1: Identify the Question Type

The question stem asks you to "explain the apparent discrepancy," so this is an Explain question. Furthermore, you know from the question stem that the mystery will involve advertisements and sales.

STEP 2: UNTANGLE THE STIMULUS

The stimulus should be viewed as a set of statements that present an apparent contradiction. The key words "even though" in the stimulus indicate a contrast or discrepancy. The discrepancy here is that pizza sales in December did not increase despite an increase in the number of emailed advertisements.

STEP 3: PREDICT THE ANSWER

The correct answer must explain why sales remained flat despite the fact that thousands of people were offered a two-for-one deal on sheet pizzas. There may be some reason this deal was unappealing to the people who received the emails. Alternatively, perhaps many people who took advantage of the sale would normally have bought pizzas at full price, so overall revenues did not increase.

STEP 4: EVALUATE THE CHOICES

(D) states that the emails were sent only to customers who were already loyal customers and already getting special deals on pizza. This explains why they did not increase their pizza purchases and is the correct answer. **(A)** does not account for the advertisement's lack of effect on sales because the emails promoted a special price and not the variety of pizzas available. **(B)** mentions that a new coffee shop opened nearby, but because it's a very different kind of restaurant, it would not be a direct competitor to the pizza shop. Therefore, its presence does not explain the lack of appeal of two-for-one pizzas. The fact that some people in the area don't have email doesn't explain why the advertisement failed to attract those who do have email, so **(C)** doesn't explain the mystery. **(E)** mentions that the two other pizza shops in town offer more expensive gourmet pizzas. This would explain why not everyone would buy pizza at this pizza shop, but it doesn't explain why emails offering a special deal failed to attract more business from people who don't want more expensive pizza.

Practice Set: Inference Questions

14. (D)

Hyperkalemia occurs when the body contains an excessive amount of potassium. In severe circumstances, hyperkalemia can lead to abnormal heart rhythms. Lowering potassium levels is essential to treating those who suffer from hyperkalemia. However, patients with severe hyperkalemia are initially given an injection of calcium, even though calcium does not lower the body's potassium levels. Instead, the calcium protects the heart from the negative effects of excess potassium. Patients are then given doses of a medicine, such as insulin or albuterol, that help reduce potassium levels.

The information given, if true, most strongly supports which of the following?

○ If an injection of calcium is not given first, medicines such as insulin or albuterol could exacerbate the conditions of severe hyperkalemia.

○ Patients with mild to moderate hyperkalemia are not given calcium to protect their heart.

○ Patients given calcium injections cannot be given insulin until the calcium has provided its full effect.

○ Not all treatments for hyperkalemia are intended to address the root cause of the condition.

○ Patients cannot reduce their potassium levels without a sufficient intake of calcium.

STEP 1: IDENTIFY THE QUESTION TYPE

The stimulus will contain information that "strongly supports" the correct answer. Therefore, this is an Inference question.

STEP 2: UNTANGLE THE STIMULUS

The author provides some information about hyperkalemia. The author mentions what it is (a condition in which the body has too much potassium), its potential effects (heart problems), and the treatment for severe circumstances (calcium to protect the heart, followed by insulin or albuterol to reduce potassium).

STEP 3: PREDICT THE ANSWER

There are lot of details here and thus a lot of potential inferences. So it's not worth trying to predict an exact answer. Instead, focus on the general ideas: the condition can be dangerous, and various treatments are given. One (calcium) addresses the potential effects of the condition, while others (insulin and albuterol) treat the cause of the condition itself. Test the choices and be wary of answers that require outside information or are not directly addressed by the information given.

STEP 4: EVALUATE THE CHOICES

(D) is correct. The treatment with calcium does not address the root cause of hyperkalemia—excess potassium. Instead, calcium helps protect against the effects of hyperkalemia. **(A)** is not supported. The calcium is said to protect the heart from excess potassium, not from insulin or albuterol. There is no evidence that the insulin or albuterol would be harmful without the calcium. **(B)** is not supported. The author claims that people with severe hyperkalemia are given calcium, but calcium could also be given to other people, including those with mild or moderate hyperkalemia. **(C)** is extreme. While the insulin is said to be given at some point after the calcium, the author doesn't say how long after. The author never suggests that the calcium has to be *fully* effective before the insulin is given. **(E)** is a 180. While calcium helps protect the heart, calcium does not reduce potassium levels. Thus, it is certainly not necessary for reducing potassium levels.

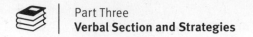

15. (E)

A local department store hires college students for one month every spring to audit its unsold inventory. It costs the department store 20 percent less to pay wages to students than it would cost to hire outside auditors from a temporary service. Even after factoring in the costs of training and insuring the students against work-related injury, the department store spends less money by hiring its own auditors than it would by hiring auditors from the temporary service.

The statements above, if true, best support which of the following assertions?

○ The amount spent on insurance for college-student auditors is more than 20 percent of the cost of paying the college students' basic wages.

○ It takes 20 percent less time for the college students to audit the unsold inventory than it does for the outside auditors.

○ The department store pays its college-student auditors 20 percent less than the temporary service pays its auditors.

○ By hiring college students, the department store will cause 20 percent of the auditors at the temporary service to lose their jobs.

○ The cost of training its own college-student auditors is less than 20 percent of the cost of hiring auditors from the temporary service.

STEP 1: IDENTIFY THE QUESTION TYPE

Since the question stem is asking you to make an assertion supported by the statements in the stimulus, this is an Inference question.

STEP 2: UNTANGLE THE STIMULUS

Sometimes Critical Reasoning questions look like math word problems. Any time you see numbers and statistics, you need to pay close attention, especially to the distinction between actual numbers and percentages. For this question, the stimulus confirms that what the department store pays student auditors in wages is 20 percent less than the cost of hiring outside auditors. You also know that even after you add the costs of training and insuring the students (costs not involved with hiring outside auditors), the cost to the store is still less than hiring the outside auditors.

STEP 3: PREDICT THE ANSWER

Based on the statements here, it must be true that the costs of training and insuring the students are not more than 20 percent of the cost of hiring the outside auditors. If they were, then the 20 percent savings in wages would be outweighed by those extra costs, and hiring outside auditors would be cheaper.

STEP 4: EVALUATE THE CHOICES

(E) matches the prediction and is the correct answer. **(A)** mentions the relationship between the students' wages and the cost of their insurance, but this relationship is not mentioned in the stimulus, so you can't infer anything about it. By the same token, **(B)** can be eliminated because it discusses the amount of time the employees take to audit the inventory, when the stimulus only concerns the cost to the department store. **(C)** distorts the 20 percent statistic from the stimulus. That statistic compares what the department store spends on student employees to what the store spends on outside auditors. What the temp service pays the auditors is totally irrelevant. **(D)** is yet another distortion of the 20 percent statistic. You can't say for sure that *any* of the outside auditors will lose their jobs if they are not hired by the department store.

16. (C)

The Internal Revenue Service (IRS) has a mandate to operate more efficiently. However, if taxpayers did not have a respectful fear of the IRS, the timely collection of taxes could not be maintained. For the last 10 years, polls have shown that most American taxpayers fear the fines and late fees that can follow an IRS audit.

The statements above, if true, would best serve as an argument that

- ○ most American taxpayers are not concerned with receiving tax credits or refunds
- ○ those American taxpayers who comply voluntarily with the tax laws do not fear the potential consequences of an audit
- ○ projecting a friendlier public image would likely be counterproductive for the IRS
- ○ more American taxpayers fear the IRS today than feared it 10 years ago
- ○ collecting delinquent taxes costs the IRS more than does collecting taxes on time

STEP 1: IDENTIFY THE QUESTION TYPE

The question stem indicates that the stimulus should be read as evidence for a conclusion you'll find in the answer choices. Since you're drawing a conclusion based on statements in the stimulus, this is an Inference question.

STEP 2: UNTANGLE THE STIMULUS

The author asserts that the IRS needs to operate more efficiently. The author also says that if taxpayers were not so afraid of the agency, it would have more difficulty collecting taxes. Fortunately (for the IRS), taxpayers report they are afraid of IRS audits.

STEP 3: PREDICT THE ANSWER

Connecting the dots between the statements in the stimulus, you can conclude that taxpayer fear is important for the IRS's efficient operation. The correct answer will align with this idea.

STEP 4: EVALUATE THE CHOICES

(C) matches the prediction and is correct. (A) introduces the idea of credits and refunds. Although the stimulus says most taxpayers are concerned about late fees and penalties, this does not mean they aren't also interested in credits and refunds. (B) is not supported by the stimulus. Be wary of sensible-sounding statements that are not based on the text. The author does not suggest that the people who are afraid of audits are not complying with the law. (D) is not supported because the stimulus provides no evidence for how people felt more than 10 years ago; the only evidence is from polls during the last 10 years. (E) is an irrelevant comparison. The stimulus speaks to whether or not taxes can be collected on time but says nothing about the costs of tax collection.

Practice Set: Bolded Statement Questions

17. (E)

The use of fingerprint analysis to identify criminal suspects dates back to the late 1800s, although the theory behind the technique existed long before it was actually used in practice. **In fact, the hypothetical possibility was so intriguing to Mark Twain that he used fingerprint identification as a plot device in his quasi-memoir *Life on the Mississippi* nearly a decade before fingerprints were used to solve a crime in real life.** Since then, fingerprint analysis has become a standard law enforcement technique for real and fictional detectives alike. Yet, despite its widespread use, the practice has never been subjected to rigorous scientific study, and some of the assumptions that underpin its use—such as the notion that each person has a unique set of fingerprints—may not be accurate. **The time has come for the legal community to acknowledge that fingerprint analysis is an unsubstantiated forensic science and to advocate for more research in the field.**

In the argument given, the two portions in boldface play which of the following roles?

○ The first is a detail that supports the author's main idea, and the second raises a contrary opinion.

○ The first is a detail that supports one opinion, and the second is a contrary opinion held by the author.

○ The first introduces an opinion, and the second contradicts that opinion.

○ The first is a detail that supports the author's main idea, and the second is additional evidence for the author's main idea.

○ The first is a detail that supports a claim made in the argument, and the second is the author's main point.

STEP 1: IDENTIFY THE QUESTION TYPE

Because the question stem asks you to identify the roles of statements in boldface, this is a Bolded Statement question.

STEP 2: UNTANGLE THE STIMULUS

The stimulus begins by providing some history about the use of fingerprint analysis and states that, over time, the technique has become a routine component of police investigations in real life and in popular culture. The key word "[y]et" signals an important shift: despite the widespread use of fingerprint analysis, it isn't a well-studied science. From here, the author pivots to her recommendation that the legal community do more to encourage scientific research into the reliability of fingerprint analysis.

STEP 3: PREDICT THE ANSWER

The first bolded statement is part of the history of fingerprint analysis presented by the author. The author uses it as an example to support the claim made in the previous sentence that the theory of fingerprint identification predates its actual use. The second bolded statement is a recommendation made by the author. Because the other information presented in the stimulus build toward this recommendation, it is the author's main point.

STEP 4: EVALUATE THE CHOICES

(E) matches the prediction and is correct. (A) incorrectly states that the second statement is "contrary" to the author's main idea, when in fact the opposite is true. (B) is incorrect because the first statement is supporting a factual claim, not an opinion, and the second statement is not a "contrary" opinion. Similarly, (C) claims that the first statement is an opinion, but it's actually a supporting detail, and that the second statement "contradicts" the first, but there is no conflict between them. Finally, (D) is incorrect because it asserts that the second statement is evidence, but it is actually the author's main point or conclusion.

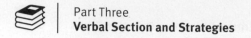
18. (B)

> Historian: It is often claimed that in many ancient societies, spices were used to disguise the taste of spoiled meat. This claim should, however, be evaluated in its full economic context. **In the early days of the Roman Empire, a pound of ginger could cost as much as 5,000 times the average daily wage.** Surely, anyone who could afford such a luxury would simply buy fresh meat rather than attempting to hide unpleasant flavors in rotten meat.

In the above argument, the statement in **boldface** plays which of the following roles?

- ○ It is data in support of a claim that the historian is attempting to refute.
- ○ It is evidence that supports the historian's conclusion.
- ○ It is the conclusion of the historian's argument.
- ○ It is a claim that the historian is attempting to refute.
- ○ It is data whose accuracy the historian questions.

STEP 1: IDENTIFY THE QUESTION TYPE

Since this asks you to identify the role played by a statement in boldface, it's a Bolded Statement question.

STEP 2: UNTANGLE THE STIMULUS

The stimulus opens with a claim that spices were often used to cover up spoiled meat; note that the historian does not claim this view as her own. Instead, she states that it should be evaluated in light of the conditions of the time. The bolded statement then provides data that relates to the exorbitant price of ginger in Ancient Rome. Based on that evidence, the historian then presents her own conclusion: that it would not make sense to use such an expensive spice, since anyone who could afford it would just buy unspoiled meat.

STEP 3: PREDICT THE ANSWER

Since the bolded statement is historical data, it's evidence. However, since there are two claims in this stimulus, you need to predict which claim the evidence supports. In this case, it's the historian's claim.

STEP 4: EVALUATE THE CHOICES

(B) states that the statement is evidence for the historian's conclusion, so it's correct. **(A)** correctly states that the bolded statement supports a claim, but for the wrong conclusion. **(C)** mischaracterizes the statement as the historian's conclusion rather than evidence. Similarly, **(D)** incorrectly states that it's the claim that the historian is trying to refute; the refuted claim appears in the first sentence of the stimulus. **(E)** claims that the historian questions the accuracy of the data in the bolded statement; however, since it's evidence to support her own conclusion, her argument rests on the veracity of the evidence.

Advanced Strategies for Critical Reasoning

In Chapter 6, you learned about the standard Critical Reasoning question types on the GMAT. Recognizing these questions, which the test maker asks over and over very predictably, enables you to read strategically—that is, to read for the details that make the difference between right and wrong answers. But the arguments in CR stimuli follow patterns as well. Recognizing common argument structures will allow you to analyze stimuli and predict correct answers more efficiently.

These advanced techniques are no substitute for knowing how to identify the conclusion, evidence, and assumptions in arguments—the ability to break down arguments into their component parts remains essential—but the three special cases we are about to discuss can help you zero in on the author's central assumption with speed and accuracy. When you understand the kind of argument an author is making, you can anticipate what kind of assumptions he or she is likely to make.

The three special cases are Causality; Representativeness; and Plans, Proposals, and Predictions. Causality and Representativeness are classic argument structures, and Plans, Proposals, and Predictions are classic argument conclusions that function in predictable ways.

Let's begin by discussing how to identify a causal argument and use that knowledge to your advantage on Critical Reasoning questions.

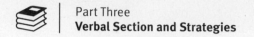
Special Case #1: Causality

A causal argument is an assertion that a certain cause produced a certain effect. In other words, X caused Y, X made Y happen, or Y is the result of X. The author's assertion of causality may be explicit (e.g., "The drought led to large-scale crop failures," or "The new city plan is responsible for these underdeveloped downtown blocks") or implicit (e.g., "Since the introduction of the new radiator design, brand X cars have seen an 8 percent increase in incidents of overheating. Customer dissatisfaction will remain high until we announce a redesign"). Examine the following example of a conclusion that contains a claim of causality:

> Married people have been shown in several important studies to have higher levels of happiness than single people. Therefore, marriage causes happiness.

This argument draws its validity from a stated cause-effect relationship (namely, that marriage causes happiness). A conclusion that X caused Y relies on certain assumptions: (1) that nothing else—A, B, C, etc.—could have caused Y; (2) that Y was not the cause of X; and (3) that the apparent relationship between X and Y wasn't just a coincidence. An author who makes any of these assumptions may be confusing correlation and causation.

Causal conclusions often appear in Weaken stimuli. There are three ways to weaken causal arguments based on the assumptions listed above. Let's try them out with the following cause-effect statement:

"Marriage causes happiness."

X = cause (marriage); Y = effect (happiness)

Consider the following patterns when asked to weaken a causal argument:

Alternative explanation: It wasn't X that caused Y; it was actually Z that caused Y.

"Marriage doesn't cause happiness; in fact, financial security (which correlates strongly with marriage) was the real cause of the happiness reported in the surveys."

Causality reversed: It wasn't X that caused Y; it was actually Y that caused X.

"Marriage doesn't cause happiness; in fact, people who are already happy are significantly more likely to marry."

Coincidence: It wasn't X that caused Y; any correlation between X and Y is a coincidence, since they have no direct relationship.

"Marriage doesn't cause happiness; other studies that looked at the same group of people over time found that people reported similar levels of happiness before and after getting married. Any seeming correlation between marriage and happiness is coincidental or based on other factors."

In Weaken questions involving causality, the first of these three weakeners (alternative explanation) is the most common. It can be difficult to predict the specific alternative cause that will appear in the correct answer. You do know, however, that the right answer will provide a plausible explanation other than the one the author assumes to be true. The introduction of a plausible alternative cause undermines the author's conclusion.

Applying the Kaplan Method: Causality

Now let's use the Kaplan Method for Critical Reasoning to solve a question involving causality:

> For the past year, a network television talk-show host has been making fun of the name of a particular brand of chainsaw, the Tree Toppler. The ridicule is obviously taking its toll: in the past 12 months, sales of the Tree Toppler have declined by 15 percent, while the sales of other chainsaws have increased.
>
> Which of the following, if true, casts the most serious doubt on the conclusion drawn above?
>
> O   The talk-show host who is ridiculing the Tree Toppler name actually owns a Tree Toppler.
>
> O   The number of product complaints from owners of the Tree Toppler has not increased in the past year.
>
> O   The average price of all chainsaws has increased by 10 percent in the past year.
>
> O   The number of stores that sell the Tree Toppler has remained steady for the past year.
>
> O   A year ago, a leading consumer magazine rated the Tree Toppler as "intolerably unsafe."

STEP 1: IDENTIFY THE QUESTION TYPE

Because this stem asks you to "cast doubt" on the conclusion, this is a Weaken question.

STEP 2: UNTANGLE THE STIMULUS

For the last year, a talk-show host has been ridiculing Tree Toppler chainsaws. Over that time, Tree Toppler sales have fallen while other chainsaws' sales have risen. The author concludes that the talk-show host's jokes must have caused the declining Tree Toppler sales.

STEP 3: PREDICT THE ANSWER

To weaken an argument in which X is claimed to have caused Y, consider whether Y might actually have caused X (i.e., reversal) or whether something else might have caused Y (i.e., alternative cause). In this case, it seems unlikely that the decline in sales caused the on-air ridicule; the host is making fun of the chainsaw's name, not its declining sales. Therefore, the correct answer to this Weaken question will probably offer some alternative explanation for the decline in Tree Toppler sales.

STEP 4: EVALUATE THE CHOICES

(E) provides that alternative explanation. If a prominent magazine rates a chainsaw as unsafe, that could certainly deter people from purchasing it, and a subsequent decline in sales would be reasonable to expect. **(E)** matches the prediction and is the correct answer.

If you hadn't immediately recognized **(E)** as a match for your prediction, you could still find the right answer by eliminating answer choices that miss the mark. Even if the talk-show host actually owns a Tree Toppler, as **(A)** says, the decline in sales could still be caused by the host's on-air ridicule; **(A)** is irrelevant. **(B)** is a 180 because it actually strengthens the argument by eliminating a potential alternative explanation for the decline in sales. **(C)** might be tempting, but the argument actually mentions that sales of other chainsaws have

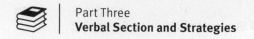
increased, so an increase in the purchase price of *all* chainsaws is not a reasonable alternative explanation. **(D)** also strengthens the argument by eliminating another alternative explanation for the decline in sales (that fewer stores are carrying the Tree Toppler).

Note that relevant alternative explanations for a causal relationship may, at first glance, appear to have no bearing on the argument. But this is precisely because the author failed to recognize that there was an alternative possibility. Before you move to the answer choices, come up with two or three specific alternative explanations. Focus on the *effect* each answer choice has on the alleged causal relationship. By weakening the causal relationship, the correct answer choice will undermine the logic of the argument.

TAKEAWAYS: CAUSALITY

When a GMAT argument uses evidence of a correlation to support a conclusion of causation ($X \rightarrow Y$), consider whether:

1. Something else is the cause of one or both of the correlated items ($Z \rightarrow Y$; or $Z \rightarrow X$ and Y)

2. Causality is reversed; the purported effect is actually the cause ($Y \rightarrow X$)

3. The correlation is mere coincidence (X and Y are unrelated)

Practice Set: Causality

1. Our architecture schools must be doing something wrong. Almost monthly we hear of domes and walkways collapsing in public places, causing serious injuries. In their pursuit of some dubious aesthetic, architects design buildings that sway, crumble, and even shed windows into our cities' streets. This kind of incompetence will disappear only when the curricula of our architecture schools devote less time to so-called artistic considerations and more time to the basics of good design.

    Which of the following, if true, would most seriously weaken the argument above?

    O   All architecture students are given training in basic physics and mechanics.

    O   Most of the problems with modern buildings stem from poor construction rather than poor design.

    O   Less than 50 percent of the curriculum at most architecture schools is devoted to aesthetics.

    O   Most buildings manage to stay in place well past their projected life expectancies.

    O   Architects study as long and as intensively as most other professionals.

2. Studies have shown that the number of books read in elementary school is correlated with later academic success. In the past year, local elementary students have read an average of 10 fewer books than the nationwide elementary student average of 35 books per year, while 90 percent of those local students report playing sports at least twice a week. If these students participated less in sports, they would read more books.

    Which of the following, if true, would most effectively weaken the argument?

    O   A nationwide survey of middle school students determined that if given a choice between reading a book and playing a sport, most of these students would choose reading a book.

    O   Participating in sports in elementary school has been shown to be as highly correlated as reading books to later academic success.

    O   The attention spans of elementary school students do not allow these children to read for as long as older students and adults are expected to read.

    O   The local elementary school is in a rural area in which there is no bookstore or public library and internet service is unreliable.

    O   Some local elementary school students who used to enjoy reading have said they no longer choose to read books, preferring to play sports at least twice a week.

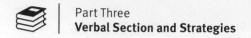
3. Attempts to blame the mayor's policies for the growing inequality of wages are misguided. The sharp growth in the gap in earnings between college and high school graduates in this city during the past decade resulted from overall technological trends that favored the skills of more educated workers. The mayor's response to this problem cannot be criticized, as it would hardly be reasonable to expect him to attempt to slow the forces of technology.

Which of the following, if true, casts the most serious doubt on the conclusion drawn in the last sentence above?

○   The mayor could have initiated policies that would have made it easier for less-educated workers to receive the education necessary for better-paying jobs.

○   Rather than cutting the education budget, the mayor could have increased the amount of staff and funding devoted to locating employment for graduating high school seniors.

○   The mayor could have attempted to generate more demand for products from industries that paid high blue-collar wages.

○   Instead of reducing the tax rate on the wealthiest earners, the mayor could have ensured that they shouldered a greater share of the total tax burden.

○   The mayor could have attempted to protect the earnings of city workers by instituting policies designed to reduce competition from foreign industries.

Special Case #2: Representativeness

> **LEARNING OBJECTIVE**
>
> In this section, you will learn how to:
>
> • Explain what it means for the sample in a survey or study to be representative of the population in the conclusion

When GMAT arguments include evidence in the form of surveys, studies, polls, anecdotes, or experiments, a key issue is often the representativeness of the group used as evidence. You may be familiar with the idea of representativeness from a statistics or research methods class. This concept is no different on the GMAT. In order to be representative, a sample must be large enough, the survey length must have covered an adequate amount of time, and the population surveyed cannot be biased in some flawed way.

In GMAT arguments, the author always believes that her evidence leads to her conclusion. Therefore, the author who uses statistical evidence always assumes the data are relevant to the conclusion. But for this to be the case, the sample used in the evidence must be representative of the group to which the conclusion is applied. Oftentimes on GMAT questions, the sample will fail to provide sufficient evidence to fully support the conclusion.

Applying the Kaplan Method: Representativeness

Now let's use the Kaplan Method for Critical Reasoning to solve a question involving representativeness:

> Candidate A was widely believed to be the favorite in her state's gubernatorial race. Candidate B, the incumbent governor, had figured prominently in a corruption scandal during the previous year. Although he was ultimately never charged with a crime, Candidate B received very negative coverage in local and national media. A poll of registered voters in the state showed that a majority supported Candidate A and would vote for her. In fact, election day exit polls of those who voted showed that most had voted for Candidate A, so she was expected to win. However, once the votes were counted, Candidate B was shown to have won a narrow victory. Clearly, respondents to the polls were not being honest when they claimed to have supported Candidate A.
>
> The argument above depends on which of the following assumptions?

- ○ It is difficult to predict the degree to which an incumbent candidate's support will be affected by negative media coverage.

- ○ The negative media coverage made supporters of Candidate B reluctant to express their views in public, and so they claimed to support Candidate A when they actually had voted for Candidate B.

- ○ No voter ever changes his or her mind about whom to vote for.

- ○ Candidate B successfully used the fact that he had not been charged with a crime to restore his good image with the voting public.

- ○ The sample of voters surveyed in the exit poll was representative of those who voted in the election.

STEP 1: IDENTIFY THE QUESTION TYPE

This question directs you to find an assumption on which the argument depends, so this is definitely an Assumption question.

STEP 2: UNTANGLE THE STIMULUS

The argument concludes that respondents to recent election exit polls and preelection polls were not being honest when they claimed to have supported Candidate A for governor. The evidence for this is that despite a strong showing in these polls, Candidate A still lost the election.

STEP 3: PREDICT THE ANSWER

This conclusion is based in part on the results of two polls, so those polls need to have been conducted with representative samples in order for the conclusion to be valid. After all, what if the polls had both been conducted outside campaign rallies for Candidate A or in Candidate A's hometown? The sample group for the polls needs to be an adequate cross section of the voting population, and since this argument stakes its conclusion on the polls, the author of the argument must be assuming that the sample is indeed representative.

This question shows you that Kaplan's strategy for representativeness is not restricted to Strengthen and Weaken questions. On Test Day, if you're asked an Assumption question and you notice that the stimulus focuses on a study, survey, poll, or experiment, know that a choice that essentially says, "The sample was representative" is likely to be correct.

STEP 4: EVALUATE THE CHOICES

(E) matches this prediction perfectly and is the correct answer. If you used the Denial Test to negate **(E)**, by stating that the poll's sample group was *not* representative, then the author's conclusion that voters must have lied can no longer be valid. If the people who participated in the polls were not representative of the larger voting population, then there would be no particular reason to expect the poll and voting results to be similar. **(E)** is therefore a necessary assumption of the argument.

(A) is not necessary to the argument because the author doesn't base her conclusion on a prediction drawn from the press coverage. Rather, the author bases her conclusion on a prediction drawn from the polling data. **(B)**, if true, would strengthen the argument, but this isn't a Strengthen question; the right answer to an Assumption question must be something upon which the argument relies. While the argument asserts that people polled lied about whom they voted for, it does not depend on any particular reason why they did so. **(C)** is far too extreme; the argument's point that the polls' respondents lied is not undone if one or two people simply changed their minds. As for **(D)**, the author doesn't necessarily assume anything about *how* Candidate B was able to eke out a victory.

TAKEAWAY: REPRESENTATIVENESS

When you see an argument based on the findings of a study, survey, experiment, or analogy, compare the population of the evidence with that of the conclusion.

Practice Set: Representativeness

4. Loneliness is commonly reported in elderly populations. A study of elderly people found that those who owned dogs reported feeling less lonely than those who did not own dogs. Clearly, an elderly person who adopts a pet will be less likely to suffer feelings of loneliness than an elderly person without a pet.

   Which of the following, if true, would most strengthen the argument above?

   ○ Owning a pet has been linked to several health benefits, including lower blood pressure.

   ○ Some people feel that cats do not engage socially with their owners as much as dogs do.

   ○ The number of elderly people who own pets is projected to rise in the coming years.

   ○ A large percentage of elderly dog owners report taking their dogs for walks and to dog parks.

   ○ Pets other than dogs provide the same benefits of companionship as do dogs.

5. A social worker surveyed 200 women, each of whom had recently given birth to her first child. Half of the women surveyed had chosen to give birth in a hospital or obstetrics clinic; the other half had chosen to give birth at home under the care of certified midwives. Of the 100 births that occurred at home, only 5 presented substantial complications, whereas 17 of the hospital births presented substantial complications. The social worker concluded from the survey that the home is actually a safer environment in which to give birth than a hospital or clinic.

   Which of the following, if true, most seriously calls the social worker's conclusion into question?

   ○ Women who give birth in hospitals and clinics often have shorter periods of labor than do women who give birth at home.

   ○ Many obstetricians discourage patients from giving birth at home.

   ○ All of the women in the study who had been diagnosed as having a high possibility of delivery complications elected to give birth in a hospital.

   ○ Women who give birth at home tend to experience less stress during labor than women who deliver in hospitals.

   ○ Pregnant doctors prefer giving birth in a hospital.

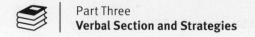

6. A team of pediatricians recently announced that pet birds are more likely to bite children under age 13 than people of any other age group. The team's finding was based on a study showing that the majority of all bird bites requiring medical attention involved children under 13. The study also found that the birds most likely to bite are cockatiels and parakeets.

    Which of the following, if true, would most weaken the pediatricians' conclusion that birds are more likely to bite children under age 13 than people of any other age group?

    O   More than half of bird bites not requiring medical attention, which exceed the number requiring such attention, involve people aged 13 and older.

    O   The majority of bird bites resulting in the death of the bitten person involve people aged 65 and older.

    O   Many serious bird bites affecting children under age 13 are inflicted by birds other than cockatiels and parakeets.

    O   Most bird bites in children under age 13 that require medical attention are far less serious than they initially appear.

    O   Most parents can learn to treat bird bites effectively if they avail themselves of a small amount of medical information.

Special Case #3: Plans, Proposals, and Predictions

Once you start identifying plans, proposals, and predictions in Critical Reasoning stimuli, you'll realize that many arguments contain conclusions in these forms. All three have a future orientation and indicate the author's opinion.

Plans and proposals are found in conclusions that begin, "Thus, we should…" or "It's in the company's best interest to…" When a conclusion takes the form of a plan or proposal, the author is likely assuming that the plan or proposal is helpful and practical under the current circumstances. GMAT questions often test whether we realize that it may not be helpful or currently practical.

Critical Reasoning stimuli involving plans or proposals generally offer only one reason for the plan or proposal. In other words, because of X, we should do Y.

So what must the author be assuming about that evidence? That it's the only, or at least the most important, factor to consider. Thus, any answer that introduces an alternative and competing consideration weakens the argument. Any answer that rules out a possible alternative consideration strengthens it.

Think about how you might weaken the following proposal:

> Sam often oversleeps because he reaches over and turns off the alarm before he's fully awake. To fix this problem, Sam proposes buying a second alarm clock.

Sam's proposal is inherently flawed because it fails to consider some important factors: Sam might put the second clock right next to the first one and just shut it off, too. Alternatively, Sam might have to plug the second clock in too far from his bed. Then he won't hear it, so it won't be of any help. Either way, there's an intervening consideration that suggests the plan will fail or will be self-defeating.

There may not be any evidence at all; the author may simply state that the plan will lead to a certain outcome. For example, the stimulus might just contain a proposal that can be paraphrased as "X will lead to increased profits." Even though there's no evidence given to support this outcome, the author is still making the general assumption that conditions exist that are conducive to success of the plan. The problem is not that the author is unreasonable in claiming that proposal X would increase profits—it might, in fact, do so. However, the proposal could be weakened by showing evidence that could undermine proposal X's chance of success; for instance, while X may lead to increased revenue, it may also increase costs.

Predictions are no different in CR questions than they are in real life; they use the future tense: "So-and-so will win the Oscar," "The economy will show modest growth," or "We will not be able to meet the production deadline." GMAT authors base their predictions on past and current trends or situations. In order to weaken such a conclusion, you want to find an answer choice that says that the trend will change. To strengthen it, look for an answer choice that says, "Future events will unfold as expected."

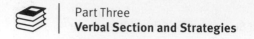

Applying the Kaplan Method: Plans, Proposals, and Predictions

Now let's use the Kaplan Method for Critical Reasoning to solve a question involving a plan, proposal, or prediction:

> Several people have died while canoeing during high water on a nearby river in recent years. The local police have proposed a ban on canoeing when the river reaches flood stage. Opponents of the ban argue that the government should ban an activity only if it harms people other than those who willingly participate in the activity, and they therefore conclude that the proposed ban on high-water canoeing is unwarranted.
>
> Which of the following, if true, most seriously weakens the opponents' conclusion?
>
> O   Sailboats are not allowed on a nearby lake when winds exceed 50 miles per hour.
>
> O   Several other local governments have imposed similar bans on other rivers.
>
> O   Several police officers have been seriously injured while trying to rescue canoeists who were stranded on the river while attempting to canoe during high water.
>
> O   More canoeists drown while canoeing rivers at normal water levels than while canoeing rivers at high water levels.
>
> O   Statistics provided by the U.S. National Park Service show that fewer people drown on rivers with high-water canoeing bans than on rivers without such bans.

STEP 1: IDENTIFY THE QUESTION TYPE

The stem contains the obvious key word "weakens," but it also asks you to weaken the opponents' conclusion in particular. Keep this information in mind—there may be more than one argument in the stimulus.

STEP 2: UNTANGLE THE STIMULUS

The government shouldn't ban an activity that poses no risk to people who don't voluntarily participate. Therefore, the opponents argue, the government should not ban high-water canoeing.

STEP 3: PREDICT THE ANSWER

To weaken the argument, you need an answer choice that explains why the opponents' proposal should, on its own terms, be rejected. Here, the opponents assume that high-water canoeing does not harm anyone who does not willingly participate in the canoeing. To weaken the conclusion, look for an answer choice suggesting that canoeing during flood stage does in fact threaten people other than those who have chosen to canoe.

STEP 4: EVALUATE THE CHOICES

(C) offers such a suggestion by stating that police officers, none of whom consented to expose themselves to the dangers of canoeing in high water, were in fact harmed as a result of such canoeing. **(C)** is the correct answer.

(A) has no bearing on the argument; it isn't clear how sailing on a lake during high wind is relevant to canoeing on a river during high water. This statement tells us nothing about whether high-water canoeing poses risks to non-canoers. And just because, as **(B)** says, other governments have also enacted the bans, that doesn't mean that the bans are necessarily reasonable. The opponents might still have a valid argument. Therefore, **(B)** is also irrelevant. **(D)** offers an irrelevant comparison: that more canoeists drown while the river is at normal levels may simply be due to the fact that there are more canoeists at that time to begin with. That has no bearing on whether canoeing should be banned when water levels are high. And (**E**) might be tempting, but it doesn't show that the opponents' proposal to abolish the ban won't work *on its own terms*. (**E**) doesn't give an example of non-canoeists harmed by the canoeing.

TAKEAWAYS: PLANS, PROPOSALS, AND PREDICTIONS

When you see a question regarding a statement about the future, identify assumptions about the feasibility, usefulness, and relevance of the future conditions.

- To weaken an argument whose conclusion is a plan or proposal, show that the plan or proposal, on its own terms, will not work.

- To weaken an argument whose conclusion is a prediction, show why the prediction is unlikely to come to pass.

- To weaken an objection to a plan, proposal, or prediction, seek evidence that it *will* work or come true.

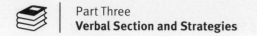

Practice Set: Plans, Proposals, and Predictions

7. A team of researchers at a university hospital has developed a chemical test that detects breast tumors in the early stages of development. In order to save lives, the researchers want to make the test a routine part of examinations at the hospital. However, a spokesperson for the hospital argued that because virtually all breast tumors are detectable by self-examination, the chemical test would have little impact on the breast cancer death rate.

    Which of the following, if true, would most seriously weaken the hospital spokesperson's argument?

    O   Fatal breast tumors are often not revealed by self-examination until it is too late for effective treatment.

    O   Breast tumors are usually discovered at an earlier stage of development than are lung tumors.

    O   Mammograms are currently in wide use as a breast cancer test and cost much less than the chemical test.

    O   Because men are not typically victims of breast cancer, the new test would benefit only half of the population.

    O   Most women learn how to check for signs of breast cancer from magazines and not from doctors.

8. Occupational safety advocate: Logging is one of the most dangerous occupations in the United States. A company has developed a chainsaw that will instantly shut off if there is kickback of the chain, which studies have shown to be the most common cause of chainsaw injuries. The logging industry should adopt this new chainsaw as standard equipment in order to prevent most of the logging-related deaths that occur each year.

    Which of the following statements, if true, most seriously weakens the occupational safety advocate's argument?

    O   Loggers are sometimes killed by problems with chainsaws other than the kickback of the chain.

    O   Injuries from falling trees cause the vast majority of deaths in the logging industry.

    O   The new chainsaw is inexpensive and easy to learn how to use.

    O   There are other, equally safe chainsaws available, but the logging industry has not adopted them.

    O   The chainsaw manufacturer's claims about its product are supported by a study conducted by a government agency.

9. According to a recent study, advertisements in medical journals often contain misleading information about the effectiveness and safety of new prescription drugs. The medical researchers who wrote the study concluded that the advertisements could result in doctors' prescribing inappropriate drugs to their patients.

   The researchers' conclusion would be most strengthened if which of the following were true?

   O Advertisements for new prescription drugs are an important source of revenue for medical journals.

   O Editors of medical journals are often unable to evaluate the claims made in advertisements for new prescription drugs.

   O Doctors rely on the advertisements as a source of information about new prescription drugs.

   O Advertisements for new prescription drugs are typically less accurate than medical journal articles evaluating those same drugs.

   O The Food and Drug Administration, the government agency responsible for drug regulation, reviews advertisements for new drugs only after the ads have already been printed.

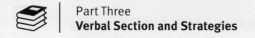

Answer Key

Practice Set: Causality

1. B
2. D
3. A

Practice Set: Representativeness

4. E
5. C
6. A

Practice Set: Plans, Proposals, and Predictions

7. A
8. B
9. C

Answers and Explanations

Practice Set: Causality

1. **(B)**

Our architecture schools must be doing something wrong. Almost monthly we hear of domes and walkways collapsing in public places, causing serious injuries. In their pursuit of some dubious aesthetic, architects design buildings that sway, crumble, and even shed windows into our cities' streets. This kind of incompetence will disappear only when the curricula of our architecture schools devote less time to so-called artistic considerations and more time to the basics of good design.

Which of the following, if true, would most seriously weaken the argument above?

- O   All architecture students are given training in basic physics and mechanics.
- O   Most of the problems with modern buildings stem from poor construction rather than poor design.
- O   Less than 50 percent of the curriculum at most architecture schools is devoted to aesthetics.
- O   Most buildings manage to stay in place well past their projected life expectancies.
- O   Architects study as long and as intensively as most other professionals.

STEP 1: IDENTIFY THE QUESTION TYPE

The phrase "most seriously weaken" in the question stem tells you that you have a Weaken question.

STEP 2: UNTANGLE THE STIMULUS

The stimulus will contain an argument; you need to pick out the conclusion, evidence, and assumption. The conclusion is the last sentence, which states that a shift away from aesthetics in architecture schools' curricula is necessary for buildings to be more soundly constructed. The evidence is the frequency with which parts of buildings collapse. Note that this is a causal argument: the author assumes that architecture schools' artistic considerations, rather than something else, are directly responsible for the crumbling buildings because the time devoted to them prevents architects from learning good design principles.

STEP 3: PREDICT THE ANSWER

The correct answer for this Weaken question will contradict the assumption that aesthetic considerations are causing buildings to be poorly designed and thus to crumble. Simply scan the choices for one that provides an alternate cause for the decay of the city's buildings.

STEP 4: EVALUATE THE CHOICES

(B) provides an alternate cause, poor building construction, and is thus the correct answer. **(A)** is irrelevant. Even if students are currently instructed in basic physics and mechanics, they may not be spending enough time learning good design principles. **(C)** is incorrect because you have no information to indicate how great a percentage of time spent studying aesthetics the author of this argument would consider too much. Perhaps "less than 50 percent" is still too much. **(D)** is incorrect because it fails to provide any new and relevant information. The author merely complains that some buildings are collapsing. The fact that "most" are not collapsing does not take away the fact that some are falling down. Finally, **(E)** is an irrelevant comparison between architects and other professionals.

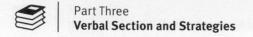

2. **(D)**

Studies have shown that the number of books read in elementary school is correlated with later academic success. In the past year, local elementary students have read an average of 10 fewer books than the nationwide elementary student average of 35 books per year, while 90 percent of those local students report playing sports at least twice a week. If these students participated less in sports, they would read more books.

Which of the following, if true, would most effectively weaken the argument?

○ A nationwide survey of middle school students determined that if given a choice between reading a book and playing a sport, most of these students would choose reading a book.

○ Participating in sports in elementary school has been shown to be as highly correlated as reading books to later academic success.

○ The attention spans of elementary school students do not allow these children to read for as long as older students and adults are expected to read.

○ The local elementary school is in a rural area in which there is no bookstore or public library and internet service is unreliable.

○ Some local elementary school students who used to enjoy reading have said they no longer choose to read books, preferring to play sports at least twice a week.

STEP 1: IDENTIFY THE QUESTION TYPE

Since the word "weaken" appears in the question stem, this is a Weaken question.

STEP 2: UNTANGLE THE STIMULUS

The conclusion is that if the local elementary school students played sports less, they would read more books. The evidence is that almost all of these students play sports two or more times a week, while the average number of books they read is lower than the national average. The author assumes that playing sports is causing students to read relatively fewer books. Note that the first sentence of the stimulus functions as background information rather than as evidence; it tells you why reading books might be important, but it is not used to support the claim that the students would read more books if they played sports less.

STEP 3: PREDICT THE ANSWER

Whenever you're asked to weaken a causal argument, consider the three classic alternative explanations: (1) cause and effect may be reversed ("reading fewer books leads to playing sports more often"), (2) there may be an alternative cause of the effect ("many local students have little access to books"), or (3) the apparent link between two events is coincidental ("whatever the cause of reading fewer books, it isn't playing sports"). You don't know exactly what the right answer will say, but you can expect it to fall into one of these three categories.

STEP 4: EVALUATE THE CHOICES

(D) weakens the argument by proposing another reason local children don't read books and do play sports. Since books are hard to get, if the children weren't allowed to play sports, they might just be bored rather than read more. Thus, **(D)** is correct. **(A)** is irrelevant because the argument is concerned with local elementary school students, not middle school students from across the country. The author's conclusion is about what would cause students to read more books, not about the effect their not reading books will eventually have, so **(B)** does not weaken the argument. **(C)** presents an irrelevant comparison. The argument specifically compares local elementary school students to a national population of elementary school students, so how younger children compare to older readers is irrelevant. **(E)** is a 180. It strengthens the argument, suggesting that indeed playing sports caused these students to read fewer books.

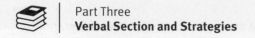
3. **(A)**

Attempts to blame the mayor's policies for the growing inequality of wages are misguided. The sharp growth in the gap in earnings between college and high school graduates in this city during the past decade resulted from overall technological trends that favored the skills of more educated workers. The mayor's response to this problem cannot be criticized, as it would hardly be reasonable to expect him to attempt to slow the forces of technology.

Which of the following, if true, casts the most serious doubt on the conclusion drawn in the last sentence above?

○   The mayor could have initiated policies that would have made it easier for less-educated workers to receive the education necessary for better-paying jobs.

○   Rather than cutting the education budget, the mayor could have increased the amount of staff and funding devoted to locating employment for graduating high school seniors.

○   The mayor could have attempted to generate more demand for products from industries that paid high blue-collar wages.

○   Instead of reducing the tax rate on the wealthiest earners, the mayor could have ensured that they shouldered a greater share of the total tax burden.

○   The mayor could have attempted to protect the earnings of city workers by instituting policies designed to reduce competition from foreign industries.

STEP 1: IDENTIFY THE QUESTION TYPE

When you're asked to "cast doubt" on an argument, you're being asked to weaken it.

STEP 2: UNTANGLE THE STIMULUS

The argument concludes that the mayor's policies are not responsible for the growing inequality of wages in the city. The argument instead attempts to blame overall technological trends that favored the skills of more educated workers and thus enabled college graduates to earn more money than high school grads.

STEP 3: PREDICT THE ANSWER

To weaken an argument in which an author says that *X* did *not* cause *Y*, think about strengthening the idea that *X did* cause *Y*. Since the author is attempting to blame technological trends and not the mayor's policies, try to find an answer indicating that the mayor's policies did play a role.

STEP 4: EVALUATE THE CHOICES

This is exactly what **(A)** does, making **(A)** the correct answer. If the mayor's policies neglected to even the playing field between better-educated workers and their less-educated counterparts, then the mayor does share some of the responsibility for the wage gap, and the author's argument is severely impaired. **(B)** misses the point. The point is not that the less-educated workers are unemployed; it's that the jobs they do have don't pay as much as those of better-educated workers. **(C)** takes too many leaps to be correct: it requires you to assume that less-educated workers were all concentrated in blue-collar jobs and that creating more demand for products from those blue-collar industries would result in higher wages for blue-collar employees. **(D)** introduces the tax rate, which is irrelevant to the argument, and **(E)** deals with city workers, which doesn't help or hurt the argument because city workers aren't necessarily better or less educated than other workers, so you don't know whether city workers are even a part of the wage gap problem.

Practice Set: Representativeness

4.   (E)

Loneliness is commonly reported in elderly populations. A study of elderly people found that those who owned dogs reported feeling less lonely than those who did not own dogs. Clearly, an elderly person who adopts a pet will be less likely to suffer feelings of loneliness than an elderly person without a pet.

Which of the following, if true, would most strengthen the argument above?

- O   Owning a pet has been linked to several health benefits, including lower blood pressure.
- O   Some people feel that cats do not engage socially with their owners as much as dogs do.
- O   The number of elderly people who own pets is projected to rise in the coming years.
- O   A large percentage of elderly dog owners report taking their dogs for walks and to dog parks.
- O   Pets other than dogs provide the same benefits of companionship as do dogs.

STEP 1: IDENTIFY THE QUESTION TYPE

The word "strengthen" indicates that you should read to identify the author's conclusion and evidence, then think about what additional evidence would support the argument's conclusion, making its central assumption more likely to be true.

STEP 2: UNTANGLE THE STIMULUS

The conclusion is signaled by the key word "[c]learly" in the last sentence: an elderly person with a pet is less likely to be lonely than one without a pet. The evidence is a study that found less loneliness in elderly dog owners than in elderly non–dog owners.

STEP 3: PREDICT THE ANSWER

Whenever an argument references a sample or a study, suspect a representativeness issue. The heart of representativeness is the assumption that a group mentioned in the evidence is representative of the group mentioned in the conclusion. In this argument, the author is assuming that the benefit conferred by dogs upon elderly owners—namely the easing of loneliness—is representative of the benefit conferred on elderly owners by pets of any kind. To strengthen the argument, look for the answer choice that supports this assumption.

STEP 4: EVALUATE THE CHOICES

(E) matches the prediction and is correct. **(A)** is incorrect because the argument is only about whether owning a pet will help with loneliness; other benefits of owning pets are irrelevant. If **(B)** said that cats actually don't engage socially with their owners as much as dogs, this choice would weaken the argument (not strengthen it) by providing evidence that not all pets are as good as dogs at alleviating loneliness. Since it talks only about how some people perceive cats, it has no effect on the argument; since it does not strengthen the argument, it can be eliminated. **(C)** is incorrect because ownership projections are irrelevant to the conclusion. Finally, **(D)** provides more evidence for the utility of dogs as companion animals and possible facilitators of companionship (one might conceivably meet other people while walking the dog or at the dog park), but it does not support the conclusion about the efficacy of pets in general.

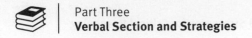

5.   (C)

A social worker surveyed 200 women, each of whom had recently given birth to her first child. Half of the women surveyed had chosen to give birth in a hospital or obstetrics clinic; the other half had chosen to give birth at home under the care of certified midwives. Of the 100 births that occurred at home, only 5 presented substantial complications, whereas 17 of the hospital births presented substantial complications. The social worker concluded from the survey that the home is actually a safer environment in which to give birth than a hospital or clinic.

Which of the following, if true, most seriously calls the social worker's conclusion into question?

- ○   Women who give birth in hospitals and clinics often have shorter periods of labor than do women who give birth at home.
- ○   Many obstetricians discourage patients from giving birth at home.
- ○   All of the women in the study who had been diagnosed as having a high possibility of delivery complications elected to give birth in a hospital.
- ○   Women who give birth at home tend to experience less stress during labor than women who deliver in hospitals.
- ○   Pregnant doctors prefer giving birth in a hospital.

STEP 1: IDENTIFY THE QUESTION TYPE

Since you need to call the social worker's conclusion into question, you need to weaken it.

STEP 2: UNTANGLE THE STIMULUS

The social worker's conclusion is that it is safer to give birth at home than at a hospital or clinic. The evidence for this is a survey in which some women chose to give birth at a hospital and others chose home birth. Overall, the hospital births presented more substantial medical complications than did the home births.

STEP 3: PREDICT THE ANSWER

You can successfully undermine the social worker's conclusion if you undermine the evidence on which it's based, namely, the study. If you find an answer choice that tells you that the survey is invalid or that the sample studied in the survey is unrepresentative, then any conclusion based on the survey would be in doubt.

STEP 4: EVALUATE THE CHOICES

(C) tells you that the hospital births presented more complications simply because the women who chose to give birth at the hospital were predisposed to complications. This suggests that these women would have had complications no matter where they gave birth, which undermines the conclusion that a hospital is less safe than a home as a place to give birth. Thus, **(C)** is the correct answer. **(A)** is irrelevant. A shorter labor can still be more dangerous, so this isn't a valid weakener. Just because obstetricians discourage home birth, as **(B)** says, doesn't mean that the home is more or less safe than a hospital; there could be plenty of reasons why the obstetricians would discourage home birth. **(D)** strengthens the argument by telling you that women who give birth at home experience less stress, which could potentially make their births go more smoothly. **(E)** also has no bearing on the argument. Pregnant doctors might prefer to give birth in a hospital simply because they are more familiar with the hospital environment, not because a hospital is necessarily safer.

6.   (A)

A team of pediatricians recently announced that pet birds are more likely to bite children under age 13 than people of any other age group. The team's finding was based on a study showing that the majority of all bird bites requiring medical attention involved children under 13. The study also found that the birds most likely to bite are cockatiels and parakeets.

Which of the following, if true, would most weaken the pediatricians' conclusion that birds are more likely to bite children under age 13 than people of any other age group?

○   More than half of bird bites not requiring medical attention, which exceed the number requiring such attention, involve people aged 13 and older.

○   The majority of bird bites resulting in the death of the bitten person involve people aged 65 and older.

○   Many serious bird bites affecting children under age 13 are inflicted by birds other than cockatiels and parakeets.

○   Most bird bites in children under age 13 that require medical attention are far less serious than they initially appear.

○   Most parents can learn to treat bird bites effectively if they avail themselves of a small amount of medical information.

STEP 1: IDENTIFY THE QUESTION TYPE

This stem contains a wealth of helpful information. Not only do you see the telltale key word "weaken" indicating the question type, but the conclusion of the argument is stated directly in the stem. Part of your job is already done.

STEP 2: UNTANGLE THE STIMULUS

The conclusion of the pediatricians is that pet birds are more likely to bite young children than bite older people. The evidence for this is a study, which should ring alarm bells for representativeness issues. The study indicates that most bird-bite injuries that required medical attention were to young children.

STEP 3: PREDICT THE ANSWER

But not all bird bites necessarily require medical attention, so in order for this study's results to prove that birds are more likely to bite young children *overall*, you need proof that the bird bites requiring medical attention are representative of all bird bites. So to weaken this argument, find a choice that essentially says, "Bites that require medical attention are *not* representative of bites in general."

STEP 4: EVALUATE THE CHOICES

You'll then be drawn to (**A**): looking at *all* bird-bite injuries reveals that most of them don't require medical attention, and of those that don't, more than half of them are suffered by people over the age of 13. (**A**) indicates that birds are just as likely, if not more likely, to bite people over the age of 13 as to bite younger children. Thus, (**A**) is the correct answer. Just because senior citizens are more likely to die from bird bites, as (**B**) says, doesn't mean that they're more likely to be bitten in the first place. (**C**) improperly seizes on the last sentence of the argument, which is a tangential statement that has no bearing on the overall conclusion. (**D**) is off base because the argument deals with the likelihood that a bird will bite someone, not with the likelihood that the bite is serious. (**E**) commits a similar error by dealing with treatment; this argument is only concerned with the relative frequency of bird bites occurring in the first place and not with the treatment plans for bites that have already occurred.

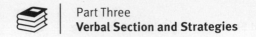

Practice Set: Plans, Proposals, and Predictions

7. **(A)**

A team of researchers at a university hospital has developed a chemical test that detects breast tumors in the early stages of development. In order to save lives, the researchers want to make the test a routine part of examinations at the hospital. However, a spokesperson for the hospital argued that because virtually all breast tumors are detectable by self-examination, the chemical test would have little impact on the breast cancer death rate.

Which of the following, if true, would most seriously weaken the hospital spokesperson's argument?

O   Fatal breast tumors are often not revealed by self-examination until it is too late for effective treatment.

O   Breast tumors are usually discovered at an earlier stage of development than are lung tumors.

O   Mammograms are currently in wide use as a breast cancer test and cost much less than the chemical test.

O   Because men are not typically victims of breast cancer, the new test would benefit only half of the population.

O   Most women learn how to check for signs of breast cancer from magazines and not from doctors.

STEP 1: IDENTIFY THE QUESTION TYPE

In addition to using the word "weaken" to signal the question type, this question stem points you to the "spokesperson's argument."

STEP 2: UNTANGLE THE STIMULUS

The spokesperson's conclusion is a prediction that the chemical test will have little impact on the breast cancer death rate. The spokesperson's evidence is that virtually all breast tumors are detectable by self-examination.

STEP 3: PREDICT THE ANSWER

The spokesperson assumes that the chemical test has no advantage over self-examination. Because this is a Weaken question, you need the answer choice that contradicts this assumption—so scan for a choice that cites an advantage of the chemical test.

STEP 4: EVALUATE THE CHOICES

(A) suggests a possible advantage of the chemical test and is the correct answer. The stimulus states that the chemical test "detects breast tumors in the early stages of development." If it is true that self-examination reveals those same tumors too late for effective treatment, then the chemical test might in fact have an impact on the breast cancer death rate, and the conclusion is weakened. **(B)** is an irrelevant comparison between breast tumors and lung tumors. **(C)** introduces a different diagnostic tool, mammograms, which are irrelevant to the question of whether the chemical test would have any positive impact relative to self-examination. **(D)** is incorrect because the fact that men typically do not contract breast cancer is irrelevant to the question of whether the chemical test would positively impact the breast cancer death rate. **(E)** is again irrelevant. Where women learn to do breast exams has no bearing on the assumption that the chemical test has no advantage over those exams.

8. (B)

Occupational safety advocate: Logging is one of the most dangerous occupations in the United States. A company has developed a chainsaw that will instantly shut off if there is kickback of the chain, which studies have shown to be the most common cause of chainsaw injuries. The logging industry should adopt this new chainsaw as standard equipment in order to prevent most of the logging-related deaths that occur each year.

Which of the following statements, if true, most seriously weakens the occupational safety advocate's argument?

- ○ Loggers are sometimes killed by problems with chainsaws other than the kickback of the chain.
- ○ Injuries from falling trees cause the vast majority of deaths in the logging industry.
- ○ The new chainsaw is inexpensive and easy to learn how to use.
- ○ There are other, equally safe chainsaws available, but the logging industry has not adopted them.
- ○ The chainsaw manufacturer's claims about its product are supported by a study conducted by a government agency.

STEP 1: IDENTIFY THE QUESTION TYPE

The word "weakens" in the question stem tells you this is a Weaken question.

STEP 2: UNTANGLE THE STIMULUS

The argument you're asked to weaken claims that the logging industry should adopt a new chainsaw to prevent most of the logging-related deaths each year. The author's evidence is that this chainsaw shuts off if there is a kickback, thus preventing injuries. The author assumes that chainsaw injuries cause the majority of logging-related deaths.

STEP 3: PREDICT THE ANSWER

The word "should" means this conclusion is a proposal, so think about common problems with proposals on the GMAT. The author must assume that the proposed solution to the problem will work. However, if at least half of deaths in the logging industry are caused by something other than chainsaws, then greater chainsaw safety won't eliminate most logging industry deaths. Look in the choices for evidence that most deaths are not chainsaw related.

STEP 4: EVALUATE THE CHOICES

(B) is a match for the prediction and is correct. If most deaths are caused by falling trees, not chainsaws, then safer chainsaws won't prevent the majority of deaths. Just the fact that fatal injuries are *sometimes* caused by something other than kickbacks isn't enough to say that the new chainsaw will not prevent *most* deaths. It might be that 99% of logging fatalities are the result of chainsaw kickbacks, in which case the argument is still valid. If anything, **(C)** might strengthen the argument. If the new chainsaw is cheap and easy to use, the industry might be more willing to embrace it, and then chainsaw injuries would decrease. Even so, this statement fails to connect chainsaw injuries to logging deaths. **(D)** is irrelevant, as the argument is not about any chainsaw other than the new one. And finally, **(E)** is similar to **(C)** in that it potentially strengthens the argument for adopting the chainsaw but still does not show that chainsaws cause deaths among loggers.

9. **(C)**

According to a recent study, advertisements in medical journals often contain misleading information about the effectiveness and safety of new prescription drugs. The medical researchers who wrote the study concluded that the advertisements could result in doctors' prescribing inappropriate drugs to their patients.

The researchers' conclusion would be most strengthened if which of the following were true?

○ Advertisements for new prescription drugs are an important source of revenue for medical journals.

○ Editors of medical journals are often unable to evaluate the claims made in advertisements for new prescription drugs.

○ Doctors rely on the advertisements as a source of information about new prescription drugs.

○ Advertisements for new prescription drugs are typically less accurate than medical journal articles evaluating those same drugs.

○ The Food and Drug Administration, the government agency responsible for drug regulation, reviews advertisements for new drugs only after the ads have already been printed.

STEP 1: IDENTIFY THE QUESTION TYPE

The phrase "most strengthened" tells you that this is a Strengthen question.

STEP 2: UNTANGLE THE STIMULUS

The researchers' argument concludes with a prediction: doctors will prescribe inappropriate drugs to their patients. This is apparently because advertisements in medical journals often contain misleading information about certain drugs.

STEP 3: PREDICT THE ANSWER

To strengthen this argument, you want a choice that gives a reason or reasons why the prediction will come to pass. What circumstances would lead to inappropriate prescriptions? Since the inaccurate information comes from medical journals, doctors will probably be more likely to prescribe inappropriate drugs if they base their decisions on what they read in the journals.

STEP 4: EVALUATE THE CHOICES

If doctors rely on the ads in medical journals to learn about new drugs, as **(C)** suggests, then inaccurate information could very well lead to faulty prescriptions. So **(C)** is correct. **(A)** tells you why the journals carry the ads, but it doesn't strengthen the idea that doctors will use them to make inappropriate prescriptions. **(B)** could explain why the ads are published despite the inaccurate and misleading information contained in them, but like **(A)**, **(B)** does not provide a bridge to doctors' inappropriate prescriptions. **(D)** makes an irrelevant comparison between the accuracy of ads and that of articles. **(E)**, like **(B)**, explains how an ad can make it to print with inaccurate information, but **(E)** doesn't tell you how an inaccurate ad necessarily translates to a faulty prescription by a doctor, so **(E)** can't strengthen the researchers' prediction.

CHAPTER 8

Critical Reasoning: Putting It All Together

LEARNING OBJECTIVES

After studying this chapter, you will be able to:

- Immediately recognize the format of a Critical Reasoning question and apply the Kaplan Method for Critical Reasoning

- Quickly determine which question type is in play and consider nuances to the Kaplan Method for Critical Reasoning that will be helpful for the specific question type

- Demonstrate the ability to evaluate your performance on Critical Reasoning questions

This quiz is designed to give you practice with a mix of Critical Reasoning question types, just like the mix of CR questions you'll see on Test Day. Take this quiz after you have studied the different Critical Reasoning question types and common stimulus patterns and practiced applying the Kaplan Method for Critical Reasoning to them.

How to Take This Quiz

By the time you take this quiz, you are hopefully well on your way to mastery of Critical Reasoning, so set a timer. Give yourself 2 minutes per question. So if you do all 11 questions at once, set the timer for 22 minutes; if you decide to do fewer questions than that in one sitting, set the timer accordingly.

Make sure to use the steps of the Kaplan Method on every question. Students are often tempted to skip step 1 and not bother identifying the question type. They get some questions right without doing this task, so they reason that it's not important. But they would get even more questions right if they were crystal clear about the task before reading the stimulus. Students are also prone to skip step 3, making a prediction, finding it easier to look in the answer choices for ideas about what might be the right answer. By leaning on the test to do their thinking for them, however, they risk falling for cleverly worded wrong-answer traps.

Furthermore, remember that on Test Day, you can't take notes on the computer screen or skip forward and back between questions. So challenge yourself now not to take notes in this book (use separate scratch paper or an erasable noteboard like the one you'll use at the testing center) and to do the questions in order.

After you've finished the quiz and are reviewing the explanations, make sure you not only can explain why the right answer is correct but also can articulate why each wrong answer is incorrect. Being able to clearly identify why wrong choices are wrong will help you avoid picking them.

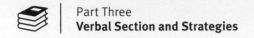

In addition, if you missed a question, understand *why* you missed it. There is always a reason! The Kaplan Method can be a useful checklist to diagnose where you went wrong.

- Did you misunderstand the task set by the question stem?
- Did you misunderstand a key pattern or detail of the stimulus?
- Was your prediction off base or too specific (or too general), or did you omit making a prediction?
- Were you tempted by a choice that did not actually match your prediction, perhaps because you could have read more carefully or because you fell for a common wrong-answer trap?

If you know why you missed a question, you can avoid making that error again.

Above all, be patient and forgiving with yourself. Practice for the GMAT is not about judging yourself. It's about making mistakes so you can learn from them and improve your score. Need more practice? Check out the Critical Reasoning quizzes and Qbank questions in your online resources.

GO ONLINE

kaptest.com/login

Critical Reasoning Quiz

1. To avoid the appearance of conflicts of interest, the board of a major U.S. stock exchange is considering a new policy that would ban former top executives of the exchange from taking positions at publicly traded companies for a period of two years after leaving the stock exchange. Critics of the plan say the policy is unfair because it would likely prevent former top executives of the exchange from earning a decent living.

    Which of the following statements, if true, would most strengthen the prediction made by the critics of the proposed company policy?

    O   The labor union that represents most of the stock exchange's employees has made public statements that threaten a strike if the policy is adopted.

    O   Former employees of the exchange most often work for publicly traded companies after leaving the exchange.

    O   Low-level managers at the exchange have an average tenure of 13 years, one of the longest in the industry.

    O   Low-level managers at the exchange most often leave their jobs for positions with the state or federal government.

    O   Former top executives of the exchange have a particular set of skills such that they are usually only able to find work with publicly traded companies.

2. The increase in taxes on cigarettes next month will not limit the use of addictive tobacco products to the extent that health advocates hope. Many cigarette smokers will shift their spending to cigars and chewing tobacco when the law takes effect.

    Which of the following, if true, would most strongly weaken the argument above?

    O   Cigars and chewing tobacco can satisfy the nicotine cravings of most cigarette smokers.

    O   The taste, smell, and texture of cigars and chewing tobacco are sufficiently different from those of cigarettes to deter cigarette smokers from using them.

    O   Many health advocates themselves use tobacco products.

    O   The government might also impose significant taxes on cigars and chewing tobacco over the course of two years.

    O   Cigars and chewing tobacco are often more expensive than cigarettes.

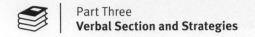

3. The percentage of local businesses with more than 10 employees is higher in Grandview City than in any other city in the state. However, the percentage of local businesses with 15 employees or more is higher in Lakeshore City, which is in the same state, than in any other city in the state.

    If the statements above are true, then which of the following must also be true?

    O   The percentage of local businesses with more than 18 employees is higher in Lakeshore City than in any other city in the state.

    O   The state has more local businesses with more than 10 employees than any other state in the country.

    O   The number of local businesses with 15 or more employees is greater in Lakeshore City than in Grandview City.

    O   Some local businesses in Grandview City have 11 to 14 employees.

    O   The average number of employees per business is higher in Lakeshore City than in Grandview City.

4. It appears that the number of people employed by a typical American software firm decreased in the 1980s and 1990s. This trend is borne out by two studies, conducted 20 years apart. In a large 1980 sample of randomly chosen American software firms, the median size of the firms' workforce populations was 65. When those same firms were studied again in 2000, the median size was 57.

    Which of the following points to the most serious logical flaw in the reasoning above?

    O   The median number of employees in American firms in many industries decreased during the 1980s and 1990s.

    O   During the 1980s and 1990s, many software firms increased the extent to which they relied on subcontractors to write code.

    O   The data in the studies refer only to companies that existed in 1980.

    O   The studies focused on the number of employees, but there are many ways of judging a firm's size, such as revenues and profits.

    O   The median number of employees is not as sound a measure of the number of employees employed in an industry as is the mean number of employees, which accounts for the vast size of the few large firms that dominate most industries.

5. The Ministry of Tourism in country X began an expensive television advertising campaign in country Y two years ago. Since that time, the number of visitors to country X from country Y has increased by more than 8 percent. Clearly, the Ministry of Tourism's campaign is responsible for the increase.

   Which of the following, if true, would most weaken the argument above?

   O The advertisements sponsored by the Ministry of Tourism in country X were panned by the country Y media for lack of imagination.

   O A devaluation of the currency in country X two years ago made travel there more affordable for residents of country Y.

   O Increasing political turmoil in country X will lead to a decrease in visitors from country Y next year.

   O The number of visitors from country Y to country Z increased by more than 8 percent over the past two years.

   O Over the past two years, the advertisement campaign launched by the Ministry of Tourism in country X cost more money than residents of country Y spent traveling in country X.

6. A corporation's recent financial report indicates that customers in its Quarx stores, which play upbeat music through an in-store audio system, spend on average 25 percent more per shopping trip than customers in its Cublx stores, which advertise specials over the audio system. Clearly, hearing music has a greater impact than hearing advertisements on how much money customers spend when shopping.

   Which of the following, if true, would most strengthen the argument above?

   O A study conducted by a psychologist found that hearing music makes shoppers feel financially secure, so they are more likely to make impulse purchases.

   O Customers who hear advertisements for things they dislike form a negative association between their shopping experience and what they heard, making them less likely to return to the store where they heard the advertisement.

   O Stores that play music tend to carry products that are essential to daily life, while those that advertise specials often stock unessential, fun items that the stores hope consumers will decide to buy on a whim if offered a special price.

   O An economist who studied consumer shopping habits found that about half the population likes to listen to music while shopping, while the other half reports either disliking music or not noticing that music is playing.

   O According to a recent sociological study, customers say that hearing specials announced while they are shopping is irritating, but they often take advantage of the discounts offered in those announcements.

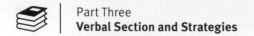

7. Cable television executive: **Our service and reliability have increased dramatically over the past year.** Our customer service line is receiving 30 percent fewer reports of interrupted service, and the number of subscribers canceling their accounts is barely half of what it was last year.

    Cable television customer: That doesn't mean your service and reliability have improved. **It's possible that customers don't bother to call your customer service line to report problems because they never get any assistance when they do.** And the drop-off in the number of canceled accounts could reflect the fact that nearly all of your dissatisfied customers have already canceled their accounts.

    In the argument above, the two portions in boldface play which of the following roles?

    ○   The first is evidence designed to lead to a conclusion; the second offers further evidence in support of that conclusion.

    ○   The first is evidence designed to lead to a conclusion; the second offers evidence designed to cast doubt on that conclusion.

    ○   The first is a conclusion; the second offers evidence in support of that conclusion.

    ○   The first is a conclusion; the second offers evidence designed to cast doubt on that conclusion.

    ○   The first is a conclusion; the second is an alternative conclusion based on the same evidence.

8. Opponents of the laws prohibiting the use of nonprescription narcotic drugs in Leffingwell argue that in a free society, people should have the right to take risks as long as the risks do not constitute a harm to others who have not elected to take such risks. These opponents conclude that people should have the legal right to make the decision whether or not to use narcotic drugs.

    Which of the following is an assumption required by the argument?

    ○   Some narcotic drugs have been shown to have medicinal qualities.

    ○   There are laws in Leffingwell that govern the use of prescription drugs.

    ○   People who use nonprescription narcotic drugs are no more likely to perpetrate a violent crime when under the influence of these drugs than when sober.

    ○   People who use certain types of narcotic drugs are no more likely to die of an overdose than of natural causes.

    ○   The rate of drug overdoses is lower in countries that do not have laws governing the use of narcotic drugs than in Leffingwell.

9. In a survey of undergraduates, two-fifths admitted to having cheated on an exam at least once during their education. However, the survey may underestimate the proportion of undergraduates who have cheated because _____.

    Which of the following best completes the passage above?

    ○   some undergraduates who have cheated at least once might have claimed on the survey never to have cheated

    ○   some undergraduates who have never cheated might have claimed on the survey to have cheated

    ○   some undergraduates who claimed on the survey to have cheated at least once may have cheated on multiple occasions throughout their education

    ○   some undergraduates who claimed on the survey to have cheated at least once may have been answering honestly

    ○   some students who are not undergraduates have probably cheated at least once during their education

10. During the last 18 years, the number of people who live or work in the Dry River Valley, which is prone to flash flooding, has continually increased, as has traffic on local roads and bridges. However, the number of people caught in flash floods has decreased, even though the annual number of floods has increased slightly.

    Which of the following, if true, best explains the decrease described above?

    ○   Flash floods are more likely to happen in the first hour of a rainstorm than afterward.

    ○   Flash floods killed some people in the Dry River Valley in every one of the last 18 years.

    ○   Better meteorological technology, combined with a better understanding of the conditions conducive to flash flooding, has improved local authorities' ability to predict when and where flash floods will occur.

    ○   Many people work in the Dry River Valley but live elsewhere.

    ○   A law that went into effect 18 years ago mandated that all new homes built in the valley be built on raised foundations, making those homes much less susceptible to flood damage.

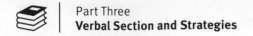

11. Colleges in Tycho City have failed to prepare their students for the business world. A recent study revealed that the majority of college graduates in Tycho City could not write a simple business letter.

Which of the following, if true, would provide additional evidence in support of the claim above?

- ○ A majority of students attending colleges in Tycho City are business majors.
- ○ The state college in neighboring Twyla Township has recently improved its business program by adding courses in business writing.
- ○ Most Tycho City college graduates move outside the Tycho City area after they graduate.
- ○ Most Tycho City college students live in on-campus dormitories.
- ○ The majority of college graduates living in Tycho City received their college degrees from institutions located in Tycho City.

Answers and explanations follow on the next page ▶ ▶ ▶

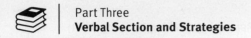

Answer Key

Critical Reasoning Quiz

1. E
2. B
3. D
4. C
5. B
6. A
7. D
8. C
9. A
10. C
11. E

Answers and Explanations

Critical Reasoning Quiz

1. (E)

To avoid the appearance of conflicts of interest, the board of a major U.S. stock exchange is considering a new policy that would ban former top executives of the exchange from taking positions at publicly traded companies for a period of two years after leaving the stock exchange. Critics of the plan say the policy is unfair because it would likely prevent former top executives of the exchange from earning a decent living.

Which of the following statements, if true, would most strengthen the prediction made by the critics of the proposed company policy?

○ The labor union that represents most of the stock exchange's employees has made public statements that threaten a strike if the policy is adopted.

○ Former employees of the exchange most often work for publicly traded companies after leaving the exchange.

○ Low-level managers at the exchange have an average tenure of 13 years, one of the longest in the industry.

○ Low-level managers at the exchange most often leave their jobs for positions with the state or federal government.

○ Former top executives of the exchange have a particular set of skills such that they are usually only able to find work with publicly traded companies

STEP 1: IDENTIFY THE QUESTION TYPE

You're looking to strengthen the argument here—specifically the prediction made by the critics of a policy. So as you examine the stimulus, the critics' argument will be most helpful.

STEP 2: UNTANGLE THE STIMULUS

A new policy would ban former top executives of a major stock exchange from working for publicly traded companies for two years after leaving the exchange. Critics of the policy contend that the policy will prevent the top executives from earning a decent living.

STEP 3: PREDICT THE ANSWER

Since you're strengthening the prediction, look for an answer choice that makes it more likely that the former top execs can't earn a decent living. A good prediction is *something that explains why top executives must work at publicly traded companies in order to make a decent living.*

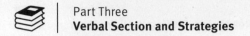

STEP 4: EVALUATE THE CHOICES

Choose **(E)**, which states that former top executives of the firm can usually only find work at publicly traded companies because of their particular skill set. If this were true, then a two-year ban on working for publicly traded companies would mean no work for most former top executives (and by extension, no decent living), thus strengthening the prediction stated by critics of the plan. Whether or not the union strikes has no bearing on the effect the new policy would have on the former executives if enacted; thus, **(A)** is incorrect. **(B)** simply states that most former employees of the exchange work for publicly traded companies; it does not tell you that they could not make a decent living elsewhere if need be. **(C)** and **(D)** refer to low-level managers, and the prediction only discusses top executives; thus, both choices are irrelevant and incorrect.

2. **(B)**

The increase in taxes on cigarettes next month will not limit the use of addictive tobacco products to the extent that health advocates hope. Many cigarette smokers will shift their spending to cigars and chewing tobacco when the law takes effect.

Which of the following, if true, would most strongly weaken the argument above?

- ○ Cigars and chewing tobacco can satisfy the nicotine cravings of most cigarette smokers.
- ○ The taste, smell, and texture of cigars and chewing tobacco are sufficiently different from those of cigarettes to deter cigarette smokers from using them.
- ○ Many health advocates themselves use tobacco products.
- ○ The government might also impose significant taxes on cigars and chewing tobacco over the course of two years.
- ○ Cigars and chewing tobacco are often more expensive than cigarettes.

STEP 1: IDENTIFY THE QUESTION TYPE

The wording is a little strange ("most strongly weaken"), but this is ultimately a Weaken question.

STEP 2: UNTANGLE THE STIMULUS

The conclusion in this argument is a prediction. According to the conclusion, many current cigarette smokers will shift their spending to cigars and chewing tobacco because of an impending increase in taxes on cigarettes. You could also look at this as a causality argument, as it asserts that the price of cigarettes affects smoking behavior.

STEP 3: PREDICT THE ANSWER

If you are using the plan/proposal/prediction approach, your prediction would be *something that explains why cigarette smokers won't use cigars or chewing tobacco, even though taxes on cigarettes will increase.* And if you are approaching this argument focusing on causality, your prediction would likely be *another factor that affects smoking behavior.* (The other two ways of weakening causality aren't very reasonable here—smoking behavior doesn't affect the price one pays for cigarettes, and you know from the stimulus that the price of cigarettes isn't set by coincidence.)

STEP 4: EVALUATE THE CHOICES

(B) effectively weakens the author's prediction: if the differences in taste, smell, and texture will deter smokers from using cigars and chewing tobacco, then it is unlikely that cigarette smokers will shift their spending to them even if taxes are raised. They may find cigarette smoking prohibitively expensive, but they won't be likely to switch to other tobacco products, no matter how much cheaper those products are. And if you were looking for a new factor that affects smoking behavior, here there are three: taste, smell, and texture. **(A)** is a 180. It strengthens the author's prediction in the last sentence: if cigars and chewing tobacco satisfy the same nicotine cravings as cigarettes, then it is likely that cigarette smokers will buy them instead if taxes on cigarettes are raised. **(C)** is incorrect because the personal habits of health advocates have no bearing on the author's prediction. **(D)** is similarly irrelevant: the author's prediction is concerned only with the spending of consumers next month, not in two years. **(E)** is tempting at first glance, but it doesn't provide enough information to weaken the argument. Will cigars and chewing tobacco still be more expensive than cigarettes after the tax increase? Without more specific information, **(E)** doesn't weaken the argument.

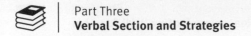

3. (D)

The percentage of local businesses with more than 10 employees is higher in Grandview City than in any other city in the state. However, the percentage of local businesses with 15 employees or more is higher in Lakeshore City, which is in the same state, than in any other city in the state.

If the statements above are true, then which of the following must also be true?

○ The percentage of local businesses with more than 18 employees is higher in Lakeshore City than in any other city in the state.

○ The state has more local businesses with more than 10 employees than any other state in the country.

○ The number of local businesses with 15 or more employees is greater in Lakeshore City than in Grandview City.

○ Some local businesses in Grandview City have 11 to 14 employees.

○ The average number of employees per business is higher in Lakeshore City than in Grandview City.

STEP 1: IDENTIFY THE QUESTION TYPE

This question asks you to choose the answer that makes a valid deduction from the stimulus, so it is an Inference question.

STEP 2: UNTANGLE THE STIMULUS

Usually, the stimulus of an Inference question will not include an argument. You just need to read and understand the statements in the stimulus and take note of any connections between them. This stimulus really just provides two related pieces of information: Grandview has the highest percentage of businesses with 11+ employees, while Lakeshore has the highest percentage with 15+.

STEP 3: PREDICT THE ANSWER

Grandview has the highest percentage of businesses with 11+ employees, but not the highest percentage with 15+. The only way that's possible is if Grandview has at least a few businesses with 11–14 employees. You might use picking numbers to make this deduction more obvious. For instance, say that both Grandview and Lakeshore have 100 businesses. If Grandview has 25 businesses with 11+ employees, and Lakeshore has 20 businesses with 15+ employees, Lakeshore could still have the higher percentage of 15+ employee businesses if Grandview has more than 5 businesses with 11–14 employees. What "must be true" is that Grandview has at least a few businesses with 11–14 employees. You'll be looking for an answer choice that says so.

STEP 4: EVALUATE THE CHOICES

(D) matches the prediction and is the correct answer. **(A)** is incorrect because businesses with more than 18 employees have no bearing on the stimulus. **(B)** introduces an irrelevant comparison between states. You're only interested in two specific cities within one state, not in any other states. **(C)** is a bit tricky, but the actual number of businesses is irrelevant; you're concerned only with percentages, not raw numbers. Finally, **(E)** wintroduces another irrelevant point. You care only about businesses with very specific numbers of employees, not about the average number of employees per business.

4. (C)

It appears that the number of people employed by a typical American software firm decreased in the 1980s and 1990s. This trend is borne out by two studies, conducted 20 years apart. In a large 1980 sample of randomly chosen American software firms, the median size of the firms' workforce populations was 65. When those same firms were studied again in 2000, the median size was 57.

Which of the following points to the most serious logical flaw in the reasoning above?

- O The median number of employees in American firms in many industries decreased during the 1980s and 1990s.
- O During the 1980s and 1990s, many software firms increased the extent to which they relied on subcontractors to write code.
- O The data in the studies refer only to companies that existed in 1980.
- O The studies focused on the number of employees, but there are many ways of judging a firm's size, such as revenues and profits.
- O The median number of employees is not as sound a measure of the number of employees employed in an industry as is the mean number of employees, which accounts for the vast size of the few large firms that dominate most industries.

STEP 1: IDENTIFY THE QUESTION TYPE

Since the question stem asks for a "logical flaw," you're dealing with a Flaw question here.

STEP 2: UNTANGLE THE STIMULUS

The argument concludes that the typical American software firm employs fewer people in the 2000s than it did in the 1980s and 1990s. This conclusion is supported by two studies; in order for the conclusion to be valid, both studies need to be representative.

STEP 3: PREDICT THE ANSWER

The sample in the 1980 study seems legitimate: it was large and randomly chosen. However, notice the problem with the 2000 study: it uses the same firms as in the 1980 study. The firms are no longer randomly chosen, nor does the sample size account for the many software firms that presumably sprang up between 1980 and 2000. In other words, the sample in the second survey was not representative of all American software firms.

STEP 4: EVALUATE THE CHOICES

This prediction matches (C), which pinpoints a problem with the representativeness of the 2000 survey. If wthe firms surveyed included only those that also existed 20 years ago, then no information is included about firms that have come into existence since then. If the survey is not based on information about all American software firms, including those that have come into existence over the last 20 years, then the survey is not representative, and any conclusions drawn from those results are called into question. (A)'s focus on many industries is irrelevant to the argument, which is concerned only with the number of people employed by a typical American software firm. (B) gives a plausible explanation of why the median size of firms is decreasing, but it fails to describe a flaw in the argument. (D) is irrelevant: the survey is concerned with the firm's size in terms of workforce population. All other measures of a firm's size are irrelevant. Finally, (E) is not a flaw in this argument. While it may be true that the mean is a better measure for total workforce population in an industry, this argument concerns the number of employees in *a typical firm* in one industry, not across the industry as a whole.

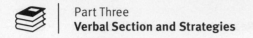
5. (B)

The Ministry of Tourism in country X began an expensive television advertising campaign in country Y two years ago. Since that time, the number of visitors to country X from country Y has increased by more than 8 percent. Clearly, the Ministry of Tourism's campaign is responsible for the increase.

Which of the following, if true, would most weaken the argument above?

○   The advertisements sponsored by the Ministry of Tourism in country X were panned by the country Y media for lack of imagination.

○   A devaluation of the currency in country X two years ago made travel there more affordable for residents of country Y.

○   Increasing political turmoil in country X will lead to a decrease in visitors from country Y next year.

○   The number of visitors from country Y to country Z increased by more than 8 percent over the past two years.

○   Over the past two years, the advertisement campaign launched by the Ministry of Tourism in country X cost more money than residents of country Y spent traveling in country X.

STEP 1: IDENTIFY THE QUESTION TYPE

The question stem clearly indicates that this is a Weaken question.

STEP 2: UNTANGLE THE STIMULUS

The conclusion is that the Ministry of Tourism's ad campaign is responsible for the increase in the number of visitors from country Y to country X. The evidence is that since the ad campaign began running, the number of visitors from country Y to country X has gone up by more than 8%.

STEP 3: PREDICT THE ANSWER

This is a very straightforward causal argument. While there are three classic alternatives to a causal argument (reverse cause and effect, find an alternative cause, or suggest coincidence), the most common way of weakening a causal argument is to exploit the second alternative—citing another possible cause for the phenomenon. So look for an answer choice that offers another explanation for the increase of tourism from country Y.

STEP 4: EVALUATE THE CHOICES

(B) offers that alternative explanation, making it the correct answer. If travel to country X became more affordable at the same time that tourism to country X increased, it is possible that the devaluation in currency is responsible for this increase rather than the Ministry of Tourism's ad campaign. While it does not *disprove* that the ad campaign was the cause of the increase, it certainly weakens the author's argument by presenting another potential cause of the increase. **(A)** does not effectively weaken the argument. Just because the media panned the ads does not mean they could not have spurred the increase in tourism. The prediction in **(C)** is irrelevant to the author's argument about the past efficacy of the Ministry of Tourism's ad campaign. **(D)** brings up tourism in country Z, which has no bearing on the argument. And **(E)** is likewise irrelevant: the author is only concerned with establishing a causal relationship between the ad campaign and increased tourism, not with whether the campaign was cost-effective.

6. **(A)**

A corporation's recent financial report indicates that customers in its Quarx stores, which play upbeat music through an in-store audio system, spend on average 25 percent more per shopping trip than customers in its Cubix stores, which advertise specials over the audio system. Clearly, hearing music has a greater impact than hearing advertisements on how much money customers spend when shopping.

Which of the following, if true, would most strengthen the argument above?

- O A study conducted by a psychologist found that hearing music makes shoppers feel financially secure, so they are more likely to make impulse purchases.

- O Customers who hear advertisements for things they dislike form a negative association between their shopping experience and what they heard, making them less likely to return to the store where they heard the advertisement.

- O Stores that play music tend to carry products that are essential to daily life, while those that advertise specials often stock unessential, fun items that the stores hope consumers will decide to buy on a whim if offered a special price.

- O An economist who studied consumer shopping habits found that about half the population likes to listen to music while shopping, while the other half reports either disliking music or not noticing that music is playing.

- O According to a recent sociological study, customers say that hearing specials announced while they are shopping is irritating, but they often take advantage of the discounts offered in those announcements.

STEP 1: IDENTIFY THE QUESTION TYPE

The question stem asks for the answer choice that will most strengthen the argument, making this a Strengthen question.

STEP 2: UNTANGLE THE STIMULUS

This is a causality argument. It concludes that playing music increases customer spending more than advertising specials over an in-store audio system. The evidence given is a report on two chains of stores. According to the report, Quarx stores play music on their audio systems and saw customers buy 25% more, on average, than customers at Cubix stores, which advertise specials on their audio systems.

STEP 3: PREDICT THE ANSWER

The correct answer will either make it more likely that hearing music causes customers to increase their spending or make it less likely that some other factor caused Quarx customers to outspend Cubix customers.

STEP 4: EVALUATE THE CHOICES

(A) strengthens the conclusion. The study found a direct link between how music makes customers feel and their willingness to spend more than they initially planned, supporting the conclusion that music increases how much money is spent. **(B)** does not say anything about how much is spent at the time the ads are heard. Since the argument is about what is spent on a particular shopping trip, future shopping trips are irrelevant. **(C)** does not strengthen (or weaken) the conclusion because it doesn't link this information about product selection to how much money customers spend. **(D)** does not provide any information about the impact customers' opinions of hearing music while shopping has on how much money customers spend. Finally, **(E)** also fails to establish any connection to how much is spent. Furthermore, it fails to mention music at all.

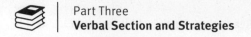
7. **(D)**

Cable television executive: **Our service and reliability have increased dramatically over the past year.** Our customer service line is receiving 30 percent fewer reports of interrupted service, and the number of subscribers canceling their accounts is barely half of what it was last year.

Cable television customer: That doesn't mean your service and reliability have improved. **It's possible that customers don't bother to call your customer service line to report problems because they never get any assistance when they do.** And the drop-off in the number of canceled accounts could reflect the fact that nearly all of your dissatisfied customers have already canceled their accounts.

In the argument above, the two portions in boldface play which of the following roles?

- ○ The first is evidence designed to lead to a conclusion; the second offers further evidence in support of that conclusion.
- ○ The first is evidence designed to lead to a conclusion; the second offers evidence designed to cast doubt on that conclusion.
- ○ The first is a conclusion; the second offers evidence in support of that conclusion.
- ○ The first is a conclusion; the second offers evidence designed to cast doubt on that conclusion.
- ○ The first is a conclusion; the second is an alternative conclusion based on the same evidence.

STEP 1: IDENTIFY THE QUESTION TYPE

This stem offers standard language for a Bolded Statement question—it asks you to determine the roles played in the arguments by each of the boldface statements.

STEP 2: UNTANGLE THE STIMULUS

The cable television executive uses evidence of fewer customer complaints and cancellations to conclude that the cable company's service has improved over the past year. The customer disagrees, providing an alternative explanation for the executive's evidence. According to the customer, there are fewer cancellations because all the dissatisfied customers have already canceled their accounts; the decreased number of complaints indicates that frustrated customers have simply given up.

STEP 3: PREDICT THE ANSWER

The first bolded statement is the cable executive's conclusion, and the second bolded statement is evidence from the customer that would support a contradictory conclusion.

STEP 4: EVALUATE THE CHOICES

(D) is correct; the second statement is designed to cast doubt on the validity of the conclusion in the first. Since the first bolded statement represents the executive's conclusion, you can eliminate **(A)** and **(B)**, which characterize this statement as evidence. The customer clearly disagrees with the executive, so you can eliminate **(C)**. **(E)** may be tempting; the second statement does provide an alternate explanation of some of the evidence, but the second statement is not a conclusion, merely a possible interpretation. Always read diligently so that you can avoid half-right, half-wrong answer choices.

8. **(C)**

Opponents of the laws prohibiting the use of nonprescription narcotic drugs in Leffingwell argue that in a free society, people should have the right to take risks as long as the risks do not constitute a harm to others who have not elected to take such risks. These opponents conclude that people should have the legal right to make the decision whether or not to use narcotic drugs.

Which of the following is an assumption required by the argument?

- ○ Some narcotic drugs have been shown to have medicinal qualities.
- ○ There are laws in Leffingwell that govern the use of prescription drugs.
- ○ People who use nonprescription narcotic drugs are no more likely to perpetrate a violent crime when under the influence of these drugs than when sober.
- ○ People who use certain types of narcotic drugs are no more likely to die of an overdose than of natural causes.
- ○ The rate of drug overdoses is lower in countries that do not have laws governing the use of narcotic drugs than in Leffingwell.

STEP 1: IDENTIFY THE QUESTION TYPE

This is an Assumption question.

STEP 2: UNTANGLE THE STIMULUS

As in all argument-based questions, you need to find the conclusion and evidence. The conclusion is the last sentence: use of nonprescription narcotic drugs should be everyone's personal decision. The evidence is that people have the right to take risks as long as taking those risks doesn't hurt anyone besides themselves.

STEP 3: PREDICT THE ANSWER

If narcotics could harm non-users, then narcotic use would not be a permissible risk, according to this argument; individuals would no longer have the right to use those drugs. The opponents of these laws, then, are assuming that nonprescription narcotics pose risks only to the people who use them. Look for a choice that paraphrases this assumption.

STEP 4: EVALUATE THE CHOICES

(C) does the job perfectly. If people are no more likely to commit violent crimes while under the influence of drugs, then others aren't at risk from the drug use. This choice is more specific than the prediction, but it is certainly one thing that the author assumes. **(A)** is incorrect because it introduces the idea of medicinal qualities, which is irrelevant to the argument. The author focuses on harm caused by drug-using behavior, not potential benefits. The prescription drugs in **(B)** are likewise irrelevant to the argument, which is concerned only with nonprescription drugs. While **(D)** does establish that certain drugs may not cause overdoses, this information has no bearing on the argument since it concerns a risk to the user of the drug, not a risk to others. Finally, **(E)** is an irrelevant comparison. The overdose rate in other countries without such laws has no bearing on the argument because rates of overdose indicate only personal risk, not risk to others.

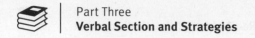

9. **(A)**

In a survey of undergraduates, two-fifths admitted to having cheated on an exam at least once during their education. However, the survey may underestimate the proportion of undergraduates who have cheated because _____.

Which of the following best completes the passage above?

○   some undergraduates who have cheated at least once might have claimed on the survey never to have cheated

○   some undergraduates who have never cheated might have claimed on the survey to have cheated

○   some undergraduates who claimed on the survey to have cheated at least once may have cheated on multiple occasions throughout their education

○   some undergraduates who claimed on the survey to have cheated at least once may have been answering honestly

○   some students who are not undergraduates have probably cheated at least once during their education

STEP 1: IDENTIFY THE QUESTION TYPE

Here, you have a question that asks you to complete the final sentence of a brief argument. The key word before the blank is "because," an evidence key word; since the missing information is evidence that would support the author's point of view, it's a Strengthen question.

STEP 2: UNTANGLE THE STIMULUS

The author's conclusion is that the survey may have underestimated the proportion of undergraduates who cheated. You know from the first sentence that two-fifths of the students *reported* having cheated at least once. The author implies that there are additional, unreported cheaters out there.

STEP 3: PREDICT THE ANSWER

The one correct answer will provide a reason to think that there are additional, unreported cheaters among the undergraduate population.

STEP 4: EVALUATE THE CHOICES

(A) is a match for the prediction and is correct: some undergrads may have cheated but lied about it on the survey. If you were looking for a reason why the survey might *overestimate* the proportion of undergrads cheating, **(B)** would be correct. **(C)** refers to multiple cases of cheating per student; the survey is only dealing with the proportion of students who have cheated at least once. **(D)** gives a reason why the survey might be accurate, which is the opposite of what you want, and **(E)** introduces students who are not undergrads, which is out of the scope of the survey.

10. (C)

During the last 18 years, the number of people who live or work in the Dry River Valley, which is prone to flash flooding, has continually increased, as has traffic on local roads and bridges. However, the number of people caught in flash floods has decreased, even though the annual number of floods has increased slightly.

Which of the following, if true, best explains the decrease described above?

- ○ Flash floods are more likely to happen in the first hour of a rainstorm than afterward.
- ○ Flash floods killed some people in the Dry River Valley in every one of the last 18 years.
- ○ Better meteorological technology, combined with a better understanding of the conditions conducive to flash flooding, has improved local authorities' ability to predict when and where flash floods will occur.
- ○ Many people work in the Dry River Valley but live elsewhere.
- ○ A law that went into effect 18 years ago mandated that all new homes built in the valley be built on raised foundations, making those homes much less susceptible to flood damage.

STEP 1: IDENTIFY THE QUESTION TYPE

This is an Explain question. You can anticipate seeing a paradox or unusual coincidence described in the stimulus. Your task is to resolve the seemingly disparate pieces of information in order to explain the anomalous result.

STEP 2: UNTANGLE THE STIMULUS

The stimulus tells you about two increases—the number of people and the number of flash floods—in the Dry River Valley. The key word "[h]owever" signals the seeming discrepancy: despite those increases, the number of people caught in flash floods has gone down. Think critically about how you can reconcile these facts.

STEP 3: PREDICT THE ANSWER

The stimulus involves numbers (of residents, floods, and flood victims), but it doesn't state any actual values. Picking numbers can help you visualize the situation in the stimulus.

Pick numbers that are permissible and manageable. Say that 18 years ago, there were 1,000 people, 10 floods, and 100 flood victims in the valley. Following the information in the stimulus, say there are now 2,000 people, 20 floods, and 50 victims.

	18 years ago	**Now**
People	1,000	2,000
Floods	10	20
People caught in floods	100	50

This shows that the floods are now less dangerous.

	18 years ago	**Now**
Proportion of people caught in floods	1 in 10	1 in 40
People caught per flood	10	2.5

The correct answer will explain this change. It will provide a reason why the floods have been less dangerous.

STEP 4: EVALUATE THE CHOICES

(C) gives you the explanation you need and is correct: more accurate advance notice of floods allows local authorities to better prevent people from getting caught. **(A)** may be true of flash flooding in general, but it doesn't give you any difference between the floods now and those 18 years ago. **(B)** is irrelevant to the argument, which deals with people *caught* in the floods, not people killed by them. **(D)** doesn't explain the difference either, as there's no reason to think that flash floods somehow selectively avoid commuters. **(E)** is also irrelevant, since the argument does not focus on property damage.

11. (E)

Colleges in Tycho City have failed to prepare their students for the business world. A recent study revealed that the majority of college graduates in Tycho City could not write a simple business letter.

Which of the following, if true, would provide additional evidence in support of the claim above?

○   A majority of students attending colleges in Tycho City are business majors.

○   The state college in neighboring Twyla Township has recently improved its business program by adding courses in business writing.

○   Most Tycho City college graduates move outside the Tycho City area after they graduate.

○   Most Tycho City college students live in on-campus dormitories.

○   The majority of college graduates living in Tycho City received their college degrees from institutions located in Tycho City.

STEP 1: IDENTIFY THE QUESTION TYPE

To "provide additional evidence in support" of an argument is to strengthen it, so this is a Strengthen question.

STEP 2: UNTANGLE THE STIMULUS

The argument concludes that colleges in Tycho City don't do a good job of preparing their grads for the business world, because the majority of college grads living in Tycho City couldn't write a simple business letter. Since this argument is based on a study, there is likely a representativeness problem.

STEP 3: PREDICT THE ANSWER

In this argument, the author makes a scope shift between the evidence and the conclusion: the evidence is based on "college graduates in Tycho City," while the conclusion refers to the supposed failings of "colleges in Tycho City." In order for the conclusion to hold, it must be true that the college grads in the study are representative of colleges in Tycho City—that is, that those people actually attended school in Tycho City. Look for an answer that bolsters that assumption.

STEP 4: EVALUATE THE CHOICES

(E) properly strengthens the argument by reinforcing the assumption. In other words, **(E)** demonstrates that the sample studied is actually representative of colleges in Tycho City. **(A)** has no effect on the argument. While the argument concerns whether students are prepared for the business world, it is not relevant what the students are majoring in. **(B)** is irrelevant. What some other college is doing does not affect an argument about the effectiveness of Tycho City college programs. **(C)** actually weakens the argument. If most Tycho City college graduates leave the Tycho City area after graduation, then it is unlikely that a study of graduates in Tycho City is representative of graduates of Tycho City colleges. Be careful of 180 answers in Strengthen/Weaken questions. Finally, **(D)** is irrelevant, since where the students live has no effect on whether or not they're adequately prepared for the business world.

GMAT by the Numbers: Critical Reasoning

Now that you've learned how to approach Critical Reasoning questions on the GMAT, let's add one more dimension to your understanding of how they work.

Take a moment to try this question. Following is performance data from thousands of people who have studied with Kaplan over the decades. Through analyzing this data, we will show you how to approach questions like this one most effectively and how to avoid similarly tempting wrong answer choice types on Test Day.

Wunderlich Park has a strict regulation that requires mountain bicyclists to wear helmets. Recently, a group of bicyclists acknowledged that helmets may prevent injuries to the wearer but protested, claiming the park should only regulate activities that may hurt a third party. Hence, the bicyclists argued that they should have the right to refrain from wearing helmets.

Which of the following, if true, most seriously weakens the conclusion in the passage?

- Ninety percent of bicyclists who use Wunderlich Park prefer to wear a helmet to protect themselves in case of an accident.

- Lawyers for Wunderlich Park have warned that the repeal of the helmet regulation would lead to an increase in general admission park entrance fees to cover the legal expenses associated with personal injury lawsuits.

- Motorcyclists in a neighboring county are required to wear a helmet while on the road.

- Parks that require the use of helmets have a lower percentage of accidents resulting in deaths than parks that don't require the use of helmets.

- More bicyclists who do not wear helmets are seriously injured in accidents than bicyclists who do wear helmets.

Explanation

The argument's conclusion is presented in the final sentence, introduced by the key word "[h]ence": the bicyclists claim that they shouldn't have to wear helmets in the park. But despite the wording of the question, it isn't really the *conclusion* itself that the test maker wants you to weaken—rather, you must weaken the *logic supporting that conclusion*. According to this argument, the reason why cyclists shouldn't be made to wear helmets is that the park should not restrict an activity that doesn't harm others. The right answer, therefore, will show how not wearing a helmet actually does harm someone else.

The correct answer—**(B)**—does just that; it shows how cyclists' not wearing helmets would in fact harm non-cyclists: the harm would be financial.

Question Statistics

10% of test takers choose **(A)**

46% of test takers choose **(B)**

2% of test takers choose **(C)**

23% of test takers choose **(D)**

19% of test takers choose **(E)**

Sample size = 3,132

The three most commonly selected wrong answers are wrong because they do not address the entire argument, only the general sense of the conclusion. **(D)** and **(E)** both give good reasons to wear a helmet, but they suggest that only the cyclist is at risk, not someone else. **(A)** discusses cyclists' preferences, but the argument about when to permit regulation has to do only with whether others would be harmed, not with personal preference. You can see that answers that ignore an argument's reasoning are popular, and as such are very common. Learn to avoid them, and you'll go a long way to improving your GMAT score.

More GMAT by the Numbers...

To see more questions, be sure to review the full-length CATs in your online resources.

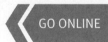

GO ONLINE

kaptest.com/login

CHAPTER 9

Reading Comprehension Strategy

LEARNING OBJECTIVES

After studying this chapter, you will be able to:

- Describe the format of Reading Comprehension questions
- State the steps of the Kaplan Method for Reading Comprehension questions
- Explain what strategic reading is and describe how it will help with Reading Comprehension questions

Below is a typical Reading Comprehension question. For now, don't worry that we haven't given you the passage this question refers to. In this chapter, we'll look at how to apply the Kaplan Method to this question, discuss the types of questions the GMAT asks about reading passages, and go over the basic principles and strategies that you want to keep in mind on every Reading Comprehension question.

> The passage suggests that Ferguson would be most likely to agree with which of the following claims about the "multiplier effect" (line 4)?
>
> O   It was unlikely to have generated the returns for the European national economies that Behrman claims.
>
> O   It may have been helpful to the European national economies, but it was not the most important outcome of the Marshall Plan.
>
> O   It was the most controversial aspect of the Marshall Plan, generating intense resistance from those countries that chose not to participate.
>
> O   It was a crucial part of the Marshall Plan, being substantially responsible for the recovery of participating Western European economies.
>
> O   It was designed primarily to assist the recovery of industry in the United States, despite its benefits to Western European national economies.

Before you move on, take a minute to think about what you see in the structure of this question and answer some questions about how you think it works:

- What does it mean to draw an inference from a GMAT passage?
- How much are you expected to know about the subject matter of the passages before you take the test?

- What can you expect to see in a GMAT passage that discusses two related theories?
- What GMAT Core Competencies are most essential to success on this question?

Previewing Reading Comprehension

> **LEARNING OBJECTIVES**
>
> In this section, you will learn how to:
>
> - Explain what it means for a statement to be supported by the passage and thus a valid Reading Comprehension inference
> - Describe how Critical Thinking, Pattern Recognition, Paraphrasing, and Attention to the Right Detail are helpful skills in Reading Comprehension

Here we'll answer the questions we just asked you to consider.

What Does It Mean to Draw an Inference from a GMAT Passage?

You may remember from the Critical Reasoning chapter the definition of an "inference" on the GMAT: an inference is something that *must* be true, based on the information provided. There are two important parts to this definition:

(1) A valid GMAT inference *must* be true based on what is stated in the text. This sets a high standard for what you consider a valid inference. It is sometimes difficult to determine whether a statement in an answer choice must always be true, but you can also approach these questions by eliminating the four answer choices that *could* be false. Keep both of these tactics in mind for questions that ask for an inference.

(2) A valid GMAT inference is based on the passage. By definition, an inference won't be explicitly stated in the passage; you will have to understand the passage well enough to read between the lines. But just because it isn't directly stated doesn't mean an inference could be anything under the sun. On the GMAT, any inference you draw will be unambiguously supported by one or more ideas stated in the passage. It may take some Critical Thinking to figure out, but you will always be able to pinpoint exactly why a valid inference must be true.

How Much Are You Expected to Know About the Subject Matter of the Passages Before You Take the Test?

Familiarity with the subject matter is not required. GMAT passages contain everything you need to answer GMAT questions. In fact, some Reading Comp questions contain wrong answer choices based on information that is actually true but not mentioned in the passage. So if you know the subject, be careful not to let your prior knowledge influence your answer. And if you don't know the subject, be happy—some wrong answer traps won't be tempting to you!

Reading Comprehension is designed to test not your prior knowledge but your critical reading skills. Among other things, it tests whether you can do the following:

- Summarize the main idea of a passage
- Understand logical relationships between facts and concepts
- Make inferences based on information in a text
- Analyze the logical structure of a passage
- Deduce the author's tone and attitude about a topic from the text

Note that none of these objectives relies on anything other than your ability to understand and apply ideas found in the passage. This should be a comforting thought: everything you need is right there in front of you. In this chapter, you will learn strategic approaches to help you make the best use of the information the test makers provide.

What Can You Expect to See in a GMAT Passage That Discusses Two Related Theories?

Because the GMAT cannot ask you purely factual questions that might reward or punish you for your outside knowledge, it tends to focus its questions on the opinions or analyses contained in the passages. Since the question at the beginning of this chapter asks you about Ferguson's attitude toward the "multiplier effect," that individual must have an opinion about it, and the passage will describe the "multiplier effect" in enough detail that you can understand Ferguson's opinion on it. You can anticipate, moreover, that at least one other person will likely have a different opinion about it.

This is a common structure for a GMAT passage: the author discusses more than one viewpoint on the same phenomenon, describing each in turn or perhaps comparing them directly, usually summarizing the relevant evidence and explaining why disagreement exists among the viewpoints' proponents. When a passage contains multiple opinions, keep track of who is making each assertion and how the assertion relates to the other opinions in the passage: does it contradict, agree with, or expand upon what came before? Another important thing to note is whether the author takes a side—does the author prefer one viewpoint to another? Does he offer his own competing argument?

What GMAT Core Competencies Are Most Essential to Success on These Questions?

Since the GMAT constructs Reading Comprehension passages in similar ways and asks questions that conform to predictable "types," you can learn to anticipate how an author will express her ideas and what the GMAT test makers will ask you about a passage. The more you practice and the more you focus on structure as you read, the stronger your Pattern Recognition skills will become.

Critical Thinking is also essential. As you read, you should ask why the author is including certain details and what the author's choice of transition key words implies about how the ideas in the passage are related.

The best test takers learn how to pay Attention to the Right Detail. Reading Comp passages are typically filled with more details than you could reasonably memorize—and more, in fact, than you will ever need to answer the questions. Since time is limited, you must prioritize the information you assimilate from the passage, focusing on the big picture but allowing yourself to return to the passage to research details as needed.

Practice Paraphrasing constantly as you read, both to keep yourself engaged and to make sure you understand what's being discussed. Developing this habit will make taking notes much easier, since you've already distilled and summarized the most important information in your head. You'll learn later in this chapter how to take concise and well-organized notes in the form of a passage map.

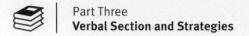
Question Format and Structure

The directions for Reading Comprehension questions look like this:

> **Directions:** The questions in this group are based on the content of a passage. After reading the passage, choose the best answer to each question. Base your answers only on what is stated or implied in the text.

In Reading Comp, you are presented with a reading passage (in an area of business, social science, biological science, or physical science) and then asked three or four questions about that text. You are not expected to be familiar with any topic beforehand—all the information you need is contained in the text in front of you. In fact, if you happen to have some previous knowledge about a given topic, it is important that you not let that knowledge affect your answers. Naturally, some passages will be easier to understand than others, though each will present a challenge. The passages will have the tone and content that one might expect from a scholarly journal.

You will see four Reading Comp passages—most likely two shorter passages with 3 questions each and two longer passages with 4 questions each, for a total of approximately 14 questions. However, as is usual for the computer-adaptive GMAT, you will see only one question at a time on the screen, and you will have to answer each question before you can see the next question. The passage will appear on the left side of the screen. It will remain there until you've answered all of the questions that relate to it. If the text is longer than the available space, you'll be given a scroll bar to move through it. Plan to take no longer than 4 minutes to read and make notes on the passage and a little less than 1.5 minutes to answer each question associated with the passage.

> **TAKEAWAYS: QUESTION FORMAT AND STRUCTURE**
>
> - GMAT passages consist of one to five paragraphs and are up to 350 words in length.
> - You will usually see two shorter and two longer passages in the Verbal section.
> - Usually, you will get three questions on a shorter passage and four questions on a longer passage. You can answer only one at a time and can't go back to previous questions.
> - The passages usually have the tone and content that one might expect from a scholarly journal.
> - You are not expected to have prior knowledge of the subject matter in the passage.
> - The passage stays on the screen for all questions that pertain to it.
> - You should spend 4 minutes per passage and a little less than 1.5 minutes per question.

The Basic Principles of Reading Comprehension

LEARNING OBJECTIVES

In this section, you will learn how to:

- Draw upon strategic reading skills to quickly take the measure of the passage topic and scope, as well as the central ideas of each paragraph
- Utilize key words to map the structure of a passage
- Distinguish between significant ideas and minor details in Reading Comprehension passages

In daily life, most people read to learn something or to pass the time pleasantly. Neither of these goals has much to do with the GMAT. On Test Day, you have a very specific goal—to get as many right answers as you can. So your reading needs to be tailored to that goal. There are really only two things a Reading Comp question can ask you about: the "big picture" of the passage or its "little details."

Since the passage is right there on the screen, you don't need to worry much about the little details as you read. (In fact, doing so may hinder your ability to answer questions, as you'll soon see.) So your main goal as you read is to prepare yourself to get the big-picture questions right, while leaving yourself as much time as possible to find the answers to the little-detail questions.

Here are the four basic principles you need to follow to accomplish this goal.

Look for the Topic and Scope of the Passage

Think of the topic as the first big idea that comes along. Almost always, it will be right there in the first sentence. It will be something broad, far too big to discuss in the 150–350 words that most GMAT passages contain. Here's an example of how a passage might begin:

> The great migration of European intellectuals to the United States in the second quarter of the 20th century prompted a transmutation in the character of Western social thought.

What's the topic? The migration of European intellectuals to the United States in the second quarter of the 20th century. It would also be okay to say that the topic is the effects of that migration on Western social thought. Topic is a very broad concept, so you really don't need to worry about how exactly you word it. You just need to get a good idea of what the passage is talking about so you feel more comfortable reading.

Now consider scope. Think of scope as a narrowing of the topic. You're looking for an idea that the author might reasonably focus on for the length of a GMAT passage. If the topic is the "migration of European intellectuals to the United States in the second quarter of the 20th century," then perhaps the scope will be *some of the effects of that migration upon Western social thought*. It will likely be even more specific: *one aspect of Western social thought affected by the migration*. But perhaps something unexpected will come along. Might the passage compare two different migrations? Or contrast two different effects? Think critically about what's coming and look for clues in the text that let you know on what specific subject(s) the author intends to focus.

Finding the scope is critically important to doing well on Reading Comp. Many Reading Comp wrong answers are wrong because the information that would be needed to support them is simply not present in the passage. It's highly unlikely that there will be a topic sentence that lays out plainly what the author intends to write about—but the first paragraph probably will give some indication of the focus of the rest of the passage.

Note that some passages are only one paragraph long. In these cases, the topic can still appear in the first sentence. The passage will probably (but not necessarily) narrow in scope somewhere in the first third of the paragraph, as the author doesn't have much text to work with and needs to get down to business quickly.

Get the Gist of Each Paragraph and Its Structural Role in the Passage

The paragraph is the main structural unit of any passage. At first, you don't yet know the topic or scope, so you have to read the first paragraph pretty closely. But once you get a sense of where the passage is going, all you need to do is understand what role each new paragraph plays. Ask yourself the following:

- Why did the author include this paragraph?
- What's discussed here that's different from the content of the paragraph before?
- What bearing does this paragraph have on the author's main idea?
- What role do the details play?

Notice that last question—don't ask yourself, "What does this mean?" but rather, "Why is it here?" Many GMAT passages try to swamp you with tedious, dense, and sometimes confusing details. Consider this paragraph, which might appear as part of a difficult science-based passage:

> The Burgess Shale yielded a surprisingly varied array of fossils. Early chordates were very rare, but there were prodigious numbers of complex forms not seen since. *Hallucigenia*, so named for a structure so bizarre that scientists did not know which was the dorsal and which the ventral side, had fourteen legs. *Opabinia* had five eyes and a long proboscis. This amazing diversity led Gould to believe that it was highly unlikely that the eventual success of chordates was a predictable outcome.

This is pretty dense stuff. But if you don't worry about understanding all of the science jargon and instead focus on the gist of the paragraph and *why* the details are there, things get easier. The first sentence isn't that bad:

> The Burgess Shale yielded a surprisingly varied array of fossils.

A quick paraphrase is that the "Burgess Shale," whatever that is, had a lot of different kinds of fossils. The passage continues:

> Early chordates were very rare, but there were prodigious numbers of complex forms not seen since. *Hallucigenia*, so named for a structure so bizarre that scientists did not know which was the dorsal and which the ventral side, had fourteen legs. *Opabinia* had five eyes and a long proboscis.

When you read this part of the passage strategically, asking what its purpose is in context, you see that this is just a list of the different kinds of fossils and some facts about them. There were not a lot of "chordates," whatever they are, but there was lots of other stuff.

> This amazing diversity led Gould to believe that it was highly unlikely that the eventual success of chordates was a predictable outcome.

Notice that the beginning of this sentence tells us *why* those intimidatingly dense details are there; they are the facts that led Gould to a belief—namely that the rise of "chordates" couldn't have been predicted. So, on your noteboard, you'd jot down something like this:

> Evidence for Gould's belief—chordate success not predictable.

Notice that you don't have to know what any of these scientific terms mean in order to know why the author brings them up. Taking apart every paragraph like this allows you to create a map of the passage's overall structure. We'll call this a *passage map* from here on—we'll discuss passage mapping in detail later in this chapter. Making a passage map will help you acquire a clear understanding of the big picture. It will give you a sense of mastery over the passage, even when it deals with a subject you don't know anything about.

To break down paragraphs and understand the structural function of each part, look for key words, or structural words or phrases that link ideas to one another. You got an overview of the categories of key words in the Verbal Section Overview chapter of this book. Let's now dig a little deeper into how key words can help you distinguish the important things (such as opinions) from the unimportant (such as supporting examples) and to understand why the author wrote each sentence.

Types of key words:

- **Contrast** key words such as *but, however, nevertheless,* and *on the other hand* tell you that a change or disagreement is coming.

- **Continuation** key words such as *moreover, also,* and *furthermore* tell you that the author is continuing on the same track or general idea.

- **Logic** key words, which you've seen to be very important in Critical Reasoning stimuli, alert you to an author's reasoning. **Evidence** key words let you know that something is being offered in support of a particular idea. The specifics of the support are usually unimportant for the first big-picture read, but you do want to know what the idea is. Examples of evidence key words are *since, because,* and *as.* **Conclusion** key words such as *therefore* and *hence* are usually *not* associated with the author's main point in Reading Comp. Rather, they indicate that the next phrase is a logical consequence of the sentence(s) that came before.

- **Illustration** key words let you know that what follows is an example of a broader point. One example, of course, is *example. For instance* is another favorite in GMAT passages.

- **Sequence/Timing** is a broader category of key words. These are any words that delineate lists or groupings. *First, second,* and *third* are obvious examples. But you could also get a chronological sequence (*17th century, 18th century,* and *today*). Science passages may also group complicated phenomena using simpler sequence key words (*at a high temperature* and *at a low temperature*, for example).

- **Emphasis** and **Opinion** key words can be subtler than those in the other categories, but these are perhaps the most important key words of all. Emphasis key words are used when the author wants to call attention to a specific point. These come in two varieties: generic emphasis key words, such as *very* and *critical,* and charged emphasis key words, such as *beneficial* or *dead end.* Opinion key words point to the ideas in a passage; these opinions are frequently the focus of GMAT questions. Be sure to distinguish between the author's opinions and those of others. Others' opinions are easier to spot and will be triggered by words such as *believe, theory,* or *hypothesis.* The author's opinion is more likely to reveal itself in words that imply a value judgment, such as *valid* or *unsupported.* (If the passage expresses something in the first person, such as *I disagree,* that's also a clear sign.)

As you might have guessed, reading the passage strategically doesn't mean simply going on a scavenger hunt for key words. Rather, it means using those key words to identify the important parts of the passage—its opinions and structure—so you can focus on them and not on little details. Key words also help you predict the function of the text that follows. Let's see how this works by taking a look at a simple example. Say you saw a passage with the following structure on Test Day. What kinds of details can you anticipate would fill each of the blanks?

> Kelley is eagerly awaiting the release of the new season of her favorite show
>
> because _____. Furthermore, _____.
>
> Moreover, _____. However, _____.

You learn about Kelley's attitude toward the upcoming release through the words "eagerly" and "favorite," which are emphasis key words. After "because" (a logic key word) will be a reason that Kelley enjoys the show. After "[f]urthermore" and "[m]oreover" (continuation key words) will be additional reasons or elaborations of the reason in the first sentence. After "[h]owever," you'll read about some drawback or counterexample that undermines the previous string of good things about the show. You can't predict the exact details that fill the blanks, but you can predict the tone and purpose of the details. Reading this way is valuable because the GMAT test makers are more likely to ask you why the author put the details in, not what's true about them.

Reading for key words seems straightforward when the passage deals with subject matter that's familiar or easy to understand. But what if you were to see the following passage about a less familiar topic? How can you decode the structure of the following paragraph?

> Quantum-enabled communication systems—communication systems based on
>
> the principles of quantum mechanics—are theoretically impervious to hacking
>
> because _____. Furthermore, _____.
>
> Moreover, _____. However, _____.

Here, the emphasis key phrase "impervious to hacking" lets you know why the author cares about quantum-enabled communication systems: they're tough to undermine. The details that would fill these blanks are probably dense and intimidating for the non-physicist, but the strategic reader will still be able to understand the passage well enough to answer GMAT questions correctly. Notice that the structure is identical to that of the paragraph about Kelley, so the details that fill the blanks will serve the same purpose as those you predicted previously. You can anticipate what they will be and why the author is including them. Reading strategically allows you to take control of the passage; you will know where the author is going and what the GMAT will consider important, even if you know nothing about the subject matter of the passage.

Look for Opinions, Theories, and Points of View—Especially the Author's

An important part of strategic reading is distinguishing between factual assertions and opinions or interpretations. It's the opinions and interpretations that Reading Comp questions are most often based on, so you should pay the most attention to them. Let's say you come upon a paragraph that reads:

> The coral polyps secrete calcareous exoskeletons, which cement themselves into an
> underlayer of rock, while the algae deposit still more calcium carbonate, which reacts with
> sea salt to create an even tougher limestone layer. All of this accounts for the amazing
> renewability of the coral reefs despite the endless erosion caused by wave activity.

In a sense, this is just like the Burgess Shale paragraph; it begins with a lot of scientific jargon and later tells us why that jargon is there. In this case, it shows us how coral reefs renew themselves. But notice a big difference—the author doesn't tell us how someone else interprets these facts. He could have written "scientists believe that these polyps account for…," but he didn't. This is the author's own interpretation.

It's important to differentiate between the author's own voice and other people's opinions. GMAT authors may disagree with other people but won't contradict themselves. So the author of the Burgess Shale passage might well disagree with Gould in the next paragraph. But the author of the Coral Reef passage has laid his cards on the table—he definitely thinks that coral polyps and algae are responsible for the renewability of coral reefs.

Spotting the opinions and theories also helps you to accomplish the goal of reading for structure. Once you spot an idea, you can step back from the barrage of words and use Critical Thinking to dissect the passage, asking, "Why is the author citing this opinion? Where's the support for this idea? Does the author agree or disagree?"

Consider how you would read the following paragraph strategically:

> Abraham Lincoln is traditionally viewed as an advocate of freedom because he issued the Emancipation Proclamation and championed the Thirteenth Amendment, which ended legal slavery in the United States. And indeed this achievement cannot be denied. But he also set uncomfortable precedents for the curtailing of civil liberties.

A strategic reader will zero in on the passage's key words and analyze what each one reveals about the structure of the passage and the author's point of view. Here, the key word "traditionally" lets you know how people usually think about Lincoln. You might already anticipate that the author is setting up a contrast between the traditional view and her own. Sure enough, the key word "but" makes the contrast clear: the author asserts that despite his other accomplishments, Lincoln in fact restricted civil liberties. And the word "uncomfortable" is an opinion key word indicating that the author is not at all pleased with Lincoln because of it. However, the author already tempered her criticism with the phrase "this achievement cannot be denied," meaning that she won't go so far as to say that Lincoln was an enemy of freedom.

At this point, the strategic reader can anticipate where the passage's structure will lead. Given how this opening paragraph ends, you can predict that the author will spend at least one paragraph describing these "uncomfortable precedents" and how they restricted civil liberties. It might even be possible, since she uses the word "precedents," that she goes on to describe how later governments or leaders used Lincoln's actions as justification for their own restrictions.

This is the power of predictive, strategic reading: by using key words to anticipate where the author is heading, you will not only stay more engaged as you read, but you'll also develop a better understanding of the structure of the passage and the author's point of view—the very things that pay off in a higher GMAT score.

Put together, the passage's structure and the opinions and theories it contains will lead you to understand the author's primary purpose in writing the passage. This is critical, as most GMAT passages have a question that directly asks for that purpose. For the Lincoln passage, you might get a question like this:

> Which of the following best represents the main idea of the passage?
>
> O   The Emancipation Proclamation had both positive and negative effects.
>
> O   Lincoln's presidency laid the groundwork for future restrictions of personal freedoms.
>
> O   The traditional image of Lincoln as a national hero must be overturned.
>
> O   Lincoln used military pressure to influence state legislatures.
>
> O   Abraham Lincoln was an advocate of freedom.

Just from a strategic reading of the first few sentences, you could eliminate **(A)** as being a distortion of the first and third sentences, **(C)** as being too extreme because of the "cannot be denied" phrase, **(D)** as irrelevant—either too narrow or just not present in the passage at all, and **(E)** as missing the author's big point—that Lincoln helped restrict civil liberties. And just like that, you can choose **(B)** as the right answer and increase your score.

Don't Obsess over Details

On the GMAT, you'll need to read only for short-term—as opposed to long-term—retention. When you finish the questions about a certain passage, that passage is over and done with. You're promptly free to forget everything about it.

What's more, there's certainly no need to memorize—or even fully comprehend—details. You *do* need to know why they are there so that you can answer big-picture questions, but you can always go back and reread them in greater depth if you're asked a question that hinges on a detail. And you'll find that if you have a good sense of the passage's scope and structure, the ideas and opinions in the passage, and the author's purpose, then you'll have little problem navigating through the text as the need arises.

Furthermore, you can even hurt your score by reading the details too closely. Here's how:

- **Wasted time.** Remember, there will only be three or four questions per passage. The test makers can't possibly ask you about all the little details. So don't waste your valuable time by focusing on minutiae you will likely not need to know. If you do, you won't have nearly enough time to deal with the questions.

- **Tempting wrong answers.** Attempting to read and understand fully every last detail can cause your mind to jumble all the details—relevant and irrelevant alike—together in a confusing mess. Since most of the wrong answers in GMAT Reading Comp are simply distortions of details from the passage, they will sound familiar and therefore be tempting to uncritical readers. The strategic reader doesn't give those details undue importance and thus isn't tempted by answer choices that focus on them. Instead, he takes advantage of the open-book nature of the test to research specific details only when asked.

- **Losing the big picture.** It's very easy to miss the forest for the trees. If you get too drawn into the small stuff, you can pass right by the emphasis and opinion key words that you'll need to understand the author's main purpose.

Here's a great trick for cutting through confusing, detail-laden sentences: focus on the subjects and verbs first, throwing away modifying phrases, and don't worry about fancy terminology. Let's revisit some dense text from before:

> The coral polyps secrete calcareous exoskeletons, which cement themselves into an underlayer of rock, while the algae deposit still more calcium carbonate, which reacts with sea salt to create an even tougher limestone layer. All of this accounts for the amazing renewability of the coral reefs despite the endless erosion caused by wave activity.

Now look at what happens if you paraphrase these sentences, distilling them to main subjects and verbs, ignoring modifiers, and not worrying about words you don't understand:

> Coral polyps (whatever they are) secrete something . . . and algae deposit something. This accounts for the amazing renewability of the coral reefs.

The structure of this paragraph has suddenly become a lot more transparent. Now the bulkiness of that first sentence won't slow you down, so you can understand its role in the big picture.

> ## TAKEAWAYS: THE BASIC PRINCIPLES OF READING COMPREHENSION
>
> The basic principles of Reading Comprehension are the following:
>
> - Look for the topic and scope of the passage.
> - Get the gist of each paragraph and its structural role in the passage.
> - Look for opinions, theories, and points of view—especially the author's.
> - Don't obsess over details.

Let's now put all these basic principles together to analyze a passage similar to one you may see on Test Day. However, unlike passages you'll see on Test Day, the following text has been formatted to approximate the way a strategic reader might see it—important key words and phrases are in bold, the main ideas are in normal type, and the supporting details are grayed out. Take a moment to read only the bold and regular text: identify what the key words tell you about the structure, paraphrase the crucial text, and practice predicting what the grayed-out portions contain.

The Federal Aviation Administration, commonly known as the FAA, is the government agency tasked with regulating civil aviation in the United States. One of the FAA's **more prominent** functions is to regulate the safety of the airline industry, which it does by creating and enforcing rules that govern the manufacture and operation of

5   commercial aircraft. **However**, the FAA is also charged with a number of other responsibilities, including a mandate to promote civil aviation. Many of the FAA's **critics have argued** that this role is directly incompatible with the agency's primary duty to regulate safety and have called on Congress to redefine the FAA's mission to exclude the duty to promote civil aviation from the agency's list of

10   responsibilities.

The critics' concern is that the safety of the airline industry cannot be adequately regulated by the same agency that is supposed to promote the industry as a whole. **According to the critics**, if a safety issue were to arise, the FAA would have to weigh the potential harm that the airline industry would suffer due to increased regulation

15   against the benefits of remedying the safety concern, which might lead to inaction by the FAA. **For example**, several leading safety advocates have recommended that the FAA prohibit the practice of allowing infants under two years old to fly as "lap children" and instead require a separate seat for all passengers regardless of age. **Because** many parents would opt out of flying if they were required to purchase

20   separate tickets for their young children, the advocates' recommendation would, if adopted, lead to a decline in airline ticket sales. The failure of the FAA to act on this proposal is, **to many critics**, a sign that the agency is more concerned with the potential loss of revenue to the airline industry than the potential loss of a young child's life.

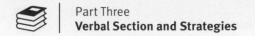

The critics' claim is not entirely without merit, as it is common for the FAA to
25 consider potential financial consequences when contemplating a new regulation.
However, the critics fundamentally misunderstand the role that this cost-benefit
analysis plays in the agency's decision-making process. If the FAA enacts
regulations that make plane tickets prohibitively expensive, people will instead
travel by car, statistically a much more dangerous mode of transportation than flying.
30 **Thus**, when the FAA declines to revise its "lap child" policy, it does so not to
protect the airline industry's revenues but to reduce the risks associated with
travel for children and their parents. **Moreover**, there is a built-in safeguard
to prevent the FAA from protecting revenues at the expense of travelers' safety:
if the FAA failed to act on a significant safety concern, the public would lose
35 confidence in airline travel, causing harm to the industry itself. **Ultimately**, the
FAA's duty to promote commercial aviation serves to reinforce its safety mission
rather than undermine it.

This passage starts with a neutral, factual tone as it describes the major functions of the FAA. The contrast key word "[h]owever" in line 5 offers the first indication of a potential conflict within the FAA's list of responsibilities, and the next sentence offers an opinion related to it: some believe that two of the FAA's missions—regulating safety and promoting civil aviation—are incompatible. Note that the author attributes this viewpoint to the "critics," so you don't yet know whether the author agrees with it. As you continue to read the passage, be on the lookout for key words that indicate the author's opinion.

On Test Day, you would take some brief notes on your notepad about the main idea of the first paragraph before moving on:

¶1: Critics: FAA has incompatible duties of safety and promotion

At the beginning of the next paragraph, the phrase "critics' concern" indicates that the author will now provide further information about the critics' point of view. Since you already know the critics' core position from the first paragraph, you don't need to get too invested in the additional explanation here. Read the second paragraph briskly and jot down a quick note before moving on:

¶2: Explanation of critics' position; example

In the third paragraph, the author finally gives her opinion. While the author says that the critics claim has some "merit," the use "[h]owever" and "fundamentally misunderstand" in the second sentence indicates that the author essentially disagrees with the critics' position. Indeed, the rest of the paragraph explains why the author believes that the FAA's responsibilities are not incompatible. Again, you don't need to worry about the details; just focus on the broad strokes in your notes:

¶3: Author: FAA's duties are not incompatible

Just from this quick analysis, notice how much you already understand about the structure of the passage and the author's point of view. You effectively know what the grayed-out parts of the passage accomplish, even though you can't recite the details they contain. You are now in a strong position to approach the questions that accompany this passage, knowing that you can always return to the passage to clarify your understanding of any relevant details. Let's look at this first question:

Which of the following best describes the author's main idea?

○ The FAA's mandate to promote civil aviation is fundamentally incompatible with its duty to regulate the safety of commercial airline travel.

○ The FAA is the government agency that oversees commercial aviation within the United States.

○ In response to the critics' claim that the FAA has incompatible mandates, Congress should remove the duty to promote civil aviation from the FAA's list of responsibilities.

○ Despite claims to the contrary, the FAA's duty to promote civil aviation is not incompatible with its responsibility to regulate airline safety.

○ The FAA's decision to continue the practice of allowing lap children will ultimately save lives.

This question asks for the author's main idea. Fortunately, you already have information about the author's position in your notes, so there's no need to go back to the passage itself to answer this question. In the third paragraph, the author rebuts the critics' claim and asserts that the FAA's duties are not fundamentally incompatible. (D) matches this prediction and is the correct answer.

If you weren't sure about the answer, you could eliminate incorrect answer choices by finding the specific faults they contain. (A) is the critics' position, not the author's, so it cannot be correct. (B) is incorrect because the author's main idea is not to describe the FAA but to give her opinion about whether or not the FAA has incompatible responsibilities. (C) is incorrect because this is a belief held by some of the critics, not by the author. Finally, while the author would agree with the statement in (E), it is included as an example that supports the author's reasoning, not as the author's main idea.

Let's look at one more question about this passage:

The author refers to the "cost-benefit analysis" (see lines 26–27) undertaken by the FAA most likely in order to

○ summarize the primary responsibilities of the FAA

○ explain the rationale that underpins a policy decision made by the FAA

○ question the ability of the FAA to balance two competing obligations

○ criticize a policy decision made by the FAA

○ defend the FAA's ability to successfully manage its list of responsibilities

This question asks why the author discusses the FAA's "cost-benefit analysis," and the line reference places this quoted text in the third paragraph. Once again, this question does not require any additional research beyond the notes you've already taken. According to your notes, the third paragraph introduces and explains the author's position, which is that the FAA's duties are not incompatible. Because this is a defense of the FAA against the critics who claim that the agency is incapable of managing its competing responsibilities, (E) is the correct answer.

(A) is incorrect because the author's summary of the FAA's responsibilities is in the first paragraph, not the third. (B) is incorrect because the author's primary concern in the third paragraph is to defend the FAA, not merely to explain a lone policy decision. While the author offers a justification for the FAA's position on lap children, she does so in order to support her broader point, which is that the agency is able to balance its responsibilities. (C) and (D) are incorrect because the author does not "question" or "criticize" the FAA in the third paragraph. Those characterizations are more closely aligned with the critics, whose opinions are discussed in the first and second paragraphs.

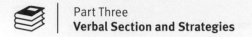

The Kaplan Method for Reading Comprehension

> **LEARNING OBJECTIVES**
>
> In this section, you will learn how to:
>
> - List the steps of the Kaplan Method for Reading Comprehension
> - Explain the purpose of each step in the Reading Comprehension method
> - Perform the steps of the method on a Reading Comprehension passage and its questions

Many test takers read the entire passage closely from beginning to end, taking detailed notes and making sure that they understand everything, and then try to answer the questions from memory. But this is *not* what the best test takers do.

The best test takers attack the passages and questions critically in the sort of aggressive, energetic, and goal-oriented way you've learned earlier. Working this way pays off because it's the kind of pragmatic and efficient approach that the GMAT rewards—the same type of approach that business schools like their students to take when faced with an intellectual challenge.

To help this strategic approach become second nature to you, Kaplan has developed a Method that you can use to attack each and every Reading Comp passage and question.

> **THE KAPLAN METHOD FOR READING COMPREHENSION**
>
> 1. Read the passage strategically.
> 2. Analyze the question stem.
> 3. Research the relevant text.
> 4. Make a prediction.
> 5. Evaluate the answer choices.

STEP 1: READ THE PASSAGE STRATEGICALLY

Like most sophisticated writing, the prose you will see on the GMAT doesn't explicitly reveal its secrets. Baldly laying out the *why* and *how* of a passage up front isn't a hallmark of GMAT Reading Comprehension passages. And even more important (as far as the test makers are concerned), if the ideas were blatantly laid out, the test makers couldn't ask probing questions about them. So to set up the questions—to test how you think about the prose you read—the GMAT uses passages in which authors hide or disguise their reasons for writing and challenge you to extract them.

This is why it's essential to start by reading the passage strategically, staying on the lookout for structural key words and phrases. With this strategic analysis as a guide, you should construct a passage map—a brief summary of each paragraph and its function in the passage's structure. You should also note the author's topic, scope, and purpose. Start by identifying the topic and then hunt for scope, trying to get a sense of where the passage is going, what the author is going to focus on, and what role the first paragraph is playing. As you finish reading each paragraph, jot down a short note about its structure and the role it plays in the passage. This process is similar to how you took notes on each paragraph of the National Park Service passage. When you finish reading the passage, double-check that you got the topic and scope right (sometimes passages can take unexpected turns) and note the author's overall purpose.

The topic will be the first big, broad idea that comes along. Almost always, it will be right there in the first sentence. There's no need to obsess over exactly how you word the topic; you just want a general idea of what the author is writing about so the passage gets easier to understand.

The scope is the narrow part of the topic that the author focuses on. If the author expresses his own opinion, then the thing he has an opinion about is the scope. Your statement of the scope should be as narrow as possible while still reflecting the passage as a whole. Your scope statement should also answer the question "What about this topic interests the author?" Identifying the scope is crucial because many wrong answers are unsupported by the facts the author has actually chosen to provide. Remember that even though the first paragraph usually narrows the topic down to the scope, there probably won't be a "topic sentence" in the traditional sense.

The purpose is what the author is seeking to accomplish by writing the passage. You'll serve yourself well by picking an active verb for the purpose. Doing so helps not only by setting you up to find the right answer—many answer choices contain active verbs—but also by forcing you to consider the author's opinion. Here are some verbs that describe the purpose of a neutral author: *describe, explain, compare*. Here are some verbs for an opinionated author: *advocate, argue, rebut, analyze*.

After you finish reading, your passage map should look something like this example:

¶1: Critics: FAA has incompatible duties of safety and promotion

¶2: Explanation of critics' position; example

¶3: Author: FAA's duties are not incompatible

Topic: Federal Aviation Administration's responsibilities

Scope: Tension between ensuring safety & promoting industry

Purpose: To argue that these responsibilities are not in conflict

You don't want to take any more than 4 minutes to read and write your passage map. After all, you get points for answering questions, not for creating nicely detailed passage maps. The more time you can spend working on the questions, the better your score will be. But creating a passage map and identifying the topic, scope, and purpose will prepare you to handle those questions efficiently and accurately.

It generally works best to create your passage map paragraph by paragraph. Don't write while you're reading, since you'll be tempted to write too much. But it's also not a good idea to wait until you've read the whole passage before writing anything, since it will be more difficult for you to recall what you've read. Analyze the structure as you read and take a few moments after you finish each paragraph to summarize the main points. Include details that are provided as evidence only when key words indicate their importance. A line or two of paraphrase is generally enough to summarize a paragraph.

Your passage map can be as elaborate or as brief as you need it to be. Don't waste time trying to write out entire sentences if fragments and abbreviations will do. And notice in the above example how effective arrows can be. For example, there's no sense writing out the purpose as "Describe two solutions to the National Park Service's dilemma resulting from the dual imperative to keep lands unimpaired and also to allow for their recreational use," when some simple notes with arrows are just as helpful to you.

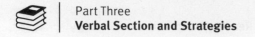

STEP 2: ANALYZE THE QUESTION STEM

Only once you have read the passage strategically and jotted down your passage map should you read the first question stem. The second step of the Kaplan Method is to identify the question type; the most common question types are Global, Detail, Inference, and Logic. We will cover each of these question types in detail in the next chapter. For now, know that you will use this step to ask yourself, "What should I do on this question? What is being asked?" Here are some guidelines for identifying each of the main question types:

- **Global.** These question stems contain language that refers to the passage as a whole, such as "primary purpose," "main idea," or "appropriate title for the passage."

- **Detail.** These question stems contain direct language such as "according to the author," "the passage states explicitly," or "is mentioned in the passage."

- **Inference.** These question stems contain indirect language such as "most likely agree," "suggests," or "implies."

- **Logic.** These question stems ask for the purpose of a detail or paragraph and contain language such as "in order to," "purpose of the second paragraph," or "for which of the following reasons."

In addition to identifying the question type, be sure to focus on *exactly* what the question is asking. Let's say you see this question:

> The passage states which of the following about the uses of fixed nitrogen?

Don't look for what the passage says about "nitrogen" in general. Don't even look for "fixed nitrogen" alone. Look for the *uses* of fixed nitrogen. (And be aware that the GMAT may ask you to recognize that *application* is a synonym of *use*.)

Finally, the GMAT occasionally asks questions that do not fall into one of the four major categories. These outliers make up only about 8 percent of GMAT Reading Comp questions, so you will probably see only one such question or maybe none at all. If you do see one, don't worry. These rare question types usually involve paraphrasing or analyzing specific points of reasoning in the passage. Often, they are extremely similar to question types you know from GMAT Critical Reasoning. Because you can use your passage map to understand the passage's structure and Kaplan's strategies for Critical Reasoning to deconstruct the author's reasoning, you will be prepared to handle even these rare question types.

STEP 3: RESEARCH THE RELEVANT TEXT

Since there just isn't enough time to memorize the whole passage, you shouldn't rely on your memory to answer questions. Treat the GMAT like an open-book test, knowing you can return to the passage as needed. However, don't let that fact make you overreliant on research in the passage. Doing so could lead to lots of rereading and wasted time. For some question types, you are just as likely to find all the information you need to answer the question correctly using only your passage map. Here is how you should focus your research for each question type:

- **Global.** The answer will deal with the passage as a whole, so you should review your passage map and the topic, scope, and purpose you noted.

- **Detail.** Use the specific reference in the question stem to research the text. Look for the detail to be associated with a key word.

- **Inference.** For questions that include specific references, research the passage based on the clues in the question stem. For open-ended questions, refer to your topic, scope, and purpose; you may need to research in the passage as you evaluate each answer choice.
- **Logic.** Use the specific reference in the question stem to research the text. Use key words to understand the passage's structure. Refer to your passage map for the purpose of a specific paragraph.

STEP 4: MAKE A PREDICTION

As you have seen in the Critical Reasoning chapter of this book, predicting the answer before you look at the answer choices is a powerful strategy to increase your efficiency and accuracy. The same is true for GMAT Reading Comp. Making a prediction allows you to know what you're looking for before you consider the answer choices. Doing so will help the right answer jump off the screen at you. It will also help you avoid wrong answer choices that might otherwise be tempting. Here is how you should form your prediction for each question type:

- **Global.** Use your passage map and topic, scope, and purpose as the basis of your prediction.
- **Detail.** Predict an answer based on what the context tells you about the detail.
- **Inference.** Remember that the right answer *must* be true based on the passage. (Since many valid inferences could be drawn from even one detail, it's often best not to make your prediction more specific than that.)
- **Logic.** Predict an answer that focuses on *why* the paragraph or detail was used, not on *what* it says.

STEP 5: EVALUATE THE ANSWER CHOICES

Hunt for the answer choice that matches your prediction. If only one choice matches, it's the right answer.

If you can't find a match for your prediction, if more than one choice seems to fit your prediction, or if you weren't able to form a prediction at all (this happens for some open-ended Inference questions), then you'll need to evaluate each answer choice, looking for errors. If you can prove four answers wrong, then you can confidently select the one that remains, even if you aren't completely sure what you think about it. This is the beauty of a multiple-choice test—knowing how to eliminate the four wrong answers is as good as knowing how to identify the correct one.

Here are some common wrong answer traps to look out for:

- **Global.** Answers that misrepresent the scope or purpose of the passage and answers that focus too heavily on details from one part of the passage
- **Detail.** Answers that distort the context or focus on the wrong details entirely
- **Inference.** Answers that include extreme language or exaggerations of the author's statements, distortions of the passage's meaning, or the exact opposite of what might be inferred
- **Logic.** Answers that get the specifics right but the purpose wrong

Look out for unsupported answer choices and for "half-right/half-wrong" choices, which are fine at the beginning but then take a wrong turn. Some answer choices are very tempting because they have the correct details and the right scope, but they have a *not*, *doesn't*, or other twist that flips their meanings to the opposite of what the question asks for. Watch out for these 180s.

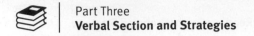

Applying the Kaplan Method for Reading Comprehension

Now try to apply the Kaplan Method to an actual GMAT-length passage and a couple of its questions. One of the following questions is the same one you saw at the beginning of the chapter. Read the passage strategically and practice making a passage map. Then compare your map to the one below the passage. Did you capture the gist of the text in your notes? Next, try your hand at the questions. For now, don't worry if you're not quite sure how to identify the question types; we will cover those thoroughly in the next chapter. Concentrate on analyzing what the question asks of you and using the Kaplan Method to take the most efficient path from question to correct answer. Ask yourself whether your reading of the passage prepared you well to research the answers to the questions. Compare your step-by-step approach to that of a GMAT expert in the explanations that follow each question.

Questions 1–2 are based on the following passage.

Many historians consider the Marshall Plan one of the United States' major foreign policy successes of the last century. Behrman argues that the financial support provided by the United States was largely responsible for the recovery of the participating European economies after the Second World War. He credits the "multiplier effect" with generating
5   four to six additional dollars of European production for each Marshall Plan dollar distributed. Farmers, shopkeepers, and manufacturers would purchase equipment and materials through their national banks, which would then submit a request for Marshall Plan funds. Upon approval, the U.S. supplier would be paid from the Marshall Plan, and the national bank would retain the local currency, which could be used for infrastructure
10   repair and other national recovery efforts.

However, other scholars are more critical. Although Ferguson concedes Behrman's economic analysis, he disputes Behrman's claim that the Marshall Plan was crucial to Europe's recovery by outlining the many other programs and policies that were already in place. Ferguson identifies the political impact of the Marshall Plan as the most significant
15   result; the citizens of Western Europe saw the United States as assisting them through the difficult process of economic restoration and strengthened their connections with their transatlantic ally. LaFeber and other revisionist historians are even more critical, describing the Marshall Plan as economic imperialism, a way to bind Western Europe's economy to that of the United States and to assist the recovery of U.S. industry, which had to return
20   to producing domestic needs after several years of manufacturing armaments and military supplies, rather than as a mechanism for the restoration of the Western European national economies.

STEP 1: READ THE PASSAGE STRATEGICALLY

Here's an example of how the passage should be analyzed. The passage is presented as seen through the lens of strategic reading. On the left is the text as you might read it, with key words and important points in bold. On the right is what you might be thinking as you read.

PASSAGE	ANALYSIS
Many historians consider the Marshall Plan one of the United States' **major** foreign policy successes of the last century.	Here's an opinion (and opinions are heavily tested). The prevailing view is that the Marshall Plan was a success. When an opinion is presented as being held by "many" people, expect that another point of view is coming up.
Behrman argues that the financial support provided by the United States was **largely** responsible for the recovery of the participating European economies after the Second World War. He **credits** the "multiplier effect" with generating four to six additional dollars of European production for each Marshall Plan dollar distributed. Farmers, shopkeepers, and manufacturers would purchase equipment and materials through their national banks, which would then submit a request for Marshall Plan funds. Upon approval, the U.S. supplier would be paid from the Marshall Plan, and the national bank would retain the local currency, which could be used for infrastructure repair and other national recovery efforts.	Behrman is one of the "many historians" who are in favor of the Marshall Plan. His evidence that the plan was a success is detailed here. Behrman thinks that the economic "multiplier effect" was important. Read the details quickly, note the location, and come back and read carefully only if needed for a question.
However, other scholars are more critical. **Although Ferguson concedes Behrman's** economic analysis, he **disputes** Behrman's claim that the Marshall Plan was crucial to Europe's recovery by outlining the many other programs and policies that were already in place. **Ferguson identifies** the political impact of the Marshall Plan as the **most significant** result; the citizens of Western Europe saw the United States as assisting them through the difficult process of economic restoration and strengthened their connections with their transatlantic ally. **LaFeber** and other revisionist historians are **even more critical**, describing the Marshall Plan as economic imperialism, a way to bind Western Europe's economy to that of the United States and to assist the recovery of U.S. industry, which had to return to producing domestic needs after several years of manufacturing armaments and military supplies, **rather than** as a mechanism for the restoration of the Western European national economies.	Here's the other opinion, as expected. "Other scholars" disagree. Ferguson is one of these "others." Ferguson thinks Behrman has the economics right, but he disagrees with Behrman's conclusion. Ferguson says that the political effect is most important. Ferguson's explanation; again, there's no need to grasp the details now. Wait until you need them for a question. LaFeber, another of these "other" historians, is "even more critical." Note the gist of his reasoning (the plan was intended to benefit the U.S., not Europe). Note that the author never expresses an opinion as to which historian's analysis is most likely to be correct.

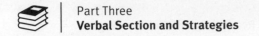
Your passage map would look something like this:

> ¶1: Many hists think MP success, e.g., B: economic "mult effect"
>
> ¶2: F: B econ is right, but MP not crucial, good relations most imp. LaF: MP for US, not Eur
>
> Topic: Marshall Plan
>
> Scope: Historians' views of success of MP
>
> Purpose: Describe three historians' views

This isn't the only way to word the passage map, of course. Anything along these lines would work—so long as you note that there are three opinions and that the author doesn't prefer one over the others. After analyzing the passage, you are well prepared to apply steps 2–5 to the questions.

1. The passage suggests that Ferguson would be most likely to agree with which of the following claims about the "multiplier effect" (line 4)?

   O It was unlikely to have generated the returns for the European national economies that Behrman claims.

   O It may have been helpful to the European national economies, but it was not the most important outcome of the Marshall Plan.

   O It was the most controversial aspect of the Marshall Plan, generating intense resistance from those countries that chose not to participate.

   O It was a crucial part of the Marshall Plan, being substantially responsible for the recovery of participating Western European economies.

   O It was designed primarily to assist the recovery of industry in the United States, despite its benefits to Western European national economies.

STEP 2: ANALYZE THE QUESTION STEM

The key word "suggests" identifies this as an Inference question. The correct answer will be fully supported by information in the passage about Ferguson's point of view on the "multiplier effect."

STEP 3: RESEARCH THE RELEVANT TEXT

The additional context clue "multiplier effect" and the line number in the question direct your research to the first paragraph. The first words of the sentence in line 2 identify the description of the "multiplier effect" that follows as that of Behrman, not Ferguson. Skim this section to refresh your memory of the "multiplier effect." The passage map locates Ferguson's opinion in the beginning of the second paragraph, so reread that section as well, specifically looking for Ferguson's view of Behrman's discussion of the "multiplier effect."

STEP 4: MAKE A PREDICTION

Behrman describes the "multiplier effect" as the mechanism by which each dollar of distributed Marshall Plan funds resulted in an additional four to six dollars made available for use by the European national banks. Lines 11–12 state "Ferguson concedes Behrman's economic analysis," but Ferguson goes on to dispute Behrman's conclusion. Predict that the correct answer will include "the multiplier effect is valid," "Behrman's conclusion is incorrect," or both. Notice that, once you clearly understand the relationship of the two historians' views, a detailed understanding of the mechanism of the "multiplier effect" is unnecessary.

STEP 5: EVALUATE THE ANSWER CHOICES

(B) matches both concepts in the prediction and is correct. (A) is a distortion of Ferguson's view. Ferguson agrees with Behrman's economic analysis, but not Behrman's assessment of the impact of the "multiplier effect." (C) is not mentioned in the passage and is incorrect. Be careful if you happen to know that some nonparticipating countries were hostile to the Marshall Plan; the text only discusses the United States and the participating Western European countries. (D) and (E) are misused details from the passage that answer the wrong question. (D) is Behrman's view, and (E) is LaFeber's view; neither is Ferguson's.

2. Which of the following statements best describes the function of the last sentence in the passage?

   ○ It provides evidence that might undermine the viewpoint of the historians mentioned in the first sentence.

   ○ It resolves the conflict over the efficacy of the Marshall Plan introduced in the first paragraph.

   ○ It clarifies some of the reasons the Marshall Plan is generally considered to have been a success.

   ○ It qualifies a claim made earlier in the passage about return earned on each dollar spent by the Marshall Plan.

   ○ It supports a claim made earlier in the passage about the importance of the Marshall Plan to the economic recovery of Western Europe.

STEP 2: ANALYZE THE QUESTION STEM

The phrase "best describes the function . . . " identifies this as a Logic question. The correct answer to a Logic question will explain how or why the author uses a feature of the passage, not the content of the feature. The context clue "last sentence in the passage" identifies the feature.

STEP 3: RESEARCH THE RELEVANT TEXT

Always begin the research for a Logic question with the purpose of the passage; then predict the relationship of the specified feature to the author's purpose. From the passage map, the author's purpose is to "describe three historians' views" of the Marshall Plan. The final sentence is one of those views, that of LaFeber, who is described as critical of the motives of the United States in offering the Marshall Plan; he believes the Marshall Plan was primarily intended to bind the U.S. and European economies and to revitalize industry in the United States. Consult the passage map to refresh your memory of the opinions of the other two historians: "Many historians" think it was very good; Behrman is firmly in the "Marshall Plan was a success" camp; and Ferguson is somewhere in the middle.

STEP 4: MAKE A PREDICTION

A good prediction would be *to describe a historian's view that is critical of the Marshall Plan.*

STEP 5: EVALUATE THE ANSWER CHOICES

(A) matches the prediction and is correct. The "many" historians in the first sentence believe the Marshall Plan was a major foreign policy success. LaFeber's view undermines this idea by pointing out the possibility that the intended benefit of the Marshall Plan devolved to the United States, not Europe. (B) is not discussed in the passage and is incorrect. The author simply presents the differing views of the historians and does not "resolve" them. (C) and (E) are 180, or opposite, choices. In the last sentence, LaFeber is challenging, not supporting, the idea that the Marshall Plan was a foreign-policy success. (D) is a misused detail from the text. The passage discusses the "multiplier effect" that impacted the return on the dollars spent on the Marshall Plan, but LaFeber's view on the "multiplier effect" is not mentioned.

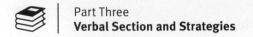

Practice Set: The Kaplan Method for Reading Comprehension

Questions 1–4 are based on the following passage.

Bog bodies, most of them dating from between 500 BCE and 100 CE, have been found across northwestern Europe. They are remarkably well preserved in many cases, sometimes down to wrinkles and scars on their leathery, reddish-brown skin. They have not been kept intact in the same way as Egyptian mummies, deliberately embalmed
5 through painstaking human technique, but have likely been perpetuated by an accident that archaeologists who study the Iron Age might call a happy one.

The wetlands in which the bodies are found are exclusively sphagnum moss bogs. These exist in temperate climes where the winter and early spring weather is cold, leaving the water in the bogs below 40°F during those months, and the bogs are all near sources of
10 salt water. Together these elements create the perfect environment for the preservation of skin and internal organs.

The biochemistry of preservation in bogs has several components. Both the cold temperatures and dense peat from the moss, which constitutes a mostly anaerobic environment, prevent significant bacterial growth in the water. As layers of moss die and
15 deteriorate in the water, they create humic acid, also known as bog acid; the acidic environment further inhibits bacteria. Interestingly, this acid often erodes the bones of bog bodies, leaving only the skin and organs, in a process quite the opposite of that which acts upon bodies outside of bogs. The dead layers of moss also release sphagnan, a carbohydrate that attaches itself to the skin of the bodies, preventing rot and
20 water damage.

Besides bodies, bogs have also preserved books, boats, and even bread and "bog butter"—waxy dairy- or meat-based substances sometimes found stored in barrels in the bogs, which likely served as the equivalent of Iron Age refrigerators, preserving food just as they preserve human skin. Much can be learned about our ancestors from the Iron
25 Age and even earlier due to the unique ability of sphagnum moss bogs to preserve so thoroughly that which has fallen into them: scholars have studied such diverse features of early human life as medical conditions like arthritis and parasitic infection, diet, and how far from home people traveled. The bogs offer a fascinating window into the past.

1. According to the passage, all of the following conditions are conducive to the preservation of bog bodies EXCEPT

    O   long winters

    O   low air temperatures

    O   proximity to salt water

    O   cool water

    O   sphagnum moss

2. The primary purpose of the passage is to

   O   explain the ways in which bog bodies are different from other preserved bodies, such as mummies

   O   challenge the position that the preservation of bodies in bogs is probably the result of intentional effort

   O   discuss the characteristics of sphagnum moss bogs that allow bodies to be found in a condition that permits unique study

   O   argue that scholars would not understand significant aspects of human life during the Iron Age had bog bodies not been discovered

   O   analyze the differences between sphagnum moss bogs and the types of environments in which bodies decay

3. In the context of the passage as a whole, the third paragraph serves primarily to

   O   evaluate the relative importance of the elements discussed in the second paragraph

   O   provide support for an argument presented in the fourth paragraph about the significance of the subject of the passage

   O   outline the creation of the environment that produces the effect that is the topic of the passage

   O   elaborate on the mechanisms underlying an effect achieved by elements introduced in the second paragraph

   O   explain the prominence of a particular academic discipline in the study of the topic of the passage

4. According to the passage, bacterial growth is inhibited by all of the following EXCEPT

   O   an anaerobic environment

   O   the presence of sphagnum moss

   O   breakdown of layers of dead moss

   O   cold water temperature

   O   release of sphagnan from dead moss

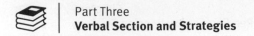
Questions 5–8 are based on the following passage.

Women around the world graduate from college at higher rates than men. However, women's participation in the workforce, especially in the ranks of senior management, continues to lag far behind that of men. Research indicates that, as women marry and start families, their earnings and opportunities for promotion decrease. While the difficulties

5 that women encounter as they attempt to balance work and family life are frequently discussed, and are beginning to be addressed by employers, it is interesting to note that the difficulties faced by working married men are seldom raised.

Scott Coltrane, a researcher at the University of Oregon, has found that, while the earnings of women tend to go down with each additional child, the earnings of

10 married men not only exceed those of both unmarried men and divorced men but also tend to go up with each additional child. One reason for this disparity may be that, as the size of the family grows, men rely on women to manage most of the responsibilities of housekeeping and child raising. While within the past few decades men have assumed a greater share of household responsibilities, in

15 the United States, women still spend nearly twice as much time as men do in caring for children and the home. The time diaries of highly educated dual-income U.S. couples show that men enjoy three and a half times the leisure time as their female partners do.

If married men earn higher salaries and have more leisure time than their female

20 counterparts do, what difficulties do these working men face? Research indicates three possible problems. First, the perceived responsibility of providing for a family drives men to work more hours and strive for promotion. Many men report feeling dissatisfied because the level of performance that is required to earn promotions and higher salaries prevents them from spending time with their families. Second, these demands on men also

25 contribute to higher levels of marital discord. In a 2008 survey, 60 percent of U.S. fathers reported work-family conflicts, compared to 47 percent of mothers.

The pressure to be perceived as a good provider contributes to the third reason that married men may struggle. While women's decisions to use family leave benefits, move to part-time employment, or leave the workforce to care for children are seen as valuable

30 contributions to family life and, by extension, society, men's decisions to do the same are frequently viewed by their employers as signs of weakness. Studies suggest that men who take advantage of paternity leave policies are viewed as weak or inadequate by both women and men. Research conducted in Australia found that men's requests to work flexibly were denied at twice the rate of those of women.

5. The author of the passage is primarily concerned with

    O   advocating changes in employers' practices regarding female employees with children

    O   examining some of the reasons that married men may experience problems related to their employment

    O   describing the psychological consequences for men of earning high salaries

    O   taking issue with those who believe that women should not earn more than men

    O   analyzing the indirect effects of discrimination against women on married men

6. The passage provides information in support of which of the following assertions about married men who work?

    O   The ability to provide for their families is the most important aspect of employment for married men.

    O   Married men in high-status positions are easily able to integrate their careers and family lives.

    O   Married men who achieve greater earnings while having a larger family are more satisfied on average than their wives.

    O   The perceived demands on men to earn enough income to support a family may have harmful effects on family life.

    O   As married men achieve higher earnings, they are able to take more time off from work to spend with their families.

7. The author of the passage discusses Coltrane's research primarily in order to

    O   illustrate the benefits that employers extend to their married male employees

    O   identify a benefit of work that married men experience that is accompanied by some potential costs

    O   defend the family leave policies and flexible work schedules that some employers offer

    O   modify the prevailing view that women experience disadvantages in the workplace after marrying and having children

    O   point out several ways in which women experience discrimination in the workplace

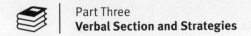
8. According to the passage, married men generally receive higher salaries and have a better chance of being promoted than do single men because

    ○ employers consider married men to be more diligent and responsible than single men

    ○ married men have usually accrued more experience than have single men

    ○ married men may be able to rely on their spouses to address child care and household responsibilities

    ○ higher pay typically corresponds with greater job security and enhanced benefits

    ○ employers recognize the difficulties of providing for a larger number of children and seek to ease this burden

Answers and explanations follow on the next page. ▶ ▶ ▶

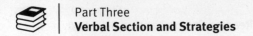

Answer Key

Practice Set: The Kaplan Method for Reading Comprehension

Bog Bodies

1. A
2. C
3. D
4. E

Working Married Men

5. B
6. D
7. B
8. C

Answers and Explanations

Practice Set: The Kaplan Method for Reading Comprehension

Bog Bodies

STEP 1: READ THE PASSAGE STRATEGICALLY

On the left, we've shown how key words help to identify the major elements of the passage and its structure and what you could skim over. On the right, we've shown what you might be thinking as you read the passage strategically.

Passage for Questions 1–4

PASSAGE	ANALYSIS
Bog bodies, most of them dating from between 500 BCE and 100 CE, have been found across northwestern Europe. They are **remarkably** well preserved in many cases, sometimes down to wrinkles and scars on their leathery, reddish-brown skin. They have **not** been kept intact in the same way as Egyptian mummies, deliberately embalmed through painstaking human technique, **but** have likely been perpetuated by an accident that archaeologists who study the Iron Age might call a happy one.	This introduces the topic of the passage: bog bodies are preserved, probably accidentally.
The wetlands in which the bodies are found are **exclusively** sphagnum moss bogs. These exist in temperate climes where the winter and early spring weather is cold, leaving the water in the bogs below 40°F during those months, and the bogs are all near sources of salt water. **Together** these elements create the **perfect environment** for the preservation of skin and internal organs.	This paragraph provides details on the conditions that promote preservation in the bogs where bodies are found.
The biochemistry of preservation in bogs has **several components**. Both the cold temperatures and dense peat from the moss, which constitutes a mostly anaerobic environment, prevent significant bacterial growth in the water. As layers of moss die and deteriorate in the water, they create humic acid, also known as bog acid; the acidic environment **further** inhibits bacteria. **Interestingly**, this acid often erodes the bones of bog bodies, leaving only the skin and organs, in a process quite the opposite of that which acts upon bodies outside of bogs. The dead layers of moss **also** release sphagnan, a carbohydrate that attaches itself to the skin of the bodies, preventing rot and water damage.	Here, you'll find scientific details on how chemical processes in the bog interact with bodies to preserve them. Skim them for now and come back to read in depth if needed for a question.

Besides bodies, bogs have **also** preserved books, boats, and even bread and "bog butter"—waxy dairy- or meat-based substances sometimes found stored in barrels in the bogs, which likely served as the equivalent of Iron Age refrigerators, preserving food just as they preserve human skin. **Much can be learned** about our ancestors from the Iron Age and even earlier due to the unique ability of sphagnum moss bogs to preserve so thoroughly that which has fallen into them: scholars have studied such diverse features of early human life as medical conditions like arthritis and parasitic infection, diet, and how far from home people traveled. The bogs offer a fascinating window into the past.

This paragraph describes the scholarly value of bog bodies and artifacts.

Passage Map

Here is an example of the notes that you might have made as you read:

¶1: Bog bodies = accidentally preserved?

¶2: Conditions of bogs

¶3: Biochemistry that allows preservation

¶4: Other things preserved; value for learning

Topic: Bog bodies

Scope: How sphagnum moss bogs preserve ⎯⎯⎯↑

Purpose: Describe and explain ⎯⎯⎯↑

1. **(A)**

   According to the passage, all of the following conditions are conducive to the preservation of bog bodies EXCEPT

   - ◯ long winters
   - ◯ low air temperatures
   - ◯ proximity to salt water
   - ◯ cool water
   - ◯ sphagnum moss

STEP 2: ANALYZE THE QUESTION STEM

The phrase "[a]ccording to the passage" indicates that this is a Detail question, but "EXCEPT" means that the four incorrect choices will be supported by the passage, while the right answer will not be.

STEP 3: RESEARCH THE RELEVANT TEXT

The necessary conditions for preserving bodies are discussed in the second paragraph: sphagnum moss, cold temperatures that lead to cool water, and nearby salt water "[t]ogether ... create the perfect environment."

STEP 4: MAKE A PREDICTION

You can't predict something that's not in the passage, but you can expect that the details you found in your research will show up in the incorrect answer choices.

STEP 5: EVALUATE THE ANSWER CHOICES

While a cold winter and early spring are important for preservation, the passage does not say the length of this season is a factor, so **(A)** is correct. The other choices are the factors that promote the preservation of bodies that you found in your research.

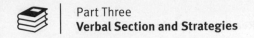

2.   **(C)**

The primary purpose of the passage is to

○   explain the ways in which bog bodies are different from other preserved bodies, such as mummies

○   challenge the position that the preservation of bodies in bogs is probably the result of intentional effort

○   discuss the characteristics of sphagnum moss bogs that allow bodies to be found in a condition that permits unique study

○   argue that scholars would not understand significant aspects of human life during the Iron Age had bog bodies not been discovered

○   analyze the differences between sphagnum moss bogs and the types of environments in which bodies decay

STEP 2: ANALYZE THE QUESTION STEM

This question asks for the primary purpose of the passage, so it's a Global question.

STEP 3: RESEARCH THE RELEVANT TEXT

Use the author's purpose in the passage map, rather than reviewing the passage itself, to predict the correct answer.

STEP 4: MAKE A PREDICTION

According to the passage map, the author's purpose was to explain how bog bodies are preserved in sphagnum moss. Look for an answer choice that encapsulates this idea.

STEP 5: EVALUATE THE ANSWER CHOICES

(C) is a neat summation of the purpose and is correct. While the author mentions at the beginning of the passage a presumed difference between bog bodies and mummies, contrasting bog bodies with other remains isn't the purpose of the passage, eliminating **(A)**. Similarly, while the author mentions that bog bodies were probably preserved by accident, the author never implies that anyone thinks any differently, let alone mounts an argument for the idea; **(B)** can be eliminated. **(D)** reflects only a few details from the last paragraph of the passage and not the passage as a whole. Moreover, while the passage says that bog bodies have helped scholars understand the lives of Iron Age humans, it does not go so far as to claim that this information would be unknown if not for the bog bodies. The passage explains what is distinct about sphagnum moss bogs but never discusses other environments, so analyzing differences between them, as in **(E)**, cannot be the primary purpose.

3.   **(D)**

In the context of the passage as a whole, the third paragraph serves primarily to

○   evaluate the relative importance of the elements discussed in the second paragraph

○   provide support for an argument presented in the fourth paragraph about the significance of the subject of the passage

○   outline the creation of the environment that produces the effect that is the topic of the passage

○   elaborate on the mechanisms underlying an effect achieved by elements introduced in the second paragraph

○   explain the prominence of a particular academic discipline in the study of the topic of the passage

STEP 2: ANALYZE THE QUESTION STEM

The question asks for the purpose of the third paragraph, so this is a Logic question.

STEP 3: RESEARCH THE RELEVANT TEXT

According to the passage map, the third paragraph discusses the biochemistry of the bogs that are involved in preservation. Research of the paragraph itself shows that it describes the ways in which the moss and cold water, first mentioned in the preceding paragraph, produce the relatively inert environment of the bog.

STEP 4: MAKE A PREDICTION

The right answer will be about how the bogs work to preserve the bodies found within them.

STEP 5: EVALUATE THE ANSWER CHOICES

(D), though phrased in more abstract language, matches this prediction and is correct. The author doesn't indicate that some factors are more important than others, so **(A)** is out. The author does say in the last paragraph that bog bodies are important, but the third paragraph does not provide support for this assertion; eliminate **(B)**. In **(C)**, "the environment… that produces the effect that is the topic" is the bog, but this paragraph describes how the bog works on bodies, not how the bog is formed. **(E)** distorts the author's use of "biochemistry"; while a grasp of biochemistry is undoubtedly helpful to understand how sphagnum moss bogs preserve bodies, the role of this paragraph is not to explain the importance of biochemistry but to explain how certain bogs preserve bodies.

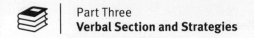

4. **(E)**

According to the passage, bacterial growth is inhibited by all of the following EXCEPT

- ○ an anaerobic environment
- ○ the presence of sphagnum moss
- ○ breakdown of layers of dead moss
- ○ cold water temperature
- ○ release of sphagnan from dead moss

STEP 2: ANALYZE THE QUESTION STEM

This is a Detail EXCEPT question.

STEP 3: RESEARCH THE RELEVANT TEXT

"[B]acterial growth" is mentioned in the third paragraph, so research this part of the text. Cold temperatures, the creation by the dense sphagnum moss of "a mostly anaerobic environment," and the release of humic or "bog" acid by the deterioration of dead layers of moss all inhibit bacterial growth.

STEP 4: MAKE A PREDICTION

Since this is an EXCEPT question, use your research as a guide to eliminate any choices that are supported.

STEP 5: EVALUATE THE ANSWER CHOICES

(E) is mentioned in the passage. However, sphagnan prevents "rot and water damage" by binding to the skin. The text does not say it acts against bacteria. This is the correct answer. **(A)**, **(B)**, **(C)**, and **(D)** all match relevant details in the passage and can be eliminated.

Working Married Men

STEP 1: READ THE PASSAGE STRATEGICALLY

On the left, we've shown how key words help to identify the major elements of the passage and its structure and what you could skim over. On the right, we've shown what you might be thinking as you read the passage strategically.

Passage for Questions 5–8

PASSAGE	ANALYSIS
Women around the world graduate from college at higher rates than men. **However**, women's participation in the workforce, especially in the ranks of senior management, continues to lag far behind that of men. **Research indicates** that, as women marry and start families, their earnings and opportunities for promotion decrease. **While** the difficulties that women encounter as they attempt to balance work and family life are frequently discussed, and are beginning to be addressed by employers, **it is interesting to note** that the difficulties faced by working married men are seldom raised.	The passage starts by introducing the difficulties faced by working women, but the contrast key word "[h]owever" introduces the actual topic of the passage: the difficulties faced by working married men.
Scott Coltrane, a researcher at the University of Oregon, has found that, **while** the earnings of women tend to go down with each additional child, the earnings of married men **not only** exceed those of both unmarried men and divorced men **but also** tend to go up with each additional child. **One reason** for this disparity may be that, as the size of the family grows, men rely on women to manage most of the responsibilities of housekeeping and child raising. While within the past few decades men have assumed a greater share of household responsibilities, in the United States, women still spend nearly twice as much time as men do in caring for children and the home. The time diaries of highly educated dual-income U.S. couples show that men enjoy three and a half times the leisure time as their female partners do.	Married men earn more with additional children. One reason is provided. The rest of the paragraph expands on that reason.

If married men earn higher salaries and have more leisure time than their female counterparts do, what difficulties do these working men face? Research indicates **three possible problems**. **First**, the perceived responsibility of providing for a family drives men to work more hours and strive for promotion. Many men report feeling dissatisfied because the level of performance that is required to earn promotions and higher salaries prevents them from spending time with their families. **Second,** these demands on men also contribute to higher levels of marital discord. In a 2008 survey, 60 percent of U.S. fathers reported work-family conflicts, compared to 47 percent of mothers.

The opening question signals a return to the topic introduced in the first paragraph.

Three reasons married men are struggling will be discussed.

First reason: married men work harder and longer to provide for their families, so they lose family time.

Second reason: more marital problems.

The pressure to be perceived as a good provider contributes to the **third reason** that married men may struggle. **While** women's decisions to use family leave benefits, move to part-time employment, or leave the workforce to care for children are seen as valuable contributions to family life and, by extension, society, men's decisions to do the same are frequently viewed by their employers as signs of weakness. Studies suggest that men who take advantage of paternity leave policies are viewed as weak or inadequate by both women and men. Research conducted in Australia found that men's requests to work flexibly were denied at twice the rate of those of women.

Third reason: men's decisions to limit work are not valued like those of women.

Passage Map

Here is an example of the notes that you might have made as you read:

¶1: Married men (MM) face difficulties in the workplace

¶2: Research: MM earn more, have more leisure

¶3: MM work harder and longer to support families, experience more marital discord

¶4: MM don't get same flexibility in workplace

Topic: Working married men

Scope: Difficulties faced by ↑

Purpose: Explain the reasons behind ↑

5.   **(B)**

The author of the passage is primarily concerned with

- O   advocating changes in employers' practices regarding female employees with children
- O   examining some of the reasons that married men may experience problems related to their employment
- O   describing the psychological consequences for men of earning high salaries
- O   taking issue with those who believe that women should not earn more than men
- O   analyzing the indirect effects of discrimination against women on married men

STEP 2: ANALYZE THE QUESTION STEM

Since this asks for what the author is "primarily concerned" with, it's a Global question.

STEP 3: RESEARCH THE RELEVANT TEXT

Consult the purpose in the passage map to find out what the main idea of the passage is.

STEP 4: MAKE A PREDICTION

The correct answer to a question about the primary concern of the passage must reflect the passage as a whole. Your prediction for the answer would be something like *explaining the difficulties that are faced by working married men*.

STEP 5: EVALUATE THE ANSWER CHOICES

(B) matches the prediction and is correct. A quick vertical scan of the first words in choices would show that **(A)** and **(D)** are wrong; the passage does not advocate or take issue with anything. There'd be no need to read the rest of these choices on Test Day, but for the record, **(A)** incorrectly addresses the difficulties that women face; while these issues are mentioned in the passage, the author discusses them to contrast women's issues with those of married men. **(D)** is simply not discussed in the passage. **(C)** misstates the main idea of the passage. The focus of the text is on the issues that are faced by working married men, only some of whom happen to earn high salaries. **(E)** is also not discussed in the passage, which does not attribute the difficulties of married men to discrimination against women.

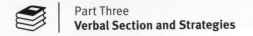
6. **(D)**

The passage provides information in support of which of the following assertions about married men who work?

○ The ability to provide for their families is the most important aspect of employment for married men.

○ Married men in high-status positions are easily able to integrate their careers and family lives.

○ Married men who achieve greater earnings while having a larger family are more satisfied on average than their wives.

○ The perceived demands on men to earn enough income to support a family may have harmful effects on family life.

○ As married men achieve higher earnings, they are able to take more time off from work to spend with their families.

STEP 2: ANALYZE THE QUESTION STEM

The question asks for something that's supported by information in the passage, so it's an Inference question.

STEP 3: RESEARCH THE RELEVANT TEXT

The passage discusses married men who work in the second, third, and fourth paragraphs, providing most details in the last two paragraphs, so support from the answer will likely come from there.

STEP 4: MAKE A PREDICTION

It's often hard to make a specific prediction for Inference questions. Instead, as you evaluate the choices, strictly compare each to the passage, keeping the author's overall purpose in writing in mind.

STEP 5: EVALUATE THE ANSWER CHOICES

Lines 9–11 and 20–21 suggest that married men earn more to provide for their families. Lines 21–25 describe two negative effects on the families of married men—that men don't have enough time to spend with their families and that those men have higher levels of marital discord. Taken together, these parts of the passage support **(D)**.

(A) goes beyond what is stated in the passage and is thus incorrect. The passage suggests that married men work more hours and earn more money to support their families as their families grow, but the passage never indicates that this is the *most* important aspect of employment for married men.

(B) is the opposite of what the passage states. The third and fourth paragraphs discuss the difficulties faced by working married men. Additionally, the passage doesn't specifically discuss men in high-status positions, just those with higher earnings.

Since the second paragraph outlines some of the advantages that married men have over their female counterparts, you may suspect that the author would agree with **(C)**, but no support for this comparison of their satisfaction levels is actually given in the passage.

(E) contradicts the passage. One of the complaints of married men, mentioned in lines 21–23, is that their job responsibilities prevent them from spending time with their families.

7.   **(B)**

The author of the passage discusses Coltrane's research primarily in order to

○   illustrate the benefits that employers extend to their married male employees

○   identify a benefit of work that married men experience that is accompanied by some potential costs

○   defend the family leave policies and flexible work schedules that some employers offer

○   modify the prevailing view that women experience disadvantages in the workplace after marrying and having children

○   point out several ways in which women experience discrimination in the workplace

STEP 2: ANALYZE THE QUESTION STEM

The words "in order to" indicate this question is asking *how* or *why* the author used a feature of the passage, not about the content of the feature itself. That means it's a Logic question.

STEP 3: RESEARCH THE RELEVANT TEXT

Coltrane's research is introduced in the second paragraph, so refer to your notes on that paragraph and consider how the author discussed the research to achieve the purpose of the passage.

STEP 4: MAKE A PREDICTION

A good prediction of the correct answer would be *to explain that earning more money may not be enough for married men to be satisfied with their jobs.*

STEP 5: EVALUATE THE ANSWER CHOICES

(B) matches the prediction and is correct.

(A) describes the content of Coltrane's research, but the primary purpose of the paragraph is not to highlight the advantages enjoyed by working married men but rather to set the stage for a discussion of the reasons married men may be dissatisfied in their jobs.

The second paragraph does not address family leave policies and flexible work schedules **(C)**; these are discussed in the fourth paragraph. Also, since the passage has a neutral tone, the author does not "defend" any particular point of view.

The author mentions some disadvantages that women face after marrying and having children **(D)**, such as lower pay with each child. The author does not argue against the idea that women experience disadvantages.

While Coltrane's research could be construed as support for the idea that discrimination against women exists in the workplace **(E)**, the author neither attributes the problems women face to discrimination in the workplace nor describes Coltrane's research as indicative of discrimination. Also, again, the purpose of discussing this research is to describe men's experiences, not women's.

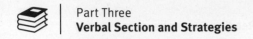
8. **(C)**

According to the passage, married men generally receive higher salaries and have a better chance of being promoted than do single men because

○   employers consider married men to be more diligent and responsible than single men

○   married men have usually accrued more experience than have single men

○   married men may be able to rely on their spouses to address child care and household responsibilities

○   higher pay typically corresponds with greater job security and enhanced benefits

○   employers recognize the difficulties of providing for a larger number of children and seek to ease this burden

STEP 2: ANALYZE THE QUESTION STEM

This asks for something that is true "[a]ccording to the passage," so it's a Detail question.

STEP 3: RESEARCH THE RELEVANT TEXT

The comparison of the salaries of married men to those of single men is found in lines 9–11, and a proposed explanation is found in lines 11–13: "One reason... may be that, as the size of the family grows, men rely on women to manage most of the responsibilities of housekeeping and child raising."

STEP 4: MAKE A PREDICTION

The right answer will paraphrase the ideas discovered while researching.

STEP 5: EVALUATE THE ANSWER CHOICES

(C) matches the prediction and is thus correct. The remaining choices may be plausible in everyday life, but none of them are mentioned in the passage, so they are all incorrect.

Reading Comprehension Question Types

Though you might be inclined to classify Reading Comp according to the kinds of passages that appear—business, social science, biological science, or physical science—it's more effective to do so by question type. While passages differ in their content, you can read them in essentially the same way, employing the same strategic reading techniques for each.

Now that you're familiar with the basic principles of Critical Reasoning and the Kaplan Method, let's look at the most common types of questions. Certain question types appear again and again on the GMAT, so it pays to understand them beforehand.

The four main question types on GMAT Reading Comp are Global, Detail, Inference, and Logic. Let's walk through each of these question types in turn, focusing on what they ask and how you can approach them most effectively.

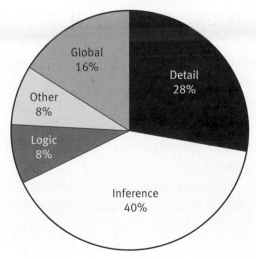

The Approximate Distribution of GMAT Reading Comprehension Questions

Global Questions

Any question that explicitly asks you to consider the passage as a whole is a Global question. Here are some examples:

- Which of the following best expresses the main idea of the passage?
- The author's primary purpose is to...
- Which of the following best describes the organization of the passage?
- Which of the following would be an appropriate title for this passage?

The correct answer will be consistent with the passage's topic, scope, purpose, and structure. If you've jotted these down on your notepad (and you should!), then it will take only a few seconds to select the right answer.

The GMAT will probably word the answer choices rather formally, so by "few seconds," we mean closer to 45 than to 10. But that's still significantly under your average time per question, giving you more time for questions that require more research.

Most wrong answers will either get the scope wrong (too narrow or too broad) or misrepresent the author's point of view. Be wary of Global answer choices that are based on details from the first or last paragraph. These are traps laid for those who wrongly assume that GMAT passages are traditional essays with "topic sentences" and "concluding sentences."

Often, answer choices to Global questions asking about the author's purpose will begin with verbs; in this case, the most efficient approach is to scan vertically to eliminate choices with verbs that are inconsistent with the author's purpose. Common wrong answers misrepresent a neutral author by using verbs that indicate an opinionated stance.

TAKEAWAYS: GLOBAL QUESTIONS

- Step 1 of the Kaplan Method provides you with the information you need to predict the answer to Global questions.
- Use your passage map, topic, scope, and purpose to predict an answer. Then search the answer choices.
- If you can't find your prediction among the answer choices, eliminate wrong answer choices that misrepresent the scope.
- When all of the answer choices start with a verb, try a vertical scan, looking for choices that match your prediction or looking to eliminate choices that misrepresent the author's purpose.

Detail Questions

LEARNING OBJECTIVES

In this section, you will learn how to:

- Identify a Detail question by the question stem
- Use content clues and your passage map to locate relevant details for answering Detail questions
- Articulate strategies for eliminating wrong answer choices in Detail questions

Detail questions ask you to identify what the passage explicitly says. Here are some sample Detail question stems:

- According to the passage, which of the following is true of X?
- The author states that...
- The author mentions which of the following in support of X?

It would be impossible to keep track of all of the details in a passage as you read through it the first time. Fortunately, Detail stems will always give you clues about where to look to find the information you need. Many Detail stems include specific words or phrases that you can easily locate in the passage. A Detail stem might even highlight a sentence or phrase in the passage itself. Using these clues, you can selectively reread parts of the passage to quickly zero in on the answer—a more efficient approach than memorization.

So between highlighting, references to specific words or phrases, and your passage map, locating the detail that the GMAT is asking about is usually not much of a challenge. What, then, could these questions possibly be testing? They are testing whether you understand that detail *in the context of the passage*. The best strategic approach, then, is to read not only the sentence that the question stem sends you to but also the sentences before and after it. Consider the following question stem:

> According to the passage, which of the following is true of the guinea pigs discussed in the highlighted portion of the passage?

Let's say that the highlighted portion of the passage goes like this:

> ...a greater percentage of the guinea pigs that lived in the crowded, indoor, heated area survived than did the guinea pigs in the outdoor cages.

If you don't read for context, you might think that something like this could be the right answer choice:

> ○   Guinea pigs survive better indoors.

But what if you read the full context, starting one sentence before?

> Until recently, scientists had no evidence to support the hypothesis that low temperature alone, and not other factors such as people crowding indoors, is responsible for the greater incidence and severity of influenza in the late fall and early winter. Last year, however, researchers uncovered several experiment logs from a research facility whose population of guinea pigs suffered an influenza outbreak in the winter of 1945; these logs documented that a greater percentage of the guinea pigs that lived in the crowded, indoor, heated area survived than did the guinea pigs in the outdoor cages.

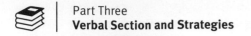
Now you could identify this as the right answer:

○ Researchers discovered that some guinea pigs survived better indoors than outdoors during a flu outbreak.

By reading not just the highlighted portion of the passage but the information before it, you realize that it's not necessarily true that guinea pigs always survive better indoors; only a specific subset did. If you had picked an answer that matched the first prediction, you would be distorting the facts—you need to understand the information *in context*.

Make sure that you read entire sentences when answering Detail questions. Notice here that the question stem sends you to the end of the last sentence, but it's the "no evidence" and "however" at the *beginning* of the sentences that form the support for the right answer.

TAKEAWAYS: DETAIL QUESTIONS

- On Detail questions, use your passage map to locate the relevant text in the passage. If necessary, read that portion of the passage again. Then predict an answer.
- On Detail questions, never pick an answer choice just because it sounds familiar. Wrong answer choices on Detail questions are often distortions of actual details in the passage.
- All of the information needed to answer Detail questions is in the passage.

Inference Questions

LEARNING OBJECTIVES

In this section, you will learn how to:

- Explain what an inference is in the context of Reading Comprehension
- Identify an Inference question by its question stem
- Articulate strategies for assessing which answer choices are supported by the passage and eliminating wrong answers, using your passage map and your understanding of the author's opinions

Reading Comp Inference questions, like Critical Reasoning Inference questions, ask you to find something that must be true based on the passage but that is not mentioned *explicitly* in the passage. In other words, you need to read "between the lines." Here are some sample Inference question stems:

- Which of the following is suggested about X?
- Which of the following can be most reasonably inferred from the passage?
- The author would most likely agree that . . .

Inference questions come in two types. The first uses key phrases or highlighting to refer to a specific part of the passage. To solve this kind of question, find the relevant detail in the passage and consider it in the context of the material surrounding it. Then make a flexible prediction about what the correct answer will state.

Consider the following Inference question, once again asking about the guinea pigs we discussed earlier:

> Which of the following is implied about the guinea pigs mentioned in the highlighted portion of the passage?

Just like last time, you want to review the context around the highlighted portion. Doing so, you'll find that "until recently," there was "no evidence" that temperature affected the flu; "however," last year these guinea pig records appeared. The logical inference is not explicitly stated, but you can easily put the information from the two sentences together. The answer will be something like this:

○   Their deaths provided new evidence that influenza may be more dangerous in lower temperatures.

Other Inference questions make no specific references, instead asking what can be inferred from the passage as a whole or what opinion the author might hold. Valid inferences can be drawn from anything in the passage, from big-picture issues like the author's opinion to any of the little details. But you will probably be able to eliminate a few answers quickly because they contradict the big picture.

Then you'll investigate the remaining answers choice by choice, looking to put each answer in one of three categories—(1) proved right, (2) proved wrong, or (3) not proved right but not proved wrong either. It's distinguishing between the second and third categories that will lead to success on Inference questions. Don't throw away an answer because you aren't sure about it or "don't like it."

If you can't find material in the passage that proves an answer choice wrong, don't eliminate it. Since the correct answer to an Inference question is something that *must* be true based on the passage, you can often find your way to the correct answer by eliminating the four choices that *could* be false.

TAKEAWAYS: INFERENCE QUESTIONS

- On Inference questions, search for the answer choice that follows from the passage.
- When it's difficult to predict a specific answer to an Inference question, you still know that the right answer *must* be true based on the passage.
- Wrong answer choices on Inference questions often use extreme language or exaggerate views expressed in the passage.

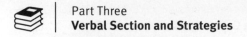
Logic Questions

Logic questions ask why the author does something—why he cites a source, why he includes a certain detail, why he puts one paragraph before another, and so forth. Another way of thinking of Logic questions is that they ask not for the purpose of the passage as a whole but for the purpose of a part of the passage. As a result, any answer choice that focuses on the actual content of a detail will be wrong.

Here are some sample Logic question stems:

- The author mentions X most probably in order to…
- Which of the following best describes the relationship of the second paragraph to the rest of the passage?
- What is the primary purpose of the third paragraph?

Most Logic questions can be answered correctly from your passage map—your written summary of each paragraph and the passage's overall topic, scope, and purpose. If the question references a detail, as does the first sample question stem above, then you should read the context in which that detail appears as well—just as you should for any Detail or Inference question that references a specific detail.

TAKEAWAYS: LOGIC QUESTIONS

- On Logic questions, predict the correct answer using the author's purpose and your passage map.
- Answer choices that focus too heavily on specifics are usually wrong—it's not content that's key in Logic questions but the author's motivation for including the content.

"Other" Questions

> **LEARNING OBJECTIVES**
>
> In this section, you will learn how to:
>
> - Identify questions that do not fall into one of the major categories of Reading Comprehension question types
> - Carefully evaluate the question stem to determine what is being asked
> - Use your passage map; the author's topic, scope, and purpose; and your ability to draw inferences to answer any question posed

As you saw from the pie chart earlier, approximately 8 percent of Reading Comp questions will not fall neatly into the four main categories described above. On such questions, strategic reading of the question stem becomes even more important, since you'll need to define precisely what the question is asking you to do and you may not be able to identify any specific pattern that the question falls into. But even within these rare "Other" question types, you can prepare yourself to see questions of the following varieties.

"Critical Reasoning" Questions

Occasionally in Reading Comp, you will be asked a question that seems more like one of the common Critical Reasoning question types, such as an **Assumption**, **Strengthen**, **Weaken**, or **Flaw** question. These questions refer to arguments, just as they do in Critical Reasoning—although unlike in Critical Reasoning, a particular argument will usually be confined to just one paragraph or portion of the Reading Comp passage, rather than the entire passage focusing on a single argument.

When you see questions like this, you should research the portion of the passage that includes the argument referenced by the question stem. Just as you would in Critical Reasoning, identify the conclusion and relevant evidence; then use the central assumption to form a prediction for the right answer.

Parallelism Questions

These questions ask you to take the ideas in a passage and apply them through analogy to a new situation. For example, a passage might describe a chain of economic events that are related causally, such as reduced customer spending leading to a slowdown of industrial production, which in turn leads to the elimination of industrial jobs. A Parallelism question might then ask you the following:

> Which of the following situations is most comparable to the economic scenario described in the passage?

In this case, the correct answer will describe a scenario that is logically similar to the one in the passage. Don't look for a choice that deals with the same subject matter as the passage, as such choices are often traps. Parallelism questions are more concerned with structure than substance, so the correct answer will provide a chain of causally connected events, such as water pollution from a factory causing the death of a certain type of algae, which in turn causes a decline in the fish population that relied on that type of algae as its primary food source.

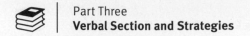

Application Questions

Application questions ask you to identify an example or application of something described in the passage. For instance, if the passage describes a process for realigning a company's management structure, an Application question could give you five answer choices, each of which describes the structure of a given company. Only the correct answer choice will accurately reflect the process described in the passage.

Application questions function similarly to Parallelism questions, except that whereas Parallelism questions ask you to identify an analogous logical situation (irrespective of subject matter), Application questions ask you to apply information or ideas directly, within the same subject area (rather than by analogy or metaphor).

Question Type Identification Exercise

LEARNING OBJECTIVE

In this section, you will learn how to:

- Identify which type of Reading Comprehension question has been asked based on the question stem

Answers are on the page following this exercise.

Identifying the question type during step 2 of the Kaplan Method for Reading Comprehension is a chance for you to put yourself in control of the entire process that follows: how to research, what to predict, and, thus, how to evaluate answer choices.

In this exercise, analyze key words in the question stem to determine what the question is asking you to do. Then choose the correct question type from the list of choices.

1. The passage implies which of the following about XXXXXXX?

   O   Global
   O   Detail
   O   Inference
   O   Logic
   O   Other

2. According to the passage, each of the following is true of XXXXXXX EXCEPT

   O   Global
   O   Detail
   O   Inference
   O   Logic
   O   Other

3. The author mentions XXXXXXX in order to

   O   Global
   O   Detail
   O   Inference
   O   Logic
   O   Other

4. The author's primary objective in the passage is to

   O   Global
   O   Detail
   O   Inference
   O   Logic
   O   Other

5. The author makes which of the following statements concerning XXXXXXX?

   O   Global
   O   Detail
   O   Inference
   O   Logic
   O   Other

6. An appropriate title for the passage would be

   O   Global
   O   Detail
   O   Inference
   O   Logic
   O   Other

7. Which of the following statements about XXXXXXX can be inferred from the passage?

   O   Global

   O   Detail

   O   Inference

   O   Logic

   O   Other

8. Which of the following, if true, would most weaken the theory proposed by XXXXXXX?

   O   Global

   O   Detail

   O   Inference

   O   Logic

   O   Other

9. Which of the following best states the central idea of the passage?

   O   Global

   O   Detail

   O   Inference

   O   Logic

   O   Other

10. Which of the following situations is most comparable to XXXXXXX as it is presented in the passage?

   O   Global

   O   Detail

   O   Inference

   O   Logic

   O   Other

11. The passage provides support for which of the following assertions about XXXXXXX?

   O   Global

   O   Detail

   O   Inference

   O   Logic

   O   Other

12. The author indicates explicitly that which of the following has been XXXXXXX?

   O   Global

   O   Detail

   O   Inference

   O   Logic

   O   Other

13. The author would most likely agree with which of the following?

   O   Global

   O   Detail

   O   Inference

   O   Logic

   O   Other

14. The author refers to XXXXXXX most probably in order to

   O   Global

   O   Detail

   O   Inference

   O   Logic

   O   Other

15. Which of the following represents the clearest application of XXXXXXX's theory as described in the passage?

   O   Global

   O   Detail

   O   Inference

   O   Logic

   O   Other

16. The passage is primarily concerned with

   O   Global

   O   Detail

   O   Inference

   O   Logic

   O   Other

Question Type Identification Exercise: Answers

1. C

When you see "implies" or "suggests," know that you're facing an Inference question.

2. B

When you see direct, categorical language like "according to the passage," know that you're facing a Detail question.

3. D

The phrase "in order to" means that this is a Logic question. Logic questions deal with the author's motivations. If a question asks you why the author includes a paragraph, brings up a detail, or cites a source, know that you are facing a Logic question.

4. A

The phrase "primary objective" means that this is a Global question.

5. B

The phrase "makes which of the following statements" signals that this is a Detail question.

6. A

The phrase "title for the passage" means that you must base your answer on the whole passage, so this is a Global question.

7. C

The word "inferred" means that this is an Inference question.

8. E (Weaken)

The word "weaken" means that this is a Weaken question, common in Critical Reasoning but one of the rarer question types in Reading Comp.

9. A

The phrase "central idea of the passage" means that this is a Global question.

10. E (Parallelism)

The phrase "most comparable to" means that this is a Parallelism question.

11. C

The phrase "passage provides support for" means that this is an Inference question.

12. B

The phrase "indicates explicitly" means that this is a Detail question.

13. C

The phrase "most likely agree" signals an Inference question.

14. D

The phrase "in order to" means that this is a Logic question.

15. E (Application)

The phrase "represents the clearest application of" means that this is an Application question. Application questions ask you to find the answer choice that is most consistent with a description, theory, or process described in the passage.

16. A

The phrase "passage is primarily concerned with" means that this is a Global question.

CHAPTER 11

Reading Comprehension: Putting It All Together

This quiz is designed to give you practice with a mix of Reading Comprehension passages and question types, just like the mix of RC passage sets you'll see on Test Day. Take this quiz after you have studied the different types of questions the test maker asks and practiced applying the Kaplan Method for Reading Comprehension, including the strategic reading that the test rewards.

How to Take This Quiz

By the time you take this quiz, you are hopefully well on your way to mastery of Reading Comprehension, so set a timer. Give yourself 3–4 minutes per passage and 1 minute 15 seconds per question. So if you do all seven passages and 35 questions in this set at once, set the timer for 68 minutes; if you decide to do fewer passage sets than that in one sitting, set the timer accordingly.

Make sure to use the steps of the Kaplan Method on every question. Students are often tempted to give step 1 short shrift, reading through the passage quickly so they can get to the questions. While you certainly want to read *efficiently*, investing the time in taking some summary notes will ensure you absorb the main points the author is making, the location of key examples, the structure of the passage, and any opinions expressed—all material you're likely to see questions on. Students are also prone to skip step 4, making a prediction, finding it easier to search the choices for an answer that "sounds right." However, you're much more likely to find the answer you want—the correct answer—if you know what you're looking for before you look for it.

Note that the GMAT will typically give you three or four questions per passage, drawing those questions adaptively from a larger pool of up to six to eight questions. (The computer considers both your current score level and the distribution of question types you've seen so far.) For several passages on this quiz, we've given you more than four questions so that you can see the full range of questions the GMAT might ask about a given passage. But remember that on Test Day, you'll probably see only three or four.

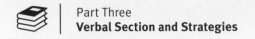
Furthermore, remember that on Test Day, you can't take notes on the computer screen or skip forward and back between questions. So challenge yourself now not to take notes in this book (use separate scratch paper or an erasable notepad like the one you'll use at the testing center) and to do the questions in order.

After you've finished the quiz and are reviewing the explanations, make sure you not only can explain why the right answer is correct but also can articulate why each wrong answer is incorrect. Being able to clearly identify why wrong choices are wrong will help you avoid picking them.

In addition, if you missed a question, understand *why* you missed it. There is always a reason! The Kaplan Method can be a useful checklist to diagnose where you went wrong.

- After reading the passage, had you mapped it well enough to avoid extensive rereading as you answered the questions?
- Did you identify the task set by the question?
- Were you able to efficiently research the context clue in the question stem either in your passage map or the passage itself?
- Was your prediction off base or too specific (or too general), or did you omit making a prediction?
- Were you tempted by a choice that did not actually match your prediction, perhaps because you could have read more carefully or because you fell for a common wrong-answer trap?

If you know why you missed a question, you can avoid making that error again.

Above all, avoid judging yourself. The only evaluation of your skill that actually matters is the one on Test Day. So if you make mistakes, resolve to learn from them and improve your score. Need more practice? Check out the Reading Comprehension quizzes and Qbank questions in your online resources.

GO ONLINE

kaptest.com/login

Reading Comprehension Quiz

Questions 1–3 refer to the following passage.

It is believed that half or more of the languages spoken on Earth will be extinct within a century. The United Nations Educational, Scientific, and Cultural Organization (UNESCO), which monitors endangered languages, says that "with each vanishing language, an irreplaceable element of human thought in its multiform variations is lost forever."
5 As the world becomes more interconnected, many languages, as well as the culture captured within them, may be lost.

There is a strong link between language and cultural identity. In nineteenth-century Japan, attempts to assimilate the Ainu people into Japanese culture included banning their language; some indigenous languages in both North America and Australia suffered
10 the same fate. Many of those languages are lost or dying. With loss of language comes loss of links to the past and feelings of belonging to a community, which research has linked to mental health. One study of Aboriginal communities found that youth suicide rates dropped to almost zero when the residents had conversational knowledge of native languages.

15 One problem endangered languages face is lack of official recognition. Residents of a country are expected to know its official language or languages, but many countries do little to recognize minority regional languages. Take Basque, a language spoken in both Spain and France. In France, only French is recognized as an official language. In Spain, the constitution allows for regional recognition of official languages besides Spanish, so
20 in Basque-speaking parts of the country, both Spanish and Basque are official languages. It is not surprising, therefore, that UNESCO cites Basque as "vulnerable" in Spain but "critically endangered" in France.

Consider, in contrast, the case of Finnish. This tongue is not endangered, even though Finland was ruled from the Middle Ages until 1917 by first Sweden and then Russia
25 and, during this period, Swedish was used as the language of administration and government. In 1919, a newly independent Finland constitutionally adopted both Finnish and Swedish as official languages, legally recognizing its native language as important to its burgeoning national identity. As of 2013, Finnish was spoken by 89 percent of the population of Finland.

30 In order to preserve languages that will otherwise be lost, linguists have proposed creating a database of endangered languages. But how would an academic repository serve the often marginalized groups that speak such languages? While directed toward a noble goal, this project would fail to address the issue of language's critical role in preserving a sense of cultural identity.

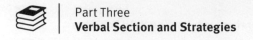

1. According to the passage, Basque is more endangered in France than in Spain because

    ○   France has suppressed Basque in order to maintain a French cultural identity

    ○   there are more Basque speakers in Spain than in France

    ○   Basque has no governmental recognition as an official language in France

    ○   multiple languages are recognized as official throughout Spain

    ○   Basque-speaking regions in Spain have developed a separate cultural identity

2. Which of the following statements, if true, would support the assertion that Finnish was "important to [Finland's] burgeoning national identity" (lines 26–27)?

    ○   Speaking Finnish after 1919 became a point of pride for those in Finland, whereas it previously had often been a source of shame.

    ○   Both Swedish and Finnish were taught in Finnish schools after 1919, just as they had been before the new constitution was adopted.

    ○   Finland adopted a new flag and national anthem after the new constitution was approved in 1919.

    ○   Some people in Finland continued to use Swedish as their preferred language even after Finnish was adopted as an official language.

    ○   Those who worked to modernize Finnish in the late nineteenth century so it would achieve broader acceptance favored the western dialect over the eastern.

3. Which of the following statements most clearly exemplifies the aspect of language extinction that UNESCO considers problematic?

    ○   As one of the world's oldest languages, Basque is worth preserving as a living historical artifact as well as a modern spoken language.

    ○   Because scholars have been unable to translate the Linear A script, the intellectual capital of the culture that produced it remains inaccessible.

    ○   Because Socrates did not leave behind any written works, his ideas have been preserved only through secondhand sources.

    ○   Most linguists term Korean a "language isolate" because it is not known to be related to any other languages.

    ○   Because it has no equivalent word in many languages, "serendipity" is a particularly difficult term to translate.

Questions 4–6 refer to the following passage.

Unlike vaccinations for polio, measles, mumps, and many other virus-borne diseases, which yield lifetime protection with one vaccination or a short series of vaccinations, vaccinations combating the influenza virus must be administered annually, and even then they may not be fully successful in preventing illness. The reason for this striking
5   difference is the ability of the influenza virus to evolve quickly. The antigens, the parts of the influenza virus recognized by the human body, include two important surface proteins, hemagglutinin and neuraminidase. Hemagglutinin is involved in the invasion of a cell within the human body, and neuraminidase assists in the release of new viruses from the cell after the viruses are replicated. As hemagglutinin is
10 copied, it is not replicated exactly, so the human immune system does not recognize the mutation as the same protein it has encountered before and does not inaugurate the immune response. In this process, called antigenic drift, the known strains of influenza are recognized and effectively combated, but, unchallenged by the immune system, mutated viruses are able to reproduce freely and, thus, form a new strain
15 of influenza.

Researchers in immune therapy are working on a variety of innovations to improve influenza vaccinations such as faster methods of production of vaccines and improvements to existing vaccines to strengthen the immune response of the human body. By far the most intriguing of these efforts are researchers' attempts
20 to produce vaccines that would target the evolutionarily conserved areas of the influenza virus. The stem that attaches hemagglutinin to the virus, the neuraminidase protein, and M2—a protein found in the membrane of the influenza virus—all appear to be nearly identical across virus strains and seem to evolve slowly. While much work remains to be done, a vaccine targeting one of these may be the key to a
25 one-time immunization protocol that would provide efficacious protection against most influenza strains.

4.   The primary purpose of the passage is to

   O   explain the process by which the influenza virus mutates quickly, thus making the development of a single vaccination impossible

   O   identify the action of hemagglutinin within the influenza virus that causes the virus to evolve rapidly

   O   compare and contrast the influenza virus with the viruses that cause polio, measles, mumps, and other virus-borne diseases

   O   discuss the reason influenza vaccinations are administered annually and recent innovations in research that may address this anomaly

   O   describe the mechanism of antigenic drift and how this process affects the human immune system

5. It can be inferred from the passage that the author believes which of the following to be true about a vaccine that could provide permanent protection against influenza with a single immunization protocol?

    O   Research into such a vaccine is promising, and the vaccine will be available soon if tests are completed successfully.

    O   The vaccine could affect neuraminidase or other areas of the virus that do not mutate rapidly.

    O   Such a vaccine cannot be effective because hemagglutinin antigens evolve too quickly.

    O   The vaccine will most likely target hemagglutinin antigens because their rapid mutation makes them susceptible to the defenses of the human immune system.

    O   The vaccine will have a similar mechanism to that of the vaccines now administered for polio, measles, mumps, and other virus-borne diseases.

6. According to the passage, each of the following is true of the influenza virus EXCEPT:

    O   The rapid evolution of hemagglutinin on the surface of the virus can prevent the human immune system from recognizing and attacking the virus.

    O   Some of the surface proteins on the influenza virus have different functions.

    O   The antigenic drift of the influenza virus means that a vaccine against influenza must change frequently.

    O   Annual immunization is not always effective protection against the influenza virus.

    O   The influenza virus is remarkable in its ability to mutate more rapidly than any other known virus.

Questions 7–12 refer to the following passage.

Responding to the negative, one-dimensional representation of African Americans in the Hollywood films of the 1970s, the women of Delta Sigma Theta, an African American service sorority, embarked on an ambitious project to produce a feature film that would challenge these stereotypes. Filmmaker S. Torriano Berry recounts in his documentary on
5   the sorority's efforts how, unfortunately, what could have been a historic project with the power to transform the U.S. entertainment industry failed due to the sorority's reliance on the major movie studios' traditional marketing and distribution system.

Lillian Benbow, the president of Delta Sigma Theta, and the sorority's Arts and Letters committee headed the effort to raise money for the production of the film,
10   *Countdown at Kusini*, from donations. While most of the funds were contributed by the thousands of sorority members across the United States, African American entertainment luminaries not only supported the project financially but also donated their talent and expertise. However, after arriving on location in Nigeria, the producers found that lack of qualified technicians, editors, film crews, equipment, and cinematic
15   support services within the country meant that unexpected costs quickly added up, drastically exceeding the initial budget.

Even with the cost overruns, the movie could have paid for itself and perhaps even turned a modest profit if the sorority's initial marketing proposal had been followed. When preparing the budget, Delta Sigma Theta expected to use a four-wall marketing
20 plan, in which the sorority's extensive membership would rent local theaters across the country, then sell tickets to other members, friends, and family. Additional screenings would be held as demand warranted. As one of the oldest and most extensive service sororities, Delta Sigma Theta had enough members in enough cities to at least recoup production costs. However, a major Hollywood film company became aware of
25 the project and approached the sorority with an offer to distribute the film. Buoyed by the interest of the mainstream media, the sorority believed that the film company's expertise in marketing and distribution would lead to broader exposure and greater opportunities for success. Unfortunately, when the film was released through traditional channels, without any coordination with the local chapters of
30 the sorority, it quickly failed.

Despite the film's commercial failure, the project is remarkable for its prescience, providing an early example of crowdfunding and media activism. Delta Sigma Theta took active steps to counter the limited range of stereotypes of African Americans in Hollywood films, and it funded these efforts through numerous small contributions.
35 Moreover, the film's ultimate impact may not be only historical but also tangible in the modern Nigerian film industry, second in size only to that of India. When *Countdown at Kusini* was produced, there was no filmmaking infrastructure in Nigeria. While some of the production equipment was brought back to the United States, much was left behind, as well as the newly developed expertise of the local technicians,
40 editors, actors, and production staff who were trained on the film. One of the most intriguing questions surrounding *Countdown at Kusini* may be that of its effect on the nascent Nigerian film industry.

7. The primary purpose of the passage is to

O   criticize Hollywood's depictions of African Americans in the films of the 1970s

O   compare and contrast the presentations of African Americans in *Countdown at Kusini* with those found in Hollywood films

O   explain how *Countdown at Kusini* transformed the film industry, particularly in Nigeria

O   chronicle the reasons for the production of *Countdown at Kusini* and the film's significance

O   describe the technical difficulties encountered in the production of *Countdown at Kusini* and how they were overcome

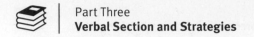
8.　The author's reference to a "four-wall marketing plan" in lines 19–20 serves primarily to

○　explain the factors that contributed to the successful release of the film

○　illustrate the characteristics of a traditional Hollywood film release

○　contrast the original marketing strategy with the one that subsequently failed

○　indicate the reasons the sorority's plan proved to be unworkable

○　demonstrate why the film was unlikely to recover its production costs

9.　According to the passage, the sorority agreed to the Hollywood film company's marketing plan for which of the following reasons?

○　The sorority believed that cost overruns in the production of the film demanded higher sales in order for the film to recover those costs.

○　The sorority determined the four-wall marketing plan would not be feasible.

○　The sorority thought that, since the Hollywood film company had more resources and experience, the film company's plan would be more effective.

○　The sorority members were not able to rent sufficient theaters to ensure the success of the four-wall marketing strategy.

○　The sorority members were concentrated in a limited number of geographic locations and needed the broader distribution channels the company was able to provide.

10.　Which of the following best describes the purpose of the fourth paragraph of the passage?

○　To explain several significant aspects of the film that indicate its historic importance

○　To provide further evidence of the failure of the film's marketing strategy

○　To present a comprehensive analysis of the effects of the Hollywood film company's marketing plan

○　To contrast the commercial failure of the film with the exceptional effort of the producers

○　To introduce facts that contradict S. Torriano Berry's opinion of the film's significance

11. The passage suggests that many of the members of Delta Sigma Theta responded to the 1970s Hollywood films featuring African Americans in which of the following ways?

   ○ They appreciated the employment opportunities offered by the introduction of major films with primarily African American actors.

   ○ They accepted the limited portrayal of African American characters as a first step toward broader media exposure.

   ○ They organized campaigns across the country protesting the limited range of stereotypical depictions of African American life in Hollywood films.

   ○ They mobilized their financial resources and organizational skills in an effort to present an alternative image of African Americans.

   ○ They became aware of the many advantages of mainstream media exposure to challenge negative stereotypes.

12. It can be inferred from the passage that which of the following is one of the reasons S. Torriano Berry considers *Countdown at Kusini* a historic African American film?

   ○ *Countdown at Kusini* is the first recorded instance of crowdfunding.

   ○ *Countdown at Kusini* introduced Hollywood studios to the marketing of privately produced films.

   ○ *Countdown at Kusini* was the first successful film to present a more realistic portrayal of African Americans.

   ○ *Countdown at Kusini* was successful as an educational film despite its commercial failure.

   ○ *Countdown at Kusini* may have been instrumental in the establishment of the Nigerian film industry.

Questions 13–17 refer to the following passage.

Parfleche is the French name for the Plains peoples' *hoemskot 'eo*—an envelope-shaped rawhide container for storing clothes, food, and personal items. The *parfleche* served not only as a practical and durable storage solution, but also as a decorative object of spiritual significance. Among certain tribes, most notably
5　the Cheyenne and Arapaho, *parfleches* were decorated by the women's painting society, whose members among the Cheyenne were known as *moneneheo*, the Selected Ones. Although similar in their economic and social importance to craftsmen's guilds in medieval and Renaissance Western Europe, the painting society also had a spiritual or religious nature. The shamanistic society required application for
10　admission and held its members to high artistic and moral standards. The society further displayed its importance by defining aspects of Cheyenne wealth and status. Painting on rawhide was fraught with challenges. If painting was attempted while the prepared hide was too moist, the applied paint bled, but if the hide was too dry, the skin did not absorb the pigments. This restricted the time frame in which
15　painting could best be completed, which meant that designs had to be visualized

fully before the work started. Moreover, every aspect of creating a *parfleche* was
a sacred act. Each design element, for instance, was a syntagma—a linguistic or
visual unit intended to convey meaning—freighted with symbolic referents. For
example, diamond shapes represented the *ha 'kot*, the grasshopper, an abundant
20 grass eater itself symbolic of the bison, the sacred source of food, shelter, tools,
and clothing. The tools used were also symbolic: the shape of the "flesher" used to
prepare the hide represented lightning bolts—emblematic of the masculine essence
of spirit. The flesher removed the flesh from the hide, transforming it into a spiritual
container that would hold earthly matter (the people's material goods).
25 Even the position of the *parfleche* in the lodge held symbolic significance. It
was stored beneath the bed of older women, not only because they were careful
guardians, but also because they were closer to Grandmother Earth, from whose
union with the lightning spirit the animals and plants of the middle world came to
provide food and shelter. The symbolism of every aspect of the *parfleche,* therefore,
30 from the interpretable design work on its outside to its storage place within the
lodge, reflects the Cheyenne belief in a complementary worldview: the blending of
the masculine spirit and the feminine physical matter.

13. According to the passage, one reason why there was a limited time frame in which to paint a
prepared rawhide was that

   O   the pigments dried quickly and thus had to be applied with speed to avoid cracking

   O   if the hide was too dry, it absorbed too much paint

   O   if the hide was too moist, it rejected the pigments

   O   the designs had to be fully visualized before painting was started

   O   if the hide was too moist, the paint bled

14. The main purpose of the passage is to

   O   describe a tool used among Native Americans when working with rawhide

   O   rebut a commonly held view about the symbolism of the *parfleche* for the Plains peoples

   O   analyze the societies of the Cheyenne and Arapaho people

   O   propose a new method for analyzing the use of symbolism in Native American art

   O   discuss the spiritual and symbolic importance of a rawhide container and its decorations to
       several Plains tribes

15. According to the author, the Cheyenne women's painting society was unlike Western European guilds of the Middle Ages and the Renaissance in that

    O   application for membership was required

    O   the group had significant economic standing in the community

    O   the group had significant social standing in the community

    O   the women's painting society was religious in nature

    O   the society had an influence on social standing and material valuation

16. You can most reasonably conclude that the Cheyenne definition of the term *moneneheo* (line 6) reflects

    O   the high status some women enjoyed as artists in Cheyenne culture

    O   the shamanistic spiritual origins of the women's painting society

    O   the notion that artists were chosen by the gods to perform their tasks

    O   the self-restrictive nature of the women's painting society

    O   a woman's skill in using rawhide tools such as the "flesher"

17. The author describes the symbolic meanings of the diamond shape most likely in order to

    O   indicate how precious the completed *parfleche* was to its owner

    O   prove that the grasshopper was superior to the bison in Cheyenne religion

    O   illustrate the visual complexity of the abstract forms used in creating a *parfleche*

    O   provide an example of the many layers of symbolism involved in creating a *parfleche*

    O   demonstrate the relationship between the symbolic shapes of the tools and the abstract designs used in creating a *parfleche*

Questions 18–23 refer to the following passage.

A one-child policy was implemented in China in 1979, and for nearly 40 years, until the policy was amended to allow two children in 2015, some Han Chinese families could legally have only one child. This rule was implemented in an attempt to slow continued growth of a population that had almost doubled since 1949. The Chinese
5   government claimed that the policy prevented 400 million births, though some have suggested that the decline may be at least partly due to economic reasons, not legal ones.

One result of the policy seems to be the birth and survival of significantly more boys than girls. One study found that China had 33 million more boys than girls under the age of
10   20, and it is believed that by 2030, 25 percent of Chinese men in their late 30s will never have been married. Research has shown that an excess of men of marriageable age is

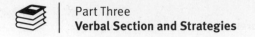
linked to higher rates of psychological problems, as it creates a marginalized underclass, and history would suggest such situations may correlate with increased aggression and violence, both inside and outside a country's borders.

15 Economist Amartya Sen wrote in 1990 of the phenomenon of "missing women" in population data, noting that in China, "the survival prospects of female children clearly have been unfavorably affected by restrictions on the size of the family." In a society that has traditionally strongly favored sons, it has been suggested that sex-specific pregnancy terminations and infanticide account for the discrepancy in numbers. But
20 others have countered this argument, believing that disease might better explain the phenomenon, either by making women more likely to give birth to male children or by making it more likely that female children will die prenatally or when very young. For at least some of the missing girls, however, a less sinister explanation may prove the correct one: parents who already had a child, or who wanted to be able to have another
25 in an attempt to have a son, simply never registered their daughters with government officials. A recent study found evidence that as many as 25 million girls were not registered at birth, some of them officially "existing" only many years later and others perhaps never officially existing at all.

18. The primary purpose of the passage is to

O   criticize the accepted explanation for missing girls in China since the implementation of the one-child policy

O   show why the expected population decline in China due to the one-child policy was not due to a decrease in the number of males

O   demonstrate how China's one-child policy has influenced past and future birth rates

O   explore the phenomenon of missing girls in China during the years of the one-child policy

O   argue that the expected population decline in China due to the one-child policy was due entirely to a decrease in the number of women

19. According to the passage, which of the following is true of societies in which there are not enough female partners for men of marriageable age?

O   They occurred historically but are not known to occur in the modern day.

O   They may be at increased risk of international conflict.

O   They are more likely to develop when a significant proportion of the population is psychologically damaged.

O   They are not known to have occurred prior to the modern day.

O   They can result in the disappearance of women from official records.

20. The last paragraph in the passage serves primarily to

    ○ present multiple potential explanations for a phenomenon described in the second paragraph

    ○ offer a critique of explanations put forward for the outcome of the policy in which the author is primarily interested

    ○ demonstrate that the least sinister explanation of a troubling phenomenon is the correct one

    ○ explain fully the phenomenon described in the second paragraph

    ○ outline why social attitudes may explain the result of the policy that is the topic of the passage

21. According to the passage, each of the following is a possible reason for missing girls in China EXCEPT:

    ○ Disease may cause more boys to be born than girls.

    ○ The one-child policy does not require girls to be registered.

    ○ Disease may cause more girls to die prenatally than boys.

    ○ Infanticide of female children occurs because families prefer sons.

    ○ Some girls are not registered so that parents can have another child.

22. Based on information in the passage, which of the following outcomes would have been most likely to occur if a Han Chinese family had a baby daughter prior to 2015?

    ○ The parents are eventually pleased to have had a daughter, because there are so many marriageable men.

    ○ Because disease may kill the daughter, the parents have another child in hopes of having a son.

    ○ The parents appeal to the authorities to approve an exception to the number of children allowed.

    ○ Because a pregnancy is more likely to result in a son than a daughter, the parents have another child.

    ○ The parents fail to officially register the daughter, and they have another child.

23. The author mentions a "marginalized underclass" (line 12) most likely in order to

   ○   show one potential societal risk of the one-child policy

   ○   give an example of why there are more men than women in China

   ○   demonstrate that men are inherently more violent than women

   ○   argue that widespread poverty may cause people to value boys more than girls

   ○   illustrate the effect of the one-child policy on average family income

Questions 24–29 refer to the following passage.

Generally, interspecific matings represent an evolutionary dead end, producing sterile offspring, if any at all. For some species of birds, however, such pairings may indeed bring evolutionary advantages to the participants. In the case of the female collared flycatchers of Gotland, three distinct factors may work to make interspecific
5   pairings with pied flycatcher males reproductively beneficial.

In many instances, female collared flycatchers nest with male pied flycatchers while continuing to mate with other collared flycatchers, in effect parasitizing the pied flycatchers, who invest in rearing and fledging any offspring. Often, more than half of the offspring raised by interspecific flycatcher pairs are, in fact, not hybrids.
10   Furthermore, an estimated 65 percent of the hybrid offspring of the resident pied flycatcher male are male. Because hybrid females are sterile and males are not, this male bias minimizes the primary disadvantage of interspecific matings: sterile offspring. Habitat specialization may be a third mechanism: these pairings tend to occur in the late spring when the coniferous woods favored by the pied flycatcher
15   provide a greater availability of food than the deciduous woods where the collared flycatchers tend to live. Together, these factors form a mechanism to improve substantially the reproductive success of female collared flycatchers beyond what would be expected of interspecific mating with pied flycatcher males.

Although all three of these mechanisms appear to act in concert to form a single
20   elaborate mechanism specifically evolved to circumvent the usual disadvantages of interspecific mating, studies have shown similar motivations for the behavior of female collared flycatchers mating within the species. According to Professor Siever Rohwer, collared flycatcher females will choose to nest with subordinate collared flycatcher males that inhabit good territory because collared flycatcher females
25   must pair-bond in order to be successful in raising offspring. To engender the best offspring, however, the females will continue to copulate with higher-quality collared males with whom they are not paired. Thus, females seem to be nesting with males of any species with the best territories available at the time, but they will continue to mate with more attractive males outside of their pair bonds.

30   A highly unusual behavior, interspecific mating seems to provide certain reproductive advantages to the collared flycatcher female. However, it remains unclear whether the mating behavior of female collared flycatchers evolved to

circumvent the usual problems with interspecific mating or whether the behavior is
simply an extension of how female collared flycatchers behave when mating within
35   their own species.

24.   The author's primary purpose is to

   O   criticize the basis of a scientific theory

   O   defend a hypothesis concerning bird-mating behaviors

   O   point out the need for further study of female collared flycatchers

   O   describe two possible explanations for the interspecific mating behavior of female
        collared flycatchers

   O   defend an unpopular view of a natural phenomenon

25.   According to the passage, female collared flycatchers' mating with male pied flycatchers could be
      explained by any of the following reasons EXCEPT:

   O   Food is more available in pied flycatcher territories during the mating season.

   O   Male pied flycatchers can help raise offspring successfully, even if the offspring are not
        theirs.

   O   Male pied flycatchers sire more female offspring than do collared flycatcher males,
        increasing the reproductive success of the female collared flycatcher.

   O   Females are known to nest with subordinate males while pursuing extra-pair copulation
        with higher-quality males.

   O   Females enjoy greater reproductive success by pair-bonding with an inferior male than by
        not pair-bonding at all.

26.   The bias toward male offspring resulting from the mating of collared flycatcher females and pied
      flycatcher males is presented as evidence that

   O   collared flycatcher females that mate with pied flycatcher males have more dominant
        male offspring

   O   the offspring from extra-pair matings with collared flycatcher males are more frequently
        male

   O   female flycatchers are not deterred from interspecific pairing by the likelihood of sterile
        hybrid offspring

   O   males are produced to reduce interspecific inbreeding in future generations

   O   interspecific breeding is normal in all varieties of flycatchers

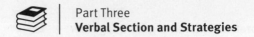

27. It can be inferred from the passage that

   O   food resources are an important determinant of success in raising offspring

   O   having 50 percent male offspring is not optimal for collared flycatcher pairs

   O   flycatchers generally mate for life

   O   males do not vary in the benefits they provide to their offspring

   O   over half of all females engage in extra-pair matings

28. Professor Rohwer would most likely agree with which of the following statements?

   O   All traits related to particular functions have evolved only for those particular functions.

   O   Flycatchers represent the best population for studies of bird-mating behavior.

   O   Behaviors may appear functional even under conditions other than those under which the behaviors evolved.

   O   Evolution has played no role in shaping the behavior of interspecifically paired flycatchers.

   O   Hybridization is generally beneficial.

29. The mating behavior of female collared flycatchers paired with subordinate male flycatchers is offered as

   O   an unwarranted assumption behind the adaptive explanation of interspecific matings

   O   an alternative explanation for pair matings of collared females with pied males

   O   evidence supporting the hypothesis of adaption for interspecific breeding

   O   a discredited mainstream explanation for why hybridization is a dead end

   O   proof in support of the theory that collared and pied flycatchers are separate species

Questions 30–35 refer to the following passage.

Rainbows have long been a part of religion and mythology in cultures around the globe, appearing as bridges between the heavens and the earth, as messages from the gods, or as weapons wielded by divine powers. Some cultures have viewed rainbows themselves as deities, or even as demonic beings from which to hide children. But in the early
5   fourteenth century, Theodoric of Freiburg, a German friar, and Kamal al-Din al-Farisi, a Persian scientist, independently turned a scientific eye to the study of rainbows.

Theodoric and al-Farisi were thousands of miles apart, but both had studied Ibn al-Haytham's *Book of Optics*. Each concluded that a rainbow's appearance is the result of sunlight refracting and reflecting through water droplets left after a rainfall. They
10   conducted experiments to provide support for their conclusions, successfully re-creating

the conditions necessary to make a rainbow appear; al-Farisi used a sphere and a camera obscura, while Theodoric used flasks and globes.

Both scholars were, as modern physics has shown, correct in their assessments. When light hits a water droplet, the water causes the light's speed to decrease. Furthermore,
15 the light refracts—or changes direction—upon entering the droplet, and some of the light reflects off the back of the droplet, refracting again as it exits. The angle of refraction depends on the wavelength of the light; thus, refraction "breaks" white light into multiple wavelengths—a phenomenon called dispersion—which appear as different colors.

But for a rainbow to fill the sky with color, more is needed. A single droplet of water will
20 disperse the entire visible light spectrum, with each wavelength leaving at a different angle, but it alone cannot create a rainbow. Only a little of the light from a particular droplet reaches the eye of the human observer, striking the eye from a particular angle. For the observer to perceive the rainbow's characteristic banded arc of different colors, a multitude of droplets suspended in the air, refracting and dispersing light, are needed,
25 with the shorter wavelengths and shallower angles of indigo and violet appearing to the observer at the bottom and the longer wavelengths and steeper angles of red and orange appearing at the top.

30. The author mentions the angle at which light leaves water droplets (lines 19–21) primarily in order to

O   describe how refraction causes light to disperse as it leaves a water droplet

O   show that indigo and violet appear at the bottom of rainbows because those colors have shallower angles

O   illustrate that a change in the angle of light changes the wavelength of the light

O   explain that the human eye perceives a rainbow only when light is refracted from multiple points

O   introduce evidence that may help solve a long-standing mystery about the physics of refraction

31. Based on the passage, it can be inferred that the rainbow's middle colors of yellow, green, and blue

O   are not broken into separate bands by the dispersion of light leaving a droplet of water

O   have longer wavelengths than do the red and orange light at the top of the rainbow

O   have wavelengths that all strike the eye of a human observer at the same angle

O   have wavelengths that are refracted at shallower angles than the wavelengths of indigo and violet light

O   have wavelengths that are shorter than those of red and orange light and longer than those of indigo and violet light

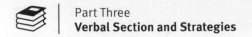

32. According to the passage, the refraction of light upon entering and leaving a water droplet

    ○ changes the angle at which light leaves the water droplet, thereby altering the light's wavelength

    ○ causes the light to be reflected and thus intensify, becoming more visible to the human observer

    ○ disperses white light, allowing it to be seen as its different component colors

    ○ causes the light to slow and thus more readily disperse according to its different wavelengths

    ○ alters the light's wavelengths so they fall within the visible spectrum

33. The primary purpose of the passage is to

    ○ explain why rainbows are a relatively rare phenomenon

    ○ describe religious and scientific explanations for the appearance of rainbows

    ○ raise doubts about a historical explanation for the appearance of rainbows

    ○ explore the reasons that the refraction of light causes it to appear as different colors

    ○ examine the physics underlying the appearance of rainbows to the human observer

34. It can be inferred that the author of the passage would most likely agree with which of the following statements about the study of rainbows?

    ○ Scientific experiments performed hundreds of years ago sometimes provided accurate results.

    ○ Cultures that associate rainbows with divinity do not approve of scientific inquiry into the nature of rainbows.

    ○ The experiments of Theodoric and al-Farisi established that refraction of light occurs in water droplets but did not examine larger volumes of water.

    ○ In societies in which the results of scientific studies of rainbows are widely accepted, rainbows are no longer associated with spiritual meaning.

    ○ Studies such as Theodoric's and al-Farisi's now have no value because modern science has shown them to be simplistic.

35. The primary function of the second paragraph is to

- ◯ discuss a challenge to the conception of rainbows as a religious symbol
- ◯ evaluate two historical methods for observing rainbows
- ◯ describe the difficulties early scholars overcame in their attempts to understand rainbows
- ◯ support the idea that medieval science is similar in value to modern science
- ◯ outline historical attempts to understand the scientific basis of rainbows

Answer Key

Reading Comprehension Quiz

Endangered Languages

1. C
2. A
3. B

Influenza Vaccination

4. D
5. B
6. E

Countdown at Kusini

7. D
8. C
9. C
10. A
11. D
12. E

Parfleche

13. E
14. E
15. D
16. A
17. D

One-Child Policy

18. D
19. B
20. A
21. B
22. E
23. A

Flycatchers

24. D
25. C
26. C
27. A
28. C
29. B

Rainbows

30. D
31. E
32. C
33. B
34. A
35. E

Answers and Explanations

Reading Comprehension Quiz

Endangered Languages

STEP 1: READ THE PASSAGE STRATEGICALLY

On the left, we've shown how key words help you to identify the major elements of the passage and its structure and what you could skim over. On the right, we've shown what you might be thinking as you read the passage strategically.

Passage for Questions 1–3

PASSAGE	ANALYSIS
It is believed that half or more of the **languages** spoken on Earth will be extinct within a century. The United Nations Educational, Scientific, and Cultural Organization (UNESCO), which monitors endangered languages, says that "with each vanishing language, an irreplaceable element of human thought in its multiform variations is lost forever." As the world becomes more interconnected, many languages, as well as the **culture** captured within them, may be **lost**.	Topic: many languages/cultures are in danger of extinction.
There is a **strong link** between **language** and **cultural identity**. In nineteenth-century Japan, attempts to assimilate the Ainu people into Japanese culture included banning their language; some indigenous languages in both North America and Australia suffered the same fate. Many of those languages are lost or dying. **With** loss of language comes loss of links to the past and feelings of belonging to a community, which research has linked to mental health. **One study** of Aboriginal communities found that youth suicide rates dropped to almost zero when the residents had conversational knowledge of native languages.	Language and identity are linked. There are examples given.
One problem endangered languages face is lack of official recognition. Residents of a country are expected to know its official language or languages, **but** many countries do little to recognize minority regional languages. **Take Basque**, a language spoken in both Spain and France. In France, only French is recognized as an official language. In Spain, the constitution allows for regional recognition of official languages besides Spanish, so in Basque-speaking parts of the country, both Spanish and Basque are official languages. It is not surprising, **therefore**, that UNESCO cites Basque as "vulnerable" in Spain but "critically endangered" in France.	This paragraph identifies one problem: lack of official recognition for regional language; Basque is given as an example.

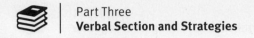
Consider, **in contrast**, the case of Finnish. This tongue is not endangered, **even though** Finland was ruled from the Middle Ages until 1917 by first Sweden and then Russia and, during this period, Swedish was used as the language of administration and government. In 1919, a newly independent Finland constitutionally adopted **both** Finnish and Swedish as official languages, legally recognizing its native language as **important** to its burgeoning national identity. As of 2013, Finnish was spoken by 89 percent of the population of Finland.

A contrast from the problem described in the previous paragraph. A language's connection to national identity can help it survive; Finnish is an example.

In order to preserve languages that will otherwise be lost, linguists have **proposed** creating a database of endangered languages. **But** how would an academic repository serve the often marginalized groups that speak such languages? **While** directed toward a noble goal, this project would **fail** to address the issue of language's **critical** role in preserving a sense of cultural identity.

One proposed solution: saving endangered languages in a database. But it wouldn't help those who will lose their native tongue/cultural identity.

Passage Map

¶1: Languages/culture endangered

¶2: Language = cultural identity

¶3: Official/not official; ex: Basque in Fr & Sp

¶4: Finnish; made official

¶5: Database won't preserve cultural identity

Topic: Language and cultural identity

Scope: Preservation of both

Purpose: Explain importance and problems & argue against one solution

1. **(C)**

According to the passage, Basque is more endangered in France than in Spain because

- ○ France has suppressed Basque in order to maintain a French cultural identity
- ○ there are more Basque speakers in Spain than in France
- ○ Basque has no governmental recognition as an official language in France
- ○ multiple languages are recognized as official throughout Spain
- ○ Basque-speaking regions in Spain have developed a separate cultural identity

STEP 2: ANALYZE THE QUESTION STEM

This asks for something that's true "[a]ccording to the passage," so it's a Detail question.

STEP 3: RESEARCH THE RELEVANT TEXT

Basque is mentioned in the third paragraph, so research the answer there. This paragraph is about the importance of official recognition to the survival of a language.

STEP 4: MAKE A PREDICTION

Basque is officially recognized in Spain but not in France, and the author links this difference to Basque's status as "vulnerable" in Spain but "critically endangered" in France, so the correct answer will reflect this distinction.

STEP 5: EVALUATE THE ANSWER CHOICES

(C) states the reason for Basque's more precarious situation in France and is correct. While France does not recognize Basque as an official language, nothing in the passage suggests Basque has been actively suppressed there, eliminating **(A)**. Nothing is said of how many speakers there are in each country, so **(B)** can be eliminated. **(D)** and **(E)** may or may not be true, but neither is a reason why, according to the passage, Basque is more endangered in France than in Spain.

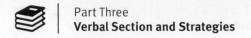

2. **(A)**

Which of the following statements, if true, would support the assertion that Finnish was "important to [Finland's] burgeoning national identity" (lines 26–27)?

O Speaking Finnish after 1919 became a point of pride for those in Finland, whereas it previously had often been a source of shame.

O Both Swedish and Finnish were taught in Finnish schools after 1919, just as they had been before the new constitution was adopted.

O Finland adopted a new flag and national anthem after the new constitution was approved in 1919.

O Some people in Finland continued to use Swedish as their preferred language even after Finnish was adopted as an official language.

O Those who worked to modernize Finnish in the late nineteenth century so it would achieve broader acceptance favored the western dialect over the eastern.

STEP 2: ANALYZE THE QUESTION STEM

This question asks for something that supports a particular assertion, so it's a Strengthen question.

STEP 3: RESEARCH THE RELEVANT TEXT

Research the line reference, reading the entire sentence for context. The author states that the acknowledgment of Finnish as key to national identity took place in 1919, when the new constitution was adopted.

STEP 4: MAKE A PREDICTION

The correct answer will be a piece of evidence that shows that the use of the Finnish language was associated with a revitalization of national pride.

STEP 5: EVALUATE THE ANSWER CHOICES

(A) describes a key change in feelings about Finnish, from negative to positive, in 1919 and supports the assertion; this is correct. **(B)** and **(D)** are examples of the status quo continuing after Finnish was adopted, so neither adds support to the assertion that the language was important to developing nationalism. **(C)** notes national symbols that may have expressed or promoted nationhood, but this choice does not support the idea that the Finnish language was important. If anything, **(E)** would be a weakener as it implies cultural divisions within Finland instead of national unity.

3. (B)

Which of the following statements most clearly exemplifies the aspect of language extinction that UNESCO considers problematic?

O   As one of the world's oldest languages, Basque is worth preserving as a living historical artifact as well as a modern spoken language.

O   Because scholars have been unable to translate the Linear A script, the intellectual capital of the culture that produced it remains inaccessible.

O   Because Socrates did not leave behind any written works, his ideas have been preserved only through secondhand sources.

O   Most linguists term Korean a "language isolate" because it is not known to be related to any other languages.

O   Because it has no equivalent word in many languages, "serendipity" is a particularly difficult term to translate.

STEP 2: ANALYZE THE QUESTION STEM

This question asks you to evaluate a statement that is not in the passage in terms of how well it reflects an idea that is in the passage. That means it's an Application question.

STEP 3: RESEARCH THE RELEVANT TEXT

UNESCO's assertion about the dangers of language loss comes in the first paragraph, so research there to see what its position is.

STEP 4: MAKE A PREDICTION

UNESCO's assertion can be paraphrased as *When a language is lost, ideas are also lost.* The correct answer will reflect this idea.

STEP 5: EVALUATE THE ANSWER CHOICES

In (**B**), the inability to translate a script has resulted in the loss of the ideas of the people who wrote it. This matches the prediction and is correct. (**A**) speaks only about the value of the language itself, not about the value of the ideas it communicates. (**C**) is a counterexample to UNESCO's concern; though there is no way to read the thoughts of Socrates in his own words, his ideas are preserved in the writings of others, diminishing the importance of whether his original language has survived. (**D**) and (**E**) are not related to losing language or the ideas that it carries. Ideas expressed in Korean are accessible to those who learn that language, and the concept expressed by "serendipity" is accessible to those who understand the word; both Korean and the English word "serendipity" are alive and well.

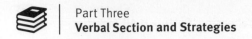

Influenza Vaccination

STEP 1: READ THE PASSAGE STRATEGICALLY

On the left, we've shown how key words help you to identify the major elements of the passage and its structure and what you could skim over. On the right, we've shown what you might be thinking as you read the passage strategically.

Passage for Questions 4–6

PASSAGE	ANALYSIS
Unlike vaccinations for polio, measles, mumps, and many other virus-borne diseases, which yield lifetime protection with one vaccination or a short series of vaccinations, vaccinations combating the influenza virus **must** be administered annually, and **even then** they may not be fully successful in preventing illness. The **reason** for this **striking** difference is the ability of the influenza virus to **evolve quickly**. The antigens, the parts of the influenza virus recognized by the human body, include two important surface proteins, hemagglutinin and neuraminidase. Hemagglutinin is involved in the invasion of a cell within the human body, and neuraminidase assists in the release of new viruses from the cell after the viruses are replicated. As hemagglutinin is copied, it is not replicated exactly, so the human immune system does not recognize the mutation as the same protein it has encountered before and does not inaugurate the immune response. In this process, called antigenic drift, the known strains of influenza are recognized and effectively combated, but, unchallenged by the immune system, mutated viruses are able to reproduce freely and, thus, form a new strain of influenza.	Comparison between vaccinations for many virus-borne diseases and… Vaccinations for influenza. You have to get flu shot every year, and it may not work. The passage will discuss the reason for this, and here it is: flu evolves rapidly. And this is the mechanism for how it does it. Skim these details, and if you need these details for a question, come back and read this more carefully.

Researchers in immune therapy are working on a variety of **innovations** to improve influenza vaccinations such as faster methods of production of vaccines and improvements to existing vaccines to strengthen the immune response of the human body. By far the **most intriguing** of these efforts are researchers' attempts to produce vaccines that would target the evolutionarily conserved areas of the influenza virus. The stem that attaches hemagglutinin to the virus, the neuraminidase protein, and M2—a protein found in the membrane of the influenza virus—all appear to be nearly identical across virus strains and seem to evolve slowly. **While** much work remains to be done, a vaccine targeting one of these **may be the key** to a one-time immunization protocol that would provide efficacious protection against most influenza strains.

The second paragraph is about new ways to improve flu shots: (1) make them faster, (2) make them stronger.

But the author really likes option (3): new vaccines that would work differently.

How new vaccines might work—again, speed up and reread this section if you need it to answer a question.

Nothing final yet, but may be possible.

Passage Map

¶1: Influenza vs. other virus-borne diseases. Flu vaccines annual, not 100% effective

   Reason: flu mutates quickly

¶2: New flu vaccine possibilities:

   (1) make faster

   (2) make stronger

   (3) new mechanism, au favorite, promising, but not yet

Topic: Influenza vaccination

Scope: Problem w/existing flu vaccinations

Purpose: To explain why flu vaccinations have to be given annually and discuss possible improvements

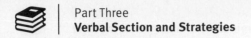

4.   **(D)**

The primary purpose of the passage is to

- ○   explain the process by which the influenza virus mutates quickly, thus making the development of a single vaccination impossible
- ○   identify the action of hemagglutinin within the influenza virus that causes the virus to evolve rapidly
- ○   compare and contrast the influenza virus with the viruses that cause polio, measles, mumps, and other virus-borne diseases
- ○   discuss the reason influenza vaccinations are administered annually and recent innovations in research that may address this anomaly
- ○   describe the mechanism of antigenic drift and how this process affects the human immune system

STEP 2: ANALYZE THE QUESTION STEM

The key phrase "primary purpose" identifies this as a Global question.

STEP 3: RESEARCH THE RELEVANT TEXT

Refer to the passage map to refresh your memory of the purpose of the passage.

STEP 4: MAKE A PREDICTION

Use the identified purpose, "to explain why influenza vaccinations must be given annually, and discuss possible improvements," as the prediction.

STEP 5: EVALUATE THE ANSWER CHOICES

(D) matches the prediction and is correct. **(A)** is half-right, half-wrong. The first part of the passage does explain why the influenza virus mutates rapidly, but the passage goes on to identify new approaches that may make it possible for a single vaccination to provide permanent protection. **(B)** is too narrow. The errors in replication of hemagglutinin are discussed, but the passage uses this information as a basis for discussion of the developments that could yield a one-time vaccination. **(C)** is also too narrow. Other virus-borne diseases are mentioned to contrast the small number of vaccinations needed for protection against them to the need for annual influenza vaccinations, but this is the only comparison between the diseases mentioned in the passage. **(E)** is a distortion of information in the passage. While the process of antigenic drift is discussed, the text only states that the mutated viruses produced are not recognized by the immune system. The effect of mutated viruses on the immune system is not discussed.

5. **(B)**

It can be inferred from the passage that the author believes which of the following to be true about a vaccine that could provide permanent protection against influenza with a single immunization protocol?

O   Research into such a vaccine is promising, and the vaccine will be available soon if tests are completed successfully.

O   The vaccine could affect neuraminidase or other areas of the virus that do not mutate rapidly.

O   Such a vaccine cannot be effective because hemagglutinin antigens evolve too quickly.

O   The vaccine will most likely target hemagglutinin antigens because their rapid mutation makes them susceptible to the defenses of the human immune system.

O   The vaccine will have a similar mechanism to that of the vaccines now administered for polio, measles, mumps, and other virus-borne diseases.

STEP 2: ANALYZE THE QUESTION STEM

The key word "inferred" identifies this as an Inference question. The correct answer will be the only choice that is supported by the passage.

STEP 3: RESEARCH THE RELEVANT TEXT

The context clue, "a vaccine that could provide permanent protection against influenza with a single immunization protocol," directs your research to the second paragraph. Within that paragraph, the emphasis key words "By far the most intriguing" identify the characteristics of possible new vaccines.

STEP 4: MAKE A PREDICTION

Lines 19–23 state that researchers are investigating neuraminidase, M2, the stem of hemagglutinin, and other surface proteins that are "nearly identical . . . and evolve slowly." Keep these ideas in mind and compare the choices to these lines in the passage.

STEP 5: EVALUATE THE ANSWER CHOICES

(B) paraphrases the description of the new vaccine and is correct. **(A)** is extreme. The last sentence of the passage states "much work remains to be done" and does not describe the vaccine as available "soon." **(C)** is a distortion of information presented in the text. Hemagglutinin does evolve quickly, but this is a reason the new vaccine will likely target other areas of the virus, not a reason why the new vaccine would be ineffective. **(D)** is a 180, or opposite, choice. The rapid evolution of hemagglutinin makes it less, not more, likely to be identified and targeted by the immune system. **(E)** is not mentioned in the passage. No comparison is made between the mechanisms of the two different types of vaccines. The way the measles, mumps, and polio vaccines operate is never discussed.

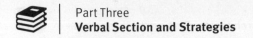

6.   **(E)**

According to the passage, each of the following is true of the influenza virus EXCEPT:

○   The rapid evolution of hemagglutinin on the surface of the virus can prevent the human immune system from recognizing and attacking the virus.

○   Some of the surface proteins on the influenza virus have different functions.

○   The antigenic drift of the influenza virus means that a vaccine against influenza must change frequently.

○   Annual immunization is not always effective protection against the influenza virus.

○   The influenza virus is remarkable in its ability to mutate more rapidly than any other known virus.

STEP 2: ANALYZE THE QUESTION STEM

The key phrases "according to the passage" and "is true" identify this as a Detail question. "Except" means the four incorrect choices will be stated in the passage. The one correct choice will either contradict or not be mentioned in the passage.

STEP 3: RESEARCH THE RELEVANT TEXT

The details of the influenza virus are found in the first paragraph.

STEP 4: MAKE A PREDICTION

Because the correct answer can be anything that is not stated in the passage, predict the sorts of details that will appear in the wrong answers. According to your passage map, the gist of the first paragraph is that the influenza virus mutates rapidly, quickly rendering vaccines obsolete. Eliminate any choice that matches this idea and be prepared to check choices against the first paragraph.

STEP 5: EVALUATE THE ANSWER CHOICES

The text never identifies influenza as the virus that evolves *most* rapidly, but only as a virus that evolves faster than the viruses that cause measles, mumps, and polio. Confirm this by reading starting at line 1, where these other diseases are mentioned, through lines 4–5: "The reason for this striking   difference is the ability of the influenza virus to evolve quickly." So the flu virus changes faster than the other viruses mentioned, but not necessarily faster than all other viruses in the world. This makes **(E)** extreme and thus the correct answer to this "except" question.

(A) seems consistent with the gist of the paragraph. Research to confirm the activity of hemagglutinin. Sure enough, lines 9–12 state, "As hemagglutinin is copied, it is not replicated exactly, so the human immune system does not recognize the mutation as the same protein it has encountered before and does not inaugurate the immune response." The virus evolves because the mistakes made as hemagglutinin is replicated keep the immune system from correctly identifying the virus, so the new virus survives in a slightly different form. This idea is stated in **(A)** so eliminate that choice.

For **(B)**, you find details about different antigens of the flu virus in lines 7–9: "Hemagglutinin is involved in the invasion of the cell within the human body, and neuraminidase assists in the release of new viruses from the cell after the viruses are replicated." Since these two proteins are identified as serving different functions in the replication of the virus, eliminate **(B)**.

(C) expresses the gist of the paragraph. Find the specific reference to "antigenic drift" in lines 12–15: "In this process, called antigenic drift... mutated viruses are able to reproduce freely and, thus, form a new strain of influenza." The purpose of the first paragraph is to discuss why the immunizations for influenza need to be administered more frequently that those of other virus-borne diseases, and these lines name that process as "antigenic drift." Eliminate (C).

(D) also aligns with the basic message of paragraph 1. Confirm by researching what the paragraph says about vaccinations. Lines 3–4 state, "vaccinations combating the influenza virus must be administered annually, and even then, they may not be fully successful in preventing illness." If the vaccine is not completely successful in preventing influenza, then a person who gets immunized with that vaccine may still get sick, so eliminate (D).

Countdown at Kusini

STEP 1: READ THE PASSAGE STRATEGICALLY

On the left, the bolded key words indicate the major elements and the structure of the passage. On the right is a sample mental narrative of an expert GMAT test taker to show what you might be thinking as you read the passage strategically.

Passage for Questions 7–12

PASSAGE	ANALYSIS
Responding to the **negative, one-dimensional** representation of African Americans in the Hollywood films of the 1970s, the women of Delta Sigma Theta, an African American service sorority, embarked on an **ambitious** project to produce a feature film that would challenge these stereotypes. Filmmaker **S. Torriano Berry** recounts in his documentary on the sorority's efforts how, **unfortunately**, what could have been a historic project with the power to transform the U.S. entertainment industry failed **due to** the sorority's reliance on the major movie studios' traditional marketing and distribution system.	The topic is going to be a response to images the author considers "negative." "Ambitious" has a positive connotation. The author approves of the sorority's effort. Berry thinks project was important ("historic") and its failure unfortunate. Project failed because traditional marketing was used.
Lillian Benbow, the president of Delta Sigma Theta and the sorority's Arts and Letters committee, headed the effort to raise money for the production of the film *Countdown at Kusini* from donations. **While** most of the funds were contributed by the thousands of sorority members across the United States, African American entertainment luminaries **not only** supported the project financially **but also** donated their talent and expertise. **However**, after arriving on location in Nigeria, the producers found that a lack of qualified technicians, editors, film crews, equipment, and cinematic support services within the country meant that unexpected costs quickly added up, **drastically** exceeding the initial budget.	How they raised the money. *Countdown at Kusini* is the topic! "Most" money from many small donations, but some stars helped. But costs were much higher than expected.

Even with the cost overruns, the movie could have paid for itself and perhaps even turned a modest profit **if** the sorority's initial marketing proposal had been followed. When preparing the budget, Delta Sigma Theta expected to use a four-wall marketing plan, in which the sorority's extensive membership would rent local theaters across the country, then sell tickets to other members, friends, and family. Additional screenings would be held as demand warranted. As one of the oldest and most extensive service sororities, Delta Sigma Theta had enough members in enough cities to at least recoup production costs. **However**, a major Hollywood film company became aware of the project and approached the sorority with an offer to distribute the film. **Buoyed** by the interest of the mainstream media, the sorority **believed** that the film company's expertise in marketing and distribution would lead to broader exposure and greater opportunities for success. **Unfortunately**, when the film was released through traditional channels, without any coordination with the local chapters of the sorority, it quickly failed.

The movie could have broken even, if the initial was followed. Expect to find details on this plan in the rest of the paragraph.

Ah! Initial plan was "4-wall" marketing.

Explanation of 4-wall marketing. Read this quickly, if there's a question about it, come back here to research the answer.

But wooed by Hollywood.

Sorority changed its mind.

Film failed because no local support.

Despite the film's commercial failure, the project is **remarkable** for its prescience, providing an early **example** of crowdfunding and media activism. Delta Sigma Theta took active steps to counter the limited range of stereotypes of African Americans in Hollywood films, and it funded these efforts through numerous small contributions. **Moreover**, the film's ultimate impact may **not be only** historical **but also** tangible in the modern Nigerian film industry, second in size only to that of India. When *Countdown at Kusini* was produced, there was no filmmaking infrastructure in Nigeria. **While** some of the production equipment was brought back to the United States, much was left behind, as well as the newly developed expertise of the local technicians, editors, actors, and production staff who were trained on the film. One of the **most intriguing questions** surrounding *Countdown at Kusini* may be that of its effect on the nascent Nigerian film industry.

Author's point of view on the film is positive.

Reasons: forerunner of crowdfunding, media activism

It benefitted the Nigerian film industry.

CAK may have started Nigerian film industry.

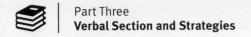
Passage Map

¶1: Film CAK, ambitious, historic, but failed commercially

¶2: How funded

¶3: Marketing: sorority (4-wall) vs. H'wood, H'wood fails

¶4: Reasons film is still notable

Topic: CAK (Countdown at Kusini)

Scope: How/why made, impact

Purpose: Describe the production, marketing, and importance of CAK

7. (D)

The primary purpose of the passage is to

○ criticize Hollywood's depictions of African Americans in the films of the 1970s

○ compare and contrast the presentations of African Americans in *Countdown at Kusini* with those found in Hollywood films

○ explain how *Countdown at Kusini* transformed the film industry, particularly in Nigeria

○ chronicle the reasons for the production of *Countdown at Kusini* and the film's significance

○ describe the technical difficulties encountered in the production of *Countdown at Kusini* and how they were overcome

STEP 2: ANALYZE THE QUESTION STEM

The phrase "primary purpose" in the question stem identifies this as a Global question.

STEP 3: RESEARCH THE RELEVANT TEXT

Use the passage map—particularly the topic, scope, and purpose—to predict the correct answer without rereading any of the passage.

STEP 4: MAKE A PREDICTION

From the scope and purpose, predict that the correct answer will say that the author is *discussing* Countdown at Kusini *and its implications.*

STEP 5: EVALUATE THE ANSWER CHOICES

(D) matches the prediction and is the correct answer. **(A)** is extreme. While the text mentions these depictions, and describes the film as responding to them, the passage does not go on to criticize Hollywood's portrayal of African Americans. **(B)** is a distortion of information in the passage. The text does not provide the details of the presentations of African Americans in *Countdown at Kusini*, nor does it compare them to those in the Hollywood films. **(C)** is a 180, or opposite, choice with respect to the U.S. film industry; in the first paragraph, the author laments the failure of the film to transform the industry. Although the movie did transform the Nigerian movie industry, this is just one way in which the film was significant; the purpose of the passage is broader than this. **(E)** is too narrow. While the production difficulties were a detail discussed in the passage, this choice ignores the author's focus on the historic significance of the film.

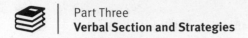
8. (C)

The author's reference to a "four-wall marketing plan" in lines 19–20 serves primarily to

○ explain the factors that contributed to the successful release of the film

○ illustrate the characteristics of a traditional Hollywood film release

○ contrast the original marketing strategy with the one that subsequently failed

○ indicate the reasons the sorority's plan proved to be unworkable

○ demonstrate why the film was unlikely to recover its production costs

STEP 2: ANALYZE THE QUESTION STEM

The key word phrase "serves primarily" identifies this as a Logic question; a question that asks how or why the author used a specific piece of information. The question stem provides the specific reference—"a four-wall marketing plan"—to guide your research.

STEP 3: RESEARCH THE RELEVANT TEXT

The reference from the question stem leads to the third paragraph, where the passage map describes four-wall marketing as the sorority's original plan. This paragraph goes on to discuss why the sorority adopted Hollywood's methods instead, methods that ultimately failed.

STEP 4: MAKE A PREDICTION

Predict that the correct answer will say that the author included the details of the paragraph in order to show a marketing approach that might have worked but wasn't used.

STEP 5: EVALUATE THE ANSWER CHOICES

The prediction matches very nicely with **(C)**; this is the correct answer. **(A)** is a 180, or opposite, choice. The passage explains that the movie was a commercial failure, so the release was not successful. **(B)** is also a 180, as four-wall marketing was the sorority's proposed marketing plan, not the traditional Hollywood approach. **(D)** is not mentioned in the passage. Since the sorority did not use the four-wall strategy, whether it would have worked or not is not addressed. **(E)** is another 180 choice. Although the film did not recover its production costs, the four-wall marketing plan was presented as the way the movie might have been able to break even.

9.   **(C)**

According to the passage, the sorority agreed to the Hollywood film company's marketing plan for which of the following reasons?

O   The sorority believed that cost overruns in the production of the film demanded higher sales in order for the film to recover those costs.

O   The sorority determined the four-wall marketing plan would not be feasible.

O   The sorority thought that, since the Hollywood film company had more resources and experience, the film company's plan would be more effective.

O   The sorority members were not able to rent sufficient theaters to ensure the success of the four-wall marketing strategy.

O   The sorority members were concentrated in a limited number of geographic locations and needed the broader distribution channels the company was able to provide.

STEP 2: ANALYZE THE QUESTION STEM

The phrase "according to" in the stem signals a Detail question. The correct answer will be explicitly stated in the passage. Also notice the context clue: you're looking for the reason the sorority agreed to the film company's marketing plan.

STEP 3: RESEARCH THE RELEVANT TEXT

The passage map focuses your research on the third paragraph. Skim the first part of the paragraph describing the sorority's four-wall marketing plan and slow down when the contrast key word "[h]owever" introduces the Hollywood film company's plan. Lines 26–28 provide the answer. "the sorority believed that the film company's expertise in marketing and distribution would lead to broader exposure and greater opportunities for success."

STEP 4: MAKE A PREDICTION

The correct answer will restate the idea expressed in lines 26–28.

STEP 5: EVALUATE THE ANSWER CHOICES

(C) is a perfect match and the correct answer. **(A)** is a faulty use of an accurate detail from the passage. Although there were cost overruns, and it is likely the sorority wanted to recover those costs, these were not the reason the sorority changed marketing plans. The first sentence of the third paragraph indicates that the sorority believed it would recover even the increased costs with the four-wall marketing plan, so there must have been another reason why it switched to the Hollywood film company's plan. **(B)** is a 180, or opposite, choice. The first sentence of the third paragraph indicates that the four-wall marketing plan would likely have been successful. **(D)** is not mentioned in the passage; the text never discusses the members' inability to acquire sufficient theaters. **(E)** is another 180 choice. The passage states in lines 23–24 that the sorority's membership was extensive enough to recoup the film's production costs.

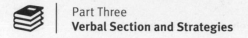

10. (A)

Which of the following best describes the purpose of the fourth paragraph of the passage?

○ To explain several significant aspects of the film that indicate its historic importance

○ To provide further evidence of the failure of the film's marketing strategy

○ To present a comprehensive analysis of the effects of the Hollywood film company's marketing plan

○ To contrast the commercial failure of the film with the exceptional effort of the producers

○ To introduce facts that contradict S. Torriano Berry's opinion of the film's significance

STEP 2: ANALYZE THE QUESTION STEM

This question stem asks for the purpose not of the whole passage, but of one of its parts. That makes this a Logic question. The stem makes clear reference to the fourth paragraph.

STEP 3: RESEARCH THE RELEVANT TEXT

As the question asks about the whole of the fourth paragraph, research in the passage map.

STEP 4: MAKE A PREDICTION

The passage map note will serve as a good prediction: the fourth paragraph provides the reasons the film is still notable, despite its commercial failure.

STEP 5: EVALUATE THE ANSWER CHOICES

(A) matches the prediction and is correct. **(B)** is a 180, or opposite, choice. The contrast key word "[d]espite" at the start of the paragraph indicates a change of direction from the discussion of the film's commercial failure. **(C)** is extreme. The text does not provide a "comprehensive analysis of the effects" of the marketing plan. The passage simply indicates that the marketing plan failed. **(D)** is incorrect because the "exceptional effort of the producers" is never discussed in the text. **(E)** is another 180 choice. Since Berry chose to document the film, and since the author describes his view of the film's failure as unfortunate, the fourth paragraph is supporting Berry's opinion, not contradicting it.

11. (D)

The passage suggests that many of the members of Delta Sigma Theta responded to the 1970s Hollywood films featuring African Americans in which of the following ways?

○ They appreciated the employment opportunities offered by the introduction of major films with primarily African American actors.

○ They accepted the limited portrayal of African American characters as a first step toward broader media exposure.

○ They organized campaigns across the country protesting the limited range of stereotypical depictions of African American life in Hollywood films.

○ They mobilized their financial resources and organizational skills in an effort to present an alternative image of African Americans.

○ They became aware of the many advantages of mainstream media exposure to challenge negative stereotypes.

STEP 2: ANALYZE THE QUESTION STEM

The key word "suggests" makes this an Inference question, so the correct answer *must* be true based on the passage but is likely not mentioned explicitly. The context clue "members... responded to the 1970s Hollywood films featuring African Americans" directs attention to the first paragraph.

STEP 3: RESEARCH THE RELEVANT TEXT

The "1970s films featuring African Americans" are mentioned in the first paragraph, where the author describes the sorority's response as an "ambitious" and "historic" feature film.

STEP 4: MAKE A PREDICTION

A good prediction would be *they made a movie* or some other straightforward summary of that idea.

STEP 5: EVALUATE THE ANSWER CHOICES

(D) paraphrases the prediction in different words and is correct. The choice includes more details discussed in the passage, but the meaning is identical to that of the prediction. All the remaining choices are responses that might be true but are not mentioned in the passage. Specifically, "employment opportunities" **(A)** and "broader media exposure" **(B)** are never discussed. **(C)** is also extreme. While the sorority had members across the country, the only "campaign" mentioned is the production and marketing plan for the film. **(E)**'s use of mainstream media to challenge stereotypes is also never mentioned.

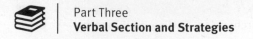
12. (E)

It can be inferred from the passage that which of the following is one of the reasons S. Torriano Berry considers *Countdown at Kusini* a historic African American film?

○   *Countdown at Kusini* is the first recorded instance of crowdfunding.

○   *Countdown at Kusini* introduced Hollywood studios to the marketing of privately produced films.

○   *Countdown at Kusini* was the first successful film to present a more realistic portrayal of African Americans.

○   *Countdown at Kusini* was successful as an educational film despite its commercial failure.

○   *Countdown at Kusini* may have been instrumental in the establishment of the Nigerian film industry.

STEP 2: ANALYZE THE QUESTION STEM

The key word "inferred" identifies this as an Inference question, and the context clue "one of the reasons S. Torriano Berry considers *Countdown at Kusini* an historic African American film" directs you to the section of the passage that will provide the support for the correct answer.

STEP 3: RESEARCH THE RELEVANT TEXT

S. Torriano Berry is identified in the first paragraph as the documentarian who considered the film one that "could have been a historic project with the power to transform the U.S. entertainment industry." The reasons for the project's eventual significance are outlined in the fourth paragraph, and the emphasis key word phrase "most intriguing" highlights the discussion of *Countdown at Kusini*'s possible impact on the Nigerian film industry.

STEP 4: MAKE A PREDICTION

Any of the three reasons mentioned in the fourth paragraph would be the correct answer. Predict *crowdfunding*, *media activism*, and *effect on the nascent Nigerian film industry* alone or in any combination.

STEP 5: EVALUATE THE ANSWER CHOICES

(E) matches the third prediction and is correct. **(A)** is extreme. The film is identified as an early example of crowdfunding, but not necessarily as the first. **(B)** is not mentioned in the passage, as a connection between *Countdown at Kusini* and other privately produced films is not discussed. **(C)** is a 180, or opposite, choice. The film was a commercial failure, not a success. **(D)** is incorrect because the educational aspect of the film was not mentioned in the text.

Parfleche

STEP 1: READ THE PASSAGE STRATEGICALLY

On the left, we've shown how key words help you to identify the major elements of the passage and its structure and what you could skim over. On the right, we've shown what you might be thinking as you read the passage strategically.

Passage for Questions 13–17

PASSAGE	ANALYSIS
Parfleche is the French name for **the Plains peoples'** *hoemskot 'eo*—an envelope-shaped rawhide container for storing clothes, food, and personal items. The *parfleche* served **not only** as a **practical** and durable storage solution, **but also** as a decorative object of **spiritual significance**. Among certain tribes, **most notably** the Cheyenne and Arapaho, *parfleches* were decorated by the women's painting society, whose members among the Cheyenne were known as *moneneheo*, the Selected Ones. **Although similar** in their **economic and social** importance to craftsmen's guilds in medieval and Renaissance Western Europe, the painting society **also** had a **spiritual or religious** nature. The shamanistic society required application for admission and held its members to **high artistic and moral standards**. The society **further** displayed its importance by defining aspects of Cheyenne wealth and status.	The topic, the *parfleche*, is addressed and defined in the first sentence. The "not only… but also" structure indicates that the author will focus on the spiritual significance of the *parfleche*. Another contrast: the group that made *parfleche* was economic/social but also spiritual/religious.
Painting on rawhide was **fraught with challenges**. If painting was attempted while the prepared hide was too moist, the applied paint bled, but if the hide was too dry, the skin did not absorb the pigments. This restricted the time frame in which painting could best be completed, which meant that designs had to be visualized fully before the work started. **Moreover, every aspect** of creating a *parfleche* was a **sacred** act. Each design element, **for instance**, was a syntagma—a linguistic or visual unit intended to convey meaning—freighted with symbolic referents. **For example**, diamond shapes represented the *ha 'kot*, the grasshopper, an abundant grass eater itself symbolic of the bison, the sacred source of food, shelter, tools, and clothing. The tools used were **also symbolic**: the shape of the "flesher" used to prepare the hide represented lightning bolts—emblematic of the masculine essence of spirit. The flesher removed the flesh from the hide, transforming it into a spiritual container that would hold earthly matter (the people's material goods).	Making of *parfleche*: difficult; highly symbolic. Even tools symbolic.

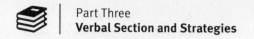

Even the **position** of the *parfleche* in the lodge held **symbolic** significance. It was stored beneath the bed of older women, **not only because** they were careful guardians, **but also because** they were closer to Grandmother Earth, from whose union with the lightning spirit the animals and plants of the middle world came to provide food and shelter. The symbolism of every aspect of the *parfleche*, **therefore**, from the interpretable design work on its outside to its storage place within the lodge, reflects the Cheyenne belief in a complementary worldview: the blending of the masculine spirit and the feminine physical matter.

Parfleche kept by mature women (considered spiritual people).

Conclusion: *parfleche* reflects masculine/feminine blend.

Passage Map

¶1: Intro to the parfleche and the people who created it

¶2: The process and symbolism involved in making the parfleche

¶3: The parfleche as a symbol of the Cheyenne worldview

Topic: The parfleche

Scope: The spiritual significance of the production, decoration, and use of the parfleche

Purpose: To explain the cultural and spiritual significance of the parfleche to the Plains peoples

13. (E)

According to the passage, one reason why there was a limited time frame in which to paint a prepared rawhide was that

○   the pigments dried quickly and thus had to be applied with speed to avoid cracking

○   if the hide was too dry, it absorbed too much paint

○   if the hide was too moist, it rejected the pigments

○   the designs had to be fully visualized before painting was started

○   if the hide was too moist, the paint bled

STEP 2: ANALYZE THE QUESTION STEM

The phrase "According to the passage..." indicates that this is a Detail question. The stem gives you a clear reference for your research: "limited time frame in which to paint a prepared rawhide."

STEP 3: RESEARCH THE RELEVANT TEXT

Using your passage map, you can refer to the second sentence of the second paragraph, where the author was discussing the difficulties in creating the *parfleche*.

STEP 4: MAKE A PREDICTION

The second sentence of paragraph 2 provides everything you need for a prediction of the correct answer: "If painting was attempted while the prepared hide was too moist, the applied paint bled, but if the hide was too dry, the skin did not absorb the pigments."

STEP 5: EVALUATE THE ANSWER CHOICES

(E) agrees perfectly with the first half of this statement and is correct. (A) is unsupported by the passage. (B) and (C) are both 180 wrong answer traps, since the sentence actually said that when the hides are too dry, they would not absorb paint. (D) is a distortion; it reverses the cause-and-effect relationship described in the passage. The reason that the designs had to be visualized in advance was the limited time during which the hides could be painted, not the other way around.

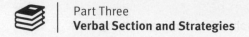
14. (E)

The main purpose of the passage is to

- ○ describe a tool used among Native Americans when working with rawhide
- ○ rebut a commonly held view about the symbolism of the *parfleche* for the Plains peoples
- ○ analyze the societies of the Cheyenne and Arapaho people
- ○ propose a new method for analyzing the use of symbolism in Native American art
- ○ discuss the spiritual and symbolic importance of a rawhide container and its decorations to several Plains tribes

STEP 2: ANALYZE THE QUESTION STEM

The wording here—"main purpose of the passage"—makes this one of the most common Global question stems that appear on the GMAT.

STEP 3: RESEARCH THE RELEVANT TEXT

Since you paraphrased the author's purpose while creating your passage map, you can simply refer to that; there is no need to go back to the passage itself.

STEP 4: MAKE A PREDICTION

The passage map tells you that the author wrote this passage to explain the *parfleche* and its "spiritual significance" to certain Indian tribes.

STEP 5: EVALUATE THE ANSWER CHOICES

(E) best summarizes this and properly reflects the author's tone. (E) is the correct answer. Notice that (E) doesn't use the word "*parfleche*" but rather its definition. Looking for the right words in Reading Comp answer choices is misguided; always look for the answer choice that matches the meaning or idea that you've predicted. (A) is too narrow in scope; it reflects only one detail from the text instead of the passage as a whole. (C) is too broad in scope; the author is focused on one aspect of Cheyenne culture. (B) and (D) are not correct because the author of this passage does not take a stand on or disagree with anyone about the symbolism of the *parfleche* or the methods used for studying it.

15. (D)

According to the author, the Cheyenne women's painting society was unlike Western European guilds of the Middle Ages and the Renaissance in that

- O   application for membership was required
- O   the group had significant economic standing in the community
- O   the group had significant social standing in the community
- O   the women's painting society was religious in nature
- O   the society had an influence on social standing and material valuation

STEP 2: ANALYZE THE QUESTION STEM

This is another Detail question, again with a clear reference point for research during the upcoming step 3. Here, you are asked what, in the author's words, distinguished the Cheyenne women's society that made the *parfleche* from medieval guilds.

STEP 3: RESEARCH THE RELEVANT TEXT

As expected, the contrast is highlighted by a key word—in this case, "[a]lthough"—in the passage. The Cheyenne group was similar to guilds in economic and social importance, but different because the Cheyenne painters' group was "spiritual or religious."

STEP 4: MAKE A PREDICTION

The correct answer will highlight the Cheyenne group's spiritual side.

STEP 5: EVALUATE THE ANSWER CHOICES

Thus, **(D)** is the correct answer choice. **(A)** is unsupported by this passage, since while you know that the women's painting society required application for membership, you do not know that the guilds were any different in their requirements. **(B)**, **(C)**, and **(E)** all describe ways in which the women's painting society was similar to the Western European guilds.

16. (A)

You can most reasonably conclude that the Cheyenne definition of the term *moneneheo* (line 6) reflects

- ○ the high status some women enjoyed as artists in Cheyenne culture
- ○ the shamanistic spiritual origins of the women's painting society
- ○ the notion that artists were chosen by the gods to perform their tasks
- ○ the self-restrictive nature of the women's painting society
- ○ a woman's skill in using rawhide tools such as the "flesher"

STEP 2: ANALYZE THE QUESTION STEM

The wording of this question stem is a bit unusual, but a moment's reflection tells you that this is an Inference question. Inference questions ask what must be true based on the passage. In this case, the passage gives you information indicating why the Cheyenne would refer to the women's painting society members as *moneneheo*. The question simply wants you to paraphrase that information accurately.

STEP 3: RESEARCH THE RELEVANT TEXT

The question stem refers to the word *moneneheo* in line 6, where the author tells you that it refers to the members of the women's painting society and translates as "the Selected Ones." The author goes on to explain the society's high importance and the "high artistic and moral standards" required for admission and membership.

STEP 4: MAKE A PREDICTION

Predicting an answer to the question, say that the Cheyenne term reflects respect for the society members' status, talent, importance, etc. Remember, you aren't trying to predict the *words* of the answer but, rather, its meaning.

STEP 5: EVALUATE THE ANSWER CHOICES

(A), with its emphasis on status, matches the prediction nicely and is correct. Although you are told that the *moneneheo* is a shamanistic organization, you learn nothing about its origins, so **(B)** is unsupported. **(C)** requires a leap from the use of "selected" to the notion that the gods do the selecting. Nothing the author writes supports this leap. The author mentions no sense in which the term *moneneheo* refers to anything "self-restrictive" on the part of the women's painting society; **(D)** is unsupported. The author draws no association between the term and the skinning tool or "flesher" (which is, in any case, not mentioned until the end of paragraph 2); thus, **(E)** is also unsupported.

17. (D)

The author describes the symbolic meanings of the diamond shape most likely in order to

- ○ indicate how precious the completed *parfleche* was to its owner
- ○ prove that the grasshopper was superior to the bison in Cheyenne religion
- ○ illustrate the visual complexity of the abstract forms used in creating a *parfleche*
- ○ provide an example of the many layers of symbolism involved in creating a *parfleche*
- ○ demonstrate the relationship between the symbolic shapes of the tools and the abstract designs used in creating a *parfleche*

STEP 2: ANALYZE THE QUESTION STEM

This is an archetypal GMAT Logic question. You are referred to a detail—here, the "diamond shape"—and asked why the author includes it in the passage. Notice that the wording of the question, ending with "in order to…" means that the answer choices must begin with verbs.

STEP 3: RESEARCH THE RELEVANT TEXT

The diamond shape was among the symbols mentioned in the second paragraph. It is located in a sentence that begins with the illustration key words "[f]or example." The sentence goes on to tell you that the diamond represents the grasshopper, which in turn represents the bison, which in turn is sacred, and so on.

STEP 4: MAKE A PREDICTION

Your research tells you that this answer must begin with a verb meaning "illustrate" or "give an example of" and continue by saying something about the symbolic meanings of the *parfleche*.

STEP 5: EVALUATE THE ANSWER CHOICES

(D) matches the prediction and is correct. Given the verbs that begin each answer choice, only **(C)** and **(D)** are really in the running. **(C)** distorts the purpose of the diamond-shape example beyond what you read in the passage. Closer reading shows answers **(A)**, **(B)**, and **(E)**, already suspect for having the wrong purpose verbs, to be even worse. **(A)** addresses the value of the *parfleche* to its owner, a topic touched on nowhere in the passage. **(B)** suggests an unsupported, and rather ridiculous, comparison between the grasshopper and bison as characterized in Cheyenne culture. **(E)** tries to apply the diamond-shape example to the tool-use example that comes later in the paragraph.

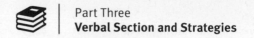

One-Child Policy

STEP 1: READ THE PASSAGE STRATEGICALLY

On the left, we've shown how key words help you to identify the major elements of the passage and its structure and what you could skim over. On the right, we've shown what you might be thinking as you read the passage strategically.

Passage for Questions 18–23

PASSAGE	ANALYSIS
A **one-child policy** was implemented in China in 1979, and for nearly 40 years, until the policy was amended to allow two children in 2015, some Han Chinese families could legally have only one child. This rule was implemented in **an attempt** to slow continued growth of a population that had almost doubled since 1949. The Chinese government **claimed** that the policy prevented 400 million births, **though** some have suggested that the decline may be at least partly due to economic reasons, **not** legal ones.	The first sentence announces the topic: the one-child policy in China. "Claimed" is a flag that there may be a dispute, and "though" signals another point of view or evidence to the contrary. Government claims one thing; "some" claim another explanation.
One result of the policy **seems** to be the birth and survival of significantly more boys than girls. **One study found** that China had 33 million more boys than girls under the age of 20, and it is believed that by 2030, 25 percent of Chinese men in their late 30s will never have been married. **Research has shown** that an excess of men of marriageable age is linked to higher rates of psychological problems, as it creates a marginalized underclass, **and history would suggest** such situations may correlate with increased aggression and violence, both inside and outside a country's borders.	A result of the one-child policy: more boys born/survive than girls. Research links this to psychological problems. History shows excess male population correlates with increased violence, but this seems more speculative.

Economist Amartya Sen wrote in 1990 of the phenomenon of "missing women" in population data, noting that in China, "the survival prospects of female children clearly have been unfavorably affected by restrictions on the size of the family." In a society that has traditionally strongly favored sons, it has been **suggested** that sex-specific pregnancy terminations and infanticide account for the discrepancy in numbers. **But** others have **countered** this argument, believing that disease might better explain the phenomenon, either by making women more likely to give birth to male children or by making it more likely that female children will die prenatally or when very young. **For at least some** of the missing girls, however, a **less sinister** explanation may prove the correct one: parents who already had a child, or who wanted to be able to have another in an attempt to have a son, simply never registered their daughters with government officials. **A recent study** found evidence that as many as 25 million girls were not registered at birth, some of them officially "existing" only many years later and others perhaps never officially existing at all

There are "missing women." Some believe this is due to deliberate actions.

Others believe there is a natural explanation.

Third possible explanation: not registering with government officials, per a recent study.

Author takes no stance on any of the theories.

Passage Map

¶1: China's one-child policy

¶2: Result of policy: more boys born/survive than girls; potential negative results

¶3: Three theories about why: deliberate (prefer son), natural (disease), lack of government registration

Topic: China's one-child policy

Scope: Result of the policy = missing girls?

Purpose: Examine one apparent result of the one-child policy and three potential explanations for it

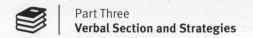

18. (D)

The primary purpose of the passage is to

○ criticize the accepted explanation for missing girls in China since the implementation of the one-child policy

○ show why the expected population decline in China due to the one-child policy was not due to a decrease in the number of males

○ demonstrate how China's one-child policy has influenced past and future birth rates

○ explore the phenomenon of missing girls in China during the years of the one-child policy

○ argue that the expected population decline in China due to the one-child policy was due entirely to a decrease in the number of women

STEP 2: ANALYZE THE QUESTION STEM

This Global question asks for the primary purpose of the passage as a whole.

STEP 3: RESEARCH THE RELEVANT TEXT

There's no need to go back to the passage itself. Review the purpose in the passage map.

STEP 4: MAKE A PREDICTION

The author discussed one result of the one-child policy (missing girls) and three potential explanations for that result. The correct answer will reflect this.

STEP 5: EVALUATE THE ANSWER CHOICES

(D), while phrased in broader terms than the purpose in the passage map, nonetheless encapsulates the passage as a whole and is the correct answer. The author does not criticize any of the potential explanations for the missing girls, so **(A)** is out. While the author does discuss the fact that more boys than girls apparently are born and survive (lines 8–9), nothing is said about whether the population of males declined. That population may have declined just as predicted, or even more than predicted; all that is known based on the passage is that the policy appears to have impacted women more than men. Eliminate **(B)**. The author does not discuss future birth rates, so eliminate **(C)**. **(E)** is extreme and has a similar problem as **(B)**: based on the information in the passage, it cannot be said that population decline occurred *only* because there were fewer women. Moreover, the author is neutral rather than making an argument. So **(E)**, too, can be eliminated.

19. (B)

According to the passage, which of the following is true of societies in which there are not enough female partners for men of marriageable age?

- ○ They occurred historically but are not known to occur in the modern day.
- ○ They may be at increased risk of international conflict.
- ○ They are more likely to develop when a significant proportion of the population is psychologically damaged.
- ○ They are not known to have occurred prior to the modern day.
- ○ They can result in the disappearance of women from official records.

STEP 2: ANALYZE THE QUESTION STEM

This is a Detail question. The correct answer will be something discussed in the passage.

STEP 3: RESEARCH THE RELEVANT TEXT

The question stem refers to a gender imbalance, which is one result of the one-child policy. According to the passage map, results are discussed in the second paragraph, so research the answer there. The author says that having more men than women of marriageable age is "linked to higher rates of psychological problems" and "increased aggression and violence, both inside and outside a country's borders."

STEP 4: MAKE A PREDICTION

Based on the research, the correct answer will be about psychological problems or increased conflict, or both.

STEP 5: EVALUATE THE ANSWER CHOICES

While the author says there is only historical evidence of a correlation between international violence ("violence… outside a country's borders") and a society with more men than women, such conflict is a possibility. The qualified language of **(B)** ("may be") is a match to the text, and this choice is correct. The passage is discussing a potential modern-day example of such a society, proving such societies did not exist only in the past, so **(A)** can be eliminated. **(C)** confuses cause and effect. The passage indicates that the psychological damage occurs as a result of the society, not that the society develops as a result of psychological damage. **(D)** is the reverse of **(A)** and is also incorrect. While the author is primarily discussing a possible modern example of such a society, potential historical occurrences are also mentioned and so are not unknown. **(E)** is not supported by the passage. If women disappear from official records, their absence would create the appearance of a society in which men outnumber women, but in no way does such a society cause women to disappear.

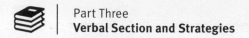

20. (A)

The last paragraph in the passage serves primarily to

- ○ present multiple potential explanations for a phenomenon described in the second paragraph
- ○ offer a critique of explanations put forward for the outcome of the policy in which the author is primarily interested
- ○ demonstrate that the least sinister explanation of a troubling phenomenon is the correct one
- ○ explain fully the phenomenon described in the second paragraph
- ○ outline why social attitudes may explain the result of the policy that is the topic of the passage

STEP 2: ANALYZE THE QUESTION STEM

This question asks you for the function of the final paragraph and is thus a Logic question. Think of it as being similar to a Global question about the author's purpose, but on a smaller scale. Instead of asking for the primary purpose of the passage as a whole, it asks for the purpose of one paragraph. Keep in mind that each paragraph supports the fulfillment of the author's overall purpose in writing.

STEP 3: RESEARCH THE RELEVANT TEXT

Rather than reviewing the entire paragraph, review the passage map for a summary. The final paragraph discusses theories about why there are fewer girls than boys in China. The missing girls are initially discussed in the second paragraph.

STEP 4: MAKE A PREDICTION

The correct answer will summarize that the last paragraph provides explanations without evaluating their relative merits.

STEP 5: EVALUATE THE ANSWER CHOICES

(A) matches the prediction and is correct. The "phenomenon described in the second paragraph" is the fact that in China, the number of boys who are born and survive seems to exceed the number of girls. "Present" matches the author's neutral tone. **(B)**, with "offer a critique," misses the mark, as the author of the passage doesn't evaluate the various explanations other people have put forward. While the author does describe the last explanation given as "less sinister," nowhere is it implied that this makes it more likely to be correct, so **(C)** is incorrect. The function of the final paragraph is to present several explanations offered by other people that may account for some or all of the missing girls, not to "fully explain" their absence as in **(D)**. Finally, **(E)** paraphrases one reason discussed in the last paragraph, a strong preference for sons, but the purpose of the paragraph is to offer several reasons, not just this one.

21. (B)

According to the passage, each of the following is a possible reason for missing girls in China EXCEPT:

O   Disease may cause more boys to be born than girls.

O   The one-child policy does not require girls to be registered.

O   Disease may cause more girls to die prenatally than boys.

O   Infanticide of female children occurs because families prefer sons.

O   Some girls are not registered so that parents can have another child.

STEP 2: ANALYZE THE QUESTION STEM

"According to the passage" indicates that this is a Detail question. The "EXCEPT" means that each incorrect answer will be found in the passage, while the correct answer will not.

STEP 3: RESEARCH THE RELEVANT TEXT

The third paragraph gives possible reasons for the missing girls: societal preference for boys, disease, or parents' failure to register the births of girls.

STEP 4: MAKE A PREDICTION

For an EXCEPT question, you can't predict what the correct answer will be, but you can predict the incorrect answers. In this case, the incorrect answers that you'll eliminate will reflect the reasons identified in step 2.

STEP 5: EVALUATE THE ANSWER CHOICES

(B) is not mentioned in the passage. While the final paragraph says that it is possible some of the missing girls are not registered, it suggests that parents avoid registering children to deceive the government and thus that parents are in fact supposed to register their daughters. Thus, **(B)** is the correct answer. **(A)**, **(C)**, **(D)**, and **(E)** are all stated in the passage and so are incorrect.

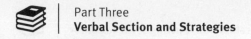

22. (E)

Based on information in the passage, which of the following outcomes would have been most likely to occur if a Han Chinese family had a baby daughter prior to 2015?

- ○ The parents are eventually pleased to have had a daughter, because there are so many marriageable men.

- ○ Because disease may kill the daughter, the parents have another child in hopes of having a son.

- ○ The parents appeal to the authorities to approve an exception to the number of children allowed.

- ○ Because a pregnancy is more likely to result in a son than a daughter, the parents have another child.

- ○ The parents fail to officially register the daughter, and they have another child.

STEP 2: ANALYZE THE QUESTION STEM

This question presents a hypothetical situation and asks you to apply information from the passage to select the most likely outcome from those listed. Thus, this is an Application question. The words "[b]ased on information in the passage" are key: do not imagine what might be true but instead choose an outcome that the passage discusses.

STEP 3: RESEARCH THE RELEVANT TEXT

Han Chinese are mentioned in the first paragraph, where the author says that before 2015, some were allowed to have only one child. The rest of the passage discusses various consequences of this law, and actions that parents might take are mentioned in the third paragraph.

STEP 4: MAKE A PREDICTION

As no exact prediction can be made, be prepared to research each choice individually, knowing that the correct answer will most likely be supported by information in the last paragraph.

STEP 5: EVALUATE THE ANSWER CHOICES

(E) is supported by the final paragraph, which suggests that some parents indeed fail to register girls in order to have another child. This is the correct choice. The passage never discusses how parents come to feel about their children after the passage of time or whether a dearth of marriageable men is changing attitudes toward having daughters. Therefore, **(A)** is unsupported and incorrect. **(B)** is also unsupported, as the passage gives disease as a possible reason for a smaller than expected number of female children, but it does not imply that fear a daughter might die would lead parents to having another child. **(C)** can be eliminated because the passage provides no information about whether parents may appeal for an exception. **(D)** distorts the information that disease may cause more boys than girls to be born; it's never suggested that this phenomenon, if it is true, motivates parents to have a second child.

23. (A)

The author mentions a "marginalized underclass" (line 12) most likely in order to

○   show one potential societal risk of the one-child policy

○   give an example of why there are more men than women in China

○   demonstrate that men are inherently more violent than women

○   argue that widespread poverty may cause people to value boys more than girls

○   illustrate the effect of the one-child policy on average family income

STEP 2: ANALYZE THE QUESTION STEM

The phrase "in order to" indicates that this is a Logic question. Specifically, the question asks *why* the author mentions a "marginalized underclass."

STEP 3: RESEARCH THE RELEVANT TEXT

The question stem refers to line 12, but the preceding line is also part of the relevant text: "Research has shown that an excess of men of marriageable age is linked to higher rates of psychological problems, as it creates a marginalized underclass…"

STEP 4: MAKE A PREDICTION

The phrase appears as part of the evidence of the potential negative impact of having significantly more men than women.

STEP 5: EVALUATE THE ANSWER CHOICES

(A) matches the prediction and is the correct answer. For (B), while the passage says that more boys are being born/surviving than girls, it doesn't mention a "marginalized underclass" as a reason for this. This underclass does not cause, but may be caused by, the population discrepancy. (C) is a distortion. The passage says it is possible that violence will rise if there are significantly more men of marriageable age than women, but not that men are innately more violent. Regardless, violence is listed alongside the psychological issues that are caused by a "marginalized underclass" and so is not the reason the author uses that phrase. For (D), the author is not attempting to make an argument at all; the passage is neutral in presentation. At any rate, there is no indication that attitudes toward boys and girls are caused by poverty. (E) is incorrect because while the one-child policy may result in unmarried and thus marginalized men, nothing is said about "average family income" across China.

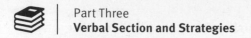
Flycatchers

STEP 1: READ THE PASSAGE STRATEGICALLY

On the left, we've shown how key words help you to identify the major elements of the passage and its structure and what you could skim over. On the right, we've shown what you might be thinking as you read the passage strategically.

Passage for Questions 24–29

PASSAGE	ANALYSIS
Generally, interspecific matings represent an evolutionary **dead end**, producing sterile offspring, if any at all. For some species of birds, **however**, such pairings may indeed bring evolutionary advantages to the participants.	"Generally" implies that there will be an exception. Usually, interspecific mating doesn't work.
In the case of the female collared flycatchers of Gotland, **three distinct factors** may work to make interspecific pairings with pied flycatcher males reproductively **beneficial**.	The female collared flycatcher is the exception. You're going to see three reasons why.
In many instances, female collared flycatchers nest with male pied flycatchers while continuing to mate with other collared flycatchers, in effect parasitizing the pied flycatchers, who invest in rearing and fledging any offspring. **Often**, more than half of the offspring raised by interspecific flycatcher pairs are, **in fact**, not hybrids.	Why interspecific mating works for female collared flycatchers: 1. They get pied flycatchers to raise their collared flycatcher offspring.
Furthermore, an estimated 65 percent of the hybrid offspring of the resident pied flycatcher male are male. **Because** hybrid females are sterile and males are not, this male bias minimizes the primary disadvantage of interspecific matings: sterile offspring. Habitat specialization may be **a third mechanism**: these pairings tend to occur in the late spring when the coniferous woods favored by the pied flycatcher provide a greater availability of food than the deciduous woods where the collared flycatchers tend to live.	2. The offspring aren't all sterile. 3. Pied flycatchers live where the food is.
Together, these factors form a mechanism to **improve substantially** the reproductive success of female collared flycatchers beyond what would be expected of interspecific mating with pied flycatcher males.	These factors seem to work together.

Although all three of these mechanisms appear to act in concert to form a single elaborate mechanism specifically evolved to circumvent the usual disadvantages of interspecific mating, **studies have shown similar motivations** for the behavior of female collared flycatchers mating within the species. **According to** Professor Siever Rohwer, collared flycatcher females will choose to nest with subordinate collared flycatcher males that inhabit good territory **because** collared flycatcher females must pair-bond in order to be successful in raising offspring. To engender the best offspring, **however**, the females will continue to copulate with higher-quality collared males with whom they are not paired. **Thus**, females **seem to** be nesting with males of any species with the best territories available at the time, **but they will** continue to mate with more attractive males outside of their pair bonds.

"Although…similar motivations": female collared flycatchers act the same way when mating with male collared flycatchers.

Pair with males that have good nests; mate with others, too.

A **highly unusual** behavior, interspecific mating **seems to provide** certain reproductive **advantages** to the collared flycatcher female. **However**, it **remains unclear** whether the mating behavior of female collared flycatchers evolved to circumvent the usual problems with interspecific mating or whether the behavior is simply an extension of how female collared flycatchers behave when mating within their own species.

The author is wrapping up.

"However" shows the central unanswered question: did female collared flycatchers evolve this way because of interspecific mating or just because they act this way generally?

Passage Map

¶1: Interspecific mating—usually evolutionary dead end/sterile offspring; FCF is exception

¶2: 3 advantages of interspecific mating for FCF

¶3: FCF nests/mates same way intraspecifically, too. Same advantages

¶4: Question—did FCF evolve this way for interspecific mating or just in general?

Topic: Interspecific mating—female collared flycatcher exception

Scope: FCF's interspecific and intraspecific mating behaviors and their evolutionary advantages

Purpose: Describe FCF's mating/nesting behavior and pose an unanswered question about its origins

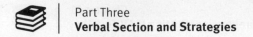
24. (D)

The author's primary purpose is to

- ○ criticize the basis of a scientific theory
- ○ defend a hypothesis concerning bird-mating behaviors
- ○ point out the need for further study of female collared flycatchers
- ○ describe two possible explanations for the interspecific mating behavior of female collared flycatchers
- ○ defend an unpopular view of a natural phenomenon

STEP 2: ANALYZE THE QUESTION STEM

"Primary purpose" signals that this is a Global question.

STEP 3: RESEARCH THE RELEVANT TEXT

No research within the passage is required. You just need to consult the passage map, specifically the statement of the author's purpose.

STEP 4: MAKE A PREDICTION

The statement of the author's purpose said that the author was describing the mating behavior of the female collared flycatcher and posing a question about it. Two possible explanations are presented: (1) interspecies mating brings distinct benefits, and (2) interspecies mating is just an extension of normal behavior. With that background, you're more than ready to assess the choices.

STEP 5: EVALUATE THE ANSWER CHOICES

(D) summarizes the author's purpose and is correct. **(A)** is incorrect because the author never takes a stand on either explanation and so does not "criticize" anything. Similarly, **(B)** and **(E)** are wrong because the author does not "defend" anything. The author never calls for further research, so **(C)** is not correct either.

25. (C)

According to the passage, female collared flycatchers' mating with male pied flycatchers could be explained by any of the following reasons EXCEPT:

○   Food is more available in pied flycatcher territories during the mating season.

○   Male pied flycatchers can help raise offspring successfully, even if the offspring are not theirs.

○   Male pied flycatchers sire more female offspring than do collared flycatcher males, increasing the reproductive success of the female collared flycatcher.

○   Females are known to nest with subordinate males while pursuing extra-pair copulation with higher-quality males.

○   Females enjoy greater reproductive success by pair-bonding with an inferior male than by not pair-bonding at all.

STEP 2: ANALYZE THE QUESTION STEM

"According to the passage" is a clear indication that this is a Detail question. Just make sure you didn't miss the "EXCEPT" at the end of the stem. Here, the four wrong answers will all have been cited in the text. The correct answer will not. Remember, the correct answer to a Detail EXCEPT question may contradict the text or not be mentioned in the passage. The right answer might also repeat a piece of information that appears in the text but that has no relevance to the question posed in the stem (i.e., make a faulty use of detail). Here, the wrong answers will give possible explanations for the female collared flycatcher's unusual mating behavior.

STEP 3: RESEARCH THE RELEVANT TEXT

The female collared flycatcher's nesting and mating behaviors are explained in the second and third paragraphs. While the question asks specifically about explanations for the interspecific mating behaviors, remember that the third paragraph told you that the motivations for intraspecific mating behaviors were similar.

STEP 4: MAKE A PREDICTION

You cannot predict what the correct answer will say, but the four wrong answers will be supported by text from paragraphs 2 or 3. Be prepared to eliminate these; what's left will be correct.

STEP 5: EVALUATE THE ANSWER CHOICES

The passage says that pied males mating with collared females father more males than females. Thus, **(C)** directly contradicts paragraph 2, making **(C)** the correct answer. The coniferous forests where the pied flycatchers live are indeed richer in food late in the season, as **(A)** suggests. Females may use the pied males for their help in rearing young—including those sired by other males—as **(B)** says. **(D)** and **(E)** are both supported by paragraph 3.

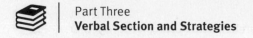
26. (C)

The bias toward male offspring resulting from the mating of collared flycatcher females and pied flycatcher males is presented as evidence that

- ○ collared flycatcher females that mate with pied flycatcher males have more dominant male offspring
- ○ the offspring from extra-pair matings with collared flycatcher males are more frequently male
- ○ female flycatchers are not deterred from interspecific pairing by the likelihood of sterile hybrid offspring
- ○ males are produced to reduce interspecific inbreeding in future generations
- ○ interspecific breeding is normal in all varieties of flycatchers

STEP 2: ANALYZE THE QUESTION STEM

The language of the question stem indicates that this is a Logic question. This stem goes out of its way to be helpful, though, by telling you that the detail at issue—the predominance of male offspring from male pied and female collared flycatcher mates—is presented as evidence. Your job will simply be to research what it is used as evidence for.

STEP 3: RESEARCH THE RELEVANT TEXT

The reference to the offspring of male pied and female collared flycatcher mates leads you to paragraph 2. You're told that the male offspring are not sterile, thus minimizing a typical downside to interspecies mating.

STEP 4: MAKE A PREDICTION

The correct answer will tell you that the male offspring bias is evidence that a typical disadvantage—sterile offspring—of interspecies mating is not present when female collared flycatchers and male pied flycatchers mate.

STEP 5: EVALUATE THE ANSWER CHOICES

(C) matches the prediction nicely. It is correct. (A) is simply not mentioned in the passage; the dominance of offspring is not discussed. (B) is a distortion; it is the interspecific hybrids, not pure collared flycatchers, that show a male bias in their offspring. (D) is incorrect because no argument is ever made about future generations of interspecific breeding. And (E) is incorrect because the passage does not comment on the regularity of interspecific breeding by any bird other than the female collared flycatcher.

27. (A)

It can be inferred from the passage that

- ○ food resources are an important determinant of success in raising offspring
- ○ having 50 percent male offspring is not optimal for collared flycatcher pairs
- ○ flycatchers generally mate for life
- ○ males do not vary in the benefits they provide to their offspring
- ○ over half of all females engage in extra-pair matings

STEP 2: ANALYZE THE QUESTION STEM

Here's an open-ended Inference question. The stem references no specific detail or part of the passage. Begin your evaluation of the answers with reference to what you know about the topic, scope, and purpose overall.

STEP 3: RESEARCH THE RELEVANT TEXT

Given that there is no reference to guide your research within the passage, simply review your topic, scope, and purpose summaries. You may have to do further research choice by choice.

STEP 4: MAKE A PREDICTION

Lacking a point of reference in the passage, you cannot make a prediction beyond saying that the correct answer will follow from the passage and agree with the author. That should be enough to help you find the correct answer or, at least, eliminate one or more of the wrong ones.

STEP 5: EVALUATE THE ANSWER CHOICES

The second paragraph points out that the greater abundance of food in pied flycatcher habitats late in the mating season is a mechanism that makes interspecies pairings reproductively beneficial. If food were not relevant to the success of raising offspring, it could not be a mechanism to make interspecific mating reproductively beneficial. So **(A)** is true based on the passage; this is the exact criterion for the correct answer in an Inference question.

All four wrong answers are either unsupported by anything addressed by the passage or out-and-out contradict the passage. **(B)** is not mentioned—the percentage of male offspring is discussed only in relation to interspecific pairs. Mating for life is never mentioned either, so **(C)** is incorrect. The fact that females *do* choose males on the basis of reproductive benefits makes **(D)** incorrect; it contradicts what the passage implies. Lastly, you have no basis for knowing the proportion of females that engage in extra-pair matings, so **(E)** is unsupported.

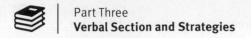
28. (C)

Professor Rohwer would most likely agree with which of the following statements?

○ All traits related to particular functions have evolved only for those particular functions.

○ Flycatchers represent the best population for studies of bird-mating behavior.

○ Behaviors may appear functional even under conditions other than those under which the behaviors evolved.

○ Evolution has played no role in shaping the behavior of interspecifically paired flycatchers.

○ Hybridization is generally beneficial.

STEP 2: ANALYZE THE QUESTION STEM

This is also an Inference question, as signaled by the phrase "most likely agree with…" The key is to spot that it is Professor Rohwer's opinion that you are drawing your inference from.

STEP 3: RESEARCH THE RELEVANT TEXT

Rohwer's opinion is discussed in the third paragraph, where the passage demonstrates the similarities between the female collared flycatcher's interspecies and intraspecies mating behavior. Rohwer's point is that pair-bonding is essential to the female collared flycatcher's success in rearing young. The implication is that the female collared flycatcher will nest with one male and mate with others regardless of whether she is engaged in intra- or interspecies mating.

STEP 4: MAKE A PREDICTION

The correct answer will have to address the context in which the author cites Rowher. The point is that it may be the necessity of pair-bonding, rather than an adaptation that favors interspecific mating, that drives the birds' behavior.

STEP 5: EVALUATE THE ANSWER CHOICES

The prediction supports **(C)** as the correct answer. **(B)** and **(E)** are unsupported: the relative benefits of studying flycatchers rather than other birds is not discussed, nor is Rohwer's opinion on the benefits of hybridization. **(A)** and **(D)** contradict, at least by implication, the message of the passage; they also include the phrases "*all* traits" and "played *no* role," which flag extreme statements.

29. (B)

The mating behavior of female collared flycatchers paired with subordinate male flycatchers is offered as

- ○ an unwarranted assumption behind the adaptive explanation of interspecific matings
- ○ an alternative explanation for pair matings of collared females with pied males
- ○ evidence supporting the hypothesis of adaption for interspecific breeding
- ○ a discredited mainstream explanation for why hybridization is a dead end
- ○ proof in support of the theory that collared and pied flycatchers are separate species

STEP 2: ANALYZE THE QUESTION STEM

Here is another Logic question. Like all Logic stems, this one gives you a clear reference to guide your research. The female collared flycatchers that pair with subordinates are mentioned in the third paragraph. Remember that Logic questions ask *why* the author included the detail, not *what* she said about it.

STEP 3: RESEARCH THE RELEVANT TEXT

The third paragraph is about the female collared flycatcher's intraspecies nesting and mating behaviors. The specific fact highlighted by the author was that the female collared flycatcher behaves similarly when mating with male collared flycatchers as it does when mating with pied males. The author's point is that the female collared flycatcher's behavior may not have evolved exclusively in support of interspecies mating.

STEP 4: MAKE A PREDICTION

While you don't know the wording that the correct answer will use, you can anticipate that it will address the position that the female collared flycatcher's behavior is possibly explained by more than just adaptation to interspecific mating.

STEP 5: EVALUATE THE ANSWER CHOICES

The prediction leads to **(B)**, which is the correct answer. Paragraph 2 had explained how the female collared flycatcher's behavior is well adapted to the special problems of interspecies mating, so paragraph 3 qualifies as an "alternative explanation." Stated evidence can never be an assumption (which is unstated), so **(A)** is incorrect. The evidence in question does not support the adaptive explanation for interspecies breeding—in fact, it does just the opposite—so **(C)** is a wrong answer choice. This evidence is also not an explanation for why hybridization is a dead end; thus, **(D)** is wrong. Lastly, that the collared and pied flycatchers are separate species is a given in the passage; otherwise, the pairing of pied males and collared females could not be called interspecific. Moreover, this evidence has nothing to do with this issue, making **(E)** incorrect.

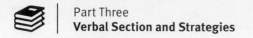

Rainbows

STEP 1: READ THE PASSAGE STRATEGICALLY

On the left, we've shown how key words help you to identify the major elements of the passage and its structure and what you could skim over. On the right, we've shown what you might be thinking as you read the passage strategically.

Passage for Questions 30–35

PASSAGE	ANALYSIS
Rainbows have long been a part of religion and mythology in cultures around the globe, appearing as bridges between the heavens and the earth, as messages from the gods, or as weapons wielded by divine powers. Some cultures have viewed rainbows themselves as deities, or even as demonic beings from which to hide children. **But** in the early fourteenth century, Theodoric of Freiburg, a German friar, and Kamal al-Din al-Farisi, a Persian scientist, independently turned a **scientific** eye to the study of rainbows.	The topic of the passage is rainbows. Presence in religion/mythology. "But" signals shift of focus: scientific study.
Theodoric and al-Farisi were thousands of miles apart, **but both** had studied Ibn al-Haytham's *Book of Optics*. **Each** concluded that a rainbow's appearance is the result of sunlight refracting and reflecting through water droplets left after a rainfall. They conducted experiments to provide **support for their conclusions**, successfully re-creating the conditions necessary to make a rainbow appear; al-Farisi used a sphere and a camera obscura, while Theodoric used flasks and globes.	14th-c studies: very far apart, but both men reached same conclusion about rainbows, and both were able to re-create a rainbow in experiments.
Both scholars were, as **modern physics** has shown, **correct** in their assessments. When light hits a water droplet, the water causes the light's speed to decrease. Furthermore, the light **refracts**—or changes direction—upon entering the droplet, and some of the light reflects off the back of the droplet, **refracting again** as it exits. The angle of refraction depends on the wavelength of the light; thus, refraction "breaks" white light into multiple wavelengths—a phenomenon called **dispersion**—which appear as different colors.	Jumps to modern knowledge. Refraction = light waves change direction. Dispersion = light breaks into separate wavelengths (colors).

But for a rainbow to fill the sky with color, **more** is needed. A **single droplet** of water will disperse the entire visible light spectrum, with each wavelength leaving at a different angle, **but** it alone cannot create a rainbow. **Only** a little of the light from a particular droplet reaches the eye of the human observer, striking the eye **from a particular angle**. For the observer to perceive the rainbow's characteristic banded arc of different colors, a **multitude of droplets** suspended in the air, refracting and dispersing light, are **needed**, with the shorter wavelengths and shallower angles of indigo and violet appearing to the observer at the bottom and the longer wavelengths and steeper angles of red and orange appearing at the top.

Just refraction and dispersion aren't enough; angle also important.

Rainbow = many drops refracting/reflecting light.

Passage Map

¶1: Rainbows in religion/myth & 14th-c. science

¶2: Medieval studies of rainbows by Theodoric/al-Farisi—different methods, same conclusion

¶3: Physics of rainbows confirms T & al-F's thinking; refraction/dispersion

¶4: More physics of rainbows (angle of observation); many droplets needed for rainbow

Topic: Rainbows

Scope: Explanations of rainbows in myth & science

Purpose: To describe supernatural and scientific explanations of rainbows

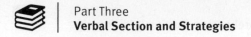

30. (D)

The author mentions the angle at which light leaves water droplets (lines 19–21) primarily in order to

○ describe how refraction causes light to disperse as it leaves a water droplet

○ show that indigo and violet appear at the bottom of rainbows because those colors have shallower angles

○ illustrate that a change in the angle of light changes the wavelength of the light

○ explain that the human eye perceives a rainbow only when light is refracted from multiple points

○ introduce evidence that may help solve a long-standing mystery about the physics of refraction

STEP 2: ANALYZE THE QUESTION STEM

This is a Logic question that asks why the author included information about the angle of light leaving water droplets.

STEP 3: RESEARCH THE RELEVANT TEXT

The cited lines are in the last paragraph. First consult the passage map to review the main point of the paragraph, which is to explain why lots of droplets are needed for someone to see a rainbow. Then review the text, including a little above and below the cited lines. The author says that light emerges from a droplet at various angles, but light from that droplet only strikes the human eye at one angle, and this is why light from many droplets is needed for a rainbow to appear.

STEP 4: MAKE A PREDICTION

The correct answer will associate the information about angles with the way light is perceived by the human observer.

STEP 5: EVALUATE THE ANSWER CHOICES

(D) matches the prediction and is thus the correct answer. **(A)** relates to the discussion of refraction in the third paragraph, and dispersion of light is associated with the angles at which light leaves the water droplet. However, describing refraction is not why the author mentions the angle of light in the fourth paragraph. **(B)** is also found in the passage: later in the same paragraph, the author says that different angles of light are associated with different colors of the rainbow, but showing this to be true is not why the author discusses the angle of light in the cited lines. **(C)** misstates information in the passage; light's wavelength affects its angle of refraction, not the other way around. As for **(E)**, based on the passage, refraction is well understood, but even if it weren't, nothing in the passage implies that the angle of light is the key to understanding refraction.

31. (E)

Based on the passage, it can be inferred that the rainbow's middle colors of yellow, green, and blue

- ○ are not broken into separate bands by the dispersion of light leaving a droplet of water
- ○ have longer wavelengths than do the red and orange light at the top of the rainbow
- ○ have wavelengths that all strike the eye of a human observer at the same angle
- ○ have wavelengths that are refracted at shallower angles than the wavelengths of indigo and violet light
- ○ have wavelengths that are shorter than those of red and orange light and longer than those of indigo and violet light

STEP 2: ANALYZE THE QUESTION STEM

This is an Inference question asking what you can reasonably conclude, based on the passage, about the three middle colors of the rainbow.

STEP 3: RESEARCH THE RELEVANT TEXT

The middle colors of yellow, green, and blue are not directly mentioned in the passage, but what colors *are* mentioned? The final sentence says that red and orange have the longest wavelengths and refract at the sharpest angles, and they appear at the top of the rainbow; by contrast, indigo and violet have the shortest wavelengths and refract at the shallowest angles, and they appear at the bottom of the rainbow.

STEP 4: MAKE A PREDICTION

Based on the research, you can infer that the colors in the middle of the rainbow are also in the middle when it comes to wavelengths and angles of refraction. The correct answer should include one or both of these ideas.

STEP 5: EVALUATE THE ANSWER CHOICES

(E) matches the prediction and is correct: the three middle colors can be inferred to have wavelengths that are shorter than those of orange and red and longer than those of indigo and violet. **(A)** is not supported by the passage, which never indicates that some colors' wavelengths do not disperse. **(B)** is a 180. The passage indicates that longer wavelengths are associated with higher positions on the rainbow, so the middle colors cannot have longer wavelengths than do red or orange. **(C)** also contradicts what the passage implies, which is that light of different colors refracts at different angles. **(D)**, like **(B)**, is a 180. The passage indicates that shallower angles are associated with lower positions on the rainbow, so the middle colors cannot have shallower angles than do indigo and violet.

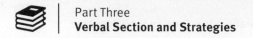

32. (C)

According to the passage, the refraction of light upon entering and leaving a water droplet

- ○ changes the angle at which light leaves the water droplet, thereby altering the light's wavelength
- ○ causes the light to be reflected and thus intensify, becoming more visible to the human observer
- ○ disperses white light, allowing it to be seen as its different component colors
- ○ causes the light to slow and thus more readily disperse according to its different wavelengths
- ○ alters the light's wavelengths so they fall within the visible spectrum

STEP 2: ANALYZE THE QUESTION STEM

The phrase "[a]ccording to the passage" indicates this is a Detail question. Here you are asked for something the passage says about refraction.

STEP 3: RESEARCH THE RELEVANT TEXT

Refraction is defined in the third paragraph as the changing of direction of a light wave upon entering or leaving a droplet of water. How much the light changes direction depends on its wavelength. White light consists of different wavelengths, so it is broken up, or dispersed, by refraction, and light at different wavelengths is seen as different colors.

STEP 4: MAKE A PREDICTION

As discovered in step 3, the passage presents several facts about refraction, and the correct answer will match one or more of these.

STEP 5: EVALUATE THE ANSWER CHOICES

(C) paraphrases the last sentence of the third paragraph and is correct. **(A)** is half right, but it says that refraction changes the light's wavelength. In fact, the light's wavelength affects the angle of refraction, so **(A)** can be eliminated. Some light is reflected in the droplet, and while this allows the light to be refracted a second time, it is not caused by refraction, nor is anything said about "intensifying" the light. Eliminate **(B)**. As for **(D)**, the light wave does slow down when it hits a water droplet, and this is also when refraction occurs, but it's not said whether one causes the other. And finally, while refraction separates light according to its wavelengths, nothing is said about wavelengths being altered, and certainly refraction is not said to make invisible light visible. Eliminate **(E)**.

33. **(B)**

The primary purpose of the passage is to

- ○ explain why rainbows are a relatively rare phenomenon
- ○ describe religious and scientific explanations for the appearance of rainbows
- ○ raise doubts about a historical explanation for the appearance of rainbows
- ○ explore the reasons that the refraction of light causes it to appear as different colors
- ○ examine the physics underlying the appearance of rainbows to the human observer

STEP 2: ANALYZE THE QUESTION STEM

This is a Global question, asking for the primary purpose of the passage as a whole.

STEP 3: RESEARCH THE RELEVANT TEXT

There's no need to review the whole passage. Use the passage map to find the purpose: to describe explanations for rainbows (mythology/science).

STEP 4: MAKE A PREDICTION

The correct answer will reflect the purpose in your passage map.

STEP 5: EVALUATE THE ANSWER CHOICES

(B) matches the prediction and is correct. Whether or not rainbows are rare is not mentioned in the passage, so **(A)** is incorrect. **(C)** is a 180, as the author confirms that the two historical explanations discussed are borne out by modern physics. **(D)** can be eliminated because this is merely a detail from the passage; the author is interested in explaining rainbows, not the refraction of light. Finally, **(E)** only addresses the last two paragraphs and is not the purpose of the passage as a whole.

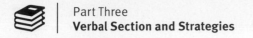
34. (A)

It can be inferred that the author of the passage would most likely agree with which of the following statements about the study of rainbows?

○ Scientific experiments performed hundreds of years ago sometimes provided accurate results.

○ Cultures that associate rainbows with divinity do not approve of scientific inquiry into the nature of rainbows.

○ The experiments of Theodoric and al-Farisi established that refraction of light occurs in water droplets but did not examine larger volumes of water.

○ In societies in which the results of scientific studies of rainbows are widely accepted, rainbows are no longer associated with spiritual meaning.

○ Studies such as Theodoric's and al-Farisi's now have no value because modern science has shown them to be simplistic.

STEP 2: ANALYZE THE QUESTION STEM

This is an Inference question, asking for the statement with which the author would most likely agree.

STEP 3: RESEARCH THE RELEVANT TEXT

Since most of the passage is about the study of rainbows, review the passage map to have the structure of the passage fresh in your mind as you review the answer choices. Plan to research each choice as needed to accept or eliminate it.

STEP 4: MAKE A PREDICTION

No precise prediction of the correct answer is possible here. However, based on the passage map, you know that humans have observed rainbows for a long time and come up with various ideas about them, at least two medieval scholars conducted scientific experiments to understand rainbows, and modern physics—which explains rainbows in terms of light wavelengths and their refraction—validates the medieval research. The correct answer will align with one or more of these key ideas.

STEP 5: EVALUATE THE ANSWER CHOICES

(A) is supported by the passage and is correct. Fourteenth-century science is first mentioned in the first paragraph and elaborated on in the second. Then, at the beginning of the third paragraph, the author says that modern physics has shown the findings of Theodoric and al-Farisi to be accurate. Thus, the author would agree that some experiments performed hundreds of years ago produced accurate results.

(B) can be researched in the first paragraph, where such cultures are discussed. While some of the ideas seem unscientific, the author never says that such peoples did not approve of scientific studies. **(C)** is not supported. The passage only discusses these researchers' work with water droplets, so whether they studied larger volumes of water is unknown. **(D)** is similar to **(B)** in that the author never implies that a scientific understanding of rainbows voids a belief in their spiritual significance. **(E)** is a 180. The author specifically mentions the accuracy of Theodoric and al-Farisi's work, thereby implying its value.

35. (E)

The primary function of the second paragraph is to

- ○ discuss a challenge to the conception of rainbows as a religious symbol
- ○ evaluate two historical methods for observing rainbows
- ○ describe the difficulties early scholars overcame in their attempts to understand rainbows
- ○ support the idea that medieval science is similar in value to modern science
- ○ outline historical attempts to understand the scientific basis of rainbows

STEP 2: ANALYZE THE QUESTION STEM

This Logic question asks for the purpose of the second paragraph.

STEP 3: RESEARCH THE RELEVANT TEXT

Since the question asks about the second paragraph, review it in the passage map. The second paragraph is concerned with "medieval studies of rainbows by Theodoric/al-Farisi—different methods, same conclusion."

STEP 4: MAKE A PREDICTION

The correct answer will align with the summary of the second paragraph in the passage map.

STEP 5: EVALUATE THE ANSWER CHOICES

(E) matches the prediction and is the correct answer. (A) might be a tempting choice, since Theodoric and al-Farisi and their scientific approach to rainbows are introduced in the first paragraph with the contrast key word "[b]ut." However, while the author indicates their approach differed from a religious or mythological approach, the passage never goes so far as to imply they sought to purge the use of rainbows as a symbol in their religions. The author does evaluate the two scholars' methods in a general way but at the beginning of the third paragraph, which states that the researchers' findings agree with those of modern physics. This is not the function of the second paragraph, so eliminate (B). Nothing is said about any difficulties Theodoric or al-Farisi may have faced, so (C) can be eliminated. (D) is extreme. While the author indicates that in this case, findings from the fourteenth century agree with those of modern physicists, the passage in no way implies that medieval science as a whole is similar in value to modern science.

GMAT by the Numbers: Reading Comprehension

Now that you've learned how to approach Reading Comprehension questions on the GMAT, let's add one more dimension to your understanding of how they work.

Take a few minutes to read this passage and try the questions associated with it. Following the questions is performance data from thousands of people who have studied with Kaplan over the decades. Through analyzing this data, we will show you how to approach questions like these most effectively and how to avoid similarly tempting wrong answer choice types on Test Day.

Introduced in 1978, video optical discs were technologically more advanced than video cassettes—they offered better picture quality without degradation over time—yet video cassettes and recorders were far more successful commercially, at least in part because relatively few movies were ever released on optical discs. As this example illustrates, superior technology is no guarantee of success in the home audio and video market.

In home audio, vinyl records were the dominant format until the 1970s, when audio cassette tapes were introduced. Cassette tapes offered no better sound quality than vinyl records (in fact, some believed they offered lower quality), yet this format became widely successful for reasons having little to do with technical advancements in sound quality. Cassettes were more portable than records, and the ability to record from records onto cassettes made the two formats complementary. In addition to buying prerecorded records and tapes, consumers could now make copies of vinyl records and listen to them outside the home. Thus, cassette tape sales grew even as vinyl remained a popular format.

The rise of audio compact discs (CDs) was quite different. Introduced in 1983, CDs clearly offered higher sound quality than records or cassettes, yet they were not an immediate success. However, CDs were persistently and aggressively marketed by the industry, and by the 1990s they had become the most popular audio format. The dominant position of CDs was further cemented later in the 1990s by the advent of new technology that allowed consumers to create their own CDs at home—thus combining one of the best features of audio cassettes with the higher sound quality of CDs.

In home video, after the failure of optical discs, video cassettes remained the dominant format until the advent of digital video discs (DVDs). Introduced in 1997, DVDs quickly gained widespread popularity. These discs were based on a technology similar to that of optical discs and offered several clear advantages over video cassettes, including better picture quality and better search features. Yet perhaps the real key to their rapid rise was the fact that manufacturers quickly made many titles available on DVD. This combination of better technology and smart marketing helped the DVD avoid the fate of the optical disc.

1. The passage is primarily concerned with which of the following?

   ○ Contrasting the success of DVDs with the failure of optical discs

   ○ Describing the crucial role played by technology in the home audio and video market

   ○ Questioning the wisdom of introducing new audio or video formats

   ○ Illustrating that there is more than one path to success in the home audio and video market

   ○ Proving that good marketing is the only way to guarantee success in the home audio and video market

2. The author of this passage would most likely agree that

   ○ better technology alone will never cause the success of a new audio or video format

   ○ a combination of better technology and good marketing is the best way to ensure success when introducing a new format

   ○ there is no perfectly reliable way to predict the success or failure of new audio and video formats

   ○ companies in the home audio or video industry should invest less in product research and development than in marketing

   ○ consumer behavior is inherently irrational

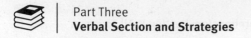
3. According to the passage, which strategy is LEAST likely to produce a successful media format?

    O Aggressively marketing a brand-new format

    O Cautiously testing the market by releasing titles sparingly

    O Relying on word-of-mouth advertising

    O Creating a new format based on earlier technology

    O Introducing a product that works with existing products

Explanation: Question 1

It is crucial not to get lost in the details of a Reading Comprehension passage but to keep your eyes focused on the author's main idea. The last sentence of the first paragraph makes it clear that the passage will focus on how superior technology does not guarantee commercial success. Each body paragraph contains an example to support this point of view. The paragraphs describe many technical details but also provide other reasons for commercial success: flexibility of use (cassettes), aggressive marketing (CDs), wide availability (DVDs). The correct answer, **(D)**, reflects the idea that success is determined by several factors.

Question Statistics

8% of test takers choose **(A)**

19% of test takers choose **(B)**

2% of test takers choose **(C)**

64% of test takers choose **(D)**

7% of test takers choose **(E)**

Sample size = 2,163

Many test takers focus too much on what the details say, rather than what idea the details support. The test makers understand this tendency, and they craft answer choices that reflect only the details. The most tempting wrong answer, **(B)**, accurately describes the details but misses the overall point that factors other than technology have an important influence. Also note how the second- and third-most popular wrong answers also miss the overall point by focusing on individual paragraphs instead of the entire passage: **(A)** focuses only on the fourth paragraph and **(E)** on the third. Although not a commonly selected wrong answer on this question, **(C)** is also wrong because it misconstrues the main idea, claiming that improved formats are not a good idea rather than simply insufficient for success.

Explanation: Question 2

Despite the vague wording of this question stem, the GMAT has a very specific standard for what defines the correct answer to Inference questions such as this one—and knowing that standard allows you to successfully avoid the common traps. From the test maker's point of view, an inference is valid only if it unambiguously *must* be true. So the right answer will be something that the author *must* agree with. If there's any room for doubt, or if it's possible that the author might not agree, the choice is wrong.

> ## Question Statistics
>
> **29%** of test takers choose (**A**)
>
> **46%** of test takers choose (**B**)
>
> **23%** of test takers choose (**C**)
>
> **1%** of test takers choose (**D**)
>
> **1%** of test takers choose (**E**)
>
> Sample size = 2,150

It's easy to see why unpopular choices (**D**) and (**E**) are wrong. The author neither makes directives to companies nor casts aspersions on consumers. But why are the two most commonly selected answers wrong? The reason is that they are too extreme.

It's very easy for an all-or-nothing statement to be possibly false. (**A**) claims that better technology will never cause the success of a new format. But the author only says that better technology "is no guarantee of success." A lack of a guarantee doesn't mean that something will "never" happen, so (**A**) is incorrect. (**B**) also goes too far by claiming that superior technology and good marketing is the "best" way to ensure success. The author clearly thinks that combining good technology with good marketing is better than having good technology alone. But this doesn't rule out the possibility that some other approach might be better still. In fact, marketing is not mentioned as part of the reason for the success of audio cassettes.

Notice how (**C**) uses more cautious wording, saying that no formula for success is "perfectly reliable." Given that the author mentions three different ways that new formats succeeded (flexibility of use, aggressive marketing, wide availability of titles), it makes sense for the author to agree that there's no one perfect way. That's why (**C**) is correct. Learn to avoid extreme language like "never" and "best" and to embrace hedged language like "no perfectly reliable," and you'll be well ahead of your competition and well on the way to a higher GMAT score.

Explanation: Question 3

Notice that the question explicitly tells you to base your answer on the content of the passage. Many test takers let their own opinions cloud their analysis and thus wander into traps. This question asks you to find the strategy most likely to fail. The first and fourth paragraphs both mention that the optical disc probably failed because not enough titles were available. That makes a cautious, slow release of titles a recipe for failure, which is why **(B)** is correct.

Question Statistics

3% of test takers choose **(A)**

70% of test takers choose **(B)**

18% of test takers choose **(C)**

6% of test takers choose **(D)**

3% of test takers choose **(E)**

Sample size = 2,122

(A) and **(E)** are mentioned in the passage as reasons that new formats succeeded—CDs were aggressively marketed, and cassettes complemented vinyl—so it's no wonder that few test takers choose those answers. Neither **(C)** nor **(D)** is mentioned in the passage, which is why these choices are wrong—there's no support for either. But you can see from the question statistics that **(C)** is a popular choice. That is because you might look at "word-of-mouth advertising" and think that it isn't a sufficiently "aggressive" marketing strategy. This may be true in the real world (although if you're a savvy buzz marketer, you might disagree), but there is nothing *in the passage* to suggest that a word-of-mouth marketing campaign couldn't be aggressive. Stick with what's supported by the passage, and you'll be successful on Test Day.

More GMAT by the Numbers...

To see more questions, be sure to review the full-length CATs in your online resources.

GO ONLINE

kaptest.com/login

CHAPTER 12

Sentence Correction Strategy

LEARNING OBJECTIVES

After studying this chapter, you will be able to:

- Recognize Sentence Correction questions by their format
- State the steps of the Kaplan Method for Sentence Correction
- Describe the extent to which you need to study formal grammar rules for success on the GMAT

Below is a typical Sentence Correction question. In this chapter, we'll look at how to apply the Kaplan Method to this question, discuss the grammar rules being tested, and go over the basic principles and strategies that you want to keep in mind on every Sentence Correction question.

Several years ago, a leading packaged food manufacturer, seeking to appeal to consumers who increasingly favor fresh foods, <u>has acquired a company that specializes in freezing produce immediately after harvest as a subsidiary.</u>

- ○ has acquired a company that specializes in freezing produce immediately after harvest as a subsidiary
- ○ has acquired as a subsidiary a company that specializes in freezing produce immediately after harvest
- ○ acquired like a subsidiary a company that specializes in freezing produce immediately after harvest
- ○ acquired as a subsidiary a company that specializes in freezing produce immediately after harvest
- ○ acquired a company specializing in the freezing of harvested produce immediately afterward as a subsidiary

Before you move on, take a minute to think about what you see in this question and answer some questions about how you think it works:

- What skills and concepts does this question test?
- How does answer choice (**A**) relate to the given sentence?
- What other patterns do you notice in the answer choices?
- What GMAT Core Competencies are most essential to success on this question?

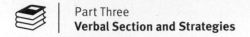

Previewing Sentence Correction

Below you'll find answers to the questions you just considered.

What Skills and Concepts Does This Question Test?

Many students, upon seeing Sentence Correction questions for the first time, think of them as "grammar" questions. It's true that correct answers often fix grammar mistakes, but you don't need to know the names of grammar rules or of different verb conjugations. What is it that you're being asked to do on Sentence Correction questions? These questions ask you to pick the answer that most clearly, correctly, or effectively gets across the idea of the sentence.

Sentence Correction questions cover a range of grammatical errors, some of which are so obscure that even good writers commit them. However, you don't have to be a grammar expert to do well on this section. All you need is a mode of attack and some knowledge about what does—and does not—constitute good GMAT grammar. Most of this chapter focuses on these common errors and how you can identify the answer choice that the GMAT considers correct.

Another key element in GMAT Sentence Correction is style, or what the directions for this question type call "effectiveness of expression." That means English that is clear and exact and without awkwardness, ambiguity, or redundancy. (Note that it doesn't have to be interesting. In fact, the test is set up to see whether you get worn down by difficult, often boring prose or whether you rise above that to stay involved—and awake.)

How Does Answer Choice (A) Relate to the Given Sentence?

Each Sentence Correction sentence will contain an underlined portion and ask you which of the choices best fits in place of that underlined portion. Choice (**A**) will always repeat exactly that underlined part of the sentence. So (**A**) is correct when there's no error. Recognizing this pattern means that you never need to spend any time reading (**A**) once you've read the original sentence. Given the statistically random distribution of correct answers across the five choices, you can anticipate that (**A**)—the sentence is correct as written—will be correct approximately 20 percent of the time.

What Other Patterns Do You Notice in the Answer Choices?

Spotting patterns in how the answer choices are presented is the bedrock of the Kaplan Method for Sentence Correction. As you scan through these answer choices, you'll see that they split into groups based on the varying ways they handle the grammatical issues in the sentence. Two of the choices start with "has acquired" and three with "acquired."

We will return to analyze this question fully once we've learned the Kaplan Method, but for now just know that we call this phenomenon a "split"—certain patterns in how the answer choices are constructed allow you to place them into groups, sometimes even eliminating two or three answer choices solely on the basis of this categorization. The differences that allow you to group choices most often occur at the beginnings of the choices, but not infrequently you'll find useful differences at the ends of choices. If you become adept at vertically scanning choices for differences of grammar and usage, you may sometimes find key distinctions in the middle of choices. Most Sentence Correction questions have at least one 3-2 or 2-2-1 split. This strategic, pattern-oriented approach will allow you to narrow the choices down to the one correct answer with the confidence and speed of an expert.

What GMAT Core Competencies Are Most Essential to Success on This Question?

Pattern Recognition and Attention to the Right Detail are the Core Competencies central to Sentence Correction questions. The typical Sentence Correction question contains two or more errors. The test makers reward you for being able to quickly spot and correct these problems that impair effective communication. Time is of the essence with these questions; the sentences vary in length and complexity, so you'll have to move considerably faster on the short ones to leave time for the long ones. Knowing the main types of grammatical errors that show up repeatedly on Sentence Correction questions and being able to analyze the patterns in how the answer choices are presented will help you move through these questions efficiently and accurately.

Question Format and Structure

> **LEARNING OBJECTIVE**
>
> In this section, you will learn how to:
>
> * Describe what it means for a sentence to follow the rules of standard written English

The GMAT Verbal Reasoning section includes about 13 Sentence Correction questions, which are mixed in with Critical Reasoning and Reading Comprehension.

The directions for Sentence Correction questions look like this:

> **Directions:** Each Sentence Correction question presents a sentence, part or all of which is underlined. Below each sentence, you will find five ways to phrase the underlined portion. The first answer choice repeats the original version, while the other four choices are different. If the original seems best, choose the first answer choice. If not, choose one of the revisions.
>
> In choosing an answer, follow the norms of standard written English: grammar, word choice, and sentence construction. Choose the answer that produces the most effective sentence, aiming to eliminate awkwardness, ambiguity, redundancy, and grammatical error.

Sentence Correction tests your command of standard written English—the rather formal language that is used in textbooks and scholarly periodicals. It's the language that's used to convey complex information precisely, as opposed to the casual language that we use for everyday communication. The good news is that you do *not* need to know every grammar rule for these questions. Errors reflecting certain rules show up repeatedly on the GMAT. Focus on mastering these commonly tested rules—that's how to get the biggest bang for your study-time buck.

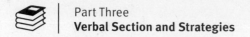

The Kaplan Method for Sentence Correction

LEARNING OBJECTIVES

In this section, you will learn how to:

- List the steps of the Kaplan Method for Sentence Correction questions
- Explain the purpose of each step in the Sentence Correction Method
- Perform the steps of the Method to answer Sentence Correction questions

Now it's time to learn how to bring together all of the strategies you read about above into a consistent protocol for approaching Sentence Correction questions. Kaplan has developed a Method for Sentence Correction that you can use to attack each and every Sentence Correction question. Through regular practice, this Method will become second nature by Test Day.

THE KAPLAN METHOD FOR SENTENCE CORRECTION

1. Read the original sentence carefully, looking for errors.
2. Scan and group the answer choices.
3. Eliminate choices until only one remains.

STEP 1: READ THE ORIGINAL SENTENCE CAREFULLY, LOOKING FOR ERRORS

Read the sentence. Look for things that sound wrong but also keep your eyes peeled for signs of the classic errors that the GMAT loves to repeat. If you spot an error, eliminate **(A)** immediately but keep reading, because there may be more than one error that the correct choice needs to fix. If you don't spot an error the first time through, or if you're not sure whether something is wrong, a quick vertical scan of the beginnings and ends of the answer choices will give you a strong clue about what sorts of grammatical issues the question is testing. This information will help you focus on these issues and possibly spot an error, or realize there is no error, in the sentence. If the choices don't vary with regard to a certain part of the sentence, then that part can't possibly be an error.

But don't spend too long here. After your initial analysis of the sentence, you're no more likely to spot a problem from further analysis—especially because there may not be an error at all! Instead, move straight to step 2.

STEP 2: SCAN AND GROUP THE ANSWER CHOICES

Instead of wasting time reading each answer choice individually, quickly scan and compare the answers with one other. If you spotted an error in step 1, sort the answer choices into two groups: those that do not fix the error (which you can eliminate) and those that appear to fix it.

If you *didn't* spot an error, try to zero in on a grammatical or stylistic difference that splits the answer choices into distinct groups. This will let you identify one of the issues that the question is testing. Once you know what is being tested, you can apply your knowledge of English grammar to determine which group is correct—thereby eliminating multiple answers at once.

STEP 3: ELIMINATE CHOICES UNTIL ONLY ONE REMAINS

If more than one choice remains, go back to step 2 and scan again to find another difference. Then eliminate accordingly. Repeat this process until only one answer remains. Finally, before heading to the next question, read your choice back into the sentence and make sure the entire sentence makes sense. By doing this, you'll make sure that all elements in the underlined portion match up with the non-underlined text.

Important Pacing Tip: If more than one choice remains after you have eliminated all of the answers that you are sure are wrong, just go with your best guess. If you don't know the rule by Test Day, you probably won't successfully teach it to yourself while taking the exam. You'll get a much higher score by investing that time in other questions. If you are working on a quiz or a practice test, of course, reading the answer explanation closely will help you to learn the important rules so you can use them successfully on Test Day.

Applying the Kaplan Method for Sentence Correction

Now let's apply the Kaplan Method to the Sentence Correction question you saw earlier:

> Several years ago, a leading packaged food manufacturer, seeking to appeal to consumers who increasingly favor fresh foods, <u>has acquired a company that specializes in freezing produce immediately after harvest as a subsidiary.</u>

- ○ has acquired a company that specializes in freezing produce immediately after harvest as a subsidiary
- ○ has acquired as a subsidiary a company that specializes in freezing produce immediately after harvest
- ○ acquired like a subsidiary a company that specializes in freezing produce immediately after harvest
- ○ acquired as a subsidiary a company that specializes in freezing produce immediately after harvest
- ○ acquired a company specializing in the freezing of harvested produce immediately afterward as a subsidiary

STEP 1: READ THE ORIGINAL SENTENCE CAREFULLY, LOOKING FOR ERRORS

The underlined portion of the sentence says what the food manufacturer did "[s]everal years ago." It begins with the verb "has acquired." This is the present perfect verb tense, which is used to describe an action that began in the past and is still occurring. In this case, the acquisition of the subsidiary happened entirely in the past—"[s]everal years ago"—so this verb tense is incorrect.

Keep reading to see whether there are other errors the correct answer must fix. At the end is the modifying phrase "as a subsidiary." Logically, this phrase describes how the company was acquired. Because of its placement, however, it describes how the company freezes produce. The placement of this phrase too far from the action it modifies is a modification error, so your answer choice must also fix this problem.

As soon as you found a problem with this sentence, you could eliminate (**A**) as a potential choice. The correct answer will fix the verb tense and modification problems without introducing other errors.

STEP 2: SCAN AND GROUP THE ANSWER CHOICES

Now quickly do a vertical scan of the choices, looking for any that repeat the error. There's a 3-2 split at the beginnings of the choices. Along with (**A**), (**B**) repeats the verb error, since it begins with "has acquired."

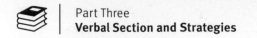

Note that if you hadn't spotted the verb error when reading the original sentence in step 1, the fact that the choices differ by verb tense would be a signal to consider this grammatical issue and double-check whether the tense used in the sentence is correct, essentially returning to step 1. At this point, you'd look for clues to the time frame of the action and determine that you need a verb that puts the action entirely in the past.

STEP 3: ELIMINATE CHOICES UNTIL ONLY ONE REMAINS

Eliminate (**A**) and (**B**) for using the wrong verb tense.

The three remaining choices all begin the same way, but they differ at the end. (**C**) and (**D**) end with "immediately after harvest," while (**E**) ends with "immediately afterward as a subsidiary." If you spotted the modification error in step 1, you already know that (**E**)'s placement is incorrect. Otherwise, you can figure it out now: the modifying words here should be describing the freezing of the produce, and the fact that the acquired company fits into its parent's organizational structure as a subsidiary has nothing to do with how it freezes green beans. Eliminate (**E**).

Now read (**C**) and (**D**) in parallel. With "acquired *like* a subsidiary," (**C**) seems to be saying that the acquired company is similar to a subsidiary but not actually a subsidiary, which does not make sense. This word choice introduces a comparison that the author is not trying to make. Eliminate (**C**).

That leaves only one choice, (**D**). Read this answer back into the sentence to confirm there are no errors: "Several years ago, a leading packaged food manufacturer, seeking to appeal to consumers who increasingly favor fresh foods, <u>acquired as a subsidiary a company that specializes in freezing produce immediately after harvest</u>."

TAKEAWAYS: THE KAPLAN METHOD FOR SENTENCE CORRECTION

- If you don't spot an error in the sentence, immediately scan the answer choices for differences. Focus on one error at a time. Usually you will find a 3-2 or 2-2-1 split, often at the beginnings or ends of the choices.

- Some differences will provide an easier basis by which to eliminate than others. If you see a difference but can't determine which alternative is better, see if there are other differences that you can use.

- Knowing how to spot the differences in the answer choices is only half the battle. Learning the test makers' favorite errors, so that you can figure out which version is correct, is the other half.

Practice Set: The Kaplan Method for Sentence Correction

1. Although the contingent of self-described experts who are in attendance at the International Symposium on Unexplained Phenomena in Deep Space Studies <u>have written an open letter stating that the newly discovered interstellar object is an alien space probe, most astronomers</u> who have studied the object closely agree that it is a comet.

    ○   have written an open letter stating that the newly discovered interstellar object is an alien space probe, most astronomers

    ○   have written an open letter stating that the interstellar object, newly discovered, is an alien space probe, most astronomers

    ○   has written an open letter stating that the newly discovered interstellar object is an alien space probe, but most astronomers

    ○   has written an open letter stating that the discovery of a new interstellar object is an alien space probe, most astronomers

    ○   has written an open letter stating that the newly discovered interstellar object is an alien space probe, most astronomers

2. The green flash, an atmospheric refractive phenomenon whereby the top edge of a setting sun will momentarily turn green, rarely is seen by the naked eye, primarily <u>on account of requiring</u> specific favorable conditions to occur.

    ○   on account of requiring

    ○   on account of their requiring

    ○   because they require

    ○   because it requires

    ○   because of requiring

3. The new hummingbird species, which was discovered only recently, <u>had been categorized as critically endangered due to its habitat being limited</u> and the low estimated size of its population.

    ○   had been categorized as critically endangered due to its habitat being limited

    ○   had been categorized as critically endangered because it has a limited habitat

    ○   has been categorized as critically endangered because it has limited its habitat

    ○   has been categorized as critically endangered because of its limited habitat

    ○   will be categorized as critically endangered due to its limiting of its habitat

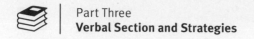
4. Fitness experts say that the weighted barbell squat or the weighted hip thrust, each part of a family of training maneuvers called compound movements, <u>is one of the best exercises for isolating and building the gluteal muscles</u>.

   ○ is one of the best exercises for isolating and building the gluteal muscles

   ○ are among the best exercises to isolate and for building the gluteal muscles

   ○ is one of the best exercises for isolating and to build the gluteal muscles

   ○ are among the best exercises for isolating and building the gluteal muscles

   ○ is one of the best exercises to isolate and for building the gluteal muscles

5. Although <u>they contain many repeated themes and depict multiple characters with strikingly similar traits</u>, the anthology consists of stories written by a diverse group of authors representing several different genres.

   ○ they contain many repeated themes and depict multiple characters with strikingly similar traits

   ○ they contain many themes repeatedly and depict multiple characters with similar traits strikingly

   ○ it contains many repeated themes and depicts multiple characters with strikingly similar traits

   ○ it contains many repeated themes and characters that depict multiple strikingly similar traits

   ○ it contains many themes repeatedly that depict multiple characters with strikingly similar traits

Answers and explanations follow on the next page. ▶ ▶ ▶

Answer Key

Practice Set: The Kaplan Method for Sentence Correction

1. E
2. D
3. D
4. A
5. C

Answers and Explanations

Practice Set: The Kaplan Method for Sentence Correction

1. **(E)**

   Although the contingent of self-described experts who are in attendance at the International Symposium on Unexplained Phenomena in Deep Space Studies <u>have written an open letter stating that the newly discovered interstellar object is an alien space probe, most astronomers</u> who have studied the object closely agree that it is a comet.

   - O   have written an open letter stating that the newly discovered interstellar object is an alien space probe, most astronomers

   - O   have written an open letter stating that the interstellar object, newly discovered, is an alien space probe, most astronomers

   - O   has written an open letter stating that the newly discovered interstellar object is an alien space probe, but most astronomers

   - O   has written an open letter stating that the discovery of a new interstellar object is an alien space probe, most astronomers

   - O   has written an open letter stating that the newly discovered interstellar object is an alien space probe, most astronomers

STEP 1: READ THE ORIGINAL SENTENCE CAREFULLY, LOOKING FOR ERRORS

The underlined portion of the sentence begins with the verb "have written," and a quick scan of the choices reveals that some retain this verb, while others change it to the singular form "has written." This 3-2 split signals that the sentence may lack proper subject-verb agreement. To check for this error, go back to the sentence and find the subject for the verb "have written." While the word "experts" is immediately before the verb, "experts" is not the subject because it is part of a prepositional phrase ("of self-described experts"). The subject is the group of people who wrote the letter, which in this case is "the contingent." Because "contingent" is a singular noun, the verb should be in its singular form ("has written").

STEP 2: SCAN AND GROUP THE ANSWER CHOICES

(A) and **(B)** use "have written," while **(C)**, **(D)**, and **(E)** use "has written."

STEP 3: ELIMINATE CHOICES UNTIL ONLY ONE REMAINS

(B) retains the original error, so both **(A)** and **(B)** can be eliminated immediately. **(C)** adds the contrast key word "but" before the phrase "most astronomers," but this is incorrect because the original sentence starts with a similar key word ("[a]lthough") that fully explains the relationship between the two clauses. **(D)** changes the meaning of the sentence, suggesting that is it the "discovery" rather than the object itself that is an alien space probe. **(E)** fixes the original mistake without making any new ones, and thus is correct. Read it into the sentence to verify:

Although the contingent of self-described experts who are in attendance at the International Symposium on Unexplained Phenomena in Deep Space Studies <u>have written an open letter stating that the newly discovered interstellar object is an alien space probe, most astronomers</u> who have studied the object closely agree that it is a comet.

2.   **(D)**

The green flash, an atmospheric refractive phenomenon whereby the top edge of a setting sun will momentarily turn green, rarely is seen by the naked eye, primarily <u>on account of requiring</u> specific favorable conditions to occur.

- ○   on account of requiring
- ○   on account of their requiring
- ○   because they require
- ○   because it requires
- ○   because of requiring

STEP 1: READ THE ORIGINAL SENTENCE CAREFULLY, LOOKING FOR ERRORS

The GMAT prefers concise constructions. This underlined piece sounds awkward. Moreover, *-ing* constructions such as "of requiring" are generally suspect on the GMAT. Seek an answer choice that is less wordy and that removes the phrase "of requiring."

STEP 2: SCAN AND GROUP THE ANSWER CHOICES

(A) and **(B)** keep "on account of." **(C)**, **(D)**, and **(E)** all use "because."

STEP 3: ELIMINATE CHOICES UNTIL ONLY ONE REMAINS

"Because" is certainly shorter and more concise than "on account of," so eliminate **(A)** and **(B)**. **(C)** uses the pronoun "they," but it refers to the "green flash," so the pronoun should be singular. Hence, **(C)** cannot be correct. **(D)** uses the pronoun "it," which agrees with its antecedent, the "green flash." This choice is concise and grammatically correct and is thus the correct answer. **(E)** is incorrect because it uses the phrase "of requiring," which sounds awkward in the original sentence. **(D)** is the correct answer. Read it back into the sentence to confirm:

The green flash, an atmospheric refractive phenomenon whereby the top edge of a setting sun will momentarily turn green, rarely is seen by the naked eye, primarily <u>because it requires</u> specific favorable conditions to occur.

3.   (D)

The new hummingbird species, which was discovered only recently, <u>had been categorized as critically endangered due to its habitat being limited</u> and the low estimated size of its population.

- ○   had been categorized as critically endangered due to its habitat being limited
- ○   had been categorized as critically endangered because it has a limited habitat
- ○   has been categorized as critically endangered because it has limited its habitat
- ○   has been categorized as critically endangered because of its limited habitat
- ○   will be categorized as critically endangered due to its limiting of its habitat

STEP 1: READ THE ORIGINAL SENTENCE CAREFULLY, LOOKING FOR ERRORS

The underlined portion begins with the verb phrase "had been categorized." A quick vertical scan of the choices reveals a "had been/has been/will be" split, suggesting that verb tense is being tested. The current form ("had been") is in the past perfect tense, which suggests that this event (categorizing) happened before another past event in the sentence. However, the other past event is that the hummingbird was discovered. Using "had been" here suggests that the bird was categorized as endangered before it was even discovered, which is illogical.

Also, the underlined portion is followed by the word "and," indicating there are two reasons for labeling the bird endangered. What comes before the "and" should be parallel in form to what comes after the "and." However, the action "being limited" is not parallel to the noun "estimated size." As the phrase "estimated size" is not underlined, it cannot be changed. So the correct answer should change "its habitat being limited" to a noun phrase (e.g., "its limited habitat").

STEP 2: SCAN AND GROUP THE ANSWER CHOICES

(A) and (B) begin with "had been," (C) and (D) use "has been," and (E) uses "will be."

STEP 3: ELIMINATE CHOICES UNTIL ONLY ONE REMAINS

Because "had been" was identified as an error, (A) and (B) can be eliminated. However, it can't be determined for sure whether the categorization has already happened or will happen in the future, so either "has been" or "will be" is possible. Now, consider the parallelism at the end. Eliminate (C) because it implies that the hummingbird is responsible for limiting its own habitat. Also, it still uses a verb ("limited") that is not parallel to the noun "size." Eliminate (E) because it adds the possessive pronoun "its" before "limiting," again implying that the hummingbird is responsible for limiting the habitat. (E) also uses a verb form ("limiting") that is not parallel to the noun "size." (D) is correct, using the present perfect tense at the beginning and providing a noun ("limited habitat") to match up with the noun "size." Read this choice back into the sentence to verify that it is correct:

The new hummingbird species, which was discovered only recently, <u>has been categorized as critically endangered because of its limited habitat</u> and the low estimated size of its population.

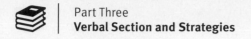

4. **(A)**

Fitness experts say that the weighted barbell squat or the weighted hip thrust, each part of a family of training maneuvers called compound movements, <u>is one of the best exercises for isolating and building the gluteal muscles</u>.

- ○ is one of the best exercises for isolating and building the gluteal muscles
- ○ are among the best exercises to isolate and for building the gluteal muscles
- ○ is one of the best exercises for isolating and to build the gluteal muscles
- ○ are among the best exercises for isolating and building the gluteal muscles
- ○ is one of the best exercises to isolate and for building the gluteal muscles

STEP 1: READ THE ORIGINAL SENTENCE CAREFULLY, LOOKING FOR ERRORS

Whenever a sentence contains an underlined verb, look for subject-verb agreement. In this sentence, the verb "is" is singular. The subject of the sentence is composed of the names of two exercises, connected by the conjunction "or." When a compound subject is connected by "or" and the last noun in the subject is singular, it takes a singular verb, meaning that "is" is correct. The rest of the sentence proceeds logically and without error.

STEP 2: SCAN AND GROUP THE ANSWER CHOICES

(A), **(C)**, and **(E)** retain the verb "is." **(B)** and **(D)** contain the verb "are."

STEP 3: ELIMINATE CHOICES UNTIL ONLY ONE REMAINS

Since "is" is the correct verb, eliminate **(B)** and **(D)**. Of the remaining choices, **(C)** and **(E)** do not use a parallel structure in the phrase at the end, using "for isolating and to build" and "to isolate and for building," respectively. That leaves **(A)** as the correct answer.

5.   **(C)**

Although <u>they contain many repeated themes and depict multiple characters with strikingly similar traits</u>, the anthology consists of stories written by a diverse group of authors representing several different genres.

- ○   they contain many repeated themes and depict multiple characters with strikingly similar traits

- ○   they contain many themes repeatedly and depict multiple characters with similar traits strikingly

- ○   it contains many repeated themes and depicts multiple characters with strikingly similar traits

- ○   it contains many repeated themes and characters that depict multiple strikingly similar traits

- ○   it contains many themes repeatedly that depict multiple characters with strikingly similar traits

STEP 1: READ THE ORIGINAL SENTENCE CAREFULLY, LOOKING FOR ERRORS

The underlined portion begins with a pronoun: "they." This is the focus of the modifying clause at the beginning of the sentence, so "they" should refer to the subject being modified. The subject of the sentence comes immediately after the comma: "the anthology," a singular noun. Even though the anthology consists of multiple stories, the opening modifying phrase refers to the singular anthology and should thus use "it," not "they."

As for the rest of the underlined portion, the adjective "repeated" correctly describes the noun "themes," and the adverb "strikingly" correctly modifies the adjective "similar."

STEP 2: SCAN AND GROUP THE ANSWER CHOICES

(A) and **(B)** use "they" at the beginning, while **(C)**, **(D)**, and **(E)** use "it."

STEP 3: ELIMINATE CHOICES UNTIL ONLY ONE REMAINS

Because "they" has been identified as incorrect, eliminate **(A)** and **(B)**. Of the remaining choices, **(C)** and **(D)** use "repeated themes," while **(E)** uses "contains… repeatedly." Eliminate **(E)** because it should be the themes that are repeated. Using the adverb "repeatedly" suggests that the act of containing is repeated, as if the anthology keeps containing things over and over. Further, by placing "that depict" after "themes," **(E)** suggests the themes depict characters, but this is something the anthology does. Between the remaining choices, eliminate **(D)** because it moves "that depict" after the "characters." Again, it's the anthology that depicts something, not the characters. Also, by moving the word "multiple," **(D)** changes the meaning to claim that there are multiple traits that are similar, not multiple characters who have similar traits. **(C)** is correct. Read this choice back into the sentence to verify that it is correct:

Although <u>it contains many repeated themes and depicts multiple characters with strikingly similar traits</u>, the anthology consists of stories written by a diverse group of authors representing several different genres.

Sentence Correction: Commonly Tested Grammar

LEARNING OBJECTIVES

After studying this chapter, you will be able to:

- Describe the commonly tested areas of grammar and usage on the GMAT
- Identify commonly tested grammar and usage errors in a sentence
- Apply the Kaplan Method for Sentence Correction to sentences with a variety of grammar and usage errors or no error

---

Doing well on Sentence Correction questions begins with knowing how to approach them and then learning the errors that appear most frequently. Test takers who learn the most commonly tested patterns on GMAT Sentence Correction will be able to answer these questions confidently and efficiently. In this section, you'll learn about the seven most commonly tested areas of grammar and usage:

1. Verbs
2. Pronouns
3. Modification
4. Parallel Structure
5. Comparisons
6. Usage/Idioms
7. Clauses and Connectors

Keep in mind that many questions, particularly those of higher difficulty, will test multiple issues. Many questions involve more than one error. Using the Kaplan Method for Sentence Correction will give you an efficient way to focus on one error at a time. With both knowledge of these commonly tested areas and mastery of the Kaplan Method, you'll be able to handle even the toughest Sentence Correction questions.

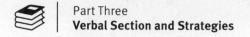
Verbs

LEARNING OBJECTIVES

In this section, you will learn how to:

- Explain what it means for the subject and verb to agree in a sentence
- Use logic and sequence of events to determine the proper tense for each verb in a sentence
- Apply the Kaplan Sentence Correction Method to sentences that may have subject-verb agreement or verb tense errors

---

The GMAT tests verbs in two ways: does the verb agree with its subject, and is the verb in the correct tense?

Subject-Verb Agreement

A sentence is defined as an independent sequence of words that contains a subject and a verb. Verbs must agree with their subjects. Singular subjects have singular verbs, and plural subjects have plural verbs. If you're a native English speaker, this is probably so automatic that you may wonder why the GMAT tests it at all. But the test makers often craftily separate subject and verb with lots of text to make it harder to recognize whether the subject and verb agree. Also, it is sometimes hard to tell whether the subject is singular or plural. You should look out for the following common subject-verb agreement issues:

- Long modifying phrases or clauses following the subject
- Phrases and clauses in commas between the subject and the verb
- Subjects joined by *either/or* and *neither/nor*
- Sentences in which the verb precedes the subject
- Collective nouns, such as *majority, committee, audience, team, group, flock, family*, especially when preceded by *the* and followed by a prepositional phrase containing a plural noun (*the group of legislators*):
  - Collective nouns take a singular verb when the members of the collective act as a unit (*the flock of geese is flying south*) or are uncountable (*a lot of water was spilled*).
  - When the members of the collective act as individuals, the collective noun takes a plural verb (*a majority of voters mail their ballots*; *a number of solutions are possible*).

Subject-Verb Agreement Exercise

Answers are on the following page.

Correct each of the following subject-verb errors.

1. The depletion of natural resources, in addition to the rapid increase in utilization of these resources, have encouraged many nations to conserve energy.

2. There is, without a doubt, many good reasons to exercise.

3. Among the many problems plaguing suburbanites is the ubiquity of shopping malls, the increasing cost of gasoline, and the unavailability of mortgages.

4. The neighbors told police investigators that neither Annette nor her brother are capable of telling the truth.

5. The assembly of delegates intend to scrutinize the governor's policy decisions.

Subject-Verb Agreement Exercise: Answers

1. "Depletion" is the subject. Correct by changing "have" to *has* or by changing "in addition to" to *and*.

2. There *are* many good reasons. A good strategy for checking subject-verb agreement is to ignore, temporarily, any parts of the sentence that are set off by commas.

3. If the sentence ended at "malls," "is" would be correct. But because there is more than one problem listed, *are* is the correct verb here.

4. "Neither Annette nor her brother *is* capable." In *or/nor* constructions, the verb agrees with the subject it is closer to. So if this read *Neither Annette nor her friends*, then *are* would be called for.

5. Even though "delegates" is plural, the subject of the sentence, "assembly," is a singular noun referring collectively to the group. "Assembly" therefore takes a singular verb: "The assembly *intends* to scrutinize."

Verb Tense

A verb tense indicates the order in which separate actions or events occur. Deciding which verb tense is appropriate in a given situation isn't just a matter of grammar; it's also a question of logic. Many GMAT sentences are long and complicated, involving or implying several different actions. The correct tenses make the sequence of events clear.

To determine whether the verbs in a sentence are in the proper tenses, pick one event as a standard and measure every other event against it. Ask yourself whether the other events are supposed to have happened before the standard event took place, after it took place, or while it took place. Those aren't mutually exclusive options, by the way: it is possible in English to have one action start before a second action and continue during that second action.

A frequent GMAT verb error is the inappropriate use of *-ing* forms: *I am going, I was going, I had been going,* and so on. As far as the GMAT is concerned, the only reason to use an *-ing* form is to emphasize that an action is continuing or that two actions are occurring simultaneously. To remember this rule, think of the word *during* and its *-ing* ending. Other than that, pick a simpler tense—one that doesn't use the *-ing* form. In other words, avoid *-ing* forms as much as possible.

Most Commonly Tested Verb Tenses

- **Simple Present**—*I am*—Used for an action happening now, with no contextual information about when it started.

- **Simple Past**—*I was*—Used for an action that happened at a specified time in the past.

- **Simple Future**—*I will*—Used for an action that will happen in the future.

- **Past Perfect**—*I had been*—Used for an action that happened *before* another past action (e.g., *I had been on the subway for 30 minutes before I realized that I was going the wrong direction*).

- **Present Perfect**—*I have been*—Used for an action that started in the past but is still continuing now (e.g., *I have been on the subway for two hours now, and I still don't know where I'm going!*) or for past events that happened at an unspecified time (e.g., *He has read* Don Quixote *seven times*).

There are other verb tenses in the English language, but these are the ones that are tested most often on the GMAT.

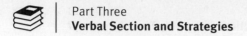

Verb Tense Exercise

Answers are on the following page.

Correct the verb tenses in each sentence.

1. The criminal escaped from custody and is believed to flee the country.

2. Some archaeologists believe that the Minoans of 3,700 years ago had practiced a religion that involved human sacrifice.

3. If the experiment works, it will be representing a quantum leap forward for pharmaceutical chemistry.

4. He had seen that movie recently, so he doesn't want to see it tonight.

5. By the time she retires, she will save enough money to allow her to live comfortably.

6. She already closed the door behind her when it occurred to her that she wasn't able to get back in later.

Verb Tense Exercise: Answers

1. "The criminal escaped" correctly uses simple past tense to refer to an event that happened at a specific time. The believing happens now, so simple present "is believed" is correct. However, the fleeing happened at an unknown and unspecified time in the past, so the present perfect should be used: . . . *is believed to have fled the country.*

2. Here, there's no indication the Minoans practiced human sacrifice for a while and then did something else. So use the simple past *practiced* instead of the past perfect "had practiced."

3. The experiment won't "be representing" a quantum leap; it will *represent* a quantum leap.

4. "Had" plus a past tense verb is used to indicate which of two things that went on in the past occurred earlier. That's not necessary in this sentence. *He saw that movie recently, so he doesn't want to see it tonight.* (*He had seen the movie recently, so he didn't want to see it tonight* also works, although it changes the meaning of the sentence to indicate that the desire happened earlier tonight instead of happening now.)

5. Here, we're indicating an action that began in the past but will end in the future. Think of it this way: at some future time, what will have happened? *She will have saved enough money.*

6. "Closed," "occurred," and "wasn't able to get back in" are all in the simple past tense. But you need to indicate that she first closed the door and then something occurred to her—namely, that she wouldn't be able to do something in the future. *She had already closed the door behind her when it occurred to her that she wouldn't be able to get back in later.*

Applying the Kaplan Method: Verbs

Now let's use the Kaplan Method on a Sentence Correction question dealing with verbs:

The governor's approval ratings <u>has been extremely high until</u> a series of corruption scandals rocked his administration last year.

- ○ has been extremely high until
- ○ have been extremely high until
- ○ had been extremely high until
- ○ were extremely high as
- ○ had been extremely high as

STEP 1: READ THE ORIGINAL SENTENCE CAREFULLY, LOOKING FOR ERRORS

Whenever a sentence contains an underlined verb, you need to make sure that it agrees with its subject and is in the correct tense. Here, the underlined portion contains a singular verb, "has been," that disagrees with the plural subject, "ratings." The verb is also in the wrong tense—"has been" indicates that the ratings are still high, but the sentence contradicts that. You can eliminate answer choice (**A**) immediately.

STEP 2: SCAN AND GROUP THE ANSWER CHOICES

Now it's time to look for a split in the answer choices. You see that the choices begin with many different verb forms: two "had been," one "were," one "have been," and one "has been." That's not a very helpful split. If you don't find a split at the beginnings of the answer choices, look for a split at the ends. Answer choices (**A**), (**B**), and (**C**) end with "until," whereas (**D**) and (**E**) end with "as"; this is a 3-2 split.

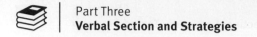
STEP 3: ELIMINATE CHOICES UNTIL ONLY ONE REMAINS

You eliminated answer choice (**A**) because the subject, "ratings," is plural, so the singular verb, "has been," cannot be correct. But verb tense is also at issue here. The correct verb tense is "had been extremely high," because the past perfect tense is used to indicate that something had already happened in the past before something else happened in the past. Here, the governor's ratings *had been* high, until scandals "rocked" his administration. This eliminates (**B**) and (**D**). And (**E**) can be eliminated, since changing the preposition from "until" to "as" loses the sense that the scandals occurred before, and led to, the reversal in the governor's approval ratings. For the record, note that (**D**) also contains this error. The GMAT will often give you multiple opportunities to eliminate answer choices. This leaves (**C**) as the only flawless answer. Read this choice back into the sentence to confirm:

The governor's approval ratings <u>had been extremely high until</u> a series of corruption scandals rocked his administration last year.

TAKEAWAYS: VERBS

- A complete sentence consists, at minimum, of a subject and a verb.
- The verb must agree with the subject of the sentence; plural subjects take plural verbs and singular subjects take singular verbs.
- The verb tense must relate that action to the time frame of other actions and the sentence as a whole.
- Don't fall for needlessly complicated verb tenses. Go for the simplest verb tense that makes sense given the time frame of the sentence.
- Use the past perfect tense (*had done, had seen*) to indicate something that happened prior to another past event.
- Use the present perfect tense for an action that happened at an unspecified time in the past (*have read, has said*) or an action that started in the past and has continued until the present time (*have lived, has been, have had*).
- Use the present perfect continuous tense (*have been studying, has been waiting*) for an action that started in the past and is still continuing now.

Practice Set: Verbs

1. The string section, which included more than 30 violinists and violists as well as more than a dozen cellists and bassists, <u>were justly praised for the tremendous passion they invoked</u> in last night's performance of Stravinsky's *Rite of Spring*.

    ○   were justly praised for the tremendous passion they invoked

    ○   were justly praised for invoking their tremendous passion

    ○   were justly praised for the passion they were tremendous in invoking

    ○   was justly praised for invoking tremendous passion

    ○   was justly praised for the tremendous passion they invoked

2. Galileo Galilei <u>had discovered four moons orbiting Jupiter, including Ganymede, the largest moon in the solar system</u>, by the time Christiaan Huygens discovered Titan, the largest moon of Saturn, in 1655.

    ○   had discovered four moons orbiting Jupiter, including Ganymede, the largest moon in the solar system

    ○   had discovered four moons orbiting Jupiter, which includes Ganymede, being the largest moon in the solar system

    ○   will have discovered four moons, including Ganymede, orbiting Jupiter, which is the largest moon in the solar system

    ○   will have discovered four moons orbiting Jupiter, the largest moon in the solar system including Ganymede

    ○   has discovered four moons orbiting Jupiter, with the largest moon in the solar system being Ganymede

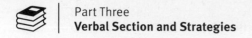
3. While Thomas Edison is often credited with inventing the incandescent light bulb, historians note that <u>several people have designed and created similar light bulbs before Edison received his patent</u>.

    O   several people have designed and created similar light bulbs before Edison received his patent

    O   several people having designed and created similar light bulbs before Edison receiving his patent

    O   several people had designed and created similar light bulbs before Edison received his patent

    O   similar light bulbs had been designed and created by several people before Edison receives his patent

    O   similar light bulbs having been designed and created by several people before Edison received his patent

4. Discovered by a French soldier in 1799, the Rosetta Stone was inscribed with three distinct scripts in two languages, Egyptian and Greek, <u>and were instrumental in helping scholars decipher the hieroglyphs used by ancient Egyptians</u>.

    O   and were instrumental in helping scholars decipher the hieroglyphs used by ancient Egyptians

    O   instrumental in helping scholars decipher the hieroglyphs being used by ancient Egyptians

    O   which was instrumental in helping scholars decipher the hieroglyphs the ancient Egyptians have used

    O   and was instrumental in helping scholars decipher the hieroglyphs used by ancient Egyptians

    O   and was instrumental in its deciphering of ancient Egyptian hieroglyphs, which helped scholars

Advanced Practice Set: Verbs

5. Companies need to ensure that the language in all of their financial reports <u>are reviewed carefully by a team of legal experts</u> since any errors can lead to serious problems for employees as well as shareholders and other investors.

- ○ are reviewed carefully by a team of legal experts
- ○ being reviewed by a careful team of legal experts
- ○ is reviewed carefully by a team of legal experts
- ○ was reviewed carefully by a legal team of experts
- ○ were reviewed by a legal team of experts carefully

6. While the skeleton of a typical human adult <u>will contain 206 bones, that of a newborn human baby usually has approximately 270, some of which fused together as the baby's body grew.</u>

- ○ will contain 206 bones, that of a newborn human baby usually has approximately 270, some of which fused together as the baby's body grew
- ○ contains 206 bones, that of a newborn human baby usually has approximately 270, some of which fuse together as the baby's body grows
- ○ contained 206 bones, that of a newborn human baby usually will have approximately 270, some of which fuse together as the baby's body grows
- ○ contains 206 bones, that of a newborn human baby usually has approximately 270, some of which fused together as the baby's body grew
- ○ will contain 206 bones, that of a newborn human baby usually has approximately 270, some of which fuse together as the baby's body grows

7. There is a booming tourism industry in Scotland centered around the so-called Loch Ness monster; however, evidence that tends to support the existence of the monster, such as grainy photographs that purport to show the creature, <u>is outweighed by the evidence that supports</u> the idea that there is no such monster.

- ○ is outweighed by the evidence that supports
- ○ are outweighed by the evidence that supports
- ○ are outweighed by evidence that supports
- ○ is outweighed by evidence for supporting
- ○ is outweighed by evidence that supports

Pronouns

LEARNING OBJECTIVES

In this section, you will learn how to:

- Define *pronoun* and describe what it means for a pronoun to be ambiguous

- Describe how pronouns must agree with their antecedents

- Apply the Kaplan Method for Sentence Correction to sentences that may have ambiguous pronouns or pronoun-antecedent agreement errors

---

Pronoun errors are one of the most common Sentence Correction issues on the GMAT. Luckily, the GMAT doesn't test every kind of pronoun error. Common errors fall into two categories: reference and agreement.

Pronoun Reference

Pronoun reference errors mean that a given pronoun does not refer to—or stand for—a specific noun or pronoun in the sentence (its antecedent). The pronouns that cause the most trouble on the GMAT are *it, its, they, their, them, who, whom, which,* and *that.* Be aware that these *are* pronouns and therefore need antecedents.

A common pattern is to use *which* or *that* to refer to an action that is not represented in the sentence as a noun. Take this sentence, for example: *The executive spoke eloquently at the annual meeting, which won him much praise.* The author means to say that the executive's eloquent speech earned praise, but what the author has actually said is that the annual meeting won the executive praise. Just because what the author means to say is obvious does not mean the author has actually said that.

Another reference error to be on the alert for is the use of *which* or *that* to refer to a person. People are represented by *who* or *whom.* Here's an example: *The journalist that/who spoke at the symposium answered many questions after her speech.* The correct pronoun is *who.*

Pronoun Agreement

For pronoun agreement errors, it's a question of numbers: perhaps a pronoun that refers to a singular noun is not in singular form, or a pronoun that refers to a plural noun is not in plural form.

As usual, the GMAT presents camouflaged examples of these two mistakes. Whenever you see a pronoun in the underlined portion of a sentence, look out for the following:

- Pronouns, such as *it* and *they*, that are often misused on the GMAT (and in everyday life)

- Pronouns that don't agree in number with their antecedents

Pronoun Reference and Agreement Exercise

Answers are on the following page.

Correct the following common pronoun reference and agreement errors.

1. Beatrix Potter's stories depict animals in an unsentimental and humorous manner, and she illustrated them with delicate watercolor paintings.

2. There is no known cure for certain forms of hepatitis; they hope, though, that a cure will be found soon.

3. If the partners cannot resolve their differences, the courts may have to do it.

4. In order to boost their name recognition, the Green Party sent canvassers to a busy shopping mall.

5. It is now recognized that the dangers of nuclear war are much graver than that of conventional warfare.

6. One of the men complained about the noise in the hallway, and they don't want to identify themselves.

Pronoun Reference and Agreement Exercise: Answers

1. "She" is clearly intended to refer to *Beatrix Potter*, but notice that the proper noun *Beatrix Potter* doesn't appear anywhere in this sentence; a pronoun cannot refer to a modifier, even a possessive modifier such as "Beatrix Potter's." There's a second problem as well: it's not clear whether the "them" that are illustrated are the stories or the animals. Here's a rewrite that solves all the problems: *Beatrix Potter not only wrote stories that depicted animals in an unsentimental and humorous manner, but also illustrated each story with delicate watercolor paintings.*

2. It's unclear what "they" refers to. The only plural noun is "forms," but it can't be the "forms of hepatitis" that are hoping for a cure. It must be *scientists* or some other group of people: *scientists hope to find a cure soon.*

3. "It" is the unclear pronoun here. There's no singular noun in the sentence for "it" to refer to. The main clause should read: ... *the courts may have to do so.*

4. A pronoun or possessive should match the form of the noun it refers to. Use *its* and not "their" in place of the Green Party, because *party*, like *audience*, is a singular noun that stands for a collective group: *In order to boost its name recognition, the Green Party...*

5. "Dangers" is plural, so the pronoun "that" should be plural as well: ... *than those of conventional warfare.*

6. The antecedent of "they" and "themselves" is "[o]ne," so the pronouns do not agree in number or gender with their antecedent. Because the gender of "[o]ne" is male ("[o]ne of the men"), the pronouns should be changed to *he* and *himself*, and the verb "don't" should be changed to the singular *doesn't.*

Applying the Kaplan Method: Pronouns

Now let's use the Kaplan Method on a Sentence Correction question dealing with pronouns:

Despite <u>the platform of the opposition party supporting the measure, they keep</u> voting against campaign finance reform in Congress.

○   the platform of the opposition party supporting the measure, they keep

○   the opposition party's platform supporting the measure, they keep

○   the opposition party's platform which supports the measure, it keeps

○   support of the measure being in the opposition party's platform, it keeps

○   the opposition party's platform supporting the measure, party members keep

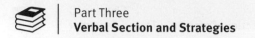

STEP 1: READ THE ORIGINAL SENTENCE CAREFULLY, LOOKING FOR ERRORS

Pattern Recognition and Attention to the Right Detail are essential to spotting pronoun issues in Sentence Correction. Here, you should be paying attention to the word "they" in the underlined portion of the sentence. Colloquially, it's common to use "they" as a nebulous pronoun with no clear antecedent. On the GMAT, though, such usage is always wrong. In this sentence, it isn't clear who "they" refers to, so you know that's an issue that needs to be fixed by the correct answer.

STEP 2: SCAN AND GROUP THE ANSWER CHOICES

The beginnings of the answer choices don't yield much in the way of splits, but the ends definitely do: **(A)** and **(B)** end with "they," **(C)** and **(D)** end with "it," and **(E)** dispenses with pronouns entirely. You have a 2-2-1 split.

STEP 3: ELIMINATE CHOICES UNTIL ONLY ONE REMAINS

The pronoun use here is wrong, because the sentence does not contain an antecedent plural noun to which "they" could refer. So **(A)** and **(B)** are incorrect. **(C)** and **(D)** contain the singular pronoun "it"—but once again, the pronoun reference is confusing and wrong. It's not the *party platform* that keeps voting against the measure, as these choices imply. Both **(C)** and **(D)** can be eliminated. Only **(E)**, which avoids faulty pronoun reference and makes it clear that "party members" keep voting against the measure, makes sense and is the correct answer.

TAKEAWAYS: PRONOUNS

- A pronoun is a word that stands for a noun.
- A pronoun must refer unambiguously to a specific noun, known as its *antecedent*.
- A pronoun must agree in number and gender with the noun it replaces.
- When you see a pronoun underlined in the original sentence, focus on that pronoun and determine whether it is being used correctly.
- The pronouns that cause the most trouble on the GMAT are *it, they, its, their, them, which,* and *that*.
- Never use *they* to refer to a third-person singular noun on the GMAT, even if you don't know or don't want to specify gender.

Practice Set: Pronouns

8. Although her X-ray photographs <u>had laid the foundation for describing the structure of DNA, Rosalind Franklin, an accomplished chemist, did not receive the Nobel prize when it was awarded for this achievement</u> in 1962.

    ○   had laid the foundation for describing the structure of DNA, Rosalind Franklin, an accomplished chemist, did not receive the Nobel prize when it was awarded for this achievement

    ○   had laid the foundation for its description, the structure of DNA did not result in accomplished chemist Rosalind Franklin receiving the Nobel prize awarded for it

    ○   of the structure of DNA had laid the foundation for their description, the accomplished chemist Rosalind Franklin was not awarded the Nobel prize for this achievement

    ○   were the foundation for describing the structure of DNA, the Nobel prize was not awarded to accomplished chemist Rosalind Franklin for It

    ○   were an achievement by Rosalind Franklin, an accomplished chemist, it did not receive the Nobel prize for laying the foundation for describing the structure of DNA

9. Film critics often cite the example of Nicolas Cage's winning the Academy Award for Best Actor as a reason that <u>an actor should not automatically be classified as elite if they win an Academy Award.</u>

    ○   an actor should not automatically be classified as elite if they win an Academy Award

    ○   an actor automatically classified as elite because they won an Academy Award should not always be classified as such

    ○   actors automatically classified as elite because they won an Academy Award should not always be classified as such

    ○   actors should not automatically be classified as elite if they win an Academy Award

    ○   actors should not be classified as automatically elite if they win an Academy Award

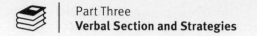

10. <u>As one step in their plan to engender greater goodwill in the community, the town council organized a series of public meetings when residents could air grievances about the opacity of decision making, a tendency to award contracts to cronies, and their failure to follow through on promised reforms.</u>

○ As one step in their plan to engender greater goodwill in the community, the town council organized a series of public meetings when residents could air grievances about the opacity of decision making, a tendency to award contracts to cronies, and their failure to follow through on promised reforms.

○ As one step in its plan to engender greater goodwill in the community, the town council organized a series of public meetings at which residents could air grievances about the opacity of decision making, a tendency to award contracts to cronies, and a failure to follow through on promised reforms.

○ As one step in its plan to engender greater goodwill in the community, the town council organized a series of public meetings at which residents could air grievances about the opacity of decision making, tendency to award contracts to cronies, and failing to follow through on promised reforms.

○ As one step in its plan to engender greater goodwill in the community, a series of public meetings was organized by the town council so that residents could air grievances about the opacity of decision making, a tendency to award contracts to cronies, and a failure to follow through on promised reforms.

○ The town council, as one step in their plan to engender greater goodwill in the community, organized a series of public meetings for residents at which they could air grievances about their opacity of decision making, tendency to award contracts to cronies, and failure to follow through on promised reforms.

Advanced Practice Set: Pronouns

11. The visiting lecturer presented some lesser-known facts about snowflakes: for example, <u>they are not white, they have exactly six sides, they do not all have a unique pattern, and they—along with ice—constitutes</u> about 75 percent of Earth's freshwater.

    ○ they are not white, they have exactly six sides, they do not all have a unique pattern, and they—along with ice—constitutes

    ○ it is not white, all snowflakes have exactly six sides, not all snowflakes have a unique pattern, and snow—along with ice—constitute

    ○ it is not white, it has exactly six sides, not all of it has a unique pattern, and it—along with ice—constitutes

    ○ they are not white, all have exactly six sides, not all have a unique pattern, and they—along with ice—constitute

    ○ they are not white, all has exactly six sides, not all has a unique pattern, and it—along with ice—constitutes

12. The defense attorneys wanted to interview the jurors following the guilty verdict, but a gag order issued by the judge prohibited <u>them from discussing the trial even after it had concluded</u>.

    ○ them from discussing the trial even after it had concluded

    ○ the jurors from discussing the trial even after it is concluded

    ○ them from discussing the trial even after it is concluded

    ○ the jurors from discussing the trial even after it had concluded

    ○ the jurors to discuss the trial even after it had concluded

13. One often referenced online dictionary's definition of *nut* as "a hard-shelled dry fruit or seed with a separable rind or shell and interior kernel" indicates that <u>it does not include almonds, cashews, peanuts, pistachios, or walnuts</u>.

    ○ it does not include almonds, cashews, peanuts, pistachios, or walnuts

    ○ almonds, cashews, peanuts, pistachios, and walnuts are not examples of nuts

    ○ almonds, cashews, peanuts, pistachios, and walnuts are not included as examples of them

    ○ almonds, cashews, peanuts, pistachios, and walnuts are not included

    ○ they do not include almonds, cashews, peanuts, pistachios, or walnuts

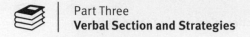
Modification

A modifier is a word, phrase, or clause that describes another part of the sentence. It should be placed as close as possible to whatever it is modifying. Adjectives modify nouns; adverbs modify verbs, adjectives, or other adverbs. Modifiers describe the word that they are right next to. (The only exception is the case of two modifiers; one has to be first.) The GMAT often creates modification errors by making a modifier appear to describe a word that it actually doesn't. Use Pattern Recognition to help you spot modification errors on the GMAT.

Modifiers and Their Placement

The most common GMAT modification error is a long modifier at the beginning of the sentence. It should modify the subject of the sentence but will likely not do so properly. Another common modification error is a long modifier that appears in the middle or at the end of a sentence. Often, such a modifier on the GMAT will logically describe something elsewhere in the sentence, but grammatically a modifying phrase must modify the word that comes immediately before or after it. The result of a misplaced modifier is a nonsensical sentence. Also look out for the following:

- Sentences beginning or ending with descriptive phrases
- *That/which* clauses, especially ones that come at the end of sentences

Modification Exercise

Answers are on the following page.

In each of the following sentences, first identify what each clause or phrase is modifying. Then, fix each error you find.

1. Upon landing at the airport, the hotel sent a limousine to pick us up.
2. Based on the most current data available, the company made plans to diversify its holdings.
3. Small and taciturn, Joan Didion's presence often goes unnoticed by those she will later write about.
4. I took several lessons to learn how to play tennis without getting the ball over the net even once.
5. The house overlooked the lake, which was set back from the shore.

Modification Exercise: Answers

1. The sentence seems to be saying that the *hotel* landed at the airport. Your common sense will tell you that "[u]pon landing at the airport" really intends to modify the unnamed *we*, instead. So you could say, *Upon landing at the airport, we were met by a limousine the hotel had sent.*

2. As written, it sounds as though the company was based on current data. "Based on the most current data available" modifies the subject "company." Obviously, though, what was based on the data were the "plans," not the company. *Based on the most current data available, plans were made to diversify the company's holdings.*

3. It's Joan Didion—not her presence—who is small and taciturn. *Small and taciturn, Joan Didion often goes unnoticed…*

4. As written, "without getting the ball over the net" is describing "how to play tennis." The intended meaning is much more likely to be *I took many tennis lessons before I could get the ball over the net even once.*

5. The misplaced modifying clause produces an absurd image: a lake that's set back from its own shore. Of course, the "which" clause should follow "[t]he house": *The house, which was set back from the shore, overlooked the lake.*

Applying the Kaplan Method: Modification

Now let's use the Kaplan Method on a Sentence Correction question dealing with modification:

<u>Subjects tend to be vividly but disturbingly portrayed in Egon Schiele's portraits, often his closest friends and relatives.</u>

○   Subjects tend to be vividly but disturbingly portrayed in Egon Schiele's portraits, often his closest friends and relatives.

○   Subjects tend to be vividly but disturbingly portrayed in Egon Schiele's portraits, who were often his closest friends and relatives.

○   Subjects of Egon Schiele's portraits, often his closest friends and relatives, tend to be vividly but disturbingly portrayed.

○   In Egon Schiele's portraits, the subjects, often his closest friends and relatives, tend to be vividly but disturbingly portrayed.

○   Vividly but disturbingly, the subjects portrayed in Egon Schiele's portraits tended to be his closest friends and relatives.

STEP 1: READ THE ORIGINAL SENTENCE CAREFULLY, LOOKING FOR ERRORS

The entire sentence is underlined, but don't let that intimidate you. Use the Kaplan Method as you normally would and look for common errors. In this case, the error is a misplaced modifier at the end of the sentence. (Keep in mind that misplaced modifiers can occur anywhere in a sentence, not just at the beginning.) Here, the modifier is the final phrase set off by a comma, "often his closest friends and relatives." This phrase should refer to "subjects," but it's placed right next to "portraits." Always ask yourself when you see a modifier, "What should this word or phrase refer to? Is it as close to that word or phrase as possible?"

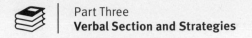

STEP 2: SCAN AND GROUP THE ANSWER CHOICES

As you scan, be on the lookout for where the modifier is placed. In these answer choices, the modifying phrase appears in several different positions. Any choice placing it far from the word it modifies—"subjects"—should be eliminated. In **(B)**, the modifying clause "who were often his closest friends and relatives" seems to refer to "portraits" rather than "subjects." Choice **(B)** retains the same problem as **(A)**, so you can eliminate it. Choice **(D)** places the modifier immediately after "subjects," so this is likely to be your answer.

STEP 3: ELIMINATE CHOICES UNTIL ONLY ONE REMAINS

In choice **(C)**, "subjects of Egon Schiele's portraits" seems to be one syntactical unit, so the phrase "often his closest friends and relatives" appears correctly to modify "subjects," even though it is not directly adjacent to "subjects." However, **(C)** is wrong because it is unclear whether "tend to be vividly but disturbingly portrayed" refers to how these subjects are displayed in the portraits or elsewhere; perhaps biographers of Schiele depict them in this manner.

Finally, choice **(E)** is incorrect because the adverbial phrase "[v]ividly but disturbingly" appears to refer to the verb "tended" rather than to the adjective "portrayed," making it seem as if the subjects' tendency to be Egon's friends is what's vivid and disturbing. Only **(D)** properly addresses this misplaced modifier problem; it is therefore your correct answer. Moreover, **(D)**, unlike **(C)**, makes it clear that the vivid but disturbing portrayal is in the portraits themselves.

TAKEAWAYS: MODIFICATION

- Adjectives modify nouns; adverbs modify verbs, adjectives, or other adverbs.
- A modifying phrase must clearly refer to what it modifies. To this end, it should be placed as close as possible to what it modifies.
- Many GMAT modification errors involve misplaced modifiers at the beginning of the sentence. When there is a modifying phrase at the beginning of the sentence, make sure that the thing the phrase describes follows the comma.
- Misplaced modifiers can also occur in the middle and at the end of a sentence, and they may or may not be set off by commas.
- When a modifying word or phrase appears in many different positions in the answer choices, determine what it is meant to modify and pick the choice that places it where it belongs.

Practice Set: Modification

14. Despite being called one of the founding members of the Impressionist movement, <u>Edgar Degas's paintings often depicted interior scenes as opposed to the landscapes depicted by most other Impressionists, and he publicly rejected the label.</u>

- ○ Edgar Degas's paintings often depicted interior scenes as opposed to the landscapes depicted by most other Impressionists, and he publicly rejected the label

- ○ Edgar Degas's paintings were unlike most other Impressionists in that they often depicted interior scenes as opposed to landscapes, and he publicly rejected the label

- ○ Edgar Degas publicly rejected the label and often depicted interior scenes in his paintings instead of landscapes, which were unlike most other Impressionists

- ○ Edgar Degas publicly rejected the label and, unlike most other Impressionists, often depicted interior scenes in his paintings instead of landscapes

- ○ the interior scenes depicted by Edgar Degas, who rejected the label, were unlike the landscapes depicted by most other Impressionists

15. The superb lyrebird is known for <u>the producing of elaborate songs, including astounding mimicry of other birds and even non-bird animals such as dingoes, which it often uses as part of a complex courtship ritual.</u>

- ○ the producing of elaborate songs, including astounding mimicry of other birds and even non-bird animals such as dingoes, which it often uses as part of a complex courtship ritual

- ○ producing elaborate songs, which are often used as part of a complex courtship ritual and can include astounding mimicry of other birds and even non-bird animals such as dingoes

- ○ their elaborate songs, which can include both astounding mimicry of other birds and even non-bird animals such as dingoes, and also is used as part of a complex courtship ritual

- ○ its elaborate songs and astounding mimicry of both other birds as well as non-bird animals such as dingoes, which are often used as part of a complex courtship ritual

- ○ the elaborate songs, which they produce, often being used as a part of a complex courtship ritual, including an astounding mimicry of other birds and even non-bird animals such as dingoes

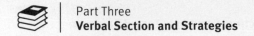

16. Believing in 1958 that Alaska and Hawaii would soon become part of the United States, <u>high school student Bob Heft, for a history class project, designed a flag with 50 stars; approved by President Eisenhower, that design became the American flag.</u>

    ○ high school student Bob Heft, for a history class project, designed a flag with 50 stars; approved by President Eisenhower, that design became the American flag

    ○ for a history class project, high school student Bob Heft designed a flag with 50 stars; approved by President Eisenhower, that design became the American flag

    ○ the American flag, designed by high school student Bob Heft with 50 stars for a history class project, was approved by President Eisenhower

    ○ high school student Bob Heft, for a history class project, designed a flag with 50 stars; approved by President Eisenhower, the American flag was what that design became

    ○ for a history class project, high school student Bob Heft designed a flag with 50 stars; approved by President Eisenhower, the American flag was what that design became

17. Consisting of surreal, nightmarish dreamscapes, <u>H. R. Giger created artwork that often inspires feelings of unease and dread in those who view it, and these reactions are why it was</u> chosen as the basis for the design of the title creature in the 1979 horror movie *Alien*.

    ○ H. R. Giger created artwork that often inspires feelings of unease and dread in those who view it, and these reactions are why it was

    ○ the artwork of H. R. Giger often inspires feelings of unease and dread in those who view it, and these reactions are why it is

    ○ H. R. Giger created artwork that often inspired feelings of unease and dread in those who view it, and these reactions are why it is

    ○ the artwork of H. R. Giger often inspires feelings of unease and dread in those who view it, and these reactions are why it was

    ○ the artwork of H. R. Giger often inspired feelings of unease and dread in those who view it, and these reactions are why it was

Advanced Practice Set: Modification

18. The recently discovered planet Kepler-90i was found via machine learning, a form of artificial intelligence in which <u>the identification of planets learned by computers is done from data by finding in the Kepler telescope instances of recorded signals from planets</u> beyond our solar system, known as exoplanets.

    O   the identification of planets learned by computers is done from data by finding in the Kepler telescope instances of recorded signals from planets

    O   computers learn to identify planets by finding in the Kepler telescope instances of recorded signals from planets beyond our solar system

    O   computers learn to identify planets by finding in data from the Kepler telescope instances of the planet's recorded signals from

    O   computers learn to identify planets by finding in data from the Kepler telescope instances of recorded signals from planets

    O   the identification of planets is learned by computers by finding in data from the Kepler telescope instances of recorded signals from planets

19. <u>Closely interrelated concepts, a change in macroeconomic policy tends to affect numerous microeconomic transactions, and the accumulation of microeconomic decisions typically influences the focus of macroeconomic studies, so</u> any economics curriculum requires considerable study of both macroeconomic and microeconomic concepts.

    O   Closely interrelated concepts, a change in macroeconomic policy tends to affect numerous microeconomic transactions, and the accumulation of microeconomic decisions typically influences the focus of macroeconomic studies, so

    O   A change in macroeconomic policy tends to affect microeconomic transactions numerously, and the accumulation of microeconomic decisions influences the focus of macroeconomic studies typically; since the concepts of macroeconomics and microeconomics are related closely,

    O   A change in macroeconomic policy tends to affect numerous microeconomic transactions, and the accumulation of microeconomic decisions typically influences the focus of macroeconomic studies as a closely related concept, so

    O   A change in macroeconomic policy tends to affect numerous microeconomic transactions, and the accumulation of microeconomic decisions typically influences the focus of macroeconomic studies; given these closely related concepts,

    O   A change in macroeconomic policy tends to affect numerous microeconomic transactions, and the accumulation of microeconomic decisions typically influences the focus of macroeconomic studies; since the concepts of macroeconomics and microeconomics are closely related,

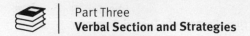
20. <u>Noticing the fact that the three students were arguing while they were writing a joint science report over the proper use of semicolons, their discussion was interrupted by the teacher</u> to give them a quick lesson on punctuation.

   ○ Noticing the fact that the three students were arguing while they were writing a joint science report over the proper use of semicolons, their discussion was interrupted by the teacher

   ○ Noting that the three students were arguing while they were writing a joint science report over the proper use of semicolons, their discussion was interrupted by the teacher

   ○ Noting that the three students were arguing over the proper use of semicolons while they were writing a joint science report, the teacher interrupted their discussion

   ○ Noticing the fact that the three students were arguing over the proper use of semicolons while they were writing a joint science report, the teacher interrupted their discussion

   ○ Noting that the three students were arguing over the proper use of semicolons while writing a joint science report, the teacher interrupted their discussion

Parallelism

> **LEARNING OBJECTIVES**
>
> In this section, you will learn how to:
>
> - Define *parallelism* and recognize grammatical structures that require parallelism
> - Apply the Kaplan Method for Sentence Correction to sentences that may have non-parallel constructions

The basic concept behind parallelism is pretty simple: ideas with the same importance and function—nouns, verbs, phrases, or whatever—should be expressed in the same grammatical form. There are two types of constructions that test parallel structure on the GMAT:

1. Lists of items or a series of events
2. Two-part constructions such as *from X to Y, both X and Y, either X or Y, prefer X to Y, not only X but also Y,* and *as much X as Y*

Parallel Construction

Prepositions, articles, and auxiliaries can begin a list without needing to be repeated throughout. But if they are repeated, they must be in every element of the list.

- Correct: "Will you travel by plane, car, or boat?"
- Also correct: "Will you travel by plane, by car, or by boat?"
- Incorrect: "Will you travel by plane, car, or by boat?"

Analogies, similes, and other comparisons all require parallel structure.

- He was as brazen as his brother was diffident.
- Seeing her smile was like feeling the warmth of the sun.

Parallelism Exercise

Answers are on the following page.

For each of the following sentences, put parallel items into the same form.

1. The city's decay stems from governmental mismanagement, increasing unemployment, and many businesses are relocating.
2. Tourists' images of France range from cosmopolitan to the pastoral.
3. Excited about visiting New York, Jasmine minded neither riding the subways nor to cope with the crowded sidewalks.
4. To visualize success is not the same as achieving it.
5. I remember my aunt making her own dandelion wine and that she played the fiddle.
6. In my favorite Armenian restaurant, the menu is fascinating and the entrées exquisite.

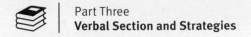

Parallelism Exercise: Answers

1. "[M]any businesses are relocating" should be written as *business relocation* to parallel "governmental mismanagement" and "increasing unemployment."

2. If you say "the pastoral," you have to say *the cosmopolitan*. Or you could say ... *from cosmopolitan to pastoral*.

3. To parallel "riding," you need *coping*—not "to cope."

4. "To visualize" should be *visualizing* to parallel "achieving." Alternately, "achieving" could be written as *to achieve* to be in parallel with "[t]o visualize."

5. Change "my aunt making" to *that my aunt made* to be parallel with "that she played." Another possibility is to change "that she played" to *playing* to match "making."

6. "[T]he menu" is singular, but "entrées" is plural, so you must say *are exquisite* to parallel the phrase "is fascinating."

Applying the Kaplan Method: Parallelism

Now let's use the Kaplan Method on a Sentence Correction question dealing with parallelism:

Pablo Picasso's genius is only fully revealed when one considers the various facets of his work as they developed through many artistic phases, beginning with his Red <u>period, continuing through his Blue period, and finishing with his period of Cubism</u>.

- ○ period, continuing through his Blue period, and finishing with his period of Cubism
- ○ period, continuing through his Blue period, and finishing with his Cubist period
- ○ period, and continuing through his Blue period and his Cubist period
- ○ period phase, his Blue period phase, and his phase of Cubism
- ○ period, his Blue period, and his period of Cubism

STEP 1: READ THE ORIGINAL SENTENCE CAREFULLY, LOOKING FOR ERRORS

The original sentence contains a list, so your Pattern Recognition skills should tell you to check for parallel structure. Because the first two items in the list contain "Red period" and "Blue period," you should expect the third item in the list to follow the adjective-noun pattern and contain "Cubist period." Instead, this sentence ends with "period of Cubism," breaking the pattern and making choice (**A**) incorrect.

STEP 2: SCAN AND GROUP THE ANSWER CHOICES

Choices (**B**) and (**C**) end with "his Cubist period," while (**A**) and (**E**) reference "his period of Cubism" and (**D**) ends with the similar construction "his phase of Cubism." You have a 3-2 split.

STEP 3: ELIMINATE CHOICES UNTIL ONLY ONE REMAINS

You've established that (**A**) is incorrect, so eliminate (**D**) and (**E**) as well. This leaves only (**B**) and (**C**) with the correct parallel construction "Cubist period." The list should also contain the parallel phrases "beginning...continuing...and finishing." (**C**) is wrong because it drops "finishing," which alters the meaning and also destroys the parallel structure. Only (**B**) exhibits parallel structure throughout the list and is the correct answer. Read it back into the sentence to confirm there are no errors:

Chapter 13
Sentence Correction: Commonly Tested Grammar

Pablo Picasso's genius is only fully revealed when one considers the various facets of his work as they developed through many artistic phases, beginning with his Red <u>period, continuing through his Blue period, and finishing with his Cubist period.</u>

TAKEAWAYS: PARALLELISM

- Items in a list must have parallel form.

- Many two-part constructions set up parallel elements. Examples: "not only A but also B," "from A to B," and "either A or B."

- The key to handling parallel structure questions is consistency.

- Analogies, metaphors, similes, and other comparisons all require parallel structure.

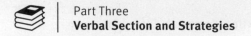

Practice Set: Parallelism

21. Although carotene and xanthophyll are present in leaves throughout the year, these pigments are not usually visible until <u>the days shorten, temperature drops, and the breaking down of the chlorophyll in the leaves reveals</u> the yellow and orange colors.

   ○ the days shorten, temperature drops, and the breaking down of the chlorophyll in the leaves reveals

   ○ the days shorten, the temperature drops, and the chlorophyll breakdown in the leaves is to reveal

   ○ the days shorten, the temperature drops, and the chlorophyll in the leaves breaks down, revealing

   ○ the days are shorter, the temperature is lower, and less chlorophyll in the leaves due to breakdown reveals

   ○ the days shorten, the temperature drops, and chlorophyll breaks down, revealing in the leaves

22. By conducting a national study of opioid abuse on college campuses, researchers hope to determine where students purchase opioids, how frequently students abuse opioids on average, and <u>which college stressors most commonly contribute to opioid abuse among students</u>.

   ○ which college stressors most commonly contribute to opioid abuse among students

   ○ which are the college stressors common to students who are likely to be turning to opioid abuse

   ○ the common stressors of college that are likely to contribute to opioid abuse among students

   ○ the stressors of college common among students who turn to opioid abuse

   ○ the types of college stressors that are common to students who are likely to turn to opioid abuse

23. Although deciding the outcome of an election by chance may seem antiquated, <u>a toss of a coin, playing a round of poker, and drawing straws are all methods that have been used</u> within the span of 15 years to determine the winner of a deadlocked election somewhere in the United States.

  ○ a toss of a coin, playing a round of poker, and drawing straws are all methods that have been used

  ○ the tossing of a coin, playing a round of poker, and drawing straws are all methods that have been used

  ○ tossing a coin, playing a round of poker, and drawing straws are all methods that would have been used

  ○ a toss of a coin, playing a round of poker, and drawing straws are all methods that had been used

  ○ tossing a coin, playing a round of poker, and drawing straws are all methods that have been used

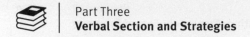

Advanced Practice Set: Parallelism

24. According to one nutrition consultant, healthy adults should not hesitate to consume eggs, since this food contains six grams of high-quality protein, all nine essential amino acids, <u>vitamins B12 and D, and is a source of various other nutrients</u> as well.

    ○ vitamins B12 and D, and is a source of various other nutrients

    ○ vitamins B12 and D, and including various other nutrients

    ○ vitamins B12 and D, and various other nutrients are included

    ○ and vitamins B12 and D, and it is a source of various other nutrients

    ○ the vitamins B12 and D, and provides various other nutrients

25. *In Cold Blood* <u>is not only often considered</u> Truman Capote's most popular novel but also the first "nonfiction novel," a literary genre that uses techniques of fictional storytelling to depict actual people and events.

    ○ is not only often considered

    ○ is as often not only considered

    ○ is often considered not only

    ○ not only is often considered to be

    ○ not only is considered as often

26. The self-portraits of Frida Kahlo can be considered both introspective explorations of a psyche that ranged free, unbounded by historical notions of cultural identity and <u>feminine, as well as subverting</u> traditional European portraiture.

    ○ feminine, as well as subverting

    ○ being feminine, and subverted

    ○ that was feminine, and subversions of

    ○ the femininity, as well as subverted

    ○ femininity, and subversions of

Comparisons

> **LEARNING OBJECTIVES**
>
> In this section, you will learn how to:
>
> - Identify faulty comparisons involving comparison words, modifying phrases, and parallelism
> - Apply the Kaplan Method for Sentence Correction to sentences that may have illogical or malformed comparisons

Faulty comparisons account for a significant number of errors in GMAT Sentence Correction questions. Most relate to the very simple idea that you can't compare apples to oranges. Of course, you want to compare things that are grammatically similar, but you also want to compare things that are logically similar. You can't logically compare, say, a person to a quality or an item to a group. You have to compare one individual to another, one quality to another, one group to another.

Three Kinds of Comparison Errors

Use Attention to the Right Detail and Pattern Recognition to keep an eye out for the following:

- Key comparison words such as *like, as, compared to, less than, more than, other than, that of,* and *those of* may be used incorrectly.

- Long modifying phrases between compared elements can distract from comparison errors. Ignore the modifying phrase at first so you can see the compared elements clearly.

- Compared items must be parallel in terms of construction. If a preposition, article, or auxiliary is in one compared item, it needs to be in the other.
  - Incorrect: I would do anything for my mother but not my boss.
  - Correct: I would do anything for my mother but not for my boss.

Comparisons Exercise

Answers are on the following page.

Fix the comparisons in the sentences below.

1. Like a black bear that I once saw in the Buenos Aires Zoo, the Central Park Zoo polar bear's personality strikes me as being sadly neurotic.
2. The article questioned the popularity of jazz compared to classical music.
3. The challenger weighed 20 pounds less than that of the defender.
4. The Boston office contributes less to total national sales than any other U.S. branch.
5. The host paid more attention to his celebrity guest than the others.

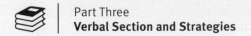

Comparisons Exercise: Answers

1. "Like" creates a comparison, and you can compare only similar things. Here, you have to compare bears to bears or personalities to personalities. *Like a black bear I once saw in the Buenos Aires Zoo, the Central Park Zoo polar bear strikes me as being sadly neurotic.*

2. *The article questioned the popularity of jazz compared to* that *of classical music.*

3. *The challenger weighed 20 pounds less than the defender did*, or *The challenger's weight was 20 pounds less than that of the defender.*

4. There are two ways to read this sentence as it's written. We could be comparing the Boston office's contribution to national sales and other branches' contributions, but we also could be comparing the Boston office's contribution to national sales and the Boston office's contribution to those other branches. The former comparison is more logical, so we clarify: *. . . than any other U.S. branch* does.

5. A similar problem—you need to repeat the verb after "than" (*than* he *paid to the others*) or refer to the verb by placing *to* after "than" (*than to the others*).

Applying the Kaplan Method: Comparisons

Now let's use the Kaplan Method on a Sentence Correction question dealing with comparisons:

<u>Like most other marsupial species and all other kangaroo species, the diet of the swamp wallaby consists</u> of leaves and other sorts of vegetation.

O   Like most other marsupial species and all other kangaroo species, the diet of the swamp wallaby consists

O   Like those of most other marsupial species and all other kangaroo species, the diets of the swamp wallaby consists

O   Just like the diet of most other marsupial species and all other kangaroo species, the diet of the swamp wallaby consists

O   Similar to the diets of most other marsupial species and all other kangaroo species, the swamp wallabies have a diet which consists

O   Like most other marsupial species and all other kangaroo species, the swamp wallaby has a diet consisting

STEP 1: READ THE ORIGINAL SENTENCE CAREFULLY, LOOKING FOR ERRORS

This sentence begins with the word "[l]ike," which signals that you have a comparison to check. Look at the items being compared and make sure they are comparable. In the original sentence, "species" are compared to a "diet." That's an incorrect comparison.

STEP 2: SCAN AND GROUP THE ANSWER CHOICES

All the answer choices contain "[l]ike" or "[s]imilar to," so they all contain comparisons. As you examine each choice, look to ensure that it makes a proper comparison. Notice how Attention to the Right Detail—to the words that signal a comparison—has helped you to quickly form a strategy for this question.

STEP 3: ELIMINATE CHOICES UNTIL ONLY ONE REMAINS

The incorrect comparison in the original sentence means that you would automatically eliminate **(A)**. Aside from sounding awkward, **(B)** contains a subject/verb agreement problem—the plural noun "diets" takes the singular verb "consists," which is incorrect. **(C)** should be eliminated because in the introductory phrase "diet" should be plural; also, there's no reason to use "[j]ust like" rather than "[l]ike." In addition, "[l]ike" is preferable to "[s]imilar to" in **(D)**, which also incorrectly compares "diets" to "wallabies." Only **(E)** correctly compares the swamp wallaby to other species. Read this choice back into the sentence to confirm it is correct:

<u>Like most other marsupial species and all other kangaroo species</u>, the swamp wallaby has a diet consisting of leaves and other sorts of vegetation.

TAKEAWAYS: COMPARISONS

- Items being compared must be both grammatically and logically comparable.
- Compared items must have parallel form.
- The key to handling comparison questions is to make sure that the comparisons are correct and avoid any possibility of ambiguity.
- Don't let intervening phrases or clauses distract you from what is being compared.

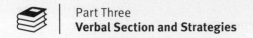

Practice Set: Comparisons

27. Determining which animal on Earth is the largest depends on one's reference point: while the blue whale's body is indeed larger than <u>the sperm whale, the sperm whale's brain is actually larger than the blue whale</u>.

  ○   the sperm whale, the sperm whale's brain is actually larger than the blue whale

  ○   that of the sperm whale, the sperm whale's brain is actually larger than that of the blue whale

  ○   that of the sperm whale, the sperm whale's brain is actually larger than the blue whale

  ○   the sperm whale's brain, the sperm whale's body is actually larger than the blue whale's brain

  ○   that of the sperm whale, the sperm whale's brain nevertheless is larger than that of the blue whale

28. <u>No less significant than</u> international pressures are the constraints that domestic culture and ideology impose on decision making by national political figures.

  ○   No less significant than

  ○   The things that are just as significant as

  ○   Just like the significant

  ○   Not lesser than the significance of

  ○   What are as significant as

29. Establishing goals for a nonprofit organization is often different <u>than setting</u> goals for a profit-making enterprise because the stakeholders of the former may be more varied.

  ○   than setting

  ○   than the setting of

  ○   from

  ○   from setting

  ○   from the setting of

Advanced Practice Set: Comparisons

30. Reducing the population of Japanese beetles is done <u>most easily by applying pesticides to turf-dwelling young larva in late summer than applications</u> to mature larva in spring or adult beetles at any time of year.

    ○ most easily by applying pesticides to turf-dwelling young larva in late summer than applications

    ○ most easily by the application of pesticides to turf-dwelling young larva in late summer than that

    ○ more easily by applying pesticides to turf-dwelling young larva in late summer than

    ○ easier through the application of pesticides to turf-dwelling young larva in late summer than

    ○ more easily by applying pesticides to turf-dwelling young larva in late summer rather than applying

31. With an elaborate menu featuring innovative dishes from a variety of world cuisines <u>as well as serving its signature breakfast fare, Penelope's Pancake Palace, an established downtown eatery, offers a more diverse selection of food than does any restaurant</u> in the city.

    ○ as well as serving its signature breakfast fare, Penelope's Pancake Palace, an established downtown eatery, offers a more diverse selection of food than does any restaurant

    ○ as well as its signature breakfast fare, Penelope's Pancake Palace, an eatery established downtown, offers a more diverse selection of food than does any restaurant

    ○ as well as with serving its signature breakfast fare, Penelope's Pancake Palace, an established downtown eatery, offers a more diverse selection of food than does any other restaurant

    ○ as well as its signature breakfast fare, Penelope's Pancake Palace, an established downtown eatery, offers a more diverse selection of food than does any other restaurant

    ○ as well as its signature breakfast fare, Penelope's Pancake Palace, an established downtown eatery, offers more of a diverse selection of food as any other restaurant

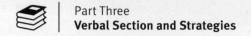

32. The United States' trade deficit with China rose in 2003 to $123 billion, <u>which is 17 percent more than the previous year</u> and more than ten times the U.S.-China trade deficit in 1998.

   ○   which is 17 percent more than the previous year

   ○   which is 17 percent higher than it was the previous year

   ○   17 percent higher than the previous year's figure was

   ○   an amount that is 17 percent more than the previous year was

   ○   an amount that is 17 percent higher than the previous year's figure

Usage and Idioms

The principle of **usage** concerns the "right" way to use words to say things as determined by users of English over time. There is no overarching grammar rule that applies across situations; each word or phrase is governed by its own rule.

Idioms are combinations of words that together have a meaning distinct from the definition of each word. For example, at the supermarket, you *pick up some bread* and *pick out a kind of frozen pizza*. The meanings of *pick up* and *pick out* are not much related to the meanings of *up* and *out*.

How to Recognize Errors Involving Usage and Idioms

Usage and idioms are likely to show up on a handful of Sentence Correction questions. If you have had consistent exposure to "standard" written English, as generally defined in academic and journalistic circles, then you will be able to trust your ear to tell you what sounds right, and what sounds wrong, in a sentence. For example, if someone were to say, "I am aware about these problems, because I saw the newscast yesterday," you'd pick up on the error right away. The correct idiom is "aware *of*," not "aware *about*."

Even so, issues of usage and idiom frequently involve small, seemingly unimportant words, like prepositions, so it is easy to overlook these errors if you don't keep alert for them—especially under time pressure as on the GMAT. Therefore, Attention to the Right Detail is important for success on questions involving usage and idioms.

Moreover, there may be commonly tested words and phrases that you've simply been using wrong all your life. Kaplan GMAT teachers often get a surprise or two as they master this material! Some idioms are commonly used incorrectly in informal, everyday English. For example, your brother says to you, "Here's a tip—Mom prefers platinum over gold." Did you spot the error? The correct idiom is "prefers X *to* Y." So it's a good idea to keep an eye out for unfamiliar idioms during your GMAT studies and in all your reading so you can jot them down and learn them.

If you have not had long-standing exposure to standard written English, then you won't be able to trust your ear as much. In this case, you'll definitely want to learn the commonly tested words and phrases that appear in this chapter and in your online resources. Making flashcards with these words and phrases can help. You might pattern your flashcards after the exercises in this section, putting a sentence with a blank in it on the front of the card and the correct word or phrase to fill in the blank on the back.

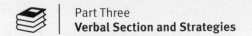

Common Errors of Usage and Idioms

When answering Sentence Correction questions on the GMAT, look out for the following:

- Prepositions (*to, from, at, over*, etc.) in the underlined portion of the sentence. Their usage is often dictated by idiomatic rules.

- Verbs whose idiomatic usage you've seen frequently tested. Common examples are *prefer, credit*, and *regard*.

- Comparisons that aren't expressed with the correct combination of words. One example is *as many X as Y*. It would be incorrect to say, for example, *You know as many idioms than you need.*

See the Usage and Idioms exercises later in this section for practice with these and other constructions in which errors often lurk.

Also keep a lookout for sentences that use more words than necessary, as well as those that seem to bury the important idea behind less important wording. The GMAT prefers active voice and a clear, direct style. That said, sometimes the correct answer on the test will not be the way you would write the sentence but will be the only grammatically correct choice: grammar is a more important criterion than style when it comes to choosing correct answers. Nonetheless, sentences that demonstrate any of the following are unlikely to be correct:

- Unnecessary passive voice: *The letter was written by John* is not wrong, but better is *John wrote the letter.*

- Unnecessary wordiness and redundancy. For example, the word *because* is better than the phrase *in view of the fact that*.

- Awkward, choppy, or clunky phrasing: if you can trust your "ear," use it to identify sentences and phrases that simply don't read well.

Finally, here's a specific tip: be alert for verbs that trigger the subjunctive mood. The subjunctive mood is called for in two situations:

1. **Orders and recommendations:** With verbs such as *order, demand, insist, recommend, ask, suggest,* etc. or sentences that indicate a request or requirement, what follows the verb should be *that*, a new subject, and the infinitive form of a verb but without the *to*. Examples:

   - He *asked* that the door *be* left open.
   - She *suggests* that her clients *read* all documents carefully.
   - It is *important* that applicants *pass* a background check.

2. **Hypothetical situations:** When contemplating hypothetical or contrary-to-fact situations in the present, use *were* (singular and plural) and *would*. For such situations in the past, change the verb tense accordingly. Examples:

   - If I *were* rich, I *would* quit my job.
   - If only I *were* there with you, I *would* be happy.
   - If James *had been* in charge, he *would* not have allowed excess expenditures.

Usage and Idioms Exercise, Part I

Answers are on the following page.

Fill in the blank with the correct word or phrase that completes the idiom correctly in the sentence. In some cases, the correct idiom may not require any additional words.

1. He modestly *attributed* his business's success _____ good luck.

2. My dictionary *defines* "idiom" _____ the usual way in which the words of a particular language are joined together.

3. Alexander Graham Bell is *credited* _____ inventing the telephone.

4. Some people with color-blindness cannot *distinguish* red _____ green.

5. Other people with color-blindness cannot *distinguish* _____ yellow _____ blue.

6. Although his story seems incredible, I *believe* it _____ the truth.

7. She is *regarded* _____ an expert on public health policy.

8. He is *considered* _____ a close friend of the president.

9. I like to *contrast* my plaid pants _____ a lovely paisley jacket.

10. According to Aristotle, contentment is *different* _____ happiness.

11. The oldest rocks on Earth are *estimated* _____ 4.6 billion years old.

12. Louisiana's legal system is *modeled* _____ the Napoleonic code.

13. I don't mean for my comments to be *perceived* _____ criticism.

14. Cigarette ads *aimed* _____ children have been banned by the FDA.

15. The mass extinction of dinosaurs has been *linked* _____ a large meteor impact.

16. Don't *worry* _____ all the idioms that might appear on the GMAT. Just learn the ones you come across between now and Test Day.

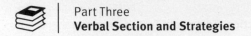
Usage and Idioms Exercise, Part I: Answers

1. He modestly *attributed* his business's success **to** good luck.

2. My dictionary *defines* "idiom" **as** the usual way in which the words of a particular language are joined together.

3. Alexander Graham Bell is *credited* **with** inventing the telephone.

4. Some color-blind people cannot *distinguish* red **from** green.

5. Other color-blind people cannot *distinguish* **between** yellow **and** blue.

6. Although his story seems incredible, I *believe* it **to be** the truth.

7. She is *regarded* **as** an expert on public health policy.

8. He is *considered* a close friend of the president. *[**This blank takes nothing.**]*

9. I like to *contrast* my plaid pants **with** a lovely paisley jacket.

10. According to Aristotle, contentment is *different* **from** happiness.

11. The oldest rocks on Earth are *estimated* **to be** 4.6 billion years old.

12. Louisiana's legal system is *modeled* **after** the Napoleonic code.

13. I don't mean for my comments to be *perceived* **as** criticism.

14. Cigarette ads *aimed* **at** children have been banned by the FDA.

15. The mass extinction of dinosaurs has been *linked* **to** a large meteor impact.

16. Don't *worry* **about** all the idioms that might appear on the GMAT. Just learn the ones you come across between now and Test Day.

Usage and Idioms Exercise, Part II

Answers are on the following page.

Fill in the blank with the correct word or phrase that completes the idiom correctly in the sentence. In some cases, choose the option that correctly completes the idiom.

1. I sold more glasses of lemonade _____ my neighbor sold.
2. She sold as many glasses of lemonade _____ she could.
3. The bigger they come, _____ they fall, or so it is said.
4. According to my diet, I can have either cake or/and ice cream, but not both.
5. Given my choice, I would have both cake _____ ice cream.
6. I must decide between one _____ the other.
7. Neither the coach _____ the players was/were happy with the team's performance.
8. I couldn't decide if/whether he was kidding or not.
9. Between/Among the three candidates, he has the more/most impressive record.
10. There are less/fewer students in class today than there were yesterday.
11. However, the amount/number of students enrolled in this class has increased.
12. People are forbidden from entering/to enter the park at night.
13. The ruling prohibits the defendant from discussing/to discuss the case.
14. Most politicians do not want to be seen associating with/among convicted felons.
15. We should treat others as/like we would want them to treat us.
16. I would prefer a salty treat like/such as potato chips over/to a candy bar.
17. The annual meeting was a situation where/in which the leadership team needed to use its influence.
18. My great-grandmother was born sometime/somewhere around 1880.
19. Scores on the GMAT range from 200 _____ 800.
20. Most local residents view the monument _____ an eyesore.
21. In the United States, there is less opposition _____ the use of genetically modified foods than in Europe.
22. Stress can lower one's resistance _____ cold and flu viruses.
23. The rise in inflation has become so significant _____ constitute a threat to the economic recovery.
24. The actress's performance was so poignant _____ the entire audience was moved to tears.
25. Just try _____ do as well as you can on the test.

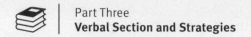
Usage and Idioms Exercise, Part II: Answers

1. I sold more glasses of lemonade *than* my neighbor sold.
2. She sold as many glasses of lemonade *as* she could.
3. The bigger they come, *the harder* they fall, or so it is said.
4. According to my diet, I can have either cake *or* ice cream, but not both.
5. Given my choice, I would have both cake *and* ice cream.
6. I must decide between one *and* the other.
7. Neither the coach *nor* the players *were* happy with the team's performance.
8. I couldn't decide *whether* he was kidding or not.
9. *Among* the three candidates, he has the *most* impressive record.
10. There are *fewer* students in class today than there were yesterday.
11. However, the *number* of students enrolled in this class has increased.
12. People are forbidden *to enter* the park at night.
13. The ruling prohibits the defendant *from discussing* the case.
14. Most politicians do not want to be seen associating *with* convicted felons.
15. We should treat others *as* we would want them to treat us.
16. I would prefer a salty treat *such as* potato chips *to* a candy bar.
17. Scores on the GMAT range from 200 *to* 800.
18. The annual meeting was a situation *in which* the leadership team needed to use its influence.
19. My great-grandmother was born *sometime* around 1880.
20. Most local residents view the monument *as* an eyesore.
21. In the United States, there is less opposition *to* the use of genetically modified foods than in Europe.
22. Stress can lower one's resistance *to* cold and flu viruses.
23. The rise in inflation has become so significant *as to* constitute a threat to the economic recovery.
24. The actress's performance was so poignant *that* the entire audience was moved to tears.
25. Just try *to* do as well as you can on the test.

Applying the Kaplan Method: Usage and Idioms

Now let's use the Kaplan Method on a Sentence Correction question dealing with usage and idioms:

> Growth in the industry is at an all-time low, with <u>less than 68,000 people employed and fewer</u> opportunity in the field than there has been during any of the past ten years.

- O   less than 68,000 people employed and fewer
- O   fewer than 68,000 people employed and fewer
- O   lesser than 68,000 people employed and fewer
- O   fewer than 68,000 people employed and less
- O   less than 68,000 people employed, and there is less

STEP 1: READ THE ORIGINAL SENTENCE CAREFULLY, LOOKING FOR ERRORS

Notice that the underlined portion of the sentence contains the words "less" and "fewer." These words are often tested on the GMAT because they are often used incorrectly. "Less" can only refer to non-countable items, such as soup or confidence. "Fewer" must refer to countable items, such as chairs or peanuts. In this sentence, since "people" can be counted, there are "fewer" people, and since "opportunity" cannot be counted, there is "less" opportunity.

STEP 2: SCAN AND GROUP THE ANSWER CHOICES

Even if that didn't occur to you as the issue in the sentence, you should note that some of the choices use "less" (or "lesser") and others use "fewer," and group accordingly into a 3-2 split. This step should prompt you to think about the associated usage rule.

STEP 3: ELIMINATE CHOICES UNTIL ONLY ONE REMAINS

Eliminate choice (**A**) because the original sentence misuses "less" and "fewer." Choices (**C**) and (**E**) make similar errors. Choice (**C**)'s "lesser than" would be unidiomatic in any context. In addition to using "less" in front of "people," (**E**) breaks off "opportunity in the field" into a new independent clause, adding unnecessary extra words and an awkward repetition of "there." Choice (**B**) uses "fewer" correctly to refer to the people but also uses it to refer to the uncountable "opportunity," so eliminate this choice. That leaves (**D**), which is correct: it uses "fewer" to describe the countable noun "people" and "less" to describe "opportunity." Read (**D**) back into the original sentence:

Growth in the industry is at an all-time low, with <u>fewer than 68,000 people employed and less</u> opportunity in the field than there has been during any of the past ten years.

TAKEAWAYS: USAGE AND IDIOMS

- Avoid using more words when a choice that uses fewer words to express the same meaning is available.
- Passive voice is not wrong, but if all else is equal, choose active voice over passive.
- Avoid clunky, choppy, or awkward-sounding sentences.
- Be alert for incorrect idiomatic usage. Idioms are word combinations that, based on common usage, have established themselves as correct in standard written English. Many GMAT idiom questions require you to use the right prepositions.

Practice Set: Usage and Idioms

33. In addition to winning the Nobel Prize in Physics for his accomplishments in quantum electro-dynamics, Richard Feynman worked on both the Manhattan Project in Los Alamos <u>as well as the Rogers Commission, which investigated</u> the space shuttle *Challenger* disaster in 1986.

    ○   as well as the Rogers Commission, which investigated

    ○   and also on the Rogers Commission that investigated

    ○   and on the Rogers Commission, which investigated

    ○   and the Rogers Commission, which is investigating

    ○   and the Rogers Commission, which investigated

34. To boost the nation's economy, it is <u>at least as important for businesses to focus</u> on developing worker productivity than it is for them to hire new employees.

    ○   at least as important for businesses to focus

    ○   at least as important for businesses focusing

    ○   no less important for businesses to focus

    ○   no less important that businesses focusing

    ○   as important, if not more important, for businesses to focus

35. The "Mpemba effect" refers to the fact that hot water freezes <u>more quickly in comparison to cold water; the researchers who investigated this effect also discovered that cold water heats more quickly in relation to warm water</u> and named that phenomenon the "inverse Mpemba effect."

- O more quickly in comparison to cold water; the researchers who investigated this effect also discovered that cold water heats more quickly in relation to warm water

- O faster; the researchers who investigated this effect also discovered that cold water heats faster

- O more quickly than cold water; the researchers who investigated this effect also discovered that cold water would heat more quickly than warm water

- O faster than cold water; the researchers who investigated this effect also discovered that cold water heats faster than warm water

- O faster than cold water; the researchers who investigated this effect also discovered that the opposite is true

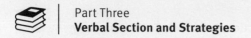

Advanced Practice Set: Usage and Idioms

36. The entrepreneurs credited the website that helped owners of small businesses find suppliers <u>to keep their new enterprise viable when cash flow was neither ample or steady</u>.

    ○　to keep their new enterprise viable when cash flow was neither ample or steady

    ○　toward keeping their new enterprise viable at a time when cash flow was not ample or steady

    ○　with keeping their new enterprise viable when cash flow was neither ample nor steady

    ○　to keeping their new enterprise viable when cash flow was neither ample nor steady

    ○　with keeping their new enterprise viable when there was not ample or steady cash flow

37. All parents who wish to hold a leadership position in the Boy Scouts are required, regardless of whether or not their child is a member, <u>for taking youth protection training</u>.

    ○　for taking youth protection training

    ○　for making sure youth protection training is taken

    ○　to take youth protection training

    ○　to have taken of the youth protection training

    ○　of taking youth protection training

38. The United States <u>would achieve a 10 percent reduction in gasoline consumption if Congress will raise</u> fuel economy standards to 31.3 miles per gallon for passenger cars and to 24.5 miles per gallon for light trucks.

    ○　would achieve a 10 percent reduction in gasoline consumption if Congress will raise

    ○　will achieve a 10 percent reduction in gasoline consumption if Congress were to raise

    ○　will have achieved a 10 percent reduction in gasoline consumption if Congress will raise

    ○　would achieve a 10 percent reduction in gasoline consumption if Congress were to raise

    ○　would achieve a 10 percent reduction in gasoline consumption if Congress were raising

Clauses and Connectors

LEARNING OBJECTIVES

In this section, you will learn how to:

- Explain the ways in which clauses are often incorrectly joined in Sentence Correction questions
- Apply the Kaplan Method for Sentence Correction to sentences whose parts may be connected incorrectly

The GMAT uses compound and complex sentences to test your knowledge of clauses and connectors. Recall that a clause is a group of words that contains a subject and a verb. When the underlined portion of a sentence includes a junction between ideas, make sure the ideas are joined correctly.

How to Recognize Errors Involving Clauses and Connectors

Clauses should be connected by one, and only one, connector (*because*, *although*, *as*, *but*, etc.). Be alert for choices that result in an omission of any connector. At the same time, avoid choices that result in the use of two connectors that indicate the same relationship between the same two ideas; the sentence only needs one.

Furthermore, the connector used should make sense given the logical relationship between the clauses. If you have not already done so, review the discussion of key words in Chapter 9: Reading Comprehension Strategy. Contrast, continuation, and logic (evidence, conclusion) key words are particularly apt to be a source of error on Sentence Correction questions. Wrong answer choices may change connector words in a way that changes the meaning of the sentence from what the author intended or that produce an illogical meaning.

Clauses and Connectors Exercise

Answers are on the following page.

For each of the following sentences, correct the error related to clauses and connectors.

1. Although the vice president ordered all employees to work through the weekend, but some employees went home.

2. Many citizens agree that austerity measures are necessary, few are happy about the ones that have been enacted.

3. Several new restaurants have recently opened next to Carlotta's Bistro on Main Street, and also a yoga studio has opened in the same building as Carlotta's too.

4. As a result of the raging wildfire, many residents were forcibly evacuated, so the fire is still out of control.

5. Since the manager is competent, nonetheless she has been promoted repeatedly.

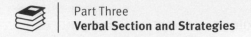

Clauses and Connectors Exercise: Answers

1. "Although" establishes a contrast between clauses, and so does "but." Only one of these words should be in the sentence.

2. The two clauses in this sentence need to be related by a connector: *Many citizens agree that austerity measures are necessary, although few are happy about the ones that have been enacted.*

3. The "and" is sufficient to connect the clause about the new restaurants to the clause about the yoga studio. The words "also" and "too" are unnecessary and should be omitted.

4. This sentence starts out with a logical cause-and-effect sequence, but then "so" indicates the fire is out of control because the residents were evacuated. This does not make sense, especially since the sentence has already said the residents were evacuated because of the fire. The word "so" should be replaced by "and" or some other logical connector.

5. "Since" indicates a reason why something happened. It's logical to say that the manager has been promoted because of her competence. The contrast key word "nonetheless" is at odds with the logical relationship between these clauses and should be deleted.

Applying the Kaplan Method: Clauses and Connectors

Now use the Kaplan Method on a Sentence Correction question dealing with clauses and connectors:

> More and more couples wait before trying to start a family, the average age of first-time parents is increasing.

- More and more couples wait before trying to start
- As more and more couples wait before trying to start
- As more and more couples wait before trying and starting
- Although more and more couples wait before trying to start
- Being that more and more couples are waiting before trying to start

STEP 1: READ THE ORIGINAL SENTENCE CAREFULLY, LOOKING FOR ERRORS

This sentence contains two complete clauses, each with its own subject and verb. The subject of "wait" is "couples," and the subject of "is increasing" is "age." Two complete clauses should be joined with a conjunction, but this sentence has no conjunction and is thus a run-on. The correct answer will provide the sentence with a conjunction. Moreover, the logical relationship between clauses is one of cause and effect. The delay in starting a family in the first clause logically leads to an increase in the average age. So look for a choice that establishes that relationship. Finally, note that the junction between the clauses is not underlined, so the connector word cannot go there; it will have to place the first clause into the correct relationship with the second.

STEP 2: SCAN AND GROUP THE ANSWER CHOICES

Choices (**B**) and (**C**) introduce "[a]s" at the beginning of the sentence. Choice (**D**) substitutes "[a]lthough," and (**E**) uses "[b]eing that."

STEP 3: ELIMINATE CHOICES UNTIL ONLY ONE REMAINS

Eliminate **(A)** for omitting a connecting word. "Being that" is a weak, awkward construction, and on the GMAT an answer choice containing it will be wrong; eliminate **(E)**. Choice **(D)** adds the conjunction "[a]lthough," which indicates a contrast and therefore doesn't make logical sense. **(B)** and **(C)** both start with "[a]s," meaning "because," which does make logical sense as a conjunction for this sentence. **(C)** changes "trying to start" to "trying and starting," which is idiomatically incorrect. The correct answer is **(B)**, which adds an appropriate conjunction and does not create any new errors. Read **(B)** back into the sentence to confirm:

<u>As more and more couples wait before trying to start</u> a family, the average age of first-time parents is increasing.

TAKEAWAYS: CLAUSES AND CONNECTORS

- Be aware of how different parts of the sentence relate to each other.
- Make sure that connections between clauses are formed in a logical way.
- Avoid choices that result in missing or redundant connectors.

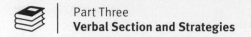
Practice Set: Clauses and Connectors

39. <u>Due to countries in a monetary union having to issue debt in a joint currency over which they lack full control, therefore</u> investors become nervous about the financial health of a country, that nation may not be able to finance its debt at the same rate enjoyed by its neighbors and thus will experience the liquidity crisis that investors fear.

   ○ Due to countries in a monetary union having to issue debt in a joint currency over which they lack full control, therefore

   ○ It is because countries in a monetary union have to issue debt in a joint currency they do not fully control, as

   ○ Because countries in a monetary union must issue debt in a joint currency over which they lack full control, if

   ○ Countries that are in a monetary union have to issue debt in a joint currency over which they lack full control, causing

   ○ In a monetary union, countries have to issue debt in a joint currency over which they fully lack control, so

40. Kererū pigeons, of the species *Hemiphaga novaeseelandiae*, <u>which won the Bird of the Year award in New Zealand in 2018, can become intoxicated when they eat fermented fruit from the forest floor and, if they consume enough, may</u> fall from the trees where they roost.

   ○ which won the Bird of the Year award in New Zealand in 2018, can become intoxicated when they eat fermented fruit from the forest floor and, if they consume enough, may

   ○ winners of New Zealand's 2018 Bird of the Year award, can become intoxicated when they eat fermented fruit from the forest floor but, if they consume enough, may

   ○ which won the Bird of the Year award in New Zealand in 2018, becoming intoxicated if they were to eat fermented fruit from the forest floor if they were to consume enough, and may

   ○ winners of the Bird of the Year award in New Zealand in 2018, can become intoxicated when it eats fermented fruit from the forest floor and, if it consumes enough, may

   ○ which won the Bird of the Year award in New Zealand in 2018, can become intoxicated when they eat fermented fruit from the forest floor and, if they consume enough, then they may

41. Science fiction has been described as the genre that, by addressing the future, <u>that it concerns ideas of large scope rather than the ephemeral thoughts</u> and emotions of individuals.

    ○ that it concerns ideas of large scope rather than the ephemeral thoughts

    ○ that concerns ideas of large scope instead of the ephemeral thoughts

    ○ concerns ideas of large scope rather than the ephemeral thoughts

    ○ so concerns ideas of large scope instead of the ephemeral thinking

    ○ it concerns ideas of large scope but not the ephemeral thoughts

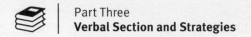
Advanced Practice Set: Clauses and Connectors

42. Although staff at one fast-food chain, in an effort to encourage children to eat healthier, proposed that the company create a <u>vegetable taste</u> like bubblegum, the company's chief executive officer ultimately reported that children who had tried the food expressed confusion about its flavor.

   O   vegetable taste

   O   vegetable tastes

   O   taste for a vegetable

   O   vegetable that has a taste

   O   vegetable that tastes

43. During the latter stages of the insurrection, the revolution's leaders resorted to ever more violent means, including public execution of members of the upper class, <u>to establish their authority, and they suppressed</u> dissent ruthlessly.

   O   to establish their authority, and they suppressed

   O   that established their authority, and it suppressed

   O   of establishing their authority and to suppress

   O   to establish their authority, and they were suppressing

   O   so that their authority was established, and it suppressed

44. <u>Either stocks or bonds have advantages: stocks can increase in value and give investors more income over time, while bonds can not only provide predictable income but also are guarantees of</u> the return of investors' principal.

   O   Either stocks or bonds have advantages: stocks can increase in value and give investors more income over time, while bonds can not only provide predictable income but also are guarantees of

   O   Both stocks and bonds have advantages: stocks can increase in value and give investors more income over time, while bonds can not only provide predictable income but also guarantee

   O   Both stocks have advantages and so do bonds: stocks can increase in value and give investors more income over time, while bonds not only can provide predictable income but also guarantee

   O   Advantages are to be had from either stocks or from bonds: stocks can increase in value and give investors more income over time, while bonds can not only provide predictable income but also guarantee

   O   Both stocks and bonds have advantages: stocks can increase in value and give investors more income over time, while bonds can not only provide predictable income but also can guarantee

Answer Key

Practice Set: Verbs

1. D
2. A
3. C
4. D

Advanced Practice Set: Verbs

5. C
6. B
7. E

Practice Set: Pronouns

8. A
9. D
10. B

Advanced Practice Set: Pronouns

11. D
12. D
13. D

Practice Set: Modification

14. D
15. B
16. A
17. D

Advanced Practice Set: Modification

18. D
19. E
20. C

Practice Set: Parallelism

21. C
22. A
23. E

Advanced Practice Set: Parallelism

24. D
25. C
26. E

Practice Set: Comparisons

27. B
28. A
29. D

Advanced Practice Set: Comparisons

30. C
31. D
32. E

Practice Set: Usage and Idioms

33. E
34. C
35. D

Advanced Practice Set: Usage and Idioms

36. C
37. C
38. D

Practice Set: Clauses and Connectors

39. C
40. A
41. C

Advanced Practice Set: Clauses and Connectors

42. E
43. A
44. B

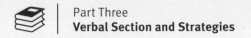

Answers and Explanations

Practice Set: Verbs

1.   (D)

The string section, which included more than 30 violinists and violists as well as more than a dozen cellists and bassists, <u>were justly praised for the tremendous passion they invoked</u> in last night's performance of Stravinsky's *Rite of Spring*.

- ○   were justly praised for the tremendous passion they invoked
- ○   were justly praised for invoking their tremendous passion
- ○   were justly praised for the passion they were tremendous in invoking
- ○   was justly praised for invoking tremendous passion
- ○   was justly praised for the tremendous passion they invoked

STEP 1: READ THE ORIGINAL SENTENCE CAREFULLY, LOOKING FOR ERRORS

The underlined portion begins with the verb phrase "were justly praised." While there are many individual musicians, the praise is given to the "string section," a singular subject. It is not correct to say "the string section were." Similarly, the pronoun "they" at the end of the underlined portion refers to the same singular subject, so that is equally problematic.

STEP 2: SCAN AND GROUP THE ANSWER CHOICES

(A), **(B)**, and **(C)** begin with "were," while **(D)** and **(E)** begin with "was."

STEP 3: ELIMINATE CHOICES UNTIL ONLY ONE REMAINS

As "were" was identified as mistaken, eliminate **(A)**, **(B)**, and **(C)**. These choices also use a plural pronoun ("they" or "their"), which is improper. Furthermore, **(B)** makes the pronoun possessive, making it sound like the passion was the musicians' rather than a feeling generated in others. And **(C)** creates the unnecessarily complex phrase "the passion they were tremendous in invoking," which now describes the musicians, instead of the passion, as "tremendous."

Then, eliminate **(E)** because it continues to use the pronoun "they" to refer to the singular string section. **(D)** corrects the verb error by using the singular "was," and it also uses more direct phrasing to eliminate the pronoun error. Read this choice back into the sentence to confirm:

The string section, which included more than 30 violinists and violists as well as more than a dozen cellists and bassists, <u>was justly praised for invoking tremendous passion</u> in last night's performance of Stravinsky's *Rite of Spring*.

2. **(A)**

Galileo Galilei <u>had discovered four moons orbiting Jupiter, including Ganymede, the largest moon in the solar system</u>, by the time Christiaan Huygens discovered Titan, the largest moon of Saturn, in 1655.

- ○ had discovered four moons orbiting Jupiter, including Ganymede, the largest moon in the solar system

- ○ had discovered four moons orbiting Jupiter, which includes Ganymede, being the largest moon in the solar system

- ○ will have discovered four moons, including Ganymede, orbiting Jupiter, which is the largest moon in the solar system

- ○ will have discovered four moons orbiting Jupiter, the largest moon in the solar system including Ganymede

- ○ has discovered four moons orbiting Jupiter, with the largest moon in the solar system being Ganymede

STEP 1: READ THE ORIGINAL SENTENCE CAREFULLY, LOOKING FOR ERRORS

The underlined portion begins with "had discovered," which is the past perfect tense. If this is correct, there should be two actions that happened in the past, and the past perfect would apply to the earlier event. As it turns out, there are two past actions in the sentence: the discovery of Jupiter's moons and the discovery of Titan. The discovery of Titan happened in 1655, and Galileo's discovery happened before that, as confirmed by the phrase "by the time." So the use of past perfect tense for Galileo's discovery is correct. Furthermore, the notes about Ganymede being one of the four moons of Jupiter and being the largest moon overall are properly set off as modifying phrases. There appears to be nothing wrong with the sentence.

STEP 2: SCAN AND GROUP THE ANSWER CHOICES

(A) and **(B)** begin with "had discovered," **(C)** and **(D)** begin with "will have discovered," and **(E)** begins with "has discovered."

STEP 3: ELIMINATE CHOICES UNTIL ONLY ONE REMAINS

Eliminate **(E)** for using present perfect tense for a discovery that happened over 300 years ago. Eliminate **(C)** and **(D)** for using a future perfect tense for something that has already happened. Furthermore, the rearrangement of terms in **(C)** puts "Jupiter" before "which," incorrectly suggesting that Jupiter itself (as opposed to Ganymede) is the largest moon. **(D)** also incorrectly rearranges the phrases, putting "the largest moon" after Jupiter, again suggesting that Jupiter, and not Ganymede, is the moon in question.

As for the remaining choices, eliminate **(B)** for adding "which" after "Jupiter," making it seem as though Jupiter itself includes Ganymede. Also, **(B)** adds the unnecessary verb "being" after "Ganymede." **(A)** is correct.

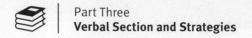
3.   (C)

While Thomas Edison is often credited with inventing the incandescent light bulb, historians note that <u>several people have designed and created similar light bulbs before Edison received his patent</u>.

- ○   several people have designed and created similar light bulbs before Edison received his patent
- ○   several people having designed and created similar light bulbs before Edison receiving his patent
- ○   several people had designed and created similar light bulbs before Edison received his patent
- ○   similar light bulbs had been designed and created by several people before Edison receives his patent
- ○   similar light bulbs having been designed and created by several people before Edison received his patent

STEP 1: READ THE ORIGINAL SENTENCE CAREFULLY, LOOKING FOR ERRORS

The underlined portion begins with the subject "several people" and the verb phrase "have designed." The verb is in the present perfect tense, so it should refer to an action that started in the past but is still occurring in the present. However, the act of designing occurred in the past and finished before another past event happened (Edison receiving his patent). Thus, this should use the past perfect tense ("had designed") instead.

STEP 2: SCAN AND GROUP THE ANSWER CHOICES

(A), **(B)**, and **(C)** begin with "several people," while **(D)** and **(E)** begin with "similar light bulbs." Either subject could be acceptable. It's more useful to note that **(A)** has the erroneous "have" paired with "designed," while **(B)** and **(E)** change "have" to "having," and **(C)** and **(D)** change it to "had."

STEP 3: ELIMINATE CHOICES UNTIL ONLY ONE REMAINS

(A) contains the mistaken "have designed," so eliminate that first. **(B)** and **(E)** change the phrase to "having designed" and "having been designed," respectively. However, the *-ing* form of "having" leaves the sentence incomplete, without an active verb. That eliminates **(B)** and **(E)**. The remaining choices correctly change the verb to "had designed." **(D)** changes the subject, which could be okay but seems suspiciously unnecessary. Then **(D)** uses the present tense verb "receives" at the end, despite the fact that the rest of the sentence puts all actions in the past. That eliminates **(D)**. **(C)** is correct. This choice provides a past perfect verb for the designing and creating that happened before Edison received his patent. Read this choice back into the sentence to verify that it is correct:

While Thomas Edison is often credited with inventing the incandescent light bulb, historians note that <u>several people had designed and created similar light bulbs before Edison received his patent</u>.

4. **(D)**

Discovered by a French soldier in 1799, the Rosetta Stone was inscribed with three distinct scripts in two languages, Egyptian and Greek, <u>and were instrumental in helping scholars decipher the hieroglyphs used by ancient Egyptians</u>.

O   and were instrumental in helping scholars decipher the hieroglyphs used by ancient Egyptians

O   instrumental in helping scholars decipher the hieroglyphs being used by ancient Egyptians

O   which was instrumental in helping scholars decipher the hieroglyphs the ancient Egyptians have used

O   and was instrumental in helping scholars decipher the hieroglyphs used by ancient Egyptians

O   and was instrumental in its deciphering of ancient Egyptian hieroglyphs, which helped scholars

STEP 1: READ THE ORIGINAL SENTENCE CAREFULLY, LOOKING FOR ERRORS

A vertical scan of the answer choices reveals various options for changing the way the underlined portion begins. In its original form, the underlined portion starts with "and were," suggesting at least a second action being performed by a subject. In this case, the subject of the sentence is the Rosetta Stone. The first action assigned to the Rosetta Stone is that it "was inscribed." However, the underlined portion uses the plural verb "were" for the second action, which is inappropriate for the singular Rosetta Stone. It should be "was." The remaining verbs in the sentence are used correctly.

STEP 2: SCAN AND GROUP THE ANSWER CHOICES

(C), **(D)**, and **(E)** change the verb at the beginning to "was," while **(A)** has "were" and **(B)** just removes the verb.

STEP 3: ELIMINATE CHOICES UNTIL ONLY ONE REMAINS

As the original sentence uses a plural verb for a singular subject, eliminate **(A)**. **(B)** eliminates the verb altogether, resulting in an incomplete thought. Further, **(B)** claims illogically that the hieroglyphs are "being used" in the present by an ancient group. **(C)** starts with "which," which refers to the object immediately before the comma: Greek. Grammatically, this is not incorrect, but it unnecessarily shifts the focus of the sentence from the stone to the Greek language. This choice also ends with the present perfect verb "have used," which is definitively not valid when talking about an ancient group. Eliminate **(C)**.

The remaining choices both go back to "and," and they both change "were" to "was," which agrees with the singular subject "the Rosetta Stone." However, **(E)** rearranges the sentence to make it sound like the Rosetta Stone deciphered the hieroglyphs and the hieroglyphs helped the scholars. That is illogical, so eliminate **(E)** and choose **(D)**. Read this choice back into the sentence to verify:

Discovered by a French soldier in 1799, the Rosetta Stone was inscribed with three distinct scripts in two languages, Egyptian and Greek, <u>and was instrumental in helping scholars decipher the hieroglyphs used by ancient Egyptians</u>.

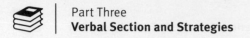

Advanced Practice Set: Verbs

5.   (C)

Companies need to ensure that the language in all of their financial reports <u>are reviewed carefully by a team of legal experts</u> since any errors can lead to serious problems for employees as well as shareholders and other investors.

    ○   are reviewed carefully by a team of legal experts

    ○   being reviewed by a careful team of legal experts

    ○   is reviewed carefully by a team of legal experts

    ○   was reviewed carefully by a legal team of experts

    ○   were reviewed by a legal team of experts carefully

STEP 1: READ THE ORIGINAL SENTENCE CAREFULLY, LOOKING FOR ERRORS

The underlined portion begins with the verb phrase "are reviewed." The object being reviewed is "the language." Although it's included in multiple reports, "the language" is still a singular noun and thus requires the singular verb phrase "is reviewed."

STEP 2: SCAN AND GROUP THE ANSWER CHOICES

Each answer begins with a different form of the opening verb phrase, so no grouping is immediately apparent. However, you might group the choices by whether the verb is singular, plural, or something else. **(A)** with "are" and **(E)** with "were" provide a plural verb, **(C)** with "is" and **(D)** with "was" provide a singular verb, and **(B)** changes the verb to the gerund "being," turning the underlined portion into a modifying phrase.

STEP 3: ELIMINATE CHOICES UNTIL ONLY ONE REMAINS

As the sentence is describing what should be done with the singular noun "the language," **(A)** and **(E)** can be eliminated for pairing that with the plural phrase "are reviewed" and "were reviewed," respectively. **(B)** changes the phrase to "being reviewed," which is not a verb. The phrase "ensure that" requires a following verb (e.g., "ensure that the language is reviewed"). Further, this choice changes the adverb "carefully" to the adjective "careful." While an adjective would be appropriate for modifying the noun "team," the sentence is saying that the *review* must be done carefully. The author is not saying that the team needs to be a "careful team" (for instance, one that tries not to spill coffee or knock over a stack of papers). Eliminate **(B)**.

The remaining choices both use an active singular verb phrase, but **(D)** uses the past tense, which does not fit the logic of the sentence. The sentence is suggesting that something should be done in the present to avoid a future problem. Besides, **(D)** also moves the adjective "legal" to describe the team, not the experts. That means the team is legal (whatever that means), and it consists of experts—but on what subject? If they're experts on dinosaurs, then that doesn't work here. **(D)** is eliminated, leaving **(C)** as the correct answer. Read this choice back into the sentence to verify:

Companies need to ensure that the language in all of their financial reports <u>is reviewed carefully by a team of legal experts</u> since any errors can lead to serious problems for employees as well as shareholders and other investors.

6. **(B)**

While the skeleton of a typical human adult <u>will contain 206 bones, that of a newborn human baby usually has approximately 270, some of which fused together as the baby's body grew</u>.

- ○ will contain 206 bones, that of a newborn human baby usually has approximately 270, some of which fused together as the baby's body grew

- ○ contains 206 bones, that of a newborn human baby usually has approximately 270, some of which fuse together as the baby's body grows

- ○ contained 206 bones, that of a newborn human baby usually will have approximately 270, some of which fuse together as the baby's body grows

- ○ contains 206 bones, that of a newborn human baby usually has approximately 270, some of which fused together as the baby's body grew

- ○ will contain 206 bones, that of a newborn human baby usually has approximately 270, some of which fuse together as the baby's body grows

STEP 1: READ THE ORIGINAL SENTENCE CAREFULLY, LOOKING FOR ERRORS

A vertical scan of the beginnings of the choices shows a mix of future, present, and past tense, so verb tense is at issue in this question. The sentence's underlined part begins with the verb "will contain." Since the author is discussing the number of bones in the human body, an "eternal truth," the present tense is needed. Read on to understand what other errors may need to be fixed, or may show up, in the answer choices: in "some of which fused together as the baby's body grew," the author seems to be talking about a specific baby who grew up in the past, but this is further discussion of the human body. The correct choice must use present tense at the beginning and toward the end.

STEP 2: SCAN AND GROUP THE ANSWER CHOICES

At the beginning of the choices, both **(A)** and **(E)** use the future tense, and **(C)** uses the past tense. Both **(B)** and **(D)** use the present tense.

STEP 3: ELIMINATE CHOICES UNTIL ONLY ONE REMAINS

Eliminate **(A)** for the reasons discussed in step 1. Since **(C)** and **(E)** also do not use the present tense "contains," eliminate these choices as well. **(C)** has the further error of using the future tense "will have" in discussing the bones a newborn baby has.

Now read **(B)** and **(D)** in parallel. They differ only after the second comma. **(D)** repeats the error of the original sentence by using the past tense to discuss a fact of human development, so eliminate this choice. Read **(B)** into the sentence to confirm that choice is correct:

While the skeleton of a typical human adult <u>contains 206 bones, that of a newborn human baby usually has approximately 270, some of which fuse together as the baby's body grows</u>.

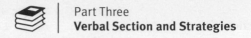
7.   (E)

There is a booming tourism industry in Scotland centered around the so-called Loch Ness monster; however, evidence that tends to support the existence of the monster, such as grainy photographs that purport to show the creature, <u>is outweighed by the evidence that supports</u> the idea that there is no such monster.

○   is outweighed by the evidence that supports

○   are outweighed by the evidence that supports

○   are outweighed by evidence that supports

○   is outweighed by evidence for supporting

○   is outweighed by evidence that supports

STEP 1: READ THE ORIGINAL SENTENCE CAREFULLY, LOOKING FOR ERRORS

The underlined portion starts with the singular verb "is," and scan of the answer choices shows a choice between "is" and the plural "are." The thing that "is outweighed by the evidence" is other "evidence." Therefore, this singular verb is correct. However, there's also a comparison here between the evidence for and against the existence of the Loch Ness monster. Comparisons must be parallel in form; here, the first part of the comparison is about "evidence," while the second is about "the evidence." Since there's a definite article in the second part but not the first, the structure of the comparison is not parallel.

STEP 2: SCAN AND GROUP THE ANSWER CHOICES

There's a 3-2 split between the choices that use "the evidence," **(A)** and **(B)**, and those that use "evidence," **(C)**, **(D)**, and **(E)**. Another 3-2 split is between the singular verb "is" in **(A)**, **(D)**, and **(E)** and the plural verb "are" in **(B)** and **(C)**. Either split is a good starting place for eliminating choices.

STEP 3: ELIMINATE CHOICES UNTIL ONLY ONE REMAINS

Eliminate **(A)** due to the comparison error identified in the original sentence and **(B)** as well because it commits the same error. **(B)** also incorrectly changes the first word in the underlined segment to the plural "are." Despite the fact that photographs are given as an example of this evidence, this verb belongs to the singular subject "evidence."

Of the three choices that fix the comparison error, **(C)** incorrectly uses "are," so it can be eliminated. **(D)** changes "that supports" to "for supporting." It would be correct to say there is *evidence for* something, and it would be correct to say there is *evidence supporting* something. However, "evidence for supporting" is not idiomatically correct usage. **(E)** is the only choice that fixes the error in the comparison without introducing a new error, so it is correct. Read it back into the sentence to confirm:

There is a booming tourism industry in Scotland centered around the so-called Loch Ness monster; however, evidence that tends to support the existence of the monster, such as grainy photographs that purport to show the creature, <u>is outweighed by evidence that supports</u> the idea that there is no such monster.

Practice Set: Pronouns

8. **(A)**

    Although her X-ray photographs <u>had laid the foundation for describing the structure of DNA, Rosalind Franklin, an accomplished chemist, did not receive the Nobel prize when it was awarded for this achievement</u> in 1962.

    O   had laid the foundation for describing the structure of DNA, Rosalind Franklin, an accomplished chemist, did not receive the Nobel prize when it was awarded for this achievement

    O   had laid the foundation for its description, the structure of DNA did not result in accomplished chemist Rosalind Franklin receiving the Nobel prize awarded for it

    O   of the structure of DNA had laid the foundation for their description, the accomplished chemist Rosalind Franklin was not awarded the Nobel prize for this achievement

    O   were the foundation for describing the structure of DNA, the Nobel prize was not awarded to accomplished chemist Rosalind Franklin for it

    O   were an achievement by Rosalind Franklin, an accomplished chemist, it did not receive the Nobel prize for laying the foundation for describing the structure of DNA

STEP 1: READ THE ORIGINAL SENTENCE CAREFULLY, LOOKING FOR ERRORS

The underlined portion begins with the past perfect verb "had laid," so first check whether this verb tense is correct. In fact it is, because the photographs "laid the foundation" before another action in the past, the awarding of the Nobel prize. That more recent past action is correctly stated with the simple past tense, "did not receive...it was awarded." The pronoun "it" appears, so make sure the pronoun unambiguously refers to a singular, nonhuman antecedent. "It" refers clearly to "the Nobel prize," so no problem there. Finally, the overall structure of the sentence is logical: her photographs laid a foundation for a scientific discovery, but Franklin did not win a prize for the discovery. There are no apparent errors, so (**A**) is likely correct, but scan the other choices to be sure.

STEP 2: SCAN AND GROUP THE ANSWER CHOICES

There's no efficient way to group the choices, so check them out one by one.

STEP 3: ELIMINATE CHOICES UNTIL ONLY ONE REMAINS

In (**B**), the final "it" seems to refer to "the structure of DNA," but describing the DNA earned the prize; the structure itself didn't earn anything. In (**C**), the plural pronoun "their" could refer only to the plural noun "photographs," but the photographs were not being described. It's hard to know what the "it" at the end of (**D**) might refer to. And the "it" in (**E**) would refer to the "photographs," but "it" is singular and "photographs" is plural; moreover, Franklin (not her photographs) would have been awarded the Nobel. Since every other choice contains an error, (**A**) is confirmed as correct.

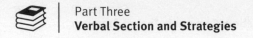

9. **(D)**

Film critics often cite the example of Nicolas Cage's winning the Academy Award for Best Actor as a reason that <u>an actor should not automatically be classified as elite if they win an Academy Award</u>.

- ○ an actor should not automatically be classified as elite if they win an Academy Award
- ○ an actor automatically classified as elite because they won an Academy Award should not always be classified as such
- ○ actors automatically classified as elite because they won an Academy Award should not always be classified as such
- ○ actors should not automatically be classified as elite if they win an Academy Award
- ○ actors should not be classified as automatically elite if they win an Academy Award

STEP 1: READ THE ORIGINAL SENTENCE CAREFULLY, LOOKING FOR ERRORS

Whenever a sentence contains an underlined pronoun, you should assess pronoun-antecedent agreement. This sentence contains the underlined pronoun "they," which is plural. Since the plural pronoun "they" refers to "an actor," which is a singular noun, the lack of agreement between the pronoun and its antecedent is an error in the sentence.

STEP 2: SCAN AND GROUP THE ANSWER CHOICES

All of the answer choices contain "they," so for the pronoun and antecedent to agree, the antecedent must be changed to something plural, such as "actors." **(A)** and **(B)** start with "an actor," while **(C)**, **(D)**, and **(E)** begin with "actors."

STEP 3: ELIMINATE CHOICES UNTIL ONLY ONE REMAINS

Eliminate **(A)** and **(B)** for the pronoun agreement error discussed above. Examining the remaining choices, note that **(C)** is wordy and subtly distorts the meaning of the original sentence; the original talks about how any actor should (not) be classified, while this choice limits the discussion to actors already classified as elite. **(E)** must be eliminated, because "automatically" should modify "should…be classified," not "elite." This leaves **(D)** as the correct answer; it fixes the pronoun agreement error and introduces no new errors.

10. (B)

As one step in their plan to engender greater goodwill in the community, the town council organized a series of public meetings when residents could air grievances about the opacity of decision making, a tendency to award contracts to cronies, and their failure to follow through on promised reforms.

○ As one step in their plan to engender greater goodwill in the community, the town council organized a series of public meetings when residents could air grievances about the opacity of decision making, a tendency to award contracts to cronies, and their failure to follow through on promised reforms.

○ As one step in its plan to engender greater goodwill in the community, the town council organized a series of public meetings at which residents could air grievances about the opacity of decision making, a tendency to award contracts to cronies, and a failure to follow through on promised reforms.

○ As one step in its plan to engender greater goodwill in the community, the town council organized a series of public meetings at which residents could air grievances about the opacity of decision making, tendency to award contracts to cronies, and failing to follow through on promised reforms.

○ As one step in its plan to engender greater goodwill in the community, a series of public meetings was organized by the town council so that residents could air grievances about the opacity of decision making, a tendency to award contracts to cronies, and a failure to follow through on promised reforms.

○ The town council, as one step in their plan to engender greater goodwill in the community, organized a series of public meetings for residents at which they could air grievances about their opacity of decision making, tendency to award contracts to cronies, and failure to follow through on promised reforms.

STEP 1: READ THE ORIGINAL SENTENCE CAREFULLY, LOOKING FOR ERRORS

When faced with choices that are this long, it is often easier to focus on one element of the sentence at a time. The opening phrase says something is happening as "one step in their plan." Whose plan? The town council's—but a council is singular and must be represented by the singular pronoun "its." If you didn't notice this error in reading the sentence, a vertical scan of the beginnings of the answer choices shows a split between "its plan" and "their plan," showing that whether this pronoun is singular or plural is one issue to consider and a good starting point.

STEP 2: SCAN AND GROUP THE ANSWER CHOICES

There's a 2-3 split; **(A)** and **(E)** use the plural pronoun "their," while **(B)**, **(C)**, and **(D)** use the singular "its."

STEP 3: ELIMINATE CHOICES UNTIL ONLY ONE REMAINS

Eliminate **(A)** and **(E)** for using the incorrect plural pronoun. Scan the remaining choices in parallel until you see a difference. **(D)** has "a series of public meetings" after the comma, indicating that the series of meetings sought to engender greater goodwill. This isn't logical, so eliminate this choice. The difference between **(B)** and **(C)** comes in the list at the end. Examine the list for parallel structure and notice the lack of parallel structure in **(C)** with "the opacity…tendency…and failing." The list in **(B)** has parallel structure, and this choice is correct.

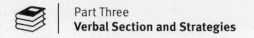

Advanced Practice Set: Pronouns

11. (D)

The visiting lecturer presented some lesser-known facts about snowflakes: for example, <u>they are not white, they have exactly six sides, they do not all have a unique pattern, and they—along with ice—constitutes</u> about 75 percent of Earth's freshwater.

- ○ they are not white, they have exactly six sides, they do not all have a unique pattern, and they—along with ice—constitutes

- ○ it is not white, all snowflakes have exactly six sides, not all snowflakes have a unique pattern, and snow—along with ice—constitute

- ○ it is not white, it has exactly six sides, not all of it has a unique pattern, and it—along with ice—constitutes

- ○ they are not white, all have exactly six sides, not all have a unique pattern, and they—along with ice—constitute

- ○ they are not white, all has exactly six sides, not all has a unique pattern, and it—along with ice—constitutes

STEP 1: READ THE ORIGINAL SENTENCE CAREFULLY, LOOKING FOR ERRORS

The underlined text begins with the plural pronoun "they," which correctly refers to "snowflakes." What follows is a list, so check that all items in the list are in parallel form. In fact, they are: "they are..., they do not have..., they...constitutes" share a subject-plus-verb structure. However, the last verb, "constitutes," does not agree with the plural pronoun "they." (The phrase between the dashes, "along with ice," does not create a compound and thus plural subject.) Therefore, this sentence is incorrect as written.

STEP 2: SCAN AND GROUP THE ANSWER CHOICES

While **(A)**, **(D)**, and **(E)** begin with "they," the other choices begin with "it."

STEP 3: ELIMINATE CHOICES UNTIL ONLY ONE REMAINS

Since **(A)** has the subject-verb agreement error noted in step 1, eliminate it. Since **(B)** and **(C)** begin with the wrong pronoun to represent "snowflakes," eliminate both of these choices as well.

Now read **(D)** and **(E)** in parallel. They differ after the first comma, where **(D)** has "all have" while **(E)** uses "all has." The pronoun "all" represents "snowflakes" and is thus plural, so the plural verb "have" is needed. Eliminate **(E)** and read **(D)** back into the sentence:

The visiting lecturer presented some lesser-known facts about snowflakes: for example, <u>they are not white, all have exactly six sides, not all have a unique pattern, and they—along with ice—constitute</u> about 75 percent of Earth's freshwater.

12. (D)

The defense attorneys wanted to interview the jurors following the guilty verdict, but a gag order issued by the judge prohibited <u>them from discussing the trial even after it had concluded</u>.

- ○ them from discussing the trial even after it had concluded
- ○ the jurors from discussing the trial even after it is concluded
- ○ them from discussing the trial even after it is concluded
- ○ the jurors from discussing the trial even after it had concluded
- ○ the jurors to discuss the trial even after it had concluded

STEP 1: READ THE ORIGINAL SENTENCE CAREFULLY, LOOKING FOR ERRORS

The underlined portion of the sentence begins with a pronoun ("them"). A quick glance at the choices reveals that three of them replace this pronoun with a noun, prompting a check for ambiguous pronoun usage. The use of "them" in the original sentence is ambiguous, because you don't know whether the judge's order prohibited the attorneys or the jurors from discussing the case after the trial.

STEP 2: SCAN AND GROUP THE ANSWER CHOICES

(A) and (C) retain the ambiguous pronoun "them," while (B), (D), and (E) replace it with "the jurors."

STEP 3: ELIMINATE CHOICES UNTIL ONLY ONE REMAINS

Because (A) and (C) retain the pronoun error, they can be eliminated. Of the remaining choices, (B) changes the the verb phrase at the end to a present tense form ("is concluded"), whereas (D) and (E) keep the original past tense phrasing ("had concluded"). Because the rest of the sentence is in past tense, it does not make sense in the context of the sentence to switch to present tense for this verb, so (B) can be eliminated as well.

The only difference between the remaining choices is that (D) retains the original language "from discussing," while (E) changes it to "to discuss." This is an idiom issue, and the right phrasing will depend on the verb that the phrase follows. In this case, the original sentence uses "prohibited," which takes the preposition "from" rather than "to." Eliminate (E) and read (D) back into the sentence to confirm:

The defense attorneys wanted to interview the jurors following the guilty verdict, but a gag order issued by the judge prohibited <u>the jurors from discussing the trial even after it had concluded</u>.

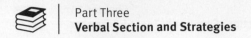

13. (B)

One often referenced online dictionary's definition of *nut* as "a hard-shelled dry fruit or seed with a separable rind or shell and interior kernel" indicates that <u>it does not include almonds, cashews, peanuts, pistachios, or walnuts</u>.

- ○ it does not include almonds, cashews, peanuts, pistachios, or walnuts
- ○ almonds, cashews, peanuts, pistachios, and walnuts are not examples of nuts
- ○ almonds, cashews, peanuts, pistachios, and walnuts are not included as examples of them
- ○ almonds, cashews, peanuts, pistachios, and walnuts are not included
- ○ they do not include almonds, cashews, peanuts, pistachios, or walnuts

STEP 1: READ THE ORIGINAL SENTENCE CAREFULLY, LOOKING FOR ERRORS

The underlined part of the sentence starts with the pronoun "it" and proceeds with a list of examples of foods. However, that pronoun could refer to any one of a number of nouns and is thus ambiguous.

STEP 2: SCAN AND GROUP THE ANSWER CHOICES

(A) and (E) begin with pronouns—"it" and "they," respectively. The other three choices start with "almonds."

STEP 3: ELIMINATE CHOICES UNTIL ONLY ONE REMAINS

Since the pronoun is ambiguous, eliminate (A). And because (E) references a nonexistent plural noun, eliminate that choice as well.

The remaining choices differ only with regard to their endings. As with (E)'s "they," (C)'s "them" refers to a nonexistent plural noun, so eliminate (C). And (D) is unclear in that it does not specify who or what does not include the listed foods. (B) is correct, since it not only fixes the original sentence's pronoun error but also does not introduce any other issues into the sentence. Read your choice back into the sentence to confirm that it is correct:

One often referenced online dictionary's definition of *nut* as "a hard-shelled dry fruit or seed with a separable rind or shell and interior kernel" indicates that <u>almonds, cashews, peanuts, pistachios, and walnuts are not examples of nuts</u>.

Practice Set: Modification

14. (D)

Despite being called one of the founding members of the Impressionist movement, <u>Edgar Degas's paintings often depicted interior scenes as opposed to the landscapes depicted by most other Impressionists, and he publicly rejected the label</u>.

- ○ Edgar Degas's paintings often depicted interior scenes as opposed to the landscapes depicted by most other Impressionists, and he publicly rejected the label

- ○ Edgar Degas's paintings were unlike most other Impressionists in that they often depicted interior scenes as opposed to landscapes, and he publicly rejected the label

- ○ Edgar Degas publicly rejected the label and often depicted interior scenes in his paintings instead of landscapes, which were unlike most other Impressionists

- ○ Edgar Degas publicly rejected the label and, unlike most other Impressionists, often depicted interior scenes in his paintings instead of landscapes

- ○ the interior scenes depicted by Edgar Degas, who rejected the label, were unlike the landscapes depicted by most other Impressionists

STEP 1: READ THE ORIGINAL SENTENCE CAREFULLY, LOOKING FOR ERRORS

The underlined portion begins with the noun "Edgar Degas's paintings." However, the modifying phrase at the beginning describes Degas himself. He—not his paintings—was called "one of the founding members of the Impressionist movement." (When a noun such as "Edgar Degas" is made possessive, it effectively becomes an adjective.) So the noun after the comma should be Degas, not his paintings. The rest of the sentence is grammatically acceptable, if a little wordy.

Step 2: Scan and Group the Answer Choices

(A) and **(B)** begin with "Edgar Degas's paintings," **(C)** and **(D)** begin with "Edgar Degas," and **(E)** begins with "the interior scenes."

STEP 3: ELIMINATE CHOICES UNTIL ONLY ONE REMAINS

(A) can be eliminated for the modification error, as can **(B)**, which fails to change the subject to Edgar Degas. Further, **(B)** illogically compares Degas's paintings to "other Impressionists." A logical comparison would compare his paintings to other artists' paintings, not to the other artists themselves. **(E)** can be eliminated, as it also provides an improper noun; the noun at the beginning should be Degas, not "the interior scenes."

The remaining choices properly change the subject to Degas. However, **(C)** ends with "which were unlike most Impressionists." This clause refers to the term immediately before it, which is "landscapes." That comparison is not logical, since it's supposed to be Degas, and not landscapes, who differs from other Impressionists. That eliminates **(C)**, leaving **(D)** as the correct answer. This choice fixes the modification error and simplifies the language by creating a compound action (Degas rejected and depicted). To confirm, read the choice back into the original sentence:

Despite being called one of the founding members of the Impressionist movement, <u>Edgar Degas publicly rejected the label and, unlike most other Impressionists, often depicted interior scenes in his paintings instead of landscapes</u>.

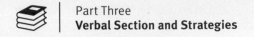
15. **(B)**

The superb lyrebird is known for <u>the producing of elaborate songs, including astounding mimicry of other birds and even non-bird animals such as dingoes, which it often uses as part of a complex courtship ritual.</u>

○ the producing of elaborate songs, including astounding mimicry of other birds and even non-bird animals such as dingoes, which it often uses as part of a complex courtship ritual

○ producing elaborate songs, which are often used as part of a complex courtship ritual and can include astounding mimicry of other birds and even non-bird animals such as dingoes

○ their elaborate songs, which can include both astounding mimicry of other birds and even non-bird animals such as dingoes, and also is used as part of a complex courtship ritual

○ its elaborate songs and astounding mimicry of both other birds as well as non-bird animals such as dingoes, which are often used as part of a complex courtship ritual

○ the elaborate songs, which they produce, often being used as a part of a complex courtship ritual, including an astounding mimicry of other birds and even non-bird animals such as dingoes

STEP 1: READ THE ORIGINAL SENTENCE CAREFULLY, LOOKING FOR ERRORS

The underlined portion begins with the awkward phrasing "the producing of elaborate songs," which could be more simply phrased as "producing elaborate songs." However, the major grammatical errors occur with the modifying phrases. The phrase that begins with "including" suggests that the mimicry of other animals is an *example* of the songs, when it's more logical to suggest that mimicry is included *as part of* the songs. And the last modifying phrase begins with "which," which seems to refer back to "dingoes." It needs to be clearer that the *songs* are used in the ritual, not the dingoes.

STEP 2: SCAN AND GROUP THE ANSWER CHOICES

As is typical of Sentence Correction questions in which modification is at issue and the underlined portion is lengthy, all of the choices have different beginnings and reorganize the content to some degree. Grouping will not be effective here.

STEP 3: ELIMINATE CHOICES UNTIL ONLY ONE REMAINS

The modifier errors allow you to eliminate **(A)**. **(B)** starts with a simpler phrase ("producing elaborate songs"). The modifying phrase beginning with "which" refers to the songs. And the modifying phrase includes a clear compound action presented in parallel form: the songs "are…used" in the ritual and "can include" mimicry. This seems like a winner.

Eliminate (**C**) for starting with the pronoun "their" to refer to the singular noun "lyrebird." Also, the word "both" in the middle phrase suggests that the song includes two things: "mimicry of other birds…and other animals." That's not right. The song doesn't include other animals; it includes mimicry of other animals. To be correct, this choice would have to read either *both the mimicry of other birds and even the mimicry of non-bird animals* or *the mimicry of both other birds and even non-bird animals*. (**D**) starts with the proper pronoun "its." However, the phrasing "both…as well as" is improper. It should be *both…and*. And this choice still uses "which" to refer to the dingoes instead of the songs. That eliminates (**D**). Lastly, (**E**) can be eliminated for using the plural pronoun "they" to refer to the singular "lyrebird." Also, the final phrase is placed as if it were modifying the ritual, but the word "including" suggests the mimicry is an example of the ritual rather than a part of the ritual. With everything else eliminated, that confirms (**B**) is correct. As a final test, read it back into the original sentence:

The superb lyrebird is known for <u>producing elaborate songs, which are often used as part of a complex courtship ritual and can include astounding mimicry of other birds and even non-bird animals such as dingoes</u>.

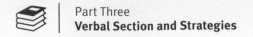
16. **(A)**

Believing in 1958 that Alaska and Hawaii would soon become part of the United States, <u>high school student Bob Heft, for a history class project, designed a flag with 50 stars; approved by President Eisenhower, that design became the American flag</u>.

- ○ high school student Bob Heft, for a history class project, designed a flag with 50 stars; approved by President Eisenhower, that design became the American flag

- ○ for a history class project, high school student Bob Heft designed a flag with 50 stars; approved by President Eisenhower, that design became the American flag

- ○ the American flag, designed by high school student Bob Heft with 50 stars for a history class project, was approved by President Eisenhower

- ○ high school student Bob Heft, for a history class project, designed a flag with 50 stars; approved by President Eisenhower, the American flag was what that design became

- ○ for a history class project, high school student Bob Heft designed a flag with 50 stars; approved by President Eisenhower, the American flag was what that design became

STEP 1: READ THE ORIGINAL SENTENCE CAREFULLY, LOOKING FOR ERRORS

The non-underlined part of the sentence is a modifying phrase describing what someone believed. Therefore, what follows the comma must be a word or phrase naming that person. "[H]igh school student Bob Heft" is that person, so the underlined portion starts off well. The next modifying phrase is "for a history class project"; this is an adverbial phrase saying when Bob designed the flag, and it is positioned next to the verb it modifies. After the semicolon, the next complete thought also begins with an introductory modifying phrase, "approved by President Eisenhower." The verbs are all correctly in the simple past tense, and there are no pronouns or comparisons, nor are there words/phrases that tend to be used incorrectly. This sentence seems to be correct as written. Check the other choices to make sure you haven't overlooked anything.

STEP 2: SCAN AND GROUP THE ANSWER CHOICES

Of the remaining choices, only **(D)** also begins with "high school student Bob Heft." **(B)** and **(E)** begin with "for a history class project," and **(C)** begins with "the American flag."

STEP 3: ELIMINATE CHOICES UNTIL ONLY ONE REMAINS

(C) starts with "the American flag," which was not capable of "[b]elieving" anything. Eliminate **(C)**.

(D) begins correctly. However, this choice ends in passive voice with "the American flag was what that design became," which is less concise and direct than the original. Eliminate **(D)**.

By placing "for a history class project" right after the introductory "[b]elieving" phrase, **(B)** and **(E)** make it sound as though Bob believed in the eventual statehood of Hawaii and Alaska as part of his history class project. That doesn't reflect the author's intended meaning, so these choices are both incorrect. Also, **(E)** has the same awkward construction at the end as **(D)**. Eliminate both and choose **(A)**.

17. (D)

Consisting of surreal, nightmarish dreamscapes, <u>H. R. Giger created artwork that often inspires feelings of unease and dread in those who view it, and these reactions are why it was</u> chosen as the basis for the design of the title creature in the 1979 horror movie *Alien*.

O   H. R. Giger created artwork that often inspires feelings of unease and dread in those who view it, and these reactions are why it was

O   the artwork of H. R. Giger often inspires feelings of unease and dread in those who view it, and these reactions are why it is

O   H. R. Giger created artwork that often inspired feelings of unease and dread in those who view it, and these reactions are why it is

O   the artwork of H. R. Giger often inspires feelings of unease and dread in those who view it, and these reactions are why it was

O   the artwork of H. R. Giger often inspired feelings of unease and dread in those who view it, and these reactions are why it was

STEP 1: READ THE ORIGINAL SENTENCE CAREFULLY, LOOKING FOR ERRORS

The opening clause of the sentence is a modifying phrase, so what comes after the comma must be the noun that phrase modifies. The modifier describes something that consists of "dreamscapes," but the underlined segment begins with the name of a person, H. R. Giger. Instead, it should begin with Giger's artwork.

Note that the underlined segment ends with a verb; this is an indication that there may be a verb-tense or subject-verb agreement error. The singular verb "was" agrees with the singular subject "artwork," and since the verb is used to describe an event that happened in the past (artwork used in a 1979 movie), the past tense is appropriate.

STEP 2: SCAN AND GROUP THE ANSWER CHOICES

There's a 3-2 split between (**B**), (**D**), and (**E**), which start with "the artwork of H. R. Giger," and (**A**) and (**C**), which start with "H. R. Giger."

STEP 3: ELIMINATE CHOICES UNTIL ONLY ONE REMAINS

Eliminate (**A**) and (**C**), which both contain the modification error you initially spotted. (**C**) also contains another error; it incorrectly changes the verb at the end of the underlined segment to the present tense. (**B**), (**D**), and (**E**) all fix the modification error, so check to see which one does so without introducing other issues.

A vertical scan of the last word shows that (**B**) introduces a verb tense error with the present tense "is" at the end, so it can be eliminated. (**E**) changes "inspires" to "inspired," which changes the meaning of the sentence. While the art was used as inspiration for a movie in the past, the sentence describes people who view the artwork, which exists in the present. Therefore, the present tense is appropriate here. (**D**) is thus correct. Confirm by reading it into the sentence:

Consisting of surreal nightmarish dreamscapes, <u>the artwork of H. R. Giger often inspires feelings of unease and dread in those who view it, and these reactions are why it was</u> chosen as the basis for the design of the title creature in the 1979 horror movie *Alien*.

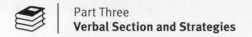
Advanced Practice Set: Modification

18. (D)

The recently discovered planet Kepler-90i was found via machine learning, a form of artificial intelligence in which <u>the identification of planets learned by computers is done from data by finding in the Kepler telescope instances of recorded signals from planets</u> beyond our solar system, known as exoplanets.

- ○ the identification of planets learned by computers is done from data by finding in the Kepler telescope instances of recorded signals from planets
- ○ computers learn to identify planets by finding in the Kepler telescope instances of recorded signals from planets beyond our solar system
- ○ computers learn to identify planets by finding in data from the Kepler telescope instances of the planet's recorded signals from
- ○ computers learn to identify planets by finding in data from the Kepler telescope instances of recorded signals from planets
- ○ the identification of planets is learned by computers by finding in data from the Kepler telescope instances of recorded signals from planets

STEP 1: READ THE ORIGINAL SENTENCE CAREFULLY, LOOKING FOR ERRORS

In the original sentence, the placement of the modifying phrase "learned by computers" makes it unclear whether the "identification" or the "planets" are learned by the computers. Furthermore, the construction "the identification of planets learned by computers is done" is passive and awkward. A scan of the beginning of the choices also shows that there's an issue of what order "computers" and "identify" should appear in the sentence. Since the computers identify planets, "computers" should come first. Moreover, the sentence states that computers found instances of recorded signals "*in* the telescope," which is illogical. A telescope is used to make observations, and it's in these data that the computer could find signals from planets.

STEP 2: SCAN AND GROUP THE ANSWER CHOICES

There's a 3-2 split here. (**B**), (**C**), and (**D**) start with "computers," while (**A**) and (**E**) start with "the identification."

STEP 3: ELIMINATE CHOICES UNTIL ONLY ONE REMAINS

Eliminate (**A**) for the errors found in step 1, and since (**E**) begins in nearly the same passive, confusing manner as (**A**), eliminate this choice. (**B**), (**C**), and (**D**) fix that error by beginning with "computers learn," so check them for other errors. Eliminate (**B**), which also has the computer finding recorded signals "in" the telescope. Eliminate (**C**) because the non-underlined phrase "known as exoplanets" must modify the noun closest to it, but the "signals from beyond our solar system" are not "known as exoplanets." (**D**) is correct. This can be confirmed by reading it back into the sentence:

The recently discovered planet Kepler-90i was found via machine learning, a form of artificial intelligence in which <u>computers learn to identify planets by finding in data from the Kepler telescope instances of recorded signals from planets</u> beyond our solar system, known as exoplanets.

19. (E)

<u>Closely interrelated concepts, a change in macroeconomic policy tends to affect numerous microeconomic transactions, and the accumulation of microeconomic decisions typically influences the focus of macroeconomic studies, so</u> any economics curriculum requires considerable study of both macroeconomic and microeconomic concepts.

○ Closely interrelated concepts, a change in macroeconomic policy tends to affect numerous microeconomic transactions, and the accumulation of microeconomic decisions typically influences the focus of macroeconomic studies, so

○ A change in macroeconomic policy tends to affect microeconomic transactions numerously, and the accumulation of microeconomic decisions influences the focus of macroeconomic studies typically; since the concepts of macroeconomics and microeconomics are related closely,

○ A change in macroeconomic policy tends to affect numerous microeconomic transactions, and the accumulation of microeconomic decisions typically influences the focus of macroeconomic studies as a closely related concept, so

○ A change in macroeconomic policy tends to affect numerous microeconomic transactions, and the accumulation of microeconomic decisions typically influences the focus of macroeconomic studies; given these closely related concepts,

○ A change in macroeconomic policy tends to affect numerous microeconomic transactions, and the accumulation of microeconomic decisions typically influences the focus of macroeconomic studies; since the concepts of macroeconomics and microeconomics are closely related,

STEP 1: READ THE ORIGINAL SENTENCE CAREFULLY, LOOKING FOR ERRORS

The underlined text before the first comma is a modifying phrase, so check whether it appropriately modifies whatever comes right after that comma: "[c]losely interrelated concepts, a change" involves an illogical modification of "a change" by "[c]losely interrelated concepts."

STEP 2: SCAN AND GROUP THE ANSWER CHOICES

Only **(A)** begins with the modifying phrase "[c]losely interrelated concepts, a change," so check toward the ends of each choice to see whether you can effectively group the answers. Like **(A)**, choice **(C)** connects the underlined portion to the clause that follows with "so." The other three choices all use a semicolon to introduce a new (presumably) complete thought. **(B)** and **(E)** start this new thought with a dependent clause beginning with "since…," while **(D)** starts it with a dependent clause beginning with "given…"

STEP 3: ELIMINATE CHOICES UNTIL ONLY ONE REMAINS

Eliminate **(A)** for the modification error noted in step 1. The word "so" is a logical connector between ideas in this sentence, so check **(C)** next. Unfortunately, in **(C)** the phrase "as a closely related concept" has been moved so that it describes only "macroeconomic studies," and it's no longer clear what macroeconomics is closely related to.

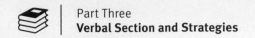

With "given," **(D)** is different from **(B)** and **(E)**, so check it next. The introductory phrase "given these closely related concepts" makes this sentence say *Because these two closely related concepts exist, they should both be in an economics curriculum*. However, the original sentence says it's *the fact that they are closely interrelated* that means they should be in the curriculum. The relatively weak key word "given" loses the meaning conveyed by the original sentence's conclusion key word "so." Eliminate **(D)**.

(B) and **(E)** end in almost the same way, and the movement of the adverb "closely" leaves it next to the participle "related" that it modifies, so this is not a problem. Look elsewhere in each choice for a problem. **(B)** inappropriately places or otherwise misuses the modifiers "numerously" (which should be the adjective *numerous* and modify the noun "microeconomic transactions" but instead is an adverb and modifies the verb "affect") and "typically" (which is too far away from "influences"). So eliminate **(B)** and read **(E)** into the sentence to confirm its correctness:

A change in macroeconomic policy tends to affect numerous microeconomic transactions, and the accumulation of microeconomic decisions typically influences the focus of macroeconomic studies; since the concepts of macroeconomics and microeconomics are closely related, any economics curriculum requires considerable study of both macroeconomic and microeconomic concepts.

20. (C)

Noticing the fact that the three students were arguing while they were writing a joint science report over the proper use of semicolons, their discussion was interrupted by the teacher to give them a quick lesson on punctuation.

- ○ Noticing the fact that the three students were arguing while they were writing a joint science report over the proper use of semicolons, their discussion was interrupted by the teacher

- ○ Noting that the three students were arguing while they were writing a joint science report over the proper use of semicolons, their discussion was interrupted by the teacher

- ○ Noting that the three students were arguing over the proper use of semicolons while they were writing a joint science report, the teacher interrupted their discussion

- ○ Noticing the fact that the three students were arguing over the proper use of semicolons while they were writing a joint science report, the teacher interrupted their discussion

- ○ Noting that the three students were arguing over the proper use of semicolons while writing a joint science report, the teacher interrupted their discussion

STEP 1: READ THE ORIGINAL SENTENCE CAREFULLY, LOOKING FOR ERRORS

The sentence starts with a modifying phrase ("Noticing the fact that…"), so the noun that this phrase is intended to modify must appear immediately after the comma. In this case, the teacher is the one who is noticing something, so it is incorrect for the clause after the comma to start with "their discussion." In addition, there is another misplaced modifier in the first clause: the students were *arguing*, not writing, over the proper use of a semicolon. The correct choice must fix both of these mistakes.

STEP 2: SCAN AND GROUP THE ANSWER CHOICES

Like (**A**), choice (**B**) retains "their discussion was interrupted by the teacher" after the comma, while (**C**), (**D**), and (**E**) change it to "the teacher interrupted their discussion."

STEP 3: ELIMINATE CHOICES UNTIL ONLY ONE REMAINS

Since the first clause is modifying the teacher, not the discussion, eliminate (**A**) and (**B**). A quick vertical scan of the remaining choices reveals a 2-1 split at the beginning of each: (**D**) keeps the original phrasing ("Noticing the fact that…"), while (**C**) and (**E**) change it to "Noting that…" Either "[n]oticing" or "[n]oting" is a correct word here, but the addition of "the fact" adds nothing. Since "[n]oting that" is more concise, eliminate (**D**).

Both (**C**) and (**E**) fix the other misplaced modifier in the original sentence, correctly moving the phrase "over the proper use of a semicolon" to follow the word it modifies ("arguing"). The only difference between them is that (**C**) uses the original language "while they were writing," while (**E**) shortens it to "while writing." You might be tempted to choose the more concise phrasing in (**E**), but omitting the words "they were" makes the meaning ambiguous: were the students arguing over the proper use of semicolons in joint science reports specifically or the proper use of semicolons in any type of writing while these particular students happened to be writing a joint science report? Because (**C**) contains no such ambiguity, it is the correct answer. Read it into the sentence to confirm:

Noting that the three students were arguing over the proper use of semicolons while they were writing a joint science report, the teacher interrupted their discussion to give them a quick lesson on punctuation and mechanics.

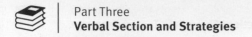

Practice Set: Parallelism

21. (C)

Although carotene and xanthophyll are present in leaves throughout the year, these pigments are not usually visible until <u>the days shorten, temperature drops, and the breaking down of the chlorophyll in the leaves reveals</u> the yellow and orange colors.

- ○ the days shorten, temperature drops, and the breaking down of the chlorophyll in the leaves reveals
- ○ the days shorten, the temperature drops, and the chlorophyll breakdown in the leaves is to reveal
- ○ the days shorten, the temperature drops, and the chlorophyll in the leaves breaks down, revealing
- ○ the days are shorter, the temperature is lower, and less chlorophyll in the leaves due to breakdown reveals
- ○ the days shorten, the temperature drops, and chlorophyll breaks down, revealing in the leaves

STEP 1: READ THE ORIGINAL SENTENCE CAREFULLY, LOOKING FOR ERRORS

Notice that the underlined portion of the sentence contains a list. This is a hint that there may be a parallelism issue at play. Items in a list must be in identical grammatical format, but the original sentence has two noun-verb pairings—"days shorten" and "temperature drops"—followed by an *-ing* construction. This is not parallel. Also, the first item is preceded by "the," the second item lacks a "the," and then "the" reappears in front of the third item.

STEP 2: SCAN AND GROUP THE ANSWER CHOICES

Due to the variation in the choices, grouping them would be inefficient. Evaluate the choices individually.

STEP 3: ELIMINATE CHOICES UNTIL ONLY ONE REMAINS

Eliminate (**A**) for the error identified in step 1. In (**B**), "is to reveal" is not parallel with "shorten" and "drops," so it's incorrect. Eliminate (**D**) due to a lack of parallelism. In the first two list items, a form of the verb "to be" is used ("are" and "is") while "reveals" is used in the third. Additionally, the phrasing of the last item makes it unclear what is breaking down to reduce the amount of chlorophyll in the leaves. (**E**) uses "the" before the first two items but drops it in the third item; also, moving "in the leaves" further from "chlorophyll" makes it less clear where the chlorophyll is. (**C**) has all items in parallel form—"shorten…drops…breaks down"—and is correct. Read it back into the original sentence to confirm:

Although carotene and xanthophyll are present in leaves throughout the year, these pigments are not usually visible until <u>the days shorten, the temperature drops, and the chlorophyll in the leaves breaks down, revealing</u> the yellow and orange colors.

22. (A)

By conducting a national study of opioid abuse on college campuses, researchers hope to determine where students purchase opioids, how frequently students abuse opioids on average, and <u>which college stressors most commonly contribute to opioid abuse among students</u>.

○   which college stressors most commonly contribute to opioid abuse among students

○   which are the college stressors common to students who are likely to be turning to opioid abuse

○   the common stressors of college that are likely to contribute to opioid abuse among students

○   the stressors of college common among students who turn to opioid abuse

○   the types of college stressors that are common to students who are likely to turn to opioid abuse

STEP 1: READ THE ORIGINAL SENTENCE CAREFULLY, LOOKING FOR ERRORS

Because this sentence has a list in the underlined portion, determine whether that list has a parallel structure. The list is "where students purchase... how frequently students... and which college stressors..." As written, the list has parallel structure, with each item beginning with a word—"where," "how," and "which"—that could begin a question (an interrogative adverb, if you're curious) followed by a noun—"students," "students," and "college stressors," respectively. Other elements worth checking are the modifying words "most commonly" before the verb "contribute" and the idiomatic usage of "contribute to." All are correct.

STEP 2: SCAN AND GROUP THE ANSWER CHOICES

(A) and (B) begin with "which," which is parallel to "where" and "how." The remaining choices begin with elements that break the parallel structure.

STEP 3: ELIMINATE CHOICES UNTIL ONLY ONE REMAINS

(C), (D), and (E) are incorrect because they begin with a word that breaks the parallel structure of the list. (B) is wrong because it is unnecessarily wordy. The sentence here is correct as written, so (A) is the answer.

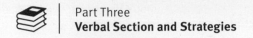

23. (E)

Although deciding the outcome of an election by chance may seem antiquated, <u>a toss of a coin, playing a round of poker, and drawing straws are all methods that have been used</u> within the span of 15 years to determine the winner of a deadlocked election somewhere in the United States.

○ a toss of a coin, playing a round of poker, and drawing straws are all methods that have been used

○ the tossing of a coin, playing a round of poker, and drawing straws are all methods that have been used

○ tossing a coin, playing a round of poker, and drawing straws are all methods that would have been used

○ a toss of a coin, playing a round of poker, and drawing straws are all methods that had been used

○ tossing a coin, playing a round of poker, and drawing straws are all methods that have been used

STEP 1: READ THE ORIGINAL SENTENCE CAREFULLY, LOOKING FOR ERRORS

Items in a list must exhibit parallel structure. The list in this sentence has one noun phrase ("a toss of a coin") and two *-ing* phrases ("playing a round of poker" and "drawing straws"). The correct choice must fix this mistake.

STEP 2: SCAN AND GROUP THE ANSWER CHOICES

All of the answer choices retain the two *-ing* verbs in the list ("playing" and "drawing"), but there is a 3-2 split on "a toss of a coin," with **(D)** retaining the original language of **(A)**, and **(B)**, **(C)**, and **(E)** replacing it with some form of "tossing a coin."

STEP 3: ELIMINATE CHOICES UNTIL ONLY ONE REMAINS

Because the items in the original sentence are not parallel as written, eliminate **(A)** and **(D)**. **(B)** adds "the…of" to the first element but not to the others, creating a new parallelism error. In addition, the phase "the tossing of a coin" is more awkward than the phrase used by the other remaining choices ("tossing a coin"). Eliminate **(B)**.

(C) and **(E)** differ only in the tense of verb used at the end of the sentence. **(C)** adds the subjunctive indicator "would," whereas **(E)** retains the original language. **(C)**'s change would make sense if the sentence were hypothetical, but it's not; these methods have actually been used. Thus, eliminate **(C)** and read **(E)** into the original to confirm:

Although deciding the outcome of an election by chance may seem antiquated, <u>tossing a coin, playing a round of poker, and drawing straws are all methods that have been used</u> within the span of 15 years to determine the winner of a deadlocked election somewhere in the United States.

Advanced Practice Set: Parallelism

24. (D)

According to one nutrition consultant, healthy adults should not hesitate to consume eggs, since this food contains six grams of high-quality protein, all nine essential amino acids, <u>vitamins B12 and D, and is a source of various other nutrients</u> as well.

- ○ vitamins B12 and D, and is a source of various other nutrients
- ○ vitamins B12 and D, and including various other nutrients
- ○ vitamins B12 and D, and various other nutrients are included
- ○ and vitamins B12 and D, and it is a source of various other nutrients
- ○ the vitamins B12 and D, and provides various other nutrients

STEP 1: READ THE ORIGINAL SENTENCE CAREFULLY, LOOKING FOR ERRORS

The underlined text includes part of a list, so examine its elements for parallelism. The first items in the list are nouns, the "grams" of protein and the "amino acids," so each succeeding item must be a noun also. "[V]itamins B12 and D" works, but the last item is not a noun. Instead, "is a source…as well" is a clause but without a subject.

STEP 2: SCAN AND GROUP THE ANSWER CHOICES

Three of the choices begin with "vitamins," while (D) and (E) begin with "and vitamins" and "the vitamins," respectively.

STEP 3: ELIMINATE CHOICES UNTIL ONLY ONE REMAINS

Eliminate (A) for its lack of parallelism. (B) also lacks a noun after "and," so eliminate it. (C) looks promising with "and…nutrients." However, the noun "nutrients" turns out not to be a noun phrase but instead a subject with a verb: "nutrients are included." This is not parallel.

Turn your attention to the two choices that vary the beginning. (E) inserts a verb after the "and." This would be correct if the sentence read "since this food contains [list of nutrients] and is a source of various other nutrients…" However, "the vitamins B12 and D" has no conjunction before it and so cannot be the last item in the series. Since the list hasn't ended, "is a source" reads as part of the list and is not parallel. That leaves (D), which uses the conjunction "and" to indicate the last item of the list, then uses "and" again to join one complete clause to another: "and it is a source…" Read (D) back into the sentence to confirm:

According to one nutrition consultant, healthy adults should not hesitate to consume eggs, since this food contains six grams of high-quality protein, all nine essential amino acids, <u>and vitamins B12 and D, and it is a source of various other nutrients</u> as well.

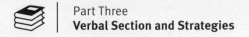

25. (C)

In Cold Blood <u>is not only often considered</u> Truman Capote's most popular novel but also the first "nonfiction novel," a literary genre that uses techniques of fictional storytelling to depict actual people and events.

- ○ is not only often considered
- ○ is as often not only considered
- ○ is often considered not only
- ○ not only is often considered to be
- ○ not only is considered as often

STEP 1: READ THE ORIGINAL SENTENCE CAREFULLY, LOOKING FOR ERRORS

The underlined portion contains the phrase "not only," which is part of the idiomatic conjunction "not only...but also." What follows both "not only" and "but also" should be in parallel form. However, "not only" is followed by a verb ("considered") while "but also" is followed by a noun ("the first 'nonfiction novel'"). Because what follows "but also" cannot be changed, the underlined portion needs to be rewritten to have "not only" followed by a noun.

STEP 2: SCAN AND GROUP THE ANSWER CHOICES

In **(A)** and **(B)**, "not only" is followed by "considered." In **(C)**, "not only" is the last part of the choice, while in **(D)** and **(E)**, it's followed by "is."

STEP 3: ELIMINATE CHOICES UNTIL ONLY ONE REMAINS

(A) can be eliminated, as can **(B)**, for having "not only" followed by a verb, which is not parallel to having "but also" followed by a noun. **(B)** also adds the word "as" before "often," which suggests there will be a comparison, but no comparison is ever drawn.

(D) and **(E)** move "not only" to the beginning of the underlined portion. However, they both still follow "not only" with a verb ("is") and so continue to commit the parallelism error. Further, **(D)** unnecessarily adds "to be" after "considered," and **(E)** uses the phrase "as often," which suggests a comparison that is never made. Those choices can be eliminated. That makes the correct answer **(C)**; by moving "not only" to the end, these words are followed by a noun (Capote's novel). To confirm, read it back into the original sentence:

In Cold Blood <u>is often considered not only</u> Truman Capote's most popular novel but also the first "nonfiction novel," a literary genre that uses techniques of fictional storytelling to depict actual people and events.

26. (E)

The self-portraits of Frida Kahlo can be considered both introspective explorations of a psyche that ranged free, unbounded by historical notions of cultural identity and <u>feminine, as well as subverting</u> traditional European portraiture.

- ○ feminine, as well as subverting
- ○ being feminine, and subverted
- ○ that was feminine, and subversions of
- ○ the femininity, as well as subverted
- ○ femininity, and subversions of

STEP 1: READ THE ORIGINAL SENTENCE CAREFULLY, LOOKING FOR ERRORS

The construction "*both* introspective explorations…" needs to be completed by *and* to be idiomatically correct, and the *and* must be followed by a noun that is parallel with "explorations." Thus, "as well as" is incorrect, and so is "subverting." Moreover, the two halves of the phrase "of cultural identity and feminine" should be in parallel form, but since "identity" is a noun and "feminine" is an adjective, this phrase is incorrect as written.

STEP 2: SCAN AND GROUP THE ANSWER CHOICES

There's too much variation in the answer choices to group effectively, so consider them one by one.

STEP 3: ELIMINATE CHOICES UNTIL ONLY ONE REMAINS

Eliminate **(A)** for the errors identified in step 1. With "being feminine," "that was feminine," and "the femininity," respectively, **(B)**, **(C)**, and **(D)** violate the parallelism of the "of cultural identity and…" phrase, so they can be eliminated. **(B)** and **(D)** also use "subverted," which is not parallel with "explorations," and **(D)** uses the unidiomatic "both… as well as." **(E)** completes both parallel constructions properly, so it is the correct answer. Read it back into the sentence to confirm:

The self-portraits of Frida Kahlo can be considered both introspective explorations of a psyche that ranged free, unbounded by historical notions of cultural identity and <u>femininity, and subversions of</u> traditional European portraiture.

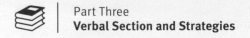

27. (B)

Determining which animal on Earth is the largest depends on one's reference point: while the blue whale's body is indeed larger than <u>the sperm whale, the sperm whale's brain is actually larger than the blue whale</u>.

- ○ the sperm whale, the sperm whale's brain is actually larger than the blue whale
- ○ that of the sperm whale, the sperm whale's brain is actually larger than that of the blue whale
- ○ that of the sperm whale, the sperm whale's brain is actually larger than the blue whale
- ○ the sperm whale's brain, the sperm whale's body is actually larger than the blue whale's brain
- ○ that of the sperm whale, the sperm whale's brain nevertheless is larger than that of the blue whale

STEP 1: READ THE ORIGINAL SENTENCE CAREFULLY, LOOKING FOR ERRORS

The underlined text both follows from and includes the comparison phrase "larger than," so check that the two comparisons are both logical and in parallel form. The first comparison involves a body (the blue whale's) and a whale (the sperm whale) and is thus illogical. The second comparison involves a brain (the sperm whale's) and a whale (the blue whale)—another illogical comparison.

STEP 2: SCAN AND GROUP THE ANSWER CHOICES

There's a 3-1-1 split here. **(A)** begins with "the sperm whale." **(B)**, **(C)**, and **(E)** begin with "that of the sperm whale." **(D)** begins with "the sperm whale's brain."

STEP 3: ELIMINATE CHOICES UNTIL ONLY ONE REMAINS

Eliminate **(A)** due to the illogical comparison identified in step 1, and since **(D)** introduces another illogical comparison—that is, between a body and a brain—eliminate that choice as well.

Now consider the remaining choices based on the sentence's second comparison. **(B)** compares the sperm whale's brain to "that [brain] of the blue whale"—a logical comparison. **(C)** compares the sperm whale's brain to the blue whale, so eliminate this choice. **(E)** compares the sperm whale's brain to "that [brain] of the blue whale" but introduces the word "nevertheless." Since the author already uses the contrast key word "while," the additional contrast key word "nevertheless" is unnecessary. Eliminate **(E)** and read **(B)** into the sentence to confirm it is correct:

Determining which animal on Earth is largest depends on one's reference point: while the blue whale's body is indeed larger than <u>that of the sperm whale, the sperm whale's brain is actually larger than that of the blue whale</u>.

28. (A)

<u>No less significant than</u> international pressures are the constraints that domestic culture and ideology impose on decision making by national political figures.

- ○ No less significant than
- ○ The things that are just as significant as
- ○ Just like the significant
- ○ Not lesser than the significance of
- ○ What are as significant as

STEP 1: READ THE ORIGINAL SENTENCE CAREFULLY, LOOKING FOR ERRORS

Because a comparison is made, check whether the comparison is valid. The original sentence contains a slightly unusual construction, but it is correct.

STEP 2: SCAN AND GROUP THE ANSWER CHOICES

There are no splits here, but be on the lookout for answer choices that alter the comparison in any way.

STEP 3: ELIMINATE CHOICES UNTIL ONLY ONE REMAINS

The original sentence appears to make a valid comparison between "international pressures" and "constraints," so **(A)** is correct. Eliminate **(B)** and **(E)** for being unnecessarily wordy. Eliminate **(C)** because it changes the meaning of the sentence slightly by leaving out the idea that the constraints are equally significant. Finally, eliminate **(D)** because it compares "significance" with "constraints."

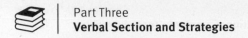

29. (D)

Establishing goals for a nonprofit organization is often different <u>than setting</u> goals for a profit-making enterprise because the stakeholders of the former may be more varied.

- ○ than setting
- ○ than the setting of
- ○ from
- ○ from setting
- ○ from the setting of

STEP 1: READ THE ORIGINAL SENTENCE CAREFULLY, LOOKING FOR ERRORS

The fact that the word "than" is underlined is a clue that there may be a comparison problem here. When one thing (a noun) is said to differ from another, the correct phrase is *different from*, not "different than." In this sentence, the *-ing* words "[e]stablishing" and "setting" are verb forms that function as nouns, so the comparison needs to use *from*, not "than."

STEP 2: SCAN AND GROUP THE ANSWER CHOICES

There's a 3-2 split between the choices that use "from," **(C)**, **(D)**, and **(E)**, and the choices that use "than," **(A)** and **(B)**.

STEP 3: ELIMINATE CHOICES UNTIL ONLY ONE REMAINS

Eliminate **(A)** and **(B)** for being on the wrong side of the split. **(C)** compares "[e]stablishing" to "goals," which would not be parallel, so this choice is incorrect. By introducing "the" and "of," **(E)** violates parallelism and is unnecessarily wordy. Thus, **(D)** is correct. Confirm this by reading it back into the sentence:

Establishing goals for a nonprofit organization is often different <u>from setting</u> goals for a profit-making enterprise because the stakeholders of the former may be more varied.

Advanced Practice Set: Comparisons

30. (C)

Reducing the population of Japanese beetles is done <u>most easily by applying pesticides to turf-dwelling young larva in late summer than applications</u> to mature larva in spring or adult beetles at any time of year.

- ○ most easily by applying pesticides to turf-dwelling young larva in late summer than applications
- ○ most easily by the application of pesticides to turf-dwelling young larva in late summer than that
- ○ more easily by applying pesticides to turf-dwelling young larva in late summer than
- ○ easier through the application of pesticides to turf-dwelling young larva in late summer than
- ○ more easily by applying pesticides to turf-dwelling young larva in late summer rather than applying

STEP 1: READ THE ORIGINAL SENTENCE CAREFULLY, LOOKING FOR ERRORS

The words at the beginning of the underlined portion, "most easily," indicate that a comparison is being made. Specifically, the comparison is about how reducing a population of insects is easier if done by attacking young larva instead of by attacking older larva or adults. This is a two-part comparison between *one way* and *other ways*, so the correct word is "more," not "most."

STEP 2: SCAN AND GROUP THE ANSWER CHOICES

There's a 2-2-1 split here. **(A)** and **(B)** use "most easily," **(C)** and **(E)** use "more easily," and **(D)** uses "easier."

STEP 3: ELIMINATE CHOICES UNTIL ONLY ONE REMAINS

Only **(C)** and **(E)** use the correct "more easily," so eliminate the other choices. One thing is done *more easily than* another, so the second part of the construction must use "than." **(E)** uses "than applying" at the end, which does not integrate correctly with the non-underlined text that follows. That leaves **(C)**, which begins with "more easily" and ends with "than," correctly forming the comparison. Read it back into the original sentence to confirm:

Reducing the population of Japanese beetles is done <u>more easily by applying pesticides</u> to turf-dwelling young larva in late summer than to mature larva in spring or adult beetles at any time of year.

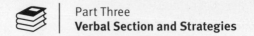
PRACTICE SET: COMPARISONS

31. (D)

With an elaborate menu featuring innovative dishes from a variety of world cuisines <u>as well as serving its signature breakfast fare, Penelope's Pancake Palace, an established downtown eatery, offers a more diverse selection of food than does any restaurant</u> in the city.

- ○ as well as serving its signature breakfast fare, Penelope's Pancake Palace, an established downtown eatery, offers a more diverse selection of food than does any restaurant

- ○ as well as its signature breakfast fare, Penelope's Pancake Palace, an eatery established downtown, offers a more diverse selection of food than does any restaurant

- ○ as well as with serving its signature breakfast fare, Penelope's Pancake Palace, an established downtown eatery, offers a more diverse selection of food than does any other restaurant

- ○ as well as its signature breakfast fare, Penelope's Pancake Palace, an established downtown eatery, offers a more diverse selection of food than does any other restaurant

- ○ as well as its signature breakfast fare, Penelope's Pancake Palace, an established downtown eatery, offers more of a diverse selection of food as any other restaurant

STEP 1: READ THE ORIGINAL SENTENCE CAREFULLY, LOOKING FOR ERRORS

The original sentence contains two phrases that require parallel and logically similar elements: "as well as" and "more…than." However, both are wrong in this sentence. The first connecting phrase joins "serving its signature breakfast fare" to either "an elaborate menu" or "featuring innovative dishes." If it's the former, the elements are not grammatically parallel because one item is a noun ("elaborate menu") and the other is an *-ing* verb ("serving"). If it's the latter, the elements are grammatically parallel ("featuring" and "serving") but illogical, because that interpretation would require the menu to be "serving" breakfast, and menus don't serve food.

Meanwhile, the "more…than" comparison is illogical because it compares Penelope's Pancake Palace to "any restaurant in the city." This construction would only make sense if Penelope's were not a restaurant or were not located in the city. But the sentence states that Penelope's is a downtown eatery, so comparing it to "*any* restaurant in the city" is, absurdly, comparing it to itself, as well as to any other restaurants.

STEP 2: SCAN AND GROUP THE ANSWER CHOICES

Choice **(C)** has the same parallelism error in the elements joined by "as well as" as does the original sentence. **(B)**, **(D)**, and **(E)** correct this lack of parallel structure by eliminating the word "serving."

You might have started with another split at the ends of the choices. Like **(A)**, choice **(B)** ends with "than does any restaurant." The other three choices compare Penelope's to "any *other* restaurant."

STEP 3: ELIMINATE CHOICES UNTIL ONLY ONE REMAINS

Eliminate **(A)** and **(C)** due to the mistake in the first construction. Then eliminate **(B)** for making a mistake in the comparison at the end. By inserting "other," **(D)** and **(E)** both compare Penelope's to other restaurants, not including itself. Finally, compare the language of **(D)** and **(E)**. The former corrects the two mistakes in the original sentence without making any additional changes, whereas the latter changes the construction of the comparison from "more…than" to "more…as." Because "more…as" is not idiomatically correct, eliminate **(E)** and read **(D)** back into the sentence to confirm:

With an elaborate menu featuring innovative dishes from a variety of world cuisines <u>as well as its signature breakfast fare, Penelope's Pancake Palace, an established downtown eatery, offers a more diverse selection of food than does any other restaurant</u> in the city.

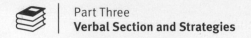
32. (E)

The United States' trade deficit with China rose in 2003 to $123 billion, <u>which is 17 percent more than the previous year</u> and more than ten times the U.S.-China trade deficit in 1998.

- ○ which is 17 percent more than the previous year
- ○ which is 17 percent higher than it was the previous year
- ○ 17 percent higher than the previous year's figure was
- ○ an amount that is 17 percent more than the previous year was
- ○ an amount that is 17 percent higher than the previous year's figure

STEP 1: READ THE ORIGINAL SENTENCE CAREFULLY, LOOKING FOR ERRORS

Because the relative pronoun "which" refers to the noun that comes immediately before it, this means the underlined segment illogically compares a sum of money, "$123 billion," to "the previous year." The correct answer must compare a sum and a sum, not a sum and a year.

STEP 2: SCAN AND GROUP THE ANSWER CHOICES

(A) and **(B)** both start with "which." **(C)** leaves out "which," while **(D)** and **(E)** substitute "an amount that" for "which."

STEP 3: ELIMINATE CHOICES UNTIL ONLY ONE REMAINS

Eliminate **(A)** because of its illogical comparison. **(B)** also bungles the comparison, thanks to its careless use of the slippery pronoun "it." Because "which" refers to "123 billion," **(B)** seems to say, nonsensically, that $123 billion is 17 percent higher than $123 billion was the previous year. **(D)** also fails to fix the illogical comparison; it compares "an amount" to "the previous year." That leaves only **(C)** and **(E)**. Both of these choices correctly compare two amounts of money. However, **(C)** adds "was" at the end, which is unnecessary and not parallel with the last part of the sentence, which does not use the verb. **(E)**, which introduces no new errors, is the correct answer. Read it back into the sentence to confirm:

The United States' trade deficit with China rose in 2003 to $123 billion, <u>an amount that is 17 percent higher than the previous year's figure</u> and more than ten times the U.S.-China trade deficit in 1998.

Practice Set: Usage and Idioms

33. (E)

In addition to winning the Nobel Prize in Physics for his accomplishments in quantum electro-dynamics, Richard Feynman worked on both the Manhattan Project in Los Alamos <u>as well as the Rogers Commission, which investigated</u> the space shuttle *Challenger* disaster in 1986.

- O   as well as the Rogers Commission, which investigated
- O   and also on the Rogers Commission that investigated
- O   and on the Rogers Commission, which investigated
- O   and the Rogers Commission, which is investigating
- O   and the Rogers Commission, which investigated

STEP 1: READ THE ORIGINAL SENTENCE CAREFULLY, LOOKING FOR ERRORS

The underlined portion begins with "as well as." However, this is part of a phrase that begins with "both." The phrasing "both…as well as" is not idiomatically correct. It should be "both…and." Note also that this two-part construction must be parallel; the phrases that follow "both" and "and" must be in the same grammatical form. In the non-underlined part, "both" is followed immediately by "the Manhattan Project," so "and" must be followed immediately by a noun as well.

STEP 2: SCAN AND GROUP THE ANSWER CHOICES

Except for (A), all of the choices make the correction to "and," although (B) adds "also on" while (C) adds "on." (D) and (E) simply replace "as well as" with "and."

STEP 3: ELIMINATE CHOICES UNTIL ONLY ONE REMAINS

(A) can be eliminated for containing the mistaken "as well as," which does not match up with "both." (B) and (C) make the correct change to "and," but they both add unnecessary words. (B) adds "also," which is redundant when paired with "both," and inserts "on" before "the Rogers Commission," violating parallelism. Also, the change from "which investigated" to "that investigated" at the end suggests there was more than one Rogers Commission. (C) can be eliminated because it adds the word "on" after "and," violating parallelism.

(D) and (E) both make the appropriate change to "and" without adding unnecessary words. However, (D) changes the verb at the end to the present "is investigating," which is not appropriate for something that is said to have taken place in the past. (E) is correct. To confirm, read it back into the original sentence:

In addition to winning the Nobel Prize in Physics for his accomplishments in quantum electrodynamics, Richard Feynman worked on both the Manhattan Project in Los Alamos <u>and the Rogers Commission, which investigated</u> the space shuttle *Challenger* disaster in 1986.

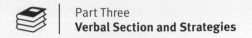

34. (C)

To boost the nation's economy, it is <u>at least as important for businesses to focus</u> on developing worker productivity than it is for them to hire new employees.

- ○ at least as important for businesses to focus
- ○ at least as important for businesses focusing
- ○ no less important for businesses to focus
- ○ no less important that businesses focusing
- ○ as important, if not more important, for businesses to focus

STEP 1: READ THE ORIGINAL SENTENCE CAREFULLY, LOOKING FOR ERRORS

The underlined portion begins with "at least as," which should idiomatically be paired with *as* (*at least as X as Y*). However, the sentence is phrased "at least as…than," which is incorrect. Because "than" cannot be changed, "at least as" must be changed to something that connects to "than."

STEP 2: SCAN AND GROUP THE ANSWER CHOICES

(A) and **(B)** start with "at least as," **(C)** and **(D)** begin with "no less," and **(E)** begins with "as."

STEP 3: ELIMINATE CHOICES UNTIL ONLY ONE REMAINS

(A) and **(B)** can be eliminated for starting with "at least as," which does not match with "than." Also, by changing "to focus" to "focusing," **(B)** removes the active verb telling what businesses need to do. Instead, it sounds as though the author is talking about businesses that are already focusing on worker productivity.

(E) changes "at least as" to the overly wordy phrase "as…if not more." However, this still does not form a correctly phrased comparison with "than," so the idiom error persists. Eliminate **(E)**.

(C) and **(D)** change "at least as" to "no less," which does match to "than" (*I am no less interested in pizza than in ice cream*). However, **(D)** changes the verb "to focus" to "focusing," which removes the active verb just as **(B)** does. That error eliminates **(D)**, leaving **(C)** as the correct answer. To confirm, read that choice into the sentence:

To boost the nation's economy, it is <u>no less important for businesses to focus</u> on developing worker productivity than it is for them to hire new employees.

35. (D)

The "Mpemba effect" refers to the fact that hot water freezes <u>more quickly in comparison to cold water; the researchers who investigated this effect also discovered that cold water heats more quickly in relation to warm water</u> and named that phenomenon the "inverse Mpemba effect."

○   more quickly in comparison to cold water; the researchers who investigated this effect also discovered that cold water heats more quickly in relation to warm water

○   faster; the researchers who investigated this effect also discovered that cold water heats faster

○   more quickly than cold water; the researchers who investigated this effect also discovered that cold water would heat more quickly than warm water

○   faster than cold water; the researchers who investigated this effect also discovered that cold water heats faster than warm water

○   faster than cold water; the researchers who investigated this effect also discovered that the opposite is true

STEP 1: READ THE ORIGINAL SENTENCE CAREFULLY, LOOKING FOR ERRORS

The underlined text does not contain any errors of grammar or meaning, so look for stylistic issues. You may already have some ideas about how you could say the same thing that the underlined text says but in fewer words, so anticipate that at least one or two choices will more concisely convey the ideas in the underlined text.

STEP 2: SCAN AND GROUP THE ANSWER CHOICES

Scan the text before the semicolon: **(A)** says "more quickly in comparison to cold water," **(B)** says "faster," **(C)** says "more quickly than does cold water," and **(D)** and **(E)** say "faster than cold water."

STEP 3: ELIMINATE CHOICES UNTIL ONLY ONE REMAINS

With respect to the first part of each choice, **(B)** is the most concise, but do not choose based on concision alone. Sometimes more words are needed. In fact, **(B)** is incorrect because it fails to complete the comparison between hot water and cold water.

Choices **(C)**, **(D)**, and **(E)** differ from each other following the phrase "discovered that." **(C)** says "cold water would heat more quickly than warm water." The use of "would" introduces the subjunctive mood, but this idea is not conditional or hypothetical. The sentence isn't saying that *cold water would heat more quickly than warm water if [some condition were met]*. So **(C)** is incorrect. By saying "the opposite is true," **(E)** changes the meaning of the sentence, seeming to say that maybe hot water doesn't freeze faster than cold water. **(D)** forms the comparisons correctly and is concise, without losing any of the author's intended meaning. Read this choice back into the sentence to confirm that it produces no errors:

The "Mpemba effect" refers to the fact that hot water freezes <u>faster than cold water; the researchers who investigated this effect also discovered that cold water heats faster than warm water</u> and named that phenomenon the "inverse Mpemba effect."

Advanced Practice Set: Usage and Idioms

36. (C)

The entrepreneurs credited the website that helped owners of small businesses find suppliers <u>to keep their new enterprise viable when cash flow was neither ample or steady</u>.

- ○   to keep their new enterprise viable when cash flow was neither ample or steady
- ○   toward keeping their new enterprise viable at a time when cash flow was not ample or steady
- ○   with keeping their new enterprise viable when cash flow was neither ample nor steady
- ○   to keeping their new enterprise viable when cash flow was neither ample nor steady
- ○   with keeping their new enterprise viable when there was not ample or steady cash flow

STEP 1: READ THE ORIGINAL SENTENCE CAREFULLY, LOOKING FOR ERRORS

There's an important clue in the non-underlined portion of this sentence. The verb "credited" is accompanied by either *to* or *with*. For example, you would *credit a high score to your good study habits* but *credit your good study habits with earning a high score*. In this question, the entrepreneurs are crediting the website *with* the success of their business. The author uses a lot of words to name the thing that the entrepreneurs credit—"the website that…suppliers"—to try to distract you from completing the idiom. The underlined portion begins with "to keep," not *with*, and so is incorrect.

Keep reading in case there are other errors the correct answer must address. At the end of the sentence, the correct construction is *neither…nor*, but this uses "neither…or." The correct choice will fix this problem as well.

STEP 2: SCAN AND GROUP THE ANSWER CHOICES

There's a 2-2-1 split in the first words of the choices, with (**A**) and (**D**) using "to," (**B**) using "toward," and (**C**) and (**E**) using "with."

STEP 3: ELIMINATE CHOICES UNTIL ONLY ONE REMAINS

Both (**B**) and (**D**) fix the "neither…nor" problem at the end in different ways, but, along with (**A**), eliminate both for not using "with." (**B**) is also unnecessarily wordy by adding "at a time"; the word "when" does the job. Now read (**C**) and (**E**) in parallel. (**E**) adopts the weak and passive "there was" construction, which places the thing of interest—the "cash flow"—at the very end of the sentence. (**C**) expresses the thought much more directly by putting "cash flow" first. (**C**) also uses "neither…nor" correctly. Read this choice back into the sentence to confirm:

The entrepreneurs credited the website that helped owners of small businesses find suppliers <u>with keeping their new enterprise viable when cash flow was neither ample nor steady</u>.

37. (C)

All parents who wish to hold a leadership position in the Boy Scouts are required, regardless of whether or not their child is a member, <u>for taking youth protection training</u>.

- ○ for taking youth protection training
- ○ for making sure youth protection training is taken
- ○ to take youth protection training
- ○ to have taken of the youth protection training
- ○ of taking youth protection training

STEP 1: READ THE ORIGINAL SENTENCE CAREFULLY, LOOKING FOR ERRORS

When analyzing this sentence, it is helpful to mentally delete the additional information between commas. The word "for" at the beginning of the underlined portion is part of the phrase "required for taking." However, saying "X is required for Y" suggests that you need X in order to have Y. That doesn't logically work in this sentence. To make it clear that taking the training is necessary, the phrase should be "required to take."

STEP 2: SCAN AND GROUP THE ANSWER CHOICES

(A) and (B) start with "for," (C) and (D) start with "to," and (E) starts with "of."

STEP 3: ELIMINATE CHOICES UNTIL ONLY ONE REMAINS

(A) and (B) can be eliminated for using "for" instead of "to." (B), in fact, makes things worse by suggesting it doesn't matter who takes the training, as long as it's taken. (E) changes "for" to "of," but that doesn't fix the problem. If it's said that "X is required of Y," then the X part is the requirement, and this sentence should say that the training is a requirement. Eliminate (E).

(C) and (D) properly use "to," but (D) unnecessarily puts the action in the past, and the word "of" does not belong. That eliminates (D), leaving (C) as the correct answer. To confirm, read it back into the original sentence:

All parents who wish to hold a leadership position in the Boy Scouts are required, regardless of whether or not their child is a member, <u>to take youth protection training</u>.

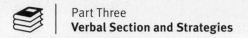

38. (D)

The United States <u>would achieve a 10 percent reduction in gasoline consumption, if Congress will raise</u> fuel economy standards to 31.3 miles per gallon for passenger cars and to 24.5 miles per gallon for light trucks.

- ○ would achieve a 10 percent reduction in gasoline consumption, if Congress will raise
- ○ will achieve a 10 percent reduction in gasoline consumption, if Congress were to raise
- ○ will have achieved a 10 percent reduction in gasoline consumption, if Congress will raise
- ○ would achieve a 10 percent reduction in gasoline consumption, if Congress were to raise
- ○ would achieve a 10 percent reduction in gasoline consumption, if Congress were raising

STEP 1: READ THE ORIGINAL SENTENCE CAREFULLY, LOOKING FOR ERRORS

The word "if" in the underlined part of this sentence signals a hypothetical situation, so you need the subjunctive mood; you must use "were" and "would." "Would achieve" is correct, but "will raise" is not. Rule out **(A)**.

STEP 2: SCAN AND GROUP THE ANSWER CHOICES

(B) and **(C)** start with "will." **(D)** and **(E)** start with "would."

STEP 3: ELIMINATE CHOICES UNTIL ONLY ONE REMAINS

(B) is incorrect because "will achieve" is ordinary future tense, not subjunctive. Similarly, **(C)** is incorrect because "will have achieved" is also not subjunctive. **(D)** and **(E)** both use "would achieve," which is the proper subjunctive mood. The difference between them comes at the end. **(D)** uses "if Congress were to raise," while **(E)** has "if Congress were raising." The final phrase in **(E)** sounds a bit odd and is in fact grammatically incorrect. The proper subjunctive construction calls for the verb that follows "were" to be in the infinitive, not the -*ing* form. **(E)** is thus incorrect, and **(D)**, which contains the proper "were"-plus-infinitive construction, is the correct answer. Here it is, read back into the sentence:

The United States <u>would achieve a 10 percent reduction in gasoline consumption, if Congress were to raise</u> fuel economy standards to 31.3 miles per gallon for passenger cars and to 24.5 miles per gallon for light trucks.

Practice Set: Clauses and Connectors

39. (C)

> Due to countries in a monetary union having to issue debt in a joint currency over which they lack full control, therefore investors become nervous about the financial health of a country, that nation may not be able to finance its debt at the same rate enjoyed by its neighbors and thus will experience the liquidity crisis that investors fear.

○ Due to countries in a monetary union having to issue debt in a joint currency over which they lack full control, therefore

○ It is because countries in a monetary union have to issue debt in a joint currency they do not fully control, as

○ Because countries in a monetary union must issue debt in a joint currency over which they lack full control, if

○ Countries that are in a monetary union have to issue debt in a joint currency over which they lack full control, causing

○ In a monetary union, countries have to issue debt in a joint currency over which they fully lack control, so

STEP 1: READ THE ORIGINAL SENTENCE CAREFULLY, LOOKING FOR ERRORS

The main clause in this sentence starts after the second comma. Therefore, the preceding clauses must be subordinate, and their subordinating conjunctions must make them relate in a logical way to the rest of the sentence. The underlined clause before the comma starts with "[d]ue to," attributing causality to the condition of having to issue debt in a joint currency. The "therefore" at the end of the underlined portion is unnecessary. Also, "therefore" is an adverb, not a conjunction, and fails to connect the clause about the nervous investors to the rest of the sentence. (**A**) is incorrect.

STEP 2: SCAN AND GROUP THE ANSWER CHOICES

Each choice begins and ends with a different word, and there is no pattern by which you can group the choices. Therefore, evaluate each one, keeping in mind the need to connect the clauses in a logical way.

STEP 3: ELIMINATE CHOICES UNTIL ONLY ONE REMAINS

You've already determined that (**A**) is incorrect. (**B**) begins with the weak "[i]t is," which is not a fatal flaw, but then this choice uses "as" after the comma. This word can mean either "because" or "while," but either way it fails to logically connect the clauses. (**D**) starts off with clear, direct prose. However, when you read it back into the sentence, you get "causing investors become nervous," which would only be idiomatic if it were *causing investors to become nervous*. And then there is no connection between the first two clauses and the main clause at all. Eliminate (**D**). In (**E**), the "so" at the end is no improvement over the "therefore" in the original. This choice also changes the adjective "full," which modifies "control," to the adverb "fully," which modifies "lack"; this choice changes the meaning of the sentence. Only (**C**), by introducing the conditional "if," gives each clause a proper role in the sentence. Confirm that (**C**) is correct by reading it back into the sentence:

> Because countries in a monetary union must issue debt in a joint currency over which they lack full control, if investors become nervous about the financial health of a country, that nation may not be able to finance its debt at the same rate enjoyed by its neighbors and thus will experience the liquidity crisis that investors fear.

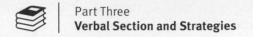

40. (A)

Kererū pigeons, of the species *Hemiphaga novaeseelandiae*, <u>which won the Bird of the Year award in New Zealand in 2018, can become intoxicated when they eat fermented fruit from the forest floor and, if they consume enough, may</u> fall from the trees where they roost.

- ○ which won the Bird of the Year award in New Zealand in 2018, can become intoxicated when they eat fermented fruit from the forest floor and, if they consume enough, may

- ○ winners of New Zealand's 2018 Bird of the Year award, can become intoxicated when they eat fermented fruit from the forest floor but, if they consume enough, may

- ○ which won the Bird of the Year award in New Zealand in 2018, becoming intoxicated if they were to eat fermented fruit from the forest floor if they were to consume enough, and may

- ○ winners of the Bird of the Year award in New Zealand in 2018, can become intoxicated when it eats fermented fruit from the forest floor and, if it consumes enough, may

- ○ which won the Bird of the Year award in New Zealand in 2018, can become intoxicated when they eat fermented fruit from the forest floor and, if they consume enough, then they may

STEP 1: READ THE ORIGINAL SENTENCE CAREFULLY, LOOKING FOR ERRORS

The underlined text begins with "which," a word that typically refers to the noun immediately before it. Here, "which" refers appropriately to the species, so there's no pronoun error.

"[W]hich" introduces a modifying phrase set off by commas, as does "if they consume enough" later in the sentence. In this second dependent clause, confirm that the plural pronoun "they" is correct. In fact it is, as it clearly refers to the "pigeons."

Now try reading the sentence without these asides to see whether the parts fit together correctly: "Kererū pigeons…can become intoxicated when they eat fermented fruit from the forest floor and…may fall from the trees where they roost." This sentence has a correctly formed compound predicate: "can become…and…may fall" is parallel, and both verbs are in the correct simple present tense to describe actions that are generally true. The conjunction "and" expresses the correct relationship between the two actions.

The sentence seems correct as written. Suspect that **(A)** is the answer but check the other choices to be sure.

STEP 2: SCAN AND GROUP THE ANSWER CHOICES

(A), **(C)**, and **(E)** begin with "which won," while **(B)** and **(D)** start with "winners." Either could be correct.

A more useful split occurs at the end, where **(A)**, **(B)**, and **(D)** use "may" while **(C)** uses "and may" and **(E)** uses "then they may." Evaluating this connection to the next thought will be helpful. In addition, there's a difference in the verb after the modifying phrase, where four of the choices use "can become" and one, **(C)**, uses "becoming." Evaluating this verb may be helpful.

STEP 3: ELIMINATE CHOICES UNTIL ONLY ONE REMAINS

With "becoming…and may," **(C)** is not parallel and in effect loses the main verb of the sentence. In **(E)**, the "then they" is superfluous; eliminate this choice. Now move on to **(B)** and **(D)**, which use "may" at the end. **(B)** replaces the conjunction "and" with "but." This is incorrect because the fact that the pigeons become intoxicated and the fact that sometimes they fall out of the trees should be joined by a continuation key word, not a contrast key word. **(D)** replaces the plural pronoun "they" with the singular "it," which doesn't correctly refer to the "pigeons." **(A)** is correct.

41. (C)

Science fiction has been described as the genre that, by addressing the future, <u>that it concerns ideas of large scope rather than the ephemeral thoughts</u> and emotions of individuals.

- ○ that it concerns ideas of large scope rather than the ephemeral thoughts
- ○ that concerns ideas of large scope instead of the ephemeral thoughts
- ○ concerns ideas of large scope rather than the ephemeral thoughts
- ○ so concerns ideas of large scope instead of the ephemeral thinking
- ○ it concerns ideas of large scope but not the ephemeral thoughts

STEP 1: READ THE ORIGINAL SENTENCE CAREFULLY, LOOKING FOR ERRORS

The clause starting "that it concerns ideas" and going all the way to the end of the sentence describes the genre of science fiction. Since the part of the sentence before the comma already has a "that," which stands for the word right before it, "genre," there is no need for another "that" after the comma or for the pronoun "it."

STEP 2: SCAN AND GROUP THE ANSWER CHOICES

The choices can be grouped with a 2-2-1 split. **(A)** and **(B)** both keep "that." **(C)** and **(D)** get rid of both "that" and "it," while **(E)** gets rid of "that" but keeps "it."

STEP 3: ELIMINATE CHOICES UNTIL ONLY ONE REMAINS

Since you determined in step 1 that both "that" and "it" were unnecessary, eliminate **(A)**, **(B)**, and **(E)**. To see clearly what sort of connector is needed, try reading the sentence without the unessential prepositional phrase "by addressing the future." In fact, no connector words are needed after the comma. "Science fiction has been described as the genre that…concerns ideas…" **(D)** uses "so" improperly and changes "thoughts" to "thinking," which is not parallel with its partner "emotions," so it can be eliminated. **(C)** is correct. This can be confirmed by reading it back into the sentence:

Science fiction has been described as the genre that, by addressing the future, <u>concerns ideas of large scope rather than the ephemeral thoughts</u> and emotions of individuals.

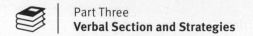

Advanced Practice Set: Clauses and Connectors

42. (E)

Although staff at one fast-food chain, in an effort to encourage children to eat healthier, proposed that the company create a <u>vegetable taste</u> like bubblegum, the company's chief executive officer ultimately reported that children who had tried the food expressed confusion about its flavor.

- ○ vegetable taste
- ○ vegetable tastes
- ○ taste for a vegetable
- ○ vegetable that has a taste
- ○ vegetable that tastes

STEP 1: READ THE ORIGINAL SENTENCE CAREFULLY, LOOKING FOR ERRORS

The sentence refers to a bubblegum-flavored vegetable. The underlined text contains a subject-verb disagreement issue, because "vegetable" is a singular subject while "taste" is a plural verb. You might initially interpret this part of the sentence as using "vegetable" attributively to describe "taste." However, reading the rest of the sentence clarifies that "vegetable" is, in this context, the food being created. The confusion is brought about by a connector error—the author does not establish the correct relationship between the two underlined words.

STEP 2: SCAN AND GROUP THE ANSWER CHOICES

Four of the choices begin with "vegetable," while (C) starts with "taste." Check the ends of the four "vegetable" choices to try to find another split: (A) and (D) contain "taste," while (B) and (E) contain "tastes."

STEP 3: ELIMINATE CHOICES UNTIL ONLY ONE REMAINS

Eliminate (A) based on the subject-verb disagreement. While (B) uses the correct singular verb "tastes," it maintains the connection problem, inappropriately making "vegetable" a subject that tastes something instead of a food with a certain taste.

(C) introduces an unclear comparison. With this choice, the author would seem to be saying that the target vegetable is "like bubblegum" and some unspecified flavor is being created for this food. The correct answer will make clear that that flavor is like that of bubblegum.

Both (D) and (E) specify that people experienced the taste of the vegetable as that of bubblegum, but (E) more concisely conveys this idea. So eliminate (D) and read (E) into the sentence to confirm its correctness:

Although staff at one fast-food chain, in an effort to encourage children to eat healthier, proposed that the company create a <u>vegetable that tastes</u> like bubblegum, the company's chief executive officer ultimately reported that children who had tried the food expressed confusion about its flavor.

43. (A)

During the latter stages of the insurrection, the revolution's leaders resorted to ever more violent means, including public execution of members of the upper class, <u>to establish their authority, and they suppressed</u> dissent ruthlessly.

- ○ to establish their authority, and they suppressed
- ○ that established their authority, and it suppressed
- ○ of establishing their authority and to suppress
- ○ to establish their authority, and they were suppressing
- ○ so that their authority was established, and it suppressed

STEP 1: READ THE ORIGINAL SENTENCE CAREFULLY, LOOKING FOR ERRORS

The revolution's leaders committed violent acts for the purpose of establishing their authority—"to establish their authority"—and they also suppressed dissent. The infinitive form "to establish" is idiomatically correct, the plural pronouns "their" and "they" correctly refer to "leaders," and "suppressed" is in the correct past tense to be parallel with "resorted" in the first clause. The various elements of the sentence are logically connected to convey the intended meaning, and there do not appear to be any errors. Suspect that **(A)** is correct as you evaluate the choices.

STEP 2: SCAN AND GROUP THE ANSWER CHOICES

(A), **(B)**, and **(E)** all end with the past tense "suppressed," while **(C)** and **(D)** use different tenses.

STEP 3: ELIMINATE CHOICES UNTIL ONLY ONE REMAINS

Eliminate **(C)** and **(D)** for using the wrong verb at the end. By changing "of establishing" to "to establish" and "suppressed" to "to suppress," **(C)** changes the structure of the sentence; this incorrectly transforms the suppression of dissent from an independent action to another effect of the executions. **(D)** uses the past progressive "were suppressing," which would only be correct to describe an action that was ongoing when another action happened; the leaders "resorted" to violence and "suppressed" dissent in the same time frame, and both take the simple past tense.

(B) and **(E)** both use the incorrect singular pronoun "it" to refer to the plural "leaders." As written, these sentences seem to say that the leaders' "authority" suppressed dissent, but it was the leaders themselves who did so. In addition, **(E)**'s "so that their authority was established" is unnecessarily in passive voice. **(A)** is correct.

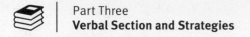
44. (B)

Either stocks or bonds have advantages: stocks can increase in value and give investors more income over time, while bonds can not only provide predictable income but also are guarantees of the return of investors' principal.

○ Either stocks or bonds have advantages: stocks can increase in value and give investors more income over time, while bonds can not only provide predictable income but also are guarantees of

○ Both stocks and bonds have advantages: stocks can increase in value and give investors more income over time, while bonds can not only provide predictable income but also guarantee

○ Both stocks have advantages and so do bonds: stocks can increase in value and give investors more income over time, while bonds not only can provide predictable income but also guarantee

○ Advantages are to be had from either stocks or from bonds: stocks can increase in value and give investors more income over time, while bonds can not only provide predictable income but also guarantee

○ Both stocks and bonds have advantages: stocks can increase in value and give investors more income over time, while bonds can not only provide predictable income but also can guarantee

STEP 1: READ THE ORIGINAL SENTENCE CAREFULLY, LOOKING FOR ERRORS

The underlined text contains two issues. The coordinate conjunction "not only…but also" requires what follows each part to be in parallel form. Here, the author has written "not only provide…but also are guarantees of," which is not parallel. The other problem is one of logical connection. The first clause before the colon indicates that either stocks or bonds, but not both, have advantages. However, what follows the colon describes advantages of both types of investments. Therefore, the "either…or" conjunction is an illogical connector. The right answer will fix both problems.

STEP 2: SCAN AND GROUP THE ANSWER CHOICES

One way to group the choices is by whether they use "either…or" or "both…and" in the first clause. **(A)** says "[e]ither…or," and **(D)** also uses this phrasing, though burying it a little deeper in the sentence. **(B)**, **(C)**, and **(E)** begin with "[b]oth stocks and bonds."

STEP 3: ELIMINATE CHOICES UNTIL ONLY ONE REMAINS

Eliminate **(A)** for the errors identified in step 1. Eliminate **(D)** for also using "either…or" and for violating parallelism. In "from either stocks or from bonds," the word "from" changes position with respect to the conjunctions—it's before "either" in the first part but after "or" in the second part. In addition, this choice rephrases the initial clause in a needlessly passive way.

The "both…and" construction needs to be parallel. **(C)**'s "[b]oth stocks have advantages and so do bonds" puts the first part in noun-verb order ("stocks have") and the second part in verb-noun order ("do bonds"), so this is incorrect. **(B)** and **(E)** are identical until near the end. **(E)** has "bonds *can not only provide* predictable income *but also can guarantee*"; the position of "can" moves with respect to the conjunction, so this is not parallel. Eliminate **(E)** and read **(B)** into the sentence to confirm it's correct:

Both stocks and bonds have advantages: stocks can increase in value and give investors more income over time, while bonds can not only provide predictable income but also guarantee the return of investors' principal.

Sentence Correction: Putting It All Together

This quiz is designed to give you practice with a mix of Sentence Correction questions, just like the variety of Sentence Correction questions you'll see on Test Day. Take this quiz after you have studied the different types of grammar and usage issues that show up in Sentence Correction and practiced applying the Kaplan Method for Sentence Correction.

How to Take This Quiz

By the time you take this quiz, you are hopefully well on your way to mastery of Sentence Correction, so set a timer. Give yourself 1 minute per question. So if you do all 15 questions in this set at once, set the timer for 15 minutes; if you decide to do fewer questions than that in one sitting, set the timer accordingly.

Make sure to use the steps of the Kaplan Method on every question. Students are often drawn into reading through the original sentence and all the choices from beginning to end, giving every word and phrase equal weight. Instead, use a mental checklist of GMAT-tested errors, based on the errors taught in the previous chapter, to focus your reading on potential problems with the sentence.

Furthermore, remember that on Test Day, you can't skip forward and back between questions, so challenge yourself to do the questions in order.

After you've finished the quiz and are reviewing the explanations, make sure you can explain why each wrong answer is incorrect. Being able to clearly identify the errors of grammar and usage in the four wrong choices will help you avoid picking them.

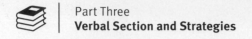
In addition, if you missed a question, understand *why* you missed it. There is always a reason! The Kaplan Method can be a useful checklist to diagnose where you went wrong.

- Were you unable to identify the error in the original sentence or recognize that there was no error?

- Did you have difficulty scanning the answer choices and grouping them in a meaningful way?

- When seeking to eliminate choices, did you have to rely on what "sounded wrong" rather than being able to point to an error that definitely made the choice wrong?

If you know why you missed a question, you can avoid making that error again.

Above all, be patient with yourself. If you make a mistake, feeling bad about it will not improve your score. Just learn from it and make a plan to address whatever skill or knowledge you still need through more study and practice. Want more questions? Check out the Sentence Correction quizzes and Qbank questions in your online resources.

GO ONLINE

kaptest.com/login

Sentence Correction Quiz

1. <u>The private companies that managed airport screening during the twentieth century</u> allowed travelers to bring a considerable variety of items through the security checkpoint, did not focus as much on travelers' physical or behavioral characteristics as on security risk factors, and did not maintain terrorism watch lists.

   ○ The private companies that managed airport screening during the twentieth century

   ○ Managing airport screening during the twentieth century, there were private companies that

   ○ Private companies during the twentieth century, which managed airport screening,

   ○ During the twentieth century, the airport screening that was managed by private companies

   ○ Private companies managed airport screening during the twentieth century, which

2. Completed in 1951 and designated a National Historic Landmark in 2006, <u>the International Style of architecture is prominently exemplified by the Farnsworth House, which was designed by Ludwig Mies van der Rohe.</u>

   ○ the International Style of architecture is prominently exemplified by the Farnsworth House, which was designed by Ludwig Mies van der Rohe

   ○ Ludwig Mies van der Rohe designed the Farnsworth House, a prominent example for the International Style of architecture

   ○ Ludwig Mies van der Rohe has designed the Farnsworth House, a prominent example of the International Style of architecture

   ○ the Farnsworth House was designed by Ludwig Mies van der Rohe and serves as a prominent example of the International Style of architecture

   ○ the Farnsworth House was prominently exemplified by the International Style of architecture, which was designed by Ludwig Mies van der Rohe

3. While the *deus ex machina*, a plot device involving a sudden and unlikely resolution to a seemingly unsolvable problem, has often been ridiculed for being contrived and unartistic, <u>they have, on occasion, been used effectively, according to some critics.</u>

   ○ they have, on occasion, been used effectively, according to some critics

   ○ they have occasionally been used effectively, according to some critics

   ○ it occasionally, according to some critics, has been used effectively

   ○ according to some critics, and effectively, as it has been occasionally used

   ○ it has, according to some critics, occasionally being used effectively

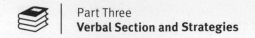

4. Inspired by the circumstances he witnessed and documented during the Polish-Soviet War of 1920, Isaac Babel wrote *Red Cavalry*, a short story collection that is filled, as <u>are many of Babel's writings, of</u> brutal and often horrific depictions of war.

   ○ are many of Babel's writings, of

   ○ are many of Babel's writings, with

   ○ Babel did in many of his writings, of

   ○ many of Babel's writings did, with

   ○ was done in many of Babel's writings, of

5. On the Scottish island of Uist, conservationists have spent many years working on plans <u>for trapping European hedgehogs, which are</u> invasive to Uist and have been blamed for reducing the population of several wading birds, and relocate them to the mainland.

   ○ for trapping European hedgehogs, which are

   ○ for the trapping of European hedgehogs, which are

   ○ to trap European hedgehogs, being

   ○ to trap European hedgehogs, which are

   ○ to trap European hedgehogs,

6. Many scholars dismiss the view that Hephaestus, son of Zeus and god of fire, is to Greek mythology <u>just like Thor, son of Odin and god of thunder, is to</u> Norse mythology, despite observations that both deities are typically depicted wielding a hammer.

   ○ just like Thor, son of Odin and god of thunder, is to

   ○ the same as Thor, son of Odin and god of thunder, relates to

   ○ what Thor, son of Odin and god of thunder, is to

   ○ as Thor, son of Odin and god of thunder, is part of

   ○ the way that Thor is, as son of Odin and god of thunder, to

7. <u>In 2017, completing the journey in six less days than was previously done, the record for sailing around the world alone was broken by French sailor François Gabart.</u>

    ○ In 2017, completing the journey in six less days than was previously done, the record for sailing around the world alone was broken by French sailor François Gabart.

    ○ Completing the journey in six fewer days than was previously done, the record for sailing around the world alone in 2017 was broken by French sailor François Gabart.

    ○ Completing the journey in six fewer days than the previous record, the record for sailing around the world alone was broken by French sailor François Gabart in 2017.

    ○ In 2017, completing the journey in six fewer days than the previous record holder, French sailor François Gabart broke the record for sailing around the world alone.

    ○ In 2017, completing the journey in six less days than the previous record, French sailor François Gabart broke the record for sailing around the world alone.

8. In a standard crossword puzzle, the black boxes are placed to make the grid diagonally symmetric, and each empty box gets filled with a single letter that is <u>part of both an across word, which is entered horizontally, and of a down word, which is</u> entered vertically.

    ○ part of both an across word, which is entered horizontally, and of a down word, which is

    ○ part of both an across word, which is entered horizontally, and a down word, which is

    ○ part of both an across word entered horizontally and of a down word

    ○ both part of an across word entered horizontally and of a down word

    ○ both part of an across word entered horizontally as well as a down word

9. Brand management in the personal care industry, <u>like any industry, is the art of defining consumer perceptions of the utility and value promised by the product line</u> and the personality projected by the company.

    ○ like any industry, is the art of defining consumer perceptions of the utility and value promised by the product line

    ○ similar to how any industry does it, is the art of defining consumer perceptions of the utility and value promised by the product line

    ○ like brand management in any industry, is the artistic defining of consumer perceptions of the product line's promises of utility and value

    ○ as in any industry, is artfully defining consumer perceptions of the utility and value promised by the product line

    ○ as in any industry, is the art of defining consumer perceptions of the utility and value promised by the product line

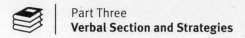
10. The principle residence of French royalty from 1682 to 1789, the Palace of Versailles is now one of the most frequently visited historic monuments in Europe and is often celebrated for its impressive Baroque <u>architecture, the extravagant decor in such rooms as the the Hall of Mirrors, and the</u> elaborate and expansive gardens that surround the palace.

   ○ architecture, the extravagant decor in such rooms as the Hall of Mirrors, and the

   ○ architecture, for the extravagant decor in such rooms as the Hall of Mirrors, and it has

   ○ architecture, the extravagant decor in such rooms as the Hall of Mirrors, and for having

   ○ architecture and extravagant decor in such rooms as the Hall of Mirrors, also having

   ○ architecture as well as for having extravagant decor in such rooms as the Hall of Mirrors, and the

11. Like some humans, some adult cats lack a sufficient quantity of the enzyme lactase to digest milk; as a result of drinking <u>it, such cats become sick, as evidenced by their</u> vomiting or excreting diarrhea or gas.

   ○ it, such cats become sick, as evidenced by their

   ○ milk, such cats become sick, as evidenced by its

   ○ milk, such cats become sick, as evidenced by those cats'

   ○ it, they become sick, as evidenced by their

   ○ milk, such cats become sick, as evidenced by their

12. Since 2007, the Department of Defense has maintained a program designed to investigate unidentified flying objects, <u>despite the views of many scientists who considered</u> that these phenomena will be found to have natural explanations.

   ○ despite the views of many scientists who considered

   ○ despite the views of many scientists who consider

   ○ despite the views of many scientists believe

   ○ despite the views of many scientists who believe

   ○ although scientists believed

13. The rise of alternative funding opportunities, such as microloans, crowdfunding, and peer-to-peer networks, <u>have enabled many small entrepreneurs to rapidly grow successful companies specializing in products that are of interest only to niche markets</u>.

    ○ have enabled many small entrepreneurs to rapidly grow successful companies specializing in products that are of interest only to niche markets

    ○ have enabled many small entrepreneurs to rapidly grow successful companies only specializing in products that are of interest to niche markets

    ○ has enabled many small entrepreneurs to rapidly grow successful companies specializing in products that are of interest only to niche markets

    ○ has enabled many small entrepreneurs to rapidly grow only successful companies specializing in products that are of interest to niche markets

    ○ has enabled many small entrepreneurs to grow successful companies specializing rapidly in products that are of interest only to niche markets

14. Nina Simone, <u>whose distinctive technique is credited as to her early classical training, is known to be famous for</u> her renditions of blues, jazz, and folk compositions as well as for her impassioned civil rights activism.

    ○ whose distinctive technique is credited as to her early classical training, is known to be famous for

    ○ whose distinctive technique is credited to her early classical training, is known for

    ○ who had a distinctive technique that is credited with her early classical training, is known for

    ○ credited with a distinctive technique due to her early classical training, is known for

    ○ who is credited to her early classical training on account of her technique, is famously known as

15. Despite rising interest rates, real estate sales in the neighborhood this summer were <u>5 percent higher than they were last summer</u>.

    ○ 5 percent higher than they were last summer

    ○ 5 percent higher than last summer

    ○ 5 percent more than last summer was

    ○ higher than 5 percent last summer

    ○ more than 5 percent higher last summer

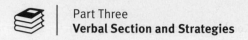

Answer Key

Sentence Correction Quiz

1. A	6. C	11. E
2. D	7. D	12. D
3. C	8. B	13. C
4. B	9. E	14. B
5. D	10. A	15. A

Answers and Explanations

Sentence Correction Quiz

1. **(A)**

   The private companies that managed airport screening during the twentieth century allowed travelers to bring a considerable variety of items through the security checkpoint, did not focus as much on travelers' physical or behavioral characteristics as on security risk factors, and did not maintain terrorism watch lists.

   ○ The private companies that managed airport screening during the twentieth century

   ○ Managing airport screening during the twentieth century, there were private companies that

   ○ Private companies during the twentieth century, which managed airport screening,

   ○ During the twentieth century, the airport screening that was managed by private companies

   ○ Private companies managed airport screening during the twentieth century, which

STEP 1: READ THE ORIGINAL SENTENCE CAREFULLY, LOOKING FOR ERRORS

The underlined text "that managed airport screening" appropriately modifies "private companies," telling which private companies are being discussed. Then "during the twentieth century" correctly modifies "managed airport screening," telling when this action occurred. The verb "managed" is correctly in the simple past tense, and there are no other issues. Suspect that (**A**) is correct but skim the other choices in case you overlooked an error.

STEP 2: SCAN AND GROUP THE ANSWER CHOICES

As is common in questions that test modification, each choice arranges the elements differently. Suspect that some modifiers will not be near the thing they modify. There is no effective way to group these choices, so just proceed to evaluate them one by one.

STEP 3: ELIMINATE CHOICES UNTIL ONLY ONE REMAINS

In (**B**), the passive construction "there were" leaves unclear what was managing airport screening. This sentence loses the original's clear, direct connection between the private companies and their function. (**C**) makes it sound as though either all private companies in the twentieth century managed airport screening or the twentieth century managed airport screening. Either reading is illogical. (**D**) opts for the less preferred passive voice and, in the process, says that the airport screening itself did various things. However, as the original sentence makes clear, the *companies* that ran the screening set various policies; it's not right to say the screening itself did these things. Finally, (**E**) says that the twentieth century performed the list of actions; eliminate (**E**). Choice (**A**) is indeed correct.

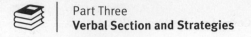

2.   (D)

Completed in 1951 and designated a National Historic Landmark in 2006, <u>the International Style of architecture is prominently exemplified by the Farnsworth House, which was designed by Ludwig Mies van der Rohe</u>.

- ○   the International Style of architecture is prominently exemplified by the Farnsworth House, which was designed by Ludwig Mies van der Rohe
- ○   Ludwig Mies van der Rohe designed the Farnsworth House, a prominent example for the International Style of architecture
- ○   Ludwig Mies van der Rohe has designed the Farnsworth House, a prominent example of the International Style of architecture
- ○   the Farnsworth House was designed by Ludwig Mies van der Rohe and serves as a prominent example of the International Style of architecture
- ○   the Farnsworth House was prominently exemplified by the International Style of architecture, which was designed by Ludwig Mies van der Rohe

STEP 1: READ THE ORIGINAL SENTENCE CAREFULLY, LOOKING FOR ERRORS

The underlined portion is preceded by a modifying phrase. An opening modifier should be followed immediately by the person or object being modified. However, the underlined portion makes that "the International Style of architecture." But that wasn't completed and designated a landmark—the Farnsworth House was. The underlined phrase should begin with "the Farnsworth House."

STEP 2: SCAN AND GROUP THE ANSWER CHOICES

(A) starts with the International Style. **(B)** and **(C)** change the opening to Ludwig Mies van der Rohe. And **(D)** and **(E)** change the opening to the Farnsworth House.

STEP 3: ELIMINATE CHOICES UNTIL ONLY ONE REMAINS

(A), **(B)**, and **(C)** can be eliminated for putting the wrong subject immediately after the opening modifier. Furthermore, **(B)** uses the idiomatically incorrect phrase "example for" instead of "example of." And **(C)** uses the present perfect "has designed" for something that was completed in 1951.

(D) and **(E)** provide the right noun after the opening modifier, but **(E)** flips the logic of the sentence. **(E)** suggests that the architectural style is an example of the house, and it also suggests that Mies van der Rohe designed the architectural style instead of the house. Eliminate **(E)**. **(D)** is the correct answer. To confirm this, read it back into the original sentence:

Completed in 1951 and designated a National Historic Landmark in 2006, <u>the Farnsworth House was designed by Ludwig Mies van der Rohe and serves as a prominent example of the International Style of architecture</u>.

3. (C)

While the *deus ex machina*, a plot device involving a sudden and unlikely resolution to a seemingly unsolvable problem, has often been ridiculed for being contrived and unartistic, <u>they have, on occasion, been used effectively, according to some critics</u>.

- ○ they have, on occasion, been used effectively, according to some critics
- ○ they have occasionally been used effectively, according to some critics
- ○ it occasionally, according to some critics, has been used effectively
- ○ according to some critics, and effectively, as it has been occasionally used
- ○ it has, according to some critics, occasionally being used effectively

STEP 1: READ THE ORIGINAL SENTENCE CAREFULLY, LOOKING FOR ERRORS

The underlined portion is the primary sentence, with the first portion being an extended modifying phrase. The modifying phrase is talking about a plot device called *deus ex machina*. However, when the underlined portion starts, it refers to that singular item with a plural pronoun (they). That needs to be changed. (If the phrase *deus ex machina* is unfamiliar, there are clues in the non-underlined portion to indicate its singular nature. First, it is referred to as "a plot device." Also, the verb "has...been ridiculed" is in the singular form.)

STEP 2: SCAN AND GROUP THE ANSWER CHOICES

(A) and (B) begin with "they," while (C) and (E) begin with "it." (D) moves the subject of the sentence but eventually uses "it."

STEP 3: ELIMINATE CHOICES UNTIL ONLY ONE REMAINS

(A) and (D) can be eliminated for using the word "they" to refer to the singular subject. The remaining choices properly change the pronoun to "it." However, (D) moves the phrases around and, with the word "and," puts the modifier "effectively" in the same series with "contrived and unartistic." The positive descriptor "effectively" needs to be contrasted with the negative descriptors, so (D) can be eliminated. By substituting "being used" for "been used," (E) fails to provide an active verb to connect with "has," leaving the sentence incomplete. Eliminate (E). That leaves (C) as the correct answer. To be sure, read it back into the original sentence:

While the *deus ex machina*, a plot device involving a sudden and unlikely resolution to a seemingly unsolvable problem, has often been ridiculed for being contrived and unartistic, <u>it occasionally, according to some critics, has been used effectively</u>.

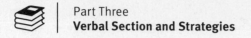

4.   **(B)**

Inspired by the circumstances he witnessed and documented during the Polish-Soviet War of 1920, Isaac Babel wrote *Red Cavalry*, a short story collection that is filled, as <u>are many of Babel's writings, of</u> brutal and often horrific depictions of war.

- ○   are many of Babel's writings, of
- ○   are many of Babel's writings, with
- ○   Babel did in many of his writings, of
- ○   many of Babel's writings did, with
- ○   was done in many of Babel's writings, of

STEP 1: READ THE ORIGINAL SENTENCE CAREFULLY, LOOKING FOR ERRORS

The underlined portion contains the verb "are," which correctly refers to Babel's writings. The word "as" indicates a comparison, which is logically drawn (the one book is filled in the same way as other writings are). However, the last word of the underlined portion is "of," which is connected to the verb "filled." That's the wrong idiomatic expression. A book is filled *with* certain details, not filled *of* those details.

STEP 2: SCAN AND GROUP THE ANSWER CHOICES

The beginning of each choice does not allow for easy grouping. However, **(A)**, **(C)**, and **(E)** all end with "of," while **(B)** and **(D)** end with "with."

STEP 3: ELIMINATE CHOICES UNTIL ONLY ONE REMAINS

(A) can be eliminated for using the word "of" instead of "with." **(C)** contains the same error and changes the wording of the modifying phrase, shifting the action from passive (the book is filled) to active (Babel filled his other books). That's not parallel. Eliminate **(C)**. And the wordier passiveness of **(E)** does not make up for the improper use of "of" at the end. Eliminate **(E)**.

(B) and **(D)** change the "of" to "with," but **(D)** changes the modifying phrase to make it sound as if Babel's writings *did* something, which they didn't. The writings didn't fill themselves. That eliminates **(D)**, leaving **(B)** as the correct answer. To confirm, read it back into the original sentence:

Inspired by the circumstances he witnessed and documented during the Polish-Soviet War of 1920, Isaac Babel wrote *Red Cavalry*, a short story collection that is filled, as <u>are many of Babel's writings, with</u> brutal and often horrific depictions of war.

5. (D)

On the Scottish island of Uist, conservationists have spent many years working on plans <u>for trapping European hedgehogs, which are</u> invasive to Uist and have been blamed for reducing the population of several wading birds, and relocate them to the mainland.

- ○ for trapping European hedgehogs, which are
- ○ for the trapping of European hedgehogs, which are
- ○ to trap European hedgehogs, being
- ○ to trap European hedgehogs, which are
- ○ to trap European hedgehogs,

STEP 1: READ THE ORIGINAL SENTENCE CAREFULLY, LOOKING FOR ERRORS

The underlined portion begins with "for trapping European hedgehogs," which is the first of two actions that are part of the conservationists' plan. The second action comes at the end of the sentence: "relocate them." (To see this two-part construction, it may help to read the sentence without the modifying "which…" clause between commas.) However, "for trapping" and "relocate" are not parallel. Furthermore, the phrase "plans for trapping" is incorrect. Idiomatically, it's proper to say *plans to do something* instead of *plans for doing something*.

STEP 2: SCAN AND GROUP THE ANSWER CHOICES

(A) and (B) use "for trapping," while (C), (D), and (E) use "to trap."

STEP 3: ELIMINATE CHOICES UNTIL ONLY ONE REMAINS

Eliminate (A) for using "for trapping," which is idiomatically incorrect and not parallel to "relocate" at the end. (B) adds some unnecessary words that do nothing to fix either issue. Eliminate (B).

(C), (D), and (E) begin with "to trap," which properly creates the parallel construction "plans to trap… and relocate." However, (C) changes "which are" to "being." This creates the phrase "being invasive… and have been blamed," which is not parallel. Eliminate (C). And (E) removes the verb altogether, creating the phrase "invasive… and have been blamed." That's an illogical combination of an adjective and a verb. Eliminate (E). (D) remains and is the correct answer. Read it back into the original sentence to confirm:

On the Scottish island of Uist, conservationists have spent many years working on plans <u>to trap European hedgehogs, which are</u> invasive to Uist and have been blamed for reducing the population of several wading birds, and relocate them to the mainland.

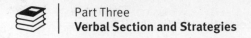
6. **(C)**

Many scholars dismiss the view that Hephaestus, son of Zeus and god of fire, is to Greek mythology just like Thor, son of Odin and god of thunder, is to Norse mythology, despite observations that both deities are typically depicted wielding a hammer.

- ○ just like Thor, son of Odin and god of thunder, is to
- ○ the same as Thor, son of Odin and god of thunder, relates to
- ○ what Thor, son of Odin and god of thunder, is to
- ○ as Thor, son of Odin and god of thunder, is part of
- ○ the way that Thor is, as son of Odin and god of thunder, to

STEP 1: READ THE ORIGINAL SENTENCE CAREFULLY, LOOKING FOR ERRORS

The underlined portion begins with "just like," which suggests a comparison. Before that, the sentence uses the structure *A is to B* (Hephaestus is to Greek mythology). However, the construct *A is to B just like C is to D* is not idiomatically correct. Instead of "just like," the word "what" is needed.

STEP 2: SCAN AND GROUP THE ANSWER CHOICES

Each choice begins with a different phrase, so there is no effective way to group the choices. Evaluate them one at a time.

STEP 3: ELIMINATE CHOICES UNTIL ONLY ONE REMAINS

(A) can be eliminated because "just like" is idiomatically incorrect. **(B)** and **(E)** can be eliminated for changing "just like" to "the same as" and "the way that," respectively, neither of which creates a correct idiomatic expression. Furthermore, **(B)** removes parallelism by changing the end from "is" to "relates to." **(E)** disrupts the parallelism by moving the placement of the modifying phrase ("as son of Odin and god of thunder"); also, the addition of "as" in this phrase is unnecessary and unparallel. **(D)** replaces "just like" with "as," which can be used in certain circumstances. However, **(D)** ultimately fails by changing the ending to "is part of," which is not parallel to the first half of the comparison. Eliminate **(D)**. That makes **(C)**, the only answer to properly create the *A is to B what C is to D* pattern without adding any new errors, the correct answer. To confirm, read it back into the original sentence:

Many scholars dismiss the view that Hephaestus, son of Zeus and god of fire, is to Greek mythology what Thor, son of Odin and god of thunder, is to Norse mythology, despite observations that both deities are typically depicted wielding a hammer.

7. (D)

In 2017, completing the journey in six less days than was previously done, the record for sailing around the world alone was broken by French sailor François Gabart.

- In 2017, completing the journey in six less days than was previously done, the record for sailing around the world alone was broken by French sailor François Gabart.

- Completing the journey in six fewer days than was previously done, the record for sailing around the world alone in 2017 was broken by French sailor François Gabart.

- Completing the journey in six fewer days than the previous record, the record for sailing around the world alone was broken by French sailor François Gabart in 2017.

- In 2017, completing the journey in six fewer days than the previous record holder, French sailor François Gabart broke the record for sailing around the world alone.

- In 2017, completing the journey in six less days than the previous record, French sailor François Gabart broke the record for sailing around the world alone.

STEP 1: READ THE ORIGINAL SENTENCE CAREFULLY, LOOKING FOR ERRORS

The original sentence contains several errors. An efficient approach when a large amount of text is underlined is to focus on one error, evaluate the choices, and then proceed to the next error. Because days are countable, the sentence should state that the journey was completed in six *fewer* days.

STEP 2: SCAN AND GROUP THE ANSWER CHOICES

There's a 3-2 split between (B), (C), and (D), which use "fewer," and (A) and (E), which use "less."

STEP 3: ELIMINATE CHOICES UNTIL ONLY ONE REMAINS

Since you identified "less" as an error in step 1, eliminate (A) and (E). To evaluate the three remaining answer choices, consider the modifying phrase between commas, "completing the journey... done." It must refer to the first noun that follows the phrase, but "the record" did not complete the journey; it was François Gabart as written in (D). Eliminate (B) and (C) for committing this error. (D) is correct.

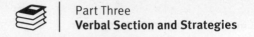
8. **(B)**

In a standard crossword puzzle, the black boxes are placed to make the grid diagonally symmetric, and each empty box gets filled with a single letter that is <u>part of both an across word, which is entered horizontally, and of a down word, which is</u> entered vertically.

○   part of both an across word, which is entered horizontally, and of a down word, which is

○   part of both an across word, which is entered horizontally, and a down word, which is

○   part of both an across word entered horizontally and of a down word

○   both part of an across word entered horizontally and of a down word

○   both part of an across word entered horizontally as well as a down word

STEP 1: READ THE ORIGINAL SENTENCE CAREFULLY, LOOKING FOR ERRORS

The underlined portion contains the word "both." When listing two items, the word "both" should be paired with the word "and" (*both X and Y*), and the two items should be presented in parallel form. The word "and" is used properly, but the structure is not parallel. There's already an "of" before "both," so the "of" distributes to both items. There's no reason to repeat the "of" before "a down word." It should be "part of both an across word… and a down word."

STEP 2: SCAN AND GROUP THE ANSWER CHOICES

(A), **(B)**, and **(C)** start with "part of both," while **(D)** and **(E)** start with "both part of." Either arrangement could work, so the correction will be made elsewhere in the choices. Furthermore, grouping by other parts of the choices can be counterproductive because the correct format will be based on how the underlined portion starts.

STEP 3: ELIMINATE CHOICES UNTIL ONLY ONE REMAINS

(A) is eliminated for repeating the "of" and making a non-parallel *part of both X and of Y* structure. It should be *part of both X and Y*, without the added "of." **(C)** contains the same problematic "of," so **(C)** can be eliminated. **(B)** makes the quick fix by getting rid of the offending "of." To make sure this is the correct answer, confirm that the remaining choices have errors.

(D) and **(E)** move the phrase "part of" to after the word "both." That would be fine, as long as there were still parallelism. The rest of the sentence would have to read: *both part of X and part of Y*. However, **(D)** leaves out the second "part," reading "a single letter is of a down word" instead of "a single letter is *part* of a down word." Then **(E)** leaves out "part of" entirely while also creating the structure *both X . . . as well as Y*, which is not idiomatically correct. The conjunction is *both X . . . and Y*. **(D)** and **(E)** can be eliminated, confirming **(B)** as the correct answer. As a final step, read it back into the original sentence:

In a standard crossword puzzle, the black boxes are placed to make the grid diagonally symmetric, and each empty box gets filled with a single letter that is <u>part of both an across word, which is entered horizontally, and a down word, which is</u> entered vertically.

9.   **(E)**

Brand management in the personal care industry, <u>like any industry, is the art of defining consumer perceptions of the utility and value promised by the product line</u> and the personality projected by the company.

○   like any industry, is the art of defining consumer perceptions of the utility and value promised by the product line

○   similar to how any industry does it, is the art of defining consumer perceptions of the utility and value promised by the product line

○   like brand management in any industry, is the artistic defining of consumer perceptions of the product line's promises of utility and value

○   as in any industry, is artfully defining consumer perceptions of the utility and value promised by the product line

○   as in any industry, is the art of defining consumer perceptions of the utility and value promised by the product line

STEP 1: SCAN THE ANSWER CHOICES, LOOKING FOR CLUES

The word "like" that begins the underlined portion of the sentence indicates that the sentence is comparing two things. Comparisons must be logical and parallel. Here, "[b]rand management" should logically be compared to some kind of management, but instead it is compared to "any industry."

STEP 2: READ THE ORIGINAL SENTENCE CAREFULLY, LOOKING FOR ERRORS

(A) and **(C)** start with "like," **(D)** and **(E)** start with "as in," and **(B)** starts with "similar to."

STEP 3: GROUP THE CHOICES AND ELIMINATE UNTIL ONLY ONE REMAINS

Eliminate **(A)** for the errors identified in step 1. **(C)** starts with "like" as **(A)** does, but it solves the comparison problem by inserting the term "brand management" into the second part of the comparison. However, when one thing "is" another, the two things must be expressed in parallel form, and "[b]rand management... is the artistic defining" is not parallel. Eliminate **(C)**. **(B)** substitutes "similar to" for "like" but still doesn't compare "management" to management, so it's incorrect.

(D) and **(E)** solve the comparison problem by using "as" to compare how brand management is in one industry to how brand management is in any industry. However, **(D)** breaks parallelism after the comma with "[b]rand management... is artfully defining," since "brand management" is a regular noun while "defining" is an *-ing* verb form acting as a noun. **(E)** uses the same noun form in both parts of the structure—"brand management... is the art"—so it is correct. Read it back into the sentence to confirm:

Brand management in the personal care industry, <u>as in any industry, is the art of defining consumer perceptions of the utility and value promised by the product line</u> and the personality projected by the company.

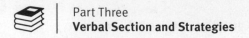

10. (A)

The principle residence of French royalty from 1682 to 1789, the Palace of Versailles is now one of the most frequently visited historic monuments in Europe and is often celebrated for its impressive Baroque <u>architecture, the extravagant decor in such rooms as the the Hall of Mirrors, and the</u> elaborate and expansive gardens that surround the palace.

○ architecture, the extravagant decor in such rooms as the Hall of Mirrors, and the

○ architecture, for the extravagant decor in such rooms as the Hall of Mirrors, and it has

○ architecture, the extravagant decor in such rooms as the Hall of Mirrors, and for having

○ architecture and extravagant decor in such rooms as the Hall of Mirrors, also having

○ architecture as well as for having extravagant decor in such rooms as the Hall of Mirrors, and the

STEP 1: READ THE ORIGINAL SENTENCE CAREFULLY, LOOKING FOR ERRORS

In the underlined portion, the sentence is listing features of the Palace of Versailles that are often celebrated. When items are listed, they should be in parallel form. In this case, there are three features: architecture, decor, and gardens. Each is described by at least one adjective (impressive Baroque; extravagant; elaborate and expansive), so everything is consistent. There appears to be no error.

STEP 2: SCAN AND GROUP THE ANSWER CHOICES

(A), **(B)**, and **(C)** have a comma after "architecture," creating a list. **(D)** and **(E)** remove the comma, creating a combined element of architecture and decor.

STEP 3: ELIMINATE CHOICES UNTIL ONLY ONE REMAINS

(B) and **(C)** both keep the list format of the original sentence. However, **(B)** adds "for" and "it has," creating a for X..., for Y..., and it has Z structure that is not parallel. Eliminate **(B)**. Similarly, **(C)** adds "for" to the end, creating a for X..., Y..., and for Z structure. That extra "for" leaves the middle item nonparallel, so **(C)** can be eliminated.

(D) and **(E)** change the structure completely, combining the architecture and decor components. This unnecessarily separates the third component (the gardens), a phrasing that would technically be okay if the choices didn't also contain grammatical errors. **(D)** leaves the final portion dangling at the end with the verb "having," which has no clear subject and is not parallel to anything else in the sentence. And **(E)** starts the last phrase with "and the...," creating a whole new clause that fails to include an active verb. **(D)** and **(E)** are eliminated, confirming that the sentence was correct as written. **(A)** is the correct answer.

11. (E)

Like some humans, some adult cats lack a sufficient quantity of the enzyme lactase to digest milk; as a result of drinking <u>it, such cats become sick, as evidenced by their</u> vomiting or excreting diarrhea or gas.

- ○ it, such cats become sick, as evidenced by their
- ○ milk, such cats become sick, as evidenced by its
- ○ milk, such cats become sick, as evidenced by those cats'
- ○ it, they become sick, as evidenced by their
- ○ milk, such cats become sick, as evidenced by their

STEP 1: READ THE ORIGINAL SENTENCE CAREFULLY, LOOKING FOR ERRORS

The underlined text begins with the pronoun "it," which could refer to either "lactase" or "milk." The pronoun is thus ambiguous. Read on for other errors or potential errors to watch for in the answer choices. The last underlined word is another pronoun, "their." This clearly refers to "cats" and is correct.

STEP 2: SCAN AND GROUP THE ANSWER CHOICES

Like **(A)**, **(D)** begins with the pronoun "it." **(B)**, **(C)**, and **(E)** begin with the noun "milk."

STEP 3: ELIMINATE CHOICES UNTIL ONLY ONE REMAINS

Since **(D)** repeats **(A)**'s error by using the ambiguous pronoun "it," eliminate both choices.

To compare **(B)**, **(C)**, and **(E)**, note how their endings differ from each other: **(B)** says "its," **(C)** says "those cats," and **(E)** says "their." Since the author's intent is to say that *cats* experience various signs of illness after drinking milk, eliminate **(B)** for inappropriately referring to only one cat. And since the text that immediately follows the semicolon refers to "such cats" becoming sick, clearly indicating *the cats without enough lactase to digest milk*, the phrase "those cats" in **(C)** is unnecessarily repetitive. The more concise "their" in **(E)** can refer only to the sick cats and thus is unambiguous. Eliminate **(C)** and read **(E)** into the sentence to confirm that it is correct:

Like some humans, some adult cats lack a sufficient quantity of the enzyme lactase to digest milk; as a result of drinking <u>milk, such cats become sick, as evidenced by their</u> vomiting or excreting diarrhea or gas.

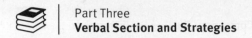

12. **(D)**

Since 2007, the Department of Defense has maintained a program designed to investigate unidentified flying objects, <u>despite the views of many scientists who considered</u> that these phenomena will be found to have natural explanations.

- ○ despite the views of many scientists who considered
- ○ despite the views of many scientists who consider
- ○ despite the views of many scientists believe
- ○ despite the views of many scientists who believe
- ○ although scientists believed

STEP 1: READ THE ORIGINAL SENTENCE CAREFULLY, LOOKING FOR ERRORS

The phrase "[s]ince 2007" is a clue that verb tenses are being tested. "Since 2007" and "has maintained" indicate the program began in the past and is still continuing, so the past tense "considered" at the end of the underlined segment is incorrect. Another issue is the idiomatic usage of "consider." On the GMAT, "consider" is used without a following connecting word or phrase. A correct use of "consider" in this sentence would be *many scientists who consider these phenomena to have natural explanations.*

STEP 2: SCAN AND GROUP THE ANSWER CHOICES

There's a 3-2 split between **(A)** and **(E)**, which use past tense verbs at the end of the underlined segment, and **(B)**, **(C)**, and **(D)**, which use present tense verbs.

STEP 3: ELIMINATE CHOICES UNTIL ONLY ONE REMAINS

(A) and **(E)** can be eliminated for being on the wrong side of the split. Since "that" is not underlined and can't be changed, eliminate **(B)** and seek a choice that doesn't end with a form of the verb "consider." **(C)** incorrectly states "the views… believe…" The *views* don't believe; the *scientists* believe. **(D)** is correct. Confirm this by reading it back into the sentence:

Since 2007, the Department of Defense has maintained a program designed to investigate unidentified flying objects, <u>despite the views of many scientists who believe</u> that these phenomena will be found to have natural explanations.

13. (C)

The rise of alternative funding opportunities, such as microloans, crowdfunding, and peer-to-peer networks, <u>have enabled many small entrepreneurs to rapidly grow successful companies specializing in products that are of interest only to niche markets</u>.

○ have enabled many small entrepreneurs to rapidly grow successful companies specializing in products that are of interest only to niche markets

○ have enabled many small entrepreneurs to rapidly grow successful companies only specializing in products that are of interest to niche markets

○ has enabled many small entrepreneurs to rapidly grow successful companies specializing in products that are of interest only to niche markets

○ has enabled many small entrepreneurs to rapidly grow only successful companies specializing in products that are of interest to niche markets

○ has enabled many small entrepreneurs to grow successful companies specializing rapidly in products that are of interest only to niche markets

STEP 1: READ THE ORIGINAL SENTENCE CAREFULLY, LOOKING FOR ERRORS

The original sentence contains an error in subject-verb agreement. The subject "rise" requires the singular verb "has enabled" at the beginning of the underlined portion, rather than the plural verb "have enabled." This error may be hard to spot with the intervening phrase containing plural nouns, but a vertical scan of the answer choices shows that some use "have" and some use "has," highlighting this verb error.

STEP 2: SCAN AND GROUP THE ANSWER CHOICES

There's a 2-3 split between "have" and "has." **(A)** and **(B)** use the plural verb, while **(C)**, **(D)**, and **(E)** all use the singular verb.

STEP 3: ELIMINATE CHOICES UNTIL ONLY ONE REMAINS

Eliminate **(A)** and **(B)** for being on the wrong side of the split. Read the remaining three choices in parallel. The first difference is in the position of "rapidly." **(E)** moves "rapidly" to describe the rate of specialization instead of the rate of growth, changing the meaning of the sentence; thus, it can be eliminated. Continue reading **(C)** and **(D)**. By placing "only" before "successful companies," **(D)** says that entrepreneurs have started nothing but successful companies, but the intention of the original sentence is that these companies are successful even though their products have limited markets. Reading **(C)** back into the sentence shows that it's correct:

The rise of alternative funding opportunities, such as microloans, crowdfunding, and peer-to-peer networks, <u>has enabled many small entrepreneurs to rapidly grow successful companies specializing in products that are of interest only to niche markets</u>.

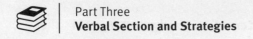
14. (B)

Nina Simone, <u>whose distinctive technique is credited as to her early classical training, is known to be famous for</u> her renditions of blues, jazz, and folk compositions as well as for her impassioned civil rights activism.

○ whose distinctive technique is credited as to her early classical training, is known to be famous for

○ whose distinctive technique is credited to her early classical training, is known for

○ who had a distinctive technique that is credited with her early classical training, is known for

○ credited with a distinctive technique due to her early classical training, is known for

○ who is credited to her early classical training on account of her technique, is famously known as

STEP 1: READ THE ORIGINAL SENTENCE CAREFULLY, LOOKING FOR ERRORS

The underlined portion of the sentence includes an unidiomatic phrase, "credited as to." When a quality of a person is being attributed to a source, the correct form is *credited to*. Here's another example: *He credited his high GMAT score to his diligent study habits.* The original sentence also includes the redundant "known to be famous for." Someone can be *known for* or *famous for* something, but not both.

STEP 2: SCAN AND GROUP THE ANSWER CHOICES

Three choices, **(B)**, **(C)** and **(D)**, use "known for" at the end, while **(A)** and **(E)** use different constructions.

STEP 3: ELIMINATE CHOICES UNTIL ONLY ONE REMAINS

(A) can be eliminated for the errors found in step 1. **(E)** uses "known as," which eliminates the redundancy but introduces an illogical comparison, comparing Simone to her "renditions" of music; it can be eliminated as well. The remaining three choices all correctly use "known for," so check them for other errors. The first part of **(C)** is wordier than the original, and "credited with" gives credit for her classical training to her technique, when the relationship is the other way around. **(D)** rearranges the words to say that Simone is given credit for a distinctive technique because she received classical training; this distorts the original's meaning. **(B)** uses the correct "credited to" and the succinct "known for." This choice is correct, which can be confirmed by reading it back into the sentence:

Nina Simone, <u>whose distinctive technique is credited to her early classical training, is known for</u> her renditions of blues, jazz, and folk compositions as well as for her impassioned civil rights activism.

15. **(A)**

Despite rising interest rates, real estate sales in the neighborhood this summer were <u>5 percent higher than they were last summer</u>.

- ○ 5 percent higher than they were last summer
- ○ 5 percent higher than last summer
- ○ 5 percent more than last summer was
- ○ higher than 5 percent last summer
- ○ more than 5 percent higher last summer

STEP 1: READ THE ORIGINAL SENTENCE CAREFULLY, LOOKING FOR ERRORS

The underlined portion contains a comparison, "higher than," which is idiomatically correct (*X is higher than Y*). In addition, the pronoun "they" makes the comparison parallel and logical: the author compares last summer's sales to this summer's sales. The sentence appears to have no error, so suspect **(A)** is correct. Check the other choices just to confirm you haven't overlooked anything.

STEP 2: SCAN AND GROUP THE ANSWER CHOICES

(A), **(B)**, and **(C)** start with "5 percent," while **(D)** and **(E)** change that to "higher than 5 percent" and "more than 5 percent," respectively.

STEP 3: ELIMINATE CHOICES UNTIL ONLY ONE REMAINS

The first thing being compared is sales from this summer. They should be compared to sales from another time period. **(B)** and **(C)** make the comparison between one season's sales and another season rather than another season's sales. Eliminate **(B)** and **(C)**.

By moving the phrase "higher than," **(D)** suggests that this summer's total sales were over 5%—but 5% of what? Sales should be a figure, not a percentage. Further, this choice suggests that this summer's sales somehow occurred last summer. Eliminate **(D)**. Unlike **(D)**, **(E)** correctly identifies the sales as 5% higher. However, **(E)** still suggests that this summer's increase occurred last summer. Eliminate **(E)**. There was never any error to fix, so the correct answer is **(A)**.

GMAT by the Numbers: Sentence Correction

Now that you've learned how to approach Sentence Correction questions on the GMAT, let's add one more dimension to your understanding of how they work.

Take a moment to try this question. Following is performance data from thousands of people who have studied with Kaplan over the decades. Through analyzing this data, we will show you how to approach questions like this one most effectively and how to avoid similarly tempting wrong answer choice types on Test Day.

The European Union announced that cod and mackerel are the only fish that <u>exceeds their new requirements for dioxin level and that they allow</u> fishermen to catch.

- ○ exceeds their new requirements for dioxin level and that they allow
- ○ exceed its new requirements for dioxin level and that they allow
- ○ exceeds its new requirements for dioxin level and that it allows
- ○ exceed its new requirements for dioxin level and that it allows
- ○ exceed their new requirements for dioxin level and that they allow

Explanation

Attention to the Right Detail and Pattern Recognition are both essential to success on Sentence Correction questions. You want to check the sentence very carefully for errors, giving special consideration to the recurring patterns that the GMAT test maker is so fond of. In this sentence, there are two underlined pronouns plus an underlined verb. Both underlined pronouns, "their" and "they," refer to the European Union, which is a singular noun. These pronouns are therefore incorrect; the sentence should use "its" and "it," respectively. Only **(C)** and **(D)** get both pronouns right, so one of these choices has to be the correct answer. The difference between **(C)** and **(D)** is the use of "exceeds" versus "exceed." Since there are two kinds of fish, "cod and mackerel," you need the plural verb. Choice **(D)** is correct.

Question Statistics

2% of test takers choose **(A)**

6% of test takers choose **(B)**

14% of test takers choose **(C)**

56% of test takers choose **(D)**

22% of test takers choose **(E)**

Sample size = 4,437

Note that the two most popular wrong choices, **(C)** and **(E)**, each correct one of the two errors in the sentence but not both. Many test takers will spot an answer choice that fixes the one mistake they were scanning for and think, "Aha—that's the answer!" and move on without actually reading the answer back into the sentence. The test maker is aware of this tendency. So beware of trap answers that correct just one of two or more errors, as well as trap answers that fix one mistake but introduce another. Always read your choice back into the sentence. It only takes a few seconds and prevents careless mistakes.

More GMAT by the Numbers . . .

To see more questions with answer choice statistics, be sure to review the full-length CATs in your online resources.

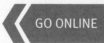
GO ONLINE

kaptest.com/login

PART FOUR

Quantitative Section and Strategies

CHAPTER 15

Quantitative Section Overview

LEARNING OBJECTIVES

After studying this chapter, you will be able to:

- List important attributes of the Quantitative section including question formats, timing, and scoring
- Articulate how knowledge of key math concepts and quantitative analysis can help you manage the Quantitative section

---

Brushing up your knowledge of math facts and formulas is important for success on the GMAT Quantitative section, but equally important is understanding how the GMAT will ask you about math concepts. Also, it is vital that you manage your time on the section to earn the highest possible score.

Composition of the Quantitative Section

LEARNING OBJECTIVE

In this section, you will learn how to:

- Name the different question formats and enumerate how many questions of each type are found in the Quantitative section

---

Slightly less than half of the multiple-choice questions that count toward your overall score appear in the Quantitative (math) section. You'll have 62 minutes to answer 31 Quantitative questions in two formats: Problem Solving and Data Sufficiency. These two types of questions are mingled throughout the Quantitative section, so you never know what's coming next. Here's what you can expect to see:

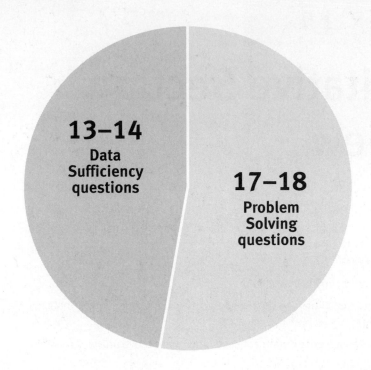

The Approximate Mix of Questions on the GMAT Quantitative Section

You may see more of one question type and fewer of the other due to the test's somewhat random selection of questions.

What the Quantitative Section Tests

LEARNING OBJECTIVES

In this section, you will learn how to:

- Identify the broad areas of math content tested on the GMAT and explain how the GMAT makes these topics challenging
- Articulate effective pacing and guessing strategies for the Quantitative section
- Describe the nature and purpose of experimental questions

Of course, the GMAT tests your math skills. So you will have to work with concepts that you may not have used for the last few years. Calculator use is not permitted on the Quantitative section, and even if you use math all the time, it's probably been a while since you were unable to use a calculator or computer to perform computations. So refreshing your fundamental math skills is definitely a crucial part of your prep.

Math Content Knowledge

Fortunately, the range of math topics tested is fairly limited. The GMAT covers only the math that U.S. students usually see during or before their first two years of high school. No trigonometry, no advanced algebra, no calculus. As you progress in your GMAT prep, you'll see that the same concepts are tested again and again in remarkably similar ways.

Areas of math content tested on the GMAT include the following: algebra, arithmetic, number properties, proportions, basic statistics, certain specific math formulas, and geometry. Algebra and arithmetic are the most commonly tested topics—they are tested either directly or indirectly on a majority of GMAT Quantitative questions. Geometry questions account for fewer than one-sixth of all GMAT math questions, but they can often be among the most challenging for test takers, so you may benefit from thorough review and practice with these concepts.

A large part of what makes the GMAT Quantitative section so challenging, however, is not the math content itself but rather how the test makers combine the different areas of math to make questions more challenging. Rare is the question that tests a single concept; more commonly, you will be asked to integrate multiple skills to solve a question. For instance, a question that asks you about triangles could also require you to solve a formula algebraically and apply your understanding of ratios to find the correct answer.

Quantitative Analysis

Most of the math tests you've taken before—even other standardized tests like the SAT and the ACT—ask questions in a fairly straightforward way. You know pretty quickly how you should solve the problem, and the only thing holding you back is how quickly or accurately you can do the math.

But the GMAT is different. Often the most difficult part of a GMAT Quantitative problem is figuring out which math skills to use in the first place. In fact, the GMAT's hardest Quantitative problems are about 95 percent analysis, 5 percent calculation. You'll have to do the following:

- Understand complicated or awkward phrasing
- Process information presented out of order
- Analyze incomplete information
- Simplify complicated information

In the next few chapters, we'll show you how to approach Quant problems strategically so you can do the analysis that will lead to efficient solutions, correct answers, and a high score. But first, let's look at some techniques for managing the Quantitative section as a whole.

Pacing on the Quantitative Section

The best way to attack the computer-adaptive GMAT is to exploit the way it determines your score. Here's what you're dealing with:

- **Penalties:** If you run out of time at the end of the section, you receive a penalty that's about twice what you'd have received if you got all those answers wrong. *And* there's an extra penalty for long strings of wrong answers at the end.

- **No review:** There is no going back to check your work. You cannot move backward to double-check your earlier answers or skip past a question that's puzzling and return to try it again later. So if you finish early, you won't be able to use that remaining time.

- **Difficulty level adjustment:** Questions get harder or easier, depending on your performance. Difficult questions raise your score more when you get them right and hurt your score less when you get them wrong. Easier questions are the opposite—getting them right helps your score less, and getting them wrong hurts your score more.

Obviously, the best of both worlds is being able to get the early questions mostly right, while taking *less than 2 minutes per question* on average so that you have a little extra time to think about those harder questions later on. To achieve that goal, you need to do three things:

1. **Know your math basics cold.** Don't waste valuable time on Test Day sweating over how to add fractions, reverse-FOIL quadratic equations, or use the rate formula. When you do math, you want to feel right at home.

2. **Look for strategic approaches.** Most GMAT problems are susceptible to multiple possible approaches. So the test makers deliberately build in shortcuts to reward critical thinkers by allowing them to move quickly through the question, leaving them with extra time. We'll show you how to find these most efficient approaches.

3. **Practice, practice, practice.** Do lots of practice problems so that you get as familiar as possible with the GMAT's most common analytical puzzles. That way you can handle them quickly (and correctly!) when you see them on Test Day. We've got tons in the upcoming chapters.

If you follow this advice, you'll do more than just set yourself up to manage your pacing well. You'll also ensure that most of the questions fall into a difficulty range that's right for you. If you struggle on a few hard questions and are sent back down to the midrange questions, that's OK! You'll get them correct, which will send you right back up to the high-value hard questions again.

During the test, do your best not to fall behind early on. Don't rush, but don't linger. Those first 5 questions shouldn't take more than 10 minutes total, and the first 10 questions shouldn't take more than 20 minutes. Pay attention to your timing as you move through the section. If you notice that you are falling behind, try to solve some questions more quickly (or if you're stuck, make strategic guesses) to catch up.

Strategic Guessing

Since missing hard questions doesn't hurt your score very much but not finishing definitely does, making a few guesses on the hardest questions will give you the chance to finish on time and earn your highest possible score.

Occasionally, you'll find that you have to make a guess, but don't guess at random. Narrowing down the answer choices first is imperative. Otherwise, your odds of getting the right answer will be pretty slim. Follow this plan when you guess:

1. **Eliminate answer choices you know are wrong.** You can often identify wrong answer choices after a little calculation. For instance, on Data Sufficiency questions, you can eliminate at least two answer choices by determining the sufficiency of just one statement.

2. **Avoid answer choices that make you suspicious.** You can get rid of these without doing any work on the problem! These answer choices either don't make logical sense with the problem or conform to common wrong-answer types. For example, if only one of the answer choices in a Problem Solving question is negative, chances are that it will be incorrect.

3. **Choose one of the remaining answer choices.** The fewer options you have to choose from, the higher your chances of selecting the right answer. You can often identify the correct answer using estimation, especially if the answer choices are spaced widely apart.

Experimental Questions

Some questions on the GMAT are experimental. These questions are not factored into your score. They are questions that the test maker is evaluating for possible use on future tests. To get good data, the test makers have to test each question against the whole range of test takers—that is, high and low scorers. Therefore, you could be on your way to an 800 and suddenly come across a question that feels out of line with how you think you are doing.

Don't panic; just do your best and keep on going. The difficulty level of the experimental questions you see has little to do with how you're currently scoring. Remember, there is no way for you to know for sure whether a question is experimental or not, so approach every question as if it were scored.

Keep in mind that it's hard to judge the true difficulty level of a question. A question that seems easy to you may simply be playing to your personal strengths and be very difficult for other test takers. So treat every question as if it counts. Don't waste time trying to speculate about the difficulty of the questions you're seeing and what that implies about your performance. Rather, focus your energy on answering the question in front of you as efficiently as possible.

How the Quantitative Section Is Scored

LEARNING OBJECTIVE

In this section, you will learn how to:

- Describe the process by which the GMAT's computer-adaptive test (CAT) functions to score your performance

The Quantitative section of the GMAT is quite different from the math sections of paper-and-pencil tests you may have taken. The major difference between the test formats is that the GMAT computer-adaptive test adapts to your performance. Each test taker is given a different mix of questions, depending on how well he or she is doing on the test. In other words, the questions get harder or easier depending on whether you answer them correctly or incorrectly. Your GMAT score is not determined by the number of questions you get right but rather by the difficulty level of the questions you get right.

When you begin a section, the computer:

- Assumes you have an average score (about 590)
- Gives you a medium-difficulty question. About half the people who take the test will get this question right, and half will get it wrong. What happens next depends on whether you answer the question correctly.

If you answer the question correctly:

- Your score goes up
- You are given a slightly harder question

If you answer the question incorrectly:

- Your score goes down
- You are given a slightly easier question

This pattern continues for the rest of the section. As you get questions right, the computer raises your score and gives you harder questions. As you get questions wrong, the computer lowers your score and gives you easier questions. In this way, the computer homes in on your score.

If you feel like you're struggling at the end of the section, don't worry! Because the CAT adapts to find the outer edge of your abilities, the test will feel hard; it's designed to be difficult for everyone, even the highest scorers.

Core Competencies on the Quantitative Section

LEARNING OBJECTIVE

In this section, you will learn how to:

* Describe how the Core Competencies of Critical Thinking, Pattern Recognition, Paraphrasing, and Attention to the Right Detail are relevant to the Quantitative section

Unlike most subject-specific tests you have taken throughout your academic career, the scope of knowledge that the GMAT requires of you is fairly limited. In fact, you don't need any background knowledge or expertise beyond fundamental math and verbal skills. While mastering those fundamentals is essential to your success on the GMAT—and this book is concerned in part with helping you develop or refresh those skills— the GMAT does *not* primarily seek to reward test takers for content-specific knowledge. Rather, the GMAT is a test of high-level thinking and reasoning abilities; it uses math and verbal subject matter as a platform to build questions that test your critical thinking and problem solving capabilities. As you prepare for the GMAT, you will notice that similar analytical skills come into play across the various question types and sections of the test.

Kaplan has adopted the term "Core Competencies" to refer to the four bedrock thinking skills rewarded by the GMAT: Critical Thinking, Pattern Recognition, Paraphrasing, and Attention to the Right Detail. The Kaplan Methods and strategies presented throughout this book will help you demonstrate these all-important skills. Let's dig into each of the Core Competencies in turn and discuss how each applies to the Quantitative section.

Critical Thinking

Most potential MBA students are adept at creative problem solving, and the GMAT offers many opportunities to demonstrate this skill. You probably already have experience assessing situations to see when data are inadequate; synthesizing information into valid deductions; finding creative solutions to complex problems; and avoiding unnecessary, redundant labor.

In GMAT terms, a critical thinker is a creative problem solver who engages in critical inquiry. One of the traits of successful test takers is their skill at asking the right questions. GMAT critical thinkers first consider what they're being asked to do, then study the given information and ask the right questions, especially, "How can I get the answer in the most direct way?" and "How can I use the question format to my advantage?"

For instance, the answer choices in a GMAT Problem Solving question often give clues to the solution. Use them. As you examine a Problem Solving question, you'll ask the test maker: "What are you really looking for in this math problem?" or "Why have you set things up in this way?" You might even discover opportunities to find the answer to a difficult question by plugging the answer choices into the information in the question—a strategy Kaplan calls "backsolving."

Likewise, as you examine a Data Sufficiency question, you'll learn to ask: "What information will I need to answer this question?" or "How can I determine whether more than one solution is possible?"

Those test takers who learn to ask the right questions become creative problem solvers—and GMAT champs. Let's see how to apply the GMAT Core Competency of Critical Thinking to a sample Problem Solving question:

1. If the perimeter of a rectangular property is 46 meters, and the area of the property is 76 square meters, what is the length of each of the shorter sides?

    ○   4

    ○   6

    ○   9

    ○   18

    ○   23

This question is a perfect example of one that can be answered with minimal calculations, provided the test taker understands how to use the test format to his advantage.

Here you are asked for the shorter sides of a rectangle. Recalling the formula for the area of a rectangle ($Area = Length \times Width$) may help you see a shorter path to the solution here. Rather than set up a complicated system of equations, remember that the property is 76 square meters in size. Since you're looking for the shorter side, you're looking for the smaller number that, when multiplied by a larger number, yields 76. You can immediately eliminate 9, 18, and 23 as possible answers, since multiplying any of those numbers by something larger than itself will give a result bigger than 76. Out of the two remaining choices, 4 divides evenly into 76. If the shorter sides measure 4, the larger sides would measure 19. And if the dimensions of the rectangle are 4 and 19, then the perimeter does equal 46. Therefore, choice (**A**) is correct.

This isn't to say that all questions are amenable to such amazing shortcuts. But it is true that almost every question on the Quantitative section of the GMAT could be solved using more than one approach. The time constraints on the GMAT are designed to reward those test takers who, through Critical Thinking and practice, have honed their ability to identify and execute the most efficient approach to every problem they might see on Test Day.

Pattern Recognition

Most people fail to appreciate the level of constraint that standardization places on test makers. Because the test makers must give reliable, valid, and comparable scores to many thousands of students each year, they're forced to reward the same skills on every test. They do so by repeating the same kinds of questions with the same traps and pitfalls, which are susceptible to the same strategic solutions.

Inexperienced test takers treat every problem as if it were a brand-new task, whereas the GMAT rewards those who spot the patterns and use them to their advantage. Of course Pattern Recognition is a key business skill in its own right: executives who recognize familiar situations and apply proven solutions to them will outperform those who reinvent the wheel every time.

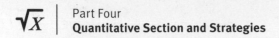

Even the smartest test taker will struggle if she approaches each GMAT question as a novel exercise. But the GMAT features nothing novel—just repeated patterns. Kaplan knows this test inside and out, and we'll show you which patterns you will encounter on Test Day. You will know the test better than your competition does. Let's see how to apply the GMAT Core Competency of Pattern Recognition to a sample Problem Solving question:

2. If $x > 7$, which of the following is equal to $\dfrac{x^2 + 8x + 16}{x^2 - 16}$?

    ○ $\dfrac{x + 4}{4(x - 4)}$

    ○ $\dfrac{x - 4}{x + 4}$

    ○ $\dfrac{x - 2}{x + 4}$

    ○ $\dfrac{x + 4}{x - 4}$

    ○ $\dfrac{x - 8}{x - 4}$

This question features one of the many patterns that is repeated over and over in the Quantitative section. The Kaplan-trained test taker looks at this problem and sees two "classic quadratics": the square of a binomial in the numerator and the difference of squares in the denominator. Factoring these expressions allows you to rewrite them as follows:

$$\frac{(x + 4)(x + 4)}{(x + 4)(x - 4)}$$

You can then cancel an $(x + 4)$ on the top and bottom and choose the correct answer, choice (**D**). As you practice with more and more GMAT questions, stay attuned to patterns you see; certain math concepts appear regularly enough on the GMAT to warrant memorization.

Paraphrasing

The third Core Competency is Paraphrasing: the GMAT rewards those who can reduce difficult, abstract, or polysyllabic prose to simple terms. Paraphrasing is, of course, an essential business skill: executives must be able to define clear tasks based on complicated requirements and accurately summarize mountains of detail.

In the Quantitative section of the GMAT, you will often be asked to paraphrase English as "math" or to simplify complicated equations using arithmetic or algebraic properties. Let's see how to apply the GMAT Core Competency of Paraphrasing to a sample Problem Solving question:

3. A basketball team plays games only against the other five teams in its league and always in the following order: Croton, Darby, Englewood, Fiennes, and Garvin. If the team's final game of the season is against Fiennes, which of the following could be the number of games in the team's schedule?

    ○   18

    ○   24

    ○   56

    ○   72

    ○   81

Rather than become intimidated by the complicated wording of this question, a smart test taker will ask, "How might I rephrase this question more simply?" A good paraphrase looks something like this: a team plays five other teams over and over in the same order, but the season stops at Fiennes. This is the fourth game of the sequence; what could the total number of games be?

With this paraphrase in hand, it's time to employ some Critical Thinking. Suppose the team plays a full round, and the next round is interrupted after the fourth game—what will the total number of games be? $5 + 4 = 9$. Suppose there are two full rounds before the interruption? $5 + 5 + 4 = 14$. Three rounds? $5 + 5 + 5 + 4 = 19$. Thinking through these scenarios causes the pattern to emerge: the answer must end in 4 or 9. The correct choice is **(B)**, which represents four full rounds plus a set of four games ending with Fiennes.

Notice how this convoluted word problem becomes manageable once paraphrased. Putting GMAT prose into your own words helps you get a handle on the situation being described and know what to do next.

Attention to the Right Detail

Details present a dilemma: missing them can cost you points. But if you try to absorb every fact in a complicated word problem all at once, you may find yourself swamped, delayed, and still unable to determine the best approach, because you haven't sorted through the information to determine what's most important. Throughout this book, you will learn how to discern the essential details from those that can slow you down or confuse you. The GMAT test makers reward examinees for paying attention to "the right details"—the ones that make the difference between right and wrong answers.

Attention to the Right Detail distinguishes great administrators from poor ones in the business world as well. Just ask anyone who's had a boss who had the wrong priorities or who was so bogged down in minutiae that the department stopped functioning.

Not all details are created equal, and there are mountains of them on the test. Learn to target only what will turn into correct answers. Let's see how to apply the GMAT Core Competency of Attention to the Right Detail to a sample Problem Solving question:

4. A drought decreased the amount of water in city X's reservoirs from 118 million gallons to 96 million gallons. If the reservoirs were at 79 percent of total capacity before the drought began, approximately how many million gallons were the reservoirs below total capacity after the drought?

    O   67

    O   58

    O   54

    O   46

    O   32

There are a lot of words in this problem, but there's one that's more important than all the others. Recognizing the word "approximately" is crucial to being able to take a strategic approach to this question.

Attention to the Right Detail on the Quantitative section also means defining precisely what the question is asking you to solve for. Here you need the current (post-drought) difference between capacity and holdings. Identifying up front what you need to solve for is important on the GMAT because the answer choices will often include options that represent "the right answer to the wrong question": the value you might come up with if you did all the math correctly but solved accidentally for a different unknown in the problem (for instance, the number of gallons below capacity the reservoir was *before* the drought).

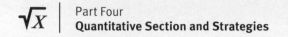
This question gives information on the pre- and post-drought holdings, as well as on the pre-drought percentage of capacity. Use that info to approximate the current shortage. To start, figure out the total capacity before the drought. You know that 118 million was 79 percent of capacity. Because approximation is perfectly fine in this case, you can round these numbers to 120 million and 80 percent, respectively, to make the math easier. Then use the percent formula:

$$120 = 0.80(\text{Total capacity})$$
$$120 = \frac{4}{5}(\text{Total capacity})$$
$$120\left(\frac{5}{4}\right) = \text{Total capacity}$$
$$150 = \text{Total capacity}$$

The question states that the current volume is 96 million gallons, which is 54 million gallons under capacity. Choice (**C**) is correct.

Think of how much time you saved by noticing that the question asked for an approximate value, thereby allowing you to avoid precise calculation with unwieldy numbers. Moreover, Attention to the Right Detail ensured that you did not select a trap answer choice: if you had accidentally solved for the total capacity and then subtracted 118 (the amount of water originally in the reservoir), you would have selected incorrect choice (**E**).

CHAPTER 16

Problem Solving Strategy

LEARNING OBJECTIVES

After studying this chapter, you will be able to:

- Describe the format of a Problem Solving question
- State the steps of the Kaplan Method for Problem Solving questions
- Explain how strategic thinking can be as important as math knowledge when solving Problem Solving questions

Below is a typical Problem Solving question. In this chapter, we'll look at how to apply the Kaplan Method to this question, discuss the math concepts being tested, and go over the basic principles and strategies that you want to keep in mind on every Problem Solving question.

George's drawer has 10 loose black socks, 15 loose blue socks, and 8 loose white socks. If George takes socks out of the drawer at random, how many would he need to take out to be sure that the removed socks include at least one matching pair?

- ○ 3
- ○ 4
- ○ 9
- ○ 15
- ○ 31

Before you move on, take a minute to think about what you see in this question and answer some questions about how you think it works:

- What mathematical concepts are being tested by this question?
- How is this different from a typical math question you may have seen in high school?
- How can you use the answer choices to your advantage?
- What GMAT Core Competencies are most essential to success on this question?

Previewing Problem Solving

Here are the answers to the questions you just considered.

What Mathematical Concepts Are Being Tested by This Question?

At first, the question at the beginning of this chapter appears to be setting up a situation involving probability. George is randomly selecting socks from a drawer whose contents are described in the question. But then the question takes an unexpected turn—rather than asking for the probability of choosing a certain combination of socks, it instead asks for the minimum number of socks George would need to draw in order to be sure of having a matching pair. There's no formula to follow here or algebraic equation to solve. This question is testing your ability to reason through the situation and choose the correct answer.

Problem Solving questions test basic math skills and an understanding of some elementary mathematical concepts—ones such as algebra, arithmetic, and geometry that most U.S. students have learned by 10th grade. Most importantly, they test the ability to reason quantitatively. All GMAT Quantitative questions depend at least as much on logical analysis as on math skills. Most rely more on logic than on math. Some, like this one, rely purely on logic and require no math skills beyond the ability to count.

Think about it this way: if business schools wanted to know how much math you knew, they could easily look at your college transcript to see what math classes you took and how you fared in them. So why require the GMAT? Because they want to look at something else. In business school, you will be given *a lot* of information, especially in the form of case studies. One of the biggest challenges you'll face will be figuring out how to think about all that information—deciding how it fits together, what deductions you can make from it, and how it pertains to business challenges.

So the Quantitative section presents you with microcosms of that task—mathematical puzzles in which the data are often presented in a confusing or misleading way, demanding that you first figure out how you can solve the puzzles before beginning any calculations. Hence the name "Problem Solving" instead of just "Math."

The most advanced questions rarely involve math that is much more difficult than the math used in intermediate-range questions. Rather, the task of analyzing the problem to figure out what math to use becomes harder.

How Is This Different from a Typical Math Question You May Have Seen in High School?

Besides the emphasis on logic mentioned above, there's another important characteristic of GMAT Problem Solving that distinguishes it from the math you have likely been required to do on exams throughout your educational career: all that the GMAT requires is that you choose the correct answer. There's no math teacher looking over your shoulder to verify that you are completing each step precisely and showing your work fully. There is no extra or partial credit for finding a mathematically elegant solution. It may seem obvious, but it bears emphasizing: the sole goal on a Problem Solving question is getting the question correct and earning your points.

What that means for the savvy test taker is that a range of paths to the solution are available. Of course, you can do the straightforward math, but you can also use other strategies such as the ones you will learn in this chapter. The value of a strategic approach is that you can often get to the answer more quickly and accurately than if you had relied on classroom math.

The challenge is that the classroom math approach has probably been so impressed upon you throughout school that you are likely to favor that approach automatically, even when it's not the best way to a solution. So as you practice, one of the best things you can do for your ultimate success on Test Day is get into the habit of Critical Thinking: always ask yourself what approaches are available to you and which one will work best on that particular question. Since the GMAT is a timed test and the adaptive format ensures that you will see questions you will find difficult, finding opportunities to increase your efficiency is of paramount importance to your score.

How Can You Use the Answer Choices to Your Advantage?

One of the big advantages you have on Problem Solving questions is the presence of the five answer choices, one of which *must* be correct. Especially when those answers are simple numbers, as they are in this question, you can often find your way to the correct answer by plugging the answer choices back into the situation described in the problem to see which one works. This is a strategy called backsolving, and you will learn later in this chapter how to apply it.

In this question, you can't literally substitute the answer choices back into the problem, since there's very little math to do here. But in this case, you can use the answer choices to help think through the basic scenario you are given. For instance, try choice (A) on for size: if George has three types of socks, is he guaranteed to pull out a matching pair when he draws only three socks? No, of course not; he could end up drawing one sock of each color. At the other end of the spectrum, what about choice (E)? If he pulls out 31 of his 33 socks, will he end up with a matching pair? Surely he will; in fact, he'll have many matching pairs. So the correct answer will be smaller than 31. If you aren't sure at first how to approach a question, thinking through the answer choices you are given will often guide you toward a game plan.

What GMAT Core Competencies Are Most Essential to Success on This Question?

The first step of the Kaplan Method for Problem Solving is to analyze the question. This analysis up front helps you find the most efficient approach to the question.

Attention to the Right Detail comes into play in step 2 of the Method when you identify the task that the question requires of you. It's all too easy to be in a hurry and solve for a value other than what the question asks for. The GMAT test makers know this and include such trap answers among the answer choices.

Pattern Recognition is essential to determining what math topic a question is testing and recognizing what formulas or rules will get you to the answer. Since the GMAT structures questions similarly from test to test, you'll become familiar with the common tasks and traps as you practice. Remember that the goal of your practice is never simply to find the correct answer. You won't see your practice questions on Test Day, but you will likely see questions very similar to them; if you keep your eyes open to patterns, you will feel prepared for any question the GMAT can throw at you.

Finally, you will benefit from Paraphrasing the information given to you by Problem Solving questions. Sometimes the given information is complicated or presented in a less-than-helpful order. Other times, the information is in the form of a word problem that must be "translated" into math. In all cases, you will distill the given information into scratchwork, which should be simple, accurate, and well organized.

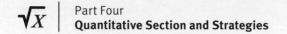

Question Format and Structure

> **LEARNING OBJECTIVE**
>
> In this section, you will learn how to:
>
> - Describe the rules related to real numbers and diagrams in Problem Solving questions

The instructions for the Problem Solving questions look like this:

> **Directions:** Solve the problems and choose the best answer.
>
> **Note:** Unless otherwise indicated, the figures accompanying questions have been drawn as accurately as possible and may be used as sources of information for answering the questions.
>
> All figures lie in a plane except where noted.
>
> All numbers used are real numbers.

There are about 17 Problem Solving questions on each GMAT Quantitative section. Happily, the format of the questions is simple enough: each Problem Solving question consists of the question stem—which gives you information and defines your task—and five answer choices. To answer a question, select the choice that correctly answers the question.

The directions indicate that some diagrams on the GMAT are drawn to scale, which means that you can use them to estimate measurements and size relationships. Other diagrams are labeled "Not drawn to scale," so you can't eyeball them. In fact, when a diagram says "Not drawn to scale," working past the confusing picture is often the key to the problem.

The directions also let you know that you won't have to deal with imaginary numbers, such as $\sqrt{-1}$, and that you'll be dealing with flat figures, such as squares and circles, unless a particular question says otherwise.

The Basic Principles of Problem Solving

> **LEARNING OBJECTIVES**
>
> In this section, you will learn how to:
>
> - Apply analytical skills to approach Problem Solving questions effectively
> - Strategically evaluate what is being asked in order to focus attention on the right details
> - Use alternative, logical approaches to Problem Solving questions in addition to performing calculations

By adopting a methodical approach to Problem Solving, you will have a clear, strategic way to think your way to a response. You won't waste time by attacking a question in a tentative or haphazard manner, nor will you get stuck doing inefficient math. A systematic approach will ensure that you find the most efficient solution to the problem and that you make as few careless and unnecessary errors as possible. Here are some ways you can optimize your Problem Solving performance by employing the Core Competencies.

In the next section, we'll show you a Method that codifies this approach to Problem Solving questions so you can use the same productive approach over and over throughout the Quantitative section.

Analyze and Simplify Before Solving

The biggest mistake test takers make on GMAT Problem Solving is doing the math right after reading the problem (or even more dangerously, *while* still reading the problem). Problem Solving questions are written to be confusing, and the approach that the question might seem to be talking you into may not be the most efficient. Consider this problem:

> At a certain diner, Joe ordered 3 doughnuts and a cup of coffee and was charged $2.25. Stella ordered 2 doughnuts and a cup of coffee and was charged $1.70. What is the price of 2 doughnuts?
>
> O $0.55
>
> O $1.00
>
> O $1.10
>
> O $1.30
>
> O $1.80

If you started doing math right away, you might immediately jot down something like $J = 3d + c$, thereby making the problem a lot tougher by introducing a variable, J, that really doesn't need to be part of the solution. If you used x and y instead of d and c, you would make your job even harder, as a part of your brain that could be used to solve the problem would be taken up remembering whether x stood for doughnuts or coffee.

However, if you analyzed the question before getting into math, you would realize that the orders are very similar. In fact, they differ by only 1 doughnut. So the price of a doughnut could be calculated simply by subtracting the prices of the orders. Instead of wasting time writing out $S = 2d + c$, you have almost completely solved the problem. Time invested in analysis usually pays off in a much more efficient solution and in less time spent on the question overall.

Here's another example of the benefit of analysis and simplification:

> What is the product of all the possible values of x if $x^2(x + 2) + 7x(x + 2) + 6(x + 2) = 0$?
>
> O -29
>
> O -12
>
> O 12
>
> O 29
>
> O 168

If you did math before any analysis, you'd distribute the multiplication and get $x^3 + 9x^2 + 20x + 12 = 0$. You might then be stuck not knowing what to do next to simplify this equation.

But if you analyzed first, you'd realize that distribution would lead to a complicated cubic equation. Looking for an easier way, you might notice that if the multiple occurrences of $(x + 2)$ were gone, you'd have a normal quadratic. You could factor out the occurrences of $(x + 2)$ and be on your way to solving:

$$x^2(x + 2) + 7x(x + 2) + 6(x + 2) = 0$$

Factor:	$(x + 2)(x^2 + 7x + 6) = 0$
Reverse-FOIL:	$(x + 2)(x + 6)(x + 1) = 0$
Solve for x:	$x = -2$ or -6 or -1
Multiply:	$-2 \times -6 \times -1 = -12$

Focus on What's Asked

Go back to the problem with the doughnuts and the coffee. Did you spot the trap? The question doesn't ask for the price of a doughnut but rather for the price of *two* doughnuts. Sure enough, one of the answer choices gives the cost of only one.

Focusing on what's asked will also help you to choose an efficient approach. Consider this question:

If $4x + y = 8$ and $y - 3x = 7$, then what is the value of $x + 2y$?

- $\frac{1}{7}$
- 3
- 15
- $\frac{52}{7}$
- $\frac{60}{7}$

You might just rush into solving for x and y and then plug them in, but focus on what you are being asked for: not x or y individually but rather $x + 2y$. How could you solve for *that*? Looking at the equations, you might notice that one equation has $4x$ and the other $-3x$, and together, that's x. Each has one y, so together you have $2y$. You can add the equations together.

Rearrange $y - 3x = 7$ to $-3x + y = 7$ so things line up nicely. Then combine the equations:

$$4x + y = 8$$
$$\underline{+[-3x + y = 7]}$$
$$x + 2y = 15$$

In the end, the math was quick because you focused on what the question asked.

Note that in this question, answer choices (**A**) and (**D**) represent the values of the individual variables. Right answers to the wrong questions are the most common wrong answer type in Problem Solving, so it pays to define the task in step 2 of the Kaplan Method.

Consider Alternative Approaches

You just saw three questions that were all most easily solved in a manner other than the math that might first occur to you. You added equations in the $x + 2y$ problem, factored instead of multiplied in the $x + 2$ problem, and realized that all you needed to do on the diner problem was find the difference in cost between the two orders.

The takeaway from these examples: it pays to *think* about what you're doing before diving into math. Most problems can be solved many different ways, some easy and some not so easy. The GMAT test maker writes the questions in such a way that the first approaches that occur to you are usually of the not-so-easy variety. So turn the problem over in your mind until you find an approach that will work. Trust your intuition—if you're thinking of a solution that involves lots of difficult math, then look for a different approach.

Here's how you might approach a more difficult question, considering different approaches until you find one that works:

$$\begin{array}{r} AB \\ +BA \\ \hline 121 \end{array}$$

In the addition problem above, A and B represent digits in two different two-digit numbers. What is the sum of A and B?

- ○ 6
- ○ 8
- ○ 9
- ○ 11
- ○ 14

This question may seem intimidating, so approach it calmly and methodically. Start as always by analyzing the question stem. You are told that A and B represent digits in two different two-digit numbers. Recall that a digit is any of the integers 0 through 9 and that a two-digit number is a number that has digits in the tens place and the units place, like 42 or 11. This means that AB is a two-digit number with A in the tens place and B in the units place. For example, if A is 3 and B is 5, then AB is 35.

Now, how do you solve for A and B? You could just experiment with different possibilities, plugging different combinations of digits in until you get $AB + BA = 121$. But since there are 10 digits, there'd be something like 100 different possible combinations. You don't have time for that. And you know that when you find yourself beginning a drawn-out, tedious process like this, there's usually an easier way to solve the problem.

This is where Critical Thinking can help. You know that you can sometimes solve for an expression without figuring out the individual variables. The sum of A and B is $A + B$, and that is in fact what you are being asked to solve for. Look back at the question stem, and see if you can find $A + B$:

$$\begin{array}{r} AB \\ +BA \\ \hline 121 \end{array}$$

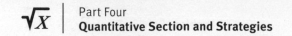

$A + B$ is the sum of the digits in the tens place. Is the answer 12? You know that it can't be, because 12 isn't an answer choice. It's possible that the $A + B$ in the tens column is getting spillover from the $B + A$ in the units column, which would mean $A + B$ is less than 12, but you can't know the amount. At the very least, though, you've established that choice (**E**) is too large, since the answer is either 12 or something less.

By now, or before now, you've realized that $B + A$ is the same as $A + B$. So the answer is also the sum of the digits in the units places:

$$\begin{array}{r} AB \\ +BA \\ \hline 121 \end{array}$$

So the units digit of the answer has to be 1. Having recognized this pattern, you can look at the answer choices and see that only (**D**) has a 1 in the units place. The answer has to be (**D**).

Note that you didn't need the exact values of A and B to solve this problem. In fact, many different pairs of digits would satisfy this equation.

Don't be put off by the challenging presentation of a problem, even when you're not sure at first how you're going to solve it. As with this problem, separate what you know from what you don't, so you don't feel over-whelmed. Always consider multiple possible approaches, reevaluating them if they get too hard to follow or seem not to be working. Use what you know about the GMAT to help you, and look everywhere for clues to the solution—both in the question stem and in the answer choices.

TAKEAWAYS: THE BASIC PRINCIPLES OF PROBLEM SOLVING

- Most GMAT word problems do not present the information in the most straightforward way. You will need to read strategically to understand the problem.
- Focusing on the question first:
  - Helps you understand what to look for in the problem
  - Allows you to avoid solving for "the right answer to the wrong question"—a common GMAT mistake

The Kaplan Method for Problem Solving

LEARNING OBJECTIVES

In this section, you will learn how to:

- List the steps of the Kaplan Method for Problem Solving
- Explain the purpose of each step of the Kaplan Method for Problem Solving
- Perform the steps of the Method to answer Problem Solving questions

---

Now that you've seen how Problem Solving questions are constructed, let's look at how to handle them. Kaplan has developed a Method for Problem Solving that you can use to attack each and every question of this type.

THE KAPLAN METHOD FOR PROBLEM SOLVING

1. Analyze the question.
2. State the task.
3. Approach strategically.
4. Confirm your answer.

STEP 1: ANALYZE THE QUESTION

Begin your analysis of the problem by getting an overview. If it's a word problem, what's the basic situation? Or is this an algebra problem? An overlapping sets problem? A permutations problem? Getting a general idea of what's going on will help you to organize your thinking and know which rules or formulas you'll have to use.

If there's anything that can be quickly simplified, do so—but don't start solving yet. For example, if a question stem gives you the classic quadratic $x^2 - y^2 = 64$, it would be fine to rewrite it immediately in your scratch-work as $(x + y)(x - y) = 64$. But you wouldn't want to start solving for values just yet; doing so would likely cause you to miss an important aspect of the problem or to overlook an efficient alternative solution.

Also, make sure to glance at the answer choices. Can they help you choose an approach? If they are variable expressions, you can use picking numbers (a strategy we'll cover later in this chapter). If they are widely spread, you can estimate. If they are numerical values, you might be able to plug them back into the question, a strategy we call backsolving. Looking at the choices may trigger an important strategic insight for you.

STEP 2: STATE THE TASK

Before you choose your approach, make sure you know what you're solving for. The most common wrong answer trap in Problem Solving is the right answer—but to the wrong question. And perhaps you won't have to do as much work as you might think—you may be able to solve for what you need without calculating the value of every single variable involved in the problem.

STEP 3: APPROACH STRATEGICALLY

The operative word here is *strategically*. Resist the temptation to hammer away at the problem, hoping for something to work. Use your analysis from steps 1 and 2 to find the most straightforward approach that allows you to make sense of the problem.

There is rarely a single "right approach." Choose the easiest for you given the current problem. Broadly speaking, there are three basic approaches.

Approach 1: A Kaplan Strategy. Frequently there will be a more efficient strategic approach to the math for those who analyze the problem carefully. Consider picking numbers or backsolving, which you will learn about later in this chapter. These approaches can simplify some tough problems and should always be on your mind as possible alternatives.

Approach 2: Straightforward Math. Sometimes simply doing the math is the most efficient approach. But remember, only do math that feels *straightforward*. To be sure, the hardest problems will make you sweat during the *analysis*, but you should never find yourself performing extremely complicated calculations.

Remember, the only thing that matters is that you select the correct answer. There is no human GMAT grader out there who's going to give you extra points for working out a math problem the hard way.

Approach 3: Guess Strategically. If you notice that estimation or simple logic will get you the answer, use those guessing techniques. They will often be faster than doing the math. If you have spent 60 to 90 seconds analyzing the problem and still haven't found a straightforward path to a solution, make a guess. You only have an average of 2 minutes per question, so you need to keep moving.

And if you have fallen behind pace, you need to guess strategically to get back on track. Hunt actively for good guessing situations and guess quickly on them (within 20–30 seconds). Don't wait until you fall so far behind that you are forced into random guesses or forced to guess on questions that you could otherwise have easily solved. Never try to make up time by rushing!

STEP 4: CONFIRM YOUR ANSWER

Because the GMAT is adaptive, you aren't able to return to questions you've already seen to check your work, so you need to build that step into your process on each question. The most efficient way to do this is to reread the question stem as you select your answer. If you notice a wrinkle in the problem that you missed earlier, you should redo the problem (if you have time) or change your answer. If you got everything right the first time, move on to the next problem with confidence.

Applying the Kaplan Method: The Basic Principles of Problem Solving

Now let's use the Kaplan Method and the strategic principles of Problem Solving to answer a sample question:

> In a certain town, there are four times as many people who were born in the town's state as there are people who were born in another state or country. The ratio of those residents born in the town's state to the town's total population is
>
> ○   1 to 4
>
> ○   1 to 3
>
> ○   1 to 2
>
> ○   3 to 4
>
> ○   4 to 5

STEP 1: ANALYZE THE QUESTION

The phrase "total population" near the end of the question stem should stand out as key. One of the classic tricks used by the GMAT test makers is to give you a part-to-part ratio and ask for an answer expressed as a part-to-whole ratio.

STEP 2: STATE THE TASK

You need to use the ratio of those born in-state to those born out-of-state to determine the ratio of those born in-state to the total population.

STEP 3: APPROACH STRATEGICALLY

Having four times as many people born in-state as out-of-state means a ratio of 4:1. You are looking for the ratio of those born in the state to the total. You are told that 4 is the part of the ratio for those who were born in the state. You can find the total by adding the two parts, in-state (4) and out-of-state (1), getting 5. The part-to-whole ratio is then 4:5, choice (**E**).

STEP 4: CONFIRM YOUR ANSWER

A good natural-language paraphrase of the information is "Four of every five residents were born in-state." That matches choice (**E**). You need to avoid traps that restate or distort the part-to-part information. Be wary of answer choice (**A**), which is just a distortion of the original ratio.

Now, let's apply the Kaplan Method for Problem Solving to the question you saw at the beginning of this chapter:

> George's drawer has 10 loose black socks, 15 loose blue socks, and 8 loose white socks. If George takes socks out of the drawer at random, how many would he need to take out to be sure that the removed socks include at least one matching pair?
>
> ○ 3
>
> ○ 4
>
> ○ 9
>
> ○ 15
>
> ○ 31

STEP 1: ANALYZE THE QUESTION

George has a bunch of unpaired socks and is pulling them out at random. This doesn't sound like the best way to get dressed, but that's the situation the question gives you.

STEP 2: STATE THE TASK

What's the smallest number of socks George has to remove to be sure of getting a matching pair? In other words, how many socks does George need to pick before he is guaranteed to have 2 matching socks? The question doesn't specify which color, so any matching color will do.

STEP 3: APPROACH STRATEGICALLY

There's no equation to set up here. Despite the fact that the question starts off sounding like a probability question, you're not asked to calculate probabilities directly.

So think logically. Obviously, George can't have a matching pair of socks if he only removes 1 sock. You need at least 2 for a pair. So what if George removes 2 socks? He *could* get a pair, of course; there's nothing stopping him from randomly drawing, for example, 2 blue socks. But he also *could* get an unmatched pair—1 blue and 1 black, perhaps—so removing 2 socks doesn't *guarantee* a matching pair.

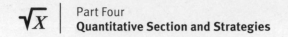
What if he takes 3 socks? Again, he *could* match a color—1 blue and 2 whites, for example. But could he still have no match with 3 socks? Yes, as it's possible (and happily you are not asked to calculate exactly *how* possible) for him to get 1 of each color—1 white, 1 blue, and 1 black.

But after that, he's guaranteed to match 1 of the colors. After all, there are only 3 colors. So even if he didn't have a match after taking out 3 (1 white, 1 blue, and 1 black), he's guaranteed to have a pair when he selects a 4th sock. You can't know whether that pair will be white, blue, or black, but the question didn't ask you to get a specific color... any one will do. The correct answer is (**B**).

STEP 4: CONFIRM YOUR ANSWER

Reread the question stem, making sure that you didn't miss anything about the problem or give the right answer to the wrong question—a common GMAT trap. For example, (**E**) is what you would have selected if you solved for the total number of socks minus 1 pair.

TAKEAWAYS: THE KAPLAN METHOD FOR PROBLEM SOLVING

- The Kaplan Method is a tested, proven way to approach Problem Solving questions consistently, efficiently, and confidently.

- Through practice, the Kaplan Method will become second nature by Test Day.

- Always be on the lookout for the most strategic approach; some Problem Solving questions require more logical analysis than mathematical calculation.

Practice Set: The Kaplan Method for Problem Solving

1. A machine manufactures notebooks in a series of 5 colors: red, blue, black, white, and yellow. After producing a notebook of 1 color from that series, it produces a notebook of the next color. Once 5 are produced, the machine repeats the same pattern. If the machine began a day producing a red notebook and completed the day by producing a black notebook, how many notebooks could have been produced that day?

    ○ 27
    ○ 34
    ○ 50
    ○ 61
    ○ 78

2. Youssef lives x blocks from his office. It takes him 1 minute per block to walk to work and 20 seconds per block to ride his bicycle to work. If it takes him exactly 10 minutes more to walk to work than to ride his bicycle, then x equals

    ○ 4
    ○ 7
    ○ 10
    ○ 15
    ○ 20

3. A book club rented the party room of a local restaurant to meet and discuss its current novel over dinner. The total charge, including food and service, was $867.50. If each member of the club paid at least $42, then what is the greatest possible number of members in the club?

    ○ 19
    ○ 20
    ○ 21
    ○ 23
    ○ 25

4. A team won 50 percent of its first 60 games in a particular season and 80 percent of its remaining games. If the team won a total of 60 percent of its games that season, what was the total number of games that the team played?

    ○ 180
    ○ 120
    ○ 90
    ○ 85
    ○ 30

5. A local restaurant recently renovated its dining space, purchasing new tables and chairs to use in addition to the original tables and chairs. The new tables each seat 6 customers, while the original tables each seat 4 customers. Altogether, the restaurant now has 40 tables and is capable of seating 220 customers. How many more new tables than original tables does the restaurant have?

    ○ 10
    ○ 20
    ○ 30
    ○ 34
    ○ 36

Step 3: Approach Strategically—Picking Numbers

> **LEARNING OBJECTIVES**
>
> In this section, you will learn how to:
>
> - Articulate how the Picking Numbers strategy works
> - Identify situations in which it may be helpful to use Picking Numbers
> - Apply the Picking Numbers strategy to appropriate Problem Solving questions

In the previous sections, you learned about the attitude that all great GMAT test takers share: that there must be a straightforward way to solve and there's no need to panic if you don't find it right away. And even if you don't use the algebra-based approach that your high school math teacher would have preferred, you will get the right answer and you will raise your score.

Identifying a more efficient alternative approach involves staying open to possibilities that might not occur to you immediately. Two such approaches—picking numbers and backsolving—are so straightforward, can eliminate so much math, and can be used so often that they deserve special mention.

Picking numbers is a powerful alternative to solving problems by brute force. Rather than trying to work with unknown variables, you pick concrete values for the variables. In essence, you're transforming algebra or abstract math rules into basic arithmetic, giving yourself a much simpler task. Pick numbers to stand in for the variables or unknowns.

How does picking numbers work?

- Pick **permissible** numbers. Some problems have explicit rules such as "x is odd." Other problems have implicit rules. For example, if a word problem says, "Betty is 5 years older than Tim," don't pick $b = -2$ and $t = -7$; these numbers wouldn't work in the problem.

- Pick **manageable** numbers. Some numbers are simply easier to work with than others. For example, $d = 2$ will probably be a more successful choice than will $d = 492\sqrt{\pi}$. The problems themselves will tell you what's manageable. For instance, $d = 2$ wouldn't be a great pick if an answer choice were $\frac{d}{12}$. (The number 12, 24, or even 120 would be much better in that case, since each is divisible by 12.)

- Once you've picked numbers to substitute for unknowns, approach the problem as basic arithmetic instead of algebra or number properties.

- Test every answer choice—sometimes certain numbers will yield a "false positive" in which a wrong answer looks right. If you get more than one "right answer," just pick a new set of numbers. The truly correct answer must work for all permissible numbers.

Note that it's just fine to pick the numbers 0 or 1 for most questions. The GMAT sometimes writes questions based on the special properties of 0 and 1, so if you aren't considering these numbers, you won't get the right answer to those questions. Furthermore, they are the most manageable numbers in all of math. Imagine picking numbers for the following problem with anything other than $b = 0$ or $b = 1$:

$$7^b + 7^b + 7^b + 7^b + 7^b + 7^b + 7^b =$$

- ○ 7^b
- ○ 7^{b+1}
- ○ 7^{7b}
- ○ 8^b
- ○ 49^b

Picking $b = 1$ makes short work of this exponents question:

$$7^b + 7^b + 7^b + 7^b + 7^b + 7^b + 7^b$$
$$= 7^1 + 7^1 + 7^1 + 7^1 + 7^1 + 7^1 + 7^1$$
$$= 7 + 7 + 7 + 7 + 7 + 7 + 7$$
$$= 49$$

Plugging $b = 1$ into the answer choices yields:

(A) $7b = 7^1 = 7$

(B) $7^{b+1} = 7^{1+1} = 7^2 = 49$

(C) $7^{7b} = 7^7$ Whatever that is, it's a lot bigger than 49.

(D) $8^b = 8^1 = 8$

(E) $49^b = 49^1 = 49$

Two answer choices match the desired result of 49, so you need to pick a new number. Try $b = 0$. First, plug it into the expression in the question stem.

$$7^b + 7^b + 7^b + 7^b + 7^b + 7^b + 7^b$$
$$= 7^0 + 7^0 + 7^0 + 7^0 + 7^0 + 7^0 + 7^0$$
$$= 1 + 1 + 1 + 1 + 1 + 1 + 1$$
$$= 7$$

Now you only need to plug $b = 0$ into **(B)** and **(E)**, the only two answer choices that worked when $b = 1$. Doing so yields:

(A) $7^{b+1} = 7^{0+1} = 7^1 = 7$

(B) $49^b = 49^0 = 1$

The answer is **(B)**.

PICKING NUMBERS

There are four signals that picking numbers will be a possible approach to the problem:

- Variables in the question stem
- Percents in the answer choices
- Variables in the answer choices
- Must be/could be/cannot be

These aren't in any particular order. You'll see many instances of each case on Test Day. We'll start with the first.

Picking Numbers with Variables in the Question Stem

If you see a question that has variables in the question stem or asks about a fraction of an unknown whole, pick numbers to represent the unknown(s) in the question stem and walk through the arithmetic of the problem. Look in the question stem and the answer choices for clues about what the most manageable numbers might be.

Example:

Carol spends $\frac{1}{4}$ of her savings on a stereo and $\frac{1}{3}$ less than she spent on the stereo for a television. What fraction of her savings did she spend on the stereo and television?

○ $\frac{1}{4}$

○ $\frac{2}{7}$

○ $\frac{5}{12}$

○ $\frac{1}{2}$

○ $\frac{7}{12}$

Lowest common denominators of fractions in the question stem are good choices for numbers to pick. So are numbers that appear frequently as denominators in the answer choices. In this case, the common denominator of the fractions in the stem is 12, so let the number 12 represent Carol's total savings (12 dollars).

That means she spends $\frac{1}{4} \times 12$ dollars, or 3 dollars, on her stereo and $\frac{2}{3} \times 3$ dollars, or 2 dollars, on her television. That comes out to be $3 + 2 = 5$ dollars; that's how much she spent on the stereo and television combined. You're asked what *fraction* of her savings she spent. Because her total savings was 12 dollars, she spent $\frac{5}{12}$ of her savings; (**C**) is correct. Notice how picking a common denominator for the variable (Carol's savings) made it easy to convert each of the fractions $\left(\frac{1}{4} \text{ and } \frac{2}{3} \times \frac{1}{4} \text{ of her savings}\right)$ to a simple integer.

A tricky part of this question is understanding how to determine the price of the television. The television does not cost $\frac{1}{3}$ of her savings. It costs $\frac{1}{3}$ *less* than the stereo; that is, it costs $\frac{2}{3}$ as much as the stereo.

By the way, some of these answers could have been eliminated quickly using basic logic. (**A**) is too small; the stereo alone costs $\frac{1}{4}$ of her savings. (**D**) and (**E**) are too large. The television costs *less* than the stereo, so the two together must cost less than $2 \times \frac{1}{4}$, or half, of Carol's savings. We'll look more at using logic to eliminate answers later in this chapter.

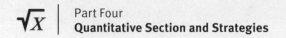
Applying the Kaplan Method: Picking Numbers with Variables in the Question Stem

Now let's use the Kaplan Method on a Problem Solving question that involves picking numbers with variables in the question stem:

> If $w > x > y > z$ on the number line, y is halfway between x and z, and x is halfway between w and z, then $\dfrac{y - x}{y - w} =$
>
> ○ $\dfrac{1}{4}$
>
> ○ $\dfrac{1}{3}$
>
> ○ $\dfrac{1}{2}$
>
> ○ $\dfrac{3}{4}$
>
> ○ 1

STEP 1: ANALYZE THE QUESTION

This question presents a very complicated relationship among four variables. Since there are multiple variables in the problem, picking numbers is a possible approach. The answer choices are all numbers, so you won't have to test each answer choice—you'd just plug numbers into the question. Since the phrase *number line* appears, you may want to consider drawing a number line to help visualize the situation:

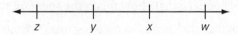

STEP 2: STATE THE TASK

The question asks you to evaluate a rather complicated fraction: $\dfrac{y - x}{y - w}$. The question stem gives you no actual values for the variables, but the answer choices are numbers. This means that the value of the fractional expression must always be the same, as long as the values of the variables follow the rules described in the question stem.

STEP 3: APPROACH STRATEGICALLY

The math seems like it would be difficult and time-consuming. You'd have to translate each rule that states a relationship between variables into a separate algebraic equation and then somehow combine them to solve for the fraction in the stem. Picking numbers, on the other hand, will be much more straightforward.

The rules are pretty complicated, so pick numbers one at a time, making sure the numbers you pick are permissible (follow the rules in the stem) and manageable (easy to work with). x and z each appear twice in the rules, so starting with those two numbers would seem to make sense.

Let's go with $z = 1$ and $x = 3$ to leave room for y.

y is halfway between 3 and 1, so $y = 2$.

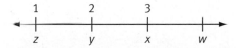

x, or 3, is halfway between w and 1, so $w - 5$.

Once you've picked a set of permissible numbers, it's time to plug these numbers into the expression in the stem:

$$\frac{y - x}{y - w} = \frac{2 - 3}{2 - 5} = \frac{-1}{-3} = \frac{1}{3}$$

The answer is (**B**). Picking numbers can often take you to the correct answer much more directly than algebra.

STEP 4: CONFIRM YOUR ANSWER

Look back at the question stem and make sure you understood all the rules and picked permissible numbers. "y is halfway between x and z." Check. "x is halfway between w and z." Check. Another potential error would have been to make w the smallest variable instead of the largest. (Did you notice how the question stem puts w on the left of the inequality statement, even though it belongs on the right-hand side of the number line?) That's another potential mistake you could catch in this step.

TAKEAWAYS: PICKING NUMBERS WITH VARIABLES IN THE QUESTION STEM

- Most people find it easier to perform calculations with numbers than to perform calculations with variables.
- Variables may be letters (n, x, t, etc.) or unspecified values (e.g., "a factory produces some number of units of a product each month").
- When picking numbers, be sure that the numbers are permissible and manageable.

Practice Set: Picking Numbers with Variables in the Question Stem

6. If $\dfrac{4y - 4x}{z - x} = 2$, then $\dfrac{2(z - x)}{z - y} =$

   ○ −1

   ○ 1

   ○ 2

   ○ 3

   ○ 4

7. DeShawn set aside some of his savings to make charitable donations. If he gives $\dfrac{1}{8}$ of the money to Charity A and $\dfrac{1}{5}$ of the remainder to Charity B, what fraction of the original amount that he set aside does DeShawn have left to distribute to other charities?

   ○ $\dfrac{3}{10}$

   ○ $\dfrac{3}{5}$

   ○ $\dfrac{27}{40}$

   ○ $\dfrac{7}{10}$

   ○ $\dfrac{11}{13}$

8. During a sale, a store sells 20 percent of its remaining stock each day, without replenishment. After 4 days, what fraction of its original stock has it sold?

○ $\dfrac{1}{625}$

○ $\dfrac{256}{625}$

○ $\dfrac{61}{125}$

○ $\dfrac{64}{125}$

○ $\dfrac{369}{625}$

Picking Numbers with Percents in the Answer Choices

Picking numbers also works well on Problem Solving questions for which the answer choices are given in percents. When the answers are in percents, 100 will almost always be the most manageable number to pick. Using 100 not only makes your calculations easier, but it also simplifies the task of expressing the final value as a percent of the original.

Example:

> The manufacturer of Sleep-EZ mattresses is offering a 10 percent discount on the price of its king-size mattress. Some retailers are offering additional discounts. If a retailer offers an additional 20 percent discount, then what is the total discount available at that retailer?
>
> ○ 10%
> ○ 25%
> ○ 28%
> ○ 30%
> ○ 35%

Since the answers are in percents, pick $100 as the original price of the mattress. (Remember, realism is irrelevant—only permissibility and manageability matter.) The manufacturer offers a 10% discount: 10% of $100 is $10. So now the mattress costs $90.

Then the retailer offers an additional 20% discount. Since the price has fallen to $90, that 20% is taken off the $90 price. A 20% discount is now a reduction of $18. The final price of the mattress is $90 − $18, or $72.

The mattress has been reduced to $72 from an original price of $100. That's a $28 reduction. Since you started with $100, you can easily calculate that $28 is 28% of the original price. Choice (**C**) is correct.

Notice that choice (**D**) commits the error of simply adding the two percents given in the question stem. An answer choice like (**D**) will never be correct on a question that gives you information about multiple percent changes.

Applying the Kaplan Method: Picking Numbers with Percents in the Answer Choices

Now let's use the Kaplan Method on a Problem Solving question that involves picking numbers with percents in the answer choices:

> In 1998, the profits of Company N were 10 percent of revenues. In 1999, the revenues of Company N fell by 20 percent, but profits were 15 percent of revenues. The profits in 1999 were what percent of the profits in 1998?
>
> ○ 80%
> ○ 105%
> ○ 120%
> ○ 124.2%
> ○ 138%

STEP 1: ANALYZE THE QUESTION

Profits and revenues are both changing over time. Since the answer choices are percents, picking 100 is a good idea.

STEP 2: STATE THE TASK

The profits in 1999 were what percent of the profits in 1998?

You'll have to compare the profits of the two years. The year 1998 is the basis of the comparison. You're not solving for the increase or decrease, just the relative amount.

In other words, you want this fraction, $\dfrac{\text{1999 profits}}{\text{1998 profits}}$, expressed as a percent.

STEP 3: APPROACH STRATEGICALLY

You should start with the original profits, since the question presents its 1999 information as a change from the 1998 information. You read this about 1998 profits: "In 1998, the profits of Company N were 10 percent of revenues." So you'll know profits if you know revenues. You're given no information about revenue at all, so just pick a number. Given the percents in the answer choices, pick $100. That makes profits in 1998 equal to $10.

Now, what about 1999 profits? You read, "In 1999... profits were 15 percent of revenues." So you have to know revenues in 1999 to know profits. What does the question say about 1999's revenues? "In 1999, the revenues of Company N fell by 20 percent." Revenues were $100, so they fell $20 to $80. Profits, then, were 15% of $80, or $0.15(\$80) = \$12$.

By the way, you don't have to calculate that directly. You can use Critical Thinking and say:

$$15\% \text{ of } 80 = 10\% \text{ of } 80 + 5\% \text{ of } 80$$
$$15\% \text{ of } 80 = 10\% \text{ of } 80 \ + \ \text{half of } (10\% \text{ of } 80)$$
$$15\% \text{ of } 80 = 8 \ + \ \text{half of } 8$$
$$15\% \text{ of } 80 = 8 \ + \ 4$$
$$15\% \text{ of } 80 = 12$$

Plugging your results back into the question yields $\dfrac{\text{1999 profits}}{\text{1998 profits}} = \dfrac{12}{10} = 1.2$.

Just multiply by 100% to convert the decimal to a percent: $1.2 \times 100\% = 120\%$. Choice (**C**) is correct.

STEP 4: CONFIRM YOUR ANSWER

Make sure to reread the question stem to confirm that you interpreted the relationships correctly.

TAKEAWAYS: PICKING NUMBERS WITH PERCENTS IN THE ANSWER CHOICES

- On a question involving multiple changes in percent, one of the trap answers will most likely involve simply adding or subtracting the percents.

- When you see a percent question with unspecified values, pick 100 for the unknown value. Doing so will make the calculations much easier.

Practice Set: Picking Numbers with Percents in the Answer Choices

9. If a bicyclist in motion increases his speed by 30 percent and then increases this speed by 10 percent, what percent of the original speed is the total increase in speed?

   ○ 10%
   ○ 40%
   ○ 43%
   ○ 64%
   ○ 140%

10. A driver delivered food from a restaurant to a customer's home by way of a certain route. If the driver then completed 20 percent of the return trip by way of the same route before the delivery vehicle broke down, what percent of the round trip did the driver complete?

    ○ 10%
    ○ 20%
    ○ 60%
    ○ 70%
    ○ 80%

11. Sofia runs a business delivering boxes of frequently used household supplies to monthly subscribers. After hiring a workflow manager, she delivered 20 percent more boxes per month while working 20 percent fewer hours herself each month. Hiring a workflow manager increased Sofia's personal productivity per hour by what percent?

    ○ 40%
    ○ 50%
    ○ 60%
    ○ 140%
    ○ 150%

Picking Numbers with Variables in the Answer Choices

Whenever the answer choices contain variables, you should consider picking numbers. The correct answer choice is the one that yields the result that you got when you plugged the same number(s) into the question stem. Make sure that you test each answer choice, just in case more than one answer choice produces the desired result. In such a case, you will need to pick a new set of numbers and repeat the process only for the answer choices that worked out the first time.

Example:

If $a > 1$, which of the following is equal to $\dfrac{2a + 6}{a^2 + 2a - 3}$?

○ a

○ $a + 3$

○ $\dfrac{2}{a - 1}$

○ $\dfrac{2a}{a - 3}$

○ $\dfrac{a - 1}{2}$

The question says that $a > 1$, so the most manageable permissible number will probably be 2. Then $\dfrac{2(2) + 6}{2^2 + 2(2) - 3} = \dfrac{4 + 6}{4 + 4 - 3} = \dfrac{10}{5} = 2$.

Now substitute 2 for a in each answer choice, looking for choices that equal 2 when $a = 2$. Eliminate choices that do not equal 2 when $a = 2$.

Choice (**A**): $a = 2$. Choice (**A**) is possibly correct.

Choice (**B**): $a + 3 = 2 + 3 = 5$. This is not 2. Discard.

Choice (**C**): $\dfrac{2}{a - 1} = \dfrac{2}{2 - 1} = \dfrac{2}{1} = 2$. Possibly correct.

Choice (**D**): $\dfrac{2a}{a - 3} = \dfrac{2(2)}{2 - 3} = \dfrac{4}{-1} = -4$. This is not 2. Discard.

Choice (**E**): $\dfrac{a - 1}{2} = \dfrac{2 - 1}{2} = \dfrac{1}{2}$. This is not 2. Discard.

You're down to (**A**) and (**C**). When more than one answer choice remains, you must pick another number. Try $a = 3$. Then $\dfrac{2(3) + 6}{3^2 + 2(3) - 3} = \dfrac{6 + 6}{9 + 6 - 3} = \dfrac{12}{12} = 1$.

Now work with the remaining answer choices.

Choice (**A**): $a = 3$. This is not 1. Discard.

Now that all four incorrect answer choices have been eliminated, you know that (**C**) must be correct. Check to see whether it equals 1 when $a = 3$.

Choice (**C**): $\dfrac{2}{a - 1} = \dfrac{2}{3 - 1} = \dfrac{2}{2} = 1$. Choice (**C**) does equal 1 when $a = 3$.

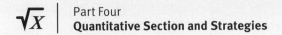

This approach to picking numbers also applies to many confusing word problems on the GMAT. Picking numbers can resolve a lot of that confusion. The key to picking numbers in word problems is to reread the question stem after you've picked numbers, substituting the numbers in place of the variables.

Example:

> A car rental company charges for mileage as follows: x dollars per mile for the first n miles and $x + 1$ dollars per mile for each mile over n miles. How much will the mileage charge be, in dollars, for a journey of d miles, where $d > n$?
>
> ○ $d(x + 1) - n$
>
> ○ $xn + d$
>
> ○ $xn + d(x + 1)$
>
> ○ $x(n + d) - d$
>
> ○ $(x + 1)(d - n)$

Suppose that you pick $x = 4$, $n = 3$, and $d = 5$. Now the problem would read like this:

A car rental company charges for mileage as follows: $4 per mile for each of the first 3 miles and $5 per mile for each mile over 3 miles. How much will the mileage charge be, in dollars, for a journey of 5 miles?

All of a sudden, the problem has gotten much more straightforward. The first 3 miles are charged at $4/mile. So that's $4 + $4 + $4, or $12. There are 2 miles remaining, and each one costs $5. So that's $5 + $5, for a total of $10. If the first 3 miles cost $12 and the next 2 cost $10, then the total charge is $12 + $10, which is $22.

Plugging $x = 4$, $n = 3$, and $d = 5$ into the answer choices, you get

(A) $d(x + 1) - n = 5(4 + 1) - 3 = 22$

(B) $xn + d = 4 \times 3 + 5 = 17$

(C) $xn + d(x + 1) = 4 \times 3 + 5(4 + 1) = 37$

(D) $x(n + d) - d = 4(3 + 5) - 5 = 27$

(E) $(x + 1)(d - n) = (4 + 1)(5 - 3) = 10$

Only **(A)** yields the same number you got when you plugged these numbers into the question stem, so **(A)** is the answer. No need for algebra at all.

Applying the Kaplan Method: Picking Numbers with Variables in the Answer Choices

Now let's use the Kaplan Method on a Problem Solving question that involves picking numbers with variables in the answer choices:

> Cindy paddles her kayak upstream at m kilometers per hour, and then returns downstream the same distance at n kilometers per hour. How many kilometers upstream did she travel if she spent a total of p hours for the round trip?
>
> ○ mnp
>
> ○ $\dfrac{mn}{p}$
>
> ○ $\dfrac{m+n}{p}$
>
> ○ $\dfrac{mnp}{m+n}$
>
> ○ $\dfrac{pm}{n} - \dfrac{pn}{m}$

STEP 1: ANALYZE THE QUESTION

Cindy is going upstream and then the same distance back downstream. Notice that the answer choices contain variables. Whenever the answer choices have variable(s), consider picking numbers as an approach.

STEP 2: STATE THE TASK

The question asks, "How many kilometers upstream did she travel if she spent a total of p hours for the round trip?" You're solving not for the total distance of her round trip, just one leg of it.

STEP 3: APPROACH STRATEGICALLY

It will be hard to pick all the variables at once, so don't try to do so. You can always go one variable at a time. It's often easiest to start with the variable that appears most often, as that value often has the greatest influence over what numbers will be manageable. In this problem, that's the distance upstream (it appears twice, since she goes the same distance downstream). So if you picked that distance to be, say, 6 kilometers, you could then easily pick manageable numbers for m and n.

But for the sake of argument, let's say you didn't see that you needed to pick distance. That's OK. If you start by picking two manageable numbers for m and n—for example, $m = 2$ and $n = 3$—then the question becomes this:

> Cindy paddles her kayak upstream at 2 kilometers per hour, and then returns downstream the same distance at 3 kilometers per hour. How many kilometers upstream did she travel if she spent a total of p hours for the round trip?

To figure out the time, you'd need the distance. As none is given, you can pick one. If the speeds are 2 kilometers per hour and 3 kilometers per hour, a distance of 6 kilometers works nicely. Now the question is this:

> Cindy paddles her kayak 6 kilometers upstream at 2 kilometers per hour, and then returns downstream 6 kilometers at 3 kilometers per hour. How many kilometers upstream did she travel if she spent a total of p hours for the round trip?

Now the time is very straightforward to calculate. Six kilometers upstream at 2 kilometers per hour means a total of 3 hours. Six kilometers downstream at 3 kilometers per hour means a total of 2 hours. That's $3 + 2 = 5$ hours for the round trip.

Now plug $m = 2$, $n = 3$, and $p = 5$ into the answer choices to see which yields 6 for the number of kilometers traveled upstream.

(A) $mnp = 2 \times 3 \times 5 = 30$. Eliminate.

(B) $\dfrac{mn}{p} = \dfrac{(2 \times 3)}{5} = \dfrac{6}{5}$. Eliminate.

(C) $\dfrac{m+n}{p} = \dfrac{(3+2)}{5} = \dfrac{5}{5} = 1$. Eliminate.

(D) $\dfrac{mnp}{m+n} = \dfrac{(2 \times 3 \times 5)}{(2+3)} = \dfrac{(2 \times 3 \times 5)}{5} = 2 \times 3 = 6$. **(D)** could be right, but you need to test **(E)** to make sure.

(E) $\dfrac{pm}{n} - \dfrac{pn}{m} = \dfrac{5 \times 2}{3} - \dfrac{5 \times 3}{2} = \dfrac{10}{3} - \dfrac{15}{2} = \dfrac{20}{6} - \dfrac{45}{6} = -\dfrac{25}{6}$. Eliminate.

Only choice **(D)** remains, so it is correct.

STEP 4: CONFIRM YOUR ANSWER

Make sure to reread the question stem to confirm that you interpreted the information correctly.

Picking numbers can make word problems much easier to understand, so it's important that you don't hastily start writing down equations. Were you to immediately start writing down algebraic equations for this question, you'd wind up with six variables: speed upstream, speed downstream, time upstream, time downstream, distance for each leg of the trip, and total time. That's a lot to deal with. See how picking numbers simplifies things.

TAKEAWAYS: PICKING NUMBERS WITH VARIABLES IN THE ANSWER CHOICES

- Questions with variables in the answer choices comprise the majority of situations in which test takers should consider picking numbers.

- After picking numbers, reread the question stem, substituting your number(s) for the variable(s).

- When picking numbers with variables in the answer choices, check each answer choice to make sure the numbers you picked don't happen to work for more than one choice.

  · Exception: For "could be" questions (e.g., "Which of the following could be odd?"), you can safely choose the first answer choice that works.

Practice Set: Picking Numbers with Variables in the Answer Choices

12. If $n \neq 1$, $j \neq 0$, $k \neq 0$, and $m \neq 0$ and if $n = \dfrac{jkm}{jk + jm + km}$, then $\dfrac{1}{n-1} =$

    ○ $\dfrac{1}{j} + \dfrac{1}{k} + \dfrac{1}{m}$

    ○ $\dfrac{jk + jm + km}{jkm - jk - jm - km}$

    ○ $\dfrac{jk + jm + km}{jkm}$

    ○ $\dfrac{jkm - jk - jm - km}{jk + jm + km}$

    ○ $j + k + m$

13. In 15 minutes, Jyoti can read p pages of her economics book. How many minutes will it take her to read r pages of her marketing book, if she reads both books at the same rate?

    ○ $\dfrac{r}{15p}$

    ○ $\dfrac{15r}{p}$

    ○ $\dfrac{15}{rp}$

    ○ $\dfrac{15p}{r}$

    ○ $\dfrac{p}{15r}$

14. To raise money for a charity, v volunteers each pledge to contribute an equal portion of the total goal of d dollars. If r more volunteers join the fund-raising campaign and agree with the original volunteers to contribute equally to the goal, how much less must each original donor give?

   ○ $\dfrac{d}{2v + r}$

   ○ $\dfrac{dv}{2v + r^2}$

   ○ $\dfrac{dr}{v^2 + vr}$

   ○ $\dfrac{dv}{r^2 + vr}$

   ○ $\dfrac{d(v + r)}{2(vr)^2}$

Picking Numbers on Must Be/Could Be/Cannot Be Questions

This is a slightly different style of question that asks things like "Which of the following must be an even integer?" or "Which of the following CANNOT be true?" These questions are usually based not on algebra or arithmetic but rather on the properties of the numbers themselves. Some of these questions can be very abstract, so picking numbers really helps. Just as with word problems, making a number properties question concrete helps you to understand it.

Example:

If a and b are odd integers, which of the following must be an even integer?

○ $a(b - 2)$

○ $ab + 4$

○ $(a + 2)(b - 4)$

○ $3a + 5b$

○ $a(a + 6)$

You can run through the answer choices quite quickly using the picking numbers strategy. Try $a = 1$, $b = 3$. Only (**D**), $3 + 15 = 18$, is even.

Another approach that works well for many "must be/could be/cannot be" problems is to pick different numbers for each answer choice, looking to eliminate the wrong answers. The principle of focusing on what's asked is particularly important here, as you need a clear idea of what you're looking for in a wrong answer. Always characterize what you're looking for among the answer choices before you dive in and start testing them. For instance, in the example you just saw, any expression that comes back even may be the correct answer, but any expression that comes back odd must certainly be incorrect and should be eliminated.

Knowing how to test the answer choices on "must be/could be/cannot be" questions is essential to your success on these questions. As you just saw, on a "must be" question, it's not enough to stop when you reach the first answer choice that works with the numbers you picked. If an answer choice works, that only proves that it *could* be true, not that it *must* be true every time. To be sure you're choosing the right answer to a "must be" or "cannot be" question, pick numbers to eliminate all four incorrect answers. However, for a "could be" question (e.g., "Which of the following could be odd?"), you can safely choose the first answer choice that works. If none of the answer choices work using the numbers you picked, you will need to pick another set of numbers and test the choices again. Always think critically about what the question stem is asking and *how* to pick numbers to find the answer most efficiently.

Roman numeral questions often feature must be/could be/cannot be language in their question stems. Let's look at how to handle one of these questions.

Example:

If integers x and y are distinct factors of 24, then which of the following CANNOT be a factor of 24?

I. $(x + y)^2$

II. $x^2 - y^2$

III. $xy + y^2$

○ I only

○ I and II

○ II and III

○ II only

○ III only

Roman numeral questions are rare but can be big time wasters if you don't work strategically. Evaluate statements one at a time, eliminating answer choices as you go. Usually you should start with the statement that appears most frequently in the answer choices.

This question asks you to figure out which statement or statements can never be a factor of 24. That means you can eliminate a statement if it could ever possibly equal a factor of 24. If you pick some numbers that don't yield a factor of 24, all that means is that the statement *might* be part of the right answer. But if you pick numbers that do yield a factor of 24, you know that any answer choice that includes that statement can be eliminated. It's much more straightforward, therefore, to prove answers wrong rather than to prove them right.

Since the question involves factors of 24, it's a good idea to list these factors out. Anytime a question deals with a small set of specific numbers, write them down. You'll find keeping track of the options to be much easier:

$$1, 2, 3, 4, 6, 8, 12, 24$$

Statement II appears three times among the answer choices, so if you can eliminate it, you'll be down to two choices right away. Squaring something large like 24 or 12 is going to produce a large number, which wouldn't be a factor of 24. So choose smaller numbers instead: $x = 4$ and $y = 2$, perhaps. Then $x^2 - y^2$ would equal $16 - 4$, or 12. Because 12 is a factor of 24, you can eliminate any answer choice containing Statement II. That leaves only (**A**) and (**E**).

Look at Statement III next. Not only are you squaring and multiplying, but you're also adding, so this number is going to get big fast. To keep it in your target range, pick the smallest numbers on your list, $x = 1$ and $y = 2$. Then $xy + y^2$ would equal $1(2) + 4$, or 6. That's a factor of 24, so (**E**) is eliminated. You know that (**A**) is the right answer without ever having to evaluate Statement I.

Applying the Kaplan Method: Picking Numbers on Must Be/Could Be/Cannot Be Questions

Now let's use the Kaplan Method on a Problem Solving question that involves picking numbers with "must be/could be/cannot be" questions:

> If j and k are integers, and $2j + k = 15$, which of the following must be true?
>
> O $j + k$ is odd.
>
> O $j + k$ is even.
>
> O j is odd.
>
> O k is odd.
>
> O $k > j$

STEP 1: ANALYZE THE QUESTION

You're given the equation $2j + k = 15$ and told that j and k are integers. Those two variables also show up in the answer choices. Whenever the answer choices contain variables, consider picking numbers.

STEP 2: STATE THE TASK

You're looking for an answer that MUST be true. Since you know to characterize the answer choices on "must be/could be/cannot be" problems, you know to remind yourself that if an answer choice could be false, even in one case, it can be eliminated.

STEP 3: APPROACH STRATEGICALLY

Pretend for a moment that you weren't able to confidently pick different numbers, trying to see whether each answer could be false and thus eliminated. You'll have to pick one set of numbers and plug them into all the choices.

Let's say that you start with $j = 4$ and $k = 7$.

(A) $4 + 7$ is odd. True. Can't be eliminated.

(B) $4 + 7$ is even. False. Eliminate.

(C) 4 is odd. False. Eliminate.

(D) 7 is odd. True. Can't be eliminated.

(E) $7 > 4$. True. Can't be eliminated.

Now you'd have to try a different set of numbers, hoping to eliminate some more. **(E)** looks like the easiest one to target, as you just have to think of a j that's greater than or equal to k. You could choose $j = 5$ and $k = 5$. There's no need to test **(C)** or **(B)**, as they've already been eliminated.

(A) $5 + 5$ is odd. False. Eliminate.

(D) 5 is odd. True. Can't be eliminated.

(E) $5 > 5$. False. Eliminate.

Only **(D)** wasn't eliminated, so it must be the correct answer.

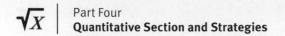

STEP 4: CONFIRM YOUR ANSWER

Make sure to reread the question stem to confirm that you interpreted the stem correctly.

TAKEAWAYS: PICKING NUMBERS ON MUST BE/COULD BE/CANNOT BE QUESTIONS

- On these questions, you can pick numbers and plug them into every answer choice…

- … or you can pick different numbers for each answer choice, trying either to eliminate it or to confirm it.

- Characterizing what you're looking for in the answer choices will help you to pick numbers.

- On Roman numeral questions, start eliminating answer choices by either testing the options that appear most often in the choices or testing the options that are easiest to evaluate.

Practice Set: Picking Numbers on Must Be/Could Be/Cannot Be Questions

15. If integers a and b are distinct factors of 30, which of the following CANNOT be a factor of 30?

       I. $ab + b^2$

      II. $(a + b)^2$

     III. $a + b$

   ○   I only

   ○   II only

   ○   III only

   ○   I and II only

   ○   I, II, and III

16. The integer a is less than -1, and the integer d is greater than 1. If $-1 < b < 0$ and $0 < c < 1$, then which of the following must be the greatest negative number?

   ○ $b - a$

   ○ $b - c$

   ○ $b - d$

   ○ $c - a$

   ○ $a - c$

17. In the set S of consecutive integers from 1 to 10, inclusive, D is the subset of all odd numbers, M is the subset of all prime numbers, and Q is the subset of all numbers whose positive square root is also a member of set S. If d is an element of D, m is an element of M, and q is an element of Q, which of the following could be true?

○ $d = \sqrt{mq}$

○ $d = \dfrac{q}{m}$

○ $m = q$

○ $q = \dfrac{m}{d^2}$

○ $q = \sqrt{dm}$

Step 3: Approach Strategically—Backsolving

> **LEARNING OBJECTIVES**
>
> In this section, you will learn how to:
>
> - Describe how the backsolving strategy is performed
> - Identify Problem Solving questions to which you can apply a backsolving strategy
> - Apply backsolving to appropriate Problem Solving questions

Backsolving is just like picking numbers, except instead of coming up with the number yourself, you use the numbers in the answer choices. You'll literally work backward through the problem, looking for the answer choice that agrees with the information in the question stem. This is a good approach whenever the task of plugging a choice into the question would allow you to confirm its details in a straightforward way.

You want to backsolve systematically, not randomly. Start with either (**B**) or (**D**). If the choice you pick isn't correct, you'll often be able to figure out whether you need to try a number that's larger or one that's smaller. Since numerical answer choices will always be in ascending or descending order, you'll be able to eliminate several choices at once.

Backsolving can save you a great deal of time. It is also an exceptional approach when you have no idea how to begin a problem.

Backsolving with Word Problems

Example:

> Ron begins reading a book at 4:30 p.m. and reads at a steady pace of 30 pages per hour. Michelle begins reading a copy of the same book at 6:00 p.m. If Michelle started 5 pages behind the page that Ron started on and reads at an average pace of 50 pages per hour, at what time would Ron and Michelle be reading the same page?
>
> ○   7:00 p.m.
>
> ○   7:30 p.m.
>
> ○   7:45 p.m.
>
> ○   8:00 p.m.
>
> ○   8:30 p.m.

You could perhaps set up a complex system of equations to solve this problem. Even if you knew exactly what those equations would be and how to solve them, that's not a very efficient use of your time. Backsolving will work better here. Pick an answer choice and see whether Michelle and Ron are on the same page at that time. There's no compelling reason to prefer one choice to another. So just quickly choose (**B**) or (**D**).

Let's say you choose (**B**). On what page is Ron at 7:30 p.m.? He started reading at 4:30 p.m., so he's been reading for 3 hours. His pace is 30 pages per hour. So he's read 30 × 3, or 90 pages. Since Michelle started 5 pages behind Ron, she'd need to read 95 pages to be at the same place. She's been reading since 6:00 p.m., so she's read for 1.5 hours. At 50 pages per hour, she's read 75 pages. That's 20 short of what she needs. So (**B**) is not the right answer.

Since Michelle is reading faster than Ron, she'll catch up to him with more time. Therefore, they'll be on the same page sometime later than 7:30 p.m., so you should try an answer choice that gives a later time. The most strategic answer choice to turn to at this point is choice (**D**). If (**D**) ends up being correct, you can choose it and move on. If (**D**) is too late, then (**C**) must be the answer. If (**D**) is too early, then the correct choice must be (**E**).

Let's try out (**D**). At 8:00 p.m., Ron has read for 3.5 hours. At a pace of 30 pages per hour, he's read 30 × 3.5, or 105 pages. Since Michelle started 5 pages behind, she'd need to read 110 pages to be at the same place. She's been reading for 2 hours at this point; at 50 pages per hour, she's read 100 pages. That's still 10 short of what she needs to catch up. So (**D**) is also not the right answer, and you need a later time than 8:00 p.m.—choice (**E**) must be correct.

When you start with either (**B**) or (**D**), you'll have picked the right answer 20% of the time. Another 20% of the time, you'll know the right answer by process of elimination without ever having to test another choice.

Sometimes you may have to test more than one choice. But as you saw above, you should never have to test more than two answer choices. Stick to (**B**) or (**D**), and you'll save valuable time and worry.

Example:

> A crate of apples contains 1 bruised apple for every 30 apples in the crate. Three out of every 4 bruised apples are considered not fit to sell, and every apple that is not fit to sell is bruised. If there are 12 apples not fit to sell in the crate, how many apples are there in the crate?
>
> O 270
>
> O 360
>
> O 480
>
> O 600
>
> O 840

Start backsolving with choice (**B**). Suppose that there are 360 apples in the crate. Then $\frac{360}{30}$ apples, or 12 apples, are bruised. Then $\frac{3}{4}$ of those 12 apples, or 9 apples, are unsalable. This is too few unsalable apples. So (**B**) is too small. The answer must be larger than 360, so (**A**) and (**B**) are eliminated. Regardless of what you might suspect the answer to be, you should next test (**D**). If (**D**) is not right, you'll know whether it's too large—in which case (**C**) would be correct—or too small—in which case (**E**) would be correct. No matter what, you'll only have to test one more choice.

Testing (**D**), suppose that there are 600 apples in the crate. Then $\frac{600}{30}$ apples, or 20 apples, are bruised. Of those 20, $\frac{3}{4}$, or 15, are unsalable. That's too many. So (**D**) and (**E**) are both out, proving that (**C**) is correct.

Backsolving works for more than just word problems. You can use it whenever you're solving for a single variable in the question stem.

Example:

What is the value of x if $\dfrac{x+1}{x-3} - \dfrac{x+2}{x-4} = 0$?

○   −2

○   −1

○   0

○   1

○   2

Since (**D**) looks easier to work with than (**B**), start with that choice.

$$\frac{1+1}{1-3} - \frac{1+2}{1-4} = \frac{2}{-2} - \frac{3}{-3} = -1 - (-1) = 0$$

Therefore, (**D**) is correct, and you don't have to test any more choices.

Applying the Kaplan Method: Backsolving

Now let's use the Kaplan Method on a Problem Solving question that lends itself to backsolving:

At a certain zoo, the ratio of sea lions to penguins is 4 to 11. If there are 84 more penguins than sea lions at the zoo, how many sea lions are there?

○   24

○   36

○   48

○   72

○   132

STEP 1: ANALYZE THE QUESTION

A zoo has more penguins than sea lions, and you're given both a ratio and a numerical difference between them.

STEP 2: STATE THE TASK

You need to figure out the number of sea lions. You should jot this down in your scratchwork to help you keep track of the task.

STEP 3: APPROACH STRATEGICALLY

Backsolving is an option whenever you can manageably plug an answer choice into the question stem. After doing so, you merely confirm whether that value is consistent with the other values given in the stem.

Let's say you start by backsolving choice (**B**). You're pretending that there are, in fact, 36 sea lions. So "the ratio of sea lions to penguins is 4 to 11" becomes "the ratio of 36 to penguins is 4 to 11," or 36:*penguins* is 4:11. If you don't see the number of penguins right away, consider rewriting the ratio vertically:

sea lions : penguins

4 : 11

36 : penguins

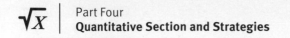

You multiply the proportional value (4) by 9 to get the actual value (36). So the actual number of penguins is $11 \times 9 = 99$.

Is that consistent with the rest of the information? There should be 84 more penguins than sea lions, but $99 - 36 = 63$. If (**B**) were correct, there would be only 63 more penguins. You can eliminate (**B**). Do you need more or fewer sea lions? Well, you need to increase the difference between them. Since the animals are in a ratio of 4:11, every time you remove 4 sea lions, you'd remove 11 penguins, *shrinking* the difference between them by 7. So you definitely need *more* sea lions—every time you add 4 sea lions, you add 11 penguins, increasing the difference by 7. Eliminate (**A**) as well and test (**D**).

$$\text{sea lions} : \text{penguins}$$
$$4 : 11$$
$$72 : \text{penguins}$$

You multiply the proportional value (4) by 18 to get the actual value (72). So the actual number of penguins is $11 \times 18 = 198$. (Or you could more simply say that since you've doubled the number of sea lions from what you had in choice (**B**), you must double the number of penguins as well.)

Is that consistent with the rest of the information? There should be 84 more penguins than sea lions. But $198 - 72 = 126$. If (**D**) were correct, there would be 126 more penguins. That's too many more, so (**D**) is eliminated. You need a smaller difference, which means you need a smaller number of sea lions. The answer must be (**C**).

STEP 4: CONFIRM YOUR ANSWER

If you had accidentally answered (**E**), which is the number of penguins, this step would save you from a wrong answer.

Did you start this problem by adding 84 to the number of sea lions in one of the answer choices and then checking whether it was consistent with the given ratio? That's fine, too. If you had trouble figuring out whether you needed to increase or decrease the number of sea lions, you could have either checked all five answer choices, stopping when you found the right ratio, or changed your approach to the question.

TAKEAWAYS: BACKSOLVING

- Like picking numbers, backsolving allows you to plug numbers into the problem. In this case, the numbers are those in the answer choices.

- To backsolve, plug in a value from an answer choice and solve the problem arithmetically. If your calculations are consistent with the question stem, then the answer is correct.

- The most efficient way to backsolve is to plug in either (**B**) or (**D**) first. If your first choice isn't correct, consider whether the correct answer is larger or smaller.

- Testing the answer choices strategically allows you to find the answer after testing, at most, two answer choices.

Practice Set: Backsolving

18. If $\left(\frac{1}{64}\right)^x = 4,096$, $x =$

   ○ $-\frac{1}{3}$

   ○ $-\frac{1}{2}$

   ○ $-\sqrt{2}$

   ○ -2

   ○ -3

19. The length of a rectangle is twice as long as the width, and the rectangle's area is greater than 72 and less than 200. Which of the following could be the length of the rectangle?

   ○   8

   ○   12

   ○   16

   ○   20

   ○   24

20. In a certain beanbag game, players toss beanbags at a board with a hole in it. If the beanbag falls into the hole, the player scores 5 points. A beanbag that lands on the board but misses the hole is worth 2 points. If a toss misses the board entirely, 1 point is deducted from the player's score. Julianna had 20 tosses and missed the board with 3 throws. Her total score was 52. How many times did she toss the beanbag into the hole?

   ○   5

   ○   6

   ○   7

   ○   8

   ○   9

Step 3: Approach Strategically—Estimating and Guessing

LEARNING OBJECTIVES

In this section, you will learn how to:

- Describe how guessing can be an effective strategy for Problem Solving questions
- Describe what it means to estimate an answer using critical thinking skills
- Apply effective guessing and estimating strategies to appropriate questions

A well-placed guess can sometimes be the best thing you can do on a problem. Because of the severe penalty exacted on those who fail to finish a section, you need to stay on a steady pace. If you fall behind, it's a good idea to guess on the hardest problems. That way you'll get back lost time instead of falling further behind. And while you shouldn't be afraid to guess, you *should* be afraid to rush! The GMAT builds in twists and writes problems in complicated ways; rushing almost always leads to a misperception of the problem. The test makers base many wrong answers on the most common misperceptions. So rushing through a problem virtually guarantees a wrong answer. It's far better to guess as needed than to rush through an entire section.

Sometimes you just have no idea how to approach a problem. Instead of throwing away 3 or 4 minutes getting frustrated, make a guess. If you didn't know how to approach the problem, you weren't likely to choose the right answer in any case, and you can use the time you save to solve other problems that you stand a better chance of answering correctly.

Lastly, there are some problems that are *best* solved using guessing techniques. The two keys to good guessing are (1) elimination of likely wrong answers by using your knowledge of the problem and of the GMAT's tendencies and (2) maintaining your focus on the "big picture"—remembering that your performance on the section as a whole matters much more than your performance on two or three questions. Better to make a guess in 1 minute and be done with a hard problem than spend 6 minutes before guessing; the extra time will pay off.

Also, keep in mind that the hardest questions are the ones you'll be most likely to need to guess on—and are also the ones that will hurt your score the *least* when you get them wrong. So don't be afraid to guess!

There are five guessing strategies that you can apply to Problem Solving:

1. Use critical thinking
2. Estimate the answer
3. Eliminate numbers appearing in the question stem
4. Eliminate the oddball
5. Eliminate uncritical solutions

You won't be able to use all of these strategies on every problem. But if you run through the checklist and eliminate whatever choices you can, you'll make your best possible guess in the least possible amount of time. Let's look at the strategies.

Use Critical Thinking

Some answers are simply logically impossible. By analyzing and simplifying before attempting to solve, you may learn enough about the problem to eliminate many wrong answer choices. Consider this problem:

A container holding 12 ounces of a solution that is 1 part alcohol to 2 parts water is added to a container holding 8 ounces of a solution that is 1 part alcohol to 3 parts water. What is the ratio of alcohol to water in the resulting solution?

O   2:5

O   3:7

O   3:5

O   4:7

O   7:3

It seems a challenging problem at first glance. But the simplified version of the problem is that you're adding a 1:2 solution to a 1:3 solution. So logically, the right answer has to be between 1:3 (or $\frac{1}{3}$, or 0.333 ...) and 1:2 (or $\frac{1}{2}$, or 0.5). (**A**) and (**B**) are both in that range, but all the others are above 1:2. So you can make a guess—with 50% odds of being right—just by analyzing the problem logically.

In case you were curious, the answer is (**B**). The 12-ounce solution has 4 ounces of alcohol and 8 ounces of water. The 8-ounce solution has 2 ounces of alcohol and 6 ounces of water. Add the amounts of alcohol and water to get 6 ounces of alcohol and 14 ounces of water for a ratio of 3:7 alcohol to water.

Also, note that Roman numeral questions are good candidates for logic-based guessing. If you can evaluate only one statement, you can still logically eliminate several answers.

Estimate the Answer

The GMAT asks some questions that are intended to be solved via estimation. When a question stem includes a word like *approximately*, that's a clear signal that estimation is the best approach you can take.

Example:

The product of all positive even numbers less than or equal to 20 is closest to which of the following?

O 10^6

O 10^7

O 10^8

O 10^9

O 10^{10}

If you had a calculator on the Quant section, you could quickly figure out that the product in question is 3,715,891,200. But with no calculator, what can you do? The keys to the solution are the word "closest" and the big spread of values in the answer choices—each is 10 times the nearest value. This problem has "estimation" written all over it.

Jot down the numbers in question:

$$2 \times 4 \times 6 \times 8 \times 10 \times 12 \times 14 \times 16 \times 18 \times 20$$

Now, how to estimate these values? Since each answer is a power of 10, you should estimate each value in a way that easily relates to 10:

$$2 \times 4 \times 6 \times 8 \times 10 \times 12 \times 14 \times 16 \times 18 \times 20$$

$$2 \times 4 \times 6 \times 10 \times 10 \times 10 \times 10 \times 20 \times 20 \times 20$$

What about the small ones? $2 \times 4 \times 6 = 48$, which is very close to 50.

$$50 \times 10 \times 10 \times 10 \times 10 \times 20 \times 20 \times 20$$

Continuing to look for tens:

$$(5 \times 10) \times 10 \times 10 \times 10 \times 10 \times (2 \times 10) \times (2 \times 10) \times (2 \times 10)$$

That's eight 10s, one 5, and three 2s:

$$2 \times 2 \times 2 \times 5 \times 10^8$$

$$(2 \times 2) \times (2 \times 5) \times 10^8$$

$$4 \times 10 \times 10^8$$

$$4 \times 10^9$$

That's closer to 10^9 than to 10^{10}, so (**D**) is the correct answer. No calculator needed, just the willingness to estimate!

Eliminate Numbers Appearing in the Question Stem

The test makers lay psychological traps as well as mathematical ones, and this guessing principle helps you to stay out of them. It's part of human psychology to deal with being lost by looking for familiar things. When you get lost in a problem, you tend to grab hold of familiar numbers, such as those you've just seen in the question stem. The GMAT doesn't like to reward people who get lost with right answers, so such numbers tend to be wrong.

Eliminate the Oddball

This is psychology again. Our eyes are attracted to difference. (Next time you watch a movie or a TV show, notice how often no one else is dressed in the same color as the main character—it's a subtle trick to keep your attention where the director wants it.) Random guessers, then, will be attracted to uniqueness. As the GMAT does not like to reward random guessing, the oddballs should be eliminated.

A word of warning about this technique: the GMAT also uses a little reverse psychology. The test makers know that people tend to be afraid of answers that seem *too* out of line with the others. These outlying values, then, will sometimes be *correct*. What Kaplan means by an "oddball," then, is *not* a number that's notably bigger or smaller but an answer choice that is structurally unique—the only fraction or the only negative number, for example.

Look at these five answer choices, for example:

○ $\sqrt{2}$

○ 2

○ 4

○ 16

○ 2,056

In this case, the answer choice 2,056 is *not* an oddball and should not be eliminated. But $\sqrt{2}$ is and should be.

Eliminate Uncritical Solutions

Because the GMAT is a test of critical thinking, answers that you'd get just by mashing numbers together are usually wrong. Consider this question:

A bag holds 2 red marbles and 3 green marbles. If you removed 2 randomly selected marbles from the bag, without replacement, what is the probability that both would be red?

○ $\frac{1}{10}$

○ $\frac{1}{5}$

○ $\frac{3}{10}$

○ $\frac{2}{5}$

○ $\frac{1}{2}$

It's true that you want 2 of the 5 marbles in the bag. But GMAT questions usually require a little more math than just that, so $\frac{2}{5}$ isn't likely to be correct. (In fact, it's the odds of getting *1* red marble when selecting 1; the probability of getting 2 red when selecting 2 is actually $\frac{1}{10}$.)

Stay Alert for Guessing Opportunities

Believe it or not, there are some GMAT problems for which a guessing strategy—most notably Logic or Estimation—is the best approach you could take. Remember that the test makers aren't trying to judge your math skills alone; they are also testing your ability to find efficient solutions to problems. Every so often, they give you a set of choices with only one logically possible answer. Make sure to look at the answer choices before you choose your approach. Otherwise, you might not realize that you can estimate.

Example:

If a store owner increases a product's price by 20 percent and then increases this price by another 15 percent, what percent of the original price is the total price increase?

○   20%

○   35%

○   38%

○   65%

○   135%

It's true that you could pick the original price to be $100, but you can do better here by thinking logically about the question and the answer choices. The price goes up 20% and then up another 15%. That 15% increase is being applied not to the original price but to the price after the first increase. If it were 15% of the original, then the total increase would be 20% + 15% = 35% (that's the "uncritical solution"). But since the second increase is based on a higher starting price, the total increase will be a little more than 35%. Only one answer, choice (**C**), fits the bill, so it must be correct.

If applied strategically, guessing will be a great tool for you on Test Day. It will help keep you out of time management trouble, help you to feel confident and in charge of the test, and occasionally reward you with a very quick right answer.

Answers and explanations follow on the next page. ▶ ▶ ▶

Answer Key

Practice Set: The Kaplan Method for Problem Solving

1. E
2. D
3. B
4. C
5. B

Practice Set: Picking Numbers with Variables in the Question Stem

6. E
7. D
8. E

Practice Set: Picking Numbers with Percents in the Answer Choices

9. C
10. C
11. B

Practice Set: Picking Numbers with Variables in the Answer Choices

12. B
13. B
14. C

Practice Set: Picking Numbers on Must Be/ Could Be/Cannot Be Questions

15. B
16. B
17. B

Practice Set: Backsolving

18. D
19. C
20. C

Answers and Explanations

Practice Set: The Kaplan Method for Problem Solving

1. **(E)**

    A machine manufactures notebooks in a series of 5 colors: red, blue, black, white, and yellow. After producing a notebook of 1 color from that series, it produces a notebook of the next color. Once 5 are produced, the machine repeats the same pattern. If the machine began a day producing a red notebook and completed the day by producing a black notebook, how many notebooks could have been produced that day?

    ○ 27
    ○ 34
    ○ 50
    ○ 61
    ○ 78

STEP 1: ANALYZE THE QUESTION

A machine makes notebooks in 5 colors, following a repeating pattern: red, blue, black, white, and yellow. You might abbreviate this in your scratchwork as R, Blu, Bla, W, Y. The machine starts on R and ends on Bla.

STEP 2: STATE THE TASK

How many notebooks could the machine have made? The question makes it clear that there's more than one possible number of notebooks produced, but since this is a multiple-choice question, you know that the answer choices contain only one possible value and four impossible values.

STEP 3: APPROACH STRATEGICALLY

So what do you know about what's possible or impossible for this machine?

The numerical answers are so high that it would probably take a long time to count each notebook one by one. Instead, look for a pattern or rule that tells you what kinds of numbers are possible or impossible answers.

The machine always follows the same pattern: R, Blu, Bla, W, Y. Since it starts on R, the third notebook will be Bla. Sadly, 3 is not an answer. The machine will make 2 more (W and Y) before the pattern is set to repeat. Then, as before, 3 new notebooks are made before you get Bla. So after the first 3, the machine needs to make 5 more to get another Bla. Since the pattern repeats, it does the same thing over and over again. So while you don't know exactly how many times the pattern repeats, you know that each time it does, 5 notebooks get made.

In other words, you've reconceptualized the pattern from "repeat {R, Blu, Bla, W, Y}" to "R, Blu, Bla + repeat {W, Y, R, Blu, Bla}."

To get a Bla notebook, then, make 3 notebooks and then any repetition of 5 notebooks. So the correct answer will be "some multiple of 5" + 3. This means the correct answer will end in either a 3 or an 8. Only (**E**), 78, which is 75 + 3, is possible.

STEP 4: CONFIRM YOUR ANSWER

Reread the question stem, making sure that you didn't miss anything about the problem. For example, if the machine had started on a W notebook, then the answer would have been "some multiple of 5" without the "plus 3."

2.   **(D)**

Youssef lives x blocks from his office. It takes him 1 minute per block to walk to work and 20 seconds per block to ride his bicycle to work. If it takes him exactly 10 minutes more to walk to work than to ride his bicycle, then x equals

- ○   4
- ○   7
- ○   10
- ○   15
- ○   20

STEP 1: ANALYZE THE QUESTION

Youssef walks a block in 1 minute and bikes a block in 20 seconds. As the answer choices are all in minutes, convert the bike rate to 3 blocks per minute. It takes Youssef 10 minutes longer to walk x blocks than to bike x blocks. Such a setup implies the need for algebra, but that might not be the best way to solve.

STEP 2: STATE THE TASK

Find the value of x, which is the number of blocks Youssef walks in the scenario.

STEP 3: APPROACH STRATEGICALLY

Setting up the algebra will get complicated quickly, but the answer choices are whole numbers that represent the number of blocks Youssef might have traveled to work, so backsolving is the best approach. Backsolving is an option whenever you can manageably plug an answer choice into the question stem.

As it takes Youssef 10 more minutes to walk than bike, start with (**D**). If Youssef lives 15 blocks from his office, it would take him 15 minutes to walk (at 1 block per minute) and 5 minutes to bike (at 3 blocks per minute). That's a difference of $15 - 5 = 10$ minutes. A 10-minute difference is exactly what you were looking for, so (**D**) is the correct answer.

STEP 4: CONFIRM YOUR ANSWER

Walking takes Youssef 10 minutes longer than biking. Since it takes Youssef a minute to walk each block, the correct answer must be greater than 10. That allows you to quickly eliminate (**A**), (**B**), and (**C**). (**E**) results in a biking time that isn't a whole number of minutes, which would lead to an answer choice that isn't a whole number. You can therefore confirm that (**D**) is correct.

3. **(B)**

A book club rented the party room of a local restaurant to meet and discuss its current novel over dinner. The total charge, including food and service, was $867.50. If each member of the club paid at least $42, then what is the greatest possible number of members in the club?

○ 19

○ 20

○ 21

○ 23

○ 25

STEP 1: ANALYZE THE QUESTION

For word problems, you need to get a logical sense of the situation so that you can understand how the information fits together. This question tells you that some unknown number of people split a bill of $867.50 and that each person paid at least $42—meaning that some could have paid more than $42 but no one could have paid less.

STEP 2: STATE THE TASK

Figure out the greatest possible number of club members. The phrase "greatest possible" tells you that there's probably no way to calculate the exact number, but there is some way to set an upper limit on the number.

STEP 3: APPROACH STRATEGICALLY

Since you're asked about the number of club members, see what the question stem tells you about club members. You're only told that each one paid a minimum of $42. So you'll know something about the total number of members if you learn something about the total amount paid. The question tells you that the total paid was $867.50.

The bigger the number of members, the less each one would have to pay to cover the tab (e.g., if there were 868 members, each would pay a little less than $1). The least each member can pay is $42. So if you split the total of $867.50 into portions of $42, you'll figure out how many members you need to have to cover those portions.

You can do this calculation with a few easy steps: $42 × 10 yields $420. Twice that is $42 × 20 = $840. One more $42, or $42 × 21, yields $882. That's too much money. If there were 21 members, and each paid no less than the minimum of $42, then they'd have paid more than the question stem says they did. So there can be at most 20 members (some will have to pay a little more than $42 to meet the bill, but the question allows for that).

Since you have numbers in the answer choices, backsolving is also a great strategy to use here. Start with (**B**), since 20 is a nice round number. You have 20 members, each of whom pays a minimum of $42, and in total they pay a minimum of $42 × 20 = $840. If there were one more member paying the minimum of $42, then together they all would have paid $840 + $42 = $882, which is too much. So (**B**) is the right answer.

STEP 4: CONFIRM YOUR ANSWER

Reread the question stem, making sure that you didn't miss anything about the problem. For example, if you misread the question stem to think that each member paid exactly $42, you may not have selected (**B**). But then when you reread, you'd see the "at least" and realize that you had to rethink your answer choice.

4.   (C)

A team won 50 percent of its first 60 games in a particular season and 80 percent of its remaining games. If the team won a total of 60 percent of its games that season, what was the total number of games that the team played?

- ○   180
- ○   120
- ○   90
- ○   85
- ○   30

STEP 1: ANALYZE THE QUESTION

You are given many different pieces of information about a team. First, the team won 50% of its first 60 games, for a total of 30 wins. Then you are told that the team won 80% of the remaining games after the initial 60. Finally, you know that the team won 60% of its games overall.

STEP 2: STATE THE TASK

What was the total number of games the team played throughout the entire season?

STEP 3: APPROACH STRATEGICALLY

The quickest way to solve this problem is to use backsolving. Start with (**B**). If the total number of games is equal to 120, you know that the team played 60 more games after the initial 60. They won 80% of the latter 60 games, for a total of 48 games. Adding the initial 30 games won to the 48 games won in the second part of the season, you get 78 games won out of a total of 120 games. You are told the winning percentage is 60% overall, but $\frac{78}{120} = 0.65$, or 65%. This number is too high, so you can eliminate (**B**).

Think strategically about which answer choice to try next. The first portion of games has a 50% winning average, while the second portion has an 80% winning average. Since the percentage you calculated for (**B**) was too high and the second portion of games has the higher winning percentage, (**B**) has too much weight on the later portion of games. You need fewer games in the second portion and therefore fewer games total. Eliminate both (**A**) and (**B**).

(**D**) gives a total number of games equaling 85. You have already accounted for the first 60 games, so focus on the remaining 25. If the team won 80% of those games, they won 20 more games. In total, the team would have won $\frac{50}{85} \approx 0.59$, or 59%. Since (**D**) is too small (less than 60%) and (**B**) is too big (greater than 60%), you know without calculating that the correct answer is (**C**).

STEP 4: CONFIRM YOUR ANSWER

To confirm your answer, backsolve for (**C**). If there are 90 total games, then there are 30 games in the second portion of the season. The team won 80% of those games, or 24 games. In total, the team would have won $\frac{54}{90} = 0.6$, or 60%.

5. (B)

A local restaurant recently renovated its dining space, purchasing new tables and chairs to use in addition to the original tables and chairs. The new tables each seat 6 customers, while the original tables each seat 4 customers. Altogether, the restaurant now has 40 tables and is capable of seating 220 customers. How many more new tables than original tables does the restaurant have?

- ○ 10
- ○ 20
- ○ 30
- ○ 34
- ○ 36

STEP 1: ANALYZE THE QUESTION

This is an algebra word problem with two variables. You should also note that you are told that the restaurant has more new tables than old and that the correct answer will represent the difference between those two numbers.

STEP 2: STATE THE TASK

Your task is to determine the difference between the number of new tables and the number of old tables. You will need to find the number of each and then subtract.

STEP 3: APPROACH STRATEGICALLY

You could solve this problem by translating the information directly into equations and then combining or substituting the variables to determine the number of each type of table. But backsolving provides a more efficient route to the correct answer here. When backsolving, begin with (**B**) or (**D**), since this will require checking at most two answers. Remembering that we have a total of 40 tables, begin with (**D**). A difference of 34 would mean that the restaurant has 37 new tables and 3 old tables. With 37 tables seating 6 diners each ($37 \times 6 = 222$), you are already over the seating capacity of 220. That means you need fewer of the new tables in the mix. Try (**B**). A difference of 20 means 30 new tables and 10 original tables: $30 \times 6 = 180$ and $10 \times 4 = 40$. Adding 180 and 40 gives you 220, the seating capacity indicated in the question stem. (**B**) is correct.

STEP 4: CONFIRM YOUR ANSWER

The easiest way to go wrong in a problem like this one is to solve for the wrong thing. Both the number of new tables (30) and the number of old tables (10) are present in an answer choice. A quick check of the question to confirm that the correct answer represents the *difference* between the table types is worthwhile before selecting the answer and moving on.

Practice Set: Picking Numbers with Variables in the Question Stem

6. **(E)**

   If $\dfrac{4y - 4x}{z - x} = 2$, then $\dfrac{2(z - x)}{z - y} =$

   ○ −1

   ○ 1

   ○ 2

   ○ 3

   ○ 4

STEP 1: ANALYZE THE QUESTION

You are given one algebraic expression set equal to 2 and asked to solve for the value of another expression. Note that the numerator of the first expression can be factored to the same format as the numerator of the second expression: $\dfrac{4(y - x)}{z - x} = 2$.

STEP 2: STATE THE TASK

Determine the value of the second expression.

STEP 3: APPROACH STRATEGICALLY

The given equation has three variables and you are asked to solve for a second expression that uses the same variables. Rather than trying to isolate variables or use substitution (which could get complicated with three variables), try picking numbers. Make sure that the numbers are permissible, meaning that they fit the given equation.

Looking at the term in the numerator, $4(y - x)$, it would be convenient if $y - x = 1$, since multiplying by 1 has no effect. So set $y = 2$ and $x = 1$ and the numerator becomes $4(2 - 1) = 4$. Since the numerator is 4 and the entire expression must be equal to 2, the denominator must be equal to 2. So set $z = 3$ so that the denominator is $3 - 1 = 2$. Once you have chosen these numbers, plug them into the second expression: $\dfrac{2(3 - 1)}{3 - 2} = 4$. This corresponds to (**E**).

STEP 4: CONFIRM YOUR ANSWER

If time permits, go back through your math. Check that when the numbers are substituted into the initial equation, you get 2, and that when they are substituted into the second equation, you get 4. If both of these are true, the answer is confirmed.

7. (D)

DeShawn set aside some of his savings to make charitable donations. If he gives $\frac{1}{8}$ of the money to Charity A and $\frac{1}{5}$ of the remainder to Charity B, what fraction of the original amount that he set aside does DeShawn have left to distribute to other charities?

○ $\frac{3}{10}$

○ $\frac{3}{5}$

○ $\frac{27}{40}$

○ $\frac{7}{10}$

○ $\frac{11}{13}$

STEP 1: ANALYZE THE QUESTION

DeShawn allocates portions of a fund to two charities and has money left over. No information is given about the amounts of money involved. A quick glance at the answer choices shows that they are fractions, not dollar values or variable expressions.

STEP 2: STATE THE TASK

Determine the fraction of DeShawn's savings that remains after the two donations. You are comparing a part (the money he has left) with the whole (all the savings he set aside for charity).

STEP 3: APPROACH STRATEGICALLY

Whenever a question gives you fractions or percents of an unknown total, consider picking numbers. Be sure to pick a permissible and manageable number for the money that DeShawn set aside to give to charities. Since the fractions you'll need to work with are $\frac{1}{8}$ and $\frac{1}{5}$, a number divisible by both 8 and 5 will be most manageable. Their product, 40, is a logical choice. You might also note that in the answer choices, four out of five of the denominators are either 40 or a number 40 might reduce to, so choosing 40 as the "whole" is likely to make the math easy.

The $\frac{1}{8}$ portion that DeShawn gives to Charity A becomes $\frac{40}{8} = 5$. His donation to Charity B is not $\frac{1}{5}$ of the total but rather $\frac{1}{5}$ of "the remainder," so you need to know what that is. Because $40 - 5 = 35$, that gift is $\frac{35}{5} = 7$.

What's left after donations of 5 and 7 is $40 - 5 - 7 = 28$. The question asks for this amount as a fraction of the original amount, so that is $\frac{28}{40} = \frac{7}{10}$. **(D)** is correct.

STEP 4: CONFIRM YOUR ANSWER

Be certain that you read all aspects of the question correctly. Had you calculated that DeShawn gave $\frac{1}{5}$ of the *total amount* rather than $\frac{1}{5}$ of what was left, you would have selected (**C**). Mistakenly selecting the amount given away rather than what was left would have led you to choose (**A**).

DeShawn allocates portions of a fund to two charities and has money left over. No information is given about the amounts of money involved. A quick glance at the answer choices shows that they are fractions, not dollar values or variable expressions.

8. (E)

During a sale, a store sells 20 percent of its remaining stock each day, without replenishment. After 4 days, what fraction of its original stock has it sold?

- ○ $\dfrac{1}{625}$
- ○ $\dfrac{256}{625}$
- ○ $\dfrac{61}{125}$
- ○ $\dfrac{64}{125}$
- ○ $\dfrac{369}{625}$

STEP 1: ANALYZE THE QUESTION

For 4 days, a store sells the same percentage of its remaining stock each day. In other words, it's not selling the same amount each day but the same proportion of each day's stock.

We're given no way to know exactly how much stock the store starts with. But the answer choices don't have any variables. Whenever variables cancel, leaving only numbers in the answer choices, picking numbers is an approach you should consider. Note that the answers are fractions. So despite the word "percent" in the question stem, 100 might not be as safe a choice when picking numbers as would a common denominator.

STEP 2: STATE THE TASK

Determine the fraction of its original stock the store has sold after 4 days.

STEP 3: APPROACH STRATEGICALLY

Instead of picking 100 for the stock, pick a common denominator. A good choice seems to be 625. Not only is it the denominator of three of the answer choices, but the number in the other two denominators (125) is a factor of 625.

There's a lot to keep track of—starting stock, stock sold, stock remaining for the next day, all on 4 different days—so jotting down a chart on your scratch paper would not be a bad idea:

Day	Start	Sold	Remains
1	625	125	500
2	500	100	400
3	400	80	320
4	320	64	256

You can calculate the total amount sold either by adding $125 + 100 + 80 + 64$ or by subtracting the eventual remains from the original amount ($625 - 256$). Whichever approach you take, 369 is the result.

The store sold $\dfrac{369}{625}$ of its original stock, so (**E**) is correct.

STEP 4: CONFIRM YOUR ANSWER

Had you accidentally answered (**B**), which is how much stock remained, or (**D**), which resembles how much was sold on the fourth day, this step would save you from a wrong answer.

Practice Set: Picking Numbers with Percents in the Answer Choices

9. (C)

If a bicyclist in motion increases his speed by 30 percent and then increases this speed by 10 percent, what percent of the original speed is the total increase in speed?

- ○ 10%
- ○ 40%
- ○ 43%
- ○ 64%
- ○ 140%

STEP 1: ANALYZE THE QUESTION

The question gives you information about two increases to the speed of a bicyclist.

STEP 2: STATE THE TASK

Determine the total percent increase.

STEP 3: APPROACH STRATEGICALLY

When faced with percentages in the question stem and in the answer choices, use the strategy of picking numbers and pick 100. If the bicyclist is initially riding at 100 (the units aren't mentioned in this problem, and in any case, your numbers don't need to be realistic—just permissible and manageable) and then increases his speed by 30%, he is now riding at 130. To increase 130 by 10%, find 10% of 130, which is 13, and add it to 130, making his final speed 143. That is an increase of 43 over his original speed of 100. Since you chose 100 as your initial number, 43 is simply 43% of the original, (**C**).

STEP 4: CONFIRM YOUR ANSWER

When confirming the answer for questions that ask about multiple percent changes, make sure that you calculated the percent changes appropriately and didn't simply add the percentages given in the question, as (**B**) does. Also, check to make sure that you solved for the correct value, the increase in speed as a percentage of the original speed. (**E**) is a trap answer because it makes the same mistake as (**B**) but is close to the final speed of 143.

10. (C)

A driver delivered food from a restaurant to a customer's home by way of a certain route. If the driver then completed 20 percent of the return trip by way of the same route before the delivery vehicle broke down, what percent of the round trip did the driver complete?

- ○ 10%
- ○ 20%
- ○ 60%
- ○ 70%
- ○ 80%

STEP 1: ANALYZE THE QUESTION

The question stem says that a driver makes part of a round trip, and the answer choices represent the portion completed, written as a percentage.

STEP 2: STATE THE TASK

Determine the percentage of the round trip that the driver completed.

STEP 3: APPROACH STRATEGICALLY

Since the answer choices contain percentages and the question stem does not provide any actual quantities (e.g., distances traveled), pick 100 to represent the round-trip distance.

If the round-trip distance is 100 miles, then when the driver completed the first half or first 50% of the trip, the driver traveled 50 miles. The driver then made part of the return trip, so the correct answer must be greater than 50%. Eliminate (**A**) and (**B**) just on that basis. More specifically, the driver traveled 20% of the 50 remaining miles, or $(0.2)(50 \text{ miles}) = 10$ miles. So the driver traveled a total of $(50 + 10) = 60$ miles out of 100 total miles. The fraction $\frac{60}{100}$ is 60%, so (**C**) is correct.

STEP 4: CONFIRM YOUR ANSWER

Ensure that you included the driver's distance for the first half of the trip. If you took into account only the 20% of the return trip, that was (**A**) 10% of the total. Also make sure you took 20% of just the return trip and not the whole trip; if you added 50% and 20%, you got (**D**) 70%.

11. (B)

Sofia runs a business delivering boxes of frequently used household supplies to monthly subscribers. After hiring a workflow manager, she delivered 20 percent more boxes per month while working 20 percent fewer hours herself each month. Hiring a workflow manager increased Sofia's personal productivity per hour by what percent?

- ○ 40%
- ○ 50%
- ○ 60%
- ○ 140%
- ○ 150%

STEP 1: ANALYZE THE QUESTION

Sofia is running her business more efficiently since hiring a workflow manager. No numbers of boxes or hours are given, only percents of unknown totals. The answer choices are also percents. Pick 100 for the starting number of boxes delivered and the starting number of hours Sofia works.

STEP 2: STATE THE TASK

Use the percent change formula to determine how much having a workflow manager increases Sofia's productivity, that is, her boxes delivered per hour.

STEP 3: APPROACH STRATEGICALLY

There's a fair amount of information here, so setting up a table to keep it organized will help you avoid errors. To start with, Sofia delivers 100 boxes in 100 hours, so she is delivering 1 box per hour. Since hiring a workflow manager results in an increase in deliveries of 20%, the new number is $100 + 20 = 120$. Since Sofia's hours decrease by 20%, her new number of hours is $100 - 20 = 80$. Now her boxes per hour is $\frac{120}{80} = \frac{3}{2} = 1.5$.

	Boxes delivered	Hours worked	Boxes/hour	Change
Before	100	100	1	
After	120	80	1.5	

Now calculate the amount of change and then the percent change. Her productivity has increased by 0.5 boxes per hour.

	Boxes delivered	Hours worked	Boxes/hour	Change
Before	100	100	1	
After	120	80	1.5	0.5

The base or original value was 1 box per hour. Set up the percent change formula:

$$\text{Percent change} = \frac{\text{Amount of change}}{\text{Base amount}}(100\%) = \frac{0.5}{1}(100\%) = 50\%$$

Her productivity increased by 50%, so (**B**) is correct.

STEP 4: CONFIRM YOUR ANSWER

Make sure you solved for percent increase, which is not the same as *what percent of the old value is the new value*? (**E**) is Sofia's new rate of work (1.5 boxes/hour) as a percentage of her old rate (1 box/hour). Note also that questions with multiple percent changes are never answered by simply adding or subtracting the percents, so (**A**) is incorrect.

Practice Set: Picking Numbers with Variables in the Answer Choices

12. (B)

If $n \neq 1$, $j \neq 0$, $k \neq 0$, and $m \neq 0$ and if $n = \dfrac{jkm}{jk + jm + km}$, then $\dfrac{1}{n-1} =$

$\bigcirc \quad \dfrac{1}{j} + \dfrac{1}{k} + \dfrac{1}{m}$

$\bigcirc \quad \dfrac{jk + jm + km}{jkm - jk - jm - km}$

$\bigcirc \quad \dfrac{jk + jm + km}{jkm}$

$\bigcirc \quad \dfrac{jkm - jk - jm - km}{jk + jm + km}$

$\bigcirc \quad j + k + m$

STEP 1: ANALYZE THE QUESTION

The question stem states that the variable n equals a fraction containing various combinations of three other variables: j, k, and m. The answer choices are other expressions with these three variables. The restrictions on the variables avoid division by zero. Furthermore, you can deduce that since n doesn't equal 1, the numerator and denominator of the fraction are not equal ($jkm \neq jk + jm + km$).

STEP 2: STATE THE TASK

Use the given equation to determine the value of $\dfrac{1}{n-1}$ in terms of j, k, and m.

STEP 3: APPROACH STRATEGICALLY

The algebraic manipulation here is daunting and difficult to accomplish within the time constraints of the GMAT, so consider picking numbers for j, k, and m. Choose manageable numbers that don't break the question's rules. For example, if $j = 2$, $k = 2$, and $m = 2$, then $(2)(2)(2) \neq 2(2) + 2(2) + 2(2)$, meaning that n does not equal 1 and making these values permissible.

Substituting 2 for j, k, and m yields $n = \dfrac{jkm}{jk + jm + km} = \dfrac{(2)(2)(2)}{2(2) + 2(2) + 2(2)} = \dfrac{8}{12} = \dfrac{2}{3}$. So $n - 1 = -\dfrac{1}{3}$

and $\dfrac{1}{n-1} = \dfrac{1}{-\dfrac{1}{3}} = -3$. Test each answer choice, looking for those that produce a value of -3 when 2 is

plugged in for j, k, and m. As soon as you determine the value is not -3, stop calculating and move on.

(A) $\frac{1}{2} + \frac{1}{2} + \frac{1}{2} \neq -3$; eliminate (A).

(B) $\dfrac{(2)(2) + (2)(2) + (2)(2)}{(2)(2)(2) - (2)(2) - (2)(2) - (2)(2)} = \dfrac{12}{8 - 12} = -\dfrac{12}{4} = -3.$

    This value is a match, but test the remaining choices to make sure no others also equal -3.

(C) This fraction is just the reciprocal of that in the question stem, so (C) is $\dfrac{1}{n}$ or $\dfrac{3}{2}$ with your picked numbers; eliminate (C).

(D) This fraction is the reciprocal of that in (B), so its value with your picked numbers is $-\dfrac{1}{3}$; eliminate (D).

(E) $j + k + m = 2 + 2 + 2 \neq -3$, so eliminate (E).

The correct answer is (B).

STEP 4: CONFIRM YOUR ANSWER

Ensure that you determined the value of $\dfrac{1}{n-1}$, not of n, $n-1$, $\dfrac{1}{n}$, or something else.

13. (B)

In 15 minutes, Jyoti can read p pages of her economics book. How many minutes will it take her to read r pages of her marketing book, if she reads both books at the same rate?

○ $\dfrac{r}{15p}$

○ $\dfrac{15r}{p}$

○ $\dfrac{15}{rp}$

○ $\dfrac{15p}{r}$

○ $\dfrac{p}{15r}$

STEP 1: ANALYZE THE QUESTION

You're told that Jyoti can read p pages of her economics book in 15 minutes and that she reads her marketing book at the same rate. In other words, if she could read 5 pages of her economics book in 15 minutes, she could also read 5 pages of her marketing book in 15 minutes.

Notice that the answer choices contain variables. Whenever this is the case, you can consider picking numbers.

STEP 2: STATE THE TASK

Determine how long, in minutes, it will take her to read r pages of her marketing book.

STEP 3: APPROACH STRATEGICALLY

Since the answer choices are in terms of p and r, you can pick values for these variables and see which of the choices provides the correct rates for those numbers. Note that most of the answer choices divide p by r or vice versa, so make one value a multiple of the other. Say Jyoti reads $p = 5$ pages of her economics book in 15 minutes. Then she reads $r = 10$ pages of her marketing book in twice as much time, 30 minutes.

Now, plug in $p = 5$ and $r = 10$ to see which choices yield a time of 30 minutes. As soon as you know a choice does not equal 30, stop calculating.

(A) is $\dfrac{r}{15p} = \dfrac{10}{15(5)}$. There's no need to work out the denominator; since 15 is already greater than 10, multiplying it by 5 will result in a larger number. This is thus a fraction less than 1, so eliminate it.

(B) is $\dfrac{15r}{p} = \dfrac{15(10)}{5} = 3(10) = 30$. This could be right, but remember that you need to test the remaining choices, since more than one could appear to be right for the numbers you picked.

(C) is $\dfrac{15}{rp} = \dfrac{15}{10(5)}$. This is, again, a fraction less than 1. Eliminate.

(D) is $\dfrac{15p}{r} = \dfrac{15(5)}{10} = \dfrac{75}{10} = 7\dfrac{1}{2}$. Eliminate.

(E) is $\dfrac{p}{15r} = \dfrac{5}{15(10)}$. Another fraction less than 1, so eliminate it.

(B) is the only choice that gives the right answer, so it's correct.

If you feel comfortable setting up proportions, doing this algebra is another efficient approach to this problem. She reads both books at the same rate, and she reads p pages in 15 minutes and r pages in an unknown number of minutes. Set up the proportion $\dfrac{\text{pages}}{\text{minutes}} = \dfrac{p}{15} = \dfrac{r}{?}$, where ? represents the unknown value. Then cross multiply: $(p)(?) = 15r$. Finally, isolate the unknown by dividing both sides by p: ? $= \dfrac{15r}{p}$. That's (**B**).

STEP 4: CONFIRM YOUR ANSWER

Reread the question stem to confirm that you interpreted the information correctly and solved for the right value: the difference in how much money each person had to give.

14. (C)

To raise money for a charity, v volunteers each pledge to contribute an equal portion of the total goal of d dollars. If r more volunteers join the fund-raising campaign and agree with the original volunteers to contribute equally to the goal, how much less must each original donor give?

○ $\dfrac{d}{2v + r}$

○ $\dfrac{dv}{2v + r^2}$

○ $\dfrac{dr}{v^2 + vr}$

○ $\dfrac{dv}{r^2 + vr}$

○ $\dfrac{d(v + r)}{2(vr)^2}$

STEP 1: ANALYZE THE QUESTION

The question describes a scenario in which a group of people divide a total amount equally and then more people divide up the same total amount. Because more people are raising the same amount of money, each person will have to give less. All the numbers of people and the amount of money are given as variables, not numbers, and the answer choices are expressed in variables.

STEP 2: STATE THE TASK

Solve for the difference in the contribution per person due to the addition of volunteers.

STEP 3: APPROACH STRATEGICALLY

Because of all the variables in this question, picking numbers may be the most efficient way to solve. Pick some numbers for v, d, and r, making sure that the numbers you pick are manageable and permissible. The total donations are first divvied up among a small group and then among a larger group, so the calculations will be simpler if the total amount is divisible by both the original and new numbers of volunteers.

You could choose 3 for the original number of volunteers, $v = 3$, and 2 for the increase in the number of volunteers, $r = 2$. This means that the numbers of volunteers are 3 and 5, so set the goal d as $3 \times 5 = 15$ (remember that the object is not to pick "realistic" numbers, just numbers that are easy to work with).

Now the problem becomes one of arithmetic with small numbers. If 3 people agreed to contribute a total of 15, then each would contribute 5; if the total is split among 5 people, then each would contribute 3. So the reduction in the contribution would be $5 - 3 = 2$. Plug the numbers picked into each of the answer choices to see which one(s) equals 2.

(A) is $\dfrac{15}{2(3)+2} = \dfrac{15}{8}$. Eliminate.

(B) is $\dfrac{15(3)}{2(3)+2^2} = \dfrac{45}{10}$. Eliminate.

(C) is $\dfrac{15(2)}{3^2+3(2)} = \dfrac{30}{15} = 2$. Possibly correct.

(D) is $\dfrac{15(3)}{2^2+3(2)} = \dfrac{45}{10}$. Eliminate.

(E) is $\dfrac{15(3+2)}{2(3\times 2)^2} = \dfrac{75}{2(36)} = \dfrac{75}{72}$. Eliminate.

Only (**C**) remains as a possible choice, so it is correct.

Alternatively, you could have used algebra to determine the solution. The original pledge amount is the total divided by the number of volunteers, $\dfrac{d}{v}$. The reduced amount is $\dfrac{d}{v+r}$, so the amount of the reduction is $\dfrac{d}{v} - \dfrac{d}{v+r}$. In order to combine the terms, create a common denominator:

$$\dfrac{(v+r)(d)}{(v+r)(v)} - \dfrac{(v)(d)}{(v)(v+r)} - \dfrac{dv+dr-dv}{v^2+vr} = \dfrac{dr}{v^2+vr}.$$

STEP 4: CONFIRM YOUR ANSWER

Reread the question stem to confirm that you interpreted the information correctly and solved for the right value, which is the difference in how much money each original person had to give.

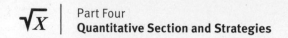

Practice Set: Picking Numbers on Must Be/Could Be/Cannot Be Questions

15. (B)

If integers a and b are distinct factors of 30, which of the following CANNOT be a factor of 30?

    I. $ab + b^2$

    II. $(a + b)^2$

    III. $a + b$

  ○ I only

  ○ II only

  ○ III only

  ○ I and II only

  ○ I, II, and III

STEP 1: ANALYZE THE QUESTION

You are given two integers, a and b, and are then told that they are distinct factors of 30. This means that a cannot equal b. Before working out the problem, jot down the factors of 30: 1, 2, 3, 5, 6, 10, 15, 30.

STEP 2: STATE THE TASK

Determine which of the Roman numeral statements cannot be a factor of 30.

STEP 3: APPROACH STRATEGICALLY

Start with Statement I, not because it is first but because it appears in the most answer choices. Since variables in the expression are multiplied together or squared, the value could get quite large; you should therefore pick small numbers for a and b. Let's choose $a = 1$ and $b = 2$. Substituting into the equation, you get $1(2) + 2^2 = 2 + 4 = 6$. Since 6 is a factor of 30, Statement I can be a factor of 30. Because you are looking for the choice that CANNOT be a factor of 30, you can eliminate any answer choice containing Statement I: (**A**), (**D**), and (**E**) cannot be correct.

Since Statements II and III each appear once in the remaining answer choices, pick the easier expression to evaluate, Statement III. If you again pick $a = 1$ and $b = 2$, you will get $1 + 2 = 3$. Because 3 is a factor of 30, you can eliminate (**C**). Without even needing to evaluate Statement II, you know the correct answer is (**B**).

STEP 4: CONFIRM YOUR ANSWER

You can check your answer by reviewing your substitutions and checking that all expressions were solved correctly.

Alternatively, you can verify that Statement II CANNOT be a factor of 30 by picking numbers. If $a = 1$ and $b = 2$, you get $(1 + 2)^2 = 3^2 = 9$, which is not a factor of 30. However, one instance of not being a factor of 30 doesn't mean this expression can never equal a factor of 30. Try the next smallest possible set of numbers that would produce a distinct result: $a = 1$ and $b = 3$. Plugging these in, you get $(1 + 3)^2 = 4^2 = 16$, also not a factor of 30. Trying a third set, $a = 2$ and $b = 3$, you get $(2 + 3)^2 = 5^2 = 25$. Again, this is not a factor of 30. One more set is all you need here; if $a = 1$ and $b = 5$, you get $(1 + 5)^2 = 6^2 = 36$. Since this is higher than 30, any other number combination you plug in will also be higher than 30 and therefore not a factor. You have confirmed that (**B**) is correct.

16. (B)

The integer a is less than -1, and the integer d is greater than 1. If $-1 < b < 0$ and $0 < c < 1$, then which of the following must be the greatest negative number?

○ $b - a$

○ $b - c$

○ $b - d$

○ $c - a$

○ $a - c$

STEP 1: ANALYZE THE QUESTION

The question provides quite a bit of information, so translating that information into a simpler form can be helpful: "The integer a is less than -1... $-1 < b < 0$" becomes $a \leq -2 < -1 < b < 0$, and "the integer d is greater than 1... $0 < c < 1$" becomes $0 < c < 1 < 2 \leq d$. Combining these two statements yields the following single statement: $a \leq -2 < -1 < b < 0 < c < 1 < 2 \leq d$, in which a and d are integers.

STEP 2: STATE THE TASK

Determine which answer choice must be the greatest negative number, meaning the negative number that is closest to 0 on the number line.

STEP 3: APPROACH STRATEGICALLY

Examine the answers logically one by one, picking numbers as needed to confirm the possible ranges of the answer choices:

(A) Subtracting a smaller number from a larger one always yields a positive result. Because $a < b$, $b - a$ is positive; eliminate **(A)**.

(B) First consider the case where b and c are as close together as possible. Pick numbers: say $b = -0.01$ and $c = 0.01$. Then $b - c$ is -0.02. So when b and c are close together, $b - c$ is a negative number very close to 0. Now consider the case where b and c are as far apart as possible. Again pick numbers: say $b = -0.99$ and $c = 0.99$. Now $b - c = -1.98$. So when b and c are as far apart as possible, $b - c$ is just above -2. So $-2 < b - c < 0$. Keep **(B)** for now.

(C) Since $b < 0$ and d is at least 2, $b - d < -2$. This value must be less than **(B)**; eliminate.

(D) For the same reason as in **(A)**, $c - a$ is positive; eliminate **(D)**.

(E) Since a is no greater than -2 and c is positive, $a - c < -2$. This value must be less than **(B)**; eliminate.

(B) is the correct answer.

STEP 4: CONFIRM YOUR ANSWER

Ensure that you answered the right question, finding the expression that represents the greatest negative number, which is the negative number closest to zero. A common error would be to choose the negative number with the greatest magnitude (absolute value), which is actually the smallest number.

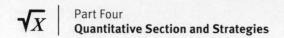
17. (B)

In the set S of consecutive integers from 1 to 10, inclusive, D is the subset of all odd numbers, M is the subset of all prime numbers, and Q is the subset of all numbers whose positive square root is also a member of set S. If d is an element of D, m is an element of M, and q is an element of Q, which of the following could be true?

○ $d = \sqrt{mq}$

○ $d = \dfrac{q}{m}$

○ $m = q$

○ $q = \dfrac{m}{d^2}$

○ $q = \sqrt{dm}$

STEP 1: ANALYZE THE QUESTION

The information in the question stem can be summarized as follows: the set of consecutive integers is $\{1, 2, 3, \ldots, 9, 10\}$; subsets include $D = \{1, 3, 5, 7, 9\}$, $M = \{2, 3, 5, 7\}$, and $Q = \{1, 4, 9\}$. (Subset Q consists of integers from 1 to 10 whose positive square roots are integers from 1 to 10—in other words, perfect squares.) The answer choices are equations relating members of these subsets.

STEP 2: STATE THE TASK

Determine which of the statements in the answer choices *could* be true. The implication here is that, once you have found a choice that works, you can select it without having to concern yourself with any of the others; each of those is *never* true.

STEP 3: APPROACH STRATEGICALLY

Since there are variables in both the question stem and choices and the choices don't lend themselves to efficient analysis using number properties rules, consider picking numbers to test only as many choices as needed to find one equation that can be true. Pick numbers for d, m, and q that are members of the variables' respective subsets.

(A) Since this choice states that the square root of mq is an integer d, mq must be a perfect square that equals d^2. However, there is no m-value that, when multiplied by any q-value, results in a perfect square. For example, if $m = 2$, then $2 \times 1 = 2$, $2 \times 4 = 8$, and $2 \times 9 = 18$, none of which is a perfect square. Run through the remaining possible pairs of m and d in the same way and eliminate **(A)**, since it cannot be true.

(B) This choice says that when q is divided by m, the result is an integer d, so m must be a factor of q. Start with $m = 2$ and look at subset Q: it contains 4, which is a multiple of 2, so the equation would be $d = \frac{4}{2} = 2$, but that value is not in D. However, if $m = 3$ and $q = 9$, then $d = \frac{9}{3} = 3$, and that value is in D. **(B)** is thus the correct answer.

While there is no need to test the remaining choices, here is what you would have found:

(C) This choice indicates that a term from M equals a term from Q. However, no such match exists, so **(C)** cannot be true; eliminate it.

(**D**) Since q is an integer, for this equation to be true, d^2 must be a factor of m. Check $d = 1$: $d^2 = 1$. Any value m divided by 1 is unchanged, and no values of m are in q, so $q \neq \frac{m}{1^2}$ and d cannot equal 1. Then check $d = 3$: $3^2 = 9$, which is greater than any possible value of m, so d cannot equal 3 or any larger value. Since (**D**) cannot be true, eliminate it.

(**E**) This choice is similar to (**A**) in that the product of two numbers must be a perfect square. In this choice, dm must be a perfect square that equals q^2. Although it is possible to create a perfect square from one member of D and one member of M (i.e., 3^2, 5^2, and 7^2), none of these perfect squares matches the square of any element of Q. Since (**E**) cannot be true, eliminate it.

STEP 4: CONFIRM YOUR ANSWER

Make sure that you found the choice that could be true, not that must be false! Also, make sure that you plugged in numbers from the right subset for each variable when testing the choices.

Practice Set: Backsolving

18. (D)

If $\left(\frac{1}{64}\right)^x = 4{,}096$, $x =$

○ $-\frac{1}{3}$

○ $-\frac{1}{2}$

○ $-\sqrt{2}$

○ -2

○ -3

STEP 1: ANALYZE THE QUESTION

The question stem provides an equation containing a fraction that is raised to an unknown number x. The choices, each of which is a number, represent potential values of x.

STEP 2: STATE THE TASK

Determine the value of x.

STEP 3: APPROACH STRATEGICALLY

Each choice is a negative value, so you are really raising the number 64 to the positive version of each $\left(\text{e.g.,} \left(\frac{1}{64}\right)^{-\frac{1}{3}} = \frac{1}{\left(\frac{1}{64}\right)^{\frac{1}{3}}} = 64^{\frac{1}{3}}\right)$. Since raising a positive integer to a fractional exponent does not result in a larger number, eliminate (**A**) and (**B**). Also, since raising an integer to $\sqrt{2}$ results in a non-integer, eliminate (**C**).

Now, since the remaining choices (**D**) and (**E**) are small integers, consider using the backsolving strategy. You'll need to test only one of these two choices to arrive at the correct answer. Since 2 is a smaller number than 3 and thus makes for easier math, test (**D**): $\left(\frac{1}{64}\right)^{-2} = 64^2 = 64(64) = 4{,}096$. This outcome matches that in the question stem, so you have found the correct answer: (**D**).

STEP 4: CONFIRM YOUR ANSWER

Ensure that you did not make any careless math errors in testing the answer choices.

19. (C)

The length of a rectangle is twice as long as the width, and the rectangle's area is greater than 72 and less than 200. Which of the following could be the length of the rectangle?

○ 8

○ 12

○ 16

○ 20

○ 24

STEP 1: ANALYZE THE QUESTION

The question stem refers to a rectangle and says that the length is twice the width. The rectangle's area, which is length times width, is between 72 and 200 exclusive. The answer choices are relatively small integers.

STEP 2: STATE THE TASK

Determine a possible value of the rectangle's longer side.

STEP 3: APPROACH STRATEGICALLY

Since the answer choices are numbers and you must determine a single value, you can use the backsolving strategy. The question asks for the length and stipulates that this is the longer side, so consider testing the larger of (**B**) and (**D**) first. That's (**D**), which is 20.

If the length measures 20, the width, which is half of the length, measures 10. The rectangle's area would then be $(20)(10) = 200$. The area needs to be less than 200, so eliminate (**D**). (**E**) would produce an even larger area, so eliminate this choice as well.

Next, test (**B**) to see whether that value could work as the rectangle's length. If the length measures 12, the width measures 6, so the rectangle's area would be $(12)(6) = 72$. The area needs to be greater than 72, so eliminate (**B**) as well as (**A**).

(**C**) is correct.

STEP 4: CONFIRM YOUR ANSWER

Make sure that you solved for the length, not the width, which is (**A**). If you have time, you could plug 16 into the question, find the width is equal to 8, and multiply to find the area is a permissible 128.

20. (C)

In a certain beanbag game, players toss beanbags at a board with a hole in it. If the beanbag falls into the hole, the player scores 5 points. A beanbag that lands on the board but misses the hole is worth 2 points. If a toss misses the board entirely, 1 point is deducted from the player's score. Julianna had 20 tosses and missed the board with 3 throws. Her total score was 52. How many times did she toss the beanbag into the hole?

- ○ 5
- ○ 6
- ○ 7
- ○ 8
- ○ 9

STEP 1: ANALYZE THE QUESTION

Julianna scored 52 points on 20 attempts in a game in which points are awarded for tossing a beanbag onto a board or into a hole in the board, but points are deducted for missing the board, which Julianna did 3 times. The answer choices, which represent the number of tosses that landed in the hole, are small integers.

STEP 2: STATE THE TASK

Find the number of times she tossed the beanbag into the hole, earning 5 points per toss.

STEP 3: APPROACH STRATEGICALLY

You could solve this problem algebraically, but seeing whole numbers in the answer choices is a clue that it might be easier to backsolve this one instead. Backsolving is an option whenever you can manageably plug an answer choice into the question stem.

Julianna had 3 misses; without those misses, she would have had $20 - 3 = 17$ attempts and a score of $52 + 3 = 55$. Select one of the choices for the number of beanbags that she tossed into the hole, calculate her score, and compare the result to 55.

You could start with either (**B**) or (**D**). If you choose (**B**), then 6 tosses in the hole would have been worth 5 points each for a total of 30 points. There would have been $17 - 6 = 11$ tosses that stayed on the board. These would be worth 2 points each for a score of 22 points. Her total score of $30 + 22 = 52$ points (ignoring the penalized tosses) is less than 55, so (**B**) is not enough tosses into the hole. Eliminate (**A**) and (**B**).

Try (**D**). Eight successes at 5 points each would be 40 points. There would be $17 - 8 = 9$ tosses at 2 points each, for a total of 18 points. Therefore, 8 tosses into the hole would have resulted in a score before penalties of $40 + 18 = 58$ points. Thus, (**D**) is too great, and the correct choice is (**C**).

STEP 4: CONFIRM YOUR ANSWER

Calculate the score with 7 tosses into the hole: $5(7) + 2(21 - 7 - 3) - 1(3) = 35 + 20 - 3 = 52$.

GMAT by the Numbers: Problem Solving

Now that you've learned how to approach Problem Solving questions on the GMAT, let's add one more dimension to your understanding of how they work.

Take a moment to try this question. Following is performance data from thousands of people who have studied with Kaplan over the decades. Through analyzing this data, we will show you how to approach questions like this one most effectively and how to avoid similarly tempting wrong answer choice types on Test Day.

> The number x of cars sold each week varies with the price y in dollars according to the equation $x = 800,000 - 50y$, where $y \leq 16,000$. What would be the total weekly revenue, in dollars, from the sale of cars priced at $15,000?

- ○ 50,000
- ○ 750,000
- ○ 850,000
- ○ 7,500,000
- ○ 750,000,000

Explanation

The first—and in many ways most important—step in Problem Solving is to understand what you're solving for. This problem gives you an equation: $x = 800{,}000 - 50y$, with x representing the number of cars sold and y representing their price. You're given the price, so $y = 15{,}000$. But you aren't solving for x. Rather, you're solving for the total revenue. You'll therefore find the number of cars sold (x), then multiply by their price ($15{,}000).

Substituting 15,000 for y in the equation, you get:

$$x = 800{,}000 - 50y$$
$$x = 800{,}000 - 50(15{,}000)$$
$$x = 800{,}000 - 750{,}000$$
$$x = 50{,}000$$

Multiplying 50,000 cars by $15,000 yields revenue of $750,000,000. **(E)** is correct.

Question Statistics

30% of test takers choose **(A)**

18% of test takers choose **(B)**

3% of test takers choose **(C)**

5% of test takers choose **(D)**

44% of test takers choose **(E)**

Sample size = 4,464

Notice that the math involved here is not extremely challenging, yet fewer than half of test takers select the right answer. That's because two wrong answers are actually right answers—but to the wrong questions. **(A)**, the most popular incorrect choice, is the value of x. It's easy to assume that you're solving for a variable given by the problem, but often you won't be. **(B)**, the other commonly selected wrong answer, is the value of $50y$. These "intermediate values" that you generated on your way to the right answer make for very tempting wrong answers—so tempting in this problem that more test takers choose them than the right answer! Be clear about what you need to solve for, and you'll avoid the biggest Problem Solving pitfall.

More GMAT by the Numbers...

To see more questions with answer choice statistics, be sure to review the full-length CATs in your online resources.

 GO ONLINE

kaptest.com/login

CHAPTER 17

Data Sufficiency Strategy

LEARNING OBJECTIVES

After studying this chapter, you will be able to:

- Describe the format of a Data Sufficiency question
- State the steps of the Kaplan Method for Data Sufficiency questions
- Explain how to solve a Data Sufficiency question by determining whether calculations could be performed, without performing the calculations

---

Below is a typical Data Sufficiency question. In this chapter, we'll look at how to apply the Kaplan Method to this question, discuss how to tackle this question type, and go over the basic principles and strategies that you want to keep in mind on every Data Sufficiency question.

Is the product of x, y, and z equal to 1?

(1) $x + y + z = 3$

(2) x, y, and z are each greater than 0.

- ○ Statement (1) ALONE is sufficient, but Statement (2) is not sufficient.
- ○ Statement (2) ALONE is sufficient, but Statement (1) is not sufficient.
- ○ BOTH statements TOGETHER are sufficient, but NEITHER statement ALONE is sufficient.
- ○ EACH statement ALONE is sufficient.
- ○ Statements (1) and (2) TOGETHER are NOT sufficient.

Before you move on, take a minute to think about what you see in this question and answer some questions about how you think it works:

- How is the structure of this question different from that of a typical math question?
- What mathematical concepts are tested in this question?
- How can you use the answer choices to your advantage?
- What GMAT Core Competencies are most essential to success on this question?

Previewing Data Sufficiency

Here are answers to the questions we just asked you to think about.

How Is the Structure of This Question Different from That of a Typical Math Question?

The problem at the beginning of this chapter starts off with the question stem, which asks whether the product of x, y, and z equals the value of 1. But then there's no other information in the question stem. So how are you supposed to answer the question? A Data Sufficiency question stem will never give you enough information to solve for an answer, which is very different from typical math problems. You're probably used to having a lot of information presented up front, followed by the actual question. But Data Sufficiency works differently: the other data are presented *after* the initial question; these are called the "statements." Your goal in a Data Sufficiency question is to determine whether the data in the statements are enough to allow you to answer the question.

Sound unusual? Absolutely. Confusing? It doesn't have to be. As just noted, all you need to do is determine whether the data are sufficient to be able to answer the question. What is *not* your goal? To do a lot of time-consuming calculations. Business schools don't care about how many advanced math classes you took. They care about something else: they want to know that you're able to assimilate a lot of information and make deductions from that information. Many Data Sufficiency questions can be solved without finding the specific answer to the question presented in the stem.

What Mathematical Concepts Are Tested in This Question?

At first, it appears that this question tests only some fairly basic arithmetic concepts: namely, multiplication (in the question stem), addition (in the first statement), and inequalities (in the second statement). But as is often the case on GMAT Quantitative questions, what's *not* stated is also important. This is not merely an arithmetic question. It's testing number properties: how numbers with certain characteristics behave in predictable ways. A careless test taker might take for granted that x, y, and z are integers. But unless the question stem says so, never assume that variables must be integers—or even positive numbers, for that matter. Training your mind to think like this on the GMAT will take time and practice, but using the Kaplan Method for Data Sufficiency and remembering how to apply the Core Competencies will help you through even the toughest Data Sufficiency questions.

How Can You Use the Answer Choices to Your Advantage?

Earlier you read that Data Sufficiency questions don't necessarily require you to solve the problem. This is because the answer choices are in a fixed format. All five of the answer choices have to do with the "sufficiency" or "insufficiency" of the statements. In other words, does one of the statements alone provide enough information to answer the question? Do both of them? Do both of them, but only when combined? Or is there just not enough information? Again, the answer choices will never give you actual values or expressions, such as "35,612" or "$4x^3 - 15y$." We'll show you how to use this fixed format to your advantage.

What GMAT Core Competencies Are Most Essential to Success on This Question?

For all Data Sufficiency questions, Critical Thinking is crucial. Mastering the format and structure will put you at an advantage over your competition, since Data Sufficiency is notoriously one of the greatest challenges for most GMAT test takers. By understanding how these questions are constructed and what the potential traps are, you will know how to get at the heart of what the test makers are asking you to do.

Attention to the Right Detail is also key to your success on Data Sufficiency. Most importantly, don't fail to consider the details that *aren't* mentioned or the restrictions that *don't* exist. Never assume anything in a Data Sufficiency question.

Question Format and Structure

> **LEARNING OBJECTIVE**
>
> In this section, you will learn how to:
>
> - Describe some key features of Data Sufficiency questions and answer choices

The instructions for Data Sufficiency questions on the GMAT look like this:

> **Directions:** In each of the problems, a question is followed by two statements containing certain data. You are to determine whether the data provided by the statements are sufficient to answer the question. Choose the correct answer based upon the statements' data, your knowledge of mathematics, and your familiarity with everyday facts (such as the number of minutes in an hour or cents in a dollar). You must indicate whether:
>
> O Statement (1) ALONE is sufficient, but Statement (2) is not sufficient.
>
> O Statement (2) ALONE is sufficient, but Statement (1) is not sufficient.
>
> O BOTH statements TOGETHER are sufficient, but NEITHER statement ALONE is sufficient.
>
> O EACH statement ALONE is sufficient.
>
> O Statements (1) and (2) TOGETHER are NOT sufficient.
>
> **Note:** Diagrams accompanying problems agree with information given in the question but may not agree with additional information given in Statements (1) and (2).
>
> All numbers used are real numbers.

The GMAT is the only test featuring Data Sufficiency questions, and beginners often misunderstand the format. On the Quantitative section, you'll see about 14 Data Sufficiency questions, which ask you to assess whether certain statements provide enough information to answer a question. Often, the question requires little or no mathematical work. The key to solving the question is understanding how the question type is structured and using that knowledge to work efficiently.

The directions may seem confusing at first, but they become clear with use. Let's walk through a simple example:

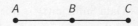

What is the length of segment *AC*?

(1) *B* is the midpoint of *AC*.

(2) *AB* = 5

○ Statement (1) ALONE is sufficient, but Statement (2) is not sufficient.

○ Statement (2) ALONE is sufficient, but Statement (1) is not sufficient.

○ BOTH statements TOGETHER are sufficient, but NEITHER statement ALONE is sufficient.

○ EACH statement ALONE is sufficient.

○ Statements (1) and (2) TOGETHER are NOT sufficient.

The diagram tells you that there is a line segment *AC* with point *B* somewhere between *A* and *C*. You're asked to figure out the length of *AC*.

Statement (1) tells you that *B* is the midpoint of *AC*, so *AB* = *BC* and *AC* = 2*AB* = 2*BC*. Since Statement (1) does not give an actual value for *AB* or *BC*, you cannot answer the question using Statement (1) alone.

Statement (2) says that *AB* = 5. Since Statement (2) does not give you any information about *BC*, the question cannot be answered using Statement (2) alone.

Using both of the statements together, you can find a value for both *AB* and *BC*; therefore, you can solve for the length of *AC*, and the answer to the question is choice (**C**).

The Basic Principles of Data Sufficiency

LEARNING OBJECTIVES

In this section, you will learn how to:

● Systematically eliminate wrong answers

● Explain that Data Sufficiency statements should not be tested for validity because they are always true, even though they may or may not provide enough information to answer the question

● Describe the importance of focusing on sufficiency, not calculation, to answer Data Sufficiency questions

Especially because this question type is more abstract than Problem Solving, it's essential to have a strategic approach to every Data Sufficiency question. Don't waste time or mental energy doing unnecessary calculations. A systematic approach will ensure that you find the most efficient solution to the problem and that you make as few careless and avoidable errors as possible. Here are some ways you can optimize your Data Sufficiency performance.

In the next section, you'll learn a Method that will structure your approach to these questions. By using the Kaplan Method for Data Sufficiency, you'll be able to incorporate these principles into your solution of every Data Sufficiency question you encounter on the Quantitative section.

Know How to Eliminate Data Sufficiency Answer Choices

As you've already learned, the directions and answer choices for Data Sufficiency questions never change, so it's to your advantage to memorize them. But you can take this approach one step further by learning how to eliminate answer choices as you work through Data Sufficiency problems.

As you evaluate the two statements, use your erasable notepad to keep track of which answer choices you have ruled out as incorrect. Use the following patterns to guide your elimination:

If Statement (1) is sufficient, the answer could only be **(A)** or **(D)**. *Eliminate* **(B)**, **(C)**, *and* **(E)**.

If Statement (1) is insufficient, the answer could only be **(B)**, **(C)**, or **(E)**. *Eliminate* **(A)** *and* **(D)**.

If Statement (2) is sufficient, the answer could only be **(B)** or **(D)**. *Eliminate* **(A)**, **(C)**, *and* **(E)**.

If Statement (2) is insufficient, the answer could only be **(A)**, **(C)**, or **(E)**. *Eliminate* **(B)** *and* **(D)**.

As you'll learn in the section on "The Kaplan Method for Data Sufficiency" later in this chapter, using the mnemonic device 12TEN will help you keep track of the five answer choices. Eliminating choices after evaluating each statement will allow you to attack the question more efficiently, without considering an answer choice you've already ruled out.

You also want to avoid a common mistake on Data Sufficiency: choosing **(C)** when the answer is actually **(A)**, **(B)**, or **(D)**. Remember: if either statement *by itself* is sufficient, then of course the two statements *together* will also be sufficient, since the statements are always true and never contradict each other. But **(C)** can be correct *only* when each statement alone is insufficient and combining the statements is necessary to obtain sufficiency.

You should consider the statements together only if each is insufficient on its own. When you evaluate the statements together, keep in mind that each statement is true. So if you're picking numbers to evaluate the statements combined, you must choose values that are permitted by *both* statements.

The Statements Are Always True

The statements are new pieces of data that apply to the problem and are always true. Don't waste time trying to verify a statement.

The fact that the statements are always true has an important corollary that will help you catch careless errors: the statements will never contradict each other. Although they won't always be sufficient to answer the question, they'll never be mutually exclusive. If it appears that two statements are in disagreement with each other, you should recheck your work, because you have made an error.

Example:

What is the value of *t*?

(1) $t^2 = t$

(2) $t + 6 = 6$

This is a straightforward Value question for which you need a value of *t*. Let's say that you made an error in your analysis of Statement (1) and thought that *t* had to equal 1. You'd think that Statement (1) was sufficient.

Then you'd look at Statement (2). Simplifying, you'd learn that t equals 0. That's also sufficient. So you'd think that the answer would be (D). However, according to your analysis, the statements contradict each other:

(1) $t = 1$

(2) $t = 0$

That isn't possible. So you'd know to go back and recheck your work. Statement (2) pretty obviously says that $t = 0$, so you would recheck your work on Statement (1). Is 1 the only number that equals itself when squared? Substitute the 0 from Statement (2) and you get $0^2 = 0 \times 0 = 0$. So Statement (1) actually permits *two* values and is therefore insufficient.

(1) $t = 0$ or 1

(2) $t = 0$

The correct answer is (B), not (D).

It's All About the Question Stem

On Data Sufficiency questions, if you rush past the question and dive into the statements, you risk doing a whole bunch of unnecessary—and possibly misleading—math. It's essential that you understand the question stem before you analyze the statements. For one thing, as you'll read about in depth later in this chapter, there's a huge difference between a question that asks for a value (a Value question) and a question that asks for an answer of yes or no (a Yes/No question). Consider this identical pair of statements:

(1) $x^3 = x$

(2) $x^2 = x$

(1) $x^3 = x$

(2) $x^2 = x$

Here's how they evaluate:

(1) $x = -1$, 0, or 1

(2) $x = 0$ or 1

(1) $x = -1$, 0, or 1

(2) $x = 0$ or 1

But you still have no idea what the answers are without seeing the question stems:

What is the value of x?   Is $x < -1$?

(1) $x = -1$, 0, or 1   (1) $x = -1$, 0, or 1

(2) $x = 0$ or 1   (2) $x = 0$ or 1

For the question on the left, a Value question, Statement (1) is insufficient because there are three possible values of x. Statement (2) is also insufficient because it permits two possible values. Even when the statements are considered together, x could be either 0 or 1. That's two values, which is insufficient for a Value question. The answer is (E).

But the question on the right is a Yes/No question, so you will need to evaluate it differently. This question asks whether x is less than -1. First, look at Statement (1). Is $-1 < -1$? No. Is $0 < -1$? No. Is $1 < -1$? No. Always no:

this statement is sufficient. The same for Statement (2): both values answer the question with a no, so it's sufficient, as well. The answer is (**D**).

That's as different as two Data Sufficiency answers can be, and it had *nothing* to do with the statements, which were identical. It's all about the question stem.

But as you begin to attack a Data Sufficiency question, you want to look for more than just whether the question is a Value or a Yes/No question. You saw how Problem Solving questions get much easier with some analysis and simplification before an approach is chosen. So too with Data Sufficiency.

Example:

If $w \neq x$, $w \neq z$, and $x \neq y$, is $\dfrac{(x-y)^3(w-z)^3}{(w-z)^2(x-y)(w-x)^2} > 0$?

(1) $x > y$

(2) $w > z$

This is a Yes/No question that asks about a fraction containing multiple variable expressions as factors. At first glance, this may look like a scary question stem. But take a closer look at that fraction. There are a lot of shared terms in the numerator and the denominator. Using the laws of exponents, you can cancel the $(w-z)^2$ and the $(x-y)$ in the denominator:

If $w \neq x$, $w \neq z$, and $x \neq y$, is $\dfrac{(x-y)^{\cancel{3}^2}(w-z)^{\cancel{3}^1}}{\cancel{(w-z)^2}\ \cancel{(x-y)}(w-x)^2} > 0$?

That simplifies the question to this:

If $w \neq x$, $w \neq z$, and $x \neq y$, is $\dfrac{(x-y)^2(w-z)}{(w-x)^2} > 0$?

This is looking better already. You can simplify even further by thinking logically about the question. You aren't asked for the value of anything, just whether this complicated fraction is positive. Without knowing anything about the values of w, x, y, and z, what can you already know about the answer to this question stem? Well, for one thing, you know that a squared term cannot be negative. So there's no way that $(x-y)^2$ or $(w-x)^2$ is negative. In fact, since $w \neq x$ and $x \neq y$, they can't be zero, either. So those two terms are both positive, which is the only thing that matters to the question. You can simplify the question even further, to this:

Is $\dfrac{(\text{positive})(w-z)}{\text{positive}} > 0$?

Since multiplying and/or dividing $(w-z)$ by anything positive will not change its sign, you have this:

Is $w - z > 0$?

Now *that's* a much simpler question. Look at how much easier the statements have become to evaluate:

(1) $x > y$

(2) $w > z$

Statement (1) is totally irrelevant to whether $w - z > 0$. This statement is insufficient.

Statement (2) tells you that w is bigger than z, so $w - z$ must be positive. (Subtract z from both sides of the inequality, and you get $w - z > 0$.) That's a definite yes. This is sufficient, so the answer is (**B**).

The more analysis and simplification you do with the question stem, the easier dealing with the statements will become.

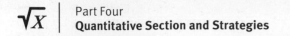
Think About Sufficiency, Not Calculation

Get into the habit of thinking about what's needed for *sufficiency*, rather than doing arithmetic calculations. One of the ways that the GMAT makes a Data Sufficiency question harder is to make the numbers scarier. But if you aren't worrying about arithmetic, you won't be fazed by this. Let's take a look at two important math concepts that can help you avoid number crunching in Data Sufficiency.

The *N*-Variables, *N*-Equations Rule

Perhaps one of the most powerful tools to evaluate sufficiency is the *n*-variables, *n*-equations rule. If you have at least as many distinct, linear equations as you have variables, you will be able to solve for the unique numerical values of all the variables. If there are two variables, you need at least two equations to solve for all the values. If you have three variables, you need at least three equations. If you have four variables, you need at least four equations, and so on.

Note that when you apply the *n*-variables, *n*-equations rule, you must be alert to the exact definition of the word *distinct*: each equation must provide new, different information. For instance, even though the equations $x + 3y = 5$ and $2x + 6y = 10$ look different, they are not in fact distinct—the second equation is merely the first equation multiplied by 2. Another example is the following system of equations: $x + 2y - 3z = 8$, $2y + 6z = 2$, and $x + 4y + 3z = 10$. These may also initially seem to be distinct, but a closer look reveals that the third equation is merely the sum of the first two. It therefore adds no new information, so this system of equations cannot be solved for unique numerical values for each variable.

Example:

> A souvenir shop made $2,400 in revenue selling postcards. If a large postcard costs twice as much as a small postcard, the shop sold 950 large postcards, and it sold no other type of postcard besides these two sizes, then how many small postcards did it sell?
>
> (1) A large postcard costs $2.
> (2) If the shop had sold 20 percent fewer small postcards, its revenue would have been reduced by $4\frac{1}{6}$ percent.

There are four factors that affect the outcome of this problem: (1) the price of a small postcard, (2) the price of a large postcard, (3) the number of small postcards sold, and (4) the number of large postcards sold. That's four variables, so four distinct linear equations would enable you to solve for any of the variables. How many equations do you have already? Well, something-or-other equals $2,400 (that's one), there's a relationship between the prices (that's two), and you get the number of large postcards (that's three). With three equations for four variables, *any new equation* will be sufficient, as long as it is distinct and it doesn't introduce a new variable.

Statement (1) is a new equation and is therefore sufficient. Statement (2) is a more complicated equation, and it would likely be time-consuming to calculate. But it is still a new, distinct equation, and it is therefore sufficient. The answer is (**D**).

Imagine how much time it would take to work through these equations. Using the *n*-variables, *n*-equations rule, it need take no longer than a minute.

One word of caution, though: having the same number of distinct linear equations guarantees sufficiency, but having fewer does *not* guarantee insufficiency. The GMAT will set up equations so that you can sometimes solve for what's asked even though you can't solve for every variable individually.

Example:

> A fruit stand sells apples, pears, and oranges. If oranges cost $0.50 each, then what is the cost of 5 oranges, 4 apples, and 3 pears?
>
> (1) The cost of 1 apple is $0.30.
>
> (2) The cost of 8 apples and 6 pears is $3.90.

There are three variables in this problem (the cost of an orange, the cost of an apple, and the cost of a pear), so three distinct equations could solve for everything. You're given only one (the exact price of an orange). So two additional distinct equations will guarantee sufficiency. But you should keep your eyes open for a way to answer your question with fewer. Since you already know the price of an orange, the only thing you'd need to answer your question is the price of 4 apples and 3 pears.

Statement (1) is insufficient, as you still do not know anything about the price of a pear. Statement (2) is only one equation, but if you divided it by 2, you'd get the cost of 4 apples and 3 pears, which is exactly what you need. This statement is sufficient, so the correct answer is (**B**).

Proportions

Another common way that the GMAT allows you to get sufficiency without knowing all the individual values is to ask questions based on proportions (ratios, percents, averages, rates/speed, etc.). The goal of the following exercise is to get you to think about what kind of information can be sufficient to answer a question, even though you can't calculate the exact value of every variable involved. Read the question stem and each of the following statements, asking yourself whether it gives you enough information to answer. Don't waste time trying to come up with the actual value.

> What was the percent increase in profits for Company X between 1991 and 1993?

Do the following statements provide sufficient information?

> (1) The company earned 20 percent less profit in 1991 than in 1993.
>
> (2) The average annual profit from 1991 to 1993 was 12.5 percent higher than the profit in 1991.
>
> (3) The average of the annual profits of 1991 and 1993 was 12.5 percent higher than the profit in 1991.
>
> (4) In 1991, the profit was $4.5 million less than in 1993.

Let's evaluate each statement on its own:

Statement (1) is sufficient. You could "reverse" the math and figure out percent increase from the given decrease. Let the 1993 profit equal P_{1993} and the 1991 profit equal P_{1991}. The statement can be translated as $P_{1991} = 0.8\,(P_{1993})$, which is $P_{1991} = \frac{4}{5}(P_{1993})$. That means $P_{1993} = \frac{5}{4}P_{1991} = 1.25(P_{1991})$. That's 125% of 1991, or a 25% increase.

Statement (2) is insufficient because you don't know anything about the profit in 1992, and this information would be necessary to set up the calculation.

Statement (3) is sufficient because you are given a proportional relationship between the two years' profits: $\left(\dfrac{P_{1991} + P_{1993}}{2} = 1.125(P_{1991})\right)$. The question asks you for a proportional relationship, so this is exactly what you need.

Statement (4) is insufficient because you aren't given the total; you don't know what percentage a $4.5 million difference represents.

TAKEAWAYS: THE BASIC PRINCIPLES OF DATA SUFFICIENCY

The basic principles of Data Sufficiency are the following:

- Know the Data Sufficiency answer choices cold.
- The statements are always true.
- It's all about the question stem.
- Think about sufficiency, not calculation.

The Kaplan Method for Data Sufficiency

LEARNING OBJECTIVES

In this section, you will learn how to:

- State the steps of the Kaplan Method for Data Sufficiency questions
- Explain the purpose of each step of the Kaplan Method for Data Sufficiency
- Perform the steps of the Method on Data Sufficiency questions

This Method is the essential systematic approach to mastering Data Sufficiency. Use this approach for every Data Sufficiency question. It will allow you to answer questions quickly and will guarantee that you avoid the common Data Sufficiency mistake of subconsciously combining the statements instead of considering them separately at first.

THE KAPLAN METHOD FOR DATA SUFFICIENCY

1. Analyze the question stem.
   - Determine Value or Yes/No.
   - Simplify.
   - Identify what is needed to answer the question.
2. Evaluate the statements using 12TEN.

STEP 1: ANALYZE THE QUESTION STEM

There are three things you should accomplish in this step:

- **Determine Value or Yes/No.** Which type of Data Sufficiency question is this? Depending on whether the question is a Value question or a Yes/No question, the rules for sufficiency are a little different. If you treat the two types the same way, you probably won't get the right answer. Later in this chapter, you'll learn the critical differences between these two types.

- **Simplify.** If the given information is an equation that can be simplified, you should do so up front. Likewise, any word problems should be translated into math or otherwise paraphrased in your scratchwork. When a question asks for the value of a specific variable and gives you a multi-variable equation, isolate the variable being asked for so you can more clearly see what kind of information you need in order to solve.

- **Identify What Is Needed to Answer the Question.** What kind of information would get you the answer to the question? The more you think up front about what information would be sufficient, the better you'll be able to evaluate the statements.

Don't rush through this step, even for seemingly simple questions. The more you glean from the question stem, the easier it will be to find the right answer.

STEP 2: EVALUATE THE STATEMENTS USING 12TEN

Since the answer choices depend on considering each statement alone, don't let the information you learn from one statement carry over into your analysis of the other. Consider each statement separately, in conjunction with the question stem. Remember that each statement is always true. Don't waste time verifying the statements; just evaluate whether this information lets you answer the question.

On Test Day, you don't want to spend even a second reading the answer choices or thinking about which answer choice is which. They will never change, so you will save yourself much time and confusion by memorizing what the answer choices mean and working with them until you've fully internalized them.

A helpful way to remember how the answer choices are structured is to use the acronym **1-2-TEN**.

1   Only Statement **(1)** is sufficient.

2   Only Statement **(2)** is sufficient.

T   You must put the statements **together** for them to be sufficient.

E   **Either** statement alone is sufficient.

N   **Neither** separately nor together are the statements sufficient.

In fact, it's so important to memorize the answer choices that after this initial sample question, we will no longer print the choices along with the questions. For each practice question, you should follow the routine you will use on Test Day: write 12TEN in your scratchwork for each question and cross out the incorrect answer choices as you eliminate them. We'll teach you patterns for eliminating answer choices later in this chapter.

Applying the Kaplan Method for Data Sufficiency

Now, let's apply the Kaplan Method for Data Sufficiency to the question you saw at the beginning of this chapter:

Is the product of x, y, and z equal to 1?

(1) $x + y + z = 3$

(2) x, y, and z are each greater than 0.

○   Statement (1) ALONE is sufficient, but Statement (2) is not sufficient.

○   Statement (2) ALONE is sufficient, but Statement (1) is not sufficient.

○   BOTH statements TOGETHER are sufficient, but NEITHER statement ALONE is sufficient.

○   EACH statement ALONE is sufficient.

○   Statements (1) and (2) TOGETHER are NOT sufficient.

STEP 1: ANALYZE THE QUESTION STEM

This is a Yes/No question. If $xyz = 1$, then the answer is yes. If $xyz \neq 1$, then the answer is no. Either answer—yes or no—would be sufficient. There's nothing that needs to be simplified in this step; all variables are in their simplest terms, and there are no common variables to combine. It's often worth thinking about how you could get the yes or no that you're looking for. For instance, if x, y, and z all equal 1, you would get an answer of yes. But is this the only way? This question is short but definitely not simple, since there may be many other possibilities to consider.

STEP 2: EVALUATE THE STATEMENTS USING 12TEN

Picking numbers for Statement (1), you can readily see how to get a yes: $x = 1$, $y = 1$, and $z = 1$. Can you pick numbers in such a way that the sum is 3 but the product is not 1? Not if you only consider positive integers. But if you consider different kinds of numbers, you can easily find some. Zero doesn't alter a sum, but it forces a product to be 0. So $x = 3$, $y = 0$, and $z = 0$, while they follow the restrictions given in Statement (1), will give you an answer of no to the original question. Since you can get both a yes and a no, Statement (1) is insufficient. Eliminate **(A)** and **(D)**—or choices "1" and "E," if you've written 12TEN in your scratchwork.

Now that you've reached a verdict on Statement (1) on its own, completely put Statement (1) out of your mind as you evaluate Statement (2) independently. Statement (2) rules out the possibility of using 0 but not the possibility of using fractions or decimals. So $x = 1$, $y = 1$, and $z = 1$ is also permissible here, but so is something like $x = 100$, $y = 100$, and $z = 100$. So xyz could equal 1, but it could also equal 1,000,000. So you can get both a yes and a no here, as well. Statement (2) is also insufficient, so you can eliminate **(B)**—which is the "2" of 12TEN.

Since each statement is insufficient on its own, you need to consider them together. Can you pick numbers that add to 3 and are all positive? Again, $x = 1$, $y = 1$, and $z = 1$ makes the cut and answers the question with a yes. Can you think of numbers that *don't* multiply to 1 that also are consistent with both statements? Once again, you have to expand your thinking to include other types of numbers besides positive integers. Fractions and decimals make things bigger when added but smaller when multiplied. For example, $x = 2.8$, $y = 0.1$, and $z = 0.1$ fit the bill. They are all positive and sum to 3. Their product is $2.8(0.1)(0.1) = 0.028$; this answers the question with a no. Since you can get both a yes and a no answer, the statements are insufficient to answer the question even when combined. The answer is **(E)**—which corresponds to the "N" of 12TEN.

Now take a few minutes and answer the questions in the following practice set. Don't worry if they're challenging at first; you're only getting started working with this unique question type. For now, do not concentrate on speed—or even on getting the correct answer in the end—but rather on building your technique for approaching Data Sufficiency questions systematically using the Method. You'll get much more practice with these questions throughout the chapter.

Practice Set: The Kaplan Method for Data Sufficiency

1. How many employees of Company R are surveyors?

    (1) Exactly $\frac{5}{8}$ of the employees of Company R are not surveyors.

    (2) The 18 architects in Company R constitute 25 percent of the company's total employees.

2. If $a^5 \geq -32$ and a is an integer, what is the value of a?

    (1) $6a + 18 \leq 12$

    (2) $a^2 > 2$

3. If $3b - |a| = 27$, what is the value of b?

    (1) $a^2 = 81$

    (2) $a^3 > 0$

4. The nth term of a sequence of distinct positive integers is determined by $a_n = (k^{a_{n-2}})(a_{n-1})$, where $n \geq 3$ and k is a constant. If $a_2 = 4$, and $a_3 = 36$, what is the value of a 5?

    (1) $a_1 = 2$

    (2) $k = 3$

5. A ferry crosses a lake and then returns to its starting point by the same route. The first time it crosses the lake, the ferry travels at 15 kilometers per hour. The ferry's return trip takes 3 hours. How many hours does the ferry take for the first leg of the trip?

    (1) The ferry's average speed for the entire round trip is 12 kilometers per hour.

    (2) The distance the ferry covers to cross the lake once is 30 kilometers.

Know the Two Types of Data Sufficiency Questions

There are two broad types of Data Sufficiency questions, and they play by slightly different rules. The two types are Value questions and Yes/No questions. During step 1 of the Kaplan Method for Data Sufficiency, you need to determine which type of question you're dealing with, since this will determine your approach.

Value Questions

A Value question will ask you for the exact value of something. If a statement narrows the possibilities down to exactly one number, then it is sufficient. Otherwise, it is not. Of the Data Sufficiency questions you'll see on Test Day, approximately two-thirds will be Value questions.

Let's take a closer look at how this question type functions using a sample question.

Example:

What is the value of x?

(1) $x^2 - 7x + 6 = 0$
(2) $5x = 30$

STEP 1: ANALYZE THE QUESTION STEM

This is a Value question, meaning you need to find the value of x to obtain sufficiency. There's nothing that needs to be simplified in this step, since there's just one variable: x. Before you evaluate the statements, remember that sufficiency is obtained when you can identify one, and *only* one, possible value for x.

STEP 2: EVALUATE THE STATEMENTS USING 12TEN

Statement (1) can be reverse-FOILed to $(x - 1)(x - 6) = 0$, which means that there are two possible values for x, either 1 or 6. But you don't even need to calculate these two values; once you know there is more than one possible value, you know that Statement (1) must be insufficient.

Statement (2) is a linear equation, containing a single variable. Therefore, there can only be one possible result (in this case, $x = 6$), and it is sufficient.

Since Statement (1) is insufficient and Statement (2) is sufficient by itself, the answer is **(B)**.

Practice Set: Value Questions

6. What is the value of $4n - 5m$?

   (1) $\dfrac{n}{5} = \dfrac{m}{4}$

   (2) $\dfrac{n}{4} = \dfrac{m}{5}$

7. What is the value of $\dfrac{st}{u}$?

   (1) $s - \dfrac{3t}{4}$ and $u = 2t$

   (2) $s = u - 10$ and $u = s + t + 2$

8. If z is an integer, what is the units digit of z^3?

   (1) z is a multiple of 5.

   (2) $\sqrt{z}$ is an integer.

9. If d is the product of exactly two distinct prime factors, what is the value of the larger of those prime factors?

   (1) $100 \le d \le 120$

   (2) d is an even number.

Yes/No Questions

Yes/No questions are, simply put, questions that call for a yes or a no answer. A key difference between Value questions and Yes/No questions is that a range of values can establish sufficiency for Yes/No questions. For example, if a question asks, "Is $x > 10$?" a statement saying $x < 9$ will be sufficient.

Note that in this example, the answer to the question in the stem is, "No, x is never greater than 10." Don't confuse an answer of yes to the question "Is Statement (1) sufficient?" with a yes to the question in the stem; they are not the same. This mistake is the most common pitfall test takers face on Yes/No questions. You can avoid this pitfall by remembering that any answer of "ALWAYS yes" or "ALWAYS no" is sufficient; only "sometimes yes, sometimes no" answers are insufficient. The definitiveness of your answer to the question stem is more important in determining sufficiency than whether the answer itself happens to be yes or no.

Sometimes Yes/No questions don't appear to call for a yes or no answer. Suppose a Data Sufficiency question asks which employee, Jane or Sam, earned more in 2017. Ask yourself, "Do I really need to know the specific earnings of Jane and Sam?" As it turns out, you don't. You should handle this question the same way as you would a Yes/No question that asked, "Did Jane earn more than Sam last year?" In both cases, you have sufficient information when you determine that only one answer is possible—Jane or Sam—even if you don't know a precise value for either Jane's earnings or Sam's earnings. Again, you can determine sufficiency knowing only ranges of values (for example, it's sufficient to know that Jane earned more than $20,000 and that Sam earned less than $16,000).

Let's take a closer look at how this question type functions using a sample question:

Example:

> If x is an integer, and $0 < x < 4$, is x prime?
>
> (1) $x > 1$
> (2) x is even.

STEP 1: ANALYZE THE QUESTION STEM

This is a Yes/No question, meaning you need to determine whether x is prime or not. According to the question stem, x could be 1, 2, or 3. You know that 2 and 3 are prime but 1 is not. In order to attain a definite yes answer, x must be either 2 or 3, and to obtain a definite no answer, x must be equal to 1. In other words, you could restate the question as "Does x equal 2 or 3?"

STEP 2: EVALUATE THE STATEMENTS USING 12TEN

Start with Statement (1). Knowing that x is greater than 1 rules out 1, leaving only 2 and 3 as possible values of x. Since both 2 and 3 are prime, you have an answer: definitely yes. This statement is sufficient. Notice that you don't know which of those two values x equals, but for a Yes/No question, knowing a precise value is irrelevant; you can still have sufficiency as long as you know the answer is "always yes" or "always no." Eliminate choices **(B)**, **(C)**, and **(E)**.

Now set aside Statement (1) and move on to Statement (2). Of the possible values of x—1, 2, and 3—only one of them is even. You've determined that x must be 2. Because 2 is prime, the statement gives you a definite yes. Statement (2) is also sufficient, so the answer is **(D)**.

Practice Set: Yes/No Questions

10. Is $\frac{z}{12} - 9$ an integer?

    (1) $\frac{z + 24}{12}$ is an integer.

    (2) z is a multiple of 6.

11. If p and z are positive integers, is pz odd?

    (1) $p \mid z$ is even.

    (2) z^p is even.

12. Is $0 < \frac{a}{b} < 1$?

    (1) $ab > 1$

    (2) $a - b < 1$

13. If the integer $y > 6$, is $x^3 y > 56$?

    (1) $4 < x^2 \leq 9$

    (2) $x^3 + x > x^3$

Here are the key facts about the two types of Data Sufficiency questions:

- Value questions ask for a numeric value, and sufficient information would allow you to calculate exactly one value for the unknown quantity.

- Yes/No questions present a binary choice, such as between "Yes, x is positive" or "No, x is not positive" or between "Swimmer A won the race" or "Swimmer B won the race," and sufficient information would allow you to determine that the answer to the question is *definitely yes* or *definitely no* (*definitely Swimmer A* or *definitely Swimmer B*).

Data Sufficiency Strategy

LEARNING OBJECTIVES

In this section, you will learn how to:

- Identify Data Sufficiency questions for which the Picking Numbers strategy is helpful and apply Picking Numbers efficiently

- Combine statements when neither statement alone is sufficient and evaluate the sufficiency of the statements together

- Use strategic guessing when appropriate to manage your pacing on Data Sufficiency questions

Now that you're familiar with how Data Sufficiency questions are constructed, let's look at two important strategic approaches to these questions. The first you're already familiar with from the Problem Solving chapter: we'll start by looking at how to effectively use the Picking Numbers strategy. After that, we'll discuss in greater detail how to most effectively combine statements.

Picking Numbers in Data Sufficiency

You've already seen the power of the Kaplan strategy of picking numbers for Problem Solving questions. You can also use this strategy for many Data Sufficiency questions that contain variables, unknown quantities, or percents of an unknown whole. When using this strategy, you always pick at least two different sets of numbers, trying to prove that the statements are *insufficient* by producing two different results. It's usually easier to prove insufficiency than sufficiency. But as you practice this strategy, the Core Competency of Pattern Recognition will also come into play. You will become adept at recognizing the types of numbers that can produce different results: positives vs. negatives, fractions vs. integers, odds vs. evens, and so on. Also, don't hesitate to use the numbers 0 and 1, as they have unique properties that make them great candidates for the picking numbers strategy.

Applying the Kaplan Method: Picking Numbers in Data Sufficiency

Now let's use the Kaplan Method on a Data Sufficiency question that involves picking numbers:

If $a + b = 20$, then what is the value of $c - d$?

(1) $ac - bd + bc - ad = 60$

(2) $d = 4$

STEP 1: ANALYZE THE QUESTION STEM

Here's a Value question, so you need one, and *only* one, value for the expression $c - d$. There's nothing much to simplify here, but keep in mind that you are given a value for another expression, $a + b$. To obtain sufficiency, you'll need values for both c and d or a way to relate the equation $a + b = 20$ to the expression $c - d$.

STEP 2: EVALUATE THE STATEMENTS USING 12TEN

As always, think strategically. Since the GMAT doesn't present the statements in any particular order, it's sometimes wise to start by evaluating Statement (2) if it looks easier to evaluate than Statement (1). Here, Statement (2) gives you a value for d but not for c. There's also no way to relate the equation $a + b = 20$ to the expression $c - d$. Eliminate **(B)** and **(D)**. Notice that you've eliminated 50 percent of the wrong answer choices very quickly.

Now let's tackle Statement (1), remembering to use the information it provides in conjunction with the question stem. You're given $a + b = 20$, so let's use picking numbers here. Pick $a = 10$ and $b = 10$.

Now, Statement (1) reads:	$10c - 10d + 10c - 10d = 60$
Combine the like terms:	$20c - 20d = 60$
Factor out the 20:	$20(c - d) = 60$
Divide out the 20:	$c - d = 3$

So the expression $c - d$ can equal 3. But you're not finished yet. You have to pick a different set of numbers to see whether you can produce a different answer.

What permissible numbers might be likely to produce a different answer? Since Statement (1) involves subtraction, try negative numbers. Try $a = 25$ and $b = -5$.

Now Statement (1) reads:	$25c - (-5)d + (-5)c - 25d = 60$
Move the common terms next to each other:	$25c + (-5)c - (-5)d - 25d = 60$
Simplify the positive and negative signs:	$25c - 5c + 5d - 25d = 60$
Combine like terms:	$20c - 20d = 60$
Factor out the 20:	$20(c - d) = 60$
Divide out the 20:	$c - d = 3$

After picking two sets of numbers that have different properties and receiving the same result, you can say with reasonable confidence that Statement (1) is sufficient. Eliminate **(C)** and **(E)**. The correct answer is **(A)**.

TAKEAWAYS: PICKING NUMBERS IN DATA SUFFICIENCY

- To evaluate a statement (or the statements combined), you must pick at least two sets of numbers.
- When picking the second set of numbers, try to produce a different answer than that given by the first set.

Practice Set: Picking Numbers in Data Sufficiency

14. Each of *A*, *B*, and *C* represents a single digit in the positive number *ABC*. If the hundreds digit is twice the units digit, is $B > A$?

    (1) $C < 2$
    (2) $B = 9$

15. Does the integer *a* have 4 or more distinct prime factors?

    (1) *a* is divisible by 36.
    (2) *a* is divisible by 35.

16. Is $|15 - m| + |m - 15| > 15$?

    (1) $m > 6$
    (2) $m < 7$

Combining Statements

If—and *only* if—each statement on its own is insufficient, you must then consider the statements together. The best way to do this is to think of the statements as one long sentence. At this stage, you can essentially approach the question as you would a Problem Solving question, using all the information you're given to answer the question. The main difference is that, since this is still Data Sufficiency, you will stop solving as soon as you know that you *can* solve. The time saved by avoiding unnecessary calculations is better spent on questions later in the section.

As you've learned earlier in this chapter, information is always consistent between the statements. The statements never contradict each other. For example, you'll never see a question in which Statement (1) says that x must be negative and Statement (2) says that x is positive. You might, however, learn from Statement (1) that x is greater than -5 and learn from Statement (2) that it's positive. Learning to recognize how one statement does or does not limit the information in the other is the key in deciding between choices (**C**) and (**E**).

Combining Statements Exercise

Answers are on the following page.

The following exercise contains a single question stem—"What is the value of x?"— and many sets of sample statements, which have already been simplified and evaluated for you. Imagine that you had analyzed the statements and gotten the possible values for x listed below: Which statements, either separately or combined, are sufficient to answer the question? Choose the appropriate Data Sufficiency answer choice—(**A**), (**B**), (**C**), (**D**), or (**E**)—for each pair of statements.

What is the value of x?

1.	(1)	$x = -1, 0, 1$	4.	(1)	$x = 1, 1$	7.	(1)	$x = 1, 1$
	(2)	$x = 0, 1$		(2)	$x = 1, 2$		(2)	$x = -1$
2.	(1)	$x < 3$	5.	(1)	$x < 4$	8.	(1)	$x \geq 2$
	(2)	$x > 1$		(2)	$x < 2$		(2)	$x \leq 2$
3.	(1)	$x = -1, 0$	6.	(1)	$x = -1, 0$	9.	(1)	x is even.
	(2)	$x < 0$		(2)	$x = -1, 0$		(2)	x is prime.

Combining Statements Exercise: Answers

1. **(E)**; x could be 0 or 1.

2. **(E)**; x could be any number between (but not including) 1 and 3. Don't assume that variables are integers.

3. **(C)**; $x = -1$.

4. **(C)**; $x = 1$.

5. **(E)**; x could be any number smaller than 2.

6. **(E)**; x could be 0 or -1. Statements that give redundant information are never sufficient when combined.

7. **(B)**; Statement (2) is sufficient. Note that you would never combine statements in this case.

8. **(C)**; $x = 2$.

9. **(C)**; $x = 2$.

Applying the Kaplan Method: Combining Statements

Now let's use the Kaplan Method on a Data Sufficiency question that involves picking numbers:

If x and y are positive integers, is $\dfrac{2x}{y}$ an integer?

(1) Some factors of y are also factors of x.

(2) All distinct prime factors of y are also prime factors of x.

STEP 1: ANALYZE THE QUESTION STEM

First, this is a Yes/No question. Any statement that gives you a "sometimes yes, sometimes no" answer is insufficient. Now, how can you paraphrase the question in the stem? You can say either, "Is $2x$ a multiple of y?" or "Does $2x$ divide evenly by y?"

STEP 2: EVALUATE THE STATEMENTS USING 12TEN

Use the Kaplan strategy of picking numbers. Pick permissible, manageable numbers. If you pick $x = 5$ and $y = 5$, that will give you a yes to the original question, since $2x$, or 10, divided by y, or 5, will yield an integer. But if you pick a different set of numbers, say $x = 2$ and $y = 42$, that will yield a fraction. Statement (1) is insufficient; eliminate **(A)** and **(D)**.

Pick numbers for Statement (2), making sure they're permissible. For example, 36 and 6 have the same distinct prime factors: 2 and 3. Picking the numbers $x = 36$ and $y = 6$ gives you an integer; choosing $x = 6$ and $y = 36$, on the other hand, gives you a fraction. Therefore, Statement (2) is insufficient; eliminate **(B)**.

Now, combining the statements, you will notice something interesting. Statement (2) is more restrictive than Statement (1). So as you combine the statements, ask yourself, "Will any numbers that satisfy Statement (2) also satisfy Statement (1)?" Yes, they will. For instance, $x = 36$ and $y = 6$, which you picked for Statement (2), also work for Statement (1): these numbers will again yield a yes answer. And $x = 6$ and $y = 36$ also work for Statement (1), yielding a no answer. Since combining the statements didn't add any new information and the information presented was insufficient, the answer must be **(E)**. Even combined, you get a "sometimes yes, sometimes no" answer to the question in the stem.

TAKEAWAYS: COMBINING STATEMENTS

- Each data statement is true. Therefore, when combining statements, look for values that are permitted by both statements.
- Treat combined statements as one long statement.
- Never combine statements unless each statement is insufficient on its own.

Practice Set: Combining Statements

17. Is $y^2 < 1$?

    (1) $y > -1$

    (2) $y < 1$

18. A taqueria has exactly two items on its menu, a taco and a burrito. On a particular day, it sold 600 items, exactly half of which were tacos. What was the taqueria's revenue on that day?

    (1) The average price of an item on the menu is $4.50.

    (2) A burrito costs twice as much as a taco.

19. If a and b are positive, what is the value of $a - b$?

    (1) $a^2 + 2ab + b^2 = 36$

    (2) $a^2 - b^2 = 12$

Strategic Guessing

When you run into a very complicated question, like the following, don't forget to use a sound Data Sufficiency guessing strategy. That means perhaps skipping a statement that looks too daunting and trying to eliminate some answer choices by looking at the easier statement. Try your hand at the difficult question below. Don't try to solve it; instead, see if you can narrow down the possibilities quickly.

Example:

What was the maximum temperature in City A on Saturday, May 14?

(1) The average (arithmetic mean) of the maximum daily temperatures in City A from Sunday, May 8, to Saturday, May 14, was 72 degrees, which was 2 degrees less than the average (arithmetic mean) of the maximum daily temperatures in City A from Monday, May 9, to Friday, May 13.

(2) The maximum temperature in City A on Saturday, May 14, was 5 degrees greater than the maximum temperature in City A on Sunday, May 8.

STEP 1: ANALYZE THE QUESTION STEM

This is a Value question. To obtain sufficiency, you need an exact maximum temperature.

STEP 2: EVALUATE THE STATEMENTS USING 12TEN

Statement (1) is long and complicated. Skip it and go straight to Statement (2); it's much easier.

Statement (2) tells you that the value you're looking for is 5 degrees more than the temperature on some other day. Without knowing the temperature on that other day, you don't have the information you need. This statement is insufficient. You can eliminate **(B)** and **(D)** and give yourself a one-in-three chance to get the right answer without even evaluating Statement (1).

Perhaps you feel comfortable evaluating Statement (1). Perhaps you don't. But let's pretend for a moment that you aren't sure how to evaluate Statement (1). Keep in mind that on the GMAT, complicated or hard-to-evaluate statements are more likely to be sufficient than insufficient. For this reason, you should avoid **(E)** and lean toward **(A)**, unless you have a logical reason to suspect that Statement (1) alone is insufficient. Of course, this doesn't guarantee you a correct answer, but if you're falling behind on time, it will help you move through the Quantitative section most efficiently. Remember, no one particular question will make or break your GMAT score, but spending too much time on one question and having to rush through several others just to make up for the lost time will hurt your score. As it turns out, **(C)** is the right answer to this particular problem.

Fortunately, you're unlikely to run into anything as complicated as Statement (1) on Test Day. The point of this exercise is to show you that even if you do encounter something this difficult, you're still in control. If you work the odds and look for the strategic approach, you will increase your likelihood of picking up the points even for questions you're not sure how to solve.

For the record, let's analyze Statement (1). If the average maximum temperature from May 8 to May 14 was 72 degrees, then the sum of the maximum temperatures of those days is $7 \times 72 = 504$ degrees. If the average maximum temperature from May 9 to May 13 was $72 + 2$, or 74 degrees, then the sum of the maximum temperatures of those days was $5 \times 74 = 370$ degrees.

The difference between those two sums is simply the sum of the maximum temperature on May 8, which you can call x, and the maximum temperature on May 14, which you can call y (since these two days were left out of the second time period). So $x + y = 504 - 370 = 134$. Statement (1) by itself is insufficient. But Statement (2) tells you that $y - x = 5$. You have the two distinct linear equations, $x + y = 134$ and $y - x = 5$. These equations can be solved for a single value for y, so the statements taken together are sufficient: choice (**C**).

This example demonstrates how guessing can be a good alternative approach for certain questions. By looking at only one statement, you can narrow down the possibilities to two or three choices. This can be a great help, particularly on difficult or time-consuming problems for which you think you might have to guess. But you must be sure you know the rules for eliminating answer choices absolutely cold by Test Day.

Answers and explanations follow on the next page. ▶ ▶ ▶

Answer Key

Practice Set: The Kaplan Method for Data Sufficiency

1. C
2. C
3. A
4. D
5. D

Practice Set: Value Questions

6. A
7. C
8. E
9. E

Practice Set: Yes/No Questions

10. A
11. B
12. E
13. C

Practice Set: Picking Numbers in Data Sufficiency

14. B
15. C
16. B

Practice Set: Combining Statements

17. C
18. A
19. C

Answers and Explanations

Practice Set: The Kaplan Method for Data Sufficiency

1. **(C)**

   How many employees of Company R are surveyors?

   (1) Exactly $\frac{5}{8}$ of the employees of Company R are not surveyors.

   (2) The 18 architects in Company R constitute 25 percent of the company's total employees.

STEP 1: ANALYZE THE QUESTION STEM

The question asks how many employees of a particular company are surveyors, so it's a Value question. A statement will be sufficient if it provides enough information to calculate the exact number of surveyors. There's no other information to simplify here, so move on to the statements.

STEP 2: EVALUATE THE STATEMENTS USING 12TEN

Statement (1) says that $\frac{5}{8}$ of the employees are not surveyors, which means the remaining $\frac{3}{8}$ of the employees are surveyors. However, there is no way to calculate an actual number of surveyors. Eliminate **(A)** and **(D)**.

Statement (2) is enough to find the total number of employees ($18 = 0.25R$, so $R = 72$), but not how many of the employees are surveyors. Statement (2) by itself is insufficient, so eliminate **(B)**. Since neither statement worked by itself, try combining them.

Combining Statements (1) and (2), you know the total number of employees (72) from Statement (2), and you know what fraction of those employees are surveyors $\left(\frac{3}{8}\right)$ from Statement (1). You could thus calculate the total number of employees who are surveyors (for the record, the calculation is $\frac{3}{8} \times 72 = 27$). **(C)** is correct.

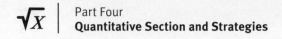

2. (C)

If $a^5 \geq -32$ and a is an integer, what is the value of a?

(1) $6a + 18 \leq 12$

(2) $a^2 > 2$

STEP 1: ANALYZE THE QUESTION STEM

From the question stem, you know that a must be an integer greater than or equal to $\sqrt[5]{-32}$. Having some powers of 2 memorized is helpful here: because $2^5 = 32$, $-2^5 = -32$, and $\sqrt[5]{-32} = -2$. Thus, the question stem is saying that $a \geq -2$. To have sufficiency, you need information that will allow you to narrow this range down to one possible value for a.

STEP 2: EVALUATE THE STATEMENTS USING 12TEN

Statement (1) gives an inequality that you could solve for a: subtracting 18 from both sides results in $6a \leq -6$, which simplifies to $a \leq -1$. Combine this with the information from the question stem that $a \geq -2$ and that a is an integer, and you know that a could be either -1 or -2. That's two values, so eliminate **(A)** and **(D)**.

Statement (2), $a^2 > 2$, means that $a > 1$ or that $a < -1$. The information in the question stem, $a^5 \geq -32$, tells you that $a \geq -2$. So a could either be any integer greater than 1, or it could be -2. (If you have trouble seeing this, sketch the possible values of a on a number line and see where they overlap.) Eliminate **(B)**. Since neither statement alone was sufficient, try combining the statements.

Combining Statements (1) and (2), you know from Statement (1) that $a \leq -1$ and from Statement (2) that either $a = -2$ or $a > 1$. The only integer value that works in both statements is -2, so this must be the value of a. **(C)** is correct.

3.   (A)

If $3b - |a| = 27$, what is the value of b?

(1) $a^2 = 81$

(2) $a^3 > 0$

STEP 1: ANALYZE THE QUESTION STEM

This is a Value question, which means that sufficiency requires one and only one value for b. A value for $|a|$ is needed in order to solve for b. Since absolute value is always positive, only the magnitude of a is needed, not its sign.

STEP 2: EVALUATE THE STATEMENTS USING 12TEN

Statement (1) gives a value for a^2; although a itself could be either positive or negative, taking the absolute value of either will have the same result. Therefore, this statement is sufficient, eliminating **(B)**, **(C)**, and **(E)**.

Statement (2) indicates that a^3 is positive. Since a negative number or zero raised to an odd exponent would not be positive, this shows that a is positive, but many values of a are still possible. This is insufficient, eliminating **(D)**.

Therefore, Statement (1) alone is sufficient, and the correct choice is **(A)**.

Note that using the Kaplan Method will keep you from falling into a trap laid by the test maker. If you thought from the first statement that having two possible values—one positive and one negative—for a meant that the information was insufficient to get one value, you might have thought you needed the information in Statement (2) to get one value for a. However, by determining what you need for sufficiency before looking at the statements, you realized that it does not matter whether you have the positive or negative value of a, as either allows solving for one and only one value for b.

4. (D)

The nth term of a sequence of distinct positive integers is determined by $a_n = \left(k^{a_{n-2}}\right)(a_{n-1})$, where $n \geq 3$ and k is a constant. If $a_2 = 4$, and $a_3 = 36$, what is the value of a 5?

(1) $a_1 = 2$

(2) $k = 3$

STEP 1: ANALYZE THE QUESTION STEM

The question stem defines a sequence by providing a relationship among three consecutive terms $(a_{n-2}, a_{n-1},$ and $a_n)$, and it asks for the value of a_5, or the fifth number in the sequence. Since this is not Problem Solving, do not be overly concerned with interpreting the sequence notation to solve for a value. Just know that the subscript represents a value's position in the sequence, so to solve for the fifth term, you'd use the equation $a_5 = \left(k^{a_3}\right)(a_4)$. You are given the values of the second and third terms, so knowing the value of k would allow you to solve for the fourth term. Then you would know the values of the third and fourth terms and k, and you'd be able to solve.

Simplify the given information to make it easier to see what is needed to determine k's value:

$$a_3 = \left(k^{a_1}\right)(a_2)$$
$$36 = \left(k^{a_1}\right)(4)$$
$$k^{a_1} = 9$$

If you know the value of a_1, you can solve for k.

STEP 2: EVALUATE THE STATEMENTS USING 12TEN

Statement (1) tells you the value of the first term in the sequence. From that value, you could determine the value of k. Then, as described in step 1, you could determine the value of a_4 and then of a_5. Since this is a Data Sufficiency question, knowing that you could determine the value of a_5 is enough—don't spend precious time actually calculating it! Eliminate **(B)**, **(C)**, and **(E)**.

Statement (2) tells you the value of k. This would allow calculation of a_4 and then a_5. This statement is also sufficient.

Since either statement on its own provides enough information to determine the value of a_5, the correct choice is **(D)**.

5.　(D)

A ferry crosses a lake and then returns to its starting point by the same route. The first time it crosses the lake, the ferry travels at 15 kilometers per hour. The ferry's return trip takes 3 hours. How many hours does the ferry take for the first leg of the trip?

(1)　The ferry's average speed for the entire round trip is 12 kilometers per hour.

(2)　The distance the ferry covers to cross the lake once is 30 kilometers.

STEP 1: ANALYZE THE QUESTION STEM

This question asks for a value: how long is the first leg of the trip? This question involves one of the common math formulas you should memorize for Test Day: Distance = Rate × Time.

Make a table to organize the information you know from the question stem:

	Distance	Rate (kph)	Time (hr)
First leg	d	15	t
Second leg	d	r	3

The question asks for the time (t) of the first leg of the trip; using the distance formula, you can set up an equation involving t: $d = 15t$. Information that provides a value for d or that provides a second equation with d and t will be sufficient to solve.

STEP 2: EVALUATE THE STATEMENTS USING 12TEN

Statement (1) gives the average speed for the entire trip, allowing you to write a second equation involving d and t. Although you wouldn't do the math on Test Day, here's how it works.

	Distance	Rate (kph)	Time (hr)
First leg	d	15	t
Second leg	d	r	3
Total journey	$2d$	12	$t + 3$

Since Total distance = Average speed × Total time, $2d = 12 \times (t + 3) = 12t + 36$. From the first leg of the trip, you know that $d = 15t$, so substitute $15t$ for d to find that $2(15t) = 12t + 36$, $30t = 12t + 36$, $18t = 36$, and $t = 2$. Thus, with two variables and two equations, you could solve for each of the variables. Eliminate (**B**), (**C**), and (**E**).

Statement (2) gives a value for d, which is exactly what you need to solve directly for t. Since both statements are sufficient individually, (**D**) is correct.

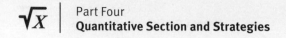

Practice Set: Value Questions

6.   (A)

What is the value of $4n - 5m$?

(1) $\dfrac{n}{5} = \dfrac{m}{4}$

(2) $\dfrac{n}{4} = \dfrac{m}{5}$

STEP 1: ANALYZE THE QUESTION STEM

This Value question requires one and only one value for the expression $4n - 5m$. You will either need to find the value for that expression or find the values of n and m individually.

STEP 2: EVALUATE THE STATEMENTS USING 12TEN

Statement (1) may not look like much help at first, but cross multiplying results in the equation $4n = 5m$. Subtract $5m$ from both sides to find that $4n - 5m = 0$. This is one and only one value for the expression in the question stem, so this statement is sufficient. Eliminate **(B)**, **(C)**, and **(E)**.

Statement (2) looks very similar to Statement (1), but cross multiplying here results in the equation $5n = 4m$. From this, there is no way to figure out the values of n or m (you would need two distinct equations to do that, given that there are two variables) and no way to isolate $4n - 5m$. Statement (2) is therefore insufficient, so you can eliminate **(D)**.

Statement (1) alone is sufficient, so the correct answer is **(A)**.

7. (C)

What is the value of $\frac{st}{u}$?

(1) $s = \frac{3t}{4}$ and $u = 2t$

(2) $s = u - 10$ and $u = s + t + 2$

STEP 1: ANALYZE THE QUESTION STEM

This is a Value question. The stem for this item includes three variables. Therefore, either three distinct equations involving these variables or specific values for each of the variables would be sufficient to get one value for the entire expression.

STEP 2: EVALUATE THE STATEMENTS USING 12TEN

Statement (1) gives you restatements of two of the variables—s and u—in terms of the third variable, t. However, this provides two distinct equations, not three. If you cannot satisfy yourself from inspection that there's no way to combine the equations to eliminate all the variables, then do the math. Replace s and u in the expression in the question stem with the expressions given in the statement:

$$\frac{st}{u} = \frac{\left(\frac{3t}{4}\right)t}{2t} = \frac{\frac{3t^2}{4}}{2t} = \frac{3t^2}{4} \times \frac{1}{2t} \times \frac{3t^2}{8t} = \frac{3}{8}t$$

The variable t is not eliminated, so you cannot solve for the value of $\frac{st}{u}$. This statement is not sufficient, so eliminate **(A)** and **(D)**.

Statement (2) also provides two equations and not three. You are told that $s - u = 10$ and that $u = s + t + 2$. Substituting $u - 10$ for s in the second equation, you find:

$$u = u - 10 + t + 2$$
$$8 = t$$

Substitute the value of 8 for t and substitute $u - 10$ for s:

$$\frac{st}{u} = \frac{(u - 10)(8)}{u} = \frac{8u - 80}{u}$$

Unfortunately, this doesn't eliminate the variable u, so Statement (2) is insufficient and you can eliminate **(B)**.

Combining the statements, you now have four distinct equations, which is more than enough to determine the values of the three variables. Don't do so! Simply knowing that you could do so is enough. The correct answer is **(C)**: neither statement alone is sufficient, but the statements combined are sufficient.

In case you're curious, from Statement (1) you know that $\frac{st}{u} = \frac{3}{8}t$. If you substitute the value of 8 for the variable t—from Statement (2)—you find that $\frac{st}{u} = 3$.

8. **(E)**

If z is an integer, what is the units digit of z^3?

(1) z is a multiple of 5.

(2) $\sqrt{z}$ is an integer.

STEP 1: ANALYZE THE QUESTION STEM

In this Value question, to have sufficiency, you need to know either the value of integer z or something about z that would enable you to determine the units digit of its cube.

STEP 2: EVALUATE THE STATEMENTS USING 12TEN

Statement (1) tells you that z is a multiple of 5. Multiples of 5 have units digits of either 0 or 5. Cubes of numbers with units digits of 0 or 5 keep the same units digit (e.g., the cube of 10 is 1,000; the cube of 5 is 125). The statement is insufficient because it gives you two possible answers to the question stem. Eliminate **(A)** and **(D)**.

Statement (2) tells you that the square root of z is an integer. This means that z is a perfect square. The statement is insufficient because there are perfect squares with many different units values. Eliminate **(B)**.

Because each of the statements is insufficient on its own, combine the statements. Combined, you know that z is both a multiple of 5 and a perfect square. If you can find examples for z that are perfect squares ending in each of the values from Statement (1), then the combined statements are insufficient. If $z = 25$, it is a multiple of 5 and its square root is an integer, and the answer to the question stem is 5. If $z = 100$, then both statements are true, and the answer to the question is 0. Since more than one answer to the question is possible, the two statements taken together are insufficient. Eliminate **(C)**. **(E)** is the correct answer.

9.   (E)

If d is the product of exactly two distinct prime factors, what is the value of the larger of those prime factors?

(1) $100 \le d \le 120$

(2) d is an even number.

STEP 1: ANALYZE THE QUESTION STEM

This is a Value question, so sufficiency will exist if there's enough information to determine one exact numeric value for d. Start with the question stem: since d is the product of *exactly* two distinct prime factors, d must be an integer whose only factors besides 1 and d are those two prime factors.

STEP 2: EVALUATE THE STATEMENTS USING 12TEN

Statement (1) gives a range of possible values. Thus, you need to determine whether more than one of those values is the product of two prime factors. In fact, several are: $2 \times 53 = 106$, $5 \times 23 = 115$, and $7 \times 17 = 119$, to name a few. Thus, there are a number of different values within the range that are the product of two prime factors, and you can't establish a single value for the larger factor. Statement (1) is insufficient. Eliminate (**A**) and (**D**).

Statement (2) only tells you that d is even. You know from the question stem that d is the product of two prime factors, so if d is even, one of those two prime factors must be 2 (because all other prime numbers are odd, and the product of any two odd numbers is odd, whereas the product of an even times an odd will always be even). However, there's no way to establish an exact value for d. Eliminate (**B**).

Now consider the statements together. Treating (1) and (2) as one long statement, d has a value from 100 to 120, and it's even. Knowing that one of the prime factors of d is 2, you can reconsider the value range established by Statement (1) in terms of multiples of 2: $(2 \times 50) \le d \le (2 \times 60)$. List out the numbers between 50 and 60 and eliminate those that aren't prime: 50, 51, 52, 53, 54, 55, 56, 57, 58, 59, 60. Since no prime number besides 2 is even, you can cross off all of the even values, which leaves 51, 53, 55, 57, and 59. Eliminate 55, since it's a multiple of 5. Since 51 has digits that sum to a multiple of 3 ($5 + 1 = 6$), 51 is a multiple of 3. Eliminate it. And 57 also has digits that sum to a multiple of 3 ($5 + 7 = 12$), so it is also not prime. That leaves 53 and 59. Both of these are prime (if you have the primes up to 100 memorized, you'll recognize this; if not, some testing will establish that both are prime). Thus, either might be the larger prime factor of d, so there's no way to establish a single value for this larger prime factor, and the two statements in combination are insufficient. The correct choice is (**E**).

Practice Set: Yes/No Questions

10. (A)

Is $\frac{z}{12} - 9$ an integer?

(1) $\frac{z + 24}{12}$ is an integer.

(2) z is a multiple of 6.

STEP 1: ANALYZE THE QUESTION STEM

This Yes/No question asks whether $\frac{z}{12} - 9$ is an integer. Sufficiency means showing that the value of the expression is definitely an integer or definitely not an integer. Recall that the difference between two integers is an integer. Since 9 is an integer, the other number, $\frac{z}{12}$, must also be an integer to answer this question with a yes. If $\frac{z}{12}$ is definitely not an integer, then the answer to the question is no. Thus, you only need to consider whether $\frac{z}{12}$ is an integer to determine sufficiency.

STEP 2: EVALUATE THE STATEMENTS USING 12TEN

Statement (1) presents a fraction that can be split into $\frac{z}{12} + \frac{24}{12}$, which is $\frac{z}{12} + 2$. Since this sum is an integer and 2 is an integer, $\frac{z}{12}$ must also be an integer. This answers the question with a definite yes, so Statement (1) is sufficient. Eliminate **(B)**, **(C)**, and **(E)**.

Statement (2) narrows the value of z to multiples of 6. Picking numbers can help determine whether this is sufficient. If $z = 6$, then $\frac{z}{12}$ is not an integer, but if $z = 12$, then $\frac{z}{12}$ is an integer. There is no definite yes or no outcome for the given expression, so this statement is insufficient. **(A)** is correct.

11. (B)

If p and z are positive integers, is pz odd?

(1) $p + z$ is even.

(2) z^p is even.

STEP 1: ANALYZE THE QUESTION STEM

This is a Yes/No question about whether the product pz is odd, given that p and z are both positive whole numbers. For pz to be odd, making the answer to the question yes, both p and z must be odd. If either p or z is even, then the answer to the question is no. Examine the statements to see whether they provide either piece of information.

STEP 2: EVALUATE THE STATEMENTS USING 12TEN

Statement (1) says that the sum $(p + z)$ is even. If two integers sum to an even number, the two integers can be either both even or both odd. For example, the sum of $1 + 3$ is 4, and the sum of $2 + 4$ is 6. If the two integers are both even, pz is not odd, so the answer to the question is no; if the two integers are both odd, pz is odd, so the answer is yes. Since different answers to the question are possible based on Statement (1), that statement is insufficient; eliminate (**A**) and (**D**).

Statement (2) says that raising one of the integers to the other gives an even answer. Since z^p involves multiplying p of the z's together, the only way for z^p to be even is if z is even. You can pick numbers to test this. If $z = 2$, then no matter what p is, the result will be even. But if $z = 3$, then no matter what p is, the result will be odd. Thus, to conform to Statement (2), z must be an even number. Then, since multiplying any integer by an even number always gives an even product, pz must be even. Statement (2) provides sufficient information to answer the question (always no), so (**B**) is correct.

12. (E)

Is $0 < \frac{a}{b} < 1$?

(1) $ab > 1$

(2) $a - b < 1$

STEP 1: ANALYZE THE QUESTION STEM

This is a Yes/No question. For sufficiency, a definite yes would show that $\frac{a}{b}$ is always a positive fraction less than 1, or a definite no would show that $\frac{a}{b}$ is always something other than a positive fraction less than 1. Picking numbers will help simplify this.

STEP 2: EVALUATE THE STATEMENTS USING 12TEN

Statement (1) tells you that ab is greater than 1. That means either that a and b are both positive or that they are both negative. Pick some numbers to test out the possibilities:

Case 1:	$a = -3, b = -2$	$(-3)(-2) > 1$	Stem question: No
Case 2:	$a = 2, b = 3$	$(2)(3) > 1$	Stem question: Yes

Because you can pick numbers that follow the rules of the statement without giving a clear yes or no answer to the question stem, the statement is insufficient. Eliminate **(A)** and **(D)**.

Statement (2) tells you that $a - b$ is less than 1. The same pairs of numbers you tested for Statement (1) apply here as well, making the statement insufficient.

Case 1:	$a = -3, b = -2$	$(-3) - (-2) < 1$	Stem question: No
Case 2:	$a = 2, b = 3$	$2 - 3 < 1$	Stem question: Yes

Eliminate **(B)**.

Because each of the statements is insufficient on its own, combine the statements. Since the same cases applied to both statements, combining the statements adds no new information to the analysis, and the combined statements are therefore insufficient. The answer must be **(E)**.

13. (C)

If the integer $y > 6$, is $x^3y > 56$?

(1) $4 < x^2 \leq 9$

(2) $x^3 + x > x^3$

STEP 1: ANALYZE THE QUESTION STEM

This is a Yes/No question. The stem tells you that y is an integer greater than 6, meaning its minimum value is 7, and it asks whether x^3y is greater than 56. Substituting 7 into the second expression reads, "Is $7x^3$ greater than 56?" Simplify further by dividing both sides by 7: "Is x^3 greater than 8?" And finally, take the cube root of both sides, "Is x greater than 2?" If you can answer this question for certain, with either a yes or a no, you'll have sufficiency.

STEP 2: EVALUATE THE STATEMENTS USING 12TEN

Statement (1) says that $4 < x^2 \leq 9$. If you take the square root of all parts of this inequality, you get two possible value ranges for x: either $2 < x \leq 3$ or $3 \leq x < -2$ (since you must consider negative as well as positive square roots). Since x itself might be either positive or negative, x^3 could be either positive or negative (because a negative number cubed remains negative). Therefore, x^3 could be greater than 8 but not greater than 27 *or* it could be less than -8 but not less than -27. Thus, you don't know whether x is greater than 2 and it's not possible to determine whether $x^3y > 56$; since y is positive, if x^3 is negative, x^3y will be negative, and if x^3 is positive, x^3y will be positive as well. Statement (1) is insufficient, so eliminate (A) and (D).

Statement (2) tells you that $x^3 + x > x^3$. Remembering that the statements are always true, pick some positive and negative numbers here to see which are permissible. If $x = 3$, then $x^3 + x = 27 + 3 = 30$, and the statement is true, since $30 > 27$; therefore, x could equal 3. Not only that, but the sum of any positive number and the cube of that number will be greater than the cube alone. However, if $x = -3$, then $x^3 + x = -27 + (-3) = -30$, and the inequality is no longer true, since -30 is not greater than -27. This example demonstrates that adding a negative number to its cube results in a value smaller than the cube. Thus, Statement (2) establishes that x is a positive number. However, that's all it establishes about the value of x, which could be 3, or 100, or 0.005, or any other positive value. Therefore, this statement doesn't provide enough information to determine whether x^3y is greater than 56. Eliminate (B).

Now consider the two statements together: Statement (1) establishes a pair of value ranges for x: $2 < x \leq 3$ or $-2 > x \geq -3$, and Statement (2) establishes that the range of values for x can only be positive. Thus, you know that $x > 2$, which is sufficient to answer the question. The correct choice is (C).

Practice Set: Picking Numbers in Data Sufficiency

14. (B)

Each of *A*, *B*, and *C* represents a single digit in the positive number *ABC*. If the hundreds digit is twice the units digit, is $B > A$?

(1) $C < 2$

(2) $B = 9$

STEP 1: ANALYZE THE QUESTION STEM

This Yes/No question stem says that a three-digit positive number's hundreds digit *A* is twice the number's units digit *C*. To simplify this information, you could represent the three digits of *ABC* with three blanks:

— — —

Then fill in each blank with what you know:

twice *C* *B* *C*

Thus, to answer the question about whether *B* is greater than *A*, a statement would need to allow you to establish a consistent numeric relationship between *A* and *B*.

STEP 2: EVALUATE THE STATEMENTS USING 12TEN

Statement (1) says that *C* is less than 2. This means that *C* is equal to 1 and therefore *A* is equal to $(2)(1) = 2$. (Note that *C* cannot be 0, since the hundreds digit would then be $(2)(0) = 0$, resulting in a two-digit, not a three-digit, number.) The middle digit *B*, by contrast, can be any digit between 0 and 9 inclusive. To determine whether Statement (1) is sufficient, pick some permissible numbers for *B* and compare them to *A*. If *B* is 3, $B > A$. But if $B = 1$, *B* is not greater than *A*. This statement is insufficient, so eliminate **(A)** and **(D)**.

Statement (2) says that $B = 9$. This time, pick some permissible numbers for *C* to determine the resulting *A*-values. As noted for Statement (1), if $C = 1$, then $A = 2$. The value 2 is less than 9, so the answer to the question is yes. Now pick another number for *C* to see whether you can generate an *A*-value that's greater than 9. The largest permissible *C*-value is 4, because if *C* is 5, then *A* would equal $(2)(5) = 10$, and 10 is not a digit. Larger values for *C* create the same problem. So pick 4 for *C*: if $C = 4$, then $A = (2)(4) = 8$, which is still less than $B = 9$. Since there is no way that *A* can be greater than *B*, the answer to the question is always yes.

Only Statement (2) is sufficient, so **(B)** is correct.

15. (C)

Does the integer a have 4 or more distinct prime factors?

(1) a is divisible by 36.

(2) a is divisible by 35.

STEP 1: ANALYZE THE QUESTION STEM

This is a Yes/No question, so you don't need to know the exact value of the number of distinct prime factors of a, just whether there are 4 or more. Notice that the question specifies distinct (different) prime factors.

Recall that every non-prime number can be rewritten as a series of prime numbers multiplied together; those are the number's prime factors. You may not be used to thinking about numbers in terms of their distinct prime factors, so picking numbers now, before considering the statements, can help you do a little thought experiment and make this question more concrete. If a is $2 \times 3 \times 5 = 30$, then it has 3 distinct prime factors, but if a is $2 \times 3 \times 5 \times 7 = 210$, then it has 4 distinct prime factors. There are many other possible combinations of 4 distinct prime factors and less than 4 distinct prime factors, but thinking of two examples may help you understand what is being asked.

STEP 2: EVALUATE THE STATEMENTS USING 12TEN

Statement (1): Pick the simplest number that's divisible by 36, namely 36 itself. That number is 6×6, which means that the prime factors are $2 \times 3 \times 2 \times 3$. Although there are 4 prime factors of 36, there are only 2 distinct prime factors. So if the number is exactly 36, the answer is no. However, the statement only says that a is divisible by 36, so a could be something like $36 \times 5 \times 7 = 1,260$, in which case it *would* have 4 distinct prime factors and the answer would be yes. Statement (1) is insufficient, so eliminate **(A)** and **(D)**.

Statement (2): Now pick the simplest number that's divisible by 35, namely 35 itself. The prime factors of 35 are 5×7. So if $a = 35$, the answer is no. However, similar to Statement (1), a could be $35 \times 2 \times 3 = 210$, in which case there would be 4 distinct prime factors. So Statement (2) is also insufficient. Eliminate **(B)** and evaluate the statements together.

If a is divisible by both 36 and 35, it would have to be the product of all the prime factors of both numbers. Since 36 has the distinct prime factors 2 and 3, and 35 has the distinct prime factors 5 and 7, any number a that is divisible by both 36 and 35 must have *at least* the 4 distinct prime factors 2, 3, 5, and 7. So considering the statements together, the answer is definitely yes. **(C)** is correct.

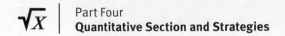

16. (B)

Is $|15 - m| + |m - 15| > 15$?

(1) $m > 6$

(2) $m < 7$

STEP 1: ANALYZE THE QUESTION STEM

In this Yes/No question, sufficiency means proving that $|15 - m| + |m - 15|$ is either definitely greater than 15 or definitely less than or equal to 15. As the question stem is dealing with a range, picking numbers will help in evaluating the statements.

STEP 2: EVALUATE THE STATEMENTS USING 12TEN

Statement (1) restricts m to values greater than 6. When picking numbers to evaluate statements, remember to always pick at least two sets of numbers to see if you can get more than one possible answer to the question—in this case, pick one number near the start of the range and one much farther away. First try $m = 7$.

$$|15 - m| + |m - 15| = |15 - 7| + |7 - 15|$$
$$= |8| + |-8|$$
$$= 8 + 8$$
$$= 16$$

Since 16 is greater than 15, $m = 7$ results in a yes answer to the question. Now try $m = 15$.

$$|15 - m| + |m - 15| = |15 - 15| + |15 - 15|$$
$$= |0| + |0|$$
$$= 0 + 0$$
$$= 0$$

Since 0 is less than 15, $m = 15$ results in a no. As $m > 6$ sometimes means yes and sometimes means no, this statement is insufficient. Eliminate **(A)** and **(D)**.

Statement (2) restricts m to values less than 7. You'll need to pick at least two values once again, so start with $m = 6$.

$$|15 - m| + |m - 15| = |15 - 6| + |6 - 15|$$
$$= |9| + |-9|$$
$$= 9 + 9$$
$$= 18$$

Because 18 is greater than 15, that's a yes. Try $m = 0$.

$$|15 - m| + |m - 15| = |15 - 0 + |0 - 15|$$
$$= |15| + |-15|$$
$$= 15 + 15$$
$$= 30$$

Not only is that a yes, but also the value is actually getting larger as m gets smaller, so this statement will always return an answer of yes to the question. Eliminate **(C)** and **(E)**.

Statement (2) alone is sufficient, so the correct answer is **(B)**.

Practice Set: Combining Statements

17. **(C)**

   Is $y^2 < 1$?

   (1) $y > -1$
   (2) $y < 1$

STEP 1: ANALYZE THE QUESTION STEM

In this Yes/No question, sufficiency means determining that y^2 is either definitely less than 1 or definitely greater than or equal to 1. All squares are non-negative—so how could it be that y^2 is less than 1? The only way this could happen is if y fell somewhere between 1 and -1 on the number line. The square of $\frac{1}{2}$, for instance, is $\frac{1}{4}$; the square of $-\frac{1}{2}$ is also $\frac{1}{4}$. Likewise, the square of 0 is 0. So the question stem can be simplified to "Is y less than 1 and greater than -1?"

STEP 2: EVALUATE THE STATEMENTS USING 12TEN

Statement (1) states that $y > -1$. Picking numbers will make this easier: $y = 0$ leads to a yes answer, as y^2 would be less than 1. However, $y = 2$ leads to an answer of no, as y^2 would be greater than 1. This statement is insufficient, so we can eliminate **(A)** and **(D)**.

Statement (2) states that $y < 1$. As we saw above, $y = 0$ leads to a yes answer. However, $y = -2$ would lead to a no answer, as y^2 would be greater than 1. This statement is insufficient, so eliminate **(B)**.

Combining the statements results in the inequality $-1 < y < 1$. That effectively limits the range of values for y to 0 and fractions whose absolute value is less than 1. Squaring any fraction whose absolute value is less than 1 will always result in a positive fraction less than 1, producing a yes answer, and you've already seen that $y = 0$ produces a yes answer. Therefore, combining the statements will produce a definite answer of yes to the question, and the correct answer is **(C)**.

18. (A)

A taqueria has exactly two items on its menu, a taco and a burrito. On a particular day, it sold 600 items, exactly half of which were tacos. What was the taqueria's revenue on that day?

(1) The average price of an item on the menu is $4.50.

(2) A burrito costs twice as much as a taco.

STEP 1: ANALYZE THE QUESTION STEM

This is a Value question. Translate the English into math and set up an equation. The taqueria sells two menu items, and the question asks for the revenue on a day when equal numbers of the two items were sold, for a total of $600. If t represents the price of a taco and b the price of a burrito, then, since 300 of each were sold, the revenue would be given by the expression $300t + 300b$. Factor out the common term to get $300(t + b)$. Thus, to answer this question, either the individual prices or their sum is needed.

STEP 2: EVALUATE THE STATEMENTS USING 12TEN

Statement (1) doesn't give enough to determine the individual price of each item, but remember that the average formula can be rearranged to Sum of the terms = Average × Number of terms. The average price ($4.50) and the number of items on the menu (2) are known, so the sum of the prices of the items can be determined. That sum can be plugged into the revenue expression to yield the answer, so Statement (1) is sufficient. Eliminate **(B)**, **(C)**, and **(E)**.

Statement (2) gives a ratio for the prices of the two menu items, but a number of different actual prices are possible that conform to this ratio, each one of which would give a different revenue total for the day. Statement (2) is insufficient, so eliminate **(D)**. The answer is **(A)**.

If you thought that you needed Statement (2) to determine the individual price of each item, you would have answered **(C)**. Since Statement (1) provides enough information by itself to answer the question, however, there is no need to combine statements.

19. (C)

If a and b are positive, what is the value of $a - b$?

(1) $a^2 + 2ab + b^2 = 36$

(2) $a^2 - b^2 = 12$

STEP 1: ANALYZE THE QUESTION STEM

In this Value question, to have sufficiency, you must have enough information to find one and only one value for $a - b$. Note that this does not necessarily mean knowing the values of a and b individually. You're told that both variables are positive.

STEP 2: EVALUATE THE STATEMENTS USING 12TEN

Statement (1) provides a classic quadratic form, $a^2 + 2ab + b^2 = 36$, which can be factored into the binomial form $(a + b)(a + b) = 36$. Thus, $(a + b)^2 = 36$ and, since a and b are positive, $a + b = 6$. While this establishes a value for $a + b$, there's no way to find $a - b$; it could be that $a = 5$ and $b = 1$, or that $a = 2$ and $b = 4$, or any other combination of positive values that sums to 6, and each would yield a different value for $a - b$. Therefore, this statement is insufficient. Eliminate (A) and (D).

Statement (2) provides another classic quadratic, which can be translated into the factored form $(a + b)(a - b) = 12$. This again is not enough either to determine exact values for a and b individually or to find the value of $a - b$. Therefore, this statement is insufficient. Eliminate (B).

Combining the statements tells you that $a + b = 6$ and $(a + b)(a - b) = 12$. Substituting 6 in for $(a + b)$ in the second equation yields $6(a - b) = 12$. Thus, $(a - b)$ must equal 2. Combining the statements creates sufficiency, so the correct answer is (C).

GMAT by the Numbers: Data Sufficiency

Now that you've learned how to approach Data Sufficiency questions on the GMAT, let's add one more dimension to your understanding of how they work.

Take a moment to try this question. Following is performance data from thousands of people who have studied with Kaplan over the decades. Through analyzing this data, we will show you how to approach questions like this one most effectively and how to avoid similarly tempting wrong answer choice types on Test Day.

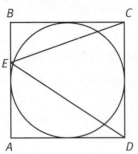

In the figure above, a circle is inscribed in square *ABCD*. What is the area of Δ*CDE*?

(1) The circle has a radius of length 3.

(2) *CDE* is isosceles.

○ Statement (1) ALONE is sufficient, but Statement (2) is not sufficient.

○ Statement (2) ALONE is sufficient, but Statement (1) is not sufficient.

○ BOTH statements TOGETHER are sufficient, but NEITHER statement ALONE is sufficient.

○ EACH statement ALONE is sufficient.

○ Statements (1) and (2) TOGETHER are NOT sufficient.

Explanation

You're asked to find the area of triangle *CDE*. The area of a triangle is equal to $\frac{1}{2}$ Base × Height. You can use *CD* as a base, and the height would be the length of a perpendicular drawn from point *E* to *CD*. Since that perpendicular line would be equal in length to *BC*, you only need to learn the length of the sides of square *ABCD* to know the length of both the base (*CD*) and the height (equal to *BC*) of triangle *CDE*.

Statement (1) says that the radius of the inscribed circle is 3, so its diameter is 6. That diameter equals the length of the sides of the square, which is what you need to answer the question. So Statement (1) is sufficient. Statement (2) gives no measurements to work with. It does allow you to figure out that point *E* bisects *AB*, but that's irrelevant to the question. Statement (2) is insufficient. Since Statement (1) is sufficient but Statement (2) is not, the correct answer is (**A**).

Question Statistics

44% of test takers choose (**A**)

2% of test takers choose (**B**)

32% of test takers choose (**C**)

1% of test takers choose (**D**)

21% of test takers choose (**E**)

Sample size = 4,242

The question statistics reveal two very common habits that lead to wrong answers. Many test takers select (**C**), believing that the statements are sufficient only when combined. Statement (1) alone does not tell you the placement of point *E*, but you don't need that information to find the triangle's area. You don't always need to know *everything* to be able to answer the question that's asked.

Also, some people struggle to relate the data about the circle to the square and then to the triangle. They look at Statement (1) and think, "I don't know how to solve with this," so they treat the statement as insufficient, leading in this question to (**E**). But to do so is to equate "I don't know how to solve this" with "This can't be solved"—not the same thing at all! You can see from the question statistics that this is a common line of thinking—and not one that the GMAT likes to reward. Be wary of guessing that a statement is insufficient unless you can see exactly why it doesn't lead to a clear answer.

More GMAT by the Numbers...

To see more questions with answer choice statistics, be sure to review the full-length CATs in your online resources.

GO ONLINE

kaptest.com/login

CHAPTER 18

Algebra on the GMAT

LEARNING OBJECTIVES

After studying this chapter, you will be able to:

- Describe which topics in algebra are tested on the GMAT
- Identify questions that feature algebra
- Apply the Kaplan Methods for Problem Solving and Data Sufficiency in questions testing various algebra skills

Below is a typical Problem Solving algebra question. In this chapter, we'll look at how to apply the Kaplan Method to this question, discuss the algebra rules being tested, and go over the basic principles and strategies that you want to keep in mind on every Quantitative question involving algebra.

If $x + y = 2$ and $x^2 - xy - 10 - 2y^2 = 0$, what does $x - 2y$ equal?

- ○ 0
- ○ 1
- ○ 2
- ○ 5
- ○ 10

Before you move on, take a minute to think about what you see in this question and answer some questions about how you think it works:

- What mathematical concepts are being tested in this question?
- What does the format of the answer choices tell you about this question?
- Do you need to know the exact values of x and y to answer this question?
- What GMAT Core Competencies are most essential to success on this question?

Previewing Algebra on the GMAT

> **LEARNING OBJECTIVES**
>
> In this section, you will learn how to:
>
> * Describe how to use the format of the answer choices to help tackle questions with algebraic concepts
> * Explain how the Core Competency of Pattern Recognition is helpful for algebra questions in the Quantitative section

There won't be that many problems that involve only algebra—maybe 20 percent of the Quantitative section. But a majority of the questions on the Quantitative section will involve algebra in some way. This makes algebra a necessary skill on the GMAT—mastering some frequently tested algebra concepts could yield large improvements on your Quant score. This chapter will guide you through the basics and give you practice applying algebra concepts to GMAT questions ranging from the simple to the most advanced. We'll start by examining the questions we just asked.

What Mathematical Concepts Are Being Tested in This Question?

For those who find algebra intimidating, this question can seem complicated and abstract at first. Unlike a word problem, which gives you a story to relate to, this question directly measures your ability to use algebraic rules to manipulate unknown terms, or variables. The first step of the Kaplan Method for Problem Solving is to analyze the question stem, and often the best way to start is to "inventory" the question to determine which math skills you will have to use to solve it.

In the question that opens this chapter, you see two algebraic equations, one of which has variables raised to the second power. If you recognized that factoring quadratic equations will be important here, congratulations! If not, don't worry—you will learn and practice those topics later in this chapter. You are being asked to solve for the algebraic expression $x - 2y$, so you can anticipate that you will manipulate these two equations to isolate (in other words, put by itself on one side of the equal sign) the expression $x - 2y$.

What Does the Format of the Answer Choices Tell You About This Question?

This may seem like a somewhat obvious deduction, but it's a crucial—and potentially reassuring—one: the answer choices here are all numbers, so this means it *is* possible to solve for a single numerical value for $x - 2y$. The GMAT can't ask you a trick question, so you can rest assured that there must be a way to use combination or substitution on these two equations to answer the question. You can think of it like a puzzle, and the test makers have given you all the pieces; it's up to you to put them together.

Do You Need to Know the Exact Values of *x* and *y* to Answer This Question?

A common mistake that test takers make in approaching a question like this one is to think they need to solve for exact values of x and y. While it's true that values for those two variables would enable you to solve for the expression $x - 2y$, they are not necessary—in fact, they may be time-consuming or even impossible to solve for. For instance, if $x = 8$ and $y = 3$, you would come up with the same value for the expression $(x - 2y = 2)$ as you would if $x = -10$ and $y = -6$. An infinite number of values are possible for x and y that would all yield the same result for this expression. Stay focused on the specific task and keep an open mind about how you can use the given information to find the correct answer; often the best path to the solution won't be the most obvious one.

What GMAT Core Competencies Are Most Essential to Success on This Question?

Here the test maker rewards Pattern Recognition; certain algebraic concepts are tested over and over on the GMAT, and you will learn and practice the most important ones in this chapter. On this question, the test taker who recognizes the opportunity to factor the quadratic equation will answer this question efficiently and accurately. Those test takers who are not as comfortable with the algebraic structures that appear frequently on the GMAT could spend a long time with a question like this one just figuring out where to begin.

How Do I Apply the Kaplan Methods to GMAT Algebra?

Now let's apply the Kaplan Method for Problem Solving to the algebra question you saw earlier:

> If $x + y = 2$ and $x^2 - xy - 10 - 2y^2 = 0$, what does $x - 2y$ equal?
>
> ○   0
>
> ○   1
>
> ○   2
>
> ○   5
>
> ○   10

Don't worry if the math is unfamiliar to you; you will have an opportunity to learn it later in the chapter. For now, focus on the basics of applying the Kaplan Method to find the most efficient approach to a GMAT algebra problem.

STEP 1: ANALYZE THE QUESTION

The GMAT will reward you for recognizing patterns. Here, you are given two variables and two equations, one of which is not linear. When you see an equation that resembles one of the quadratic patterns you know, try factoring it using reverse-FOIL. Odds are the problem will be greatly simplified.

STEP 2: STATE THE TASK

You need to solve for $x - 2y$. Notice that you are asked for the value of an expression, not an individual variable. Don't waste time solving for all the variables individually if it's not necessary.

STEP 3: APPROACH STRATEGICALLY

If you add 10 to both sides of the second equation, you get $x^2 - xy - 2y^2 = 10$. Now the left side looks like an expression that you can factor with reverse-FOIL. Since you could get the x^2 term by multiplying x and x, you know both factors will contain x:

$$(x)(x) = 10$$

Next, determine what two factors multiplied together will equal $-2y^2$. You need either $-2y$ and y or $2y$ and $-y$. Since the coefficient of the xy term is negative, choose $-2y$ and y. Then the sum of the outer and inner products will give you $-xy$. Thus, the factorization of $x^2 - xy - 2y^2$ is:

$$(x + y)(x - 2y)$$

Now, notice that both factors of $x^2 - xy - 2y^2$ appear in the question stem. You are told that $x + y = 2$, and you are asked to find the value of $x - 2y$.

You can find the value of $x - 2y$ by returning to the equation you've already factored. You know that $(x + y)$ $(x - 2y) = 10$. Since $x + y = 2$, you can replace $(x + y)$ with 2, giving you $2(x - 2y) = 10$, or $(x - 2y) = 5$. So **(D)** is the correct answer.

Did you get to $2(x - 2y) = 10$ and then go further to $2x - 4y = 10$ or to $x = 5 + 2y$? If so, you lost sight of what was asked. You may find it helpful to write down what's asked on your noteboard so it's always in your line of sight.

STEP 4: CONFIRM YOUR ANSWER

Reread the question stem to check that you have answered the right question. Here, confirm that you have solved for $x - 2y$ and not x or y. When you have done that, you can move on.

Now let's look at each of the six most important algebra topics that show up on the GMAT Quantitative section, starting with translating words into expressions and equations.

Translating Words into Expressions and Equations

> **LEARNING OBJECTIVES**
>
> In this section, you will learn how to:
>
> - Translate words into their mathematical equivalents
> - Break up word problem statements into smaller, more manageable parts
> - Apply the Kaplan Method for Problem Solving to word problem questions

Often, the most frustrating aspect of word problems is the odd way in which information is presented. Don't get frustrated. Just break down the information into small pieces and take things one step at a time. Word problems can usually be translated from left to right, but not always. Say you see this sentence: "There are twice as many dollars in George's wallet as the amount that is 5 dollars less than the amount in Bill's wallet." Instead of trying to translate it into math all in one go, approach it piecemeal.

Whenever possible, choose letters for your variables that make sense in the context of the problem. You could start by calling the amount in George's wallet G and the amount in Bill's wallet B. Now, think about the relationship between the two amounts: G is not compared to B but to 5 dollars less than B, or $(B - 5)$. You can now say that G is twice as large as $(B - 5)$. So if you were to set them *equal* to each other, you'd have to multiply $(B - 5)$ by 2. The equation is $G = 2(B - 5)$.

If you had tried to translate it in the order it's written, you might have come up with something like $2G = 5 - B$, and you can be sure that there'd be a wrong answer choice waiting to take advantage of that. So think carefully before you translate.

Words and Their Math Equivalents

The hardest part of word problems is the process of taking the English sentences and extracting the math from them. The actual math in word problems tends to be the easiest part. The following translation table should help you start dealing with English-to-math translation.

Word Problems Translation Table	
English	**Math**
equals, is, was, will be, has, costs, adds up to, the same as, as much as	$=$
times, of, multiplied by, product of, twice, double, by	$\times$
divided by, per, out of, each, ratio	$\div$
plus, added to, and, sum, combined	$+$
minus, subtracted from, smaller than, less than, fewer, decreased by, difference between	$-$
a number, how much, how many, what	x, n, etc.

Take a look at the following example:

Beatrice's wage	**is**	**3 dollars more than**	**twice Alan's wage**
↓	↓	↓	↓
B	$=$	$3 +$	$2A$

Start by breaking the problem down into smaller, more manageable pieces:

- Define the variables: B for Beatrice, A for Alan.
- Break the sentence into shorter phrases: the information about Beatrice and the information about Alan.
- Translate each phrase into an expression: B for Beatrice's wage, $3 + 2A$ for three more than twice Alan's wage.
- Put the expressions together to form an equation: $B = 3 + 2A$.

Always take the time to make sure you are translating the problem correctly. Improper translation will cost you points.

Translation Exercise

Answers are on the following page.

Translate the following sentences into algebra. When names are used, use the first letter of each person's name as the appropriate variable.

1. w is x less than y.
2. The ratio of $3x$ to $8y$ is 5 to 7.
3. The product of x decreased by y and one-half the sum of x and twice y.
4. Mike's score on his geometry test was twice Lidia's score.
5. Samantha is 4 years older than Jeannette.
6. Jamie is 5 years older than Charlie was 3 years ago.
7. Giuseppa's weight is 75 pounds more than twice Jovanna's weight.
8. Luigi has 17 fewer dollars than Sean has.

9. In 5 years, Sandy will be 4 years younger than twice Tina's age.

10. The sum of Richard's age and Cindy's age in years is 17 more than the amount by which Tim's age is greater than Kathy's age.

11. If Mack's salary were increased by $5,000, then the combined salaries of Mack and Andrea would be equal to three times what Mack's salary would be if it were increased by one-half of itself.

Translation Exercise: Answers

1. $w = y - x$

2. $\dfrac{3x}{8y} = \dfrac{5}{7}$

3. $(x - y)\left[\dfrac{1}{2}(x + 2y)\right]$

4. $M = 2L$

5. $S = J + 4$

6. $J = (C - 3) + 5$

7. $G = 2J + 75$

8. $L = S - 17$

9. $S + 5 = 2(T + 5) - 4$

10. $R + C = (T - K) + 17$

11. $(M + 5,000) + A = 3\left(M + \dfrac{1}{2}M\right)$

In-Format Question: Translating Words into Expressions and Equations on the GMAT

Now let's use the Kaplan Method on a Problem Solving question dealing with translating words into expressions and equations:

> Charles's and Sarah's current ages are C years and S years, respectively. If 6 years from now, Charles will be at least as old as Sarah was 2 years ago, which of the following must be true?
>
> O $C + 6 < S - 2$
>
> O $C + 6 \leq S + 2$
>
> O $C + 6 = S - 2$
>
> O $C + 6 > S - 2$
>
> O $C + 6 \geq S - 2$

STEP 1: ANALYZE THE QUESTION

This problem may look complicated at first, but it's really just asking you to translate the English sentence into math. Once the word problem has been translated, you can apply basic algebra to simplify the statement to match the correct answer choice.

STEP 2: STATE THE TASK

You need to translate the word problem into math.

STEP 3: APPROACH STRATEGICALLY

Look at the word problem and work from left to right to extract your algebraic statements. Rather than picking x and y for your variables, use C for Charles's age and S for Sarah's age:

Six years from now, Charles's age will be $C + 6$.

Two years ago, Sarah's age was $S - 2$.

Now connect these two algebraic statements. You are told that in 6 years, Charles will be at least as old as Sarah was 2 years ago. The phrase "will be at least as old as" implies that Charles could be exactly the same age as Sarah 2 years ago, or he could be older. Therefore, use the "greater than or equal to" sign between the two statements:

$$C + 6 \geq S - 2$$

The correct answer is **(E)**.

STEP 4: CONFIRM YOUR ANSWER

This translation directly matches **(E)**, but be careful to check that the variables are in the correct order and that you have used the correct inequality sign.

TAKEAWAYS: TRANSLATING WORDS INTO EXPRESSIONS AND EQUATIONS

- Word problems can be translated into math, usually one phrase at a time and from left to right.

- Don't automatically choose x and y for everything. Pick letters (or groups of letters) whose meaning will be clear at a glance.

Practice Set: Translating Words into Expressions and Equations on the GMAT

1. Machine A produces *r* paper clips per hour. Machine B produces *s* paper clips per hour. If *s* is 30 greater than *r*, which expression represents the number of paper clips the two machines working together produce in *t* hours?

    ○ $r + s + 30$

    ○ $t(r + s) + 30$

    ○ $t(r + s + 30)$

    ○ $t(2s + 30)$

    ○ $t(2r + 30)$

2. The youngest of 4 children has siblings who are 3, 5, and 8 years older than she is. If the average (arithmetic mean) age of the 4 siblings is 21, what is the age of the youngest sibling?

    ○ 17

    ○ 18

    ○ 19

    ○ 21

    ○ 22

Isolating a Variable

> **LEARNING OBJECTIVES**
>
> In this section, you will learn how to:
>
> - Perform key algebraic operations using mathematical laws and the order of operations
> - Apply the Kaplan Method for Problem Solving to solve questions that deal with isolating a variable

A **term** is a numerical constant or the product of a numerical constant and one or more variables. Examples of terms are 5, $3x$, $4x^2yz$, and $2ac$.

An **algebraic expression** is a combination of one or more terms. Terms in an expression are separated by either $+$ or $-$ signs. Examples of expressions are $3xy$, $4ab + 5cd$, and $x^2 - 1$.

In the term $3xy$, the numerical constant 3 is called a **coefficient**. In a simple term such as z, 1 is the coefficient. A number without any variables is called a **constant term**. An expression with one term, such as $3xy$, is called a **monomial**; one with two terms, such as $4a + 2d$, is a **binomial**; one with three terms, such as $xy + z - a$, is a **trinomial**. The general name for expressions with more than one term is **polynomial**.

Substitution

Substitution is a method that you can employ to evaluate an algebraic expression or to express an algebraic expression in terms of other variables.

Example: Evaluate $3x^2 - 4x$ when $x = 2$.

Replace every x in the expression with 2 and then carry out the designated operations. Remember to follow the order of operations (PEMDAS):

$$\mathbf{P} = \text{Parentheses}$$
$$\mathbf{E} = \text{Exponents}$$
$$\left.\begin{array}{l}\mathbf{M} = \text{Multiplication}\\ \mathbf{D} = \text{Division}\end{array}\right\} \quad \text{in order from left to right}$$
$$\left.\begin{array}{l}\mathbf{A} = \text{Addition}\\ \mathbf{S} = \text{Subtraction}\end{array}\right\} \quad \text{in order from left to right}$$

$$3x^2 - 4x$$
$$= 3(2)^2 - 4(2)$$
$$= 3 \times 4 - 4 \times 2$$
$$= 12 - 8$$
$$= 4$$

Example: Express $\dfrac{a}{b - a}$ in terms of x and y if $a = 2x$ and $b = 3y$.

Here, replace every a with $2x$ and every b with $3y$:

$$\frac{a}{b - a} = \frac{2x}{3y - 2x}$$

Operations with Polynomials

All of the laws of arithmetic operations, such as the commutative, associative, and distributive laws, are also applicable to polynomials.

The **commutative law** applies to addition and to multiplication. The order of the terms does not matter.

$$2x + 5y = 5y + 2x$$
$$5a \times 3b = 3b \times 5a = 15ab$$

The **associative law** means that when only addition and/or subtraction are involved or only multiplication and/or division are involved, the order of operations does not matter.

$$2x - 3x + 5y + 2y = (2x - 3x) + (5y + 2y) = -x + 7y$$
$$(-2x)\left(\frac{1}{2}x\right)(3y)(-2y) = \left(-x^2\right)\left(-6y^2\right) = 6x^2y^2$$

Note that the process of simplifying an expression by subtracting or adding together those terms with the same variable component is called **combining like terms**.

The **distributive law** is important because it allows you to express expressions with two or more terms in different forms, which can facilitate solving.

$$3a(2b - 5c) = (3a \times 2b) - (3a \times 5c) = 6ab - 15ac$$
$$5xy - 10y = (5y)(x) - (5y)(2) = 5y(x - 2)$$

The product of two binomials can be calculated by applying the distributive law twice.

Example: $(y + 5)(y - 2)$

$$= y(y - 2) + 5(y - 2)$$
$$= (y \times y) + (y \times -2) + (5 \times y) + (5 \times -2)$$
$$= y^2 - 2y + 5y - 10$$
$$= y^2 + 3y - 10$$

You multiply the First terms first, then the Outer terms, then the Inner terms, and finally the Last terms. A simple mnemonic for this is the word **FOIL**.

Factoring Algebraic Expressions

Factoring a polynomial means expressing it as a product of two or more simpler expressions.

Common Monomial Factor

When there is a monomial factor common to every term in the polynomial, it can be factored out by using the distributive law.

Example: $2a + 6ac = 2a(1 + 3c)$

Here, $2a$ is the greatest common factor of $2a$ and $6ac$.

Making problems look more complicated than they are by distributing a common factor is a classic GMAT trick. Whenever algebra looks scary, check whether common factors could be factored out.

Equations

An **equation** is an algebraic sentence that says that two expressions are equal to each other. The two expressions consist of numbers, variables, and arithmetic operations to be performed on these numbers and variables.

Solving Equations

To solve for some variable, you can manipulate the equation until you have isolated that variable on one side of the equal sign, leaving any numbers or other variables on the other side. Of course, you must be careful to manipulate the equation only in accordance with the equality postulate: *whenever you perform an operation on one side of the equation, you must perform the same operation on the other side.* Otherwise, the two sides of the equation will no longer be equal.

The steps for isolating a variable are as follows:

1. Eliminate any **fractions** by multiplying both sides by the least common denominator.
2. Put all terms with the variable you're solving for on one **side** by adding or subtracting on both sides.
3. **Combine** like terms.
4. **Factor** out the desired variable.
5. **Divide** to leave the desired variable by itself.

Linear, or First-Degree, Equations

These are equations in which all the variables are raised to the first power (e.g., there are no squares or cubes). To solve such an equation, you'll need to perform operations on both sides of the equal sign in order to get the variable you're solving for alone on one side. The operations you can perform without upsetting the balance of the equation are addition and subtraction, as well as multiplication or division by a number other than 0. At each step in the process, you'll need to use the reverse of the operation that's being applied to the variable in order to isolate the variable.

Example: If $-x + 2 = 3x - 6$, what is the value of x?

1. Put all the terms with the variable on one side of the equation. Put all constant terms on the other side of the equation.

$$-x + x + 2 + 6 = 3x + x + 6 - 6$$
$$2 + 6 = 3x + x$$

2. Combine like terms.

$$4x = 8$$

3. Divide to leave the desired variable by itself.

$$\frac{4x}{4} = \frac{8}{4}$$
$$x = 2$$

Note above that since eliminating fractions (step 1) and factoring out the desired variable (step 4) were not necessary, those steps were not mentioned. If a particular step is irrelevant to a GMAT question, just proceed to the next step!

You can easily check your work when solving this kind of equation. The answer you arrive at represents the value of the variable that makes the equation hold true. Therefore, to check that it's correct, just substitute this value for the variable in the original equation. If the equation holds true, you've found the correct answer. In the previous example, you got a value of 2 for x. Replacing x with 2 in your original equation results in $-2 + 2 = 3(2) - 6$, which simplifies to $0 = 0$. That's a true statement, so 2 is indeed the correct value for x.

Equations with Fractions

The GMAT loves to make algebra problems look harder than they need to be by using fractions. Whenever you see a fraction in an algebra question, always get rid of the fraction as your first step. Let's see how to solve such a problem.

Example: Solve $\dfrac{x-2}{3} + \dfrac{x-4}{10} = \dfrac{x}{2}$

1. Eliminate fractions by multiplying both sides of the equation by the least common denominator (LCD). Here the LCD is 30.

$$30\left(\dfrac{x-2}{3}\right) + 30\left(\dfrac{x-4}{10}\right) = 30\left(\dfrac{x}{2}\right)$$
$$10(x-2) + 3(x-4) = 15(x)$$
$$10x - 20 + 3x - 12 = 15x$$

2. Put all terms with the variable on one side by adding or subtracting on both sides. Put all constant terms on the other side of the equation.

$$-20 - 12 = 15x - 10x - 3x$$

3. Combine like terms.

$$-32 = 2x$$

4. Divide to leave the desired variable by itself.

$$x = \dfrac{-32}{2}$$
$$x = -16$$

Literal Equations

On some problems involving more than one variable, you cannot find a specific value for a variable; you can only solve for one variable in terms of the others. To do this, try to get the desired variable alone on one side and all the other variables on the other side.

Example: In the formula $V = \dfrac{PN}{R + NT}$, solve for N in terms of P, R, T, and V.

1. Eliminate fractions by cross multiplying.

$$\dfrac{V}{1} = \dfrac{PN}{R + NT}$$
$$V(R + NT) = PN$$

2. Remove parentheses by distributing.

$$VR + VNT = PN$$

3. Put all terms containing N on one side and all other terms on the other side.

$$VNT - PN = -VR$$

4. Factor out the common factor N.

$$N(VT - P) = -VR$$

5. Divide by $(VT - P)$ to get N alone.

$$N = \dfrac{-VR}{VT - P}$$

Note: You can reduce the number of negative terms in the answer by multiplying both the numerator and the denominator of the fraction on the right-hand side by -1.

$$N = \dfrac{VR}{P - VT}$$

In-Format Question: Isolating a Variable on the GMAT

Now let's use the Kaplan Method on a Problem Solving question dealing with isolating a variable:

If $\dfrac{5}{2 + \dfrac{3}{n}} = 2$, then $n =$

○ $\dfrac{1}{2}$

○ 1

○ $\dfrac{3}{2}$

○ 3

○ 6

STEP 1: ANALYZE THE QUESTION

Follow the steps for isolating a variable carefully and methodically. In this question, the variable you need to isolate is buried under two fractions. When working with fractions, you can often simplify the work by one of two strategies: (1) multiplying by a common denominator or (2) cross multiplying the equation. For this question, use cross multiplication to isolate n.

STEP 2: STATE THE TASK

Your task is to bring the variable n to one side of the equation and the rest of the terms to the other side.

STEP 3: APPROACH STRATEGICALLY

Begin by cross multiplying the equation, which results in this equation:

$$5(1) = 2\left(2 + \frac{3}{n}\right)$$

Now simplify the equation:

$$5 = 2(2) + 2\left(\frac{3}{n}\right)$$
$$5 = 4 + \frac{6}{n}$$

Combine like terms:

$$5 - 4 = \frac{6}{n}$$
$$1 = \frac{6}{n}$$
$$n = 6$$

The correct answer is **(E)**.

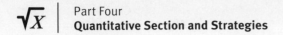
STEP 4: CONFIRM YOUR ANSWER

You can check your calculations by simply plugging $n = 6$ into the original equation. If the expression on the left side is equal to 2, the calculations are correct. You could have also used backsolving, but since there isn't an easy way to know whether you must select an answer choice that is larger or smaller than the one you started with, algebra is the most efficient way to get the answer here.

> **TAKEAWAYS: ISOLATING A VARIABLE**
>
> - Simplify equations with fractions by first eliminating the fractions.
> - To solve for a variable, isolate that variable on one side of the equation and put all constants on the other side of the equation.
> - If a problem involves more than one variable, put the desired variable alone on one side of the equation and all the other variables and constants on the other side.

Practice Set: Isolating a Variable on the GMAT

3. If $\dfrac{3a - 2ce}{3} = \dfrac{4b - 2de}{2}$, then $\dfrac{e}{3} =$

    ○ $\dfrac{9a - 8b}{6c - 4d}$

    ○ $\dfrac{6a - 3b}{2c - 3d}$

    ○ $\dfrac{3a - 6b}{2c - 3d}$

    ○ $\dfrac{a - 2b}{6c - 9d}$

    ○ $\dfrac{a - 2b}{2c - 3d}$

4. If $2\left(s - r\right) = -2\left(\dfrac{r^2 - s^2}{s^2 \quad r^2}\right)$ and $s^2 - r^2 \neq 0$, then $s - r =$

    ○ −2

    ○ −1

    ○ 0

    ○ 1

    ○ 2

5. A laptop computer uses s fewer watts of electricity than a desktop computer does. In combination, the 2 computers use t watts of electricity. Which of the following expressions represents the desktop computer's electricity usage, in watts?

    ○ $\dfrac{t}{2} - s$

    ○ $\dfrac{t + s}{2}$

    ○ $t(s - 1)$

    ○ $t - \dfrac{s}{2}$

    ○ $t - 2s$

Quadratic Equations

> **LEARNING OBJECTIVES**
>
> In this section, you will learn how to:
>
> - Identify the most common forms of quadratic expressions found on the GMAT
> - Solve quadratic equations by factoring
> - Apply the Kaplan Methods for Problem Solving and Data Sufficiency to questions involving quadratic equations

The term *quadratic* refers to a mathematical expression in the form $ax^2 + bx + c$, where a, b, and c are constants and a does not equal zero. The algebraic rules you learned for solving a linear equation still apply to quadratics, but there are also some specific things to know about handling quadratic equations. On the GMAT, you will find that questions dealing with quadratics use the same patterns over and over.

Factoring Quadratic Expressions

Earlier in this chapter, you learned that two binomials can be multiplied together by applying the distributive law twice; in other words, you use FOIL (multiplying the First terms first, then the Outer terms, then the Inner terms, and finally the Last terms) to "expand" the expression. The result is often a quadratic expression in the form $ax^2 + bx + c$.

Example: $(y + 5)(y - 2)$

$$= y(y - 2) + 5(y - 2)$$
$$= (y \times y) + (y \times -2) + (5 \times y) + (5 \times -2)$$
$$= y^2 - 2y + 5y - 10$$
$$= y^2 + 3y - 10$$

Factoring is the reverse of this process of expanding the expression. Factoring can be thought of as applying the FOIL method backward, or using "reverse-FOIL." Below you will learn how to factor the most common forms of quadratic expression on the GMAT.

Polynomials of the Form $x^2 + bx + c$

Many quadratic polynomials can be factored into a product of two binomials. The product of the first term in each binomial must equal the first term of the polynomial. The product of the last term of each binomial must equal the last term of the polynomial. The sum of the remaining products must equal the second term of the polynomial.

Example: $x^2 - 3x + 2$

Using reverse-FOIL, you can factor this into two binomials, each containing an x term. Start by writing down what you know.

$$x^2 - 3x + 2 = (x \quad)(x \quad)$$

In each binomial on the right, you need to fill in the missing term. The product of the two missing terms will be the last term in the polynomial: 2. The sum of the two missing terms will be the coefficient of the second term of the polynomial: -3. Try the possible factors of 2 until you get a pair that adds up to -3. There are two possibilities: 1 and 2 or -1 and -2. Since $(-1) + (-2) = -3$, you can fill -1 and -2 into the empty spaces.

Thus, $x^2 - 3x + 2 = (x - 1)(x - 2)$.

If the coefficient of the constant (the last term) is negative, then your binomials will have different signs (one + and one −). If the coefficient of the constant is positive, then your binomials will both have the same sign as the coefficient in the middle term (two +'s or two −'s). Check out the previous example: both binomials have a minus sign because of the −3 coefficient of the term −3x.

Note: Whenever you factor a polynomial, you can check your answer by using FOIL to obtain the original polynomial.

Classic Quadratics

The process of reverse-FOIL works on the quadratics you will find on the GMAT. However, there also exist some patterns called "classic quadratics," which you can factor more quickly by recognizing the pattern than by using reverse-FOIL.

Difference of Two Perfect Squares

The difference of two squares can be factored into the product of two binomials: $a^2 - b^2 = (a + b)(a - b)$.

In the case of equations written as the difference of two squares, you don't need to go through all the steps of factoring using reverse-FOIL; just recognize the pattern.

Example: $d^2 - 16 = (d + 4)(d - 4)$

Polynomials of the Form $a^2 + 2ab + b^2$

This type of polynomial is also a pattern that appears frequently enough on the GMAT to warrant memorization. Any polynomial of this form is equivalent to the square of a binomial. Notice that according to FOIL, $(a + b)^2 = a^2 + 2ab + b^2$.

Factoring such a polynomial using reverse-FOIL is just reversing this procedure.

Example: $x^2 + 6x + 9 = (x)^2 + 2(x)(3) + (3)^2 = (x + 3)^2$

Polynomials of the Form $a^2 - 2ab + b^2$

Any polynomial of this form is equivalent to the square of a binomial as in the previous example. Here though, the binomial is the difference of two terms: $(a - b)^2 = a^2 - 2ab + b^2$.

Example: $x^2 - 10x + 25 = (x)^2 - 2(x)(5) + (5)^2 = (x - 5)^2$

The GMAT uses these three "classic quadratics" over and over. Review them thoroughly and look out for them as you practice. Notice that all the forms begin and end in a perfect square:

$$a^2 - b^2$$

$$a^2 + 2ab + b^2$$

$$a^2 - 2ab + b^2$$

Picking up on these patterns will save you lots of work, especially in the difficult questions. Imagine seeing this expression show up on the test:

$$4x^4 + 52x^2 + 169$$

This may look daunting at first glance. But if you realize that 169 is 13^2, and $4x^4$ is $(2x^2)^2$, you can then make the educated guess that this polynomial factors as $(2x^2 + 13)^2$. You then only have to confirm that $52x^2 = 2 \times 2x^2 \times 13$ (which it is) to start making the problem easier.

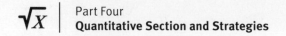

Solving Quadratic Equations

If the expression $ax^2 + bx + c$ is set equal to zero, there is a special name for it: a quadratic equation. Since it is an equation, you can find the value or values for x that make the equation work. You can do so by using the factored form of the equation obtained through reverse-FOIL.

Example: $x^2 - 3x + 2 = 0$

To find the solutions, or **roots**, start by factoring using reverse-FOIL. Factor $x^2 - 3x + 2$ into $(x - 1)(x - 2)$, making the quadratic equation:

$$(x - 1)(x - 2) = 0$$

You now have a product of two binomials that is equal to zero. When does a product of two terms equal zero? The only time that happens is when at least one of the terms is zero. If the product of $(x - 1)$ and $(x - 2)$ is equal to zero, that means either the first term equals zero or the second term equals zero. So to find the roots, you just need to set the two binomials equal to zero. That gives you:

$$x - 1 = 0 \text{ or } x - 2 = 0$$

Solving for x, you get $x = 1$ or $x = 2$. As a check, you can plug in 1 and 2 into the equation $x^2 - 3x + 2 = 0$, and you'll see that either value makes the equation work.

In-Format Question: Quadratic Equations on the GMAT

Now let's use the Kaplan Method on a Problem Solving question dealing with quadratic equations:

> If $(a - 3)^2 = 5 - 10a$, then which of the following is the value of a?
>
> O   −3
>
> O   −2
>
> O   0
>
> O   2
>
> O   3

STEP 1: ANALYZE THE QUESTION

When you are asked to solve for a variable that is squared, the most efficient solution is typically to factor the equation into two binomials. Remember that in order to factor the equation, you must bring all of the terms to one side of the equation and have only zero on the other side.

STEP 2: STATE THE TASK

You need to solve for the value of a. To do this, you'll need to first simplify the equation in the question stem to fit the standard quadratic equation format needed to factor $(ax^2 + bx + c = 0)$; then determine the factors for the equation.

STEP 3: APPROACH STRATEGICALLY

You are given the equation in the form $(a - 3)^2 = 5 - 10a$.

You can simplify the equation by subtracting 5 from both sides and adding $10a$ to both sides:

$$(a - 3)^2 - 5 + 10a = 0$$

Next, multiply out the far left expression using FOIL and simplify:

$$(a-3)(a-3)-5+10a=0$$
$$a^2-3a-3a+9-5+10a=0$$
$$a^2-6a+9-5+10a=0$$
$$a^2+4a+4=0$$

Now use reverse-FOIL to factor the quadratic expression on the left:

$$(a+2)(a+2)=0$$

To solve for *a*, set each of the binomials equal to zero. In this case, there is only one binomial, so $a+2=0$, and $a=-2$. Choice **(B)** is correct.

You can also use backsolving, although this may not be the most efficient solution, since it would be difficult to know after testing an incorrect answer choice whether the right answer should be larger or smaller, and you could end up testing several choices before finding the correct one. Even in such situations, backsolving can still help you find the right answer when you aren't sure how to solve algebraically. Let's say you start with choice **(B)**.

$$(-2-3)^2 = 5-10(-2)$$
$$(-5)^2 = 5-(-20)$$
$$25 = 25$$

In this case, you got lucky and found the correct answer on the first try. If you hadn't, you could then proceed to test the other choices (in order of their manageability) until you found one that works.

STEP 4: CONFIRM YOUR ANSWER

You can plug your calculated value for *a* into the equation in the question stem to confirm that the calculations are correct.

TAKEAWAYS: QUADRATIC EQUATIONS

- FOIL = First, Outer, Inner, Last
  - $(a+b)(c+d) = ac+ad+bc+bd$
- To solve a quadratic equation, rewrite the equation in the form $ax^2+bx+c=0$, then perform reverse-FOIL.
- Following are three classic quadratics that often appear on the GMAT. Recognize them to avoid spending time performing FOIL or reverse-FOIL on Test Day.
  - $a^2-b^2=(a+b)(a-b)$
  - $(a+b)^2=(a+b)(a+b)=a^2+2ab+b^2$
  - $(a-b)^2=(a-b)(a-b)=a^2-2ab+b^2$
- Quadratic equations usually have two roots (solutions). Suppose the quadratic equation has been written so that the right side is zero. If both factors involving a variable on the left side are the same (see classic quadratics 2 and 3 above), then there is only one distinct root.

Practice Set: Quadratic Equations on the GMAT

6. Is $x > 0$?

   (1) $x^2 - 8x + 16 = 0$

   (2) $x^2 - x - 12 = 0$

7. Which of the following expressions could be equal to 0 when $n^2 - 4n = 12$?

   ○ $n^2 - 2n - 15$

   ○ $n^2 - 2n + 1$

   ○ $n^2 + 4n - 12$

   ○ $n^2 - 5n - 6$

   ○ $n^2 + 6n + 5$

8. Which of the following could equal zero for some value of x?

   I. $3x^2 - 12$

   II. $x^2 + x^4 + 1$

   III. $x^2 + 7x + 6$

   ○ I only

   ○ III only

   ○ I and II only

   ○ I and III only

   ○ I, II, and III

Systems of Linear Equations

LEARNING OBJECTIVES

In this section, you will learn how to:

- Identify whether substitution or combination is more efficient for solving a given system of linear equations
- Apply the techniques of substitution and combination
- Apply the Kaplan Methods for Problem Solving and Data Sufficiency to questions involving systems of linear equations

In general, if a problem has multiple variables and you want to find unique numerical values for all of the variables, you will need as many distinct equations as you have variables. If you are given two distinct equations with two variables, you can combine the equations to obtain a unique solution set. Don't be intimidated by calculating values, since usually—though not always—the GMAT will give integer answers for the variables. Focus instead on looking for opportunities to combine equations. The GMAT rewards those who find clever combinations with quick solutions.

Note that the word *distinct* means that each equation must provide new, different information. In other words, each additional equation must contain information you couldn't have derived using the equation(s) you already have.

Two Approaches to Solving Systems of Linear Equations

There are two commonly used ways to solve a system of linear equations: substitution and combination. Some systems of equations will be more efficiently solved with substitution and others with combination. Learn both approaches so you are ready to use either one on the questions you see on Test Day.

Substitution

Isolate one variable in one equation. Then plug the expression that it equals into its place in the other equation.

Example: Find the values of m and n if $m = 4n + 2$ and $3m + 2n = 20$.

1. You know that $m = 4n + 2$. Substitute $4n + 2$ for m in the second equation.

   $$3(4n + 2) + 2n = 20$$

2. Solve for n.

   $$12n + 6 + 2n = 20$$
   $$14n + 6 = 20$$
   $$14n = 14$$
   $$n = \frac{14}{14} = 1$$

3. To find the value of m, substitute 1 for n in the first equation and solve.

   $$m = 4n + 2$$
   $$m = 4(1) + 2$$
   $$m = 4 + 2 = 6$$

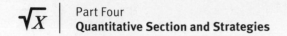

Combination

Add or subtract whole equations from each other to eliminate a variable.

Example: Find the values of x and y if $4x + 3y = 27$ and $3x - 6y = -21$.

There's no obvious isolation/substitution to be done, since all variables have coefficients. But if you multiplied the first equation by 2, you'd be able to get rid of the y's.

$$2(4x + 3y) = 2(27)$$
$$\text{Distribute}: \quad 8x + 6y = 54$$

Now add the new equation to the second equation, carefully lining them up to combine like terms:

$$
\begin{array}{r}
8x + 6y = 54 \\
+\ [3x - 6y = -21] \\
\hline
11x \qquad = 33
\end{array}
$$

Divide by 11: $x = 3$

This value can now be substituted back into either equation to yield the other value.

$$4x + 3y = 27$$
$$4(3) + 3y = 27$$
$$12 + 3y = 27$$
$$3y = 15$$
$$y = 5$$

In-Format Question: Systems of Linear Equations on the GMAT

Now let's use the Kaplan Method on a Problem Solving question dealing with systems of linear equations:

If $x + y = 5y - 13$ and $x - y = 5$, then $x =$

   ◯   11

   ◯   12

   ◯   13

   ◯   14

   ◯   15

STEP 1: ANALYZE THE QUESTION

You have two distinct linear equations and two variables, so you will be able to solve for x. Remember that there are two techniques for solving distinct linear equations: (1) substitution and (2) combination. Since these equations look easy to simplify, substituting one equation into the other will be the most efficient approach here.

STEP 2: STATE THE TASK

Substitute one linear equation into the other to eliminate y and solve for x.

STEP 3: APPROACH STRATEGICALLY

Simply the first equation:

$$x + y = 5y - 13$$
$$x - 4y = -13$$

Simplify the second equation:

$$x - y = 5$$
$$-y = 5 - x$$
$$y = x - 5$$

Substitute the second equation into the first and solve for x:

$$x - 4(x - 5) = -13$$
$$x - 4x + 20 - -13$$
$$-3x = -33$$
$$x = 11$$

Choice **(A)** is correct.

STEP 4: CONFIRM YOUR ANSWER

You can confirm your work by substituting $x = 11$ into either equation to find a value for y. This value for y can then be substituted into the other equation to ensure that $x = 11$.

TAKEAWAYS: SYSTEMS OF LINEAR EQUATIONS

- In a system of equations with n distinct variables, you must have at least n distinct linear equations to be able to solve for each variable.
- Use one of the following two ways to solve a system of linear equations:
  - Substitution: Solve one equation for one of the variables and substitute that value into the other equation.
  - Combination: Add or subtract one equation from the other to cancel out one of the variables.

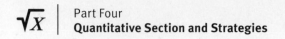

Practice Set: Systems of Linear Equations on the GMAT

9. A photographer has visited exactly 42 countries, all of which have been in Africa, Europe, or Asia. If the photographer has been to 6 more countries in Europe than in Asia, and twice as many in Africa as in Europe, how many countries in Asia has the photographer visited?

    ○ 4

    ○ 6

    ○ 12

    ○ 18

    ○ 24

10. Paula has a collection of used books worth $104. How many are histories?

    (1) Paula has only mysteries and histories; each mystery is worth $1, and each history is worth $25.

    (2) Paula has exactly 4 mysteries in her collection that together are worth a total of $4.

11. In 8 years, Leonard will be twice as many years old as Mikala is now. If Leonard were twice as old as he was 2 years ago, and if Mikala were five times as old as she was 2 years ago, the sum of their ages would be 51. What will be the sum of their ages in 3 years?

    ○ 12

    ○ 14

    ○ 19

    ○ 22

    ○ 25

Special Cases in Systems of Linear Equations

> **LEARNING OBJECTIVE**
>
> In this section, you will learn how to:
>
> - Identify cases in which it may not be necessary to have as many equations as variables in a system of equations

On the GMAT, it is not always necessary to solve for each variable to answer a question. Some questions will ask you to solve for a sum, difference, or other relationship between variables rather than for the variables themselves. In such a case, rather than attempting to solve for both x and y, you will solve for values for expressions such as $(x + y)$ or $(x - y)$, the average of x and y, or the ratio between the two variables. Questions involving special cases reward test takers who seek out opportunities to use Critical Thinking and Pattern Recognition in GMAT questions.

Special cases in systems of linear equations appear most frequently in problems involving sums, differences, averages, and ratios. You will see them appear more often in Data Sufficiency questions than in Problem Solving questions, because Data Sufficiency questions require you to recognize whether you have enough information to determine a relationship. Don't assume that you can't answer a question just because there are more variables present than there are equations. By simplifying the equation, you may be able to cancel out one or more variables entirely.

In-Format Question: Special Cases in Systems of Linear Equations on the GMAT

Let's look at a Data Sufficiency question that involves special cases in systems of linear equations.

What is the value of $x - y$?

(1) $3x + 3y = 31$
(2) $3x - 3y = 13$

STEP 1: ANALYZE THE QUESTION STEM

First, look at your question stem and recognize that this is a special situation. You are not asked for the value of x or y; rather, you are asked for the value of $x - y$. Next, determine whether there is enough information to find the value of $x - y$. Keep in mind that you do not have to know the values of each of the variables x and y to be able to find the value of $x - y$. Because the question stem does not provide any information for finding the value of $x - y$, look at the statements.

STEP 2: EVALUATE THE STATEMENTS USING 12TEN

Statement (1) is $3x + 3y = 31$. There is no way to rearrange this equation to find the value of $x - y$. Therefore, Statement (1) is insufficient. You can eliminate **(A)** and **(D)**.

Statement (2) is $3x - 3y = 13$. Factoring 3 from the left side of this equation, you have $3(x - y) = 13$. Dividing both sides of this equation by 3, you have $x - y = \frac{13}{3}$, and Statement (2) is sufficient to find the value of $x - y$. Choice **(B)** is correct.

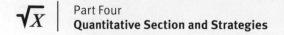
TAKEAWAYS: SPECIAL CASES IN SYSTEMS OF LINEAR EQUATIONS

- Use Critical Thinking and Pattern Recognition to solve problems involving special cases in systems of linear equations.

- When you are asked to solve for the sum/difference/product/quotient of variables, you may not need to solve for each variable. Don't assume that you can't answer a question just because there are more variables present than there are equations.

- Make sure to cancel out or combine variables before you determine that there are more variables than equations.

Practice Set: Special Cases in Systems of Linear Equations on the GMAT

12. What is the value of b?

    (1) $5b - a = 3b + 5a$

    (2) $4(b - a) = 12 - 4a$

13. What is the value of $a + b$?

    (1) $5a + 2b = 22$

    (2) $3b = 30 - 6a$

14. If the average (arithmetic mean) of x and y is 30 and $3y + z = 180$, what is the value of $\frac{z}{x}$?

    ◯ $\frac{1}{6}$

    ◯ $\frac{1}{3}$

    ◯ 1

    ◯ 3

    ◯ 6

Sequences

A sequence is an ordered list of numbers a_{n-1}, a_n, a_{n+1}, where n denotes where in the sequence the number is located. Sequence-based questions on the GMAT can look complicated, but once you learn to break down the notation, they're not that tricky.

Example: If $n = 2$, a_2 is the 2nd number,

$a_{2+1} = a_3$ is the 3rd number,

$a_{2-1} = a_1$ is the 1st number, and so on.

Before you dive into statement and answer evaluation, make sure you understand what you are looking for. Use Paraphrasing to state the information in the question in your own words. Then apply Critical Thinking to identify the pattern in the sequence you're given. (Since this is the GMAT, there will always be a discernible pattern to the sequence even if it isn't transparent immediately.)

Once you have a thorough understanding of the question stem and the sequence, look at the statements and answers. Picking numbers is a useful strategy if you're not given concrete values for the terms in a sequence.

With a little patience and a strategic approach, you can attack even the most intimidating sequence questions effectively.

In-Format Question: Sequences on the GMAT

Now let's use the Kaplan Method on a Problem Solving question dealing with sequences:

> In an increasing sequence of 8 consecutive even integers, the sum of the first 4 integers is 268. What is the sum of all the integers in the sequence?
>
> O   552
>
> O   568
>
> O   574
>
> O   586
>
> O   590

STEP 1: ANALYZE THE QUESTION

You are asked to determine the sum of all the integers in the sequence, and you are given the sum of the first 4 of 8 integers. As discussed in the Statistics chapter of this book, half of the numbers in a consecutive sequence with an even number of terms must be greater than and half must be less than the mean.

STEP 2: STATE THE TASK

Since you are given the sum of the first half of the sequence, you can use the average formula to solve this strategically.

STEP 3: APPROACH STRATEGICALLY

Since the sum of 4 terms is 268, the average is $268 \div 4 = 67$, which means the 4 even integers must be 64, 66, 68, and 70. This means that the next 4 must be 72, 74, 76, and 78. The sum of all 8 is 568, and that's your answer. You could also apply Critical Thinking and realize that since the numbers in the sequence are consecutive even integers, the first term in the second group will be 8 larger than the first term in the first group, the second term in the second group 8 larger than the second term in the first group, and so on. This means that the final 4 numbers add up to $268 + (8 + 8 + 8 + 8)$, or 300. Then $268 + 300 = 568$. Choice (**B**) is correct.

STEP 4: CONFIRM YOUR ANSWER

The numbers in the answer choices here are not very spread out, so estimation is not likely to be very helpful. A quick double-check, especially using the alternative method above, will confirm that you didn't make any mistakes.

TAKEAWAY: SEQUENCES

- Sequences can look complicated, and their descriptions can be confusingly worded. Paraphrase, simplify, and stay attuned to the patterns.

Practice Set: Sequences on the GMAT

15. *l, m, n, o, p*

An arithmetic sequence is a sequence in which each term after the first is equal to the sum of the preceding term and a constant. If the list of letters shown above is an arithmetic sequence, which of the following must also be an arithmetic sequence?

   I. $3l, 3m, 3n, 3o, 3p$
   II. l^2, m^2, n^2, o^2, p^2
   III. $l - 5, m - 5, n - 5, o - 5, p - 5$

   ○   I only
   ○   II only
   ○   III only
   ○   I and III
   ○   II and III

16. In a certain sequence of positive integers, the term t_n is given by the formula $t_n = 3(t_{n-2}) + 2(t_{n-1}) - 1$ for all $n \geq 1$. If $t_6 = 152$ and $t_5 = 51$, what is the value of t_2?

   ○   1
   ○   2
   ○   3
   ○   6
   ○   17

17. In the infinite sequence S, each term S_n after S_2 is equal to the sum of the two terms S_{n-1} and S_{n-2}. If S_1 is 4, what is the value of S_2?

   (1) $S_3 = 7$
   (2) $S_4 = 10$

Functions and Symbolism

LEARNING OBJECTIVES

In this section, you will learn how to:

- Describe the GMAT's use of nontraditional notation symbols
- Apply the Kaplan Methods for Problem Solving and Data Sufficiency to questions involving functions and symbolism

---

The GMAT uses classic function notation that you may recall from your later high school algebra classes. It also uses some untraditional notation, such as $\diamond$, $\spadesuit$, or $\otimes$. Both types boil down to substitution.

The basic idea is that these questions ask you to substitute values or operations in a unique way described by the problem. Here's a classic function problem.

Example: What is the minimum value of the function $f(x) = x^2 - 1$?

What this problem is telling you is that whatever number is between those parentheses gets substituted in place of x in $x^2 - 1$. For instance, $f(2) = 2^2 - 1 = 3$.

A strategic way to solve would be to substitute whatever answer choices the GMAT gives you as the answer to the function. Some may not be possible; others will be. For example, $x^2 = -4$ isn't possible, since the GMAT uses only real numbers and the square of a real number must be non-negative. The smallest of the possible answer choices would be the correct response.

You could solve this question logically, too. The value of the function will be smallest when x^2 is smallest. Squaring a negative number produces a positive number, so x^2 can never be negative. The smallest result you could get is $x^2 = 0$. So the smallest $x^2 - 1$ can be is $0 - 1$, or -1.

Some questions offer strange symbols but work basically the same way—as rules for how to substitute.

Example: If $x \spadesuit y = 3x - y^2$, then what is the value of $8 \spadesuit 2$?

The given equation is really just a rule for substitution. Whatever is to the left of the $\spadesuit$ symbol is x and should be substituted in place of x in $3x - y^2$. Similarly, anything to the right of $\spadesuit$ is y and should be substituted for y.

$$x \spadesuit y = 3x - y^2$$
$$8 \spadesuit 2 = 3(8) - (2)^2$$
$$8 \spadesuit 2 = 24 - 4$$
$$8 \spadesuit 2 = 20$$

For the most part, symbols on the GMAT define operations (i.e., the process that one or more numbers must be put through). Occasionally, the GMAT will use symbols to stand in for digits, but this isn't as common.

In-Format Question: Functions and Symbolism on the GMAT

Now let's use the Kaplan Method on a Data Sufficiency question dealing with functions and symbolism:

> The symbol ♣ represents one of the following operations: addition, subtraction, multiplication, or division. What is the value of 6 ♣ 2?
>
> (1)   0 ♣ 3 = 0
> (2)   2 ♣ 1 = 2

STEP 1: ANALYZE THE QUESTION STEM

You need to determine whether there is sufficient information to find the value of 6 ♣ 2, and you are told that the symbol ♣ can stand for any one of the four operations of addition, subtraction, multiplication, or division.

Now, since there is no further information in the question stem, look at the statements.

STEP 2: EVALUATE THE STATEMENTS USING 12TEN

Statement (1) tells you that 0 ♣ 3 = 0. The potential operations that yield this value are:

$$\text{Multiplication: } 0 \times 3 = 0$$

$$\text{Division: } 0 \div 3 = 0$$

So ♣ could stand for multiplication or division. However, $6 \times 2 = 12$ and $6 \div 2 = 3$, so there is more than one possible answer to the question. Statement (1) is insufficient. Eliminate **(A)** and **(D)**.

Statement (2) tells you that 2 ♣ 1 = 2. The potential operations that yield this value are:

$$\text{Multiplication: } 2 \times 1 = 2$$

$$\text{Division: } 2 \div 1 = 2$$

So again, ♣ could be multiplication or division; as you saw in evaluating the first statement, the value of 6 ♣ 2 changes depending on whether the symbol represents multiplication or division. More than one answer is possible for the question, so Statement (2) is insufficient. Eliminate **(B)**.

Taking the statements together, you still know only that ♣ could be multiplication or division. However, since each of these operations yields a different value, the two statements taken together are insufficient. Therefore, **(E)** is correct.

TAKEAWAYS: FUNCTIONS AND SYMBOLISM

- GMAT symbolism questions define symbols and then ask test takers to apply those definitions.
- The definitions given in a GMAT symbolism question apply only to the particular GMAT question at hand.
- Symbolism questions are usually solved by substitution.
- In most GMAT symbolism questions, symbols represent operations, but in some GMAT symbolism questions, symbols represent numbers.

Practice Set: Functions and Symbolism on the GMAT

18. Let $\boxed{x} = \dfrac{x^2 + 1}{2}$ and $\widehat{y} = \dfrac{3y}{2}$, for all integers x and y. If $m = 2$, $\boxed{\widehat{m}}$ is equal to which of the following?

   ○ $\dfrac{13}{8}$

   ○ 3

   ○ $\dfrac{15}{4}$

   ○ 5

   ○ $\dfrac{37}{2}$

19.

   In the multiplication problem above, each of the symbols ◇, △, and ● represents a positive digit. If ◇ > △, what is the value of ◇?

   (1) △ = 1
   (2) ● = 9

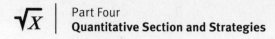
20. For all positive numbers x and y, the operation $x \blacklozenge y$ is defined by $x \blacklozenge y = \dfrac{x^2 - x}{2xy}$. If $x \blacklozenge 5 = 2$, then $x =$

   ○ 1

   ○ 5

   ○ 11

   ○ 20

   ○ 21

21. The operation $\flat\, x$ is defined by the equation $\flat\, x = ax - b(x - 1) + c$, where a, b, and c are constants that are positive integers. The value of $\flat\, 0$ is 7. What is the value of b?

   (1) $a = 3$

   (2) $c = 5$

Answers and explanations follow on the next page. ▶ ▶ ▶

Answer Key

Practice Set: Translating Words into Expressions and Equations on the GMAT

1. E
2. A

Practice Set: Isolating a Variable on the GMAT

3. E
4. D
5. B

Practice Set: Quadratic Equations on the GMAT

6. A
7. D
8. D

Practice Set: Systems of Linear Equations on the GMAT

9. B
10. C
11. E

Practice Set: Special Cases in Systems of Linear Equations on the GMAT

12. B
13. C
14. D

Practice Set: Sequences on the GMAT

15. D
16. B
17. D

Practice Set: Functions and Symbolism on the GMAT

18. D
19. B
20. E
21. B

Answers and Explanations

Practice Set: Translating Words into Expressions and Equations on the GMAT

1. **(E)**

    Machine A produces r paper clips per hour. Machine B produces s paper clips per hour. If s is 30 greater than r, which expression represents the number of paper clips the two machines working together produce in t hours?

    ○ $r + s + 30$

    ○ $t(r + s) + 30$

    ○ $t(r + s + 30)$

    ○ $t(2s + 30)$

    ○ $t(2r + 30)$

STEP 1: ANALYZE THE QUESTION

The sentences in this word problem can be translated into algebraic statements to determine the total number of paper clips produced by both machines over a given number of hours. Alternatively, numbers could be picked for r and t and arithmetic could be done, but algebra is the more efficient approach if you are comfortable with it.

STEP 2: STATE THE TASK

Find the expression that represents the number of paper clips both machines working together produce in t hours.

STEP 3: APPROACH STRATEGICALLY

Translate the phrase "s is 30 greater than r" as $s = r + 30$. Thus, the two machines produce $r + r + 30 = 2r + 30$ paper clips in each hour. In t hours, that would be $t(2r + 30)$. That's **(E)**.

STEP 4: CONFIRM YOUR ANSWER

If you solve using algebra, you could pick numbers to confirm: say $r = 10$, then $s = 10 + 30 = 40$. Together, the machines produce $10 + 40 = 50$ paper clips each hour. If $t = 2$, then the machines produce $50 \times 2 = 100$ paper clips in 2 hours. When you plug the numbers you picked into the answer choices, only **(E)** equals 100.

2.   **(A)**

The youngest of 4 children has siblings who are 3, 5, and 8 years older than she is. If the average (arithmetic mean) age of the 4 siblings is 21, what is the age of the youngest sibling?

- ○ 17
- ○ 18
- ○ 19
- ○ 21
- ○ 22

STEP 1: ANALYZE THE QUESTION

You can apply the translation rules to this word problem to convert the question into a manageable algebraic equation.

STEP 2: STATE THE TASK

Once the word problem has been translated, apply basic algebra to simplify the statement to match the correct answer choice.

STEP 3: APPROACH STRATEGICALLY

Let x be the age of the youngest sibling in years. Then the ages of the other siblings, who are 3, 5, and 8 years older than the youngest sibling, are $x + 3$, $x + 5$, and $x + 8$, respectively. The average age of the four siblings is 21. Therefore, the average of x, $x + 3$, $x + 5$, and $x + 8$ is 21.

The average formula is $\text{Average} = \dfrac{\text{Sum of the terms}}{\text{Number of terms}}$. So you can write the equation

$\dfrac{x + (x + 3) + (x + 5) + (x + 8)}{4} = 21.$

Solve the equation for x:

$$\frac{x + (x + 3) + (x + 5) + (x + 8)}{4} = 21$$

$$\frac{x + x + 3 + x + 5 + x + 8}{4} = 21$$

$$\frac{4x + 16}{4} = 21$$

$$4x + 16 = 84$$

$$4x = 68$$

$$x = \frac{68}{4} = 17$$

The correct answer is **(A)**.

STEP 4: CONFIRM YOUR ANSWER

For Average questions, an easy way to confirm your answer is to plug your value for x into the average formula and see if the same answer comes out on both sides. If not, go back over your calculations.

Practice Set: Isolating a Variable on the GMAT

3. **(E)**

If $\dfrac{3a - 2ce}{3} = \dfrac{4b - 2de}{2}$, then $\dfrac{e}{3} =$

○ $\dfrac{9a - 8b}{6c - 4d}$

○ $\dfrac{6a - 3b}{2c - 3d}$

○ $\dfrac{3a - 6b}{2c - 3d}$

○ $\dfrac{a - 2b}{6c - 9d}$

○ $\dfrac{a - 2b}{2c - 3d}$

STEP 1: ANALYZE THE QUESTION

You are provided with an equation with fractions in terms of the variables a, b, c, d, and e. The answer choices are also fractions with variables.

STEP 2: STATE THE TASK

Use algebra to manipulate the equation so that $\dfrac{e}{3}$ is on one side and all other terms are on the other side.

STEP 3: APPROACH STRATEGICALLY

To isolate the variable e, cross multiply the given equation to eliminate the fractions: $2(3a - 2ce) = 3(4b - 2de)$. Distributing 2 on the left side of the equation and 3 on the right side gives $6a - 4ce = 12b - 6de$.

Add $6de$ to both sides so that all terms that contain e are on one side of the equation: $6a - 4ce + 6de = 12b$.

Subtract $6a$ from both sides so that only terms with e are on the left: $-4ce + 6de = -6a + 12b$.

Factoring out e yields $e(-4c + 6d) = -6a + 12b$.

Dividing both sides by $(-4c + 6d)$ results in $e = \dfrac{-6a + 12b}{-4c + 6d}$. Simplify the fraction on the right by dividing each term by 2: $e = \dfrac{-3a + 6b}{-2c + 3d}$.

Your task is not to solve for e but for $\dfrac{e}{3}$. Thus, $\dfrac{e}{3} = \dfrac{1}{3}e = \left(\dfrac{1}{3}\right)\left(\dfrac{-3a + 6b}{-2c + 3d}\right) = \dfrac{-a + 2b}{-2c + 3d}$. None of the choices match, but **(E)** is close. Multiplying this expression by $\dfrac{-1}{-1}$ does not change its value but does change the sign of each term, resulting in $\dfrac{a - 2b}{2c - 3d}$. Thus, **(E)** is correct.

STEP 4: CONFIRM YOUR ANSWER

Double-check that you solved for the right expression; **(C)** represents the value of e rather than $\dfrac{e}{3}$.

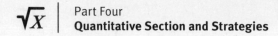

4. **(D)**

If $2(s - r) = -2\left(\dfrac{r^2 - s^2}{s^2 - r^2}\right)$ and $s^2 - r^2 \neq 0$, then $s - r =$

- ○ −2
- ○ −1
- ○ 0
- ○ 1
- ○ 2

STEP 1: ANALYZE THE QUESTION

The question provides a complicated-looking equation in terms of two variables. Since the answer choices are all numbers, however, there must be a way to find a numerical value for the requested expression.

STEP 2: STATE THE TASK

Find the value of $s - r$.

STEP 3: APPROACH STRATEGICALLY

The fact that $x - y = -(y - x)$ is an important idea for the GMAT. For example, you may use this property to reexpress algebraic expressions to match the given answer choices. Here, a variation can be used to simplify the equation in the question stem, $2(s - r) = -2\left(\dfrac{r^2 - s^2}{s^2 - r^2}\right)$, to solve for $s - r$. Begin by dividing both sides by 2:

$$s - r = -1\left(\frac{r^2 - s^2}{s^2 - r^2}\right)$$

To multiply the numerator by -1, simply reverse the terms:

$$s - r = \frac{s^2 - r^2}{s^2 - r^2}$$

Cancel common factors:

$$s - r = 1$$

(D) is correct.

STEP 4: CONFIRM YOUR ANSWER

If you have time, double-check your algebra.

5. **(B)**

A laptop computer uses s fewer watts of electricity than a desktop computer does. In combination, the 2 computers use t watts of electricity. Which of the following expressions represents the desktop computer's electricity usage, in watts?

- $\dfrac{t}{2} - s$
- $\dfrac{t+s}{2}$
- $t(s-1)$
- $t - \dfrac{s}{2}$
- $t - 2s$

STEP 1: ANALYZE THE QUESTION

You're given a relationship between the desktop computer's electricity usage and the laptop computer's electricity usage in terms of a variable, and you're also given the combined electricity usage in terms of another variable. Either straight algebra or picking numbers could work here.

Call the desktop computer's usage D and the laptop's usage L.

Because the laptop uses s fewer watts than the desktop, the $L = D - s$.

Because the sum of the desktop's usage and the laptop's usage is t watts, you have the equation $D + L = t$. You also know that $L = D - s$, so you can use substitution to rewrite this equation as $D + (D - s) = t$.

STEP 2: STATE THE TASK

Isolate the desktop computer's electricity usage in terms of the given variables.

STEP 3: APPROACH STRATEGICALLY

Now that you've translated the facts of the problem into math expressions, you can solve the equation for D:

$$D + (D - s) = t$$
$$D + D - s = t$$
$$2D - s = t$$
$$2D = t + s$$
$$D = \frac{t+s}{2}$$

Thus, **(B)** is correct.

Alternatively, you could pick numbers. Say the combined electricity usage, t, is 100 watts and the desktop uses 70 watts. This means the laptop uses 30 watts, or 40 fewer watts than the laptop; therefore, $s = 40$. Plug these values of $t = 100$ and $s = 40$ into the answer choices to see which choice matches the desktop's wattage of 70:

(A): $\frac{100}{2} - 40 = 10$. Eliminate.

(B): $\frac{100 + 40}{2} = 70$. Keep for now and check the remaining answers.

(C): $100(40 - 1) = 3,900$. Eliminate.

(D): $100 - \frac{40}{2} = 80$. Eliminate.

(E): $100 - (2 \times 40) = 20$. Eliminate. So **(B)** is correct.

STEP 4: CONFIRM YOUR ANSWER

If you solved algebraically, be sure you correctly translated the words into mathematical expressions. If you picked numbers, check that each variable is assigned the correct value.

Practice Set: Quadratic Equations on the GMAT

6. (A)

Is $x > 0$?

(1) $x^2 - 8x + 16 = 0$

(2) $x^2 - x - 12 = 0$

STEP 1: ANALYZE THE QUESTION STEM

In this Yes/No question, sufficiency means determining that x is either definitely positive or definitely not positive (zero or negative).

STEP 2: EVALUATE THE STATEMENTS USING 12TEN

Statement (1) provides a quadratic equation in which the sign of the constant term (16) is positive. A plus sign here means the quadratic has roots (value(s) of x) that are either both positive or both negative. Thus, this statement is sufficient to answer the question with either a clear yes or no. Don't take the time to find the value of x, but if you did, you would reverse-FOIL to find that $x^2 - 8x + 16 = (x - 4)(x - 4) = 0$, meaning that $x - 4 = 0$ and $x = 4$; the answer to the question is yes. Eliminate **(B)**, **(C)**, and **(E)**.

Statement (2) provides a quadratic equation in which the sign of the constant term (-12) is negative. You don't need to factor the equation to determine whether this is sufficient, because a negative sign in this position of a quadratic guarantees that it has two roots—one positive and one negative. This statement is therefore insufficient. Eliminate **(D)** and choose **(A)**.

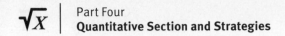

7. (D)

Which of the following expressions could be equal to 0 when $n^2 - 4n = 12$?

- ◯ $n^2 - 2n - 15$
- ◯ $n^2 - 2n + 1$
- ◯ $n^2 + 4n - 12$
- ◯ $n^2 - 5n - 6$
- ◯ $n^2 + 6n + 5$

STEP 1: ANALYZE THE QUESTION

The question stem provides the equation $n^2 - 4n = 12$, which can be restated as the quadratic equation $n^2 - 4n - 12 = 0$.

STEP 2: STATE THE TASK

The question asks which of the answer choices could be equal to zero, given the values of n that are consistent with the equation in the stem.

STEP 3: APPROACH STRATEGICALLY

When a quadratic equation is set equal to 0 and factored, one of the factors must be equal to 0 and the possible values of the variable are derived from that fact. Therefore, if an expression in the choices shares a common factor with the given equation, that expression could be equal to 0.

The equation in the question stem factors to $(n - 6)(n + 2) = 0$. So factor the choices to determine whether they have either $n - 6$ or $n + 2$ as a factor. If they do, they could be equal to zero.

(A) is $n^2 - 2n - 15 = (n + 3)(n - 5)$. Eliminate.

(B) is $n^2 - 2n + 1 = (n - 1)(n - 1)$. Eliminate.

(C) is $n^2 + 4n - 12 = (n - 2)(n + 6)$. Be careful here! The factors of this expression reverse the signs of the factors of the given equation. Eliminate.

(D) is $n^2 - 5n - 6 = (n - 6)(n + 1)$. The factor $(n - 6)$ is shared by the given equation, so **(D)** is correct.

For the record, **(E)** is $n^2 + 6n + 5 = (n + 5)(n + 1)$. Eliminate.

(D) shares a factor with the given equation, so it is correct.

STEP 4: CONFIRM YOUR ANSWER

When factoring quadratics, an easy way to check your work is to expand the binomials back into their original form by applying the FOIL technique. If time permits, do this for every quadratic expression you factor to avoid calculation errors.

8. **(D)**

Which of the following could equal zero for some value of x?

    I. $3x^2 - 12$

    II. $x^2 + x^4 + 1$

    III. $x^2 + 7x + 6$

   ○   I only

   ○   III only

   ○   I and II only

   ○   I and III only

   ○   I, II, and III

STEP 1: ANALYZE THE QUESTION

This is a Roman numeral question involving equations with x raised to various exponents; expect that you'll have to do some factoring.

STEP 2: STATE THE TASK

Determine which of the equations could be equal to 0.

STEP 3: APPROACH STRATEGICALLY

No statement is markedly easier to work with than the others, and Statement I shows up the most in the choices, so start there. Factor the expression into $3(x^2 - 4) = 3(x + 2)(x - 2)$. If x is 2 or -2, the expression is 0. Statement I must be part of the correct answer, so eliminate **(B)**.

Evaluate Statement II next. Notice that both variable terms, x^2 and x^4, will never be negative, since any real base raised to an even exponent is either zero or positive. Therefore, this expression cannot be less than the constant term, 1. Eliminate **(C)** and **(E)**.

Evaluate Statement III by factoring $x^2 + 7x + 6$ into $(x + 6)(x + 1)$. The expression will be 0 if $x = -6$ or $x = -1$. **(D)** is correct.

STEP 4: CONFIRM YOUR ANSWER

In Roman numeral questions, make sure you pick the choice that includes all the valid statements and none of the invalid statements.

Practice Set: Systems of Linear Equations on the GMAT

9.   (B)

A photographer has visited exactly 42 countries, all of which have been in Africa, Europe, or Asia. If the photographer has been to 6 more countries in Europe than in Asia, and twice as many in Africa as in Europe, how many countries in Asia has the photographer visited?

- ○   4
- ○   6
- ○   12
- ○   18
- ○   24

STEP 1: ANALYZE THE QUESTION

The question provides information about the 42 countries a photographer has been to, which are on 3 continents. The number of visited countries on each continent can be represented by a variable, and there's enough information to set up three equations. Thus, you're able to solve for any of the three variables.

STEP 2: STATE THE TASK

Use a system of linear equations to determine the number of countries in Asia that the photographer has visited.

STEP 3: APPROACH STRATEGICALLY

Let S represent the number of countries in Asia, F the number in Africa, and E the number in Europe. Since there are 42 countries total, $F + E + S = 42$. Also, since the photographer has been to 6 more countries in Europe than in Asia, $E = S + 6$. Twice as many in Africa as in Europe gives $F = 2E$.

It follows that, since $E = S + 6$, $F = 2E = 2(S + 6)$. So by substitution:

$$F + E + S = 42$$
$$2(S + 6) + (S + 6) + S = 42$$
$$2S + 12 + S + 6 + S = 42$$
$$4S + 18 = 42$$
$$4S = 24$$
$$S = 6$$

Therefore, the photographer has been to 6 countries in Asia, and the answer is **(B)**.

STEP 4: CONFIRM YOUR ANSWER

As always, be sure to answer the right question. **(C)** is the number of countries visited in Europe, and **(E)** is the number visited in Africa. If time permits, plug 6 back into the word problem as the number of countries in Asia and see whether you come up with 42 total countries: Asia = 6; Europe = 6 + 6 = 12; Africa = 2 × 12 = 24. Finally, 6 + 12 + 24 = 42.

10. (C)

Paula has a collection of used books worth $104. How many are histories?

(1) Paula has only mysteries and histories; each mystery is worth $1, and each history is worth $25.

(2) Paula has exactly 4 mysteries in her collection that together are worth a total of $4.

STEP 1: ANALYZE THE QUESTION STEM

This is a Value question. The question stem says that Paula's used book collection is worth $104 and asks how many are histories, but there is no information about any other books or their worth.

STEP 2: EVALUATE THE STATEMENTS USING 12TEN

Statement (1) tells you that Paula has only mysteries at $1 apiece and histories at $25 apiece. If m is the number of mysteries and h is the number of histories, the total worth can be stated as the number of each type of book times the unit worth: $104 = 1m + 25h$. Since you have one equation with two variables, this is insufficient. Eliminate **(A)** and **(D)**.

Statement (2) states that there are exactly 4 mysteries with a total worth of $4. Thus, the worth of each mystery is $1, and the total worth of the histories is $104 – $4 = $100. Lacking information about the worth per history book, this statement is also insufficient. Eliminate **(B)** and evaluate the statements together.

Statement (1) says that history books are worth $25 each, and from Statement (2), you know that the history books are worth $100 each. This is sufficient to determine the number of history books, so **(C)** is correct.

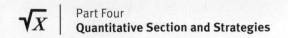
11. (E)

In 8 years, Leonard will be twice as many years old as Mikala is now. If Leonard were twice as old as he was 2 years ago, and if Mikala were five times as old as she was 2 years ago, the sum of their ages would be 51. What will be the sum of their ages in 3 years?

- ○ 12
- ○ 14
- ○ 19
- ○ 22
- ○ 25

STEP 1: ANALYZE THE QUESTION

The question provides information about two people's ages at varying points in time. The answer choices are integers, but because they represent a sum of *two* unknown ages, backsolving would not be an efficient strategy here.

STEP 2: STATE THE TASK

Determine the sum of the two people's ages 3 years from now, or $(L + 3) + (M + 3) = L + M + 6$. You'll need to translate the words into algebraic equations and then solve the system of equations for the unknown.

STEP 3: APPROACH STRATEGICALLY

That Leonard's age in 8 years will be twice Mikala's current age can be written as $L + 8 = 2M$. Note that you age Leonard by 8 years by adding 8 to L, but you don't add any years to M because this statement deals with Mikala's current age. Because the task is to find the sum of their ages, rearrange this so the L and M terms are on the same side of the equal sign: $L - 2M = -8$.

Leonard's age 2 years ago is $L - 2$, so twice that age is $2(L - 2)$. And 2 years ago, Mikala's age was $M - 2$, so five times that age is $5(M - 2)$. The equation for the second sentence is thus $2(L - 2) + 5(M - 2) = 51$. Distribute the 2 and 5 across the parentheses: $2L - 4 + 5M - 10 = 51$. Simplify: $2L + 5M = 65$.

There is no way to directly add or subtract these equations to find $L + M$, but if you add the equations, the two terms have the same coefficient, which can then be divided out. Thus, combination is an efficient approach.

$$L - 2M = -8$$
$$+[2L + 5M = 65]$$
$$\overline{3L + 3M = 57}$$
$$L + M = 19$$

The question asks for the sum of the two ages in 3 years: $L + M + 6 = 19 + 6 = 25$. **(E)** is correct.

STEP 4: CONFIRM YOUR ANSWER

Be certain that you correctly untangled the question stem and that you answered the question that was asked. **(C)** is the sum of the ages now. **(D)** is the sum of the ages plus 3 years, but both Leonard and Mikala will be 3 years older, so 3 needs to be added twice.

Practice Set: Special Cases in Systems of Linear Equations on the GMAT

12. (B)

What is the value of b?

(1) $5b - a = 3b + 5a$

(2) $4(b - a) = 12 - 4a$

STEP 1: ANALYZE THE QUESTION STEM

This Value question stem gives no information about b. Thus, move on to the statements. For sufficiency, a statement must supply information that would allow you to calculate a single value for b.

STEP 2: EVALUATE THE STATEMENTS USING 12TEN

Statement (1) is $5b - a = 3b + 5a$. Simplifying this equation yields $2b = 6a$, which is $b = 3a$, but neither variable cancels out. Thus, you have one equation with two variables, and you can't solve for the value of either variable. Therefore, there is not enough information to find the value of b. Statement (1) is insufficient. Eliminate **(A)** and **(D)**.

Statement (2) is $4(b - a) = 12 - 4a$. Simplify this equation to see whether a variable cancels out. Multiplying out the left side of the equation gives $4b - 4a = 12 - 4a$. Adding $4a$ to both sides yields $4b = 12$, so the variable a cancels out in the simplification, leaving you with one linear equation containing only one variable, b, which you could solve for. Thus, Statement (2) is sufficient, and **(B)** is correct.

If you see a question like this one on Test Day, don't be too quick to assume that you need two equations to solve for the value of either variable—be sure to simplify the equation first.

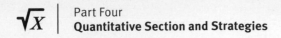
13. (C)

What is the value of $a + b$?

(1) $5a + 2b = 22$

(2) $3b = 30 - 6a$

STEP 1: ANALYZE THE QUESTION STEM

In this Value question, you must determine whether there is sufficient information to determine the value of $a + b$. Note that this may not require finding the individual values of a and b; solving for the value of the entire expression would suffice. Because no information is given in the question stem, move on to the statements.

STEP 2: EVALUATE THE STATEMENTS USING 12TEN

Statement (1) provides one equation with two variables, $5a + 2b = 22$. Because the number of variables is greater than the number of different equations, there's no way to solve for the values of a and b. Moreover, there's no way to isolate $a + b$ on one side. Thus, Statement (1) is insufficient. Eliminate **(A)** and **(D)**.

Statement (2) gives $3b = 30 - 6a$, which is one equation with the two variables a and b. Rearranging this gives $6a + 3b = 30$; dividing each term by 3 yields $2a + b = 10$. Again, because the number of variables is greater than the number of different equations, and because there's no way to simplify for the value of $a + b$, Statement (2) is insufficient. Eliminate **(B)**.

Now look at the statements together. You have two distinct linear equations and two variables, so you can solve for their values. Therefore, the two statements taken together are sufficient, and **(C)** is correct. For the record, here's the math: if you rearrange the equation in Statement (2) by adding $6a$ to both sides, you get $6a + 3b = 30$. Now use combination, subtracting one equation from the other, to solve for $a + b$ in one step:

$$\begin{aligned} 6a + 3b &= 30 \\ -[5a + 2b &= 22] \\ \hline a + b &= 8 \end{aligned}$$

14. (D)

If the average (arithmetic mean) of x and y is 30 and $3y + z = 180$, what is the value of $\frac{z}{x}$?

- $\frac{1}{6}$
- $\frac{1}{3}$
- 1
- 3
- 6

STEP 1: ANALYZE THE QUESTION

You're given the average of x and y and the value of $3y + z$. There are two equations and three variables, so look for a way to eliminate y, which is not part of the value you're solving for.

STEP 2: STATE THE TASK

Find the value of $\frac{z}{x}$.

STEP 3: APPROACH STRATEGICALLY

Translate "the average of x and y is 30" as $\frac{x + y}{2} = 30$. Multiply both sides by 2 to find that $x + y = 60$. Since you need the value of $\frac{z}{x}$, isolate each of these variables: $x + y = 60$, so $x = 60 - y$, and $3y + z = 180$, so $z = 180 - 3y$. Therefore, $\frac{z}{x} = \frac{180 - 3y}{60 - y}$. Factoring out a 3 from the numerator yields $\frac{z}{x} = \frac{3(60 - y)}{60 - y} = 3$. The correct choice is **(D)**.

Here's another approach. After getting $x + y = 60$, multiply this equation by 3 to get $3x + 3y = 180$. Since $3y + z = 180$, you can set the two equations equal to each other: $3x + 3y = 3y + z$. Subtract $3y$ from both sides to find $3x = z$. Now divide both sides by x: $3 = \frac{z}{x}$.

STEP 4: CONFIRM YOUR ANSWER

Confirm that you've found $\frac{z}{x}$ and not $\frac{x}{z}$, which is **(B)**. You can also pick numbers to confirm: since the average of x and y is 30, choose $x = 30$ and $y = 30$. Then $3y = 90$, so since $z = 180 - 3y$, $z = 90$. Then $\frac{z}{x} = \frac{90}{30} = 3$.

Practice Set: Sequences on the GMAT

15. (D)

l, m, n, o, p

An arithmetic sequence is a sequence in which each term after the first is equal to the sum of the preceding term and a constant. If the list of letters shown above is an arithmetic sequence, which of the following must also be an arithmetic sequence?

    I. $3l, 3m, 3n, 3o, 3p$

    II. l^2, m^2, n^2, o^2, p^2

    III. $l - 5, m - 5, n - 5, o - 5, p - 5$

○ I only

○ II only

○ III only

○ I and III

○ II and III

STEP 1: ANALYZE THE QUESTION

You are provided with the definition of an arithmetic sequence and told that *l, m, n, o, p* is one such sequence. As this is a Roman numeral question with variables, expect to use picking numbers and don't forget to check the Roman numeral statements in the most efficient order. In this question, you will want to begin with Statement III, as it shows up the most in the answer choices.

STEP 2: STATE THE TASK

Determine which of the Roman numeral statements are true.

STEP 3: APPROACH STRATEGICALLY

Statement III: To test this statement, say the original arithmetic sequence is 6, 9, 12, 1 5, 18 (adding a constant of 3 each time). Statement III would have you subtract 5 from each term, which results in the sequence 1, 4, 7, 10, 13. This is still an arithmetic sequence as each term is exactly 3 more than its preceding term, so Statement III is a true statement. Eliminate **(A)** and **(B)**.

Of the remaining statements, Statement I is easier to test. Using the same original sequence you had above, Statement I would have you multiply each term by 3. Doing so results in the sequence 18, 27, 36, 45, 54. This is still an arithmetic sequence as each term is exactly 9 more than its preceding term, so Statement I is a true statement. Eliminate **(C)** and **(E)**.

Therefore, the correct answer is **(D)**.

STEP 4: CONFIRM YOUR ANSWER

To confirm the answer, test Statement II: Using the same original sequence picked above, Statement II would have you square each term. The larger numbers can make this time-consuming, but just squaring the first three terms (36, 81, 144) should be enough to show you that Statement II does not result in an arithmetic sequence. **(D)** is confirmed.

16. **(B)**

In a certain sequence of positive integers, the term t_n is given by the formula $t_n = 3(t_{n-2}) + 2(t_{n-1}) - 1$ for all $n \geq 1$. If $t_6 = 152$ and $t_5 = 51$, what is the value of t_2?

- ○ 1
- ○ 2
- ○ 3
- ○ 6
- ○ 17

STEP 1: ANALYZE THE QUESTION

The question stem provides the formula for a sequence and the values for the fifth and sixth terms in the sequence, t_5 and t_6.

STEP 2: STATE THE TASK

Determine the value of the second term in the sequence, t_2.

STEP 3: APPROACH STRATEGICALLY

Work backward from the known values until you get to t_2. For t_6, the t_{n-2} term is t_4 and the t_{n-1} term is t_5. Plug the two known values into the formula for the series to get $152 = 3(t_4) + 2(51) - 1$. This simplifies to $3(t_4) = 51$, so $t_4 = 17$. For t_5, the formula is $51 = 3(t_3) + 2(17) - 1$. Thus, $3(t_3) = 18$ and $t_3 = 6$. One more to go! For t_4, $17 = 3(t_2) + 2(6) - 1$. So $3(t_2) = 6$ and $t_2 = 2$, which is **(B)**.

STEP 4: CONFIRM YOUR ANSWER

(D) is t_3 and (E) is t_4. Checking your scratchwork to make sure you've calculated through to the correct number in the sequence will help you avoid these wrong answer traps.

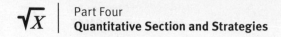
17. (D)

In the infinite sequence S, each term S_n after S_2 is equal to the sum of the two terms S_{n-1} and S_{n-2}. If S_1 is 4, what is the value of S_2?

(1) $S_3 = 7$

(2) $S_4 = 10$

STEP 1: ANALYZE THE QUESTION STEM

This is a Value question. You must determine what information is needed to solve directly for the term S_2. The question stem says that if S_n is the nth term of the sequence, then for $n > 2$, you have $S_n = S_{n-1} + S_{n-2}$. That is, after the second term in the sequence, the next term is equal to the sum of the two previous terms. For example, the third term is equal to the sum of the first and second terms.

You also know that S_1 is 4. Because $S_3 = S_2 + S_1$, $S_3 = S_2 + 4$. So you have one linear equation with two variables, S_3 and S_2. To find the value of S_2, you need more information that will lead to a single possible value for S_2.

You could find the value of S_2 if you were given the value of S_3. You could also find the value of S_2 if you were given another linear equation with the variables S_3 and S_2 that is different from the first equation. Look at the statements.

STEP 2: EVALUATE THE STATEMENTS USING 12TEN

Statement (1) says that $S_3 = 7$. Because $S_3 = S_2 + 4$, you have the equation $7 = S_2 + 4$. From this equation, you can find the single possible value of S_2. Statement (1) is sufficient. Eliminate **(B)**, **(C)**, and **(E)**.

Statement (2) says that $S_4 = 10$. Because $S_4 = S_3 + S_2$, you have the equation $S_3 + S_2 = 10$. This is another linear equation containing the terms S_2 and S_3. Because the two equations are distinct, you have enough information to determine the values for both S_3 and S_2. Statement (2) is sufficient. **(D)** is correct.

Practice Set: Functions and Symbolism on the GMAT

18. (D)

Let $\boxed{x} = \dfrac{x^2+1}{2}$ and $\textcircled{y} = \dfrac{3y}{2}$, for all integers x and y. If $m = 2$, $\boxed{\textcircled{m}}$ is equal to which of the following?

- ○ $\dfrac{13}{8}$
- ○ 3
- ○ $\dfrac{15}{4}$
- ○ 5
- ○ $\dfrac{37}{2}$

STEP 1: ANALYZE THE QUESTION

This is a symbolism problem containing two definitions and a nested function. You will need to begin with the innermost function and work your way outward.

STEP 2: STATE THE TASK

Find the value of $\boxed{\textcircled{m}}$.

STEP 3: APPROACH STRATEGICALLY

Symbolism problems may look frighteningly complicated, so it's important to remember that they are nothing more than dressed-up equations for which you are asked to plug in a value. In this question, you are given two definition equations and a nested function (a function within a function). You're also told that $m = 2$. With nested functions, you start with the innermost equation and work outward, so begin by plugging 2 in for the variable in the circle equation: $\dfrac{3y}{2} = \dfrac{3(2)}{2} = 3$. Now take the result, 3, and plug that into the square equation:

$$\frac{x^2+1}{2} = \frac{3^2+1}{2}$$
$$= \frac{9+1}{2}$$
$$= \frac{10}{2}$$
$$= 5$$

The value of $\boxed{\textcircled{m}}$ is 5, so the correct answer is **(D)**.

STEP 4: CONFIRM YOUR ANSWER

When working with nested functions, remember to always work from the inside out. Doing so allows you to avoid trap choices like **(C)**, which is the result of working from the outside in.

19. (B)

$$\begin{array}{r} \diamond \\ \times\, \underline{\triangle} \\ \bullet \end{array}$$

In the multiplication problem above, each of the symbols $\diamond$, $\triangle$, and $\bullet$ represents a positive digit. If $\diamond > \triangle$, what is the value of $\diamond$?

(1) $\triangle = 1$

(2) $\bullet = 9$

STEP 1: ANALYZE THE QUESTION STEM

Before beginning the solution, note for clarity that a positive digit is one of the integers 1, 2, 3, 4, 5, 6, 7, 8, and 9. You are given in the question stem that the product of the digits $\diamond$ and $\triangle$ is $\bullet$ and that $\diamond > \triangle$. You want to know if there is sufficient information to determine the value of the digit $\diamond$.

STEP 2: EVALUATE THE STATEMENTS USING 12TEN

Statement (1) says that $\triangle = 1$. So the product of $\diamond$ and 1 is $\bullet$. Because the product of any number and 1 is that number, the product of $\diamond$ and 1 is $\diamond$. So $\diamond = \bullet$. You know from the question stem that $\diamond > \triangle$, and because Statement (1) says that $\triangle = 1$, you have $\diamond > 1$. However, you do not know the value of the digit. So $\diamond$ could be any of the eight remaining positive digits 2, 3, 4, 5, 6, 7, 8, and 9. Because there is more than one possible value for $\diamond$, Statement (1) is insufficient. Eliminate **(A)** and **(D)**.

Statement (2) says that $\bullet = 9$. So the product of $\diamond$ and $\triangle$ is 9. There are two ways to write 9 as the product of two digits, 9×1 and 3×3. Because $\diamond \times \triangle = 9$ and you must have $\diamond > \triangle$, it must be the case that $\diamond = 9$ and $\triangle = 1$. So $\diamond$ has only one possible value, 9. Statement (2) is sufficient. **(B)** is correct.

20. (E)

For all positive numbers x and y, the operation $x \blacklozenge y$ is defined by $x \blacklozenge y = \dfrac{x^2 - x}{2xy}$. If $x \blacklozenge 5 = 2$, then $x =$

○ 1

○ 5

○ 11

○ 20

○ 21

STEP 1: ANALYZE THE QUESTION

You're told that $x \blacklozenge y$ is defined by the expression $\dfrac{x^2 - x}{2xy}$. Translated into English, this means that when you "diamond" two numbers, you square the first number, then subtract the first number from this square, and divide the result by 2 times the product of the first and second numbers. You also know that when y (the second number) equals 5 in this expression, the result is 2.

STEP 2: STATE THE TASK

Determine the value of x based on the definition.

STEP 3: APPROACH STRATEGICALLY

Because you know that $x \blacklozenge 5 = 2$, replace y with 5 in the defining equation and set it equal to 2: $\dfrac{x^2 - x}{(2x)5} = 2$. Combine factors in the denominator: $\dfrac{x^2 - x}{10x} = 2$. Next, multiply both sides by $10x$: $x^2 - x = 20x$. Subtract $20x$ from both sides to yield $x^2 - 21x = 0$. Now factor out an x from each term on the left: $x(x - 21) = 0$. Thus, either $x = 21$ or $x = 0$. The question stem specifies that x is positive, so you're left with $x = 21$. The correct choice is **(E)**.

STEP 4: CONFIRM YOUR ANSWER

Check that you substituted numbers correctly into the definition and verify your calculations, making sure you solve for the value of x and not y. If you plugged in 5 for x and solved for y, you probably chose **(A)**.

21. (B)

The operation ♪ x is defined by the equation ♪ $x = ax - b(x - 1) + c$, where a, b, and c are constants that are positive integers. The value of ♪ 0 is 7. What is the value of b?

(1) $a = 3$

(2) $c = 5$

STEP 1: ANALYZE THE QUESTION STEM

The stem describes an operation performed on the variable x as ♪ $x = ax - b(x - 1) + c$, where a, b, and c are positive integers. The additional information that ♪ $0 = 7$ is provided. Therefore, substitute 0 for x into the function and set it equal to 7: $a(0) - b(0 - 1) + c = 7$; this simplifies to $b + c = 7$.

Simplified, the question stem provides two variables but only one equation. Each additional value for ♪ x would enable you to create an equation in terms of a, b, and c, just as you did when you translated ♪ $0 = 7$ into $b + c = 7$. So two more values for ♪ x or some other information that enables you to determine a value for c would be sufficient.

STEP 2: EVALUATE THE STATEMENTS USING 12TEN

Statement (1) says that $a = 3$. This information, unlike a value for ♪ x, does not enable you to write another equation, nor does a appear in the equation $b + c = 7$. Thus, Statement (1) is insufficient. Eliminate **(A)** and **(D)**.

Statement (2) informs you that $c = 5$. This information also does not enable you to write another equation, so you do not have enough information to determine the value of *all* the variables. However, you can plug this value into $b + c = 7$ to get the value of b. Therefore, Statement (2) is sufficient to solve for the value of b, and **(B)** is correct.

GMAT by the Numbers: Algebra

Now that you've learned how to approach algebra questions on the GMAT, let's add one more dimension to your understanding of how they work.

Take a moment to try this question. Following is performance data from thousands of people who have studied with Kaplan over the decades. Through analyzing this data, we will show you how to approach questions like this one most effectively and how to avoid similarly tempting wrong answer choice types on Test Day.

What is the value of g?

(1) $f + g = 9$

(2) $3f - 27 = -3g$

○ Statement (1) ALONE is sufficient, but Statement (2) is not sufficient.

○ Statement (2) ALONE is sufficient, but Statement (1) is not sufficient.

○ BOTH statements TOGETHER are sufficient, but NEITHER statement ALONE is sufficient.

○ EACH statement ALONE is sufficient.

○ Statements (1) and (2) TOGETHER are NOT sufficient.

Explanation

This question asks you to find the value of *g*. Neither statement by itself can give you that value, since each contains the variable *f* as well.

Question Statistics

0% of test takers choose **(A)**

2% of test takers choose **(B)**

25% of test takers choose **(C)**

1% of test takers choose **(D)**

72% of test takers choose **(E)**

Sample size = 4,242

It's tempting to think as one-fourth of test takers did: the statements together will be sufficient because you can rewrite Statement (1) as $f = 9 - g$, substitute into Statement (2), and then solve for *g*. But that's only tempting to a test taker who doesn't first simplify Statement (2):

$$3f - 27 = -3g$$

$$3f + 3g = 27$$

$$f + g = 9$$

This is the same equation as Statement (1), so it doesn't add any new information. Knowing that $f + g = 9$ isn't enough to know the value of *g*, so the statements are insufficient even when combined. Choice **(E)** is correct.

GMAT questions rarely give you algebraic statements in their most useful form. It's a safe bet that you'll need to simplify or reexpress almost all the algebra you see on Test Day. Doing so will help you steer clear of common wrong answers and keep you on the road to a higher score.

More GMAT by the Numbers...

To see more questions with answer choice statistics, be sure to review the full-length CATs in your
online resources.

 GO ONLINE

kaptest.com/login

CHAPTER 19

Arithmetic on the GMAT

> **LEARNING OBJECTIVES**
>
> After studying this chapter, you will be able to:
>
> - Describe which arithmetic topics are tested on the GMAT
> - Identify questions that involve arithmetic concepts
> - Apply the Kaplan Methods for Problem Solving and Data Sufficiency to questions testing a variety of arithmetic concepts

Below is a typical Problem Solving arithmetic question. In this chapter, we'll look at how to apply the Kaplan Method to this question, discuss the arithmetic rules being tested, and go over the basic principles and strategies that you want to keep in mind on every Quantitative question involving arithmetic.

> If x is a number such that $-2 \leq x < 2$, which of the following has the largest possible absolute value?
>
> ○ $3x - 1$
> ○ $x^2 - x$
> ○ $3 - x$
> ○ $x - 3$
> ○ $x^2 + 1$

Before you move on, take a minute to think about what you see in this question and answer some questions about how you think it works:

- What mathematical concepts are being tested in this question?
- What do you notice about the answer choices?
- How do the math concepts in the question relate to the answer choices?
- What GMAT Core Competencies are most essential to success on this question?

Previewing Arithmetic on the GMAT

Most of the Quantitative questions you will see on the GMAT involve arithmetic to some extent. The GMAT frequently increases the difficulty level of questions by combining various topics, such as absolute value, inequalities, exponents, and fractions, and often incorporating these topics into questions that involve algebra, geometry, or proportions. You will be in a much stronger position on Test Day if you have these definitions and operations down cold, freeing up your brain to focus on the more complex critical thinking tasks these difficult and often abstract questions require. This chapter will guide you through the basics and give you practice applying arithmetic concepts to GMAT questions ranging from the simple to the most advanced. First, let's dive into the questions you just considered.

What Mathematical Concepts Are Being Tested in This Question?

As is often the case with GMAT Quantitative questions, a couple of different yet related concepts are involved within this single question. Here, the question gives a range of possible values of x. So you're looking at inequalities, dealing with both positive and negative numbers. The question itself asks about absolute value, a different topic, but very much related to inequalities, as you'll see later in this chapter.

What Do You Notice About the Answer Choices?

Each answer choice contains one variable, x, which makes the question seem a little more straightforward. However, note that a few of the answer choices contain x^2, which introduces more complexity, in that you must understand the behavior of exponential expressions.

How Do the Math Concepts in the Question Relate to the Answer Choices?

Absolute value is the measure of a number's distance from zero on the number line. (Because 5 and -5 are the same distance from zero—5 units—both numbers have the same absolute value: 5.) When squaring a term, the result will always be non-negative. So even though the possible values of x are both positive and negative, certain answer choices will test your ability to recognize this property of terms raised to even exponents.

What Core Competencies Are Most Essential to Success on This Question?

Here, the test maker rewards those who understand how paying Attention to the Right Detail is important to answering the question correctly. Despite the basic nature of some of the math topics, the GMAT ultimately rewards test takers who not only know the rules but can apply them to answer questions most efficiently.

How Do I Apply the Kaplan Methods to GMAT Arithmetic?

Now let's apply the Kaplan Method for Problem Solving to the arithmetic question you saw earlier:

> If x is a number such that $-2 \leq x \leq 2$, which of the following has the largest possible absolute value?
>
> ○ $3x - 1$
>
> ○ $x^2 - x$
>
> ○ $3 - x$
>
> ○ $x - 3$
>
> ○ $x^2 + 1$

STEP 1: ANALYZE THE QUESTION

This is an abstract question for which the answer choices contain variables, so picking numbers will be an efficient strategy to use. Since you are asked to find the answer choice that yields the largest absolute value, you should pick numbers at the ends of the range of possible values for x. For each value of x you test, you will need to check all the answer choices in case some have the same value.

STEP 2: STATE THE TASK

Evaluate each answer choice, using both $x = 2$ or $x = -2$ (the values for x with the greatest possible absolute value), in order to determine which choice will produce the largest absolute value.

STEP 3: APPROACH STRATEGICALLY

You'll need to plug in those values of x, but first notice choices (C) and (D): $3 - x$ and $x - 3$ are negatives of each other, which means they have the same absolute value. Since the question asks for the choice that has the largest possible absolute value, you can eliminate both of these choices. Notice also that with choice (E), the absolute value will be the same if using 2 or -2, since squaring the x-term will give the same value.

Since the question tests absolute value, plug in -2 first for x in each of the remaining answer choices. Choice (A) gives $3(-2) - 1$, which equals -7. The absolute value of -7 is equal to 7. Choice (B) gives $(-2)^2 - (-2) = 4 - (-2) = 6$, which has an absolute value of 6. Choice (E) gives $(-2)^2 + 1 = 4 + 1 = 5$, which has an absolute value of 5. You already know that choice (E) will yield the same absolute value when $x = 2$, so eliminate choice (E); you already found that choices (A) and (B) give a larger possible absolute value.

Try $x = 2$ with the remaining two answer choices. In choice (A), $3(2) - 1 = 6 - 1 = 5$, and the absolute value of 5 is equal to 5. For choice (B), $(2)^2 - 2 = 4 - 2 = 2$, and the absolute value of 2 is equal to 2. The largest absolute value you found was for choice (A), when $x = -2$. Therefore, (A) is correct.

STEP 4: CONFIRM YOUR ANSWER

Confirm that your calculations are correct and that your answer makes sense.

Arithmetic Operations

> **LEARNING OBJECTIVES**
>
> In this section, you will learn how to:
>
> - Outline the order of operations
> - Explain how understanding the laws of operations will help you on the Quantitative section

Order of Operations

$$\mathbf{P} = \text{Parentheses}$$
$$\mathbf{E} = \text{Exponents}$$
$$\left.\begin{array}{l}\mathbf{M} = \text{Multiplication}\\ \mathbf{D} = \text{Division}\end{array}\right\} \text{ in order from left to right}$$
$$\left.\begin{array}{l}\mathbf{A} = \text{Addition}\\ \mathbf{S} = \text{Subtraction}\end{array}\right\} \text{ in order from left to right}$$

If an expression has parentheses within parentheses, work from the innermost out. This mnemonic will help you remember the order of operations: Please Excuse My Dear Aunt Sally (PEMDAS).

Example: $30 - 5 \times 4 + (7 - 3)^2 \div 8$

First, perform any operations within **parentheses**.	$30 - 5 \times 4 + 4^2 \div 8$
Next, raise to any powers indicated by **exponents**.	$30 - 5 \times 4 + 16 \div 8$
Then, do all **multiplication** and **division** in order from left to right.	$30 - 20 + 2$
Last, do all **addition** and **subtraction** in order from left to right.	$10 + 2$
Answer:	12

Laws of Operations

These laws will not be tested directly on the GMAT (you won't need to define what each law is). Focus rather on understanding how to manipulate numbers using the various laws listed below.

Commutative Law

It doesn't matter in what order the operation is performed. Addition and multiplication are both commutative, while division and subtraction are not commutative.

Example:
$$5 + 8 = 8 + 5$$
$$2 \times 6 = 6 \times 2$$
$$3 - 2 \neq 2 - 3$$
$$6 \div 2 \neq 2 \div 6$$

Associative Law

The terms can be regrouped without changing the result. Addition and multiplication are also associative, while division and subtraction are not.

Example: $(a+b)+c = a+(b+c)$ $\quad$ $(a \times b) \times c = a \times (b \times c)$

$$(3+5)+8 = 3+(5+8) \quad (4 \times 5) \times 6 = 4 \times (5 \times 8)$$

$$8+8 = 3+13 \qquad\qquad 20 \times 6 = 4 \times 30$$

$$16 = 16 \qquad\qquad\qquad 120 = 120$$

Distributive Law

The distributive law allows you to "distribute" a factor among the terms being added or subtracted. In general, $a(b+c) = ab + ac$.

Example: $4(3+7) = 4 \times 3 + 4 \times 7$

$$4 \times 10 = 12 + 28$$

$$40 = 40$$

Division can be distributed in a similar way.

Example: $\dfrac{4+6}{2} = \dfrac{4}{2} + \dfrac{6}{2}$

$$\dfrac{10}{2} = 2+3$$

$$5 = 5$$

However, when the sum or difference is in the **denominator**, no distribution is possible.

Example. $\dfrac{9}{4+5}$ is *not* equal to $\dfrac{9}{4} + \dfrac{9}{5}$.

Factoring

The technique called *factoring* uses the distributive law in its reverse form. You can factor to simplify some calculations.

Example: $11 + 22 + 33 + 44$

$$= (11 \times 1) + (11 \times 2) + (11 \times 3) + (11 \times 4)$$

$$= 11 \times (1+2+3+4)$$

$$= 11 \times 10$$

$$= 110$$

Fractions and Decimals

> **LEARNING OBJECTIVES**
>
> In this section, you will learn how to:
>
> - Perform operations with fractions, mixed numbers, and decimals
> - Convert between fractions and decimals
> - Predict whether fractions or decimals will be easier to work with in a given problem
> - Apply the Kaplan Methods for Problem Solving and Data Sufficiency to questions involving fractions and decimals

Fractions

4 ← numerator (also known as the *dividend*)

— ← fraction bar (means *divided by*)

5 ← denominator (also known as the *divisor*)

Equivalent Fractions

When you multiply the numerator and denominator by the same number (any number other than zero), the fraction is unchanged. You simply get an equivalent fraction.

Example: $\dfrac{1}{2} = \dfrac{1 \times 2}{2 \times 2} = \dfrac{2}{4}$

Similarly, dividing the top and bottom by the same nonzero number leaves the fraction unchanged.

Example: $\dfrac{5}{10} = \dfrac{5 \div 5}{10 \div 5} = \dfrac{1}{2}$

The GMAT often uses this technique to change the form of fractions that have radicals in the denominator.

Example: $\dfrac{9}{\sqrt{2}} = \dfrac{9 \times \sqrt{2}}{\sqrt{2} \times \sqrt{2}} = \dfrac{9\sqrt{2}}{2}$

Canceling and Reducing Fractions

Generally speaking, when you work with fractions on the GMAT, you'll need to put them in the **lowest terms**. That means that the numerator and the denominator are not divisible by any common integer greater than 1.

Example: The fraction $\dfrac{1}{2}$ is in lowest terms, but the fraction $\dfrac{3}{6}$ is not, since 3 and 6 are both divisible by 3.

The method you use to take a fraction and put it in lowest terms is called **reducing**. That simply means to factor and divide out any **common multiples** from both the numerator and denominator. This process is also commonly called **canceling**. Canceling is particularly useful to avoid time-consuming calculation.

Example: Reduce $\dfrac{15}{35}$ to lowest terms.

First, determine the largest common factor of the numerator and denominator. Then, divide the top and bottom by that number to reduce.

$$\frac{15}{35} = \frac{3 \times 5}{7 \times 5} = \frac{3 \times \cancel{5}}{7 \times \cancel{5}} = \frac{3}{7}$$

Adding and Subtracting Fractions

We can't add or subtract two fractions directly unless they have the same, or a *common*, denominator.

A common denominator is just a **common multiple** of the denominators of the fractions. The **least common denominator** (LCD) is the **least common multiple** (LCM): the smallest positive number that is a multiple of all the terms.

Example: $\frac{3}{5} + \frac{2}{3} - \frac{1}{2}$

Denominators are 5, 3, 2.

Least common denominator (LCD) = 30.

For each fraction, divide the LCD by the denominator.

$$30 \div 5 = 6$$
$$30 \div 3 = 10$$
$$30 \div 2 = 15$$

Then, multiply the numerator and denominator by that result.

Combine the numerators by adding or subtracting and keep the LCD as the denominator.

$$\left(\frac{3}{5} \times \frac{6}{6}\right) + \left(\frac{2}{3} \times \frac{10}{10}\right) - \left(\frac{1}{2} \times \frac{15}{15}\right)$$
$$= \frac{18}{30} + \frac{20}{30} - \frac{15}{30}$$
$$= \frac{18 + 20 - 15}{30} = \frac{23}{30}$$

Multiplying Fractions

To multiply fractions, simply multiply the numerators together and the denominators together. Often, this process can be sped up by canceling common factors before you multiply.

Example: $\frac{10}{9} \times \frac{3}{4} \times \frac{8}{15}$

First, reduce (cancel) diagonally and vertically.

$$\frac{^2 \cancel{10}}{_3 \cancel{9}} \times \frac{^1 \cancel{3}}{_1 \cancel{4}} \times \frac{\cancel{8}^2}{\cancel{15}_3}$$

In this case, divide both 10 in the numerator and 15 in the denominator by their common factor 5. Likewise, 3 in the numerator and 9 in the denominator can be reduced by factoring out a 3. Finally, 8 in the numerator and 4 in the denominator can be divided by the common factor 4.

Then multiply the numerators together and the denominators together.

$$\frac{2 \times 1 \times 2}{3 \times 1 \times 3} = \frac{4}{9}$$

Dividing Fractions

To divide one fraction by another, you actually multiply the first fraction by the **reciprocal** of the divisor (the second fraction).

To get the reciprocal of a fraction, invert it. Simply switch around the numerator and the denominator.

For example, the reciprocal of the fraction $\frac{3}{7}$ is $\frac{7}{3}$.

Example: $\frac{4}{3} \div \frac{4}{9}$

Invert the divisor, then multiply as usual.

$$\frac{4}{3} \div \frac{4}{9}$$

$$= \frac{4}{3} \times \frac{9}{4}$$

$$= \frac{{}^1\cancel{4}}{{}_1\cancel{3}} \times \frac{\cancel{9}^3}{\cancel{4}_1}$$

$$= \frac{1 \times 3}{1 \times 1} = \frac{3}{1}$$

$$= 3$$

Complex Fractions

A complex fraction is a fraction that contains one or more fractions in its numerator or denominator. There are two methods for simplifying complex fractions.

Method I: Use the distributive law. Find the least common multiple of all the denominators and multiply all the terms in the top and bottom of the complex fraction by the LCM. This will eliminate all the denominators, greatly simplifying the calculation.

Example:

$$\frac{\frac{7}{9} - \frac{1}{6}}{\frac{1}{3} + \frac{1}{2}}$$

The LCM of all the denominators is 18.

$$= \frac{18 \times \left(\frac{7}{9} - \frac{7}{6}\right)}{18 \times \left(\frac{1}{3} + \frac{1}{2}\right)}$$

$$= \frac{\frac{{}^2\cancel{18}}{1} \times \frac{7}{\cancel{9}_1} - \frac{{}^3\cancel{18}}{1} \times \frac{1}{\cancel{6}_1}}{\frac{{}^6\cancel{18}}{1} \times \frac{1}{\cancel{3}_1} + \frac{{}^9\cancel{18}}{1} \times \frac{1}{\cancel{2}_1}}$$

$$= \frac{2 \times 7 - 3 \times 1}{6 \times 1 + 9 \times 1}$$

$$= \frac{14 - 3}{6 + 9}$$

$$= \frac{11}{15}$$

Method II: Treat the numerator and denominator separately. Combine the terms in each to get a single fraction on top and a single fraction on bottom. You are left with the division of two fractions, which you perform by multiplying the top fraction by the reciprocal of the bottom one. This method is preferable when it is difficult to get an LCM for all of the denominators.

Example:

$$\cfrac{\dfrac{5}{11} - \dfrac{5}{22}}{\dfrac{7}{16} + \dfrac{3}{8}}$$

The LCM of the numerator is 22.

The LCM of the denominator is 16.

$$= \cfrac{\dfrac{10}{22} - \dfrac{5}{22}}{\dfrac{7}{16} + \dfrac{6}{16}} = \cfrac{\dfrac{5}{22}}{\dfrac{13}{16}} = \dfrac{5}{11 \,\cancel{22}} \times \dfrac{\cancel{16}^{8}}{13} = \dfrac{40}{143}$$

Comparing Positive Fractions

If the numerators are the same, the fraction with the smaller denominator will have the larger value, since the numerator is divided into a smaller number of parts.

Example: $\dfrac{4}{5} > \dfrac{4}{7}$

If the denominators are the same, the fraction with the larger numerator will have the larger value.

Example: $\dfrac{5}{8} > \dfrac{3}{8}$

If neither the numerators nor the denominators are the same, express all of the fractions in terms of some common denominator. The fraction with the largest numerator will be the largest.

One version of this method is to multiply the numerator of the left fraction by the denominator of the right fraction and vice versa (similar to cross multiplying). Then compare the products obtained this way. If the left product is greater, then the left fraction was greater to start with.

Example. Compare $\dfrac{5}{7}$ and $\dfrac{9}{11}$.

Compare 5×11 and 9×7.

Because $55 < 63$, $\dfrac{5}{7} < \dfrac{9}{11}$.

Example: Compare $\dfrac{22}{19}$ and $\dfrac{11}{9}$.

As before, the comparison can be made by cross multiplying.

Compare 22×9 and 11×19.

Because $198 < 209$, $\dfrac{22}{19} < \dfrac{11}{9}$.

You can also convert the fractions to percents or decimals for easy comparison. This technique is especially useful when finding a common denominator seems time-consuming.

Example: Compare $\dfrac{5}{8}$, $\dfrac{2}{3}$, and $\dfrac{7}{11}$.

$\dfrac{5}{8} = 0.625$, $\dfrac{2}{3} = 0.66666\ldots$, and $\dfrac{7}{11} = 0.636363\ldots$

Because $0.625 < 0.636363\ldots < 0.66666\ldots$, $\dfrac{5}{8} < \dfrac{7}{11} < \dfrac{2}{3}$.

Converting fractions to decimals or percents frequently comes up on the GMAT. Often, the problem gives you fractions in the question but percents in the answer choices. It's a good idea to memorize the common fraction-to-decimal equivalencies for Test Day.

Another way to compare fractions is to find a "benchmark value" against which the fractions can be compared, particularly when dealing with large numbers.

Example: Compare $\frac{13}{24}$ and $\frac{33}{68}$.

Both are very close to $\frac{1}{2}$.

$\frac{1}{2} = \frac{12}{24}$ and $\frac{1}{2} = \frac{34}{68}$.

Because $\frac{13}{24} > \frac{1}{2}$ and $\frac{33}{68} < \frac{1}{2}, \frac{13}{24} > \frac{33}{68}$.

Mixed Numbers

Fractions whose numerators are greater than their denominators may be converted into mixed numbers and vice versa. Mixed numbers consist of an integer and a fraction. For example, $3\frac{1}{4}$, $12\frac{2}{5}$, and $5\frac{7}{8}$ are all mixed numbers.

Example: Convert $\frac{23}{4}$ to a mixed number.

$$\frac{23}{4} = \frac{20}{4} + \frac{3}{4}$$
$$= 5\frac{3}{4}$$

Example: Convert $2\frac{3}{7}$ to a fraction.

$$2\frac{3}{7} = 2 + \frac{3}{7}$$
$$= \frac{14}{7} + \frac{3}{7}$$
$$= \frac{17}{7}$$

Decimals

Decimals can be converted to common fractions with a power of 10 in the denominator.

Example: $0.053 = \frac{53}{10^3} = \frac{53}{1,000}$

Numbers are made up of digits in specific places. The GMAT occasionally asks questions using the terms **digit** and **place**, so you should be familiar with the naming convention:

hundreds	tens	units	tenths	hundredths	thousandths
3	1	5	.2	4	6

When a GMAT question specifies that a variable is a digit, the only possible values are the integers between 0 and 9, inclusive.

Comparing Decimals

To compare decimals, add zeros after the last digit to the right of the decimal point until all the decimals have the same number of digits. Doing this will make all the denominators of the fractions the same. Therefore, comparing the numerators will determine the order of values.

Example: Arrange in order from smallest to largest: 0.7, 0.77, 0.07, 0.707, and 0.077.

$$0.7 = 0.700 = \frac{700}{1,000}$$

$$0.77 = 0.770 = \frac{770}{1,000}$$

$$0.07 = 0.070 = \frac{70}{1,000}$$

$$0.707 = 0.707 = \frac{707}{1,000}$$

$$0.077 = 0.077 = \frac{77}{1,000}$$

Because $70 < 77 < 700 < 707 < 770$, $0.07 < 0.077 < 0.7 < 0.707 < 0.77$.

Adding and Subtracting Decimals

When adding or subtracting decimals, make sure that the decimal points are lined up, one under the other. This will ensure that the corresponding places are added: that is, tenths are added to tenths, hundredths to hundredths, etc.

Example: $0.5 + 0.05 + 0.005 =$

0.5	(1 decimal place)
0.05	(2 decimal places)
+ 0.005	+ (3 decimal places)
0.555	(3 decimal places)

Multiplying and Dividing Decimals

To multiply two decimals, initially multiply them as you would integers and ignore the decimal places. The number of decimal places in the product will be the sum of the number of decimal places in the factors that are multiplied together.

Example: $0.675 \times 0.42 =$

0.675	(3 decimal places)
$\times 0.42$	+ (2 decimal places)
1350	
+ 27000	
0.28350	(5 decimal places)

Division—Method I: When dividing a decimal by another decimal, multiply each by a power of 10 such that the divisor becomes an integer; that is, move the decimal point of each the same number of places. (This doesn't change the value of the quotient.) Then carry out the division as you would with integers, placing the decimal point in the quotient directly above the decimal point in the dividend.

Example: $0.675 \div 0.25 =$ Move the decimal point over two places to the right to make 0.25 an integer.

$67.5 \div 25 =$

$$\begin{array}{r} 2.7 \\ 25\overline{)67.5} \\ -50 \\ \hline 175 \\ -175 \\ \hline 0 \end{array}$$

Division—Method II: Turn the division problem into a fraction. It is best when the numbers have common factors. Move the decimal point in the numerator and the denominator an equivalent number of places to make both numbers integers. Then cancel common factors.

Example: $0.675 \div 0.25$

$$\frac{0.675}{0.25}$$

$$\frac{675}{250}$$

$$\frac{\overset{135}{\cancel{675}}}{\underset{50}{\cancel{250}}} = \frac{\overset{27}{\cancel{135}}}{\underset{10}{\cancel{50}}} = \frac{27}{10} = 2.7$$

In-Format Question: Fractions and Decimals on the GMAT

Now let's use the Kaplan Method on a Problem Solving question dealing with fractions:

$$\frac{1}{3} + \left(\frac{2}{3}\right)^2 =$$

- ○ $\frac{5}{12}$
- ○ $\frac{17}{27}$
- ○ $\frac{7}{9}$
- ○ 1
- ○ $\frac{5}{3}$

STEP 1: ANALYZE THE QUESTION

You're given an expression with two fractions, one of which is raised to an exponent. Attention to the Right Detail is important here; in this case, note the use of the parentheses around only one of the fractions.

STEP 2: STATE THE TASK

Follow the order of operations (PEMDAS); start with the parentheses, then add the fractions by finding a common denominator.

STEP 3: APPROACH STRATEGICALLY

First, square both the numerator and denominator of $\frac{2}{3}$, giving a value of $\frac{4}{9}$. Then find a common denominator for the two fractions $\frac{1}{3}$ and $\frac{4}{9}$. Multiply the numerator and denominator of $\frac{1}{3}$ by 3, which yields $\frac{3}{9}$. Now that the denominators are the same, you can add the two fractions $\frac{3}{9} + \frac{4}{9}$, which gives you the answer, $\frac{7}{9}$, choice **(C)**.

STEP 4: CONFIRM YOUR ANSWER

Take a moment to verify your math, particularly making sure you followed the order of operations and accurately converted fractions into forms that have a common denominator. Note that **(D)** would be a tempting wrong answer if you had first added the two fractions and then squared the result.

TAKEAWAYS: FRACTIONS AND DECIMALS

- When adding or subtracting fractions, you must have a common denominator.

- $\frac{a}{b} \times \frac{c}{d} = \frac{ac}{bd}$

- $\dfrac{\left(\dfrac{a}{b}\right)}{\left(\dfrac{c}{d}\right)} = \frac{a}{b} \times \frac{d}{c} = \frac{ad}{bc}$

- Knowing common fraction-to-decimal equivalencies will help save you time on Test Day.

Practice Set: Fractions and Decimals on the GMAT

1. If x and y are positive numbers, is $\dfrac{x^2}{y} > \dfrac{x}{y^2}$?

    (1) $\dfrac{x}{y} > 1$

    (2) $xy > 1$

2. If a and b are positive numbers, is $8a < 3b$?

    (1) $\dfrac{a}{b} < 0.374$

    (2) $b > 2.671a$

3. The equation $\dfrac{5a}{2b} + \dfrac{10}{3} = 5$ is equivalent to each of the following EXCEPT:

    ○ $3a = 2b$

    ○ $5a - 2b = \dfrac{4b}{3}$

    ○ $\dfrac{5a}{2b} + 1 = \dfrac{8}{3}$

    ○ $3a + 2b - 1 = 2a + 3b$

    ○ $\dfrac{a}{2b} = \dfrac{1}{3}$

Exponents

LEARNING OBJECTIVES

In this section, you will learn how to:

- Manipulate expressions and perform operations using exponent rules
- Correctly describe the parts of an exponent term using the terms *coefficient*, *base*, and *exponent*
- Apply the Kaplan Methods for Problem Solving and Data Sufficiency to questions with exponents

Rules of Operations with Exponents

In the term $3x^2$, 3 is the **coefficient**, x is the **base**, and 2 is the **exponent**. The exponent refers to the number of times the base is multiplied by itself. For instance, in 4^3, you multiply 4 by itself 3 times: $4^3 = 4 \times 4 \times 4 = 64$.

Accurately distinguishing among these elements is important. For instance, in the expression $3x^2$, only the x is being squared (x is the base), not the 3 (3 is the coefficient). In other words, $3x^2 = 3(x^2)$. If you wanted to square the 3 as well, you would need to rewrite the term as $(3x)^2$ to make 3 part of the base. Remember that in the order of operations, you raise to a power *before* you multiply, so in $3x^2$, you square x and *then* multiply by 3.

A number multiplied by itself is called the **square** of that number (e.g., 5×5 or 5^2 is 5 squared).

A number multiplied by itself two times is called the **cube** of that number (e.g., $4 \times 4 \times 4$ is 4^3 or 4 cubed)

To multiply two terms with the same base, keep the base and add the exponents.

Example:

$$2^2 \times 2^3 = 2^{2+3}$$
$$= 2^5$$

To divide two terms with the same base, keep the base and subtract the exponent of the denominator from the exponent of the numerator.

Example:

$$\frac{4^4}{4^2} = 4^{4-2}$$
$$= 4^2$$

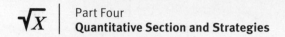

To raise a power to another power, multiply the exponents.

Example:

$$\left(3^2\right)^4 = 3^{2 \times 4}$$
$$= 3^8$$

To multiply two terms with the same exponent but different bases, multiply the bases together and keep the exponent.

Example:

$$\left(2^3\right)\left(3^3\right) = (2 \times 3)^3$$
$$= 6^3$$

Any number raised to the first power equals itself: $a^1 = a$.

Any number except zero that is raised to the zero power is equal to 1: $a^0 = 1$. The exception to this rule is when the base is also equal to zero (0^0 is undefined).

A negative exponent indicates a reciprocal. To arrive at an equivalent expression, take the reciprocal of the base and change the sign of the exponent.

$$a^{-n} = \frac{1}{a^n} \text{ or } \left(\frac{1}{a}\right)^n$$

Example: $2^{-3} = \frac{1}{2^3} = \frac{1}{8}$

When raising a fraction to an exponent, you can solve in one of two ways: either by raising the numerator and the denominator to the exponent separately, or by multiplying the whole fraction by itself the number of times indicated by the exponent. Either approach yields the same result.

Example: $\left(\frac{2}{3}\right)^2 = \frac{2^2}{3^2} = \frac{4}{9}$

$\left(\frac{2}{3}\right)^2 = \frac{2}{3} \times \frac{2}{3} = \frac{2 \times 2}{3 \times 3} = \frac{4}{9}$

Note that the squared value here, $\frac{4}{9}$, is less than the base, $\frac{2}{3}$. Raising a positive fraction less than 1 to a positive exponent greater than 1 results in a smaller value. The higher the exponent, the smaller the result.

Bases of 10

The exponent of a base of 10 tells you how many zeros the number would contain if written out.

Example: $10^6 = 1,000,000$ (6 zeros), since 10 multiplied by itself 6 times is equal to 1,000,000.

When multiplying a number by a power of 10, move the decimal point to the right the same number of places as in the exponent; that is, the number of zeros in that power of 10.

When dividing by a power of 10, move the decimal point the corresponding number of places to the left. (Note that dividing by 10^4 is the same as multiplying by 10^{-4}.)

In-Format Question: Exponents on the GMAT

Now let's use the Kaplan Method on a Data Sufficiency question dealing with exponents:

Does $a = b$?

(1) $a^2 - b^2 = 0$

(2) $1 - \dfrac{a^3}{b^3} = 0$

STEP 1: ANALYZE THE QUESTION STEM

This is a Yes/No question. You need to determine whether there is enough information to answer the question "Does $a = b$?" There is no information provided in the question stem, so look at the statements.

STEP 2: EVALUATE THE STATEMENTS USING 12TEN

Statement (1) says that $a^2 - b^2 = 0$, which is the same as saying $a^2 = b^2$. Now if $a^2 = b^2$, then either $a = b$ or $a = -b$. You can test a few cases by picking numbers. If $a = 5$ and $b = 5$, then $a^2 = b^2$, so Statement (1) is true and $a = b$. The answer to the question is yes.

If $a = 5$ and $b = -5$, then $a^2 = b^2$ because $5^2 = (-5)^2 = 25$, so Statement (1) is true and a is not equal to b. The answer to the question is no. Because more than one answer to the question is possible, Statement (1) is insufficient. You can eliminate **(A)** and **(D)**.

Statement (2) tells you that $1 - \dfrac{a^3}{b^3} = 0$, which can be simplified as $1 - \dfrac{a^3}{b^3} = 0$, or $a^3 = b^3$. In the equation $a^3 = b^3$, both a and b are raised to the same odd exponent. Remembering the rules governing exponents, you know that when raised to an odd power, positive numbers yield positive results and negative numbers yield negative results. So if $a^3 = b^3$, you can now conclude that $a = b$. The answer to the question is always yes, and Statement (2) is sufficient. The correct answer is **(B)**.

If you weren't sure about the rules of exponents, you could use picking numbers to evaluate Statement (2). In order for a^3 to equal b^3, a and b must have the same value. For instance, if $a = -5$ and $b = -5$, then $a^3 = b^3$ because $(-5)^3 = (-5)^3 = -125$. You cannot pick numbers such as $a = 5$ and $b = -5$, since $5^3 = 125 \neq (-5)^3 = -125$. Since it's impossible to pick different numbers for a and b, the answer to the question is always yes, and you can choose **(B)**.

Note how the Core Competency of Attention to the Right Detail plays a big role in answering the question correctly. It's easy to be misled into thinking that if $a^2 = b^2$, then a must be equal to b. Pay attention to whether exponents are even or odd when confronted with a similar problem.

TAKEAWAYS: EXPONENTS

- Exponents count the number of times something is multiplied by itself.
- $a^b \times a^c = a^{b+c}$
- $\dfrac{a^b}{a^c} = a^{b-c}$
- $\left(a^b\right)^c = a^{b \times c}$
- $\left(a^b\right)\left(c^b\right) = (a \times c)^b$
- $a^{-b} = \dfrac{1}{a^b}$
- Raising a positive fraction less than 1 to a positive exponent greater than 1 results in a smaller value. The higher the exponent, the smaller the result.
- When a negative number is raised to an even exponent, the result is positive. When a negative number is raised to an odd exponent, the result is negative.
- When multiplying a number by a power of 10, the exponent just represents the number of places to move the decimal.

Practice Set: Exponents on the GMAT

4. At Car Part Corporation, there is a machine that produces brake pads. As the machine works, a wheel assembly turns. After the wheel assembly turns 4.09×10^6 times, the machine needs maintenance. Since being installed, the machine has received maintenance 30 times. Approximately how many total turns had the wheel assembly made when the machine last received maintenance?

   ○ 1.3×10^5

   ○ 1.2×10^7

   ○ 1.2×10^8

   ○ 4.1×10^7

   ○ 7.0×10^8

5. If $\dfrac{2^{5x}}{8^{2x-2}} = 8$, what is the value of x?

   ○ 1

   ○ 2

   ○ 3

   ○ 4

   ○ 5

6. If x is a positive integer, then $9^x + 3^{2x+1} =$

   ○ $3(3^{2x+1})$

   ○ 3^{4x-1}

   ○ 3^{4x+1}

   ○ $4(3^{2x})$

   ○ 12^{2x}

Radicals

Fractions as Exponents

A fractional exponent indicates a root. So $(a)^{\frac{1}{n}} = \sqrt[n]{a}$ (read "the nth root of a"). If no specific n is present, the radical sign means a square root. If the numerator in the fractional exponent is a different integer, raise the resulting term to that exponent.

Example: $\qquad 8^{\frac{1}{3}} = \sqrt[3]{8} = 2$

Example: $\qquad 8^{\frac{2}{3}} = \left(\sqrt[3]{8}\right)^2 = 2^2 = 4$

Rules of Operations with Radical Symbols

By convention, the symbol $\sqrt{}$ (called *radical*) means the *positive* square root only. Even though there are two different numbers whose square is 9 (both 3 and -3), when you see $\sqrt{9}$ on the GMAT, it refers to the positive number 3 only.

Example: $\qquad \sqrt{9} = +3; \ -\sqrt{9} = -3$

When it comes to the four basic arithmetic operations, you treat radicals in much the same way you would treat variables.

Addition and Subtraction

Only like radicals can be added to or subtracted from one another.

Example: $\qquad 2\sqrt{3} + 4\sqrt{2} - \sqrt{2} - 3\sqrt{3} = \left(4\sqrt{2} - \sqrt{2}\right) + \left(2\sqrt{3} - 3\sqrt{3}\right)$ [Note: $\sqrt{2} = 1\sqrt{2}$]

$$= 3\sqrt{2} + \left(-\sqrt{3}\right)$$

$$= 3\sqrt{2} - \sqrt{3}$$

Multiplication and Division

To multiply or divide one radical by another, multiply or divide the numbers outside the radical signs, then the numbers inside the radical signs.

Example: $\qquad \left(6\sqrt{3}\right) \times \left(2\sqrt{5}\right) = (6 \times 2) \times \left(\sqrt{3} \times \sqrt{5}\right) = 12\sqrt{3 \times 5} = 12\sqrt{15}$

Example: $\qquad 12\sqrt{15} \div 2\sqrt{5} = (12 \div 2) \times \left(\sqrt{15} \div \sqrt{5}\right) = 6\sqrt{\frac{15}{5}} = 6\sqrt{3}$

Example: $\qquad \dfrac{4\sqrt{18}}{2\sqrt{6}} = \left(\dfrac{4}{2}\right)\left(\dfrac{\sqrt{18}}{\sqrt{6}}\right) = 2\sqrt{\dfrac{18}{6}} = 2\sqrt{3}$

If the number inside the radical is a multiple of a perfect square, the expression can be simplified by factoring out the perfect square.

Example: $$\sqrt{72} = \sqrt{36 \times 2} = \sqrt{36} \times \sqrt{2} = 6\sqrt{2}$$

Warning: You *cannot* "split up" addition underneath a radical sign, although the GMAT will try to trick you into thinking you can.

Example:
$$\sqrt{100} = 10$$
$$\sqrt{100} = \sqrt{36 + 64}$$
$$\sqrt{100} \ne \sqrt{36} + \sqrt{64}$$
$$\sqrt{100} \ne 6 + 8$$
$$\sqrt{100} \ne 14$$

Exponents and Powers of 10 with Radicals

If an exponent is under the square root sign, just divide the exponent by 2. If an exponent is under a cube root sign, divide it by 3.

Example:
$$\sqrt{13^4} = 13^2$$
$$\sqrt[3]{7^6} = 7^2$$

If a decimal is under a square root sign, take the square root of the number and divide the number of decimal places by 2. Likewise, if a decimal is under a cube root sign, take the cube root of the number and divide the number of decimal places by 3.

Example:
$$\sqrt{0.0009} = 0.03$$
$$\sqrt[3]{0.000125} = 0.05$$

In-Format Question: Radicals on the GMAT

Now let's use the Kaplan Method on a Problem Solving question dealing with radicals:

$$\left(\sqrt{3} + \sqrt{7}\right)\left(\sqrt{3} - \sqrt{7}\right) =$$

○ $-7 - 2\sqrt{3}$

○ -4

○ 3

○ $2\sqrt{7} + 3$

○ $7 + 2\sqrt{3}$

STEP 1: ANALYZE THE QUESTION

You have to multiply two expressions with square roots in the terms. Note that the numbers under the radical signs are the same; this may be a signal to look at the question more strategically.

STEP 2: STATE THE TASK

To begin, recall that $\sqrt{a} + \sqrt{b}$ does *not* equal $\sqrt{a+b}$. Also, $\sqrt{a} - \sqrt{b}$ does not equal $\sqrt{a-b}$. Thus, in this question, you cannot combine the radicals inside the parentheses; instead, you need to multiply the expressions $\sqrt{3} + \sqrt{7}$ and $\sqrt{3} - \sqrt{7}$ using FOIL.

STEP 3: APPROACH STRATEGICALLY

If you've memorized the classic quadratic equations, you might recognize the expression in the stem as the factors of the difference of two squares. Recognizing this pattern will save you time, since you can avoid going through the entire process of applying FOIL.

Remember that $(a + b)(a - b) = a^2 - b^2$.

Substitute $\sqrt{3}$ for a, and $\sqrt{7}$ for b. Then you have $\sqrt{3}^2 - \sqrt{7}^2$, or $3 - 7$, which equals -4.

If you hadn't noticed the shortcut, you could have applied FOIL:

$$\left(\sqrt{3} + \sqrt{7}\right)\left(\sqrt{3} - \sqrt{7}\right) = \left(\sqrt{3}\right)\left(\sqrt{3}\right) - \left(\sqrt{3}\right)\left(\sqrt{7}\right) + \left(\sqrt{7}\right)\left(\sqrt{3}\right) - \left(\sqrt{7}\right)\left(\sqrt{7}\right)$$

Now, $\left(\sqrt{3}\right)\left(\sqrt{3}\right) = 3$ and $\left(\sqrt{7}\right)\left(\sqrt{7}\right) = 7$, so you are left with $3 - 0 - 7 = -4$.

Either way, **(B)** is correct.

STEP 4: CONFIRM YOUR ANSWER

Quickly double-check the last calculation step, and you're done.

TAKEAWAYS: RADICALS

- Radicals follow the same rules as exponents.
- $\sqrt{ab} = \sqrt{a} \times \sqrt{b}$
- $\sqrt{\dfrac{a}{b}} = \dfrac{\sqrt{a}}{\sqrt{b}}$
- $\sqrt{a+b} \neq \sqrt{a} + \sqrt{b}$
- $\sqrt{a-b} \neq \sqrt{a} - \sqrt{b}$
- $\left(\sqrt{a}\right)^2 = a$
- $\sqrt{a^2} = |a|$
- $a^{\frac{1}{2}} = \sqrt{a}$
- $a^{\frac{b}{c}} = \left(\sqrt[c]{a}\right)^b$

Practice Set: Radicals on the GMAT

7. If a positive number A is equal to 3^x and A, when squared, is equal to the cube root of 27 raised to the fourth power, what is the value of x?

    ○   81
    ○   27
    ○   9
    ○   2
    ○   1

8   If $r > 0$, is $\sqrt{r}$ an integer?

    (3) r^2 is an integer.

    (4) $r = m^2$, where m is an integer.

9. $\sqrt{36 - \dfrac{3 \times 23}{4}} =$

    ○ $6 - \dfrac{\sqrt{69}}{2}$

    ○ $\dfrac{3\sqrt{5}}{2}$

    ○ $\dfrac{5\sqrt{3}}{2}$

    ○ $12 - \dfrac{\sqrt{69}}{2}$

    ○ $\dfrac{25\sqrt{3}}{4}$

Absolute Value

The **absolute value** of a number is the number's distance from zero on the number line. It is denoted by two vertical lines. Since absolute value is a distance, it is always non-negative. For instance, both $+3$ and -3 are 3 units from zero, so their absolute values are both 3.

Example: $|-3| = 3$

$\qquad\qquad |+3| = 3$

The GMAT will increase the difficulty of an absolute value question (and therefore the benefit of getting it right) by using variables.

Example: $|z| = 3$

You don't know what z equals. Since z is 3 units from 0, you can deduce that it either equals $+3$ or -3.

So you can rewrite this one equation as two:

$$z = 3 \text{ OR } z = -3$$

Another way to conceptualize this is as follows:

$$|z| = 3$$

$$\pm z = 3$$

$$+z = 3 \text{ OR } -z = 3$$

$$z = 3 \text{ OR } z = -3$$

These problems are fairly straightforward when only one number is involved. But what about expressions? Treat the absolute value bars as parentheses and figure out the value of what's inside *before* you perform the operation. Needless to say, the GMAT will base wrong answers on performing these operations in the wrong order.

INCORRECT: $|-3| + |5| = |-3 + 5| = |2| = 2$

CORRECT: $|-3| + |5| = 3 + 5 = 8$

Now, let's look at what happens when you are given expressions with variables.

Example: $|x - 3| = 3$

Believe it or not, this isn't any different from the earlier example:

$$|z| = 3$$

$$z = 3 \text{ OR } z = -3$$

Think of it this way:

$$|{<}{<}chunk{>}{>}| = 3$$

$${<}{<}chunk{>}{>} = 3 \text{ OR } {<}{<}chunk{>}{>} = -3$$

Since the $<<chunk>>$ here is $x - 3$, that gives you the following:

$$|x - 3| = 3$$

$$x - 3 = 3 \text{ OR } x - 3 = -3$$

$$x = 6 \text{ OR } x = 0$$

The GMAT sometimes adds another layer of complexity to absolute value questions by including inequalities. The key is to remember that when considering the possible negative value, the inequality sign changes direction:

$$|x - z| > 3$$

$$x - z > 3 \text{ OR } x - z < -3$$

Don't worry if that concept seems a little strange to you right now. We'll explore this idea further when we discuss inequalities later in this chapter.

In-Format Question: Absolute Value on the GMAT

Now let's use the Kaplan Method on a Problem Solving question dealing with absolute value:

How many possible integer values are there for x, if $|4x - 3| < 6$?

- O One
- O Two
- O Three
- O Four
- O Five

STEP 1: ANALYZE THE QUESTION

You're asked for the number of integers that could satisfy an inequality. The inequality includes an expression with an absolute value.

STEP 2: STATE THE TASK

You'll have to evaluate the inequality, find the range of x on the number line, and then count the number of integers that could be acceptable values of x. Remember that the correct answer is not any particular value of x but the number of possible integer values.

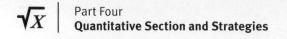

STEP 3: APPROACH STRATEGICALLY

Since you have an absolute value in an expression, you have to consider two possibilities: either $4x - 3 < 6$ or $-(4x - 3) < 6$. Multiply both sides of the second inequality by -1, remembering to reverse the inequality sign: the second inequality can be written as $4x - 3 > -6$. Combine these two statements to analyze the expression more quickly: $-6 < 4x - 3 < 6$. Adding 3 to each of the three members, you have $-3 < 4x < 9$. Dividing each of the three members by 4 gives you $-\frac{3}{4} < x < \frac{9}{4}$. The possible integer values of x such that $-\frac{3}{4} < x < \frac{9}{4}$ are 0, 1, and 2. There are three such values, and **(C)** is correct.

STEP 4: CONFIRM YOUR ANSWER

Confirm that your calculations are correct. Quickly sketch the range of x on a number line to confirm your count of the number of possible integer values of x.

TAKEAWAYS: ABSOLUTE VALUE

- Use these three tools to solve absolute value problems:
  1. Interpret absolute value as the expression's distance from zero on the number line.
  2. Draw a number line.
  3. Write two equations for every equation with an absolute value; one or the other of these new equations must be true.
- When there is an absolute value sign, there is a high likelihood of a trap answer for those who assume the quantity inside can only be positive.

Practice Set: Absolute Value on the GMAT

10. Which of the following could be the value of x, if $|12 - 4x| + 2 = 6$?

    ○ -4

    ○ -2

    ○ 1

    ○ 3

    ○ 4

11. If x and y are integers and $z = |x - 2| - |y + 2|$, does $z = 0$?

    (1) $\dfrac{9}{5} < x < \dfrac{7}{2}$ and $-3 \leq y < -\dfrac{21}{11}$

    (2) $2 \leq x < \dfrac{7}{3}$ and $-\dfrac{22}{7} < y < -\dfrac{13}{7}$

12. If $\left|\dfrac{7 - 3j}{2}\right| \leq 4$, then which of the following must be true?

    ○ $j \leq -\dfrac{1}{3}$

    ○ $j \leq \dfrac{3}{7}$

    ○ $j \leq 5$

    ○ $j \geq -\dfrac{3}{7}$

    ○ $j \geq 5$

Inequalities

LEARNING OBJECTIVES

In this section, you will learn how to:

- Properly interpret the meaning of inequality symbols and use a number line to plot ranges
- Solve inequalities, including three-part inequalities
- Apply the Kaplan Methods for Problem Solving and Data Sufficiency to questions dealing with inequalities

---

Inequality Symbols

$>$ greater than

$<$ less than

$\geq$ greater than or equal to

$\leq$ less than or equal to

Example: $x > 4$ means x is greater than 4.

Example: $x < 0$ means x is less than zero (x is a negative number).

Example: $x \geq -2$ means x can be -2 or any number greater than -2.

Example: $x \leq \frac{1}{2}$ means x can be $\frac{1}{2}$ or any number less than $\frac{1}{2}$.

A range of values is often expressed on a number line. Two ranges are shown below.

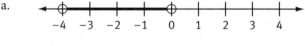

(a) represents the set of all numbers between -4 and 0, excluding the endpoints -4 and 0, or $-4 < x < 0$.

(b) represents the set of all numbers greater than -1, up to and *including* 3, or $-1 < x \leq 3$.

Sketching a number line is a great way to help yourself to visualize inequalities on Test Day.

Solving Inequalities

To solve inequalities, you use the same methods as used in solving equations with one exception: if the inequality is multiplied or divided by a negative number, the direction of the inequality is reversed.

If the inequality $-3x < 2$ is multiplied by -1, the resulting inequality is $3x > -2$.

Example: Solve for x and represent the solution set on a number line: $3 - \frac{x}{4} \geq 2$

1. Multiply both sides by 4.

2. Subtract 12 from both sides.

3. Divide both sides by -1 and change the direction of the sign.

$$12 - x \geq 8$$

$$-x \geq -4$$

$$x \leq 4$$

Note that the solution set to an inequality is not a single value but a range of possible values. Here, the values include 4 and all numbers less than 4.

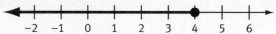

Example: Describe the possible values for x if $|2x - 5| < 3$.

With an absolute value, you must split the inequality into two: one with a positive number and one with a negative number. But you *must reverse the direction of the inequality sign in the negative case*:

$$|2x - 5| < 3$$

$2x - 5 < 3$	AND	$2x - 5 > -3$
$2x < 8$	AND	$2x > 2$
$x < 4$	AND	$x > 1$
	$1 < x < 4$	

You also need to watch out for this possibility when multiplying or dividing by variables.

Example: Simplify $3b < 2b^2$.

$$3b < 2b^2$$

Divide both sides by b: Before you can do so, you must know whether b is negative.

Write down both possibilities:

if b is neg.	OR	if b is pos.
$3 > 2b$	OR	$3 < 2b$

Divide by 2:

$$\frac{3}{2} > b \quad \text{OR} \quad \frac{3}{2} < b$$

All negative numbers are less than $\frac{3}{2}$, so b could equal any negative number at all or any positive number greater than $\frac{3}{2}$.

$$b < 0 \quad \text{OR} \quad \frac{3}{2} < b$$

Three-Part Inequalities

If you are given a three-part inequality, you can still perform calculations on it. But instead of saying, "What I do to one side, I must also do to the other," you say, "What I do to one part, I must do to *all* parts."

Example: Simplify $-11 < 2x - 5 < 1$.

$$-11 < 2x - 5 < 1$$

Add 5 to all parts:	$-11 + 5 < 2x - 5 + 5 < 1 + 5$
Combine like terms:	$-6 < 2x < 6$
Divide all parts by 2:	$-3 < x < 3$

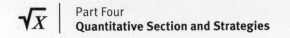

In-Format Question: Inequalities on the GMAT

Now let's use the Kaplan Method to solve a Problem Solving question dealing with inequalities:

> If $x > 4$ and $3x - 2y = 0$, then which of the following must be true?
>
> ○ $y < -6$
> ○ $y < -4$
> ○ $y = 6$
> ○ $y < 6$
> ○ $y > 6$

STEP 1: ANALYZE THE QUESTION

You're given an equation with two variables and an inequality giving you a range of values for one of the variables. Using this information, and scanning the answer choices, you need to determine what will always be true of y for the equation and the inequality to be true.

STEP 2: STATE THE TASK

Solve the equation for x in terms of y, then substitute the resulting expression for x into the inequality. Finally, evaluate the answer choices and determine which must be true.

STEP 3: APPROACH STRATEGICALLY

You should start by solving the equation for x as follows:

$$3x - 2y = 0$$
$$3x = 2y$$
$$x = \frac{2}{3}y$$

Because you know that $x > 4$, you can replace x with the value of the equation, so $\frac{2}{3}y > 4$. You can plow through with the calculations here, but by applying Critical Thinking, you can actually get the right answer now. Since multiplying y by a proper fraction must be larger than 4, then y itself must be larger than 4 as well. Since there's no other limitation, find the answer choice that gives you a range of results that are all larger than 4. The only choice that does that is choice (**E**).

STEP 4: CONFIRM YOUR ANSWER

You can confirm your answer using traditional math: multiply both sides of the inequality $\frac{2}{3}y > 4$ by 3.

So $2y > 12$. Next, divide both sides of this inequality by 2, which leads to the conclusion that $y > 6$. Answer choice (**E**) is correct.

TAKEAWAYS: INEQUALITIES

Inequalities should be treated exactly as equations, with two exceptions:

1. When you multiply or divide an inequality by a negative number, you must reverse the direction of the inequality sign.

2. Single-variable equations are usually solved for a specific value, whereas inequalities can only be solved for a range of values.

Practice Set: Inequalities on the GMAT

13. Is $a > 5$?

    (1) $8a \geq 40$

    (2) $4a + 6 \leq 25$

14. How many integers n are there such that $-145 < -\left|-n^2\right| < -120$?

    ○   0

    ○   2

    ○   4

    ○   11

    ○   12

15. If $\dfrac{a - b}{c} > 0$, is $c < 0$?

    (1) $a^2 < b^2$

    (2) $\dfrac{b}{c} < \dfrac{a}{c}$

Answers and explanations follow on the next page. ▶ ▶ ▶

Answer Key

Practice Set: Fractions and Decimals on the GMAT

1. B
2. D
3. D

Practice Set: Exponents on the GMAT

4. C
5. C
6. D

Practice Set: Radicals on the GMAT

7. D
8. B
9. C

Practice Set: Absolute Value on the GMAT

10. E
11. E
12. C

Practice Set: Inequalities on the GMAT

13. B
14. C
15. E

Answers and Explanations

Practice Set: Fractions and Decimals on the GMAT

1. **(B)**

   If x and y are positive numbers, is $\dfrac{x^2}{y} > \dfrac{x}{y^2}$?

   (1) $\dfrac{x}{y} > 1$

   (2) $xy > 1$

STEP 1: ANALYZE THE QUESTION STEM

This is a Yes/No question. It is given that x and y are positive, so each side of the inequality can be multiplied or divided by x or y without having to flip the sign. The fractions can be eliminated by multiplying both sides by y^2:

$$\frac{x^2}{y}\left(y^2\right) > \frac{x}{y^2}\left(y^2\right)$$

$$x^2 y > x$$

This can then be simplified further by dividing both sides by x:

$$\frac{x^2 y}{x} > \frac{x}{x}$$

$$xy > 1$$

Simplified this way, the question can be interpreted as asking whether the product of x and y is greater than 1.

STEP 2: EVALUATE THE STATEMENTS USING 12TEN

Statement (1) indicates that x divided by y is greater than 1. As y is positive, you can multiply both sides of this statement by y to get rid of the fraction:

$$\frac{x}{y}(y) > 1(y)$$

$$x > y$$

However, knowing that that x is greater than y does nothing to confirm whether their product is greater than 1. It's possible that x is 2 and y is 1, resulting in a product of 2. However, it's also possible that x is 2 and y is 0.1, resulting in a product of 0.2. The product can be greater than or less than 1, making this statement insufficient. Eliminate **(A)** and **(D)**.

Statement (2) directly confirms that the product of x and y is indeed greater than 1. Thus, this is sufficient. Eliminate **(C)** and **(E)**.

There is no need to combine the statements. The second statement is sufficient by itself, but not the first statement. The correct answer is **(B)**.

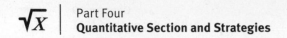

2.　(D)

If a and b are positive numbers, is $8a < 3b$?

(1)　$\dfrac{a}{b} < 0.374$

(2)　$b > 2.671a$

STEP 1: ANALYZE THE QUESTION STEM

This is a Yes/No question. Because a and b are positive, both sides of the inequality can be multiplied or divided by either variable without having to switch the sign. Because the inequality can be rearranged in several ways, take a look ahead at the statements to determine what approach will be most useful. As each statement provides a different arrangement of the variables, it will be better to rearrange the given inequality twice, each time mimicking the arrangement in the statement being tested.

STEP 2: EVALUATE THE STATEMENTS USING 12TEN

Statement (1) provides information about the fraction $\dfrac{a}{b}$, so manipulate the inequality in the question stem to get the same fraction for easier comparison. Start by dividing both sides by b:

$$\frac{8a}{b} < \frac{3b}{b}$$

$$\frac{8a}{b} < 3$$

Then divide both sides by 8:

$$\frac{8a}{b(8)} < \frac{3}{8}$$

$$\frac{a}{b} < \frac{3}{8}$$

As a decimal, $\dfrac{3}{8} = 0.375$. So the question is asking whether $\dfrac{a}{b}$ is less than 0.375. If $\dfrac{a}{b}$ is less than 0.374, as Statement (1) indicates, then it must also be less than 0.375. That makes Statement (1) sufficient. Eliminate **(B)**, **(C)**, and **(E)**.

Statement (2) provides an inequality about b. Again, manipulate the inequality in the question stem to get b by itself for easier comparison. Divide both sides by 3 and translate the resulting fraction into a decimal:

$$\frac{8a}{3} < \frac{3b}{3}$$

$$2\frac{2}{3}(a) < b$$

$$2.\overline{6}a < b$$

So the question is asking whether b is greater than $2.\overline{6}a$. If b is greater than $2.671a$, as Statement (2) indicates, then it is certainly greater than $2.\overline{6}a$. That makes Statement (2) sufficient. That eliminates **(A)**.

Combining the statements will not be necessary. Each statement is sufficient by itself, making **(D)** the correct answer.

3. **(D)**

The equation $\frac{5a}{2b} + \frac{10}{3} = 5$ is equivalent to each of the following EXCEPT:

- ○ $3a = 2b$
- ○ $5a - 2b = \frac{4b}{3}$
- ○ $\frac{5a}{2b} + 1 = \frac{8}{3}$
- ○ $3a + 2b - 1 = 2a + 3b$
- ○ $\frac{a}{2b} = \frac{1}{3}$

STEP 1: ANALYZE THE QUESTION

The question states that four of the answer choices are equivalent to $\frac{5a}{2b} + \frac{10}{3} = 5$ and one isn't. Simplify that equation to make it easier to compare to the choices. There are a couple of routes you might take. You might first subtract $\frac{10}{3}$ from both sides: $\frac{5a}{2b} + \frac{10}{3} - \frac{10}{3} = \frac{15}{3} - \frac{10}{3}$. So $\frac{5a}{2b} = \frac{5}{3}$. Cross multiply to get $15a = 10b$. Then divide by 5 so that $3a = 2b$.

Alternatively, you might have cleared the fractions first by multiplying each term by $(2b)(3)$:

$$\frac{5a\,(2b)\,(3)}{2b} + \frac{10(2b)\,(3)}{3} = 5(2b)(3)$$

$$15a + 20b = 30b$$

$$15a = 10b$$

$$3a = 2b$$

STEP 2: STATE THE TASK

Determine which of the answer choices is *not* equivalent to the given equation. This means that the same values that produce an equality in the stated equation do *not* produce an equality for the correct choice.

STEP 3: APPROACH STRATEGICALLY

Rearranging the given equation in lots of different ways until you've satisfied yourself that it's equivalent to four of the choices could be time-consuming. Fortunately, picking numbers will be an efficient approach. Since $3a = 2b$, $a = 2$ and $b = 3$ would be good choices.

Because you've already simplified the given equation to $3a = 2b$, you know that (**A**) is equivalent and is not the correct choice.

(**B**): Since $5a - 2b = 5(2) - 2(3) = 10 - 6 = 4$ and $\frac{4b}{3} = \frac{4(3)}{3} = 4$, this choice is equivalent to the original. Eliminate.

(**C**): Plug the numbers into this equation: $\frac{5(2)}{2(3)} + 1 = \frac{10}{6} + \frac{6}{6} = \frac{16}{6} = \frac{8}{3}$. This also works. Eliminate.

(**D**): $3a + 2b - 1 = 3(2) + 2(3) - 1 = 11$, but $2a + 3b = 2(2) + 3(3) = 13$. This is not a valid equation, so (**D**) is correct.

Since this is an EXCEPT question, there is no need to check (**E**). For the record, $\frac{2}{2(3)} = \frac{2}{6} = \frac{1}{3}$.

STEP 4: CONFIRM YOUR ANSWER

Confirm that your calculations for (**D**) are correct and that you chose an answer that is *not* a valid equation.

Practice Set: Exponents on the GMAT

4. (C)

At Car Part Corporation, there is a machine that produces brake pads. As the machine works, a wheel assembly turns. After the wheel assembly turns 4.09×10^6 times, the machine needs maintenance. Since being installed, the machine has received maintenance 30 times. Approximately how many total turns had the wheel assembly made when the machine last received maintenance?

- ○ 1.3×10^5
- ○ 1.2×10^7
- ○ 1.2×10^8
- ○ 4.1×10^7
- ○ 7.0×10^8

STEP 1: ANALYZE THE QUESTION

This question states that after a machine's wheel assembly turns 4.09×10^6 times, the machine needs maintenance. The machine has received maintenance 30 times.

STEP 2: STATE THE TASK

Find the approximate total number of turns that the wheel assembly had made at the time of its last maintenance.

STEP 3: APPROACH STRATEGICALLY

Because the machine received maintenance 30 times, the total turns must be 30 times 4.09×10^6. Since the question asks for an approximate value, round 4.09 to 4. Notice that the answer choices are written in terms of powers of 10. Therefore, rewrite 30 as 3×10. Then calculate:

$$3 \times 10^1 \times 4 \times 10^6$$

$$3 \times 4 \times 10^1 \times 10^6$$

$$12 \times 10^7$$

Looking at the answer choices, notice that the leading value 12 is not among the options. However, 12 can be rewritten as 1.2×10, giving $1.2 \times 10^1 \times 10^7 = 1.2 \times 10^8$. **(C)** is correct.

STEP 4: CONFIRM YOUR ANSWER

Reread the question stem, making sure that you translated the scenario correctly into math. For example, dividing 4.09×10^6 by 30 would result in **(A)**. Also, make sure you accurately kept track of the exponent and the decimal places in your answer.

5. **(C)**

If $\dfrac{2^{5x}}{8^{2x-2}} = 8$, what is the value of x?

- ○ 1
- ○ 2
- ○ 3
- ○ 4
- ○ 5

STEP 1: ANALYZE THE QUESTION

You need to solve for x in an equation with exponents in the numerator and denominator of a fraction. The bases in the numerator and denominator are not the same, but one of the bases, 8, is equal to the other one, 2, raised to the third power.

STEP 2: STATE THE TASK

Because of the complexity of the expression with the variable and the potentially large values of the numbers, backsolving is unlikely to be efficient. Instead, use algebra and the rules for exponents to solve for x.

STEP 3: APPROACH STRATEGICALLY

Start by cross multiplying to eliminate the denominator of the fraction: $2^{5x} = (8^{2x-2}) \times 8 = (8^{2x-2})(8^1) = 8^{2x-2+1} = 8^{2x-1}$.

Now the equation is $2^{5x} = 8^{2x-1}$. As written, the two bases are different, so it's necessary to make them the same before solving for x. Since $8 = 2^3$, you can substitute 2^3 for 8 in the equation: $2^{5x} = (2^3)^{2x-1}$. Further simplifying on the right yields $2^{5x} = 2^{6x-3}$.

When exponential expressions with the same base have equal values, where the base is not 1, 0, or -1, the exponents must also have equal values. Therefore, $5x = 6x - 3$, so $x = 3$. **(C)** is correct.

STEP 4: CONFIRM YOUR ANSWER

Check that you properly multiplied exponents when converting the larger base to the smaller one.

6. **(D)**

If x is a positive integer, then $9^x + 3^{2x+1} =$

○ $3(3^{2x+1})$

○ 3^{4x-1}

○ 3^{4x+1}

○ $4(3^{2x})$

○ 12^{2x}

STEP 1: ANALYZE THE QUESTION

The question involves an expression that adds two numbers that have different bases and different exponents. Both exponents contain the variable x. Recall that you can only add or subtract numbers with exponents when both the bases and the exponents are the same.

STEP 2: STATE THE TASK

Determine which of the answer choices is equal to the given expression.

STEP 3: APPROACH STRATEGICALLY

To solve this question algebraically, first convert both terms to a common base. Since $9 = 3^2$, the expression becomes $(3^2)^x + 3^{2x+1}$, which further simplifies to $3^{2x} + 3^{2x+1}$. Now consider that 3^{2x+1} can be restated as $(3^1)(3^{2x})$. Now the expression reads $3^{2x} + 3(3^{2x})$, which is $4(3^{2x})$. **(D)** is correct.

You could also use the picking numbers strategy. For a question with variables in the answer choices, all four incorrect choices must be eliminated because sometimes one or more incorrect choices will work for the particular value that you choose.

Try $x = 1$. Then $9^x + 3^{2x+1} = 9^1 + 3^{2+1} = 9 + 27 = 36$. Now substitute 1 for x into each answer choice. Any choice that does not equal 36 when $x = 1$ can be eliminated.

(A) $3(3^{2x+1}) = 3(3^3) = 3^4 = 81$. Eliminate **(A)**.

(B) $3^{4x-1} = 3^{4-1} = 3^3 = 27$. Eliminate **(B)**.

(C) $3^{4x+1} = 3^5 =$ something greater than 81 of **(A)**. Eliminate **(C)**.

(D) $4(3^{2x}) = 4(3^2) = 4(9) = 36$. This *could* be the correct choice.

(E) $12^{2x} = 12^2 = 144$. Eliminate **(E)**.

(D) is correct.

STEP 4: CONFIRM YOUR ANSWER

Confirm that your application of the exponent rules and your calculations are correct.

Practice Set: Radicals on the GMAT

7. **(D)**

If a positive number A is equal to 3^x and A, when squared, is equal to the cube root of 27 raised to the fourth power, what is the value of x?

- ○ 81
- ○ 27
- ○ 9
- ○ 2
- ○ 1

STEP 1: ANALYZE THE QUESTION

The question stem first says that $A = 3^x$. Translate each component of the next part of the sentence to arrive at the equation $A^2 = \sqrt[3]{27}^4$. Because you are being asked to find the value of x, look for a way to set the term with x in it equal to the numeric value on the right of the second equation. If $A = 3^x$, then $A^2 = \left(3^x\right)^2 = 3^{2x}$.

Now you have A^2 equal to two different terms, so you can set them equal to each other: $3^{2x} = \sqrt[3]{27}^4$.

STEP 2: STATE THE TASK

Strategically apply exponent and radical rules to solve for x.

STEP 3: APPROACH STRATEGICALLY

If you happen to know that the cube root of 27 is 3 (because $3^3 = 27$), then you can substitute 3^3 for 27 and simplify to $3^{2x} = 3^4$. Because the bases are the same, you can set the exponents equal and solve: $2x = 4$ and $x = 2$.

You can also use radical sign rules, which tell you that $\sqrt[3]{27}^4 = 27^{\frac{4}{3}}$. Then substitute 3^3 for 27 to make this $\left(3^3\right)^{\frac{4}{3}}$. When you raise a power to a power, you multiply the exponents; $3 \times \frac{4}{3} = 4$, so the right side of your equation is 3^4. Now $3^{2x} = 3^4$, $2x = 4$, and $x = 2$.

This matches choice **(D)**.

STEP 4: CONFIRM YOUR ANSWER

Backsolving is a great way to confirm your choice. Plug in 2 for x to find that $A = 9$ and therefore $A^2 = 81$. This is indeed equal to 3 (the cube root of 27) to the fourth power.

8.   **(B)**

   If $r > 0$, is $\sqrt{r}$ an integer?

   (1) r^2 is an integer.

   (2) $r = m^2$, where m is an integer.

STEP 1: ANALYZE THE QUESTION STEM

This is a Yes/No question. Here you are given that r is positive, and you need to find out whether you have sufficient information to determine whether $\sqrt{r}$ is an integer. There is no information in the question stem that you can use to determine whether or not $\sqrt{r}$ is an integer, so look at the statements.

STEP 2: EVALUATE THE STATEMENTS USING 12TEN

Statement (1) says that r^2 is an integer. If $r = 4$, then $r^2 = 4^2 = 16$ is an integer, so Statement (1) is true. In this case, $\sqrt{r} = \sqrt{4} = 2$ is an integer, and the answer to the question is yes. If $r = 5$, then $r^2 = 5^2 = 25$ is an integer, so Statement (1) is true. In this case, $\sqrt{r} = \sqrt{5}$ is not an integer, and the answer to the question is no. Because different answers to the question are possible, this statement is insufficient. You can eliminate **(A)** and **(D)**.

Now look at Statement (2). If $r = m^2$, where m is an integer, then $\sqrt{r} = \sqrt{m^2} = |m|$. Thus, $\sqrt{r}$ must always be an integer, since you are told that m is an integer. Statement (2) is sufficient, so **(B)** is correct.

9. **(C)**

$$\sqrt{36 - \frac{3 \times 23}{4}} =$$

- ○ $6 - \frac{\sqrt{69}}{2}$
- ○ $\frac{3\sqrt{5}}{2}$
- ○ $\frac{5\sqrt{3}}{2}$
- ○ $12 - \frac{\sqrt{69}}{2}$
- ○ $\frac{25\sqrt{3}}{4}$

STEP 1: ANALYZE THE QUESTION

You are given a complicated radical expression with numbers but no variables.

STEP 2: STATE THE TASK

Use the rules of radicals to simplify the given expression.

STEP 3: APPROACH STRATEGICALLY

Straightforward math is the best approach here. Subtraction under the radical sign cannot be "split up" under separate radical signs, so the first step is to combine the two terms into one fraction using a common denominator.

$$\sqrt{36 - \frac{3 \times 23}{4}} = \sqrt{\frac{144}{4} - \frac{69}{4}}$$

$$= \sqrt{\frac{144 - 69}{4}}$$

$$= \sqrt{\frac{75}{4}}$$

Now simplify by finding the factors of 75 and 4 that are perfect squares. Since all that is left under the radical sign is multiplication and division, you can split up the factors to facilitate simplification.

$$\sqrt{\frac{75}{4}}$$

$$= \frac{\sqrt{25 \times 3}}{\sqrt{4}}$$

$$= \frac{\sqrt{25} \times \sqrt{3}}{\sqrt{4}}$$

$$= \frac{5\sqrt{3}}{2}$$

The answer is $\frac{5\sqrt{3}}{2}$, so **(C)** is correct.

STEP 4: CONFIRM YOUR ANSWER

Check your application of the rules for radicals and your arithmetic. The GMAT will try to trick you into forgetting that you cannot split up subtraction and addition under the radical sign. Notice that **(A)** is the trap answer that awaits those who forget this rule.

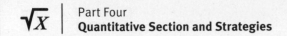

Practice Set: Absolute Value on the GMAT

10. **(E)**

Which of the following could be the value of x, if $|12 - 4x| + 2 = 6$?

- ○ −4
- ○ −2
- ○ 1
- ○ 3
- ○ 4

STEP 1: ANALYZE THE QUESTION

You are given an equation that has an absolute value. Recall that when absolute value is involved, you need to set up two equations, one for a positive value inside the absolute value bars and one for a negative value inside the bars.

STEP 2: STATE THE TASK

The question asks you to find what *could be* the value of x. This implies that x potentially has multiple values, although only one will be in the answer choices.

STEP 3: APPROACH STRATEGICALLY

First, deal with the term outside the absolute value bars by subtracting 2 from both sides of the equation to get $|12 - 4x| = 4$. Now, $12 - 4x$ could equal 4 or −4. Solve for each of the cases separately.

If the expression equals 4, the equation is $12 - 4x = 4$. Solve for the value of x:

$$12 - 4x = 4$$
$$-4x = -8$$
$$x = 2$$

Because this is not an answer choice, solve for the value of x when the expression equals −4:

$$12 - 4x = -4$$
$$-4x = -16$$
$$x = 4$$

This is choice **(E)**.

STEP 4: CONFIRM YOUR ANSWER

To confirm your answer, you can backsolve, plugging 4 in for x in the original equation: $|12 - 4(4)| + 2 = |12 - 16| + 2 = |-4| + 2 = 4 + 2 = 6$. **(E)** is confirmed as correct.

11. (E)

If x and y are integers and $z = |x - 2| - |y + 2|$, does $z = 0$?

(1) $\frac{9}{5} < x < \frac{7}{2}$ and $-3 \le y < -\frac{21}{11}$

(2) $2 \le x < \frac{7}{3}$ and $-\frac{22}{7} < y < -\frac{13}{7}$

STEP 1: ANALYZE THE QUESTION STEM

This is a Yes/No question asking whether $z = 0$. Given the equation $z = |x - 2| - |y + 2|$, if $z = 0$, then $|y + 2| = |x - 2|$. So if the answer to the question is yes, x and y have the same magnitude but different signs. For example, if $x = -2$, y must equal 2 so that $|2 + 2| = |-2 - 2| = 4$. If $x = 0$, then y must equal 0 so that $|0 + 2| = |0 - 2| = 2$. So for sufficiency, the statements will need to provide enough information to determine whether x and y meet that condition. The question stem says that x and y are integers, so while the statements have inequalities involving scary fractions, you'll only need to consider integer values in those ranges.

STEP 2: EVALUATE THE STATEMENTS USING 12TEN

In Statement (1), the only integers in the range for x are 2 and 3, and the only integers in the range for y are -3 and -2. Thus, the values of x and y could, but do not necessarily have to be, opposites of each other. Eliminate **(A)** and **(D)**.

From Statement (2), you can conclude that x must equal 2 and that y must equal -3 or -2. Thus, y's value could be but does not necessarily have to be the opposite value of x. Eliminate **(B)**.

Combining Statements (1) and (2), you know that x must equal 2 because that is the only value for x that works for both statements. However, in both statements, y could equal -3 or -2. Since y's value could be -2 and the opposite of x, but y could also be -3, the correct answer is **(E)**.

12. (C)

If $\left|\dfrac{7-3j}{2}\right| \leq 4$, then which of the following must be true?

○ $j \leq -\dfrac{1}{3}$

○ $j \leq \dfrac{3}{7}$

○ $j \leq 5$

○ $j \geq -\dfrac{3}{7}$

○ $j \geq 5$

STEP 1: ANALYZE THE QUESTION

This question involves an inequality with an absolute value. The solution to an inequality will have a range of values, and solving for an absolute value means writing two inequalities, one if the value between the bars is positive and one if it is negative. Note that the question wants a statement that *must* be true, not one that *could* be true.

STEP 2: STATE THE TASK

Evaluate the inequality to find the range of values for j. Check this result against the answer choices to see which *must* hold true.

STEP 3: APPROACH STRATEGICALLY

Rewrite the given inequality as two inequalities: $\dfrac{7-3j}{2} \leq 4$ and $\dfrac{7-3j}{2} \geq -4$. Remember to flip the inequality sign for the negative case. Evaluate both equations to find the range for j.

Evaluate the first inequality. Reverse the inequality sign when dividing by a negative number.

$$\frac{7-3j}{2} \leq 4$$
$$7 - 3j \leq 8$$
$$-3j \leq 1$$
$$j \leq -\frac{1}{3}$$

Evaluate the second inequality:

$$\frac{7-3j}{2} \geq -4$$
$$7 - 3j \geq -8$$
$$-3j \geq -15$$
$$j \leq 5$$

Therefore, the full range of values for j is $-\dfrac{1}{3} \leq j \leq 5$.

Evaluate the choices to see which *must* be true. **(A)** and **(E)** contain numbers that appear in the inequality for the full range of values for *j*, but both are incorrect because they use the opposite inequality symbols. **(B)** and **(D)** *could* both be true, but do not have to be true, as there are permissible values of *j* that are both less than and greater than $\frac{3}{7}$. However, it is true that *j* must be less than 5, and **(C)** is correct.

STEP 4: CONFIRM YOUR ANSWER

A good way to check your answer to questions involving inequalities is to sketch the solutions to the inequalities on a number line so you can see the range of the solutions.

Practice Set: Inequalities on the GMAT

13. (B)

Is $a > 5$?

(1) $8a \geq 40$

(2) $4a + 6 \leq 25$

STEP 1: ANALYZE THE QUESTION STEM

In this Yes/No question, sufficiency means demonstrating that a is either definitely greater than 5 or that a is definitely less than or equal to 5.

STEP 2: EVALUATE THE STATEMENTS USING 12TEN

Simplify Statement (1). If $8a \geq 40$, then $a \geq 5$. This means that a can be greater than 5 or equal to 5, so this statement is insufficient. Eliminate **(A)** and **(D)**.

Statement (2) says that $4a + 6 \leq 25$, which simplifies to $4a \leq 19$ and $a \leq (19 \div 4)$. Since $19 \div 4 < 5$, a must be less than 5. This means that the answer to the stem question is unequivocally no, so Statement (2) alone is sufficient. **(B)** is correct.

14. (C)

How many integers n are there such that $-145 < -\left|-n^2\right| < -120$?

- ○ 0
- ○ 2
- ○ 4
- ○ 11
- ○ 12

STEP 1: ANALYZE THE QUESTION

The variable n is defined as an integer, and several operations are performed on n in the given inequality, which includes an absolute value expression.

STEP 2: STATE THE TASK

Solve the inequality to determine n's total possible number of integer values.

STEP 3: APPROACH STRATEGICALLY

Since each part of the inequality has a negative sign, start by multiplying each term by -1 to make it positive. Remember to reverse the direction of each inequality sign because you are multiplying by a negative number: $145 > \left|-n^2\right| > 120$. Also, this may be easier to read if you write it with the smallest value on the left, just as numbers are placed on the number line: $120 < \left|-n^2\right| < 145$. Now based on the general rule that $|-x| = |x|$, $\left|-n^2\right| = \left|n^2\right|$, simplify the inequality further to $120 < \left|n^2\right| < 145$.

The question stem says that n is an integer, so n^2 is a perfect square. Since 120 is 1 less than the perfect square 121 $(= 11^2)$ and 145 is 1 greater than the perfect square 144 $(= 12^2)$, both 121 and 144 are within the range of permissible values for n^2. Therefore, you can rewrite the inequality as $11^2 \leq \left|n^2\right| \leq 12^2$. Thus, the perfect square n^2 could equal only 11^2 or 12^2.

If $n^2 = 11^2$, $n = \pm\sqrt{11^2} = \pm11$; if $n^2 = 12^2$, $n = \pm\sqrt{12^2} = \pm12$. So n could equal ±11 or ±12 for a total of four possible values. Thus, **(C)** is correct.

STEP 4: CONFIRM YOUR ANSWER

Ensure that you determined the entire total number of possible values for n, including the negative square roots of both 121 and 144.

15. (E)

If $\dfrac{a-b}{c} > 0$, is $c < 0$?

(1) $a^2 < b^2$

(2) $\dfrac{b}{c} < \dfrac{a}{c}$

STEP 1: ANALYZE THE QUESTION STEM

This is a Yes/No question that asks whether c is negative, given an inequality that contains c along with two other variables. That expression is positive, so $(a - b)$ and c are either both positive or both negative. Thus, a statement that gives information on the sign of the expression $(a - b)$ would provide sufficient information to answer the question.

STEP 2: EVALUATE THE STATEMENTS USING 12TEN

Statement (1) does not provide any information on c, so see what, if anything, you can deduce about a and b by rewriting Statement (1) to more closely resemble the $(a - b)$ expression from the question stem.

$$a^2 < b^2$$
$$a^2 - b^2 < 0$$
$$(a + b)(a - b) < 0$$

Since the product of $(a + b)$ and $(a - b)$ is negative, either $(a + b)$ is positive and $(a - b)$ is negative, or $(a + b)$ is negative and $(a - b)$ is positive. The value of $(a + b)$ is completely unknown, so you cannot determine whether $(a - b)$ is positive or negative, and thus you don't know whether c is positive or negative. Statement (1) is insufficient; eliminate **(A)** and **(D)**.

Statement (2) can be rewritten as follows.

$$\frac{a}{c} - \frac{b}{c} > 0$$
$$\frac{a - b}{c} > 0$$

Since this inequality matches that from the question stem, Statement (2) does not provide any new information and is thus insufficient. Eliminate **(B)**.

Now combine the statements. Since you already determined that Statement (2) just repeats what the question stem already says and that Statement (1) does not tell you the sign of either c or $(a - b)$, the statements are insufficient even when combined. Thus, **(E)** is correct.

GMAT by the Numbers: Arithmetic

Now that you've learned how to approach arithmetic questions on the GMAT, let's add one more dimension to your understanding of how they work.

Take a moment to try this question. Following is performance data from thousands of people who have studied with Kaplan over the decades. Through analyzing this data, we will show you how to approach questions like this one most effectively and how to avoid similarly tempting wrong answer choice types on Test Day.

What is the value of integer n?

(1) $n = n^4$
(2) $1^n \neq n$

○ Statement (1) ALONE is sufficient, but Statement (2) is not sufficient.

○ Statement (2) ALONE is sufficient, but Statement (1) is not sufficient.

○ BOTH statements TOGETHER are sufficient, but NEITHER statement ALONE is sufficient.

○ EACH statement ALONE is sufficient.

○ Statements (1) and (2) TOGETHER are NOT sufficient.

Explanation

This question asks for the value of n and tells you only that it's an integer. This leaves *all* integers as possible values—an important observation because some integers behave differently in certain arithmetic operations than others. The values 1, 0, and negative numbers all have special properties that are often crucial to consider.

> ## Question Statistics
>
> **19%** of test takers choose **(A)**
>
> **9%** of test takers choose **(B)**
>
> **48%** of test takers choose **(C)**
>
> **3%** of test takers choose **(D)**
>
> **21%** of test takers choose **(E)**
>
> Sample size = 4,200

Statement (1) tells you that $n = n^4$. It may be tempting to think that n must equal 1, but 0 also equals its own fourth power: 0. The question statistics reveal that test takers often overlook this possibility, choosing **(A)**, so it's no surprise that the test maker creates questions that exploit this error. Since n could equal either 1 or 0, Statement (1) is insufficient.

Statement (2) tells you only that $1^n \neq n$. No matter what exponent 1 is raised to, the value will remain 1. For example, $1^2 = 1$, as do 1^3 and 1^4. So the only value of n that Statement (2) excludes is $n = 1$. Alone, this statement is certainly insufficient. But when combined with Statement (1), you have an answer. Statement (1) permits only $n = 1$ and $n = 0$. Statement (2) removes $n = 1$ from consideration, leaving $n = 0$ as the only possibility. The correct answer is **(C)**.

Considering different values, such as 0, will help you to avoid traps. Also noteworthy is how many test takers select **(E)** on this problem. Such a response reflects a common error on difficult Data Sufficiency questions: these two statements are abstract, so many test takers—unsure of how to handle them—decide that they are insufficient. Correct these common assumptions—that values are positive integers and that abstract statements don't contain useful information—and you'll see a much higher score on Test Day.

More GMAT by the Numbers . . .

To see more questions with answer choice statistics, be sure to review the full-length CATs in your online resources.

GO ONLINE

kaptest.com/login

Number Properties on the GMAT

Below is a typical Data Sufficiency question dealing with number properties. In this chapter, we'll look at how to apply the Kaplan Method to this question, discuss the number properties rules being tested, and go over the basic principles and strategies that you want to keep in mind on every Quantitative question involving number properties.

> Each of the 600 elements of Set X is a distinct integer. How many of the integers in Set X are positive odd integers?
>
> (1) Set X contains 150 even integers.
>
> (2) 70 percent of the odd integers in Set X are positive.

Before you move on, take a minute to think about what you see in this question and answer some questions about how you think it works:

- What does it mean that each of the elements is a distinct integer?
- How are integers related to even and odd numbers?
- How are positive integers different from non-negative integers?
- What GMAT Core Competencies are most essential to success on this question?

Previewing Number Properties on the GMAT

Number properties are all about categories and rules. Certain kinds of numbers behave the same ways in all cases. When discussing number properties, don't assume that they apply exclusively to integers. Integers are one subset of numbers: namely, positive and negative whole numbers and zero. The concept of number properties is perfect fodder for the GMAT test makers because it allows them to reward you for using the Core Competencies of Pattern Recognition and Critical Thinking to draw inferences about how numbers behave, based on certain characteristics they possess. That's why number properties questions appear on the Quant section with greater frequency than other topics: these questions constitute approximately 20 percent of GMAT Problem Solving questions and nearly 30 percent of Data Sufficiency questions. Let's start by discussing each of the questions we just asked you to think about.

What Does It Mean That Each of the Elements Is a Distinct Integer?

Distinct simply means "different." So in this question, all 600 integers are different—there are no integers that show up more than once in the set. Don't assume that a set of integers always contains only distinct integers. This concept often comes into play with questions dealing with variables. Just because x and y are different letters does not necessarily mean that they represent different values.

How Are Integers Related to Even and Odd Numbers?

All integers are either odd or even. Students often forget that 0 is an even number. All integers ending with the digit 0, 2, 4, 6, or 8 are considered even numbers, and all integers ending with the digit 1, 3, 5, 7, or 9 are considered odd numbers. When a number is classified as even or odd, it must also be an integer; non-integers are not considered odd or even.

How Are Positive Integers Different from Non-Negative Integers?

Basically, the only difference is the number zero. Zero is the only number that is neither positive nor negative. This is a great example of how number properties questions test your Attention to the Right Detail. A question that asks about negative numbers does not include zero as a possibility, but a question that asks for non-positive numbers does include zero. You can bet that considering zero when it shouldn't be considered, or vice versa, can lead to a wrong answer on Test Day.

What GMAT Core Competencies Are Most Essential to Success on This Question?

As mentioned earlier, because number properties deal with the expected behavior of numbers based on certain rules, Pattern Recognition is an essential Core Competency for these questions. Also, you should use Critical Thinking in two ways: by remembering the abstract rules of number properties and by using the Kaplan strategy of picking numbers to make those properties more concrete in your mind on Test Day.

How Do I Apply the Kaplan Methods to GMAT Number Properties?

Now let's apply the Kaplan Method for Data Sufficiency to the number properties question you saw earlier:

> Each of the 600 elements of Set X is a distinct integer. How many of the integers in Set X are positive odd integers?
>
> (1) Set X contains 150 even integers.
>
> (2) 70 percent of the odd integers in Set X are positive.

STEP 1: ANALYZE THE QUESTION STEM

This is a Value question. To have sufficiency, you need a single value for the number of positive odd integers in Set X. The question stem tells you that the total number of integers in the set is 600 and that they are all distinct, or different from each other.

STEP 2: EVALUATE THE STATEMENTS USING 12TEN

Once you are sure you understand the information in the question stem, move on to the statements. Statement (1) tells you the number of even integers in Set X, from which you could determine the number of odd integers in Set X. But you don't know the number of these odd integers that are positive. Statement (1) is insufficient. Eliminate **(A)** and **(D)**.

Statement (2) tells you the percentage of the odd integers in Set X that are positive. But Statement (2) tells you nothing about the number of odd or even integers in Set X. Statement (2) is insufficient. Eliminate **(B)**.

Now combine the statements. From the two statements together, you could determine the number of odd integers and the percentage of those odd integers that are positive. Together, the two statements are sufficient. Choice **(C)** is correct.

Now let's look at each of the six areas of number properties that show up on the GMAT Quantitative section, starting with integers and non-integers.

Integers and Non-Integers

LEARNING OBJECTIVES

In this section, you will learn how to:

- Define *integer* and describe the number properties pertaining to integers that are commonly tested on the GMAT
- Distinguish different types of integers and non-integers
- Apply the Kaplan Method for Data Sufficiency to questions involving integers and non-integers

Integers are a particularly useful number properties category for the GMAT test makers, since questions that focus on the rules governing integers force test takers to discriminate between different categories of numbers (whole numbers versus fractions or decimals) and since integers include positives, negatives, and zero. Additionally, integers can be easily combined with other number properties to make more difficult questions (e.g., saying that the square root of a number is an integer means that the number is a perfect square, or saying that the quotient of two numbers is an integer means that the numbers are multiples/factors of one another).

These questions also contain an important trap that you must learn to avoid: never assume a number is an integer unless you're told that it is. The absence of information in a GMAT question can be just as important as its inclusion.

Types of Integers and Non-Integers

Real Numbers

All numbers on the number line. All of the numbers on the GMAT are real.

Integers

All of the numbers with no fractional or decimal parts: in other words, all multiples of 1. Negative numbers and 0 are also integers.

Rational Numbers

All of the numbers that can be expressed as the ratio of two integers (all integers and fractions).

Irrational Numbers

All real numbers that are not rational, both positive and negative (e.g., π, $-\sqrt{3}$).

On the GMAT, it's highly unlikely that you'll get a question that uses the terms **rational** or **irrational**, but you will see many questions that use the term **integer**. Both positive and negative whole numbers are integers. Zero is also an integer. Keep in mind that if a question doesn't say a number is an integer, then the number could be a fraction. Some Data Sufficiency answers depend upon this possibility.

Two rules are important to remember when performing operations with integers:

- When an integer is added to, subtracted from, or multiplied by another integer, the result is an integer.
- An integer divided by an integer may or may not result in an integer.

As with all number properties questions, picking numbers for questions about integers and non-integers can make them easier to tackle.

In-Format Question: Integers and Non-Integers on the GMAT

Now let's use the Kaplan Method on a Data Sufficiency question dealing with integers and non-integers:

> Is z an integer?
>
> (1) $2z$ is an even integer.
> (2) $4z$ is an even integer.

STEP 1: ANALYZE THE QUESTION STEM

This is a Yes/No question, so remember that either "always yes" or "always no" is required for sufficiency. The stem asks you whether z is an integer. It doesn't provide any other information, so move on to the statements.

STEP 2: EVALUATE THE STATEMENTS USING 12TEN

Statement (1): If $2z$ is an even number, z must be an integer because all even numbers can be evenly divided by 2. You can use picking numbers to test this. For instance, if $2z = 2$, then $z = 1$. If $2z = -122$, then $z = -61$. You can pick any even integer for $2z$ and always find that z is an integer, so Statement (1) is sufficient. Eliminate **(B)**, **(C)**, and **(E)**.

Statement (2) looks similar to Statement (1), but you can use picking numbers to be sure. If $4z = 4$, then $z = 1$, which is an integer. But if $4z = 6$, then $z = 1.5$, which is *not* an integer. So you can't say that z is always or never an integer. Statement (2) is insufficient, and **(A)** is correct.

TAKEAWAYS: INTEGERS AND NON-INTEGERS

- The term *integer* refers to positive whole numbers, zero, and negative whole numbers.

- When an integer is added to, subtracted from, or multiplied by another integer, the result is an integer. An integer divided by an integer may or may not result in an integer.

- When *integer* is a central word in a question, you have a number properties question. Take note of whether you are using rules or picking numbers.

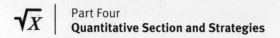

Practice Set: Integers and Non-Integers on the GMAT

1. If each of d, q, and r is a positive integer such that $dq + r = 3$, what is the value of d?

    (1) The number $\frac{r}{d}$ is less than $0.\overline{66}$.

    (2) The integer $\frac{q}{r}$ is less than 2.

2. If f and g are positive integers, is $\frac{f + g}{f}$ an integer?

    (1) $g = 5f - 4$

    (2) $f = \frac{1}{3}g$

3. If n is a positive integer, is $\frac{\sqrt{n}}{3}$ an integer?

    (1) $\sqrt{\frac{n}{3}}$ is an integer.

    (2) $\sqrt{14n}$ is NOT an integer.

Odds and Evens

LEARNING OBJECTIVES

In this section, you will learn how to:

- Explain the rules for odds and evens
- Apply the Kaplan Methods for Problem Solving and Data Sufficiency to questions dealing with odd and even numbers

---

The terms **odd** and **even** apply only to integers. Even numbers are integers that are divisible by 2, and odd numbers are integers that are not. Odd and even numbers may be negative; 0 is even. A number needs just a single factor of 2 to be even, so the product of an even number and any integer will always be even.

The GMAT tests the same odds and evens rules over and over. The rules are simple, and putting a little effort into memorizing them now will save you precious time on Test Day.

Rules for Odds and Evens

$$\text{Odd} \pm \text{Odd} = \text{Even} \qquad \text{Odd} \times \text{Odd} = \text{Odd}$$
$$\text{Even} \pm \text{Even} = \text{Even} \qquad \text{Even} \times \text{Even} = \text{Even}$$
$$\text{Odd} \pm \text{Even} = \text{Odd} \qquad \text{Odd} \times \text{Even} = \text{Even}$$

Applying these rules, we notice some important implications for odd and even numbers raised to exponents:

Exponent Rules for Odds and Evens

$$\text{Odd}^{\text{any positive integer}} = \text{Odd}$$

$$\text{Even}^{\text{any positive integer}} = \text{Even}$$

Knowing these rules cold will free up your mind so you can strategize when answering questions. As with all number properties questions, picking numbers is a useful strategy to use for questions that deal with odds and evens.

In-Format Question: Odds and Evens on the GMAT

Now let's use the Kaplan Method on a Data Sufficiency question dealing with odds and evens:

> If x is an integer, is x odd?
>
> (1) $x + 4$ is an odd integer.
>
> (2) $\frac{x}{3}$ is NOT an even integer.

STEP 1: ANALYZE THE QUESTION STEM

This is a Yes/No question. You are told that x is an integer. You want to determine whether there is enough information to answer the question "Is x odd?" Now look at the statements.

STEP 2: EVALUATE THE STATEMENTS USING 12TEN

Statement (1) says that $x + 4$ is an odd integer. So x is equal to an odd integer minus 4. Because 4 is an even integer, x is an odd integer minus an even integer. Because an odd minus an even is odd, x must be odd. Statement (1) is sufficient. You can eliminate **(B)**, **(C)**, and **(E)**.

Statement (2) says that $\frac{x}{3}$ is not an even integer. To determine sufficiency, pick a number for x. If $x = 3$, then $\frac{x}{3} = \frac{3}{3} = 1$ is an odd integer, so $\frac{x}{3}$ is not an even integer, and Statement (2) is true. In this case, $x = 3$ is odd, so the answer to the question is yes.

If $x = 2$, then $\frac{x}{3} = \frac{2}{3}$ is not an even integer; in fact, it is not an integer at all. And that is fine, because nowhere in the question does it state that $\frac{x}{3}$ is an integer. So Statement (2) is true. In this case, $x = 2$ is even, not odd, and the answer to the question is no.

Because more than one answer to the question is possible, Statement (2) is insufficient. Choice **(A)** is correct.

TAKEAWAYS: ODDS AND EVENS

- Most questions about odd and even numbers can be solved by using a few simple rules:

$$\text{Odd} \pm \text{Odd} = \text{Even} \qquad \text{Odd} \times \text{Odd} = \text{Odd}$$
$$\text{Even} \pm \text{Even} = \text{Even} \qquad \text{Even} \times \text{Even} = \text{Even}$$
$$\text{Odd} \pm \text{Even} = \text{Odd} \qquad \text{Odd} \times \text{Even} = \text{Even}$$

Practice Set: Odds and Evens on the GMAT

4. Set S contains 5 integers, labeled A, B, C, D, and E. If the sum of all of the elements of set S is odd, how many of the elements of set S are even?

    (1) The sum of A and B is odd.

    (2) The product of B, C, and D is odd.

5. If a and b are integers and a is odd, is b even?

    (1) $(a^3 + 1) \times b$ is even.

    (2) $\dfrac{a^2}{b} = b - 4$

6. If m is an odd number and p is a prime number, which of the following must be odd?

    ○ mp

    ○ $m(m + p)$

    ○ $m - p$

    ○ $m^2 + 2p^2 + 1$

    ○ $m^2(m + 2p)$

Positives and Negatives

LEARNING OBJECTIVES

In this section, you will learn how to:

- Describe the properties of positive and negative numbers
- Perform operations with positive and negative numbers
- Apply the Kaplan Methods for Problem Solving and Data Sufficiency to questions dealing with positives and negatives

---

Some GMAT questions hinge on whether the numbers involved are positive or negative. These properties are especially important to keep in mind when picking numbers on a Data Sufficiency question. If both positives and negatives are permissible for a given question, make sure you test both possibilities, since doing so will often yield noteworthy results. Take the same approach that you've been learning to use for other number properties: spend some time memorizing the rules but always keep your eye out for strategic opportunities.

Numbers with Special Properties

Properties of Zero

Adding or subtracting zero from a number does not change the number.

Examples: $2 + 0 = 2$
   $4 - 0 = 4$

Any number multiplied by zero equals zero.

Example: $12 \times 0 = 0$

Division by zero is **undefined**. When given an algebraic expression, be sure that the denominator is not zero. The fraction $\frac{0}{0}$ is likewise undefined.

Properties of 1 and −1

Multiplying or dividing a number by 1 does not change the number.

Examples: $4 \times 1 = 4$
   $-3 \div 1 = -3$

Multiplying or dividing a number by −1 changes the sign, but not the absolute value.

Examples: $6 \times (-1) = -6$
   $-2 \div (-1) = -(-2) = 2$

Note: The sum of a number and −1 times that number is equal to zero.

The **reciprocal** of a number is 1 divided by the number. The product of a number and its reciprocal is 1. Zero has no reciprocal, since $\frac{1}{0}$ is undefined.

Properties of Numbers Between −1 and 1

The reciprocal of a number between 0 and 1 is greater than the number itself.

Example: The reciprocal of $\frac{2}{3}$ is $\frac{1}{\frac{2}{3}}$.

$$\frac{1}{\frac{2}{3}} = 1 \div \frac{2}{3} = 1 \times \frac{3}{2} = \frac{3}{2}$$

$$\frac{3}{2} > \frac{2}{3}$$

(You can also easily get the reciprocal of a fraction by switching the numerator and denominator. The result will be the same. For example, the reciprocal of $\frac{2}{3}$ is $\frac{3}{2}$.)

The reciprocal of a number between −1 and 0 is less than the number itself.

Example: The reciprocal of $-\frac{2}{3}$ is $\frac{1}{-\frac{2}{3}}$.

$$\frac{1}{-\frac{2}{3}} = 1 \div -\frac{2}{3} = 1 \times -\frac{3}{2} = -\frac{3}{2}$$

$$-\frac{3}{2} < -\frac{2}{3}$$

The square of a number between 0 and 1 is less than the number itself.

Example: $\left(\frac{1}{2}\right)^2 = \frac{1}{2} \times \frac{1}{2} = \frac{1}{4}$, which is less than $\frac{1}{2}$.

Multiplying any positive number by a fraction between 0 and 1 gives a product smaller than the original number.

Example: $6 \times \frac{1}{4} = \frac{6}{4} = \frac{3}{2}$, which is less than 6.

Multiplying any negative number by a fraction between 0 and 1 gives a product greater than the original number.

Example: $-3 \times \frac{1}{6} = -\frac{3}{6} = -\frac{1}{2}$, which is greater than −3.

The special properties of −1, 0, and 1 make them important numbers to consider when you are picking numbers for Data Sufficiency questions, as well as for the "could be/must be" kinds of Problem Solving questions. Because numbers between −1 and 1 can make things larger or smaller in different ways than do other numbers, they are good numbers to pick when testing whether one expression always has to be less than or greater than another.

All these properties can best be seen by observation rather than by memorization.

Operations with Positives and Negatives

Addition

With Like Signs: Add the absolute values and keep the same sign. Adding a negative number is the same as subtracting a positive number.

Example: $(-6) + (-3) = -9$

With Unlike Signs: Take the difference of the absolute values and keep the sign of the number with the larger absolute value.

Example: $(-7) + (+3) = -4$

Subtraction

Subtraction is the inverse operation of addition, so subtracting a negative number is the same as adding a positive number.

Example: $(-5) - (-10)$
$$= (-5) + (+10)$$
$$= 5$$

Multiplication and Division

The product or the quotient of two numbers with the same sign is positive.

Examples: $(-2) \times (-5) = +10$ and $\frac{-50}{-5} = +10$

The product or the quotient of two numbers with opposite signs is negative.

Examples: $(-2) \times (+3) = -6$ and $\frac{-6}{2} = -3$

Keep in mind that it doesn't matter whether the negative sign is in the numerator or in the denominator. The fraction $\frac{-6}{2}$ is the same as $\frac{6}{-2}$ and $-\frac{6}{2}$.

In-Format Question: Positives and Negatives on the GMAT

Now let's use the Kaplan Method on a Data Sufficiency question dealing with positives and negatives:

> Is $x - 2y + z$ greater than $x + y - z$?
>
> (1) y is positive.
>
> (2) z is negative.

STEP 1: ANALYZE THE QUESTION STEM

This is a Yes/No question. The question stem asks, "Is $x - 2y + z > x + y - z$?" Don't miss an opportunity to use Critical Thinking to find a more efficient solution to this problem. You can simplify this inequality to make it easier to work with:

$$x - 2y + z > x + y - z$$
$$-2y + z > y - z$$
$$z > 3y - z$$
$$2z > 3y$$

This simplified inequality is equivalent to the original inequality. Now you can work with the equivalent question stem, "Is $2z > 3y$?" Look at the statements next.

STEP 2: EVALUATE THE STATEMENTS USING 12TEN

Statement (1) says that y is positive. However, you're given no information about z, so this statement is insufficient. You can test this by picking numbers. For example, if $y = 1$ and $z = 5$, then y is positive, so Statement (1) is true. You have $2z = 2(5) = 10$ while $3y = 3(1) = 3$. In this case, $2z$ is greater than $3y$, and the answer to the question is yes.

However, if $y = 1$ and $z = -4$, then y is positive, so Statement (1) is true. You have $2z = 2(-4) = -8$ while $3y = 3(1) = 3$. In this case, $2z$ is less than $3y$, and the answer to the question is no.

Because more than one answer to the question is possible, Statement (1) is insufficient. You can eliminate **(A)** and **(D)**.

Statement (2) says that z is negative. However, you have no information about y, so this statement is insufficient. For example, if you pick numbers so that $y = -4$ and $z = -1$, then z is negative, so Statement (2) is true. You have $2z = 2(-1) = -2$, while $3y = 3(-4) = -12$. In this case, $2z$ is greater than $3y$, and the answer to the question is yes.

However, if $y = 1$ and $z = -4$, which are the values that you worked with when you considered Statement (1), then z is negative, so Statement (2) is true. Again, $2z = 2(-4) = -8$ while $3y = 3(1) = 3$, so in this case, $2z$ is less than $3y$, and the answer to the question is no. Because more than one answer to the question is possible, Statement (2) is insufficient. You can eliminate **(B)**.

Taking the statements together, as y is positive, $3y$ is positive. Because z is negative, $2z$ is negative. Because $2z$ is negative and $3y$ is positive, $2z$ is less than $3y$. It is not true that $2z > 3y$. You can answer the question with a definite no. The two statements taken together are sufficient. **(C)** is correct.

TAKEAWAYS: POSITIVES AND NEGATIVES

- When multiplying or dividing numbers with the same sign, the result is always positive. When multiplying or dividing two numbers with different signs, the result is always negative.

- Subtracting a negative number is the same as adding a positive number.

Practice Set: Positives and Negatives on the GMAT

7. If $x - y = 8$, which of the following must be true?

    I.   Both x and y are positive.

    II. If x is positive, y must be positive.

    III. If x is negative, y must be negative.

    ○ I only

    ○ II only

    ○ III only

    ○ I and II

    ○ II and III

8. If $b \neq 0$ and $-1 < \dfrac{a}{b} < 1$, which of the following CANNOT be true?

    ○ $a + b < 0$

    ○ $(a + b)(a - b) > 0$

    ○ $a - b > 0$

    ○ $(a + b)(a - b) < 0$

    ○ $a + b > 0$

9. Is $\dfrac{s - t}{st} < 0$?

    (1) $t < 0 < s$

    (2) $\dfrac{st}{s - t} < -1$

Factors and Multiples

Factors and multiples are relatively simple concepts used to make some fairly difficult GMAT problems. Multiples—the products of a given integer and other integers—boil down to the numbers you list when counting by a certain number. For example, the multiples of 5 are 5, 10, 15, 20, and so on. Factors—those integers that divide another integer without leaving a remainder—are a little trickier, but this section and the next, on remainders and primes, will show you some ways to determine the factors of a number on Test Day.

A **multiple** is the product of a given integer and another integer. An integer that is divisible by another integer without a remainder is a multiple of that integer.

Example: 12 is a multiple of 3, since 12 is divisible by 3.

The **least common multiple** of two or more numbers is the smallest integer that is a multiple of all the numbers or the smallest integer that is divisible by the numbers.

Example: The least common multiple of 6 and 8 is 24, since that is the smallest multiple of 6 that is also divisible by 8 and vice versa.

The **factors**, or **divisors**, of a number are the positive integers that divide into that number without a remainder (or a remainder of 0).

Example: The number 36 has nine positive factors: 1, 2, 3, 4, 6, 9, 12, 18, and 36.

You can group these factors in pairs: $1 \times 36 = 2 \times 18 = 3 \times 12 = 4 \times 9 = 6 \times 6$.

These rules can be synthesized into one: $\dfrac{\text{Multiple}}{\text{Factor}} = \text{Integer}$.

The **greatest common factor**, or **greatest common divisor**, of a pair of numbers is the largest factor shared by the two numbers.

As with all number properties questions, picking numbers is a useful strategy to use with questions about factors and multiples. When picking numbers, keep in mind the following:

- Every number is both a factor and a multiple of itself.
- 1 is a factor of every number.
- 0 is a multiple of every number.

In-Format Question: Factors and Multiples on the GMAT

Now let's use the Kaplan Method on a Problem Solving question dealing with factors and multiples:

> If p, q, and r are positive integers such that q is a factor of r, and r is a multiple of p, which of the following must be an integer?
>
> ○ $\dfrac{p+q}{r}$
>
> ○ $\dfrac{r+p}{q}$
>
> ○ $\dfrac{p}{q}$
>
> ○ $\dfrac{pq}{r}$
>
> ○ $\dfrac{r(p+q)}{pq}$

STEP 1: ANALYZE THE QUESTION

You are given the information that q is a factor of r, so you know that r is a multiple of q. The question stem also says that r is a multiple of p. Thus, r is a multiple of both p and q. This question is very abstract, so picking numbers that are permissible will help you make quick work of the answer choices.

STEP 2: STATE THE TASK

You need to pick numbers for p, q, and r and apply them to the answer choices. Pay Attention to the Right Detail: you are looking for the answer choice that is an integer. Eliminate any answer choices that do not yield an integer.

STEP 3: APPROACH STRATEGICALLY

Based on work in Step 1, you know that r is a multiple of both p and q. So if $p = 2$ and $q = 3$, then $r = 12$ meets the criteria stated in the question stem.

You can now substitute these values into the answer choices. Because this is a "which of the following" question, begin with (E).

Choice (E): $\dfrac{r(p+q)}{pq} = \dfrac{12(2+3)}{2(3)} = \dfrac{12(5)}{6} = 10$. The answer is an integer, so possibly correct.

Choice (D): $\dfrac{pq}{r} = \dfrac{2(3)}{12} = \dfrac{6}{12}$. Not an integer. Eliminate.

Choice (C): $\dfrac{p}{q} = \dfrac{2}{3}$. Not an integer. Eliminate.

Choice (B): $\dfrac{r+p}{q} = \dfrac{12+2}{3} = \dfrac{14}{3}$. Not an integer. Eliminate.

Choice (A): $\dfrac{p+q}{r} = \dfrac{2+3}{12} = \dfrac{5}{12}$. Not an integer. Eliminate.

STEP 4: CONFIRM YOUR ANSWER

If all other four answer choices can give non-integers, (**E**) must be the answer. Note that if you had originally picked different numbers, you may have ended up with more than one answer choice that produced an integer value. Whenever this is the case, you would need to pick a new set of numbers and test only the answer choices that worked out the first time.

(**E**) also makes logical sense because it equals $\dfrac{rp + rq}{pq} = \dfrac{rp}{pq} + \dfrac{rq}{pq} = \dfrac{r}{q} + \dfrac{r}{p}$, and according to the question

stem, q and p are both factors of r, so $\dfrac{r}{q}$ and $\dfrac{r}{p}$ are both integers. Therefore, their sum must also be an integer.

TAKEAWAYS: FACTORS AND MULTIPLES

- A *multiple* is the product of a given integer and another integer.
- A factor is an integer that divides another integer without leaving a remainder.

Practice Set: Factors and Multiples on the GMAT

10. If a certain number is divisible by 18 and 24, it must also be divisible by which of the following?

   ○ 30
   ○ 36
   ○ 72
   ○ 216
   ○ 432

11. What is the greatest positive integer x such that 9^{6x} is a factor of 81^{10+x}?

   ○ 2
   ○ 4
   ○ 5
   ○ 6
   ○ 15

12. How many positive integers less than 70 are multiples of either 3 or 4 but not both?

   ○ 17
   ○ 18
   ○ 23
   ○ 30
   ○ 35

Remainders and Primes

> **LEARNING OBJECTIVES**
>
> In this section, you will learn how to:
>
> - Define *remainder* and explain how to find it
> - Use prime factorization to find the lowest common multiple
> - Apply the Kaplan Methods for Problem Solving and Data Sufficiency to questions dealing with remainders and primes

These two topics—remainders and prime numbers—are math concepts that you may not use a lot in day-to-day life. Although you may be rusty on these concepts, there's no need to be intimidated. The most important thing for you to understand is what a remainder is and how it differs from a quotient. In most areas of life and work, you likely perform division using a calculator, which automatically calculates the decimal places. Remainders are tested on the GMAT, in part, because they are distinctly *not* what calculators give you.

Remainders

The **remainder** is what is left over in a division problem. A remainder is always smaller than the number you are dividing by.

Example: 17 divided by 3 is 5 with a remainder of 2.

The GMAT sometimes asks questions that require you to identify numbers that when divided by a given number produce a certain remainder. For example, "*n* is a number that when divided by 7 has a remainder of 2." Most GMAT remainder problems like this one are best solved by the strategy of picking numbers.

Prime Numbers

A **prime number** is an integer greater than 1 that has only two positive factors, 1 and itself. The number 1 is not considered a prime. The number 2 is the first prime number and the only even prime. (Do you see why? Any other even number has 2 as a factor and, therefore, is not prime.) The GMAT expects test takers to recognize the prime numbers up to 50. They are 2, 3, 5, 7, 11, 13, 17, 19, 23, 29, 31, 37, 41, 43, and 47.

Prime Factorization

The **prime factorization** of a number is the expression of the number as the product of its prime factors. No matter how you factor a number, its prime factors will always be the same.

Example: $36 = 6 \times 6 = 2 \times 3 \times 2 \times 3 = 2^2 \times 3^2$

Example:
$$480 = 48 \times 10 = 8 \times 6 \times 2 \times 5$$
$$= 4 \times 2 \times 2 \times 3 \times 2 \times 5$$
$$= 2 \times 2 \times 2 \times 2 \times 3 \times 2 \times 5$$
$$= 2^5 \times 3 \times 5$$

The easiest way to determine a number's prime factorization is to figure out a pair of factors of the number and then determine their factors, continuing the process until you're left with only prime numbers. Those primes will be the prime factorization.

Example: Find the prime factorization of 1,050.

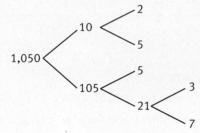

So the prime factorization of 1,050 is $2 \times 3 \times 5^2 \times 7$.

Prime factorization is one of the most valuable tools for the entire Quantitative section. Any question about multiples or factors is really, at its heart, a question about prime factors. Quickly jotting down the prime factorizations of the numbers in such questions can provide the key to the solution. Prime factorization is often the key to dealing with scary exponents as well. If a GMAT problem gives you 35^8, rewriting it as $(5 \times 7)^8 = 5^8 \times 7^8$ is almost certainly the way to go.

Distinct Prime Factors

The GMAT asks not only about prime factors, but also about distinct prime factors. *Distinct* simply means "different." Thus, $1,050 = 2 \times 3 \times 5 \times 5 \times 7$, five numbers with 5 repeating once; it has five prime factors, but only four distinct ones.

Divisibility Tests

Several tests can quickly determine whether a given number is a multiple of 2, 3, 4, 5, 7, 8, 9, 10, and 11.

A number is divisible by 2 if its units digit is even.

> 138 is divisible by 2 because 8 is even.

> 177 is not divisible by 2 because 7 is not even.

A number is divisible by 3 if the sum of its digits is divisible by 3.

> 4,317 is divisible by 3 because $4 + 3 + 1 + 7 = 15$ and 15 is divisible by 3.

> 32,872 is not divisible by 3 because $3 + 2 + 8 + 7 + 2 = 22$ and 22 is not divisible by 3.

A number is divisible by 4 if its last two digits compose a two-digit number that is itself divisible by 4.

> 1,732 is divisible by 4 because 32 is divisible by 4.

> 1,746 is not divisible by 4 because 46 is not divisible by 4.

A number is divisible by 5 if its units digit is either a 5 or a 0.

> 26,985 is divisible by 5.

> 55,783 is not divisible by 5.

A number is divisible by 7 if the difference between its units digit multiplied by 2 and the rest of the number is a multiple of 7.

> 147 is divisible by 7 because $14 - 7(2) = 0$, which is divisible by 7.

> 682 is not divisible by 7 because $68 - 2(2) = 64$, which is not divisible by 7.

A number is divisible by 8 if its last three digits compose a three-digit number that is itself divisible by 8.

76,848 is divisible by 8 because 848 is divisible by 8.

65,102 is not divisible by 8 because 102 is not divisible by 8.

A number is divisible by 9 if the sum of its digits is divisible by 9.

16,956 is divisible by 9 because $1 + 6 + 9 + 5 + 6 = 27$, and 27 is divisible by 9.

4,317 is not divisible by 9 because $4 + 3 + 1 + 7 = 15$, and 15 is not divisible by 9.

A number is divisible by 10 if its units digit is zero.

67,890 is divisible by 10.

56,432 is not divisible by 10.

A number is divisible by 11 if the difference between the sum of its odd-placed digits and the sum of its even-placed digits is divisible by 11.

5,181 is divisible by 11 because $(5 + 8) - (1 + 1) = 11$, which is divisible by 11.

5,577 is a multiple of 11 because $(5 + 7) - (5 + 7) = 0$, which is divisible by 11.

827 is not divisible by 11 because $(8 + 7) - 2 = 13$, which is not divisible by 11.

Bonus rule for 11: If the digit in the tens place of a three-digit number is equal to the sum of the digits in that number's hundreds and units places, then that number is divisible by 11.

Furthermore, the quotient of the number divided by 11 will be a two-digit number composed of the digits in the original number's hundreds and units places. Divisibility by 11 shows up with surprising regularity in the GMAT's tougher Quantitative problems.

341 is divisible by 11 because $3 + 1 = 4$. Furthermore, $341 = 31 \times 11$.

792 is divisible by 11 because $7 + 2 = 9$. Furthermore, $792 = 72 \times 11$.

This rule *cannot* be used to rule out divisibility, only to rule it in:

715 is divisible by 11, even though $7 + 5 \neq 1$ ($715 = 65 \times 11$).

You can combine these rules above with factorization to figure out whether a number is divisible by other numbers.

To be divisible by 6, a number must pass the divisibility tests for both 2 and 3, since $6 = 2 \times 3$.

534 is divisible by 6 because 4 is divisible by 2 *and* $5 + 3 + 4 = 12$, which is divisible by 3.

To be divisible by 44, a number must pass the divisibility tests for both 4 and 11, since $44 = 4 \times 11$.

1,848 is divisible by 44 because 48 is divisible by 4 *and* $(1 + 4) - (8 + 8) = -11$, which is divisible by 11.

Note that combining rules to test divisibility only works when the separate numbers you are testing do not have any factors in common (as is the case with 2 and 3 and with 4 and 11 above).

In-Format Question: Remainders and Primes on the GMAT

Now let's use the Kaplan Method on a Problem Solving question dealing with remainders and primes:

If *a* and *b* are prime numbers, which of the following CANNOT be the value of *ab*?

- ○ 9
- ○ 14
- ○ 21
- ○ 23
- ○ 25

STEP 1: ANALYZE THE QUESTION

Given that *a* and *b* are prime numbers, you are looking for the one answer choice that cannot be the product of two prime numbers. Note though that when the question is testing prime numbers, remember to test the special case of the number 2, since 2 is both the smallest prime number and also the only even prime number.

STEP 2: STATE THE TASK

Pick numbers that are permissible and systematically apply the numbers to the answer choices. Eliminate answer choices that cannot be the product of the two prime numbers.

STEP 3: APPROACH STRATEGICALLY

This is a "which of the following" question, so you can start with (**E**) and test the choices.

Choice (**E**): The product is 25, which can be created by multiplying 5 × 5. Because 5 is a prime number, 25 can be the product of two primes and, thus, cannot be the correct choice. Notice that the question stem requires only that *a* and *b* be prime numbers, not that they be distinct prime numbers. Eliminate.

Choice (**D**): The number 23 is prime; its only factors are 1 and 23. Because 1 is not a prime number, 23 cannot be the product of two prime numbers. Therefore, (**D**) is correct.

STEP 4: CONFIRM YOUR ANSWER

Use Critical Thinking to check your work. Logically, it makes sense that the correct answer would be a prime number, since *a* and *b*, as prime numbers, must both be greater than 1, making it impossible for *ab* to be a prime number.

TAKEAWAYS: REMAINDERS AND PRIMES

- A *remainder* is the number left over when one integer is divided by another.
- A *prime number* is a positive integer greater than 1 that is divisible only by 1 and itself.

Practice Set: Remainders and Primes on the GMAT

13. If n is an integer such that $12 \le n \le 24$, is n a prime number?

   (1) The remainder when n is divided by 4 is 1.

   (2) The remainder when n is divided by 6 is 1.

14. If $x = 12$, $y = 35$, and $x^2 y^2 = 21 \times 28 \times 30 \times z$, what is the value of z?

   ○　10

   ○　12

   ○　15

   ○　21

   ○　30

15. If $a = 5m + 2$ and $b = 5n + 13$, and m and n are positive integers, what is the remainder when $a + b$ is divided by 5?

   ○　0

   ○　1

   ○　2

   ○　3

   ○　4

Answer Key

Practice Set: Integers and Non-Integers on the GMAT

1. D
2. B
3. A

Practice Set: Odds and Evens on the GMAT

4. C
5. B
6. E

Practice Set: Positives and Negatives on the GMAT

7. C
8. B
9. D

Practice Set: Factors and Multiples on the GMAT

10. C
11. C
12. D

Practice Set: Remainders and Primes on the GMAT

13. B
14. A
15. A

Answers and Explanations

Practice Set: Integers and Non-Integers on the GMAT

1. **(D)**

   If each of d, q, and r is a positive integer such that $dq + r = 3$, what is the value of d?

   (1) The number $\frac{r}{d}$ is less than $0.\overline{66}$.

   (2) The integer $\frac{q}{r}$ is less than 2.

STEP 1: ANALYZE THE QUESTION STEM

This question gives an equation with three variables, each defined as a positive integer. It asks for the value of one of the variables.

Before heading to the two statements, simplify the information in the question stem. Since each variable is a positive integer, dq is a positive integer. Since $dq + r = 3$, only two possibilities exist.

- If $dq = 1$, $r = 2$. In this case, both d and q must equal 1.
- If $dq = 2$, $r = 1$. Here, either $d = 1$ and $q = 2$, or $d = 2$ and $q = 1$.

So far, you have enough information to determine that d equals either 1 or 2. A statement that provides enough information to limit d to just one of those two values would be sufficient.

STEP 2: EVALUATE THE STATEMENTS USING 12TEN

Statement (1) essentially says that $\frac{r}{d}$ is a fraction that is less than $\frac{2}{3}$. For this to be true, r must be less than d, so r would equal 1 and d would equal 2. This statement is sufficient, so eliminate **(B)**, **(C)**, and **(E)**.

Statement (2) says that $\frac{q}{r}$ is an integer that is less than 2. This means that $\frac{q}{r} = 1$, which can be rewritten as $q = r$. Now test the possibilities for q and r in relation to d:

- If $q = r = 1$, $d = 2$.
- If $q = r = 2$, the question stem's equation becomes $dq + r = 2d + 2 = 3$, which would mean that d was not an integer—and this is not permitted according to the question stem.

Therefore, d can equal only 2. This statement is sufficient, so **(D)** is correct.

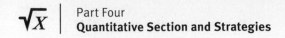

2.   **(B)**

If f and g are positive integers, is $\dfrac{f+g}{f}$ an integer?

(1) $g = 5f - 4$

(2) $f = \dfrac{1}{3}g$

STEP 1: ANALYZE THE QUESTION STEM

This Yes/No question states that f and g are positive integers and asks whether the fraction $\dfrac{f+g}{f}$ is an integer.

While multiplication, addition, and subtraction of integers all result in an integer, when an integer is divided by an integer, the numerator must be a multiple of the denominator for the result to be an integer. Thus, you need enough information to determine whether $f + g$ is a multiple of f.

STEP 2: EVALUATE THE STATEMENTS USING 12TEN

Statement (1) informs you that $g = 5f - 4$. Substitute that into the fraction in the question stem to get $\dfrac{f + 5f - 4}{f} = \dfrac{6f - 4}{f} = 6 - \dfrac{4}{f}$. This is an integer only if 4 is a multiple of f. There is not enough information to determine whether that is true, so eliminate **(A)** and **(D)**.

Statement (2), $f = \dfrac{1}{3}g$, can be rearranged as $3f = g$. Substitute that into the fraction to get $\dfrac{f + 3f}{f} = \dfrac{4f}{f} = 4$. This is, indeed, an integer, so **(B)** is correct.

3. **(A)**

If n is a positive integer, is $\frac{\sqrt{n}}{3}$ an integer?

(1) $\sqrt{\frac{n}{3}}$ is an integer.

(2) $\sqrt{14n}$ is NOT an integer.

STEP 1: ANALYZE THE QUESTION STEM

This is a Yes/No question. You are told that n is a positive integer. You need to determine whether there is enough information to determine whether $\frac{\sqrt{n}}{3}$ is an integer. Since the square root of 9 is 3, in order for the answer to be yes, n would have to be 9 multiplied by a perfect square (a perfect square with 9 as a factor).

To see this, you can pick numbers:

If $n = 9 \times 1$, then $\frac{\sqrt{n}}{3} = \frac{\sqrt{9 \times 1}}{3} = \frac{\sqrt{9}\sqrt{1}}{3} = \frac{3 \times 1}{3} = 1$.

If $n = 9 \times 4 = 36$, then $\frac{\sqrt{n}}{3} = \frac{\sqrt{9 \times 4}}{3} = \frac{\sqrt{9}\sqrt{4}}{3} = \frac{3 \times 2}{3} = 2$.

And if $n = 9 \times 9 = 81$, then $\frac{\sqrt{n}}{3} = \frac{\sqrt{9 \times 9}}{3} = \frac{\sqrt{9}\sqrt{9}}{3} = \frac{3 \times 3}{3} = 3$.

You can see that this pattern always yields an integer.

But if $n = 3$, $\frac{\sqrt{n}}{3} = \frac{\sqrt{3}}{3}$, which is not an integer. If $n = 9 \times 3 = 27$, then $\frac{\sqrt{n}}{3} = \frac{\sqrt{27}}{3} = \frac{3\sqrt{3}}{3} = \sqrt{3}$, which is not an integer. So if n is some number other than 9 multiplied by a perfect square, the answer to the question is no.

STEP 2: EVALUATE THE STATEMENTS USING 12TEN

You can either use logic and the number property rules or pick numbers to evaluate the statements.

Statement (1) tells you that $\sqrt{\frac{n}{3}}$ is an integer. This means that $n = 3x$, where x is some unknown integer that is a perfect square. If none of the factors of x is 3, then there is no way that n can be 9 times a perfect square, so the answer would be no. If, on the other hand, x *does* have a factor of 3, because x is a perfect square, it must have an *even* number of factors of 3. Consequently, n, which is $3x$, would have an *odd* number of factors of 3 and its square root would not even be an integer, let alone an integer that is divisible by 3. Statement (1) is sufficient to answer the question with a no. Eliminate **(B)**, **(C)**, and **(E)**.

As an alternative to the above solution, you could have plugged in some numbers for n into $\sqrt{\frac{n}{3}}$. Use 9×1, 9×4, and 9×9, since those values mean that $\frac{\sqrt{n}}{3}$ is an integer. Plugging in $9 \times 1 = 9$ results in $\sqrt{\frac{n}{3}} = \sqrt{\frac{9}{3}} = \sqrt{3}$, which is not an integer and, therefore, not a permitted value of n. Plugging in $9 \times 4 = 36$ gives you $2\sqrt{3}$, and plugging in $9 \times 9 = 81$ results in $3\sqrt{3}$. Continuing with greater values for n will just continue this pattern. None of the values that would answer the question with a yes are permissible values for Statement (1). Thus, the answer to the question must be no, and this statement is sufficient.

Statement (2) tells you that $\sqrt{14n}$ is not an integer. For any value of n that is not a multiple of 14, that radical is not an integer. However, the question asks whether $\frac{\sqrt{n}}{3}$ is an integer. So n could be 9 and $\frac{\sqrt{n}}{3}$ would be an integer. On the other hand, there are a myriad of values for which neither $\frac{\sqrt{n}}{3}$ nor $\sqrt{14n}$ is an integer. Eliminate **(D)**. The correct choice is **(A)**.

Practice Set: Odds and Evens on the GMAT

4. **(C)**

Set S contains 5 integers, labeled A, B, C, D, and E. If the sum of all of the elements of set S is odd, how many of the elements of set S are even?

(1)   The sum of A and B is odd.

(2)   The product of B, C, and D is odd.

STEP 1: ANALYZE THE QUESTION STEM

This is a Value question. You need to determine whether there's enough information to figure out how many of the integers in set S are even, and you know that the sum of all five integers in set S is odd. If the sum of the integers is odd, there has to be an odd number of odd integers in the set. Therefore, set S must contain either 1, 3, or 5 odd integers.

STEP 2: EVALUATE THE STATEMENTS USING 12TEN

Statement (1) says that the sum of A and B is odd. When two integers sum to an odd number, one must be even and the other odd (because the sum of two even integers or two odd integers will always be even). Therefore, there cannot be five odd integers in the set. Since $A + B$ is odd, and the sum of all the integers in the set is odd, the sum of C, D, and E must be even. However, that could mean that two of these three are odd and one is even, or it could mean that all three are even. Thus, Statement (1) is insufficient. Eliminate **(A)** and **(D)**.

Statement (2) says that the product of B, C, and D is odd. An odd product can have only odd factors, never any even ones, so for $B \times C \times D$ to be odd, B, C, and D must each be odd. However, this statement says nothing about A or E, which could both be even or both be odd for all five integers in the set to sum to an odd number. Therefore, this statement is insufficient and you can eliminate **(B)**.

Now take the statements together. You've already determined from information in the question stem and from Statement (1) that there must be either one or three odd integers in set S. From Statement (2), you know that B, C, and D are all odd. Thus, the two statements together prove that there must be exactly three odd integers in set S, and therefore two even integers. **(C)** is correct.

5. **(B)**

If a and b are integers and a is odd, is b even?

(1) $(a^3 + 1) \times b$ is even.

(2) $\dfrac{a^2}{b} = b - 4$

STEP 1: ANALYZE THE QUESTION STEM

In this Yes/No question, you are told that a is an odd integer and asked whether b is even. If you can answer either "definitely yes" or "definitely no" to this question, you'll have sufficiency. Therefore, sufficiency means showing that b is either always even or always odd.

STEP 2: EVALUATE THE STATEMENTS USING 12TEN

Statement (1) provides an expression that's even. Evaluate it one piece at a time. Since a is odd, a^3 must also be odd (because odd × odd is always odd); therefore, $a^3 + 1$ must be even (because odd + odd = even). Since an even times any other integer will always be even, b could be either even or odd and the statement would still hold true. Therefore, Statement (1) is insufficient. Eliminate **(A)** and **(D)**.

Statement (2) offers an algebraic equation that expresses the relationship between a and b. Solve this to see if there's enough information to determine whether b is even or odd:

$$\frac{a^2}{b} = b - 4$$

$$a^2 = b(b - 4)$$

$$a^2 = b^2 - 4b$$

There's no need to simplify further. Instead, use the rules of odds and evens; since a is odd, again a^2 must be odd, because odd × odd = odd. Thus, you can say that $b^2 - 4b$ must also be odd. Because any even number times any other integer is always even, $4b$ must be even. Therefore, you can say that $b^2 -$ even = odd.

Since an odd minus an even will always yield an odd, but an even minus an even will always be even, b^2 must be odd. Because two integers multiplied together (in this case, $b \times b$) that produce an odd product must both be odd, b itself must be odd. Thus, Statement (2) is sufficient, and **(B)** is correct.

6. **(E)**

If m is an odd number and p is a prime number, which of the following must be odd?

○ mp

○ $m(m + p)$

○ $m - p$

○ $m^2 + 2p^2 + 1$

○ $m^2(m + 2p)$

1: ANALYZE THE QUESTION

In this abstract number properties question, m must be an odd number and p must be a prime number. A prime number is a positive integer with exactly two factors: 1 and itself. Examples of prime numbers include 2, 3, 5, and 7. Note that 2 is even (2 is the only even prime number), so p may be even or odd.

STEP 2: STATE THE TASK

Determine which answer choice must always be odd or, in other words, eliminate any answer choices that can be even.

STEP 3: APPROACH STRATEGICALLY

For some number properties questions, picking numbers is an efficient strategy.

Since m is an odd number, let m be a small, easy-to-manage value such as 1. While 1 can be a poor choice for picking numbers in a Problem Solving question where you are solving for a numeric value, it is a fine choice when you are finding an expression with a particular number property, since 1 behaves the same way as any other odd number. Since p is a prime number, 5 is a good choice. Evaluate each answer choice by plugging in these values and eliminating any choice that produces an even value.

(A) $mp = (1)(5) = 5$. Keep **(A)**.

(B) $m(m + p) = 1(1 + 5) = 1(6) = 6$. Eliminate **(B)**.

(C) $m - p = 1 - 5 = -4$. Eliminate **(C)**.

(D) $m^2 + 2p^2 + 1 = 1^2 + 2(5)^2 + 1 = 1 + 50 + 1 = 52$. Eliminate **(D)**.

(E) $m^2(m + 2p) = 1^2(1 + 2 \times 5) = 1(1 + 10) = 1(11) = 11$. Keep **(E)**.

Since both **(A)** and **(E)** produced odd values, they both can be odd. But *must* they be odd? Pick numbers one more time. Pick 2 for p to test an even number for this variable. Keep $m = 1$ since all other permissible values for m are also odd and will not affect the result.

(A) $mp = (1)(2) = 6$. Eliminate **(A)**.

Therefore, **(E)** is correct.

STEP 4: CONFIRM YOUR ANSWER

You can verify that **(E)** is correct: $m^2(m + 2p) = 1^2(1 + 2 \times 2) = 1(1 + 4) = 1(5) = 5$. Also, you can check **(E)** by applying the rules for odds and evens. Since m^2 is an odd value squared, this is an odd $\times$ odd, which is always odd. Then $2p$ is even for any p value, and $m + 2p$ is then an odd + even, which is odd. Lastly, multiplying two odd values, m^2 and $m + 2p$, yields an odd product.

Practice Set: Positives and Negatives on the GMAT

7.   **(C)**

If $x - y = 8$, which of the following must be true?

    I.   Both x and y are positive.

    II. If x is positive, y must be positive.

    III. If x is negative, y must be negative.

O   I only

O   II only

O   III only

O   I and II

O   II and III

STEP 1: ANALYZE THE QUESTION

You know that $x - y = 8$. As this is a Roman numeral question with variables, expect to use picking numbers and don't forget to check the Roman numeral statements in the most efficient order. In this question, begin with Statement II, as it shows up the most in the answer choices.

STEP 2: STATE THE TASK

Determine which of the Roman numeral statements are true.

STEP 3: APPROACH STRATEGICALLY

Statement II: If x is positive, y must be positive. To test whether this statement needs to be true, try to pick some numbers for x and y where the result is false. The key is to pick numbers such that the condition is true but the result is false. If $x - 6$ and $y = -2$, then $x - y$ does equal 8. The condition is true, yet you were able to make the result false, so Statement II does not need to be true. Eliminate **(B)**, **(D)**, and **(E)**.

Of the remaining statements, Statement I (Both x and y are positive) is the easier one to test because the numbers picked for x and y can be used to invalidate this statement as well. Eliminate **(A)**.

Therefore, the correct answer is **(C)**.

STEP 4: CONFIRM YOUR ANSWER

Confirm the answer by checking Statement III: If x is negative, y must be negative. In the equation $x - y = 8$, if x is negative and y is positive, then the result would simply get more negative. The only way to arrive at a positive answer when x is negative is for y to also be negative. Choice **(C)** is confirmed.

8.   (B)

If $b \neq 0$ and $-1 < \dfrac{a}{b} < 1$, which of the following CANNOT be true?

○ $a + b < 0$

○ $(a + b)(a - b) > 0$

○ $a - b > 0$

○ $(a + b)(a - b) < 0$

○ $a + b > 0$

STEP 1: ANALYZE THE QUESTION

The question tells you that $\dfrac{a}{b}$ is a fraction between -1 and 1. The answer choices compare various expressions to 0, so you'll be considering positive and negative number properties as you evaluate the choices. The inequality in the question stem means that the absolute value of a is less than the absolute value of b (a is closer to 0); the two values may have the same or different signs.

STEP 2: STATE THE TASK

Find the answer choice that cannot be true, no matter what permissible values of a and b are used.

STEP 3: APPROACH STRATEGICALLY

Evaluate each choice to see whether or not it can be true; since there's no need to go in order, pick statements that seem easy to evaluate. **(A)** and **(E)** are very similar and relatively easy to evaluate. Since both a and b could be negative, their sum could be less than 0, which means **(A)** could be true; since they could be positive, their sum could be greater than 0, which means **(E)** could be true. Eliminate both of these choices.

(C) is a good one to tackle next. This statement is true if $a > b$. The inequality in the question stem allows for a to be positive while b is negative (e.g., $a = 1$ and $b = -2$), so this choice could be true—eliminate it.

(B) and **(D)** contain the same quadratic expression: $(a + b)(a - b)$. Restate this as $a^2 - b^2$. Any non-zero value raised to an even exponent is positive, so the fact that a and/or b could be negative can be ignored. The absolute value of b is greater than that of a, so $b^2 > a^2$. Thus, $a^2 - b^2$ must be negative and cannot be positive. The statement $(a + b)(a - b) > 0$ cannot be true, so **(B)** is correct.

STEP 4: CONFIRM YOUR ANSWER

If needed, you can pick permissible numbers to quickly check that **(B)** cannot be true.

9. **(D)**

Is $\dfrac{s-t}{st} < 0$?

(1) $t < 0 < s$

(2) $\dfrac{st}{s-t} < -1$

STEP 1: ANALYZE THE QUESTION STEM

This is a Yes/No question that asks whether an algebraic expression is negative. The answer will be yes if $(s - t)$ and st have opposite signs, and the answer will be no if they have the same sign. Thus, a statement would need to provide the values of the individual variables or the signs of both $(s - t)$ and st to provide sufficient information to answer the question.

STEP 2: EVALUATE THE STATEMENTS USING 12TEN

Statement (1) says that s is positive and t is negative. Therefore, $(s - t)$ involves subtracting a negative number from a positive number. Subtracting a negative number is the same as adding a positive number, so since s is already positive, $(s - t)$ is really a positive number plus another positive number, which must be positive.

Additionally, st is a positive number times a negative number, so st is negative. So $\dfrac{s-t}{st} = \dfrac{\text{positive number}}{\text{negative number}} = $ negative number. The answer to the question is thus a definite yes, and Statement (1) is sufficient; eliminate **(B)**, **(C)**, and **(E)**.

Statement (2) says that the reciprocal of the given expression is less than -1. Whether a negative fraction is written as $\dfrac{a}{b}$ or as $\dfrac{b}{a}$ the fraction is still negative. So $\dfrac{s-t}{st}$ is also negative, making Statement (2) sufficient; **(D)** is correct.

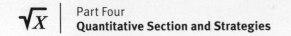

Practice Set: Factors and Multiples on the GMAT

10. (C)

If a certain number is divisible by 18 and 24, it must also be divisible by which of the following?

- ○ 30
- ○ 36
- ○ 72
- ○ 216
- ○ 432

STEP 1: ANALYZE THE QUESTION

The question states that a number is divisible by both 18 and 24, meaning that 18 and 24 divide into the number with no remainder. This is the same as saying that this number is a multiple of both 18 and 24.

STEP 2: STATE THE TASK

By asking which choice the number is "divisible by," the question is asking which of the choices divides into the number with no remainder. This is the same as asking which of the choices must be a factor of the number.

STEP 3: APPROACH STRATEGICALLY

To think about what this number could be, you can count by 18s and 24s until you find a number that is on both lists. So it's 18, 36, 54, 72 . . . and it's 24, 48, 72 . . . The smallest number that's divisible by both 18 and 24 is 72. Numbers smaller than this aren't divisible by both 18 and 24, and while the number could be a larger multiple of 72 (for example, $2 \times 72 = 144$ is divisible by both 18 and 24), it isn't necessarily greater than 72. Thus, you know that the number must be divisible by 72, and **(C)** is correct. Note that 72 is the least common multiple of 18 and 24.

If you don't feel comfortable counting by 18s and 24s (or if you encounter a problem with larger numbers that you definitely don't feel comfortable counting by), another way to find the least common multiple is to use prime factorization, discussed in depth in the next section. The prime factorization of 18 is $2 \times 3 \times 3$, so this number must have at least one 2 and two 3s as factors. The prime factorization of 24 is $2 \times 2 \times 2 \times 3$. You already know the number has a 3 as a factor (in fact, it has two 3s), but now you also know it must have not just one but three 2s as factors. So the number in question *must* have prime factors of 2, 2, 2, 3, and 3. It *could* have other factors as well, but these are the only ones you can be sure of.

If you go the prime factorization route, the next step is to determine the prime factors of each choice and compare them to the prime factors 2, 2, 2, 3, and 3. The prime factors of 30 are 2, 3, and 5, but the number does not necessarily have a prime factor of 5. Eliminate **(A)**. The prime factorization of 36 is $2 \times 2 \times 3 \times 3$. Since the number in the question requires three factors of 2, eliminate **(B)**. The prime factorization of 72 is $2 \times 2 \times 2 \times 3 \times 3$. All of these prime factors must be in the given number, so **(C)** is correct.

STEP 4: CONFIRM YOUR ANSWER

Be certain that you answered the question that was asked. A common error is to multiply 18 by 24 to get 432 and choose **(E)**. However, while it is possible that the number is 432 or a multiple of 432, it does not have to have all these factors; it could be a smaller common multiple of 18 and 24.

11. (C)

What is the greatest positive integer x such that 9^{6x} is a factor of 81^{10+x}?

- ○   2
- ○   4
- ○   5
- ○   6
- ○   15

STEP 1: ANALYZE THE QUESTION

This question states that 9^{6x} can be a factor of 81^{10+x}. Because x is a positive integer, both exponent terms are positive integers. The answer choices are possible values of x.

STEP 2: STATE THE TASK

Use the rules of exponents and an understanding of factors and multiples to find the largest possible exponent x that will make 9^{6x} a factor of 81^{10+x}.

STEP 3: APPROACH STRATEGICALLY

First, to work more easily with the two exponent terms, give them the same base. Since 81 is 9^2, 81^{10+x} is $(9^2)^{10+x} = 9^{20+2x}$.

Now the task is to find the largest x such that 9^{6x} is a factor of 9^{20+2x}. Recall that the largest factor of a positive integer is that integer (e.g., the greatest factor of 5 is 5, and the greatest factor of 100 is 100). So the largest factor of 81^{10+x} is a value equivalent to 81^{10+x}. Therefore, find the x value that makes 9^{6x} equal to 9^{20+2x}. Since the bases are the same, set the exponents equal to each other and solve for x.

$$6x = 20 + 2x$$

$$4x = 20$$

$$x = 5$$

When $x = 5$, 9^{6x} equals 81^{10+x} and is its greatest possible factor. **(C)** is correct.

STEP 4: CONFIRM YOUR ANSWER

Plugging 5 back in for x shows that the two exponent terms are equal. You get $9^{6\times 5}$ and 81^{10+5}, or 9^{30} and 81^{15}. Because $81 = 9^2$, $81^{15} = (9^2)^{15} = 9^{30}$. The two values are equal, and 9^{6x} is as large as it can be to still be a factor of 81^{10+x}; x can't be any greater than 5.

12. **(D)**

How many positive integers less than 70 are multiples of either 3 or 4 but not both?

○ 17

○ 18

○ 23

○ 30

○ 35

STEP 1: ANALYZE THE QUESTION

This question involves multiples of 3 and multiples of 4 or, in other words, numbers that are divisible by 3 or by 4. When dealing with divisibility, remember that prime factorization can often provide an efficient path to the solution.

STEP 2: STATE THE TASK

Find the number of multiples of 3 that are less than 70 and take out the values that are multiples of both 3 and 4. Find the number of multiples of 4 that are less than 70 and take out the values that are multiples of both 3 and 4. Add the two values together.

STEP 3: APPROACH STRATEGICALLY

The prime factorization of 3 is 3 because it is already a prime number. The prime factorization of 4 is 2×2. Since there are no overlaps in the prime factors needed to make up the two numbers, a number that is a multiple of both 3 and 4 is a multiple of $2 \times 2 \times 3 = 12$.

Dividing 3 into 70 yields 23 and a remainder. Therefore, there are 23 multiples of 3 among the positive integers less than 70. Dividing 12 into 70 yields 5 and a remainder, which means there are 5 positive integers less than 70 that are multiples of both 3 and 4. Subtracting 5 from 23 yields 18, which represents the number of positive integers less than 70 that are multiples of 3 but not 4.

Dividing 4 into 70 yields 17 and a remainder. Therefore, there are 17 multiples of 4 among the positive integers less than 70. You have already found that there are 5 positive integers less than 70 that are multiples of both 3 and 4. Subtracting 5 from 17 yields 12, which represents the number of positive integers less than 70 that are multiples of 4 but not 3.

The question asks for the number of multiples of 3 or 4 but not both. This is equal to the number of multiples of 3 but not 4 plus the number of multiples of 4 but not 3, the two values previously computed. Adding 18 and 12 yields 30, making **(D)** correct.

STEP 4: CONFIRM YOUR ANSWER

To confirm the answer, you could write out all of the multiples of 3 under 70, then cross out any that are multiples of 4. Next, write out all the multiples of 4 under 70 and cross out any that are multiples of 3. The total number of numbers that are not crossed out is 30, so **(D)** is confirmed.

Practice Set: Remainders and Primes on the GMAT

13. **(B)**

If n is an integer such that $12 \leq n \leq 24$, is n a prime number?

(1) The remainder when n is divided by 4 is 1.

(2) The remainder when n is divided by 6 is 1.

STEP 1: ANALYZE THE QUESTION STEM

This Yes/No question states that n is an integer between 12 and 24 inclusive, and it asks whether n is a prime number. Information that allows you to determine that n definitely is prime, or definitely is not prime, will be sufficient.

STEP 2: EVALUATE THE STATEMENTS USING 12TEN

Statement (1) tells you that dividing n by 4 leaves a remainder of 1, meaning that n is 1 greater than a multiple of 4. The multiples of 4 within the range are 12, 16, 20, and 24, and 1 more than 24 is outside the range. Thus, the possible values of n are 13, 17, and 21. The first two are, indeed, prime numbers, but 21 is divisible by 3 and 7. Therefore, Statement (1) is insufficient. Eliminate **(A)** and **(D)**.

Statement (2) says that dividing n by 6 leaves a remainder of 1. Thus, according to this statement, n could be 13 or 19. Both of these are prime numbers, so Statement (2) is sufficient. **(B)** is correct.

14. (A)

If $x = 12$, $y = 35$, and $x^2y^2 = 21 \times 28 \times 30 \times z$, what is the value of z?

- ○ 10
- ○ 12
- ○ 15
- ○ 21
- ○ 30

STEP 1: ANALYZE THE QUESTION

The question gives the values of x and y and says that x^2y^2 is the product of three integers and a third variable, z. You need to determine the value of z. When the GMAT presents large-scale multiplication or division that seems overly complicated, look for a faster way. This question is a great candidate for prime factorization, since you need to factor a large product to determine the unknown factor z.

STEP 2: STATE THE TASK

Determine the prime factors of the given expression and of each term in the product; then cancel out all the common terms. Those that remain will be the prime factors of z.

STEP 3: APPROACH STRATEGICALLY

Find the prime factorization of x^2 and y^2:

$$12^2 = (2 \times 2 \times 3)(2 \times 2 \times 3)$$
$$35^2 = (5 \times 7)(5 \times 7)$$

Thus, you can say that $x^2y^2 = 2 \times 2 \times 2 \times 2 \times 3 \times 3 \times 5 \times 5 \times 7 \times 7$. Now find the prime factors of 21, 28, and 30:

$$21 = 3 \times 7$$
$$28 = 2 \times 2 \times 7$$
$$30 = 2 \times 3 \times 5$$

Therefore, $21 \times 28 \times 30 \times z = 2 \times 2 \times 2 \times 3 \times 3 \times 5 \times 7 \times 7 \times z$. Now compare the two lists of prime factors you've found and cancel out prime factors that are shared to determine what is left over; these will be the factors of z:

$$x^2y^2 = \cancel{2} \times \cancel{2} \times \cancel{2} \times 2 \times \cancel{3} \times \cancel{3} \times \cancel{5} \times 5 \times \cancel{7} \times \cancel{7}$$
$$x^2y^2 = \cancel{2} \times \cancel{2} \times \cancel{2} \times \cancel{3} \times \cancel{3} \times \cancel{5} \times \cancel{7} \times \cancel{7} \times z$$
$$z = 2 \times 5 = 10$$

(A) is correct.

STEP 4: CONFIRM YOUR ANSWER

When using prime factorization, be careful to list all of the prime factors, including ones that repeat, such as $2 \times 2 \times 2 \times 2$ or 5×5.

15. (A)

If $a = 5m + 2$ and $b = 5n + 13$, and m and n are positive integers, what is the remainder when $a + b$ is divided by 5?

- ○ 0
- ○ 1
- ○ 2
- ○ 3
- ○ 4

STEP 1: ANALYZE THE QUESTION

This question tests your ability to think critically about the characteristics of remainders in division.

STEP 2: STATE THE TASK

Use the two equations given to find the remainder when $a + b$ is divided by 5.

STEP 3: APPROACH STRATEGICALLY

Start by determining the value of $a + b$ by adding the two given equations: $a + b = 5m + 2 + 5n + 13 = 5m + 5n + 15$. Notice that all three terms have a common factor of 5, so $a + b = 5(m + n + 3)$. Thus, $(a + b) \div 5 = m + n + 3$. Since m and n are integers, $m + n + 3$ must be an integer. So when $a + b$ is divided by 5, the result is an integer; this means that $a + b$ is a multiple of 5. Since $a + b$ is a multiple of 5, there is no remainder when $a + b$ is divided by 5, and **(A)** is correct.

STEP 4: CONFIRM YOUR ANSWER

To double-check your work, you could pick numbers. Using 2 for m and n will make the arithmetic easy. Now $a = 5(2) + 2 = 12$ and $b = 5(2) + 13 = 23$. Thus, $a + b = 12 + 23 = 25$, which is evenly divisible by 5.

GMAT by the Numbers: Number Properties

Now that you've learned how to approach number properties questions on the GMAT, let's add one more dimension to your understanding of how they work.

Take a moment to try this question. Following is performance data from thousands of people who have studied with Kaplan over the decades. Through analyzing this data, we will show you how to approach questions like this one most effectively and how to avoid similarly tempting wrong answer choice types on Test Day.

If a and b are positive integers, is $3a^2b$ divisible by 60?

(1) a is divisible by 10.
(2) b is divisible by 18.

○   Statement (1) ALONE is sufficient, but Statement (2) is not sufficient.

○   Statement (2) ALONE is sufficient, but Statement (1) is not sufficient.

○   BOTH statements TOGETHER are sufficient, but NEITHER statement ALONE is sufficient.

○   EACH statement ALONE is sufficient.

○   Statements (1) and (2) TOGETHER are NOT sufficient.

Explanation

This Yes/No question asks whether $3a^2b$ is divisible by 60. In other words, it asks whether $\frac{3a^2b}{60}$ is an integer. The 3 in the numerator cancels out a factor of 3 from the denominator, so it's really asking whether $\frac{a^2b}{20}$ is an integer. For this expression to be an integer, the remaining factors in the denominator will have to be canceled out by the numerator. Since $20 = 2 \times 2 \times 5$, you're really being asked whether a^2b contains two 2s and one 5 among its factors.

Statement (1) says that a is divisible by 10. Since $10 = 2 \times 5$, you know that a contains at least one 2 and at least one 5 among its factors. Therefore, the a^2 in the numerator must have at least two 2s and at least two 5s. It doesn't matter what factors b contains, since a^2 alone provides all the factors needed to cancel out the 20. Statement (1) is therefore sufficient.

Since $18 = 2 \times 3 \times 3$, Statement (2) tells you that b has at least one 2 and at least two 3s among its factors. By itself, b does not guarantee two factors of 2, let alone any factor of 5. Therefore, Statement (2) is insufficient.

Since Statement (1) alone is sufficient but Statement (2) is not, **(A)** is correct.

Question Statistics

49% of test takers choose **(A)**

3% of test takers choose **(B)**

37% of test takers choose **(C)**

3% of test takers choose **(D)**

8% of test takers choose **(E)**

Sample size = 5,507

As the question statistics reveal, many test takers automatically assume that they need information about every variable in order to answer a question. Knowing this, the test maker often writes statements that provide sufficient information despite not telling you about each variable. Don't automatically think that you need information on all the variables—analyze the question stem carefully to see what you *really* need, and you'll put yourself well ahead of your competition.

More GMAT by the Numbers . . .

To see more questions with answer choice statistics, be sure to review the full-length CATs in your online resources.

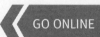 GO ONLINE

kaptest.com/login

CHAPTER 21

Ratios and Proportions on the GMAT

LEARNING OBJECTIVES

After studying this chapter, you will be able to:

- Describe how ratios and proportions are tested on the GMAT
- Identify questions that involve ratios and proportions
- Apply the Kaplan Methods for Problem Solving and Data Sufficiency in questions that test ratios and proportions

Below is a typical Problem Solving proportions question. In this chapter, we'll look at how to apply the Kaplan Method to this question, discuss the proportions rules being tested, and go over the basic principles and strategies that you want to keep in mind on every Quantitative question involving ratios and proportions.

> A baseball team won 45 percent of the first 80 games it played. How many of the remaining 82 games will the team have to win in order to have won exactly 50 percent of all the games it played?
>
> ○ 36
> ○ 45
> ○ 50
> ○ 55
> ○ 81

Before you move on, take a minute to think about what you see in this question and answer some questions about how you think it works:

- What are the various ways you can express 45 percent (as a decimal, fraction, or ratio)?
- What are two different ways to solve this question? Which one is most efficient?
- What trap answer choices might the test makers include for those who misread the question?
- What GMAT Core Competencies are most essential to success on this question?

Previewing Ratios and Proportions on the GMAT

LEARNING OBJECTIVES

In this section, you will learn how to:

- Express proportionality using a decimal, a fraction, or a ratio
- Explain how the Core Competencies of Critical Thinking, Attention to the Right Detail, and Paraphrasing are useful on questions involving proportionality

---

Proportionality shows up on the GMAT in the form of fractions, ratios, decimals, and percents. Fundamentally, proportions represent relationships. You deal with proportionality every day, even if you might not realize it. Rates and speeds, for example, are expressed as ratios: a car travels 30 miles per hour, or a worker earns $80 per task. You can use these proportional relationships to determine how many miles a car travels at this speed over a given length of time or how many tasks a worker must complete in order to earn a given amount of money. Prices are also ratios: a certain item costs $4.50, so the ratio of items to dollars is 1:4.5. Then you could use a proportion to discover how much 24 of the same item would cost. Note that knowing the proportional relationship of one thing to another does not tell you how many things you have. For example, if the ratio of gerbils to parrots in a pet store is 2:3, you don't know the exact number of gerbils or parrots. However, you do know that for every 2 gerbils the store has, there are 3 parrots as well.

Often the GMAT tests proportions in the form of word problems, so the translation skills you learned in the Algebra chapter (a form of Paraphrasing) will continue to be valuable here as you cut through the seeming novelty of the given "story" to understand the underlying proportional relationships being described.

Here are the answers to the questions you were asked to consider.

What Are the Various Ways You Can Express 45 Percent (as a Decimal, Fraction, or Ratio)?

One of the most important skills you can develop for dealing with proportions questions on the GMAT is the ability to convert quickly among percent, decimal, fractional, and ratio forms of the same value. This skill is so crucial because GMAT problems often mix these various formats within the same problem—getting all the values expressed in the same way will make them easier to handle. Also, certain values are just easier to work with in one format or another. For instance, you'd much rather perform arithmetic operations with the fraction $\frac{1}{7}$ than you would with the unwieldy decimal 0.1428571 . . .

In this problem, you may choose to express 45 percent as a decimal (0.45); as a fraction ($\frac{45}{100}$, which reduces to $\frac{9}{20}$); or as a ratio (45:100, which reduces to 9:20), depending on which is easiest to work with at the time. Remembering that *percent* simply means "out of 100" is the key to making these conversions. Later in this chapter, you will find a chart to help you memorize some of the common conversions you're most likely to need on Test Day.

What Are Two Different Ways to Solve This Question? Which One Is Most Efficient?

A lot of information is given in this question, so it is especially important that you organize your scratch-work effectively. You are asked for the number of games a team still needs to win in order to achieve a certain winning percentage. You are given the team's winning percentage so far, the number of games it's played so far, and the number of games it still needs to play, so you have all the information you need to solve arithmetically.

As is usual on the GMAT, this question doesn't necessarily give you the information in the most convenient form, so you will have to do some calculating to figure out the actual number of games the team has won so far and the total number of games the team will have played, but these calculations are possible, so you can solve this question arithmetically. (We will return to this question and solve it using the Kaplan Method later this chapter.)

If that approach was the one that first occurred to you, that's fine—and you're not alone. You have likely been rewarded all your academic life for knowing how to do the "schoolroom math," and this approach can get you the correct answer on the GMAT as well. What might not have occurred to you initially is the other strategy you could use to solve this problem: backsolving. Whenever you are asked to solve for a single value (here, it's the number of games the team still needs to win) and the answer choices are all simple numerical values, it may be quicker and easier to answer the question by plugging the values in the answer choices into the scenario described in the question stem.

More guidance on backsolving is available in the Problem Solving chapter of this book; it's a highly efficient strategy, and it's well worth becoming comfortable with, even if you are generally expert at solving using "classroom math."

What Trap Answer Choices Might the Test Makers Include for Those Who Misread the Question?

There are various unknowns in this question that the unwary test taker might mistakenly choose as the correct answer—but to the wrong question. As you practice, never choose an answer choice simply because you recognize that number from your calculations; some of these choices are likely to be traps.

This question asks you for the number of additional games the team must win. Possible trap answers are the number of wins so far—choice (A)—and the total number of wins the team needs—choice (E).

The final step of the Kaplan Method for Problem Solving is to confirm your answer; by double-checking that you are answering the question that was asked, you will avoid this all-too-common mistake.

What GMAT Core Competencies Are Most Essential to Success on This Question?

As you've seen throughout the Quant section, Critical Thinking is necessary for deciding on the most efficient strategic approach, and Attention to the Right Detail will ensure that you answer the question that is asked instead of falling for trap answers. Specifically on proportions questions, you will use your skill in Paraphrasing to convert ratios into the form that's easiest for that problem. You will also pay Attention to the Right Detail so that you don't confuse different types of ratios such as part-to-part and part-to-whole.

How Do I Apply the Kaplan Methods to GMAT Ratios and Proportions?

Now let's apply the Kaplan Method for Problem Solving to the proportions question you saw earlier:

> A baseball team won 45 percent of the first 80 games it played. How many of the remaining 82 games will the team have to win in order to have won exactly 50 percent of all the games it played?
>
> ○ 36
>
> ○ 45
>
> ○ 50
>
> ○ 55
>
> ○ 81

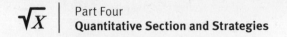

STEP 1: ANALYZE THE QUESTION

You are given the percentage of games a team has won for the first 80 games and the number of games it has yet to play (82). You are asked to calculate how many more games the team needs to win to have a 50% win record.

STEP 2: STATE THE TASK

You need to calculate the total number of games that will be played, then the total number of those that need to be won for a 50% record. Then calculate how many games have already been won and subtract that from the total number of wins needed.

STEP 3: APPROACH STRATEGICALLY

First, add the 80 games that have already been played to the number of remaining games to get the total games: $80 + 82 = 162$. To win 50% of the games, the team would need to win half of these, or 81. You can use the percentage given to calculate how many games the team has already won: 45% of 80.

The number of the games the team still needs to win is $81 - 36 = 45$. Choice **(B)** is correct. 45% can be expressed as $\frac{45}{100} = \frac{9}{20}$. Use this fraction when multiplying: $\frac{9}{20} \times 80 = 9 \times 4 = 36$.

The answer choices are small, manageable numbers, so you may want to use backsolving, especially if you're not sure how to set up the arithmetic. If you choose to backsolve, remember to think about exactly what the answer choices represent: the number of additional games the team needs to win. Start with choice **(B)**, 45 games. Calculate the games already won, 45% of $80 = \frac{9}{20} \times 80 = 36$, and add the 45 additional games: $36 + 45 = 81$.

Now you can ask yourself, is 81 half (or 50%) of all the games? The team's already played 80, and there are 82 left to play, so $80 + 82 = 162$ and, yes, choice **(B)** is 50% of 162.

If you had instead backsolved starting with **(D)**, you would have ended up with too high a proportion of games won (91 of 162) and known that you needed a smaller number of wins during the second part of the season in order to end up with a winning percentage of 50%.

STEP 4: CONFIRM YOUR ANSWER

Review your calculations to be sure they're correct. You can also verify that your answer is logical using Critical Thinking: the team would need more than 40 additional wins to make up for the fact that it won less than 50% of its first 80 games.

Now let's look at each of the areas of proportions that show up on the GMAT Quantitative section, starting with how ratios relate to proportions.

Ratios

LEARNING OBJECTIVES

In this section, you will learn how to:

- Describe various types of ratios including part to part, part to whole, and those with two or more terms
- Articulate an effective guessing strategy for working with questions that involve ratios
- Apply the Kaplan Methods for Problem Solving and Data Sufficiency to questions dealing with ratios

A ratio is a comparison of two quantities by division. Ratios may be written with a fraction bar $\left(\dfrac{x}{y}\right)$, with a colon ($x{:}y$), or in English ("the ratio of x to y"). Ratios can (and in most cases, should) be reduced to lowest terms, just as fractions are reduced.

Example: Joe is 16 years old and Mary is 12. The ratio of Joe's age to Mary's age is 16 to 12.

$$\frac{16}{12} = \frac{4}{3} \text{ or } 4{:}3$$

In a ratio of two numbers, the numerator is often associated with the word *of* and the denominator with the word *to*.

$$\text{Ratio} = \frac{\text{Of}\ldots}{\text{To}}$$

Example: In a box of doughnuts, 12 are sugar and 18 are chocolate. What is the ratio of sugar doughnuts to chocolate doughnuts?

$$\text{Ratio} = \frac{\text{Of sugar}}{\text{To chocolate}} = \frac{12}{18} = \frac{2}{3}$$

Part-to-Part Ratios and Part-to-Whole Ratios

A ratio represents the proportional relationship between quantities or numbers. A ratio can compare either a part to another part or a part to a whole. One type of ratio can readily be converted to the other only if all the parts together equal the whole and there is no overlap among the parts (that is, if the whole is equal to the sum of its parts).

Example: The ratio of domestic sales to foreign sales of a certain product is 3:5. What fraction of the total sales are the domestic sales?

First, note that this is the same as asking for the ratio of the amount of domestic sales to the amount of total sales.

In this case, the whole (total sales) is equal to the sum of the parts (domestic and foreign sales). You can convert from a part:part ratio to a part:whole ratio. For every 8 sales of the product, 3 are domestic and 5 are foreign. The ratio of domestic sales to total sales is then $\dfrac{3}{8}$ or 3:8.

Example: The ratio of domestic to European sales of a certain product is 3:5. What is the ratio of domestic sales to total sales?

> Here you cannot convert from a part:part ratio (domestic sales:European sales) to a part:whole ratio (domestic sales:total sales) because you don't know whether there are any other sales besides domestic and European sales. The question doesn't say that the product is sold only domestically and in Europe, so you cannot assume there are no other sales. The ratio asked for here cannot be determined.

Ratios with More Than Two Terms

Some GMAT questions deal with ratios that have three or more terms. Always represent them with colons (e.g., *x:y:z*).

Even though they convey information about more relationships, ratios involving more than two terms are governed by the same principles as two-term ratios. Ratios involving more than two terms are usually ratios of various parts, and it is usually the case that the sum of these parts equals the whole, making it possible to find part-to-whole ratios as well.

Example: Given that the ratio of men to women to children in a room is 4:3:2, what other ratios can be determined?

> The whole here is the number of people in the room, and since every person is either a man, a woman, or a child, you can determine part:whole ratios for each of these parts. Of every nine $(4 + 3 + 2 = 9)$ people in the room, 4 are men, 3 are women, and 2 are children. This gives you three part:whole ratios as follows:
>
> Ratio of men:total people = 4:9. or $\frac{4}{9}$.
>
> Ratio of women:total people = 3:9 = 1:3 or $\frac{1}{3}$.
>
> Ratio of children:total people = 2:9 or $\frac{2}{9}$.
>
> In addition, from any ratio of more than two terms, you can determine various two-term ratios among the parts.
>
> Ratio of women:men = 3:4 or $\frac{3}{4}$.
>
> Ratio of men:children = 4:2 = 2:1 or $\frac{2}{1}$.
>
> Ratio of children:women = 2:3 or $\frac{2}{3}$.
>
> And finally, if you were asked to establish a relationship between the number of adults and the number of children in the room, this would also be possible. For every 2 children, there are 4 men and 3 women, which is $4 + 3 = 7$ adults. Thus,
>
> Ratio of children:adults = 2:7 or $\frac{2}{7}$.
>
> Ratio of adults:children = 7:2 or $\frac{7}{2}$.

Naturally, a GMAT question will require you to determine only one or at most two of these ratios, but knowing how much information is contained within a given ratio will help you to determine quickly which questions are solvable and which, if any, are not.

Ratios Versus Actual Numbers

Ratios are always reduced to simplest form. If a team's ratio of wins to losses is 5:3, this does not necessarily mean that the team has won exactly 5 games and lost exactly 3. For instance, if a team has won 30 games and lost 18, its ratio is still 5:3. Unless you know the actual number of games played (or the actual number won or lost), you can't know the actual values of the parts in the ratio.

Example: In a classroom of 30 first-grade students, the ratio of the 5-year-olds in the class to students in the class is 2:5. How many students are 5 years old?

You are given a part-to-whole ratio (5-year-olds:students). This ratio can also be expressed as a fraction. Multiplying this fraction by the whole gives the value of the corresponding part. There are 30 students, and $\frac{2}{5}$ of them are 5 years old, so the number of 5-year-olds (5YOs) must be $\frac{2}{5} \times 30$.

$$\frac{2 \text{ 5YOs}}{1 \cancel{5} \text{ students}} \times \cancel{30}^{6} \text{ students} = 2 \times 6 \text{ 5YOs} = 12 \text{ 5YOs}$$

For many problems, you can make some deductions about the actual values, even when you aren't given a total directly. Often, this is the key to solving a challenging proportions question.

Let's say that a car dealership has used and new cars in stock in a ratio of 2:5. You don't know the actual number. You know that if there are 2 used cars, there will be 5 new cars. And if there are 4 (or 2 × 2) used cars, there will be 10 (or 5 × 2) new cars. If there are 6 used cars (2 × 3), then there are 15 new cars (5 × 3). In other words, the actual numbers will always equal the figures in the ratio multiplied by the same (unknown) factor.

You can translate from ratios into algebra:

$$\text{used} : \text{new} = 2 : 5$$
$$\text{used} = 2x; \text{new} = 5x$$

Example: A homecoming party at College Y is initially attended by students and alumni in a ratio of 1 to 5. But after two hours, 36 more students arrive, changing the ratio of students to alumni to 1 to 2. If the number of alumni did not change over those two hours, how many people were at the party when it began?

Besides the 36 additional students who arrive, nowhere are actual numbers referred to directly. But you can jot down the two ratios you're given in a slightly more useable form:

$$\begin{array}{cc} S:A & s+36:A \\ 1:5 & 1:2 \end{array}$$

Translate into algebra. Let x be the number of students initially at the party.

$$\begin{array}{cc} S:A & s+36:A \\ 1:5 & 1:2 \\ x:5x & x+36:2(x+36) \end{array}$$

Now you've got some equations to work with:

$$A = 5x$$
$$A = 2x + 72$$

You now have two different expressions for A that are equal. Thus:

$$5x = 2x + 72$$
$$3x = 72$$
$$x = 24$$

Now you know that there were 24 students initially.

Substitute 24 for x to solve for alumni:

$$A = 5 \times 24$$
$$A = 120$$

The party started with 24 students and 120 alumni, for a total of 144 people.

Guessing with Ratios

You may have noticed that many GMAT ratio problems involve things like students, women, children, cars, and so forth—things that cannot really exist as non-integer values. (You can't have $43\frac{1}{5}$ people at a party, for instance!)

There's a valuable deduction to be made here—if the entities in a problem cannot logically be non-integers, then the factor by which the ratio is multiplied must be an integer. Therefore, *the actual number of something must be a multiple of its value in the ratio.*

Example:

A movie buff stores movies on the internet and on her personal computer in a ratio of 7:2. If she purchases 6 new movies and downloads them to her personal computer, that ratio would change to 11:4. If she stores movies in no other locations, what was the original number of movies she owned before the purchase of new movies?

- ○ 22
- ○ 28
- ○ 77
- ○ 99
- ○ 105

The question asks for the whole of the ratio for which you are initially given only two parts. The question specifies that there are no other parts to the whole, so you can add the two parts together:

Internet : Computer : Total

7:2:9

There's no such thing as "a fraction of a movie," so the common factor by which you'd multiply 7, 2, and 9 to find the actual numbers must be an integer. That means the number of movies stored on the internet is a multiple of 7, the number of movies stored on the computer is a multiple of 2, and the total—what you're looking for—must be a multiple of 9.

Take a look at the answers—only (**D**) is a multiple of 9, so there's no need to do any more math; (**D**) must be the answer.

In-Format Question: Ratios on the GMAT

Now let's use the Kaplan Method on a Problem Solving question dealing with ratios:

> The ratio of two quantities is 2:3. If each of the quantities is increased by 6, what is the ratio of the new quantities?
>
> O 2:3
>
> O 6:7
>
> O 8:9
>
> O 8:3
>
> O It cannot be determined from the information given.

STEP 1: ANALYZE THE QUESTION

For ratio questions, keep careful track of which values are ratios and which are actual quantities. You are told that the ratio of quantities is 2:3. So the smallest value for quantity A is 2 and for quantity B is 3. You could also have any multiple of this ratio, so you could have quantity A = 4 and quantity B = 6, for example.

STEP 2: STATE THE TASK

Now that you have a clear picture of the information, pay Attention to the Right Detail. You are given the ratio of the two quantities, not the exact number of each. Without the actual total value or one of the quantities' values, you can't determine the new values. The correct answer is (**E**).

If you weren't able to apply this rule so directly, you could solve this question by picking numbers for the possible quantities.

STEP 3: APPROACH STRATEGICALLY

First, test the smallest possible quantities, since these will be the most manageable: quantity A = 2 and quantity B = 3. Adding 6 to each quantity, you get the following new values: quantity A = 8 and quantity B = 9. The new ratio would be 8:9.

Before you select (**C**), however, you must test a second case. If quantity A = 4 and quantity B = 6, then after adding 6 to each quantity, you get the following new values: quantity A = 10 and quantity B = 12. The new ratio would be 10:12, or 5:6.

You can get two distinct results depending on the original values you choose for the actual quantities, so the correct answer must be (**E**).

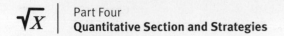

STEP 4: CONFIRM YOUR ANSWER

In ratio questions, if you change the actual quantities through multiplication or division, the resulting ratio will be the same, regardless of the starting values of the quantities. However, the same ratio may not be preserved if you add or subtract from the quantities. Knowing this rule is a great way to confirm your answer. Note, by the way, that while this was a Problem Solving question, the GMAT likes to test your understanding of this rule with Data Sufficiency questions in which you need to determine whether you have enough information to solve.

TAKEAWAYS: RATIOS

- A ratio represents the proportional relationship between quantities or numbers.
- If you are given the number of each item, you can determine the ratio.
- If you are given a ratio and the actual number of items that corresponds to one element of the ratio, you can determine the number of items represented by each of the other elements of the ratio.
- The actual number of items is always a multiple of the number representing that item in the ratio.
- The GMAT can describe ratios in various forms. For example, "the ratio of x to y" = $\dfrac{x}{y} = x : y$.

Practice Set: Ratios on the GMAT

1. At a certain university, the football program receives 4 times more funding than does the basketball program. Together, the football and basketball programs receive 3 times as much funding as do all other sports programs combined. What is the ratio of funding for the basketball program to funding for all other sports programs, not including the football program?

   ○   1:5
   ○   1:4
   ○   3:5
   ○   3:4
   ○   5:3

2. If $\frac{a}{b} = \frac{c}{d}$, what is the numerical ratio of b to d?

   (1) $\frac{a}{b} = \frac{3c}{2b}$
   (2) $a = 2$ and $d = 4$.

3. If the ratio of a to b is 4 to 3 and the ratio of b to c is 1 to 5, what is the ratio of a to c?

   ○ $\frac{4}{15}$
   ○ $\frac{1}{3}$
   ○ $\frac{2}{5}$
   ○ $\frac{4}{5}$
   ○ $\frac{7}{6}$

Applying Fractions to Proportions

> **LEARNING OBJECTIVES**
>
> In this section, you will learn how to:
>
> - Solve proportion problems using cross multiplication
> - Apply the Kaplan Methods for Problem Solving and Data Sufficiency to questions dealing with fractions and proportions

As you saw in the previous section, the GMAT will frequently ask you to deal with proportional relationships by working with fractions used to represent ratios. Let's look at how to apply the skills you learned in the Arithmetic chapter for dealing with fractions to questions that ask about proportions.

A proportion is a comparison of two ratios. Usually, a proportion consists of an equation in which two ratios (expressed as fractions) are set equal to each other. You can set up proportions whenever you are given a relationship between more than one fraction or ratio and are asked to solve for the missing part. Fractions in proportions represent part-to-part or part-to-whole relationships. When dealing with proportions, pay close attention to what something is a proportion of. A common "twist" is to use different denominators in the same problem.

In the proportion $\frac{a}{b} = \frac{c}{d}$, a and d are identified as the **extremes**, and c and b are identified as the **means**. These terms stem from the alternate notation for these ratios, $a{:}b = c{:}d$, in which the extremes occupy the end positions of the equation. But despite that terminology, it's usually easier to express proportions as fractions when solving GMAT problems.

To solve a proportion, use cross multiplication to multiply the numerator from the first ratio by the denominator from the second ratio, then the denominator from the first ratio by the numerator of the second ratio, and set the values equal to each other. In other words, set the product of the means equal to the product of the extremes. After this step, divide both sides of this new equation to isolate the variable you're solving for.

Example: Solve for m: $\frac{6}{11} = \frac{m}{33}$.

> Using cross multiplication, the equation becomes $6 \times 33 = m \times 11$. Before you spend time multiplying out 6×33, notice that you can instead divide both sides of the equation by 11. This simplifies to $6 \times 3 = m$. Thus, $m = 18$.

In word problems, set up the proportions so that units of the same type are either one above the other or directly across from one another.

Example: The ratio of T-shirts to sweaters in a closet is 4:5. If there are 12 T-shirts in the closet, how many sweaters are there?

Set up a proportion to solve this question, being careful to line up the units. There are different ways you can approach this problem to get the correct answer. One possible proportion would be $\frac{4 \text{ T-shirts}}{5 \text{ sweaters}} = \frac{12 \text{ T-shirts}}{x \text{ sweaters}}$. Note that the label of T-shirts appears in both numerators and the label of sweaters appears in both denominators. Another possible proportion would be $\frac{4 \text{ T-shirts}}{12 \text{ T-shirts}} = \frac{5 \text{ sweaters}}{x \text{ sweaters}}$, where the numbers corresponding with T-shirts appear on the left side and the values corresponding with sweaters appear on the right side. Either way, cross multiplying the means and the extremes results in the equation $4x = 60$. Therefore, $x = 15$. There are 15 sweaters in the closet.

In-Format Question: Applying Fractions to Proportions on the GMAT

Now let's use the Kaplan Method on a Data Sufficiency question that involves applying fractions to proportions:

After 360 liters of fuel were added to a container, the amount of fuel in the container was $\frac{5}{8}$ of the tank's capacity. What is the capacity of the container?

(1) After the 360 liters were added, the container had 108 liters less than $\frac{3}{4}$ of the tank's capacity.

(2) Before the 360 liters were added, there were 180 liters of fuel in the container.

STEP 1: ANALYZE THE QUESTION STEM

First, recognize that this is a Value question. You need an exact value of the capacity of the container after 360 liters of fuel are added to it. Next, take control of the question by setting up an equation. Call the capacity of the container C liters and say that before the 360 liters of fuel were added, there were N liters of fuel in the container. Since after the 360 liters of fuel were added, the amount of fuel in the container was $\frac{5}{8}$ of the tank's capacity, write the equation $N + 360 = \frac{5}{8}C$. Now look at the statements.

STEP 2: EVALUATE THE STATEMENTS USING 12TEN

Start with Statement (2), which looks like the more straightforward of the two. Statement (2) says that before the 360 liters were added, there were 180 liters of fuel in the container. After the 360 liters were added, there were $180 + 360 = 540$ liters. Since after the 360 liters were added, the amount of fuel in the container was $\frac{5}{8}$ of the tank's capacity, you can write the equation $540 = \frac{5}{8}C$. This is a first-degree equation, so it must lead to exactly one value for C. Don't waste time calculating to find the exact value. All you need to know is that Statement (2) is sufficient. Eliminate **(A)**, **(C)**, and **(E)**.

Now look at Statement (1). Statement (1) says that after the 360 liters were added, the container had 108 liters less than $\frac{3}{4}$ of the tank's capacity. You can translate this as $N + 360 = \frac{3}{4}C - 108$. Since you know from the question stem that $N + 360 = \frac{5}{8}C$, you can say that $\frac{5}{8}C = \frac{3}{4}C - 108$. This is a first-degree equation, so it must lead to exactly one value for C. Statement (1) is sufficient. Eliminate choice **(B)**.

If you want to check your work, you can solve the equation $\frac{5}{8}C = \frac{3}{4}C - 108$ for C to be sure that there is just one solution. Multiplying both sides by 8, you have $8\left(\frac{5}{8}C\right) = 8\left(\frac{3}{4}C - 108\right)$, $5C = 8\left(\frac{3}{4}C\right) - 8(108)$, and $864 = C$. You see that there is indeed just one solution. This statement is sufficient.

Either statement is sufficient, making **(D)** the correct answer.

Notice that both statements lead to the same capacity of 864 liters for the container. The statements in a Data Sufficiency question will never contradict one another, so if each statement alone is sufficient, the two statements will always answer the question in the same exact way. You can use this fact to double-check whether you are applying the statements correctly.

TAKEAWAYS: APPLYING FRACTIONS TO PROPORTIONS

- Fractions in proportions represent the part-to-part or part-to-whole relationships in a question.
- To solve a question that asks for the missing part of a ratio, set up a proportion by setting two equivalent fractions equal to each other; then use cross multiplication to solve for the missing piece.

Practice Set: Applying Fractions to Proportions on the GMAT

4. The weight of a certain type of cable is always directly proportional to its length. If 560 meters of this cable weighs 84 kilograms, what is the weight, in kilograms, of 110 meters of the same cable?

    ○   11.5
    ○   16.5
    ○   22
    ○   24.5
    ○   26

5. The ratio of the cost of a wooden plank to the length of a wooden plank is constant. A plank measuring 6 feet long costs $96. Jordan wants to buy planks that measure 10 feet in length, and Kristen wants to buy planks that are 7.5 feet in length. How much more, in dollars, will Jordan pay per plank?

    ○   40
    ○   45
    ○   120
    ○   135
    ○   160

6. There are chips of four different colors distributed in stacks as follows: $\frac{1}{2}$ are white, $\frac{1}{6}$ are green, $\frac{1}{5}$ are blue, and the remaining 12 chips are red. What is the total number of chips in the four stacks?

    ○   60
    ○   75
    ○   90
    ○   100
    ○   125

Percents with Specified Values

> **LEARNING OBJECTIVES**
>
> In this section, you will learn how to:
>
> - Convert between fractions, percents, and decimals
> - Calculate a percentage change
> - Apply the Kaplan Methods for Problem Solving and Data Sufficiency to questions dealing with percents when values are specified

In the Problem Solving chapter of this book, you learned how to use the picking numbers strategy to deal with questions that involve taking percents of unspecified values. Questions that specify the exact values are often more straightforward, but they require your familiarity with several formulas for dealing with fractions and percents.

Key to these questions is the fact that *percent* is just another word for "per one hundred."

Therefore, 19 percent (or 19%) means 19 hundredths

or $\dfrac{19}{100}$

or 0.19

or 19 out of every 100 things

or 19 parts out of a whole of 100 parts.

Converting Percents, Fractions, and Decimals

GMAT questions will often require that you convert among percents, decimals, fractions, and ratios. Below you will learn the process for making each of these conversions, but they all boil down to using the percent formula:

$$\text{Percent} = \frac{\text{Part}}{\text{Whole}} \times 100\%$$

Plug in the information you have and solve for the missing pieces.

To make a percent from a decimal or fraction, multiply by 100 percent. Since 100 percent means 100 hundredths, or 1, multiplying by 100 percent will not change the number.

Example: $0.17 = 0.17 \times 100\% = 17\%$

Example: $\dfrac{1}{4} = \dfrac{1}{4} \times 100\% = 25\%$

To drop a percent, divide by 100 percent. Once again, dividing by 100 percent, which is equivalent to 1, will not change the number.

Example: $32\% = \dfrac{32\%}{100\%} = \dfrac{32}{100} = \dfrac{8}{25}$

Example: $\dfrac{1}{2}\% = \dfrac{\frac{1}{2}\%}{100\%} = \dfrac{1}{200}$

To change a percent to a decimal, just drop the percent sign and move the decimal point two places to the left. (This is the same as dividing by 100 percent.)

Example: $0.8\% = 0.008$

Being familiar with the following fraction-to-percent equivalents can save you a lot of time on questions that require you to perform such conversions.

Common Fraction-to-Percent Equivalents

$$\frac{1}{20} = 5\% \qquad \frac{1}{11} = 9\frac{1}{11}\% \qquad \frac{1}{10} = 10\% \qquad \frac{1}{9} = 11\frac{1}{9}\% \qquad \frac{1}{8} = 12\frac{1}{2}\%$$

$$\frac{1}{6} = 16\frac{2}{3}\% \qquad \frac{1}{5} = 20\% \qquad \frac{1}{4} = 25\% \qquad \frac{1}{3} = 33\frac{1}{3}\% \qquad \frac{1}{2} = 50\%$$

$$10\% = \frac{1}{10} \qquad\qquad 12\frac{1}{2}\% = \frac{1}{8} \qquad\qquad 16\frac{2}{3}\% = \frac{1}{6}$$

$$20\% = \frac{2}{10} = \frac{1}{5} \qquad\qquad 25\% = \frac{2}{8} = \frac{1}{4} \qquad\qquad 33\frac{1}{3}\% = \frac{2}{6} = \frac{1}{3}$$

$$30\% = \frac{3}{10} \qquad\qquad 37\frac{1}{2}\% = \frac{3}{8} \qquad\qquad 50\% = \frac{3}{6} = \frac{1}{2}$$

$$40\% = \frac{4}{10} = \frac{2}{5} \qquad\qquad 50\% = \frac{4}{8} = \frac{2}{4} = \frac{1}{2} \qquad\qquad 66\frac{2}{3}\% = \frac{4}{6} = \frac{2}{3}$$

$$50\% = \frac{5}{10} = \frac{1}{2} \qquad\qquad 62\frac{1}{2}\% = \frac{5}{8} \qquad\qquad 83\frac{1}{3}\% = \frac{5}{6}$$

$$60\% = \frac{6}{10} = \frac{3}{5} \qquad\qquad 75\% = \frac{6}{8} = \frac{3}{4}$$

$$70\% = \frac{7}{10} \qquad\qquad 87\frac{1}{2}\% = \frac{7}{8}$$

$$80\% = \frac{8}{10} = \frac{4}{5}$$

$$90\% = \frac{9}{10}$$

$$100\% = \frac{10}{10} = 1$$

Percent Problems

Percent problems will usually give you two of the terms from the formula below and ask for the third. It is usually easiest to change the percent to a common fraction before performing the calculation. Most percent problems can be solved by plugging into a variant of the percent formula:

$$\text{Percent} \times \text{Whole} = \text{Part}$$

In percent problems, the whole generally will be associated with the word *of*, and the part will be associated with the word *is*. The percent can be represented as the ratio of the part to the whole, or the *is* to the *of*.

Example: What is 25 percent of 36?

Here you are given the percent and the whole. To find the part, change the percent to a fraction, then multiply. Use the following formula:

$$x\% \text{ of } y = \frac{x}{100} \times y$$

Since $25\% = \frac{1}{4}$, you are really being asked what one-fourth of 36 is.

$$\frac{1}{4} \times 36 = 9$$

Example: 13 is $33\frac{1}{3}$ percent of what number?

Recall that

$$33\frac{1}{2} = \frac{1}{3}$$

$$13 = \frac{1}{3}$$

$$39 = n$$

Example: 18 is what percent of 3?

$$m \times 3 = 18$$

$$m = 6$$

$$6 \times 100\% = 600\%$$

Other problems will ask you to calculate "percent greater than" or "percent less than." In these cases, it is the number that follows the word *than* to which the percentage is applied.

You may find it faster to convert *percent greater/less than* to *percent of*. As an example, "*x* percent greater than" becomes "$(100 + x)\%$ of." And "*x* percent less than" becomes "$(100 - x)\%$ of."

Example: If *n* is 15 percent less than 60, what is the value of *n*?

$$n = 60 - (15\% \times 60)$$

$$n = 60 - \left(\frac{15}{100} \times 60\right)$$

$$n = 60 - 9$$

$$n = 51$$

Example: What is the price of a television that costs 28 percent more than a $50 radio?

Let *t* equal the price of the television and *r* equal the price of the radio.

$$t = r + (28\% \times r)$$

$$t = 50 + \left(\frac{28}{100} \times 50\right)$$

$$t = 50 + \frac{28}{2}$$

$$t = 50 + 14$$

$$t = \$64$$

Percent Increase and Decrease

$$\text{Percent decrease} = \frac{\text{Amount of decrease}}{\text{Original whole}} \times 100\%$$

$$\text{Percent decrease} = \frac{\text{Amount of decrease}}{\text{Original whole}} \times 100\%$$

$$\text{New whole} = \text{Original whole} \pm \text{Amount of change}$$

When dealing with percent increase and percent decrease, always be careful to put the amount of increase or decrease over the *original* whole, not over the new whole.

Example: If a dress is offered for a discounted price of $120, what is the percent discount if the regular price is $150?

$$\text{Percent decrease} = \frac{\text{Amount of decrease}}{\text{Original whole}} \times 100\%$$

You're asked to calculate the discount, so you'll use the regular selling price of $150 as the original whole. The difference in prices is $150 − $120, or $30.

$$\text{Percent discount} = \frac{\$30}{\$150} \times 100\%$$

$$\text{Percent discount} = \frac{1}{5} \times 100\% = 20\%$$

Combining Percents: On some problems, you'll need to find more than one percent, or a percent of a percent. Be careful: you can't just add percents, unless the percents are of the same whole. Let's look at an example.

Example: The price of an antique is reduced by 20 percent, and then this discount price is further reduced by 10 percent. If the antique originally cost $200, what is its final price?

First, you know that the price is reduced by 20%. That's the same thing as saying that the price becomes (100% − 20%), or 80% of what it originally was. Eighty percent of $200 is equal to $\frac{8}{10} \times \$200$ or $160. Then, *this price* is reduced by 10%. So 10% × $160 = $16, and the final price of the antique is $160 − $16 = $144

A common error in this kind of problem is to assume that the final price is simply a 30% reduction of the original price. That would mean that the final price is 70% of the original, or 70% × $200 = $140. But, as you've just seen, this is *not* correct. Adding or subtracting percents directly only works if those percents are being taken of the same whole. In this example, since you took 20% of the original price and then 10% of the reduced price, you can't just add the percents together.

Note that in this example, a 20% reduction followed by a 10% reduction does not equal a 30% reduction but rather one of 28%. This will always happen—two decreases cause a total percent decrease of less than the sum of the two individual percents. This is because the second percent decrease is taken from a smaller starting value. Likewise, two increases cause a total increase of more than the sum of the two individually, since the second percent increase is calculated based on a higher starting point. You can use this fact to estimate an answer quickly.

In-Format Question: Percents with Specified Values on the GMAT

Now let's use the Kaplan Method on a Problem Solving question that involves percents with specified values:

> A pet store regularly sells pet food at a discount of 10 percent to 30 percent from the manufacturer's suggested retail price. If during a sale, the store discounts an additional 20 percent from the discount price, what would be the lowest possible price of a container of pet food that had a manufacturer's suggested retail price of $20.00?

- ○ $10.00
- ○ $11.20
- ○ $14.40
- ○ $16.00
- ○ $18.00

STEP 1: ANALYZE THE QUESTION

This question is asking for the lowest possible price of pet food that has been marked down twice. Another way to phrase the question is that you want the maximum possible discount. So you'll take the maximum discount at each stage of the markdown to determine the lowest price.

Since the question gives you an actual starting value for the price, you cannot pick numbers to make the calculations easier. Notice that you could backsolve this question, since the answer choices are all numbers, but since this question involves multiple discounts, backsolving could result in lots of calculation. The more efficient approach here is to use what you know about percent decrease.

STEP 2: STATE THE TASK

Using the starting value of $20, you must apply the two maximum discounts, one after the other.

STEP 3: APPROACH STRATEGICALLY

The original price for the pet food was $20, and the maximum reduction the store gives is 30%. You can approach the reduction calculation in two ways:

1. You could determine 30% of $20 and then subtract this amount from $20:

$$\$20 \times 0.3 = \$6; \$20 - \$6 = \$14$$

2. You can find the new price directly. Since $100\% - 30\% = 70\%$, the new price is 70% of $20:

$$\$20 \times 0.7 = \$14$$

Regardless of the approach, you find that the first reduced price is $14.

Now, you need to take the 20% discount off this reduced price. Again, you could apply either approach to calculate this value, but the second approach is more efficient: $14 \times 0.8 = \$11.20$. **(B)** is correct.

STEP 4: CONFIRM YOUR ANSWER

Since there wasn't much arithmetic, you can quickly check for any careless errors. Also, reread the question stem to make sure that you didn't misinterpret anything and that you solved for the correct value.

TAKEAWAYS: PERCENTS WITH SPECIFIED VALUES

- $x\% = \dfrac{x}{100}$

- $x\%$ of $y = \dfrac{x}{100} \times y$

- Percent $= \dfrac{\text{Part}}{\text{Whole}} \times 100\%$

- Final as percent of original $= \dfrac{\text{Final}}{\text{Original}} \times 100\%$

- Percent change $= \dfrac{\text{Difference}}{\text{Original}} \times 100\%$

Practice Set: Percents with Specified Values on the GMAT

7.   Four different batches of concrete are combined in a large mixing vat. Batch A, which weighs 1,000 kilograms, contains 30 percent gravel by weight. Batch B, which is twice the weight of batch A, is made up of 40 percent gravel. Batch C weighs 25 percent less than batch B and contains 50 percent gravel. Finally, batch D, which is half the weight of batch A, contains 60 percent gravel. What is the percentage of gravel in the concrete when the four batches are mixed together?

  ○   40%

  ○   43%

  ○   45%

  ○   50%

  ○   55%

8.   In the first quarter of the year, a certain entrepreneur sold 36 percent of the 75 crafts that she put for sale online. In the second quarter of that year, she sold one-fourth of the remaining crafts. What was the percent decrease from the first quarter to the second in the number of crafts the entrepreneur sold?

  ○   12%

  ○   25%

  ○ $55\frac{5}{9}$%

  ○   61%

  ○ $66\frac{2}{3}$%

9. **Survey of Student Preferences**

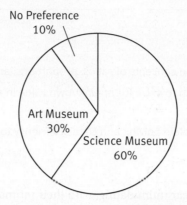

No Preference
10%

Art Museum
30%

Science Museum
60%

The administration of a certain school surveys all 120 students to plan a field trip. Each student can express a preference for only one destination: the science museum, the art museum, or neither. The results of the student survey are shown above. Assuming that the maximum number of students who are allowed to visit their preferred museum visit that museum for the field trip, how many students who have a preference do not visit their preferred museum?

(1) Due to transportation constraints, the maximum number of students who can take a field trip to the science museum is 55.

(2) Due to high demand, the art museum can accommodate a maximum of 50 students.

Mixtures

Problems involving mixtures may appear intimidating, with their intimations of chemistry, but really they are just proportion, ratio, and percentage problems in disguise. Most mixture questions will ask you to combine two portions that are themselves subdivided into portions. At other times, the question stem may prescribe the ratio of elements in a mixture and then add or remove some or all of one of those portions, asking you to recalculate the new ratio that results. Recognize the familiar patterns at work and you will be a step ahead on the GMAT.

Mixtures on the GMAT are most commonly mixtures of liquids.

Example: You currently have 10 ounces of a solution that is 14 percent alcohol and the rest water. How much water would you have to add to the solution to make the alcohol content equal to 10 percent?

If the solution is 14% alcohol now, that means there are $10 \text{ oz} \times \dfrac{14}{100} = 1.4$ oz of alcohol in the initial solution. The rest of the solution is water.

Think critically about this situation, since it's one that occurs often in mixtures problems: When water is added, the amount of alcohol in the mixture remains constant at 1.4 oz. However, you are told that this same amount of alcohol represents 10% of the resulting mixture.

Since 1.4 is 10% of 14, the final mixture must have a total volume of 14 oz. The difference in volume between the old and new mixtures is accounted for solely by the addition of water, so you'd need to add $14 - 10 = 4$ oz of water to make a 10% alcohol solution.

Notice that the only real difference between this and a lot of the proportion or ratio questions that you've seen so far in this chapter is that it deals with a liquid, rather than with cars, students, adults, or children. Mixture problems involve many of the same skills you use on other ratio problems, except they require you to keep track of amounts rather than numbers.

In-Format Question: Mixtures on the GMAT

Now let's use the Kaplan Method on a Problem Solving question dealing with mixtures:

> Two brands of detergent are to be combined. Detergent X contains 20 percent bleach and
> 80 percent soap, while Detergent Y contains 45 percent bleach and 55 percent soap. If the
> combined mixture is to be 35 percent bleach, what percent of the final mixture should be
> Detergent X?

- ○ 10%
- ○ $32\frac{1}{2}$%
- ○ 35%
- ○ 40%
- ○ 60%

STEP 1: ANALYZE THE QUESTION

This is a complex question, but there is a straightforward solution. You are creating a new mixture from two others, X and Y. X is 20% bleach, and Y is 45% bleach. The new mixture is to be 35% bleach.

In other words, some amount of a 20% bleach mixture plus some amount of a 45% bleach mixture will balance each other out to form a 35% bleach mixture.

STEP 2: STATE THE TASK

Because this question involves finding a particular balance between Detergents X and Y, you can use the balanced average approach to solve. You could also use algebra or backsolving, but the balanced average approach will be the most efficient. This will let you calculate the proportion of Detergent X in the final mixture.

STEP 3: APPROACH STRATEGICALLY

The question does not state how many parts of Detergent X are used, so call this x. And the question does not state how many parts of Y are used, so call this y. Here's how it balances:

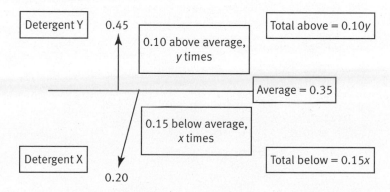

Since the amount above the average has to equal the amount below the average, $0.10y = 0.15x$. To solve for a proportional amount, you can view this as a ratio. Divide both sides by y and by 0.15 to get the ratio of x to y:

$$0.10y = 0.15x$$

$$\frac{0.10}{0.15} = \frac{x}{y}$$

$$\frac{10}{15} = \frac{x}{y}$$

$$\frac{2}{3} = \frac{x}{y}$$

So x:y is 2:3. Add the total to the ratio to determine how x relates to the total: x:y:total = 2:3:5.

Thus, x:total = 2:5. That means x makes up $\frac{2}{5}$, or 40%, of the total mixture. Choice (**D**) is correct.

STEP 4: CONFIRM YOUR ANSWER

Review your calculations for this question. Also, confirm that your answer choice makes sense in the context of the question.

TAKEAWAYS: MIXTURES

- For mixture problems, translate the given information into ratios.
- For questions that involve altering a given mixture, identify whether any of the amounts remain constant between the old and new mixtures.

Practice Set: Mixtures on the GMAT

10. A display case contains a certain number of donuts, some chocolate, some jelly filled, and the rest plain. One-sixth of the donuts are chocolate. How many chocolate donuts must be added so that one-fourth of the total donuts are chocolate?

    (1) There are 40 plain donuts in the case.

    (2) The ratio of plain donuts to jelly-filled donuts is 2:1.

11. A farmer who grows only two crops, corn and soybeans, has the same combined target output by weight every year. This year, corn makes up 40 percent of the crop and weighs 24 tons. Next year, however, the farmer wants corn to be only 15 percent of the total tonnage. How many more tons of soybeans must the farmer grow next year to maintain the same target output?

    ○ 9
    ○ 15
    ○ 25
    ○ 36
    ○ 51

12. If an amount of a solution containing 10 percent Chemical A is combined with twice as much of a solution that is 30 percent Chemical A and four times as much of a solution that is 35 percent Chemical A, what is the concentration of Chemical A in the resulting solution?

    ○ 17.5%
    ○ 20%
    ○ 25%
    ○ 27.5%
    ○ 30%

Answer Key

Practice Set: Ratios on the GMAT

1. C
2. A
3. A

Practice Set: Applying Fractions to Proportions on the GMAT

4. B
5. A
6. C

Practice Set: Percents with Specified Values on the GMAT

7. B
8. C
9. C

Practice Set: Mixtures on the GMAT

10. C
11. B
12. E

Answers and Explanations

Practice Set: Ratios on the GMAT

1. **(C)**

    At a certain university, the football program receives 4 times more funding than does the basketball program. Together, the football and basketball programs receive 3 times as much funding as do all other sports programs combined. What is the ratio of funding for the basketball program to funding for all other sports programs, not including the football program?

    ○ 1:5

    ○ 1:4

    ○ 3:5

    ○ 3:4

    ○ 5:3

STEP 1: ANALYZE THE QUESTION

The question gives you enough information to set up two ratios. The football program gets 4 times as much funding as basketball, so the ratio $f{:}b$ is 4:1. Football and basketball combined get 3 times as much funding as the other sports, so the ratio $(f + b){:}s$ is 3:1. However, no actual values are given.

STEP 2: STATE THE TASK

Find the ratio of basketball's funding to funding for other sports (not including football).

STEP 3: APPROACH STRATEGICALLY

Picking numbers is a great strategy to answer ratio questions when no actual values are given. Numbers need not be realistic; pick easy-to-use values. Let the funding for basketball be \$3. Since football receives 4 times as much, its funding is \$12. Together, these two programs have \$15 in funding, which is 3 times as much as that of all of the other sports combined. Therefore, the other programs receive \$5. Finally, the ratio of funding for basketball to that for all other sports is 3:5.

Alternatively, select variables to represent the funding unknowns (such as f for football, b for basketball, and s for other sports programs). Then, $f = 4b$, since football gets 4 times more than basketball. Together, these two teams' funding is $f + b$, and, substituting $4b$ for f, the total amount is $4b + b = 5b$. That's 3 times the amount given to the other programs, s, so $5b = 3s$. Rewriting the equation to solve for $b{:}s$, you obtain the ratio 3:5.

Solving with either method shows that the correct answer is **(C)**.

STEP 4: CONFIRM YOUR ANSWER

In a ratio question where the answer represents a part:part ratio, make sure the answer you pick represents the right parts in the right order.

2.   **(A)**

If $\frac{a}{b} = \frac{c}{d}$, what is the numerical ratio of b to d?

(1) $\frac{a}{b} = \frac{3c}{2b}$

(2) $a = 2$ and $d = 4$.

STEP 1: ANALYZE THE QUESTION STEM

This Value question stem provides a proportion with four variables and asks for a numerical value of the ratio of b to d. Rearranging the proportion to put b over d on one side may help you visualize what is needed: cross multiply to get $ad = bc$; divide both sides by d to get $a = \frac{bc}{d}$, and divide both sides by c to get $\frac{a}{c} = \frac{b}{d}$. Therefore, you need the ratio of a to c in order to determine the ratio of b to d.

STEP 2: EVALUATE THE STATEMENTS USING 12TEN

Statement (1) says that $\frac{a}{b} = \frac{3c}{2b}$. Cross multiply to find that $2ab = 3bc$. Divide both sides by b: $2a = 3c$. This means that $\frac{a}{c} = \frac{3}{2}$. You've already determined that this is also the ratio of $\frac{b}{d}$. This statement is sufficient, so eliminate **(B)**, **(C)**, and **(E)**.

Plug the values in Statement (2) into the equation: $\frac{2}{b} = \frac{c}{4}$. Cross multiplying results in $bc = 8$. Although the statement provides a value for d, you can't determine the value of b, so this statement is insufficient. **(A)** is correct.

3.   (A)

If the ratio of a to b is 4 to 3 and the ratio of b to c is 1 to 5, what is the ratio of a to c?

- $\frac{4}{15}$
- $\frac{1}{3}$
- $\frac{2}{5}$
- $\frac{4}{5}$
- $\frac{7}{6}$

STEP 1: ANALYZE THE QUESTION

You are given two ratios, a to b and b to c, and are asked to solve for the ratio of a to c.

STEP 2: STATE THE TASK

Produce the ratio a to c. You can do so by picking numbers or by translating the given information into equations and combining them.

STEP 3: APPROACH STRATEGICALLY

Translating the first equation, you have $\frac{a}{b} = \frac{4}{3}$.

Translating the second equation, you have $\frac{b}{c} = \frac{1}{5}$.

You can calculate $\frac{a}{c}$ by multiplying $\frac{a}{b}$ by $\frac{b}{c}$:

$$\frac{a}{c} = \left(\frac{a}{b}\right)\left(\frac{b}{c}\right) = \left(\frac{4}{3}\right)\left(\frac{1}{5}\right) = \frac{4}{15}$$

(A) is correct.

Had you used picking numbers, the most straightforward values to choose are $a = 4$ and $b = 3$. If $b = 3$, then the only permissible value of c is 15. That makes the ratio of a to c equal to $\frac{4}{15}$.

STEP 4: CONFIRM YOUR ANSWER

When you are given two ratios, their product or quotient will always produce a third ratio. Be sure to confirm the order of the words in the question stem ratios to ensure that you have translated the ratios correctly.

Practice Set: Applying Fractions to Proportions on the GMAT

4.   **(B)**

The weight of a certain type of cable is always directly proportional to its length. If 560 meters of this cable weighs 84 kilograms, what is the weight, in kilograms, of 110 meters of the same cable?

- ○   11.5
- ○   16.5
- ○   22
- ○   24.5
- ○   26

STEP 1: ANALYZE THE QUESTION

The first sentence of the question, with "directly proportional," is a strong clue that you can set up an equation to relate the length of the cable to its weight.

STEP 2: STATE THE TASK

Create a proportion using the known length-to-weight relationship to find the weight of 110 meters of the cable.

STEP 3: APPROACH STRATEGICALLY

Let w equal the unknown weight of 110 meters of the cable. The cable's weight is proportional to its length, so set up a proportion:

$$\frac{84}{560} = \frac{w}{110}$$

While it's important to know how to calculate such proportions mathematically, using critical thinking and estimation can often make your life easier on Test Day.

Note the relationship between 560 and 110: 110 is *about a fifth* of 560 (that's because $110 \times 5 = 550$, which is very close to 560). Therefore, you can say that the unknown weight of 110 meters of cable must be *about a fifth* of 84. A fifth of 100 would be 20; a fifth of 75 would be 15; a fifth of 84 must be between 15 and 20. Among the answer choices, only 16.5 is close to one-fifth of 84. Thus, **(B)** is correct.

If you didn't spot this opportunity to estimate, you could do the math like this:

$$\frac{84}{560} = \frac{w}{110}$$
$$(84)(110) = 560w$$
$$(84)(11) = 56w$$
$$(21)(11) = 14w$$
$$(3)(11) = 2w$$
$$33 = 2w$$
$$w = 16.5$$

STEP 4: CONFIRM YOUR ANSWER

Plug the value you calculated for w back into the original proportion you set up to confirm that the relationship among values makes sense.

5. (A)

The ratio of the cost of a wooden plank to the length of a wooden plank is constant. A plank measuring 6 feet long costs \$96. Jordan wants to buy planks that measure 10 feet in length, and Kristen wants to buy planks that are 7.5 feet in length. How much more, in dollars, will Jordan pay per plank?

- ○ 40
- ○ 45
- ○ 120
- ○ 135
- ○ 160

STEP 1: ANALYZE THE QUESTION

You're given a ratio of length of a plank to cost of that plank. You're also told the lengths of two planks that will be purchased. You can express this ratio as a fraction and reduce: $\dfrac{\text{length}}{\$} = \dfrac{6}{96} = \dfrac{1}{16}$.

STEP 2: STATE THE TASK

You're asked for the difference between the two people's costs. Use the fixed (proportional) relationship between length and cost to find the cost of the difference between their planks.

STEP 3: APPROACH STRATEGICALLY

The plank that Jordan wants to buy is $10 - 7.5 = 2.5$ feet longer than the plank that Kristen wants to buy. Let x be the cost of the 2.5-foot difference and set up the following proportion:

$$\frac{1}{16} = \frac{2.5}{x}$$

The equation after you cross multiply is $x = 16 \times 2.5$, so $x = 40$. (One way to do this mental arithmetic efficiently is to first multiply 16 by 2 to get 32, then multiply 16 by 0.5 to get 8, and finally to add 32 and 8 to get 40.)

This matches **(A)**.

STEP 4: CONFIRM YOUR ANSWER

You can confirm your answer by solving for the separate amounts that Jordan and Kristen pay and then taking the difference. Since they pay \$16 per 1 foot, Jordan pays $10 \times \$16 = \$160$ and Kristen pays $7.5 \times \$16 = \$120$. That's a difference of \$40.

6.   (C)

There are chips of four different colors distributed in stacks as follows: $\frac{1}{2}$ are white, $\frac{1}{6}$ are green, $\frac{1}{5}$ are blue, and the remaining 12 chips are red. What is the total number of chips in the four stacks?

- ○   60
- ○   75
- ○   90
- ○   100
- ○   125

STEP 1: ANALYZE THE QUESTION

This question presents colored chips as parts that make up a whole. Most of the parts are identified as fractions of the whole, while one part is identified as a specific quantity. If you note that the actual number of each color of chips as well as the total number of chips must be integers, this insight will help you backsolve efficiently. (Things that normally come whole, such as chips, people, pets, etc., will never be broken into pieces in proportions questions on the GMAT.)

STEP 2: STATE THE TASK

Use the information given about chips of different colors to determine the total number of chips.

STEP 3: APPROACH STRATEGICALLY

There is more than one way to approach this question. One strategy is to determine what fraction of the total are the 12 red chips and then use that information to calculate the total number. Convert the three given fractions to the common denominator of 30 and add those rewritten fractions:

$$\left(\frac{15}{15}\right)\left(\frac{1}{2}\right) + \left(\frac{5}{5}\right)\left(\frac{1}{6}\right) + \left(\frac{6}{6}\right)\left(\frac{1}{5}\right) = \frac{15}{30} + \frac{5}{30} + \frac{6}{30} = \frac{26}{30}$$

So the rest of the chips, $\frac{30}{30} - \frac{26}{30} = \frac{4}{30} = \frac{2}{15}$, are the 12 red ones. Solve for the total number of chips, x, by setting up the proportion of part-to-whole ratios, $\frac{12}{x} = \frac{2}{15}$. Cross multiply: $2x = 180$. Thus, $x = 90$, and **(C)** is correct.

Alternatively, you could backsolve. Since $\frac{1}{2}$, $\frac{1}{6}$, and $\frac{1}{5}$ of the chips are integers, the total number of chips must be divisible by 2, 5, and 6. Thus, the total is divisible by the least common multiple of 2, 5, and 6, which is 30. Since the total number of chips must be divisible by 30, eliminate **(B)**, **(D)**, and **(E)**. Select one of the two remaining choices to backsolve. For **(A)**, 60, there would be $\frac{1}{2} \times 60 = 30$ white chips, $\frac{1}{6} \times 60 = 10$ green chips, and $\frac{1}{5} \times 60 = 12$ blue chips. Thus, $60 - 30 - 10 - 12 = 8$ chips would be red if 60 were the correct total. Since there are actually 12 red chips, the correct choice must be **(C)**, 90.

STEP 4: CONFIRM YOUR ANSWER

As a quick check that you determined the correct total, use the fact that when a fraction is taken of a whole, the fraction is multiplied by the whole. Thus, multiply the fractions given in the question stem by 90 and then sum those values along with the 12 red chips. The result should equal 90:

$$\frac{1}{2}(90) + \frac{1}{6}(90) + \frac{1}{5}(90) + 12 = 45 + 15 + 18 + 12 = 90$$

Practice Set: Percents with Specified Values on the GMAT

7. (B)

Four different batches of concrete are combined in a large mixing vat. Batch A, which weighs 1,000 kilograms, contains 30 percent gravel by weight. Batch B, which is twice the weight of batch A, is made up of 40 percent gravel. Batch C weighs 25 percent less than batch B and contains 50 percent gravel. Finally, batch D, which is half the weight of batch A, contains 60 percent gravel. What is the percentage of gravel in the concrete when the four batches are mixed together?

- O 40%
- O 43%
- O 45%
- O 50%
- O 55%

STEP 1: ANALYZE THE QUESTION

The question provides the percentage of gravel in four different batches of concrete that are combined into one large mixture. Batch A weighs 1,000 pounds. The weights of the other batches are given in relative terms. Batch B is twice the weight of batch A, or 2,000 kilograms. Batch C weighs 25% less than batch B, so batch C is 1,500 kilograms. Batch D is half the weight of batch A, or 500 kilograms.

STEP 2: STATE THE TASK

Determine the percentage of gravel in the final mixture.

STEP 3: APPROACH STRATEGICALLY

Calculate the total weight of gravel and the total weight of the complete mixture. Then divide the weight of gravel by that total weight and convert to a percentage. Batch A, which weighs 1,000 kilograms (kg), contains 30% gravel, so that is $1,000 \times 0.30 = 300$ kg. Batch B contains $2,000 \times 0.40 = 800$ kg of gravel. The weight of the gravel in batch C is $1,500 \times 0.50 = 750$ kg, and the weight of the gravel in batch D is $500 \times 0.60 = 300$ kg.

The total weight of gravel is $300 + 800 + 750 + 300 = 2,150$ kg, and the weight of the complete mixture is $1,000 + 2,000 + 1,500 + 500 = 5,000$ kg. Therefore, the percentage of gravel is $\frac{2,150}{5,000} \times 100\% = 43\%$. One efficient way to do the division in your head is to think of $\frac{2,150}{5,000}$ as being equal to $\frac{2,000}{5,000} + \frac{150}{5,000} = \frac{2}{5} + \frac{3}{100}$. Then convert each of these fractions to 0.40 and 0.03, respectively, and add to get 0.43. **(B)** is correct.

STEP 4: CONFIRM YOUR ANSWER

Be certain that you calculated a weighted average; the unweighted simple average is **(C)** 45%. If you were pressed for time, you could have made an educated guess. By noting that the two largest batches contained 40% and 50% gravel, you could have logically narrowed the choices down to **(B)** and **(C)**.

8. (C)

In the first quarter of the year, a certain entrepreneur sold 36 percent of the 75 crafts that she put for sale online. In the second quarter of that year, she sold one-fourth of the remaining crafts. What was the percent decrease from the first quarter to the second in the number of crafts the entrepreneur sold?

- ○ 12%
- ○ 25%
- ○ $55\frac{5}{9}$%
- ○ 61%
- ○ $66\frac{2}{3}$%

STEP 1: ANALYZE THE QUESTION

This question stem contains information about two periods of sales, one as a percent of a total and the other as a fraction of the remaining total. You are asked to calculate the percent decrease in sales from one quarter to the next. To determine this value, you need the number of crafts sold in each quarter.

STEP 2: STATE THE TASK

Translate the question stem into three equations to determine (1) number of crafts sold in the first quarter, (2) number of crafts sold in the second quarter, and (3) percent decrease in the number of crafts sold.

STEP 3: APPROACH STRATEGICALLY

Translating the first sentence (first quarter), you have 36% × 75 crafts = 0.36 × 75. This arithmetic looks time-consuming. However, 0.75 × 36 produces the same result, and 0.75 is equal to three-fourths. So there were $\frac{3}{\cancel{4}^1} \times \cancel{36}^9 = 27$ crafts sold.

Next, she sold one-fourth of the remaining crafts. The number of crafts remaining is 75 − 27 = 48. Therefore, she sold $\frac{1}{\cancel{4}^1} \times \cancel{48}^{12} = 12$.

The percent change formula is this:

$$\text{Percent change} = \frac{\text{Difference in values}}{\text{Original value}} \times 100\%$$

Plug in the values:

$$\text{Percent change} = \frac{27-12}{27} \times 100\% = \frac{15}{27} \times 100\% = \frac{5}{9} \times 100\% = 55\frac{5}{9}\%$$

(C) is correct.

STEP 4: CONFIRM YOUR ANSWER

Make sure you translated each part of the scenario correctly, especially the sentence about the second quarter sales, which describes one-fourth of the *remaining* crafts. Then double-check your work, especially in setting up the percent change calculation.

9. **(C)**

Survey of Student Preferences

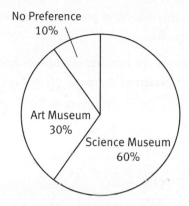

No Preference
10%

Art Museum
30%

Science Museum
60%

The administration of a certain school surveys all 120 students to plan a field trip. Each student can express a preference for only one destination: the science museum, the art museum, or neither. The results of the student survey are shown above. Assuming that the maximum number of students who are allowed to visit their preferred museum visit that museum for the field trip, how many students who have a preference do not visit their preferred museum?

(1) Due to transportation constraints, the maximum number of students who can take a field trip to the science museum is 55.

(2) Due to high demand, the art museum can accommodate a maximum of 50 students.

STEP 1: ANALYZE THE QUESTION STEM

This is a Value question. When presented with a chart, take a quick look at the information in it and consider the types of calculations that can be made using that information. This circle graph displays the results of the student survey. Since there are 120 students, the number of students who prefer the science museum is 120×0.60, the number of students who prefer the art museum is 120×0.30, and the number of students who prefer neither museum is 120×0.10.

The question stem asks how many students will *not* be able to visit their preferred museum. This question implies that there is some limitation on the number of students who can attend each museum. You can ignore the students who have no preference as they are irrelevant to this question.

STEP 2: EVALUATE THE STATEMENTS USING 12TEN

Statement (1) indicates that no more than 55 students can visit the science museum for the field trip. Comparing 55 to the number of students who prefer the science museum would allow determination of how many of these students won't get their first choice. (If you're curious, $120 \times 0.60 = 72$ students would like to go, so $72 - 55 = 17$ students who don't get their first choice.) However, this statement alone provides no information about how many students who want to visit the art museum will be denied the opportunity to attend that museum. Eliminate (**A**) and (**D**).

Statement (2) says that the limitation for the art museum is 50. Again, comparing 50 to the number of students who wish to visit the art museum would allow determination of the number thwarted in their desire. (The number who prefer the art museum is $120 \times 0.30 = 36$, so all these students get their first choice and the number denied is 0.) By itself, however, this statement provides no information about the students who want to visit the science museum, so eliminate **(B)**.

Together, the statements allow calculation of the number of students from the science museum group and the art museum group who will not get their preferred museum. All students who have expressed a preference are accounted for. Thus, **(C)** is correct.

Practice Set: Mixtures on the GMAT

10. (C)

A display case contains a certain number of donuts, some chocolate, some jelly filled, and the rest plain. One-sixth of the donuts are chocolate. How many chocolate donuts must be added so that one-fourth of the total donuts are chocolate?

(1) There are 40 plain donuts in the case.

(2) The ratio of plain donuts to jelly-filled donuts is 2:1.

STEP 1: ANALYZE THE QUESTION STEM

For this Value question, your first step is to translate the words into math. Let c equal the number of chocolate donuts, j equal the number of jelly donuts, and p equal the number of plain donuts. If T is the total number of donuts, then $c + j + p = T$ and $c = \frac{1}{6}T$. You want to know how many more chocolate donuts (x) need to be added to make the case consist of one-quarter chocolate donuts. When x chocolate donuts are added, this also adds to the total number of donuts, so $c + x = \frac{1}{4}(T + x)$. Substituting $\frac{1}{6}T$ for c makes the equation $\frac{1}{6}T + x = \frac{1}{4}(T + x)$. Thus, if you had enough information to determine how many donuts are in the case (T), you could solve for x.

STEP 2: EVALUATE THE STATEMENTS USING 12TEN

Statement (1): While this tells you the number of plain donuts in the case, the fact that $p = 40$ doesn't tell you how many donuts there are in total. Thus, Statement (1) is insufficient. Eliminate **(A)** and **(D)**.

Now evaluate Statement (2), which provides a ratio between plain donuts and jelly-filled donuts. This tells you how the $\frac{5}{6}$ of donuts that aren't chocolate are divvied up between plain and jelly, but since there is no actual number of any of the donut types, this statement does not allow calculation of T or c. Statement (2) is not sufficient. Eliminate **(B)**.

Now combining the statements, you can say that $p = 40$ and that $\frac{p}{j} = \frac{2}{1}$, so you can set up a proportion to determine how many jelly-filled donuts there are: $\frac{40}{j} = \frac{2}{1}$, so $40 = 2j$ and $j = 20$. Thus, there are $40 + 20 = 60$ non-chocolate donuts in the case. You know that $60 = \frac{5}{6}$ of the total donuts (because $\frac{1}{6}$ of the donuts are chocolate), so $T = 60 \div \frac{5}{6} = 60 \times \frac{6}{5} = 12 \times 6 = 72$. You've determined that finding this is enough to answer the question, so the statements together are sufficient, and the correct choice is **(C)**.

While you only need to know that you have sufficient information to find a value to answer a Data Sufficiency value question, if you're curious, here's what the math would look like. You're starting with 72 total donuts, so $T = 72$:

$$\frac{1}{6}T + x = \frac{1}{4}(T + x)$$

$$\frac{1}{6}(72) + x = \frac{1}{4}(72 + x)$$

$$12 + x = 18 + \frac{1}{4}x$$

$$\frac{3}{4}x = 6$$

$$x = 8$$

So you start with 72 total donuts, 12 of which are chocolate. Adding 8 chocolate donuts yields 20 chocolate donuts and 80 total donuts, and the number of chocolate donuts is now $\frac{1}{4}$ of the total.

11. (B)

A farmer who grows only two crops, corn and soybeans, has the same combined target output by weight every year. This year, corn makes up 40 percent of the crop and weighs 24 tons. Next year, however, the farmer wants corn to be only 15 percent of the total tonnage. How many more tons of soybeans must the farmer grow next year to maintain the same target output?

- O 9
- O 15
- O 25
- O 36
- O 51

STEP 1: ANALYZE THE QUESTION

The question describes that a particular farmer always has the same total target output for crops each year, growing only corn and soybeans. This year, 24 tons of corn makes up 40% of the output; next year, she wants to grow the same total output but have only 15% be corn. Since the total output remains the same, she is going to grow less corn and more soybeans.

STEP 2: STATE THE TASK

Translate the information into equations to determine how many more tons of soybeans the farmer must grow to reach the desired output level.

STEP 3: APPROACH STRATEGICALLY

First, use the fact that 24 tons of corn makes up 40% of the target output to find the target output amount t:

$$0.40t = 24$$
$$\frac{4}{10}t = 24$$
$$4t = 240$$
$$t = 60$$

The total output is 60 tons. Next year, corn will only be 15% of the total output, so that will be 0.15×60. You can do this arithmetic quickly in your head: 10% of 60 is 6, and 5% of 60 is half that, or 3. Then $(10\% + 5\%)$ of 60 is $6 + 3$, or 9 tons. This is 15 fewer tons than for the current year. Therefore, to maintain the target output, the farmer will need to grow 15 more tons of soybeans.

STEP 4: CONFIRM YOUR ANSWER

Make sure you've answered the right question. **(A)** represents the amount of corn the farmer will grow next year, **(D)** represents the total amount of soybeans grown this year, and **(E)** represents the total amount of soybeans to be grown next year.

12. (E)

If an amount of a solution containing 10 percent Chemical A is combined with twice as much of a solution that is 30 percent Chemical A and four times as much of a solution that is 35 percent Chemical A, what is the concentration of Chemical A in the resulting solution?

○   17.5%

○   20%

○   25%

○   27.5%

○   30%

STEP 1: ANALYZE THE QUESTION

The question provides the relative amounts of solutions containing different stated concentrations of a chemical. These different solutions are combined. The ratio of the solutions is 1:2:4. No actual amounts of solution are given, but since the answer choices are percents, not amounts, you don't need amounts to solve.

STEP 2: STATE THE TASK

Determine the concentration of Chemical A in the total solution.

STEP 3: APPROACH STRATEGICALLY

You can determine the final concentration by first calculating the total relative amounts of Chemical A and of the combined solution and then dividing the amount of Chemical A by the total amount of solution.

One unit of the 10% solution contains $1 \times 0.1 = 0.1$ units of Chemical A; 2 units of the 30% solution contain $2 \times 0.3 = 0.6$ units; 4 units of the 35% solution contain $4 \times 0.35 = 1.4$ units. So the total amount of Chemical A is $0.1 + 0.6 + 1.4 = 2.1$ units. The total volume of the combined solution is $1 + 2 + 4 = 7$ units. Thus, the resulting concentration is $\frac{2.1}{7} = 0.3 = 30\%$. **(E)** is correct.

STEP 4: CONFIRM YOUR ANSWER

You can check your result of 30% using the balance approach. One unit of the 10% solution is $1(30 - 10) = 20$ below the overall 30%. The 30% solution is the same as the overall concentration, and 4 units of the 35% solution are $4(35 - 30) = 20$ above the overall 30%. Thus, the concentrations are "in balance" when the average of 30% is used.

GMAT by the Numbers: Ratios and Proportions

Now that you've learned how to approach proportions questions on the GMAT, let's add one more dimension to your understanding of how they work.

Take a moment to try this question. Following is performance data from thousands of people who have studied with Kaplan over the decades. Through analyzing this data, we will show you how to approach questions like this one most effectively and how to avoid similarly tempting wrong answer choice types on Test Day.

> The price of a certain car this year is $42,000, which is 25 percent greater than the cost of the car last year. What was the price of the car last year?
>
> O $27,000
> O $28,000
> O $31,500
> O $33,600
> O $34,500

Explanation

The test makers often set up percentage problems to reward those who do two important things. The first is to be careful about what number the percentage is applied to. The second is to remember to look for ways to simplify calculations.

Question Statistics

1% of test takers choose **(A)**

1% of test takers choose **(B)**

19% of test takers choose **(C)**

74% of test takers choose **(D)**

5% of test takers choose **(E)**

Sample size = 3,799

This problem tells you that an increase of 25% raises the price of a car to $42,000. Be careful to apply that 25% increase to the unknown original price, not the $42,000. Decreasing $42,000 by 25% yields $31,500, which is the most common wrong answer. Avoid that one error, and your odds of getting the right answer go up dramatically.

If you set up the arithmetic the way the GMAT presents it, you get:

$$\text{Original price} \times 1.25 = 42,000$$

This would have you dividing 42,000 by 1.25—a simple task for a calculator but a time-consuming one for a person. On the GMAT, you'll often have more success by converting percentages to fractions. An increase of 25% means an increase of $\frac{1}{4}$, bringing the total up to $\frac{5}{4}$ of the original:

$$\text{Original price} \times \frac{5}{4} = 42,000$$

$$\text{Original price} = 42,000 \times \frac{4}{5}$$

$$\text{Original price} = 8,400 \times 4$$

$$\text{Original price} = 33,600$$

Choice **(D)** is correct.

More GMAT by the Numbers...

To see more questions with answer choice statistics, be sure to review the full-length CATs in your online resources.

GO ONLINE

kaptest.com/login

CHAPTER 22

Math Formulas on the GMAT

LEARNING OBJECTIVES

After studying this chapter, you will be able to:

- Identify questions that require the use of commonly tested math formulas
- Translate a word problem into the appropriate formula and solve for the unknown value
- Apply the Kaplan Methods for Problem Solving and Data Sufficiency to a variety of questions that involve formulas

---

Below is a typical Problem Solving question dealing with a commonly tested math formula. In this chapter, we'll look at how to apply the Kaplan Method to this question, discuss the common math formulas tested on the GMAT, and go over the basic principles and strategies that you want to keep in mind on every Quantitative question involving math formulas.

If the average (arithmetic mean) of x, 25, y, and 30 is $x + y$, which of the following equals the value of x?

- ○ $18\frac{1}{3}y$

- ○ $18\frac{1}{3} + y$

- ○ $18 - \frac{3}{y}$

- ○ $y - 18\frac{1}{3}$

- ○ $18\frac{1}{3} - y$

Before you move on, take a minute to think about what you see in this question and answer some questions about how you think it works:

- What math formula is being tested in this question?
- What does the format of the answer choices tell you about your task?
- What can you infer about how the GMAT constructs questions based on common math formulas?
- What GMAT Core Competencies are most essential to success on this question?

Previewing Math Formulas on the GMAT

Following are answers to the questions you just considered.

What Math Formula Is Being Tested in This Question?

This question tests your understanding of the formula to solve for the average, or arithmetic mean, of a group of values. In this case, you are told the average $(x + y)$ and are asked to solve for a missing term (x).

What Does the Format of the Answer Choices Tell You About Your Task?

The answer choices are algebraic expressions, not numerical values, so you can infer that the question must not supply enough information to solve for the actual value of x. Rather, what you will solve for is x "in terms of y." All this means is that the actual value of x will vary depending on the value of y.

From the format of the answer choices, you can glean that your task on this question is to set up the average formula, plug in the information provided by the question stem into the appropriate positions in the formula, and use what you know about solving algebraic equations to isolate the variable x on one side and everything else on the other.

What Can You Infer About How the GMAT Constructs Questions Based on Common Math Formulas?

The GMAT assumes that you have a working knowledge of several classic formulas. You should be comfortable using these so that you don't have to waste time trying to remember them on Test Day.

The GMAT tests these formulas by giving you some information that relates to a known formula and asking you for a different, missing piece of information that can be solved for using that formula.

Many of the formulas commonly tested on the GMAT have three parts. For example:

$$\text{Rate} = \frac{\text{Quantity A}}{\text{Quantity B}}$$

$$\text{Speed} = \frac{\text{Distance}}{\text{Time}}$$

$$\text{Average} = \frac{\text{Sum of terms}}{\text{Number of terms}}$$

This chapter will cover the formulas listed above, plus others. The important thing to remember is that when you are given two parts of any three-part formula, you can always solve for the missing part. Keep this in mind when you encounter a question that seems to have you stumped. Always start by figuring out what formula is at issue; then figure out what parts of the given information can be substituted into that formula. At this point, the path to the solution will usually become clear.

What GMAT Core Competencies Are Most Essential to Success on This Question?

As with all questions that hinge on standard mathematical formulas, you must first use your Pattern Recognition skills to identify the relevant formula. Once you've done so, Critical Thinking becomes important as you determine how the given information applies to the formula at hand. The GMAT often presents information in a less-than-intuitive way, forcing you to decode the meaning and relevance of that information to the solution.

How Do I Apply the Kaplan Methods to GMAT Formulas?

Now let's apply the Kaplan Method for Problem Solving to the math formulas question you saw earlier:

> If the average (arithmetic mean) of x, 25, y, and 30 is $x + y$, which of the following equals the value of x?
>
> ○ $18\frac{1}{3}y$
>
> ○ $18\frac{1}{3} + y$
>
> ○ $18 - \frac{3}{y}$
>
> ○ $y - 18\frac{1}{3}$
>
> ○ $18\frac{1}{3} - y$

STEP 1: ANALYZE THE QUESTION

This question gives you a lot of information. You are told that the average of the four terms, x, 25, y, and 30, is $x + y$. A quick glance at the answer choices reveals that you are being asked to solve for x in terms of y.

STEP 2: STATE THE TASK

You'll need to set up the average formula and then isolate x. But don't rush to the conclusion that you have to do a lot of algebra here.

STEP 3: APPROACH STRATEGICALLY

Think critically about how you can approach this problem to save time. Picking numbers is almost always a simple way to handle problems in which you need to solve for one variable in terms of another. Once you put the terms in the average formula, you can pick a number for x, solve the problem for y, and then plug that number into the answer choices to get the one that matches your choice for x. The average formula is the sum of terms divided by the number of terms. Here, that would look like this: $\frac{x + 25 + y + 30}{4} = x + y$. Multiplying both sides by 4 results in $x + 25 + y + 30 = 4(x + y)$. Distribute the 4 and you have $x + 25 + y + 30 = 4x + 4y$.

Now pick an easy number to substitute for x. Let's have $x = 1$. That gives you $1 + 25 + y + 30 = 4 + 4y$. Combine like terms, and you have $56 + y = 4 + 4y$. Doing the subtraction necessary to get y and the numbers on different sides of the equation leaves you with $52 = 3y$. Divide each side by 3, and you find that $y = 17\frac{1}{3}$. Since you chose 1 to stand in for x, all you need to do is substitute $17\frac{1}{3}$ in for y and find the answer choice that equals 1. That's choice (**E**).

You could also have solved algebraically. Taking the equation above, $x + 25 + y + 30 = 4x + 4y$, you can continue to simplify by combining like terms until you get $55 = 3x + 3y$. Factoring out a 3 from the right side gives you $55 = 3(x + y)$, and dividing both sides by 3 results in $\frac{55}{3}$. Isolating x and converting $\frac{55}{3}$ to a mixed number results in $x = 18\frac{1}{3} - y$, which corresponds to choice (**E**).

STEP 4: CONFIRM YOUR ANSWER

Using picking numbers can save you valuable time on this problem. You can also solve it with pure algebra, of course, and that approach can be used to confirm your answer if you initially solve by picking numbers.

Now let's look at each of the common math formulas that show up on the GMAT Quantitative section, starting with averages.

Averages

> **LEARNING OBJECTIVES**
>
> In this section, you will learn how to:
>
> - Apply the average formula and the balance approach to find an average
> - Explain what a weighted average is and when to use it
> - Apply the Kaplan Methods for Problem Solving and Data Sufficiency to questions dealing with averages

The average (arithmetic mean) of a group of numbers is defined as the sum of the values divided by the number of values.

$$\text{Average value} = \frac{\text{Sum of values}}{\text{Number of values}}$$

Example: Henry buys 3 items costing $2.00, $0.75, and $0.25. What is the average price?

$$\begin{aligned}
\text{Average price} &= \frac{\text{Sum of prices}}{\text{Number of prices}} \\
&= \frac{\text{Total price}}{\text{Number of prices}} \\
&= \frac{\$2.00 + \$0.75 + \$0.25}{3} \\
&= \frac{\$3.00}{3} \\
&= \$1.00
\end{aligned}$$

The Balance Approach to Averages

You can save yourself a lot of laborious and error-prone calculation if you think of the average as a "balancing point" between the numbers in the series. That is, the difference between the average and every number below it will equal the difference between the average and every number above it. The "balanced average" approach dramatically reduces the difficulty of the arithmetic.

You've already seen that the average of $2.00, $0.75, and $0.25 is $1.00. Here's how that balances:

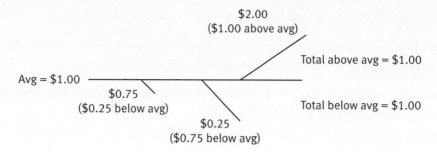

Now let's use this approach to solve a problem.

Example: The average of 43, 44, 45, and x is 45. What is the value of x?

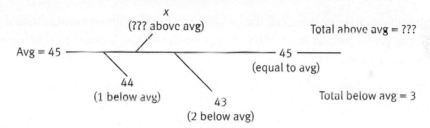

Since the amount above the average must equal the amount below the average, the amount above must be 3. Therefore, x is 3 above the average: $3 + 45 = 48$; $x = 48$.

Weighted Average

A further way to calculate averages on the GMAT is to use the "weighted average" formula:

Weighted average of n terms $= (\text{Percent}_1)(\text{Average}_1) + (\text{Percent}_2)(\text{Average}_2) + \ldots + (\text{Percent}_n)(\text{Average}_n)$

Weighted averages are useful when you know the average of different portions of the whole. For example, if two-fifths of the students in a class have a GPA of 79 and the remaining three-fifths have an average of 84, you could set up the weighted average formula as follows:

$$\text{Weighted average} = (0.4)(79) + (0.6)(84)$$
$$= 31.6 + 50.4$$
$$= 82$$

Notice the average of the whole class comes out to be closer to 84 than to 79. This will always be the case when the portions of the whole are of different sizes. In fact, this is where the term "weighted average" comes from; the larger the portion of the whole, the more heavily "weighted" that portion is when calculating the overall average. Note that you can use the weighted average formula as long as you have averages for all portions adding up to 100 percent of the whole.

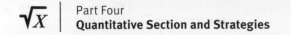

In-Format Question: Averages on the GMAT

Now let's use the Kaplan Method on a Data Sufficiency question dealing with averages:

> If each of the bowlers in a tournament bowled an equal number of games, what is the average (arithmetic mean) score of all the games bowled in the tournament?
>
> (1) Of the bowlers, 70 percent had an average (arithmetic mean) score of 120, and the other 30 percent had an average score of 140.
>
> (2) Each of the 350 bowlers in the tournament bowled 3 games.

STEP 1: ANALYZE THE QUESTION STEM

First, determine the type of Data Sufficiency question you're dealing with. You need one exact value for the average score of the games, so this a Value question.

There's no direct simplification to be done, but the fact that you're asked for an average should alert you to the possibility that you can get the answer in a variety of ways—either through direct calculation of the scores or through a weighted average approach.

To answer the question, you'll need either the number of games and the total of the scores or some way to calculate a weighted average.

STEP 2: EVALUATE THE STATEMENTS USING 12TEN

Statement (2) is very straightforward, so starting there makes sense. This tells you the number of games but nothing about the scores. Insufficient. Eliminate **(B)** and **(D)**.

Statement (1) doesn't allow you to figure out exactly the number of games or the exact sum of the scores. But since the proportions add up to 100% of the total, and since all the bowlers bowled the same number of games, you can calculate the overall average using the weighted average approach. Sufficient. The answer is **(A)**.

Remember, you don't actually want to calculate the average, just know that you could. That calculation would be: overall average $= 0.7(120) + 0.3(140)$.

The GMAT rewards those who think critically and find the most efficient approach to a problem. By using the weighted average approach, you avoided messy calculations and saved valuable time.

TAKEAWAYS: AVERAGES
• Average $= \dfrac{\text{Sum of the terms}}{\text{Number of terms}}$
• Balanced average approach: the sum of the differences between each term and the average must be zero. You can solve some average questions using this fact alone.
• Weighted average of n terms $= (\text{Percent}_1)(\text{Average}_1) + (\text{Percent}_2)(\text{Average}_2) + \ldots + (\text{Percent}_n)(\text{Average}_n)$

Practice Set: Averages on the GMAT

1. Bradley's grade in his science class is determined by his scores on 5 tests that each count an equal amount toward his grade. He has received scores of 67, 76, 78, and 94 on the 4 science tests thus far. If the last test consists of 20 equally weighted questions and is graded out of 100 points, how many questions does he need to answer correctly on the last test in order to average an 80 in his science class?

    O   15

    O   16

    O   17

    O   18

    O   19

2.

Points	# of arrows
0	1
1	1
3	3
5	6
7	8
9	2

In a certain archery contest, archers are awarded a different number of points for each arrow, depending upon the accuracy of the shot. If an arrow hits the bull's-eye, 10 points are awarded. The results for one archer are shown in the table above, but the values do not include her bull's-eyes. If the archer's average score per arrow is 6.0, how many of her attempts were bull's-eyes?

O   0

O   1

O   2

O   3

O   4

3. An exam is given in a certain class. The average (arithmetic mean) of the highest score and the lowest score on the exam is equal to x. If the average score for the entire class is equal to y and there are z students in the class, where $z > 5$, then in terms of x, y, and z, what is the average score for the class, excluding the highest and lowest scores?

    O $\dfrac{zy - 2x}{z}$

    O $\dfrac{zy - 2}{z}$

    O $\dfrac{zx - y}{z - 2}$

    O $\dfrac{zy - 2x}{z - 2}$

    O $\dfrac{zy - x}{z + 2}$

4. The average price of Emily's 5 meals was $20. Meals with a price of $25 or more include a free dessert. How many of Emily's 5 meals included a free dessert?

    (1) The most expensive of the 5 meals had a price of $50.
    (2) The least expensive of the 5 meals had a price of $10.

Rates and Speed—Converting Rates

> **LEARNING OBJECTIVES**
>
> In this section, you will learn how to:
>
> - Determine whether something is a rate and identify the most commonly tested rate
> - Use algebra and the Picking Numbers strategy to answer questions on rate and speed
> - Apply the Kaplan Method for Problem Solving to questions dealing with converting rates

You've seen this formula before:

$$\text{Speed} = \frac{\text{Distance}}{\text{Time}}$$

The most common rate is a speed—miles per hour—but anything with the word *per* is a rate: kilometers per second, miles per gallon, ounces of cheese per party guest, and so forth. A rate is any quantity of A per quantity of B.

$$\text{Rate } A \text{ per } B = \frac{\text{Quantity of } A}{\text{Quantity of } B}$$

Most rate problems involve conversions from one rate to another. These are best handled by multiplying the various rates so that measurements cancel. You may have to invert some of the rates to make the measurements cancel.

Example: If a car averages 25 miles per gallon and each gallon of gas costs $2.40, what's the value of the gas consumed in a trip of 175 miles?

$$\frac{\$2.40}{\text{gallon}} \times \frac{\text{gallon}}{25\,\text{miles}} \times 175\,\text{miles}$$

$$\frac{\$2.40}{\cancel{\text{gallon}}} \times \frac{\cancel{\text{gallon}}}{\cancel{25}^{1}\,\cancel{\text{miles}}} \times \cancel{175}^{7}\,\cancel{\text{miles}}$$

$$\$2.40 \times 7$$

$$\$16.80$$

Here's what a GMAT question might look like that gives you a rate that you must then convert. Follow along with this example:

> If José reads at a constant rate of 2 pages every 5 minutes, how many seconds will it take him to read N pages?
>
> ○ $\frac{2}{5}N$
>
> ○ $2N$
>
> ○ $\frac{5}{2}N$
>
> ○ $24N$
>
> ○ $150N$

There are two common ways of solving rate problems: algebraically and by using the picking numbers strategy. Let's try both for the problem above.

Algebraic Solution: You can call the number of seconds that you've been asked to find T. The first hurdle that you need to clear in this problem is that you're given a rate in minutes but asked to calculate the number of seconds. Change the rate you're given to seconds so you can get that aspect of the problem out of the way. There are 60 seconds to a minute. So you need to change the rate as follows:

$$\frac{2 \text{ pages}}{5 \text{ minutes}} \times \frac{1 \text{ minute}}{60 \text{ seconds}} = \frac{2 \text{ pages}}{300 \text{ seconds}} = \frac{1 \text{ page}}{150 \text{ seconds}}$$

Since the rates are the same, N and T will be in the same proportion as the rate you are given. So you can set up this equation:

$$\frac{1}{150} = \frac{N}{T}$$

Now cross multiply to solve for T: $T = 150N$. The answer is **(E)**.

Picking Numbers Solution: Since this question asks you to solve for the amount of time it takes José to read an unspecified number of pages, you can make the situation more concrete by picking a number for N. Keep the number simple, so that it's easy to work with: try $N = 2$, since José reads exactly 2 pages every 5 minutes, or 300 seconds (5×60 seconds $= 300$ seconds). Now look for the answer choices that yield 300 when $N = 2$. The only one that does so is **(E)**, so that must be the answer.

In-Format Question: Rates and Speed—Converting Rates on the GMAT

Now let's use the Kaplan Method on a Problem Solving question dealing with converting rates:

> If the city centers of New York and London are 3,471 miles apart, which of the following is closest to the distance between the city centers in inches? (There are 5,280 feet in a mile.)
>
> ○ 1.75×10^7
> ○ 1.83×10^7
> ○ 2.10×10^8
> ○ 2.10×10^9
> ○ 2.20×10^{10}

STEP 1: ANALYZE THE QUESTION

There are some scary numbers in this question. Attention to the Right Detail can help you zero in on the most crucial piece of information: the words *closest to* let you know that you can afford to estimate, as does the fact that most answers are a whole power of 10 different from each other.

STEP 2: STATE THE TASK

Your task is to convert 3,471 miles into inches.

STEP 3: APPROACH STRATEGICALLY

The problem gives you 5,280 feet per mile, allowing you to convert miles to feet. (The GMAT will expect you to know more common conversions, such as 12 inches per foot.)

So the calculation is $3{,}471 \text{ miles} \times \dfrac{5{,}280 \text{ feet}}{\text{mile}} \times \dfrac{12 \text{ inches}}{\text{foot}}$.

That's $3{,}471 \times 5{,}280 \times 12$. Happily, you can estimate, so save time by changing that to $3{,}500 \times 5{,}000 \times 10 = 175{,}000{,}000$, or 1.75×10^8. The only answer that's remotely close (within a power of 10) is **(C)**, so **(C)** is the answer.

STEP 4: CONFIRM YOUR ANSWER

Reread the question stem, making sure that you didn't miss anything about the problem. For example, if you accidentally solved for feet instead of inches, you'd have chosen **(A)** or **(B)**. This step would save you from the error.

TAKEAWAYS: RATES AND SPEED – CONVERTING RATES

- $\text{Rate} = \dfrac{\text{Quantity of } A}{\text{Quantity of } B} = \text{Quantity of } A \text{ per Quantity of } B$

- $\text{Speed} = \dfrac{\text{Distance}}{\text{Time}}$
- When solving a conversion algebraically, set up the equation so that units cancel.

- Keep track of the units of measurement. Rate questions often involve converting minutes to hours or days to weeks.

Practice Set: Rates and Speed—Converting Rates on the GMAT

5. A group of friends rent a small bus to go sightseeing. The rate for the bus and driver is $90 per hour, and the total distance of the sightseeing tour is 112 miles. If the total charge for the trip is $420, what is the average speed of the bus in miles per hour?

   ○ 16.7

   ○ 21.0

   ○ 22.5

   ○ 24.0

   ○ 25.8

6. Pierre's European car measures fuel economy in terms of liters per kilometer. If the car averages $\frac{1 \text{ liter}}{10 \text{ kilometers}}$ on a trip, what is the car's approximate fuel economy in terms of the standard U.S. measurement of miles per gallon? (Note: 1 gallon is approximately 3.78 liters, and 1 mile is approximately 1.61 kilometers.)

   ○ 4

   ○ 16

   ○ 24

   ○ 30

   ○ 40

7. A student can complete x homework questions in h hours. According to his calculations, it will take him 4 days to complete his latest assignment if he works m minutes a day. How many questions are on his latest assignment?

   ○ $\frac{mx}{60h}$

   ○ $\frac{15x}{mh}$

   ○ $\frac{4xh}{m}$

   ○ $\frac{mx}{15h}$

   ○ $\frac{4mx}{15h}$

Rates and Speed—Multi-Part Journeys

The GMAT often uses scenarios involving multi-part journeys in order to ask questions about "average rates." In such cases, the test makers will give you information that includes two or more different rates or speeds. So far in this chapter, you've learned about both averages and rates, so it's understandably tempting in this situation simply to average the different individual rates you're given.

Don't fall for this trap. Just as you cannot use the averages of two different portions of a group to determine the group's overall average (unless you know the weights of the portions), you also cannot find the average speed of a journey from the speeds of two parts unless you know the proportion of time spent or distance traveled in those parts. The GMAT's biggest trap with multi-part journeys or tasks is to offer an answer choice that fails to account for the weighting of the averages and simply splits the difference between the two portions. The GMAT writes its problems so that this is *never* the correct solution. Instead, you'll need to use the average rate formula.

Average Rate

$$\text{Average } A \text{ per } B = \frac{\text{Total } A}{\text{Total } B}$$

Example: John travels 30 miles in 2 hours and then 60 miles in 3 hours. What is his average speed in miles per hour?

$$\text{Average miles per hour} = \frac{\text{Total miles}}{\text{Total hours}}$$

$$= \frac{(30 + 60) \text{ miles}}{2 + 3 \text{ hours}} = \frac{90 \text{ miles}}{5 \text{ hours}} = 18 \text{ miles/hour}$$

Notice how you can check your work on this question by applying some Critical Thinking: John's first rate was 15 miles per hour, and his second rate was 20 miles per hour, so his average rate will fall somewhere between 15 and 20 miles per hour. You can estimate effectively on this question, as on most average rate questions, by identifying the rate at which John spent more time traveling. In this case, John spent more time traveling at 20 miles per hour, so his average rate should be closer to 20 than to 15. Indeed, 18 miles per hour is consistent with the direction in which the average rate should be weighted.

Average rate problems on the GMAT can become quite complex. If your paraphrase of the question stem is anything like "First this person moves at one speed, then at another," then you're dealing with a multi-part journey problem. There is frequently a lot of information to deal with.

To organize the data on complicated multi-part journey problems, try jotting down this chart on your notepad:

	Rate	Time	Distance
Part 1 of trip			
Part 2 of trip			
Entire trip			

This chart folds many equations into one:

- Rate × Time = Distance; each row of boxes multiplies across.
- Time (part 1) + Time (part 2) = Time (entire trip); time boxes add down.
- Distance (part 1) + Distance (part 2) = Distance (entire trip); distance boxes add down.
- Rates *do not* add down; they are calculated by dividing distance by time. If you need to calculate the speed for the entire trip, use the average speed formula:

$$\text{Average speed} = \frac{\text{Total distance}}{\text{Total time}}$$

Let's go through a sample question, and you'll see how the chart helps you.

> A powerboat crosses a lake at 18 miles per hour and returns at 12 miles per hour. If the time taken turning the boat around was negligible and it returns by the same route, then what was the boat's average speed for the round trip, in miles per hour?

When you notice that you have a multi-part journey problem, jot down the chart, using a question mark to indicate the value that the question asks you for:

	Rate (mph)	Time (hr)	Distance (miles)
Part 1 of trip			
Part 2 of trip			
Entire trip	?		

Now fill in the data given by the problem:

	Rate (mph)	Time (hr)	Distance (miles)
Part 1 of trip	18		
Part 2 of trip	12		
Entire trip	?		

Now you clearly have to get some information about either the time or the distance to be able to solve for much of anything. The only other piece of information you have is that the boat traveled the same route both times. That means the distance must have been the same. You could use the variable *D*, but the math will get fairly complicated if you do. Instead, keep it simple and pick numbers. A number that's a multiple both of 18 and of 12 will make the math work out nicely, so let's say the lake was 36 miles across:

	Rate (mph)	Time (hr)	Distance (miles)
Part 1 of trip	18		36
Part 2 of trip	12		36
Entire trip	?		

Now you can solve for the times and the total distance:

	Rate (mph)	Time (hr)	Distance (miles)
Part 1 of trip	18	2	36
Part 2 of trip	12	3	36
Entire trip	?		72

And finally for total time:

	Rate (mph)	Time (hr)	Distance (miles)
Part 1 of trip	18	2	36
Part 2 of trip	12	3	36
Entire trip	?	5	72

Now you have what you need to solve for average rate. It's $\dfrac{\text{Total distance}}{\text{Total time}} = \dfrac{72}{5} = 14.4$ mph. This answer makes logical sense, since the two rates are 18 and 12 miles per hour and the boat spent more time traveling at the lower speed, so the average is closer to 12 than to 18.

In-Format Question: Rates and Speed—Multi-Part Journeys on the GMAT

Now let's use the Kaplan Method on a Data Sufficiency question dealing with a multi-part journey:

> What was the average speed of a runner in a race from Point X to Point Z?
>
> (1) The runner's average speed from Point X to Point Y was 10 miles per hour.
>
> (2) The runner's average speed from Point Y to Point Z was 8 miles per hour.

STEP 1: ANALYZE THE QUESTION STEM

This is a Value question, so you need one exact speed for the trip from Point X to Point Z.

Use Critical Thinking: there's no direct simplification to be done, but since you can sometimes calculate exact speeds with unknown distance or time, there might be a way to solve for speed without knowing the exact distance and time.

To answer the question, you'll need either the exact distance and time or some information about distance or time that allows you to calculate speed.

STEP 2: EVALUATE THE STATEMENTS USING 12TEN

Statement (1) gives you some data about the trip from X to Y but nothing about X to Z. Insufficient. Eliminate **(A)** and **(D)**. Likewise, Statement (2) gives you data about the trip from Y to Z but nothing about X to Z. Insufficient. Eliminate **(B)**.

Now you must combine. Notice that something crucial is missing—information relating either the times or the distances of the X-to-Y and the Y-to-Z leg. If the X-to-Y distance were 10 miles and the Y-to-Z distance were 10 inches, the average speed would be essentially 10 mph. And if it's the other way around, with the X-to-Y distance 10 inches and the Y-to-Z distance 10 miles, the average speed would be essentially 8 mph. The combined statements are insufficient, so the answer is **(E)**.

TAKEAWAYS: RATES AND SPEED—MULTI-PART JOURNEYS

- In average rate and average speed questions, one wrong answer choice involves not accounting for the weighting of the averages. To avoid this wrong answer, use the average rate and average speed formulas.

$$\text{Average speed} = \frac{\text{Total distance}}{\text{Total time}}$$

- For multi-part journeys, use a chart to organize data.

- In an average speed question, if you recognize the direction in which the speed should be weighted, you can rapidly eliminate incorrect answers.

Practice Set: Rates and Speed—Multi-Part Journeys on the GMAT

8. A motorcyclist started riding at highway marker A, drove 120 miles to highway marker B, and then, without pausing, continued to highway marker C, where she stopped. The average speed of the motorcyclist, over the course of the entire trip, was 45 miles per hour. If the ride from marker A to marker B lasted 3 times as many hours as the rest of the ride, and the distance from marker B to marker C was half of the distance from marker A to marker B, what was the average speed, in miles per hour, of the motorcyclist while driving from marker B to marker C?

    ○   40
    ○   45
    ○   50
    ○   55
    ○   60

9. Did Jon complete a journey of 40 kilometers in less time than it took Ann to complete the same journey?

    (1)   Jon traveled at an average speed of 30 kilometers per hour for the first 10 kilometers and then at an average speed of 15 kilometers per hour for the rest of the journey.

    (2)   Ann traveled at an average speed of 20 kilometers per hour for the entire journey.

10. A hiker walks three sections of a trail that are of equal length. The first section of the trail is flat, and on this section the hiker travels at 3 miles per hour for 1.5 hours. The second section is uphill, and on this section the hiker's pace slows by 25 percent. The third section is downhill, and here his speed doubles. What was the hiker's average speed for the entire three-section hike?

   - ○ 1.5
   - ○ 3
   - ○ 3.25
   - ○ 4.5
   - ○ 9.75

11. A truck driver drove for 2 days. On the second day, she drove 3 hours longer and at an average speed of 15 miles per hour faster than she drove on the first day. If she drove a total of 1,020 miles and spent 21 hours driving during the 2 days, what was her average speed on the first day, in miles per hour?

   - ○ 25
   - ○ 30
   - ○ 35
   - ○ 40
   - ○ 45

Combined Rates and Combined Work

> **LEARNING OBJECTIVES**
>
> In this section, you will learn how to:
>
> - Recognize questions involving two entities that are simultaneously involved in doing work
> - Perform calculations using the combined work formula and the hour-by-hour approach
> - Apply the Kaplan Method for Problem Solving to questions dealing with combined rates or combined work

Combined work questions present you with information about different people or machines that can perform the same job in different amounts of time. Rates in combined work questions are expressed in a similar way to how you'll see them expressed in other rate questions:

$$\text{Rate} = \frac{\text{Number of tasks}}{\text{Time to complete tasks}}, \text{ or number of tasks } per \text{ amount of time}$$

Combined work questions would be much more straightforward if they provided you with the rates at which people or machines work; instead, the test makers make things more complicated by giving you the information in terms of how much time it takes for each individual to complete a given task. To calculate the total time needed for everyone working together to finish the job, use this formula:

> The reciprocal of the time it takes everyone working together = The sum of the reciprocals of the times it would take each person working individually. (The reciprocal of A is $\frac{1}{A}$.)

Written algebraically, this formula comes out as follows:

$\frac{1}{\text{Total time}} = \frac{1}{A} + \frac{1}{B} + \frac{1}{C} + \ldots + \frac{1}{N}$, where A, B, C, etc. represent the time it takes the individual people or machines to do the job by themselves.

You can use this general version of the formula with any number of people or machines working together.

If, however, the question presents you with only two people or machines working together, you will save time by using the following simplified version of the combined work formula:

$$\text{Total time} = \frac{AB}{A + B}$$

Again, A and B are the times it takes the two people working alone to finish the job. By solving for the total time directly instead of for its reciprocal, you'll avoid a common trap.

Example: Bob can clean a room in 3 hours, and George can clean the same room in 2 hours. How many hours does it take Bob and George to clean the room if they work together but independently?

$$\text{Total time} = \frac{AB}{A + B} = \frac{3 \times 2}{3 + 2}$$

Total time $= \frac{6}{5}$ hours, or 1 hour 12 minutes.

Attention to the Right Detail is crucial on combined work problems in which the GMAT can give you the needed information in various forms. The Critical Thinker will be rewarded by seeing what the question requires and choosing the most strategic approach.

Let's now look at a seemingly complicated GMAT work problem and see how the formula makes things much easier.

> Working together, John, David, and Roger require $2\frac{1}{4}$ hours to complete a certain task, if each of them works at his respective constant rate. If John alone can complete the task in $4\frac{1}{2}$ hours and David alone can complete the task in 9 hours, how many hours would it take Roger to complete the task working alone?

- $\bigcirc$ $2\frac{1}{3}$

- $\bigcirc$ $4\frac{1}{2}$

- $\bigcirc$ $6\frac{3}{4}$

- $\bigcirc$ 9

- $\bigcirc$ 12

Combined Work Formula: Here's the solution, employing the combined work formula.

$$\frac{1}{T} = \frac{1}{J} + \frac{1}{D} + \frac{1}{R}$$
$$\frac{1}{2.25} = \frac{1}{4.5} + \frac{1}{9} + \frac{1}{R}$$
$$\frac{4}{9} = \frac{2}{9} + \frac{1}{9} + \frac{1}{R}$$
$$\frac{1}{9} = \frac{1}{R}$$
$$R = 9$$

Hour-by-Hour Approach: An alternative approach to this kind of problem that some find intuitive and quick is to break down the work on an hour-by-hour basis. Take David first. By himself, he could do the entire task in 9 hours. Therefore, during every single hour that these three people work together, David will complete $\frac{1}{9}$ of the task ($\frac{1}{9}$ is just the reciprocal of 9). In the second hour, he'll do another $\frac{1}{9}$. And in that extra $\frac{1}{4}$ hour, he'll do $\frac{1}{36}$ of the task. Add them up: David will be doing $\frac{1}{9} + \frac{1}{9} + \frac{1}{36} = \frac{9}{36} = \frac{1}{4}$ of the entire task during the period in question.

How about John? He's much faster than David. Working alone, he could complete the entire task in $4\frac{1}{2}$ hours (or $\frac{9}{2}$ hours). So during each hour he works, he'll do the reciprocal of $\frac{9}{2}$ (or $\frac{2}{9}$) of the task. Multiply that $\frac{2}{9}$ of a task per hour by the $2\frac{1}{4}$ hours the three men work, and you see that John himself will account for $\frac{2}{9} \times \frac{9}{4}$ or $\frac{1}{2}$ of the task.

With David and John accounting for $\frac{1}{4}$ and $\frac{1}{2}$ of the task respectively, that leaves exactly $\frac{1}{4}$ of the task to be performed by Roger. You can either see that this means that Roger and David work at the same rate—so it'll also take Roger 9 hours—or just divide $2\frac{1}{4}$ hours by $\frac{1}{4}$ task to get 9 hours per task, choice (**D**).

Some harder work problems involve tasks left undone. In those cases, you'd need to use this hour-by-hour approach, so it's worthwhile to be familiar with it.

In-Format Question: Combined Rates and Combined Work on the GMAT

Now let's use the Kaplan Method on a Problem Solving question dealing with combined rates and combined work:

> Working alone, Machine X can manufacture 1,000 nails in 12 hours. Working together, Machines X and Y can manufacture 1,000 nails in 5 hours. How many hours does it take Machine Y to manufacture 1,000 nails working alone?

- ○ $3\frac{9}{17}$
- ○ $5\frac{1}{3}$
- ○ 7
- ○ $7\frac{1}{5}$
- ○ $8\frac{4}{7}$

STEP 1: ANALYZE THE QUESTION

You have a choice of approaches for this combined work question. You can add the rates or solve with the times directly, whichever you find easier.

STEP 2: STATE THE TASK

You're asked for the time it takes Machine Y to make 1,000 nails.

STEP 3: APPROACH STRATEGICALLY

Many combined work questions have answer choices that can be logically eliminated, and this is no different. Since the machines take 5 hours together, it's hardly reasonable to think that one machine would take *fewer* than 5 hours on its own. **(A)** can't be correct. Some estimation allows you to eliminate one more—**(B)** is very, very close to the combined time. Even though Machine X isn't very fast, it's not so slow that it would save only a third of an hour. You've just eliminated two answer choices through Critical Thinking.

Since you're given times and they are all for the same-sized task (manufacturing 1,000 nails), and the task is completed, the formula $T = \dfrac{AB}{A+B}$ will apply nicely.

$$5 = \frac{12Y}{12+Y}$$
$$5(12 + Y) = 12Y$$
$$60 + 5Y = 12Y$$
$$60 = 7Y$$
$$\frac{60}{7} = Y$$
$$8\frac{4}{7} = Y$$

The answer is **(E)**.

You also could have solved this problem by adding the rates.

$$\text{Total rate} = \text{Rate } X + \text{Rate } Y$$
$$\text{Rate} = \frac{\text{Task}}{\text{Time}}$$

If the tasks are all the same, you can save yourself a lot of work by just giving one task the value of 1—in this problem, meaning "1 batch of 1,000 nails."

$$\frac{1}{5} = \frac{1}{12} + \frac{1}{Y}$$

$$\frac{12}{60} = \frac{5}{60} + \frac{1}{Y}$$

$$\frac{12}{60} - \frac{5}{60} = \frac{1}{Y}$$

$$\frac{7}{60} = \frac{1}{Y}$$

$$\frac{60}{7} = Y$$

$$8\frac{4}{7} = Y$$

STEP 4: CONFIRM YOUR ANSWER

Reread the question stem, making sure that you didn't miss anything about the problem. More complicated combined work problems will shift the size of the task halfway through the question stem.

TAKEAWAYS: COMBINED RATES AND COMBINED WORK

- When using rates in a combined work question, $\dfrac{\text{Number of tasks}}{\text{Time to complete tasks}}$.

- The combined work formula for two workers is $\dfrac{AB}{A+B}$, where T equals the time both workers take to do the task when working together, and A and B equal the time needed by each worker to do the job on his or her own, respectively.

- If more than two workers work together, use the generic formula for combined work:

$$\frac{1}{T} = \frac{1}{A} + \frac{1}{B} + \frac{1}{C} + \ldots + \frac{1}{N}$$

Practice Set: Combined Rates and Combined Work on the GMAT

12. Working at its usual constant rate, Pump A can empty a water storage tank in 3 hours. Pump B, also working at its usual constant rate, can empty half of the same tank in 4 hours. How many hours will it take both pumps working together at their usual respective constant rates to empty half of the tank?

   ○ $\frac{12}{11}$

   ○ $\frac{24}{11}$

   ○ $\frac{24}{7}$

   ○ $\frac{7}{2}$

   ○ $\frac{36}{7}$

13. Machine 1 and Machine 2 working together can produce 12,000 meters of steel cable per hour. Each machine works at a constant rate. Machine 1 by itself can produce 5,000 meters of cable per hour. How many hours would it Machine 2 working alone to produce 12,000 meters of cable?

   ○ $\frac{7}{12}$

   ○ $\frac{67}{40}$

   ○ $\frac{12}{7}$

   ○ $\frac{11}{5}$

   ○ $\frac{5}{2}$

14. Two trucks travel from Alphaburg to Betaville along the same route. The speed limit for the first 30 miles is 60 miles per hour. The speed limit for the next 10 miles is 40 miles per hour, and the limit for the final 60 miles is 55 miles per hour. Truck F has a maximum speed of 70 miles per hour, but Truck S has a speed-limiting governor installed to cap its maximum speed at 50 miles per hour. Truck S departs Alphaburg 12 minutes before Truck F. If each truck travels at the lesser of the speed limit or the maximum speed of the truck, how far from Betaville is the point where Truck F catches up with Truck S?

- O 5 miles
- O 20 miles
- O 55 miles
- O 95 miles
- O Both trucks arrive at Betaville simultaneously.

Interest Rates

Interest rates are something that you might be acutely aware of in real life, especially as they apply to mortgages and credit cards, but unless you work directly in a field that touches on loans or mortgages, you probably don't think about the formulas used to calculate them.

Fortunately, you don't have to puzzle over calculating out the interest year-by-year or step-by-step. You can memorize and apply formulas to help you manage the information from the question stem much more efficiently and accurately than by simply applying brute force to the arithmetic.

Interest rate questions rely on three important pieces of information: (1) the principal, or the amount initially invested; (2) the interest rate, or the rate at which the investment grows; and (3) the time period during which the investment accrues interest.

Attention to the Right Detail is necessary even when applying the formulas—and no detail is more important to interest rate questions than whether the interest is simple or compound. Simple and compound interest use different formulas:

Simple interest is interest applied only to the principal, not to the interest that has already accrued. Use this formula:

> **(Total of principal and interest)** = **Principal** $\times$ **(1 + *rt*)**, where *r* equals the interest rate per time period expressed as a decimal and *t* equals the number of time periods

Example: If \$100 were invested at 12 percent simple annual interest, what would be the total value of the investment after 3 years?

$$\text{Total} = \$100 \times (1 + 0.12 \times 3) = \$100(1.36) = \$136$$

Compound interest is interest applied to the principal and any previously accrued interest. Use this formula:

> **(Total of principal and interest)** = **Principal** $\times$ **(1 + *r*)**^{t}, where *r* equals the interest rate per time period expressed as a decimal and *t* equals the number of time periods

Example: If \$100 were invested at 12 percent interest compounded annually, what would be the total value of the investment after 3 years?

$$\text{Total} = \$100 \times (1 + 0.12)^3 = \$100(1.12)^3$$

Despite the GMAT's general preference for simplified values in the answer choices, you will often see answer choices for a compound interest rate problem written as expressions similar to the result above. You can be thankful that you won't have to calculate values such as 1.12^3, since you don't have the use of a calculator on the Quant section.

On Test Day, you might also encounter a more difficult question that requires dealing with annual interest but payments not on an annual basis. In this case, r equals the annual rate divided by the number of times per year it is applied, and t equals the number of years multiplied by the number of times per year interest is applied.

Example: If \$100 were invested at 12 percent annual interest, compounded quarterly, what would be the total value of the investment after 3 years?

$$\text{Total} = \$100 \times \left(1 + \frac{0.12}{4}\right)^{(3\times4)} = \$100(1.03)^{12}$$

In-Format Question: Interest Rates on the GMAT

Now let's use the Kaplan Method on a Problem Solving question dealing with interest rates:

> The number of bacteria in a petri dish increased by 50 percent every 2 hours. If there were 108 million bacteria in the dish at 2:00 p.m., at what time were there 32 million bacteria in the dish?

- ○ 6:00 p.m.
- ○ 8:00 p.m.
- ○ 6:00 a.m.
- ○ 8:00 a.m.
- ○ 10:00 a.m.

STEP 1: ANALYZE THE QUESTION

This may not look like an interest rate question at first glance, but interest rates are just percent increases applied multiple times. The number of bacteria increases 50% every 2 hours. You could think of this as 50% compounded interest applied once every 2 hours.

STEP 2: STATE THE TASK

Instead of calculating forward, you have to calculate back—if there are 108 million in the dish at 2:00 p.m., when were there 32 million?

STEP 3: APPROACH STRATEGICALLY

This problem could be solved as a straightforward percent change, but let's look at it through the lens of interest rates:

$$108 = 32 \times (1.5)^t$$
$$\frac{108}{32} = (1.5)^t$$
$$\frac{27}{8} = (1.5)^t$$
$$\frac{27}{8} = \left(\frac{3}{2}\right)^t$$
$$\frac{27}{8} = \frac{3^t}{2^t}$$
$$\frac{3^3}{2^3} = \frac{3^t}{2^t}$$

Clearly, then $t = 3$. That's three 2-hour increases for a total of 6 hours. Since there were 108 million at 2:00 p.m., there were 32 million 6 hours earlier at 8:00 a.m.

The answer is **(D)**.

This is also an excellent backsolving question, as you could easily just try out a time for 32 million and see whether that's consistent with 108 million at 2:00 p.m.

Let's say you try **(B)** first:

Time	Millions of bacteria
8:00 p.m.	32
10:00 p.m.	48
Midnight	72
2:00 a.m.	108

That's either far too soon (12 hours too soon) or far too late (12 hours too late), depending on how you envision the day. Either way, **(B)** is wrong by a lot, and just shifting 2 hours to 6:00 p.m. won't help matters. Eliminate **(A)** as well.

Now let's try **(D)**:

Time	Millions of bacteria
8:00 a.m.	32
10:00 a.m.	48
Noon	72
2:00 p.m.	108

Exactly what it should be (you might also have seen that **(D)** would be correct when you noticed that **(B)**, 8:00 p.m., was off by exactly 12 hours). The answer is **(D)**.

STEP 4: CONFIRM YOUR ANSWER

Reread the question stem, making sure that you didn't accidentally skip over any important aspects of the situation.

TAKEAWAYS: INTEREST RATES

- Simple interest:
  (Total of principal and interest) = Principal $\times (1 + rt)$, where r equals the interest rate per time period expressed as a decimal and t equals the number of time periods.

- Compound interest:
  (Total of principal and interest) = Principal $\times (1 + r)^t$, where r equals the interest rate per time period expressed as a decimal and t equals the number of time periods.

Practice Set: Interest Rates on the GMAT

15. A certain account pays 1.5 percent compound interest every 3 months. A person invested an initial amount and did not invest any more money in the account after that. If after exactly 5 years, the amount of money in the account was T dollars, which of the following is an expression for the original number of dollars invested in the account?

    ○ $(1.015)^4 T$

    ○ $(1.015)^{15} T$

    ○ $(1.015)^{20} T$

    ○ $\dfrac{T}{(1.015)^{15}}$

    ○ $\dfrac{T}{(1.015)^{20}}$

16. Binh invested \$1,000 in a certificate of deposit (CD) that matured in 4 years. The certificate paid 4 percent annual interest compounded quarterly for the original 4-year term and then 2 percent simple annual interest on the compounded amount after that until the CD was redeemed by the holder. If Binh held his CD for exactly 6 years, how much money did he receive when he redeemed it?

    ○ $1,000 \times (1.01)^{16} \times 1.04$

    ○ $1,000 \times (1.01)^{16} \times (1.02)^2$

    ○ $1,000 \times (1.04)^6$

    ○ $1,000 \times (1.01)^{24}$

    ○ $1,000 \times (1.04)^{16} \times (1.02)^2$

17. The amount of an investment will double in approximately $\frac{70}{p}$ years, where p is the percent interest, compounded annually. If Thelma invests \$40,000 in a long-term CD that pays 5 percent interest, compounded annually, what will be the approximate total value of the investment when Thelma is ready to retire 42 years later?

    ○ \$280,000

    ○ \$320,000

    ○ \$360,000

    ○ \$450,000

    ○ \$540,000

Overlapping Sets

Another classic GMAT setup involves a large group that is subdivided into two potentially overlapping sub-groups. For example, let's say that in a room of 20 people, there are 12 dog owners and 14 cat owners. Since 12 plus 14 is more than 20, the only way this situation makes any sense is if some people own both a dog and a cat. And it's possible that some own neither. Essentially, there are four different subgroups to consider: (1) those who own a dog but not a cat, (2) those who own a cat but not a dog, (3) those who own both a cat and a dog, and (4) those who own neither a cat nor a dog. You could also combine some of these groups to consider both the total number of dog owners and the total number of cat owners.

Three Approaches to Overlapping Sets

There are three ways to work these problems. Let's look at each.

Approach 1: Overlapping Sets Formula

Use the overlapping sets formula:

$$\text{Group 1} + \text{Group 2} - \text{Both} + \text{Neither} = \text{Total}$$

Example: An office manager orders 27 pizzas for a party. Of these, 15 have pepperoni, and 10 have mushrooms. If 4 pizzas have no toppings at all, and no other toppings are ordered, then how many pizzas were ordered with both pepperoni and mushrooms?

$$
\begin{aligned}
\text{Group 1} + \text{Group 2} - \text{Both} + \text{Neither} &= \text{Total} \\
\text{Pepperoni} + \text{Mushrooms} - \text{Both} + \text{Neither} &= \text{Total} \\
15 + 10 - \text{Both} + 4 &= 27 \\
29 - \text{Both} &= 27 \\
\text{Both} &= 2
\end{aligned}
$$

Approach 2: Venn Diagram

Organize the given information using a Venn diagram. This approach uses partially overlapping circles to represent the data visually:

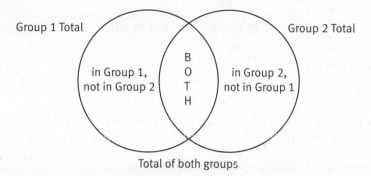

Example: All the students in a class study either Forensics or Statistics. There are 16 Forensics students, 3 of whom also study Statistics. How many Statistics students are in the class if the class has 25 students altogether?

Because 3 of the Forensics students also study Statistics, there must be 13 who study only Forensics. If the "Forensics only" and "Both" groups total 16 and there are 25 students in the class, then $25 - 16$, or 9, students study only Statistics. Thus, $9 + 3 = 12$, the total number of Statistics students. Putting all these numbers into the Venn diagram as you go helps you to see these relationships clearly:

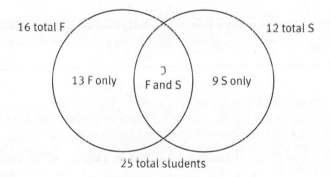

Approach 3: Chart

Organize the given information using a chart. This way works best with complicated overlapping sets problems because it has a separate place for each of the nine data points you might be given. Take your time organizing the chart, and the problem will almost solve itself:

	In Group 1	Not in Group 1	Total
In Group 2			
Not in Group 2			
Total			

Example: A company has 200 employees, 90 of whom belong to a union. If there are 95 part-time nonunion employees and 80 full-time union employees, then how many full-time employees are in the company?

Start by putting the data into the chart, using a question mark to indicate the value that the question asks for:

	In union	Not in union	Total
Full-time	80		?
Part-time		95	
Total	90		200

Now you can calculate the total number of nonunion employees ($200 - 90 = 110$) and the number of part-time union employees ($90 - 80 = 10$):

	In union	Not in union	Total
Full-time	80		?
Part-time	10	95	
Total	90	110	200

And now either calculate full-time nonunion employees ($110 - 95 = 15$) or the total number of part-time employees ($10 + 95 = 105$):

	In union	Not in union	Total
Full-time	80	15	?
Part-time	10	95	105
Total	90	110	200

Either way, you can then calculate the total number of full-time employees ($80 + 15 = 95$ or $200 - 105 = 95$):

	In union	Not in union	Total
Full-time	80	15	95
Part-time	10	95	105
Total	90	110	200

There are 95 full-time employees.

Each of the three approaches has its pluses and minuses. Your own personal thinking style will respond best to one of these over the others. Practice all of them so you get a sense of which approach you like with different problems.

Now try the following example on your own, using Critical Thinking to assess which of the three approaches will be most effective:

A group of 25 children went to the circus, 60 percent of whom liked the clowns. If the number of preschool children who liked the clowns was 3 more than the number of preschool children who did not, and the number of preschool children was 1 larger than the number of school-age children, then how many school-age children did not like the clowns?

In your overview of the problem, you can see that there are some complex relationships going on; you shouldn't try to understand them all at once. But notice that there are two ways in which children can be classified: preschool or school-age, liked or didn't like the clowns. That makes this an overlapping sets problem.

The approach that offers the most flexibility, shows the most detail, and is therefore frequently the safest to use with this question type is this chart:

	In Group 1	Not in Group 1	Total
In Group 2			
Not in Group 2			
Total			

In this problem, the two groupings are preschool or school-age and likes clowns or doesn't like clowns. So here's the chart you'd use for this problem:

	Likes clowns	Doesn't like	Total
Preschool			
School-age			
Total			

Now enter the information from the question stem:

	Likes clowns	Doesn't like	Total
Preschool	$x \mid 3$	x	$s + 1$
School-age		?	s
Total	60% of 25		25

Two calculations can be done right away: 60% of $25 = (0.6)(25) = 15$. Also, $(s + 1) + s = 25$. That means $2s + 1 = 25$, so $2s = 24$ and $s = 12$.

	Likes clowns	Doesn't like	Total
Preschool	$x + 3$	x	13
School-age		?	12
Total	15		25

The next two calculations suggested by the chart are the total number of children who don't like clowns, $25 - 15 = 10$, and the value of x. Use the equation $(x + 3) + x = 13$, or $2x + 3 = 13$. That means $2x = 10$, or $x = 5$. Then $x + 3 = 8$.

	Likes clowns	Doesn't like	Total
Preschool	8	5	13
School-age		?	12
Total	15	10	25

Now you know the answer to the question . . . the number of school-age children who didn't like the clowns is 10 − 5, or 5. You can fill in the number of school-age children who like clowns, too, just for fun.

	Likes clowns	Doesn't like	Total
Preschool	8	5	13
School-age	7	5	12
Total	15	10	25

Because this chart shows all nine possible data points in these problems, it allows you to answer any question that might be asked. Fraction of school-age kids who liked the clowns? It's $\frac{7}{12}$. Percentage of children who didn't like the clowns who were also preschoolers? It's 50%. Ratio of school-age children who liked the clowns to preschoolers who didn't? It's 7:5.

When overlapping sets questions involve proportions, be very clear about what the basis of the proportion is. For example, the number of preschoolers who didn't like the clowns could be described as 20% (of the children), 50% (of the children who didn't like clowns), or 100% (as large as the number of school-age children who didn't like the clowns).

In-Format Question: Overlapping Sets on the GMAT

Now let's use the Kaplan Method on a Problem Solving question dealing with overlapping sets:

> A polling company surveyed a certain country, and it found that 35 percent of that country's registered voters had an unfavorable impression of both of that state's major political parties and that 20 percent had a favorable impression only of Party A. If 1 registered voter has a favorable impression of both parties for every 2 registered voters who have a favorable impression only of Party B, then what percentage of the country's registered voters have a favorable impression of both parties (assuming that respondents to the poll were given a choice between favorable and unfavorable impressions only)?

- ○ 15
- ○ 20
- ○ 30
- ○ 35
- ○ 45

STEP 1: ANALYZE THE QUESTION

You're presented with a lot of information in this overlapping sets question. Don't try to digest it all at once. Notice that the total group (registered voters) can be separated into two major categories (those who like Party A and those who like Party B) and that those categories are not mutually exclusive (which means that someone could be in both categories—in this case, that someone could like both parties). That's the general setup for overlapping sets questions.

Use Critical Thinking to choose the best approach for this problem. This is a complicated question with many data points. The most powerful tool for understanding confusing or complicated overlapping sets is a chart:

	Favorable B	Not favorable B	Total
Favorable A	?		
Not favorable A			
Total			

STEP 2: STATE THE TASK

You need to calculate the percentage of registered voters who like both parties; in other words, the value in the upper left-hand box.

STEP 3: APPROACH STRATEGICALLY

Start by putting the information into the chart. For simplicity's sake, pick 100 for the total number of voters.

	Favorable B	Not favorable B	Total
Favorable A	?	20	
Not favorable A		35	
Total			100

The other piece of data is "1 registered voter has a favorable impression of both parties for every 2 registered voters who have a favorable impression only of Party B." In other words, the ratio of "favorable A and favorable B" to "favorable B and not favorable A" is 1:2. So you have something else to put in the chart—let's call that x and $2x$.

	Favorable B	Not favorable B	Total
Favorable A	x (?)	20	
Not favorable A	$2x$	35	
Total			100

Since this chart adds down (and across), you can fill in the rest easily enough:

	Favorable B	Not favorable B	Total
Favorable A	x (?)	20	$20 + x$
Not favorable A	$2x$	35	$35 + 2x$
Total	$3x$	55	100

Whether you use the Total column or the Total row, you have the same equation to solve for x:

$$3x + 55 = 100$$
$$3x = 45$$
$$x = 15$$

The answer is (A).

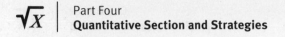

STEP 4: CONFIRM YOUR ANSWER

Reread the question stem, making sure that you didn't accidentally misread anything.

TAKEAWAYS: OVERLAPPING SETS

- Overlapping sets questions on the GMAT require you to determine the elements in a set that do, or do not, overlap with elements of other sets.

- There are three approaches for overlapping sets questions:
  - Use the overlapping sets formula: Total = Group 1 + Group 2 − Both + Neither.
  - Draw a Venn diagram and use numbers to notate areas of overlap. This often works best for questions involving three overlapping sets.
  - Jot a table on your noteboard and solve. This works best with overlapping set problems involving two binary characteristics that can readily become column and row labels.

Practice Set: Overlapping Sets on the GMAT

18. Of the 65 books released last year by a particular publishing house, 25 were no more than 200 pages. The publisher released 35 fiction books, of which 20 were more than 200 pages, and it also published nonfiction books. How many nonfiction books of no more than 200 pages did the publishing house release last year?

    ○   5

    ○   10

    ○   20

    ○   30

    ○   35

19. Three hundred students at College Q study a foreign language. Of these, 110 of those students study French and 170 study Spanish. If at least 90 students who study a foreign language at College Q study neither French nor Spanish, then the number of students who study Spanish but not French could be any number from

    ○   10 to 40

    ○   40 to 100

    ○   60 to 100

    ○   60 to 110

    ○   70 to 110

20. The *Financial News Daily* has 25 reporters covering Asia, 20 covering Europe, and 20 covering North America. Four reporters cover Asia and Europe but not North America, 6 reporters cover Asia and North America but not Europe, and 7 reporters cover Europe and North America but not Asia. How many reporters cover all three continents (Asia, Europe, and North America)?

    (1)   The *Financial News Daily* has 38 reporters in total covering at least 1 of the following continents: Asia, Europe, and North America.

    (2)   There are more *Financial News Daily* reporters covering only Asia than there are *Financial News Daily* reporters covering only North America.

Answer Key

Practice Set: Averages on the GMAT

1. C
2. D
3. D
4. C

Practice Set: Rates and Speed—Converting Rates on the GMAT

5. D
6. C
7. D

Practice Set: Rates and Speed—Multi-Part Journeys on the GMAT

8. E
9. C
10. B
11. D

Practice Set: Combined Rates and Combined Work on the GMAT

12. A
13. C
14. A

Practice Set: Interest Rates on the GMAT

15. E
16. A
17. B

Practice Set: Overlapping Sets on the GMAT

18. B
19. C
20. A

Answers and Explanations

Practice Set: Averages on the GMAT

1. **(C)**

    Bradley's grade in his science class is determined by his scores on 5 tests that each count an equal amount toward his grade. He has received scores of 67, 76, 78, and 94 on the 4 science tests thus far. If the last test consists of 20 equally weighted questions and is graded out of 100 points, how many questions does he need to answer correctly on the last test in order to average an 80 in his science class?

    ○   15

    ○   16

    ○   17

    ○   18

    ○   19

STEP 1: ANALYZE THE QUESTION

Bradley wants an average score of 80 out of 100. Four of his test scores are known, and the fifth score is unknown. His last test has 20 questions on it worth 100 points, so he will earn $\frac{100}{20} = 5$ points per question.

STEP 2: STATE THE TASK

Use the average formula to solve for the test score needed to achieve an 80 average. Then translate that into the number of questions correct out of 20.

STEP 3: APPROACH STRATEGICALLY

It's worth noting that the numbers here are relatively large, so calculating an average using the average formula, while certainly doable, is somewhat cumbersome. Using the "balanced average" strategy will let you work with smaller numbers.

The goal average is 80. Bradley currently has three scores less than 80: 67, 76, and 78, which are 13, 4, and 2 points, respectively, less than 80. Therefore, he has a sum of $13 + 4 + 2 = 19$ points to the left of the average. He has one score greater than 80: 94, which is 14 points greater than (to the right of) 80. To balance the 19 points on the left with the 14 points on the right, Bradley needs 5 points more on the right. The score that adds 5 points to the right of 80 is $80 + 5 = 85$.

Translate 85 points into questions correct on the test: $\frac{85 \text{ pts}}{5 \text{ pts/question}} = 17$ questions. **(C)** is correct.

STEP 4: CONFIRM YOUR ANSWER

To confirm your answer, you can backsolve by plugging **(C)** back into the question: if Bradley gets 17 out of 20 questions correct, he receives a score of 85. In combination with his previous test scores, his average in the class will be $\frac{85 + 67 + 76 + 78 + 94}{5} = \frac{400}{5} = 80$. This confirms choice **(C)**.

2. **(D)**

Points	# of arrows
0	1
1	1
3	3
5	6
7	8
9	2

In a certain archery contest, archers are awarded a different number of points for each arrow, depending upon the accuracy of the shot. If an arrow hits the bull's-eye, 10 points are awarded. The results for one archer are shown in the table above, but the values do not include her bull's-eyes. If the archer's average score per arrow is 6.0, how many of her attempts were bull's-eyes?

- ○ 0
- ○ 1
- ○ 2
- ○ 3
- ○ 4

STEP 1: ANALYZE THE QUESTION

This is a weighted average question that displays the frequency of each value except 10 in a table. There are a total of 21 values listed in the table. The average of all the values, including the ones not shown, is 6.0.

STEP 2: STATE THE TASK

Determine the number of 10-point arrows the archer had in order to attain her average of 6.0.

STEP 3: APPROACH STRATEGICALLY

You can backsolve or do straight-ahead math. Either way, you first find the total arrows and points scored that are shown in the table. Add the number of arrows: $1 + 1 + 3 + 6 + 8 + 2 = 21$ arrows. Then find the total points shown: $1(0) + 1(1) + 3(3) + 6(5) + 8(7) + 2(9) = 114$.

If you go the backsolving route, first note that the bull's-eyes score more than any of other arrows, so a larger number of bull's-eyes will pull the average up. You might start with **(B)**, 1 arrow that scored 10 points. In this case, the archer would have shot $21 + 1 = 22$ arrows and scored $114 + 10 = 124$ points. When you begin to divide 124 by 22, you get 5 and a remainder. You are looking for an average of 6, so this is not enough 10-point arrows. Eliminate **(A)** and **(B)** and move on to **(D)**: $21 + 3 = 24$ arrows and $114 + (3)(10) = 144$ points. When you divide 144 by 24, you get 6—which is the desired average. **(D)** is correct.

If you choose to do regular math, set up an equation using the fact that a weighted average is the sum of each value times its frequency, divided by the total number of values. Let x be the unknown number of bull's-eyes. Then:

$$6 = \frac{0(1) + 1(1) + 3(3) + 5(6) + 7(8) + 9(2) + 10(x)}{21 + x}$$

$$6 = \frac{114 + 10x}{21 + x}$$

Multiply both sides by $21 + x$ to get $126 + 6x = 114 + 10x$. This simplifies to $12 = 4x$, so $x = 3$. Again, **(D)** is correct.

STEP 4: CONFIRM YOUR ANSWER

If you did not backsolve to find the answer, compute the average with 3 bull's-eyes: $\frac{114 + 10(3)}{21 + 3} = \frac{144}{24} = 6$. If you backsolved, confirm that you correctly added the number of arrows and corresponding number of points before finding the average.

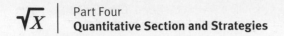

3. (D)

An exam is given in a certain class. The average (arithmetic mean) of the highest score and the lowest score on the exam is equal to x. If the average score for the entire class is equal to y and there are z students in the class, where $z > 5$, then in terms of x, y, and z, what is the average score for the class, excluding the highest and lowest scores?

- $\dfrac{zy - 2x}{z}$

- $\dfrac{zy - 2}{z}$

- $\dfrac{zx - y}{z - 2}$

- $\dfrac{zy - 2x}{z - 2}$

- $\dfrac{zy - x}{z + 2}$

STEP 1: ANALYZE THE QUESTION

This is a complicated-looking word problem with lots of variables, including variables in the answer choices. Whenever there are variables in the answer choices, consider picking numbers. When picking numbers in a question dealing with averages, pick all the numbers in a group to equal the average of that group.

STEP 2: STATE THE TASK

Your task is to calculate the average of the class after excluding the highest and lowest scores. Before rushing into the math, think logically about what the task tells you about the correct answer. Since the total size of the class is z, there will be $(z - 2)$ scores after the high score and low scores are eliminated. Since an average is the sum divided by the number of terms, the correct answer must have $(z - 2)$ as a denominator. A quick check of the answer choices reveals that only **(C)** and **(D)** might possibly be correct. If you were falling behind on time or unsure of how to approach this question, you could make a 50/50 guess pretty quickly.

Many GMAT word problems have answer choices that can be eliminated without much math.

STEP 3: APPROACH STRATEGICALLY

See what you know about the class. The average of the whole class is y, and there are z students in the class. Now what about the high and low scores? You're told nothing about them, save that their average is x.

This is all pretty abstract, so simplify things by picking numbers. Start with the number of students. It must be greater than 5, so say that it's 6 $(z = 6)$.

Now pick scores for the 6 students. You could pick all different scores, but the easiest approach of all is to let all 6 scores be equal to the average of those scores. Say that the class as a whole averages a score of 2. After all, realism doesn't matter when picking numbers, only permissibility and manageability. So $y = 2$.

scores (in order): 2, 2, 2, 2, 2, 2

Now, what are the highest and the lowest? Let's bold them below for emphasis:

scores (in order): **2**, 2, 2, 2, 2, **2**

Together, the high and low scores also average 2. We can calculate that so quickly because when all the terms in a group equal the same value, the average is also equal to that value. So $x = 2$.

Your task is to calculate the average of the class after excluding the high and low scores:

$$\text{scores (in order): } \cancel{2}, 2, 2, 2, 2, \cancel{2}$$

Looks like that average will be 2 as well. Now you just need to plug $z = 6$, $y = 2$, and $x = 2$ into the answer choices, looking for the result of 2:

(A) $\dfrac{(6 \times 2) - (2 \times 2)}{6} = \dfrac{12 - 4}{6} = \dfrac{8}{6} = \dfrac{4}{3}$. Eliminate.

(B) $\dfrac{(6 \times 2) - 2}{6} = \dfrac{12 - 2}{6} = \dfrac{10}{6} = \dfrac{5}{3}$. Eliminate.

(C) $\dfrac{(6 \times 2) - 2}{6 - 2} = \dfrac{12 - 2}{4} = \dfrac{10}{4} - \dfrac{5}{2}$. Eliminate.

(D) $\dfrac{(6 \times 2) - (2 \times 2)}{6 - 2} = \dfrac{12 - 4}{4} = \dfrac{8}{4} = 2$. Possibly correct.

(E) $\dfrac{(6 \times 2) - 2}{6 + 2} - \dfrac{12 - 2}{8} = \dfrac{10}{8} = \dfrac{5}{4}$. Eliminate.

The answer is **(D)**.

There is an algebraic solution, but you may find this approach more complicated and abstract:

$$\text{Average of non-excluded scores} = \frac{\text{Sum of non-excluded scores}}{\text{Number of non-excluded scores}}$$

$$\text{Number of non-excluded scores} = \text{Number of all scores} - \text{Number of excluded scores}$$

$$\text{Number of non-excluded scores} = z - 2$$

$$\text{Sum of non-excluded scores} = \text{Sum of all scores} - \text{Sum of excluded scores}$$

$$\text{Average of all scores} = \frac{\text{Sum of all scores}}{\text{Number of all scores}}$$

$$y = \frac{\text{Sum of all scores}}{z}$$

$$zy = \text{Sum of all scores}$$

$$\text{Average of excluded scores} = \frac{\text{Sum of excluded scores}}{\text{Number of excluded scores}}$$

$$x = \frac{\text{Sum of excluded scores}}{2}$$

$$2x = \text{Sum of excluded scores}$$

$$\text{Sum of non-excluded scores} = zy - 2x$$

$$\text{Average of non-excluded scores} = \frac{\text{Sum of non-excluded scores}}{\text{Number of non-excluded scores}}$$

$$\text{Average of non-excluded scores} = \frac{zy - 2x}{z - 2}$$

This expression matches **(D)**, which is the correct answer.

Picking numbers can reduce some of the most complicated average questions to very simple arithmetic.

STEP 4: CONFIRM YOUR ANSWER

Reread the question stem, making sure that you didn't miss anything about the problem.

4. **(C)**

The average price of Emily's 5 meals was $20. Meals with a price of $25 or more include a free dessert. How many of Emily's 5 meals included a free dessert?

(1) The most expensive of the 5 meals had a price of $50.

(2) The least expensive of the 5 meals had a price of $10.

STEP 1: ANALYZE THE QUESTION STEM

This is a Value question. Since the average price of Emily's 5 meals was $20, the sum of the prices of all 5 meals was $5 \times \$20 = \$100$. You're also told that meals with a price of $25 or more include a free dessert. You need to determine whether there's enough information to find how many of Emily's meals included a free dessert. Thus, you'll have sufficient information if you can determine the exact number of meals that had a price of at least $25.

STEP 2: EVALUATE THE STATEMENTS USING 12TEN

Look at Statement (1). The most expensive meal had a price of $50, and the sum of all 5 prices was $100, so the prices of the other 4 meals must have had a sum of $100 − \$50 = \$50$. However, there's no way to determine how that $50 was distributed among the remaining 4 meals; it could be that 1 of the meals was $25 or more and each of the other 3 was less than $25, or it could be that each of the 4 meals was less than $25. Because there's insufficient information in this statement to determine an exact number of meals costing $25 or more, eliminate **(A)** and **(D)**.

Statement (2) tells you that the least expensive of the 5 meals had a price of $10. Since the prices of the 5 meals sum to $100, the prices of the 4 most expensive meals sum to $90. Now, consider the possibilities: it could be that 3 of these 4 meals are $25 each and the fourth is $15, or that 1 meal is $45 and the other 3 are $15 each, or some other combination of prices that sum to $90. Since there is more than one possibility for the number of meals that cost at least $25, this statement is insufficient. Eliminate **(B)**.

Now, consider the statements together. If the most expensive meal were $50 and the least expensive meal were $10, then the sum of the remaining 3 meals was $100 − \$50 − \$10 = \$40$. How might this $40 be distributed among the remaining 3 meals? Since Emily's least expensive meal was $10, each of these 3 remaining meals must cost more than $10, so 2 of the 3 together must cost over $20; therefore, the third cannot be as much as $25 (for example, if 2 of these 3 remaining meals were $10.50 each, there would only be $40 − \$10.50 − \$10.50 = \$19$ left for the third meal). Therefore, it's only possible for 1 meal (the $50 one, which is the most expensive) to have a price of at least $25. Thus, the two statements combined are sufficient to determine an exact number of meals that cost at least $25, and the correct choice is **(C)**.

Practice Set: Rates and Speed—Converting Rates on the GMAT

5. **(D)**

A group of friends rent a small bus to go sightseeing. The rate for the bus and driver is $90 per hour, and the total distance of the sightseeing tour is 112 miles. If the total charge for the trip is $420, what is the average speed of the bus in miles per hour?

○ 16.7

○ 21.0

○ 22.5

○ 24.0

○ 25.8

STEP 1: ANALYZE THE QUESTION

You are provided with three pieces of information about a trip: the per-hour rate to rent a bus and driver, the distance traveled, and the total charge.

STEP 2: STATE THE TASK

Use rate calculations to determine the average speed of the bus.

STEP 3: APPROACH STRATEGICALLY

There are three different units in the question: dollars, hours, and miles. Pay close attention to these units in order to obtain a rate in terms of miles per hour. You can start by determining the duration of the trip in hours: $\frac{\$420/hr}{\$90} = 4\frac{2}{3}$ hrs. Since Speed $= \frac{\text{Distance}}{\text{Time}}$, convert $4\frac{2}{3}$ hrs to $\frac{14}{3}$ hrs and set up the equation Speed $= \frac{112 \text{ miles}}{\frac{14}{3} \text{ hrs}}$. Then invert the denominator and multiply to get $112 \times \frac{3}{14} = \frac{\cancel{2} \times 2 \times 2 \times 2 \times 2 \times 3}{\cancel{2} \times \cancel{2}} = 24$.

So the average speed is 24 miles per hour. **(D)** is correct.

STEP 4: CONFIRM YOUR ANSWER

Check your calculations and units.

6.   **(C)**

Pierre's European car measures fuel economy in terms of liters per kilometer. If the car averages $\frac{1\,\text{liter}}{10\,\text{kilometers}}$ on a trip, what is the car's approximate fuel economy in terms of the standard U.S. measurement of miles per gallon? (Note: 1 gallon is approximately 3.78 liters, and 1 mile is approximately 1.61 kilometers.)

○   4

○   16

○   24

○   30

○   40

STEP 1: ANALYZE THE QUESTION

You're given a rate, and it looks like you'll have to convert it. You'll have to pay close attention to the units (liters, kilometers, gallons, and miles) so that you make the right conversion. Note that the question asks for an approximate value, so you may be able to make some estimates rather than perform precise calculations.

STEP 2: STATE THE TASK

Convert $\frac{1\,\text{liter}}{10\,\text{kilometers}}$ into terms of miles per gallon. In other words, you start with this:

$$\frac{1\,\text{liter}}{10\,\text{kilometer}}$$

And you want to end up with this:

$$\frac{???\,\text{miles}}{\text{gallon}}$$

STEP 3: APPROACH STRATEGICALLY

Since the ultimate result will be in terms of $\frac{\text{distance}}{\text{volume}}$, start by inverting $\frac{1\,\text{liter}}{10\,\text{kilometers}}$ to get $\frac{10\,\text{kilometers}}{1\,\text{liter}}$. Convert the terms one by one to avoid confusion. Start with distance. Since 1 mile = 1.61 kilometers,

$10\,\text{kilometers} \times \frac{1\,\text{mile}}{1.61\,\text{kilometers}} \approx 6\,\text{miles}$ (since the question asks for the approximate fuel economy, you can round). Given that 1 gallon = 3.78 liters, $1\,\text{liter} \times \frac{1\,\text{gallon}}{3.78\,\text{liters}} \approx 0.25\,\text{gallons}$. Finally, $\frac{6\,\text{miles}}{0.25\,\text{gallons}} = \frac{24\,\text{miles}}{1\,\text{gallon}}$.

(C) is correct.

STEP 4: CONFIRM YOUR ANSWER

Reread the question stem, making sure that you didn't miss any important details in the problem. Be certain that you payed close attention to the units throughout your calculations.

7.   (D)

A student can complete x homework questions in h hours. According to his calculations, it will take him 4 days to complete his latest assignment if he works m minutes a day. How many questions are on his latest assignment?

○ $\dfrac{mx}{60h}$

○ $\dfrac{15x}{mh}$

○ $\dfrac{4xh}{m}$

○ $\dfrac{mx}{15h}$

○ $\dfrac{4mx}{15h}$

STEP 1: ANALYZE THE QUESTION

This question gives you two rates expressed in variables (x questions per h hours, m minutes per 1 day) and a time as a number (4 days). It's worth noting the variety of units in the question stem; converting units will definitely be a part of solving.

STEP 2: STATE THE TASK

This question asks for the number of questions on the student's assignment given his rate of work and the amount of time he works.

STEP 3: APPROACH STRATEGICALLY

With so many variables involved, this question can seem abstract, and setting up the algebra may be daunting. Picking numbers is a good strategy here.

Since there are 60 minutes in 1 hour, let $m = 60$. So he works for 60 minutes (1 hour) each day. Then pick small numbers for x and h that are factors/multiples of each other and of 60, since rates involve division. You might let $x = 6$ and $h = 2$. Based on the numbers picked, the student completes 6 questions every 2 hours, or 3 questions an hour. The student is going to work 1 hour a day for 4 days, or 4 hours total. That means there must be $\dfrac{3 \text{ questions}}{1 \text{ hour}} \times 4 \text{ hours} = 12$ questions on the latest assignment.

Plug the numbers you picked into the answer choices to see which yields the same answer of 12:

(A) $\dfrac{mx}{60h} = \dfrac{60(6)}{60(2)} = \dfrac{6}{2} \neq 12$. Eliminate.

(B) $\dfrac{15x}{mh} = \dfrac{15(6)}{60(2)} = \dfrac{1(3)}{4(1)} \neq 12$. Eliminate.

(C) $\dfrac{4xh}{m} = \dfrac{4(6)(2)}{60} = \dfrac{4 \times 2}{10} = \dfrac{8}{10} \neq 12$. Eliminate.

(D) $\dfrac{mx}{15h} = \dfrac{(60)(6)}{15(2)} = \dfrac{(4)(3)}{1(1)} = 12$. Keep this one.

(E) $\dfrac{4mx}{15h} = \dfrac{4(60)(6)}{15(2)} = \dfrac{4(4)(3)}{1(1)} \neq 12$. Eliminate.

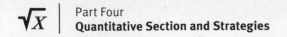
Note that you must plug the chosen values into every choice in case more than one gives you a matching result. In this case, only choice (**D**) yields a result of 5.

Alternatively, this question can be solved via dimensional analysis. The student will work m minutes per day. Because *per* indicates a rate, and rates can be represented as fractions, you have the fraction $\dfrac{m \text{ minutes}}{1 \text{ day}}$.

Another rate in this question is the rate at which the student works. Because he completes x questions in h hours, the rate can be represented as $\dfrac{x \text{ questions}}{h \text{ hours}}$.

The student will be working on this assignment for 4 days. Multiply rates together so that units cancel and yield a final answer in terms of number of questions.

$$4 \text{ days} \times \frac{m \text{ minutes}}{1 \text{ day}} \times \frac{1 \text{ hour}}{60 \text{ minutes}} \times \frac{x \text{ questions}}{h \text{ hours}} = \frac{4mx}{60h} = \frac{mx}{15h} \text{ questions}$$

This matches (**D**).

STEP 4: CONFIRM YOUR ANSWER

You can confirm your answer by picking a different set of numbers or by using the strategy you did not originally use (picking number vs. dimensional analysis).

Practice Set: Rates and Speed—Multi-Part Journeys on the GMAT

8. **(E)**

A motorcyclist started riding at highway marker A, drove 120 miles to highway marker B, and then, without pausing, continued to highway marker C, where she stopped. The average speed of the motorcyclist, over the course of the entire trip, was 45 miles per hour. If the ride from marker A to marker B lasted 3 times as many hours as the rest of the ride, and the distance from marker B to marker C was half of the distance from marker A to marker B, what was the average speed, in miles per hour, of the motorcyclist while driving from marker B to marker C?

- ○ 40
- ○ 45
- ○ 50
- ○ 55
- ○ 60

STEP 1: ANALYZE THE QUESTION

A motorcyclist rides from highway marker to highway marker for different distances and durations and at different speeds. With so many pieces of information given for this multi-stage journey, you should be prepared to track it all with a table.

STEP 2: STATE THE TASK

Find the average speed, in miles per hour (mph), of the motorcyclist while driving from marker B to marker C.

STEP 3: APPROACH STRATEGICALLY

With so much information to keep track of, the best way to approach this problem is first to organize all of the given concrete information into a table:

	Rate (mph)	Time (hr)	Distance (miles)
Marker A to marker B			120
Marker B to marker C	?		
Total	45		

You're told that the ride from marker A to marker B took 3 times as long as the ride from marker B to marker C and that the distance from marker B to marker C is half the distance from marker A to marker B. Using t for the amount of time, in hours, that it took to ride from marker B to marker C, you can now fill in your table with the following:

	Rate (mph)	Time (hr)	Distance (miles)
Marker A to marker B		3t	120
Marker B to marker C	?	t	60
Total	45	4t	180

It took $4t$ hours to go 180 miles at 45 miles per hour, so t must equal 1. You can now finish the table:

	Rate (mph)	Time (hr)	Distance (miles)
Marker A to marker B	40	3	120
Marker B to marker C	60	1	60
Total	45	4	180

You're looking for the average speed from marker B to marker C, which, according to the table, is 60 miles per hour. The correct choice is (**E**).

STEP 4: CONFIRM YOUR ANSWER

When using a table to organize information, check to ensure that the given pieces of information are filled into the correct parts of the table. Also remember that unlike time and distance, for which the values in the columns sum to get the total, the only way to calculate rate is to divide the distance for that row by the corresponding time.

9. **(C)**

Did Jon complete a journey of 40 kilometers in less time than it took Ann to complete the same journey?

(1) Jon traveled at an average speed of 30 kilometers per hour for the first 10 kilometers and then at an average speed of 15 kilometers per hour for the rest of the journey.

(2) Ann traveled at an average speed of 20 kilometers per hour for the entire journey.

STEP 1: ANALYZE THE QUESTION STEM

This is a Yes/No question. The stem asks you to compare the time it took two people to complete the same journey of 40 kilometers. Remember that $\dfrac{\text{Distance}}{\text{Time}}$. Since you're given the distance in the question stem, you'll need information adequate to determine both travelers' rates of speed.

STEP 2: EVALUATE THE STATEMENTS USING 12TEN

Statement (1) gives you Jon's speed. Together with the question stem, this is enough information to determine the time required by Jon to complete the journey. But you get no information about Ann. Statement (1) is insufficient. You can eliminate **(A)** and **(D)**.

Statement (2) and the question stem together give enough information to determine the time Ann took to complete the journey but nothing about Jon. Statement (2) is also insufficient. Eliminate **(B)**.

Combining the two statements, you have enough to determine both the time Jon took to complete the journey and the time Ann took to complete the journey. Note that you don't need to calculate their times; knowing that you could calculate them is enough. **(C)** is correct.

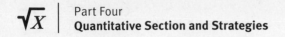
10. (B)

A hiker walks three sections of a trail that are of equal length. The first section of the trail is flat, and on this section the hiker travels at 3 miles per hour for 1.5 hours. The second section is uphill, and on this section the hiker's pace slows by 25 percent. The third section is downhill, and here his speed doubles. What was the hiker's average speed for the entire three-section hike?

- ○ 1.5
- ○ 3
- ○ 3.25
- ○ 4.5
- ○ 9.75

STEP 1: ANALYZE THE QUESTION

A journey consists of three parts of equal distance, traveled at different speeds. You know both the speed and the time needed to cover the first section, so you can derive the distance of each section from this information. The speeds for the second and third parts of the journey are given in terms of the speed for the previous part.

STEP 2: STATE THE TASK

Use the average rate formula to calculate the hiker's average speed for the entire journey.

STEP 3: APPROACH STRATEGICALLY

To find the average rate of speed for the entire journey, you'll need the total distance hiked and the total time the hike took.

To find the distance of the first section of the hike, use the distance formula: Distance = Rate × Time. In this case, that means distance = 3 mph × 1.5 hours = 4.5 miles. Since each section is the same length, each section of the hike is 4.5 miles, and the total hike is 3 × 4.5 miles.

Now calculate the time needed for the second section of the hike. This will be distance divided by speed. The hiker's speed on the second section is 25% less than the speed on the first section, which is 100% − 25% = 75% of the starting speed; calculate 0.75 × 3 mph = 2.25 mph. (Be careful here! You have to apply the percentage to the hiker's rate, not his time.) Thus, the time needed for the second section of the hike is 4.5 miles ÷ 2.25 mph = 2 hours.

For the third section, apply the same process: the hiker's rate is twice his rate on the second section, so that's 2 × 2.25 mph = 4.5 mph. Again the distance is 4.5 miles, so the time needed is 4.5 miles ÷ 4.5 mph = 1 hour. Therefore, the time for the entire hike is 1.5 hours + 2 hours + 1 hour = 4.5 hours.

Finally, calculate the average rate for the journey:

$$\frac{3 \times 4.5 \text{ miles}}{4.5 \text{ hours}} = 3 \text{ mph}$$

You might find it helpful to organize the information in a table and fill in each piece of information as you find it:

	Rate (mph)	Time (hr)	Distance (miles)
Part 1 of hike	3	1.5	$3 \times 1.5 = 4.5$
Part 2 of hike			4.5
Part 3 of hike			4.5
Entire hike	?		

Now calculate the data for each cell:

	Rate (mph)	Time (hr)	Distance (miles)
Part 1 of hike	3	1.5	$3 \times 1.5 = 4.5$
Part 2 of hike	$0.75 \times 3 = 2.25$	$4.5 \div 2.25 = 2$	4.5
Part 3 of hike	$2 \times 2.25 = 4.5$	$4.5 \div 4.5 = 1$	4.5
Entire hike	?		3×4.5

Finally, find the time and then the rate for the entire trip:

	Rate (mph)	Time (hr)	Distance (miles)
Part 1 of hike	3	1.5	$3 \times 1.5 = 4.5$
Part 2 of hike	$0.75 \times 3 = 2.25$	$4.5 \div 2.25 = 2$	4.5
Part 3 of hike	$2 \times 2.25 = 4.5$	$4.5 \div 4.5 = 1$	4.5
Entire hike	$(3 \times 4.5) \div 4.5 = 3$	$1.5 + 2 + 1 = 4.5$	3×4.5

The correct choice is (**B**).

STEP 4: CONFIRM YOUR ANSWER

Be sure that you've properly applied the percent adjustments to the appropriate speeds for each section of the hike and that you used the correct formula, Average rate = Total distance ÷ Total time, to find the final answer.

11. (D)

A truck driver drove for 2 days. On the second day, she drove 3 hours longer and at an average speed of 15 miles per hour faster than she drove on the first day. If she drove a total of 1,020 miles and spent 21 hours driving during the 2 days, what was her average speed on the first day, in miles per hour?

- ○ 25
- ○ 30
- ○ 35
- ○ 40
- ○ 45

STEP 1: ANALYZE THE QUESTION

This is another multi-stage journey question. So despite the intimidating presentation, you know that you will transfer the data from the question stem into this chart:

	Rate (mph)	Time (hr)	Distance (miles)
Day 1	?		
Day 2			
Entire trip			

STEP 2: STATE THE TASK

Solve for speed on the first day, which is the top-left box of the chart.

STEP 3: APPROACH STRATEGICALLY

Before you get too worried about what your solution will be, plug the data into the chart to help organize your thinking. The first thing you read is "On the second day, she drove 3 hours longer . . . than she drove on the first day." You know the total time will be 21 hours, so you can't just pick a number. Use t for time on the first day. That makes time on the second day $t + 3$.

Similarly, "On the second day, she drove . . . at an average speed of 15 miles per hour faster than she drove on the first day" allows you to say that if r is speed on the first day, then $r + 15$ is speed on the second day. The rest of the data is simply numerical:

	Rate (mph)	Time (hr)	Distance (miles)
Day 1	r (?)	t	
Day 2	$r + 15$	$t + 3$	
Entire trip		21	1,020

Since the total of the 2 days' times will be the time for the entire trip, you can say:

$$t + (t + 3) = 21$$

$$2t + 3 = 21$$

$$2t = 18$$

$$t = 9$$

Put that into the chart:

	Rate (mph)	Time (hr)	Distance (miles)
Day 1	r (?)	9	
Day 2	$r + 15$	12	
Entire trip		21	1,020

That allows you to find distance for each day by multiplying (Rate × Time = Distance).

	Rate (mph)	Time (hr)	Distance (miles)
Day 1	r (?)	9	$9r$
Day 2	$r + 15$	12	$12(r + 15)$
Entire trip		21	1,020

Now you have an equation that will allow you to solve for r, which is what you're looking for—speed on Day 1. Since the total of the 2 days' distances will be the distance for the entire trip, you can say:

$$9r + 12(r + 15) = 1,020$$

$$9r + 12r + 180 = 1,020$$

$$21r = 840$$

$$r = 40$$

The answer is **(D)**.

STEP 4: CONFIRM YOUR ANSWER

Reread the question stem, making sure that you didn't miss anything about the problem. For example, if you inverted some information about the 2 days, you could end up with **(A)**.

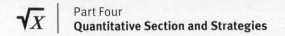

Practice Set: Combined Rates and Combined Work on the GMAT

12. (A)

Working at its usual constant rate, Pump A can empty a water storage tank in 3 hours. Pump B, also working at its usual constant rate, can empty half of the same tank in 4 hours. How many hours will it take both pumps working together at their usual respective constant rates to empty half of the tank?

- ○ $\frac{12}{11}$
- ○ $\frac{24}{11}$
- ○ $\frac{24}{7}$
- ○ $\frac{7}{2}$
- ○ $\frac{36}{7}$

STEP 1: ANALYZE THE QUESTION

Pump A takes 3 hours to empty a tank, and Pump B takes 4 hours to empty half of the same tank—that is, it would take Pump B 8 hours to empty the whole tank.

STEP 2: STATE THE TASK

Use an understanding of combined rates to find the number of hours it would take both pumps, working together at their respective rates, to empty half the tank.

STEP 3: APPROACH STRATEGICALLY

While you could calculate this problem using the combined work formula, some critical thinking can go far here. Since Pump A by itself can empty the tank in 3 hours, it stands to reason that Pump A and Pump B working together must be able to empty the tank in fewer than 3 hours. Notice that **(C)**, **(D)**, and **(E)** are all greater than 3, so eliminate all of them. Furthermore, you're trying to find how long it would take the two pumps to empty only half of the tank, so logically, that must be less than half of 3 hours, or 1.5 hours. Since **(B)** is greater than 1.5, you can eliminate it as well. Thus, the correct answer is the only remaining choice, **(A)**.

STEP 4: CONFIRM YOUR ANSWER

If you used the logical approach above, then to confirm your answer, use the combined work formula, $T = \frac{AB}{A+B}$ (If you used the formula in the first place, then check your answer against the logic of the situation.)
In this case, T is the time Pump A and Pump B take to empty the entire tank when working together, and A and B are the respective amounts of time that it takes each pump to empty the tank individually. Plug the given times into this formula and solve:

$$T = \frac{AB}{A+B}$$
$$T = \frac{3 \times 8}{3+8}$$
$$T = \frac{24}{11}$$

So it takes Pump A and Pump B working together $\frac{24}{11}$ hours to empty the whole tank. Since you need to find how long it would take to empty just half the tank, that's $\frac{24}{11} \div 2 = \frac{12}{11}$ hours.

13. (C)

Machine 1 and Machine 2 working together can produce 12,000 meters of steel cable per hour. Each machine works at a constant rate. Machine 1 by itself can produce 5,000 meters of cable per hour. How many hours would it Machine 2 working alone to produce 12,000 meters of cable?

- ○ $\frac{7}{12}$
- ○ $\frac{67}{40}$
- ○ $\frac{12}{7}$
- ○ $\frac{11}{5}$
- ○ $\frac{5}{2}$

STEP 1: ANALYZE THE QUESTION

This is a combined work problem with a twist. Rather than being given the time each machine can complete the job separately, you're given the time it takes the two machines together to complete the job and the portion of the job one of the two machines can do in the same amount of time.

STEP 2: STATE THE TASK

Find how long it will take the second machine, working alone, to complete the entire job.

STEP 3: APPROACH STRATEGICALLY

You can use the combined work formula, $T = \dfrac{AB}{A + B}$. In this formula, A and B are the times that each machine can do the job in time T. You're given that Machine 1 and Machine 2 together can produce 12,000 meters of cable in 1 hour, so in this scenario, $T = 1$.

You're also given that Machine 1 by itself can produce 5,000 meters of cable in 1 hour. From this, you can find how long it would take Machine 1 to complete the entire 12,000 meters: Machine 1 can complete $\dfrac{5{,}000}{12{,}000} = \dfrac{5}{12}$ of the job in 1 hour. Therefore, Machine 1 will take 1 hour $\div \dfrac{5}{12}$ hours/job $= \dfrac{12}{5}$ hours to complete the entire job.

Now plug this information into the combined work formula:

$\dfrac{\frac{12}{5}B}{\frac{12}{5} + B} = 1$. Multiply both sides by the denominator to simplify: $\frac{12}{5}B = \frac{12}{5} + B$. Multiply each term by 5 to clear the fractions: $12B = 12 + 5B$. Then $7B = 12$, and $B = \dfrac{12}{7}$. This is the time it would take Machine 2 to make 12,000 meters of cable, and **(C)** is correct.

STEP 4: CONFIRM YOUR ANSWER

You can confirm your answer with an alternative approach. Once you've determined that Machine 1 can do $\dfrac{5}{12}$ of the job (producing 12,000 meters of cable) in 1 hour, you can deduce that Machine 2 must be able to complete $\dfrac{12}{12} - \dfrac{5}{12} = \dfrac{7}{12}$ of the job in 1 hour. Set up a proportion of jobs to hours and solve for the hours for 1 job:

$$\frac{\text{jobs}}{\text{hours}} = \frac{\frac{7}{12}}{1} = \frac{1}{x}$$

Cross multiply: $\frac{7}{12}x = 1$, and $x = \dfrac{12}{7}$.

14. **(A)**

Two trucks travel from Alphaburg to Betaville along the same route. The speed limit for the first 30 miles is 60 miles per hour. The speed limit for the next 10 miles is 40 miles per hour, and the limit for the final 60 miles is 55 miles per hour. Truck F has a maximum speed of 70 miles per hour, but Truck S has a speed-limiting governor installed to cap its maximum speed at 50 miles per hour. Truck S departs Alphaburg 12 minutes before Truck F. If each truck travels at the lesser of the speed limit or the maximum speed of the truck, how far from Betaville is the point where Truck F catches up with Truck S?

- ○ 5 miles
- ○ 20 miles
- ○ 55 miles
- ○ 95 miles
- ○ Both trucks arrive at Betaville simultaneously.

STEP 1: ANALYZE THE QUESTION

Because two trucks are traveling the same route and the slower truck sets out on the journey before the faster truck, this is an overtaking problem. The relative speed of the two trucks is the *difference* between their speeds; this is the rate at which the faster truck catches up with the slower truck. There are limiting factors included in the question, including the speed limits on the roads and the maximum speeds of the trucks.

- For the first 30 miles, Truck F travels at 60 mph and Truck S at 50 mph, so F is gaining on S at the rate of 10 mph.

- Both trucks travel the next 10 miles at 40 mph.

- For the final 60 miles, Truck F travels at 55 mph and Truck S at 50 mph, so F is traveling 5 mph faster than S.

STEP 2: STATE THE TASK

Determine the distance from Betaville to the point where Truck F overtakes Truck S.

STEP 3: APPROACH STRATEGICALLY

Since there are different speeds involved in the three segments of the journey, analyze this piece by piece. The first leg is 30 miles. Using the formula Distance = Rate × Time rearranged as $\text{Time} = \dfrac{\text{Distance}}{\text{Rate}}$, Truck S traverses this leg in $\dfrac{30}{50} = 0.6$ hours. Truck F starts 12 minutes later, or $\dfrac{12}{60} = \dfrac{1}{5} = 0.2$ hours later. It completes this leg in $\dfrac{30}{60} = 0.5$ hours, which is 0.1 hours less than the time for S. However, since Truck F started 0.2 hours after Truck S, Truck F arrives at the end of the 30-mile leg $0.2 - 0.1 = 0.1$ hour after Truck S.

The trucks will complete the 10-mile segment in the same amount of time since they both are limited to 40 mph, so Truck F will begin the final 60-mile leg 0.1 hour after Truck S does.

For the last 60 miles, Truck F overtakes Truck S at a rate of 5 mph. Truck S starts this leg 0.1 hour before Truck F. Traveling at 50 mph, that is a $50 \times 0.1 = 5$-mile head start. So given that F is traveling 5 mph faster, it would catch up with S in exactly an hour. The point at which this occurs would be 1 hour $\times$ 55 mph = 55 miles from the start of the leg. Because the entire segment is 60 miles long, this point is $60 - 55 = 5$ miles from Betaville. **(A)** is correct.

STEP 4: CONFIRM YOUR ANSWER

The tricky part of this question is all the details presented regarding distances and speeds. Reread the question stem, making sure that you used the correct values, and check your calculations. **(B)** is the distance the trucks traveled on the last leg before F catches up to S. **(D)** is the correct distance from Alphaburg rather than from Betaville.

Practice Set: Interest Rates on the GMAT

15. (E)

A certain account pays 1.5 percent compound interest every 3 months. A person invested an initial amount and did not invest any more money in the account after that. If after exactly 5 years, the amount of money in the account was T dollars, which of the following is an expression for the original number of dollars invested in the account?

- ○ $(1.015)^4 T$
- ○ $(1.015)^{15} T$
- ○ $(1.015)^{20} T$
- ○ $\dfrac{T}{(1.015)^{15}}$
- ○ $\dfrac{T}{(1.015)^{20}}$

STEP 1: ANALYZE THE QUESTION

The question addresses compound interest. It's worth noting that the interest is not annual interest but is compounded every 3 months. Since there are 12 months per year, the interest compounds 4 times per year.

Although there are variables in the answer choices, picking numbers probably won't be needed, as the answers are just various ways that the interest formula might be constructed.

STEP 2: STATE THE TASK

Solve for the original amount in the account. Call it P for principal.

STEP 3: APPROACH STRATEGICALLY

Since the question seems all about whether you can properly construct the compound interest formula, make sure that you carefully set up each part. The general formula is this:

$$T = P(1 + r)^t$$

All of the answer choices use 1.015, so you know for certain—if you didn't already—that inside the parentheses must be 1.015:

$$T = P(1.015)^t$$

Since interest is compounded 4 times per year for 5 years, $t = 4 \times 5 = 20$.

$$T = P(1.015)^{20}$$

$$\frac{T}{(1.015)^{20}} = P$$

The answer is **(E)**.

STEP 4: CONFIRM YOUR ANSWER

Reread the question stem, making sure that you didn't accidentally skip over any important aspects of the situation. For example, if you initially missed the "every 3 months" part of the stimulus, you would have been looking for an answer with an exponent of 4. This step gives you the chance to catch such errors.

16. (A)

Binh invested $1,000 in a certificate of deposit (CD) that matured in 4 years. The certificate paid 4 percent annual interest compounded quarterly for the original 4-year term and then 2 percent simple annual interest on the compounded amount after that until the CD was redeemed by the holder. If Binh held his CD for exactly 6 years, how much money did he receive when he redeemed it?

- ○ $1,000 \times (1.01)^{16} \times 1.04$
- ○ $1,000 \times (1.01)^{16} \times (1.02)^2$
- ○ $1,000 \times (1.04)^6$
- ○ $1,000 \times (1.01)^{24}$
- ○ $1,000 \times (1.04)^{16} \times (1.02)^2$

STEP 1: ANALYZE THE QUESTION

A $1,000 certificate of deposit paid 4% annual interest compounded quarterly until it matured in 4 years, which means that 1% was added to the principal 4 times per year. Thereafter, the certificate paid 2% annual simple interest on the compounded amount. Binh purchased such a certificate and redeemed it after 6 years.

STEP 2: STATE THE TASK

Determine which expression among the answer choices represents the value of the CD after 6 years.

STEP 3: APPROACH STRATEGICALLY

The formula for compound interest is Principal $\times (1 + r)^t$, where r is the interest rate per time period expressed as a decimal and t is the number of time periods. Since this CD had a 4% annual rate with interest compounded quarterly, $r = \frac{1}{4} \times 0.04 = 0.01$. Because the compounding occurred 4 times per year for 4 years, $t = 4 \times 4 = 16$. Thus, the value of the CD at the end of 4 years was $1,000 \times (1.01)^{16}$. This amount then amassed simple interest. The formula for simple interest is Principal $\times (1 + rt)$. In this case, the interest rate was 2%, so $r = 0.2$, and it accrued for 2 years, so $t = 2$. So Principal $\times (1 + 0.02(2)) =$ Principal $\times 1.04$. Thus, the total value after 6 years was $(1.01)^{16} \times 1.04$. **(A)** is correct.

STEP 4: CONFIRM YOUR ANSWER

Whenever an interest problem involves compounding other than annually, be certain to adjust the interest rate per compounding period and the number of times that compounding occurs. Double-check these values in your solution.

17. (B)

The amount of an investment will double in approximately $\frac{70}{p}$ years, where p is the percent interest, compounded annually. If Thelma invests $40,000 in a long-term CD that pays 5 percent interest, compounded annually, what will be the approximate total value of the investment when Thelma is ready to retire 42 years later?

- ○ $280,000
- ○ $320,000
- ○ $360,000
- ○ $450,000
- ○ $540,000

STEP 1: ANALYZE THE QUESTION

You're given a piece of information other than just interest rate and principal. How might it influence your solution? You may not be sure yet, but it's unlikely to be extraneous information. Also, the word *approximate* should make you happy: you may be able to estimate rather than calculate.

STEP 2: STATE THE TASK

What is the approximate value in 42 years of a $40,000 investment that earns 5% compound annual interest?

STEP 3: APPROACH STRATEGICALLY

This problem is a great example of why strategic reading and logical analysis should precede any math. If you rush blindly into math, you'd get Total $= \$40,000 \times (1.05)^{42}$. There's no way to solve, even approximately, without a calculator.

But what if you approached the problem strategically? You're asked for "total value of the investment." Scan through the question stem looking for information related to total value, and you find "*the amount of an investment* will double in approximately $\frac{70}{p}$ years, where p is the percent interest."

Then search for the interest and discover that it is 5%. So you now know that the investment will double every $\frac{70}{5}$ years—or every 14 years.

Now look for how many years the money is invested and see that it's 42 years: 42 is 14×3, so 42 years means 3 doublings. The total value will be approximately $\$40,000 \times 2 \times 2 \times 2 = \$40,000 \times 8 = \$320,000$.

The answer is (**B**).

STEP 4: CONFIRM YOUR ANSWER

Reread the question stem, making sure that you didn't accidentally skip over any important aspects of the situation.

Practice Set: Overlapping Sets on the GMAT

18. (B)

Of the 65 books released last year by a particular publishing house, 25 were no more than 200 pages. The publisher released 35 fiction books, of which 20 were more than 200 pages, and it also published nonfiction books. How many nonfiction books of no more than 200 pages did the publishing house release last year?

- ○ 5
- ○ 10
- ○ 20
- ○ 30
- ○ 35

STEP 1: ANALYZE THE QUESTION

This question provides you with information about a group of 65 books; every book is classified as either fiction or nonfiction and as either greater than 200 pages or less than or equal to 200 pages (to avoid having these irrelevant numbers in your head, you might paraphrase this as "long books and short books"). Plan on organizing the details in a table to keep track of them.

STEP 2: STATE THE TASK

Find the total number of nonfiction books "of no more than 200 pages"—in other words, less than or equal to 200 pages, or short nonfiction books.

STEP 3: APPROACH STRATEGICALLY

Organize all of the given information into a table:

	Fiction	Nonfiction	Total
Short		?	25
Long	20		
Total	35		65

With everything organized, fill in the blanks. Once you have two entries in a row or column, you can fill in the third entry for that row or column. If the two known values are subtotals, add them to get the total; if one of the known values is a total, subtract the known subtotal from the total to get the other subtotal.

	Fiction	Nonfiction	Total
Short	15	10	25
Long	20	20	40
Total	35	30	65

Arrive at the correct answer either by subtracting 15 short fiction books from 25 total short books in the first row or by subtracting 20 long nonfiction books from 30 total nonfiction books in the second column. The number of short nonfiction books is 10. **(B)** is correct.

STEP 4: CONFIRM YOUR ANSWER

When using a table, check to make sure that you answer with the right piece of information; three of the incorrect choices are numbers that fill in other cells in the table. Also, double-check that you answered the right question; for example, if you read the question as "How many nonfiction books of more than 200 pages" instead of "*no* more than 200 pages," you may have chosen (**C**).

19. (C)

Three hundred students at College Q study a foreign language. Of these, 110 of those students study French and 170 study Spanish. If at least 90 students who study a foreign language at College Q study neither French nor Spanish, then the number of students who study Spanish but not French could be any number from

- ○ 10 to 40
- ○ 40 to 100
- ○ 60 to 100
- ○ 60 to 110
- ○ 70 to 110

STEP 1: ANALYZE THE QUESTION

Since students are split into two potentially overlapping sets—those who study Spanish and those who study French—this is an overlapping sets problem. To help organize the data, draw a table:

	French	Not French	Total
Spanish		?	
Not Spanish			
Total			

STEP 2: STATE THE TASK

You need to find a valid range, with both an upper and lower limit, for those who are in the "Spanish and not French" category.

STEP 3: APPROACH STRATEGICALLY

You have a piece of data with a lower limit ("at least 90") but nothing with an upper limit. It's hard to know intuitively what that upper limit should be, so put in the data from the question stem so you can understand the problem more clearly:

	French	Not French	Total
Spanish		?	170
Not Spanish		at least 90	
Total	110		300

From this, you can figure out how many do *not* study each language:

	French	Not French	Total
Spanish		?	170
Not Spanish		at least 90	130
Total	110	190	300

Now that you have a clearer understanding of the situation, you can understand more about the limitations on the "at least 90" group. Since the total of the "not Spanish" row is 130, there could be no more than 130 in the "not Spanish and not French" category. (More than 130 would require a negative number of students in the "French and not Spanish" category.)

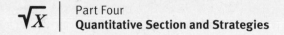

	French	Not French	Total
Spanish		?	170
Not Spanish		90 to 130	130
Total	110	190	300

The "Spanish and not French" category must add with "90 to 130" to yield 190. There could be as many as 100 (since $100 + 90 = 190$) or as few as 60 (since $60 + 130 = 190$).

The answer is **(C)**.

STEP 4: CONFIRM YOUR ANSWER

Reread the question stem, making sure that you didn't accidentally misread anything. For example, **(E)** is the value of the "Spanish and French" category.

20. (A)

The *Financial News Daily* has 25 reporters covering Asia, 20 covering Europe, and 20 covering North America. Four reporters cover Asia and Europe but not North America, 6 reporters cover Asia and North America but not Europe, and 7 reporters cover Europe and North America but not Asia. How many reporters cover all three continents (Asia, Europe, and North America)?

(1) The *Financial News Daily* has 38 reporters in total covering at least 1 of the following continents: Asia, Europe, and North America.

(2) There are more *Financial News Daily* reporters covering only Asia than there are *Financial News Daily* reporters covering only North America.

STEP 1: ANALYZE THE QUESTION STEM

This is a Value question. It is asking for the number of reporters who cover all three continents.

There's a lot of information, and it begs to be simplified. As the reporters may cover one, two, or three of the continents, this is an overlapping sets question. But with *three* sets, a chart-based approach would be too unwieldy. The best way to visualize three overlapping sets is with a Venn diagram. Take care to put the totals for each continent just outside the circles so that you don't lose the distinction between the number covering a continent and the number covering *only* that continent.

So that you know what you need, put an *x* in the "all three continents" space on the diagram.

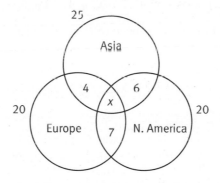

You can continue to analyze your information. A total of 25 reporters cover Asia, 6 of whom also cover only North America, 4 of whom also cover only Europe, and *x* of whom also cover both Europe and North America.

Therefore, $25 - (6 + 4 + x)$, or $15 - x$, cover only Asia.

Similarly, $20 - (4 + 7 + x)$, or $9 - x$, cover only Europe, and $20 - (7 + 6 + x)$, or $7 - x$, cover only North America.

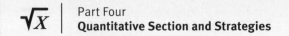

Put that into your diagram:

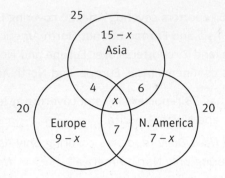

Many kinds of information, therefore, would allow you to figure out the number of reporters who cover all three continents. Any data that lets you make an equation with x would be sufficient.

STEP 2: EVALUATE THE STATEMENTS USING 12TEN

Statement (1) says that the grand total of all the reporters is 38. In other words, if you added up all the various subcategories, you'd get 38. That's sufficient, as the only variable in that equation would be x. Eliminate **(B)**, **(C)**, and **(E)**.

Although you wouldn't want to set the whole thing up (you'd stop as soon as you knew that you *could* set up the equation), here's what it would be:

$$(15 - x) + (9 - x) + (7 - x) + 4 + 7 + 6 + x = 38$$

Once the information from the question stem has been fully simplified and analyzed, you see that Statement (2) is only saying that $(15 - x) > (7 - x)$. That's just $15 > 7$, which is hardly new information. Statement (2) adds nothing and must be insufficient. **(A)** is correct

GMAT by the Numbers: Math Formulas

Now that you've learned how to approach math formulas questions on the GMAT, let's add one more dimension to your understanding of how they work.

Take a moment to try this question. Following is performance data from thousands of people who have studied with Kaplan over the decades. Through analyzing this data, we will show you how to approach questions like this one most effectively and how to avoid similarly tempting wrong answer choice types on Test Day.

In an election, candidate Smith won 52 percent of the total vote in Counties A and B. He won 61 percent of the vote in County A. If the ratio of people who voted in County A to County B is 3:1, what percent of the vote did candidate Smith win in County B?

- ○ 25%
- ○ 27%
- ○ 34%
- ○ 43%
- ○ 49%

Explanation

> **Question Statistics**
>
> **57%** of test takers choose (**A**)
>
> **16%** of test takers choose (**B**)
>
> **10%** of test takers choose (**C**)
>
> **12%** of test takers choose (**D**)
>
> **5%** of test takers choose (**E**)
>
> Sample size = 5,221

The statistics above show that this is a hard question, as many test takers get it wrong. But no single wrong answer stands out as a common trap. This is the sign of a problem that is challenging because most test takers simply don't know how to approach it. However, this question doesn't have to be difficult.

The question demonstrates the pattern in which two entities, each with a different proportion or average, are combined to form a total with a new overall proportion or average. You can make quick work of this problem using the balance approach. Smith ends up at 52%, and County A is 9 points above this at 61%. Moreover, there are 3 people in County A for every 1 person in County B, so multiply A's 9-point surplus by 3 to get a 27-point surplus. To bring the vote percentage into balance at 52%, County B has to be 27 points below 52%, or 25%. (**A**) is correct.

Or you can use a formula that handles this problem:

(Proportion A)(Weight of A) + (Proportion B)(Weight of B) = (Total proportion)(Total weight)

You can represent the proportion of the vote Smith won in County B with the variable b. Then just plug the data into the formula and solve:

$$(0.61)(3) + (b)(1) = (0.52)(3 + 1)$$
$$1.83 + b = (0.52)(4)$$
$$1.83 + b = 2.08$$
$$b = 2.08 - 1.83$$
$$b = 0.25$$

By learning these classic formulas and problem-solving techniques, you'll find yourself comfortably handling problems that stump many other test takers.

More GMAT by the Numbers...

To see more questions with answer choice statistics, be sure to review the full-length CATs in your online resources.

GO ONLINE

kaptest.com/login

CHAPTER 23

Statistics on the GMAT

LEARNING OBJECTIVES

After studying this chapter, you will be able to:

- Describe the types of statistics routinely tested on the GMAT
- Identify questions that involve statistics concepts
- Apply the Kaplan Methods for Problem Solving and Data Sufficiency to a variety of different question types that deal with statistics

---

Below is a typical Data Sufficiency question dealing with probability, one of the categories of statistics that we will discuss in this chapter. In this chapter, we'll look at how to apply the Kaplan Method to this question, discuss the probability rules being tested, and go over the basic principles and strategies that you want to keep in mind on every Quantitative question involving statistics.

Tracy has 3 bags of marbles, each bag containing at least 1 blue marble, at least 1 red marble, and no marbles of another color. If Tracy selects 1 marble at random from each bag, what is the probability that all 3 marbles that she selects will be red?

(1)   There is a total of 5 red marbles and 5 blue marbles in the 3 bags.

(2)   The ratios of red to blue marbles in the 3 bags are 2:1, 1:1, and 1:2.

Before you move on, take a minute to think about what you see in this question and answer some questions about how you think it works:

- What does probability measure?
- How can ratios help you calculate probability on this question?
- What Kaplan strategy can you use to solve this question?
- What GMAT Core Competencies are most essential to success on this question?

Previewing Statistics on the GMAT

Now we'll explore answers to the questions you just considered.

What Does Probability Measure?

Probability measures the likelihood of a certain event occurring. Probability can be expressed as a fraction or decimal between 0 and 1 or as a percentage between 0 percent and 100 percent. The lower the probability, the less likely that event is to occur. On the GMAT, the test makers often incorporate this concept into high-difficulty questions that ask about the probability of multiple events happening or not happening. In addition to learning the rules, operations, and formulas specific to probability, remember that the same rules you already know for proportions and fractions continue to apply.

How Can Ratios Help You Calculate Probability on This Question?

In a situation like the one described in this question stem, the probability of a given outcome of random selection is equal to the ratio of the items from which the selection is being made. In other words, if a bag contains only 2 red marbles and 2 blue marbles, the probability of selecting a red marble from this bag is the same as the ratio of red marbles to total marbles in the bag, which is 2:4, or $\frac{1}{2}$.

What Kaplan Strategy Can You Use to Solve This Question?

Since different scenarios are possible for how many marbles of each color are in each bag, picking numbers will help you test out the possible distributions of marbles among the bags and determine whether the information is sufficient to solve for a single answer to the question stem.

Remember that whenever you pick numbers for a Data Sufficiency question, the numbers you pick must be permissible—they must obey any rules or restrictions given in the stem and the statement you're testing. For example, if a statement tells you that there cannot be more than 6 marbles in each bag, you cannot pick the numbers red = 4 and blue = 5 for that bag.

What GMAT Core Competencies Are Most Essential to Success on This Question?

Critical Thinking will help you determine what information is necessary to calculate the desired probability: are ratios sufficient, or do you need actual numbers of the marbles? Do you need information on each bag individually, or is information about all three bags combined enough? Even though Data Sufficiency questions don't ask you to calculate an exact value for the answer to the question stem, you do need to know how you *would* calculate that answer if you needed to.

Pattern Recognition is crucial here, as it is on all statistics questions, since the GMAT often asks questions that hinge on the same concepts and formulas that you can memorize. Here, you need to remember the probability formula, as well as how to calculate the joint probability of independent events (Tracy's selection from each of the 3 bags).

Finally, Attention to the Right Detail is necessary whenever you work with probabilities, which are essentially fractions or ratios. You need to be clear whether you are dealing with part-to-part or part-to-whole ratios and keep track of which items are in the numerator and denominator.

How Do I Apply the Kaplan Methods to GMAT Statistics?

Now let's apply the Kaplan Method for Data Sufficiency to the statistics question we saw earlier:

> Tracy has 3 bags of marbles, each bag containing at least 1 blue marble, at least 1 red marble, and no marbles of another color. If Tracy selects 1 marble at random from each bag, what is the probability that all 3 marbles that she selects will be red?
>
> (3) There is a total of 5 red marbles and 5 blue marbles in the 3 bags.
> (4) The ratios of red to blue marbles in the 3 bags are 2:1, 1:1, and 1:2.

STEP 1: ANALYZE THE QUESTION STEM

This is a Value question. You are asked for the probability that when 1 marble is chosen at random from each of the 3 bags, each marble chosen is red. You know that each bag contains at least 1 blue marble, at least 1 red marble, and no other marbles of any other color. Now let's look at the statements.

STEP 2: EVALUATE THE STATEMENTS USING 12TEN

Statement (1) tells you that a total of 5 red marbles and 5 blue marbles are distributed among the 3 bags. Because there are different ways to distribute the marbles among the bags, there are different possible probabilities and, therefore, different possible answers to the question.

You can use picking numbers to test out these different scenarios; if the different permissible scenarios result in different answers to the question stem, then the statement is insufficient.

For example, let's call the bags Bag 1, Bag 2, and Bag 3. If Bag 1 contains 3 blue marbles and 3 red marbles, while Bags 2 and 3 each contain 1 blue marble and 1 red marble, then the probability that all 3 marbles chosen are red can be calculated by multiplying together the individual probabilities of selecting a red marble from each of the 3 bags:

$$\frac{\text{Bag 1 red}}{\text{Bag 1 total}} \times \frac{\text{Bag 2 red}}{\text{Bag 2 total}} \times \frac{\text{Bag 3 red}}{\text{Bag 3 total}} = \frac{1}{2} \times \frac{1}{2} \times \frac{1}{2} = \frac{1}{8}$$

If, however, Bag 1 contains 3 blue marbles and 1 red marble, Bag 2 contains 1 blue marble and 3 red marbles, and Bag 3 contains 1 blue marble and 1 red marble, then the probability that all 3 marbles chosen are red is $\frac{1}{4} \times \frac{3}{4} \times \frac{1}{2} = \frac{3}{32}$.

Because different answers to the question are possible when you pick different permissible numbers, Statement (1) is insufficient. Eliminate choices (**A**) and (**D**).

Now look at Statement (2). You are told the ratio of red to blue marbles in each bag. So you can say that the probability of picking a red marble from one bag is $\frac{2}{3}$, the probability of picking a red marble from another bag is $\frac{1}{2}$, and the probability of picking a marble from the remaining bag is $\frac{1}{3}$. The probability of picking a red marble from each of the 3 bags is $\frac{2}{3} \times \frac{1}{2} \times \frac{1}{3}$. You do not have to calculate the value of this expression. Just knowing that you *could* calculate this probability is enough. Statement (2) is sufficient, and (**B**) is correct.

Now let's look at each of the areas of statistics that show up on the GMAT Quantitative section, starting with median, mode, range, and standard deviation.

Median, Mode, Range, and Standard Deviation

Median

If an odd group of numbers is arranged in numerical order, the median is the middle value.

Example: What is the median of 4, 5, 100, 1, and 6?

First, arrange the numbers in numerical order: 1, 4, 5, 6, and 100. The middle number (the median) is 5.

If a set has an even number of terms, then the median is the average (arithmetic mean) of the two middle terms after the terms are arranged in numerical order.

Example: What is the median value of 2, 9, 8, 17, 11, and 37?

Arrange the values in numerical order: 2, 8, 9, 11, 17, 37. The two middle numbers are 9 and 11. The median is the average of 9 and 11, that is, 10.

The median can be quite different from the average. For instance, in the first set of numbers above, {1, 4, 5, 6, 100}, the median is 5, but the average is $\frac{1 + 4 + 5 + 6 + 100}{5} = \frac{116}{5} = 23.2$.

Mode

The mode is the number that appears most frequently in a set. For example, in the set {1, 2, 2, 2, 3, 4, 4, 5, 6}, the mode is 2.

It is possible for a set to have more than one mode. For example, in the set {35, 42, 35, 57, 57, 19}, the two modes are 35 and 57.

Range

The range is the positive difference between the largest term in the set and the smallest term. For example, in the set {2, 4, 10, 20, 26}, the range is 24.

Standard Deviation

Standard deviation measures the dispersion of a set of numbers around the mean. If you've worked with the standard deviation formula in high school or college, you might remember that the formula looks like this:

$$\sqrt{\frac{1}{N}\left[(x_1 - \mu)^2 + (x_2 - \mu)^2 + \ldots + (x_N - \mu)^2\right]}$$

It can be intimidating, so let's paraphrase it in plain English. Calculating the standard deviation involves the following steps:

1. Find the average (arithmetic mean) of the set.

2. Subtract the average of the set from each term in that set.

3. Square each result.

4. Take the average of those squares.

5. Calculate the positive square root of that average.

Fortunately, the GMAT will only very rarely require you to apply this formula, and only on the most difficult questions. When standard deviation is tested, all you will generally need to understand is the basic concept: standard deviation represents how close or far the terms in a list are from the average.

Thus, {1, 2, 3} and {101, 102, 103} have the same standard deviation, since they both have one term on the average and two terms exactly one unit away from the average. A quickly sketched number line can confirm this:

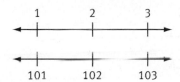

The set {1, 3, 5} will have a smaller standard deviation than {0, 3, 6}. Both sets have an average of 3, but the first has terms 2, 0, and 2 units from the average while the second has terms 3, 0, and 3 units from the average. Again, you can confirm this with a quick sketch:

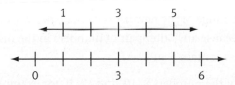

You could also calculate the standard deviation for the sets {1, 3, 5} and {0, 3, 6} to confirm:

{1, 3, 5}

mean = 3

$\sqrt{\frac{1}{3}\left[(1-3)^2 + (3-3)^2 + (5-3)^2\right]}$

$\sqrt{\frac{1}{3}\left[(-2)^2 + 0^2 + 2^2\right]}$

$\sqrt{\frac{1}{3}(4+0+4)}$

$\sqrt{\frac{1}{3}(8)}$

$\sqrt{\frac{8}{3}}$

{0, 3, 6}

mean = 3

$\sqrt{\frac{1}{3}\left[(0-3)^2 + (3-3)^2 + (6-3)^2\right]}$

$\sqrt{\frac{1}{3}\left[(-3)^2 + 0^2 + 3^2\right]}$

$\sqrt{\frac{1}{3}(9+0+9)}$

$\sqrt{\frac{1}{3}(18)}$

$\sqrt{6}$

Since 6 is larger than $\frac{8}{3}$, you can see that the standard deviation of the second, more widely spaced set of numbers is larger than that of the first set. However, you will save much time on Test Day by using your understanding of how standard deviation works to estimate rather than calculating the answers to questions such as these.

In other words, the GMAT test makers are more interested in whether you understand the concept of standard deviation and can apply Critical Thinking to situations that involve it than in whether you can perform complex mathematical calculations.

In-Format Question: Median, Mode, Range, and Standard Deviation on the GMAT

Now let's use the Kaplan Method on a Data Sufficiency question dealing with median, mode, range, and standard deviation:

> List *L* consists of 12, 8, 10, 14, and 6. If two numbers are removed from list *L*, what is the standard deviation of the new list?
>
> (1) The range of the new list is 8.
> (2) The median of the new list is 8.

STEP 1: ANALYZE THE QUESTION STEM

This is a Value question. You know that two numbers are removed from the list 12, 8, 10, 14, 6. You want to determine the standard deviation of the new list. There is no other information given, so let's look at the statements.

STEP 2: EVALUATE THE STATEMENTS USING 12TEN

Statement (1): You are told that the range of the new list is 8. The only way to have a range of 8 is for both 6 and 14 to appear in the new list, because any other pair of numbers in the original list will be closer to one another than 8. So the new list must contain 6 and 14.

The new list will also contain one of the numbers 8, 10, and 12. If, for example, the third number in the list is 10, then the list will be 6, 10, and 14. If the third number in the list is 12, then the numbers in the list will be 6, 12, and 14. The standard deviation of the list 6, 10, and 14 will be different from the standard deviation of the list 6, 12, and 14 because the two sets have different means and the numbers in the two lists are dispersed differently around the mean.

More than one standard deviation is possible, and therefore more than one answer to the question is possible. Statement (1) is insufficient. Eliminate choices **(A)** and **(D)**.

Statement (2) says that the median of the new set is 8. Because there will be an odd number (3) of members of the new list, 8 will have to appear in the list in order for 8 to be the median. Additionally, since 8 must be in the middle of the new list and there is only one possible value less than 8, you know that 6 must also be in the list. The new list could be 6, 8, 10, which has a median of 8, and the new list could also be 6, 8, 14, which also has a median of 8.

The standard deviation of the numbers in the list 6, 8, 10 is less than the standard deviation of the list 6, 8, 14. More than one standard deviation is possible, and therefore more than one answer to the question is possible. So Statement (2) is insufficient. You can eliminate choice **(B)**.

Now that you've determined that Statement (1) and Statement (2) are both insufficient on their own, look at the statements together: you know from Statement (1) that 6 and 14 must be in the list, and you know from Statement (2) that 6 and 8 must be in the list. The statements taken together tell you that the list must consist of 6, 8, and 14. Because there is only one possible list, there can only be one standard deviation. The statements taken together are sufficient. **(C)** is correct.

TAKEAWAYS: MEDIAN, MODE, RANGE, AND STANDARD DEVIATION

- In a list with an odd number of terms arranged in ascending or descending order, the median is the middle term.

- In a list with an even number of terms arranged in ascending or descending order, the median is the average of the two middle terms.

- The mode of a list of terms is the term(s) that appear(s) most frequently.

- The range is the positive difference between the largest term in the list and the smallest term.

- Standard deviation measures the dispersion of a set of numbers around the mean. The GMAT will hardly ever require you to apply the formula for standard deviation. Instead, use Critical Thinking and quick sketches of number lines to determine how close the terms in a list are from the average.

Practice Set: Median, Mode, Range, and Standard Deviation on the GMAT

1. Data set S contains the elements $\{-5, x, 2, 0, -1, 1, 9\}$. What is the value of x?

    (1) The average (arithmetic mean) of data set S is 2.

    (2) The median of data set S is 1.

2. If the range of the eight numbers 17, 8, 14, 28, 9, 4, 11, and n is 25, what is the difference between the greatest possible value of n and the least possible value of n?

    ○ 1

    ○ 3

    ○ 21

    ○ 26

    ○ 29

3. In the list of numbers $\{a, b, c\}$, a is the average (arithmetic mean) of the list and $b + c = 0$. What is the standard deviation of a, b, and c?

    (1) $b - a = 2$

    (2) $c - a = 2$

4. Given the set of even numbers $\{2, 18, 32, x, y\}$, what is the median of the set?

    (1) $y(y - 1) = 30$

    (2) $(x - y)^3 \leq 0$

Sequences of Integers

LEARNING OBJECTIVES

In this section, you will learn how to:

- Recall that in a list of consecutive values, the average (arithmetic mean) equals the median
- Find the number of terms in a list of consecutive integers
- Calculate the sum of a sequence of consecutive integers
- Apply the Kaplan Methods for Problem Solving and Data Sufficiency to questions dealing with sequences of integers

Average and Median of Consecutive Integers

The average, or mean, of a set of consecutive integers will equal its median.

Example: What is the average of 1, 2, 3, 4, and 5?

$$\frac{1 + 2 + 3 + 4 + 5}{5} = \frac{15}{5} = 3$$

For this set, 3 is both the mean and the median. This is always the case for sets of consecutive or evenly spaced integers.

There is another way to calculate the average of this set. The average of a series of consecutive or evenly spaced integers is also the same as the average of its first and last terms. For the last example, that works out to $\frac{1 + 5}{2} = \frac{6}{2} = 3$.

Sum of Numbers

If you know the average of a group of numbers and how many numbers are in the group, you can find the sum of the numbers. You can think of it as if all the numbers in the group are equal to the average value.

$$\text{Sum of values} = \text{Average value} \times \text{Number of values}$$

Example: What is the sum of all the integers between 1 and 66 inclusive?

Since this is a series of consecutive integers, you can find its average by averaging the first and last terms: $\frac{1 + 66}{2} = \frac{67}{2}$.

To find the number of terms in a set of consecutive integers, take the difference between the largest and the smallest numbers and add 1.

$$\text{Sum of values} = \text{Average value} \times \text{Number of values}$$

$$\frac{67}{2} \times 66 = \frac{67}{\cancel{2}} \times \cancel{66}^{33} = 2{,}211$$

Granted, you still have to calculate 67×33, but that is much easier than adding all 66 numbers!

You may also have to find a sum in what might seem to be a normal average problem.

Example: The average daily temperature for the first week in January was 31 degrees Fahrenheit. If the average temperature for the first six days was 30 degrees, what was the temperature on the seventh day?

The sum for all 7 days = $31 \times 7 = 217$ degrees.

The sum for the first 6 days = $30 \times 6 = 180$ degrees.

The temperature on the seventh day = $217 - 180 = 37$ degrees.

In-Format Question: Sequences of Integers on the GMAT

Now let's use the Kaplan Method on a Problem Solving question dealing with sequences of integers:

In a new housing development, trees are to be planted in a straight line along a 166-foot stretch of sidewalk. Each tree will be planted in a square plot with sides measuring 1 foot. If there must be 14 feet between each plot, what is the maximum number of trees that can be planted?

- ○ 8
- ○ 9
- ○ 10
- ○ 11
- ○ 12

STEP 1: ANALYZE THE QUESTION

Though this is not a geometry question, a quick sketch of the situation will help illustrate how to solve it.

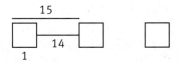

So you know that the unit of one tree and one space is 1 foot + 14 feet = 15 feet.

STEP 2: STATE THE TASK

To find how many trees can be planted, determine the feet required for a tree and the space between trees. Then divide the total length of the sidewalk by the unit of 1 tree and the space between trees.

STEP 3: APPROACH STRATEGICALLY

Each tree takes up 1 foot, and each space takes up 14 feet. Together, they take up 15 feet. Now find how many times 15 goes into the total number of feet on one side of the sidewalk:

$$166 \div 15 = 11, \text{ with a remainder of 1 foot}$$

You can plant 1 last tree in the remaining foot, bringing the total number of trees to 12. This means along the sidewalk, you can plant 12 trees with 11 spaces between them, as long as you start and end with a tree. **(E)** is correct.

STEP 4: CONFIRM YOUR ANSWER

Make sure your answer makes sense in the context of the question. Did you take into account the remainder of the division? Will an entire tree fit in the remaining space? You can use these questions to confirm your work.

TAKEAWAYS: SEQUENCES OF INTEGERS

- In a sequence of consecutive or evenly spaced integers, the average, or mean, equals the median.

- To find the number of terms in a sequence of consecutive integers, take the difference between the largest and the smallest and add 1.

- To find the sum of a sequence of consecutive or evenly spaced integers, multiply the average of the largest and the smallest term by the number of terms.

- To find the sum of any set of numbers, multiply the average by the number of terms.

Practice Set: Sequences of Integers on the GMAT

5. The sum of a sequence of consecutive integers is 1,125 and the median is 45. What is the value of the greatest integer in the sequence?

    ○   33
    ○   45
    ○   56
    ○   57
    ○   58

6. What is the sum of the multiples of 4 between 13 and 125 inclusive?

    ○   1,890
    ○   1,960
    ○   2,200
    ○   3,780
    ○   4,400

7. If z is the sum of three consecutive odd positive integers, is z evenly divisible by 9?

    (1)   When the smallest of the three numbers is divided by 3, the remainder is 1.
    (2)   The smallest of the three numbers is divisible by 7.

8. The sum of a sequence of six consecutive positive integers is Z. The sum of terms in a different sequence of five consecutive integers is Z − 5. If the greatest term of the five-number sequence is 40, what is the difference between the median term of the five-number sequence and the least term of the six-number sequence?

    ○   5
    ○   7
    ○   8
    ○   9
    ○   10

Combinations and Permutations

Some GMAT questions ask you to count the number of possible ways to select a small subgroup from a larger group. If the selection is **unordered**, then it's a combinations question. But if the selection is **ordered**, it's a permutations question.

For example, if a question asks you to count the possible number of different slates of officers who could be elected to positions in class government, then order matters—President Bob and Vice President Thelma is a different slate than President Thelma and Vice President Bob. You would use the permutations formula in this scenario. But if you had to count the number of pairs of flavors of jelly beans, you are solving a combinations question; cherry and lemon is the same pair as lemon and cherry, so order does not matter (i.e., you wouldn't count those as two different pairs).

The very first thing you need to do is use Critical Thinking to figure out whether a given question calls for an ordered or an unordered selection—otherwise, you won't know which formula to use.

Combinations

The combinations formula is used when solving for the number of k unordered selections one can make from a group of n items, where $k \leq n$. This is usually referred to as $_nC_k$, which is often said as "n choose k." Not that the GMAT is an oral exam, of course, but it's helpful to say it that way to yourself because that's what making combinations is—an act of choosing small groups from a larger group.

Here's the formula, in which $n!$, or n-factorial, is the product of n and every positive integer smaller than n (for example, $5! = 5 \times 4 \times 3 \times 2 \times 1$), where n is a positive integer:

$$_nC_k = \frac{n!}{k!(n-k)!}$$

Example: A company is selecting 4 members of its board of directors to sit on an ethics subcommittee. If the board has 9 members, any of whom may serve on the subcommittee, how many different selections of members could the company make?

Since the order in which you select the members doesn't change the composition of the committee in any way, this is a combinations question. The size of the group from which you choose is n, and the size of the selected group is k. So $n = 9$ and $k = 4$.

$$_9C_4 = \frac{9!}{4!(9-4)!}$$

$$\frac{9!}{4!5!}$$

$$\frac{9 \times 8 \times 7 \times 6 \times 5 \times 4 \times 3 \times 2 \times 1}{4 \times 3 \times 2 \times 1 \times 5 \times 4 \times 3 \times 2 \times 1}$$

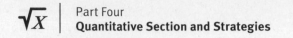

Save yourself some work. There's rarely a need to multiply out factorials, since many of the factors can quickly be canceled.

$$\frac{9 \times \cancel{8}^2 \times 7 \times \cancel{6} \times \cancel{5 \times 4 \times 3 \times 2} \times 1}{\cancel{4} \times 3 \times 2 \times 1 \times \cancel{5 \times 4 \times 3 \times 2} \times 1}$$

$$9 \times 2 \times 7 = 126$$

Sometimes the problems will be more complicated and will require multiple iterations of the formula.

Example: County X holds an annual math competition, to which each county high school sends a team of 4 students. If School A has 6 boys and 7 girls whose math grades qualify them to be on their school's team, and competition rules stipulate that the team must consist of 2 boys and 2 girls, how many different teams might School A send to the competition?

> The order of selection doesn't matter here, so you can use the combinations formula. But be careful: if you lump all the students together in a group of 13 and calculate $_{13}C_4$, you'd wind up including some all-boy teams and all-girl teams. The question explicitly says you can only select 2 boys and 2 girls. So you aren't really choosing 4 students from 13 but rather choosing 2 boys from 6 and 2 girls from 7.

$$_6C_2 \text{ and } _7C_2$$

$$\frac{6!}{2!4!} \times \frac{7!}{2!5!}$$

$$\frac{6 \times 5 \times 4 \times 3 \times 2 \times 1}{2 \times 1 \times 4 \times 3 \times 2 \times 1} \times \frac{7 \times 6 \times 5 \times 4 \times 3 \times 2 \times 1}{2 \times 1 \times 5 \times 4 \times 3 \times 2 \times 1}$$

$$\frac{\cancel{6}^3 \times 5 \times \cancel{4 \times 3 \times 2 \times 1}}{2 \times 1 \times \cancel{4 \times 3 \times 2 \times 1}} \times \frac{7 \times \cancel{6}^3 \times \cancel{5 \times 4 \times 3 \times 2 \times 1}}{\cancel{2} \times 1 \times \cancel{5 \times 4 \times 3 \times 2 \times 1}}$$

> $3 \times 5 \times 7 \times 3 = 315$ possible teams consisting of 2 boys and 2 girls.

Permutations

If the order of selection matters, you can use the permutation formulas:

> Number of permutations (arrangements) of n items $= n!$

> Number of permutations of k items selected from $n = {_nP_k} = \dfrac{n!}{(n-k)!}$

Example: How many ways are there to arrange the letters in the word ASCENT?

> Clearly, order matters here, since ASCENT is different from TNECSA. There are 6 letters in the word, so you must calculate the permutations of 6 items:

> $6! = 6 \times 5 \times 4 \times 3 \times 2 \times 1 = 720$

Another way to solve is to draw a quick sketch of the problem with blanks for the arranged items. Then write in the number of possibilities for each blank in order. Finally, multiply the numbers together. Many high-difficulty GMAT permutation questions resist formulaic treatment but are easier to complete with the "draw blanks" approach.

Here's how you would use this technique to solve the ASCENT problem:

ASCENT has 6 letters, so you need 6 blanks:

$$\underline{} \times \underline{} \times \underline{} \times \underline{} \times \underline{} \times \underline{}$$

There are 6 letters you might place in the first blank (A, S, C, E, N, or T):

$$\underline{6} \times \underline{} \times \underline{} \times \underline{} \times \underline{} \times \underline{}$$

No matter which letter you placed there, there will be 5 possibilities for the next blank:

$$\underline{6} \times \underline{5} \times \underline{} \times \underline{} \times \underline{} \times \underline{}$$

There will be 4 for the next, 3 thereafter, 2 after that, and just 1 letter left for the last:

$$\underline{6} \times \underline{5} \times \underline{4} \times \underline{3} \times \underline{2} \times \underline{1} = 720$$

Notice that you wind up reproducing the arrangements formula, $n!$. It's quite possible to solve most permutation problems without figuring out the right formula ahead of time, although knowing the formulas can save you time on Test Day.

Example: There are 6 children at a family reunion, 3 boys and 3 girls. They will be lined up single-file for a photo, alternating genders. How many arrangements of the children are possible for this photo?

You may not be sure how to approach this with a formula, so draw a picture. You know you'll have 6 "blanks," but you don't know whether to begin with a boy or with a girl. It could be either one. So try both:

bgbgbg or *gbgbgb*

$$\underline{} \times \underline{} \times \underline{} \times \underline{} \times \underline{} \times \underline{} + \underline{} \times \underline{} \times \underline{} \times \underline{} \times \underline{} \times \underline{}$$

Any of the 3 boys could go in the first spot, and any of the 3 girls in the second:

$$\underline{3} \times \underline{3} \times \underline{} \times \underline{} \times \underline{} \times \underline{} + \underline{} \times \underline{} \times \underline{} \times \underline{} \times \underline{} \times \underline{}$$

The next spot can be filled with either of the remaining 2 boys; the one after by either of the 2 remaining girls. Then the last boy and the last girl take their places:

$$\underline{3} \times \underline{3} \times \underline{2} \times \underline{2} \times \underline{1} \times \underline{1} + \underline{} \times \underline{} \times \underline{} \times \underline{} \times \underline{} \times \underline{}$$

That's the boy-first possibility. The same numbers of boys and girls apply to the girl-first possibility, and so you get:

$$\underline{3} \times \underline{3} \times \underline{2} \times \underline{2} \times \underline{1} \times \underline{1} + \underline{3} \times \underline{3} \times \underline{2} \times \underline{2} \times \underline{1} \times \underline{1}$$

$$9 \times 4 \times 1 + 9 \times 4 \times 1$$

$36 + 36 = 72$ possible arrangements of 3 boys and 3 girls, alternating genders.

Hybrids of Combinations and Permutations

Some questions involve elements of both ordered and unordered selection.

Example: How many ways are there to arrange the letters in the word ASSETS?

Earlier you saw that the rearrangement of ASCENT was a permutation. But what about ASSETS? The order of the E, the A, the T, and the S's matter . . . but the order of the 3 S's themselves does not.

Think about it this way: put a "tag" on the S's . . . $AS_1S_2ETS_3$. If you just calculated 6! again, you'd be counting $AS_1S_2ETS_3$ and $AS_3S_1ETS_2$ as different words, even though with the tags gone, you can clearly see that they aren't (ASSETS is the same as ASSETS). So you'll need to eliminate all the redundant arrangements from the 6! total.

Since there are 3 S's in the word ASSETS, there are 3! ways to rearrange those S's without changing the word. You need to count every group of 3! within the 6! total as only 1 arrangement.

So instead of 6! arrangements, as there were for ASCENT, the word ASSETS has $\frac{6!}{3!}$.

$$\frac{6!}{3!} = \frac{6 \times 5 \times 4 \times 3 \times 2 \times 1}{3 \times 2 \times 1} = 6 \times 5 \times 4 = 120$$

The same logic would apply to the arrangements of ASSESS: $\frac{6!}{4!}$.

And if two letters repeat, you need two corrections to eliminate the redundant arrangements. For instance, the number of arrangements of the letters in the word REASSESS is $\frac{8!}{4!2!}$.

Some tricky GMAT problems boil down to this "rearranging letters" problem.

Example: A restaurant is hanging 7 large tiles on its wall in a single row. How many arrangements of tiles are possible if there are 3 white tiles and 4 blue tiles?

This problem essentially asks for the arrangements of *WWWBBBB*. Remember that although there are 7 total tiles to arrange, all the white tiles are indistinguishable from one another, as are the blue tiles. Therefore, you will need to divide out the number of redundant arrangements from the 7! total arrangements:

$$\frac{7!}{3!4!} = \frac{7 \times 6 \times 5 \times 4 \times 3 \times 2 \times 1}{3 \times 2 \times 1 \times 4 \times 3 \times 2 \times 1}$$

Did you notice that $\frac{7!}{3!4!}$ is the same as $_7C_3$? Which is also the same as $_7C_4$, $\frac{7!}{4!3!}$?

Whether you think "rearrange *WWWBBBB*," "choose 4 of the 7 tiles to be blue (the rest will be white)," or "choose 3 of the 7 tiles to be white (the rest will be blue)," the result is the same. As you'll soon see, many probability questions involve just this kind of calculation.

In-Format Question: Combinations and Permutations on the GMAT

Now let's use the Kaplan Method on a Problem Solving question dealing with combinations and permutations:

> Six children, Arya, Betsy, Chen, Daniel, Emily, and Franco, are to be seated in a single row of 6 chairs. If Betsy cannot sit next to Emily, how many different arrangements of the 6 children are possible?
>
> ○ 240
> ○ 480
> ○ 540
> ○ 720
> ○ 840

STEP 1: ANALYZE THE QUESTION

You have to arrange 6 children in 6 chairs, but 2 of the children can't sit together. You're asked to calculate the number of different arrangements of children.

STEP 2: STATE THE TASK

You need to calculate the total number of possible arrangements of the children. Then you'll subtract the number of ways Betsy can sit next to Emily.

STEP 3: APPROACH STRATEGICALLY

The possible number of arrangements of 6 elements is $6! = 6 \times 5 \times 4 \times 3 \times 2 \times 1 = 720$.

Now you'll have to calculate the number of arrangements that would violate the question stem by putting Betsy next to Emily. If you number the seats from left to right, there are 5 ways they could sit together if Betsy is on the left and Emily is on the right:

Seats 1 & 2

Seats 2 & 3

Seats 3 & 4

Seats 4 & 5

Seats 5 & 6

And there are 5 more ways if Emily is on the left and Betsy is on the right, for a total of 10. Now, for any one of those 10 ways, the 4 remaining children can be seated in 4! ways: $4! = 4 \times 3 \times 2 \times 1 = 24$. So you need to subtract $24 \times 10 = 240$ ways that have Betsy and Emily sitting together from your original total of 720: $720 - 240 = 480$. The correct answer is **(B)**.

STEP 4: CONFIRM YOUR ANSWER

Verify that you understood the scenario in the question stem correctly and that your calculations are correct.

> ### TAKEAWAYS: COMBINATIONS AND PERMUTATIONS
>
> - The combination formula, $_nC_k = \dfrac{n!}{k!(n-k)!}$, gives the number of **unordered** subgroups of k items that can be selected from a group of n different items, where $k \leq n$. If n is a positive integer, $n!$ is the product of the first n positive integers.
> - The permutation formula, $_nP_k = \dfrac{n!}{(n-k)!}$, gives the number of **ordered** subgroups of k items that can be made from a set of n different items, where $k \leq n$.
> - The number of possible arrangements of n different items is $n!$.

Practice Set: Combinations and Permutations on the GMAT

9. How many organizational structures can be formed that consist of Division A; at least one of Divisions B and C; at least two of Divisions D, E, and F; and at least two of Divisions G, H, J, and K?

    ○ 60

    ○ 90

    ○ 99

    ○ 120

    ○ 132

10. Of the 5 distinguishable wires that lead into an apartment, 2 are for cable television service and 3 are for telephone service. Using these wires, how many distinct combinations of 3 wires are there such that at least 1 of the wires is for cable television?

    ○ 6

    ○ 7

    ○ 8

    ○ 9

    ○ 10

11. When cleaning her house, Carlotta discovered an old box of candles and figurines, each of which is unique. She wants to display the items on a shelf. How many different ways can she place the items in a row on the shelf if she alternates between candles and figurines?

    (1) If only the figurines were lined up, 40,320 different arrangements would be possible.

    (2) Carlotta has one more candle than figurine.

12. There are 6 identical chips, each of which has 1 red side and 1 blue side. How many more ways are there to arrange the chips with 3 red sides and 3 blue sides showing than there are to arrange the chips with 4 red sides and 2 blue sides showing?

   ○   3

   ○   5

   ○   6

   ○   15

   ○   20

Probability

LEARNING OBJECTIVES

In this section, you will learn how to:

- Describe five approaches to probability questions
- Distinguish between independent and dependent events
- Apply the Kaplan Methods for Problem Solving and Data Sufficiency to questions dealing with probability

Probability is the likelihood that a desired outcome will occur.

$$\text{Probability} = \frac{\text{Number of desired outcomes}}{\text{Number of total possible outcomes}}$$

Example: If you have 12 shirts in a drawer and 9 of them are white, the probability of picking a white shirt at random is $\frac{9}{12} = \frac{3}{4}$. The probability can also be expressed as 0.75 or 75 percent.

To find the probability that one or another of mutually exclusive events occurs, add the probabilities of the events.

Example: Of the 12 shirts in a drawer, 4 are white, 5 are blue, and 3 are green. If you choose 1 shirt at random, what is the probability that the shirt you choose is either white or green?

If you choose only 1 shirt, that shirt cannot be more than 1 color. This is what the phrase "mutually exclusive events" means; the shirt you choose will either be white, or blue, or green. In this case, the desired outcomes are white and green. The probability of picking a white shirt at random is $\frac{4}{12}$. The probability of picking a green shirt at random is $\frac{3}{12}$. The probability that the chosen shirt is either white or green is therefore $\frac{4}{12} + \frac{3}{12} = \frac{7}{12}$.

Many hard probability questions involve finding the probability of a certain outcome after multiple repetitions of the same experiment or different experiments (a coin being tossed several times, etc.).

Five Approaches to Probability

Broadly speaking, there are five approaches you can take to probability questions.

Approach 1: Multiply the Probabilities of Individual Events

This works best when you know the probability for each event and you need to find the probability of all the events occurring (e.g., the probability that the first flip of a coin lands heads up and the second flip lands tails up). Make sure to pay attention to what effect, if any, the outcome of the first event has on the second, the second on the third, and so on.

Example: If 3 students are chosen at random from a class with 6 girls and 4 boys, what is the probability that all 3 students chosen will be girls?

The probability that the first student chosen will be a girl is $\frac{6}{10}$, or $\frac{3}{5}$.

After that girl is chosen, there are 9 students remaining, 5 of whom are girls. So the probability of choosing a girl for the second student is $\frac{5}{9}$.

Finally, for the third pick, there are 8 total students remaining, 4 of whom are girls. The probability of choosing a girl for the third student is therefore $\frac{4}{8} = \frac{1}{2}$.

The probability that all 3 students chosen will be girls is $\frac{3}{5} \times \frac{5}{9} \times \frac{1}{2} = \frac{15}{90} = \frac{1}{6}$.

Approach 2: Subtract the Probability of the *Undesired* Outcomes from the Total

This approach works best when you cannot readily calculate the probability of the desired outcomes but you can readily do so for the undesired ones. In probability, the total of all possible outcomes is always 1.

Example: If a fair coin is flipped 3 times, what is the probability of getting at least 1 tail?

Note that "fair" means that every outcome is equally possible. A fair coin will land heads up 50 percent of the time.

What's desired is 1 tail, 2 tails, or 3 tails in 3 flips. That's a lot to keep track of. But what's undesired is very clear—3 heads in a row.

Total − Undesired

$1 - HHH$
$1 - \frac{1}{2} \times \frac{1}{2} \times \frac{1}{2}$

$1 - \frac{1}{8}$

$\frac{7}{8}$

The "Total − Undesired" approach works well for many kinds of GMAT questions, not just for probability. For example, if a question presented a circle inscribed in a square, it's how you'd calculate the area of the parts of the figure that were inside the square but outside the circle—you'd subtract the area of the circle from the area of the square.

Approach 3: Solve for the Probability of One Possible Desired Outcome, Then Multiply by All the Permutations of That Outcome

This works best when you need to know the probability that an event will occur a certain number of times, but the order of those occurrences doesn't matter.

Example: If a fair coin is flipped 5 times, what is the probability of getting exactly 3 heads?

It's clear what you desire—3 heads and 2 tails—but you don't have to get it in any particular order. *HTHTH* would be fine, as would *HHHTT*, *TTHHH*, and so forth. So Approach 1 wouldn't work well for this problem. But you can use Approach 1 to figure out the probability of *one* of these outcomes:

$$\frac{1}{2} \times \frac{1}{2} \times \frac{1}{2} \times \frac{1}{2} \times \frac{1}{2} = \frac{1}{32}$$

Now you can multiply this result by the number of ways you could get this outcome—in other words, by the number of ways you could rearrange the letters in *HHHTT*. You saw how to do this earlier, in our discussion of "hybrid combinations and permutations" problems a few pages ago.

Use the combinations formula to solve for the number of arrangements of *HHHTT* (which is the same as calculating the total number of arrangements, 5!, and dividing out the indistinguishable outcomes):

$$\frac{5!}{3!2!} = \frac{5 \times 4 \times 3 \times 2 \times 1}{3 \times 2 \times 1 \times 2 \times 1} = 5 \times 2 = 10$$

There are 10 different ways to get 3 heads and 2 tails. Each one of those outcomes has a probability of $\frac{1}{32}$.

The probability of getting exactly 3 heads in 5 coin flips is $\frac{1}{32} \times 10 = \frac{5}{16}$.

Approach 4: Find the Numerator and Denominator of the Probability Formula Separately

You can calculate the total number of possible outcomes and the total number of desired outcomes, then put them together in one big fraction (instead of multiplying lots of little fractions together).

Like Approach 3, this one works best when what you want is very specific but the order in which it happens is not.

Example: A bag holds 4 red marbles, 5 blue marbles, and 2 green marbles. If 5 marbles are selected one after another without replacement, what is the probability of drawing 2 red marbles, 2 blue marbles, and 1 green marble?

$$\text{Probability} = \frac{\text{Number of desired outcomes}}{\text{Number of total possible outcomes}}$$

Start by thinking about the possible outcomes. You are reaching into a bag of 11 marbles and pulling out 5. (The fact that they are pulled out one by one doesn't change anything; in the end, you still have 5 marbles.) Quite literally, this is "11 choose 5," $_{11}C_5$.

possible selections = $_{11}C_5 =$

$$\frac{11!}{5!6!} = \frac{11 \times 10 \times 9 \times 8 \times 7 \times 6 \times 5 \times 4 \times 3 \times 2 \times 1}{5 \times 4 \times 3 \times 2 \times 1 \times 6 \times 5 \times 4 \times 3 \times 2 \times 1} = 11 \times 2 \times 3 \times 7$$

Save yourself some work: don't multiply out factors that may later cancel. You can leave the expression as $11 \times 2 \times 3 \times 7$ for now.

Now, what is desired? You want 2 of the 4 red marbles, literally "4 choose 2," or $_4C_2$. You also want 2 of the 5 blue marbles ($_5C_2$) and 1 of the 2 green marbles ($_2C_1$).

desired selections = $_4C_2$ and $_5C_2$ and $_2C_1$

$$\frac{4!}{2!2!} \times \frac{5!}{2!3!} \times \frac{2!}{1!1!}$$

$$\frac{4 \times 3 \times 2 \times 1}{2 \times 1 \times 2 \times 1} \times \frac{5 \times 4 \times 3 \times 2 \times 1}{2 \times 1 \times 3 \times 2 \times 1} \times \frac{2 \times 1}{1 \times 1}$$

$$6 \times 10 \times 2$$

Now put the fraction together:

$$\frac{\text{Number of desired outcomes}}{\text{Number of total possible outcomes}} = \frac{6 \times 10 \times 2}{11 \times 2 \times 3 \times 7} = \frac{10 \times 2}{11 \times 7} = \frac{20}{77}$$

Approach 5: Don't Do Any Math—Just Count Up the Outcomes

This approach works best when the numbers involved are small. In this circumstance, there's really no need to waste time thinking of the right arithmetic calculation.

Example: If a fair coin is flipped 2 times, what is the probability of getting exactly 1 head?

Two coin flips aren't very many. List out the possible results:

HH, HT, TH, or *TT*

Of these 4 possibilities, 2 have exactly 1 head—*HT* and *TH*. So the probability of getting exactly 1 head in 2 flips is $\frac{2}{4}$, or $\frac{1}{2}$.

Take your time thinking probability questions through—often the hardest part is figuring out which approach you want to take.

In-Format Question: Probability on the GMAT

Now let's use the Kaplan Method on a Problem Solving question dealing with probability:

> Robert tossed a fair coin 3 times. What is the probability that the coin landed heads up exactly twice?

- O   0.125
- O   0.250
- O   0.375
- O   0.750
- O   0.875

STEP 1: ANALYZE THE QUESTION

As with any probability question, think carefully about your approach before you start any calculations. You know that each coin flip has a $\frac{1}{2}$ chance of being heads and a $\frac{1}{2}$ chance of being tails.

STEP 2: STATE THE TASK

You need to calculate the probability of exactly 2 heads in 3 flips. There are many approaches you could take. But even if you didn't see a math-based one, the low number of flips means that you could just count possibilities.

STEP 3: APPROACH STRATEGICALLY

You can write out all the ways of flipping a coin 3 times and count how many result in exactly 2 heads. As long as you are systematic about it, so you don't miss anything, you can get the answer well within 2 minutes. *HHH, HHT, HTH, HTT, THH, THT, TTH, TTT.* That's 8 possible outcomes, 3 of which have exactly 2 heads: $\frac{3}{8}$, or 0.375, is the answer.

Of course, there are math-based solutions as well. One is to calculate the probability of one desired outcome, then multiply by the number of desired outcomes. *HHT* has a probability of $\frac{1}{2} \times \frac{1}{2} \times \frac{1}{2} = \frac{1}{8}$, or 0.125. The number of ways of arranging 2 *H*s and 1 *T* is calculated in the same manner as the rearranged letter problems. In this case, that's:

$$\frac{3!}{2!1!} = 3$$

So the probability of getting exactly 2 heads in 3 flips is $0.125 \times 3 = 0.375$. The answer is **(C)**.

STEP 4: CONFIRM YOUR ANSWER

Whichever method you chose, there weren't many calculations to make. Double-check your arithmetic so that you avoid careless errors and quickly reread the question stem, confirming that you answered the question that was asked.

TAKEAWAYS: PROBABILITY

$$\text{Probability} = \frac{\text{Number of desired outcomes}}{\text{Total number of outcomes}}$$

- The sum of the probabilities of a complete set of mutually exclusive possible outcomes is 1.
- To find the probability that one *or* another of two mutually exclusive events will occur, add the probabilities of the two events.
- To find the probability that one *and* another of two independent events will occur, multiply the probabilities of the two events.
- Sometimes it is easier to subtract the probability of an event *not* occurring from 1, rather than to find directly the probability of the event occurring.

Practice Set: Probability on the GMAT

13. A garden shed contains a total of 8 bags of yard care supplies. There are 3 bags of fertilizer and 2 bags of grass seed, and the remaining bags are of mulch. If 3 bags are selected from the shed at random, one at a time without replacement, what is the probability that none of the bags are of mulch?

   ○ $\frac{1}{56}$

   ○ $\frac{15}{128}$

   ○ $\frac{5}{28}$

   ○ $\frac{125}{336}$

   ○ $\frac{3}{8}$

14. A bag contains 4 red marbles and 5 marbles of other colors. A second bag contains 3 red marbles and 6 marbles of other colors. If 1 marble is selected at random from each bag, what is the probability that exactly 1 of the marbles will be red?

   ○ $\frac{4}{27}$

   ○ $\frac{7}{18}$

   ○ $\frac{13}{27}$

   ○ $\frac{17}{27}$

   ○ $\frac{55}{81}$

15. A certain event has only outcomes *A* or *B*, and they are equally likely and mutually exclusive. Out of 5 random occurrences of the event, what is the probability that fewer than half result in an outcome of *A*?

    ○ $\frac{3}{16}$

    ○ $\frac{5}{16}$

    ○ $\frac{1}{3}$

    ○ $\frac{2}{5}$

    ○ $\frac{1}{2}$

16. A student is entered in a college housing lottery for two consecutive years. What is the probability that the student receives housing through the lottery for at least one of these years?

    (1) Of the students in the lottery, 80 percent do not receive housing through the lottery in any given year.

    (2) Each year, 1 of 5 students receives housing through the lottery.

Answer Key

Practice Set: Median, Mode, Range, and Standard Deviation on the GMAT

1. A
2. D
3. D
4. C

Practice Set: Sequences of Integers on the GMAT

5. D
6. B
7. A
8. C

Practice Set: Combinations and Permutations on the GMAT

9. E
10. D
11. C
12. B

Practice Set: Probability on the GMAT

13. C
14. C
15. E
16. D

Answers and Explanations

Practice Set: Median, Mode, Range, and Standard Deviation on the GMAT

1. **(A)**

   Data set S contains the elements $\{-5, x, 2, 0, -1, 1, 9\}$. What is the value of x?

   (1) The average (arithmetic mean) of data set S is 2.

   (2) The median of data set S is 1.

STEP 1: ANALYZE THE QUESTION STEM

This Value question lists the elements of a data set, including the variable x, and asks for the value of that variable.

STEP 2: EVALUATE THE STATEMENTS USING 12TEN

Statement (1): Since the mean of a group of numbers is $\dfrac{\text{Sum of values}}{\text{Number of values}}$, you could write the equation $\dfrac{-5 + x + 2 + 0 + (-1) + 1 + 9}{7} = 2$ and solve for x. This statement is sufficient, so eliminate **(B)**, **(C)**, and **(E)**.

Statement (2): In order to determine the median of a list of numbers, restate them in ascending numerical order. Begin by listing the known values: $\{-5, -1, 0, 1, 2, 9\}$. Since there are seven values, the fourth greatest value will be the median. Pick some values for x. If $x = 1$, then the median is 1; thus, x could be 1. However, if x is any value greater than 1, such as 2, then 1 is still the median. Thus, x could be any value equal to or greater than 1. This statement is insufficient, so **(A)** is correct.

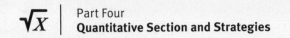
2. **(D)**

If the range of the eight numbers 17, 8, 14, 28, 9, 4, 11, and n is 25, what is the difference between the greatest possible value of n and the least possible value of n?

- ○ 1
- ○ 3
- ○ 21
- ○ 26
- ○ 29

STEP 1: ANALYZE THE QUESTION

By saying that the range of these eight numbers is 25, this question is saying that the difference between the largest and smallest value is 25. The range of the seven known numbers in the set is $28 - 4 = 24$. Thus, n must be either the largest number or the smallest number in the set.

STEP 2: STATE THE TASK

Determine how far n can be from the smallest known value and the largest known value in the set and then find the difference between those distances.

STEP 3: APPROACH STRATEGICALLY

List the known numbers in order, leaving spaces to visualize where n might be in the list: __, 4, 8, 9, 11, 14, 17, 28, __. The largest known value is 28, so if that were the largest value of all eight numbers, n would have to be $28 - 25 = 3$. On the other hand, the smallest known value is 4, so if that were the smallest value, n would have to be $4 + 25 = 29$. Thus, n could either be 3 or 29. Therefore, the difference between the largest and smallest possible values of n is $29 - 3 = 26$. The correct answer is **(D)**.

STEP 4: CONFIRM YOUR ANSWER

Review the order of numbers on your list and confirm your calculations. Finally, make sure you answered the question asked, which is not about a possible value of n—**(B)** and **(E)** represent n's possible values—but the difference between its possible values.

3. (D)

In the list of numbers $\{a, b, c\}$, a is the average (arithmetic mean) of the list and $b + c = 0$. What is the standard deviation of a, b, and c?

(1) $b - a = 2$

(2) $c - a = 2$

STEP 1: ANALYZE THE QUESTION STEM

This Value question presents three variables, a, b, and c, and tells you that a is the average of the three values. Also, b and c sum to 0. This means that b and c have the same magnitude (e.g., if $b = 2$, then $c = -2$; if $b = 0$, then $c = 0$).

Since b and c are balanced around 0 (their absolute values are equal), a must be exactly between b and c and thus equal to 0. Standard deviation is calculated by finding each number's distance from the mean as a first step. So for you to be able to determine the standard deviation of a, b, and c, a statement would need to provide either the specific value of b or c or the difference between either of those values and a.

STEP 2: EVALUATE THE STATEMENTS USING 12TEN

Statement (1) tells you the difference between b and a. Since the difference between b and the average a is 2, the distance between c and the average is 2, and the distance between a and the average is 0. These are the values you'd use to find the standard deviation, making this statement sufficient. Eliminate **(B)**, **(C)**, and **(E)**.

Statement (2) gives the difference between c and the average a. As with Statement (1), this tells you the difference between c and the mean and allows you to find the difference between b and the mean, and you already know that the mean is 0. Thus, this statement is sufficient, so **(D)** is correct.

4. (C)

Given the set of even numbers {2, 18, 32, x, y}, what is the median of the set?

(1) $y(y - 1) = 30$

(2) $(x - y)^3 \leq 0$

STEP 1: ANALYZE THE QUESTION STEM

This is a Value question. You're asked for the median of numbers in a set that includes two variables. One way to answer this question would be to find the values of both variables. You can also get to one value for the median of a set of five numbers if you can identify which number has two numbers in the set less than or equal to it and two numbers in the set greater than or equal to it. In other words, you can solve if you can find the number that must be in the middle of the set, even if you're not sure exactly what that number is.

STEP 2: EVALUATE THE STATEMENTS USING 12TEN

Since Statement (1) is a quadratic equation with one variable, you might be able solve for a single value of y. However, since this would not tell you the value of x, you wouldn't know what the median was. Eliminate **(A)** and **(D)**.

Evaluating Statement (2) and applying knowledge of number properties (specifically that a negative base raised to an odd exponent results in a negative number), there are two potential scenarios:

1. $x = y$, making $x - y = 0$ and $(x - y)^3 = 0$
2. $x < y$, making $x - y < 0$ and $(x - y)^3 < 0$

While Statement (2) provides information on the relationship between the two variables, it does not provide information about the relationship between the variables and the other numbers in the set, which makes it insufficient for the task at hand. Eliminate **(B)**.

Now try combining the statements. You were able to eliminate Statement (1) without taking the time to solve for y, but it's now worthwhile to do so:

$$y(y - 1) = 30$$
$$y^2 - y = 30$$
$$y^2 - y - 30 = 0$$
$$(y - 6)(y + 5) = 0$$
$$y = 6 \text{ or } y = -5$$

The question stem indicates that the set only contains even numbers, so you know that $y = 6$.

Based on the other numbers in the set, you know for sure that there are two numbers greater than y (the 18 and the 32). Based on Statement (2), you know that x is less than or equal to y, which would mean that, in the context of the set, y also has two numbers lesser than or equal to it. The set contains five numbers, so y (which is 6) is the median, and you can definitively answer the question. Because the statements together are sufficient, the correct answer is **(C)**.

Practice Set: Sequences of Integers on the GMAT

5. (D)

The sum of a sequence of consecutive integers is 1,125 and the median is 45. What is the value of the greatest integer in the sequence?

- ○ 33
- ○ 45
- ○ 56
- ○ 57
- ○ 58

STEP 1: ANALYZE THE QUESTION

The question states that the median of a sequence of consecutive integers is 45 and that the sum of all the integers is 1,125. In a sequence of consecutive integers, the median equals the average (arithmetic mean).

STEP 2: STATE THE TASK

Determine the value of the greatest integer in the sequence.

STEP 3: APPROACH STRATEGICALLY

Use the formula for averages to determine how many integers are in the sequence. Then use that information and the given median to find the value of the greatest number in the sequence.

Rearrange the averages formula to get Number of values $= \dfrac{\text{Sum of values}}{\text{Average value}}$. So that is $\dfrac{1{,}125}{45} = 25$. Thus, there will be 1 less than half of 25, or 12, consecutive integers less than 45 and 12 greater than 45. So the greatest value in the sequence is $45 + 12 = 57$. **(D)** is correct.

STEP 4: CONFIRM YOUR ANSWER

Double-check your calculations to ensure that you haven't made any avoidable mistakes.

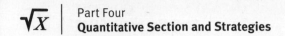
6. **(B)**

What is the sum of the multiples of 4 between 13 and 125 inclusive?

○ 1,890

○ 1,960

○ 2,200

○ 3,780

○ 4,400

STEP 1: ANALYZE THE QUESTION

When working with sets of consecutive numbers, look for ways to save time and work by recognizing patterns and first and last terms in the set.

To find the sum of terms in a set of consecutive numbers, apply the average formula:

$$\text{Average} = \frac{\text{Sum of terms}}{\text{Number of terms}}$$

$$\text{Sum of terms} = (\text{Average})(\text{Number of terms})$$

STEP 2: STATE THE TASK

To find the sum, you need to calculate the average of the terms in the set and the number of items in the set.

STEP 3: APPROACH STRATEGICALLY

First, find the smallest and largest multiple of 4 between 13 and 125. In this range, the smallest multiple of 4 is 16, and the largest is 124. Thus, the set of values in this question is really the multiples of 4 from 16 to 124 inclusive.

The average of a set of consecutive numbers equals the average of the smallest and largest terms. The average of these two numbers is $\frac{16 + 124}{2} = \frac{140}{2} = 70$. So the average of all terms in this set is 70.

Now find the number of multiples of 4 between 16 and 124 inclusive. You could simply list all of the terms in the sequence, but that would be time-consuming. A great shortcut to determine this value is to find the difference between the smallest and largest terms and add 1. Because the numbers in this set are multiples of 4, you must divide the difference by 4 before adding 1. Therefore, the number of terms in this set is $\frac{124 - 16}{4} + 1 = \frac{108}{4} + 1 = 27 + 1 = 28$.

So the average of the terms in the set is 70, and the number of terms in the set is 28. The sum of the terms in the set is the product of these two values: $28 \times 70 = 1,960$. **(B)** is correct.

STEP 4: CONFIRM YOUR ANSWER

Pay careful attention to the wording of this question stem. The set is inclusive, so confirm that you added 1 when you calculated the number of terms.

7. **(A)**

If z is the sum of three consecutive odd positive integers, is z evenly divisible by 9?

(1) When the smallest of the three numbers is divided by 3, the remainder is 1.

(2) The smallest of the three numbers is divisible by 7.

STEP 1: ANALYZE THE QUESTION STEM

This is a Yes/No question. If z is the sum of three consecutive odd positive integers, call the smallest integer x and write the other two as $(x + 2)$ and $(x + 4)$, respectively. Therefore, the sum of the three integers is $x + (x + 2) + (x + 4)$ or, combining like terms, $3x + 6$. Finally, you can factor to find that the sum is $3(x + 2)$.

So the question is really asking, "Is $3(x + 2)$ evenly divisible by 9?"

STEP 2: EVALUATE THE STATEMENTS USING 12TEN

Statement (1): You are told that when x is divided by 3, the remainder is 1. So x is 3 times some integer plus 1. Call that integer y and substitute $3y + 1$ for x in the expression above to get $3(3y + 1 + 2) = 3(3y + 3)$. When the factor is distributed, this is $9y + 9$. Since y is an integer, this expression must be divisible by 9. So the answer is always yes, and Statement (1) is sufficient. Eliminate **(B)**, **(C)**, and **(E)**.

If you prefer picking numbers to algebra, you could set $x = 1$. If $x = 1$, then the sum of the 3 numbers is $1 + 3 + 5 = 9$. Then you could try $x = 7$, the next odd number that leaves a remainder of 1 when divided by 3, and get a sum of 27, which is also divisible by 9. Each time you increase x by 6 to find the next odd integer that leaves a remainder of 1 when divided by 3, the sum increases by 18, so the relationship holds true.

Statement (2): You can check this statement for sufficiency by picking numbers. If $x = 7$, then the sum is $3(7 + 2) = 27$, which is divisible by 9. However, if $x = 21$, the next odd number divisible by 7, then the sum is $3(21 + 2) = 69$, which is not divisible by 9. Therefore, Statement (2) is insufficient. The correct choice is **(A)**.

8. **(C)**

The sum of a sequence of six consecutive positive integers is Z. The sum of terms in a different sequence of five consecutive integers is $Z - 5$. If the greatest term of the five-number sequence is 40, what is the difference between the median term of the five-number sequence and the least term of the six-number sequence?

    ○ 5

    ○ 7

    ○ 8

    ○ 9

    ○ 10

STEP 1: ANALYZE THE QUESTION

There are two sequences of integers. The sum of the sequence with six consecutive integers is Z. The second sequence consists of five consecutive integers, the sum of which is $Z - 5$. The greatest integer in this latter sequence is 40.

STEP 2: STATE THE TASK

Determine the difference between the median, or middle, term of the five-number sequence and the smallest term of the six-number sequence.

STEP 3: APPROACH STRATEGICALLY

If the greatest term in the five-number sequence is 40, that sequence must be 36, 37, 38, 39, 40. The sum of a sequence of integers is the average (arithmetic mean) times the number of terms. Since this sequence has an odd number of consecutive terms, the middle or median value, 38, is also the mean. Thus, the sum of terms in this sequence is $38 \times 5 = 190$. Since this sum is equivalent to $Z - 5, Z = 195$.

Since the sum of terms in the six-term sequence is 195, then using the formula $\text{Average} = \dfrac{\text{Sum of terms}}{\text{Number of terms}}$ yields $195 \div 6 = 32.5$. This sequence has an even number of terms, so the mean is the average of the two middle terms when all of the terms are arranged in numeric order. Therefore, the third and fourth terms in the sequence must be 32 and 33, and the entire sequence is 30, 31, 32, 33, 34, 35. Thus, the difference between the third term of the five-number sequence (38) and the smallest term of the six-number sequence (30) is 8, which is **(C)**.

STEP 4: CONFIRM YOUR ANSWER

Go back over the question stem to make sure that you didn't misread anything. Then check your determination of the sequences to make sure you selected the correct values to compare.

Practice Set: Combinations and Permutations on the GMAT

9.   (E)

How many organizational structures can be formed that consist of Division A; at least one of Divisions B and C; at least two of Divisions D, E, and F; and at least two of Divisions G, H, J, and K?

O   60

O   90

O   99

O   120

O   132

STEP 1: ANALYZE THE QUESTION

The question describes the creation of an organizational structure and the divisions that could be included in it. Since nothing indicates that order matters (for an organization to have Divisions A and B is exactly like that organization having Divisions B and A), this is a combinations question.

STEP 2: STATE THE TASK

Find the number of organizational structures that can be made according to these specifications, using the combinations formula as needed.

STEP 3: APPROACH STRATEGICALLY

Since Division A must be part of the organization, there is only 1 way to choose that unit.

If at least one of B and C must be in the organization, only B, only C, or both could be in it, making for 3 possible ways to choose from these divisions.

At least two of D, E, and F must be part of the organization. If two join, there are 3 possible outcomes: D and E, D and F, or E and F. Or all three could be included, which is 1 more outcome. So there are 4 possible ways to choose this group of units.

Finally, at least two of G, H, J, and K must be included. If two are included, $_4C_2 = \dfrac{4!}{(2!)(4-2)!} = \dfrac{4 \times 3 \times (2!)}{2 \times 1 \times (2!)} = 6$ possible outcomes. If three of these divisions are used, there are four ways to leave one division out, so that's 4 possible outcomes. If all four are included, that's 1 more outcome. Thus, there are 11 possible ways to choose divisions from this group.

To find the number of organizational structures that can be formed from these various groups, multiply the numbers of ways of selecting each group: $1 \times 3 \times 4 \times 11 = 132$.

STEP 4: CONFIRM YOUR ANSWER

Make sure you counted all of the possibilities for including the divisions in counting the number of possible organizational structures.

10. (D)

Of the 5 distinguishable wires that lead into an apartment, 2 are for cable television service and 3 are for telephone service. Using these wires, how many distinct combinations of 3 wires are there such that at least 1 of the wires is for cable television?

- ○ 6
- ○ 7
- ○ 8
- ○ 9
- ○ 10

STEP 1: ANALYZE THE QUESTION

For any question that asks you to make subsets or groups of a larger pool of items, pay careful attention to the wording of the question stem. You need to determine whether the order of the items in each subgroup matters. In this question, you are asked to make distinct combinations of 3 wires from a set of 5 wires. Because you want distinct combinations, the order of the wires will not matter, and you can apply the combinations formula to solve the question. Notice the phrase "at least" in the question stem. When questions use that phrase, solving for the total and then subtracting the undesired outcomes is usually a very efficient approach. The total is the number of ways one could select any 3 wires from 5. The undesired outcome is selecting only telephone wires.

STEP 2: STATE THE TASK

Apply the combinations formula to determine how many subsets of 3 wires can be created from the pool of 5 wires. Then determine how many ways there are to select only 3 telephone wires and subtract.

STEP 3: APPROACH STRATEGICALLY

Use the combinations formula, $\dfrac{n!}{k!(n-k)!}$, to find the total number of ways to choose 3 wires out of 5. Substituting 5 for n and 3 for k, you find that the total number of ways to choose 3 wires out of 5 is:

$$\frac{5!}{3!(5-3)!} = \frac{5!}{3!2!} = \frac{5(4)(3!)}{3!2!} = \frac{5(4)}{2} = 5(2) = 10$$

You now know that there are 10 subsets of 3 wires. Now turn your attention to what is undesired—selecting only telephone wires. Because there are only 3 telephone wires, there is only 1 possible way to choose 3 of the 5 wires such that all are telephone wires. Thus, there are $10 - 1 = 9$ ways to choose 3 wires such that at least 1 of the wires would be for cable. **(D)** is correct.

STEP 4: CONFIRM YOUR ANSWER

Pay careful attention to exactly what the question stem is asking. Notice that **(E)** is a trap for the unwary test taker who simply calculates the total number of possible outcomes.

11. (C)

When cleaning her house, Carlotta discovered an old box of candles and figurines, each of which is unique. She wants to display the items on a shelf. How many different ways can she place the items in a row on the shelf if she alternates between candles and figurines?

(1) If only the figurines were lined up, 40,320 different arrangements would be possible.

(2) Carlotta has one more candle than figurine.

STEP 1: ANALYZE THE QUESTION STEM

This Value question describes lining up different candles and figurines in such a way that no two of the same type of object are adjacent to each other and asks how many different arrangements can be made. In order to determine that value, you would need to know the exact number of each object.

STEP 2: EVALUATE THE STATEMENTS USING 12TEN

Statement (1) tells you that 40,320 arrangements can be made using only the distinct figurines. If the number of figurines is f, then the number of arrangements is $f! = 40{,}320$. You could solve this for the number of figurines, but there's no need to do so on Test Day (but for the record, $8! = 40{,}320$). However, you don't know the number of candles. The row could start and end with a candle, in which case there would be $f + 1$ candles, there could be equal numbers of candles and figures, or the row could start and end with figurines, meaning that there would be $f - 1$ candles. Thus, Statement (1) is insufficient. Eliminate **(A)** and **(D)**.

Statement (2) informs you that there's one more candle than figurine, but does not tell you how many there are. This is insufficient, so eliminate **(B)** and proceed to evaluate the statements together.

Statement (1) enables you to calculate the number of figurines and Statement (2) tells you that there's one more candle. So you know the numbers of each object, which is sufficient to determine the number of arrangements. **(C)** is correct.

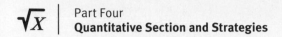
12. (B)

There are 6 identical chips, each of which has 1 red side and 1 blue side. How many more ways are there to arrange the chips with 3 red sides and 3 blue sides showing than there are to arrange the chips with 4 red sides and 2 blue sides showing?

- ○ 3
- ○ 5
- ○ 6
- ○ 15
- ○ 20

STEP 1: ANALYZE THE QUESTION

The question states that there are 6 identical chips, each with a red side and a blue side. Since the chips are identical, there is no way to distinguish among any chips with the same color showing.

STEP 2: STATE THE TASK

Determine the difference between the number of ways that 3 red-sided and 3 blue-sided chips can be arranged and the number of ways 4 red-sided and 2 blue-sided chips can be arranged.

STEP 3: APPROACH STRATEGICALLY

If the chips were all different from each other, there would be 6! ways to arrange them. However, that number must be reduced by factors that represent the number of ways that the red sides can be arranged and the blue sides can be arranged, since all of these configurations are identical.

For 3 of each color, divide 6! by 3! twice to represent the indistinguishable arrangements of 3 blue and 3 red chips. Thus, the number of ways to arrange the chips is $\frac{6!}{3!(3!)} = \frac{\cancel{6} \times 5 \times 4}{\cancel{3 \times 2} \times 1} = 5 \times 4 = 20$. Similarly, the number of ways to arrange 4 reds and 2 blues is $\frac{6!}{4!(2!)} = \frac{6 \times 5}{2 \times 1} = 3 \times 5 = 15$. Since $20 - 15 = 5$, **(B)** is correct.

STEP 4: CONFIRM YOUR ANSWER

Check that you answered the question that is actually asked. **(C)** is merely the number of chips, and **(D)** and **(E)** represent the number of arrangements for each of the two configurations.

Practice Set: Probability on the GMAT

13. (C)

A garden shed contains a total of 8 bags of yard care supplies. There are 3 bags of fertilizer and 2 bags of grass seed, and the remaining bags are of mulch. If 3 bags are selected from the shed at random, one at a time without replacement, what is the probability that none of the bags are of mulch?

- ○ $\frac{1}{56}$
- ○ $\frac{15}{128}$
- ○ $\frac{5}{28}$
- ○ $\frac{125}{336}$
- ○ $\frac{3}{8}$

STEP 1: ANALYZE THE QUESTION

Three bags are randomly chosen, without replacement, from a shed containing 3 kinds of bags. You're given the total number of bags (8) and the numbers of fertilizer (2) and grass seed (3) bags, so the starting number of non-mulch bags is $2 + 3 = 5$.

STEP 2: STATE THE TASK

Use the probability formula for dependent events to find the probability of not choosing a bag of mulch 3 times.

STEP 3: APPROACH STRATEGICALLY

Probability is $\dfrac{\text{Outcome of interest}}{\text{Total possible outcomes}}$. There are 8 total bags and 5 of them do not have mulch, so the first time you pick a bag out of the shed, there is a $\frac{5}{8}$ chance of getting a non-mulch bag.

This bag is not replaced, so now there are 7 total bags and 4 are non-mulch: that's a $\frac{4}{7}$ probability.

One more bag to pick up: this time there are 6 total bags and 3 non-mulch, so there is a $\frac{3}{6} = \frac{1}{2}$ chance of getting the desired result this time.

To achieve the desired result, you need to get 1 non-mulch bag *and* a second one *and* a third one. This means you multiply the individual events' probabilities:

$$\frac{5}{\cancel{8}^2} \times \frac{\cancel{4}^1}{7} \times \frac{1}{2} = \frac{5}{28}$$

(C) is correct.

STEP 4: CONFIRM YOUR ANSWER

Reread the question stem to ensure that you understood the scenario correctly, and double-check that you didn't make any mistakes in calculating the probabilities.

14. (C)

A bag contains 4 red marbles and 5 marbles of other colors. A second bag contains 3 red marbles and 6 marbles of other colors. If 1 marble is selected at random from each bag, what is the probability that exactly 1 of the marbles will be red?

- $\frac{4}{27}$
- $\frac{7}{18}$
- $\frac{13}{27}$
- $\frac{17}{27}$
- $\frac{55}{81}$

STEP 1: ANALYZE THE QUESTION

The question says that there are 2 different bags containing 9 marbles each. One bag contains 4 red marbles, and the other bag has 3 red marbles. A marble is selected randomly from each of the bags.

STEP 2: STATE THE TASK

Determine the probability that exactly 1 of the 2 marbles that is drawn is red.

STEP 3: APPROACH STRATEGICALLY

There are two ways to select exactly 1 red marble. One way is to select a red marble from the first bag and a non-red marble from the second bag. The other way is to select a non-red marble from the first bag and a red marble from the second bag. Since the desired result can be attained in one manner or another, add these two probabilities to get the total probability of selecting exactly 1 red marble.

The probability that the red marble is chosen from the first bag is $\frac{4}{9}$, and the probability that a non-red marble is chosen from the second bag is $\frac{9-3}{9} = \frac{6}{9}$. Since both of these outcomes must occur, multiply their probabilities to get $\frac{4}{9} \times \frac{6}{9} = \frac{24}{81}$. There is no need to simplify at this point because you will be adding this to another fraction.

The probability that a non-red marble is chosen from the first bag is $\frac{9-4}{9} = \frac{5}{9}$, and the probability that a red marble is chosen from the second bag is $\frac{3}{9}$. Since both of these outcomes must occur, multiply their probabilities to get $\frac{5}{9} \times \frac{3}{9} = \frac{15}{81}$.

Now, add the probabilities of the two desired outcomes; the probability that exactly 1 of the chosen marbles is red is $\frac{24}{81} + \frac{15}{81} = \frac{39}{81} = \frac{13}{27}$. **(C)** is correct.

STEP 4: CONFIRM YOUR ANSWER

Confirm that these two scenarios are the only two ways in which the desired outcome can occur. **(A)** is the probability that both marbles will be red, and **(D)** is the probability that one *or* both will be red.

15. (E)

A certain event has only outcomes A or B, and they are equally likely and mutually exclusive. Out of 5 random occurrences of the event, what is the probability that fewer than half result in an outcome of A?

○ $\frac{3}{16}$

○ $\frac{5}{16}$

○ $\frac{1}{3}$

○ $\frac{2}{5}$

○ $\frac{1}{2}$

STEP 1: ANALYZE THE QUESTION

The question states that an event has two equally likely outcomes and that they are mutually exclusive. In other words, every time the event happens, there's a 50% chance of outcome A and a 50% chance of outcome B.

STEP 2: STATE THE TASK

Determine the probability that fewer than half of 5 random trials result in outcome A.

STEP 3: APPROACH STRATEGICALLY

The probability that less than half of 5 trials have an outcome of A is the total of the probability of 0, 1, or 2 outcome As. Use the probability formula $P = \dfrac{\text{\# of desired outcomes}}{\text{\# of possible outcomes}}$ to determine this probability.

Since each occurrence has 2 possible outcomes, the total number of possible outcomes is $2^5 = 32$. There is only 1 way to have no As, that is, 5 Bs. There are 5 ways to have 1 A, since that singular A could occur on any 1 of the 5 trials.

There are 2 ways to find the number of ways to get 2 As. You could actually count the ways: AABBB, ABABB, ABBAB, ABBBA, BAABB, BABAB, BABBA, BBAAB, BBABA, and BBBAA, for a total of 10 different ways. Alternatively, you could use the combinations formula to find the number of combinations of 2 As out of 5 events:

$$_5C_2 = \frac{5!}{2!(3!)} = \frac{5 \times 4 \times \cancel{3} \times \cancel{2} \times \cancel{1}}{2 \times 1(\cancel{3} \times \cancel{2} \times \cancel{1})} = \frac{20}{2} = 10$$

The total number of ways to obtain the desired outcome is thus $1 + 5 + 10 = 16$, so the probability is $\frac{16}{32} = \frac{1}{2}$. **(E)** is correct.

STEP 4: CONFIRM YOUR ANSWER

Be certain that you answered the question that was asked and counted all the ways to get 2 or less outcomes of A. Although it may seem counterintuitive that the probability of getting *less* than half As is exactly $\frac{1}{2}$, you can verify that this is correct by checking to see if the probability of *all* outcomes is equal to 1. The same calculations would show that the probability for 0, 1, or 2 Bs, is also $\frac{1}{2}$. Since this corresponds to 3, 4, or 5 As, the total probability of 0, 1, 2, 3, 4, or 5 As is $\frac{1}{2} + \frac{1}{2} = 1$. Put another way, since there are 6 different numbers of As that are possible (from 0 to 5), getting 0, 1, or 2 As does in fact cover half the possibilities.

16. (D)

A student is entered in a college housing lottery for two consecutive years. What is the probability that the student receives housing through the lottery for at least one of these years?

(1) Of the students in the lottery, 80 percent do not receive housing through the lottery in any given year.

(2) Each year, 1 of 5 students receives housing through the lottery.

STEP 1: ANALYZE THE QUESTION STEM

This Value question asks for the probability that a student receives housing in at least one of two consecutive years. In order to calculate that probability, you would need to know the probability of getting housing in each year. (Another possibility that could be useful is the chance of *not* getting housing, since 1 − Undesired Probability = Desired Probability.)

STEP 2: EVALUATE THE STATEMENTS USING 12TEN

Statement (1): This gives you the probability of *not* getting into housing. An 80% chance of not getting housing each year means a 20% chance of getting housing each year. The exact answer isn't something that you need to worry about, since this isn't Problem Solving. You know an answer can be calculated, so Statement (1) is sufficient. Eliminate choices **(B)**, **(C)**, and **(E)**.

Statement (2): This isn't given in percentage form, but any proportion will serve. This gives you the likelihood of getting housing in any given year. You now know that Statement (2), which gives you the same information that Statement (1) does, must be sufficient. **(D)** is correct.

GMAT by the Numbers: Statistics

Now that you've learned how to approach statistics questions on the GMAT, let's add one more dimension to your understanding of how they work.

Take a moment to try this question. Following is performance data from thousands of people who have studied with Kaplan over the decades. Through analyzing this data, we will show you how to approach questions like this one most effectively and how to avoid similarly tempting wrong answer choice types on Test Day.

> A company plans to award prizes to its top 3 salespeople, with the largest prize going to the top salesperson, the next-largest prize to the next salesperson, and a smaller prize to the third-ranking salesperson. If the company has 12 salespeople on staff, how many different arrangements of winners are possible?
>
> ○ 1,728
> ○ 1,440
> ○ 1,320
> ○ 220
> ○ 6

Explanation

Questions that ask test takers to count possibilities are often the most frustrating. This is because most people try to shoehorn the problem into a preexisting arithmetic formula without first analyzing the problem to see whether the formula applies. Understand the question before you jump into solving.

This problem asks you to calculate the number of ways you can distribute first-, second-, and third-place prizes among 12 people. Many test takers try to apply the combinations formula here. But doing so is not appropriate because that formula counts the number of *unordered* selections one can make from a group. You're asked to *order* your selections into first, second, and third place, so you need a different approach: simply count the number of possibilities for each prize.

Any of 12 people might win first place, leaving 11 possible choices for second. This leaves 10 possible winners for third. Hence, these prizes could be awarded $12 \times 11 \times 10 = 1{,}320$ possible ways. Choice (**C**) is correct.

Question Statistics

3% of test takers choose (**A**)

4% of test takers choose (**B**)

58% of test takers choose (**C**)

33% of test takers choose (**D**)

2% of test takers choose (**E**)

Sample size = 5,473

Unsurprisingly, the only other commonly selected answer on this problem, choice (**D**), is the result of erroneously applying the combinations formula to this problem. When solving a statistics question, understand the scenario before you start any arithmetic. You'll dramatically improve your odds of avoiding the common traps and selecting the right answer.

More GMAT by the Numbers...

To see more questions with answer choice statistics, be sure to review the full-length CATs in your online resources.

GO ONLINE

kaptest.com/login

CHAPTER 24

Geometry on the GMAT

LEARNING OBJECTIVES

After studying this chapter, you will be able to:

- Describe the types of geometric concepts that are frequently tested on the GMAT
- Identify the geometry rules that are relevant to a given geometry question
- Apply the Kaplan Methods for Problem Solving and Data Sufficiency to questions dealing with geometry

Below is a typical Problem Solving geometry question. In this chapter, we'll look at how to apply the Kaplan Method to this question, discuss the geometry rules being tested, and go over the basic principles and strategies that you want to keep in mind on every Quantitative question involving geometry.

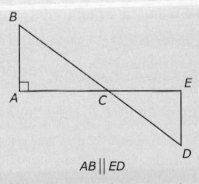

$AB \parallel ED$

Note: Figure not drawn to scale.

In the figure above, $ED = 1$, $CD = 2$, and $AE = 6\sqrt{3}$. What is the perimeter of $\triangle ABC$?

- ○ $3\sqrt{3}$
- ○ $10 + 5\sqrt{3}$
- ○ $10\sqrt{3}$
- ○ $15 + 5\sqrt{3}$
- ○ $25\sqrt{3}$

Before you move on, take a minute to think about what you see in this question and answer some questions about how you think it works:

- What types of shapes are presented in the figure?
- How does knowing that lines *AB* and *ED* are parallel help you?
- How does knowing the measure of angle *BAC* help you?
- What GMAT Core Competencies are most essential to success on this question?

Previewing Geometry on the GMAT

> **LEARNING OBJECTIVES**
>
> In this section, you will learn how to:
>
> - Describe how familiarity with key geometric concepts helps you prepare for the GMAT
> - Explain how the Core Competencies of Pattern Recognition and Paraphrasing can help you tackle a variety of questions that deal with geometry

Here we'll discuss answers to the questions asked in the previous section.

What Types of Shapes Are Presented in the Figure?

The diagram contains two triangles. More importantly, note that since the triangles meet at a common point, the angles that meet at that point (in this case, angles *BCA* and *DCE*) must be equal as well.

How Does Knowing That Lines *AB* and *ED* Are Parallel Help You?

You're given that sides *AB* and *ED* are parallel. This defines a relationship between angles *ABC* and *CDE*: they are equal. You'll see this mentioned later in this chapter, but these two are alternate interior angles, formed by a line (called a *transversal*) that intersects two parallel lines.

How Does Knowing the Measure of Angle *BAC* Help You?

Since angle *BAC* is a right angle, triangle *ABC* is a right triangle. And given that *BA* and *ED* are parallel and two pairs of angles are equal in the two triangles, the measure of angle *BAC* must also be equal to that of *CED*, and both must equal 90°. Triangles *ABC* and *CDE* are therefore similar triangles—their three angles have the same measures, and their side lengths share the same ratio.

Because right triangles have so many patterns that the test makers can write questions about, they are the most frequently tested geometric shapes on the GMAT. You'll learn later in this chapter about the relationships certain right triangles display between their side lengths and angle measurements.

What GMAT Core Competencies Are Most Essential to Success on This Question?

Pattern Recognition will play a key role here, as we'll look at how the lengths of a right triangle can often give us more information about a triangle, such as angle measurements. Additionally, even though in this case you're not translating a word problem into an equation, your ability to apply the Core Competency of Paraphrasing is important, since you can use information about one part of the figure to draw inferences about other parts. In particular, knowing how to interpret the information about the parallel lines will be the key to answering this question efficiently.

How Do I Apply the Kaplan Methods to GMAT Geometry?

Now let's apply the Kaplan Method for Problem Solving to the geometry question you saw earlier.

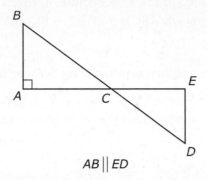

$AB \parallel ED$

Note: Figure not drawn to scale.

In the figure above, $ED = 1$, $CD = 2$, and $AE = 6\sqrt{3}$. What is the perimeter of $\triangle ABC$?

○ $3\sqrt{3}$

○ $10 + 5\sqrt{3}$

○ $10\sqrt{3}$

○ $15 + 5\sqrt{3}$

○ $25\sqrt{3}$

STEP 1: ANALYZE THE QUESTION

You're given two triangles that meet at a certain point and are told that two of the line segments that form their sides are parallel. Additionally, you're given that angle *BAC* is a right angle, which makes triangle *ABC* a right triangle. Since *AB* and *ED* are parallel, angles *ABC* and *CDE* are equal, because they are alternate interior angles formed by two parallel lines cut by a transversal. Angles *BCA* and *DCE* are also equal, since these are vertical angles. And since the measure of all interior angles of a triangle must add up to a specific number, 180, then angles *BAC* and *CED* must also be equal.

STEP 2: STATE THE TASK

You're asked to find the perimeter of triangle *ABC*. You'll need to use the information about triangle *CDE* to be able to figure out the side lengths of *ABC*. The last step will be to add up the side lengths.

STEP 3: APPROACH STRATEGICALLY

Since you know that *CDE* is a right triangle, you can use the Pythagorean theorem to first find the length of the missing side of triangle *CDE* by substituting the relevant values into the equation $(ED)^2 + (CE)^2 = (CD)^2$.

However, if you noticed that one side of the triangle, *ED*, is equal to 1 and the hypotenuse, *CD*, is equal to 2, then you may recognize that this is a special right triangle, specifically the 30-60-90 triangle. Recognizing this pattern will save you much time. If the hypotenuse is twice the length of one of the sides of the triangle, then the side lengths of the triangle will be in the ratio of $1 : \sqrt{3} : 2$. Therefore, side *CE* must have a length of $\sqrt{3}$. Since you are given that *AE* equals $6\sqrt{3}$, leg *AC* must equal $6\sqrt{3} - \sqrt{3} = 5\sqrt{3}$.

Since you established that the side lengths of triangle *CDE* are in the ratio of $1 : \sqrt{3} : 2$, and you identified that its corresponding angles are equal to those of triangle *ABC*, then the two triangles are similar, and the three sides *AB*:*AC*:*BC* must also follow the ratio of $1 : \sqrt{3} : 2$. Because *AC* equals $5\sqrt{3}$, *AB* must equal 5, and *BC* must equal 10. Therefore, the perimeter of triangle *ABC* is $5\sqrt{3} + 5 + 10$, or $15 + 5\sqrt{3}$. Choice (**D**) is correct.

STEP 4: CONFIRM YOUR ANSWER

Make sure you've paired up the angles and their corresponding side lengths correctly, using the ratio of side lengths of a 30°-60°-90° triangle.

Now let's look at each of the seven areas of geometry that show up on the GMAT Quantitative section, starting with lines and angles.

Lines and Angles

LEARNING OBJECTIVES

In this section, you will learn how to:

- Define *parallel* and *perpendicular lines*, *complementary* and *supplementary angles*, and *vertical angles*
- Calculate values of angles created by intersecting lines
- Apply the Kaplan Methods for Problem Solving and Data Sufficiency to questions dealing with lines and angles

Lines

A line is a one-dimensional abstraction—infinitely long with no width. Two points determine a straight line; given any two points, there is exactly one straight line that passes through them.

A line **segment** is a section of a straight line of finite length with two endpoints. A line segment is named for its endpoints, as in segment *AB* below. The **midpoint** is the point that divides a line segment into two equal parts.

Example:

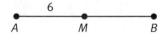

In the figure above, *A* and *B* are the endpoints of the line segment *AB*, and *M* is the midpoint ($AM = MB$). What is the length of *AB*?

Since *AM* is 6, *MB* is also 6, so *AB* is $6 + 6$, or 12.

Two lines are **parallel** if they lie in the same plane and never intersect each other regardless of how far they are extended. If line ℓ_1 is parallel to line ℓ_2, you write $\ell_1 \parallel \ell_2$.

Two lines are **perpendicular** if they intersect at a 90° angle. The shortest distance from a point to a line is the line segment drawn from the point to the line such that it is perpendicular to the line. If line ℓ_1 is perpendicular to line ℓ_2, you write $\ell_1 \perp \ell_2$. If $\ell_1 \perp \ell_2$ and $\ell_2 \perp \ell_3$, then $\ell_1 \parallel \ell_3$.

Angles

An angle is formed by two lines or line segments intersecting at a point. The point of intersection is called the **vertex** of the angle. Angles are measured in degrees (°).

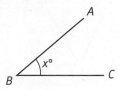

Angle x, $\angle ABC$, and $\angle B$ all denote the same angle shown in the diagram above.

Acute, Right, and Obtuse Angles

An **acute angle** is an angle whose degree measure is between 0° and 90°. A **right angle** is an angle whose degree measure is exactly 90°. An **obtuse angle** is an angle whose degree measure is between 90° and 180°. A **straight angle** is an angle whose degree measure is exactly 180° (half of a circle, which contains 360°).

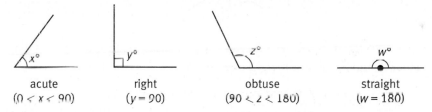

acute	right	obtuse	straight
$(0 < x < 90)$	$(y = 90)$	$(90 < z < 180)$	$(w = 180)$

Sums of Angle Measures

The sum of the measures of the angles on one side of a straight line is 180°.

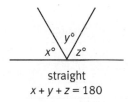

straight
$x + y + z = 180$

The sum of the measures of the angles around a point is 360°.

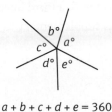

$a + b + c + d + e = 360$

Two angles are **supplementary** if together they make up a straight angle (i.e., if the sum of their measures is 180°). Two angles are **complementary** if together they make up a right angle (i.e., if the sum of their measures is 90°).

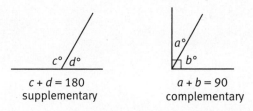

$c + d = 180$	$a + b = 90$
supplementary	complementary

A line or line segment **bisects** an angle if it splits the angle into two smaller, equal angles. Line segment BD below bisects $\angle ABC$, and $\angle ABD$ has the same measure as $\angle DBC$. The two smaller angles are each half the size of $\angle ABC$.

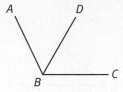

Vertical Angles

Vertical angles are a pair of opposite angles formed by two intersecting line segments. At the point of intersection, two pairs of vertical angles are formed. Angles a and c below are vertical angles, as are b and d.

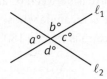

The two angles in a pair of vertical angles have the same degree measure. In the previous diagram, $a = c$ and $b = d$. In addition, since ℓ_1 and line ℓ_2 are straight lines, $a + b = c + d = a + d = b + c = 180$.

In other words, each angle is supplementary to each of its two adjacent angles.

If two parallel lines intersect with a third line (called a *transversal*), the third line will intersect each of the parallel lines at the same angle. In the figure below, $a = e$ because the transversal intersects lines ℓ_1 and ℓ_2 at the same angle. Since a and e are equal, and $c = a$ and $e = g$ (vertical angles), you know that $a = c = e = g$. Similarly, $b = d = f = h$.

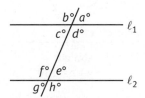

In other words, when two parallel lines intersect with a third line, all acute angles formed are equal, all obtuse angles formed are equal, and any acute angle is supplementary to any obtuse angle.

In-Format Question: Lines and Angles on the GMAT

Now let's use the Kaplan Method on a Problem Solving question dealing with lines and angles:

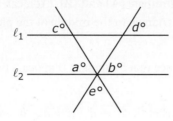

If ℓ_1 is parallel to ℓ_2 in the figure above, which of the following expressions must equal 180?

    I. $a + b$

   II. $c + e$

  III. $c + d + e$

- ○ I only
- ○ II only
- ○ III only
- ○ II and III only
- ○ I, II, and III

STEP 1: ANALYZE THE QUESTION

When analyzing a geometry question that includes a figure, you'll want to consider the question stem and the figure together. Here, the question stem tells you that ℓ_1 and ℓ_2 are parallel. This is the time to use Critical Thinking to help you come to an efficient solution. Since ℓ_1 and ℓ_2 are parallel, you know that the corresponding angles created by the transversals (intersecting lines) will be of equal measure. Specifically, that means:

$$a = c$$

$$b = d$$

Looking at the figure again, you see that angles a and b, plus that third angle between them, compose a straight line, which is $180°$. Since angle e is the "vertical angle" of that third angle, their measures are the same. So you can deduce:

$$a + b + e = 180$$

STEP 2: STATE THE TASK

Your task is to determine which of the three Roman numeral statements are equal to 180. You just deduced $a + b + e = 180$, so if a statement is equal to $a + b + e$, then it will also be equal to 180.

STEP 3: APPROACH STRATEGICALLY

Which Roman numeral statement should you check first? You could start with Statement III, which looks similar to what you're after. It also appears in the most answer choices (tying Statement II), so that's another good reason to start with Statement III.

Does $c + d + e = a + b + e$? You figured out earlier that $a = c$ and $b = d$. Substituting a for c and b for d, you confirm that $c + d + e$ does in fact equal $a + b + e$, which means that it also equals 180. The right answer must contain Statement III, so you can eliminate **(A)** and **(B)**. (You can also use Critical Thinking to note that c, d, and e are vertical angles for the triangle in the middle of the picture; the angles in a triangle always sum to 180°.)

Looking at the answers that remain, you see that Statement II appears twice, whereas Statement I appears only once. Evaluate Statement II next.

Does $c + e = a + b + e$? You deduced earlier that $c + d + e = a + b + e$. The only way, then, that $c + e$ would also equal $a + b + e$ is if $d = 0$. You have no idea what its value is, but it's definitely not 0. So Statement II is not part of the right answer. That lets you eliminate **(D)** and **(E)**, leaving only the correct answer, **(C)**.

You could also have solved by picking numbers. A Roman numeral statement will be part of the right answer only if it *must* equal 180. So if you can pick numbers to get a statement to equal something other than 180, you can eliminate it. Let's say that you pick $c = 30$ and $d = 40$. Since a and c are corresponding angles, $a = 30$. Similarly, $b = 40$. That means that the unnamed angle between a and b must equal $180 - (30 + 40)$, or 110. Since e has the same measure, $e = 110$. Quickly plugging those numbers into the Roman numeral statements gives the following:

  I. $30 + 40 = 70$. Eliminate.

  II. $30 + 110 = 140$. Eliminate.

  III. $30 + 40 + 110 = 180$. Don't eliminate.

After you eliminate Statements I and II, only choice **(C)** is possible.

STEP 4: CONFIRM YOUR ANSWER

Finally, reread the question stem, making sure that you didn't miss anything about the problem. You're looking for the angles in the figure that add up to 180. You've determined that $a + b + e = 180$ and that $a + b + e = c + d + e$. Therefore, $c + d + e = 180$, making **(C)** the only correct answer.

TAKEAWAYS: LINES AND ANGLES

- Vertical angles are equal.
- The sum of angles that form a straight line is 180°.
- When two parallel lines are intersected by a third line, the corresponding angles are equal.
- Sometimes it is possible to determine the relationship between angles without determining the degree measures of the angles.

Practice Set: Lines and Angles on the GMAT

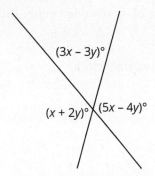

$(3x - 3y)°$

$(x + 2y)°$ $(5x - 4y)°$

Note: Not drawn to scale.

1. In the figure above, what is the value of *y*?

    ○   36
    ○   54
    ○   90
    ○   126
    ○   180

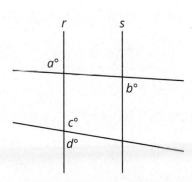

2. In the figure above, if lines *r* and *s* are parallel, what is the value of $a + b$?

    (1) $c - a = 25$
    (2) $a - d = 15$

3. A certain line segment rotates consistently in one direction in 45° increments around one of its endpoints *E*. The segment loses half of its length every 45° that it rotates, and it stops rotating when it reaches less than 5 percent of its starting length. Did the segment stop rotating?

   (1) The segment rotated at least 180°.

   (2) The segment made at most 5 movements.

Triangles

LEARNING OBJECTIVES

In this section, you will learn how to:

- Describe different types of triangles
- Recognize the significance of commonly appearing Pythagorean triples for solving questions involving right triangles
- Recognize the significance of 30-60-90 and 45-45-90 angle measurements and the corresponding side length ratios
- Calculate the area of a triangle and solve for its angle measurements and the length of its sides
- Apply the Kaplan Method for Problem Solving to questions dealing with triangles

Triangle Concepts and Formulas

A triangle is a closed figure with three angles and three straight sides.

The sum of the **interior angles** of any triangle is 180°.

Each interior angle is supplementary to an adjacent **exterior angle**. The degree measure of an exterior angle is equal to the sum of the measures of the two nonadjacent (remote) interior angles.

In the figure below, a, b, and c are interior angles. Therefore, $a + b + c = 180$. In addition, d is supplementary to c; therefore, $d + c = 180$. So $d + c = a + b + c$, and $d = a + b$. Thus, the exterior angle d is equal to the sum of the two remote interior angles a and b.

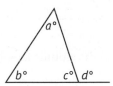

The **altitude** (or height) of a triangle is the perpendicular distance from a vertex to the side opposite the vertex. The altitude can fall inside the triangle, outside the triangle, or on one of the sides.

Altitude = AD

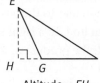

Altitude = EH

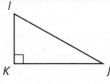

Altitude = IK

Sides and Angles

The length of any side of a triangle is less than the sum of the lengths of the other two sides, and it is greater than the positive difference of the lengths of the other two sides.

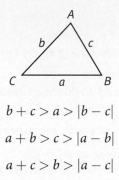

$$b + c > a > |b - c|$$
$$a + b > c > |a - b|$$
$$a + c > b > |a - c|$$

If the lengths of two sides of a triangle are unequal, the greater angle lies opposite the longer side and vice versa. In the figure above, if $\angle A > \angle B > \angle C$, then $a > b > c$.

Area of a Triangle

The formula for the area of a triangle is:

$$\frac{1}{2} \times \text{base} \times \text{height}$$

Example:

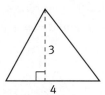

In the diagram above, the base has length 4 and the altitude length 3, so you can write:

$$A = \frac{1}{2}bh$$
$$= \frac{1}{2} \times 4 \times 3 = 6$$

Remember that the height (or altitude) is perpendicular to the base. Therefore, when two sides of a triangle are perpendicular to each other, the area is easy to find. In a right triangle, the two sides that form the $90°$ angle are called the **legs**. Then the area is one-half the product of the legs, or:

$$A = \frac{1}{2}bh$$
$$= \frac{1}{2} \times l_1 \times l_2$$

Example:

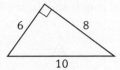

In the triangle above, you could treat the hypotenuse as the base, since that is the way the figure is drawn. If you did this, you would need to know the distance from the hypotenuse to the opposite vertex to determine the area of the triangle. A more straightforward method is to notice that this is a right triangle with legs of lengths 6 and 8, which allows you to use the alternative formula for area:

$$A = \frac{1}{2} \times l_1 \times l_2$$
$$= \frac{1}{2} \times 6 \times 8$$
$$= 24$$

Perimeter of a Triangle

The perimeter of a triangle is the distance around the triangle. In other words, the perimeter is equal to the sum of the lengths of the sides.

Example:

In the triangle above, the sides are of length 5, 6, and 8. Therefore, the perimeter is 5 + 6 + 8, or 19.

Isosceles Triangles

An isosceles triangle is a triangle that has two sides of equal length. The two equal sides are called **legs**, and the third side is called the **base**.

Since the two legs have the same length, the two angles opposite the legs must have the same measure. In the figure below, $PQ = PR$ and $\angle Q = \angle R$.

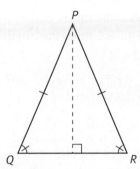

Equilateral Triangles

An equilateral triangle has three sides of equal length and three 60° angles.

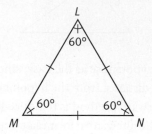

Similar Triangles

Triangles are **similar** if corresponding angles have the same measure. For instance, any two triangles whose angles measure 30°, 60°, and 90° are similar. In similar triangles, corresponding side lengths are proportional to one another. Triangles are **congruent** if corresponding angles have the same measure and corresponding sides have the same length.

Example:

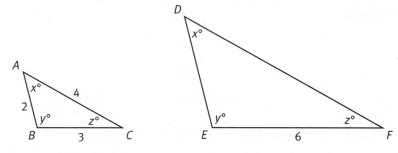

What is the perimeter of $\triangle DEF$ above?

Each triangle has an $x°$ angle, a $y°$ angle, and a $z°$ angle; therefore, the triangles are similar, and corresponding sides are proportional to one another. BC and EF are corresponding sides; each is opposite the $x°$ angle. Since EF is twice the length of BC, each side of $\triangle DEF$ will be twice the length of the corresponding side of $\triangle ABC$. Therefore, $DE = 2(AB)$ or 4, and $DF = 2(AC)$ or 8. The perimeter of $\triangle DEF$ is $4 + 6 + 8 = 18$.

The ratio of the areas of two similar triangles is the square of the ratio of corresponding lengths. For instance, in the example above, since each side of $\triangle DEF$ is 2 times the length of the corresponding side of $\triangle ABC$, $\triangle DEF$ must have 2^2 or 4 times the area of $\triangle ABC$.

$$\frac{\text{Area } \triangle DEF}{\text{Area } \triangle ABC} = \left(\frac{DE}{AB}\right)^2 = \left(\frac{2}{1}\right)^2 = 4$$

Right Triangles

A right triangle has one interior angle of 90°, which is also the largest angle of the triangle. The longest side, which lies opposite the right angle, is called the **hypotenuse**. The other two sides are called the **legs**.

Pythagorean Theorem: The **Pythagorean theorem** holds for all right triangles and states that the square of the hypotenuse is equal to the sum of the squares of the legs.

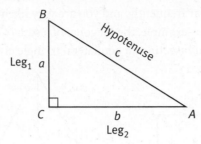

$$(\text{Leg}_1)^2 + (\text{Leg}_2)^2 = (\text{Hypotenuse})^2$$

or

$$a^2 + b^2 = c^2$$

Some sets of integers happen to satisfy the Pythagorean theorem. These sets of integers are commonly referred to as *Pythagorean triples*. One very common set that you might remember is 3, 4, and 5. Since $3^2 + 4^2 = 5^2$, you can have a right triangle with legs of lengths 3 and 4 and hypotenuse of length 5. This is the most common kind of right triangle on the GMAT. You should be familiar with the numbers so that whenever you see a right triangle with legs of 3 and 4, you will immediately know the hypotenuse must have length 5. In addition, any multiple of these lengths makes a Pythagorean triple; for instance, $6^2 + 8^2 = 10^2$, so 6, 8, and 10 also make a right triangle. One other triple that appears regularly on the GMAT is 5, 12, and 13.

Don't overuse the Pythagorean theorem. Easily recognizable right triangle patterns such as the triples allow you to avoid spending time on the formula when solving the majority of GMAT geometry problems. But from time to time, the GMAT may challenge you with a triangle that doesn't offer any convenient shortcuts, so make sure you can apply the Pythagorean theorem when necessary.

Example: What is the length of the hypotenuse of a right triangle with legs of length 9 and 10?

Use the Pythagorean theorem: the square of the length of the hypotenuse equals the sum of the squares of the lengths of the legs. Here the legs are 9 and 10, so you have

$$\text{Hypotenuse}^2 = 9^2 + 10^2$$
$$= 81 + 100 = 181$$
$$\text{Hypotenuse} = \sqrt{181}$$

Special Right Triangles: You can always use the Pythagorean theorem to find the lengths of the sides in a right triangle. There are two special kinds of right triangles, though, that always have side lengths in the same ratios:

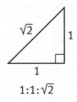

1:1:$\sqrt{2}$

(for isosceles right triangles)

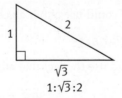

1:$\sqrt{3}$:2

(for 30-60-90 triangles)

These two special right triangles appear frequently, and you are very likely to see them. However, the GMAT can hide them in unexpected ways. For example, the diagonal of a square creates two isosceles right triangles, also known as 45-45-90 triangles. And bisecting an equilateral triangle creates two 30-60-90 triangles:

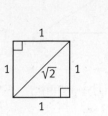 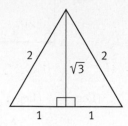

In-Format Question: Triangles on the GMAT

Now let's use the Kaplan Method on a Problem Solving question dealing with triangles:

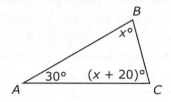

In △ABC above, x =

○ 30

○ 45

○ 60

○ 65

○ 75

STEP 1: ANALYZE THE QUESTION

This is a straightforward triangle question that tests your knowledge of basic triangle properties. As with most questions in the Quantitative section, you can solve this one by using more than one approach. You could use algebra to solve for x, or you could backsolve, plugging the answer choices for x into the figure. With either method, you'll need to remember the fact that the angles of a triangle sum to 180°.

STEP 2: STATE THE TASK

Your task is to solve for x. You could use either algebra or backsolving.

STEP 3: APPROACH STRATEGICALLY

If you solved with algebra, you'd use the fact that all the angles of a triangle sum to 180° to set up this equation:

$$30 + x + x + 20 = 180$$
$$2x + 50 = 180$$
$$2x = 130$$
$$x = 65$$

(D) is the correct answer.

If you backsolved, you could start with any answer choice, but as an example, let's say that you started with **(B)**. If you test $x = 45$, then the three angles of the triangle would be 30°, 45°, and 65°, which sum to 140°. You know triangles have 180°, so this answer choice is too small, and you can eliminate **(A)** and **(B)**. Testing **(D)** yields angles of 30°, 65°, and 85°. These angles sum to 180°, which proves that **(D)** is correct.

STEP 4: CONFIRM YOUR ANSWER

Read back over the problem to confirm that your solution accurately follows from the information in the question. You were asked to solve for x. You've done so correctly, so you can move on to the next problem.

TAKEAWAYS: TRIANGLES

- Area $= \frac{1}{2}$ (base)(height)
- The interior angles of any triangle sum to 180°.
- Every external angle of a triangle equals the sum of the two remote interior angles.
- In any triangle, a side opposite a greater angle is longer than a side opposite a smaller angle, and sides opposite equal angles are equal.
- Every side of a triangle must be longer than the difference of the lengths of the other two sides and shorter than the sum of the lengths of the other two sides.
- Some special right triangles to recognize are those with sides in the proportions 3:4:5 and 5:12:13.
- Some special right triangles to recognize are those with angle measures 30-60-90 and 45-45-90. The side lengths of these triangles are $x : x\sqrt{3} : 2x$ and $x : x : x\sqrt{2}$, respectively.
- Pythagorean theorem: In a right triangle, if the sides are a, b, and c, $a^2 + b^2 = c^2$.

Practice Set: Triangles on the GMAT

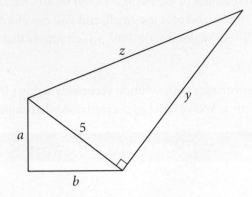

4. Based on the figure shown, which of the following could be true?

    I. $a = b$
    II. $y = z$
    III. $a^2 + b^2 = z^2 - y^2$

    ○ None
    ○ I only
    ○ II only
    ○ I and III only
    ○ I, II, and III

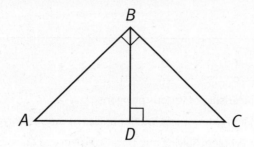

5. In the figure above, if ∠ABC is a right angle and BD bisects AC, then what is the ratio of BC to AC?

   ○ $\frac{\sqrt{2}}{4}$

   ○ $\frac{\sqrt{2}}{3}$

   ○ $\frac{1}{2}$

   ○ $\frac{\sqrt{2}}{2}$

   ○ $\sqrt{2}$

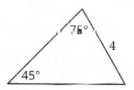

6. What is the area of the triangle in the figure above?

   ○ $2 + 2\sqrt{3}$

   ○ $4\sqrt{3}$

   ○ $6 + 2\sqrt{3}$

   ○ $6\sqrt{3}$

   ○ 12

Polygons

A polygon is a closed figure whose sides are straight line segments.

The **perimeter** of a polygon is the distance around the polygon, or the sum of the lengths of the sides.

A **vertex** of a polygon is the point where two adjacent sides meet.

A **diagonal** of a polygon is a line segment connecting two nonadjacent vertices.

A **regular** polygon has sides of equal length and interior angles of equal measure.

The number of sides determines the specific name of the polygon. A **triangle** has three sides, a **quadrilateral** has four sides, a **pentagon** has five sides, and a **hexagon** has six sides. Triangles and quadrilaterals are by far the most important polygons on the GMAT.

Interior and Exterior Angles

A polygon can be divided into triangles by drawing diagonals from a given vertex to all other nonadjacent vertices. For instance, the pentagon below can be divided into three triangles. Since the sum of the interior angles of each triangle is 180°, the sum of the interior angles of a pentagon is $3 \times 180° = 540°$.

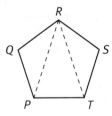

Example:

What is the measure of one interior angle of the regular hexagon above?

You need to find the sum of the interior angles and divide by the number of interior angles, or 6. Since the hexagon is regular, all angles are equal, so each of them is equal to one-sixth of the sum. Since you can draw four triangles in a six-sided figure, the sum of the interior angles will be $4 \times 180°$, or 720°. Therefore, each of the six interior angles measures $\frac{720°}{6}$ or 120°.

While splitting up polygons into triangles always works to find the sum of the interior angles, there is a formula you can memorize to speed up the process. The sum of the interior angle measures of a polygon with n sides is equal to $(n - 2)180°$. Therefore, in a regular polygon, the measure of each interior angle can be calculated using this formula: $\dfrac{(n - 2)180°}{n}$.

Quadrilaterals

The most important quadrilaterals to know for the GMAT are the rectangle and square. Anything could show up on the test, but concentrate on the most important figures and principles. The lesser-known properties can readily be deduced from the way the figure looks and from your knowledge of geometry.

Quadrilateral

A quadrilateral is a four-sided polygon. The sum of its four interior angles is 360°.

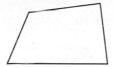

Rectangle

A rectangle is a quadrilateral with four equal angles, each a right angle.

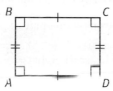

The opposite sides of a rectangle are equal in length. Also, the diagonals of a rectangle have equal length and bisect each other.

Square

A square is a rectangle with four equal sides.

Areas of Quadrilaterals

To find the area of a rectangle, you multiply the lengths of any two adjacent sides, called the length and width.

Area of a rectangle = length × width = lw.

To find the area of a square, since length and width are equal, you say:

Area of a square = (side)^2 = s^2.

In the rare event that you have to find the area of a parallelogram (a quadrilateral with equal and parallel opposite sides), multiply the base and the height.

Area of a parallelogram = base × height = bh

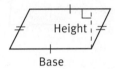

The diagonals of a parallelogram do not necessarily have equal length, but they do bisect each other.

The area of a trapezoid—a quadrilateral with exactly one pair of parallel sides—can be calculated as follows:

Area of a trapezoid = $\frac{1}{2}$ (the sum of the bases)(height) = $\frac{1}{2}(b_1 + b_2)(h)$

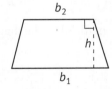

In-Format Question: Polygons on the GMAT

Now let's use the Kaplan Method on a Problem Solving question dealing with polygons:

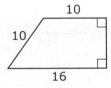

What is the perimeter of the figure above?

- ○ 43
- ○ 44
- ○ 46
- ○ 47
- ○ 48

STEP 1: ANALYZE THE QUESTION

If this were a simple square or triangle, your work would be quick. However, when given an unfamiliar shape on the GMAT, you can often split the figure into smaller, familiar shapes to calculate the needed sides or angles.

STEP 2: STATE THE TASK

The task is to solve for the perimeter of the figure, or the sum of the length of its sides. To do this, you need to determine the length of the unlabeled side.

STEP 3: APPROACH STRATEGICALLY

Pattern Recognition helps you recognize that this polygon can be broken down into smaller, more manageable figures. In this case, you can break the shape into a rectangle and a right triangle. Drop a perpendicular from the left endpoint of the top horizontal side of length 10 to the bottom horizontal side of length 16.

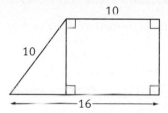

This perpendicular will divide the quadrilateral into a right triangle and a rectangle. Because the lengths of the opposite sides of a rectangle are equal, the horizontal sides of the rectangle both have a length of 10. This means that the horizontal leg of the right triangle will have a length of 16 − 10, or 6.

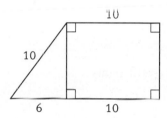

At this point, you might recognize that the right triangle is a special right triangle. It is a 3:4:5 right triangle, and each side of it is a member of the 3 to 4 to 5 ratio multiplied by 2. The leg of length 6 is 2 × 3, and the hypotenuse of length 10 is 2 × 5. So the length of the other leg is 2 × 4 = 8. Because opposite sides of a rectangle are equal, the vertical side of the rectangle at the right also has a length of 8.

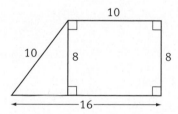

Now you can find the perimeter of the quadrilateral. The sum of the length of the figure's sides is 16 + 10 + 10 + 8 = 44. That's choice (**B**).

If you were short on time for this question, you could use Critical Thinking to strategically eliminate a few of the answer choices. In any right triangle, the hypotenuse is always the longest side of the triangle. So in the figure, the side shared by the triangle and rectangle must be less than 10, since it makes up one of the legs of the right triangle.

If the short side of the rectangle were equal to 10, then the perimeter of the total quadrilateral would be $10 + 10 + 10 + 16 = 46$. Since you know that one of the sides must be less than 10, the perimeter must be less than 46. This definitively eliminates **(C)**, **(D)**, and **(E)**, and you have a much better chance of picking the correct answer.

STEP 4: CONFIRM YOUR ANSWER

Read back over the problem, confirming that your solution accurately follows the information in the question.

TAKEAWAYS: POLYGONS

- A polygon is a closed plane figure formed by three or more line segments.
  - Perimeter = sum of all sides
- The sum of the interior angle measures of a polygon with n sides is equal to $(n - 2)180°$.
- Special case: parallelograms (quadrilaterals whose opposite sides are parallel)
  - Parallelograms include rectangles and squares.
  - Opposite sides are equal.
  - Opposite angles are equal.
  - Area = (base)(height)
  - The diagonals bisect each other.
- Special case: trapezoid
  - Area = $\frac{1}{2}$ (the sum of the bases)(height)

Practice Set: Polygons on the GMAT

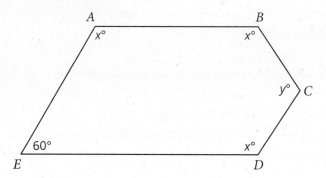

Note: Not drawn to scale.

7. In the figure shown above, *AB* and *DE* are parallel. What is the value of *y*?

   ○ 110

   ○ 120

   ○ 135

   ○ 150

   ○ 160

0. A contractor uses half of the available concrete to pour an 8-foot by 12-foot rectangular base for a monument. If she uses the rest of the concrete to create a uniform-width walkway all the way around the base of the monument, using the same amount of concrete per square foot as for the base, what is the maximum possible width of the walkway?

   ○ 1 foot

   ○ 2 feet

   ○ 3 feet

   ○ 4 feet

   ○ 6 feet

9. Is the length of a side of square *S* greater than the length of a side of equilateral triangle *T*?

   (1) The sum of the lengths of a side of *S* and a side of *T* is 22.

   (2) The ratio of the perimeter of square *S* to the perimeter of triangle *T* is 5 to 6.

Circles

Circle Concepts and Formulas

A circle is the set of all points in a plane at the same distance from a certain point. This point is called the **center** of the circle.

A circle is labeled by its center point: circle O means the circle with center point O. Two circles of different size with the same center are called **concentric**.

Diameter

A diameter is a line segment that connects two points on the circle and passes through the center of the circle. In circle O, AB is a diameter.

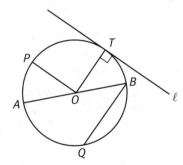

Radius

A radius is a line segment from the center of the circle to any point on the circle. The radius of a circle is one-half the length of the diameter. In circle O, OA, OB, OP, and OT are radii.

Chord

A chord is a line segment joining two points on the circle. In circle O, QB and AB are chords. A diameter of a circle is a longest chord of the circle.

Central Angle

A central angle is an angle formed by two radii. In circle O, $\angle AOP$, $\angle POB$, $\angle AOB$, along with others, are central angles.

Tangent

A line that touches only one point on the circumference of the circle is **tangent** to that circle. A line drawn tangent to a circle is perpendicular to the radius at the point of tangency. Line ℓ is tangent to circle O at point T.

Circumference and Arc Length

The distance around a circle is called the **circumference**. The number π ("pi") is the ratio of a circle's circumference to its diameter. The value of π is 3.14159265 …, usually approximated as 3.14. For the GMAT, it is usually sufficient to remember that π is a little more than 3.

Since π equals the ratio of the circumference to the diameter, a formula for the circumference is:

$$C = \pi d$$

or

$$C = 2\pi r$$

An **arc** is a portion of the circumference of a circle. In the figure below, AB is an arc of the circle that spans central angle AOB. The shorter distance between A and B along the circle is called the **minor arc**; the longer distance AXB is the **major arc**. An arc that is exactly half the circumference of the circle is called a **semicircle** (in other words, half a circle).

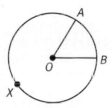

The length of an arc is the same fraction of a circle's circumference as its degree measure is of the degree measure of the circle ($360°$). For an arc with a central angle measuring n degrees:

$$\text{Arc length} = \left(\frac{n}{360}\right) \times \text{circumference}$$

$$= \frac{n}{360} \times 2\pi r$$

Example:

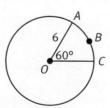

What is the length of arc ABC of the circle with center O above?

Since circumference $= 2\pi r$ and the radius is 6, the circumference is $2 \times \pi \times 6 = 12\pi$.

Since $\angle AOC$ measures $60°$, the arc is $\frac{60}{360}$, or one-sixth, of the circumference.

Therefore, the length of the arc is $\frac{1}{6} \times 12\pi$, or 2π.

Inscribed Angle and Arc Length

An **inscribed angle** is one that opens up from the edge of a circle instead of its center. Here, angle *ABC* is inscribed.

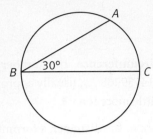

An inscribed angle also has a relationship with minor arc length. For an inscribed angle measuring *n* degrees:

$$\text{Arc length} = \left(\frac{n}{180}\right) \times \text{circumference}$$

In other words, an angle that's inscribed defines an arc twice as long as one defined by a central angle of equal angle measure.

Area of a Circle

The area of a circle is given by this formula:

$$\text{Area} = \pi r^2$$

A **sector** is a portion of the circle bounded by two radii and an arc. In the circle below with center *O*, *OAB* is a sector. To determine the area of a sector of a circle, use a similar method to the one you used to find the length of an arc: determine what fraction of 360° is in the degree measure of the central angle of the sector, then multiply that fraction by the area of the circle.

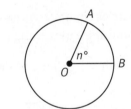

$$\text{Area of sector} = \left(\frac{n}{360}\right) \times (\text{Area of circle})$$

$$= \frac{n}{360} \times \pi r^2$$

Example:

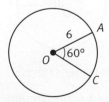

What is the area of sector *AOC* in the circle with center *O* above?

Since ∠*AOC* measures 60°, a 60° "slice" is $\frac{60}{360}$, or one-sixth, of the circle. So the sector has an area of $\frac{1}{6} \times \pi r^2 = \frac{1}{6} \times \pi(6)^2 = \frac{1}{6} \times 36\pi = 6\pi$.

In-Format Question: Circles on the GMAT

Now let's use the Kaplan Method on a Problem Solving question dealing with circles:

> If the diameter of a circle increases by 50 percent, by what percent will the area of the circle increase?

- ○ 25%
- ○ 50%
- ○ 100%
- ○ 125%
- ○ 225%

STEP 1: ANALYZE THE QUESTION

For any geometry question without a figure, it is important to draw a quick sketch of the described figure to avoid simple mistakes on Test Day. So on your notepad, you should draw two circles: (1) the original circle and (2) the circle with increased diameter.

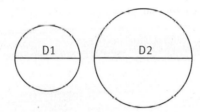

Now look at the question stem again. Notice that this is a percent question in disguise and that you are not given the original or final diameter. This is a great candidate for picking numbers.

STEP 2: STATE THE TASK

You want the percent increase of area from the small circle to the large one. If you use picking numbers, the task will be much more straightforward, as you will be solving for the increase between two numbers rather than two algebraic expressions.

STEP 3: APPROACH STRATEGICALLY

To make your calculations manageable, consider that the area of a circle is given in terms of its radius and the radius is $\frac{1}{2}$ of the diameter. So you want the diameter to be a multiple of 2. Suppose that the original diameter is 4. Then the original radius is $\frac{1}{2}(4) = 2$. Therefore, the area of the original circle is

$$\pi r^2 = \pi(2)^2 = 4\pi$$

The diameter of 4 is increased by 50%, or $\frac{1}{2}$. The new diameter is $4 + \frac{1}{2}(4) = 4 + 2 = 6$. Therefore, the new radius is $\frac{1}{2}(6) = 3$. The area of the new circle is:

$$\pi r^2 = \pi(3)^2 = 9\pi$$

To calculate the percent increase between the two circles, use the following equation:

$$\text{Percent increase} = \frac{\text{Difference}}{\text{Original}} \times 100\%$$

$$\text{Difference} = 9\pi - 4\pi = 5\pi$$

$$\text{Percent increase} = \frac{5\pi}{4\pi} \times 100\%$$

$$= \frac{5}{4} \times 100\%$$

$$= 1.25 \times 100\%$$

$$= 125\%$$

The correct answer is **(D)**.

STEP 4: CONFIRM YOUR ANSWER

Be very careful how you apply the percent increase equation. A common error is to use the wrong value in the denominator. Another is to solve not for the percent difference but for how much one amount is as a percent of another. **(E)**, for example, is the answer to "The area of the circle after the increase is what percent of its original area?" Always take a moment to confirm that your answer choice makes sense logically.

TAKEAWAYS: CIRCLES

- Area $= \pi r^2$
- Circumference $= 2\pi r$
- The length of an arc as a fraction of a circle's circumference is equal to the degree measure of the corresponding central angle as a fraction of 360.
- The area of a sector as a fraction of a circle's area is equal to the degree measure of the corresponding central angle as a fraction of 360.
- A line that has exactly one point in common with a circle is tangent to the circle and perpendicular to the radius.

Practice Set: Circles on the GMAT

10. The length of an arc on circle *C* formed by a central angle measuring 60° is 12. What is the diameter of the circle?

    ○ $\frac{18}{\pi}$

    ○ $\frac{36}{\pi}$

    ○ 6π

    ○ $\frac{72}{\pi}$

    ○ 12π

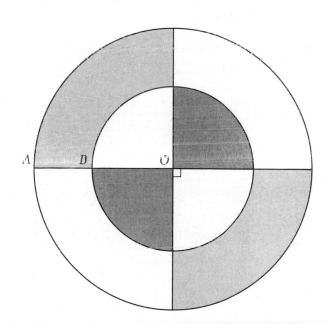

11. The figure above represents a circular garden, with center *O*. *AB* is 4 feet, and *BO* is 3 feet. The gardener plans to plant sunflowers in the two light gray sections and tulips in the two dark gray sections. How much more area, in square feet, will be covered by sunflowers than tulips?

    ○ $\frac{9}{2}\pi$

    ○ 8π

    ○ $\frac{31}{2}\pi$

    ○ 20π

    ○ 31π

12. If two circles overlap each other, what is the area of that overlap?

    (1) The edge of each circle intersects the center of the other circle.

    (2) The sum of the circumferences of the two circles is 12π.

Multiple Figures

LEARNING OBJECTIVES

In this section, you will learn how to:

- Describe the multiple-figures scenarios that commonly appear
- Break down complex figures into simpler components
- Apply the Kaplan Methods for Problem Solving and Data Sufficiency to questions dealing with multiple figures

You can expect to see some questions on the GMAT that deal with multiple figures. They test your understanding of various geometrical concepts and relationships, not just your ability to memorize a few formulas. The hypotenuse of a right triangle may be the side of a neighboring rectangle or the diameter of a circumscribed circle. Keep looking for the relationships between the different figures until you find one that leads you to the answer.

Common Multiple-Figure Scenarios

Shaded and Unshaded Regions

One common kind of multiple-figures question involves irregularly shaped regions formed by two or more overlapping figures, often with one region shaded. When you are asked to find the area of such a region, either or both of the following methods may work:

1. Break up that shaded area into smaller pieces you know the formula for; find the area of each using the proper formula; add those areas together.

2. Find the area of the whole figure and the area of the unshaded region and subtract the latter from the former.

Example:

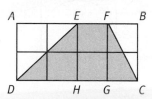

Rectangle *ABCD* above has an area of 72 and is composed of 8 equal squares. Find the area of the shaded region.

For this problem, you can use either of the two approaches. First, divide 8 into 72 to get the area of each square, which is 9. Since the area of a square equals the length of its side squared, each side of the small squares must have length 3. Now you have a choice of methods.

1. You can break up the trapezoid into right triangle *DEH*, rectangle *EFGH*, and right triangle *FGC*. The area of triangle *DEH* is $\frac{1}{2} \times 6 \times 6$, or 18. The area of rectangle *EFGH* is 3×6, or 18. The area of triangle *FGC* is $\frac{1}{2} \times 6 \times 3$, or 9. The total area is $18 + 18 + 9$, or 45. You could also use the formula for the area of a trapezoid, $\frac{1}{2}(b_1 + b_2)(h)$, to get the same result:
    $$\frac{1}{2}(3 + 12)(6) = \frac{1}{2}(15)(6) = 15 \times 3 = 45.$$

2. The area of the whole rectangle *ABCD* is 72. The area of unshaded triangle *AED* is $\frac{1}{2} \times 6 \times 6$, or 18. The area of unshaded triangle *FBC* is $\frac{1}{2} \times 6 \times 3$, or 9. Therefore, the total unshaded area is $18 + 9 = 27$. The area of the shaded region is the area of the rectangle minus the unshaded area, or $72 - 27 = 45$.

Inscribed and Circumscribed Figures

A polygon is **inscribed** in a circle if all the vertices of the polygon lie on the circle. A polygon is **circumscribed** about a circle if all the sides of the polygon are tangent to the circle.

Square *ABCD* is inscribed in circle *O*. (We can also say that circle *O* is circumscribed about square *ABCD*.)

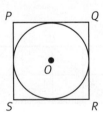

Square *PQRS* is circumscribed about circle *O*. (We can also say that circle *O* is inscribed in square *PQRS*.)

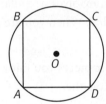

A triangle inscribed in a semicircle such that one side of the triangle coincides with the diameter of the semicircle is a right triangle.

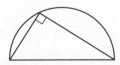

In-Format Question: Multiple Figures on the GMAT

Now let's use the Kaplan Method on a Problem Solving question dealing with multiple figures:

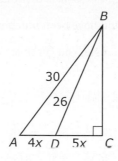

What is the length of *BC* in the figure above?

- ○ 10
- ○ 16
- ○ 18
- ○ 20
- ○ 24

STEP 1: ANALYZE THE QUESTION

As with any complicated shape on the GMAT, you can begin by breaking this figure into two simpler shapes: triangle *ABC* and triangle *DBC*. Analyze them separately first.

Triangle *ABC*: *BC* is one leg of this right triangle. The other leg, *AC*, is equal to the sum of $4x + 5x = 9x$. The hypotenuse is 30.

Triangle *DBC*: *BC* is also one leg of this right triangle. The other leg is $DC = 5x$, and the hypotenuse is 26.

Use your Pattern Recognition skills to note that the two hypotenuses are each consistent with special right triangles. The hypotenuse $BD = 26$, which is 13×2, so *DBC* might be a 5:12:13 right triangle. That would make the other sides $12 \times 2 = 24$ and $5 \times 2 = 10$.

The hypotenuse $BA = 30$, which is 5×6, so it might be part of a 3:4:5 triangle. That would make the other sides $3 \times 6 = 18$ and $4 \times 6 = 24$. If these are special right triangles, which you know the GMAT likes to use, then they'd share a side length of 24. The side they share is *BC*, so it would be reasonable to guess right now that $BC = 24$.

STEP 2: STATE THE TASK

You are solving for *BC*. Since *BC* must be 24 if these two triangles are special right triangles (again, very common on the GMAT), it would be a very good idea to guess **(E)** if you were behind on time.

STEP 3: APPROACH STRATEGICALLY

Since you already suspect that $BC = 24$, that *BDC* is a 5:12:13 triangle, and that *ABC* is a 3:4:5 triangle, you should try to confirm it. Use the special triangle ratios to see what one triangle would be if $BC = 24$ and check whether that makes sense with the other triangle. If it does, *BC* is indeed 24.

If DBC is a 5:12:13, then DC would equal 10. So $5x$ may be 10, and x may be 2. If $x = 2$, then AC, which equals $9x$, would equal 18. That's exactly what it should equal if ABC is a 3:4:5 triangle, so everything in the figure works with $BC = 24$. The correct answer is **(E)**. In essence, this was a backsolving solution.

You could have solved with algebra, but it would have been much more time-consuming.

Applying the Pythagorean theorem to each triangle, you get this:

Triangle ABC:

$$(BC)^2 + (9x)^2 = (30)^2$$
$$(BC)^2 + 81x^2 = 900$$
$$(BC)^2 = 900 - 81x^2$$

Triangle DBC:

$$(BC)^2 + (5x)^2 = (26)^2$$
$$(BC)^2 + 25x^2 = 676$$
$$(BC)^2 = 676 - 25x^2$$

To solve for BC, you must first calculate x. To do so, you can set the two equations equal to one another:

$$900 - 81x^2 = 676 - 25x^2$$
$$56x^2 = 224$$
$$x^2 = \frac{224}{56} = 4$$
$$x = 2 \text{ or } x = -2$$

Remember that in the context of a geometry question, all side lengths must be positive, so x must equal 2.

Now you can plug this value for x into either of your original equations to find BC. $BC = 24$.

Triangle ABC: The length of leg AC is $9x = 9(2) = 18$.

Since $AC = 18 = 6 \times 3$, the hypotenuse $AB = 30 = 6 \times 5$, and $BC = 24 = 6 \times 4$, you've just proved that ABC is a 3:4:5 right triangle.

Triangle DBC: The length of leg DC is $5x = 5(2) = 10$.

Since $DC = 10 = 2 \times 5$, the hypotenuse $DB = 26 = 2 \times 13$, and $BC = 24 = 2 \times 12$, you've just proved that DBC is a 5:12:13 right triangle.

The correct answer is **(E)**.

Notice how the solution that doesn't rely on using the suspected Pythagorean triples is much more complex and time-consuming. Use Critical Thinking and Pattern Recognition to your advantage here. Special right triangles are immense time-savers, and the GMAT uses them all the time—two big reasons why it makes sense to use them whenever you suspect that they appear.

STEP 4: CONFIRM YOUR ANSWER

Reread the question and the figure, making sure that you didn't misread anything or solve for the wrong measure. Beware of traps: if you'd solved for AC, you'd have selected **(C)**, and if you'd solved for DC, you'd have selected **(A)**.

TAKEAWAYS: MULTIPLE FIGURES

- Difficult geometry questions often contain complex figures. The key to answering these questions is to break the figures down into simpler figures.

- Look for measurements that are shared across figures so that you can take information about one figure and apply it to another.

Practice Set: Multiple Figures on the GMAT

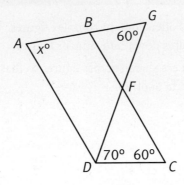

13. In the figure above, what is the value of *x*?

    (1)   *AD* ∥ *BC*

    (2)   ∠*GBC* = 70°

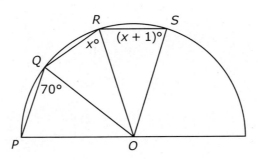

14. In the figure above, point *O* is the center of the semicircle, and *PQ* is parallel to *OS*. What is the measure of ∠*ROS*?

    ○   34°

    ○   36°

    ○   54.5°

    ○   72°

    ○   73°

15. An isosceles triangle is inscribed in a circle such that one of the triangle's sides coincides with the circle's longest chord. If the measure of another side of the triangle is 5, what is the difference between the area of the circle and the area of the triangle?

   ○ $\frac{25}{2}(1-\pi)$

   ○ $25(\pi - 1)$

   ○ $\frac{25}{2}(\pi + 1)$

   ○ $\frac{25}{2}(\pi - 1)$

   ○ $\frac{25}{4}(\pi - 1)$

Solids

A **solid** is a three-dimensional figure (a figure having length, width, and height) and is, therefore, rather difficult to represent accurately on a two-dimensional page. Figures are drawn in perspective, giving them the appearance of depth. If a diagram represents a three-dimensional figure, that fact will be specified in the accompanying text.

Fortunately, only a few types of solids appear with any frequency on the GMAT: rectangular solids (including cubes) and cylinders. These are both uniform solids (solids in which the measure of each dimension is constant through the entire object). Other types, such as spheres, may appear, but these questions typically will involve only understanding the solid's properties and not applying any special formula.

Terminology

Here are the terms used to describe the common solids:

Vertex

The vertices of a solid are the points at its corners. For example, a cube has eight vertices.

Edge

The edges of a solid are the line segments that connect the vertices and form the sides of each face of the solid. A cube has 12 edges.

Face

The faces of a solid are the polygons that are the boundaries of the solid. A cube has six faces, all squares.

Volume

The volume of a solid is the amount of space enclosed by that solid. The volume of any uniform solid is equal to the area of its base times its height.

Surface Area

In general, the surface area of a solid is equal to the sum of the areas of the solid's faces.

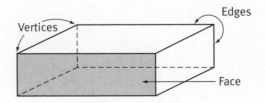

Rectangular Solid

A rectangular solid is a solid with six rectangular faces (all edges meet at right angles). Examples are cereal boxes, bricks, etc.

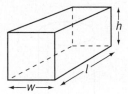

Volume = Area of base × Height = Length × Width × Height

$$V = l \times w \times h$$

Surface area = Sum of areas of faces

$$SA = 2lw + 2lh + 2wh$$

Diagonals in Rectangular Solids

It's common for difficult geometry questions to ask you to calculate the length of a rectangular solid's diagonal (one that runs from lower-front-left to upper-back right, for example).

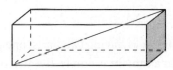

There's a simple formula to calculate the diagonal. It looks a lot like the Pythagorean theorem (in fact, it's derived using that theorem).

$$\text{Diagonal}^2 = \text{Length}^2 + \text{Width}^2 + \text{Height}^2$$

Cube

A cube is a special rectangular solid with all edges equal ($l = w = h$), such as a die or a sugar cube. All faces of a cube are squares.

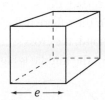

Volume = Area of base × Height = Edge³

$$V = l \times w \times h = e^3$$

Surface area = Sum of areas of faces = 6 × Edge²

$$SA = 6e^2$$

Cylinder

A cylinder is a uniform solid whose horizontal cross section is a circle. An example is a soup can. You need two pieces of information to find the volume and surface area of a cylinder: the radius of the base and the height.

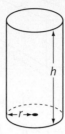

Volume = Area of base × Height

$$V = \pi r^2 \times h$$

Lateral surface area (LSA) = Circumference of base × Height

$$LSA = 2\pi r \times h$$

Total surface area = Areas of bases + LSA

$$SA = 2\pi r^2 + 2\pi rh$$

You can think of the surface area of a cylinder as having two parts: one part is the top and bottom (the circles), and the other part is the lateral surface. In a can, for example, the area of either the top or the bottom is just the area of the circle, or lid, which represents the top; hence, πr^2 for the top and πr^2 for the bottom, yielding a total of $2\pi r^2$. For the lateral surface area, the area around the can, think of removing the can's label. When unrolled, it's actually in the shape of a rectangle. One side is the height of the can, and the other side is the distance around the circle, or circumference. Hence, its area is $h \times (2\pi r)$, or $2\pi rh$. Thus, the total surface area is $2\pi r^2 + 2\pi rh$.

Sphere

A sphere is made up of all the points in space a certain distance from a center point; it's like a three-dimensional circle. The distance from the center to a point on the sphere is the radius of the sphere. A basketball is a good example of a sphere. A sphere is not a uniform solid; the cross sections are all circles, but they are of different sizes. (In other words, a slice of a basketball from the middle is bigger than a slice from the top.)

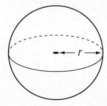

It is not important to know how to find the volume or surface area of a sphere, but occasionally a question might require you to understand what a sphere is.

In-Format Question: Solids on the GMAT

Now let's use the Kaplan Method on a Data Sufficiency question dealing with solids:

> A rectangular fish tank has uniform depth. How long does it take to fill the tank with water?
>
> (1) The tank is 4 feet wide and 10 feet long.
>
> (2) The tank is filled with water at a rate of 1.5 cubic feet per minute.

STEP 1: ANALYZE THE QUESTION STEM

This Value question requires you to determine whether there is sufficient information to find how long it takes to fill a rectangular tank with a uniform depth with water. Not only do you need the volume of the tank, but you also need the rate at which the tank is being filled.

STEP 2: EVALUATE THE STATEMENTS USING 12TEN

Statement (1) tells you that the tank is 4 feet wide and 10 feet long. Because you are not given any information about the depth, you cannot determine the volume of the tank. Furthermore, you are not given any information about the rate at which the tank is filled with water. This statement is insufficient. You can eliminate (**A**) and (**D**).

Statement (2) tells you that the tank is being filled at a rate of 1.5 cubic feet per minute. You have no information with which to determine the volume of the tank, so you cannot determine how long it will take to fill the tank with water. Eliminate (**B**).

Now you must combine statements. You know the length of the tank, the width of the tank, and the rate at which it is being filled. Because you do not know the depth of the tank, you cannot determine its volume. Because you cannot determine the volume of the tank, you cannot solve for how long it takes to fill the tank with water. The two statements taken together are insufficient, and (**E**) is correct.

TAKEAWAYS: SOLIDS

- Almost all solids on the GMAT are uniform solids (solids in which the measure of each dimension is constant through the entire object).
- To determine the volume of a uniform solid, multiply the area of the base by the height.
  - Volume of cylinder $= \pi r^2 h$
  - Volume of rectangular solid $= l \times w \times h$

Practice Set: Solids on the GMAT

16. A cylindrical tank with a height of 8 feet is completely full of gasoline. This gasoline is pumped into an empty cylindrical tank with a diameter of 24 feet and a height of 18 feet. If the gasoline reaches a height of 2 feet in this tank, what is the diameter, in feet, of the original tank?

   ○ 3
   ○ 6
   ○ 8
   ○ 10
   ○ 12

17. A rectangular solid has the dimensions 4, 5, and x. If the number of units in the solid's volume and the number of units in that solid's surface area are the same, what is the sum of the areas of the two largest faces of the solid?

   ○ 20
   ○ 40
   ○ 100
   ○ 200
   ○ 400

18. A cube with an edge length of 6 contains the largest possible sphere that completely fits inside of it. If the volume V of a sphere with radius r is given by the formula $V = \frac{4}{3}\pi r^3$, what is the volume of the empty space inside the cube?

   ○ $36(\pi^3 - 6)$
   ○ 36π
   ○ $36(6 - \pi)$
   ○ $36(\pi - 1)$
   ○ $36(4 - \pi)$

Coordinate Geometry

Concepts and Formulas in Coordinate Geometry

Slope

The slope of a line on a coordinate plane tells you how steeply that line goes up or down. If a line gets higher as you move to the right, it has a positive slope. If it goes down as you move to the right, it has a negative slope. To find the slope of a line, use the following formula:

$$\text{Slope} = \frac{\text{Rise}}{\text{Run}} = \frac{\text{Change in } y}{\text{Change in } x}$$

Rise means the difference between the y coordinate values of the two points on the line, and *run* means the difference between the x-coordinate values.

Example: What is the slope of the line that contains the points $(1,2)$ and $(4,-5)$?

$$\text{Slope} = \frac{-5-2}{4-1} = \frac{-7}{3} = -\frac{7}{3}$$

To determine the slope of a line from an equation, put the equation into slope-intercept form: $y = mx + b$, where the slope is m.

Example: What is the slope of the line given by the equation $3x + 2y = 4$?

$$3x + 2y = 4$$
$$2y = -3x + 4$$
$$y = -\frac{3}{2}x + 2, \text{ so } m \text{ is } -\frac{3}{2}$$

The word *intercept* in "slope-intercept form" is there because b is the value of the y-intercept—the point at which the line crosses the y-axis. Another way to think of that is that $(0,b)$ will be a point on the line.

Perpendicular lines have slopes that are negative reciprocals of one another. For the line in this example, with a slope of $-\frac{3}{2}$, a perpendicular line would have a slope of $\frac{2}{3}$.

Calculating Distance on the Coordinate Plane

To determine the distance between any two points on a coordinate plane, you can use the Pythagorean theorem.

Example: What is the length of *AB*?

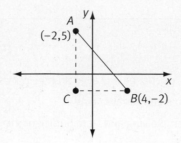

Sketch lines from points *A* and *B* parallel to the axes. They will form a right triangle, and the intersection will have the same *x*-coordinate as one point and the same *y*-coordinate as the other. Because the new lines aren't diagonal, their length is easy to figure out. In this example, the length of *AC* is 7 because the line drops down 5 from *A* to the *x*-axis and then another 2 to *C*. Similarly, the length of *BC* is 6.

Now you can use the Pythagorean theorem to calculate *AB*:

$$AB^2 = BC^2 + AC^2$$
$$AB^2 = 6^2 + 7^2$$
$$AB^2 = 36 + 49$$
$$AB^2 = 85$$
$$AB = \sqrt{85}$$

In-Format Question: Coordinate Geometry on the GMAT

Now let's use the Kaplan Method on a Data Sufficiency question dealing with coordinate geometry:

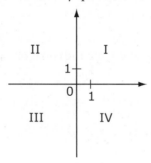

If $st > 0$, in which quadrant of the coordinate system above does the point (s, t) lie?

(1) $(s, -t)$ lies in quadrant II.

(2) s is negative.

STEP 1: ANALYZE THE QUESTION STEM

In this Value question, you are asked to determine which quadrant the point (s, t) is in. You are told in the question stem that $st > 0$, which means that *s* and *t* are either both positive or both negative. This is only true in quadrants I and III.

STEP 2: EVALUATE THE STATEMENTS USING 12TEN

Statement (1): You know that $(s, -t)$ lies in quadrant II, which tells you that s is negative and $-t$ is positive, so t must be negative. Because s and t are both negative, (s, t) is in quadrant III, and the statement is sufficient. Eliminate **(B)**, **(C)**, and **(E)**.

Statement (2): You are told that s is negative, which is also sufficient, because you already deduced from the question stem that s and t have the same sign.

The correct answer is **(D)**.

TAKEAWAYS: COORDINATE GEOMETRY

- Slope of a line $= \dfrac{\text{Rise}}{\text{Run}} = \dfrac{\text{Change in } y}{\text{Change in } x}$

- The equation of a non-vertical straight line in the two-dimensional coordinate plane is typically expressed in the form $y = mx + b$, where m is the slope and b is the point at which the line intercepts the y-axis.

- Be aware that difficult geometry questions may present lines in the form $x = cy + d$. In this equation, c is NOT the slope! You need to put the line in $y = mx + b$ form to find the slope.

- The slope of a line is the negative reciprocal of the slope of a perpendicular line.

- One way to find a distance in the coordinate plane is to use the Pythagorean theorem.

Practice Set: Lines and Angles on the GMAT

19. Line ℓ_1 is given by the equation $y = mx + 3$, and line ℓ_2 is given by the equation $y = nx - 7$, where m and n are constants. Is ℓ_1 parallel to ℓ_2?

    (1) $m^2 - n^2 = 0$

    (2) mn is positive.

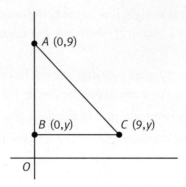

20. In the rectangular coordinate system above, triangle ABC has an area of 27 square units. Vertex A is at point $(0,9)$, vertex B is at point $(0,y)$, and vertex C is at point $(9,y)$. What is the value of y?

    ○ 1

    ○ 2

    ○ 3

    ○ 4

    ○ 6

21. In the *xy*-coordinate system, if (*m,n*) and (*m* + 2, *n* + *k*) are two points on the line with the equation *x* = 2*y* + 5, then *k* =

   ○ $\frac{1}{2}$

   ○   1

   ○   2

   ○ $\frac{5}{2}$

   ○   4

Answer Key

Practice Set: Lines and Angles on the GMAT

1. A
2. C
3. E

Practice Set: Triangles on the GMAT

4. D
5. D
6. C

Practice Set: Polygons on the GMAT

7. B
8. B
9. B

Practice Set: Circles on the GMAT

10. D
11. C
12. C

Practice Set: Multiple Figures on the GMAT

13. A
14. A
15. D

Practice Set: Solids on the GMAT

16. E
17. D
18. C

Practice Set: Coordinate Geometry on the GMAT

19. C
20. C
21. B

Answers and Explanations

Practice Set: Lines and Angles on the GMAT

1. **(A)**

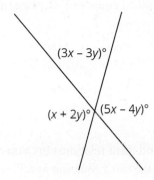

Note: Not drawn to scale.

In the figure above, what is the value of y?

- ○ 36
- ○ 54
- ○ 90
- ○ 126
- ○ 180

STEP 1: ANALYZE THE QUESTION

There are several relationships that you can deduce from the diagram:

(1) Vertical angles are equal, so $x + 2y = 5x - 4y$.

(2) Angles along a straight line add up to $180°$, so $x + 2y + 3x - 3y = 180$.

(3) By the same logic, $5x - 4y + 3x - 3y = 180$.

STEP 2: STATE THE TASK

The question only asks about the value of y. However, there are two variables, x and y, which means you need two equations to solve for the value of either individual variable.

STEP 3: APPROACH STRATEGICALLY

Any two of the relationships identified in the first step are sufficient to determine the value of y. For example, using the first two relationships, you can start by simplifying the first equation:

$$x + 2y = 5x - 4y$$
$$6y = 4x$$

Simplify the second equation as follows:

$$x + 2y + 3x - 3y = 180$$
$$4x - y = 180$$

Note that the $4x$ term appears in both simplified equations. Replace the $4x$ in the second equation with the $6y$ from the first equation and solve for y:

$$6y - y = 180$$
$$5y = 180$$
$$y = 36$$

(A) is correct.

Alternatively, if you chose to use the first and third relationships, you can use the $6y = 4x$ relationship from simplifying the first equation and simplify the third equation as follows:

$$5x - 4y + 3x - 3y = 180$$
$$8x - 7y = 180$$

Note that $8x = 2 \times 4x$, which means you can replace it with $2 \times 6y = 12y$. Plug in $12y$ for $8x$ and solve for y:

$$12y - 7y = 180$$
$$5y = 180$$
$$y = 36$$

This again matches **(A)**.

Another alternative is to use the two supplementary angle relationships. Based on the previous work, the two equations you have from simplifying the equations are $4x - y = 180$ and $8x - 7y = 180$. Double the first equation to yield $8x - 2y = 360$ so that the x term has the same coefficient in both equations. Subtract the second equation from the first and solve for y:

$$8x - 2y = 360$$
$$\underline{-[8x - 7y = 180]}$$
$$5y = 180$$
$$y = 36$$

Once more, **(A)** is correct.

STEP 4: CONFIRM YOUR ANSWER

Make sure that you copied the expressions correctly from the figure and solved for the value of y, not x, which is **(B)** 54.

2. (C)

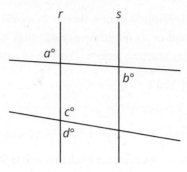

In the figure above, if lines r and s are parallel, what is the value of $a + b$?

(1) $c - a = 25$

(2) $a - d = 15$

STEP 1: ANALYZE THE QUESTION STEM

This is a Value question. You're given a figure and told that lines r and s are parallel, which makes the other lines in the figure transversals. When a transversal intersects a pair of parallel lines, all acute angles formed by that transversal are equal, and all obtuse angles formed are equal. Therefore, since angle a and angle b are both acute angles on the same transversal, they're equal to each other. So in order to determine the value of $a + b$, all you need to know is the value of either angle. Angles c and d form a straight line, so their sum is $180°$.

STEP 2: EVALUATE THE STATEMENTS USING 12TEN

Statement (1) indicates that $c - a = 25$. This doesn't give you enough information to pin down the value of any of the angles. Eliminate (**A**) and (**D**).

Statement (2) says that $a - d = 15$. Similar to Statement (1), this tells you that angle a is greater than angle d but gives no clue as to their values. Eliminate (**B**) and evaluate the statements together.

Restate the equation in Statement (2) as $a = d + 15$. Then substitute $d + 15$ for a in the equation in Statement (1) to get $c - (d + 15) = 25$, so $c - d - 15 = 25$ and $c - d = 40$. You know that $c + d = 180$. Add these two equations to eliminate the d terms:

$$
\begin{array}{r}
c - d = 40 \\
+[c + d = 180] \\
\hline
2c = 220
\end{array}
$$

You wouldn't do the math for this Data Sufficiency question, but you could then determine that $c = 110$ and plug that into $c - a = 25$ to get the value of a. From that, you would also know the value of b, since $a = b$, and you could find the sum $a + b$. So, together, the statements are sufficient. (**C**) is correct.

3. **(E)**

A certain line segment rotates consistently in one direction in 45° increments around one of its endpoints *E*. The segment loses half of its length every 45° that it rotates, and it stops rotating when it reaches less than 5 percent of its starting length. Did the segment stop rotating?

(1) The segment rotated at least 180°.

(2) The segment made at most 5 movements.

STEP 1: ANALYZE THE QUESTION STEM

Simplify the question stem by determining the number of degrees that the segment has to rotate to be less than 5% of its starting length. Consider picking 100 to represent the segment's initial length, so when the segment is 5% of its starting length, its length is 5.

- After the first 45° rotation, the segment measures one-half of 100, or 50.
- After 90°, it measures 25.
- After 135°, it measures 12.5.
- After 180°, it measures 6.25.
- After 225°, it measures half of 6.25. This is less than 5.

The segment will therefore reach less than 5% of its starting length after moving five 45° increments, or 225°. Thus, the question becomes, "Did the segment make 5 movements?" or "Did it rotate 225°?"

STEP 2: EVALUATE THE STATEMENTS USING 12TEN

Statement (1) says that the segment rotated at least 180°. If the segment rotated exactly 180°, the answer is no. However, the segment could have rotated 225°, and then the answer would be yes. Statement (1) is insufficient, so eliminate **(A)** and **(D)**.

Statement (2) says that the segment made no more than 5 movements. If the segment made 5 movements, the answer is yes, but if the segment made fewer movements, the answer is no. Statement (2) is insufficient, so eliminate **(B)** and combine the statements.

Combining Statements (1) and (2) produces this statement: the segment rotated at least 180° *and* made at most 5 movements. This leaves open the possibility that it moved 4 times (for 180°) or 5 times (for 225°). The answer to the question could still be yes or no, so **(E)** is correct.

Practice Set: Triangles on the GMAT

4. **(D)**

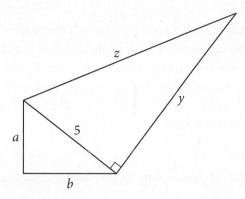

Based on the figure shown, which of the following could be true?

    I. $a = b$

    II. $y = z$

    III. $a^2 + b^2 = z^2 - y^2$

○   None

○   I only

○   II only

○   I and III only

○   I, II, and III

STEP 1: ANALYZE THE QUESTION

In this Roman numeral question, the figure consists of two triangles that share the side of length 5. One triangle's other two sides measure a and b, while the other triangle's other two sides measure y and z. Additionally, the latter triangle contains a right angle, so since z is opposite that right angle, z is that triangle's hypotenuse, and y and 5 are that triangle's legs.

STEP 2: STATE THE TASK

This question asks which Roman numeral statement(s) *could* be true, meaning that incorrect answer choices reference statements that must be false.

STEP 3: APPROACH STRATEGICALLY

Roman numeral I says that sides a and b have the same length. Since you are not given any information for that triangle other than its remaining side's length of 5, the lengths of a and b could be equal or unequal to each other. Since this statement could be true, eliminate those choices that do not contain Roman numeral I: **(A)** and **(C)**.

Consider Roman numeral II and note that since z is the triangle's hypotenuse and thus is that triangle's longest side, $z > y$. Roman numeral II therefore must be false. Eliminate any remaining choices that contain II: **(E)**.

Finally, examine Roman numeral III: $a^2 + b^2 = z^2 - y^2$. Recall the Pythagorean theorem: the sum of the squared leg lengths equals the squared hypotenuse length. So $y^2 + 5^2 = z^2$. Now subtract y^2 from both sides to obtain $z^2 - y^2 = 5^2$.

Since the two triangles share the side of length 5, see whether you could apply the Pythagorean theorem to the other triangle as well. While you are not told that the triangle with side lengths a and b is a right triangle, you are also not told that it cannot be. So if that triangle were a right triangle, you could treat the sides of lengths a and b as the triangle's legs and the side of length 5 as that triangle's hypotenuse to get $a^2 + b^2 = 5^2$. Since $z^2 - y^2$ must equal 5^2 and $a^2 + b^2$ could equal 5^2 as well, it could be true that a $a^2 + b^2 = z^2 - y^2$. Since Roman numeral III could be true, **(D)** is correct.

STEP 4: CONFIRM YOUR ANSWER

Ensure that you selected all choices that contain only Roman numeral statements that could be true.

5. (D)

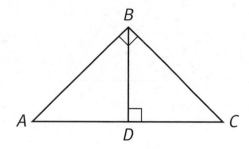

In the figure above, if $\angle ABC$ is a right angle and BD bisects AC, then what is the ratio of BC to AC?

- ○ $\dfrac{\sqrt{2}}{4}$

- ○ $\dfrac{\sqrt{2}}{3}$

- ○ $\dfrac{1}{2}$

- ○ $\dfrac{\sqrt{2}}{2}$

- ○ $\sqrt{2}$

STEP 1: ANALYZE THE QUESTION

In this geometry question, you're given a right triangle, and you're told that BD bisects the hypotenuse of the triangle. This means that it also bisects $\angle ABC$; that is, $\angle ABD$ and $\angle CBD$ both measure 45°.

STEP 2: STATE THE TASK

Find the ratio of BC to AC, that is, the ratio of one of the legs of the original right triangle to its hypotenuse.

STEP 3: APPROACH STRATEGICALLY

Line segment BD divides right triangle ABC into two right triangles. Each of the two smaller triangles consists of a 90° angle at vertex D, a 45° angle at vertex B, and a $180° - (90° + 45°) = 45°$ angle at the third vertex. Thus, the angles at vertices A and C are 45°, and the large triangle is a 45-45-90 triangle. This means that the corresponding side ratios are $x : x : x\sqrt{2}$. Leg BC is represented in this ratio by x and hypotenuse AC by $x\sqrt{2}$, making the ratio of BC to AC equal to $\dfrac{x}{x\sqrt{2}}$. Cancel the x terms and rationalize the denominator:

$$\frac{\cancel{x}\left(\sqrt{2}\right)}{\cancel{x}\sqrt{2}\left(\sqrt{2}\right)} = \frac{\sqrt{2}}{2}.$$

STEP 4: CONFIRM YOUR ANSWER

Make sure you answer with the ratio of the right sides in the right order. **(E)** is the reciprocal of the correct choice, reduced to its simplest form.

6. **(C)**

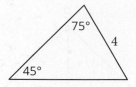

What is the area of the triangle in the figure above?

- ○ $2 + 2\sqrt{3}$
- ○ $4\sqrt{3}$
- ○ $6 + 2\sqrt{3}$
- ○ $6\sqrt{3}$
- ○ 12

STEP 1: ANALYZE THE QUESTION

To find the area of a triangle requires knowing the base and height of the triangle. An angle measurement is missing from the diagram. Since all the angles in a triangle add to 180°, the missing angle must be 180° − (45° + 75°), or 60°. Note that two of the angle measurements, 60° and 45°, are part of two of the GMAT's most commonly used shapes: the 45-45-90 special right triangle and the 30-60-90 special right triangle. If a special right triangle appears in a GMAT problem, it is probably key to the solution.

STEP 2: STATE THE TASK

You are trying to find the area, which involves using a basic triangle formula: area $= \frac{1}{2}$ base × height.

STEP 3: APPROACH STRATEGICALLY

Divide the triangle into two smaller right triangles by imagining an altitude from the 75° angle to the horizontal base. This will create a 45-45-90 triangle on the left side of the altitude and a 30-60-90 triangle on the right side of the altitude.

The 30-60-90 triangle on the right side of the altitude has a hypotenuse of 4. The ratio of sides of a 30-60-90 triangle is $x : x\sqrt{3} : 2x$, where x is the shorter leg, $x\sqrt{3}$ is the longer leg, and $2x$ is the hypotenuse. Therefore, you can deduce that the shorter leg is 2 and the longer leg (the altitude) is $2\sqrt{3}$.

You now also know the length of the sides of the 45-45-90 triangle: $2\sqrt{3}$. Therefore, the horizontal base of the large triangle is $2\sqrt{3} + 2$ and the height is $2\sqrt{3}$.

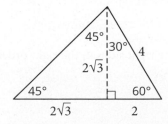

Now plug the known dimensions into the triangle area formula: area $= \frac{1}{2} \times \left(2\sqrt{3} + 2\right) \times 2\sqrt{3} =$ $\frac{1}{2} \times \left(4 \times 3 + 4\sqrt{3}\right) = 6 + 2\sqrt{3}$. Therefore, **(C)** is correct.

STEP 4: CONFIRM YOUR ANSWER

Check that you've correctly remembered the special right triangle relationships and have plugged in the correct values to the area formula.

Practice Set: Polygons on the GMAT

7.   **(B)**

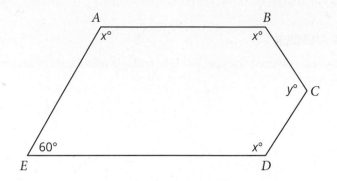

Note: Not drawn to scale.

In the figure shown above, *AB* and *DE* are parallel. What is the value of *y*?

- ○   110
- ○   120
- ○   135
- ○   150
- ○   160

STEP 1: ANALYZE THE QUESTION

You're given a pentagon that has two parallel sides, three angles that are equal (labeled $x°$) and one angle of 60°. The remaining angle is labeled $y°$. This irregular pentagon is not a figure for which there is any set formula, so look to divide it into figures for which you do know formulas.

STEP 2: STATE THE TASK

Use the given information to derive the value of *y*.

STEP 3: APPROACH STRATEGICALLY

Because two opposite sides of the pentagon are parallel, and you know one of the angles formed by one of these parallel sides, you can deduce the value of *x*, and from there, the value of *y*. Subdividing this complex polygon into simpler shapes can help with your analysis, and the 60° angle is a strong clue to make a 30-60-90 triangle. Draw an altitude to create this right triangle:

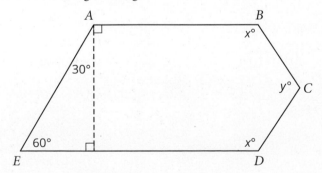

Because x is the complete angle at vertex A, you can deduce that $x = 30° + 90° = 120°$. Alternatively, you may have deduced this because AB and DE are parallel, making AE a transversal and the two angles it forms supplementary. Use this information to figure out how much all of the known angles add up to; then subtract this from the sum of interior angles of a pentagon to find y. The interior angles of a pentagon sum to 540°. (If you didn't know this, you could use the formula for the sum of interior angles of a polygon: $s = 180(n - 2)$, where s is the sum of interior angles and n is the number of sides.) Since $x = 120°$, $3x = 360°$, and you can say that $3x + 60° = 420°$. Therefore, $y = 540° - 420° = 120°$. That's **(B)**.

STEP 4: CONFIRM YOUR ANSWER

Double-check that you've properly added up the angles and used the correct value for the interior angles of a pentagon.

8. **(B)**

A contractor uses half of the available concrete to pour an 8-foot by 12-foot rectangular base for a monument. If she uses the rest of the concrete to create a uniform-width walkway all the way around the base of the monument, using the same amount of concrete per square foot as for the base, what is the maximum possible width of the walkway?

○   1 foot

○   2 feet

○   3 feet

○   4 feet

○   6 feet

STEP 1: ANALYZE THE QUESTION

The question describes a contractor using half of her concrete to make an 8- by 12-foot rectangular area. She uses the remainder of the concrete to create a uniform-width walkway around that area. Since she used half the concrete to make the inner rectangle, she uses the remaining half—or the same amount of concrete—for the walkway.

STEP 2: STATE THE TASK

Use the geometry formula for area of a rectangle to determine the maximum width of the walkway.

STEP 3: APPROACH STRATEGICALLY

Draw a sketch to illustrate the scenario:

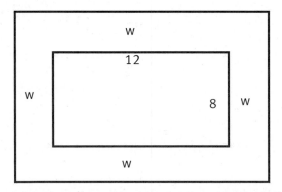

Since the amounts of concrete used for the base and the walkway are the same, the contractor will have enough concrete to make a walkway that has an area of $8 \times 12 = 96$ square feet. The area of the walkway is the area of the larger rectangle formed by the perimeter of the walkway less the area of the rectangular base. If you designate the width of the walkway as w, you can write the equation $(w + w + 12)(w + w + 8) - (8 \times 12) = 8 \times 12$, which simplifies to $(2w + 12)(2w + 8) - 96 = 96$. So $4w^2 + 40w + 96 = 192$. Because the squared term has a coefficient of 4, see if you can divide all terms by 4 to eliminate that coefficient. Indeed you can, getting $w^2 + 10w + 24 = 48$. So in standard quadratic form, $w^2 + 10w - 24 = 0$. Factor this to get $(w - 2)(w + 12) = 0$. Since w cannot be -12 (a dimension of a geometric figure cannot be negative), it must be 2. **(B)** is correct.

STEP 4: CONFIRM YOUR ANSWER

Given a width of 2, the outer dimensions of the walkway are $8 + 2 + 2 = 12$ and $12 + 2 + 2 = 16$. The area of such a rectangle is $12 \times 16 = 192$. This is, indeed, equal to the area of the monument base plus the area of the walkway, since $96 + 96 = 192$.

9. **(B)**

Is the length of a side of square S greater than the length of a side of equilateral triangle T?

(1) The sum of the lengths of a side of S and a side of T is 22.

(2) The ratio of the perimeter of square S to the perimeter of triangle T is 5 to 6.

STEP 1: ANALYZE THE QUESTION STEM

This Yes/No question requires that you determine whether there is enough information to answer the question "Is the length of a side of square S greater than the length of a side of the equilateral triangle T?" Let a be the length of a side of square S and let b be the length of a side of equilateral triangle T. Then you can paraphrase the question as "Is $a > b$?" There is no information in the question stem that you can use to determine whether or not there is sufficiency, so look at the statements.

STEP 2: EVALUATE THE STATEMENTS USING 12TEN

Statement (1) says that $a + b = 22$. Here, a could be greater, b could be greater, or a and b could be equal. If $a = 18$ and $b = 4$ (they have to be consistent with Statement (1), so they must total 22), then $a > b$, and the answer to the question is yes. However, if $a = 4$ and $b = 18$ (again, consistent with Statement (1), as they total 22), then $a < b$, and the answer to the question is no.

Because different answers to the question are possible, Statement (1) is insufficient. Eliminate **(A)** and **(D)**.

Statement (2): The ratio of the perimeter of the square to the perimeter of the triangle is 5 to 6. The perimeter of the square is $4a$. The perimeter of the equilateral triangle is $3b$. Thus, you can write the equation $\dfrac{4a}{3b} = \dfrac{5}{6}$.

Since this equation gives a proportional relationship between a and b, you know that you could simplify this equation and answer the question with a definite yes or no. Because a and b are side lengths, a and b are both positive, so this equation will describe a consistent ratio between these values. Note that you don't have to solve for the ratio in order to know that Statement (2) is sufficient. **(B)** is correct.

Practice Set: Circles on the GMAT

10. (D)

The length of an arc on circle C formed by a central angle measuring 60° is 12. What is the diameter of the circle?

- ○ $\dfrac{18}{\pi}$

- ○ $\dfrac{36}{\pi}$

- ○ 6π

- ○ $\dfrac{72}{\pi}$

- ○ 12π

STEP 1: ANALYZE THE QUESTION

The question gives you the length of the arc formed by a 60° central angle. The ratio of the central angle to the total 360° of the circle can be used to relate the arc formed by the central angle to the full circumference.

STEP 2: STATE THE TASK

Find the circumference of the circle and then use that value to determine the diameter.

STEP 3: APPROACH STRATEGICALLY

Set up a proportion to find the circumference:

$$\frac{\text{Length of arc}}{\text{Circumference}} = \frac{\text{Central angle}}{360°}$$

$$\frac{12}{\text{Circumference}} = \frac{60°}{360°}$$

$$\frac{12}{\text{Circumference}} = \frac{1}{6}$$

$$\text{Circumference} = 72$$

Because circumference $= \pi \times$ diameter, diameter $= \dfrac{\text{circumference}}{\pi} = \dfrac{72}{\pi}$. **(D)** is correct.

STEP 4: CONFIRM YOUR ANSWER

Check your logic and the setup of the proportion. Be certain that you answered the question that was asked; **(B)** is the radius, not the diameter.

11. **(C)**

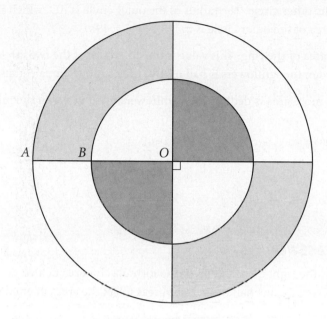

The figure above represents a circular garden, with center O. AB is 4 feet, and BO is 3 feet. The gardener plans to plant sunflowers in the two light gray sections and tulips in the two dark gray sections. How much more area, in square feet, will be covered by sunflowers than tulips?

- ○ $\frac{9}{2}\pi$
- ○ 8π
- ◔ $\frac{31}{2}\pi$
- ○ 20π
- ○ 31π

STEP 1: ANALYZE THE QUESTION

The figure contains one circle inside a larger circle. Each of the tulip regions is a quarter of the inner circle. The total area dedicated to tulips is thus $\frac{1}{4} + \frac{1}{4} = \frac{1}{2}$ of the inner circle.

Each of the sunflower regions is a quarter of the ring between the outer and inner circles. The total area dedicated to sunflowers is $\frac{1}{4} + \frac{1}{4} = \frac{1}{2}$ of the ring area. The total area of the ring is the difference between the areas of the outer and inner circles.

STEP 2: STATE THE TASK

Find the difference in areas dedicated to the two types of flowers, or the difference between half the ring area and half the inner circle area.

STEP 3: APPROACH STRATEGICALLY

First, find the area of the inner circle. The formula for the area of a circle is πr^2. From the question stem, you know that $r = 3$, so the area of the inner circle is $\pi r^2 = \pi(3)^2 = 9\pi$. Because the area in the garden for tulips is half of this, the tulip area equals $\frac{1}{2} \times 9\pi = \frac{9}{2}\pi$.

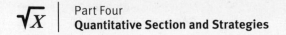
Now solve for the area of the outer circle. The radius of the outer circle is AO, which is equal to $AB + BO = 4 + 3 = 7$. Therefore, the area of the outer circle is $\pi r^2 = \pi(7)^2 = 49\pi$.

Now you can solve for the area of the ring. This value is the difference of the two circle areas: $49\pi - 9\pi = 40\pi$. Because the area in the garden for sunflowers is half of this, the sunflower area equals $\frac{1}{2} \times 40\pi = 20\pi$.

Lastly, solve for how much more area is dedicated to sunflowers by subtracting the tulip area from the sunflower area.

$$20\pi - \frac{9}{2}\pi = \frac{40}{2}\pi - \frac{9}{2}\pi$$
$$= \frac{31}{2}\pi$$

This matches **(C)**.

STEP 4: CONFIRM YOUR ANSWER

Confirm that you answered the right question, using the formulas for area of a circle (and not circumference, for example) and remembering to take half the various areas to get the areas planted with flowers.

12. (C)

If two circles overlap each other, what is the area of that overlap?

(1) The edge of each circle intersects the center of the other circle.

(2) The sum of the circumferences of the two circles is 12π.

STEP 1: ANALYZE THE QUESTION STEM

This Value question says that two circles overlap and asks for that overlap's area. To be sufficient, a statement needs to provide enough information to determine just one area value for the overlap.

STEP 2: EVALUATE THE STATEMENTS USING 12TEN

Consider sketching the scenario that Statement (1) describes. The sample sketch below names the circles A and B.

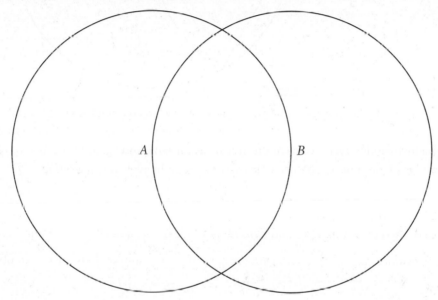

Since each circle's edge intersects the other circle's center, the circles must have the same radius. A small radius would mean small circles and a small area of overlap, while a large radius would mean large circles and a large area of overlap. Statement (1) is insufficient, so eliminate **(A)** and **(D)**.

Statement (2) says that the circles' circumferences add to 12π. Although you can determine a circle's radius from that circle's circumference, using the formula circumference = (2π)(radius), this statement tells you about both circles together, and there is no way to know whether they are congruent or one is larger than the other, or how much the two circles overlap. Therefore, finding the area of overlap is impossible. Since Statement (2) is insufficient, eliminate **(B)** and combine the two statements.

Statement (1) indicates that the circles are congruent and thus have the same radius. Statement (2) gives you the sum of the circumferences (12π), so dividing that total by 2 gives either individual circle's circumference (6π). From the circumference, you could solve for the radius using the equation $6\pi = 2\pi r$.

To determine whether knowing the radius is sufficient to answer the question, sketch radius AB and two additional radii for each circle (AD and AE for circle A and BD and BE for circle B) to create two congruent,

equilateral triangles *ADB* and *AEB* that share segment *AB* as a base. An equilateral triangle has only 60°
interior angles; the updated sketch below labels one as an example.

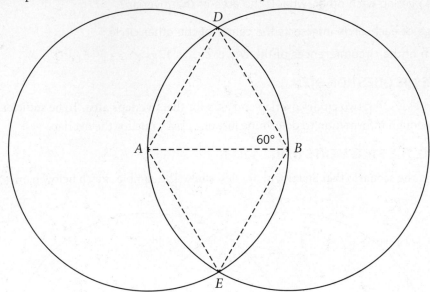

From this more complete sketch, notice that the area of overlap between circles *A* and *B* is (area of circle
A's sector *DAE*) + (area of circle *B*'s sector *DBE*) − (area of triangles *ADB* and *AEB*). Since the area of each
triangle was originally included twice, once in the area of sector *DAE* and again in the area of sector *DBE*,
their combined area must be subtracted once to leave the area of the two circles' overlap.

Each of triangles *ADB* and *AEB* is equilateral, so the sum in degrees of angles *DAB* and *EAB* is 60 + 60 = 120;
similarly, the sum in degrees of angles *DBA* and *EBA* is 120. Since 120° is one-third of the 360 total degrees
in a circle, the area of each of sectors *DAE* and *DBE* is one-third of the area of circles *A* and *B*, respectively:
$\left(\frac{1}{3}\right)\left(\pi \times \text{radius}^2\right)$. And since sectors *DAE* and *DBE* are congruent, the sum of their areas is double that of either

area alone: $(2)\left(\frac{1}{3}\right)\left(\pi \times \text{radius}^2\right)$.

The area of either triangle *ADB* or triangle *AEB* is determined by the triangle's base and its height. Add heights
CD and *CE* to triangles *ADB* and *AEB*, respectively.

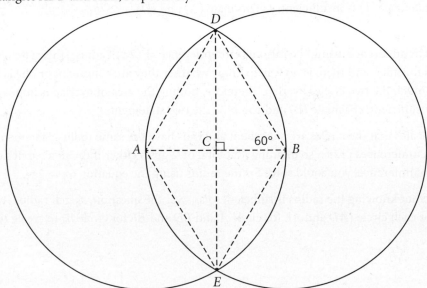

In sketching each equilateral triangle's height, you break each triangle into a pair of congruent 30°-60°-90° triangles. The lengths of the sides opposite the 30°, 60°, and 90° angles are in the ratio $x : x\sqrt{3} : 2x$. So for example, triangle DCB's base CB is half of either circle's radius AB and is multiplied by $\sqrt{3}$ to determine that triangle's height CD. Segment CD is also triangle ADB's height, so that triangle's area equals

$\left(\frac{1}{2}\right)(\text{base})(\text{height}) = \left(\frac{1}{2}\right)(\text{radius})\left(\frac{1}{2} \times \text{radius} \times \sqrt{3}\right)$. Again, since triangles ADB and AEB are congruent, triangle AEB's area is the same, so the sum of those triangles' areas is twice their individual areas:

$(2)\left(\frac{1}{2}\right)(\text{radius})\left(\frac{1}{2} \times \text{radius} \times \sqrt{3}\right)$.

Combining this information on the areas of the sectors and triangles, the area of the circles' overlap is

$(2)\left(\frac{1}{3}\right)\left(\pi \times \text{radius}^2\right) - (2)\left(\frac{1}{2}\right)(\text{radius})\left(\frac{1}{2} \times \text{radius} \times \sqrt{3}\right)$.

Since you know the radius from Statement (2), Statement (1) allows you to determine the area of the circles' overlap via the expression $(2)\left(\frac{1}{3}\right)\left(\pi \times \text{radius}^2\right) - (2)\left(\frac{1}{2}\right)(\text{radius})\left(\frac{1}{2} \times \text{radius} \times \sqrt{3}\right)$. Since this is a Data Sufficiency question, do not spend time actually calculating that area; instead, knowing that you could if you wanted to is enough to conclude that **(C)** is correct.

Practice Set: Multiple Figures on the GMAT

13. **(A)**

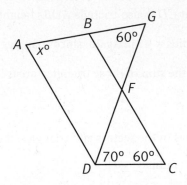

In the figure above, what is the value of *x*?

(1) *AD* || *BC*

(2) ∠*GBC* = 70°

STEP 1: ANALYZE THE QUESTION STEM

For this Value question, you can make the following observations from the figure:

In triangle *DFC*, the measure of angle *DFC* is 180° − 70° − 60° = 50°.

Angle *BFG* is vertical to angle *DFC*, so the measure of angle *BFG* is also 50°.

In triangle *FBG*, the measure of angle *GBF* is 180° − 50° − 60° = 70°.

Angle *ABF* completes a straight line with angle *GBF*, so the measure of angle *ABF* is 180° − 70° = 110°.

Angles *GFC* and *BFD* each complete a straight line with angle *DFC*, so the measure of each of these angles is 180° − 50° = 130°.

There are many things that would give you the value of *x*. You have two of the angles in quadrilateral *ABFD*, so getting the measure of angle *FDA* would give you the third and allow you to solve for *x* (all quadrilaterals have interior angles that sum to 360°). It's a complex figure, so there may be other ways to solve for *x* as well. You'll need to think carefully about any information you're given.

STEP 2: EVALUATE THE STATEMENTS USING 12TEN

Statement (1) states that *AD* is parallel to *BC*. Therefore, angle *GBF* and the angle marked *x*° must be equal. Because the measure of angle *GBF* is 70°, the measure of the angle marked *x*° must be 70°. Thus, *x* = 70. Statement (1) is sufficient. You can eliminate **(B)**, **(C)**, and **(E)**.

Statement (2) tells you that ∠*GBC* = 70°. You already concluded that ∠*GBF* = 70° when you gathered information from the figure in step 1. Because angle *GBF* is the same as angle *GBC*, this statement does not provide you with any new information and is therefore insufficient.

The correct answer is **(A)**.

14. (A)

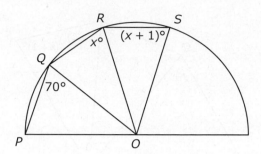

In the figure above, point *O* is the center of the semicircle, and *PQ* is parallel to *OS*. What is the measure of ∠*ROS*?

- ○ 34°
- ○ 36°
- ○ 54.5°
- ○ 72°
- ○ 73°

STEP 1: ANALYZE THE QUESTION

This question presents you with a complex figure consisting of three triangles inscribed in a semicircle. You are told that *PQ* is parallel to *OS*.

STEP 2: STATE THE TASK

Find the measure of ∠*ROS*.

STEP 3: APPROACH STRATEGICALLY

The problem looks downright daunting, but the key, as with all geometry problems that involve complex figures, is to use any concrete information given to determine the starting point. With that in mind, begin by listing what you know from the figure:

1. Two of the three sides of each of the three inscribed triangles are radii of the semicircle. That means the three inscribed triangles are isosceles.

2. Since *PQ* is parallel to *OS*, *QO* is a transversal. When a transversal intersects with a pair of parallel lines, alternate interior angles are equal. In this case, since ∠*PQO* = 70°, ∠*QOS* must also be 70°.

Add this information to your sketch of $\triangle QOR$ and $\triangle ROS$:

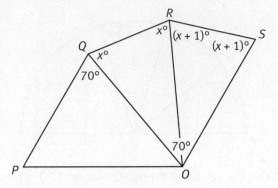

As you can't simply split angle $\angle QOS$ in half to find your answer (you can't make assumptions about the relative sizes of angles just from eyeballing the diagram), you'll instead need to solve for x. To do so, recall that a triangle's interior angles sum to $180°$. If you add up all six interior angles from $\triangle QOR$ and $\triangle ROS$, you'll have a sum of $360°$. You can now set up an equation to solve for the value of x.

$$x + x + (x + 1) + (x + 1) + 70 = 360$$
$$4x + 72 = 360$$
$$4x = 288$$
$$x = 72$$

Since $x = 72$, each of the two base angles in $\triangle ROS$ is $72 + 1 = 73°$. Therefore, the measure of $\angle ROS$ is $180 - 2(73) = 180 - 146 = 34°$. The correct answer is **(A)**.

STEP 4: CONFIRM YOUR ANSWER

If you were pressed for time, a bit of Critical Thinking would reveal that isosceles triangles with base angles of approximately $70°$ cannot possibly allow a remaining angle as large as **(C)**, **(D)**, or **(E)** would indicate.

15. (D)

An isosceles triangle is inscribed in a circle such that one of the triangle's sides coincides with the circle's longest chord. If the measure of another side of the triangle is 5, what is the difference between the area of the circle and the area of the triangle?

○ $\frac{25}{2}(1 - \pi)$

○ $25(\pi - 1)$

○ $\frac{25}{2}(\pi + 1)$

○ $\frac{25}{2}(\pi - 1)$

○ $\frac{25}{4}(\pi - 1)$

STEP 1: ANALYZE THE QUESTION

"An isosceles triangle is inscribed in a circle" means that each vertex of a triangle with at least two sides of equal length is on the circumference of a circle. Furthermore, "one of the triangle's sides coincides with the circle's longest chord" means that one side of the triangle is a diameter of the circle. When a side of a triangle that's inscribed in a circle is a diameter of the circle, the vertex across from the diameter is a right angle, so the triangle is a right triangle and the side that coincides with the diameter is its hypotenuse. You're also told that the measure of another side of this triangle is 5. Since the triangle is isosceles, the third side must also have a length of 5, and the angles that are opposite those sides must also be of equal measure. Since one angle already measures 90°, each of the other two measures 45°. Thus, the inscribed figure is a 45°-45°-90° triangle.

Sketching a figure on your notepad to visualize the figures will be helpful. Your sketch might look something like this:

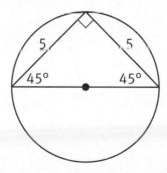

STEP 2: STATE THE TASK

Determine the difference between the circle's area and the triangle's area, or $A_C - A_T$.

STEP 3: APPROACH STRATEGICALLY

You're given a measure of one of the triangle's sides, so start by finding the area of the triangle. Since it is a right triangle, one leg is the triangle's base, and the other leg is the height. Substitute those lengths into the formula for area of a triangle:

$$\frac{1}{2}bh = \frac{1}{2}(5)(5) = \frac{25}{2}.$$

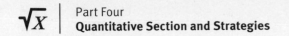
The formula for area of a circle is πr^2, so to find the area of the circle, you need to know the radius. In this figure, the radius of the circle is half the length of the triangle's hypotenuse. Because the triangle is a 45°-45°-90° triangle, the measures of the sides are in the ratio $1 : 1 : \sqrt{2}$. Thus, since each of the two legs measures 5, the hypotenuse measures $5\sqrt{2}$. This is also the circle's diameter, so the radius is half of $5\sqrt{2}$, or $\frac{5\sqrt{2}}{2}$. Thus, the circle's area is this:

$$\pi r^2 = \pi\left(\frac{5\sqrt{2}}{2}\right)^2 = \pi\left[\frac{(5)^2\left(\sqrt{2}\right)^2}{(2)^2}\right] = \pi\left(\frac{25 \times \cancel{2}}{2^{\cancel{2}}}\right) = \frac{25\pi}{2}$$

Finally, the area of the circle minus the area of the triangle is $\frac{25\pi}{2} - \frac{25}{2} = \frac{25}{2}(\pi - 1)$, which matches **(D)**—the correct choice.

On Test Day, if you were behind on time and needed to make a strategic guess, you could note that **(A)** stands out as being the only choice whose binomial factor doesn't begin with π. Indeed, because π is greater than 1, $1 - \pi$ is negative. This choice is thus the product of a positive number and a negative number, which is negative. The difference between the area of a circle and the area of a triangle inscribed within it must be positive, so you could eliminate **(A)** and guess from among the other choices.

STEP 4: CONFIRM YOUR ANSWER

Ensure that you answered the question, which asks for the difference in areas between the circle and the triangle. Potential trap answers include **(A)**, which is the area of the triangle minus the area of the circle, and **(C)**, which is the sum of the two areas.

Practice Set: Solids on the GMAT

16. (E)

A cylindrical tank with a height of 8 feet is completely full of gasoline. This gasoline is pumped into an empty cylindrical tank with a diameter of 24 feet and a height of 18 feet. If the gasoline reaches a height of 2 feet in this tank, what is the diameter, in feet, of the original tank?

- ○ 3
- ○ 6
- ○ 8
- ○ 10
- ○ 12

STEP 1: ANALYZE THE QUESTION

There are two cylindrical tanks. The first is completely full of gasoline, which is all transferred to the second. The height of the first tank is given. Both the height and the diameter of the second tank are given, but that height is actually irrelevant since you're not finding the volume of the second tank; what is relevant is the height that the gasoline reaches in that second tank. The key to such a transference problem is noting that the volume of the gasoline in the original tank must equal the volume of the gasoline in the new tank.

STEP 2: STATE THE TASK

Use the formula for volume of a cylinder to find the diameter of the original tank.

STEP 3: APPROACH STRATEGICALLY

The volume of any uniform solid is equal to the area of its base times that solid's height, so the volume of a right circular cylinder is $\pi r^2 h$. More information is given about the second cylinder, so start there. It has a diameter of 24 feet, so its radius must be 12 feet. The gasoline fills it to a height of 2 feet, so use 2 for the height. Thus, the volume of the gasoline in that tank is $\pi(12)^2(2) = 288\pi$ ft^3.

Now, plug this value back into the volume formula for the first cylinder to find its diameter: $288\pi = \pi r^2(8)$, so $r^2 = 36$ and $r = 6$ ft. Finally, double the radius to find the diameter, which is 12 ft. The answer is **(E)**.

STEP 4: CONFIRM YOUR ANSWER

As always, be sure to read the question stem carefully, noting the key details. Here, the diameter, not the radius, of the second tank's base was given and the gasoline did not reach the top of the second tank.

17. (D)

A rectangular solid has the dimensions 4, 5, and x. If the number of units in the solid's volume and the number of units in that solid's surface area are the same, what is the sum of the areas of the two largest faces of the solid?

- ○ 20
- ○ 40
- ○ 100
- ○ 200
- ○ 400

STEP 1: ANALYZE THE QUESTION

The question stem tells you that the number of units in a rectangular solid's volume and the number of units in that solid's surface area are the same. Recall that the volume of a rectangular solid is Length × Height × Width and that the surface area is the sum of the areas of all six faces. You are also given specific values (4 and 5) for two of the three dimensions of the solid.

STEP 2: STATE THE TASK

Determine the sum of the areas of the two largest faces of the solid.

STEP 3: APPROACH STRATEGICALLY

The solid's volume and surface area are equal values, so $\ell wh = 2\ell w + 2\ell h + 2wh$. Since you are not told which dimensions 4 and 5 represent, simply substitute those values into this equation in a consistent way, assigning x to the third dimension. If, say, $\ell = 4$ and $w = 5$, then $4(5)x = 2(4)(5) + 2(4)x + 2(5)x$. Now, solve for x:

$$20x = 2(4)(5) + 2(4)x + 2(5)x = 2[4(5) + 4x + 5x]$$
$$20x = 2(9x + 20)$$
$$10x = 9x + 20$$
$$x = 20$$

Because 20 is greater than 4 or 5, 20 is the largest dimension of the solid. Use that value and the second-largest dimension's measure to find the area of each of the largest faces of the solid: $20(5) = 100$. Finally, since opposite faces of a rectangular solid have the same area, double 100 to determine the sum of the areas of those two largest faces: $2(100) = 200$.

The correct choice is **(D)**.

STEP 4: CONFIRM YOUR ANSWER

Ensure that you answered the question asked. For example, if you stopped working after solving for x, you might have selected **(A)**. If you forgot to double the area in the last step, **(C)** was waiting for you.

18. (C)

A cube with an edge length of 6 contains the largest possible sphere that completely fits inside of it. If the volume V of a sphere with radius r is given by the formula $V = \frac{4}{3}\pi r^3$, what is the volume of the empty space inside the cube?

○ $36(\pi 3 - 6)$

○ 36π

○ $36(6 - \pi)$

○ $36(\pi - 1)$

○ $36(4 - \pi)$

STEP 1: ANALYZE THE QUESTION

The question stem tells you that a cube with edge 6 contains the largest possible sphere that completely fits inside of it. So the length of the sphere's diameter is the same as the length of the cube's side. There is also some empty space in the cube that is not occupied by the sphere; this is the three-dimensional equivalent of inscribing a circle in a square—there's some empty space in the corners. The formula for the volume of a sphere is given to you. Recall that the volume of a cube is the edge length cubed.

STEP 2: STATE THE TASK

Determine the volume of the empty space in the cube, which is the difference between the cube's and sphere's volumes:

$$V_{\text{empty space}} = V_{\text{cube}} - V_{\text{sphere}} = (\text{edge})^3 - \frac{4}{3}\pi r^3$$

STEP 3: APPROACH STRATEGICALLY

You're given concrete information about the cube, so start by finding its volume:

$$V_{\text{cube}} = e^3 = 6^3 = 216$$

Now use the given formula to find the volume of the sphere. Since the length of the sphere's diameter is the same as the length of the cube's edge, the sphere's radius is half the length of the cube's edge: $r = \frac{1}{2}(6) = 3$. Plug this in for r in the formula:

$$V = \frac{4}{3}\pi r^3 = \frac{4}{3}(3^3)\pi = 4(3^2)\pi = 4(9)\pi = 36\pi$$

Now, determine the volume of the empty space in the cube:

$V_{\text{cube}} - V_{\text{sphere}} = 216 - 36\pi$. This doesn't look like any of the answer choices, which all begin with a factor of 36. Factor 36 out of this expression to get $36(6 - \pi)$.

This matches **(C)**, which is the correct choice.

STEP 4: CONFIRM YOUR ANSWER

Make sure you determined the difference between the volume of the cube and the volume of the sphere and not some other value, starting with confirming that you correctly derived the sphere's radius.

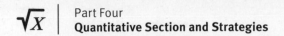

Practice Set: Coordinate Geometry on the GMAT

19. (C)

Line ℓ_1 is given by the equation $y = mx + 3$, and line ℓ_2 is given by the equation $y = nx - 7$, where m and n are constants. Is ℓ_1 parallel to ℓ_2?

(1) $m^2 - n^2 = 0$

(2) mn is positive.

STEP 1: ANALYZE THE QUESTION STEM

This is a Yes/No question asking whether two lines, each of which is represented by a unique equation, are parallel. Since two lines are parallel if they have the same slope, the statements are sufficient if they provide enough information to determine whether m and n, the slopes of lines ℓ_1 and ℓ_2, respectively, are equal.

STEP 2: EVALUATE THE STATEMENTS USING 12TEN

Statement (1) says that $m^2 - n^2 = 0$. This is one of the "classic" quadratics; it factors to $(m + n)(m - n) = 0$. This means that $m = n$ or $-n$. In other words, m and n have the same magnitude, but they could have either the same sign or opposite signs. So, if they had the same sign, the slopes would be equal and the answer to the question would be yes, but if they had opposite signs, the slopes would not be equal and the answer would be no. Thus, this statement is insufficient; eliminate **(A)** and **(D)**.

Statement (2) says that the product of m and n is positive. This means that m and n have the same sign; they're either both positive or both negative. Without more information, though, there's no way to know whether they're equal, so this statement is insufficient. Eliminate **(B)**.

Now, combine the statements. According to (1), $m = n$ or $-n$, but according to (2), m and n must have the same sign. That leaves $m = n$ as the only possibility. Even though there's not enough information to determine what the slopes are, they must be equal to each other. Choose **(C)**.

20. (C)

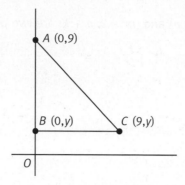

In the rectangular coordinate system above, triangle *ABC* has an area of 27 square units. Vertex *A* is at point (0,9), vertex *B* is at point (0,*y*), and vertex *C* is at point (9,*y*). What is the value of *y*?

- ○ 1
- ○ 2
- ○ 3
- ○ 4
- ○ 6

STEP 1: ANALYZE THE QUESTION

You're given the *x*- and *y*-coordinates of one of the three vertices of triangle *ABC*, the *x*-coordinates of the remaining two vertices, and the area of the triangle. Since the *y*-coordinates of the two vertices not specified are both represented by *y*, they are the same, so the side *BC* of the triangle is parallel to the *x*-axis. Additionally, side *AB* lies on the *y*-axis, so this is a right triangle.

STEP 2: STATE THE TASK

Determine the *y*-coordinate of points *B* and *C* on the graph.

STEP 3: APPROACH STRATEGICALLY

Since you are given the area of the triangle, use the formula for the area of a triangle to determine the missing coordinate:

The area of triangle $ABC = \left(\frac{1}{2}\right)$ (base)(height) $= 27$. Since the graph indicates that the base of the triangle extends from point $(0, y)$ to point $(9, y)$, the base has a length of 9, so $\left(\frac{1}{2}\right)(9)(\text{height}) = 27$. Simplifying yields $9 \times \text{height} = 54$, so height $= 54 \div 9 = 6$. Since vertex *A* lies at point $(0, 9)$, the *y*-coordinate of vertex *B* must be $9 - 6 = 3$. Thus, $y = 3$. The correct choice is **(C)**.

STEP 4: CONFIRM YOUR ANSWER

Use the height you've calculated from the *y*-coordinate you've found to check whether the area matches that in the question stem. Note also that 6 in **(E)** is a trap answer for the unwary test taker, since that's the height of the triangle, not the value of *y*.

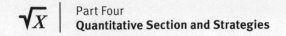
21. (B)

In the *xy*-coordinate system, if (m,n) and $(m + 2, n + k)$ are two points on the line with the equation $x = 2y + 5$, then $k =$

○ $\frac{1}{2}$

○ 1

○ 2

○ $\frac{5}{2}$

○ 4

STEP 1: ANALYZE THE QUESTION

For any question involving the equation of a line, a good place to start is the slope-intercept form of the line, $y = mx + b$. Remember that if you have two points on a line, you can derive the entire equation, and if you have an equation of the line, you can calculate any points on that line.

STEP 2: STATE THE TASK

You must solve for k, which is the amount by which the *y*-coordinate increases when the *x*-coordinate increases by 2.

STEP 3: APPROACH STRATEGICALLY

The slope of a line is the ratio between the change in *y* and the change in *x*. In other words, every time the *x*-coordinate increases by 1, the *y*-coordinate increases by the amount of the slope.

The equation of the line in the question stem is defined as $x = 2y + 5$. You must isolate *y* to have slope-intercept form:

$$x = 2y + 5$$
$$x - 5 = 2y$$
$$\frac{x - 5}{2} = y$$
$$y = \frac{1}{2}x - \frac{5}{2}$$

So the slope of this line is $\frac{1}{2}$. This means that for every change of $+1$ in the *x* direction, there is a change of $+\frac{1}{2}$ in the *y* direction. Therefore, you know that, because there is an increase of 2 units in the *x* direction when moving from *m* to $m + 2$, there must be a change of 1 unit in the *y* direction when moving from *n* to $n + k$. So $k = 1$.

Since there are variables that eventually cancel (*m* and *n* are not part of the answer choices), you can use picking numbers. Say that you choose the *y*-coordinate of the point (m,n) to be 0 to allow for easier calculations. Using the equation you're given to relate *x*- and *y*-coordinates, you can calculate the *x*-coordinate:

$$x = 2y + 5$$
$$x = 2(0) + 5$$
$$x = 5$$

So (m,n) is the point (5,0).

Now you'll plug your values of m and n into the next point: $(m + 2, n + k)$. That yields $(7,k)$. All you have to do is plug an x-coordinate of 7 into the equation to solve for k, the y-coordinate:

$$x = 2y + 5$$
$$7 = 2k + 5$$
$$2 = 2k$$
$$1 = k$$

(B) is correct.

STEP 4: CONFIRM YOUR ANSWER

Reread the question, making sure that you didn't miss anything. For example, if you thought that the original equation was $y = 2x + 5$, then you would have answered **(E)**. This step would help you to catch that error.

GMAT by the Numbers: Geometry

Now that you've learned how to approach geometry questions on the GMAT, let's add one more dimension to your understanding of how they work.

Take a moment to try this question. Following is performance data from thousands of people who have studied with Kaplan over the decades. Through analyzing this data, we will show you how to approach questions like this one most effectively and how to avoid similarly tempting wrong answer choice types on Test Day.

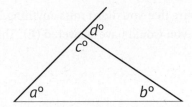

In the figure above, what is the value of *b*?

(1) $a + c + d = 225$

(2) $d - a = 55$

○ Statement (1) ALONE is sufficient, but Statement (2) is not sufficient.

○ Statement (2) ALONE is sufficient, but Statement (1) is not sufficient.

○ BOTH statements TOGETHER are sufficient, but NEITHER statement ALONE is sufficient.

○ EACH statement ALONE is sufficient.

○ Statements (1) and (2) TOGETHER are NOT sufficient.

Explanation

The key to most GMAT geometry problems is to analyze the given figure before you worry too much about how you're going to solve. In this problem, you're given a triangle and a straight line, both of which have angles that add to 180°. Hence, you can create two equations:

$$a + b + c = 180 \text{ and } d + c = 180$$

Since both $(a + b + c)$ and $(d + c)$ equal 180, you can set them equal to each other. And since you're solving for b, you'll want to first simplify the equation to isolate b:

$$a + b + c = d + c$$
$$a + b = d$$
$$b = d - a$$

To solve for b, you need only find a value for $d - a$. Having thus analyzed the question stem, you see that Statement (2) gives you exactly what you need and is sufficient and that Statement (1) does not and is insufficient. Hence, **(B)** is correct.

Question Statistics

7% of test takers choose **(A)**

25% of test takers choose **(B)**

50% of test takers choose **(C)**

5% of test takers choose **(D)**

13% of test takers choose **(E)**

Sample size = 4,597

The question statistics reveal what the test maker already knows—that the vast majority of test takers don't do much up-front analysis, thereby making their task much harder and causing them to miss what could be straightforward solutions. Make sure to analyze figures before you solve, and you'll make GMAT geometry much easier.

More GMAT by the Numbers ...

To see more questions with answer choice statistics, be sure to review the full-length CATs in your online resources.

GO ONLINE

kaptest.com/login

CHAPTER 25

Quantitative Reasoning: Putting It All Together— Advanced Practice

In this chapter, you'll find two 20-question practice sets consisting entirely of questions most test takers find challenging. The first practice set contains Problem Solving questions; the second contains Data Sufficiency questions. Following each practice set, you'll find the answer key, as well as complete explanations for every question.

How to Use These Practice Sets

Use these question sets to hone your critical thinking skills if you are aiming for a very high GMAT score. If you are not yet comfortable with the practice questions in the preceding chapters of this book, then continue to review the arithmetic, algebra, geometry, and other topics presented there until you are able to find the correct answers to most of those practice questions. Then you'll be ready to tackle the tougher questions here.

If you are ready to do so, set a timer, giving yourself 2 minutes for each question. If you decided to do five Problem Solving questions and five Data Sufficiency questions in one sitting, for example, you would put 20 minutes on the timer.

As always, be sure to *review the explanation* to every problem you do in this chapter. Noting a different way to work through a problem, even if you got that problem right, is a powerful way to enhance your critical thinking skills—and it's ultimately those skills that you will be relying on in order to achieve a very high score on Test Day.

Ready to take your Quantitative score to the next level? Then turn the page and begin work!

Advanced Problem Solving Practice Set

1. The numbers m, n, and T are all positive, and $m > n$. A weekend farm stand sells only peaches. On Saturday, the farm stand has T peaches to sell, at a profit of m cents each. Any peaches remaining for sale on Sunday will be marked down and sold at a profit of $(m - n)$ cents each. If all peaches available for sale on Saturday morning are sold by Sunday evening, how many peaches, in terms of T, m, and n, does the stand need to sell on Saturday in order to make the same profit on each day?

    ○ $\dfrac{Tm}{m - n}$

    ○ $\dfrac{Tm}{n - m}$

    ○ $\dfrac{m(m - n)}{T}$

    ○ $\dfrac{T}{m - n}$

    ○ $\dfrac{T(m - n)}{2m - n}$

2. Set X consists of at least 2 members and is a set of consecutive odd integers with an average (arithmetic mean) of 37.

    Set Y consists of at least 10 members and is also a set of consecutive odd integers with an average (arithmetic mean) of 37.

    Set Z consists of all of the members of both set X and set Y.

    Which of the following statements must be true?

    I.   The standard deviation of set Z is not equal to the standard deviation of set X.
    II. The standard deviation of set Z is equal to the standard deviation of set Y.
    III. The average (arithmetic mean) of set Z is 37.

    ○ I only
    ○ II only
    ○ III only
    ○ I and III
    ○ II and III

3. The number 10,010 has how many positive integer factors?

   ○ 31

   ○ 32

   ○ 33

   ○ 34

   ○ 35

4. A department of motor vehicles asks visitors to draw numbered tickets from a dispenser so that they can be served in order by number. Six friends have graduated from truck-driving school and go to the department to get commercial driving licenses. They draw tickets and find that their numbers are a set of evenly spaced integers with a range of 10. Which of the following could NOT be the sum of their numbers?

   ○ 1,254

   ○ 1,428

   ○ 3,972

   ○ 4,316

   ○ 8,010

5. For all values of x, y, and z, $x \Diamond y \Diamond z = x^2(y - 1)(z + 2)$.

   If $a < 0$, which of the following shows R, S, and T arranged in order from least to greatest?

   R: $1 \Diamond a \Diamond 3$

   S: $3 \Diamond a \Diamond 1$

   T: $a \Diamond 3 \Diamond 1$

   ○ R, S, T
   ○ T, S, R
   ○ R, T, S
   ○ T, R, S
   ○ S, R, T

6. If a and b are integers, and $2a + b = 17$, then $8a + b$ cannot equal which of the following?

   ○ −1
   ○ 33
   ○ 35
   ○ 65
   ○ 71

7. Two workers have different pay scales. Worker A receives $50 for any day worked plus $15 per hour. Worker B receives $27 per hour. Both workers may work for a fraction of an hour and be paid in proportion to their respective hourly rates. If Worker A arrives at 9:21 a.m. and receives the $50 upon arrival and Worker B arrives at 10:09 a.m., assuming both work continuously, at what time would their earnings be identical?

    ○   11:09 a.m.

    ○   12:01 p.m.

    ○   2:31 p.m.

    ○   3:19 p.m.

    ○   3:36 p.m.

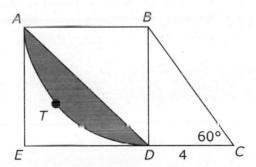

8. In the figure above, *ABDE* is a square, and arc *ATD* is part of a circle with center *B*. The measure of angle *BCD* is 60°, and line segment *CD* has a length of 4. What is the area of the shaded region?

    ○ $16\pi - 32$

    ○ $12\pi - 24$

    ○ $12\pi - 48$

    ○ $48\pi - 24$

    ○ $48\pi - 48$

9.   When the cube of a non-zero number y is subtracted from 35, the result is equal to the result of dividing 216 by the cube of that number y. What is the sum of all the possible values of y?

   ○ $\frac{5}{2}$

   ○   5

   ○   6

   ○   10

   ○   12

10.   One letter is selected at random from the five letters V, W, X, Y, and Z, and event A is the event that the letter V is selected. A fair six-sided die with sides numbered 1, 2, 3, 4, 5, and 6 is to be rolled, and event B is the event that a 5 or a 6 shows. A fair coin is to be tossed, and event C is the event that a head shows. What is the probability that event A occurs and at least one of the events B and C occurs?

   ○ $\frac{1}{30}$

   ○ $\frac{1}{15}$

   ○ $\frac{1}{10}$

   ○ $\frac{2}{15}$

   ○ $\frac{1}{5}$

11. A car traveled from Town A to Town B. The car traveled the first $\frac{3}{8}$ of the distance from Town A to Town B at an average speed of x miles per hour, where $x > 0$. The car traveled the remaining distance at an average speed of y miles per hour, where $y > 0$. The car traveled the entire distance from Town A to Town B at an average speed of z miles per hour. Which of the following equations gives y in terms of x and z?

○ $y = \dfrac{3x + 5z}{8}$

○ $y = \dfrac{5xz}{8x + 3z}$

○ $y = \dfrac{8x - 3z}{5xz}$

○ $y = \dfrac{3xz}{8x - 5z}$

○ $y = \dfrac{5xz}{8x - 3z}$

12. An ornithologist has studied a particular population of starlings and discovered that their population has increased by 400 percent every 10 years starting in 1890. If the initial population in 1890 was 256 birds, how large was the population of starlings in 1970?

○ 102,400

○ 10,000,000

○ 16,777,216

○ 20,000,000

○ 100,000,000

13. If $(x^2 + 8)yz < 0$, $wz > 0$, and $xyz < 0$, then which of the following must be true?

   I. $x < 0$
   II. $wy < 0$
   III. $yz < 0$

   ○ II only

   ○ III only

   ○ I and III only

   ○ II and III only

   ○ I, II, and III

14. If $\dfrac{61^2 - 1}{h}$ is an integer, then h could be divisible by each of the following EXCEPT

   ○ 8

   ○ 12

   ○ 15

   ○ 18

   ○ 31

15. If a, b, and c are integers such that $0 < a < b < c$, and a is even, b is prime, and c is odd, which of the following is a possible value for abc?

   ○   5

   ○   12

   ○   16

   ○   34

   ○   54

16. A fair die with sides numbered 1, 2, 3, 4, 5, and 6 is to be rolled 4 times. What is the probability that on at least one roll, the number showing will be less than 3?

   ○ $\dfrac{65}{81}$

   ○ $\dfrac{67}{81}$

   ○ $\dfrac{8}{9}$

   ○ $\dfrac{26}{27}$

   ○ $\dfrac{80}{81}$

17. There are 816 students enrolled at a certain high school. Each of these students is taking at least one of the subjects economics, geography, and biology. The sum of the number of students taking exactly one of these subjects and the number of students taking all three of these subjects is 5 times the number of students taking exactly two of these subjects. The ratio of the number of students taking only the two subjects economics and geography to the number of students taking only the two subjects economics and biology to the number of students taking only the two subjects geography and biology is 3:6:8. How many of the students enrolled at this high school are taking only the two subjects geography and biology?

- O 35
- O 42
- O 64
- O 136
- O 240

18. Working alone at a constant rate, Machine P produces a widgets in 3 hours. Working alone at a constant rate, Machine Q produces b widgets in 4 hours. If Machines P and Q work together for c hours, then in terms of a, b, and c, how many widgets will Machines P and Q produce?

- O $\frac{3ac + 4bc}{12}$
- O $\frac{4ac + 3bc}{12}$
- O $\frac{4ac + 3bc}{6}$
- O $4ac + 3bc$
- O $\frac{ac + 2bc}{4}$

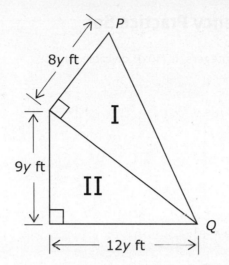

19. In the figure above, the perimeter of triangle I is 16 feet greater than the perimeter of triangle II. What is the length of PQ, in feet?

   ○ 27

   ○ 51

   ○ 68

   ○ 75

   ○ 85

20. If $x > 0$, $y > 0$, and $\dfrac{7x^2 + 72xy + 4y^2}{4x^2 + 12xy + 5y^2} = 4$, what is the value of $\dfrac{x+y}{y}$?

   ○ $\dfrac{3}{4}$

   ○ $\dfrac{4}{3}$

   ○ $\dfrac{10}{7}$

   ○ $\dfrac{7}{4}$

   ○ $\dfrac{7}{3}$

Advanced Data Sufficiency Practice Set

1. If x and y are positive even integers, is $(40x)^x$ divisible by y?

    (1) $x = \frac{1}{128}y$

    (2) y is a multiple of 160.

2. If $a \neq 0$, $\frac{x}{y} = -\frac{1}{a}$, and $\frac{y}{z} = \frac{b}{3}$, is $\frac{x}{z} > \frac{1}{2}$?

    (1) $a^2 - 2a - 3 = 0$

    (2) $b^2 - 4b + 4 = 1$

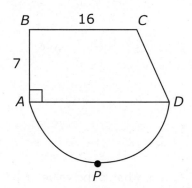

3. In the figure above, what is the area of semicircle DPA?

    (1) The area of quadrilateral $ABCD$ is 140.

    (2) The length of the line segment whose endpoints are B and D is 25.

4. Is x divisible by 39?

    (1) x divided by 65 results in a remainder of 7.

    (2) x divided by 36 results in a remainder of 15.

5. If a and b are positive integers with different units digits, and b is the square of an integer, is a also the square of an integer?

    (1) The units digit of $a + b$ is 8.

    (2) $b = 121$

6. What is the value of $8x + y$?

    (1) $3x - 2y + z = 10$

    (2) $2(x + 3y) - (y + 2z) = 25$

7. If b and c are two-digit positive integers and $b - c = 22d$, is d an integer?

    (1) The tens digit and the units digit of b are identical.

    (2) $\frac{b + c}{22} = x$, and x is an integer.

8. The integers x and y are positive, $x > y + 8$, and $y > 8$. What is the remainder when $x^2 - y^2$ is divided by 8?

    (1) The remainder when $x + y$ is divided by 8 is 7.

    (2) The remainder when $x - y$ is divided by 8 is 5.

9. If $x > y > 0$, does $3^{x+1} + 3(2^y) = 12v$?

    (1) $\dfrac{3^{2x} - 2^{2y}}{3^x - 2^y} = 4v$

    (2) $2(3^{x+2}) + 9(2^{y+1}) = 72v$

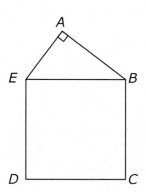

10. In the figure above, the measure of angle EAB in triangle ABE is 90°, and $BCDE$ is a square. What is the length of AB?

    (1) The length of AE is 12, and the ratio of the area of triangle ABE to the area of square $BCDE$ is $\dfrac{6}{25}$.

    (2) The perimeter of square $BCDE$ is 80 and the ratio of the length of AE to the length of AB is 3 to 4.

11. In the sequence T, the first term is the non-zero number a, and each term after the first term is equal to the non-zero number r multiplied by the previous term. What is the value of the fourth term of the sequence?

    (1) The sum of the first two terms of the sequence is 16.

    (2) The 18th term of the sequence is 81 times the 14th term of the sequence.

12. A person is to be selected at random from the group T of people. What is the probability that the person selected is a member of club E?

    (1) The probability that a person selected at random from group T is not a member of club D and is not a member of club E is $\frac{1}{4}$.

    (2) The probability that a person selected at random from group T is a member of club D and not a member of club E is $\frac{5}{12}$.

13. The population of Town X on January 1, 2010, was 56 percent greater than the population of the same town on January 1, 2005. The population of Town X on January 1, 2015, was 75 percent greater than the population of the same town on January 1, 2010. What was the population of Town X on January 1, 2005?

    (1) The population of Town X on January 1, 2015, was 21,840.

    (2) The increase in the population of Town X from January 1, 2010, to January 1, 2015, was 4,880 greater than the increase in the population of Town X from January 1, 2005, to January 1, 2010.

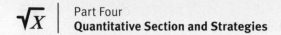
14. What is the value of $x - 3z$?

   (1) $x + 4y = 3$
   (2) $x^2 + 4xy - 3xz - 12yz = 24$

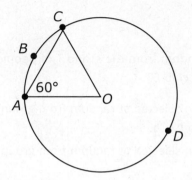

15. In the figure above, the center of the circle is O, and the measure of angle CAO is 60°. What is the perimeter of triangle OAC?

   (1)   The length of arc CDA is 16π greater than the length of arc ABC.
   (2)   The area of triangle OAC is $36\sqrt{3}$.

16. If x and y are integers and $3x > 8y$, is $y > -18$?

 (1) $-9 < x < 20$

 (2) $y = \dfrac{(x - 42)}{5}$

17. Over the course of 5 days, Monday through Friday, Danny collects a total of 76 baseball cards. Each day, he collects a different number of cards. If Danny collects the largest number of cards on Friday and the second largest number of cards on Thursday, did Danny collect more than 8 cards on Thursday?

 (1) On Friday, Danny collected 49 cards.

 (2) On one of the first 3 days, Danny collected 6 cards.

18. If $y = x^2$, is the equation $(2^{5y})(4^{120}) = 16^{20x}$ true?

 (1) $(4 - x)(12 - x) = 0$

 (2) $(x - 4)(x - 8)(x - 24) = 0$

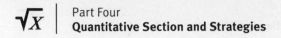
19. The ratio of the number of students in an auditorium who are seniors to the number of students in the auditorium who are not seniors is 7:5. How many students are there in the auditorium?

   (1) The ratio of the number of students who are seniors who are taking history to the number of students who are not seniors who are taking history is 21:5.

   (2) Of the students in the auditorium who are seniors, $\frac{3}{5}$ are taking history; of the students in the auditorium who are not seniors, $\frac{1}{5}$ are taking history; and the number of seniors in the auditorium who are taking history is 208 greater than the number of students in the auditorium who are not seniors and taking history.

20. If $y > 0$, is $\frac{x}{y} < 3$?

   (1) $x(x + y) - 4y(x + y) < 0$

   (2) $5(y + 8) < 20y - 3x + 40$

Answers and explanations follow on the next page. ▶ ▶ ▶

Answer Key

Advanced Problem Solving Practice Set		Advanced Data Sufficiency Practice Set	
1.	E	1.	A
2.	C	2.	E
3.	B	3.	B
4.	D	4.	A
5.	E	5.	A
6.	B	6.	C
7.	D	7.	C
8.	B	8.	C
9.	B	9.	D
10.	D	10.	B
11.	E	11.	E
12.	E	12.	C
13.	D	13.	D
14.	D	14.	C
15.	E	15.	D
16.	A	16.	B
17.	C	17.	A
18.	B	18.	A
19.	C	19.	B
20.	E	20.	E

Answers and Explanations

Advanced Problem Solving Practice Set

1. **(E)**

    The numbers m, n, and T are all positive, and $m > n$. A weekend farm stand sells only peaches. On Saturday, the farm stand has T peaches to sell, at a profit of m cents each. Any peaches remaining for sale on Sunday will be marked down and sold at a profit of $(m - n)$ cents each. If all peaches available for sale on Saturday morning are sold by Sunday evening, how many peaches, in terms of T, m, and n, does the stand need to sell on Saturday in order to make the same profit on each day?

    ○ $\dfrac{Tm}{m - n}$

    ○ $\dfrac{Tm}{n - m}$

    ○ $\dfrac{m(m - n)}{T}$

    ○ $\dfrac{T}{m - n}$

    ○ $\dfrac{T(m - n)}{2m - n}$

STEP 1: ANALYZE THE QUESTION

There are a total of T peaches, all of which are to be sold during the course of the weekend. On Saturday, the profit for each peach is m cents. On Sunday, the profit for each peach is $(m - n)$ cents.

STEP 2: STATE THE TASK

How many peaches must be sold on Saturday to make Saturday's profit equal Sunday's profit?

STEP 3: APPROACH STRATEGICALLY

Start by setting up expressions for Saturday's profit and Sunday's profit and then set those expressions equal. There's no variable given for the number of peaches sold on either day, so call the number of peaches to be sold on Saturday x. The total profit for Saturday will be (m cents per peach) times (x peaches), which is mx cents. On Sunday, there will be $(T - x)$ peaches left, each of which will bring a profit of $(m - n)$ cents. The total profit for Sunday will be $[(m - n)$ cents per peach] times $[(T - x)$ peaches], which is $(m - n)(T - x)$ cents. Saturday's profit must equal Sunday's profit: $mx = (m - n)(T - x)$. The question asks for the number of peaches to be sold on Saturday, so solve for x:

$$mx = (m - n)(T - x)$$
$$mx = mT - mx - nT + nx$$
$$2mx - nx = mT - nT$$
$$(2m - n)x = mT - nT$$
$$x = \frac{mT - nT}{2m - n}$$

None of the answer choices are written $\dfrac{mT - nT}{2m - n}$. However, $\dfrac{mT - nT}{2m - n} = \dfrac{T(m - n)}{2m - n}$.

(E) is correct.

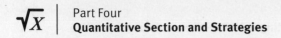

STEP 4: CONFIRM YOUR ANSWER

Confirm that your answer makes sense. Rewrite the denominator to test the size of the fraction:

$\dfrac{m-n}{2m-n} = \dfrac{m-n}{2(m-n)+n}$. It should be fairly easy to see that this is less than $\dfrac{1}{2}$. So $\dfrac{T(m-n)}{2m-n}$, which equals

$T\left(\dfrac{m-n}{2m-n}\right)$, must be less than $T\left(\dfrac{1}{2}\right)$, or $\dfrac{T}{2}$. It follows that the number of peaches sold on Saturday, which is

$\dfrac{T(m-n)}{2m-n}$, is less than half of the total number of peaches sold. That makes sense because the profit per peach is lower on Sunday than on Saturday—so fewer than half the peaches would have to be sold on Saturday in order for both days' profits to be equal.

2. **(C)**

Set X consists of at least 2 members and is a set of consecutive odd integers with an average (arithmetic mean) of 37.

Set Y consists of at least 10 members and is also a set of consecutive odd integers with an average (arithmetic mean) of 37.

Set Z consists of all of the members of both set X and set Y.

Which of the following statements must be true?

   I.   The standard deviation of set Z is not equal to the standard deviation of set X.
   II. The standard deviation of set Z is equal to the standard deviation of set Y.
   III. The average (arithmetic mean) of set Z is 37.

   O   I only
   O   II only
   O   III only
   O   I and III
   O   II and III

STEP 1: ANALYZE THE QUESTION

Set X has at least 2 members and consists of consecutive odd integers that have a mean of 37. For any set of evenly spaced numbers, the mean equals the median, so the median of set X is 37. For a set of consecutive odd integers to have an average that is an odd integer, there must be an odd number of members. So set X must actually contain at least 3 members. Thus, set X could be, for example, $\{35, 37, 39\}$ or $\{33, 35, 37, 39, 41\}$.

Set Y has the same mean and median as set X. However, set Y has a greater minimum number of members. The question says that set Y has at least 10 members. But again, for a set of consecutive odd integers to have an average that is an odd integer, there must be an odd number of members, so set Y must contain at least 11 members. Note that although set Y has a higher minimum number of terms, neither set has a maximum. This means that it's possible for set X to have more members than set Y or even for the sets to be equal to one another.

Set Z contains all the members of both set X and set Y. When sets X and Y have different numbers of members, set Z equals either set X or set Y, whichever has the greater number of members. For example, if set $X = \{35, 37, 39\}$ and set $Y = \{27, 29, 31, 33, 35, 37, 39, 41, 43, 45, 47\}$, then set Z would be equal to set Y, as the entirety of set X is contained within set Y. When sets X and Y have the same number of members (and therefore are equal), set Z equals both sets X and Y.

STEP 2: STATE THE TASK

Evaluate the three statements and determine which are always true about sets X, Y, and Z.

STEP 3: APPROACH STRATEGICALLY

Of the Roman numeral statements, III is the most frequently mentioned in the answer choices and, conveniently, also the easiest to consider. Set Z will always equal set X and/or Y, and both set X and set Y have a mean of 37. Therefore, set Z will also always have a mean of 37, and Statement III is part of the correct answer. Eliminate **(A)** and **(B)**.

The other two options involve the standard deviation of set Z. Recall that standard deviation refers to how spread out a set of numbers is. Like many GMAT questions involving standard deviation, this one does not require calculation of the actual value. Instead, recognize that sets of equally spaced integers will have different standard deviations depending on how many members are in the set. When two sets have equally spaced numbers and the spacing in both sets is the same, the set with the greater number of numbers has the greater standard deviation. While the standard deviation of set Z will always be equal to either (or both) the standard deviation of set X or Y, it is not necessarily different than the standard deviation of set X, nor is it necessarily equal to the standard deviation of set Y. This eliminates **(D)** and **(E)**, making **(C)** the correct answer.

STEP 4: CONFIRM YOUR ANSWER

Quickly confirm by recognizing that when set X has more members than set Y, both Statements I and II are not true. Statement III is the only one that is true under all circumstances.

3. (B)

The number 10,010 has how many positive integer factors?

- ○ 31
- ○ 32
- ○ 33
- ○ 34
- ○ 35

STEP 1: ANALYZE THE QUESTION

There's no information to catalogue in the question stem; there is just the number 10,010. However, the answer choices provide a clue: you need to find a way to count more than 30 factors.

STEP 2: STATE THE TASK

The question asks for the total number of positive factors, not just prime factors.

STEP 3: APPROACH STRATEGICALLY

Making a chart of all factors of a number works well for two-digit numbers, but it would require a great deal of arithmetic in this case. Instead, start by finding the prime factorization of 10,010, and then use those prime factors to find the total number of factors. The number 10,010 ends in zero, so it's divisible by 10, or 2×5. So far, you have $2 \times 5 \times 1{,}001$. Now use divisibility rules to investigate the factor 1,001. This is not an even number, so it isn't divisible by 2. Its digits do not sum to 3, so it isn't divisible by 3. It doesn't end in 5 or 0, so 5 is also not a factor. What about 7? To check whether a given number is divisible by 7, multiply the units digit by 2, subtract the result from the remaining digits, and check if the result is divisible by 7. If yes, then the original number is also divisible by 7. The units digit of 1,001 is 1. Multiply by 2 and subtract from 100: $100 - 2 = 98$. Because 98 is divisible by 7 ($98 = 7 \times 14$), 1,001 is also divisible by 7. Do the long division to find that $1{,}001 \div 7 = 143$. Now again apply divisibility rules to 143. It's not divisible by 2, 3, 5, or 7. What about 11? A number is divisible by 11 if the difference between the sum of its even-placed digits and the sum of its odd-placed digits is divisible by 11 without leaving a remainder. In the case of 143, $(1 + 3) - 4 = 0$. Zero divided by 11 is 0 without any remainder, so 143 is divisible by 11. Do the division to find that $143 \div 11 = 13$.

The full prime factorization of 10,010, then, is as follows: $2 \times 5 \times 7 \times 11 \times 13$. Once you have its prime factorization, the fastest way to determine how many factors a number has is to add 1 to each exponent in the prime factorization and multiply the resulting values. You can write the prime factorization of 10,010 as $2^1 \times 5^1 \times 7^1 \times 11^1 \times 13^1$. Now add 1 to each exponent and multiply: $(1 + 1)(1 + 1)(1 + 1)(1 + 1)(1 + 1) = (2)(2)(2)(2)(2) = 32$. The correct answer is **(B)**.

STEP 4: CONFIRM YOUR ANSWER

Do a quick check to make sure you included all the prime factors you discovered and check the exponents.

4. **(D)**

A department of motor vehicles asks visitors to draw numbered tickets from a dispenser so that they can be served in order by number. Six friends have graduated from truck-driving school and go to the department to get commercial driving licenses. They draw tickets and find that their numbers are a set of evenly spaced integers with a range of 10. Which of the following could NOT be the sum of their numbers?

- ○ 1,254
- ○ 1,428
- ○ 3,972
- ○ 4,316
- ○ 8,010

STEP 1: ANALYZE THE QUESTION

Six people draw six evenly spaced integers with a range of 10. You could pick two numbers with a range of 10, such as 1 and 11 or 2 and 12, and experiment to see how six evenly spaced integers could fit in the range. Clearly, the integers must be 2 apart.

Alternatively, the formula for the number of members in a set of evenly spaced integers is this:

$$\# \text{of numbers} = \frac{\text{Range}}{\text{Interval}} + 1$$

In this case:

$$6 = \frac{10}{\text{Interval}} + 1$$
$$6(\text{Interval}) = 10 + 1(\text{Interval})$$
$$5(\text{Interval}) = 10$$
$$\text{Interval} = 2$$

Anytime the GMAT uses a small set of evenly spaced integers, remember that a single variable is sufficient to represent the series. Thus, x can represent the first integer, and the six integers can be written $x, x + 2, x + 4, x + 6, x + 8, x + 10$. The sum of these would be $6x + 30$, or $6(x + 5)$. While you do not know the value of this expression (since you do not know the value of x), you do know it is a multiple of 6.

STEP 2: STATE THE TASK

You need to find the answer choice that *cannot* equal $6(x + 5)$. The correct answer is the one that is *not* a multiple of 6.

STEP 3: APPROACH STRATEGICALLY

Use the rule for divisibility by 6, which combines the rules for divisibility by 2 and 3. To be divisible by 2, the number must be even, and to be divisible by 3, the sum of the digits of the number must be divisible by 3.

All the answer choices are even, so use the rule for divisibility by 3.

(A): $1 + 2 + 5 + 4 = 12$. Eliminate.

(B): $1 + 4 + 2 + 8 = 15$. Eliminate.

(C): $3 + 9 + 7 + 2 = 21$. Eliminate.

(D): $4 + 3 + 1 + 6 = 14$, which is *not* divisible by 3. This is the correct answer.

For the record...

(E): $8 + 0 + 1 + 0 = 9$. Eliminate.

STEP 4: CONFIRM YOUR ANSWER

If you divide 4,316 by 6, you get 719 with a remainder of 2. Therefore, 4,316 is not divisible by 6, and **(D)** is correct.

5. (E)

For all values of x, y, and z, $x \lozenge y \lozenge z = x^2(y - 1)(z + 2)$.

If $a < 0$, which of the following shows R, S, and T arranged in order from least to greatest?

$R: 1 \lozenge a \lozenge 3$

$S: 3 \lozenge a \lozenge 1$

$T: a \lozenge 3 \lozenge 1$

- ○ R, S, T
- ○ T, S, R
- ○ R, T, S
- ○ T, R, S
- ○ S, R, T

STEP 1: ANALYZE THE QUESTION

You are given a symbolic algebra equation that describes the relationship of variables x, y, and z. Using this symbolism as a function, substitute 1, 3, and a for x, y, and z in the various orders shown. Keep in mind that a is negative.

STEP 2: STATE THE TASK

The question requires you to use the symbolic equation given and evaluate R, S, and T, placing them in order from smallest to largest.

STEP 3: APPROACH STRATEGICALLY

There are no obvious answer choices to eliminate, so calculate the values of R, S, and T and rank them in order from smallest to largest. Again, $x \lozenge y \lozenge z = x^2(y - 1)(z + 2)$.

$$R: 1 \lozenge a \lozenge 3 = 1^2(a - 1)(3 + 2)$$
$$= 1(a - 1)(5)$$
$$= 5(a - 1) = 5a - 5$$
$$S: 3 \lozenge a \lozenge 1 = 3^2(a - 1)(1 + 2)$$
$$= 9(a - 1)(3)$$
$$= 27(a - 1) = 27a - 27$$
$$T: a \lozenge 3 \lozenge 1 = a^2(3 - 1)(1 + 2)$$
$$= a^2(2)(3) = 6a^2$$

You know that T must be a positive value because the a is squared and multiplied by a positive number. Keeping in mind that a is negative, it should be clear that the expressions that result for R and S subtract a positive value from a negative value, making them both negative numbers. Therefore, T must be the greatest of the choices. Eliminate **(B)**, **(C)**, and **(D)**.

Next compare R and S. Both involve multiplying the negative value a by a constant and then subtracting a positive integer. However, both terms of S have a greater absolute value than those of R, making S less than R and **(E)** the correct answer.

STEP 4: CONFIRM YOUR ANSWER

You could pick numbers for a to confirm your answer. For example, if $a = -1$, then $R = 5a - 5 = 5(-1) - 5 = -10$, $S = 27a - 27 = 27(-1) - 27 = -54$, and $T = 6(-1^2) = 6$. For any permissible value of a, S is always less than R and T is always positive, again making **(E)** the correct answer.

6.   **(B)**

If a and b are integers, and $2a + b = 17$, then $8a + b$ cannot equal which of the following?

○   −1

○   33

○   35

○   65

○   71

STEP 1: ANALYZE THE QUESTION

Because the question asks about what $8a + b$ *cannot* equal, try to find some rule about what the expression must equal and go from there. The correct answer will violate some property represented in the given information.

STEP 2: STATE THE TASK

To find the value in the answer choices that would not work with the given information, use the equation $2a + b = 17$ in conjunction with the expression $8a + b$.

STEP 3: APPROACH STRATEGICALLY

Since you have only one equation, you can't solve for either variable, but you can still substitute and get one variable in the expression you're evaluating. Substituting for either variable would work, but it is easier to substitute for b, since all you have to do is put $2a$ on the other side of the equation. If $b = -2a + 17$, then the expression $8a + b$ becomes $8a + (-2a + 17)$, which simplifies to $6a + 17$. Because you know that a is an integer, $6a$ must be a multiple of 6. Then because you're adding 17 to a multiple of 6, the correct answer must be just that—the result of adding 17 to a multiple of 6. (If you notice that this is 1 less than a multiple of 6, evaluating the answer choices is even faster.)

(A): $-1 - 17 = -18$, a multiple of 6. Eliminate.

(B): $33 - 17 = 16$, which is not a multiple of 6. **(B)** is the correct answer.

For the record …

(C): $35 - 17 = 18$, a multiple of 6. Eliminate.

(D): $65 - 17 = 48$, a multiple of 6. Eliminate.

(E): $71 - 17 = 54$, a multiple of 6. Eliminate.

STEP 4: CONFIRM YOUR ANSWER

Using substitution, you know that $8a + b = 6a + 17$. If $6a + 17 = 33$, then $6a = 16$ and $a = \frac{8}{3}$, which is not an integer. **(B)** is correct.

7.   **(D)**

Two workers have different pay scales. Worker A receives $50 for any day worked plus $15 per hour. Worker B receives $27 per hour. Both workers may work for a fraction of an hour and be paid in proportion to their respective hourly rates. If Worker A arrives at 9:21 a.m. and receives the $50 upon arrival and Worker B arrives at 10:09 a.m., assuming both work continuously, at what time would their earnings be identical?

○   11:09 a.m.

○   12:01 p.m.

○   2:31 p.m.

○   3:19 p.m.

○   3:36 p.m.

STEP 1: ANALYZE THE QUESTION

The stem gives you a lot of information. There are two workers, each with a different pay scale as well as time arrived. It would be worth writing down the basics on your noteboard, like this:

A: 9:21 $50 + 15/hr

B: 10:09 $27/hr

STEP 2: STATE THE TASK

Even though this is about wages and money, it's a combined rates problem, just like a question that asks when two trains pass each other. The correct answer will be the time that the different rates produce the same sum of money.

STEP 3: APPROACH STRATEGICALLY

While it's possible to backsolve, it would be necessary to plug each time into two different formulas, making this approach both time-consuming and potentially error-prone. Furthermore, combining rates is usually very fast if done correctly. However, if combining the rates as described below seems too tricky and you feel confident with the arithmetic involved (and understand what result would indicate a time too late or too early), backsolving may be a good option.

Anytime the GMAT gives you different rates and asks you to find when or where they produce the same result, you can use four steps to get the answer—often in a minute or less.

The first step is to calculate any distance/work/earnings that one entity achieves when the other is not active. In this case, A works for 48 minutes before B begins, so you want to know how much money A has already made. In combined work problems, calculations are easiest if you state time as a fraction, and 48 minutes is $\frac{4}{5}$ of an hour. Thus, $15 \times \frac{4}{5} = \$12$ earned. Also, A gets $50 right off the bat, so A is $12 + $50 = $62 up when B begins working.

The second step is to combine rates. In this case, think about B catching up to A. Worker A makes $15 an hour and Worker B makes $27 an hour, so for each hour they both work, B gains on A by $12.

The third step is to divide the distance/work/earnings by the combined rate to get the time, so divide $62 by $12 per hour, and get $5\frac{2}{12}$ or $5\frac{1}{6}$ hours. A sixth of an hour is 10 minutes, so they are both working for 5 hours 10 minutes.

The last step is to add the time worked to the starting time. In this case, add 5 hours 10 minutes to the first time when both started working, 10:09 a.m., and get 3:19 p.m. **(D)** is the correct answer.

STEP 4: CONFIRM YOUR ANSWER

When taking the four steps described above leads to an answer that exactly matches one of the choices, you can feel confident that you have solved correctly. However, to confirm, you could find that Worker A worked for 5 hours 58 minutes and so, at $15 an hour, made $89.50 + $50, or $139.50. Worker B worked for 5 hours 10 minutes at $27 an hour, which also yields $139.50. Again, **(D)** is correct.

8. (B)

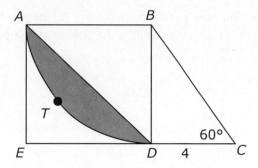

In the figure above, *ABDE* is a square, and arc *ATD* is part of a circle with center *B*. The measure of angle *BCD* is 60°, and line segment *CD* has a length of 4. What is the area of the shaded region?

- ○ $16\pi - 32$
- ○ $12\pi - 24$
- ○ $12\pi - 48$
- ○ $48\pi - 24$
- ○ $48\pi - 48$

STEP 1: ANALYZE THE QUESTION

In a shaded region question, it is important to recognize what shapes are interacting to produce the shaded region. In this case, the shaded region is the result of removing triangle *ABD*, whose area is half the area of square *ABDE*, from the sector of a circle. Additionally, you are given two important measurements for triangle *BCD*: angle *BCD* measures 60° and side *CD* has a length of 4.

STEP 2: STATE THE TASK

Subtract half the area of the square from the area of the circle sector to calculate the area of the shaded region.

STEP 3: APPROACH STRATEGICALLY

The area of a sector of a circle has the same proportional relationship to the area of the full circle as its central angle does to 360°. This sector has a central angle, which is interior angle *ABD* of the square. Since *B* is a vertex of a square, the measure of angle *ABD* is 90°. Because 90° is one-fourth of 360°, the sector defined by arc *ATD* has an area one-fourth of that of the full circle. To calculate the area of both the half square and quarter circle, determine the length of *BD*, which is both a radius of the circle and a side of the square. Triangle *BCD* is a 30-60-90 triangle, and its sides therefore have the proportion $x:\sqrt{3}x:2x$. Side *CD* is opposite the 30° angle and is therefore represented by the *x* in this proportional relationship. Side *BD* thus has a length of $4\sqrt{3}$. The area of the square is $\left(4\sqrt{3}\right)^2 = 16 \times 3 = 48$, and the area of triangle *ABD* is 24. The area of the circle is $\pi\left(4\sqrt{3}\right)^2 = 48\pi$, and the quarter circle has an area of $\frac{1}{4}(48\pi) = 12\pi$. Therefore, the area of the shaded region is $12\pi - 24$, and the correct answer is **(B)**.

STEP 4: CONFIRM YOUR ANSWER

Check that you correctly applied the 30-60-90 triangle side length ratio and performed the calculations accurately.

9. **(B)**

When the cube of a non-zero number y is subtracted from 35, the result is equal to the result of dividing 216 by the cube of that number y. What is the sum of all the possible values of y?

○ $\frac{5}{2}$

○ 5

○ 6

○ 10

○ 12

STEP 1: ANALYZE THE QUESTION

Start by translating the English into math. The cube of the number y is y^3. The result of subtracting the cube of the number y from 35 is $35 - y^3$. When the 216 is divided by y^3, the result is $\frac{216}{y^3}$. So $35 - y^3 = \frac{216}{y^3}$.

STEP 2: STATE THE TASK

Solve for all possible values of y and add them.

STEP 3: APPROACH STRATEGICALLY

Solve the equation you've written for y.

$$35 - y^3 = \frac{216}{y^3}$$

Multiply both sides by y^3: $\qquad (35 - y^3)y^3 = \left(\frac{216}{y^3}\right)y^3$

Simplify both sides: $\qquad 35y^3 - y^6 = 216$

Subtract 216 from both sides: $\quad 35y^3 - y^6 - 216 = 0$

Multiply both sides by -1: $\quad -35y^3 + y^6 + 216 = 0$

Rearrange the left side: $\quad y^6 - 35y^3 + 216 = 0$

Now simplify the equation $y^6 - 35y^3 + 216 = 0$. It helps to recognize that $y^6 = y^{3 \times 2} = (y^3)^2$. Replacing y^6 with $(y^3)^2$ in the equation $y^6 - 35y^3 + 216 = 0$ produces $(y^3)^2 - 35y^3 + 216 = 0$. Now notice that you have a quadratic equation if you consider y^3 to be the unknown. The equation $(y^3)^2 - 35y^3 + 216 = 0$ factors to $(y^3 - 8)(y^3 - 27) = 0$. So $y^3 = 8$ or $y^3 = 27$. Now $8 = 2^3$ and $27 = 3^3$. So if $y^3 = 8$, then $y = 2$, while if $y^3 = 27$, then $y = 3$. The possible values of y are 2 and 3. The sum of all the possible values of y is $2 + 3 = 5$.

(B) is correct.

STEP 4: CONFIRM YOUR ANSWER

You can check that you have the correct values of y by plugging them into the equation $35 - y^3 = \frac{216}{y^3}$. If $y = 2$, you get $35 - 8 = \frac{216}{8}$, or $27 = 27$. If $y = 3$, you get $35 - 27 = \frac{216}{27}$, or $8 = 8$.

10. **(D)**

One letter is selected at random from the five letters V, W, X, Y, and Z, and event A is the event that the letter V is selected. A fair six-sided die with sides numbered 1, 2, 3, 4, 5, and 6 is to be rolled, and event B is the event that a 5 or a 6 shows. A fair coin is to be tossed, and event C is the event that a head shows. What is the probability that event A occurs and at least one of the events B and C occurs?

○ $\frac{1}{30}$

○ $\frac{1}{15}$

○ $\frac{1}{10}$

○ $\frac{2}{15}$

○ $\frac{1}{5}$

STEP 1: ANALYZE THE QUESTION

This is a probability question with three separate and independent events.

STEP 2: STATE THE TASK

You need to calculate the probability that event A will occur *and* that either *or* both events B and C will occur.

STEP 3: APPROACH STRATEGICALLY

The probability of an event is $\dfrac{\text{Number of desired outcomes}}{\text{Number of possible outcomes}}$. For event A, one letter is selected at random from the five letters V, W, X, Y, and Z, so the probability that event A occurs is $\frac{1}{5}$. For event B, a 5 or 6 must occur from the 6 possible outcomes 1, 2, 3, 4, 5, and 6, so the probability that event B occurs is $\frac{2}{6} = \frac{1}{3}$. For event C, a head comes up out of 2 possible outcomes, heads and tails, so the probability that event C occurs is $\frac{1}{2}$.

This can be written as $P(A) = \frac{1}{5}$, $P(B) = \frac{1}{3}$, and $P(C) = \frac{1}{2}$.

The probability that event A occurs and at least one of the events B and C occurs is $P(A) \times P(B \text{ or } C)$.

Find $P(B \text{ or } C)$: Applying the generalized formula for 2 events, $P(B \text{ or } C) = P(B) + P(C) - P(B \text{ and } C)$.

The events B and C are independent, so $P(B \text{ and } C) = P(B)P(C)$.

Replacing $P(B \text{ and } C)$ with $P(B)P(C)$, you have $P(B \text{ or } C) = P(B) + P(C) - P(B)P(C)$. Then substitute in $P(B) = \frac{1}{3}$ and $P(C) = \frac{1}{2}$:

$$P(B \text{ or } C) = \frac{1}{3} + \frac{1}{2} - \frac{1}{3} \times \frac{1}{2}$$

$$= \frac{2}{6} + \frac{3}{6} - \frac{1}{6}$$

$$= \frac{4}{6} = \frac{2}{3}$$

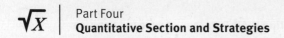

Now find the probability that event A occurs and at least one of the events B and C occurs:

$$P(A) \times P(B \text{ or } C) = \frac{1}{5} \times \frac{2}{3} = \frac{2}{15}$$

(D) is correct.

STEP 4: CONFIRM YOUR ANSWER

You can check that you have calculated $P(B \text{ or } C)$ correctly by calculating the probability that neither B nor C occurs and subtracting from 1. $P(\sim B) = \frac{2}{3}$ and $P(\sim C) = \frac{1}{2}$, so $P(B \text{ or } C) = 1 - \frac{2}{3} \times \frac{1}{2} = 1 - \frac{1}{3} = \frac{2}{3}$.

11. (E)

A car traveled from Town A to Town B. The car traveled the first $\frac{3}{8}$ of the distance from Town A to Town B at an average speed of x miles per hour, where $x > 0$. The car traveled the remaining distance at an average speed of y miles per hour, where $y > 0$. The car traveled the entire distance from Town A to Town B at an average speed of z miles per hour. Which of the following equations gives y in terms of x and z?

○ $y = \dfrac{3x + 5z}{8}$

○ $y = \dfrac{5xz}{8x + 3z}$

○ $y = \dfrac{8x - 3z}{5xz}$

○ $y = \dfrac{3xz}{8x - 5z}$

○ $y = \dfrac{5xz}{8x - 3z}$

STEP 1: ANALYZE THE QUESTION

The car moves at x mph for the first $\frac{3}{8}$ of the trip and y mph for the final $\frac{5}{8}$. Its average speed over the entire distance traveled is z mph.

STEP 2: STATE THE TASK

You want y in terms of x and z.

STEP 3: APPROACH STRATEGICALLY

Remember that Distance = Speed × Time, and that Total distance = Average speed × Total time. Call the distance from Town A to Town B d miles. Then the first $\frac{3}{8}$ of the distance from Town A to Town B is $\frac{3d}{8}$ miles. Since the car traveled the first $\frac{3d}{8}$ miles at an average speed of x miles per hour, the time that it took the car to travel the first $\frac{3d}{8}$ miles was $\dfrac{\left(\frac{3d}{8}\text{ miles}\right)}{\left(x\frac{\text{miles}}{\text{hour}}\right)} = \dfrac{3d}{8x}$ hours. The remainder of the distance from Town A to Town B, in miles, was $\frac{5d}{8}$. Since the car traveled $\frac{5d}{8}$ miles at an average speed of y miles per hour, the time that it took the car to travel the remaining $\frac{5d}{8}$ miles was $\dfrac{\left(\frac{5d}{8}\text{ miles}\right)}{\left(y\frac{\text{miles}}{\text{hour}}\right)} = \dfrac{5d}{8y}$ hours. The total time for the trip was $\left(\frac{3d}{8x} + \frac{5d}{8y}\right)$ hours. Since the car traveled a distance of d miles in $\left(\frac{3d}{8x} + \frac{5d}{8y}\right)$ hours, the average speed of the car was $\dfrac{d\text{ miles}}{\left(\frac{3d}{8x} + \frac{5d}{8y}\right)\text{hours}}$, or $\dfrac{d}{\left(\frac{3d}{8x} + \frac{5d}{8y}\right)}$ miles per hour. You know that the average speed of the car was z miles per hour. So $\dfrac{d}{\left(\frac{3d}{8x} + \frac{5d}{8y}\right)} = z$.

Now solve this equation for y in terms of x and z. The variable d is in the way, but it looks like this variable can be canceled. Factoring d out of the denominator in the left side of the equation $\dfrac{d}{\left(\dfrac{3d}{8x}+\dfrac{5d}{8y}\right)}=z$ yields

$\dfrac{d}{d\left(\dfrac{3}{8x}+\dfrac{5}{8y}\right)}=z$. Canceling d from the numerator and denominator of the left side results in $\dfrac{1}{\left(\dfrac{3}{8x}+\dfrac{5}{8y}\right)}=z$.

Multiplying both sides by the denominator $\dfrac{3}{8x}+\dfrac{5}{8y}$, you get $1=z\left(\dfrac{3}{8x}+\dfrac{5}{8y}\right)$. Multiplying out the right side produces $1=\dfrac{3z}{8x}+\dfrac{5z}{8y}$. Multiply both sides by the least common denominator on the right side, which is $8xy$, to get rid of the denominators: $8xy(1)=8xy\left(\dfrac{3z}{8x}+\dfrac{5z}{8y}\right)$, so $8xy=3yz+5xz$. Since you are trying to solve for y in terms of x and z, get all the expressions involving y on one side of the equation, and all expressions not involving y on the other side of the equation. Subtracting $3yz$ from both sides yields $8xy-3yz=5xz$. Factoring y out of the left side, $y(8x-3z)=5xz$. Dividing both sides by $8x-3z$, $y=\dfrac{5xz}{8x-3z}$.

(E) is correct.

STEP 4: CONFIRM YOUR ANSWER

Check to make sure you applied the average speed formula correctly and that you solved for the correct variable.

12. (E)

An ornithologist has studied a particular population of starlings and discovered that their population has increased by 400 percent every 10 years starting in 1890. If the initial population in 1890 was 256 birds, how large was the population of starlings in 1970?

- ○ 102,400
- ○ 10,000,000
- ○ 16,777,216
- ○ 20,000,000
- ○ 100,000,000

STEP 1: ANALYZE THE QUESTION

You know that the initial population of starlings in 1890 is 256 and that the population increases by 400% every 10 years.

STEP 2: STATE THE TASK

Find the size of the population of starlings in 1970.

STEP 3: APPROACH STRATEGICALLY

Although this question does not deal with money, it is useful to notice that the given facts fit the compound interest formula perfectly. The formula, as applied to money, is (Total of principal and interest) = Principal $\times$ $(1 + r)^t$, where r is the interest rate per time period and t is the number of time periods. In this question, the total of "principal and interest" is the final population of starlings in 1970, the "principal" is the initial population (256), the "interest rate" is the population growth rate expressed as a decimal (4.00), and t is the number of 10-year periods from 1890 to 1970 (8). Thus, you have the following:

$$1970 \text{ population} = 256 \times (1 + 4)^8 = 256 \times 5^8$$

At this point, you could do the arithmetic, but without a calculator, this approach would be time-consuming and potentially prone to errors. Remember that when seemingly complicated arithmetic arises on the GMAT, there is often a more strategic way to get to the answer. If you notice that 256 is a power of 2, you can use the exponent rules to make your task much simpler:

$$256 \times 5^8 = 2^8 \times 5^8 = (2 \times 5)^8 = 10^8 = 100,000,000$$

The correct answer is (**E**).

STEP 4: CONFIRM YOUR ANSWER

Confirm that you have applied the compound interest formula correctly.

13. (D)

If $(x^2 + 8)yz < 0$, $wz > 0$, and $xyz < 0$, then which of the following must be true?

    I. $x < 0$

    II. $wy < 0$

    III. $yz < 0$

  ◯ II only

  ◯ III only

  ◯ I and III only

  ◯ II and III only

  ◯ I, II, and III

STEP 1: ANALYZE THE QUESTION

This question concerns positive and negative number properties. Since $wz > 0$ and $xyz < 0$, each of the variables w, x, y, and z is non-zero. In the first inequality, which is $(x^2 + 8)yz < 0$, x^2 must be greater than zero because from the third inequality $xyz < 0$, you know that x is not zero. Since x^2 is positive and 8 is positive, $x^2 + 8$ is positive. Since $(x^2 + 8)yz < 0$, and since $x^2 + 8$ is positive, it must be that yz is negative. Thus, y and z have opposite signs. Since $wz > 0$, both w and z must have the same sign. Finally, in order for xyz to be negative, either one or all of the three variables x, y, and z must be negative.

STEP 2: STATE THE TASK

Determine which of three inequalities must be true.

STEP 3: APPROACH STRATEGICALLY

Usually, the most efficient way to solve this type of question is to start with the Roman numeral statement that appears most often in the answer choices; in this case, that is Statement III, $yz < 0$. You already determined that y and z have opposite signs, so this statement must be true. You can eliminate **(A)**.

Look at Statement II next. You determined that w and z have the same sign. Therefore, if y times z is negative, then y times w must also be negative, and Statement II must be true. You can now eliminate **(B)** and **(C)**.

Finally, if xyz is negative and yz is also negative, then x must be positive. Eliminate **(E)**. **(D)** is correct.

STEP 4: CONFIRM YOUR ANSWER

Check your reasoning to confirm that y has the opposite sign as w, that y has the opposite sign as z, and that x is positive.

14. (D)

If $\dfrac{61^2 - 1}{h}$ is an integer, then h could be divisible by each of the following EXCEPT

- O 8
- O 12
- O 15
- O 18
- O 31

STEP 1: ANALYZE THE QUESTION

Calculating the actual value of the numerator would be too time-consuming, but it's presented in the form of the difference of two perfect squares (61^2 and 1^2). This is one of the classic quadratics:
$61^2 - 1^2 = (61 + 1)(61 - 1)$, or $(62)(60)$.

STEP 2: STATE THE TASK

In order for $\dfrac{61^2 - 1}{h}$ to be an integer, $61^2 - 1^2$ must be a multiple of h. So the question essentially asks which factor of h would *not* divide evenly into the numerator. Four of the choices will divide evenly into the numerator; the correct answer will not.

STEP 3: APPROACH STRATEGICALLY

It would take far too much time to find the product of 60 and 62 and then divide that by each of the answer choices. Instead, remember that for h to divide evenly into the product of 60 and 62, h must share factors with 60 and/or 62. Moreover, the answer choices represent factors of h. Looking at the choices, 8 has factors of 2 and 4. Because 2 is a factor of 62 and 4 is a factor of 60, you can cross out **(A)**. Choices **(B)**, **(C)**, and **(E)** are a little more straightforward; since 12 itself is a factor of 60, 15 is also a factor of 60, and 31 is a factor of 62. The only choice that is not a factor of either number is 18. The correct answer is **(D)**.

STEP 4: CONFIRM YOUR ANSWER

You can quickly check that 18 is not a factor of the product of 60 and 62 by breaking down 18, 60, and 62 into their prime factors: $\dfrac{60 \times 62}{18} = \dfrac{2 \times 2 \times 3 \times 5 \times 2 \times 31}{2 \times 3 \times 3}$. Notice that the 2 in the denominator will cancel out one of the 2s in the numerator, but only one of the 3s in the denominator will cancel out. So the denominator will have a 3 remaining that cannot be canceled out. Therefore, the product of 60 and 62 is *not* divisible by 18, and **(D)** is correct.

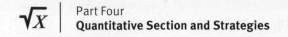
15. (E)

If a, b, and c are integers such that $0 < a < b < c$, and a is even, b is prime, and c is odd, which of the following is a possible value for abc?

- ○ 5
- ○ 12
- ○ 16
- ○ 34
- ○ 54

STEP 1: ANALYZE THE QUESTION

You know that a, b, and c are positive integers. Because b is greater than a, an even number, b must be greater than 2; then because b is a prime number greater than 2, it must be odd. Then since c is greater than at least one odd prime number, c is greater than 3, and because c is odd, it must be at least 5.

STEP 2: STATE THE TASK

Determine which of the answer choices is a *possible* value for abc. Note that this doesn't mean that the correct choice is the *only* possible value for abc.

STEP 3: APPROACH STRATEGICALLY

Given the structure of the problem, you will have to eliminate any answer choice that cannot be a possible value for abc rather than solve for a single value of abc. If you think of abc as $a \times bc$, then, regardless of the values of b and c, abc must be even since a is an even number. Eliminate **(A)**.

To deal with the remaining answer choices, since the question contains variables and the answer choices are numbers, picking numbers is a good approach. The least value possible for a is 2, the first even number greater than 0. The next largest prime number, 3, can be substituted for b. (Note that b is a prime number that has to be greater than a positive even number, meaning it can't be 2, the only even prime number.) The product of a and b would be 6, and this could be multiplied by 2 to make $abc = 12$. However, 2 is not a permissible value for c, so eliminate **(B)**. $2 \times 3 = 6$, $2 \times 5 = 10$, and $2 \times 7 = 14$ are not factors of 16, and moving up to the next even number, 4, makes the smallest possible value for ab 20, so eliminate **(C)**. Similarly, if a is 2, the only possible values of ab that are less than 34 are 6, 10, 14, 22, and 26. None of these are factors of 34, so you'll have to consider $a = 4$. Since $ab = 20$ and $ab = 28$ are not factors of 34, eliminate **(D)**. Since $6 \times 9 = 54$ and 9 is a valid value for c, 54 is indeed one possible value for abc, and **(E)** is correct.

STEP 4: CONFIRM YOUR ANSWER

Check that you used permissible values when checking the answer choices.

16. (A)

A fair die with sides numbered 1, 2, 3, 4, 5, and 6 is to be rolled 4 times. What is the probability that on at least one roll, the number showing will be less than 3?

○ $\frac{65}{81}$

○ $\frac{67}{81}$

○ $\frac{8}{9}$

○ $\frac{26}{27}$

○ $\frac{80}{81}$

STEP 1: ANALYZE THE QUESTION

Note that "less than 3" means a 1 or 2.

STEP 2: STATE THE TASK

You need the probability that *at least* 1 roll is a 1 or 2. That means the probability that 1, 2, 3, or 4 rolls result in a 1 or 2.

STEP 3: APPROACH STRATEGICALLY

Instead of calculating all those probabilities separately and adding them together, it will be easier to find the probability that *no* rolls result in a 1 or 2, and then subtract that probability from 1. Start by finding the probability that each of the 4 rolls results in at least a 3. The probability formula is as follows:

$$\text{Probability} = \frac{\text{Number of desired outcomes}}{\text{Number of possible outcomes}}$$

When rolling the die once, there are 4 desired outcomes, which are 3, 4, 5, and 6, and there are 6 possible outcomes, which are 1, 2, 3, 4, 5, and 6. The probability that when the die is rolled once, a number greater than or equal to 3 results is $\frac{4}{6} = \frac{2}{3}$. Since the results of the 4 rolls of the dice are independent of each other, the probability that all 4 rolls result in a number greater than or equal to 3 is $\frac{2}{3} \times \frac{2}{3} \times \frac{2}{3} \times \frac{2}{3} = \frac{2 \times 2 \times 2 \times 2}{3 \times 3 \times 3 \times 3} = \frac{16}{81}$.

It follows that the probability that at least 1 roll results in a number less than 3 is $1 - \frac{16}{81} = \frac{81}{81} - \frac{16}{81} = \frac{81 - 16}{81} = \frac{65}{81}$.

(A) is correct.

STEP 4: CONFIRM YOUR ANSWER

Check that you've calculated the probability of rolling a 3, 4, 5, or 6 correctly; check that you've accounted for 4 rolls; and check your subtraction.

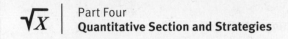

17. (C)

There are 816 students enrolled at a certain high school. Each of these students is taking at least one of the subjects economics, geography, and biology. The sum of the number of students taking exactly one of these subjects and the number of students taking all three of these subjects is 5 times the number of students taking exactly two of these subjects. The ratio of the number of students taking only the two subjects economics and geography to the number of students taking only the two subjects economics and biology to the number of students taking only the two subjects geography and biology is 3:6:8. How many of the students enrolled at this high school are taking only the two subjects geography and biology?

- ○ 35
- ○ 42
- ○ 64
- ○ 136
- ○ 240

STEP 1: ANALYZE THE QUESTION

This is a tough overlapping sets question. You are given the total number of students (816), sufficient information to set up two equations about students taking one, two, and three of the subjects and ratios of the various two-subject combinations.

STEP 2: STATE THE TASK

You need to find the number of students taking one particular two-subject combination: geography and biology.

STEP 3: APPROACH STRATEGICALLY

Start by setting up a couple of equations concerning students taking one, two, and three subjects. Say that the number of students taking exactly one of the subjects is x, say that the number of students taking exactly two of the subjects is y, and say that the number of students taking all three of the subjects is z. Since there are 816 students in the high school, $x + y + z = 816$. Since the sum of the number of students taking exactly one of the subjects and the number of students taking all three of the subjects is 5 times the number of students taking exactly two of the subjects, $x + z = 5y$. Now rewrite the equation $x + y + z = 816$ as $(x + z) + y = 816$. Substitute $5y$ for $x + z$ to find that $5y + y = 816$, $6y = 816$, and $y = \dfrac{816}{6} = 136$. Thus, the number of students taking exactly two of the subjects is 136.

Now make use of the ratios provided. The ratio of the number of students taking only economics and geography to the number of students taking only economics and biology to the number of students taking only geography and biology is 3:6:8, so the number of students taking only the two subjects geography and biology is:

$$\frac{8}{3+6+8}(136) = \frac{8}{17}(136) = 8(8) = 64$$

(C) is correct.

STEP 4: CONFIRM YOUR ANSWER

One way to confirm your answer is to calculate how many students are taking the other two-subject combinations, and then add the three values to see if they in fact sum to 136: $\dfrac{3}{17}(136) = (3)(8) = 24$ and $\dfrac{6}{17}(136) = (6)(8) = 48$. It is in fact the case that $64 + 24 + 48 = 136$.

18. (B)

Working alone at a constant rate, Machine P produces a widgets in 3 hours. Working alone at a constant rate, Machine Q produces b widgets in 4 hours. If Machines P and Q work together for c hours, then in terms of a, b, and c, how many widgets will Machines P and Q produce?

○ $\dfrac{3ac + 4bc}{12}$

○ $\dfrac{4ac + 3bc}{12}$

○ $\dfrac{4ac + 3bc}{6}$

○ $4ac + 3bc$

○ $\dfrac{ac + 2bc}{4}$

STEP 1: ANALYZE THE QUESTION

The question gives the production rates for three machines. The answer choices are given in algebraic terms.

STEP 2: STATE THE TASK

Find the number of widgets produced by two of the three machines.

STEP 3: APPROACH STRATEGICALLY

Since Machine P produces a widgets in 3 hours, it produces widgets at the rate of $\frac{a}{3}$ widgets per hour. By the same logic, Machine P produces widgets at the rate of $\frac{b}{4}$ widgets per hour. So working together, Machine P and Machine Q produce widgets at the rate of $\frac{a}{3} + \frac{b}{4}$ widgets per hour. Recall that

Work = Rate × Time. Thus, in c hours, working together, Machine P and Machine Q produce:

$$\left[\left(\frac{a}{3} + \frac{b}{4}\right)\frac{\text{widgets}}{\text{hour}}\right] \times (c \text{ hours}) = c\left(\frac{a}{3} + \frac{b}{4}\right) \text{ widgets}.$$

None of the answer choices is written as $c\left(\frac{a}{3} + \frac{b}{4}\right)$. So rewrite this expression:

$$c\left(\frac{a}{3} + \frac{b}{4}\right) = c\left(\frac{a \times 4}{3 \times 4} + \frac{b \times 3}{4 \times 3}\right)$$

$$= c\left(\frac{4a}{12} + \frac{3b}{12}\right) = c\left(\frac{4a + 3b}{12}\right) = \frac{4ac + 3bc}{12}$$

(B) is correct.

STEP 4: CONFIRM YOUR ANSWER

Double-check your calculations to make sure your algebra is correct.

19. (C)

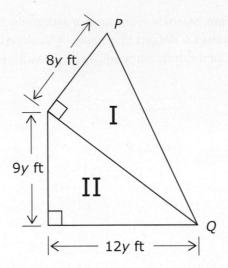

In the figure above, the perimeter of triangle I is 16 feet greater than the perimeter of triangle II. What is the length of *PQ*, in feet?

○ 27

○ 51

○ 68

○ 75

○ 85

STEP 1: ANALYZE THE QUESTION

The question shows two right triangles arranged so that the hypotenuse of one triangle is also one of the legs of the other triangle. Dimensions of some of the sides are provided in terms of the variable *y*. The question also provides information about the difference between the perimeters of the two triangles. The answer choices are numbers, not expressed in terms of *y*.

STEP 2: STATE THE TASK

Find the length of the unshared hypotenuse.

STEP 3: APPROACH STRATEGICALLY

Describe the lengths of the hypotenuses of right triangles I and II in terms of *y* and feet. Looking at right triangle II, you see that the leg of length 9*y* feet can be expressed as $3 \times (3y$ feet) and the leg of length 12*y* feet is $4 \times (3y$ feet). So right triangle II is a 3-4-5 right triangle with each member of the 3 to 4 to 5 ratio multiplied by 3*y* feet. That means the length of the hypotenuse of right triangle II is $5 \times (3y$ feet) $= 15y$ feet.

Now find the length of PQ. Triangle I is a right triangle with one leg of length $8y$ feet and the other leg (the hypotenuse of triangle II) of $15y$ feet. You may have the ratio 8:15:17 memorized, and if so, you know that PQ is $17y$ feet. Alternatively, you can use the Pythagorean theorem: $a^2 + b^2 = c^2$, or $8^2 + 15^2 = PQ^2$.

$$PQ^2 = (8y)^2 + (15y)^2$$
$$= 64y^2 + 225y^2$$
$$= (64 + 225)(y^2)$$
$$= 289y^2$$
$$PQ = \sqrt{289y^2} = 17y$$

You now know the lengths of all the sides of triangles I and II.

The perimeter of triangle I is $8y + 15y + 17y = 40y$.

The perimeter of triangle II is $9y + 12y + 15y = 36y$.

The perimeter of triangle I is 16 feet greater than the perimeter of triangle II. So $40y = 36y + 16$, $4y = 16$, and $y = 4$. The length of PQ, in feet, is $17y = 17(4) = 68$. **(C)** is correct.

STEP 4: CONFIRM YOUR ANSWER

Since PQ is the hypotenuse of the triangle that has a leg that is the hypotenuse of the other triangle, PQ must be the longest side of either triangle. The greatest length of the other sides is $15y$, so $17y$ is a logical value.

20. (E)

If $x > 0$, $y > 0$, and, $\dfrac{7x^2 + 72xy + 4y^2}{4x^2 + 12xy + 5y^2} = 4$ what is the value of $\dfrac{x+y}{y}$?

○ $\dfrac{3}{4}$

○ $\dfrac{4}{3}$

○ $\dfrac{10}{7}$

○ $\dfrac{7}{4}$

○ $\dfrac{7}{3}$

STEP 1: ANALYZE THE QUESTION

The problem presents an equation in two variables, x and y, with quadratic expressions in both the numerator and denominator. The answer choices are in the form of fractions, with no variables.

STEP 2: STATE THE TASK

Find the numeric value of an expression stated in terms of x and y.

STEP 3: APPROACH STRATEGICALLY

Begin by simplifying the equation $\dfrac{7x^2 + 72xy + 4y^2}{4x^2 + 12xy + 5y^2} = 4$.

$$7x^2 + 72xy + 4y^2 = 4\left(4x^2 + 12xy + 5y^2\right)$$

$$7x^2 + 72xy + 4y^2 = 16x^2 + 48xy + 20y^2$$

$$72xy + 4y^2 = 9x^2 + 48xy + 20y^2$$

$$24xy + 4y^2 = 9x^2 + 20y^2$$

$$24xy = 9x^2 + 16y^2$$

$$9x^2 - 24xy + 16y^2 = 0$$

$$(3x - 4y)(3x - 4y) = 0$$

Thus, $3x - 4y = 0$.

You are seeking the value of $\dfrac{x+y}{y}$. Rewrite this as $\dfrac{x+y}{y} = \dfrac{x}{y} + \dfrac{y}{y} = \dfrac{x}{y} + 1$.

Solve the equation $3x - 4y = 0$ for the value of $\frac{x}{y}$:

$$3x - 4y = 0$$
$$3x = 4y$$
$$\frac{3x}{y} = 4$$
$$\frac{x}{y} = \frac{4}{3}$$

Thus, $\frac{x+y}{y} = \frac{x}{y} + 1 = \frac{4}{3} + 1 = \frac{7}{3}$. **(E)** is correct.

STEP 4: CONFIRM YOUR ANSWER

Unfortunately, there is no easy way to plug the solution back into the problem. Check the math used to derive your answer.

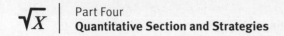
Advanced Data Sufficiency Practice Set

1. **(A)**

If x and y are positive even integers, is $(40x)^x$ divisible by y?

(1) $x = \frac{1}{128}y$

(2) y is a multiple of 160.

STEP 1: ANALYZE THE QUESTION STEM

This is a Yes/No question. Essentially, the question asks whether $\dfrac{(40x)^x}{y}$ is an integer. Note that x and y are both even. Also note that because x is even and 40 is an integer, the expression $(40x)^x$ must be even. Finally, note that x is a factor of the base as well as the exponent.

To determine that y divides evenly into $(40x)^x$, you need to know that y has no prime factors that are not found in 40 or x and that it has no prime factor raised to an exponent that is greater than the number of times that prime number is a factor of $(40x)^x$. If a statement allows you to establish both these conditions, you can answer the question with a yes, and the statement is sufficient. If you can show that either of these conditions does not exist, then the statement allows you to answer the question with a no and is likewise sufficient.

STEP 2: EVALUATE THE STATEMENTS USING 12TEN

Statement (1) tells you that $y = 128x$. Taking this statement into account, the question now becomes whether $\dfrac{(40x)^x}{128x}$ is an integer. The number 128 has only 2 as a prime factor, breaking down to 2^7. So focus on the number of times 2 is a factor of the expression $(40x)^x$. Remember that x is positive and even, so $x \geq 2$. Since x is the exponent in the expression $(40x)^x$, a greater value of x will make the number of times 2 is a factor of $(40x)^x$ greater. It follows that if $x = 2$ makes $128x$ a factor of $(40x)^x$, the answer to the question is definitively yes, and you have sufficiency. (Note that if $x > 2$, all other factors of x besides 2 will cancel in the denominator because there will be a greater number of them in the numerator due to the exponent. For instance, if $x = 6 = (2)(3)$, then there will be one factor of 3 in the denominator and six factors of 3 in the numerator.)

Substituting 2 for x yields:

$$\frac{(40x)^x}{128x} = \frac{(40 \times 2)^2}{128 \times 2} = \frac{\left(2^3 \times 5 \times 2\right)^2}{2^7 \times 2} = \frac{2^8 \times 5}{2^8} = 5$$

So $x = 2$ makes $128x$ a factor of $(40x)^x$, and Statement (1) is sufficient. Eliminate **(B)**, **(C)**, and **(E)**.

Statement (2) tells you that y is a multiple of 160 and thus has 2 and 5 as its distinct prime factors. While that may seem to align with the 40 in the exponent, y being a multiple of 160 means that it could be infinitely large and thus potentially too big to be a factor, given that you don't know the value of x. Statement (2) is insufficient.

(A) is the correct answer.

2. **(E)**

If $a \neq 0$, $\frac{x}{y} = -\frac{1}{a}$, and $\frac{y}{z} = \frac{b}{3}$, is $\frac{x}{z} > \frac{1}{2}$?

(1) $a^2 - 2a - 3 = 0$

(2) $b^2 - 4b + 4 = 1$

STEP 1: ANALYZE THE QUESTION STEM

The question stem gives two equations and asks whether a third algebraic fraction is greater than a constant, making this a Yes/No question. You can simplify the given information by combining the two equations. Note that multiplying them together will make the y cancel out: $\left(\frac{x}{y}\right)\left(\frac{y}{z}\right) = \left(-\frac{1}{a}\right)\left(\frac{b}{3}\right)$ results in $\frac{x}{z} = -\frac{b}{3a}$. The question asks about $\frac{x}{z}$, so if you can find the values of a and b, you will have sufficiency. You will also have sufficiency if you can find the value of $\frac{b}{a}$. Since $\frac{a}{b}$ is the reciprocal of $\frac{b}{a}$, you will also have sufficiency if you can find the value of $\frac{a}{b}$. Finally, you will have sufficiency if you can find that, in some other way, there is only one answer to the question regarding $\frac{x}{z}$ and $\frac{1}{2}$.

STEP 2: EVALUATE THE STATEMENTS USING 12TEN

Since each statement uses only one of the variables needed, **(A)**, **(B)**, and **(D)** can be crossed off immediately. The task then becomes determining whether the two statements taken together are sufficient or not.

Neither of the statements is simpler than the other, so begin by factoring either of them. In Statement (1), factoring the left side of the equation $a^2 - 2a - 3 = 0$ yields $(a + 1)(a - 3) = 0$, making $a = -1$ or 3. In Statement (2), subtract 1 from both sides, resulting in $b^2 - 4b + 3 = 0$. Factoring the left side of the equation $b^2 - 4b + 3 = 0$ produces $(b - 1)(b - 3) = 0$, making $b = 1$ or $b = 3$.

As noted in step 1, in order to answer the question is $\frac{x}{z} > \frac{1}{2}$, you must know the values of a and b, or you must know the value $\frac{b}{a}$, or you must know the value $\frac{a}{b}$, or you must be able to compare $\frac{x}{z}$ and $\frac{1}{2}$ in some other way. The four possible combinations of a and b are these:

$$a = -1 \text{ and } b = 1$$

$$a = -1 \text{ and } b = 3$$

$$a = 3 \text{ and } b = 1$$

$$a = 3 \text{ and } b = 3$$

Test the first pair, as it is the easiest. If $a = -1$ and $b = 1$, then $\frac{x}{z} = -\frac{b}{3a} = -\frac{1}{3(-1)} = \frac{1}{3}$, which is *not* greater than $\frac{1}{2}$. In this case, the answer to the question is no.

To try to avoid having to test all four combinations, notice that with both a and b positive, $-\frac{b}{3a}$ will be negative, and the answer will still be no. So stay with $a = -1$. You can expect a greater value for $\frac{x}{z}$ when $b = 3$ than when $b = 1$, so test $b = 3$. If $a = -1$ and $b = 3$, $\frac{x}{z} = -\frac{b}{3a} = -\frac{3}{3(-1)} = 1$. In this case, $\frac{x}{z} > \frac{1}{2}$ and the answer to the question is yes.

One possibility gives you an answer of yes to the question and a different possibility gives you an answer of no to the question, making the statements taken together insufficient to answer the question definitively. The correct answer is **(E)**.

3.   (B)

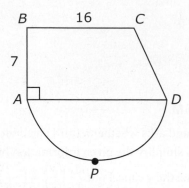

In the figure above, what is the area of semicircle *DPA*?

(1)   The area of quadrilateral *ABCD* is 140.

(2)   The length of the line segment whose endpoints are *B* and *D* is 25.

STEP 1: ANALYZE THE QUESTION STEM

This is a Value question. The question stem contains a diagram with multiple figures, and you need to be able to find a single possible area of the semicircle *DPA* to have sufficiency. In order to do that, you would need to know the length of diameter *AD* of the semicircle. *AD* is also a side of quadrilateral *ABCD*. Because a semicircle has half the area of a circle with the same diameter, knowing the length of *AD* would allow you to calculate the area of semicircle *DPA*.

STEP 2: EVALUATE THE STATEMENTS USING 12TEN

Statement (1) tells you that the area of the quadrilateral *ABCD* is 140. Using the formula for the area of a trapezoid, $\text{Area} = \dfrac{b_1 + b_2}{2} \times h$, it would appear that you could plug in the information you know from the diagram and Statement (1) (the area, the height, and b_1) to solve for b_2. However, it's important to remember that figures in Data Sufficiency questions are not necessarily drawn to scale. You are not given enough information to determine whether sides *AD* and *BC* are parallel; therefore, *ABCD* is not necessarily a trapezoid. Statement (1) is thus insufficient, and you can eliminate **(A)** and **(D)**.

Statement (2) tells you that the length of the line segment whose endpoints are *B* and *D* is 25. This line segment, if added to the figure, would be the hypotenuse of right triangle *ABD*. Since you now know two sides of a right triangle, it would be possible to calculate the length of the third side, *AD*, by using the Pythagorean theorem. As mentioned above, knowing the length of *AD* would allow you to calculate the area of the semicircle, and Statement (2) is sufficient. Therefore, the correct answer is **(B)**.

4. (A)

Is x divisible by 39?

(1) x divided by 65 results in a remainder of 7.

(2) x divided by 36 results in a remainder of 15.

STEP 1: ANALYZE THE QUESTION STEM

This is a Yes/No question. Unlike other remainder questions in which you can pick numbers, the remainders in the statements would be very tedious and time-consuming to test multiple times individually, let alone to combine. Thus, there must be a simpler way to determine divisibility. Whenever the numbers given are unwieldy, the easiest and most efficient way to establish divisibility is to find the prime factors. In this case, 39 breaks down to 3×13, so for x to be divisible by 39, it must be divisible by both 3 and 13.

STEP 2: EVALUATE THE STATEMENTS USING 12TEN

Statement (1) gives the number 65. Consider that 65 is 5×13; one of the prime factors of 39 is present. For x to be divisible by 13, the remainder itself must be a multiple of 13. The remainder 7 is not a multiple of 13, so it is impossible for x to be divisible by 13 or 39. This makes the answer to the question always no, and Statement (1) is sufficient. Eliminate choices **(B)**, **(C)**, and **(E)**.

In evaluating Statement (2), you can use the same principle. The number 36 is divisible by 3, one of the necessary primes, so the remainder must also be divisible by 3. The remainder 15 is divisible by 3, meaning that x is a multiple of 3. Since you don't know anything else about x, it's entirely possible that x is also divisible by 13, while there are certainly values that would make x not divisible by 13. Statement (2) is insufficient.

The correct answer is **(A)**.

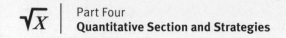

5.   **(A)**

If a and b are positive integers with different units digits, and b is the square of an integer, is a also the square of an integer?

(1)   The units digit of $a + b$ is 8.

(2) $b = 121$

STEP 1: ANALYZE THE QUESTION STEM

This is a Yes/No question. The given information provides a clue about the two numbers having different units digits and tells you that b is a perfect square. On advanced number properties questions, it's worth checking if two different types of clues work together. Units digits of certain groups of numbers often fall into consistent patterns, and squares certainly fit into that category. The units digits of the squares of 1–10 are $\{1, 4, 9, 6, 5, 6,$ $9, 4, 1, 0\}$, and this pattern will continue, since the units digits of 11–20, 21–30, and so on will be the same as those of 1–10. So a perfect square can only have one of six units digits: 0, 1, 4, 5, 6, or 9. For a to be a perfect square, its units digit must be one of those numbers.

STEP 2: EVALUATE THE STATEMENTS USING 12TEN

Evaluating Statement (1), you see that the sum of the integers a and b has a units digit of 8. Work your way through the list of possible units digits of squares of integers. Again, that list is 0, 1, 4, 5, 6, and 9. If the units digit of b is 0, then the units digit of a is 8, and 8 is not on the list. If the units digit of b is 1, the units digit of a is 7, and 7 is also not on the list. If the units digit of b is 4, the units digit of a is 4, but this is not permitted because the units digits of a and b must be different. If the units digit of b is 5, the units digit of a is 3, and 3 is not on the list. If the units digit of b is 6, the units digit of a is 2, and 2 is not on the list. If the units digit of b is 9, the units digit of a is 9, but again, the units digits of a and b must be different. It follows that the units digit of a cannot be the units digit of the square of an integer, so a cannot be the square of an integer. The answer to the question is definitively no, and Statement (1) is sufficient. Eliminate **(B)**, **(C)**, and **(E)**.

Statement (2) precludes a from having 1 as its units digit, but it does nothing else, since the only relevant limitation is that the two numbers have different units digits. Statement (2) is insufficient.

The correct answer is **(A)**.

6. **(C)**

What is the value of $8x + y$?

(1) $3x - 2y + z = 10$

(2) $2(x + 3y) - (y + 2z) = -25$

STEP 1: ANALYZE THE QUESTION STEM

This is a Value question: a statement that allows the calculation of a single value for $8x + y$ is sufficient. Simplify the equation in Statement (2):

$$2(x + 3y) - (y + 2z) = -25$$
$$2x + 6y - y - 2z = -25$$
$$2x + 5y - 2z = -25$$

STEP 2: EVALUATE THE STATEMENTS USING 12TEN

Each of the two statements is an equation with the same three variables. As neither of these equations can be solved for $8x + y$, neither statement on its own is sufficient, and you can eliminate **(A)**, **(B)**, and **(D)**.

Taken together, the two statements represent a system of equations. To solve for each variable in a system of linear equations with three variables, three distinct equations are required. Since the statements provide only two equations, **(E)** may be tempting. However, even when there are fewer equations than variables, sometimes the value of a particular variable, or the value of an expression, can be found. When a question concerns solving a system of equations for an expression, consider whether multiplying one or both equations by a constant and combining them will allow you to solve. Multiplying the equation in Statement (1) by 2 results in $6x - 4y + 2z = 20$. Adding the corresponding sides of this equation and the simplified equation in Statement (2), $2x + 5y - 2z = -25$, gives $8x + y = -5$. Since both statements together allow the calculation of $8x + y$, the correct answer is **(C)**.

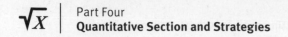

7. **(C)**

    If b and c are two-digit positive integers and $b - c = 22d$, is d an integer?

    (1) The tens digit and the units digit of b are identical.

    (2) $\frac{b+c}{22} = x$, and x is an integer.

STEP 1: ANALYZE THE QUESTION STEM

This is a Yes/No question. The question stem tells you that the variables b and c are integers between 10 and 99 inclusive and asks whether $b - c$ is a multiple of 22.

STEP 2: EVALUATE THE STATEMENTS USING 12TEN

Statement (1) merely tells you that the two digits of b are the same, so the value of b must be 11, 22, 33, etc. Since you are given no further information about c, Statement (1) by itself is insufficient, and answer choices **(A)** and **(D)** can be eliminated.

Statement (2) provides the information that $b + c$ is a multiple of 22, since $b + c = 22x$ and x is an integer. However, the question asks about $b - c$, not $b + c$, so this statement, too, is insufficient. If you were unsure, you could plug in some number pairs to verify that $b - c$ could be a multiple of 22 but need not be. Set $b = 12$ and $c = 10$; $b + c = 22$, which is divisible by 22, but $b - c = 2$, which clearly is not divisible by 22. Now try $b = 11$ and $c = 33$; $b + c = 44$ is divisible by 22, while $b - c = -22$ is divisible by 22 as well. Eliminate **(B)**.

Now look at both statements together along with the information in the question stem. Statement (1) says that the tens and units digits of b are the same, so b is a multiple of 11. From Statement (2), you know that $b + c$ is a multiple of 22. Every multiple of 22 is a multiple of 11, so $b + c$ is a multiple of 11. Since $b + c$ is a multiple of 11 and b is a multiple of 11, $(b + c) - b = c$, which is a multiple of 11. Since b and c are both multiples of 11, $b - c$ is also a multiple of 11. Since $b + c$ is a multiple of 22, $b + c$ is even. This means that both b and c are even or both b and c are odd. In either case, $b - c$ is even, or, in other words, $b - c$ is a multiple of 2. Since $b - c$ is a multiple of 11, $b - c$ is a multiple of 2, and the integers 2 and 11 have no common factor greater than 1, $b - c$ is a multiple of $11 \times 2 = 22$. The statements taken together are sufficient to answer the question definitively yes. **(C)** is correct.

8. (C)

The integers x and y are positive, $x > y + 8$, and $y > 8$. What is the remainder when $x^2 - y^2$ is divided by 8?

(1) The remainder when $x + y$ is divided by 8 is 7.

(2) The remainder when $x - y$ is divided by 8 is 5.

STEP 1: ANALYZE THE QUESTION STEM

This is a Value question. You are given two positive integers. Since y is an integer and $y > 8$, the minimum value of y is 9. Since $x > y + 8$, and the minimum value of y is 9, x must be greater than $9 + 8 - 17$. Thus, $x > 17$. Since x is an integer, the minimum value of x is 18. The question asks for the remainder when the difference of the squares of the two numbers is divided by 8. You can factor the expression $x^2 - y^2$ to its equivalent $(x + y)(x - y)$.

STEP 2: EVALUATE THE STATEMENTS USING 12TEN

Statement (1): Since the remainder when $x + y$ is divided by 8 is 7, you can represent $x + y$ as $8m + 7$, where m is an integer. Substituting this into the factored expression, $(8m + 7)(x - y)$ still doesn't tell you enough about $x - y$ to get a definite answer, so Statement (1) is insufficient. Eliminate **(A)** and **(D)**.

Statement (2): This time, you can substitute $8n + 5$ for $x - y$, where n is an integer, but now you don't know enough about $x + y$, so Statement (2) is also insufficient and you can eliminate **(B)**.

Combining the results above, can you determine with certainty the remainder when $(8m + 7)(8n + 5)$ is divided by 8?

Using FOIL, you can write the expression $(8m + 7)(8n + 5)$ as $64mn + 40m + 56n + 35$. Since the first three terms contain the coefficients 64, 40, and 56, respectively, and m and n are integers, each of these terms is evenly divisible by 8. Thus, the remainder resulting from dividing the expression $x^2 - y^2$ by 8 is the remainder when 35 is divided by 8, which is 3. So the statements together are sufficient, and **(C)** is correct.

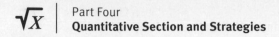

9. **(D)**

If $x > y > 0$, does $3^{x+1} + 3(2^y) = 12v$?

(1) $\dfrac{3^{2x} - 2^{2y}}{3^x - 2^y} = 4v$

(2) $2(3^{x+2}) + 9(2^{y+1}) = 72v$

STEP 1: ANALYZE THE QUESTION STEM

This is a Yes/No question. A statement is sufficient if it allows you to answer the question with either a definite yes or a definite no.

Begin by simplifying the equation $3^{x+1} + 3(2^y) = 12v$. Using the law of exponents that says that $b^a b^c = b^{a+c}$, you can rewrite 3^{x+1} as $(3^x)(3^1) = 3(3^x)$. So replace 3^{x+1} with $3(3^x)$: $3(3^x) + 3(2^y) = 12v$. Now factor a 3 out of the left side to yield $3(3^x + 2^y) = 12v$. Dividing both sides of the equation by 3 results in $3^x + 2^y = 4v$. So the question stem is asking, "If $x > y > 0$, does $3^x + 2^y = 4v$?"

STEP 2: EVALUATE THE STATEMENTS USING 12TEN

Statement (1): Rewrite the equation $\dfrac{3^{2x} - 2^{2y}}{3^x - 2^y} = 4v$ to evaluate it. There is a law of exponents that says that $(b^a)^c = b^{ac}$, so $3^{2x} = (3^x)^2$ and $2^{2y} = (2^y)^2$. It follows that $3^{2x} - 2^{2y} = (3^x)^2 - (2^y)^2$. This is one of the classic quadratics: $(3^x)^2 - (2^y)^2 = (3^x - 2^y)(3^x + 2^y)$. So Statement (1) can be written as $\dfrac{\left(3^x - 2^y\right)\left(3^x + 2^y\right)}{3^x - 2^y} = 4v$.

Cancel a factor of $3^x - 2^y$ from the numerator and denominator of the left side of the equation to find that $3^x + 2^y = 4v$. Since $3^x + 2^y = 4v$ is equivalent to $3^{x+1} + 3(2^y) = 12v$, Statement (1) allows you to answer the question with a definite yes and is sufficient. Eliminate **(B)**, **(C)**, and **(E)**.

Statement (2): Because $b^a b^c = b^{a+c}$, $3^{x+2} = (3^x)(3^2) = (3^x)(9) = 9(3^x)$. Also, $2^{y+1} = (2^y)(2^1) = (2^y)(2) = 2(2^y)$. Thus, $2(3^{x+2}) + 9(2^{y+1}) = 72v$ can be written as $2[9(3^x)] + 9[2(2^y)] = 72v$, or $18(3^x) + 18(2^y) = 72v$. Factoring 18 out of the left side of the equation gives $18(3^x + 2^y) = 72v$. Divide both sides of the equation by 18: $3^x + 2^y = 4v$. Since this is the same equation shown to be sufficient for Statement (1), Statement (2) allows you to answer the question with a definite yes and is sufficient.

(D) is correct.

10. **(B)**

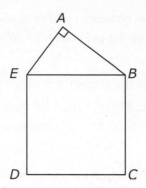

In the figure above, the measure of angle *EAB* in triangle *ABE* is 90°, and *BCDE* is a square. What is the length of *AB*?

(1)   The length of *AE* is 12, and the ratio of the area of triangle *ABE* to the area of square *BCDE* is $\frac{6}{25}$.

(2)   The perimeter of square *BCDE* is 80 and the ratio of the length of *AE* to the length of *AB* is 3 to 4.

STEP 1: ANALYZE THE QUESTION STEM

This is a Value question. The figure shows a right triangle whose hypotenuse is one side of a square, and a statement that is sufficient would allow you to find the length of side *AB*.

STEP 2: EVALUATE THE STATEMENTS USING 12TEN

Statement (1): The area of right triangle *ABE* is:

$$\frac{1}{2}(AE)(AB) = \frac{1}{2}(12)(AB) = 6(AB)$$

Since triangle *ABE* is a right triangle, the Pythagorean theorem says that
$(BE)^2 = (AB)^2 + 12^2 = (AB)^2 + 144$. Thus, $BE = \sqrt{(AB)^2 + 144}$. The area of square *BCDE* is:

$$(BE)^2 = \sqrt{(AB)^2 + 144} \times \sqrt{(AB)^2 + 144} = (AB)^2 + 144$$

Since the ratio of the area of triangle *ABE* to the area of square *BCDE* is $\frac{6}{25}$, $\frac{6(AB)}{(AB)^2 + 144} = \frac{6}{25}$. Solve this equation for *AB*:

$$\frac{y}{y^2 + 144} = \frac{1}{25}$$
$$25y = y^2 + 144$$
$$y^2 - 25y + 144 = 0$$

Factor $y^2 - 25y + 144$. With some testing, you find that $y^2 - 25y + 144 = (y - 9)(y - 16)$.
So $(y - 9)(y - 16) = 0$. Thus, it is possible that the length of *AB* is 9 or 16. Because more than one answer to the question is possible, Statement (1) is insufficient. Eliminate **(A)** and **(D)**.

Statement (2): The perimeter of square *ABCD* is 80, so the length of one side of the square is $\frac{80}{4} = 20$.
Because the ratio of *AE* to *AB* is 3 to 4, right triangle *ABE* is a 3-4-5 right triangle. Knowing the ratios of the sides and the length of the hypotenuse, you could calculate the length of side *AB*. However, since this is a Data Sufficiency question, there is no need to perform the calculations. Statement (2) is sufficient. (For the record, right triangle *ABE* has side lengths of 12, 16, and 20. *AB* is the longer leg and equals 16.)

(B) is correct.

11. (E)

In the sequence T, the first term is the non-zero number a, and each term after the first term is equal to the non-zero number r multiplied by the previous term. What is the value of the fourth term of the sequence?

(1) The sum of the first two terms of the sequence is 16.

(2) The 18th term of the sequence is 81 times the 14th term of the sequence.

STEP 1: ANALYZE THE QUESTION STEM

This is a Value question involving a geometric sequence. Each term after the first term is r times the previous term. So if the nth term is a_n, where n is an integer and $n \geq 1$, then $a_1 = a$, $a_2 = ar$, $a_3 = ar^2$, $a_4 = ar^3$, $a_5 = ar^4$, and so on. In general, if n is an integer and $n \geq 1$, then the nth term is the product of one factor of a and $n - 1$ factors of r, or $a_n = ar^{n-1}$.

STEP 2: EVALUATE THE STATEMENTS USING 12TEN

Statement (1): The sum of the first two terms is 16. Thus, $a + ar = 16$. This is one equation with two variables, and there are many possible values for a and r. Statement (1) is insufficient. Eliminate **(A)** and **(D)**.

Statement (2): This statement says that $a_{18} = 81a_{14}$. You know the following:

$$a_{15} = a_{14}r$$

$$a_{16} = a_{15}r$$

$$a_{17} = a_{16}r$$

$$a_{18} = a_{17}r$$

So $a_{18} = a_{17}r = (a_{16}r)r = a_{16}r^2 = (a_{15}r)r^2 = a_{15}r^3 = (a_{14}r)r^3 = a_{14}r^4$.

Since $a_{18} = 81a_{14}$, $a_{14}r^4 = 81a_{14}$. According to the question stem, $a \neq 0$ and $r \neq 0$, so a_{14} does not equal 0. Divide by a_{14}: $r^4 = 81$. Now $81 = 3^4$ or $(-3)^4$, so $r = 3$ or $r = -3$. This statement provides two values for r and no information about a, so the fourth term cannot be calculated. For example, if $a = 4$ and $r = 3$, then $a_4 = 4(3^{4-1}) = 4(3^3) = 4(27) = 108$. But if $a = 2$ and $r = -3$, then $a_4 = 2(-3)^{4-1} = 2(-3)^3 = 2(-27) = -54$. Since different answers to the question are possible, Statement (2) is insufficient. Eliminate **(B)**.

The statements taken together: From Statement (1), which says that the sum of the first two terms is 16, you know that $a + ar = 16$. From Statement (2), which says that $a_{18} = 81a_{14}$, you know that $r = 3$ or $r = -3$.

Consider the case where $r = 3$. Substituting 3 for r into the equation $a + ar = 16$, $a + a(3) = 16$, $a + 3a = 16$, $4a = 16$, and $a = 4$. In this case, the fourth term is $ar^{4-1} = 4(3^{4-1}) = 4(3^3) = 4(27) = 108$. Now consider the case where $r = -3$. Substituting -3 for r into the equation $a + ar = 16$, $a + a(-3) = 16$, $a - 3a = 16$, $-2a = 16$, and $a = -8$. With these values of r and a, the fourth term is $(-8)(-3)^{4-1} = (-8)(-3)^3 = (-8)(-27) = 216$. Because there is more than one possible answer to the question, the statements taken together are insufficient.

(E) is correct.

12. (C)

A person is to be selected at random from the group T of people. What is the probability that the person selected is a member of club E?

(1) The probability that a person selected at random from group T is not a member of club D and is not a member of club E is $\frac{1}{4}$.

(2) The probability that a person selected at random from group T is a member of club D and not a member of club E is $\frac{5}{12}$.

STEP 1: ANALYZE THE QUESTION STEM

This is a Value question involving the probability of a single event. A person is to be selected at random from group T, and the question asks for the probability that the person selected is a member of club E. The probability that the person selected is a member of club D can be written as $P(D)$ and the probability that the person is a member of club E as $P(E)$.

STEP 2: EVALUATE THE STATEMENTS USING 12TEN

Statement (1): The probability that the person selected is not a member of either club is $\frac{1}{4}$. The probability that an event does not occur is equal to 1 minus the probability that the event does occur, so the probability that the person chosen is a member of at least one of the two clubs—that is, $P(D \text{ or } E)$—is $1 - \frac{1}{4} = \frac{3}{4}$. In general, $P(D \text{ or } E) = P(D) + P(E) - P(D \text{ and } E)$. (This formula is worth memorizing.) In this case, you can substitute $\frac{3}{4}$ for $P(D \text{ or } E)$, so $P(D) + P(E) - P(D \text{ and } E) = \frac{3}{4}$. However, without any other information about $P(D)$ or $P(D \text{ and } E)$, you cannot find $P(E)$. Statement (1) is insufficient. Eliminate **(A)** and **(D)**.

Statement (2): Because the probability that the chosen person is a member of club D and not club E is $\frac{5}{12}$, $P(D \text{ and not } E) = \frac{5}{12}$. Since $P(D) = P(D \text{ and } E) + P(D \text{ and not } E)$, $P(D \text{ and not } E) = P(D) - P(D \text{ and } E)$. Thus, $P(D) - P(D \text{ and } E) = \frac{5}{12}$. There is no way to find $P(E)$ from this information. Statement (2) is insufficient, and **(B)** can be eliminated.

The statements taken together: from Statement (1), $P(D) + P(E) - P(D \text{ and } E) = \frac{3}{4}$. From Statement (2), $P(D) - P(D \text{ and } E) = \frac{5}{12}$. You can rearrange the equation from Statement (1): $P(D) - P(D \text{ and } E) + P(E) = \frac{3}{4}$. Using $P(D) - P(D \text{ and } E) = \frac{5}{12}$, substitute $\frac{5}{12}$ for $P(D) - P(D \text{ and } E)$ in $P(D) - P(D \text{ and } E) + P(E) = \frac{3}{4}$. Then $\frac{5}{12} + P(E) = \frac{3}{4}$, and you can solve for the probability that the person selected is a member of club E.

There is no need to do the calculation, but for the record, it would be:

$$P(E) = \frac{3}{4} - \frac{5}{12} = \frac{9}{12} - \frac{5}{12} = \frac{4}{12} = \frac{1}{3}$$

The statements taken together are sufficient.

(C) is correct.

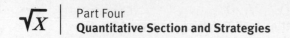

13. (D)

The population of Town X on January 1, 2010, was 56 percent greater than the population of the same town on January 1, 2005. The population of Town X on January 1, 2015, was 75 percent greater than the population of the same town on January 1, 2010. What was the population of Town X on January 1, 2005?

(1) The population of Town X on January 1, 2015, was 21,840.

(2) The increase in the population of Town X from January 1, 2010, to January 1, 2015, was 4,880 greater than the increase in the population of Town X from January 1, 2005, to January 1, 2010.

STEP 1: ANALYZE THE QUESTION STEM

This is a Value question involving multiple percent increases. Say the population of Town X on January 1, 2005, was N. Because the population of Town X on January 1, 2010, was 56% greater than the population on January 1, 2005, the population in 2010 was $N + (56\% \text{ of } N) = N + 0.56N = 1.56N$. Then because the population on January 1, 2015, was 75% greater than the population on January 1, 2010, the population in 2015 can be written as follows:

$$1.56N + 0.75(1.56N) = 1.56N + \frac{3}{4}(1.56N)$$
$$= 1.56N + 3(0.39N)$$
$$= 1.56N + 1.17N$$
$$= 2.73N$$

Note that because you know the percent increase from each of the three named years to the next, a statement that provides the population for any of those three years will be sufficient.

STEP 2: EVALUATE THE STATEMENTS USING 12TEN

Statement (1): Because the population on January 1, 2015, was $2.73N$, you can write the equation $2.73N = 21,840$. Then $N = \dfrac{21,840}{2.73}$. This equation produces just one value for N, so Statement (1) is sufficient. Eliminate **(B)**, **(C)**, and **(E)**.

Statement (2): The increase in the population from 2005 to 2010 can be written as $1.56N - N = 0.56N$. The increase in the population from 2010 to 2015 is $2.73N - 1.56N = 1.17N$. Because the increase from 2010 to 2015 was 4,880 greater than the increase from 2005 to 2010, you can write the equation $1.17N = 0.56N + 4,880$. There is one equation with one variable, so you could solve for N and Statement (2) is sufficient.

(D) is correct.

14. **(C)**

What is the value of $x - 3z$?

(1) $x + 4y = 3$

(2) $x^2 + 4xy - 3xz - 12yz = 24$

STEP 1: ANALYZE THE QUESTION STEM

This is a Value question. Knowing the values of x and z separately would be sufficient to answer the question, as would knowing the value of the entire expression $x - 3z$.

STEP 2: EVALUATE THE STATEMENTS USING 12TEN

Statement (1) is clearly insufficient, as the equation $x + 4y = 3$ does not include the variable z. Eliminate **(A)** and **(D)**.

Statement (2) provides one equation with three variables, so there will be different possible values for $x - 3z$. For example, if you let $x = 0$ and $y = 8$, then the equation $x^2 + 4xy - 3xz - 12yz = 24$ leads to $z = -\frac{1}{4}$. Plugging $x = 0$ and $z = -\frac{1}{4}$ into $x - 3z$, you have $x - 3z = 0 - 3\left(-\frac{1}{4}\right) = \frac{3}{4}$. In this case, the answer to the question is $\frac{3}{4}$. But if you let $x = 3$ and $y = 0$, the equation $x^2 + 4xy - 3xz - 12yz = 24$ leads to $z = -\frac{5}{3}$. Plugging $x = 3$ and $z = -\frac{5}{3}$ into $x - 3z$ gives you the following: $x - 3z = 3 - 3\left(-\frac{5}{3}\right) = 3 + 5 = 8$. In this case, the answer to the question is 8. Since different answers to the question are possible, Statement (2) is insufficient. Eliminate **(B)**.

To combine the statements, start by simplifying the left side of the equation in Statement (2).

$$x^2 + 4xy - 3xz - 12yz = x(x + 4y) - 3z(x + 4y) = (x + 4y)(x - 3z)$$

Thus, Statement (2) is equivalent to $(x + 4y)(x - 3z) = 24$. Statement (1) says that $x + 4y = 3$. Substitute 3 for $x + 4y$ in the equation $(x + 4y)(x - 3z) = 24$ to produce $3(x - 3z) = 24$. Dividing both sides by 3 yields $x - 3z = 8$. The statements together lead to a single possible value of 8 for $x - 3z$. The statements taken together are sufficient.

(C) is correct.

15. (D)

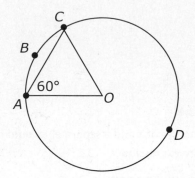

In the figure above, the center of the circle is O, and the measure of angle CAO is 60°. What is the perimeter of triangle OAC?

(1)   The length of arc CDA is 16π greater than the length of arc ABC.

(2)   The area of triangle OAC is $36\sqrt{3}$.

STEP 1: ANALYZE THE QUESTION STEM

This question asks for the perimeter of the triangle, so it is a Value question. Sides OA and OC of triangle OAC are both radii of the circle, so $OA = OC$, making the triangle isosceles so that $\angle OCA$ must also equal 60°. Because the three angles of a triangle must sum to 180°, the central angle is also 60°—in other words, triangle OAC is equilateral. So each of its three sides is equal to the circle's radius. If you can find the radius, you can find the perimeter of the triangle, and you have sufficiency.

STEP 2: EVALUATE THE STATEMENTS USING 12TEN

Statement (1): In a circle with radius r, the length L of an arc intercepted by a central angle whose measure is n degrees is given by the formula $L = 2\pi r \times \dfrac{n}{360}$. Here, the central angle intercepting arc CDA has a measure of $360° - 60° = 300°$, and the central angle intercepting arc ABC has a measure of 60°. So the length of arc CDA is $2\pi r \times \dfrac{300}{360} = 2\pi r \times \dfrac{5}{6} = \dfrac{5\pi r}{3}$, and the length of arc ABC is $2\pi r \times \dfrac{60}{360} = 2\pi r \times \dfrac{1}{6} = \dfrac{\pi r}{3}$. Since Statement (1) says that the length of arc CDA is 16π greater than the length of arc ABC, you know that $\dfrac{5\pi r}{3} = \dfrac{\pi r}{3} + 16\pi$.

That's a single equation in one variable, so you can solve for r. Statement (1) is sufficient. (For the record, dividing both sides of this equation by π and multiplying both sides by 3 yields $5r = r + 48$, so $r = 12$, and the perimeter is $3(12) = 36$.) Eliminate **(B)**, **(C)**, and **(E)**.

Statement (2) says that the area of triangle OAC is $36\sqrt{2}$. Triangle OAC is equilateral. The length of each side of triangle OAC could be called s.

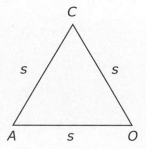

Drop an altitude from point C to side OA:

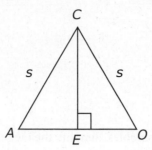

Altitude CE divides triangle OAC into two identical 30°-60°-90° right triangles.

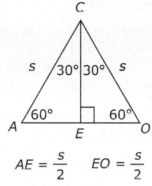

$$AE = \frac{s}{2} \qquad EO = \frac{s}{2}$$

The two identical 30°-60°-90° right triangles are triangles ACE and OCE. The side lengths in a 30°-60°-90° right triangle are in a ratio of 1 to $\sqrt{3}$ to 2. Since the length of hypotenuse AC of right triangle ACE is s, the length of leg AE, which is opposite the 30° angle must be $\frac{s}{2}$, and the length of leg CE, which is opposite the 60° angle, must be $\frac{s}{2} \times \sqrt{3} = \frac{s\sqrt{3}}{2}$. You can now describe the area of triangle OAC in terms of s. The area of any triangle is $\frac{1}{2}b \times h$. Call the base OA and the height CE. Then $OA = s$ and $CE = \frac{s\sqrt{3}}{2}$. The area of triangle OAC is:

$$\frac{1}{2} \times OA \times CE = \frac{1}{2} \times s \times \frac{s\sqrt{3}}{2} = \frac{s^2\sqrt{3}}{4}$$

Since the area of triangle OAC is given in Statement (2) to be $\frac{1}{2} \times OA \times CE = \frac{1}{2} \times s \times \frac{s\sqrt{3}}{2} = \frac{s^2\sqrt{3}}{4}$, you can write the equation $\frac{s^2\sqrt{3}}{4} = 36\sqrt{3}$. That's again a single equation in one variable. It does have a squared term, but as negative lengths are disallowed, you can stop here and declare Statement (2) sufficient. (For the record: $\frac{s^2}{4} = 36$, so $s^2 = 144$ and $s = 12$. The perimeter is again $3(12) = 36$.)

(D) is correct.

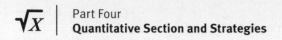
16. (B)

If x and y are integers and $3x > 8y$, is $y > -18$?

(1) $-9 < x < 20$

(2) $y = \dfrac{(x - 42)}{5}$

STEP 1: ANALYZE THE QUESTION STEM

This is a Yes/No question with two integer variables. Simplify the inequality given in the stem, $3x > 8y$, to get $y < \dfrac{3}{8}x$.

STEP 2: EVALUATE THE STATEMENTS USING 12TEN

Statement (1): The possible values of x are limited by the range of this inequality, so examine the endpoints of the range. If $x > -9$, the least value that is permissible for x is -8. Since y is less than $\dfrac{3}{8}x$, it follows that $y < -3$. Some values of y could be > -18, but there is no lower limit for y, so it could also be < -18. There is no need to evaluate the upper boundary of x. Statement (1) is insufficient, so eliminate **(A)** and **(D)**.

Statement (2): Simplify the equation by multiplying both sides by 5 to get $5y = x - 42$. Add 42 to both sides and $x = 5y + 42$. Substitute this value for x into the inequality $3x > 8y$:

$$3(5y + 42) > 8y$$
$$15y + 126 > 8y$$
$$7y + 126 > 0$$
$$7y > -126$$
$$y > -18$$

Statement (2) is sufficient to answer definitively yes.

(B) is correct.

17. **(A)**

Over the course of 5 days, Monday through Friday, Danny collects a total of 76 baseball cards. Each day, he collects a different number of cards. If Danny collects the largest number of cards on Friday and the second largest number of cards on Thursday, did Danny collect more than 8 cards on Thursday?

(1) On Friday, Danny collected 49 cards.

(2) On one of the first 3 days, Danny collected 6 cards.

STEP 1: ANALYZE THE QUESTION STEM

This is a Yes/No question that is packed with information in the stem. Danny collects a *different* number of cards each of the 5 days. He collects the *largest* number of cards on Friday and the *second largest* number on Thursday. The question asks if Danny collected *more* than 8 cards on Thursday.

STEP 2: EVALUATE THE STATEMENTS USING 12TEN

Statement (1): The largest number of cards collected on Thursday that would result in a no answer to the question is 8. Since the number of cards collected Monday, Tuesday, and Wednesday is different each day and must be less than 8, the maximum numbers of cards he could collect on those days are 5, 6, and 7. Totaling up all the days, $5 + 6 + 7 + 8 + 49 = 75$. Collecting 8 cards on Thursday does not enable Danny to collect 76 cards in total given the constraints of the question, so the information in Statement (1) means that Danny must have collected more than 8 cards on Thursday. Statement (1) is sufficient to answer "always yes," so eliminate **(B)**, **(C)**, and **(E)**.

Statement (2): If Danny collects 6 cards on one of the first 3 days, the fewest cards he could have collected on those days would be $6 + 2 + 1 = 9$, leaving $76 - 9 = 67$ cards to be collected on Thursday and Friday. Danny could have collected 7 cards on Thursday and 60 on Friday, in which case the answer to the question is no. Alternatively, he could have collected as many as 33 cards on Thursday and 34 on Friday and the answer would be yes. Therefore, Statement (2) is insufficient.

(A) is correct.

18. (A)

If $y = x^2$, is the equation $(2^{5y})(4^{120}) = 16^{20x}$ true?

(1) $(4 - x)(12 - x) = 0$

(2) $(x - 4)(x - 8)(x - 24) = 0$

STEP 1: ANALYZE THE QUESTION STEM

This question asks whether an equation is true, making it a Yes/No question. Start by simplifying the equation in the question stem. Notice that you can write all three powers with a base of 2, since $4 = 2^2$ and $16 = 2^4$. Substituting these values produces $(2^{5y})((2^2)^{120}) = (2^4)^{20x}$, which simplifies to $(2^{5y})(2^{2 \times 120}) = 2^{4 \times 20x}$, or $(2^{5y})(2^{240}) = 2^{80x}$. This, in turn, can be rewritten as $2^{5y + 240} = 2^{80x}$. When equal powers have the same base, the exponents must be equal. So $5y + 240 = 80x$. Remember that $y = x^2$, so you can substitute x^2 for y to yield $5x^2 + 240 = 80x$. Subtracting $80x$ from both sides, $5x^2 - 80x + 240 = 0$. Dividing both sides by 5, $x^2 - 16x + 48 = 0$. This factors to $(x - 4)(x - 12) = 0$. So $x - 4 = 0$ or $x - 12 = 0$, and $x = 4$ or $x = 12$.

So if $x = 4$ or $x = 12$, then the equation $(2^{5y})(4^{120}) = (16^{20x})$ is true, and the answer to the question is definitively yes. If x is neither of these values, the answer is definitively no. Either of these situations would be sufficient.

STEP 2: EVALUATE THE STATEMENTS USING 12TEN

Statement (1) says that $(4 - x)(12 - x) = 0$. When the product of a group of numbers is 0, at least one of the numbers must be 0. So if $(4 - x)(12 - x) = 0$, then $4 - x = 0$ or $12 - x = 0$. If $4 - x = 0$, then $4 = x$, or $x = 4$. If $12 - x = 0$, then $12 = x$, or $x = 12$. You've already determined that the equation $(2^{5y})(4^{120}) = (16^{20x})$ is true when $x = 4$ or $x = 12$. Statement (1) is sufficient, as the answer to the question is always yes. Eliminate **(B)**, **(C)**, and **(E)**.

Statement (2) says that $(x - 4)(x - 8)(x - 24) = 0$. Again, when the product of a group of numbers is 0, at least one of the numbers must be 0. So in this case, $x - 4 = 0$, $x - 8 = 0$, or $x - 24 = 0$. If $x - 4 = 0$, then $x = 4$. If $x - 8 = 0$, then $x = 8$. If $x - 24 = 0$, then $x = 24$. The possible values of x are 4, 8, and 24. You know that the equation $(2^{5y})(4^{120}) = (16^{20x})$ is true when $x = 4$ or $x = 12$. If $x = 4$, then the answer to the question is yes. If $x = 8$, or if $x = 24$, the answer to the question is no. Since more than one answer to the question is possible, Statement (2) is insufficient.

(A) is correct.

19. (B)

The ratio of the number of students in an auditorium who are seniors to the number of students in the auditorium who are not seniors is 7:5. How many students are there in the auditorium?

(1) The ratio of the number of students who are seniors who are taking history to the number of students who are not seniors who are taking history is 21:5.

(2) Of the students in the auditorium who are seniors, $\frac{3}{5}$ are taking history; of the students in the auditorium who are not seniors, $\frac{1}{5}$ are taking history; and the number of seniors in the auditorium who are taking history is 208 greater than the number of students in the auditorium who are not seniors and taking history.

STEP 1: ANALYZE THE QUESTION STEM

This is a Value question. Since the question asks for the total number of students, start by rewriting the part-to-part ratio in the question stem as a part-to-whole ratio. The ratio of seniors to non-seniors is 7:5, so the ratio of the students who are seniors to the total number of students is $\frac{7}{7+5} = \frac{7}{12}$, and the ratio of the students in the auditorium who are not seniors to the total number of students is $\frac{5}{7+5} = \frac{5}{12}$. Remember that there is a common multiplier in the numerator and denominator of every ratio, so you could write the ratio of seniors to total students as $\frac{7x}{12x}$ and the ratio of non-seniors to total students as $\frac{5x}{12x}$. If you can find the common multiplier x, you can find the total number of students, and you have sufficiency.

STEP 2: EVALUATE THE STATEMENTS USING 12TEN

Statement (1): You are given the ratio of the number of students who are seniors who are taking history to the number of students who are not seniors who are taking history. There is no actual number of students given, and there's no way to calculate the common multiplier in the original ratio and thus calculate the total number of students. Statement (1) is insufficient. Eliminate **(A)** and **(D)**.

Statement (2): From the ratio given in the question stem, you know that there are $7x$ seniors, $5x$ non-seniors, and $12x$ total students present in the auditorium. From Statement (2), you know that of the $7x$ seniors, $\frac{3}{5}$ are taking history. In other words, $\frac{(7x)(3)}{5} = \frac{21x}{5}$ seniors are taking history. Similarly, $\frac{1}{5}$ of the $5x$ non-seniors are taking history, so $\frac{5x}{5} = x$ non-seniors are taking history. Furthermore, the number of seniors taking history is 208 greater than the number of non-seniors taking history, so you can write an equation to solve for x: $\frac{21x}{5} = x + 208$. This is a single equation in one variable, so you can stop here and declare Statement (2) to be sufficient. (For the record: $21x = 5x + 208(5)$, $16x = 208(5)$, $x = 13(5) = 65$. There are $12x = (12)(65) = 780$ total students.)

(B) is correct.

20. (E)

If $y > 0$, is $\frac{x}{y} < 3$?

(1) $x(x + y) - 4y(x + y) < 0$

(2) $5(y + 8) < 20y - 3x + 40$

STEP 1: ANALYZE THE QUESTION STEM

Since y is positive, you can multiply both sides of the inequality $\frac{x}{y} < 3$ by the positive number y to obtain the equivalent inequality $x < 3y$. So the question is equivalent to "If $y > 0$, is $x < 3y$?"

STEP 2: EVALUATE THE STATEMENTS USING 12TEN

Statement (1): Factor $x + y$ out of the left side of the inequality to yield $x(x + y) - 4y(x + y) = (x + y)(x - 4y)$. So Statement (1) is equivalent to $(x + y)(x - 4y) < 0$. When the product of two quantities is negative, one of the quantities must be negative and the other quantity must be positive. So either (i) $x + y < 0$ and $x - 4y > 0$, or (ii) $x + y > 0$ and $x - 4y < 0$. (Keep in mind that y is positive.) In case (i), if $x + y < 0$, then $x < -y$. If $x - 4y > 0$, then $x > 4y$. So in case (i), $x < -y$ and $x > 4y$. Since y is positive, $x < -y$ means that x is less than $-y$, where $-y$ is a negative number. Since y is positive, $x > 4y$ means that x is greater than $4y$, where $4y$ is a positive number. So case (i) requires that x be less than the negative number $-y$ and also requires that x be greater than the positive number $4y$. This is impossible. So case (i), which is $x + y < 0$ and $x - 4y > 0$, cannot happen. On to case (ii), which is $x + y > 0$ and $x - 4y < 0$. (Again, keep in mind that $y > 0$.) If $x + y > 0$, then $x > -y$. If $x - 4y < 0$, then $x < 4y$. So this time, $x > -y$ and $x < 4y$. Since y is positive, $x > -y$ means that x is greater than the negative number $-y$. Since y is positive, $x < 4y$ means that x is less than the positive number $4y$. So case (ii), $x + y > 0$ and $x - 4y < 0$, is possible. In case (ii), you can conclude that $-y < x < 4y$. Because case (i) is impossible, Statement (1) is equivalent to $-y < x < 4y$. Since y is positive, $3y < 4y$. You know that $x < 4y$. However, you do not know whether or not $x < 3y$.

More than one answer to the question is possible, so Statement (1) is insufficient. Eliminate **(A)** and **(D)**.
Statement (2): Simplify the inequality $5(y + 8) < 20y - 3x + 40$.

$$5(y + 8) < 20y - 3x + 40$$
$$5y + 40 < 20y - 3x + 40$$
$$5y < 20y - 3x$$
$$3x < 15y$$
$$x < 5y$$

Statement (2) is equivalent to $x < 5y$. Since y is positive, $3y < 5y$. You know that $x < 5y$. However, you do not know whether or not $x < 3y$. Statement (2) is insufficient. Eliminate **(B)**.

The statements taken together: Statement (1) is equivalent to $-y < x < 4y$, and Statement (2) is equivalent to $x < 5y$. Because the question requires that $y > 0$, $4y < 5y$ and the range in Statement (1) is a subset of the range in Statement (2). Therefore, the statements taken together require that $-y < x < 4y$, which you have already determined to be insufficient.

(E) is correct.

PART FIVE

Analytical Writing and Integrated Reasoning Sections

Analytical Writing Assessment

The Analytical Writing Assessment (AWA) is either the first task or the last task on the GMAT, depending on which section order you choose. When the section begins, you will be presented with the Analysis of an Argument essay assignment. You will have 30 minutes to complete it.

For the essay, you will analyze a given topic and then type your essay into a simple word processing program. It allows you to do only the following basic functions:

- Insert text
- Delete text
- Cut and paste
- Undo the previous action
- Scroll up and down on the screen

Spell-check and grammar-check functions are not available in the program, so you will have to check those things carefully yourself. One or two spelling errors or a few minor grammatical errors will not lower your score. But many spelling errors can hurt your score, as can grammar errors that are serious enough to obscure your intended meaning.

Thirty minutes is not enough time to produce the same kind of essay you've written for college classes. Nor is it enough time to do a lot of trial and error as you type. It is, however, enough time to write a "strong first draft" if you plan carefully, and that's what the essay graders are looking for.

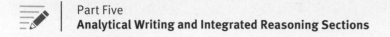
Previewing the Analytical Writing Assessment

You should practice giving yourself 30 minutes to brainstorm and type AWA essays between now and Test Day. By doing so, you will get an idea of how much you can write in the time allotted; your typing speed might also improve with practice.

Your task for the Argument essay is to assess the logic and use of evidence in an argument. It doesn't matter whether you agree or disagree with the argument's conclusion. Rather, you need to explain the ways in which the author has failed to fully support that conclusion.

Let's take a look at a sample prompt:

> The following appeared in a memo from the CEO of My Pie, a chain of pizza restaurants.
>
> "Officials in the film industry report that over half of the films released last year targeted an age 14–22 audience. Moreover, national sales data indicate that pizza is a favorite food among this age group. Since Filmmax opened a theater in a local mall last year, pizza sales at our restaurant in that mall have been higher than at any other restaurant in our chain. Because watching movies seems to stimulate pizza sales, the best way to increase our profits is to expand by opening new My Pie restaurants near every Filmmax theater."
>
> Consider how logical you find this argument. In your essay, be sure to discuss the line of reasoning and the use of evidence in the argument. For example, you may need to consider what questionable assumptions underlie the thinking and what alternative explanations or counterpoints might weaken the conclusion. You may also discuss what types of evidence would strengthen or refute the argument, what changes in the argument would make it more logically sound, and what, if anything, would help you better evaluate its conclusion.

Where are the holes in the argument? In what ways does it fail to be completely convincing? Why might the plan fail? Not only do you have to identify its major weaknesses, but you must also explain them.

How the AWA Is Scored

Your essays will be graded on a scale from 0 to 6 (highest). You'll receive one score, which will be an average of the scores that you receive from each of the two graders, rounded up to the nearest half point. This score does not contribute to your overall 200–800 score, nor is it combined with any other subscore. Business schools receive not only your score but also the text of your essay. Some schools compare your writing in your application's personal statement to your writing on the AWA to confirm that your application essay was plausibly written by you and not someone else.

Your essay will be graded by a human grader as well as a computerized essay grader (the IntelliMetric™ system). The two grade completely independently of each other—IntelliMetric™ isn't told the human's score, nor is the human told the computer's. If the two scores are identical, then that's your score. If the scores differ by one point, those scores are averaged. If they differ by more than one point, a second human will grade the essay to resolve any differences. IntelliMetric™ and the human grader agree on the same grade about 55 percent of the time and agree on identical or adjacent grades 97 percent of the time. (Only 3 percent of essays need rereading.) These figures are equivalent to how often two trained human graders agree.

IntelliMetric™ was designed to make the same judgments that a good human grader would. In fact, part of the Graduate Management Admission Council's (GMAC's) argument for the validity of IntelliMetric™ is that its performance is statistically indistinguishable from a human's. Still, you should remember that it is *not* a human and write accordingly.

IntelliMetric's™ grading algorithm was designed using 400 officially graded essays for each prompt. That's a huge sample of responses, so don't worry about whether IntelliMetric™ will understand your ideas—it's highly likely that someone out of those 400 responses made a similar point.

Before you begin to write, outline your essay. Good organization always counts, but with a computer grader, it's more important than ever. Use transitional phrases like *first, therefore, since,* and *for example* so that the computer can recognize structured analysis. The length of your essay is not a factor, as neither the computer nor the human rater counts the number of words in your response. The paragraphs in the body of your essay should develop your ideas in some depth and so should be at least several sentences long. However, the quality of your thinking and writing is much more important than the quantity of words.

Furthermore, computers are not good judges of humor or creativity. (The human judges don't reward those either. The standard is business writing, and you shouldn't be making overly witty or irreverent remarks in, say, an email to a CEO.)

Though IntelliMetric™ doesn't grade spelling per se, it could give you a lower score if it can't understand you or thinks you used the wrong words.

Here's what your essay will be graded on:

- **Structure.** Does your essay have good paragraph unity, organization, and flow?

- **Evidence.** It's not enough simply to assert good points. Do you develop them well? How strong are the examples you provide?

- **Depth of Logic.** Do you take apart the argument and analyze its major weaknesses effectively?

- **Style.** The GMAC calls this "control of the elements of standard written English." How well do you express your ideas?

Now let's take a more in-depth look at the scoring scale so you get a sense of what to aim for. This rubric shows how the GMAC will grade your essay based on the four categories of Structure, Evidence, Depth of Logic, and Style.

	1 Seriously Deficient	2 Substantially Flawed	3 Inadequate	4 Satisfactory	5 Good	6 Excellent
Structure	Lacks length and organization; *does not adhere* to topic.	Lacks length and organization; *unclear understanding* of topic.	Lacks length enough for real analysis; *strays from topic* or is partially unfocused.	Has *good basic organization* and sufficient paragraphing.	Has *well-developed paragraphs* and structure; stays on topic.	Has well-developed paragraphs and structure; *paragraphing works with examples*.
Evidence	Provides *few, if any, examples* to back up claims.	Provides *very sparse examples* to back up claims.	Provides *insufficient examples* to back up claims.	Provides *sufficient examples* to back up claims.	Provides *strong examples* to back up claims.	Provides *very strong examples* to back up claims.
Depth of Logic	Shows *very little understanding of the argument* and gives no analysis of/takes no position on it.	Presents the writer's views, but *fails to give any analytical critique*.	Analyzes somewhat, but *fails to show some key parts of the argument*.	Shows key parts of the argument adequately with *some analysis*.	Shows key parts of the argument and *analyzes them thoughtfully*.	Shows key parts of the argument and *analyzes them with great clarity*.
Style	Has *severe and persistent errors* in sentence structure and use of language; meaning is lost.	*Frequently uses language incorrectly*, and sentence structure, grammar, and usage errors inhibit meaning.	*Uses language imprecisely* and is deficient in variety; some major errors or a number of small errors.	*Controls language adequately*, including syntax and diction; a few flaws.	*Controls language with clarity*, including variety of syntax and diction; may have a flaw here and there.	*Controls language extremely well*, including variety of syntax and diction; may have a small flaw here and there.

GMAC will grade your essay holistically based on the above rubric to arrive at your final score:

- **6: Excellent.** Essays that earn the top score must be insightful, well supported by evidence, logically organized, and skillfully written. A 6 essay need not be perfect, just very good.

- **5: Good.** A 5 essay is well written and well supported but may not be as compellingly argued as a 6. There may also be more frequent or more serious writing errors than in a 6.

- **4: Satisfactory.** The important elements of the argument are addressed but not explained robustly. The organization is good, and the evidence provided is adequate. The writing may have some flaws but is generally acceptable.

- **3: Inadequate.** A 3 response misses important elements of the argument, offers little or no evidence to support its ideas, and doesn't clearly express its meaning.

- **2: Substantially Flawed.** An essay scoring a 2 has some serious problems. It may not use any examples whatsoever or support its ideas in any way. Its writing will have many errors that interfere with the meaning of the sentences.

- **1: Seriously Deficient.** These essays are rare. A 1 score is reserved for essays that provide little or no evidence of the ability to analyze an argument or to develop ideas in any way. A 1 essay will have so many writing errors that the essay may be unintelligible.

- **0: No Score.** A score of 0 signifies an attempt to avoid addressing the prompt at all, either by writing only random or repeating characters or by copying the prompt. You could also score a 0 by not writing in English or by addressing a completely different topic.

- **NR: Blank.** This speaks for itself. This is what you get if you write no essay at all. Some schools will not consider your GMAT score if your essay receives an NR.

TAKEAWAYS: HOW THE AWA IS SCORED

- Your AWA score does not count toward the 200–800 overall score, nor is it combined with any other subscore.

- Business schools receive the text of your essay along with your score report.

- The essay grading is almost pass/fail in nature: there's a clear line between 1–3 (bad) and 4–6 (good).

- A writer with a solid plan and reasonable control over language will earn a score of 4 or higher on the AWA.

The Basic Principles of Analytical Writing

LEARNING OBJECTIVES

In this section, you will learn how to:

- Describe what it means for your writing to have a logical structure

- Explain how your control of language through grammar, diction, and syntax will affect your score on the Analytical Writing Assessment

- Evaluate whether your writing is concise, forceful, and correct

You aren't being evaluated solely on the strength of your ideas. Your score will also depend on how well you express them. If your writing style isn't clear, your ideas won't come across, no matter how brilliant they are.

Good essay writing isn't just grammatically correct. It is also clear and concise. The following principles will help you express your ideas in good GMAT style.

Use a Logical Structure

Good essays have a straightforward, linear structure. The problem is that we rarely think in a straightforward, linear way. That's why it's so important to plan your response before you begin typing. If you type *while* planning, your essay will likely loop back on itself, contain redundancies, or fail to follow through on what it sets up.

Logical structure consists of three things:

Paragraph Unity

Paragraph unity means each paragraph discusses one thing and all the discussion of that one thing happens in that paragraph. Let's say that you're responding to the essay prompt we just saw and one of your points is that there may have been reasons for the success of the My Pie restaurant other than its proximity to the Filmmax theater. Your next paragraph should move on to another idea—perhaps something about the expense of opening a new My Pie restaurant near every Filmmax theater. If, in the middle of that next paragraph, you went back to your point about other possible reasons for the success of the My Pie restaurant, you'd be violating paragraph unity.

Train of Thought

This is similar to paragraph unity, but it applies to the whole essay. It's confusing to the reader when an essay keeps jumping back and forth between the different weaknesses of an argument. Discuss one point fully, and then address the next. Don't write another paragraph about a topic you've already discussed.

Flow

The basic idea of flow is that you should deliver on what you promise and not radically change the subject. If your introductory paragraph says that you will mention reasons why Hula burgers might be less popular among the 8- to 12-year-old demographic than regular hamburgers are, you need to make sure that you actually do so. Similarly, avoid suddenly expanding the scope of the essay in the last sentence.

Your Control of Language Is Important

Writing that is grammatical, concise, direct, and persuasive displays the "superior control of language" (as the test maker terms it) that earns top GMAT Analytical Writing scores. To achieve effective GMAT style in your essays, you should pay attention to the following points.

Grammar

Your writing must follow the same general rules of standard written English that are tested by Sentence Correction questions. If you're not confident of your mastery of grammar, review the Sentence Correction chapters of this book.

Diction

Diction means word choice. Do you use the words *affect* and *effect* correctly? What about *its* and *it's*, *there* and *their*, *precede* and *proceed*, *principal* and *principle*, and *whose* and *who's*? In addition to avoiding errors of usage, you will need to demonstrate your ability to use language precisely and employ a formal, professional tone.

Syntax

Syntax refers to sentence structure. Do you construct your sentences so that your ideas are clear and understandable? Do you vary the length and structure of your sentences?

Keep Things Simple

Perhaps the single most important piece of advice to bear in mind when writing a GMAT essay is to keep everything simple. This rule applies to word choice, sentence structure, and organization. If you obsess about how to use or spell an unusual word, you can lose your way. The more complicated your sentences are, the more likely they'll be plagued by errors. The more complex your organization becomes, the more likely your argument will get bogged down in convoluted sentences that obscure your point.

Keep in mind that simple does not mean *simplistic*. A clear, straightforward approach can still be sophisticated and convey perceptive insights.

Minor Grammatical Flaws Won't Harm Your Score

Many test takers mistakenly believe they'll lose points over a few mechanical errors. That's not the case. GMAT essays should be polished first drafts. This means that a couple of misplaced commas, misspellings, or other minor glitches aren't going to affect your score. Occasional mistakes of this type are acceptable and inevitable, given that you have only 30 minutes to construct your essay. In fact, according to the scoring rubric, a top-scoring essay may well have a few minor grammatical flaws.

But if your essays are littered with misspellings and grammar errors, the graders may conclude that you have a serious communication problem. Keep in mind that sentence fragments are not acceptable, nor are informal structures such as bullet points or numerical enumeration (e.g., "(1)" instead of "first"). So be concise, forceful, and correct. An effective essay wastes no words; makes its point in a clear, direct way; and conforms to the generally accepted rules of grammar and style.

GMAT Style Checklist

On the GMAT, there are three rules of thumb for successful writing: be concise, be forceful, and be correct. Following these rules is a sure way to improve your writing style—and your score. Let's look at each one in more depth.

Be Concise

- Cut out words, phrases, and sentences that don't add any information or serve a necessary purpose.
- Watch out for repetitive phrases such as "refer back" or "absolutely essential."
- Don't use conjunctions to join sentences that would be more effective as separate sentences.
- Don't use needless qualifiers such as "really" or "kind of."

Examples

Wordy: The agency is not prepared to undertake expansion at this point in time.
Concise: The agency is not ready to expand.

Redundant: All of these problems have combined together to create a serious crisis.
Concise: Combined, these problems create a crisis.

Too many qualifiers: Ferrara seems to be sort of a slow worker.
Concise: Ferrara works slowly.

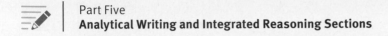
Be Forceful

- Don't refer to yourself needlessly. Avoid pointless phrases like "in my personal opinion"; even phrases such as "I agree" or "I think" are considered stylistically weak.

- Avoid jargon and pompous language; it won't impress anybody. For example, "a waste of time and money" is better than "a pointless expenditure of temporal and financial resources."

- Don't use the passive voice. Use active verbs whenever possible.

- Avoid clichés and overused terms or phrases (for example, "beyond the shadow of a doubt").

- Don't be vague. Avoid generalizations and abstractions when more specific words would be clearer.

- Don't use weak sentence openings. Be wary of sentences that begin with "there is" or "there are." For example, "There are several ways in which this sentence is awkward" should be rewritten as "This sentence is awkward in several ways."

- Don't be monotonous; vary sentence length and style.

- Use transitions to connect sentences and make your essay easy to follow.

Examples

Needlessly references self: Although I am no expert, I do not think privacy should be valued more than social concerns.
Speaks confidently: Privacy should not be valued more than social concerns.

Uses passive voice: The report was compiled by a number of field anthropologists and marriage experts.
Uses active voice: A number of field anthropologists and marriage experts compiled the report.

Opens weakly: It would be of no use to fight a drug war without waging a battle against demand for illicit substances.
Opens strongly: The government cannot fight a drug war effectively without waging a battle against the demand for illicit substances.

Uses cliché: A ballpark estimate of the number of fans in the stadium would be 120,000.
Employs plain English: About 120,000 fans were in the stadium.

Be Correct

- Observe the rules of standard written English. The most important rules are covered in the Sentence Correction chapter of this book.

Examples

Subject and verb disagree: Meredith, along with her associates, expect the sustainable energy proposal to pass.
Subject and verb agree: Meredith, along with her associates, expects the sustainable energy proposal to pass.

Uses faulty modification: Having worked in publishing for 10 years, Stokely's résumé shows that he is well qualified.
Uses correct modification: Stokely, who has worked in publishing for 10 years, appears from his résumé to be well qualified.

Uses pronouns incorrectly: A retirement community offers more activities than a private dwelling does, but it is cheaper.
Uses pronouns correctly: A retirement community offers more activities than a private dwelling does, but a private dwelling is cheaper.

Has unparallel structure: The dancer taught her understudy how to move, how to dress, and how to work with choreographers and deal with professional competition.

Has parallel structure: The dancer taught her understudy how to move, dress, work with choreographers, and deal with professional competition.

Is a fragmented sentence: There is time to invest in property. After one has established oneself in the business world, however.

Is a complete sentence: There is time to invest in property, but only after one has established oneself in the business world.

Is a run-on sentence: Antonio just joined the athletic club staff this year, however, because Barry has been with us since 1975, we would expect Barry to be more skilled with the weight-lifting equipment.

Is a correct sentence: Antonio joined the athletic club staff this year. However, because Barry has been with us since 1975, we would expect him to be more skilled with the weight-lifting equipment.

TAKEAWAYS: THE BASIC PRINCIPLES OF ANALYTICAL WRITING

- Your control of language is important.
- Keep things simple.
- Minor grammatical flaws won't harm your score.
- Use a logical structure.
- Be concise, forceful, and correct.

The Kaplan Method for Analytical Writing

LEARNING OBJECTIVES

In this section, you will learn how to:

- List the steps of the Kaplan Method for Analytical Writing
- Explain the purpose of each step of the Method for Analytical Writing
- Perform the steps of the Method for Analytical Writing

You have a limited amount of time to show the business school admissions officers that you can think logically and express yourself in clearly written English. They don't care how many syllables you can cram into a sentence or how fancy your phrases are. They care that you make sense. Whatever you do, don't hide beneath a lot of hefty words and abstract language. Make sure that everything you say is clearly written and relevant to the topic. Get in there, state your main points, back them up, and get out. The Kaplan Method for Analytical Writing—along with Kaplan's recommendations for how much time you should devote to each step of the Method—will help you produce the best essay you're capable of writing in 30 minutes.

STEP 1: TAKE APART THE ARGUMENT

- Read through the prompt to get a sense of its scope.
- Identify the author's conclusion and the evidence used to support it.
- You can take about 2 minutes on this step.

STEP 2: SELECT THE POINTS YOU WILL MAKE

- Identify at least two important gaps (assumptions) between the evidence and the conclusion.
- Think of how you'll explain or illustrate those gaps and under what circumstances the author's assumptions would not hold true.
- Think about how the author could remedy these weaknesses. This part of the Kaplan Method is very much like predicting the answer to a Critical Reasoning Strengthen or Weaken question.
- Step 2 should take about 5 minutes.

STEP 3: ORGANIZE USING KAPLAN'S ESSAY TEMPLATE

- Outline your essay.
- Lead with your best points.
- If you practice with the Kaplan template for the essay before Test Day, organizing the essay will go smoothly and predictably. Using the Kaplan template will help you turn vague thoughts about the prompt into organized, developed paragraphs.
- The organization process should take less than 1 minute.

STEP 4: WRITE YOUR ESSAY

- Be direct.
- Use paragraph breaks to make your essay easier to read.
- Use transitions and structural key words to link related ideas; they will help your writing flow.
- Finish strongly.
- You can afford no more than 20 minutes of typing. The other 10 minutes should be dedicated to planning and correcting.

STEP 5: PROOFREAD YOUR WORK

- Save enough time to read through the entire essay—2 minutes at minimum.
- Fix any spelling, grammar, syntax, or diction errors.
- Add any needed key words to improve the flow of your ideas.
- Don't add any new ideas or change the structure of your essay. There just isn't time.

ORGANIZING THE ARGUMENT ESSAY: THE KAPLAN TEMPLATE

PARAGRAPH 1:

Show that you understand the argument by putting it in your own words.

PARAGRAPH 2:

Point out one flawed assumption in the author's reasoning; explain why it is questionable.

PARAGRAPH 3:

Identify another source of the author's faulty reasoning; explain why it is questionable.

ADDITIONAL PARAGRAPHS AS APPROPRIATE:

Continue to bring in points of fault in the argument, as time permits.

> Time Valve #1:
> Skip to the next paragraph without adding any additional flaws.

SECOND-TO-LAST PARAGRAPH:

Describe evidence that would—if it were provided—strengthen the argument.

> Time Valve #2:
> Combine this paragraph with the last paragraph.

LAST PARAGRAPH:

Conclude that without such evidence, you're not persuaded.

Applying the Kaplan Method for Analytical Writing

Screen 1: General Instructions

The general instructions for the Argument essay will look like this:

Analytical Writing Assessment Instructions

Analysis of an Argument Essay

Time: 30 Minutes

In this part of the test, you will be asked to write a critical analysis of the argument in the prompt. You are not being asked to give your own views on the topic.

COMPOSING YOUR ESSAY: Before you begin to type, take a little time to look at the argument and plan your essay. Make sure your ideas are organized and clearly stated. Leave some time to read over your essay and make any changes you think are necessary. You will have 30 minutes to write your essay.

ESSAY ASSESSMENT: Qualified graders with varied backgrounds, including experience in business subject areas, will assess the overall quality of your analysis and composition. They will look at how well you:

- Identify key elements of the argument and examine them
- Arrange your analysis of the argument presented
- Give appropriate examples and reasons for support
- Master the components of written English

The instructions on Screen 1 tell you to read the argument, plan your essay before writing it, and leave a little time at the end for review. Sound familiar? The Kaplan Method mirrors these steps. While the prompts for the essay vary, the general directions are always the same. Become familiar with the essay directions now so you don't waste valuable time reading them on Test Day.

Screen 2: Specific Prompt

The next screen you go to will contain the specific essay prompt.

Read the argument and the directions that follow it, and write down any ideas that will be helpful in mapping out your essay. Begin writing your essay in the box at the bottom of this screen.

The following appeared as part of a business plan created by a management consultant hired by Comfy Food Restaurant:

"After adding several vegetarian entrees to its dinner menu late last year, Comfy Food experienced a 21 percent increase in the average number of entrees ordered each evening. Furthermore, restaurant reviewers have viewed menu innovations at other dining establishments favorably, writing positive reviews. Therefore, Comfy Food should continue to expand the vegetarian offerings on its menu by replacing several meat entrees with salads, as well as adding meatless appetizers and side dish options. Doing so will allow Comfy Food to gain a competitive advantage over other local restaurants and increase its profits."

Consider how logical you find this argument. In your essay, be sure to discuss the line of reasoning and the use of evidence in the argument. For example, you may need to consider what questionable assumptions underlie the thinking and what alternative explanations or counterpoints might weaken the conclusion. You may also discuss what types of evidence would strengthen or refute the argument, what changes in the argument would make it more logically sound, and what, if anything, would help you better evaluate its conclusion.

The only part of Screen 2 that will change is the specific prompt, which is in quotation marks. The instructions above and below it will stay the same. Again, practicing with these directions now will mean that you won't waste time reading them on Test Day.

The Stimulus

Analysis of an Argument topics will probably remind you of certain Critical Reasoning questions, in particular Strengthen/Weaken and Evaluate questions. Just as in these Critical Reasoning questions, the writer tries to persuade you of something—her conclusion—by citing some evidence. So look for these two basic components of an argument: a conclusion and supporting evidence. Furthermore, just as in Critical Reasoning, be on the lookout for assumptions—the ways the writer makes the leap from evidence to conclusion. These can often be found in mismatched terms between the evidence and conclusion and in possibilities the author has overlooked.

The Question Stem

The question stem instructs you to decide how convincing you find the argument, explain why, and discuss what might improve the argument. Note that there is a right answer here: the argument *always* has some problems. You want to focus your efforts on finding them, explaining them, and fixing them.

Exactly what are you being asked to do here? Paraphrase the following sentences of the question stem.

> Consider how logical you find this argument. In your essay, be sure to discuss the line of reasoning and the use of evidence in the argument.

Translation: Critique the argument. Discuss the ways in which it is not convincing. How and why might the evidence not fully support the conclusion?

> For example, you may need to consider what questionable assumptions underlie the thinking and what alternative explanations or counterpoints might weaken the conclusion. You may also discuss what types of evidence would strengthen or refute the argument, what changes in the argument would make it more logically sound, and what, if anything, would help you better evaluate its conclusion.

Translation: Spot weak links in the argument and offer constructive modifications that would strengthen them.

Let's use the Kaplan Method for Analytical Writing on the Analysis of an Argument topic we saw before:

> The following appeared as part of a business plan created by a management consultant hired by Comfy Food Restaurant:

> "After adding several vegetarian entrees to its dinner menu late last year, Comfy Food experienced a 9 percent increase in the average number of entrees ordered each evening. Furthermore, restaurant reviewers have viewed menu innovations at other dining establishments favorably, writing positive reviews. Therefore, Comfy Food should continue to expand the vegetarian offerings on its menu by replacing several meat entrees with salads, as well as adding meatless appetizers and side dish options. Doing so will allow Comfy Food to gain a competitive advantage over other local restaurants and increase its profits."

STEP 1: TAKE APART THE ARGUMENT

First, identify the conclusion—the point the argument is trying to make. Here, the conclusion is the recommendation in the second sentence:

> Comfy Food should continue to expand the vegetarian offerings on its menu by replacing several meat entrees with salads, as well as adding meatless appetizers and side dish options.

Next, identify the evidence—the basis for the conclusion. Here, several pieces of evidence are provided. You might jot them on your notepad like this:

- Fact: Adding veggie dinner entrees → more entrees ordered
- Fact: Other restaurants changed menus → good reviews
- Opinion: More desirable entrees + good reviews will make this restaurant more competitive relative to other restaurants
- Opinion: Attracting more customers from other restaurants will lead to greater profits

Finally, paraphrase the argument as a whole in your own words: *Comfy Foods should increase its selection of vegetarian items because doing so will be good for business.*

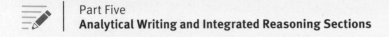

If you aren't able to put the argument in your own words, you don't yet understand it well enough to analyze it sufficiently. Don't rush this step; you can afford a full 2 minutes if you need it.

STEP 2: SELECT THE POINTS YOU WILL MAKE

Now that you've found the conclusion and evidence, think about what assumptions the author makes. What's wrong with her reasoning? What important questions does she leave unaddressed? Here are the key assumptions this author makes:

- Because adding vegetarian entrees boosted entree ordering before, adding more salads to the menu will have the same effect.
- Because other restaurants' menu changes got good reviews, Comfy Food's planned menu change will get good reviews.
- Diners who don't currently eat (or eat often) at Comfy Food will eat there (more often) in response to salads and good reviews.
- The markup on the new menu items won't be so much less than the markup on the items they are replacing that profits could go down, even if volume goes up.

You also will need to explain how these assumptions could be false or how the questions reveal weaknesses in the author's argument. Add counterexamples and reasoning to your notes. The following notes are written out so they can be easily understood by readers of this book, but on Test Day, no one needs to understand your notes but you. So use just enough words to remind yourself of your ideas, and abbreviate wherever possible.

- Because adding vegetarian entrees coincided with entree ordering before, adding more salads to the menu will have the same effect.
  - The increase in entree orders may have been due to some other factor and not the menu change.
  - The "vegetarian entrees" in the evidence weren't necessarily "salads," so there's no support for adding salads specifically to the menu. Perhaps diners who eat at Comfy Foods like hearty bean-and-rice casseroles.
  - There's no evidence that adding vegetarian appetizers and side dishes will influence customer behavior; the evidence is only about entrees.
  - Perhaps the restaurant is already providing all the vegetarian items that patrons want, so adding yet more items will do nothing for sales.
- Because other restaurants' menu changes got good reviews, Comfy Food's planned menu change will get good reviews.
  - The other restaurants may have made completely different menu changes, such as to include more locally sourced, organic ingredients or to offer different cuisines. Reviewers may not look favorably upon Comfy Food's changes.
- Diners who don't currently eat (or eat often) at Comfy Food will eat there (more often) in response to salads and good reviews.
  - The author provides evidence that people ordered more entrees when the menu was changed last year, but that doesn't necessarily mean more people visited this restaurant instead of another one. Maybe diners substituted entrees for other orders.
  - The author offers no evidence that potential customers respond to reviews. Maybe people tend to keep going to the restaurants they're already familiar with rather than trying someplace they've read about in a review.

- The markup on the new menu items won't be so much less than the markup on the items they are replacing that profits could go down, even if volume goes up.

  - Even if changing the menu attracts more customers and they order more food, that's no guarantee that the restaurant will be more profitable. If the difference between what dishes cost to make and what the restaurant can charge decreases, selling more food might result in less profit.

Then think about evidence that would make the argument stronger or more logically sound:

- Evidence, such as a customer survey, confirming that local diners want salads and meatless appetizers and side dishes

- The same survey could provide data about why diners visit one restaurant over another

- Evidence, such as from conversations with restaurant critics or research into dining trends, that the proposed menu changes will garner positive reviews

- Evidence in the form of financial projections that shows an increase in customer orders, given the new mix of menu items and their markups, will in fact result in increased profits

STEP 3: ORGANIZE USING KAPLAN'S ESSAY TEMPLATE

Look over the notes you've jotted down. Select the strongest point to be first, the next-strongest to be second, and so on. Two criteria determine whether a point is strong. One is how well you can explain it. If, for example, you aren't sure how to explain potential inertia in customer behavior, you should use that idea last—if at all. The other is how seriously the weakness undermines the argument's persuasiveness. If customers have no interest in salads, for example, the argument is in serious trouble.

Then decide how you'll arrange your points. Follow the Kaplan template. You can just number the ideas you've already brainstormed. Here's one way someone might organize this essay. Note that this person has reorganized the order of ideas from the notes above, and they've divided up the third idea—about what drives customer behavior—combining parts of it with two other ideas instead of writing about it in a separate paragraph.

¶ Restate argument and assert that it relies too heavily on assumptions

¶ Assump: increased orders = profits

¶ Assump: reviews will be positive & reviews drive customer behavior

¶ Assump: demand for salads, etc. & menu choices drive customer behavior

¶ Evidence that would strengthen argument

¶ Conclude

Remember, you may not have time to use all your points. Leaving your weakest for last means that if you run short on time, you'll leave out your weakest point instead of your best.

Here's another tip: If you're concerned about running out of time, write a strong concluding sentence that restates your thesis (that in the absence of further evidence, the argument is not persuasive) right after you write your introductory paragraph. After all, you know how your essay will end. Then spend the available time filling in the middle with body paragraphs, without the pressure of needing to leave time to write a clear conclusion.

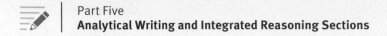

STEP 4: WRITE YOUR ESSAY

Begin typing your essay now. Keep in mind the principles of sound writing discussed earlier.

Keep your writing simple and clear. Choose words that you know how to use well. Avoid the temptation to make your writing "sound smarter" with overly complicated sentences or vocabulary that feels awkward.

Keep your eye on the clock and make sure that you don't run out of time to proofread. If you need to, leave out your last point or two. (Make sure that you include at least two main points.) Let's pretend that the writer of the following essay had only 6 minutes left on the clock after the third paragraph. She wisely chose neither to rush through her final paragraph nor to skip proofreading. Instead, she left out her point about cost.

> The business consultant recommends that Comfy Foods Restaurant change its menu, specifically by replacing some meat entrees with salads and adding other vegetarian options. This strategy will, according to the consultant, give the restaurant an advantage over other area restaurants and be more profitable. Certainly this argument would be compelling if it were credible. However, the argument relies on unsupported assumptions and is therefore unconvincing.
>
> The consultant supports this proposal in part by stating that it will increase the restaurant's profits. Even if the plan works as intended and Comfy Foods enjoys greater market share and more customers, profits may not follow. A higher volume of food orders will result in higher profits only if the total margin is greater. If these new items cost more to make than the old items, or if the restaurant cannot charge as much for them, or some combination of the two, even greater sales may not lead to greater profits. Unless data are provided to address this issue, the restaurant's management cannot be sure that this alleged benefit of the plan will come to pass.
>
> Moreover, it is far from certain that customers will respond positively to changes in the menu. The consultant implies that reviewers will write positive reviews after the changes, because they have written positive reviews about changes to the menus at other restaurants. However, no information is provided about what those changes were. Perhaps those restaurants shifted to using more locally sourced, organic ingredients, or perhaps they incorporated items from diverse cuisines into their offerings. Even if those restaurants did begin serving more vegetarian food, perhaps they prepared the food in an exceptionally delicious manner and that is what reviewers responded to—not the change to the menu itself. Finally, there is no evidence that restaurant patrons act on what they read in reviews. They may continue to visit the establishments they know and love, no matter how enticing a review may be. Without knowing more about what factors influence reviews and how reviews influence customer behavior, management should be skeptical of the effects of this plan.
>
> In addition, the consultant assumes that the restaurant's experience with adding a few unspecified vegetarian entrees to the menu supports the specific recommendation to add salads and non-entree dishes. First, there is no evidence that adding the new entrees actually increased sales of entrees, other than the fact that the two events happened at the same time. Perhaps entree sales would have gone up for some other reason, regardless of the menu change. Second, maybe Comfy Foods customers like hearty bean-and-rice casseroles and will be uninterested in salads. Finally, there is no evidence to support the idea that vegetarian side dishes and appetizers will be well received. Indeed, since the restaurant has already expanded its vegetarian offerings, perhaps customer demand for this food is already being satisfied and further offerings will have no effect.

Comfy Foods management should ask the consultant to provide more data to support her assumptions. A survey of local residents could confirm what people who dine out want to see on restaurant menus and how they decide to visit one restaurant over another. Conversations with restaurant critics or research into dining trends would give more insight into whether the proposed menu changes would garner the positive reviews that the consultant anticipates. A detailed breakdown of costs and prices of current and proposed menu items, at different volumes, would help management determine whether changing the menu would increase profits.

Unfortunately, because the consultant has not provided these types of evidence, management should not rely on her plan to improve the business.

STEP 5: PROOFREAD YOUR WORK

Save a few minutes to go back over your essay and catch any obvious errors or opportunities for improvement. The best way to improve your writing and proofreading skills is practice. When you practice responding to AWA prompts, do so on a computer—but to mimic test conditions, don't use the automatic spell-check or grammar-check. You can turn off these functions in your browser or word processor settings. Write practice essays using the prompts at the end of this chapter or those provided by the test maker at **mba.com**. The pool of prompts provided by the test maker contains the actual prompts from which the GMAT will select your essay topic on Test Day.

Practice Essays

Directions. Write an essay on each of the three topics below. The writing should be concise, forceful, and grammatically correct. After you have finished, proofread to catch any errors. Allow yourself 30 minutes to complete each essay. Practice writing under timed conditions so that you get a feel for how much you can afford to write while leaving enough time to proofread.

Essay 1

The following appeared as part of an article on an appliance repair trade association website:

"Several months ago, our association rewrote our voluntary guidelines to be more stringent. During this period, those member companies that adhered to the new, stricter guidelines reported experiencing a lower rate of callbacks per service call than during the same period last year. Since callbacks, which involve returning to the customer site after the initial visit, have a significant effect on productivity, if we were to make these guidelines mandatory, all our member companies would see improved productivity. Acme Appliance deserves special recognition: it followed the guidelines more closely than did any other participating company, so Acme's customers can be assured that their problem will be fixed during the technician's first visit, and the company must be enjoying strong productivity gains."

Consider how logical you find this argument. In your essay, be sure to discuss the line of reasoning and the use of evidence in the argument. For example, you may need to consider what questionable assumptions underlie the thinking and what alternative explanations or counterpoints might weaken the conclusion. You may also discuss what types of evidence would strengthen or refute the argument, what changes in the argument would make it more logically sound, and what, if anything, would help you better evaluate its conclusion.

After writing your essay, compare it to the sample responses that follow. Don't focus on length, as word count is not part of the grading criteria. Rather, focus on how logical the structure is and whether the essay makes its points in a clear and straightforward style.

Student Response 1 (as written, including original errors)

The writer argues that making guidelines mandatory would make the productivity of all the companies better. He also says that Acme has better productivity, and their customers are having their problems fixed during the first visit. The problem is that these conclusions are based on unsupported assumptions. The evidence is just about callbacks, but productivity is bigger than that. Also, Acme is doing better than other companies, but that doesn't mean their customers are always happy—just happy the first time more often than other companies.

This argument is also weak because all the member companies are not necessarily the same as the ones that participated. After all, the guidelines are voluntary, so only some companies did. This argument could be strengthened if the author would make sure all the other companies are similar to the ones that met the stricter guidelines and aren't different in some way. The author should also talk about productivity in general, since maybe reducing callbacks isn't the only the that following the guidelines do. Maybe copmanies that follow the guidelines also have to do things that are less productive. And the author needs to tell us more about Acme instead of just asserting that its customers are served first time and its productive. Following the guidelines closely doesn't mean these things happen, necessarily.

So this is a flawed argument. Maybe the guidelines work, but maybe they don't. More information is needed.

Analysis 1

Structure: The writer gives an evaluation of the argument in paragraph 1, where he correctly identifies conclusion and evidence as well as the key flaws in the argument's reasoning. However, the organization breaks down in paragraph 2, where the writer first names another weakness of the argument and then jumps into strengthening the argument. A better-written essay would have used several more paragraphs, identifying and explaining each flaw separately.

Evidence: The writer does not fully support his position with specific examples. Rather, he writes vaguely of different possibilities. While this is not completely wrong, it's also not the type of concrete support that is needed here.

Depth of Logic: This is probably the weakest area in the essay. The writer fails to fully develop his ideas. What does he mean by "productivity is bigger than that [callbacks]"? He should explain what some other dimensions of productivity are and how following stricter guidelines might actually make a company less productive; for example, if repair technicians must have all the tools and parts they might need on their truck at all times so they can solve every problem on the first visit, then that might tie up a lot of inventory that could be used more efficiently. As another example, the author tries to discuss the problem of representativeness at the top of paragraph 2 but fails to give examples of how companies could be "similar" or "different."

Style: The language is somewhat informal and imprecise, the sentence structure and vocabulary are basic, and there are a few outright errors. Nonetheless, the author expresses his ideas pretty clearly. While this writing style would prevent this essay from scoring a 6, it would not prevent a score of 4 or even 5 if the ideas were developed more deeply.

This essay would earn a score of 3. While the writer has some decent ideas and shows adequate writing ability, the structure of the essay is poor, the logic fails to show some parts of the author's argument, and the writer inadequately develops support for his points. Had this student used the same ideas, but developed and organized them according to the Kaplan template, he would have earned a score of 4 or better.

Student Response 2 (as written, including original errors)

The author of this article makes two claims. First, he says that because some member companies have ostensibly benefited from following the rewritten guidelines, all member companies would benefit from doing so. Second, he says that because Acme Appliance has followed the guidelines more closely than any other company, its customers are always satisfied on the technician's first visit and the company is enjoying "strong" productivity gains. These conclusions must be viewed with skepticism, however, since the author bases them on insufficient evidence, instead making a number of unfounded assumptions.

It may be true that better productivity would follow for any company that followed the stricter guidelines. However, because obeying the guidelines is voluntary, it is possible that the companies that voluntarily complied are more generally motivated to do well than are other companies in the trade association. Alternatively, the participating firms may have seen some advantage in the new guidelines that the other members did not. Thus, this sample of companies may not be representative of the larger population; specifically, these firms may have been better positioned than their peers to take advantage of rules that encouraged higher performance.

In addition, while callbacks are established as a "significant" factor in productivity, the author does not provide evidence that they are the only factor. Even if following the new guidelines would reduce the rate of callbacks for all member companies, these stricter rules might impose burdens that would actually reduce productivity. For example, the fact that they reduce callbacks suggests that technicians are fully prepared for whatever problem they need to fix at every site. If the guidelines require companies to staff each service call with several technicians, as well as a complete set of tools and parts so that every possible repair can be made, then the rate of callbacks would indeed decrease, but productivity might well be lower because of the resources devoted to each call. Thus, the prediction of increased productivity is not well supported.

Finally, the claims about Acme Appliance would need much more evidence to be plausible. There is no evidence that following the guidelines "more closely" results in large productivity gains. Perhaps just following a few of the stricter guidelines improves productivity, but at a certain point, the company sees diminishing returns from following even more of the rules. Also, there is a leap from seeing some productivity improvement from reducing callbacks to seeing "strong" productivity improvement. Moreover, the claim that Acme's customers "can be assured" of satisfaction on the first visit goes beyond the evidence, which is only that adhering to the new guidelines improves callback rates, not that it eliminates callbacks completely.

To make this argument persuasive, the author needs to present evidence that addresses his assumptions. If the writer could show that all other member companies were similar to the early adopters, then the argument that all members would enjoy lower callback rates would be strengthened. The writer should also show that the new guidelines do not impose burdens that would reduce productivity, offsetting the gains from fewer callbacks. Finally, the argument about the specific case of Acme would be stronger if the author went into more detail about how this company's greater adherence to the guidelines would affect productivity and guarantee successful first visits.

Unfortunately, because the author has not provided this additional evidence, the argument to make the new guidelines mandatory for all association members is unconvincing.

Analysis 2

Structure: The writer of this essay has clearly used the Kaplan template to her benefit. She frames the argument succinctly in the first paragraph. In each of the middle paragraphs, she lays out one major problem in the argument's reasoning and explains with clear support why it is a problem. In the next-to-last paragraph, the writer introduces evidence that would strengthen the argument. The last paragraph states her conclusion clearly.

Evidence: The evidence is solid. In particular, the writer uses counterexamples to illuminate why the argument's assumptions may not hold true.

Depth of Logic: The logic in this essay is much stronger than in the last. The organization of the essay leaves few gaps in the reasoning.

Style: The writing style is superior. Sentence structure and vocabulary are varied, and words are well chosen to convey the intended meaning. Ideas flow logically from one to another, thanks in part to the effective use of key words.

This essay would receive a score of 6 from the GMAT graders, as it is a strong essay in all four categories of evaluation. The conclusion is somewhat terse, but when the ideas have already been well developed, a brief conclusion does not detract from the score.

Essay 2

The following appeared in a memo from the regional manager of Luxe Spa, a chain of high-end salons.

"Over 75 percent of households in Parksboro have Jacuzzi bathtubs. In addition, the average family income in Parksboro is 50 percent higher than the national average, and a local store reports record-high sales of the most costly brands of hair and body care products. With so much being spent on personal care, Parksboro will be a profitable location for a new Luxe Spa—a salon that offers premium services at prices that are above average."

Consider how logical you find this argument. In your essay, be sure to discuss the line of reasoning and the use of evidence in the argument. For example, you may need to consider what questionable assumptions underlie the thinking and what alternative explanations or counterpoints might weaken the conclusion. You may also discuss what types of evidence would strengthen or refute the argument, what changes in the argument would make it more logically sound, and what, if anything, would help you better evaluate its conclusion.

After writing your essay, compare it to the sample response that follows.

Student Response (as written, including original errors)

Though it might seem at first glance that the regional manager of Luxe Spa has good reasons for suggesting that Parksboro would be a profitable location for a new spa, a closer examination of the arguments presented reveals numerous examples of leaps of faith, poor reasoning, and ill-defined terminology. In order to better support her claim, the manager would need to show a correlation between the figures she cites in reference to Parksboro's residents and a willingness to spend money at a spa with high prices.

The manager quotes specific statistics about the percentage of residents with Jacuzzis and the average income in Parksboro. She then uses these figures as evidence to support her argument. However, neither of these statistics as presented does much to bolster her claim. Just because 75 percent of homes have Jacuzzis doesn't mean those homeowners are more likely to go to a pricey spa. For instance, the presence of Jacuzzis in their houses may indicate a preference for pampering themselves at home. Parksboro could also be a planned development in the suburbs where all the houses are designed with Jacuzzis. If this is the case, than the mere ownership of a certain kind of bathtub should hardly be taken as a clear indication of a person's inclination to go to a spa. In addition, the fact that Parksboro's average family income is 50 percent higher than the national average is not enough on its own to predict the success or failure of a spa in the region. Parksboro may have a very small population, for instance, or a small number of wealthy people counterbalanced by a number of medium- to low-income families. We simply cannot tell from the information provided. In addition, the failure of the manager to provide the national average family income for comparison makes it unclear if earning 50 percent more would allow for a luxurious lifestyle or not.

The mention of a local store's record-high sales of expensive personal care items similarly provides scant evidence to support the manager's assertions. We are given no indication of what constitutes "record-high" sales for this particular store or what "most costly" means in this context. Perhaps this store usually sells very few personal care products and had one unusual month. Even if this one store sold a high volume of hair- and body-care products, it may not be representative of the Parksboro market as a whole. And perhaps "most costly" refers only to the most costly brands available in Parksboro, not to the most costly brands nationwide. The manager needs to provide much more specific information about residents' spending habits in order to provide compelling evidence that personal care ranks high among their priorities.

To make the case that Parksboro would be a profitable location for Luxe Spa, the regional manager should try to show that people there have a surplus of income and a tendency to spend it on indulging in spa treatments. Although an attempt is made to make this very argument, the lack of supporting information provided weakens rather than strengthens the memo. Information such as whether there are other high-end spas in the area and the presence of tourism in the town could also have been introduced as reinforcement. As it stands, Luxe Spa would be ill-advised to open a location in Parksboro based solely on the evidence provided here.

Analysis

Structure: The use of the Kaplan template is evident here. In the first paragraph, the writer demonstrates his understanding of the argument and gives a summary of its flaws. Each paragraph that follows elaborates on one flaw in the author's reasoning. The final paragraph introduces evidence that, if provided, would strengthen the argument.

Evidence: The evidence is strong. The writer develops his points by providing examples to explain why the author's reasoning is questionable. Some minor flaws are evident, as in the second paragraph, when the writer misses an opportunity to point out that a small population might not be enough to support a spa.

Depth of Logic: Once again, the organization of the essay enhances its depth of logic. The writer takes apart the argument methodically and provides clear analysis of each part.

Style: The writing style is smooth and controlled, and grammar and syntax errors are minimal to nonexistent.

This essay would score a 6. The writer makes a very strong showing in all four categories of the grading rubric.

Essay 3

The following appeared in a document released by a community's arts bureau:

"In a recent county survey, 20 percent more county residents indicated that they watch TV programs dedicated to the arts than was reported eight years ago. The number of visitors to our county's museums and galleries over the past eight years has gone up by a comparable proportion. Now that the commercial funding public TV relies on is facing severe cuts, which will consequently limit arts programming, it is likely that attendance at our county's art museums will also go down. Therefore, public funds that are currently dedicated to the arts should be partially shifted to public television."

Consider how logical you find this argument. In your essay, be sure to discuss the line of reasoning and the use of evidence in the argument. For example, you may need to consider what questionable assumptions underlie the thinking and what alternative explanations or counterpoints might weaken the conclusion. You may also discuss what types of evidence would strengthen or refute the argument, what changes in the argument would make it more logically sound, and what, if anything, would help you better evaluate its conclusion.

After writing your essay, compare it to the sample response that follows.

Student Response (as written, including original errors)

In a time of threatened scarcity of funding, a community arts organization is asking to shift public arts funds partly to public television. The organization cites a recent survey of county residents that shows a 20 percent self-reported increase in arts TV-watching over the last eight years concomitant with a similar, documented increase in local museum and art gallery attendance. This earnest plea is understandable, but the underlying rationale for shifting funding is flawed and lacks sufficient substantiation.

First, the author may be confusing correlation with causation. Does the survey—even if we accept its findings as valid—really indicate that people went to museums as a result of seeing arts programming on television? Its quite possible that there are alternate reasons for the increase in attendance at museums, such as partnerships with schools, discount programs for senior citizens, introduction of IMAX theaters, or popular traveling exhibits. Alternatively, people may be watching more arts programming on television as a direct result of being lured into museum attendance for reasons that have nothing to do with television.

A second reason to be hesitant to adopt the recommended funding shift is that it assumes that there are only two viable sources of funding for public television: commercial and public. Before it resorts to diverting public funds from other arts organizations, public television has the option to pursue direct fundraising from viewers; these newly enthusiastic television arts program viewers may be delighted to support such programming directly. Public television has a unique opportunity to reach its audience in a way that is more elusive to smaller art museums. It is potentially in a superior position to recover from reduced corporate funding without needing to rely more heavily on public funds.

Conversely, it is possible that the author knows more than he has shared about a connection between public television watching and local museum attendance. For instance, there may have been some specific partnerships in the last eight years between local museums and local public television stations, including specific programming designed to tie in with current museum exhibitions. The recent survey to which the author alluded may have referenced direct ties between the television programming and museum attendance. Such data would make it more likely that increasing the public funding for public television would also directly benefit local museums.

Until more information is provided to us, however, we cannot accept the authors' argument for a shift in public funds to local public television as a way to support local art museums.

Analysis

Structure: This essay is very well organized. The essayist's use of transitions is particularly strong here, as she leads the reader through the points of fault in the argument and describes evidence that could potentially strengthen the argument.

Evidence: The essayist provides multiple strong examples that strengthen her major points.

Depth of Logic: The essayist accurately identifies the assumptions inherent in the argument and develops her points by proposing plausible alternative explanations for the evidence the argument's author cites.

Style: The essayist has a few problems with misplaced apostrophes; otherwise, the grammar and syntax are strong.

This essay would score a 6. It is an excellent example of how following the Kaplan template will help you organize your ideas into a convincing essay. After the introduction, two paragraphs develop and support the author's two main points, followed by a paragraph describing how the argument could be strengthened and a clear conclusion.

Integrated Reasoning

LEARNING OBJECTIVES

After studying this chapter, you will be able to:

- Describe important attributes of the Integrated Reasoning section including format, question types, timing, and scoring
- Apply critical thinking skills to systematically approach a variety of tasks on the Integrated Reasoning section

---

The Integrated Reasoning section is either the second section or the next-to-last section of the GMAT, depending on which section order you choose. You'll have 30 minutes to complete the 12 questions it contains.

Previewing the Integrated Reasoning Section

LEARNING OBJECTIVES

In this section, you will learn how to:

- Describe the formats of and differences between the four Integrated Reasoning question types
- Explain how the user interface in Integrated Reasoning differs from that used elsewhere on the GMAT

Integrated Reasoning questions are designed to resemble the types of problems you will encounter in business school and in your business and management career. These questions focus on your ability to solve complex problems using data from multiple sources in a variety of formats.

What Are the Formats of IR Questions, and What Content Do They Test?

There are 12 questions in the Integrated Reasoning section, nearly all of which include multiple parts. For example, a single graph, discussion, or chart will be used as the basis for several parts of one question, and each question may measure a different skill set.

In the Integrated Reasoning section, you must analyze different types of data (presented in graphs, tables, and passages, among other formats), synthesize data in verbal and graphical formats, and evaluate outcomes and trade-offs. Some of the data are presented in interactive formats, such as spreadsheets. You may need to sort data within columns to determine the answer or click on multiple tabbed pages to view additional information.

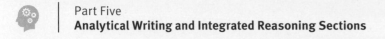

The Integrated Reasoning section consists of four question types:

1. **Graphics Interpretation** questions contain two statements that must be completed using drop-down menus. The statements pertain to a graph, scatter plot, or other form of visual information.

2. **Multi-Source Reasoning** questions provide given information in the form of text, charts, or tables spread across two or three tabbed pages. Some of the questions are traditional five-answer multiple-choice, while others consist of three true/false–style statements that must all be answered correctly in order to receive credit for the question.

3. **Table Analysis** questions present information in the form of a sortable spreadsheet. Table Analysis questions feature the same true/false question format seen in Multi-Source Reasoning questions.

4. **Two-Part Analysis** questions start out like ordinary Quant or Verbal questions, but instead of selecting one answer from five choices, you must select answers to two related questions from a common pool of five or six choices. Unless the question specifies that the two answers are different, they aren't necessarily on different rows but can be the same.

In this chapter, you will find two to three examples of each type of question set. You can practice with additional Integrated Reasoning questions, complete with answers and explanations, in the quizzes and practice tests in your online resources.

Because the questions in the Integrated Reasoning section vary greatly in form and content, flexibility will be key to success. Since Integrated Reasoning questions draw on many of the same skills you need for the Verbal and Quantitative sections, thorough practice with GMAT questions of all types is the best way to prepare for Integrated Reasoning.

How Long Is the IR Section, and How Much Time Do I Have?

The Integrated Reasoning section is 30 minutes long. Navigation on the IR section, as on the rest of the GMAT, moves forward only. You may not skip questions and go back to them later, and you may not return to questions you have already answered. If you are unsure of the answer, you need to take your best guess and keep going.

Unlike the Quantitative and Verbal sections of the GMAT, the Integrated Reasoning section is not computer adaptive. Your performance on one question will not determine the difficulty of the one that follows.

What Is the User Interface Like on the IR Section?

The Integrated Reasoning section looks very different from the rest of the GMAT. Because hands-on experience is the best way to learn the user interface, it is recommended that you practice with these question types in your Kaplan online resources.

In the Integrated Reasoning section, you will see question formats other than multiple choice. You may be required to select your answer from drop-down menus or true/false options. The new formats are straightforward and easy to use but look very different from the multiple-choice questions used in the Quantitative and Verbal sections and require some different techniques.

You will also need to understand how to navigate through spreadsheets and tabbed pages. Table Analysis questions present you with a table of data that can be sorted using a drop-down menu. Pay close attention to how the drop-down menu operates and make sure to consider all your sorting options. Multi-Source Reasoning questions require you to integrate information from several tabbed pages.

You have the use of an onscreen calculator for the Integrated Reasoning section *only*. You are not allowed to bring your own calculator into the exam. The calculator performs basic functions and can be accessed by clicking an icon on the screen. A calculator screen will then pop up over the question. The calculator looks like this:

Use caution when using the calculator. You run the risk of entering information incorrectly, resulting in a wrong answer; moreover, rounding and estimation are often much faster than the time-consuming process of entering multiple large numbers. Use the calculator only when necessary.

What GMAT Core Competencies Are Most Essential to Success on IR Questions?

Critical Thinking is key here, as you'll need to connect the dots between different pieces of information that may not have an obvious connection, since they're presented in different places and in different formats. Paraphrasing is also important, since on item after item you'll need to get the gist of a fair quantity of information and do so efficiently. Pattern Recognition will help with everything from spotting trends in the data in a table to understanding the relationship of answer choices in the two columns of a Two-Part Analysis question. And Attention to the Right Detail will help you accurately pluck the relevant piece of data from a graph, table, or text.

How the Integrated Reasoning Section Is Scored

> **LEARNING OBJECTIVE**
>
> In this section, you will learn how to:
>
> - Describe the scoring of the Integrated Reasoning section

Scoring

The Integrated Reasoning section does not contribute to the total 200–800 GMAT score. Instead, it's scored on its own scale from 1 to 8, in whole-point increments. Since there are 12 items on the IR section, there is not a one-to-one correspondence between the number of items you get right and your score on the section. This is at least in part due to the presence of some unscored experimental items. However, since you will not know which items are experimental, you should treat every item as though it counts.

While a few items in the IR section are traditional multiple-choice questions, most items require two or three selections. There is no partial credit. Thus, getting two questions right and one question wrong on a three-part Table Analysis or Multi-Source Reasoning item is exactly the same as getting all three questions wrong. For more information about scoring, see Chapter 1: Introduction to the GMAT.

The Kaplan Method for Integrated Reasoning

LEARNING OBJECTIVE

In this section, you will learn how to:

- List the steps of the Kaplan Method for Integrated Reasoning and explain the purpose of each step

Now that you've read about the format of the IR section and its four question types, it's time to learn how to approach these questions strategically. Kaplan has developed a Method for Integrated Reasoning that you can use flexibly to solve each question in this section. Approaching these questions methodically is important, given the tight time constraints you'll be working under.

THE KAPLAN METHOD FOR INTEGRATED REASONING

1. Analyze the information.
2. Approach strategically.

STEP 1: ANALYZE THE INFORMATION

All items on the IR section have this in common: they will present you with information you need to analyze before you can approach answering the question(s). In Graphics Interpretation questions, this information is presented in some sort of graph. In Table Analysis, it's given to you in a sortable mini spreadsheet. In Multi-Source Reasoning, you'll get two or three tabs of information, often a mix of text, tables, and/or graphs. And in Two-Part Analysis, you'll be given anything from a paragraph expressing an argument to a geometry figure.

In all cases, it will be critical to get the gist of this information so you don't attempt questions without all the useful facts. When a good amount of data is presented, as in a graph, in a table, or on tabs, noting where to find various details will be important so you can research them efficiently if and when you need them.

STEP 2: APPROACH STRATEGICALLY

Since time is of the essence on the IR section, you don't want to do any work you don't have to do on the road to maximizing your score. While a strategic approach takes many forms on these diverse questions, you'll always want to do three things:

1. Zero in on the exact information you need to answer the question.
2. Use the strategies you employ on the Quantitative and Verbal sections to get to the answer efficiently. These strategies include passage mapping, estimation, predicting, backsolving, and elimination of incorrect choices based on your understanding of the scenario before doing any hard work.
3. Don't be afraid to guess and go. Very few students can complete all 12 items in the IR section in the 30 minutes given. If you can quickly ascertain that a certain item does not match well to your skill set, guess on the question(s) and move on. This guessing approach will ensure that you get to all of the questions that you can get right with enough time to solve.

The Integrated Reasoning Question Types

Graphics Interpretation

Graphics Interpretation questions test your ability to interpret and analyze data presented visually in graphs or graphical images. For each question, you will see a graph with accompanying text and two questions.

As with a Reading Comprehension passage, you do not need to absorb every bit of information on the graph to answer the questions. What you *do* need to do is get the gist of the graph and what it contains so that you can efficiently find the information you need. You will then read the question stem, view the answer choices, and use the information in the graph to select the correct answer.

Graphics Interpretation questions feature many different types of graphs, including line graphs, scatter plots, Venn diagrams, and even geological timelines. Both examples in this chapter happen to focus on scatter plots, but don't take this as a sign that scatter plots are more important than any other type of graphic you may see on Test Day. We've chosen these as our examples because you're probably less familiar with scatter plots than with the other types of graphs commonly seen on the Integrated Reasoning section.

All graphics are accompanied by two incomplete sentences. Test takers must use a drop-down menu to select a word or phrase that completes the sentence according to the information presented in the graphic. There is no partial credit. Some of the sample graphs in this book are accompanied by more than two sentences in order to give you a better sense of the variety of questions you may be asked. The drop-down menus in this chapter are represented in multiple-choice format for ease of reading.

Let's take a look at some Graphics Interpretation questions.

Eruptions of the Old Faithful Geyser, Yellowstone National Park

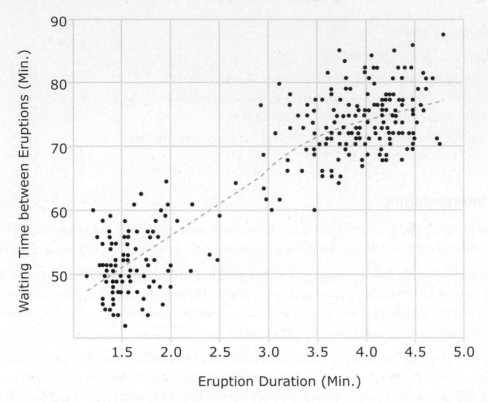

The graph above is a scatter plot with each point representing the duration of an eruption of Old Faithful, a geyser in Yellowstone National Park, and the time in minutes until the following eruption occurred. The dotted line represents a regression line. For each blank, select the answer choice that correctly completes the statement according to the information in the graph.

1a. The relationship between the duration of eruptions and the waiting time between eruptions is _____.

- O   linear and positive
- O   nonlinear and positive
- O   linear and negative
- O   nonlinear and negative

1b. The graph suggests that Old Faithful has _____ of eruption.

- O   one type
- O   two distinct types
- O   more than two distinct types

1c. For an eruption of less than two minutes, the maximum recorded wait time is _____ the minimum recorded wait time of an eruption of more than four minutes.

    O   greater than

    O   equal to

    O   less than

STEP 1: ANALYZE THE INFORMATION

Your first step with a question of this type should be to read the text that accompanies the graph. You may see only a single sentence, or you may see (as in this case) a full paragraph. This text is important. Although most Graphics Interpretation questions can be answered without reference to the text, reading will give you an overview of the information the graph contains and how it is presented. On Test Day, taking a moment to paraphrase the written information will improve your understanding of the image, speeding up your analysis and reducing your chances of committing a careless error.

Here, the paragraph tells you that the graph shows the behavior of a single geyser, Old Faithful. The graph presents two types of information: how long the eruptions of Old Faithful last and how long it then takes before the next eruption happens. Each point on the graph represents an eruption.

Next, look at the graph itself. Get a bird's-eye view of the graph by reading the title and the labels of the axes and notice how the information from the paragraph is represented in the graph. Here, you'll notice that the duration, or length, of the eruption is measured against the waiting time that follows it before the next eruption. Now look at the units of measurement that correspond to each axis and determine whether the scales are similar. In this case, both axes are measured in minutes, but the scales are very different: the x-axis is measured in 0.5-minute increments, while the y-axis is measured in 10-minute increments. Furthermore, the x-axis starts at 1.0 and ends at 5.0, while the y-axis starts at 40 and goes to 90. Then notice if there are any specific features mentioned in the accompanying paragraph that you see represented on the graph, such as a regression line.

The final step before answering the questions is to look at the data to see if they fall into a general pattern. On this scatter plot, most of the data points separate into two distinct groups. With a pattern this clear, you can anticipate that this observation will be key to answering one or more of the accompanying questions. Making these observations before analyzing the questions will help you answer each question more effectively.

STEP 2: APPROACH STRATEGICALLY

Question 1a: First, read and paraphrase the question. It asks about the relationship between the duration of eruptions and the waiting time between eruptions, which means that you are looking for a pattern in how the data points are arrayed on the graph. Before attempting to predict an answer, scan the answer choices. Here, you see the words *linear*, *nonlinear*, *positive*, and *negative*, which indicate that the pattern may take the shape and slope of a line. The regression line will help you here. There is more than one type of regression line, and in this case, the exact type of regression line has not been specified. But you should know that a regression line, however it is calculated, represents the overall trend of the points as a group. The regression line slopes upward—meaning the waiting time gets longer as the explosion duration gets longer. This is a positive relationship—both variables tend to increase and decrease together—so you can narrow the answer down to choices (**A**) and (**B**). Next, you need to determine whether the relationship is linear or nonlinear by looking at the shape of the regression line. You'll notice that the regression "line" isn't really a line, because its slope changes as the amounts of time get longer. Since the relationship isn't linear through the entire data set, the answer is (**B**).

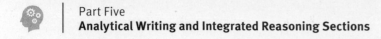
Question 1b: This question might seem a little tricky at first, since the way it's worded might make you think you need to know something qualitative about the types of eruptions the geyser experiences—perhaps something about their magnitude or geological characteristics. But the GMAT will never require you to have outside knowledge beyond high school math and general knowledge of grammar and logic. All the information you need to answer this question is contained in the graph. Begin by paraphrasing the question for yourself: does Old Faithful have one, two, or more than two distinct types of eruption? As you noticed before, the data points separate themselves into two main clusters. There are a few stray data points scattered outside these clusters, but their number is not significant. Therefore, you can infer from the graph that Old Faithful has two types of eruptions, **(B)**.

Question 1c: For this question, you need to examine the data in the graph more closely. This statement contains a comparison between two data points: the maximum wait time for an eruption that lasts less than two minutes and the minimum wait time for an eruption that lasts more than four minutes. Note that you're asked to compare the wait times of these two points—that's their height along the *y*-axis. So this question asks you to find these two points and compare their heights. The first point is the highest point to the left of the two-minute line on the *x*-axis, which looks to be just below 65 on the *y*-axis. Now find the second point, the lowest point to the right of the four-minute line on the *x*-axis. The lowest point to the right of that line appears to be just below the 70-minute mark on the *y*-axis. The first point is therefore lower than the second, so you would choose "less than," **(C)**.

We've discussed how, before attacking any Graphics Interpretation question, you need to understand what the graph contains and how it is constructed. You can then target your research to answer each question correctly and efficiently. Try using these techniques on the next set of questions.

Study of Adults' Sleep Habits

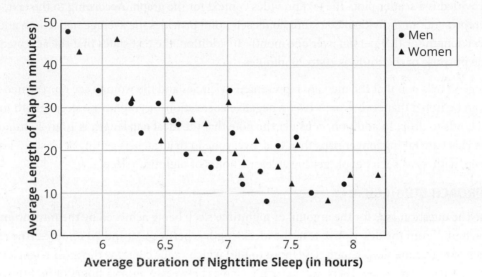

As part of a study on the napping habits of adults, several scientists asked 40 individuals who nap frequently—20 men and 20 women—to record the duration of their naps for one month. These individuals were also asked to record the amount of sleep they get at night. For the purpose of the study, the accepted ideal nap length was set at 10 to 20 minutes per nap. This length has been shown to help combat fatigue and make one feel more alert. The chart above shows the average nap duration and average nighttime sleep length for each of the individuals.

For each statement, select the option from the drop-down menu that completes the statement as accurately as possible according to the information provided.

2a. Of the women whose average nap length was in the accepted ideal range, the greatest number received an average of _____ hours of nighttime sleep.

- O between 6 and 6.5
- O between 6.5 and 7
- O between 7 and 7.5
- O between 7.5 and 8

2b. Of the men in the survey, _____ of them napped, on average, for more than 30 minutes.

- O 25%
- O 30%
- O 55%
- O 60%

STEP 1: ANALYZE THE INFORMATION

The graph provided is a scatter plot. The text provides context for the graph. According to the text, each point on the chart represents an individual in a study, and each point provides the average nap length and average nighttime sleep length for that person over one month. In addition, the text states that the accepted ideal nap length, for the purpose of the study, is 10 to 20 minutes.

The graph's legend tells you that the men are represented by circles and the women are represented by triangles. It can be noted that both groups have a negative correlation—as nighttime sleep length increases, nap duration tends to drop. In addition, consider the note that the ideal nap length is 10 to 20 minutes. Most people in this chart are taking longer naps than this. Everyone in that range is getting at least 6.5 hours of nighttime sleep, with most such people getting at least 7 hours of nighttime sleep.

STEP 2: APPROACH STRATEGICALLY

Question 2a: The question asks for the amount of nighttime sleep being achieved by the most women getting an ideal nap length. From the descriptive text, the ideal length is between 10 and 20 minutes. The choices provide ranges of nighttime sleep length. Use those to find which range contains the most triangles with nap times between 10 and 20 minutes. There are no such triangles between 6 and 6.5 hours of nighttime sleep. There's only one between 6.5 and 7 hours. There are four between 7 and 7.5 hours. And there are only three between 7.5 and 8 hours. So, it's the nighttime sleep range of 7 to 7.5 hours that contains the most women getting the ideal nap length. That makes **(C)** correct.

Question 2b: This question asks how many men had an average nap length of over 30 minutes. The men are represented by circles. Above the 30-minute line there are six circles. However, the choices are not in numbers but in percentages. According to the descriptive text, there are 20 men in total. So the percentage would be $\frac{6}{20} \times 100\% = 30\%$. That makes **(B)** correct. This could also have been estimated to save calculation and eliminate the wrong choices. Knowing that 25% would be one-fourth, or 5 out of 20, helps eliminate the first choice. And 6 out of 20 is certainly less than half, which eliminates the remaining answers.

Computer Algorithm

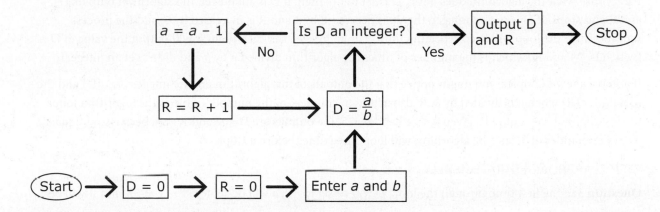

The flowchart represents a computer algorithm that takes two positive integers as the input and is intended to return two integers as the output. Each process is symbolized by an equation, such as $a = a - 1$. In this particular process, 1 is subtracted from the current value of the variable a, and the difference then becomes the value of a. For example, if the value of a is 5 before the process $a = a - 1$ is completed, then the value of a will be 4 after the process is completed. Algorithms that are incorrectly formed may sometimes get stuck in an infinite loop. An infinite loop is a sequence of instructions that never terminates. Complete the following statements by making selections from the drop-down menus in accordance with the algorithm represented by the flowchart.

3a. If 58 and 11 are entered as the values for a and b respectively, then one of the outputs of the function will be _____.

- ○ $D = 0$
- ○ $D = 4$
- ○ $D = 55$
- ○ $R = 3$
- ○ $R = 4$

3b. The algorithm will get stuck in an infinite loop

- ○ if $a > b$
- ○ if $a = b$
- ○ if $a < b$
- ○ never

STEP 1: ANALYZE THE INFORMATION

Paraphrase what the algorithm does. First, D is set to $\frac{a}{b}$. Then, if D is an integer, the algorithm outputs D and R and stops. If D is not an integer, then a is decreased by 1 and R is increased by 1, and the process repeats. Thus, the loop will keep repeating until $\frac{a}{b}$ is an integer, at which point it will output the value of D (which is $\frac{a}{b}$) and R (which is the number of times the algorithm divided a by b and didn't get an integer).

If you try a few examples, you might notice that the outputs of this algorithm are the integer part (D) and the remainder (R) when a is divided by b. R also acts as a "counter" of the number of times the algorithm loops before stopping. For example, given $a = 13$ and $b = 5$, the outputs are D $= 2$ and R $= 3$, because $\frac{13}{5}$ equals 2 with a remainder of 3, and the algorithm will loop three times before it stops.

STEP 2: APPROACH STRATEGICALLY

Question 3a: The first time through the loop, D will be set to $\frac{58}{11}$, a will be set to $58 - 1 = 57$, and R will be set to $0 + 1 = 1$. The second time through the loop, D will be set to $\frac{57}{11}$, a will be set to $57 - 1 = 56$, and R will be set to $1 + 1 = 2$. The third time through the loop, D will be set to $\frac{56}{11}$, a will be set to $56 - 1 = 55$, and R will be set to $2 + 1 = 3$. On the fourth time through the loop, D will be set to $\frac{55}{11} = 5$, which is an integer, so the algorithm will stop and the values of a and R will not be changed. Thus, the outputs are D $= 5$ and R $= 3$. D $= 5$ is not present among the selections, but R $= 3$ is. The correct answer is **(D)**.

Question 3b: If $a > b$, then you've already seen that the algorithm will stop. If $a = b$, then the algorithm will also stop, because a number divided by itself always equals 1 with a remainder of 0. If $a < b$, it may seem that the algorithm will get stuck because D will keep getting set to a fraction. For example, if $a = 9$ and $b = 10$, D will get set to $\frac{9}{10}$, then $\frac{8}{10}$, then $\frac{7}{10}$, and so on. However, a will eventually be reduced to 0, at which point $\frac{a}{b}$ will equal 0 (which is an integer) and the algorithm will stop. Thus, no matter the values of a and b, the algorithm's termination condition is always triggered. This means that it will never not stop, which is **(D)**.

Multi-Source Reasoning

As its name suggests, Multi-Source Reasoning tests your ability to synthesize information from multiple sources to answer questions. The information will be presented on two or three tabbed pages. You will have to click through the tabs to find the information you need. The data can be in the form of text, graphs, or tables.

The information on the tabs may seem overwhelming, so approach it similarly to how you approach Reading Comprehension. Get the gist of what the tabs contain and take brief notes highlighting the main points of each tab. Don't try to absorb all of the information at first, but make sure you scan all of the information on each tab so that you'll know where to find it when you answer the questions.

The tabbed pages are on the left side of the screen, and the questions appear one at a time on the right. You can get hands-on experience with tabbed pages in your online resources. Take a few minutes to become familiar with the navigation of this section. Doing so will save you valuable time when answering the questions.

Some of the questions about the tabbed information will be in the standard multiple-choice format that you're familiar with from the Verbal and Quantitative sections. Others, called multiple dichotomous choice questions, will require you to evaluate three statements or questions individually; you'll usually be choosing whether statements are true or false or whether the answer to a question is yes or no. There is no partial credit.

| Stainless Steel | Table #1 | Table #2 |

Stainless Steel Categories

Stainless steels are alloys of iron and carbon that also contain a minimum of 10.5% chromium and various amounts of other alloying materials, which may include molybdenum, manganese, and nickel, among others. Stainless steels are designated with three-digit SAE numbers generally ranging from the 200s to the 600s, sometimes followed by a single letter. The three most common categories of stainless steel are described below, and examples of seven specific varieties from within these three categories are listed in the tables that follow.

Ferritic steels contain 12.5%–17% chromium, less than 0.1% carbon, and up to 1% nickel. Ferritic steels are magnetic and can be strengthened by cold working but cannot be heat treated. They are commonly used in automotive exhaust systems, agricultural equipment, and high-heat applications such as furnaces and boilers.

Austenitic steels contain 16%–26% chromium, not more than 0.8% carbon, and 6%–15% nickel. They are nonmagnetic and are not heat treatable. Austenitic steels are the most common type of stainless steel globally, and they are commonly used in food-processing equipment, piping, and kitchen utensils.

Martensitic steels contain 10.5%–17% chromium, up to 1.2% carbon, and not more than 0.4% nickel. They are magnetic and heat treatable. Martensitic steels are commonly used in knives, cutting tools, and dental and surgical equipment.

| Stainless Steel | Table #1 | Table #2 |

Partial Composition of Various Stainless Steels

SAE number	Chromium %	Carbon %	Nickel %
304	18.0–20.0	0.08	8.0–10.5
309S	22.0–24.0	0.08	12.0–15.0
316	16.0–18.0	0.08	10.0–14.0
321	17.0–19.0	0.08	9.0–12.0
409	10.5–11.75	0.08	0.50
410	11.5–13.5	0.15	0.75
430	16.0–18.0	0.20	0.75

Stainless Steel | Table #1 | Table #2

Select Physical Properties of Various Stainless Steels

SAE number	Density (Kg/M^3)	Rockwell hardness	Heat treatable	Magnetic
304	7,900	90	No	No
309S	7,950	85	No	No
316	8,000	95	No	No
321	7,900	95	No	No
409	7,800	75	No	Yes
410	7,850	80	Yes	Yes
430	7,800	89	No	Yes

4. Consider each of the following statements. Indicate *Yes* if the given information supports the statement. Otherwise, indicate *No*.

Yes	No	
O	O	All of the listed stainless steels with a carbon content of 0.08% are Austenitic.
O	O	A stainless steel among those listed with a Rockwell hardness of at least 85 must be either Austenitic or Ferritic.
O	O	Of the steels listed, the average density of Austenitic steels is greater than the average density of Ferritic steels.

5. Based on the information in the passage and tables, the stainless steel with the highest ratio of carbon to nickel has which of the following hardness ratings?

O 80
O 85
O 89
O 90
O 95

STEP 1: ANALYZE THE INFORMATION

You approached Graphics Interpretation by first getting a general sense of how the graph works. Similarly, you need to know what is on each tabbed page before you begin answering Multi-Source Reasoning questions. Take brief notes on the content of each tab as you examine it.

In the first tab, you find a definition of stainless steel and data about three classes of stainless steel, including certain physical properties of each, such as whether it is magnetic or heat treatable, and their common uses.

On the second tab, you are given a table detailing the chromium, carbon, and nickel content ranges of seven different stainless steels, listed by their SAE numbers. Note that the content ranges are listed as percentages.

Switch to the third tab to view another table. This one shows physical properties of each of the same seven steels, including density, hardness, and whether the steel is magnetic or heat treatable.

STEP 2: APPROACH STRATEGICALLY

Question 4a: The text in Tab 1 indicates that Austenitic steels contain 16%–26% chromium, not more than 0.8% carbon, and 6%–15% nickel. These steels are also neither magnetic nor heat treatable.

The question restricts itself to steels that are 0.08% carbon, so find those steels in Tab 2. They are SAE 304 through SAE 409. Of these, all have allowable chromium percentages, but SAE 409 has only 0.5% nickel. Therefore, it is not Austenitic. Alternatively, you could check Tab 3 for the magnetic and heat-treatable characteristics. Here, you'll see that SAE 409 is magnetic and therefore not Austenitic. The answer is No.

Question 4b: Because this specifies a hardness of 85 or above, begin by examining the table in Tab 3; all of the SAE 300-series steels and SAE 430 have a hardness of 85 or higher. Next, return to the text in Tab 1 to determine what constitutes Ferritic steel: it is magnetic but not heat treatable. You've already determined from the previous question that an Austenitic steel is neither. Put another way, any steel in the table that is not heat treatable is either Austenitic or Ferritic. According to the table in Tab 3, none of the SAE 300-series steels is heat treatable and neither is SAE 430, so the answer is Yes.

Question 4c: From the first two questions in this set, you've determined from the information in the text and the table in Tab 3 that all of the SAE 300-series steels are Austenitic. You've also determined that SAE 409 and SAE 430 are Ferritic. A glance at Tab 3 will confirm that SAE 410, being both magnetic and heat treatable, is neither Austenitic nor Ferritic. Rather than doing complex calculations, notice that the two Ferritic steels, SAE 409 and SAE 430, each have a density of 7,800, while all of the Austenitic steels are above 7,850. Thus, you can conclude that the Austenitic steels have a higher average density, so the answer is Yes.

Question 5: Because this question asks for a ratio of carbon to nickel, think of carbon as the numerator of a fraction and nickel as the denominator. The highest ratio will be the fraction with the largest numerator relative to the denominator. Therefore, you can quickly eliminate all of the SAE 300-series steels, since their denominators are many times greater than any of the SAE 400-series steels while their numerators are less than or equal to those of the 400 series. Now use estimation to compare SAE 409 to SAE 410: 0.08 over 0.50 is less than 0.15 over 0.75, since 0.15 is nearly twice 0.08 but 0.75 is considerably less than twice 0.50. What about SAE 430? Since it has a bigger numerator than SAE 410 but the same denominator, it must have the highest ratio. Now find its hardness rating in the table in Tab 3: 89. Therefore, **(C)** is correct.

You've learned from working through this set of Multi-Source Reasoning questions that it's crucial to get the gist of each tabbed page and take brief notes highlighting the main points before attempting to answer any questions. Now apply these techniques to the next set of Multi-Source Reasoning questions.

| Email #1 | Email #2 | Email #3 |

*Email from **project manager** to financial officer*

August 3, 9:43 a.m.

Did all three bids arrive on time last night? We need to minimize delays on construction, so if the contractors have submitted their estimates and our research team has compiled reports on the contractors' histories, we should make a decision on which firm to hire by the end of the day.

| Email #1 | Email #2 | Email #3 |

*Email from **financial officer** in response to the project manager's August 3, 9:43 a.m. email*

August 3, 10:12 a.m.

Appaloosa Construction sent us a bid of $1.35 million. Its bid is the highest of the three, but its track record is spotless; none of the past 10 major projects it has worked on has gone over budget by more than 4 percent. Breton Construction did manage to underbid them—its representative claims that it can do the project for $1.25 million. However, in the past two years, Breton oversaw two different projects that went over budget by a full 25 percent. If our project were to exceed Breton's estimate by a comparable percentage, we would run out of funds before completion. Finally, Campolina Construction presented a $1.1 million plan, and its track record is as good as Appaloosa's. Unfortunately, although Appaloosa and Breton can both start tomorrow, Campolina would be unable to begin work until August 25, so we cannot accept Campolina's low bid.

| Email #1 | Email #2 | Email #3 |

*Email from **project manager** in response to the financial officer's August 3, 10:12 a.m. email*

August 3, 10:38 a.m.

Even though Breton's work could potentially cost less than either of the other two, that savings does not justify the risk of being unable to complete the project. But as far as Campolina is concerned, you're not considering the actual cost of a delay. It's true that we are losing money at a constant rate each day we don't start building. But even after factoring in the losses of waiting until August 25, the estimated cost of working with Campolina still ends up $50,000 below Appaloosa's bid.

6. Consider each of the following statements. Does the information in the three emails support the inferences as stated? Choose *Yes* if the statement can be accurately inferred; otherwise, choose *No*.

Yes	No	
○	○	In making their decision, the project manager and the financial officer considered how much time the contractors would spend on construction.
○	○	The project manager and the financial officer disagree about the best choice of contractors for completing the project.
○	○	The project manager is willing to wait a few days before deciding on Campolina's bid.

7. The amount of money lost each day that construction is delayed is closest to

   ○ $2,500
   ○ $10,000
   ○ $20,000
   ○ $55,000
   ○ $65,000

STEP 1: ANALYZE THE INFORMATION

First, look through the tabbed pages and notice the basics: you have three emails, sent minutes apart, between a project manager and a financial officer. Use your Reading Comprehension Passage Mapping skills to create a brief synopsis of each email in your scratchwork:

Email #1—project manager to financial officer:

- Asking about the bids
- Start construction as soon as possible
- Make a decision by the end of the day

Email #2—financial officer to project manager:

- Appaloosa—$1.35 million—great track record
- Breton—$1.25 million—usually over budget—would run out of funds before completion
- Campolina—$1.1 million—can't begin work until August 25—can't accept

Think strategically here: although the financial officer never draws an explicit conclusion about which company should be hired, his opinion is clear. Breton could cause the company to run out of money for the project, and Campolina's delayed start date is unacceptable, so the financial officer must be in favor of Appaloosa.

Email #3—project manager to financial officer:

- Breton—not worth the risk
- Reminder about the cost of delay
- Campolina is still cheaper, even with the delay

It is not necessary to jot down all of the figures and calculations from the email. Just as with Reading Comprehension, if you need the details, they will be there for you to refer to later.

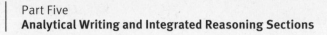

STEP 2: APPROACH STRATEGICALLY

Question 6: Notice that you have another set of yes/no questions. As always, you'll want to read the introductory sentences very carefully. Your task is to consider whether the inferences in the questions are supported by the information in the three emails. Critical Reasoning skills will help you here; you must use *only* the evidence in the three emails to determine your answers.

Question 6a: Read carefully here. Time is discussed, but it is discussed in reference to when the construction can begin, not how long it will take. There isn't any mention of the length of construction in your notes, and if you glance through the three emails, there isn't any information there either. The answer is No.

Question 6b: This question asks whether the project manager and financial officer disagree about who would be the best contractor. The answer to this question, as seen in your notes on the emails, is Yes. The project manager thinks Campolina is the best choice, and the financial officer is in favor of Appaloosa.

Question 6c: The wording of this statement is tricky, so answer it by doing some careful research in the emails. Here, the question asks whether the project manager is willing to wait a few days to decide. Glance at your notes to find relevant key words: "decision" is mentioned in the first email, and "delay," or waiting, is mentioned in the third. Going to the first email, you see that the project manager wants to reach a decision by the end of the day. This seems to contradict the inference given in the question, but don't stop just yet. Check the third email to see whether the project manager changed her mind. In the third email, the project manager discusses waiting, stating that it might be acceptable to wait to begin construction with Campolina—but there is nothing in this email about waiting to make a decision. Thus, you cannot infer that the project manager is willing to wait a few days, and the answer here is No.

Question 7: By now, you can expect that you'll need to find information in multiple emails to answer this question. Looking at your notes, you see that the delay costs are discussed in the third email. The email states that a constant amount is lost every day that construction is delayed. From the second email, you find that the other two companies can start the next day, August 4, but Campolina can't start until August 25, a delay of 21 days. Next, use the information given to determine how much money is lost in those 21 days.

The third email says that even with the delay, Campolina would cost $50,000 less than Appaloosa's $1.35 million bid, or $1.3 million. That means the cost caused by the delay would be $1.3 million − $1.1 million, or $200,000. To determine the cost per day, calculate $\frac{\$200,000}{21} \approx \$9,524$. However, since the question asks for the number that's "closest to" the amount lost per day, you can save time by estimating. Round 21 to 20 and calculate much more easily that $200,000 divided by 20 is $10,000, or **(B)**.

| Email #1 | Email #2 | Email #3 |

*Email from **CEO** to store manager*

April 10, 2:53 a.m.

I just got a call from the police. Our store on Thompson street was robbed again. This is the third time in exactly seven months. After the first robbery, you said you would heighten security, but the measures you took had no effect; 60 days later the same store was robbed. Then you said you'd install an alarm system, but I guess you never got around to that. After the second robbery, the insurance company threatened to cancel our account if the store was robbed again and we hadn't done anything to increase the security of the premises. What am I supposed to tell them?

| Email #1 | Email #2 | Email #3 |

*Email from **store manager** in response to the CEO's April 10, 2:53 a.m. message*

April 10, 3:38 a.m.

I had an alarm system installed within a week after the second robbery. It took the police exactly four minutes to get to the store after the alarm was triggered; the robber was in and out in three. The alarm company called me after calling the police, and I still beat the police to the scene. I've told the alarm company to call me first next time—I missed the robber by no more than 30 seconds.

You can tell the insurance company that the measures I undertook after the first robbery did have a major impact. We started moving inventory from the shelves to the back room before closing the store each day. This cut our losses in the second robbery by nearly 70 percent as compared to the first robbery. I've attached the exact numbers for your perusal. After the second robbery, we began leaving even less inventory on the shelves. It's too soon to tell exactly how much money we lost in this morning's robbery, but my survey indicates that the losses are about another 40 percent smaller than those of the second robbery.

| Email #1 | Email #2 | Email #3 |

*Attachment to the **store manager's** April 10, 3:38 a.m. email*

Value of Stolen Inventory				
Robbery	**Cameras**	**Tripods**	**Lenses**	**Accessories**
First	$45,652	$9,834	$2,119	$589
Second	$11,000	$4,832	$1,003	$672

8. If the manager's estimates are correct and if the tripods stolen in the third robbery account for 15 percent of the value of the stolen inventory, then the value of the stolen tripods is closest to

- ○ $800
- ○ $1,100
- ○ $1,600
- ○ $2,100
- ○ $4,800

9. For each of the following statements, select *True* if the statement can be verified to be true assuming that the information in the emails (but not necessarily the attachment) is accurate. Otherwise, select *False*.

True	False	
○	○	An alarm system was installed at the store in November.
○	○	Upon being reached by phone, the store manager can make it to the store in under five minutes.
○	○	The attachment contradicts the store manager.

10. For each of the following statements, select *Yes* if the statement can be reasonably inferred from the emails and the attachment. Otherwise, select *No*.

Yes	No	
○	○	The robbery could have been prevented if the store manager had installed shatterproof windows.
○	○	The alarm company's phone call to the police lasted less than 45 seconds.
○	○	The value of the lenses stolen in the third robbery is less than that of the second robbery.

STEP 1: ANALYZE THE INFORMATION

Email #1—CEO to store manager

- 3 robberies
- Assumes manager's security measures had no effect/weren't done.
- Problem: What to tell the insurance company?

Email #2—Store manager to CEO

- After 1st robbery, moved inventory, cutting losses in 2nd robbery.
- After 2nd robbery, had alarm installed—but robber was fast.
- After 2nd robbery, moved more inventory, cutting losses in 3rd robbery.

Attachment to email 2—Value of stolen goods in 1st vs. 2nd robbery

- As manager claims, much less overall was stolen in 2nd robbery.

STEP 2: APPROACH STRATEGICALLY

Question 8: The store manager's email states that there was an estimated 40% reduction in losses from the second robbery to the third. The total losses of the second robbery were about $18,000, so the losses of the third robbery were about $18,000 × 60%, or about $11,000. Then 15% of that is about $1,650, which is closest to **(C)**.

Question 9a: The CEO's message states that the first robbery was exactly seven months ago and that the second robbery happened 60 days later. The current day is April 10, so the first robbery happened around September 10 and the second on November 10. The store manager's email states that the alarm was installed within a week of the second robbery, so there was indeed an alarm installed in November. The answer is True.

Question 9b: According to the second email, the store manager missed the robber by 30 seconds. Since the robber was in and out in 3 minutes, the maximum time it could have taken for the store manager to reach the store was 3 minutes 30 seconds. The answer is True.

Question 9c: The total losses of the first robbery were $58,194. The total losses of the second robbery were $17,507. This is a percent change of $\frac{58,194 - 17,507}{58,194}$, or 69.9%, which confirms the store manager's claim that the reduction in losses was "nearly 70 percent." The answer is False.

Question 10a: There's no information in the tabs about how the robber broke into the store. Thus, there's no way to tell whether shatterproof windows would have made any difference. The answer is No.

Question 10b: The store manager's email states that he or she missed the robber by 30 seconds. This means that the alarm company's phone call to the police (whom they called first) lasted at least 30 seconds, but there's no way to tell whether that call was longer or shorter than 45 seconds. The answer is No.

Question 10c: According to the store manager, the total losses of the third robbery are 40% less than those of the second robbery. However, the store manager doesn't say that the losses are proportional in all categories. It's possible that decreases in losses for other goods compensated for an increase in losses for lenses. The answer is No.

Table Analysis

Table Analysis questions measure your ability to interpret and analyze information presented in a sortable table similar to a spreadsheet. You will see a table, a paragraph of text that describes it, and one set of the same three-part multiple dichotomous choice questions you saw for Multi-Source Reasoning (i.e., yes/no, true/false, etc.).

Directly above the table, you will see a Sort button that, when clicked, opens a drop-down menu of options that correspond to the column headers in the table. When you select a category from the drop-down menu, the entire chart will be sorted based on the category you select. If the information in that column is numerical, it will be sorted from lowest to highest. If the information in that column is text, it will be sorted in alphabetical order. While working through the questions in this book, decide how you would sort the information before answering each question. To gain experience sorting tables in the test interface, use the questions in your online resources.

Read the text that accompanies the table first to get an overview of the table's content. Then look at the table itself, paying special attention to the column headings. Now let's look at some Table Analysis questions.

Total Fall Enrollment in Private Degree-Granting Institutions: 2008

Sort By [Select... | ▾]

| | | Undergraduate | | | | Postbaccalaureate | | |
| | | 4-year | | 2-year | | | | |
	Total	Not-for-profit	For-profit	Not-for-profit	For-profit	Total	Not-for-profit	For-profit
Alabama	58,558	23,229	34,000	0	1,329	7,343	4,128	3,215
Arizona	291,869	3,539	275,530	0	12,800	81,066	4,507	76,559
California	264,775	136,304	76,356	2,375	49,740	147,979	129,522	18,457
Colorado	69,460	18,375	40,733	165	10,187	20,507	13,586	6,921
District of Columbia	71,465	37,967	33,498	0	0	49,061	36,575	12,486
Florida	206,477	106,089	79,732	152	20,504	56,629	48,067	8,562
Georgia	76,356	47,701	23,670	1,057	3,928	23,757	17,940	5,817
Illinois	200,263	134,075	56,676	1,126	8,386	98,568	86,235	12,333
Indiana	88,896	68,677	13,020	495	6,704	16,110	15,652	458
Iowa	113,385	45,397	67,601	151	236	16,487	10,919	5,568
Massachusetts	173,897	166,873	2,800	1,737	2,487	97,339	97,203	136
Michigan	101,252	93,562	4,649	0	3,041	23,507	22,870	637
Minnesota	78,855	50,793	25,723	106	2,233	75,567	21,232	54,335
Missouri	117,735	95,299	12,510	2,275	7,651	49,937	49,298	639
New York	390,435	341,205	24,241	6,575	18,414	168,531	166,449	2,082
North Carolina	75,228	68,524	4,635	572	1,497	18,773	18,039	734
Ohio	146,395	107,277	7,044	1,272	30,802	31,669	30,621	1,048
Pennsylvania	251,369	195,359	17,783	7,492	30,735	83,943	83,372	571
Tennessee	75,283	54,023	8,373	278	12,609	18,187	17,097	1,090
Texas	127,359	92,495	12,935	867	21,062	36,657	33,996	2,661
Virginia	90,439	59,959	24,416	0	6,064	27,236	24,789	2,447

The table above gives the 2008 enrollment in private degree-granting institutions for the 20 states with the highest total enrollment, as well as for the District of Columbia. These statistics do not include state-funded and federally funded public institutions. The data include both for-profit and not-for-profit institutions; enrollment for both of these categories is provided in addition to the total enrollment.

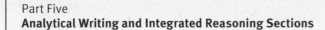
11. Consider the following statements about enrollment in the 21 locations shown in the table. For each statement, indicate whether the statement is *True* or *False*, based on the information provided in the table.

True	False	
○	○	The state with the largest number of students enrolled in for-profit four-year undergraduate programs has the smallest number of students enrolled in not-for-profit four-year undergraduate programs.
○	○	The state with the median number of students enrolled in not-for-profit four-year undergraduate programs also has the median number of students enrolled in not-for-profit two-year undergraduate programs.
○	○	More than half of the students enrolled in degree-granting programs in Minnesota attend for-profit schools.

STEP 1: ANALYZE THE INFORMATION

As with Graphics Interpretation questions, your first step should be to read the text accompanying the table. Here, the text explains that the table shows the private school enrollment numbers for various states, as well as for the District of Columbia, in 2008. It also tells you that the table distinguishes between for-profit and not-for-profit institutions.

Next, look at the table itself and read the column headings. The private institutions are split into two main categories, undergraduate and postbaccalaureate, which are further broken down into for-profit and not-for-profit schools. The undergraduate schools are also divided into two- and four-year programs. Total enrollment numbers for undergraduate and postbaccalaureate programs are also provided. This is a lot of information, and you will need to pay attention to how it is organized in order to answer the questions.

STEP 2: APPROACH STRATEGICALLY

Question 11a: Many Table Analysis questions ask you to compare pieces of information. Take each question one piece at a time. For this question, you first need to find the state with the largest enrollment in for-profit four-year undergraduate schools. Look at your table and find the column that contains that information. Here, it's easy to see that Arizona has the highest enrollment, with 275,530 students. If you weren't able to see that at a glance, you could sort the table by the for-profit four-year undergraduate column. Now that you have the first piece of information, it's time to find the second. You now know that you're looking for information about Arizona. Sort the table by the not-for-profit four-year undergraduate column, and you'll see that Arizona is by far the lowest, at 3,539 students. Arizona, the state with the largest for-profit four-year undergraduate enrollment, does in fact have the smallest not-for-profit four-year undergraduate enrollment, so the answer is True.

Question 11b: Here, you are asked again to compare two pieces of information. By now, you should be zeroing in on the key words in the statement that will tell you how to sort the table. In this case, you are looking for the "not-for-profit four-year undergraduate" column and the "not-for-profit two-year undergraduate" column. Also notice the key word "median," which appears twice. You need to sort two columns and compare the median numbers. The median number of each set will appear exactly in the middle of the set when all the terms are placed in ascending or descending order. You won't be able to eyeball the median number, so get ready to use the Sort function. First, sort by not-for-profit four-year undergraduate institutions:

Sort By [Undergraduate 4-year Not-for-profit | ▼]

		Undergraduate				Postbaccalaureate		
		4-year		2-year				
	Total	Not-for-profit	For-profit	Not-for-profit	For-profit	Total	Not-for-profit	For-profit
Arizona	291,869	3,539	275,530	0	12,800	81,066	4,507	76,559
Colorado	69,460	18,375	40,733	165	10,187	20,507	13,586	6,921
Alabama	58,558	23,229	34,000	0	1,329	7,343	4,128	3,215
District of Columbia	71,465	37,967	33,498	0	0	49,061	36,575	12,486
Iowa	113,385	45,397	67,601	151	236	16,487	10,919	5,568
Georgia	76,356	47,701	23,670	1,057	3,928	23,757	17,940	5,817
Minnesota	78,855	50,793	25,723	106	2,233	75,567	21,232	54,335
Tennessee	75,283	54,023	8,373	278	12,609	18,187	17,097	1,090
Virginia	90,439	59,959	24,416	0	6,064	27,236	24,789	2,447
North Carolina	75,228	68,524	4,635	572	1,497	18,773	18,039	734
Indiana	88,896	68,677	13,020	495	6,704	16,110	15,652	458
Texas	127,359	92,495	12,935	867	21,062	36,657	33,996	2,661
Michigan	101,252	93,562	4,649	0	3,041	23,507	22,870	637
Missouri	117,735	95,299	12,510	2,275	7,651	49,937	49,298	639
Florida	206,477	106,089	79,732	152	20,504	56,629	48,067	8,562
Ohio	146,395	107,277	7,044	1,272	30,802	31,669	30,621	1,048
Illinois	200,263	134,075	56,676	1,126	8,386	98,568	86,235	12,333
California	264,775	136,304	76,356	2,375	49,740	147,979	129,522	18,457
Massachusetts	173,897	166,873	2,800	1,737	2,487	97,339	97,203	136
Pennsylvania	251,369	195,359	17,783	7,492	30,735	83,943	83,372	571
New York	390,435	341,205	24,241	6,575	18,414	168,531	166,449	2,082

There are 21 locations in this table, so you will be looking for the 11th state. To calculate which line you're looking for in a table with an odd number of lines, you can always use the following formula: $\text{Median} = \dfrac{\text{Total} - 1}{2} + 1$.

In this example, $\dfrac{21 - 1}{2} + 1 = 10 + 1 = 11$. According to the sorted chart, the 11th state is Indiana. Once you know to focus on Indiana, sort the table by not-for-profit two-year undergraduate institutions:

Sort By | Undergraduate 2-year Not-for-profit ▾ |

		Undergraduate				Postbaccalaureate		
		4-year		**2-year**				
	Total	Not-for-profit	For-profit	Not-for-profit	For-profit	Total	Not-for-profit	For-profit
Arizona	291,869	3,539	275,530	0	12,800	81,066	4,507	76,559
Michigan	101,252	93,562	4,649	0	3,041	23,507	22,870	637
Virginia	90,439	59,959	24,416	0	6,064	27,236	24,789	2,447
District of Columbia	71,465	37,967	33,498	0	0	49,061	36,575	12,486
Alabama	58,558	23,229	34,000	0	1,329	7,343	4,128	3,215
Minnesota	78,855	50,793	25,723	106	2,233	75,567	21,232	54,335
Iowa	113,385	45,397	67,601	151	236	16,487	10,919	5,568
Florida	206,477	106,089	79,732	152	20,504	56,629	48,067	8,562
Colorado	69,460	18,375	40,733	165	10,187	20,507	13,586	6,921
Tennessee	75,283	54,023	8,373	278	12,609	18,187	17,097	1,090
Indiana	88,896	68,677	13,020	495	6,704	16,110	15,652	458
North Carolina	75,228	68,524	4,635	572	1,497	18,773	18,039	734
Texas	127,359	92,495	12,935	867	21,062	36,657	33,996	2,661
Georgia	76,356	47,701	23,670	1,057	3,928	23,757	17,940	5,817
Illinois	200,263	134,075	56,676	1,126	8,386	98,568	86,235	12,333
Ohio	146,395	107,277	7,044	1,272	30,802	31,669	30,621	1,048
Massachusetts	173,897	166,873	2,800	1,737	2,487	97,339	97,203	136
Missouri	117,735	95,299	12,510	2,275	7,651	49,937	49,298	639
California	264,775	136,304	76,356	2,375	49,740	147,979	129,522	18,457
New York	390,435	341,205	24,241	6,575	18,414	168,531	166,449	2,082
Pennsylvania	251,369	195,359	17,783	7,492	30,735	83,943	83,372	571

Again, Indiana is the median (the 11th state), so the answer to this question is True.

Question 11c: For this question, you'll be looking for information about Minnesota. Specifically, you'll need to find the number of students in that state who attend for-profit schools and then determine whether that number is more than half of Minnesota's total enrollment.

Approach strategically here—rather than add all the numbers, do some comparisons. In the four-year undergraduate programs, there are approximately 25,000 more students in not-for-profit schools. Look next at the two-year undergraduate enrollments. These numbers are probably too low to significantly affect the total, so turn your attention to the postbaccalaureate column: here, there are approximately 33,000 more students enrolled in for-profit schools. Because 33,000 is significantly higher than 25,000, you know that there are more students enrolled in the for-profit schools, making the answer to this question True.

Of course, if you have time to check your work, you can use the on-screen calculator:

For-profit: $25,723 + 2,233 + 54,335 = 82,291$

Not-for-profit: $50,793 + 106 + 21,232 = 72,131$

More than half the enrollments in Minnesota are in for-profit institutions, confirming our answer of True.

Remember, for success in Table Analysis, you need to understand what information the table contains and how it is organized before attacking the questions. Pay close attention to the column headings and use the Sort function when a vertical scan of a column is not practical, especially when finding the median. Apply this strategic approach to the next set of Table Analysis questions.

U.S. Coastal Counties Most Frequently Hit by Hurricanes: 1960–2008

Sort By | Select... ▾ |

Coastline region	State	County	Number of hurricanes	Percent change in population, 1960–2008
Gulf of Mexico	Florida	Monroe County	15	50.8
Gulf of Mexico	Louisiana	Lafourche Parish	14	67.2
Atlantic	North Carolina	Carteret County	14	104.3
Atlantic	North Carolina	Dare County	13	465.9
Atlantic	North Carolina	Hyde County	13	10.1
Gulf of Mexico	Louisiana	Jefferson Parish	12	108.9
Atlantic	Florida	Palm Beach County	12	454.7
Atlantic	Florida	Miami-Dade County	11	156.5
Gulf of Mexico	Louisiana	St. Bernard Parish	11	17.2
Gulf of Mexico	Louisiana	Cameron Parish	11	4.8
Gulf of Mexico	Louisiana	Terrebonne Parish	11	78.7

The table presents data on the 11 U.S. coastal counties that were hit by the most hurricanes between 1960 and 2008. It also lists the percent change in population for each county during the same time period. Positive percentages represent population growth.

12. Consider the following statements. For each statement, evaluate whether that statement is *True* or *False*, according to the information in the table.

True	False	
O	O	The median number of hurricanes in the Florida counties was higher than the median number of hurricanes in each of the other states' counties.
O	O	The counties listed in the table that experienced the three greatest percent changes in population during the period are all part of the coastline region whose listed counties had the greater range in number of hurricanes during the same period.
O	O	The Gulf of Mexico coastline region experienced fewer hurricanes per county listed in the table, on average, than did the Atlantic coastline region.

STEP 1: ANALYZE THE INFORMATION

This table has fewer columns than the previous one did, but don't assume that means you're in for an easy time—the questions might compensate for the graph's simplicity. They may require more thought, more math, or both. Begin as always by reading the paragraph of text that accompanies the table. It tells you that the table provides data about hurricane occurrences in U.S. coastal counties during a specific time period.

Now look at the table itself. Note that the first three columns provide geographical data and move from more general to more specific as you go from left to right. There are only two coastline regions, but they include three states, which in turn contain a total of 11 counties. The last two columns contain numerical data. Glance at the numbers in the columns to get a feel for the ranges and to see whether there are any obvious outliers. The numbers in the Hurricanes column don't vary much, but the numbers in the Percent population change column, while all positive (signifying population growth), vary widely.

STEP 2: APPROACH STRATEGICALLY

Question 12a: This statement deals with the median number of hurricanes in each state's counties. Since it compares Florida to the other states, you want to sort by State, not by County. That will allow you to see each state's counties grouped together vertically, which will make it easier to find the median for each state:

Sort By [State ▼]

Coastline region	State	County	Number of hurricanes	Percent change in population, 1960–2008
Gulf of Mexico	Florida	Monroe County	15	50.8
Atlantic	Florida	Palm Beach County	12	454.7
Atlantic	Florida	Miami-Dade County	11	156.5
Gulf of Mexico	Louisiana	Lafourche Parish	14	67.2
Gulf of Mexico	Louisiana	Jefferson Parish	12	108.9
Gulf of Mexico	Louisiana	St. Bernard Parish	11	17.2
Gulf of Mexico	Louisiana	Cameron Parish	11	4.8
Gulf of Mexico	Louisiana	Terrebonne Parish	11	78.7
Atlantic	North Carolina	Carteret County	14	104.3
Atlantic	North Carolina	Dare County	13	465.9
Atlantic	North Carolina	Hyde County	13	10.1

There are three counties in Florida: Monroe, Palm Beach, and Miami-Dade. There were 15, 12, and 11 hurricanes in those counties, respectively. Thus, the median number of hurricanes for Florida's counties was 12. Louisiana has five counties, so the median number of hurricanes will be the third one when they are listed in numerical order. Louisiana's five counties (Lafourche Parish, Jefferson Parish, St. Bernard Parish, Cameron Parish, and Terrebonne Parish) had 14, 12, 11, 11, and 11 hurricanes, respectively. Thus the median for Louisiana was 11. North Carolina's three counties (Carteret, Dare, and Hyde) had 14, 13, and 13 hurricanes, respectively, for a median of 13. Since Florida's median of 12 is lower than North Carolina's median of 13, Florida's median was not higher than the median in each of the other states' counties, and the answer is False.

Question 12b: Take a moment to think about where to begin here, because this statement relates population change, counties, *and* coastline regions. You need to figure out which counties experienced the greatest percent change in population and which coastline region had the greater range in number of hurricanes. You can work on either one first. If you start with the population growth, you can scan down the Percent change in population column and look for the three largest numbers. If you find it hard to keep track of them this way, sort the table on that column:

Sort By [Percent change in population...] [▼]

Coastline region	State	County	Number of hurricanes	Percent change in population, 1960–2008
Gulf of Mexico	Louisiana	Cameron Parish	11	4.8
Atlantic	North Carolina	Hyde County	13	10.1
Gulf of Mexico	Louisiana	St. Bernard Parish	11	17.2
Gulf of Mexico	Florida	Monroe County	15	50.8
Gulf of Mexico	Louisiana	Lafourche Parish	14	67.2
Gulf of Mexico	Louisiana	Terrebonne Parish	11	78.7
Atlantic	North Carolina	Carteret County	14	104.3
Gulf of Mexico	Louisiana	Jefferson Parish	12	108.9
Atlantic	Florida	Miami-Dade County	11	156.5
Atlantic	Florida	Palm Beach County	12	454.7
Atlantic	North Carolina	Dare County	13	465.9

The last three rows represent the counties with the greatest percent change in population: Miami-Dade County, at 156.5%, Palm Beach County, at 454.7%, and Dare County, at 465.9%. Now glance at the Coastline region column to see that all three of these counties are in the Atlantic coastline region. The question that remains is whether the counties in the Atlantic coastline region had a greater range in number of hurricanes than did the counties in the Gulf of Mexico region. Sort the table, this time on the Coastline region column:

Sort By [Coastline region... | ▼]

Coastline region	State	County	Number of hurricanes	Percent change in population, 1960–2008
Atlantic	North Carolina	Dare County	13	465.9
Atlantic	Florida	Palm Beach County	12	454.7
Atlantic	Florida	Miami-Dade County	11	156.5
Atlantic	North Carolina	Carteret County	14	104.3
Atlantic	North Carolina	Hyde County	13	10.1
Gulf of Mexico	Louisiana	Jefferson Parish	12	108.9
Gulf of Mexico	Louisiana	Terrebonne Parish	11	78.7
Gulf of Mexico	Louisiana	Lafourche Parish	14	67.2
Gulf of Mexico	Florida	Monroe County	15	50.8
Gulf of Mexico	Louisiana	St. Bernard Parish	11	17.2
Gulf of Mexico	Louisiana	Cameron Parish	11	4.8

In the Atlantic coastline region, Carteret County in North Carolina experienced the greatest number of hurricanes, at 14. Miami-Dade County in Florida experienced the smallest number of hurricanes, at 11. Thus, the range for counties in the Atlantic region was $14 - 11 = 3$. In the Gulf of Mexico region, Monroe County in Florida experienced the greatest number of hurricanes, at 15. Three counties in the region experienced 11 hurricanes, the smallest number for the region. The range for counties in the Gulf of Mexico region was therefore $15 - 11 = 4$. Since the counties with the three greatest percent changes in population were part of the Atlantic coastline region, which had a smaller range than did the Gulf of Mexico coastline region, the answer is False.

Question 12c: Since this statement compares the Gulf of Mexico coastline region to the Atlantic coastline region, sort the table again by coastline region (see the sorted table above in the explanation for Question 12b). The statement asks about the number of hurricanes per county, on average, so you'll have to calculate the average for each coastline region.

Add the number of hurricanes for the Atlantic coastline region to get $13 + 12 + 11 + 14 + 13 = 63$. There are five counties in the Atlantic coastline region, so the average number of hurricanes per county was $\frac{63}{5}$. You can simplify this to $12\frac{3}{5}$ or use the calculator to get $63 \div 5 = 12.6$. For the Gulf of Mexico coastline region, there were a total of $12 + 11 + 14 + 15 + 11 + 11 = 74$ hurricanes. There are six counties in that coastline region, so the average number of hurricanes per county was $\frac{74}{6}$. Simplify this to $12\frac{1}{3}$ or use the calculator to get $74 \div 6 = 12.3333$. Since $12.3333 < 12.6$ (or $12\frac{1}{3} < 12\frac{3}{5}$), the Gulf of Mexico coastline region did indeed experience fewer hurricanes per county, on average, than did the Atlantic coastline region, so the answer is True.

Branch Manager Performance Reviews

Sort By [Select...   ▼]

Manager	Employee satisfaction rating (%)	Yearly sales (thousands of dollars)	Percent change in sales over previous year	Underground parking	Free shipping	Size of sales force
L. Jenkins	32.3	58.4	+5.3	no	no	5
P. Parsons	44.4	92.0	−7.8	yes	yes	11
A. Yangzou	65.7	105.2	−1.2	no	yes	10
D. Xin	55.7	85.1	+10.8	yes	yes	15
M. Stover	18.0	116.9	+15.5	no	yes	12
Z. Szymes	50.1	64.7	+4.8	no	no	8
T. Emerald	64.2	77.4	+0.3	yes	no	11
O. McDonough	75.5	79.6	+31.2	no	yes	8
K. Eriksson	46.9	58.9	−20.0	no	no	13
B. Stripley	48.7	101.7	−9.4	yes	yes	16

A small furniture store chain conducted performance reviews of its 10 branch managers. The managers' performance in several metrics over the last year has been compiled in the table. The table also lists some relevant features of each manager's branch.

13. For each of the following statements, select *True* if the statement can be verified to be true based on the given information. Otherwise, select *False*.

True	False	
○	○	A majority of the managers who oversaw an increase in sales over the previous year have an employee satisfaction rating higher than the median.
○	○	There is a positive correlation between the size of a branch's sales force and that branch's change in year-over-year sales.
○	○	The branch that had the highest sales in the previous year has underground parking.

STEP 1: ANALYZE THE INFORMATION

For each of 10 branch managers, three measures of job performance are given, as well as three features of their stores.

STEP 2: APPROACH STRATEGICALLY

Question 13a: Sort the data by employee satisfaction rating to quickly find the median; it's about 49%. Six managers saw positive sales growth. Of these, four have an employee rating above 49%—Emerald, Xin, Szymes, and McDonough—and two have an employee rating below 49%—Jenkins and Stover. Four out of six is a majority. The correct answer is True.

Question 13b: The second statement asserts that as the size of a branch's sales force increases, so too does its change in year-over-year sales. This is untrue: the three smallest branches saw positive growth, while the two biggest branches saw negative growth. There is in fact no correlation between sales force and change in sales, and the second statement is False.

Question 13c: For the third statement, locate the branch that had the highest sales in the previous year. While Stover's branch had the highest sales this year, that's up 15.5% over the previous year, so Stover's sales in the previous year were under $100,000. The branch with the highest sales the previous year was Stripley's. Its $101,700 in sales this year with a 9.4% decrease over the previous year puts the previous year's sales at around $112,000. Stripley's branch does have underground parking, so this statement is True.

Two-Part Analysis

Simply put, Two-Part Analysis questions have solutions in two parts. Two-Part Analysis questions consist of a few lines of text and instructions to select choices in a table based on the given information. These questions may test quantitative or verbal skills.

Solving an algebraic Two-Part Analysis usually necessitates setting up an algebraic equation with two variables. You'll want to begin by first reading the text and identifying the two quantities, which may be provided or may need to be assigned variables. Then, you'll create one or more equations that relate the two values or variables. Once you've set up your equations, you can simplify them and look for a match (if the answer choices are algebraic equations or expressions) or start plugging in answer choices from the table until you find two corresponding values that work together.

Verbal Two-Part Analysis questions draw on many of the same logical reasoning skills, such as drawing supported inferences and finding assumptions, that you use on the Verbal section of the GMAT. For example, after reading about a type of dwelling used by a certain species of animal, you might identify from among the choices a characteristic that must be true of all dwellings of that type and a characteristic that can never be true. Alternatively, you might be asked to strengthen and weaken an author's argument.

All this will make much more sense with concrete examples, so let's take a look at some questions to see how Two-Part Analysis questions work.

14. At University X, there are 146 students who are taking economics and 97 students who are taking history.

In the table below, pick two numbers that are consistent with the information that is given. In the first column, select the row that shows the number of students at University X who are taking at least one of economics and history, and in the second column, select the row that shows the number of students at University X who are taking both economics and history.

Taking at least one of economics and history	Taking both economics and history	Possible answers
○	○	78
○	○	83
○	○	104
○	○	154
○	○	160
○	○	164

STEP 1: ANALYZE THE INFORMATION

The text in Two-Part Analysis questions is likely to be brief, so read it thoroughly before doing anything else. Here, you are given information about students at University X: the number of students who are taking economics, 146, and the number of students who are taking history, 97. The question asks you to find two numbers: first, the number of students taking at least one of these two subjects and, second, the number of students taking both.

STEP 2: APPROACH STRATEGICALLY

Start by solving for the number of students taking at least one subject. The most efficient way to determine this number is to think critically. If you add together the numbers of students taking each subject, you get: $146 + 97 = 243$. However, you know from the question stem and the column header that some students are taking both; if you rely on simple addition, you end up counting those students twice. Instead, set up an equation that relates the number of students in *at least* one subject, a, to the number of students in *both*, b.

Initial formula:	# in at least one = # in Group 1 + # in Group 2 − # in both
Fill in what you know:	$a = 146 + 97 - b$
Simplify:	$a = 243 - b$

Before you start plugging in the answer choices to find two values that satisfy this equation, think critically: Which number will be bigger? In this case, it has to be a. With that in mind, move to the answer choices.

Because your equation is $a = 243 - b$, start by plugging b into the equation to determine if there is a corresponding value for a in the chart. b must be the smaller of the two numbers, so start testing at the top of the column with $b = 78$. Your equation is now $a = 243 - 78 = 165$. Do you see 165 in the possible answer choices? Nope. The closest they get is 164, so this is not the correct answer. Once you know that 78 is not a possible answer for b, move on to 83. Plugging it into the formula, you have $a = 243 - 83 = 160$. Do you see 160 among the possible answer choices? Yes. This question format always has a single solution, so you don't need to test any further answer choices. You have your answer: $a = 160$ and $b = 83$.

Before submitting your answers, make sure that you enter each of your choices in the correct column. It would be unfortunate to do all of the work correctly, get the correct answers, and then not receive credit simply because you selected the numbers in the opposite columns. Look back at your scratchwork and remember that *a* represents the number of students in at least one subject and *b* represents the number of students in both subjects. You can now be sure that 160 belongs in the first column and 83 belongs in the second column.

Take what you've learned about solving for unknowns by using the given information to set up an equation and apply it to the next Two-Part Analysis question.

15. When Car P travels at a constant speed of *x* miles per hour for 84 minutes, and Car Q travels at an average speed of *y* miles per hour for 168 minutes, Car P travels 21 miles more than Car Q.

    In the table below, select a value for *x* and a value for *y* that together are consistent with the given information. In the first column, select the row that corresponds to the value of *x*, and in the second column, select the row that corresponds to the value of *y*.

Value of *x*	Value of *y*	Possible answers
○	○	8
○	○	14
○	○	17
○	○	29
○	○	42
○	○	49

STEP 1: ANALYZE THE INFORMATION

When reading the information, remember that your goal is to use it to create an equation that relates the two unknowns, x and y. The text gives information about two cars and states one definitive relationship between them: Car P travels 21 more miles than Car Q. That is enough to indicate that your equation will focus on distance traveled. Go back to the beginning of the question stem to determine what you can about the distance the two cars travel.

STEP 2: APPROACH STRATEGICALLY

Since the time traveled is given in terms of minutes, and speed in terms of miles per hour, you need to convert to get all of the times expressed in the same units.

$$\text{Car P time traveled} = 84 \text{ minutes} \times \frac{1 \text{ hour}}{60 \text{ minutes}} = 1.4 \text{ hours}$$

$$\text{Car Q time traveled} = 168 \text{ minutes} \times \frac{1 \text{ hour}}{60 \text{ minutes}} = 2.8 \text{ hours}$$

Since Distance = Speed × Time, the distance each car traveled, in terms of x and y, is as follows:

$$\text{Car P distance traveled} = \frac{x \text{ miles}}{\text{hour}} \times 1.4 \text{ hours} = 1.4x \text{ miles}$$

$$\text{Car Q distance traveled} = \frac{y \text{ miles}}{\text{hour}} \times 2.8 \text{ hours} = 2.8y \text{ miles}$$

Once you have determined the distance traveled by each car, use the information that Car P travels 21 miles farther to set up the following equation: $1.4x = 2.8y + 21$. Before moving to the answer choices, be sure to get one variable entirely by itself. In this case, you can divide both sides by 1.4 to get $x = 2y + 15$. You can now plug possible values for y into this equation to see what value for x would result.

To simplify the process of plugging in answer choices, first determine which value is going to be bigger. Since all of the answer choices are positive (as they would have to be, since they represent the speed a car travels), you know that x must be greater than y. This makes sense when you think about the logic of the problem, which specifies that Car P travels a greater distance than Car Q in a shorter amount of time.

Use the possible answer choices to start testing for y. As before, since you are starting with the smaller value, y, you will start plugging in numbers from the top of the list and work down. Start with $y = 8$. Substituting into the equation, you get $x = 2(8) + 15 = 31$. Since 31 is not an option in the table, you know that 8 is not the value of y. Next, try $y = 14$. In this case, the calculation would be $x = 2(14) + 15 = 43$. Again, 43 is not one of the available choices, so keep going. If $y = 17$, then $x = 2(17) + 15 = 49$. Since 49 is among the answer choices, it must be the value for x. Again, be very careful when filling in the answer choices. Your answers are $x = 49$ and $y = 17$.

Now that you are familiar with the basic format and structure of Two-Part Analysis questions, try your hand at the following question, which focuses on your reasoning skills rather than on math.

16. A father is planning to knit a striped hat and a checkered blanket for his newborn son. Each of these items will consist of four distinct colors of yarn. Since the hat and blanket are part of a matching set, they must share at least two colors. Each color of yarn is available in three types: one made with cotton fiber, one made with wool fiber, and one made with acrylic fiber. The cotton and wool yarns are made from natural fibers, while the acrylic yarn is from a synthetic fiber. Due to cost concerns, each item can contain no more than two colors of yarn in natural fibers; the other colors will be synthetic. All of the yarn of the same color in each item will be made of the same kind of fiber. He has already chosen the following styles of yarn for each item.

Hat:

    Green wool

    Yellow wool

    Blue acrylic

Blanket:

    Red acrylic

    Gray cotton

    Blue acrylic

Select a style of yarn that could be used in either the hat or the blanket, but not both. Then select a style of yarn that can be used in neither the hat nor the blanket. Make only two selections, one in each column.

Either the hat or blanket, but not both	Neither hat nor blanket	Possible yarn styles
O	O	Brown acrylic
O	O	Orange acrylic
O	O	Gray acrylic
O	O	White acrylic
O	O	Red cotton
O	O	Black acrylic

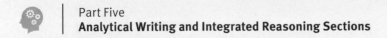
STEP 1: ANALYZE THE INFORMATION

You've got two items to be knitted; each will be made of four kinds of yarn, and the knitter has already decided on three of them for each project. Paraphrase the rules that govern selecting the fourth type of yarn: each item must have four different colors, each can have only two colors at most in natural fiber, and the two items must share two colors.

STEP 2: APPROACH STRATEGICALLY

Use the GMAT Core Competency of Attention to the Right Detail as you consider the rules governing each item. The hat already has two types of yarn made of natural fiber, so the fourth color there must be acrylic. The blanket only has one type of yarn with natural fibers, so its fourth color could be either natural (cotton or wool) or acrylic. The items already share one color, so at least one color picked to finish the items must be the same as another color in the other item in order for there to be two shared colors. On Test Day, you'd quickly paraphrase this info on your notepad.

Keep the rules in mind as you evaluate the choices. For the first column, you want to pick a style of yarn that would work for either item individually, but not work for both, and for the second column you want to pick one that can't be used in either. You already noted that an acrylic yarn would work in either item. Gray acrylic would be permissible for the hat, but not for the blanket, since that item already has gray wool yarn. Thus, gray acrylic is the answer for the first column. If the fourth color in each item were brown, orange, white, or black, then each would have four distinct colors and two shared colors. So brown, orange, white, or black acrylic yarn could be used in both items, which means they're incorrect for both columns. Red cotton can't be used for the hat, since it already has two wool yarns, and it can't be used for the blanket since it already has red acrylic yarn; this is the right answer for the second column.

Pay close attention to the column headings when filling in the answer choices. The correct answer for the first column is gray acrylic, and the correct answer for the second column is red cotton.

17. State A currently allows casino gambling while State B does not. The legislature of State B is considering a proposal under which a limited number of casino licenses would be granted within the state in order to compete with State A for gambling revenue. Given the fact that a great many citizens of State B currently visit casinos in State A, the legislature of State B would be foolish not to enact this proposal.

In the table below, select one statement that would *strengthen* the proposal and another that would *weaken* it. Make exactly two selections, one in each column.

Would strengthen proposal	Would weaken proposal	Possible statements
O	O	Some other states that have granted casino licenses have subsequently experienced an overall increase in revenue.
O	O	The residents of State B who currently visit casinos in State A travel to State A primarily to visit a nature preserve that serves as a major tourist attraction.
O	O	Currently, more State A residents than State B residents undertake international travel.
O	O	Before State A offered casinos, those residents of State B who wanted to visit casinos had to travel nearly twice as far in order to do so.
O	O	Most residents of State B who traveled to State A within the past year made the trip primarily to visit casinos.
O	O	Over the past five years, the gambling revenue that State A has taken in has more than offset the associated infrastructure costs associated with gambling tourism.

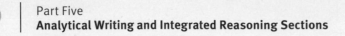

STEP 1: ANALYZE THE INFORMATION

In order to strengthen or weaken an argument, start by finding the conclusion, evidence, and assumption—exactly as you would do when attacking Strengthen or Weaken questions in Critical Reasoning. The author's conclusion is that State B should adopt the proposal to grant casino licenses. The evidence is that residents of State B currently visit casinos in State A. The author assumes that those same State B residents would visit casinos in State B if they had the opportunity to do so rather than visit the casinos in State A.

STEP 2: APPROACH STRATEGICALLY

To strengthen the argument, look for a statement that supports the assumption that State B residents would stay home if there were casinos in State B rather than travel to State A. The fifth statement does so very well: "Most residents of State B who traveled to State A within the past year made the trip primarily to visit casinos." If State B residents are traveling to State A specifically to visit casinos, they might well save themselves the trip if there were casinos in State B.

To weaken the argument, look for a statement that undercuts the assumption—that is, find a statement that makes it less likely that residents of State B would visit casinos within their own state if given the opportunity to do so. That's the second statement: "The residents of State B who currently visit casinos in State A travel to State A primarily to visit a nature preserve that serves as a major tourist attraction." If State B residents are traveling to State A in order to visit a nature preserve, then they are not traveling specifically in order to visit casinos, and perhaps their casino visits are not all that important to them. They will likely continue to travel to State A (and perhaps continue to visit the casinos there as part of their visit), but there is no reason to believe that they might make separate trips to visit casinos within State B.

The correct answers are "Most residents of State B who traveled to State A within the past year made the trip primarily to visit casinos" to strengthen the proposal and "The residents of State B who currently visit casinos in State A travel to State A primarily to visit a nature preserve that serves as a major tourist attraction" to weaken the proposal.

Note that the first choice is incorrect because even if some states did see increased revenue from casino gambling, there may be more states that did not, or that even saw revenue decreases. The third and fourth choices are wrong because international travel and what happened before State A offered casinos both have no bearing on the argument. Finally, the last choice is wrong because the argument is about revenue only; infrastructure costs have no impact.

Conclusion

As you've seen from the examples in this chapter, Integrated Reasoning questions measure many of the same skills that you use for the Quantitative and Verbal sections of the test, such as paraphrasing information, finding key words, determining whether an inference is supported, and using estimation instead of calculation. Regular review of the questions in this chapter, as well as those found in the quizzes and practice tests in your online resources, will help you get the best score you possibly can on Integrated Reasoning.

Test Day

Take Control of Test Day

In the earlier parts of this book, we looked at the content covered on the various sections of the GMAT. We also discussed the test expertise you'll need to move through those sections. Now we turn to the often overlooked topic of test mentality, that is, how to get into peak mental condition for the GMAT.

Mental Conditioning

Your frame of mind has a lot to do with the level of success you achieve. Here's what's involved in developing your best mindset for the GMAT.

Test Awareness

To do your best on the GMAT, you must always keep in mind that the test is unlike other tests that you've taken in terms of both the content and the scoring system. If you took a test in high school or college and got a quarter of the questions wrong, you'd probably receive a pretty lousy grade. But due to the adaptive nature of the GMAT, missing only a quarter of the questions would give you a very high score. The test is designed to push test takers to their limits, so people rarely get every question right. In fact, you can get a handful of questions wrong and still score in the 99th percentile.

In other words, don't let what you consider to be a subpar performance on a handful of questions ruin your performance on the rest. A couple of missed questions won't, by themselves, spoil your score. But if you allow the frustration of those questions to unnerve you, you could end up compromising your performance on other questions or on the section as a whole. Missing a few points won't ruin your score, but losing your head will.

The test is designed to find your limits, so it should feel challenging. If you feel you've done poorly on a section, don't worry—you may have done just fine. Keep in mind that the questions that you are likely to struggle on most will be the hardest ones—the ones that hurt your score *least* if you miss them. To reach your highest potential score, you must remain calm and focused. Simply do your best on each question, and once a question or section is over, forget about it and move on.

Moreover, don't try to guess which questions are unscored (experimental questions). This kind of speculation has gotten countless test takers into trouble. They have a hunch that a certain question is one that doesn't count and then don't take it seriously. You cannot know which questions are experimental, so treat each one as if it counts. That way, you're covered no matter what. Likewise, don't worry if a question you get seems "too easy." This doesn't necessarily mean that you're doing poorly; it might be experimental. Or it might happen to align well with your individual strengths. Or perhaps you are just well prepared, have great strategies, and are beating the test! Do your best, get it right, and move on with confidence.

Stamina

The GMAT is a grueling experience, and some test takers simply run out of gas when they reach the final questions. To avoid this, you must prepare by taking full-length practice tests (not skipping over any sections) so that on Test Day, the 3.5 hours of testing will seem like a breeze—or at least not a hurricane.

Your online resources include full-length CATs for just this purpose. If you finish the tests included with this book, a further option is to download the test maker's GMAT® Official Starter Kit software, which contains two full-length exams and is available free from **mba.com**. One drawback to the software is that it does not include explanations, so you will want to rely on your Kaplan materials, which include thorough explanations, for the bulk of your study. However, the test maker's CATs should give you a good indication of your score range.

Confidence

Confidence in your ability leads to quick, sure answers and a sense of poise that translates into more points. Confidence builds on itself, but unfortunately, so does self-doubt. If you lack confidence, you end up reading sentences and answer choices two, three, or four times until you confuse yourself and get off track. Or you begin to solve a math problem one way, worry that your approach won't work and jump to a different approach, and then go back to your first approach, wasting time without making progress. This uncertainty ruins your timing, perpetuating a downward spiral.

If you cultivate a positive GMAT mindset, however, you'll gear your practice toward taking control of the test. And when you have achieved that goal—armed with the techniques and strategies explained in this book— you'll be ready to face the GMAT with supreme confidence.

Positive Attitude

Those who approach the GMAT as an obstacle and who rail against the necessity of taking it usually don't fare as well as those who see the GMAT as an opportunity. Those who look forward to doing battle with the GMAT—or, at least, who enjoy the opportunity to distinguish themselves from the rest of the applicant pack— tend to score better than do those who resent or dread it.

Take our word for it: developing a positive attitude is a proven test-taking technique. Here are a few steps you can take to make sure you develop the right GMAT attitude:

- Look at the GMAT as a challenge but try not to obsess over it; you certainly don't want to psych yourself out of the game.
- Remember that, yes, the GMAT is obviously important, but contrary to popular belief, this one test will not single-handedly determine the outcome of your life—or even of your business school admissions.

- Try to have fun with the test. Learning how to match your wits against those of the test maker can be a very satisfying experience, and the critical thinking skills you'll acquire will benefit you in business school, as well as in your future career.

- Remember that you're more prepared than most people. You've trained with Kaplan. You have the tools you need, plus the ability to use those tools.

Stress Management

The countdown has begun. Your date with the test is looming on the horizon. Anxiety is on the rise. You have butterflies in your stomach, and your thinking is getting cloudy. Maybe you think you won't be ready. Maybe you already know your stuff, but you're going into panic mode anyway. Don't worry! It's possible to tame that anxiety and stress—before *and* during the test.

Remember, some stress is normal and good. Anxiety is a motivation to study. The adrenaline that gets pumped into your bloodstream when you're stressed helps you stay alert and think more clearly. But if you feel that the tension is so great that it's preventing you from using your study time effectively, here are some things you can do to get it under control.

Take Control

Lack of control is a prime cause of stress. Research shows that if you don't have a sense of control over what's happening in your life, you can easily end up feeling helpless and hopeless. Try to identify the sources of the stress you feel. Which ones can you do something about? Can you find ways to reduce the stress you're feeling from any of these sources?

Make a Study Schedule

Often, the mere realization that you're procrastinating on your GMAT study can cause stress. To help you gain control over your preparation process, make study appointments with yourself on your calendar—and then keep these appointments with yourself! Without setting aside time to study for the GMAT, it's easy to keep putting it off due to looming work deadlines, business school applications, or other commitments on your calendar. The hardest part of studying is getting started, so get started soon and start small. Even committing to working on five problems a day will produce a pleasant feeling of accomplishment and momentum, leading you to be able to make longer and longer commitments to your Test Day success.

Focus on Your Strengths

Make a list of areas of strength you have that will help you do well on the test. We all have strengths, and recognizing your own is like having reserves of solid gold in the bank. You'll be able to draw on your reserves as you need them, helping you solve difficult questions, maintain confidence, and keep test stress and anxiety at a distance. And every time you recognize a new area of strength, solve a challenging problem, or score well on a practice test, congratulate yourself—you'll only increase your reserves.

Imagine Yourself Succeeding

Close your eyes and imagine yourself in a relaxing situation. Breathe easily and naturally. Now think of a real-life situation in which you did well on an assignment. Focus on this success. Now turn your thoughts to the GMAT and keep your thoughts and feelings in line with that successful experience. Don't make comparisons between them; just imagine yourself taking the upcoming test with the same feelings of confidence and relaxed control.

Set Realistic Goals

Facing your problem areas gives you some distinct advantages. What do you want to accomplish in the study time remaining? Make a list of realistic goals. You can't help feeling more confident when you know you're actively improving your chances of earning a higher GMAT score.

Exercise Regularly

Whether it's jogging, biking, push-ups, or a pickup basketball game, physical exercise will stimulate your mind and body and improve your ability to think and concentrate. A surprising number of test takers fall out of the habit of regular exercise, ironically because they're spending so much time prepping for the exam. A little physical exertion will help you to keep your mind and body in sync and to sleep better at night.

Eat Well

Good nutrition will help you focus and think clearly. Eat plenty of fruits and vegetables; low-fat protein such as fish, skinless poultry, beans, and legumes; and whole grains such as brown rice, whole-wheat bread, and pastas. Don't eat a lot of sugary and high-fat snacks or salty foods. Note that on Test Day, you can't bring food or drink into the testing room. But you can keep a healthy snack in your locker to recharge you between sections.

Sleep Well

Every GMAT problem requires careful critical thinking. Unfortunately, that's the first mental skill to go away when you are sleep deprived. Get a full night's sleep as often as you can during your preparation, especially as Test Day approaches.

Keep Breathing

Conscious attention to breathing is an excellent way to manage stress while you're taking the test. Most of the people who get into trouble during the GMAT take shallow breaths; they breathe using only their upper chests and shoulder muscles and may even hold their breath for long periods of time. Conversely, test takers who breathe deeply in a slow, relaxed manner are likely to be in better control during the session.

Stretch

If you find yourself getting spaced out or burned out as you're studying or taking the test, stop for a brief moment and stretch. Even though you'll be pausing for a moment, it's a moment well spent. Stretching will help to refresh you and refocus your thoughts.

Stress Management Quiz

Don't be alarmed: this is not a GMAT quiz. It is important to your score, though. Imagine that there are two people with equal GMAT knowledge, skill, and practice. Why might one still outperform the other? The biggest difference will likely be that one manages stress and anxiety better than the other.

This quiz is a chance to reinforce and expand upon the ideas and advice you've read so far in this chapter. Have fun with it and think about how to apply the correct answers to your own life and study schedule.

1. What is Test Day stress?

   O A feeling of anxiety felt only by those aiming for a top score

   O Any factor, physical or psychological, that impedes my performance on the GMAT

   O A consequence of poor preparation

   O A constant fear of not getting into my first-choice school

   O Something that only poor test takers experience

2. It is most helpful to my Test Day success when my friends and family

   O push me to study more

   O tell me how much more I have to learn

   O compete with me over test scores

   O have positive attitudes about my ability to achieve my best score and help me get my mind off the test whenever I am not studying

   O care little about my performance and prevent me from getting sufficient time to prep

3. In the weeks leading up to the exam, how can I reduce stress?

   O List my weaknesses and create a study schedule to overcome them, one topic at a time

   O Get some exercise

   O Limit self-deprecating humor and keep a positive attitude

   O Get sufficient sleep

   O All of the above

4. In the final days before my exam, I should worry about all of the topics that I still have trouble with or haven't hit, rather than congratulate myself on how far I've come.

   ○ True

   ○ False

5. The night before the exam, what can I do to reduce stress?

   ○ Try to learn topics that I have not mastered yet

   ○ Go to my local bar with my friends, drink a few pitchers of beer, and try to get my mind off the exam

   ○ Briefly review the topics that I mastered but haven't looked at in a while and get a good night's sleep

   ○ Stay up all night, memorizing the grammar and math concepts

   ○ Panic

6. On Test Day, what can I do to reduce stress?

   ○ Make sure I know where the testing center is and allow plenty of time to get there early

   ○ Eat a nutritious breakfast

   ○ Dress in layers to be ready for any temperature in the testing room

   ○ Expect a lot of paperwork before the test begins

   ○ All of the above

7. During the exam, if I don't know how to answer a question and I begin to panic, I should

    O   keep rereading the question until I determine the correct approach, no matter how long it takes

    O   bite my fingernails and moan

    O   keep breathing, take a moment to get my bearings, and determine whether I should take a strategic guess or give the question another minute or two

    O   remind myself that if I miss the question, I will not get into business school, I will fail in life, and I will be forced to live with my parents forever

    O   choose an answer choice that I haven't chosen much so far in that section

8. During the GMAT, I should avoid worrying about questions that I have already answered.

    O   True

    O   False

9. What should I do next to make sure that I am prepared to overcome the natural stress that comes with taking an important test?

    O   Understand that anxiety is a sign of weakness and suppress it ruthlessly

    O   Take control of my preparation by following a study schedule and cultivating a positive attitude

    O   Forget about Test Day stress until Test Day and then figure out how to deal with it

    O   Decide not to take the GMAT

    O   Nothing—this exercise has taught me all I need to know about Test Day stress management

The Week Before Test Day

Is it starting to feel like your whole life is a buildup to the GMAT? You've known about it for years, worried about it for months, and have now spent at least a few weeks in solid preparation for it. As Test Day approaches, you may find your anxiety is on the rise. You shouldn't worry. After the preparation you've received from this book, you're in good shape for the test. To calm any jitters you may have, though, let's go over a few strategies for the days leading up to the test.

In the week or so leading up to Test Day, you should do the following:

- Visit the testing center. Sometimes seeing the actual room where your test will be administered and taking notice of little things—such as the kind of desk you'll be working on, whether the room is likely to be hot or cold, etc.—may help to calm your nerves. And if you've never been to the testing center, visiting beforehand is a good way to ensure that you don't get lost on Test Day. If you can go on the same day of the week and at the same time of day as your actual test, so much the better; you'll be able to scope out traffic patterns and parking. Remember, you must be on time—the computers at the testing centers are booked all day long. Consider using **Kaplan's Official Test Day Experience** to take a Kaplan practice test at a Pearson test center.
- Practice working on test material, preferably a full-length test, at the same time of day that your test is scheduled for as if it were the real Test Day.
- Practice using the test interface and get tips about what to expect at the test center by taking the tutorial at **mba.com/tutorial**.
- Time yourself while practicing so you don't feel as though you are rushing on Test Day.
- Evaluate where you stand. Use the time remaining before the test to shore up your weak points, rereading the appropriate sections of this book. But make sure not to neglect your strong areas; after all, those are where you'll rack up most of your points.

The Day Before Test Day

This advice might seem counterintuitive, but try to avoid intensive studying the day before the test. There's little you can do to improve your score at this late date, and you may just wind up exhausting yourself and burning out. Our advice is to review a few key concepts, get together everything you'll need for Test Day (acceptable photo identification, the names of schools to which you'd like to send your GMAT scores, directions to the testing center, a healthy snack for the break), and then take the night off entirely. Go to see a movie or watch some TV. Try not to think too much about the test; just relax and store up some energy for the big day.

On Test Day

Test Day should contain no surprises. Test takers who feel in control of the events leading up to the test take that confidence with them into the testing center.

Leave early for the testing center, giving yourself plenty of time. Read something to warm up your brain; you don't want the GMAT to be the first written material your brain tries to assimilate that day. Dress in layers for maximum comfort. That way, you'll be able to adjust to the testing room's temperature. In traveling to the testing center, leave yourself enough time for traffic or mass transit delays.

Be ready for a long day. Total testing time, remember, is a little more than 3.0 hours. When you add the administrative paperwork before and after, and the two 8-minute breaks, you're looking at an experience of 3.5 hours or more.

You will feel most prepared and confident if you have an understanding of how the logistics of Test Day will play out. Taking the full-length practice CATs in your online resources and those from **mba.com** will help you get the feel for the GMAT itself, but certain events are unique to the experience in the testing center. Here's what to expect:

At the testing center, you will . . .

- Check in.
- Place your belongings in a locker.
- Receive an erasable notepad and pen for your scratchwork.
- Go to the assigned computer. (Note that you will be videotaped as you take the test. Don't be disturbed by any video cameras facing you; this is just a tool that enables the test administrators to maintain a fair testing environment.)
- Select your score recipients. The computer will ask you where to send your results. You may send your scores to up to five schools free of charge. You should take advantage of this free service, as waiting until later has no advantage. If you specify your score recipients after the test or choose more than five schools, you will have to pay US $35 per school (as this book goes to press) to send results.
- Complete the four sections of the test, taking advantage of the two 8-minute breaks offered to visit the restroom, eat your snack, and reboot your brain.
- See your unofficial Quantitative, Verbal, and Integrated Reasoning scores.
- Choose whether to cancel or keep your scores.
- Check out.
- Remove your belongings from the locker and leave the testing facility.

Here are some strategic reminders to help guide your work on Test Day:

- Read each question stem carefully and reread it before making your final selection.
- Don't get bogged down in the middle of any section. You may find later questions more to your liking. So don't panic. Eliminate answer choices, guess, and move on.
- Don't fall behind early. Even if you get most of the first 10 questions right, you'll wind up rushing yourself into enough errors that you cancel out your early success. Keep a steady pace throughout the test and finish each section strong, avoiding the penalty for not completing all the questions.
- Don't bother trying to figure out which questions are unscored. It can't help you, and you might very well be wrong. Instead, just resolve to do your best on every question.
- Confidence is key. Accentuate the positives and don't dwell on the negatives. Your attitude and outlook are crucial to your performance on Test Day.
- During the exam, try not to speculate about how you're scoring. Imagine a baseball player who's focusing on the crowd's cheers and the sportswriters and his contract as he steps up to the plate: there's no surer way to strike out. Instead, focus on the question-by-question task of picking an answer choice. The correct answer is there. You don't have to come up with it; it's sitting right there in front of you!

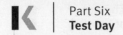
What should you do if you...

- **Start to lose confidence?** If questions seem to be getting hard, don't lose confidence; since the GMAT is adaptive, it is practically guaranteed to feel like a struggle—for everyone! Trust in your preparation and in the skills and strategies you have practiced.

- **Start to lose concentration?** If you lose your concentration, pause, take a deep breath, exhale, and go back to the test. This will help you refocus and settle back in.

- **Take too long for a break?** If you take too long at the break, the test will continue without you. When the 8-minute countdown timer hits zero, the next section of the test—and its clock—will start. So keep timing in mind, even on your breaks, and don't return to the test room late.

- **Find the test environment too distracting?** If the test environment is too distracting, tell the proctor. If the proctor can't—or won't—do anything about it, mention the problem in the exit survey.

After Test Day, you should...

- Congratulate yourself for all the hard work you've put in. Make sure you celebrate afterward—and start thinking about all of the great times you'll be having at the business school of your choice!

- Plan your approach to business school applications, including references and essays.

- Expect to wait for up to 20 days for your Official Score Report (which includes your Analytical Writing score) to be posted online, although it often appears sooner.

Cancellation and Multiple Scores Policy

On Test Day, you will be able to see your unofficial scores—Integrated Reasoning, Quantitative, Verbal, and Total—and then decide whether to accept them. You'll have two minutes to decide whether to cancel your scores. If you do not make a choice, your scores will be canceled. Canceled scores are not included in score reports; if you cancel your scores, no one will know. In addition, if you decide to cancel your scores at the test center, you can reinstate them for a $50 fee. Any scores dating from January 1, 2014, or later are eligible for reinstatement. Moreover, if you don't cancel your scores but then decide you should have, you can cancel them at **mba.com** for up to 72 hours after the test date for a $25 fee.

The bottom line: You have control over your test experience and how you present yourself to graduate programs. You can show up on Test Day with confidence, knowing that if you perform below your goals, you don't necessarily need to submit your scores to schools.

To get the most out of this flexibility, the test maker recommends that you know in advance what score you are willing to accept so that when asked whether you wish to send scores or cancel them, you have already considered your answer. We at Kaplan would echo that advice and add the following: because you only get two minutes to decide whether to cancel, and this comes after over three hours of testing that may leave you feeling exhausted and not in the best frame of mind for making high-stakes decisions, it is imperative that you enter the test knowing your lowest acceptable score. Know that if you need to, you can always take the test again and show improvement; any school you submit your scores to will be pleased to see an improvement.

However, you should not take this policy to mean that you should devote less time to studying for the exam. Remember that you can take the GMAT only once every 16 days, only five times within a calendar year, and only eight times in total. In addition, it costs $250 to take the GMAT, so canceling your scores comes at a substantial price. As always, the best option of all is to prepare sufficiently with comprehensive materials and realistic practice so that you can test just once and achieve the score you need.

TAKEAWAYS

If you cancel your scores...

- They may be reinstated for a $50 fee.
- You will not receive a refund for the test.
- No one else will know. Canceled scores are not included in score reports.

If you do not cancel your scores...

- An official score report, including your AWA score, will be available online and sent to your designated schools within 20 days after you take the test.
- Your score and any other scores from within the past five years will appear on score reports sent to business schools. Most business schools consider only your highest GMAT score, but a few may average your scores. Check with individual schools for their policies on multiple scores.

Appendixes

Appendixes

APPENDIX A

How Much Can a GMAT Score Change?

The following appendix is adapted from The GMAT Unlocked, *a white paper from Kaplan's Research Series. For more information, or if you're interested in any of our practice resources, courses, or tutoring programs, please visit us at **KaplanGMAT.com**.*

Whether you are just starting your studies or whether you have already taken the GMAT and are looking to retest, there's likely one question on your mind more than any other: how much can I improve my score?

This is an important practical question. If you have a baseline score that's far from your target, you need to know whether you can reach your target and how much work it will take. Or, you may have received a low score on the GMAT, and you're wondering how much it might go up if you retook the test in a month with a better mindset and some further study under your belt.

While the exact answer to the question of score improvement is as unique as your particular talents and circumstances, there is some information that's worth knowing. There are actually two questions regarding how much a person's GMAT score can change within a given period of time:

1. How much do scores vary?
2. How much can scores be improved?

Let's discuss some important facts related to these two questions and examine what these facts mean for your preparation.

How Much Scores Vary

Scores can vary widely, but they tend not to. The test maker presents two statistics on the subject that tell slightly different stories.

First is the reliability of the test. The GMAC says that you are 92 percent likely[1] to get the same score on the GMAT if you take the test and then retake it, unless your skills have improved or deteriorated in the interim. So there is little reason to retake the GMAT in the hope of improving your score by chance. If you retake the test, plan to do substantial preparation to improve your score.

The standard error of measurement also gives you some perspective on score improvement. Your score on the GMAT is an estimate of the "true" score of your ability, and the test maker says that "the standard error of measurement is 30–40 points" for the 200–800 score.[2] This means that your score on Test Day may well be 30 to 40 points below your "true" score, or it may be 30 to 40 points above your "true" score. Thus, a score improvement of 40 points or more constitutes a major accomplishment. In other words, 40 points may or may not sound like a lot on the GMAT scoring scale to you—but it is a lot.

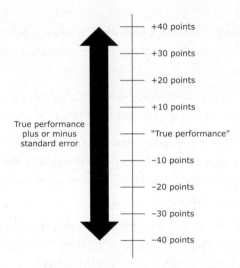

The Magic Number Is 40 When Comparing Scores to True Performance

Having a "Bad Day"

As GMAT teachers, we see applicants have a "bad day," recognize it as such, and walk away with unrealistically high hopes about how much their score will go up after a simple retake on a "good day." The figures above— the 92 percent reliability and the 30- to 40-point standard error—indicate that your score on a good day is likely to be the same as your score on a bad day. Furthermore, if your score on a good day is any higher, it's very, very unlikely to be more than 40 points higher, unless you have raised your skill level through preparation. There is hope for score improvement (we at Kaplan have seen hardworking students make tremendous score gains), but it lies along a path paved with practice.

One exception to this rule is the off day caused by sickness or a traumatic life event. If you have reason to believe that specific circumstances have caused you to underperform significantly, you should probably cancel your score on Test Day. This scenario is why it is so important to go into Test Day knowing both your goal score and the minimum score you will accept without canceling (see the section on "Cancellation and

---

[1] "Validity, Reliability, and Fairness." gmac.com/gmat-other-assessments/about-the-gmat-exam/validity-reliability-fairness.aspx

[2] *GMAT Handbook* (2018, April 16). mba.com/gmathandbook

Multiple Scores Policy" in Chapter 28 for more detail). Even if you don't cancel, you might wish to schedule another testing appointment in the near future to have a good shot at the exam. Other disruptions that may affect your performance, such as a fire alarm going off or computer malfunctions during your test, can also be good reason to cancel your scores or retake the exam. If the disruption is caused by an irregularity in testing conditions, you should report it to the test administrators immediately and follow up through the appropriate channels to make sure that the situation is remedied fairly.

The "Gamble Retake"

Maybe you had a fine day at the test, but you got a 690 and you're aiming for one of the top 10 or so programs, where the average score is around 720. You hear the standard error is about 30 points, which is almost exactly the size of the increase you'd like. So you wonder whether you should gamble on a retake—simply take the test again and hope to do better. Knowing that you can simply cancel your score if you do the same or worse on the test provides a good measure of insurance against those risks. However, when you are contemplating such an investment of money ($250 for test registration), time, and stress, it's first worth considering logically what your actual chances are of improving your score without additional dedicated study in the interim.

Here's a breakdown of the gamble retake. Let's consider three cases:

1. Say your true score (at your current skill level) is 690. In this case, you are quite likely to get a 690, or close to it, on a gamble retake. Moreover, you're as likely to get a 660 on your gamble retake as a 720.

2. Say your true score at your current skill level is a 720. This is the possibility you want to believe is the case. In this case, your 690 score was somewhat lower than your true score—not necessarily because you had a bad day but perhaps due to statistical variation in scores. In this case, on your gamble retake, you're most likely to score at or near 720.

3. Say your true score at your current skill level is a 660. This case is the mirror image of case #2. In this case, your 690 was indeed a fluke, but in your favor. You're likely to score at or near a 660 on your gamble retake, and you're just as likely to score under 660 as above 660.

There are other possibilities, of course—your true score at your current skill level could be 680 or 700 or something near this range. It could even be as far away as 600 or 780—but such cases are very unlikely (and if you'd like to gamble on those odds, you may want to dedicate your B-school tuition to playing the lottery instead). But given the statistical reliability of the GMAT, the most likely case of all is #1. Cases #2 and #3 are less likely—and each of those is as likely as the other.

So even if you are only 30, 20, or 10 points shy of your goal, the gamble retake is not a particularly good gamble. The risk posed by case #3 is entirely mitigated by the fact that if you underperform on your retake, you may simply cancel your score. Nevertheless, a straight-up gamble retake will produce the same score more often than any other result—the most likely outcome is a simple waste of time and money. In general, a retake is the right move only if you have a month or two beforehand to devote to serious study.

Improving Your Score

Devoting your time and focus to regular study, on the other hand, is no gamble; it's a proven way to gain familiarity with, and ultimately mastery over, the test. Rather than guessing at your true skill level as we discussed above, you can accurately assess your performance by looking at the range of scores after you've taken several practice CATs. While the exact score will likely vary from test to test, the scores taken together should reveal a consistent pattern of performance. As you continue to practice, look for upward trends. Keeping the standard error of measurement in mind, don't focus too minutely on the individual scores but rather on the larger picture they reveal. Use this book and your online resources to move that range upward over time. Keep working to improve your performance until you're comfortable with the score range you are seeing consistently on your CATs. With practice, you can feel confident that you will receive a score on Test Day that reflects your highest attainable level of ability.

A Closer Look at GMAT Scoring

The following appendix is adapted from The GMAT Unlocked, *a white paper from Kaplan's Research Series. For more information, or if you're interested in any of our classroom or tutoring programs, please visit our website at* **KaplanGMAT.com**.

As you have seen throughout this book, every question has a difficulty level. This fact is an important part of the adaptive algorithm through which getting questions correct is "rewarded" with harder questions.

There's a little more to this story. After all, in Chapter 2 of this book, you learned that on the computer-adaptive GMAT, the first question you see is an "average difficulty" question; that means approximately half the people get the question right and half the people get it wrong. In a sense, for all the people who got the question right, it's an easy question, and in that same sense, it's a hard question for all the people who got it wrong. The difficulty of the question can be described by this entire pattern of responses, rather than just the percentage who answered it correctly.

Every Question Has a Curve[1]

Let's take a closer look at such a pattern for a 550-level question. Imagine that a complete and representative population of GMAT test takers got to tango with this question and we tracked the results. The pattern of who got the question right and wrong would look something like this:

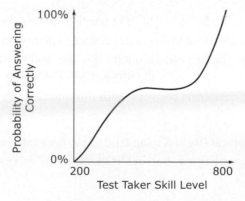

A Question Curve That Levels Around 550

---

[1] This section is based primarily on spoken remarks delivered at the 2009 and 2011 GMAC Test Prep Summits.

Notice what the axes represent in this graph. This graph shows the percentage of people who got the question correct, ordering those percentages by the test takers' ability—rather, their ability plus practice, since we know a great deal of practice goes into the test. When you count how many people get the question right at all their different skill levels, you end up with a pretty smooth curve. This curve makes a lot of sense when you examine the parts. Over on the right, where the test takers are very good, they are almost certain to get the question correct. Those individuals are destined for top-10 B-schools or to work as Kaplan faculty or both. On the left, where the test takers are at the bottom of the pool, the odds of getting the question correct are almost zero.

Finally, in the middle, the curve flattens out. The 540-, 550-, and 560-level test takers have about a 50 percent chance of getting the question right, and that's why the curve flattens out at a height corresponding to the 50 percent probability level. That part reflects what we've already said when discussing how the CAT works: a test taker who should ultimately score at the 550 level will get a question like this correct half of the time, on average. Also, the fact that the curve is nicely symmetrical indicates that when you take the entire test-taking population together, about half will get it right and half will get it wrong.

Now take a look at this one. It's a different question, so it has a different curve.

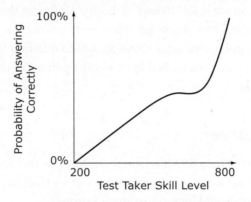

A Question Curve That Levels Around 650

It's a similar shape but stretched and shifted to the right. It's a harder question. Everyone below the 650 skill level is below the 50 percent level and therefore has a greater chance of getting this question wrong than getting it right. Also, if you look where the curve levels out for this one, you see that it's still at a height of 50 percent but that portion is now hovering at about the 650 skill level. Whereas for the first question, 550-level test takers had even odds of answering correctly, with this question, it's the 650-level test takers who have the even odds.

This conversation is getting fairly technical (we at Kaplan tend to be more interested in the behind-the-scenes details of the GMAT than our valued readers may be), but let's look at one more example, a trickier one.

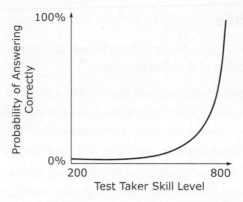

The Curve for a 750-Level Question

This curve may appear deformed at first when compared to the previous question curves. Like the other curves, it moves generally upward from left to right, but unlike the other ones, the left side seems stretched out. Like the other curves, it has a flat part, but in this case the flat part stays close to 0 percent along the *y*-axis for a long time before curving upward. And that curve is *way* to the right.

According to the science of building test questions, you never really know what kind of curve a question is going to have when your mathematicians and wordsmiths devise it; you just have to write it and then collect the data to see what its curve is. That's true for the test makers (this is the reason they include experimental questions on the GMAT), and it's also true for us at Kaplan as we write and norm our practice tests to be the most accurate study tools for Test Day.

If you were the test maker and you had a question on your hands with this curve, you'd find this question to be not as useful in some respects and especially useful in others. First, consider the test takers at skill levels of 700 and below. They all are basically doomed: 700 level? 200 level? They all tend to get it wrong, so this question does not distinguish among them very efficiently. The first question we looked at does a much better job of telling those categories apart, because basically all 200-level test takers who see that question get it wrong and basically all 700-levelers get it right.

Nevertheless, this question is very good at one thing: it can distinguish among 700-, 750-, and 800-level scorers. If you look at the 700-level portion of the axis, you can see that the curve is riding low, and test takers on that part of the curve are, most likely, going to answer this question incorrectly. If your ability level is that of a 750-scorer, you have a good chance on this one. But if you're an 800-scorer, you're likely getting this question right. Telling the difference among these groups is what this question is perfect for: once you've progressed within a section and demonstrated that you're in the 700–800 range, the test will dish up questions with curves like this one to determine whether you belong at the top or the bottom of that range.

The whole point of the GMAT is that it's meant to discern the applicants who will be able to handle the coursework at a given business school program and the ones who won't. It's all about distinguishing among a competitive set of candidates in a fair and objective way. Toward that goal, each question has a job to do, which is to help in the task of distinguishing among test takers' ability levels, and each question does that job a little bit differently, based on the unique shape of its curve.

Fair and Unfair Questions

Apart from understanding better how the CAT algorithm chooses questions, you'll also note the following practical takeaways from the discussion of question curves:

- **"Bad" questions.** How do the test makers determine whether a question is clearly written? It all comes back to the curve. Psychometricians collect information on each individual question and look at the curve for that question, and—as you've just seen—these curves give much more nuanced information than mere numbers or percentages can give. Questions that have nonsensical curves are thrown out.[2]

- **Fair and unfair questions.** This point is similar to the preceding takeaway—and it has to do with the issue of whether questions might be culturally biased or gender biased. An extremely important consideration in constructing the GMAT (so the test makers tell us) is to make a test that is fair to people from diverse geographies and backgrounds. To give an example: a vice president of Research and Development at GMAC once narrated a story to members of our team about a Critical Reasoning question previously on the test that concerned skim milk. As it so happens, while the term *skim milk* is readily understood in the United States, it does not carry equal meaning in India. Moreover, the kind of milk at stake in the question had nothing to do with the argument, the argument's conclusion, its critical assumptions, or anything substantially related to the question's correct answer. But seeing a foreign expression in the first few words of the question was distracting to some Indian test takers. That distraction was one that test takers from the United States didn't have to endure, and therefore—however slight the inequity—the question was ultimately deemed unfair.

The test makers avoid many such inequities through diligence and common sense, but unfair questions can also be identified and eradicated using the curves we discussed above. Just as the test makers can create the curve for a particular question, so can they create the curve for that question for a particular group and conduct analysis called differential item functioning (DIF). And if, for example, they see that test takers in India are getting the skim milk question wrong more than they should be, across all of the different skill levels of the Indian test takers, then the test makers have the opportunity to reexamine that question and uncover the point of cultural bias if human review hadn't already picked it up.

---

[2] For example, imagine a curve that looks like a parabola with negative concavity. This curve has a high point and then slopes downward on both sides from that point, symmetrical on the left and right, like a ∩ shape. It's an odd shape for a curve, but it can happen. The people whose skill level is at the parabola's high point (say, 670) are the ones who get the question correct most often. Then we head to the left, and the percentage who get it right drops. That part makes sense: people at lower skill levels don't do as well on the question. The confusing part is when we head to the right of the topmost point. Those people are higher in skill level, but they get the question right *less* often? There's something wrong with the curve, because the most skilled test takers are getting the question wrong and being penalized. In fact, questions with curves such as this are often phrased confusingly or inaccurately. If a question is a good 670-level question but has a small error or grounds for misinterpretation that perceptive 700+ test takers are conditioned to notice, it may reward the 670-level test takers and falsely penalize the 700+ test takers. Such a question can be deemed "unfair" on scientific grounds—based on its curve—and it never graduates from being an experimental question into the ranks of questions that count toward GMAT scores.

Not All Questions Are Worth the Same

Have you harbored a conviction all along that some GMAT questions are worth more than others? If so, you have been right, although perhaps not in exactly the way you thought. We saw in the previous examination that each question has a different curve. Each is unique in its ability to slice and dice test taker ability. And so it makes sense that each question has a different opportunity to impact your score. We saw a question above whose curve allowed it to distinguish 700-level scorers from 750- and 800-level scorers. If you are a 750-level scorer, or aspire to be, that may be one of the most important questions you see on Test Day. It will actually create a larger swing in your running score than the previous or following question will. Meanwhile, if you are a 680 scorer working to break 700 at this point, that particular question is of little relevance to you: if you see it (and you will likely not), you can get it wrong, and doing so would not do much to hurt your goal of scoring 700+.

Let's return to the first 10 questions of a Quant or Verbal section, which we discussed briefly in Chapter 2. As you've already seen, your performance on this first series of questions helps the CAT determine your rough placement on the difficulty scale. And you've also seen how questions appearing later in a section can be quite important as well, as they are the ones that are specifically targeted to evaluate your ability level compared to those test takers who will ultimately score slightly higher or lower than you.

The item curves help explain both points. Many of the questions near the beginning of the exam will have curves designed to separate 600 from 400, then 650 from 600, 670 from 630, and so on. As you progress through the test, the CAT tailors its questions to your ability level to learn more about you as a test taker. But all of these questions have a slightly different impact on your score. There are reasons to suspect that you might see questions later in a section that could make a big difference to your score. And there is every possibility that questions that could cause larger swings are inserted by the test makers later on intentionally, as the algorithm seeks to verify its estimate of your ability in different ways. As one study of an operational CAT pool found: "Findings refuted the myth that the beginning items are the most important."[3] The curves are key, not a question's placement per se.

On Test Day, you have only one choice: give every question your best effort. Give easy-looking questions a quick look for unseen pitfalls. Be open to guessing on harder-looking questions so that you can maximize the time you have available to answer all the questions you are capable of answering correctly. Take a balanced approach to time management. Don't be too quick to assume any question is one you'll definitely get right or definitely get wrong. And know that it's hard to fool a CAT. Its question selection and scoring algorithms are sophisticated, so your best defense is a good offense: practicing to improve your performance on questions across the range of difficulty levels.

---

[3] Talento-Miller, E., Han, K. T., & Guo, F. (2011). Guess again: The effect of correct guesses on scores in an operational CAT program. mba.com/~/media/Files/gmac/Research/research-report-series/guessagaintheeffectofcorrect.pdf